MW00889772

The Saban Era

The Saban Era

Alabama Crimson Tide Football Domination
2007-2023

Brad Beard

Copyright © 2024 by King's Road Enterprises, LLC. All rights reserved. No part of this publication may be reproduced, distributed, or transmitted in any form or by any means, including photocopying, recording, or other electronic or mechanical methods, without the prior written permission of the publisher, except in the case of brief quotations embodied in reviews and certain other non-commercial uses permitted by copyright law.

Cover art by Daniel A. Moore.

Published in Vestavia Hills, Alabama.

Library of Congress Control Number: 2024930828

ISBN: 9798372614093

Dedication

This book is dedicated to my family - Jill, Brooklyn, Jaclyn, and Goldie. You all mean the world to me, and I thank God for you every single day!

Acknowledgments

I would like to thank God for making this possible. Without Him, I never would have found the time, patience, and thoughts to be able to put this together. I also thank Him for this incredible era of Alabama football, especially during a time in my life where I have been blessed enough to have been able to travel to see so many games in person. And to my wife, Jill, thank you for all your support, allowing me to travel all over the country to witness history and some of the most incredible games I have ever seen in my life. I also appreciate your support as I spent countless hours at nights and on weekends putting this book together.

I cannot thank you enough, Coach Saban, for all that you have done for this program. You've brought us unforgettable games like the thriller over Clemson and 2nd-and-26 against Georgia, both for National Championships. More importantly, you've built a program centered on integrity, discipline, and developing men of character. The 2011 team's resilience after the tornado embodied your lessons on perseverance. Your commitment extends far beyond the field - from team Thanksgivings to preparing players for life. You are a model of leadership, humility, and strength. Your Nick's Kids Foundation and youth camps inspire countless lives. I'd also like to thank you, Miss Terry, for your invaluable contributions to our University. I can only imagine what all you have done behind the scenes to make all of this possible. Thank you both for your relentless work ethic - we are all better people today because of you!

I would also like to extend my gratitude to the Athletic Directors who played pivotal roles in this era. To the late Mal Moore, who showed unwavering determination in securing our head coach - may you rest in peace. Your legacy lives on through the program's continued success. To Greg Byrne, thank you for seamlessly stepping in and maintaining the strength of our program with your dedicated leadership. My sincere appreciation goes out to all coaching and administrative staff - your tireless efforts behind the scenes, though often unseen, have been instrumental in enabling the success of this era. To the players who have poured their hearts and souls into this program - your dedication is truly awe-inspiring. From grueling practices and strength training to meticulous preparation, you've given your all. Your unwavering commitment to excellence shines through in every 60-minute battle on the field. Thank you for your incredible hard work, and congratulations on your well-deserved success!

Thank you, Daniel Moore, for allowing me to put your picture of Coach Saban on the front cover of this book. When I met you and asked for your permission, you said, "I would be honored". Well, I am the one who is honored! For those of you who do not have an Alabama painting by Daniel Moore on your wall, you need to get one!

Thank you, Mom and Dad, for raising me as an Alabama fan. To my great friend, Kiker - thank you so much for always having an extra ticket for me. OBR, thank you for the tickets you got for me as well. To my fraternity brothers and fellow Bama lovers – I love all of our text threads with Bama discussions and game analysis. To my tailgate buddies - Kiker, OBR, Sham, Manderson, Joe, LB, Canada Steve, and the Laney brothers – from our tailgates when we could literally drive onto the quad by Gorgas Library to our many trips to Dallas and Atlanta, to Penn State, Texas A&M, LSU, California, Florida, Phoenix, New Orleans, NFL Draft in Chicago, tailgating on the yacht in Miami (thank you, Steve), Bourbon Trail for the Kentucky game, and so many more – we had some incredible trips to see some very memorable games! Roll Tide!

For God so loved the world that He gave His one and only Son, that whoever believes in Him shall not perish but have eternal life. -John 3:16

Contents

Introduction

After the overall game summaries, this book breaks down every year of Nick Saban's 17 years of coaching at Alabama. Each chapter starts with game summaries for the year, coaching staff, recruits, rosters, and transfers. Then each game is summarized with a box score, total yards, recap, and player stats. Finally, season stats, awards and honors, and NFL draftees conclude each chapter. After this, the next three chapters contain player career stats, all-time Alabama stats leaders, and other stats and streaks.

I spent more than 1,000 hours over the last few years researching, gathering data, verifying, updating, formatting, and putting it all together in an organized format that is very easy to view, relive, and reference. For the game summaries, I used a combination of me watching the games, the highlights, the play-by-play analysis, as well as finding write-ups online and using them as a baseline. Then I consolidated them so they would fit on a single page (well, most of them anyway) and fixed inaccuracies, spelling, and grammar errors. I added more detail in some cases, and the later years are longer because streaks occurred and records were broken, and I wanted to be sure I captured all of that information.

Some recruit positions were listed differently from different sources. Some players may have been recruited at one position but then changed positions later. Regarding the rosters, the players in **bold** indicate starters, but it's important to keep in mind that starters were sometimes fluid as some players split time and injuries changed things up throughout the season. The starters are indicated from depth charts that were produced at the beginning of the season, and some players may have transferred in/out after the rosters were released. I did my best with the data I found. Players in *italics* indicate that they transferred *to* Alabama.

This book has a page limit, and I wanted to be thorough and include everything. In order to accomplish this, some tables had to be created in small print. My apologies if you need to get your readers out to see them, but they should only apply to the tables you'll just want to reference as opposed to fully read.

Regarding the team rankings, I used the ESPN rankings which should be sourced from the Associated Press (AP) poll until the College Football Playoff rankings were released during the season (typically in November, starting in 2014). I also used the ESPN QBR formula (out of 100) in the game stats. I counted the wins/losses that Saban achieved - not after sanctions and forfeits (2007). If he beat the team, I counted it as a win. For SEC games, I counted the SEC Championship games and National Championship games against SEC opponents (so LSU in 2011 and Georgia in 2017 and 2021). Some of the game rushing stats show a non-bold row for "Team". The data in this row is the result of kneel downs that resulted in lost yardage, and these lost yards officially count as negative rushing yards.

Keep in mind that the drafts occurred in April of the year following the football season. For example, players drafted in 2011 were from the 2010 football season, so they are listed in the 2010 section. For NFL teams that changed names, I used the most current name. Note that Jalen Hurts is not listed as being drafted from the University of Alabama since the NFL officially uses the last school the player attended, which in his case is the University of Oklahoma.

Game Summaries

During Nick Saban's 17 seasons as the Alabama head coach, his record was 206-29 (88%) and 131-20 in the SEC (87%). He won six National Championships (appearing in nine) and nine SEC Championships (appearing in ten). He went 6-2 in the first round of the College Football Playoffs and 4-2 in other Bowl Games. His teams were ranked #1 in 97 different weeks.

2007[1]

Record	7-6	52/120
SEC Record	4-4	
Rank		
Points for	352	
Points against	286	
Pts/game	27.1	65/120
Opp pts/game	22	28/120
SOS	4.4	21/120

Saban's first season - time to start "The Process"

Independence Bowl

Date	Bama Rank		Opp Rank	Opponent	Bama	Opp	Result	SEC
09/01/07		vs		Western Carolina	52	6	W	
09/08/07		@		Vanderbilt	24	10	W	W
09/15/07		vs	16	Arkansas	41	38	W	W
09/22/07	16	vs	22	Georgia	23	26	L	L
09/29/07	22	N		Florida State	14	21	L	
10/06/07		vs		Houston	30	24	W	
10/13/07		@		Ole Miss	27	24	W	W
10/20/07		vs	21	Tennessee	41	17	W	W
11/03/07	17	vs	3	LSU	34	41	L	L
11/10/07	22	@		Mississippi State	12	17	L	L
11/17/07		vs		Louisiana Monroe	14	21	L	
11/24/07		@		Auburn	10	17	L	L
11/30/07		N		Colorado	30	24	W	

2008[2]

Record	12-2	6/120
SEC Record	8-1	
Rank	6	
Points for	422	
Points against	200	
Pts/game	30.1	35/120
Opp pts/game	14.3	7/120
SOS	2.93	34/120

Undefeated regular season

SEC Championship

Sugar Bowl

Date	Bama Rank		Opp Rank	Opponent	Bama	Opp	Result	SEC
08/30/08	24	N	9	Clemson	34	10	W	
09/06/08	13	vs		Tulane	20	6	W	
09/13/08	11	vs		Western Kentucky	41	7	W	
09/20/08	9	@		Arkansas	49	14	W	W
09/27/08	8	@	3	Georgia	41	30	W	W
10/04/08	2	vs		Kentucky	17	14	W	W
10/18/08	2	vs		Ole Miss	24	20	W	W
10/25/08	2	@		Tennessee	29	9	W	W
11/01/08	2	vs		Arkansas State	35	0	W	
11/08/08	1	@	16	LSU	27	21	W	W
11/15/08	1	vs		Mississippi State	32	7	W	W
11/29/08	1	vs		Auburn	36	0	W	W
12/06/08	1	N	4	Florida	20	31	L	L
01/02/09	4	N	6	Utah	17	31	L	

2009[3]

Record	14-0	1/120
SEC Record	9-0	
Rank	1	
Points for	449	
Points against	164	
Pts/game	32.1	22/120
Opp pts/game	11.7	2/120
SOS	6.62	2/120

Perfect Season, 14-0
SEC Champions (1)
National Champions (1)

SEC Championship

BCS National Championship

Date	Bama Rank		Opp Rank	Opponent	Bama	Opp	Result	SEC
09/05/09	5	N	7	Virginia Tech	34	24	W	
09/12/09	4	vs		Florida Intl.	40	14	W	
09/19/09	4	vs		North Texas	53	7	W	
09/26/09	3	vs		Arkansas	35	7	W	W
10/03/09	3	@		Kentucky	38	20	W	W
10/10/09	3	@	20	Ole Miss	22	3	W	W
10/17/09	2	vs	22	South Carolina	20	6	W	W
10/24/09	2	vs		Tennessee	12	10	W	W
11/07/09	3	vs	9	LSU	24	15	W	W
11/14/09	2	@		Mississippi State	31	3	W	W
11/21/09	2	vs		Chattanooga	45	0	W	
11/27/09	2	@		Auburn	26	21	W	W
12/05/09	2	N	1	Florida	32	13	W	W
01/07/10	1	N	2	Texas	37	21	W	

2010[4]

Stat			Date	Bama Rank		Opp Rank	Opponent	Bama	Opp	Result	SEC
Record	10-3	16/120	09/04/10	1	vs		San Jose State	48	3	W	
SEC Record	5-3		09/11/10	1	vs	18	Penn State	24	3	W	
Rank	10		09/18/10	1	@		Duke	62	13	W	
Points for	464		09/25/10	1	@	10	Arkansas	24	20	W	W
Points against	176		10/02/10	1	vs	7	Florida	31	6	W	W
Pts/game	35.7	18/120	10/09/10	1	@	19	South Carolina	21	35	L	L
Opp pts/game	13.5	3/120	10/16/10	8	vs		Ole Miss	23	10	W	W
SOS	4.69	18/120	10/23/10	8	@		Tennessee	41	10	W	W
			11/06/10	6	@	10	LSU	21	24	L	L
Never lost more than two games again			11/13/10	12	vs	19	Mississippi State	30	10	W	W
			11/18/10	11	vs		Georgia State	63	7	W	
			11/26/10	11	vs	2	Auburn	27	28	L	L
CapitalOne Bowl			01/01/11	16	N	9	Michigan State	49	7	W	

2011[5]

Stat			Date	Bama Rank		Opp Rank	Opponent	Bama	Opp	Result	SEC
Record	12-1	3/120	09/03/11	2	vs		Kent State	48	7	W	
SEC Record	8-1		09/10/11	3	@	23	Penn State	27	11	W	
Rank	1		09/17/11	2	vs		North Texas	41	0	W	
Points for	453		09/24/11	3	vs	14	Arkansas	38	14	W	W
Points against	106		10/01/11	3	@	12	Florida	38	10	W	W
Pts/game	34.8	20/120	10/08/11	2	vs		Vanderbilt	34	0	W	W
Opp pts/game	8.2	1/120	10/15/11	2	@		Ole Miss	52	7	W	W
SOS	4.21	17/120	10/22/11	2	vs		Tennessee	37	6	W	W
Avenged only loss of the season against LSU by beating them in the National Championship Game (2)			11/05/11	2	vs	1	LSU	6	9	L	L
			11/12/11	3	@		Mississippi State	24	7	W	W
			11/19/11	3	vs		GA Southern	45	21	W	
			11/26/11	2	@	24	Auburn	42	14	W	W
BCS National Championship			01/09/12	2	N	1	LSU	21	0	W	W

2012[6]

Stat			Date	Bama Rank		Opp Rank	Opponent	Bama	Opp	Result	SEC
Record	13-1	2/124	09/01/12	2	N	8	Michigan	41	14	W	
SEC Record	8-1		09/08/12	1	vs		Western KY	35	0	W	
Rank	1		09/15/12	1	@		Arkansas	52	0	W	W
Points for	542		09/22/12	1	vs		Florida Atlantic	40	7	W	
Points against	153		09/29/12	1	vs		Ole Miss	33	14	W	W
Pts/game	38.7	12/124	10/13/12	1	@		Missouri	42	10	W	W
Opp pts/game	10.9	1/124	10/20/12	1	@		Tennessee	44	13	W	W
SOS	5.51	14/124	10/27/12	1	vs	11	Mississippi State	38	7	W	W
			11/03/12	1	@	5	LSU	21	17	W	W
SEC Champions (2)			11/10/12	1	vs	15	Texas A&M	24	29	L	L
Back-to-Back National Champions (3)			11/17/12	4	vs		Western Carolina	49	0	W	
			11/24/12	2	vs		Auburn	49	0	W	W
SEC Championship			12/01/12	2	N	3	Georgia	32	28	W	W
BCS National Championship			01/07/13	2	N	1	Notre Dame	42	14	W	

2013[7]

Stat			Date	Bama Rank		Opp Rank	Opponent	Bama	Opp	Result	SEC
Record	11-2	9/125	08/31/13	1	N		Virginia Tech	35	10	W	
SEC Record	7-1		09/14/13	1	@	6	Texas A&M	49	42	W	W
Rank	7		09/21/13	1	vs		Colorado State	31	6	W	
Points for	496		09/28/13	1	vs	21	Ole Miss	25	0	W	W
Points against	181		10/05/13	1	vs		Georgia State	45	3	W	
Pts/game	38.2	17/125	10/12/13	1	@		Kentucky	48	7	W	W
Opp pts/game	13.9	4/125	10/19/13	1	vs		Arkansas	52	0	W	W
SOS	3.76	35/125	10/26/13	1	vs		Tennessee	45	10	W	W
			11/09/13	1	vs	13	LSU	38	17	W	W
Last year of the BCS era			11/16/13	1	@		Mississippi State	20	7	W	W
			11/23/13	1	vs		Chattanooga	49	0	W	
			11/30/13	1	@	4	Auburn	28	34	L	L
Sugar Bowl			01/02/14	3	N	11	Oklahoma	31	45	L	

3

2014[8]

Record	12-2	6/128
SEC Record	8-1	
Rank	4	
Points for	517	
Points against	258	
Pts/game	36.9	16/128
Opp pts/game	18.4	6/128
SOS	7.26	5/128

First year of CFP Era
SEC Champions (3)

SEC Championship
CFP Semifinal

Date	Bama Rank		Opp Rank	Opponent	Bama	Opp	Result	SEC
08/30/14	2	N		West Virginia	33	23	W	
09/06/14	2	vs		Florida Atlantic	41	0	W	
09/13/14	3	vs		Southern Mississippi	52	12	W	
09/20/14	3	vs		Florida	42	21	W	W
10/04/14	3	@	11	Ole Miss	17	23	L	L
10/11/14	7	@		Arkansas	14	13	W	W
10/18/14	7	vs	21	Texas A&M	59	0	W	W
10/25/14	4	@		Tennessee	34	20	W	W
11/08/14	5	@	16	LSU	20	13	W	W
11/15/14	5	vs	1	Mississippi State	25	20	W	W
11/22/14	1	vs		Western Carolina	48	14	W	
11/29/14	1	vs	15	Auburn	55	44	W	W
12/06/14	1	N	16	Missouri	42	13	W	W
01/01/15	1	N	4	Ohio State	35	42	L	

2015[9]

Record	14-1	1/128
SEC Record	8-1	
Rank	1	
Points for	526	
Points against	227	
Pts/game	35.1	20/128
Opp pts/game	15.1	3/128
SOS	7.46	1/128

Back-to-Back SEC Champions (4)
National Champions (4)

SEC Championship
CFP Semifinal
CFP National Championship

Date	Bama Rank		Opp Rank	Opponent	Bama	Opp	Result	SEC
09/05/15	3	N	20	Wisconsin	35	17	W	
09/12/15	2	vs		Middle Tennessee St	37	10	W	
09/19/15	2	vs	15	Ole Miss	37	43	L	L
09/26/15	12	vs		Louisiana Monroe	34	0	W	
10/03/15	13	@	8	Georgia	38	10	W	W
10/10/15	8	vs		Arkansas	27	14	W	W
10/17/15	10	@	9	Texas A&M	41	23	W	W
10/24/15	8	vs		Tennessee	19	14	W	W
11/07/15	2	vs	4	LSU	30	16	W	W
11/14/15	2	@	17	Mississippi State	31	6	W	W
11/21/15	2	vs		Charleston Southern	56	6	W	
11/28/15	2	@		Auburn	29	13	W	W
12/05/15	2	N	18	Florida	29	15	W	W
12/31/15	2	N	3	Michigan State	38	0	W	
01/11/16	2	N	1	Clemson	45	40	W	

2016[10]

Record	14-1	1/128
SEC Record	9-0	
Rank	2	
Points for	582	
Points against	195	
Pts/game	38.8	16/128
Opp pts/game	13	1/128
SOS	7.29	1/128

Third consecutive SEC Championship (5)

SEC Championship
CFP Semifinal
CFP National Championship

Date	Bama Rank		Opp Rank	Opponent	Bama	Opp	Result	SEC
09/03/16	1	N	20	USC	52	6	W	
09/10/16	1	vs		Western Kentucky	38	10	W	
09/17/16	1	@	19	Ole Miss	48	43	W	W
09/24/16	1	vs		Kent State	48	0	W	
10/01/16	1	vs		Kentucky	34	6	W	W
10/08/16	1	@	16	Arkansas	49	30	W	W
10/15/16	1	@	9	Tennessee	49	10	W	W
10/22/16	1	vs	6	Texas A&M	33	14	W	W
11/05/16	1	@	13	LSU	10	0	W	W
11/12/16	1	vs		Mississippi State	51	3	W	W
11/19/16	1	vs		Chattanooga	31	3	W	
11/26/16	1	vs	13	Auburn	30	12	W	W
12/03/16	1	N	15	Florida	54	16	W	W
12/31/16	1	N	4	Washington	24	7	W	
01/09/17	1	N	2	Clemson	31	35	L	

2017[11]

Record	13-1	2/130
SEC Record	8-1	
Rank	1	
Points for	519	
Points against	167	
Pts/game	37.1	15/130
Opp pts/game	11.9	1/130
SOS	5.46	22/130

National Champions (5)

CFP Semifinal
CFP National Championship

Date	Bama Rank		Opp Rank	Opponent	Bama	Opp	Result	SEC
09/02/17	1	N	3	Florida State	24	7	W	
09/09/17	1	vs		Fresno State	41	10	W	
09/16/17	1	vs		Colorado State	41	23	W	
09/23/17	1	@		Vanderbilt	59	0	W	W
09/30/17	1	vs		Ole Miss	66	3	W	W
10/07/17	1	@		Texas A&M	27	19	W	W
10/14/17	1	vs		Arkansas	41	9	W	W
10/21/17	1	vs		Tennessee	45	7	W	W
11/04/17	2	vs	19	LSU	24	10	W	W
11/11/17	2	@	16	Mississippi State	31	24	W	W
11/18/17	1	vs		Mercer	56	0	W	
11/25/17	1	@	6	Auburn	14	26	L	L
01/01/18	4	N	1	Clemson	24	6	W	
01/08/18	4	N	3	Georgia	26	23	W	W

2018[12]

			Date	Bama Rank		Opp Rank	Opponent	Bama	Opp	Result	SEC
Record	14-1	2/130	09/01/18	1	N		Louisville	51	14	W	
SEC Record	9-0		09/08/18	1	vs		Arkansas State	57	7	W	
Rank	2		09/15/18	1	@		Ole Miss	62	7	W	W
Points for	684		09/22/18	1	vs	22	Texas A&M	45	23	W	W
Points against	271		09/29/18	1	vs		Louisiana	56	14	W	
Pts/game	45.6	3/130	10/06/18	1	@		Arkansas	65	31	W	W
Opp pts/game	18.1	12/130	10/13/18	1	vs		Missouri	39	10	W	W
SOS	6.63	3/130	10/20/18	1	@		Tennessee	58	21	W	W
			11/03/18	1	@	3	LSU	29	0	W	W
SEC Champions (6)			11/10/18	1	vs	16	Mississippi State	24	0	W	W
			11/17/18	1	vs		Citadel	50	17	W	
			11/24/18	1	vs		Auburn	52	21	W	W
SEC Championship			12/01/18	1	N	4	Georgia	35	28	W	W
CFP Semifinal			12/29/18	1	N	4	Oklahoma	45	34	W	
CFP National Championship			01/07/19	1	N	2	Clemson	16	44	L	

2019[13]

			Date	Bama Rank		Opp Rank	Opponent	Bama	Opp	Result	SEC
Record	11-2	10/130	08/31/19	2	N		Duke	42	3	W	
SEC Record	6-2		09/07/19	2	vs		New Mexico St	62	10	W	
Rank	8		09/14/19	2	@		South Carolina	47	23	W	W
Points for	614		09/21/19	2	vs		Southern Miss	49	7	W	
Points against	242		09/28/19	2	vs		Ole Miss	59	31	W	W
Pts/game	47.2	2/130	10/12/19	1	@	24	Texas A&M	47	28	W	W
Opp pts/game	18.6	13/130	10/19/19	1	vs		Tennessee	35	13	W	W
SOS	2.81	39/130	10/26/19	1	vs		Arkansas	48	7	W	W
			11/09/19	3	vs	2	LSU	41	46	L	L
Both losses by a combined eight			11/16/19	5	@		Mississippi State	38	7	W	W
points			11/23/19	5	vs		Western Carolina	66	3	W	
			11/30/19	5	@	15	Auburn	45	48	L	L
Citrus Bowl			01/01/20	13	N	14	Michigan	35	16	W	

2020[14]

			Date	Bama Rank		Opp Rank	Opponent	Bama	Opp	Result	SEC
Record	13-0	1/127	09/26/20	2	@		Missouri	38	19	W	W
SEC Record	11-0		10/03/20	2	vs	13	Texas A&M	52	24	W	W
Rank	1		10/10/20	2	@		Ole Miss	63	48	W	W
Points for	630		10/17/20	2	vs	3	Georgia	41	24	W	W
Points against	252		10/24/20	2	@		Tennessee	48	17	W	W
Pts/game	48.5	2/127	10/31/20	2	vs		Mississippi State	41	0	W	W
Opp pts/game	19.4	13/127	11/21/20	1	vs		Kentucky	63	3	W	W
SOS	9.64	3/127	11/28/20	1	vs	22	Auburn	42	13	W	W
Perfect Season (2), SEC (7) and			12/05/20	1	@		LSU	55	17	W	W
National (6) Champions			12/12/20	1	@		Arkansas	52	3	W	W
SEC Championship			12/19/20	1	N	7	Florida	52	46	W	W
CFP Semifinal			01/01/21	1	N	4	Notre Dame	31	14	W	
CFP National Championship			01/11/21	1	N	3	Ohio State	52	24	W	

2021[15]

			Date	Bama Rank		Opp Rank	Opponent	Bama	Opp	Result	SEC
Record	13-2	4/130	09/04/21	1	N	14	Miami	44	13	W	
SEC Record	8-2		09/11/21	1	vs		Mercer	48	14	W	
Rank	2		09/18/21	1	@	11	Florida	31	29	W	W
Points for	598		09/25/21	1	vs		Southern Miss	63	14	W	
Points against	302		10/02/21	1	vs	12	Ole Miss	42	21	W	W
Pts/game	39.9	6/130	10/09/21	1	@		Texas A&M	38	41	L	L
Opp pts/game	20.1	18/130	10/16/21	5	@		Mississippi State	49	9	W	W
SOS	5.69	7/130	10/23/21	4	vs		Tennessee	52	24	W	W
			11/06/21	2	vs		LSU	20	14	W	W
Back-to-Back SEC Champions (8)			11/13/21	2	vs		New Mexico St	59	3	W	
			11/20/21	2	vs	21	Arkansas	42	35	W	W
			11/27/21	3	@		Auburn	24	22	W	W
SEC Championship			12/04/21	3	N	1	Georgia	41	24	W	W
CFP Semifinal			12/31/21	1	N	4	Cincinnati	27	6	W	
CFP National Championship			01/10/22	1	N	3	Georgia	18	33	L	L

2022[16]				Date	Bama Rank		Opp Rank	Opponent	Bama	Opp	Result	SEC
Record	11-2	6/131		09/03/22	1	vs		Utah State	55	0	W	
SEC Record	6-2			09/10/22	1	@		Texas	20	19	W	
Rank	5			09/17/22	2	vs		Louisiana Monroe	63	7	W	
Points for	537			09/24/22	2	vs		Vanderbilt	55	3	W	W
Points against	233			10/01/22	2	@	20	Arkansas	49	26	W	W
Pts/game	41.3	4/131		10/08/22	1	vs		Texas A&M	24	20	W	W
Opp pts/game	17.9	9/131		10/15/22	3	@	6	Tennessee	49	52	L	L
SOS	4.58	26/131		10/22/22	6	vs	24	Mississippi State	30	6	W	W
				11/05/22	6	@	10	LSU	31	32	L	L
Both losses by a combined four points				11/12/22	9	@	11	Ole Miss	30	24	W	W
Only missed CFP by one spot				11/19/22	8	vs		Austin Peay	34	0	W	
				11/26/22	7	vs		Auburn	49	27	W	W
Sugar Bowl				12/31/22	5	N	9	Kansas State	45	20	W	

2023[17]				Date	Bama Rank		Opp Rank	Opponent	Bama	Opp	Result	SEC
Record	12-2	6/133		09/02/23	4	vs		Middle TN State	56	7	W	
SEC Record	9-0			09/09/23	3	vs	11	Texas	24	34	L	
Rank	5			09/16/23	10	@		South Florida	17	3	W	
Points for	479			09/23/23	13	vs	15	Ole Miss	24	10	W	W
Points against	269			09/30/23	12	@		Mississippi State	40	17	W	W
Pts/game	34.2	24/133		10/07/23	11	@		Texas A&M	26	20	W	W
Opp pts/game	19.2	16/133		10/14/23	11	vs		Arkansas	24	21	W	W
SOS	6.58	3/133		10/21/23	11	vs	17	Tennessee	34	20	W	W
				11/04/23	8	vs	14	LSU	42	28	W	W
SEC Champions (9)				11/11/23	8	@		Kentucky	49	21	W	W
				11/18/23	8	vs		Chattanooga	66	10	W	
				11/25/23	8	@		Auburn	27	24	W	W
SEC Championship				12/02/23	8	N	1	Georgia	27	24	W	W
CFP Semifinal				01/01/24	4	N	1	Michigan	20	27	L	

2007

Overall

Record	7-6
SEC Record	4-4
Points for	352
Points against	286
Points/game	27.1
Opp points/game	22
SOS[1]	4.4

What I would like for every football team to do that we play is to sit there and say, 'I hate playing against these guys. I hate playing 'em. Their effort, their toughness, their relentless resiliency to go out every play and focus and play the next play and compete in the game for 60 minutes in the game - I can't handle it.' That's the kind of football team we want.
-Nick Saban

Games

Date	Bama Rank		Opp Rank	Opponent	Bama	Opp	Result	SEC
09/01/07		vs		Western Carolina	52	6	W	
09/08/07		@		Vanderbilt	24	10	W	W
09/15/07		vs	16	Arkansas	41	38	W	W
09/22/07	16	vs	22	Georgia	23	26	L	L
09/29/07	22	N		Florida State	14	21	L	
10/06/07		vs		Houston	30	24	W	
10/13/07		@		Ole Miss	27	24	W	W
10/20/07		vs	21	Tennessee	41	17	W	W
11/03/07	17	vs	3	LSU	34	41	L	L
11/10/07	22	@		Mississippi State	12	17	L	L
11/17/07		vs		Louisiana Monroe	14	21	L	
11/24/07		@		Auburn	10	17	L	L
11/30/07		N		Colorado	30	24	W	

Coaches

Name	Position	Year
Nick Saban	Head Coach	1
Major Applewhite	Offensive Coordinator / Quarterbacks	1
Burton Burns	Associate Head Coach / Running Backs	1
Curt Cignetti	Wide Receivers / Recruiting Coordinator	1
Scott Cochran	Strength and Conditioning	1
Bo Davis	Defensive Line	1
Ron Middleton	Tight Ends / Special Teams	1
Joe Pendry	Offensive Line	1
Kirby Smart	Assistant Head Coach - Defense / Secondary	1
Kevin Steele	Defensive Coordinator / Inside Linebackers	1
Lance Thompson	Outside Linebackers	1

Recruits

Name	Pos	Scout	Rivals	247 Sports	ESPN Grade	Hometown	High school / college	Height	Weight	Committed
Josh Chapman	DT	3	3	3	71	Hoover, AL	Hoover HS	6-1	280	2/6/07
Patrick Crump	OL	3	3	3	74	Hoover, AL	Hoover HS	6-3	285	9/13/06
Luther Davis	DE	4	4	4	79	West Monroe, LA	West Monroe HS	6-4	254	1/26/07
Jeremy Elder	DT	3	2	3	73	College Park, GA	North Clayton HS	6-3	270	2/4/07
Nick Fanuzzi	QB	3	3	3	78	San Antonio, TX	Winston Churchill HS	6-3	200	1/22/07
Tarence Farmer	CB	3	3	3	77	Houston, TX	St. Pius X HS	6-1	190	1/22/07
Nick Gentry	DT	3	3	3	78	Prattville, AL	Prattville HS	6-1	265	8/6/06
Brandon Gibson	WR	4	4	4	79	Mobile, AL	UMS-Wright Prep School	6-2	190	2/7/07
Demetrius Goode	RB	3	4	3	79	Chatham, VA	Hargrave Military Academy	5-11	200	1/28/07
Jeramie Griffin	RB	4	3	3	77	Batesville, MS	South Panola HS	6-0	230	1/28/07
Darius Hanks	WR	3	3	3	71	Norcross, GA	Norcross HS	6-0	168	1/29/07
Jennings Hester	ILB	2	2	3	72	Atlanta, GA	Marist School	6-3	228	6/13/06
Kareem Jackson	CB	3	4	3	40	Fork Union, VA	Fork Union Military Academy	5-10	185	1/22/07
Chris Lett	S	3	4	3	77	Pensacola, FL	Pensacola HS	6-2	195	5/25/06
Marquis Maze	WR	3	3	3	79	Tarrant, AL	Tarrant HS	5-9	160	2/7/07
Rolando McClain	ILB	4	4	4	79	Decatur, AL	Decatur HS	6-4	240	6/21/06
Alfred McCullough	DT	3	4	3	76	Athens, AL	Athens HS	6-3	297	7/9/06
Kerry Murphy	DT	4	4	4	81	Hoover, AL	Hoover HS	6-5	315	1/14/07
Michael Ricks	S	N/A	4	4	NR	Booneville, MS	NE Mississippi Community College	6-2	195	2/7/07
Jamar Taylor	RB	3	3	3	75	Lakeland, FL	Lakeland Senior HS	5-9	204	6/7/06
Chris Underwood	TE	2	2	2	40	Vestavia Hills, AL	Vestavia Hills HS	6-4	202	1/28/07
William Vlachos	OG	3	3	3	80	Mountain Brook, AL	Mountain Brook HS	6-2	287	9/13/06
Alex Watkins	DE	3	4	3	77	Brownsville, TN	Haywood HS	6-5	225	6/18/06
Chavis Williams	DE	2	3	3	75	Dora, AL	Dora HS	6-5	220	2/2/07

	Scout	Rivals	247Sports
5 Stars	0	0	0
4 Stars	5	10	5
3 Stars	15	11	18
2 Stars	3	3	1

Roster

Num	Player	Pos	Class	Height	Weight	Hometown	Last School
82	Earl Alexander	WR	FR	6-5	210	Phenix City	Central HS
32	Eryk Anders	LB	SO	6-2	225	San Antonio, TX	Smithson Valley HS
28	Javier Arenas	CB	SO	5-9	193	Tampa, FL	Robinson HS
25	Alex Benson	LB	FR	6-1	218	Trussville, AL	Hewitt-Trussville HS
50	Justin Britt	OG	SR	6-5	284	Cullman, AL	Cullman HS
81	Keith Brown	WR	SR	6-3	194	Pensacola, FL	Harrison-Central
43	Sam Burnthall	S	SO	6-2	185	Decatur, AL	Decatur HS
11	Matt Caddell	WR	SR	6-0	187	McCalla, AL	McAdory HS
59	Antoine Caldwell	OG	JR	6-3	292	Montgomery, AL	Lee HS
72	Chris Capps	OT	SR	6-6	298	Jonesboro, GA	Landmark Christian School
70	Evan Cardwell	C	SO	6-2	278	Killen, AL	Brooks HS
20	Marcus Carter	S	SR	6-0	205	Fort Payne, AL	Fort Payne HS
2	Simeon Castille	CB	SR	6-1	193	Birmingham, AL	Briarwood Christian HS
99	Josh Chapman	DL	FR	6-1	300	Hoover, AL	Hoover HS
86	Jamie Christensen	K	SR	6-0	177	Norcross, GA	Norcross / Naval Academy (RI)
22	Austin Clifford	DB	SO	5-11	182	Stuart, FL	Martin County HS
38	Glen Coffee	TB	SO	6-2	197	Fort Walton Beach, FL	For Walton Beach HS
23	Tremayne Coger	CB	FR	5-11	190	Columbia, TN	Central HS
56	Matt Collins	LB	SR	6-1	246	Clay, AL	Clay-Chalkville, AL
69	Patrick Crump	OL	FR	6-3	285	Hoover, AL	Hoover HS
65	Joshua Curry	NT	JR	6-1	314	Tuscaloosa, AL	Central HS / East Miss. CC
75	Cody Davis	OT	JR	6-6	283	Tuscaloosa, AL	Hillcrest HS
79	Drew Davis	OT	SO	6-6	268	Evergreen, AL	Sparta Academy
96	Luther Davis	DL	FR	6-4	275	West Monroe, LA	West Monroe HS
76	Marlon Davis	OG	JR	6-4	290	Columbus, GA	Carver HS
95	Brandon Deaderick	DE	SO	6-4	286	Elizabethtown, KY	Elizabethtown HS
37	Trent Dean	DB	JR	5-11	188	Decatur, AL	Decatur HS
60	Scott Deaton	OG	SO	6-6	286	Birmingham, AL	Oak Mountain HS
16	James Denton	QB	FR	6-1	205	Charlottesville, VA	St. Annes-Belfield
85	Preston Dial	TE	FR	6-3	223	Mobile, AL	UMS Wright
39	Justin Dunn	LB	FR	6-0	230	Bessemer, AL	Bessemer Academy
19	Patrick Eades	P	JR	6-2	185	Hoover, AL	Hoover HS
54	Jeremy Elder	DL	FR	6-3	270	College Park, GA	North Clayton HS
50	Cy Ellis	LB	SO	5-10	219	Killen, AL	Brooks HS
98	Brandon Fanney	LB	SO	6-4	241	Morristown, TN	Hargrave Military HS
13	Nick Fanuzzi	QB	FR	6-3	201	San Antonio, TX	Churchill HS
11	P.J. Fitzgerald	P	SO	5-11	194	Coral Springs, FL	Douglas HS
15	Andrew Friedman	K	SO	6-1	202	Fairhope, AL	UMS Wright
57	Morgan Garner	OL	JR	6-2	262	Deatsville, AL	Stanhope Elmore HS
58	Nick Gentry	DL	FR	6-3	263	Prattville, AL	Prattville HS
18	Brandon Gibson	WR	FR	6-1	192	Mobile, AL	UMS Wright
92	Wallace Gilberry	DE	SR	6-3	267	Bay Minette, AL	Baldwin County HS
33	Demetrius Goode	RB	FR	5-10	197	LaGrange, GA	LaGrange HS / Hargrave Military Academy
29	Terry Grant	TB	FR	5-10	188	Lumberton, MS	Lumberton HS
36	Eric Gray	CB	SR	6-0	195	Trinity, AL	West Morgan HS
26	Hampton Gray	DB	FR	6-1	193	Tuscaloosa, AL	Tuscaloosa County
91	Stabler Gray	DE	SO	6-5	253	Tuscaloosa, AL	Holy Spirit HS
93	Bobby Greenwood	DE	JR	6-5	267	Prattville, AL	Prattville HS
34	Jeramie Griffin	RB	FR	6-0	225	Batesville, MS	South Panola HS
22	D.J. Hall	WR	SR	6-2	195	Fort Walton Beach, FL	Choctawhatchee HS
21	Prince Hall	LB	SO	5-11	235	Moreno Valley, CA	Moreno Valley HS
86	Darius Hanks	WR	FR	6-0	190	Norcross, GA	Norcross
30	Patrick Hanrahan	FB	FR	6-0	245	Springville, AL	Springville HS
42	Jennings Hester	LB	FR	6-2	224	Atlanta, GA	Marist School
45	Charlie Higgenbotham	LB	FR	6-1	211	Birmingham, AL	Mountain Brook HS
7	Adam Hill	P	FR	5-10	188	Douglasville, GA	Chapel Hill HS
89	Charles Hoke	TE	JR	6-7	253	Birmingham, AL	Briarwood Christian HS
40	Baron Huber	FB	SO	6-3	242	Knoxville, TN	Powell HS
3	Kareem Jackson	CB	FR	5-11	185	Fork Union, VA / Macon, GA	Fork Union Military Academy / Westside HS
10	Jimmy Johns	TB	JR	6-2	233	Brookhaven, MS	Brookhaven HS
24	Marquis Johnson	CB	SO	5-11	186	Sarasota, FL	Booker HS
78	Mike Johnson	OT	SO	6-6	298	Pensacola, FL	Pine Forest HS
49	Rashad Johnson	S	JR	6-0	187	Sulligent, AL	Sulligent HS
84	Jake Jones	WR	FR	6-1	177	Birmingham, AL	Mountain Brook HS
29	Tyrone King	DB	JR	5-10	190	Birmingham, AL	Minor HS / Grambling
35	Charlie Kirschman	DL	FR	6-2	228	St. Augustine, FL	Nease HS
47	Ezekial Knight	LB	JR	6-4	235	Wedowee, AL	Randolph County HS
41	Chris Lett	DB	FR	6-2	195	Pensacola, FL	Pensacola HS
20	Jonathan Lowe	WR	JR	5-7	184	Phenix City, AL	Central HS
30	Rajiv Lundy	DB	FR	6-0	195	So. Delran, NJ	Rhode Island HS
10	Justin Martin	P	SO	5-9	203	Thomson, GA	Thompson HS

9

Num	Player	Pos	Class	Height	Weight	Hometown	Last School
4	Marquis Maze	WR	FR	5-9	167	Tarrant, AL	Tarrant HS
83	**Travis McCall**	**TE**	**JR**	**6-2**	**261**	**Prattville, AL**	**Prattville HS**
1	Rolando McClain	LB	FR	6-4	255	Decatur, AL	Decatur HS
80	Mike McCoy	WR	SO	6-3	199	Rankin, MS	Northwest HS
52	Alfred McCullough	DL	FR	6-2	317	Athens, AL	Athens HS
25	Aaron McDaniel	WR	JR	6-1	181	Fort Payne, AL	Fort Payne HS
17	Greg McElroy	QB	FR	6-3	218	Southlake, TX	Carroll HS
16	**Lionel Mitchell**	**CB**	**JR**	**6-2**	**182**	**Stone Mountain, GA**	**Hargrave Military HS**
34	Courtny Moore	DB	JR	5-10	182	Killen, AL	Bradshaw HS
66	**Brian Motley**	**DT**	**FR**	**6-2**	**280**	**Autaugaville, AL**	**Autaugaville HS**
41	Cliff Murphy	WR	SO	6-2	201	Anniston, AL	Saks HS
57	**Darren Mustin**	**LB**	**SR**	**6-2**	**235**	**Brentwood, TN**	**Brentwood Academy**
38	Joel Nix	LB	SO	5-11	232	Bessemer, AL	Hewitt-Trussville HS
7	Will Oakley	SE	JR	6-1	196	Ponte Verda Beach, FL	Nease HS
68	Taylor Pharr	OT	FR	6-6	281	Irondale, AL	Shades Valley HS
4	Tyrone Prothro	SE	SR	5-8	178	Heflin, AL	Cleburne County HS
24	Chris Pugh	WR	SO	6-4	195	Moulton, AL	Lawrence County HS
59	Mitch Ray	LB	FR	6-0	200	Birmingham, AL	Lawrence County HS
31	Forress Rayford	CB	SR	5-11	174	Mobile, AL	UMS Wright
13	Cory Reamer	LB	SO	6-4	223	Hoover, AL	Hoover
64	Layne Rinks	DT	JR	6-3	300	Leighton, AL	Bradshaw HS
8	Chris Rogers	S	SO	6-0	192	Lakeland, FL	Evangel Christian HS
74	David Ross	OG	FR	6-4	297	Homewood, AL	Homewood HS
19	Darwin Salaam	WR	SO	6-3	187	Madison, AL	Sparkman HS
94	**Keith Saunders**	**DE**	**SR**	**6-4**	**251**	**Willingboro, NJ**	**Holy Cross**
46	Zach Schreiber	LB	SO	6-1	212	Shreveport, LA	Evangel Christian
54	Brian Selman	LS	FR	6-0	210	Vestavia Hills, AL	Vestavia HS
26	Ali Sharrief	S	SO	5-9	197	Stevenson, AL	North Jackson HS
48	Travis Sikes	WR	FR	6-2	194	Nashville, TN	Christ Presbyterian HS
71	**Andre Smith**	**OT**	**SO**	**6-5**	**340**	**Birmingham, AL**	**Huffman**
94	Mike Sparks	K	FR	6-3	200	Loganville, GA	Loganville HS
61	**B.J. Stabler**	**OT**	**JR**	**6-4**	**294**	**Grove Hill, AL**	**Clark County HS**
62	Alex Stadler	OT	FR	6-5	299	Bealeton, VA	Liberty HS
6	Marcel Stamps	LB	SR	6-2	198	Brantley, AL	Brantley HS
9	Nikita Stover	SE	JR	6-0	207	Hartselle, AL	Itawamba CC
90	Milton Talbert	DE	FR	6-3	252	Hattiesburg, MS	Hattiesburg HS
9	Heath Thomas	P	FR	6-3	217	Montgomery, AL	Trinity Presbyterian
31	Leigh Tiffin	K	SO	6-1	198	Muscle Shoals, AL	Muscle Shoals HS
87	Chris Underwood	TE	JR	6-4	226	Birmingham, AL	Vestavia HS
5	Roy Upchurch	TB	SO	6-0	192	Tallahassee, FL	Godby HS
6	William Vandervoort	QB	FR	6-3	190	Anniston, AL	Donoho HS
44	Jacob Vane	FB	FR	6-1	232	Oak Ridge, TN	Oak Ridge HS
62	Lance Vickers	DL	FR	6-3	233	Athens, AL	Athens HS
73	William Vlachos	OL	FR	6-1	295	Birmingham, AL	Mountain Brook HS
44	Demarcus Waldrop	LB	SR	5-11	203	Pinson, AL	Pinson Valley HS
88	Nick Walker	TE	JR	6-5	255	Brundidge, AL	Pike County HS
77	Byron Walton	DT	SO	6-3	306	Trinity, AL	West Morgan HS
97	Lorenzo Washington	DT	SO	6-4	283	Loganville, GA	Hargrave Military HS
87	Alex Watkins	LB	FR	6-3	218	Brownsville, TN	Haywood HS
55	Chavis Williams	LB	FR	6-4	214	Dora, AL	Dora HS
45	Reyn Willis	WR	SO	6-4	212	Raleigh, NC	Virginia Episopal HS
14	**John Parker Wilson**	**QB**	**JR**	**6-2**	**213**	**Hoover, AL**	**Hoover HS**
96	Daniel Wood	TE	SO	6-4	247	McCalla, AL	McAdory HS
27	Justin Woodall	S	SO	6-2	224	Oxford, MS	Lafayette HS

Note: Starters in bold
Note: Table data from "2007 Alabama Crimson Tide football team" (18)

Games

09/01/07 - Alabama vs Western Carolina

Team	1	2	3	4	T		Passing	Rushing	Total
Western Carolina	0	3	0	3	6		171	76	247
Alabama	14	10	14	14	52		262	313	575

The Nick Saban era commenced before a sold-out, home crowd of 92,138 by defeating the Western Carolina Catamounts 52-6 for both Nick Saban's first regular season game and victory as Alabama's head coach. Redshirt freshman running back Terry Grant scored the first touchdown of the season, on the first offensive play of the game, with a 47-yard touchdown run. Grant then scored his second touchdown on a 1-yard run to give Alabama a 14-0 lead at the end of the first quarter. After a successful 34-yard Jonathon Parsons field goal by the Catamounts, Grant scored his third touchdown of the evening on a 21-yard run. Leigh Tiffin then hit a 21-yard field goal to give Alabama a 24-3 halftime lead.

Bama continued the scoring in the third quarter with another pair of touchdowns. The first came on a 1-yard Glen Coffee run and the second on a 1-yard touchdown pass from Greg McElroy to Nick Walker. After a second Parsons field goal for Western Carolina, Alabama scored touchdowns on a 1-yard Jimmy Johns run and a 25-yard Roy Upchurch run to make the final score 52-6. For his 134-yard, three touchdown performance, Terry Grant was named the SEC Freshman of the Week.[18]

Passing	C/ATT	YDS	AVG	TD	INT	QBR
JP Wilson	17/25	189	7.5	0	0	72.8
G. McElroy	8/9	73	8.1	1	0	91.5
Team	25/34	262	7.8	1	0	--

Rushing	CAR	YDS	AVG	TD	LONG
T. Grant	18	134	7.4	3	47
G. Coffee	9	76	8.4	1	20
R. Upchurch	6	55	9.2	1	25
J. Johns	8	31	3.9	1	12
JP Wilson	3	17	5.7	0	15
Team	44	313	7.1	6	47

Punting	NO	YDS	AVG	TB	IN 20	LONG
PJ Fitzgerald	1	40	40	0	0	40

Kicking	FG	PCT	LONG	XP	PTS
L. Tiffin	1/3	33.3	21	7/7	10

Receiving	REC	YDS	AVG	TD	LONG
DJ Hall	4	52	13	0	19
N. Walker	5	40	8	1	14
E. Alexander	4	40	10	0	13
G. Coffee	1	32	32	0	32
J. Johns	2	28	14	0	20
M. McCoy	2	25	12.5	0	13
T. Grant	2	13	6.5	0	9
N. Stover	1	10	10	0	10
T. McCall	1	8	8	0	8
D. Hanks	1	6	6	0	6
R. Upchurch	1	4	4	0	4
B. Huber	1	4	4	0	4
Team	25	262	10.5	1	32

Punt returns	NO	YDS	AVG	LONG	TD
J. Lowe	1	23	23	23	0
J. Arenas	2	13	6.5	8	0
Team	3	36	12	23	0

Note: Table data from "Alabama 52-6 Western Carolina (Sep 1, 2007) Box Score" (19)

11

09/08/07 - Alabama at Vanderbilt

Team	1	2	3	4	T		Passing	Rushing	Total
Alabama	10	6	0	8	**24**		150	222	**372**
Vanderbilt	3	0	0	7	**10**		175	57	**232**

For the 19th consecutive time, stretching back to the 1984 season, Alabama defeated the Vanderbilt Commodores to open conference play. In this contest, the Crimson Tide was victorious before a sold-out crowd of 39,773 at Vanderbilt Stadium 24-10 for Nick Saban's first conference victory as Alabama's head coach. After Javier Arenas returned the first punt of the game 69 yards to the 1-yard line, for the second week in a row Terry Grant scored a touchdown on Alabama's first offensive play with his 1-yard run. Leigh Tiffin hit a 20-yard field goal later in the quarter as did the Commodores' Bryant Hahnfeldt from 33 yards to make the score 10-3 at the end of the first. A pair of Tiffin field goals from 40 and 29 yards extended Bama's lead to 16-3 at the half.

After a scoreless third quarter, Grant scored his second touchdown of the afternoon on a 2-yard run early in the fourth quarter. With a successful two-point conversion pass from John Parker Wilson to Nick Walker, Alabama extended its lead to 24-3. Vanderbilt scored a late touchdown on a 15-yard Adams Mackenzi pass to George Smith to make the finals score 24-10. For his 173-yard, two touchdown performance, and for the second consecutive week, Terry Grant was named the SEC Freshman of the Week.[18]

Passing	C/ATT	YDS	AVG	TD	INT	QBR
JP Wilson	14/28	150	5.4	0	1	27.6

Rushing	CAR	YDS	AVG	TD	LONG
T. Grant	24	173	7.2	2	35
G. Coffee	11	48	4.4	0	12
JP Wilson	7	5	0.7	0	6
J. Johns	3	3	1	0	4
Team	2	-7	-3.5	0	0
Team	47	222	4.7	2	35

Interceptions	INT	YDS	TD
R. Johnson	1	0	0

Punting	NO	YDS	AVG	TB	IN 20	LONG
PJ Fitzgerald	5	208	41.6	0	0	5

Receiving	REC	YDS	AVG	TD	LONG
DJ Hall	3	67	22.3	0	30
T. Grant	3	26	8.7	0	17
G. Coffee	2	18	9	0	14
M. McCoy	3	15	5	0	9
J. Johns	1	13	13	0	13
N. Walker	2	11	5.5	0	6
Team	14	150	10.7	0	30

Kicking	FG	PCT	LONG	XP	PTS
L. Tiffin	3/5	60	40	1/1	10

Punt returns	NO	YDS	AVG	LONG	TD
J. Arenas	3	79	26.3	69	0
J. Lowe	1	0	0	0	0
Team	4	79	26.3	69	0

Note: Table data from "Alabama 24-10 Vanderbilt (Sep 8, 2007) Box Score" (20)

09/15/07 - Alabama vs Arkansas (16)

Team	1	2	3	4	T		Passing	Rushing	Total
Arkansas (16)	0	10	7	21	38		149	301	450
Alabama	21	0	10	10	41		327	123	450

In what was considered its first true test of the season, Alabama built an early 21-point lead but had to mount a come-from-behind drive in the final two minutes of the game in order to capture a 41-38 victory against the Arkansas Razorbacks. Bama took a 21-0 lead into the second quarter after a pair of D.J. Hall touchdown receptions of nine and 35 yards from John Parker Wilson and a 14-yard Glen Coffee run. The first touchdown by Hall was set up by an interception by Darren Mustin that gave the Tide the ball at their own 9-yard line. The other capped a 4-play, 80-yard drive in just 1:08. Coffee's score was in between those two, capping a 6-play, 74-yard drive that only took 1:39. The Razorbacks closed the gap to 21-10 at the half after Casey Dick threw a 40-yard touchdown pass to Crosby Tuck and Alex Tejada converted a 22-yard field goal (after grabbing an interception).

Alabama extended its lead to 31-10 in the third quarter after a 24-yard Leigh Tiffin field goal and a 2-yard Wilson touchdown pass to Nick Walker (set up by Javier Arenas' 38-yard punt return to the Arkansas 2-yard line). From this point, Arkansas scored four touchdowns to take a 38-31 lead late into the fourth quarter. Dick hit Andrew Davie for a 2-yard touchdown reception late in the third. In the fourth, Darren McFadden scored on runs of one and five yards on consecutive drives, and Peyton Hillis had a 7-yard touchdown reception to give the Razorbacks a 38-31 lead with 8:08 remaining in the game. Tiffin converted a 42-yard field goal with 4:20 remaining in the game, and then with only eight seconds remaining, Wilson hit Matt Caddell for a 4-yard, game-winning touchdown reception.

With his 172 yards receiving, D.J. Hall set a new Crimson Tide record for career receiving yardage previously held by Ozzie Newsome with 2,070 yards.[18]

Passing	C/ATT	YDS	AVG	TD	INT	QBR
JP Wilson	24/45	327	7.3	4	2	59.4

Rushing	CAR	YDS	AVG	TD	LONG
T. Grant	20	96	4.8	0	39
G. Coffee	7	34	4.9	1	14
J. Johns	2	1	0.5	0	3
JP Wilson	5	-8	-1.6	0	9
Team	34	123	3.6	1	39

Interceptions	INT	YDS	TD
D. Mustin	1	6	0

Punting	NO	YDS	AVG	TB	IN 20	LONG
PJ Fitzgerald	5	181	36.2	0	0	48

Receiving	REC	YDS	AVG	TD	LONG
DJ Hall	6	172	28.7	2	44
M. Caddell	9	91	10.1	1	19
M. McCoy	5	28	5.6	0	9
K. Brown	2	18	9	0	9
W. Oakley	1	16	16	0	16
N. Walker	1	2	2	1	2
Team	24	327	13.6	4	44

Kicking	FG	PCT	LONG	XP	PTS
L. Tiffin	2/3	66.7	42	4/4	10
A. Friedman	0/0	0	0	1/1	1
Team	2/3	66.7	51	5/5	11

Punt returns	NO	YDS	AVG	LONG	TD
J. Arenas	6	79	13.2	58	0

Note: Table data from "Alabama 41-38 Arkansas (Sep 15, 2007) Box Score" (21)

09/22/07 - Alabama (16) vs Georgia (22)

Team	1	2	3	4	OT	T		Passing	Rushing	Total
Georgia (22)	7	3	7	3	6	26		224	153	377
Alabama (16)	0	3	7	10	3	23		185	164	349

A week after upsetting Arkansas and entering both the AP and Coaches' Polls, Alabama was defeated in overtime by the Georgia Bulldogs 26-23. The Crimson Tide found themselves trailing 7-0 early in the first quarter after a 10-yard touchdown pass from Matthew Stafford to Thomas Brown. Brandon Coutu and Leigh Tiffin each added a field goal in the second quarter for their respective teams, and other than Alabama's incomplete pass on a 4th-and-1 play, both teams punted for the rest of the half, giving the Bulldogs a 10-3 lead.

In the third quarter, Alabama's John Parker Wilson scrambled for a 1-yard touchdown run, but the Bulldogs immediately answered on their next drive with a 6-yard rushing touchdown from Knowshon Moreno. Coutu connected on a 47-yard field goal as the Bulldogs extended their lead in the fourth quarter to 20-10. Alabama responded with 22-yard Tiffin field goal and a second rushing touchdown from Wilson. Wilson's 6-yard score with 1:09 left in the game capped a 10-play, 88-yard drive to force overtime.

On its first possession of overtime, Alabama failed to move the football and Leigh Tiffin connected on a 42-yard field goal. As for Georgia, Stafford connected on a 25-yard pass to Mikey Henderson on their first offensive play in overtime, and the Bulldogs left Tuscaloosa 26-23 overtime winners.[18]

Passing	C/ATT	YDS	AVG	TD	INT	QBR
JP Wilson	17/35	185	5.3	0	0	53.7

Rushing	CAR	YDS	AVG	TD	LONG
T. Grant	11	80	7.3	0	30
G. Coffee	16	62	3.9	0	13
R. Upchurch	2	19	9.5	0	10
JP Wilson	6	3	0.5	2	6
Team	35	164	4.7	2	30

Interceptions	INT	YDS	TD
R. Johnson	1	26	0
L. Mitchell	1	7	0
Team	2	33	0

Punting	NO	YDS	AVG	TB	IN 20	LONG
PJ Fitzgerald	7	270	38.6	0	0	46

Receiving	REC	YDS	AVG	TD	LONG
K. Brown	3	73	24.3	0	43
M. McCoy	6	47	7.8	0	14
DJ Hall	3	46	15.3	0	21
T. Grant	3	9	3	0	8
M. Caddell	1	5	5	0	5
N. Walker	1	5	5	0	5
Team	17	185	10.9	0	43

Punt returns	NO	YDS	AVG	LONG	TD
J. Arenas	3	9	3	9	0

Kicking	FG	PCT	LONG	XP	PTS
L. Tiffin	3/3	100	42	2/2	11

Note: Table data from "Georgia 26-23 Alabama (Sep 22, 2007) Box Score" (22)

09/29/07 - Alabama (22) at Florida State

Team	1	2	3	4	T		Passing	Rushing	Total
Alabama (22)	0	0	0	14	14		240	89	329
Florida State	0	0	7	14	21		266	82	348

In what was Alabama's first regular season game played at a neutral site since the Kickoff Classic in 1986, Alabama was defeated in the inaugural River City Showdown in Jacksonville, Florida by the Florida State Seminoles 21-14.

After a scoreless first half (12 total punts and one missed FSU field goal attempt from 46 yards), the Seminoles got on the board first in the third quarter. Florida State scored on its first play of the second half when Xavier Lee connected with De'Cody Fagg for a 7-yard touchdown reception. Alabama punted, Prince Hall intercepted Xaiver Lee, then two teams traded two more punts each. The Seminoles extended their lead to 14-0 early in the fourth quarter on a 5-yard Antone Smith touchdown run after they recorded a sack-fumble.

Alabama scored its first points of the evening late in the fourth quarter when John Parker Wilson threw a 7-yard touchdown pass to D.J. Hall to cut the Florida State lead to 14-7. This capped a long 13-play, 91-yard drive that took 3:53 off the clock. On the Seminoles' next offensive play, Lee threw a 70-yard touchdown pass to Fagg and extended their lead to 21-7. After the Tide turned the ball over on downs at the 50-yard line, they forced one last punt before cutting the lead after Wilson hit Keith Brown for a 17-yard touchdown reception. However, Alabama was unable to recover the onside kick on the ensuing kickoff and lost by the final score of 21-14.

The 85,412 fans at the game set the attendance record for Jacksonville Municipal Stadium, exceeding numbers of Super Bowl XXXIX or any of the annual Florida-Georgia rivalry games. It was the first time the teams had met since 1974, and it was the first meeting since Birmingham, Alabama native Bobby Bowden took over as head coach of the Seminoles.[18]

Passing	C/ATT	YDS	AVG	TD	INT	QBR
JP Wilson	28/53	240	4.5	2	0	40.4

Rushing	CAR	YDS	AVG	TD	LONG
T. Grant	9	36	4	0	13
G. Coffee	5	31	6.2	0	11
JP Wilson	10	21	2.1	0	18
R. Upchurch	3	1	0.3	0	3
Team	27	89	3.3	0	18

Interceptions	INT	YDS	TD
P. Hall	1	10	0

Punting	NO	YDS	AVG	TB	IN 20	LONG
PJ Fitzgerald	10	369	36.9	0	0	56

Receiving	REC	YDS	AVG	TD	LONG
DJ Hall	7	83	11.9	1	27
M. Caddell	5	41	8.2	0	25
T. Grant	3	38	12.7	0	27
K. Brown	3	34	11.3	1	17
G. Coffee	3	21	7	0	8
M. McCoy	3	12	4	0	8
N. Walker	2	11	5.5	0	8
R. Upchurch	2	0	0	0	1
Team	28	240	8.6	2	27

Punt returns	NO	YDS	AVG	LONG	TD
J. Arenas	2	0	0	0	0

Kicking	FG	PCT	LONG	XP	PTS
L. Tiffin	0/0	0	0	2/2	2

Note: Table data from "Florida State 21-14 Alabama (Sep 29, 2007) Box Score" (23)

10/06/07 - Alabama vs Houston

Team	1	2	3	4	T		Passing	Rushing	Total
Houston	0	7	3	14	24		261	143	404
Alabama	23	0	7	0	30		157	190	347

Coming on the heels of two consecutive losses, the Crimson Tide defeated the Houston Cougars on Homecoming in Tuscaloosa 30-24. After the first quarter, Alabama led Houston 23-0 after scoring a trio of touchdowns and a safety. John Parker Wilson scored the first touchdown of the afternoon on a 1-yard run to cap the opening 13-play, 80-yard drive. On the ensuing Cougar drive, Wallace Gilberry sacked Houston quarterback Blake Joseph for a safety and a 9-0 Alabama lead. The Crimson Tide then closed the first quarter with a pair of Wilson touchdown passes to take a 23-0 lead into the second quarter. The first came on a 23-yard pass to Nikita Stover (10-play, 66-yard drive) and the second on a 23-yard pass to Mike McCoy (6-play, 85-yard drive).

Holding Alabama scoreless in the second quarter, before halftime Houston managed to score its first touchdown on a 68-yard Joseph pass to Donnie Avery to make the halftime score 23-7. A 34-yard Houston field goal in the third quarter made the score 23-10 before Alabama scored its final touchdown on a 4-yard Glen Coffee run (capping a 6-play, 44-yard drive in two minutes) to make it 30-10. The game appeared over going into the fourth quarter, but Houston attempted a comeback by scoring two touchdowns to come within six points of the Tide. Houston scored a pair of touchdowns in the fourth on a 2-yard Case Keenum run and a 30-yard Keenum pass to Anthony Alridge to cut the score to 30-24. On the last play of the game, Houston almost scored another touchdown to win the game, but an interception in the end zone by Simeon Castille sealed the victory for Bama. For his 11-tackle, two sack performance, Wallace Gilberry was named SEC Defensive Line Player of the Week.[18]

Passing	C/ATT	YDS	AVG	TD	INT	QBR
JP Wilson	15/27	157	5.8	2	1	43.5

Rushing	CAR	YDS	AVG	TD	LONG
G. Coffee	30	121	4	1	9
R. Upchurch	6	32	5.3	0	22
JP Wilson	7	25	3.6	1	10
T. Grant	3	12	4	0	9
Team	46	190	4.1	2	22

Interceptions	INT	YDS	TD
R. Johnson	1	26	0
S. Castille	1	0	0
Team	2	26	0

Punting	NO	YDS	AVG	TB	IN 20	LONG
PJ Fitzgerald	7	280	40	0	0	46

Receiving	REC	YDS	AVG	TD	LONG
N. Walker	2	43	21.5	0	27
G. Coffee	6	30	5	0	8
M. McCoy	1	23	23	1	23
N. Stover	1	23	23	1	23
DJ Hall	3	19	6.3	0	10
M. Caddell	1	13	13	0	13
T. Grant	1	6	6	0	6
Team	15	157	10.5	2	27

Punt returns	NO	YDS	AVG	LONG	TD
J. Arenas	2	6	3	5	0

Kicking	FG	PCT	LONG	XP	PTS
L. Tiffin	0/0	0	0	4/4	4

Note: Table data from "Alabama 30-24 Houston (Oct 6, 2007) Box Score" (24)

16

10/13/07 - Alabama at Ole Miss

Team	1	2	3	4	T		Passing	Rushing	Total
Alabama	3	14	0	10	27		265	113	**378**
Ole Miss	7	3	14	0	24		284	136	**420**

In an unexpected offensive showcase, Alabama managed to defeat the Ole Miss Rebels 27-24 in Oxford. Both teams had very long drives in the first quarter, taking 11:23 off the clock collectively. Leigh Tiffin opened the scoring on the very first drive of the game with a 27-yard field goal to give the Crimson Tide a 3-0 lead, capping a 14-play, 61-yard drive in 6:35. The Rebels responded with an 8-yard Dexter McCluster touchdown reception from Seth Adams capping a 9-play, 80-yard drive in 4:48. Alabama was driving again when the first quarter came to a close with Ole Miss up 7-3.

In the second quarter, Alabama scored a pair of touchdowns with the first coming on a 2-yard Glen Coffee run and the second on a 1-yard John Parker Wilson run. Ole Miss added a 22-yard Joshua Shene field goal in between. Simeon Castille picked off a Seth Adams pass, Leigh Tiffin missed a 35-yard field goal, and Alabama was up 17-10 at the half.

Ole Miss took a 24-17 lead into the fourth quarter following a pair of touchdowns in the third. Adams scored on a 3-yard run then connected with Mike Hicks for a 17-yard touchdown reception in the quarter. The Crimson Tide then mounted a fourth quarter comeback. Terry Grant scored on a 3-yard run as the Tide took advantage of good field position due to a Javier Arenas 53-yard punt return to the Ole Miss 21-yard line. Leigh Tiffin kicked the game-winning field goal from 24 yards with 5:14 remaining in the game. Ole Miss attempted to score on their last drive to either force the game into overtime with a field goal or win with a touchdown. With a 4th-and-22 on Alabama's 45-yard line, Adams completed a pass to Shay Hodge at the 3-yard line. However, the call was reviewed and then reversed after Nick Saban called a timeout to give the officials more time to look at the replay. John Parker Wilson was 26-for-40 and threw an interception and no touchdowns. The defense was able to force three interceptions on the day.[18]

Passing	C/ATT	YDS	AVG	TD	INT	QBR
JP Wilson	26/40	265	6.6	0	1	60.1

Rushing	CAR	YDS	AVG	TD	LONG
T. Grant	16	62	3.9	1	22
G. Coffee	12	41	3.4	1	9
R. Upchurch	5	39	7.8	0	16
PJ Fitzgerald	1	-5	-5	0	0
JP Wilson	5	-23	-4.6	1	1
Team	1	-1	-1	0	0
Team	**40**	**113**	**2.8**	**3**	**22**

Interceptions	INT	YDS	TD
E. Knight	1	27	0
S. Castille	1	2	0
R. Johnson	1	0	0
Team	3	29	0

Punting	NO	YDS	AVG	TB	IN 20	LONG
PJ Fitzgerald	2	86	43	0	0	47

Receiving	REC	YDS	AVG	TD	LONG
DJ Hall	11	140	12.7	0	36
M. Caddell	7	49	7	0	10
G. Coffee	2	21	10.5	0	12
T. McCall	1	16	16	0	16
K. Brown	1	15	15	0	15
N. Stover	1	9	9	0	9
N. Walker	1	7	7	0	7
M. McCoy	1	6	6	0	6
R. Upchurch	1	2	2	0	2
Team	26	265	10.2	0	36

Punt returns	NO	YDS	AVG	LONG	TD
J. Arenas	2	71	35.5	54	0

Kicking	FG	PCT	LONG	XP	PTS
L. Tiffin	2/3	66.7	27	3/3	9

Note: Table data from "Alabama 27-24 Ole Miss (Oct 13, 2007) Box Score" (25)

17

10/20/07 - Alabama vs Tennessee (21)

Team	1	2	3	4	T		Passing	Rushing	Total
Tennessee (21)	7	10	0	0	17		258	103	361
Alabama	10	14	6	11	41		363	147	510

In its annual rivalry game, Alabama met the Tennessee Volunteers and was victorious 41-17 in Nick Saban's first "The Third Saturday in October" as head coach of Alabama. Saban elected to kick an onside kick on the opening kickoff that Alabama recovered. On the ensuing drive, Leigh Tiffin connected on a 39-yard field goal to give the Crimson Tide an early 3-0 lead. Bama extended its lead to 10-0 when John Parker Wilson connected with Terry Grant on a 3-yard touchdown pass after a 9-play, 84-yard drive including a nice 43-yard reception from D.J. Hall. The Volunteers scored their first points of the afternoon on the following drive on a 2-yard Arian Foster run to make the score 10-7 entering the second quarter.

Tennessee took a 14-10 lead early in the second quarter after Erik Ainge threw a 3-yard touchdown pass to Luke Stocker after Bama missed a 49-yard field goal attempt. Alabama took over after that. D.J. Hall had two second-quarter touchdown receptions on John Parker Wilson passes of 16 and two yards, capping drives of 86 and 75 yards, respectively. Daniel Lincoln then connected on a 45-yard field goal as time expired and Alabama led 24-17 at the half.

Tiffin added three more field goals in the second half to bring his total to four on the day, and Terry Grant capped a 10-play, 82-yard drive with an 8-yard touchdown run in the fourth to give Alabama the 41-17 victory after a successful two-point conversion. D.J. Hall and John Parker Wilson had career days for Alabama. Hall had 13 receptions for 185 yards and two touchdowns. Wilson was 32-of-46 for 363 yards and three touchdowns.[18]

Passing	C/ATT	YDS	AVG	TD	INT	QBR
JP Wilson	32/46	363	7.9	3	0	73.5

Rushing	CAR	YDS	AVG	TD	LONG
T. Grant	26	104	4	1	26
JP Wilson	6	28	4.7	0	7
R. Upchurch	6	15	2.5	0	4
Team	38	147	3.9	1	26

Interceptions	INT	YDS	TD
K. Jackson	2	29	0

Kicking	FG	PCT	LONG	XP	PTS
L. Tiffin	4/5	80	44	3/3	15

Punting	NO	YDS	AVG	TB	IN 20	LONG
PJ Fitzgerald	2	87	43.5	0	1	51

Receiving	REC	YDS	AVG	TD	LONG
DJ Hall	13	185	14.2	2	42
M. Caddell	4	58	14.5	0	22
T. Grant	6	31	5.2	1	12
N. Stover	2	24	12	0	19
R. Upchurch	1	22	22	0	22
T. McCall	3	21	7	0	14
M. McCoy	2	12	6	0	8
K. Brown	1	10	10	0	10
Team	32	363	11.3	3	42

Kick returns	NO	YDS	AVG	LONG	TD
J. Arenas	1	62	62	62	0
C. Rogers	1	14	14	14	0
M. Caddell	1	12	12	12	0
Team	3	88	29.3	62	0

Note: Table data from "Alabama 41-17 Tennessee (Oct 20, 2007) Box Score" (26)

11/03/07 - Alabama (17) vs LSU (3)

Team	1	2	3	4	T		Passing	Rushing	Total
LSU (3)	10	7	7	17	41		388	87	475
Alabama (17)	3	17	7	7	34		234	20	254

In the game dubbed "Saban Bowl I", in which Nick Saban's new Alabama team faced an LSU Tigers team that featured several players Saban himself had recruited during his tenure in Baton Rouge, the Tide found themselves in an SEC shootout, but lost 41-34. Alabama struck first with a 36-yard Leigh Tiffin field goal. However, the Tigers then scored 17 unanswered points. After Colt David connected on a 43-yard field goal to tie the game at 3-3, Matt Flynn connected with Early Doucet for a ten-yard touchdown reception and Jacob Hester scored from one yard out to give LSU a 17-3 lead early in the second quarter. Alabama responded with 17 points in the second quarter, and the Crimson Tide led 20-17 at halftime. The first score came on a 67-yard John Parker Wilson touchdown pass to D.J. Hall, the second on a 21-yard Tiffin field goal, and the third on a 29-yard Wilson touchdown pass to Keith Brown following an interception by Kareem Jackson.

The third quarter saw no scoring until the last two minutes. With 1:19 left, Keith Brown caught a 14-yard touchdown pass from Wilson to make the score 27-17. The Tigers quickly responded on their next drive when Flynn threw a 61-yard touchdown pass to Demetrius Byrd to bring the Tigers back to within three points of Bama. Then, with 11:21 left in the game, Colt David kicked a 49-yard field goal to tie it up at 27-27. The Crimson Tide took a 34-27 lead when Javier Arenas returned a punt for a 61-yard touchdown. With 2:49 left, LSU was able to tie the game again when Flynn threw a 32-yard touchdown pass to Doucet. It appeared the game might go into overtime until Wilson fumbled the ball and LSU recovered on the Alabama 4-yard line. Two plays later, Hester ran it in for the game-winning touchdown to make the score 41-34. The Tigers had 475 total yards compared to Alabama's 254. Alabama was able to stay in the game thanks to three interceptions the defense was able to force and 130 yards in penalties that LSU accumulated. John Parker Wilson was 14-of-40 with 234 yards, threw three touchdowns, was sacked seven times, and threw an interception.[18]

Passing	C/ATT	YDS	AVG	TD	INT	QBR
JP Wilson	14/40	234	5.9	3	1	33.7

Rushing	CAR	YDS	AVG	TD	LONG
J. Lowe	10	31	3.1	0	8
T. Grant	13	23	1.8	0	5
DJ Hall	1	0	0	0	0
JP Wilson	9	-34	-3.8	0	23
Team	33	20	0.6	0	23

Interceptions	INT	YDS	TD
K. Jackson	1	59	0
E. Knight	1	0	0
R. Johnson	1	0	0
Team	3	59	0

Punting	NO	YDS	AVG	TB	IN 20	LONG
PJ Fitzgerald	8	267	33.4	0	0	37

Receiving	REC	YDS	AVG	TD	LONG
DJ Hall	2	76	38	1	67
M. Caddell	3	55	18.3	0	32
K. Brown	2	43	21.5	2	29
T. Grant	3	29	9.7	0	15
N. Walker	2	25	12.5	0	15
M. McCoy	1	4	4	0	4
J. Lowe	1	2	2	0	2
Team	14	234	16.7	3	67

Punt returns	NO	YDS	AVG	LONG	TD
J. Arenas	3	69	23	61	1

Kicking	FG	PCT	LONG	XP	PTS
L. Tiffin	2/2	100	36	4/4	10

Note: Table data from "LSU 41-34 Alabama (Nov 3, 2007) Box Score" (27)

11/10/07 - Alabama (22) at Mississippi State

Team	1	2	3	4	T		Passing	Rushing	Total
Alabama (22)	6	3	0	3	12		121	153	274
Mississippi State	0	10	7	0	17		100	115	215

Coming a week after a tough loss to LSU, the Mississippi State Bulldogs defeated Alabama for the second consecutive season, this time by a score of 17-12. Alabama took a 9-0 lead halfway through the second quarter on Leigh Tiffin field goals of 39, 51 and 29 yards. With just over four minutes remaining in the half, Adam Carlson connected on a 35-yard field goal to cut the score to 9-3. The Bulldogs then took the lead as time expired in the first half after Anthony Johnson intercepted a John Parker Wilson pass and returned it 100 yards for a 10-9 lead.

In the third quarter, Mississippi State extended its lead to 17-9 after scoring the only offensive touchdown of the game. The score came on a 3-yard run by Anthony Dixon. Alabama scored its final points in the fourth on a 50-yard Tiffin field goal, his fourth of the afternoon.[18]

Passing	C/ATT	YDS	AVG	TD	INT	QBR
JP Wilson	16/34	121	3.6	0	2	25.3

Rushing	CAR	YDS	AVG	TD	LONG
T. Grant	19	75	3.9	0	17
J. Lowe	7	40	5.7	0	12
JP Wilson	9	37	4.1	0	15
R. Upchurch	2	1	0.5	0	1
Team	37	153	4.1	0	17

Receiving	REC	YDS	AVG	TD	LONG
M. Caddell	3	53	17.7	0	20
DJ Hall	5	46	9.2	0	15
K. Brown	2	12	6	0	7
M. McCoy	1	10	10	0	10
J. Lowe	1	5	5	0	5
T. Grant	3	0	0	0	4
N. Walker	1	-5	-5	0	0
Team	16	121	7.6	0	20

Interceptions	INT	YDS	TD
R. Johnson	1	8	0

Kicking	FG	PCT	LONG	XP	PTS
L. Tiffin	4/4	100	51	0/0	12

Punting	NO	YDS	AVG	TB	IN 20	LONG
PJ Fitzgerald	4	179	44.8	0	0	56

Note: Table data from "Mississippi State 17-12 Alabama (Nov 10, 2007) Box Score" (28)

20

11/17/07 - Alabama vs Louisiana Monroe

Team	1	2	3	4	T		Passing	Rushing	Total
Louisiana Monroe	0	14	7	0	21		161	121	**282**
Alabama	7	7	0	0	14		246	163	**409**

Coming off its second consecutive loss, Alabama suffered its worst loss of the season when the Louisiana Monroe Warhawks defeated the Crimson Tide 21-14 in Bryant-Denny Stadium. Alabama took an early 7-0 lead after a 17-yard Keith Brown touchdown reception from John Parker Wilson. The Warhawks tied the game at 7-7 on the first play of the second quarter when Calvin Dawson ran it in from one yard out. Both teams then traded touchdowns to tie the game at 14-14 at the half. Alabama scored on a 12-yard Terry Grant run and Louisiana Monroe scored on a 13-yard Frank Goodin run. The Warhawks scored what turned out to be the game-winning touchdown in the third quarter when Kinsmon Lancaster tossed an 11-yard score to Marty Humphrey to win the game for Louisiana Monroe 21-14.[18]

Nick Saban later told this story:

It was the most humiliating defeat, maybe of my entire coaching career. I think we had five guys suspended by the NCAA. We had three more suspended for disciplinary reasons. We played horrible in the game. I was almost ashamed of how we represented the university and the program. We fumbled the ball six times. So, we ended up getting beat in the game. Everybody's disappointed. Fans are disappointed. Coaches are disappointed. Players are disappointed. But when you're the coach, you have to win the locker room after the game and try to inspire the guys when they didn't perform very well. Then you have to go to the press conference and explain why you played so poorly. Then you have to go to the recruiting room and tell recruits that it's not really going to be this way in the future.

So, then, after all that, after all that humiliation, I get in my car to drive home, and I don't have any gas in the car. So, now I've got to stop at a self-serve, put some gas in the car, and I used to wear my LSU National Championship ring. So, I go to pay the guy, and the guy says, "Wow, what's that ring?" And I say, "That's a National Championship ring. And we're going to do the same thing here at Alabama." And the guy looks at me and says, "We'll never do it as long as that Nick Saban is coach." [597]

Passing	C/ATT	YDS	AVG	TD	INT	QBR
JP Wilson	21/31	246	7.9	1	2	43

Rushing	CAR	YDS	AVG	TD	LONG
T. Grant	21	96	4.6	1	15
J. Johns	4	34	8.5	0	22
J. Lowe	7	28	4	0	8
JP Wilson	3	5	1.7	0	4
Team	35	163	4.7	1	22

Kicking	FG	PCT	LONG	XP	PTS
L. Tiffin	0/1	0	0	2/2	2

Punting	NO	YDS	AVG	TB	IN 20	LONG
PJ Fitzgerald	3	110	36.7	0	0	43

Receiving	REC	YDS	AVG	TD	LONG
K. Brown	6	97	16.2	1	35
DJ Hall	3	32	10.7	0	18
M. Caddell	2	30	15	0	25
M. McCoy	3	25	8.3	0	16
T. Grant	2	24	12	0	13
P. Dial	1	21	21	0	21
J. Lowe	3	12	4	0	18
N. Stover	1	5	5	0	5
Team	21	246	11.7	1	35

Punt returns	NO	YDS	AVG	LONG	TD
J. Lowe	2	21	10.5	19	0
S. Castille	1	0	0	0	0
J. Arenas	2	-3	-1.5	0	0
Team	5	18	3.6	19	0

Note: Table data from "Louisiana Monroe 21-14 Alabama (Nov 17, 2007) Box Score" (29)

11/24/07 - Alabama at Auburn

Team	1	2	3	4	T		Passing	Rushing	Total
Alabama	0	7	0	3	**10**		113	112	**225**
Auburn	10	0	0	7	**17**		117	165	**282**

Coming off its third consecutive loss, Alabama lost in the Iron Bowl for the sixth consecutive time against the arch-rival Auburn Tigers 17-10 on "The Plains". Auburn took a 10-0 lead in the first quarter with Ben Tate scoring on a 3-yard touchdown run and Wes Byrum connecting on a 37-yard field goal while Alabama punted on its first two possessions. The Tide then cut the lead to 10-7 after a 2-yard John Parker Wilson touchdown run early in the second quarter, capping off an 11-play, 53-yard drive. After holding Auburn to a punt, Alabama missed a field goal from 44 yards. Both teams then traded interceptions (Rolando McClain for Bama and Jerraud Powers for Auburn) before halftime.

After a scoreless third quarter and seven consecutive punts, Brandon Cox extended the Tigers' lead to 17-7 on his 1-yard touchdown run with only 3:58 remaining in the game. Alabama was able to cut the lead to 17-10 after a 49-yard Leigh Tiffin field goal with 2:11 left in the game. However, the Crimson Tide was unable to recover the onside kick on the ensuing kickoff and Auburn was able to run out the clock to preserve the 17-10 victory.[18]

Passing	C/ATT	YDS	AVG	TD	INT	QBR
JP Wilson	12/26	113	4.3	0	1	51.6

Rushing	CAR	YDS	AVG	TD	LONG
G. Coffee	20	60	3	0	8
R. Upchurch	8	41	5.1	0	9
DJ Hall	1	7	7	0	7
JP Wilson	7	4	0.6	1	9
Team	36	112	3.1	1	9

Interceptions	INT	YDS	TD
R. McClain	1	23	0

Punting	NO	YDS	AVG	TB	IN 20	LONG
PJ Fitzgerald	6	218	36.3	0	0	48

Receiving	REC	YDS	AVG	TD	LONG
DJ Hall	3	29	9.7	0	13
N. Walker	2	27	13.5	0	19
N. Stover	2	25	12.5	0	18
K. Brown	1	19	19	0	19
G. Coffee	2	9	4.5	0	5
M. Caddell	1	4	4	0	4
T. McCall	1	0	0	0	0
Team	12	113	9.4	0	19

Punt returns	NO	YDS	AVG	LONG	TD
J. Lowe	2	7	3.5	7	0
M. Caddell	1	-4	-4	-4	0
Team	3	3	1.5	7	0

Kicking	FG	PCT	LONG	XP	PTS
L. Tiffin	1/2	50	49	1/1	4

Note: Table data from "Auburn 17-10 Alabama (Nov 24, 2007) Box Score" (30)

11/30/07 - Alabama at Colorado

Team	1	2	3	4	T		Passing	Rushing	Total
Alabama	20	7	0	3	**30**		256	132	**388**
Colorado	0	14	3	7	**24**		322	75	**397**

After a four-game slide to end a once promising season, Alabama defeated the Colorado Buffaloes in the 2007 Independence Bowl 30-24 to finish the season with an overall record of 7-6. Alabama scored on its opening drive on a 41-yard Leigh Tiffin field goal to lead 3-0. Colorado's first offensive play of the game resulted in an interception by Rolando McClain. Once again, Alabama relied on another field goal from Tiffin, this one from 24 yards out, to push its lead to 6-0. Later in the quarter, John Parker Wilson threw touchdown strikes of 15 yards to Keith Brown (6-play, 55-yard drive) and 34 yards to Matt Caddell (5-play, 63-yard drive) to extend the Crimson Tide lead to 20-0 after one quarter.

Early in the second quarter Wilson took the Tide 65 yards for a score in six plays, taking just 1:47 off the clock. He connected with Nikita Stover on a 31-yard touchdown pass, and the Crimson Tide lead 27-0. The Buffaloes controlled the majority of the second quarter after Wilson threw an interception to Ryan Walters with just under six minutes remaining in the half. Colorado cut the Alabama lead to 27-14 at the half on a pair of Cody Hawkins touchdown passes. The first was a 4-yard pass to Tyson DeVree and the second a 25-yard pass to Dusty Sprague.

The only score in the third quarter would come from Kevin Eberhart on a 39-yard Colorado field goal. Tiffin kicked a field goal as the Crimson Tide lead 30-17 with just over four minutes remaining in the game. Colorado responded on the following drive with a 14-yard Hawkins touchdown pass to DeVree to cut the Alabama lead to 30-24 with 3:51 remaining in the game. Alabama was able to run the clock down, and after receiving the 49-yard P.J. Fitzgerald punt, only one second remained in the game. On the final play of the game, Colorado attempted several lateral passes but would fall short of midfield. The 30-24 victory sent Alabama to a 7-6 overall record as they avoided a second consecutive losing season.[18]

Passing	C/ATT	YDS	AVG	TD	INT	QBR
JP Wilson	19/32	256	8	3	1	88.8

Rushing	CAR	YDS	AVG	TD	LONG
G. Coffee	19	72	3.8	0	15
R. Upchurch	12	34	2.8	0	9
JP Wilson	4	24	6	0	24
M. Caddell	1	12	12	0	12
N. Stover	1	-10	-10	0	0
Team	37	132	3.6	0	24

Kicking	FG	PCT	LONG	XP	PTS
L. Tiffin	3/3	100	41	3/3	12

Punting	NO	YDS	AVG	TB	IN 20	LONG
PJ Fitzgerald	4	180	45	0	0	51

Receiving	REC	YDS	AVG	TD	LONG
M. Caddell	4	76	19	1	34
DJ Hall	4	58	14.5	0	20
N. Walker	4	38	9.5	0	13
N. Stover	2	35	17.5	1	31
R. Upchurch	2	23	11.5	0	17
K. Brown	1	15	15	1	15
G. Coffee	2	11	5.5	0	7
Team	19	256	13.5	3	34

Interceptions	INT	YDS	TD
R. McClain	1	17	0
D. Mustin	1	0	0
Team	2	17	0

Note: Table data from "Alabama 30-24 Colorado (Dec 30, 2007) Box Score" (30)

Season Stats

Record	7-6	52nd of 120
SEC Record	4-4	
Points for	352	
Points against	286	
Points/game	27.1	65th of 120
Opp points/game	22	28th of 120
SOS[1]	4.4	21st of 120

Team stats (averages per game)

Split	G	Passing					Rushing				Total Offense		
		Cmp	Att	Pct	Yds	TD	Att	Yds	Avg	TD	Plays	Yds	Avg
Offense	13	20.2	36.3	55.7	224.5	1.5	37.7	149.2	4	1.5	74	373.8	5.1
Defense	13	17.8	32.9	54.2	221.3	1.5	36.2	124.2	3.4	1.1	69.1	345.5	5
Difference		2.4	3.4	1.5	3.2	0	1.5	25	0.6	0.4	4.9	28.3	0.1

Split	First Downs				Penalties		Turnovers		
	Pass	Rush	Pen	Tot	No.	Yds	Fum	Int	Tot
Offense	11.1	9.2	2.5	22.8	4.5	34.8	0.6	0.9	1.5
Defense	9.5	7.8	0.8	18.1	7.6	66.4	0.4	1.5	1.8
Difference	1.6	1.4	1.7	4.7	-3.1	-31.6	0.2	-0.6	-0.3

Passing

Rk	Player	G	Cmp	Att	Pct	Yds	Y/A	AY/A	TD	Int	Rate
1	John Parker Wilson	13	255	462	55.2	2846	6.2	5.8	18	12	114.6
2	Greg McElroy	2	8	9	88.9	73	8.1	10.3	1	0	193.7

Rushing and receiving

Rk	Player	G	Rushing				Receiving				Scrimmage			
			Att	Yds	Avg	TD	Rec	Yds	Avg	TD	Plays	Yds	Avg	TD
1	Terry Grant	11	180	891	5	8	26	176	6.8	1	206	1067	5.2	9
2	Glen Coffee	9	129	545	4.2	4	18	142	7.9	0	147	687	4.7	4
3	John Parker Wilson	13	81	104	1.3	5					81	104	1.3	5
4	Roy Upchurch	12	50	237	4.7	1	7	51	7.3	0	57	288	5.1	1
5	Jonathan Lowe	9	24	99	4.1	0	5	19	3.8	0	29	118	4.1	0
6	Jimmy Johns	12	17	69	4.1	1	3	41	13.7	0	20	110	5.5	1
7	D.J. Hall	13	2	7	3.5	0	67	1005	15	6	69	1012	14.7	6
8	Matt Caddell	13	1	12	12	0	40	475	11.9	2	41	487	11.9	2
9	P.J. Fitzgerald	13	1	-5	-5	0					1	-5	-5	0
10	Nikita Stover	10	1	-10	-10	0	10	131	13.1	2	11	121	11	2
11	Mike McCoy	12					28	207	7.4	1	28	207	7.4	1
12	Nick Walker	13					23	204	8.9	2	23	204	8.9	2
13	Keith Brown	12					22	336	15.3	5	22	336	15.3	5
14	Travis McCall	12					6	45	7.5	0	6	45	7.5	0
15	Earl Alexander	11					4	40	10	0	4	40	10	0
16	Preston Dial	9					1	21	21	0	1	21	21	0
17	Will Oakley	10					1	16	16	0	1	16	16	0
18	Darius Hanks	1					1	6	6	0	1	6	6	0
19	Baron Huber	13					1	4	4	0	1	4	4	0

Defense and fumbles

Rk	Player	G	Tackles					Def Int					Fumbles			
			Solo	Ast	Tot	Loss	Sk	Int	Yds	Avg	TD	PD	FR	Yds	TD	FF
1	Rashad Johnson	13	57	37	94	5.5	1	6	64	10.7	0					
2	Wallace Gilberry	13	47	33	80	27	10					2				2
3	Darren Mustin	12	51	28	79	8.5	1	2	6	3	0					
4	Rolando McClain	13	38	36	74	5	1	2	40	20	0					
5	Kareem Jackson	13	48	18	66	4	0	3	80	26.7	0					
6	Ezekial Knight	13	34	30	64	11	3	2	28	14	0					
7	Simeon Castille	13	40	23	63	6.5	1.5	2	0	0	0					
8	Prince Hall	11	29	29	58	0.5	0.5	1	10	10	0					
9	Marcus Carter	13	29	21	50	1.5	0					2				1
10	Lorenzo Washington	13	16	20	36	4.5	3									
11	Lionel Mitchell	12	24	9	33	1	0	1	7	7	0					
12	Keith Saunders	13	16	17	33	0	0					1				
13	Brandon Deaderick	13	10	12	22	3	2									
14	Ali Sharrief	13	17	4	21	1	0					1				
15	Bobby Greenwood	12	8	12	20	4.5	1									
16	Javier Arenas	12	13	7	20	2	0									
17	Demarcus Waldrop	11	9	4	13	0.5	0									1
18	Charlie Higgenbotham	10	8	4	12	0	0									
19	Brian Motley	9	3	8	11	2.5	0									
20	Chris Rogers	8	7	3	10	0	0									
21	Brandon Fanney	9	2	5	7	0	0									
22	Jimmy Johns	12	3	4	7	0	0									
23	Tyrone King	10	2	3	5	0	0					1				1
24	Marquis Johnson	8	3	1	4	0	0					1	1	1	0	0
25	Eryk Anders	9	4	0	4	0	0									
26	Earl Alexander	11	3	1	4	0	0									
27	Luther Davis	5	1	2	3	1	0									
28	Eric Gray	10	2	1	3	0	0									
29	Cory Reamer	12	2	0	2	0	0									
30	Chavis Williams	6	1	1	2	0	0									
31	Mike Johnson	13	2	0	2	0	0									
32	Matt Caddell	13	1	1	2	0	0									
33	Glen Coffee	9	1	1	2	0	0									
34	P.J. Fitzgerald	13	2	0	2	0	0									
35	John Parker Wilson	13	2	0	2	0	0									
36	Andre Smith	13	1	0	1	0	0									
37	Josh Chapman	1	1	0	1	0	0									
38	Alfred McCullough	1	0	1	1	0	0									
39	Forress Rayford	2	1	0	1	0	0									
40	Brian Selman	12	1	0	1	0	0									
41	Milton Talbert	4	0	1	1	0	0									
42	Terry Grant	11	1	0	1	0	0									
43	Baron Huber	13	1	0	1	0	0									
44	Travis McCall	12	1	0	1	0	0									
45	Mike McCoy	12	1	0	1	0	0									
46	Nikita Stover	10	1	0	1	0	0									
47	Roy Upchurch	12	1	0	1	0	0									

Kick and punt returns

Rk	Player	G	Kick Ret				Punt Ret			
			Ret	Yds	Avg	TD	Ret	Yds	Avg	TD
1	Javier Arenas	12	27	657	24.3	0	21	323	15.4	1
2	Jonathan Lowe	9	14	277	19.8	0	4	51	12.8	0
3	Matt Caddell	13	4	57	14.3	0	1	-4	-4	0
4	Travis McCall	12	1	11	11	0				
5	D.J. Hall	13	1	7	7	0				
6	Jimmy Johns	12	1	5	5	0				
7	Simeon Castille	13					1	0	0	0

Kicking and punting

Rk	Player	G	Kicking							Punting		
			XPM	XPA	XP%	FGM	FGA	FG%	Pts	Punts	Yds	Avg
1	Leigh Tiffin	13	36	36	100	25	34	73.5	111			
2	Andrew Friedman	1	1	1	100							
3	P.J. Fitzgerald	13								64	2475	38.7

Scoring

Rk	Player	G	Touchdowns								Kicking				
			Rush	Rec	Int	FR	PR	KR	Tot	XPM	FGM	2PM	Sfty	Pts
1	Leigh Tiffin	13								36	25			111
2	Terry Grant	11	8	1					9					54
3	D.J. Hall	13		6					6					36
4	John Parker Wilson	13	5						5			2		34
5	Keith Brown	12		5					5					30
6	Glen Coffee	9	4						4					24
7	Matt Caddell	13		2					2					12
8	Nick Walker	13		2					2					12
9	Nikita Stover	10		2					2					12
10	Javier Arenas	12					1		1					6
11	Jimmy Johns	12	1						1					6
12	Mike McCoy	12		1					1					6
13	Roy Upchurch	12	1						1					6
14	Andrew Friedman	1								1				1

Stats include bowl games
Note: Table data from "2007 Alabama Crimson Tide Stats" (1)

Awards and honors

Name	Award	Type
Terry Grant	Freshman All-SEC	SEC
Kareem Jackson	Freshman All-SEC	SEC
Rolando McClain	Freshman All-SEC	SEC
Simeon Castille	Coaches' All-SEC First Team	SEC
Wallace Gilberry	Coaches' All-SEC First Team	SEC
Rashad Johnson	Coaches' All-SEC First Team	SEC
Andre Smith	Coaches' All-SEC First Team	SEC
Antoine Caldwell	Coaches' All-SEC Second Team	SEC
D.J. Hall	Coaches' All-SEC Second Team	SEC
Rolando McClain	FWAA Freshman All-American Team	SEC
Simeon Castille	Senior Bowl	All-Star Team
Wallace Gilberry	Senior Bowl	All-Star Team
DJ Hall	Senior Bowl	All-Star Team

Note: Table data from "2007 Alabama Crimson Tide football team" (18)

2008

Overall

Record	12-2
SEC Record	8-1
Rank	6
Points for	422
Points against	200
Points/game	30.1
Opp points/game	14.3
SOS[2]	2.93

How much does this game mean to you? Because if it means something to you, you can't stand still. You understand? You play fast. You play strong. You go out there and dominate the guy you're playing against, and make his ass quit! That's our trademark! That's our M.O. as a team! That's what people know us as! -Nick Saban

Games

Date	Bama Rank		Opp Rank	Opponent	Bama	Opp	Result	SEC
08/30/08	24	N	9	Clemson	34	10	W	
09/06/08	13	vs		Tulane	20	6	W	
09/13/08	11	vs		Western Kentucky	41	7	W	
09/20/08	9	@		Arkansas	49	14	W	W
09/27/08	8	@	3	Georgia	41	30	W	W
10/04/08	2	vs		Kentucky	17	14	W	W
10/18/08	2	vs		Ole Miss	24	20	W	W
10/25/08	2	@		Tennessee	29	9	W	W
11/01/08	2	vs		Arkansas State	35	0	W	
11/08/08	1	@	16	LSU	27	21	W	W
11/15/08	1	vs		Mississippi State	32	7	W	W
11/29/08	1	vs		Auburn	36	0	W	W
12/06/08	1	N	4	Florida	20	31	L	L
01/02/09	4	N	6	Utah	17	31	L	

Coaches

Name	Position	Year
Nick Saban	Head Coach	2
Burton Burns	Associate Head Coach / Running Backs	2
Curt Cignetti	Wide Receivers / Recruiting Coordinator	2
Scott Cochran	Strength and Conditioning	2
Bo Davis	Defensive Line	2
Jim McElwain	Offensive Coordinator / Quarterbacks	1
Joe Pendry	Offensive Line	2
Freddie Roach	Assistant Strength and Conditioning	1
Kirby Smart	Defense Coordinator	2
Kevin Steele	Associate HC / Head Defensive Coach - Inside Linebackers	2
Lance Thompson	Outside Linebackers	2
Bobby Williams	Tight Ends / Special Teams	1

Recruits

Name	Pos	Scout	Rivals	247 Sports	ESPN Grade	Hometown	High school / college	Height	Weight	Committed
Mark Barron	ATH	5	4	4	80	Mobile, AL	St. Paul's Episcopal	6-2	210	8/24/07
Undra Billingsley	DE	3	3	3	74	Birmingham, AL	Woodlawn HS	6-3	265	3/24/07
Devonta Bolton	WR	4	4	4	80	Norcross, GA	Norcross HS	6-3	220	8/4/07
John Michael Boswell	OT	3	4	3	79	Northport, AL	Tuscaloosa County HS	6-6	300	4/21/07
Terrence Cody	DT	4	3	3	NR	Perkinston, MS	Mississippi Gulf Coast Community College	6-5	385	11/29/07
Marcell Dareus	DT	4	3	4	77	Birmingham, AL	Huffman HS	6-4	275	2/6/08
Robby Green	CB	4	4	4	80	River Ridge, LA	John Curtis Christian HS	6-0	170	12/11/07
Glenn Harbin	DE	3	4	3	77	Mobile, AL	McGill-Toolen Catholic HS	6-6	252	1/30/08
Jerrell Harris	OLB	4	4	4	81	Gadsden, AL	Gadsden City HS	6-3	215	2/6/08
Dont'a Hightower	DE	4	4	4	79	Lewisburg, TN	Marshall County HS	6-2	245	11/14/07
Destin Hood	WR	3	4	3	80	Mobile, AL	St. Paul's Episcopal	6-2	182	8/6/07
Mark Ingram II	RB	3	4	4	81	Flint, MI	Flint Southwestern Academy	5-10	202	2/5/08
Chris Jackson	ATH	4	3	4	80	McDonough, GA	Henry County HS	6-1	190	12/18/07
Star Jackson	QB	4	4	4	79	Lake Worth, FL	Lake Worth Community HS	6-3	205	9/4/07
Barrett Jones	OT	4	4	4	78	Cordova, TN	Evangelical Christian	6-5	270	11/6/07
Julio Jones	WR	5	5	5	95	Foley, AL	Foley HS	6-4	212	2/6/08
Chris Jordan	OLB	4	4	4	80	Brentwood, TN	Brentwood Academy	6-2	208	12/9/07
Alonzo Lawrence	CB	4	4	4	80	Lucedale, MS	George County HS	6-0	180	2/1/08
Robert Lester	S	3	4	3	80	Foley, AL	Foley HS	6-2	205	10/12/07
Brandon Lewis	DE	3	4	3	79	Pleasant Grove, AL	Pleasant Grove HS	6-3	260	3/5/07
Tyler Love	OT	5	5	5	83	Mountain Brook, AL	Mountain Brook HS	6-8	285	7/27/07
Ivan Matchett	RB	3	3	3	79	Mobile, AL	St. Paul's Episcopal	5-10	205	3/27/07
Kerry Murphy	DT	4	4	4	81	Chatham, VA	Hargrave Military Academy	6-4	300	1/13/06
Wesley Neighbors	S	3	2	3	78	Huntsville, AL	Huntsville HS	6-1	190	4/2/07
Jermaine Preyear	FB	3	3	3	77	Mobile, AL	W.P. Davidson HS	5-11	195	3/2/07
Melvin Ray	WR	4	4	4	80	Tallahassee, FL	North Florida Christian HS	6-3	202	7/28/07
B.J. Scott	ATH	4	5	5	84	Prichard, AL	Vigor HS	5-10	190	7/30/07
Brad Smelley	TE	2	3	3	77	Tuscaloosa, AL	American Christian Academy	6-3	215	5/6/07
Corey Smith	K	2	2	3	75	Bunker Hill, WV	Musselman HS	6-0	190	3/24/07
Damion Square	DE	4	3	4	79	Houston, TX	Yates HS	6-3	268	8/11/07
Courtney Upshaw	DE	4	4	4	83	Eufaula, AL	Eufaula HS	6-3	240	6/7/07
Michael Williams	DE	4	4	4	79	Reform, AL	Pickens County HS	6-6	270	2/16/07

	Scout	Rivals	247Sports
5 Stars	3	3	3
4 Stars	17	19	17
3 Stars	10	8	12
2 Stars	2	2	0

Note: Table data from "2008 Alabama Crimson Tide football team" (32)

Roster

Num	Player	Pos	Class	Height	Weight	Hometown	Last School
82	Earl Alexander	WR	SO	6-5	210	Phenix City, AL	Central
32	Eryk Anders	LB	JR	6-2	225	San Antonio, TX	Smithson Valley
28	Javier Arenas	DB	JR	5-9	193	Tampa, FL	Robinson
4	Mark Barron	DB	FR	6-2	215	Mobile, AL	St. Paul's
94	Undra Billingsley	DL	FR	6-3	275	Birmingham, AL	Woodlawn
67	John Michael Boswell	OL	FR	6-5	300	Northport,	Tuscaloosa County
46	Michael Brown	LB	FR	6-1	225	Glendale, AZ	
87	Drew Bullard	LB	FR	6-3	241	Florence, AL	Florence
59	Antoine Caldwell	OL	SR	6-3	292	Montgomery, AL	Lee HS
70	Evan Cardwell	OL	SO	6-2	278	Killen, AL	Brooks HS
99	Josh Chapman	DL	SO	6-1	300	Hoover, AL	Hoover HS
62	Terrence Cody	DL	SO	6-5	380	FortMyers,	Gulf Coast C.C.
38	Glen Coffee	RB	JR	6-2	197	Fort Walton Beach, FL	For Walton Beach HS
57	Marcell Dareus	DL	FR	6-3	280	Huffman, AL	Huffman
16	Thomas Darrah	QB	FR	6-5	190	Newnan, GA	Newnan
79	Drew Davis	OL	SO	6-7	276	Evergreen, AL	Sparta Academy
96	Luther Davis	DL	SO	6-4	275	West Monroe, AL	West Monroe
76	Marlon Davis	OL	SR	6-4	290	Columbus, GA	Carver HS
95	Brandon Deaderick	DL	JR	6-4	286	Elizabethtown, KY	Elizabethtown
60	Scott Deaton	OL	JR	6-6	286	Birmingham, AL	Oak Mountain HS
51	Michael DeJohn	LB	FR	6-0	220	Hoover, AL	Hoover
85	Preston Dial	TE	SO	6-3	223	Mobile, AL	UMS-Wright
13	Robert Ezell	QB	FR	5-9	163	Athens, AL	Athens
98	Brandon Fanney	DL	JR	6-4	241	Morristown, TN	Hargrave Military HS
18	Nick Fanuzzi	QB	SO	6-3	201	San Antonio, TX	Churchill HS
97	P.J. Fitzgerald	P	JR	5-11	194	Coral Springs, FL	Douglas HS
81	Andrew Friedman	K	JR	6-1	210	Fairhope, AL	UMS Wright
58	Nick Gentry	DL	SO	6-3	263	Prattville, AL	Prattville
11	Brandon Gibson	WR	FR	6-1	192	Mobile, AL	UMS-Wright
6	Demetrius Goode	RB	FR	5-10	197	LaGrange, GA	LaGrange HS / Hargrave Military Academy
29	Terry Grant	RB	SO	5-10	188	Lumberton, MS	Lumberton
33	Hampton Gray	DB	SO	6-1	188	Tuscaloosa, AL	Tuscaloosa County
23	Robby Green	DB	FR	6-0	180	NewOrleans,	John Curtis Christian
93	Bobby Greenwood	DL	SR	6-5	267	Prattville, AL	Prattville HS
34	Jeramie Griffin	RB	FR	6-0	225	Batesville, MS	South Panola
21	Prince Hall	LB	JR	5-11	235	Moreno Valley, CA	Moreno Valley HS
53	Daren Hallman	LB	FR	6-3	230	Lynn Haven, FL	A. C.rawford Mosley HS
15	Darius Hanks	WR	SO	6-0	190	Norcross, GA	Norcross
54	Glenn Harbin	DL	FR	6-6	245	Mobile, AL	McGill-Toolen
5	Jerrell Harris	LB	FR	6-3	215	Gadsden, AL	Gadsden City
42	Jennings Hester	LB	FR	6-2	224	Atlanta, GA	Marist School
45	Charlie Higgenbotham	LB	SO	6-1	211	Birmingham, AL	Mountain Brook HS
30	Dont'a Hightower	LB	FR	6-4	250	Lewisburg, TN	Marshall County
40	Baron Huber	RB	JR	6-3	242	Knoxville, TN	Powell
22	Mark Ingram II	RB	FR	5-10	215	Flint, MI	Southwestern Academy
19	Chris Jackson	WR	FR	6-1	190	McDonough, GA	Henry County HS
3	Kareem Jackson	DB	SO	5-11	185	Macon, GA	Fork Union Military
2	Star Jackson	QB	FR	6-3	195	Lake Worth, FL	Lake Worth
24	Marquis Johnson	DB	JR	5-11	186	Sarasota, FL	Booker
78	Mike Johnson	OL	JR	6-6	298	Pensacola, FL	Pine Forest
49	Rashad Johnson	DB	SR	6-0	187	Sulligent, AL	Sulligent HS
75	Barrett Jones	OL	FR	6-5	280	Memphis, TN	Evangelical Christian
8	Julio Jones	WR	FR	6-4	210	Foley, AL	Foley
36	Chris Jordan	RB	FR	6-2	220	Brentwood, TN	LSU
20	Tyrone King	DB	JR	5-11	204	Birmingham, AL	Grambling State
35	Charlie Kirschman	LB	SO	6-2	228	St. Augustine, FL	Nease HS
15	Alonzo Lawrence	DB	FR	6-1	190	Lucedale, MS	George County HS
56	Calvin Lee	LB	FR	6-2	215	Chapin, SC	Chapin HS
37	Robert Lester	DB	FR	6-2	210	Foley, AL	Foley
72	Tyler Love	OL	FR	6-7	290	Mountain Brook, AL	Mountain Brook
30	Jonathan Lowe	RB	JR	5-7	184	Phenix City, AL	Central
31	Ivan Matchett	RB	FR	5-10	215	Mobile, AL	St. Paul's
4	Marquis Maze	WR	FR	5-9	167	Tarrant, AL	Tarrant
83	Travis McCall	TE	SR	6-2	261	Prattville, AL	Prattville HS
25	Rolando McClain	LB	SO	6-4	255	Decatur, AL	Decatur
80	Mike McCoy	WR	JR	6-3	199	Rankin, MS	Northwest Rankin
52	Alfred McCullough	DL	SO	6-2	317	Athens, AL	Athens
12	Greg McElroy	QB	SO	6-3	218	Southlake, TX	Carroll
66	Brian Motley	DL	SO	6-2	280	Autaugaville, AL	Autaugaville HS
46	Wesley Neighbors	DB	FR	6-1	210	Huntsville, AL	Huntsville
7	Will Oakley	WR	SR	6-1	196	Ponte Vedra Beach, FL	Nease HS
10	Morgan Ogilvie	QB	FR	6-0	185	Mountain Brook, AL	Mountain Brook

29

Num	Player	Pos	Class	Height	Weight	Hometown	Last School
84	Colin Peek	TE	JR	6-6	241	Jacksonville, FL	Georgia Tech
39	Kyle Pennington	WR	FR	5-11	170	Chatom, AL	Washington County
68	Taylor Pharr	OL	SO	6-6	281	Irondale, AL	Shades Valley
57	Brad Pounds	DL	SR	6-3	280	Boaz, AL	Boaz HS
13	**Cory Reamer**	**LB**	**JR**	**6-4**	**223**	**Hoover, AL**	**Hoover**
8	Chris Rogers	DB	JR	6-0	192	Lakeland, FL	Evangel Christian
74	David Ross	OL	SO	6-4	297	Homewood, AL	Homewood
1	B.J. Scott	WR	FR	5-11	188	Prichard, AL	Vigor
86	Chris Scott	DB	SO	5-11	175	Birmingham, AL	Ramsey
50	Brian Selman	LS	JR	6-0	218	Vestavia Hills, AL	Vestavia Hills
26	Ali Sharrief	DB	JR	5-9	197	Stevenson, AL	North Jackson
48	Travis Sikes	WR	SO	6-2	194	Nashville, TN	Christ Presbyterian
17	Brad Smelley	TE	FR	6-3	218	Tuscaloosa, AL	American Christian
71	**Andre Smith**	**OL**	**JR**	**6-5**	**340**	**Birmingham, AL**	**Huffman**
44	Corey Smith	K	FR	6-0	195	Bunker Hill, WV	Musselman
45	Sam Snider	P	FR	5-10	163	Norcross, GA	Norcross
92	Damion Square	DL	FR	6-2	290	Houston, TX	Yates
9	**Nikita Stover**	**WR**	**SR**	**6-0**	**207**	**Hartselle, AL**	**Itawamba CC**
90	Milton Talbert	DL	SO	6-3	252	Hattiesburg, MS	Hattiesburg
98	Heath Thomas	P	JR	6-3	213	Montgomery, AL	Trinity
99	**Leigh Tiffin**	**K**	**JR**	**6-1**	**198**	**Muscle Shoals, AL**	**Muscle Shoals**
61	Carson Tinker	OL	FR	6-1	230	Murfreesboro, TN	Riverdale
87	**Chris Underwood**	**TE**	**FR**	**6-4**	**226**	**Birmingham, AL**	**Vestavia Hills**
5	Roy Upchurch	RB	JR	6-0	192	Tallahassee, FL	Godby
41	Courtney Upshaw	LB	FR	6-2	230	Eufaula, AL	Eufaula
73	William Vlachos	OL	SO	6-1	295	Birmingham, AL	Mountain Brook
43	A.J. Walker	WR	FR	6-1	185	Huntsville, AL	Huntsville
88	**Nick Walker**	**TE**	**SR**	**6-5**	**255**	**Brundidge, AL**	**Pike County HS**
97	**Lorenzo Washington**	**DL**	**JR**	**6-4**	**283**	**Loganville, GA**	**Hargrave Military**
91	Alex Watkins	LB	FR	6-3	218	Brownsville, TX	Haywood
55	**Chavis Williams**	**LB**	**SO**	**6-4**	**214**	**Dora, AL**	**Dora**
63	David Williams	OL	FR	6-3	272	Duncanville, AL	Hillcrest
89	Michael Williams	TE	FR	6-6	270	Reform, AL	Pickens County
14	**John Parker Wilson**	**QB**	**SR**	**6-2**	**213**	**Hoover, AL**	**Hoover HS**
27	**Justin Woodall**	**DB**	**JR**	**6-2**	**224**	**Oxford, MS**	**Lafayette HS**

Note: Starters in bold
Note: Table data from "2008 Alabama Crimson Tide Roster" (33)

30

Games

Chick-fil-A College Kickoff
Georgia Dome
Atlanta, GA

08/30/08 - Alabama (24) at Clemson (9)

Team	1	2	3	4	T		Passing	Rushing	Total
Alabama (24)	13	10	8	3	34		180	239	419
Clemson (9)	0	3	7	0	10		188	0	188

In January 2008, officials from both Clemson and Alabama announced they would open the 2008 season against each other in the inaugural Chick-fil-A College Kickoff at the Georgia Dome in Atlanta. With ESPN's College GameDay in town and Clemson, selected as the preseason favorite to win the Atlantic Coast Conference, the Crimson Tide upset the Tigers 34-10 to open the season.

After opening the scoring on a 54-yard Leigh Tiffin field goal, Cory Reamer forced a Jamie Harper fumble recovered by Dont'a Hightower at the Clemson 31. The ensuing drive resulted in a 21-yard Tiffin field goal and a 6-0 lead. After holding the Tigers to a three-and-out, the Tide reached the end zone for the first time on the evening on a 1-yard John Parker Wilson touchdown run to extend the lead to 13-0. After Mark Buchholz hit a 33-yard field goal early in the second quarter, Alabama extended its lead to 20-3 after Wilson hit Nick Walker for a 4-yard touchdown reception on the following 14-play, 83-yard drive. After a missed 52-yard Tiffin field goal, Marquis Johnson intercepted a Cullen Harper pass on the next Clemson possession to set up a 34-yard Tiffin field goal as time expired to give Alabama a 23-3 halftime lead.

Clemson opened the second half with C.J. Spiller returning the opening kickoff 96 yards for a touchdown to cut the lead to 23-10. Alabama responded later in the third quarter with a 4-yard Wilson touchdown pass to Julio Jones, extending the lead to 31-10 after the successful two-point conversion run by Mark Ingram II. Tiffin added the final points of the game on a 26-yard field goal to cap a 14-play, 78-yard drive in bringing the final score to 34-10.

James Davis and C.J. Spiller, the duo known as "Thunder and Lightning," combined for only 20 yards on the ground, while the team's rushing total was zero. Clemson's redshirt senior quarterback, Cullen Harper, completed 20-of-34 passes but had no touchdowns and one interception. Alabama's John Parker Wilson completed 22-of-30 passes with no interceptions.[32]

Passing	C/ATT	YDS	AVG	TD	INT	QBR
JP Wilson	22/30	180	6.0	2	0	90.3

Rushing	CAR	YDS	AVG	TD	LONG
M. Ingram II	17	96	5.6	0	28
G. Coffee	17	90	5.3	0	18
R. Upchurch	8	37	4.6	0	7
JP Wilson	4	19	4.8	1	15
T. Grant	4	-3	-0.8	0	2
Team	50	239	4.8	1	28

Receiving	REC	YDS	AVG	TD	LONG
N. Walker	7	67	9.6	1	21
M. McCoy	2	33	16.5	0	24
R. Upchurch	4	30	7.5	0	11
J. Jones	4	28	7	1	9
G. Coffee	1	9	9	0	9
T. McCall	1	8	8	0	8
M. Ingram II	2	5	2.5	0	4
B. Scott	1	0	0	0	0
Team	22	180	8.2	2	24

Interceptions	INT	YDS	TD
M. Johnson	1	7	0

Punt returns	NO	YDS	AVG	LONG	TD
J. Arenas	3	23	7.7	22	0

Punting	NO	YDS	AVG	TB	IN 20	LONG
PJ Fitzgerald	2	73	36.5	0	0	40

Kicking	FG	PCT	LONG	XP	PTS
L. Tiffin	4/5	80	54	2/2	14

Note: Table data from "Alabama 34-10 Clemson (Aug 30, 2008) Box Score" (34)

09/06/08 - Alabama (13) vs Tulane

Team	1	2	3	4	T		Passing	Rushing	Total
Tulane	0	3	0	3	6		232	86	318
Alabama (13)	13	0	7	0	20		73	99	172

Alabama's season home-opener saw the Crimson Tide defeat Tulane 20-6 in the 41st meeting between the two teams and the first since 1994. Alabama received the opening kickoff but went three-and-out on its first possession. After the Bama defense stopped Tulane on its opening possession, Javier Arenas ignited the crowd on an 87-yard punt return for a touchdown and a 7-0 lead. Later in the first quarter, Chris Rogers returned a blocked punt 17 yards for a touchdown, though freshman kicker Corey Smith missed the extra point, resulting in a 13-0 lead. Tulane scored the only points of the second quarter on a 35-yard Ross Thevenot field goal, bringing the halftime score to 13-3.

At the end of the third quarter, Mark Ingram II scored the lone offensive touchdown of the game on a 15-yard run, capping an 11-play, 77-yard drive. A 21-yard Thevenot field goal in the fourth quarter brought the game to its final 20-6 margin. For the game, Javier Arenas set a school record with 147 yards on punt returns, eclipsing the previous mark of 141 yards set by Harry Gilmer against Georgia in 1947. For his performance, Arenas was named the SEC Special Teams Player of the Week.[32]

Passing	C/ATT	YDS	AVG	TD	INT	QBR
JP Wilson	11/23	73	3.2	0	0	10

Rushing	CAR	YDS	AVG	TD	LONG
M. Ingram II	11	63	5.7	1	16
G. Coffee	9	55	6.1	0	21
JP Wilson	5	-18	-3.6	0	11
Team	1	-1	-1	0	0
Team	26	99	3.8	1	21

Kicking	FG	PCT	LONG	XP	PTS
L. Tiffin	0/0	0	0	2/2	2
C. Smith	0/1	0	0	0/1	0
Team	0/1	0	0	2/3	2

Punting	NO	YDS	AVG	TB	IN 20	LONG
PJ Fitzgerald	7	280	40	0	0	46

Receiving	REC	YDS	AVG	TD	LONG
M. Maze	4	22	5.5	0	12
N. Walker	1	15	15	0	15
J. Jones	1	13	13	0	13
T. Grant	1	9	9	0	9
R. Upchurch	1	7	7	0	7
M. Ingram II	1	7	7	0	7
T. McCall	1	3	3	0	3
G. Coffee	1	-3	-3	0	0
Team	11	73	6.6	0	15

Punt returns	NO	YDS	AVG	LONG	TD
J. Arenas	5	147	29.4	87	1
C. Rogers	1	17	17	17	1
R. Upchurch	1	6	6	6	0
J. Jones	1	1	1	1	0
Team	8	171	24.4	87	2

Note: Table data from "Alabama 20-6 Tulane (Sep 6, 2008) Box Score" (35)

09/13/08 - Alabama (11) vs Western Kentucky

Team	1	2	3	4	T		Passing	Rushing	Total
Western Kentucky	0	7	0	0	7		116	42	158
Alabama (11)	17	14	10	0	41		276	281	557

In week three, Alabama defeated the Western Kentucky Hilltoppers 41-7, who were playing their second season in the FBS. The Bama defense held the Hilltoppers' offense to a three-and-out on their first drive of the game. The Crimson Tide offense took over and completed a 12-play drive that ended with a 7-yard touchdown run by Mark Ingram II. WKU fumbled on the first play of its subsequent drive, and Alabama recovered the ball on the WKU 17-yard line, setting up a 22-yard field goal by Leigh Tiffin. Ingram II scored his second touchdown of the afternoon on a 5-yard run to give Alabama a 17-0 at the end of the first quarter. Alabama scored on its first possession of the second quarter on an 8-yard Terry Grant touchdown run to cap a 9-play, 78-yard drive. John Parker Wilson threw an interception on the first play of the next drive. This set up the Hilltoppers' lone score of the afternoon on a 30-yard touchdown reception by Tristan Jones from David Wolke. Alabama put one more touchdown on the scoreboard on a 2-yard Nick Walker reception from Wilson to take a 31-7 lead into halftime.

On the first drive of the second half, the Bama offense was held to a 25-yard Tiffin field goal, making the score 34-7. The defense held WKU to a three-and-out on its first possession of the second half. This set up a 7-play, 55-yard drive that ended with a 12-yard touchdown pass from Wilson to Julio Jones. Alabama benched most of its starters at the end of the third quarter, and neither team scored in the fourth quarter to make the final score 41-7.[32]

Passing	C/ATT	YDS	AVG	TD	INT	QBR
JP Wilson	17/27	215	8	2	1	72.3
G. McElroy	4/6	61	10.2	0	0	90.7
Team	21/33	276	8.4	2	1	--

Rushing	CAR	YDS	AVG	TD	LONG
G. Coffee	11	97	8.8	0	51
R. Upchurch	11	53	4.8	0	14
M. Ingram II	9	51	5.7	2	9
T. Grant	8	39	4.9	1	18
D. Goode	7	21	3	0	7
JP Wilson	3	20	6.7	0	20
Team	49	281	5.7	3	51

Interceptions	INT	YDS	TD
J. Woodall	1	1	0

Kicking	FG	PCT	LONG	XP	PTS
L. Tiffin	2/3	66.7	25	5/5	11

Receiving	REC	YDS	AVG	TD	LONG
J. Jones	5	66	13.2	1	36
E. Alexander	3	50	16.7	0	27
M. McCoy	3	42	14	0	22
M. Maze	2	25	12.5	0	23
T. Grant	1	22	22	0	22
N. Stover	1	18	18	0	18
D. Hanks	1	18	18	0	18
N. Walker	3	14	4.7	1	6
W. Oakley	1	13	13	0	13
P. Dial	1	8	8	0	8
Team	21	276	13.1	2	36

Punt returns	NO	YDS	AVG	LONG	TD
J. Arenas	2	38	19	19	0
J. Jones	1	10	10	10	0
M. Maze	1	5	5	5	0
Team	4	53	13.3	19	0

Note: Table data from "Alabama 41-7 Western Kentucky (Sep 13, 2008) Box Score" (36)

09/20/08 - Alabama (9) at Arkansas

Team	1	2	3	4	T		Passing	Rushing	Total
Alabama (9)	21	14	7	7	49		74	328	402
Arkansas	0	7	0	7	14		217	92	309

In what was Head Coach Bobby Petrino's first game against Alabama, the Crimson Tide was victorious by a final score of 49-14. The Tide received the opening kickoff and put together a 10-play, 71-yard drive with Mark Ingram II scoring on a 1-yard touchdown run. Arkansas was forced to punt on its first drive, and on the first play of the subsequent Alabama drive, Glen Coffee ran 87 yards for the Tide's second touchdown and a 14-0 lead. In the final minute of the first quarter, Javier Arenas intercepted a Casey Dick pass and returned it 63 yards for a touchdown to give Alabama a 21-0 lead at the end of the first quarter.

Arkansas started its next drive at its own 47-yard line after a 41-yard kickoff return by Dennis Johnson and drove 53 yards for a touchdown, scoring on 4th-and-1 from the Bama 12-yard line on a Dick pass to Andrew Davie. Bama responded with a 68-yard drive capped off by a 25-yard touchdown pass from John Parker Wilson to Julio Jones. Arkansas put together a steady drive on its next possession, but Justin Woodall intercepted Dick at the Bama 26-yard line and returned it 74 yards for a touchdown. Arkansas put together another solid drive, but facing a 1st-and-goal at the Bama 1-yard line, they were kept out by the stout Bama defense on a goal-line stand to close out the half with Bama up 35-7.

Arkansas received the second half kickoff, but Alabama's Marquis Johnson intercepted Dick's pass on the first play of the second half to set up a 31-yard touchdown run by Glen Coffee. By the end of the third quarter, both teams had put in their substitutes. On Alabama's first possession of the fourth quarter, backup quarterback Greg McElroy's pass was intercepted by Ramon Broadway, setting up a 10-yard touchdown pass by Arkansas second-string quarterback Tyler Wilson to Michael Smith. On the first play of Bama's next drive, Roy Upchurch ran 62 yards for Alabama's final touchdown to make the final score 49-14. The 49 points were the most points scored by Alabama in an SEC game since a 59-28 victory over Vanderbilt in 1990.[32]

Passing	C/ATT	YDS	AVG	TD	INT	QBR
JP Wilson	6/14	74	5.3	1	0	55.4
G. McElroy	0/1	0	0	0	1	0
Team	6/15	74	2.6	1	1	--

Receiving	REC	YDS	AVG	TD	LONG
E. Alexander	2	38	19	0	26
J. Jones	1	25	25	1	25
N. Walker	1	6	6	0	6
T. Grant	2	5	2.5	0	8
Team	6	74	12.3	1	26

Rushing	CAR	YDS	AVG	TD	LONG
G. Coffee	10	162	16.2	2	87
R. Upchurch	7	91	13	1	62
M. Ingram II	6	53	8.8	1	26
T. Grant	10	32	3.2	0	10
JP Wilson	2	-10	-5	0	2
Team	35	328	9.4	4	87

Punt returns	NO	YDS	AVG	LONG	TD
J. Arenas	3	16	5.3	14	0
M. Maze	1	3	3	3	0
M. Barron	1	1	1	1	0
Team	5	20	4	14	0

Kicking	FG	PCT	LONG	XP	PTS
L. Tiffin	0/0	0	0	7/7	7

Punting	NO	YDS	AVG	TB	IN 20	LONG
PJ Fitzgerald	5	226	45.2	0	0	56

Interceptions	INT	YDS	TD
J. Woodall	1	74	1
J. Arenas	1	63	1
C. Rogers	1	0	0
M. Johnson	1	0	0
Team	4	137	2

Note: Table data from "Alabama 49-14 Arkansas (Sep 20, 2008) Box Score" (37)

34

09/27/08 - Alabama (8) at Georgia (3)

Team	1	2	3	4	T		Passing	Rushing	Total
Alabama (8)	10	21	0	10	41		205	129	334
Georgia (3)	0	0	10	20	30		274	50	324

With ESPN's College Gameday in Athens and Georgia wearing black jerseys for only the third time in school history, the Crimson Tide upset the Bulldogs 41-30 in a game that will forever be known as "The Blackout". Alabama quickly took control of the game, moving the ball 73 yards before Mark Ingram II ran for a 7-yard touchdown to make the score 7-0. After the Bulldogs failed to move the ball on their first drive, the Tide again put points on the board as Leigh Tiffin kicked a 23-yard field goal with 4:51 left in the first quarter to give Alabama 10-0 lead.

After the Bulldogs' offense again failed to move the ball, Alabama began a drive at the Georgia 48-yard line. Two plays later, a 31-yard pass from John Parker Wilson to Julio Jones moved the ball inside the Georgia 5-yard line. Glen Coffee ran in from three yards for his third touchdown of the season, and Alabama led 17-0. On Georgia's next drive, quarterback Matthew Stafford completed a 16-yard pass to wide receiver A.J. Green, but he fumbled the ball and Dont'a Hightower recovered it for Alabama. After a short drive, Roy Upchurch scored Alabama's third rushing touchdown to extend its lead to 24-0. Before halftime, Wilson connected with Julio Jones for a 22-yard touchdown pass as Alabama led 31-0 at half.

In the second half, Georgia scored on its first drive when Blair Walsh kicked a 33-yard field goal. Alabama went three-and-out for the first time, forcing a P.J. Fitzgerald punt. Later in the third quarter, running back Knowshon Moreno ran for a 2-yard touchdown to cap a 58-yard drive and cut Alabama's lead to 31-10. Georgia made it a game again when Prince Miller returned a Fitzgerald punt for a 92-yard touchdown making the score 31-17. On the following drive, Alabama extended its lead to 34-17 on a 32-yard Leigh Tiffin field goal. On a crucial drive in the fourth quarter, Alabama converted when Glen Coffee gave Alabama a 41-17 lead by scoring his second rushing touchdown of the game on a 12-yard run. On the following drive, Georgia struck back when Matthew Stafford completed a 24-yard touchdown pass to Michael Moore, though failed in an attempted two-point conversion. Georgia got the ball back after a successful onside kick, starting its drive at the Alabama 40-yard line. A.J. Green caught a 21-yard touchdown pass from Stafford again for their final score of the game, as Alabama survived 41-30. With the victory, the Crimson Tide snapped a three-game losing streak to the Bulldogs dating back to the 1995 season. The 41 points were the most ever scored by the Tide against Georgia.[32]

Passing	C/ATT	YDS	AVG	TD	INT	QBR
JP Wilson	13/16	205	12.8	1	0	99.3

Rushing	CAR	YDS	AVG	TD	LONG
G. Coffee	23	86	3.7	2	15
R. Upchurch	6	18	3	1	4
M. Ingram II	7	17	2.4	1	8
JP Wilson	5	13	2.6	0	7
Team	4	-5	-1.3	0	0
Team	45	129	2.9	4	15

Punting	NO	YDS	AVG	TB	IN 20	LONG
PJ Fitzgerald	2	89	44.5	0	0	47

Receiving	REC	YDS	AVG	TD	LONG
J. Jones	5	94	18.8	1	31
R. Upchurch	2	51	25.5	0	29
M. McCoy	2	22	11	0	12
N. Stover	1	14	14	0	14
N. Walker	1	11	11	0	11
B. Scott	1	7	7	0	7
G. Coffee	1	6	6	0	6
Team	13	205	15.8	1	31

Punt returns	NO	YDS	AVG	LONG	TD
J. Arenas	2	27	13.5	17	0

Kicking	FG	PCT	LONG	XP	PTS
L. Tiffin	2/2	100	32	5/5	11

Note: Table data from "Alabama 41-30 Georgia (Sep 27, 2008) Box Score" (38)

10/04/08 - Alabama (2) vs Kentucky

Team	1	2	3	4	T	Passing	Rushing	Total
Kentucky	0	0	7	7	14	241	35	276
Alabama (2)	14	0	0	3	17	106	282	388

The Crimson Tide entered their game against the Kentucky Wildcats as the No. 2 ranked team in America, their highest ranking in fifteen years, and escaped with a 17-14 victory. After early stalled drives from each team, Alabama began its first successful drive with 12:25 left in the first quarter. Glen Coffee ran ahead for a short 3-yard gain, and on the next play, John Parker Wilson connected with Julio Jones for a 40-yard pass; however, the play was negated following a penalty. On the next play, Coffee rushed through the middle of the line for a 78-yard touchdown, his second longest and fifth rushing touchdown of the season. With under two minutes to go, Kentucky quarterback Mike Hartline fumbled while attempting a pass, and Alabama linebacker Rolando McClain recovered and returned it four yards for a touchdown. Leigh Tiffin missed the extra point, though after an offside penalty, he was given another attempt which he converted. After both offenses failed to score in the second quarter, Alabama took a 14-0 lead into the halftime break.

Halfway into the third quarter, Kentucky's offense finally got on the scoreboard when Hartline connected on a 26-yard touchdown pass to Dicky Lyons Jr. Once more, both offenses were unable to move the ball for rest of the third quarter. Early in the fourth quarter, Alabama began its second-to-last drive with 11:10 remaining, defending a 14-7 lead. The drive included 12 rushing attempts and a pass to Julio Jones as Alabama moved the ball 81 yards in just over eight minutes. After a delay of game penalty, Leigh Tiffin connected on the game-winning 24-yard field goal which gave Alabama a 17-7 lead. With 2:12 remaining, Hartline and the Kentucky offense again took the field. After a mix of successful and incomplete passes, Kentucky faced a 3rd-and-10 on the Crimson Tide 48-yard line. A 48-yard touchdown pass from Hartline to receiver DeMoreo Ford cut the Alabama lead to three. A failed onside kick attempt ended Kentucky's hope for a comeback, and Alabama escaped with a 17-14 victory.

Despite the lack of offensive points, Alabama running back Glen Coffee rushed for a season-high 218 yards on 25 attempts, including a touchdown and two fumbles. The 218 yards gained by Coffee was the most by an Alabama rusher since Shaun Alexander in 1996.[32]

Passing	C/ATT	YDS	AVG	TD	INT	QBR
JP Wilson	7/17	106	6.2	0	1	11.8

Rushing	CAR	YDS	AVG	TD	LONG
G. Coffee	25	218	8.7	1	78
M. Ingram II	11	66	6	0	36
R. Upchurch	5	19	3.8	0	8
M. Maze	1	1	1	0	1
JP Wilson	6	-20	-3.3	0	3
Team	1	-2	-2	0	0
Team	49	282	5.8	1	7

Receiving	REC	YDS	AVG	TD	LONG
J. Jones	3	52	17.3	0	23
N. Walker	2	30	15	0	24
G. Coffee	1	15	15	0	15
N. Stover	1	9	9	0	9
Team	7	106	15.1	0	24

Punt returns	NO	YDS	AVG	LONG	TD
J. Arenas	6	52	8.7	22	0
M. Johnson	1	0	0	0	0
Team	7	52	8.7	22	0

Interceptions	INT	YDS	TD
K. Jackson	1	5	0

Kicking	FG	PCT	LONG	XP	PTS
L. Tiffin	1/3	33.3	54	2/2	5

Punting	NO	YDS	AVG	TB	IN 20	LONG
PJ Fitzgerald	6	259	43.2	0	0	48

Note: Table data from "Alabama 17-14 Kentucky (Oct 4, 2008) Box Score" (39)

10/18/08 - Alabama (2) vs Ole Miss

Team	1	2	3	4	T		Passing	Rushing	Total
Ole Miss	3	0	7	10	**20**		201	158	**359**
Alabama (2)	7	17	0	0	**24**		189	107	**296**

Playing after its first bye week of the season, Alabama returned to the field and defeated its long-time rival Ole Miss Rebels 24-20. After several early failed drives in the opening quarter, Ole Miss became the first team to score on Alabama in the first quarter as well as the first to have a lead against Alabama in 2008 after a successful 25-yard Joshua Shene field goal. Alabama responded on its next drive going 73 yards in four plays ending with a 26-yard touchdown pass from John Parker Wilson to Marquis Maze to take a 7-3 lead to end the first quarter. Ole Miss had limited offense in the second quarter as the Tide defense held a shutout for the remainder of the half. The offense scored 17 points starting with a 2-yard run from Mark Ingram II on an 11-play, 60-yard drive. Two interceptions set up the next two scores, one by Justin Woodall and the other by Rashad Johnson. Leigh Tiffin kicked a 41-yard field goal, then Wilson threw a 30-yard touchdown pass to Mike McCoy to take a 24-3 at halftime.

However, the second half was different as the Crimson Tide failed to score for the remainder of the game. Ole Miss Head Coach Houston Nutt gambled on a 4th-and-goal with a fake field goal attempt as Rob Park passed to Jason Cook for a 9-yard touchdown. Several minutes into the fourth quarter, Ole Miss again cut Alabama's lead to 24-17 after Jevan Snead threw a 17-yard touchdown strike to Shay Hodge. Three minutes later, Shene hit a 35-yard field goal to cut Alabama's lead to 24-20. A stalled drive forced Alabama punter P.J. Fitzgerald to give the ball to the Rebels with 3:03 left. The Rebels moved the ball steadily down the field over the next two minutes, however they turned it over on downs after a failed 4th-and-5 on Alabama's 43-yard line. The victory pushed Alabama to 6-0, giving them bowl eligibility and was the team's fifth in a row over the Rebels.[32]

Passing	C/ATT	YDS	AVG	TD	INT	QBR
JP Wilson	15/23	189	8.2	1	0	62.4

Rushing	CAR	YDS	AVG	TD	LONG
M. Ingram II	17	73	4.3	1	19
G. Coffee	13	52	4	0	14
JP Wilson	2	-16	-8	0	0
Team	2	-2	-1	0	0
Team	**34**	**107**	**3.1**	**1**	**19**

Interceptions	INT	YDS	TD
R. Johnson	1	29	0
J. Woodall	1	12	0
Team	**2**	**41**	**0**

Punting	NO	YDS	AVG	TB	IN 20	LONG
PJ Fitzgerald	7	278	39.7	0	0	49

Receiving	REC	YDS	AVG	TD	LONG
N. Walker	5	65	13	0	40
J. Jones	3	63	21	0	40
M. McCoy	3	45	15	1	30
M. Maze	2	29	14.5	1	26
B. Smelley	1	16	16	0	16
G. Coffee	2	1	0.5	0	6
Team	**16**	**219**	**13.7**	**2**	**40**

Punt returns	NO	YDS	AVG	LONG	TD
J. Arenas	2	14	7	11	0

Kicking	FG	PCT	LONG	XP	PTS
L. Tiffin	1/1	100	41	3/3	6

Note: Table data from "Alabama 24-20 Ole Miss (Oct 18, 2008) Box Score" (40)

10/25/08 - Alabama (2) at Tennessee

Team	1	2	3	4	T		Passing	Rushing	Total
Alabama (2)	6	7	9	7	29		188	178	**366**
Tennessee	3	0	0	6	9		137	36	**173**

In its annual rivalry game, Alabama met its rival to the north in the Tennessee Volunteers and was victorious 29-9. Both teams traded field goals in the first quarter with Leigh Tiffin converting from 39 and 43 yards for Alabama and Daniel Lincoln converting one from 31 yards for Tennessee to give the Tide a 6-3 lead at the end the first quarter. In the second quarter, the Crimson Tide offense moved 66 yards down the field with Glen Coffee scoring on a 3-yard touchdown run. With 2:41 remaining in the first half, the Volunteers started their final drive of the half at their own 22-yard line. The Tennessee offense quickly moved the ball down the field with several key Nick Stephens completions. A 5-yard procedure penalty on the offense set up a 3rd-and-6 on Alabama's 19-yard line. Stephens completed a pass to Lucas Taylor; however, it did not count as Taylor was flagged for offensive pass interference. After failing to gain enough yardage on third down, the Volunteers again attempted a field goal, and after a timeout in attempt to "ice the kicker" by Nick Saban, Lincoln missed his second field goal of the game to give Alabama a 13-3 halftime lead.

The Tide quickly took control of the third quarter, forcing a three-and-out on Tennessee's first possession. Alabama responded with a 30-yard Tiffin field goal to extend its lead to 16-3. After another forced three-and-out, Alabama steadily moved the ball downfield 79 yards in 12 plays ending in a John Parker Wilson rush for a 1-yard touchdown. However, the two-point conversion was not successful, and Alabama led 22-3. Early in the fourth quarter, Roy Upchurch sealed the Alabama victory with a 4-yard touchdown run capping an 8-play, 80-yard drive. A Josh Briscoe touchdown reception from Stephens cut into the lead, but the Tide stopped the two-point conversion, giving them a 29-9 victory. It was the final game of the rivalry for Tennessee Head Coach Phillip Fulmer, who resigned ten days later.[32]

Passing	C/ATT	YDS	AVG	TD	INT	QBR
JP Wilson	17/24	188	7.8	0	0	83.3

Rushing	CAR	YDS	AVG	TD	LONG
R. Upchurch	14	86	6.1	1	19
G. Coffee	19	78	4.1	1	13
T. Grant	4	11	2.8	0	8
JP Wilson	2	2	1	1	1
M. Ingram II	4	1	0.3	0	2
Team	43	178	4.1	3	19

Kicking	FG	PCT	LONG	XP	PTS
L. Tiffin	3/3	100	43	2/2	11

Punting	NO	YDS	AVG	TB	IN 20	LONG
PJ Fitzgerald	2	94	47	0	0	48

Receiving	REC	YDS	AVG	TD	LONG
J. Jones	6	103	17.2	0	35
N. Walker	3	24	8	0	11
W. Oakley	1	14	14	0	14
M. McCoy	1	13	13	0	13
R. Upchurch	2	13	6.5	0	10
B. Smelley	1	8	8	0	8
N. Stover	1	6	6	0	6
G. Coffee	1	4	4	0	4
M. Maze	1	3	3	0	3
Team	17	188	11.1	0	35

Punt returns	NO	YDS	AVG	LONG	TD
J. Arenas	4	17	4.3	22	0

Note: Table data from "Alabama 29-9 Tennessee (Oct 25, 2008) Box Score" (41)

11/01/08 - Alabama (2) vs Arkansas State

Team	1	2	3	4	T		Passing	Rushing	Total
Arkansas State	0	0	0	0	**0**		67	91	**158**
Alabama (2)	7	7	14	7	**35**		152	205	**357**

Alabama faced the Arkansas State Red Wolves for only the second time in school history (the first being a 34-7 victory in the 1982 season) and was victorious 35-0. The Crimson Tide offense got on the scoreboard first after a stalled Red Wolves opening drive. After the Crimson Tide offense drove 89 yards in 16 plays in just under eight minutes, Glen Coffee ran for a 9-yard touchdown to give Alabama a 7-0 lead. Both offenses failed to move the ball far down field, resulting in several punts and a Wilson interception by Red Wolves defensive back Dominique Williams. Midway through the second quarter, Alabama safety Rashad Johnson intercepted a Corey Leonard pass and returned it for 32 yards and a touchdown to give the Tide a 14-0 at the half.

On Alabama's opening second half drive, Roy Upchurch ran for a 22-yard touchdown capping off a 4-play, 71-yard drive that took only 1:23 off the clock to give Alabama a 21-0 lead. Both offenses again stalled before Alabama's freshman running back Mark Ingram II ran for a 5-yard touchdown to extend the Crimson Tide lead to 28-0. Midway through the fourth quarter, Ingram II again scored on a 17-yard rush for the final score of the game. Ingram II finished the game with 12 carries for 113 yards, including two touchdowns, and for his performance was named the SEC Freshman of the Week. The following day, the Crimson Tide achieved their first regular season No. 1 ranking in the AP Poll since the 1980 season, and their first ever No. 1 BCS ranking.[32]

Passing	C/ATT	YDS	AVG	TD	INT	QBR
JP Wilson	15/28	152	5.4	0	1	37.8

Rushing	CAR	YDS	AVG	TD	LONG
M. Ingram II	12	113	9.4	2	30
G. Coffee	9	56	6.2	1	12
R. Upchurch	5	31	6.2	1	22
JP Wilson	8	7	0.9	0	8
T. Grant	2	-2	-1	0	1
Team	36	205	5.7	4	30

Interceptions	INT	YDS	TD
R. Johnson	1	32	0

Punting	NO	YDS	AVG	TB	IN 20	LONG
PJ Fitzgerald	3	121	40.3	0	0	45

Receiving	REC	YDS	AVG	TD	LONG
J. Jones	5	62	12.4	0	21
M. McCoy	3	26	8.7	0	15
M. Maze	1	24	24	0	24
B. Smelley	1	11	11	0	11
D. Hanks	1	10	10	0	10
G. Coffee	1	9	9	0	9
T. McCall	1	6	6	0	6
E. Alexander	1	2	2	0	2
M. Ingram II	1	2	2	0	2
Team	15	152	10.1	0	24

Punt returns	NO	YDS	AVG	LONG	TD
J. Arenas	6	27	6.8	13	0

Kicking	FG	PCT	LONG	XP	PTS
L. Tiffin	0/1	0	0	5/5	5

Note: Table data from "Alabama 35-0 Arkansas State (Nov 1, 2008) Box Score" (42)

11/08/08 - Alabama (1) at LSU (16)

Team	1	2	3	4	OT	T		Passing	Rushing	Total
Alabama (1)	7	7	7	0	6	27		215	138	**353**
LSU (16)	14	0	0	7	0	21		181	201	**382**

Nick Saban returned to Tiger Stadium for the first time since his tenure as the Miami Dolphins head coach. Alabama entered the game as the No. 1 ranked team in all major polls and defeated the LSU Tigers 27-21 in overtime. Alabama's offense quickly marched down to the LSU 26-yard line. John Parker Wilson passed to Earl Alexander who picked up 25 yards before fumbling out of the end zone, resulting in a touchback for the Tigers. On the first LSU possession, the Tigers ran three plays for a loss of seven yards before Alabama safety Rashad Johnson intercepted Jarrett Lee, returning it to the LSU 15. Glen Coffee moved the ball to the goal line before John Parker Wilson dove into the end zone two plays later for a 7-0 lead. The Tigers came back to tie the game on their next drive (Jarrett Lee's 30-yard TD pass to Demetrius Byrd). On the ensuing kickoff, Javier Arenas fumbled which was recovered by Josh Jasper at the Tide's 30-yard line. After a Lee incomplete pass, RB Charles Scott scored on a 30-yard rush (LSU up 14-7). After both teams punted, Rashad Johnson intercepted a pass and returned it for 54 yards and a touchdown to tie the score at 14-14 at the half.

Early in the third quarter, Alabama regained the lead 21-14 on a 3-yard Glen Coffee touchdown run capping a 7-play, 69-yard drive. Alabama punted on its next two possessions. Early in the fourth, LSU ran more than six minutes off the game clock. Charles Scott ran for his second touchdown of the game (tied 21-21). With 1:58 left in the game, Alabama received the ball on its own 41-yard line following a punt. Bama moved the ball to the LSU 11-yard line. With several seconds left on the clock, Alabama lined up for a game-winning, 29-yard field goal from Leigh Tiffin. Ricky Jean-Francois blocked it, sending the game into overtime.

On its first possession, LSU ran for a 5-yard gain. Richard Murphy rushed for a loss of one on the following play as Alabama linebacker Rolando McClain stopped him short of the line of scrimmage. On third down, Jarrett Lee threw his fourth interception of the game when Rashad Johnson again intercepted a pass. The Tide offense came out throwing as John Parker Wilson completed a 23-yard strike to Julio Jones, moving the ball to the 2-yard line of LSU. After a short rush by Glen Coffee, Wilson jumped over a pile of players to get his second rushing touchdown and preserve Alabama's unblemished record. With the win, the Crimson Tide clinched the SEC West Division and a spot in the 2008 SEC Championship Game.[32]

Passing	C/ATT	YDS	AVG	TD	INT	QBR
JP Wilson	15/31	215	6.9	0	1	67.7

Rushing	CAR	YDS	AVG	TD	LONG
G. Coffee	26	126	4.8	1	31
JP Wilson	5	7	1.4	2	6
M. Ingram II	5	6	1.2	0	2
Team	1	-1	-1	0	0
Team	37	138	3.7	3	31

Interceptions	INT	YDS	TD
R. Johnson	3	64	1
R. McClain	1	12	0
Team	4	76	1

Punting	NO	YDS	AVG	TB	IN 20	LONG
PJ Fitzgerald	7	295	42.1	0	0	53

Receiving	REC	YDS	AVG	TD	LONG
J. Jones	7	128	18.3	0	26
E. Alexander	1	26	26	0	26
G. Coffee	2	19	9.5	0	11
N. Walker	1	18	18	0	18
T. McCall	2	14	7	0	7
M. McCoy	2	10	5	0	6
Team	15	215	14.3	0	26

Punt returns	NO	YDS	AVG	LONG	TD
J. Arenas	5	23	4.6	23	0

Kicking	FG	PCT	LONG	XP	PTS
L. Tiffin	0/2	0	0	3/3	3

Note: Table data from "Alabama 27-21 LSU (Nov 8, 2008) Box Score" (43)

11/15/08 - Alabama (1) vs Mississippi State

Team	1	2	3	4	T		Passing	Rushing	Total
Mississippi State	0	7	0	0	**7**		132	35	**167**
Alabama (1)	5	7	10	10	**32**		166	198	**364**

A week after its overtime victory over LSU, Alabama returned home and defeated the Mississippi State Bulldogs 32-7. Alabama took an early 2-0 lead after a Blake McAdams punt was blocked by Kareem Jackson and recovered by State in the end zone for a safety on the Bulldogs' first offensive possession. After holding the Tide on the following series, State's Tyson Lee committed a fumble that was recovered by Brandon Fanney. The subsequent Alabama 9-play, 35-yard drive was capped with a 35-yard Leigh Tiffin field goal to give the Tide a 5-0 lead at the end of the first quarter.

After both teams punted, the Bulldogs responded early in the second quarter and took a 7-5 lead after Tyson Lee hit Jamayel Smith for a 31-yard touchdown reception capping a 7-play, 78-yard drive. Alabama punted, then Javier Arenas returned Mississippi State's punt 46 yards to the MSU 2-yard line. Alabama retook the lead 12-7 late in the second quarter and would not relinquish it again after a 1-yard John Parker Wilson touchdown run.

After holding the Bulldogs on their opening possession of the second half, the Tide extended its lead to 19-7 when Javier Arenas returned a punt 80 yards for a touchdown. Tiffin added a pair of field goals from 34 and 35 yards out respectively before Mark Ingram II scored the final points of the game on a 1-yard touchdown run late in the fourth quarter and made the final score 32-7. The 3-play drive included two big catches, one by Brad Smelley for 37 yards and the other on a 34-yard catch from Julio Jones. In the game, Javier Arenas broke both of Harry Gilmer's Alabama single game record for punt return yardage with 153 on six attempts, and the all-time record for punt return yardage in a career.[32]

Passing	C/ATT	YDS	AVG	TD	INT	QBR
JP Wilson	10/17	148	8.7	0	0	34.2
G. McElroy	2/2	18	9	0	0	99.9
Team	12/19	166	8.7	0	0	--

Rushing	CAR	YDS	AVG	TD	LONG
M. Ingram II	13	78	6	1	40
G. Coffee	17	71	4.2	0	12
J. Griffin	5	27	5.4	0	8
JP Wilson	11	19	1.7	1	11
D. Goode	2	3	1.5	0	2
Team	48	198	4.1	2	40

Kicking	FG	PCT	LONG	XP	PTS
L. Tiffin	3/3	100	35	3/3	12

Punting	NO	YDS	AVG	TB	IN 20	LONG
PJ Fitzgerald	5	215	43	0	0	46

Receiving	REC	YDS	AVG	TD	LONG
J. Jones	3	53	17.7	0	34
B. Smelley	2	46	23	0	37
D. Hanks	2	24	12	0	12
T. McCall	1	12	12	0	12
G. Coffee	1	11	11	0	11
J. Griffin	1	9	9	0	9
N. Walker	1	6	6	0	6
M. Ingram II	1	5	5	0	5
Team	12	166	13.8	0	37

Punt returns	NO	YDS	AVG	LONG	TD
J. Arenas	7	153	21.9	80	1
K. Jackson	1	8	8	8	0
Team	8	161	23	80	1

Note: Table data from "Alabama 32-7 Mississippi State (Nov 15, 2008) Box Score" (44)

11/29/08 - Alabama (1) vs Auburn

Team	1	2	3	4	T		Passing	Rushing	Total
Auburn	0	0	0	0	0		113	57	170
Alabama (1)	3	7	19	7	36		178	234	412

In the Iron Bowl, the Crimson Tide snapped a six-game losing streak against the Auburn Tigers with a 36-0 victory. Alabama took a 3-0 lead at the end of the first quarter when Leigh Tiffin connected on a 37-yard field goal following a 14-play, 77-yard drive. Glen Coffee extended the lead to 10-0 on a 41-yard touchdown run capping a 4-play, 65-yard drive. At the end of the second quarter, Auburn's Morgan Hull appeared to connect on a 39-yard field goal. However, Alabama's Nick Saban called a timeout just before the play to negate the field goal in an attempt to ice the kicker. On the re-kick, Bama's Bobby Greenwood blocked the field goal attempt to preserve a 10-0 Crimson Tide lead at the half. All five of Auburn's other first half possessions resulted in punts.

In the third quarter, Alabama scored 19 points on a trio of touchdowns. Two plays after punting, Alabama's Rolando McClain recovered a fumble setting up the Tide for the first score. It came in 12 seconds on the first play of the drive on a 39-yard Nikita Stover reception from John Parker Wilson, and after Tiffin's extra point was blocked by Mike McNeil, Bama led 16-0. Auburn fumbled again, and this time Terrence Cody scooped it up at the AU 44-yard line. Eight plays later, Mark Ingram II scored from a yard out (Alabama's two-point conversion attempt failed). Auburn punted on its next possession, then Mark Ingram II scored his third touchdown of the game from 14 yards out. Up 29-0 going into the fourth quarter, Alabama pulled most of its starters late in the game. As such, the final points of the evening came on a 34-yard touchdown pass from back-up quarterback Greg McElroy to Marquis Maze to make the final score 36-0.

The victory was Alabama's first win against the Tigers since 2001 and the first all-time victory over Auburn at Bryant-Denny Stadium.[32]

Passing	C/ATT	YDS	AVG	TD	INT	QBR
JP Wilson	8/16	134	8.4	1	0	76.9
G. McElroy	2/2	44	22	1	0	99.2
Team	10/18	178	9.9	2	0	--

Rushing	CAR	YDS	AVG	TD	LONG
G. Coffee	20	144	7.2	1	41
M. Ingram II	15	64	4.3	2	14
R. Upchurch	2	15	7.5	0	11
T. Grant	7	11	1.6	0	7
J. Griffin	1	2	2	0	2
JP Wilson	4	0	0	0	4
Team	1	-2	-2	0	0
Team	50	234	4.7	3	41

Punting	NO	YDS	AVG	TB	IN 20	LONG
PJ Fitzgerald	5	167	33.4	0	0	41

Receiving	REC	YDS	AVG	TD	LONG
N. Stover	1	39	39	1	39
J. Jones	3	36	12	0	15
M. Maze	1	34	34	1	34
M. Ingram II	1	27	27	0	27
D. Hanks	1	17	17	0	17
B. Smelley	1	10	10	0	10
T. McCall	1	9	9	0	9
N. Walker	1	6	6	0	6
Team	10	178	17.8	2	39

Punt returns	NO	YDS	AVG	LONG	TD
J. Arenas	4	20	5	14	0

Kicking	FG	PCT	LONG	XP	PTS
L. Tiffin	1/1	100	37	3/4	6

Note: Table data from "Alabama 36-0 Auburn (Nov 29, 2008) Box Score" (45)

12/06/08 - Alabama (1) at Florida (4)

Team	1	2	3	4	T	Passing	Rushing	Total
Alabama (1)	10	0	10	0	20	187	136	323
Florida (4)	7	10	0	14	31	216	142	358

In the 2008 edition of the SEC Championship Game, the Crimson Tide met the Florida Gators for the sixth time and lost 31-20. Florida took a 7-0 lead midway through the first quarter when Tim Tebow threw a 3-yard touchdown pass to Carl Moore. On the next possession, Alabama responded with a 2-play, 82-yard drive to tie the game at 7-7. The drive included a 64-yard pass play from John Parker Wilson to Julio Jones and an 18-yard touchdown run by Glen Coffee. Florida went three-and-out and punted 36 yards from its own 13-yard line, Javier Arenas returned it 19 yards, and after a 5-yard penalty, the Tide took over at the Florida 25-yard line. They were not able to get into the end zone, but they took a 10-7 lead late in the first quarter after Leigh Tiffin connected on a 30-yard field goal.

Florida was forced to punt after going three-and-out, and Alabama was stopped on fourth down at the Florida 31-yard line a couple of minutes into the second quarter. The Gators then drove 67 yards in eight plays when Jonathan Phillips connected on a 19-yard field goal. After forcing Alabama to go three-and-out, Tebow hit David Nelson for a 5-yard touchdown reception to take a 17-10 lead at the half after they held Alabama to another punt.

To start the third quarter, Alabama held Florida to another three-and-out before driving 91 yards in 15 plays. Bama tied the game at 17-17 after Mark Ingram II scored on a 2-yard touchdown run. Florida then drove 46 yards and missed a field goal while Alabama drove 65 yards and made theirs from 27 yards with eight seconds remaining in the third quarter to take a 20-17 lead.

The Gators responded with a pair of fourth-quarter touchdowns to secure a 31-20 victory. The first came on a 1-yard Jeffery Demps run and the second on a 5-yard Tebow pass to Riley Cooper. Alabama's last two possessions resulted in a punt and interception.[32]

Passing	C/ATT	YDS	AVG	TD	INT	QBR
JP Wilson	12/25	187	7.5	0	1	73

Rushing	CAR	YDS	AVG	TD	LONG
G. Coffee	21	112	5.3	1	18
M. Ingram II	8	21	2.6	1	9
JP Wilson	3	2	0.7	0	9
PJ Fitzgerald	1	1	1	0	1
Team	33	136	4.1	2	18

Punting	NO	YDS	AVG	TB	IN 20	LONG
PJ Fitzgerald	4	164	41	0	0	47

Receiving	REC	YDS	AVG	TD	LONG
J. Jones	5	124	24.8	0	64
N. Walker	3	37	12.3	0	17
D. Hanks	3	19	6.3	0	10
G. Coffee	1	7	7	0	7
Team	12	187	15.6	0	64

Punt returns	NO	YDS	AVG	LONG	TD
J. Arenas	3	20	6.7	20	0

Kicking	FG	PCT	LONG	XP	PTS
L. Tiffin	2/2	100	30	2/2	8

Note: Table data from "Florida 31-20 Alabama (Dec 6, 2008) Box Score" (46)

01/02/09 - Alabama (4) vs Utah (6)

Team	1	2	3	4	T		Passing	Rushing	Total
Utah (6)	21	0	7	3	31		336	13	349
Alabama (4)	0	10	7	0	17		177	31	208

After falling to the eventual national champion Florida Gators in the SEC Championship Game, the Crimson Tide was selected with an at-large bid to play in the 2009 Sugar Bowl against the Mountain West Conference champion Utah Utes. Before the game, Alabama's All-American left tackle Andre Smith was suspended.

Utah took a commanding 21-0 lead in the first quarter and did not relinquish it for the remainder of the game. Utah scored first on a 7-yard Brent Casteel reception from Brian Johnson, second on a 2-yard Matt Asiata run (after an interception thrown by John Parker Wilson), and third on an 18-yard Bradon Godfrey reception from Johnson. Alabama responded and cut the lead to 21-10 at the half after a 52-yard Leigh Tiffin field goal and a 73-yard Javier Arenas punt return for a touchdown (after missing a 47-yard field goal attempt).

After Dont'a Hightower sacked Brian Johnson causing a fumble that Bobby Greenwood recovered, the Crimson Tide brought the score to 21-17 early in the third when John Parker Wilson threw a 4-yard touchdown pass to Glen Coffee. However, Utah closed the game with ten unanswered points on a 28-yard David Reed touchdown reception from Johnson and a 28-yard Louie Sakoda field goal to secure its 31-17 victory. Alabama missed a 49-yard field goal in the third quarter, and its last two possessions in the fourth ended with a fumble (from a sack) and an interception.[32]

Passing	C/ATT	YDS	AVG	TD	INT	QBR
JP Wilson	18/30	177	5.9	1	2	48.4

Rushing	CAR	YDS	AVG	TD	LONG
G. Coffee	13	36	2.8	0	11
M.ngram II	8	26	3.3	0	13
JP Wilson	12	-31	-2.6	0	10
Team	33	31	0.9	0	13

Kicking	FG	PCT	LONG	XP	PTS
L. Tiffin	1/3	33.3	52	2/2	5

Punting	NO	YDS	AVG	TB	IN 20	LONG
PJ Fitzgerald	4	166	41.5	0	0	51

Receiving	REC	YDS	AVG	TD	LONG
J. Jones	7	77	11	0	30
G. Coffee	4	40	10	1	13
N. Walker	3	25	8.3	0	12
N. Stover	1	15	15	0	15
M. Ingram II	1	8	8	0	8
B. Smelley	1	7	7	0	7
E. Alexander	1	5	5	0	5
Team	18	177	9.8	1	30

Punt returns	NO	YDS	AVG	LONG	TD
J. Arenas	3	73	24.3	73	1

Note: Table data from "Utah 31-17 Alabama (Jan 2, 2009) Box Score" (47)

Season Stats

Record	12-2	6th of 120
SEC Record	8-1	
Rank	6	
Points for	422	
Points against	200	
Points/game	30.1	35th of 120
Opp points/game	14.3	7th of 120
SOS^2	2.93	34th of 120

Team stats (averages per game)

Split	G	Passing					Rushing				Total Offense		
		Cmp	Att	Pct	Yds	TD	Att	Yds	Avg	TD	Plays	Yds	Avg
Offense	14	13.9	23.9	58.4	171.1	0.8	40.6	184.6	4.6	2.3	64.4	355.8	5.5
Defense	14	17.6	33.4	52.7	189.4	1.3	27.9	74.1	2.7	0.4	61.3	263.5	4.3
Difference		-3.7	-9.5	5.7	-18.3	-0.5	12.7	110.5	1.9	1.9	3.1	92.3	1.2

Split	First Downs				Penalties		Turnovers		
	Pass	Rush	Pen	Tot	No.	Yds	Fum	Int	Tot
Offense	8	9.5	1.3	18.8	4.1	37.1	0.7	0.6	1.4
Defense	8.6	4.3	1.2	14.1	6.2	47.6	0.7	1.1	1.8
Difference	-0.6	5.2	0.1	4.7	-2.1	-10.5	0	-0.5	-0.4

Passing

Rk	Player	G	Passing								
			Cmp	Att	Pct	Yds	Y/A	AY/A	TD	Int	Rate
1	John Parker Wilson	14	187	323	57.9	2273	7	6.5	10	8	122.3
2	Greg McElroy	6	8	11	72.7	123	11.2	8.9	1	1	178.5

Rushing and receiving

Rk	Player	G	Rushing				Receiving				Scrimmage			
			Att	Yds	Avg	TD	Rec	Yds	Avg	TD	Plays	Yds	Avg	TD
1	Glen Coffee	14	233	1383	5.9	10	16	118	7.4	1	249	1501	6	11
2	Mark Ingram II	14	143	728	5.1	12	7	54	7.7	0	150	782	5.2	12
3	John Parker Wilson	14	72	-6	-0.1	5					72	-6	-0.1	5
4	Roy Upchurch	10	58	350	6	4	9	101	11.2	0	67	451	6.7	4
5	Terry Grant	13	35	88	2.5	1	4	36	9	0	39	124	3.2	1
6	Demetrius Goode	3	9	24	2.7	0					9	24	2.7	0
7	Jeramie Griffin	2	6	29	4.8	0	1	9	9	0	7	38	5.4	0
8	Marquis Maze	13	1	1	1	0	11	137	12.5	2	12	138	11.5	2
9	P.J. Fitzgerald	14	1	1	1	0					1	1	1	0
10	Julio Jones	14					58	924	15.9	4	58	924	15.9	4
11	Nick Walker	14					32	324	10.1	2	32	324	10.1	2
12	Mike McCoy	13					16	191	11.9	1	16	191	11.9	1
13	Earl Alexander	12					8	121	15.1	0	8	121	15.1	0
14	Darius Hanks	7					8	88	11	0	8	88	11	0
15	Brad Smelley	7					7	98	14	0	7	98	14	0
16	Travis McCall	14					7	52	7.4	0	7	52	7.4	0
17	Nikita Stover	13					6	101	16.8	1	6	101	16.8	1
18	Will Oakley	8					2	27	13.5	0	2	27	13.5	0
19	B.J. Scott	9					2	7	3.5	0	2	7	3.5	0
20	Preston Dial	12					1	8	8	0	1	8	8	0

Defense and fumbles

Rk	Player	G	Tackles					Def Int					Fumbles			
			Solo	Ast	Tot	Loss	Sk	Int	Yds	Avg	TD	PD	FR	Yds	TD	FF
1	Rolando McClain	14	48	47	95	12	3	1	12	12	0			4	1	
2	Rashad Johnson	14	60	29	89	5	1	5	125	25	2					
3	Brandon Fanney	14	26	40	66	9	1					1				
4	Dont'a Hightower	14	26	38	64	2.5	0						1	8	0	1
5	Javier Arenas	14	44	19	63	3.5	2	1	63	63	1					
6	Marquis Johnson	14	32	17	49	1	0	2	7	3.5	0					
7	Justin Woodall	14	33	14	47	1.5	0	4	99	24.8	1					
8	Kareem Jackson	14	28	16	44	1	0	1	5	5	0					
9	Bobby Greenwood	14	19	21	40	7	5					1	1	5	0	0
10	Brandon Deaderick	14	14	22	36	5.5	4									
11	Cory Reamer	14	16	19	35	6	1									1
12	Ali Sharrief	14	20	11	31	2.5	0					5				
13	Eryk Anders	14	14	10	24	4.5	2.5					1				2
14	Terrence Cody	12	7	17	24	4.5	0.5									1
15	Courtney Upshaw	13	12	10	22	3	0					2				
16	Prince Hall	11	7	10	17	2	0.5									1
17	Josh Chapman	10	9	7	16	4	0									
18	Mark Barron	13	9	7	16	1.5	1.5									
19	Tyrone King	13	11	4	15	0	0									2
20	Chris Rogers	13	10	3	13	0	0	1	-6	-6	0					
21	Lorenzo Washington	13	3	9	12	2.5	1									
22	Luther Davis	13	6	6	12	2.5	0									
23	Robby Green	11	4	2	6	0	0									
24	Chris Jackson	11	1	5	6	0	0									
25	Leigh Tiffin	14	3	3	6	0	0									
26	Marcell Dareus	8	1	3	4	0	0									
27	Charlie Higgenbotham	13	2	2	4	1	1									
28	P.J. Fitzgerald	14	2	2	4	0	0									
29	Chris Jordan	9	0	3	3	0	0									
30	Jerrell Harris	10	1	2	3	0	0									
31	Terry Grant	13	2	1	3	0	0									
32	Marquis Maze	13	1	2	3	0	0									
33	Roy Upchurch	10	0	3	3	0	0									
34	Milton Talbert	3	1	1	2	0	0									
35	Glen Coffee	14	1	1	2	0	0									
36	Julio Jones	14	2	0	2	0	0									
37	Travis McCall	14	2	0	2	0	0									
38	Chavis Williams	5	1	0	1	1	1									
39	Mike Johnson	14	1	0	1	0	0									
40	Nick Walker	14	1	0	1	0	0									

Kick and punt returns

Rk	Player	G	Kick Ret				Punt Ret			
			Ret	Yds	Avg	TD	Ret	Yds	Avg	TD
1	Javier Arenas	14	26	614	23.6	0	41	650	15.9	3
2	Mike McCoy	13	5	60	12	0				
3	Terry Grant	13	3	52	17.3	0				
4	Mark Ingram II	14	1	26	26	0				
5	Julio Jones	14	1	21	21	0	2	11	5.5	0
6	Marquis Maze	13	1	19	19	0	2	8	4	0
7	Baron Huber	14	1	15	15	0				
8	Travis McCall	14	1	9	9	0				
9	Kareem Jackson	14					1	8	8	0
10	Roy Upchurch	10					1	6	6	0
11	Mark Barron	13					1	1	1	0
12	Marquis Johnson	14					1	0	0	0

Kicking and punting

Rk	Player	G	Kicking							Punting		
			XPM	XPA	XP%	FGM	FGA	FG%	Pts	Punts	Yds	Avg
1	Leigh Tiffin	14	46	47	97.9	20	29	69	106			
2	Corey Smith	3	0	1	0	0	1	0	0			
3	P.J. Fitzgerald	14								59	2427	41.1

Scoring

Rk	Player	G	Touchdowns							Kicking				Pts
			Rush	Rec	Int	FR	PR	KR	Tot	XPM	FGM	2PM	Sfty	Pts
1	Leigh Tiffin	14								46	20			106
2	Mark Ingram II	14	12						12			1		74
3	Glen Coffee	14	10	1					11					66
4	John Parker Wilson	14	5						5					30
5	Javier Arenas	14			1		3		4					24
6	Julio Jones	14		4					4					24
7	Roy Upchurch	10	4						4					24
8	Marquis Maze	13		2					2					12
9	Nick Walker	14		2					2					12
10	Rashad Johnson	14			2				2					12
11	Justin Woodall	14			1				1					6
12	Mike McCoy	13		1					1					6
13	Nikita Stover	13		1					1					6
14	Rolando McClain	14				1			1					6
15	Terry Grant	13	1						1					6

Stats include bowl games
Note: Table data from "2008 Alabama Crimson Tide Stats" (2)

Awards and honors

Name	Award	Type
Antoine Caldwell	Permanent Team Captain	Team
Rashad Johnson	Permanent Team Captain	Team
John Parker Wilson	Permanent Team Captain	Team
Glen Coffee	MVP	Team
Andre Smith	Offensive Player of the Year	Team
John Parker Wilson	Offensive Player of the Year	Team
Rashad Johnson	Defensive Player of the Year	Team
Rolando McClain	Defensive Player of the Year	Team
Javier Arenas	Special Teams Player of the Year	Team
P.J. Fitzgerald	Special Teams Player of the Year	Team
Leigh Tiffin	Special Teams Player of the Year	Team
Nick Saban	Coach of the Year	SEC
Julio Jones	Freshman of the Year	SEC
Antoine Caldwell	AP All-SEC First Team	SEC
Terrence Cody	AP All-SEC First Team	SEC
Glen Coffee	AP All-SEC First Team	SEC
Rashad Johnson	AP All-SEC First Team	SEC
Rolando McClain	AP All-SEC First Team	SEC
Andre Smith	AP All-SEC First Team	SEC
Javier Arenas	AP All-SEC Second Team	SEC
Mike Johnson	AP All-SEC Second Team	SEC
Julio Jones	AP All-SEC Second Team	SEC
Antoine Caldwell	Coaches' All-SEC First Team	SEC
Terrence Cody	Coaches' All-SEC First Team	SEC
Rashad Johnson	Coaches' All-SEC First Team	SEC
Rolando McClain	Coaches' All-SEC First Team	SEC
Andre Smith	Coaches' All-SEC First Team	SEC
Javier Arenas	Coaches' All-SEC Second Team	SEC
Glen Coffee	Coaches' All-SEC Second Team	SEC
Mike Johnson	Coaches' All-SEC Second Team	SEC
Julio Jones	Coaches' All-SEC Second Team	SEC
John Michael Boswell	Freshman All-SEC	SEC
Don't'a Hightower	Freshman All-SEC	SEC
Mark Ingram II	Freshman All-SEC	SEC
Julio Jones	Freshman All-SEC	SEC
Antoine Caldwell	AFCA All-America Team	National
Terrence Cody	AFCA All-America Team	National
Rashad Johnson	AFCA All-America Team	National
Andre Smith	AFCA All-America Team	National

Name	Award	Type
Rashad Johnson	All-America Second Team	National
Rolando McClain	All-America Third Team	National
Antoine Caldwell	AP All-America First Team	National
Terrence Cody	AP All-America First Team	National
Andre Smith	AP All-America First Team	National
Nick Saban	AP Coach of the Year	National
Nick Saban	Eddie Robinson Coach of the Year	National
Nick Saban	Home Depot Coach of the Year	National
Nick Saban	Liberty Mutual Coach of the Year	National
Antoine Caldwell	Consensus All-American	National
Terrence Cody	Consensus All-American	National
Andre Smith	Consensus All-American	National
Andre Smith	Lombardi Award Finalist	National
Andre Smith	Outland Trophy	National
Antoine Caldwell	Rimington Trophy Finalist	National
Nick Saban	Sporting News College Football Coach of the Year	National
Andre Smith	Unanimous All-American	National
Andre Smith	Walter Camp All-America First Team	National
Nick Saban	Walter Camp Coach of the Year	National
Javier Arenas	Senior Bowl	All-Star Team
Terrence Cody	Senior Bowl	All-Star Team
Mike Johnson	Senior Bowl	All-Star Team
Colin Peek	Senior Bowl	All-Star Team
Leigh Tiffin	Senior Bowl	All-Star Team

NFL

Season	Year drafted	Round	Pick	Overall	Player	Position	Team
2008	2009	1	6	6	Andre Smith	OT	Cincinnati Bengals
2008	2009	3	10	74	Glen Coffee	RB	San Francisco 49ers
2008	2009	3	13	77	Antoine Caldwell	C	Houston Texans
2008	2009	3	31	95	Rashad Johnson	CB	Arizona Cardinals

Note: Table data from "2008 Alabama Crimson Tide football team" (32)

2009

Overall

Record	14-0
SEC Record	9-0
Rank	1
Points for	449
Points against	164
Points/game	32.1
Opp points/game	11.7
SOS[3]	6.62

I want everybody here to know, this is not the end. This is the beginning. -Nick Saban

Games

Date	Bama Rank		Opp Rank	Opponent	Bama	Opp	Result	SEC
09/05/09	5	N	7	Virginia Tech	34	24	W	
09/12/09	4	vs		Florida Intl	40	14	W	
09/19/09	4	vs		North Texas	53	7	W	
09/26/09	3	vs		Arkansas	35	7	W	W
10/03/09	3	@		Kentucky	38	20	W	W
10/10/09	3	@	20	Ole Miss	22	3	W	W
10/17/09	2	vs	22	South Carolina	20	6	W	W
10/24/09	2	vs		Tennessee	12	10	W	W
11/07/09	3	vs	9	LSU	24	15	W	W
11/14/09	2	@		Mississippi State	31	3	W	W
11/21/09	2	vs		Chattanooga	45	0	W	
11/27/09	2	@		Auburn	26	21	W	W
12/05/09	2	N	1	Florida	32	13	W	W
01/07/10	1	N	2	Texas	37	21	W	

Coaches

Name	Position	Year
Nick Saban	Head Coach	3
Burton Burns	Associate Head Coach / Running Backs	3
Curt Cignetti	Receivers / Recruiting Coordinator	3
Scott Cochran	Strength and Conditioning	3
Bo Davis	Defensive Line	3
Jim McElwain	Offensive Coordinator / Quarterbacks	2
Joe Pendry	Offensive Line	3
Freddie Roach	Asst. Strength and Conditioning	2
Kirby Smart	Defensive Coordinator	3
Sal Sunseri	Assistant Head Coach / Linebackers	1
Bobby Williams	Tight Ends / Special Teams	2
James Willis	Associate Head Coach / Outside Linebackers	1

Recruits

Name	Pos	Pos Rank	Scout	Rivals	247 Sports	ESPN Grade	Hometown	High school / college	Height	Weight	Committed
Jonathan Atchison	OLB	14	3	3	3	80	Atlanta, GA	Douglass HS	6-3	216	12/5/08
Kenny Bell	WR	49	4	4	4	78	Rayville, LA	Rayville HS	6-1	160	2/4/09
Chris Bonds	DT	10	3	3	3	80	Columbia, SC	Richland Northeast HS	6-2	262	11/24/08
Michael Bowman	WR	119	4	4	4	75	Rossville, GA	Ridgeland HS	6-4	206	9/13/08
James Carpenter	OT		4	4	4	NR	Coffeyville, KS	Coffeyville Community College	6-5	205	11/29/08
Quinton Dial	DT	28	3	4	3	79	Pinson, AL	Clay-Chalkville HS	6-5	308	6/9/08
D.J. Fluker	OT	1	4	5	5	86	Foley, AL	Foley HS	6-7	350	11/7/07
Nico Johnson	ILB	2	5	5	5	84	Andalusia, AL	Andalusia HS	6-3	226	9/3/08
Phelon Jones	CB			4	4		Mobile, AL	LSU	5-11	200	12/10/06
Kendall Kelly	WR	7	4	4	4	82	Gadsden, AL	Gadsden City HS	6-4	210	2/4/09
Dre Kirkpatrick	CB	1	5	5	5	92	Gadsden, AL	Gadsden City HS	6-2	180	2/4/09
Eddie Lacy	RB	17	4	4	4	81	Geismar, LA	Dutchtown HS	5-11	210	2/4/09
Mike Marrow	FB	2	3	3	3	80	Toledo, OH	Central Catholic HS	6-2	240	6/20/08
A.J. McCarron	QB	4	4	4	4	83	Mobile, AL	St. Paul's Episcopal HS	6-4	189	5/3/08
Darius McKeller	OT	30	3	3	3	78	Jonesboro, GA	Jonesboro HS	6-6	280	4/23/08
William Ming	DE	19	4	4	4	80	Athens, AL	Athens HS	6-4	265	7/22/08
Brandon Moore	DT	30	4	4	4	79	Montgomery, AL	George Washington Carver HS	6-4	313	2/4/09
Kerry Murphy	DT			4	4	81	Hoover, AL	Hoover HS	6-6	315	9/21/07
Kevin Norwood	WR	66	3	4	3	77	D'Iberville, MS	D'Iberville HS	6-3	180	12/16/08
Anthony Orr	DE	82	3	3	3	76	Harvest, AL	Sparkman HS	6-4	260	7/29/08
Tana Patrick	OLB	9	4	4	4	81	Stevenson, AL	North Jackson HS	6-3	215	2/4/09
Jermaine Preyear	FB	20		3	3	77	Mobile, AL	Davidson HS	5-11	205	
Trent Richardson	RB	1	5	5	5	91	Pensacola, FL	Escambia HS	5-11	210	2/4/09
Darrington Sentimore	DT	20	4	4	4	79	Destrehan, LA	Destrehan HS	6-3	265	10/5/08
Petey Smith	ILB	5	3	3	4	81	Seffner, FL	Armwood HS	6-0	230	1/28/09
Anthony Steen	DT	39	3	3	3	78	Clarksdale, MS	Lee Academy	6-4	297	7/29/08
Ed Stinson	DE	22	3	4	3	80	Homestead, FL	South Dade HS	6-4	227	1/30/09
Chance Warmack	OG	16	3	3	3	79	Atlanta, GA	Westlake HS	6-2	329	5/23/08
Kellen Williams	OT	79	3	3	3	75	Snellville, GA	Brookwood HS	6-3	295	4/27/08

	Scout	Rivals	247Sports
5 Stars	3	4	4
4 Stars	11	15	13
3 Stars	12	10	12
2 Stars	0	0	0

Note: Table data from "2009 Alabama Crimson Tide football team." (48)

Roster

Num	Player	Pos	Class	Height	Weight	Hometown	Last School
82	Earl Alexander	WR	JR	6-4	216	Phenix City, AL	Central
32	Eryk Anders	LB	SR	6-2	227	San Antonio, TX	Smithson Valley
28	Javier Arenas	DB	SR	5-9	198	Tampa, FL	Robinson
49	Jonathan Atchison	LB	FR	6-2	235	Atlanta, GA	Douglass
4	Mark Barron	DB	SO	6-2	215	Mobile, AL	St. Paul's
7	Kenny Bell	WR	FR	6-1	160	Rayville, LA	Rayville
44	Alex Benson	LB	SR	6-1	210	Trussville, AL	Hewitt-Trussville
86	Undra Billingsley	TE	FR	6-3	275	Birmingham, AL	Woodlawn
93	Chris Bonds	DL	FR	6-4	280	Columbia, SC	Richland Northeast
67	John Michael Boswell	OL	SO	6-5	300	Northport, AL	Tuscaloosa County
88	Michael Bowman	WR	FR	6-4	210	Rossville, GA	Ridgeland
87	Drew Bullard	LB	SO	6-3	240	Florence, AL	Florence
77	James Carpenter	OL	JR	6-5	300	Augusta, GA	Hephzibah
99	Josh Chapman	DL	SO	6-1	305	Hoover, AL	Hoover HS
62	Terrence Cody	DL	SR	6-5	365	Ft. Myers, FL	Gulf Coast C.C.
57	Marcell Dareus	DL	SO	6-3	280	Huffman, AL	Huffman
16	Thomas Darrah	QB	SO	6-6	212	Newnan, GA	Newnan
79	Drew Davis	OL	SR	6-7	305	Evergreen, AL	Sparta Academy
96	Luther Davis	DL	JR	6-3	299	West Monroe, LA	West Monroe
51	Brandon Deaderick	DL	SR	6-4	287	Elizabethtown, KY	Elizabethtown
95	Michael DeJohn	LB	JR	6-0	220	Hoover, AL	Hoover
85	Preston Dial	TE	JR	6-3	245	Mobile, AL	UMS-Wright
40	DeMarcus DuBose	LB	SO	6-1	230	Montgomery, AL	Jefferson Davis
13	Rob Ezell	WR	JR	5-10	170	Athens, AL	Athens
97	P.J. Fitzgerald	P	SR	5-11	198	Coral Springs, FL	Stoneman Douglas
76	D.J. Fluker	OL	FR	6-6	340	Foley, AL	Foley
58	Nick Gentry	DL	SO	6-1	254	Prattville, AL	Prattville
11	Brandon Gibson	WR	SO	6-1	196	Mobile, AL	UMS-Wright
6	Demetrius Goode	RB	SO	5-10	190	LaGrange, GA	Hargrave
29	Terry Grant	RB	JR	5-9	190	Lumberton, MS	Lumberton
33	Hampton Gray	DB	SR	6-1	194	Tuscaloosa, AL	Tuscaloosa County
23	Robby Green	DB	SO	6-0	180	New Orleans, LA	John Curtis Christian
34	Jeramie Griffin	RB	SO	6-2	228	Batesville, MS	South Panola
15	Darius Hanks	WR	JR	6-0	172	Norcross, GA	Norcross
54	Glenn Harbin	DL	SO	6-6	245	Mobile, AL	McGill-Toolen
5	Jerrell Harris	LB	SO	6-3	215	Gadsden, AL	Gadsden City
30	Dont'a Hightower	LB	SO	6-4	250	Lewisburg, TN	Marshall County
40	Baron Huber	RB	SR	6-3	249	Knoxville, TN	Powell
22	Mark Ingram II	RB	SO	5-10	215	Flint, MI	Southwestern Academy
3	Kareem Jackson	DB	JR	5-11	192	Macon, GA	Fork Union Military
2	Star Jackson	QB	FR	6-3	195	Lake Worth, FL	Lake Worth
24	Marquis Johnson	DB	SR	5-11	192	Sarasota, FL	Booker
78	Mike Johnson	OL	JR	6-6	305	Pensacola, FL	Pine Forest
35	Nico Johnson	LB	FR	6-3	225	Andalusia, AL	Andalusia
75	Barrett Jones	OL	SO	6-5	280	Memphis, TN	Evangelical Christian
8	Julio Jones	WR	SO	6-4	210	Foley, AL	Foley
9	Phelon Jones	DB	SO	5-11	195	Moblie, AL	LSU
36	Chris Jordan	LB	SO	6-2	220	Brentwood, TN	Brentwood Academy
81	Kendall Kelly	WR	FR	6-3	216	Gadsden, AL	Gadsden City
20	Tyrone King	DB	SR	5-11	198	Birmingham, AL	Grambling State
21	Dre Kirkpatrick	DB	FR	6-3	185	Gadsden, AL	Gadsden City
42	Eddie Lacy	RB	FR	6-0	210	Geismar, LA	Dutchtown
37	Robert Lester	DB	FR	6-2	210	Foley, AL	Foley
72	Tyler Love	OL	FR	6-7	290	Mountain Brook, AL	Mountain Brook
33	Mike Marrow	RB	FR	6-2	240	Holland, OH	Central Catholic
4	Marquis Maze	WR	SO	5-10	179	Tarrant, AL	Tarrant
10	A.J. McCarron	QB	FR	6-4	190	Mobile, AL	Saint Paul's Episcopal School
25	Rolando McClain	LB	JR	6-4	258	Decatur, AL	Decatur
80	Mike McCoy	WR	SR	6-3	215	Rankin, MS	Northwest Rankin
52	Alfred McCullough	OL	SO	6-2	292	Athens, AL	Athens
12	Greg McElroy	QB	JR	6-3	220	Southlake, TX	Carroll
56	William Ming	DL	FR	6-3	260	Athens, AL	Athens
59	Brandon Moore	DL	FR	6-5	310	Montgomery, AL	Carver
66	Brian Motley	OL	JR	6-2	289	Autaugaville, AL	Autaugaville
64	Kerry Murphy	DL	FR	6-4	323	Hoover, AL	Hargrave/Hoover
46	Wesley Neighbors	DB	SO	6-1	210	Huntsville, AL	Huntsville
83	Kevin Norwood	WR	FR	6-2	180	D'Iberville, MS	D'Iberville
10	Morgan Ogilvie	QB	SO	6-0	185	Mountain Brook, AL	Mountain Brook
2	Tana Patrick	LB	FR	6-3	235	Bridgeport, AL	North Jackson
84	Colin Peek	TE	SR	6-6	255	Ponte Vedra, FL	Georgia Tech
39	Kyle Pennington	DB	JR	5-11	177	Chatom, AL	Washington County
68	Taylor Pharr	OL	JR	6-6	290	Irondale, AL	Shades Valley

51

Num	Player	Pos	Class	Height	Weight	Hometown	Last School
54	Russell Raines	OL	FR	6-2	290	Satsuma, AL	Satsuma
13	**Cory Reamer**	**LB**	**SR**	**6-4**	**234**	**Hoover, AL**	**Hoover**
3	Trent Richardson	RB	FR	5-11	220	Pensacola, FL	Escambia
8	Chris Rogers	DB	SR	6-0	195	Lakeland, FL	Evangel Christian
74	David Ross	OL	JR	6-3	295	Homewood, AL	Homewood
1	B.J. Scott	DB	SO	5-11	188	Prichard, AL	Vigor
50	Brian Selman	DS	SR	6-0	211	Vestavia Hills, AL	Vestavia Hills
94	Darrington Sentimore	DL	FR	6-3	280	Norco, LA	Destrehan
26	Ali Sharrief	DB	SR	5-9	205	Stevenson, AL	North Jackson
94	Jeremy Shelley	PK	FR	5-10	170	Raleigh, NC	Broughton
48	Travis Sikes	WR	JR	6-2	188	Nashville, TN	Christ Presbyterian
65	Allen Skelton	OL	SO	6-1	256	Coker, AL	Tuscaloosa County
17	**Brad Smelley**	**TE**	**SO**	**6-3**	**218**	**Tuscaloosa, AL**	**American Christian**
92	Damion Square	DL	FR	6-3	273	Houston, TX	Yates
61	Anthony Steen	OL	FR	6-3	305	Lambert, MS	Lee Academy
47	Ed Stinson	DL	FR	6-4	240	Homestead, FL	South Dade
46	William Strickland	WR	SO	5-10	173	Tuscaloosa, AL	Northridge
90	Milton Talbert	DL	JR	6-4	275	Hattiesburg, MS	Hattiesburg
99	**Leigh Tiffin**	**K**	**SR**	**6-2**	**212**	**Muscle Shoals, AL**	**Muscle Shoals**
61	Carson Tinker	LS	SO	6-1	230	Murfreesboro, TN	Riverdale
87	Chris Underwood	TE	SO	6-4	231	Birmingham, AL	Vestavia Hills
5	Roy Upchurch	RB	SR	6-0	205	Tallahassee, FL	Godby
41	Courtney Upshaw	LB	SO	6-2	249	Eufaula, AL	Eufaula
44	Jacob Vane	RB	SR	6-1	232	Oak Ridge, TN	Oak Ridge HS
73	**William Vlachos**	**OL**	**SO**	**6-1**	**294**	**Birmingham, AL**	**Mountain Brook**
43	A.J. Walker	WR	SO	6-1	185	Huntsville, AL	Huntsville
65	Chance Warmack	OL	FR	6-3	301	Atlanta, GA	Westlake
97	**Lorenzo Washington**	**DL**	**SR**	**6-5**	**290**	**Loganville, GA**	**Hargrave Military**
91	Alex Watkins	LB	SO	6-3	225	Brownsville, TN	Haywood
55	Chavis Williams	LB	JR	6-4	223	Dora, AL	Dora
60	David Williams	OL	FR	6-3	272	Duncanville, AL	Hillcrest
89	Michael Williams	TE	FR	6-6	266	Reform, AL	Pickens County
9	Nick Williams	WR	FR	5-10	165	Fort Lauderdale, FL	St. Thomas Aquinas
27	**Justin Woodall**	**DB**	**SR**	**6-2**	**220**	**Oxford, MS**	**Lafayette HS**
18	Rod Woodson	DB	FR	5-11	200	Olive Branch, MS	Olive Branch

Note: Starters in bold
Note: Table data from "2009 Alabama Crimson Tide Roster" (49)

Games

09/05/09 - Alabama (5) at Virginia Tech (7)

Chick-fil-A College Kickoff
Georgia Dome
Atlanta, GA

Team	1	2	3	4	T		Passing	Rushing	Total
Alabama (5)	9	7	0	18	34		230	268	**498**
Virginia Tech (7)	7	10	0	7	24		91	64	**155**

The Tide dominated play for most of the game, outgaining Tech in total offense by 498 yards to 155, but mistakes, penalties, and poor play by the special teams allowed the Hokies to hang on until 18 fourth-quarter points sealed the 34-24 Alabama victory.

Bama scored first with field goals of 49 and 34 yards from Leigh Tiffin to take an early 6-0 lead. The Hokies responded with a 98-yard Dyrell Roberts kickoff return for a touchdown to give Tech a 7-6 lead. Following the recovery of a Ryan Williams fumble by Brian Selman deep in Hokie territory, the Tide retook the lead 9-7 on a 32-yard Tiffin field goal. Early in the second quarter, Antoine Hopkins intercepted a Greg McElroy pass. Tech led 10-9 after a successful 28-yard Matt Waldron field goal. Alabama responded by driving 76 yards for a touchdown and a 16-10 lead, with the big plays coming on a 14-yard run by Mark Ingram II, passes of 16 and 10 yards from McElroy to Julio Jones, and the score coming on a 19-yard Roy Upchurch run. On the next Virginia Tech possession, three personal fouls and a pass interference penalty carried the Hokies downfield with Williams scoring on a 1-yard touchdown run. The score remained 17-16 (Hokies) at the half after Tiffin missed a 36-yard field goal at the end of the second quarter.

In the third quarter Roy Upchurch fumbled the ball at the Virginia Tech 9-yard line after a long run, negating the lone scoring opportunity in the quarter. Still down by a point in the fourth, McElroy hit Marquis Maze for a 48-yard completion to the Virginia Tech 6-yard line, and Ingram II scored a TD on the next play. A successful two-point conversion pass from McElroy to Colin Peek gave Alabama a 24-17 lead. Davon Morgan fumbled on the kickoff, and Chris Rogers recovered for the Tide at the Tech 21-yard line. The following Alabama drive stalled at the 3-yard line, but Tiffin's fourth field goal made the score 27-17. Poor kickoff coverage and penalties set up a 32-yard Williams run that cut the lead to 27-24. Alabama quickly struck back as Ingram II rushed for 39 yards, McElroy completed a 19-yard pass to Peek, and then threw to Ingram II for an 18-yard touchdown. The Hokies never threatened to score again, and Alabama won 34-24. Ingram II led the Tide with 150 yards rushing on 26 carries and a pair of touchdowns, and he was named the SEC Offensive Player of the Week.[48]

Passing	C/ATT	YDS	AVG	TD	INT	QBR
G. McElroy	15/30	230	7.7	1	1	78.5

Rushing	CAR	YDS	AVG	TD	LONG
M. Ingram II	26	150	5.8	1	39
R. Upchurch	7	90	12.9	1	34
G. McElroy	8	28	3.5	0	9
T. Richardson	3	10	3.3	0	6
T. Grant	2	2	1	0	2
M. Maze	1	-1	-1	0	0
J. Jones	1	-1	-1	0	0
Team	1	-10	-10	0	0
Team	49	268	5.5	2	39

Punting	NO	YDS	AVG	TB	IN 20	LONG
PJ Fitzgerald	5	224	44.8	0	0	53

Receiving	REC	YDS	AVG	TD	LONG
M. Maze	2	57	28.5	0	48
D. Hanks	3	55	18.3	0	35
J. Jones	4	46	11.5	0	16
C. Peek	3	37	12.3	0	19
M. Ingram II	3	35	11.7	1	18
Team	15	230	15.3	1	48

Kick returns	NO	YDS	AVG	LONG	TD
J. Arenas	3	55	18.3	22	0
T. Grant	2	44	22	29	0
Team	5	99	19.8	29	0

Punt returns	NO	YDS	AVG	LONG	TD
J. Arenas	6	35	5.8	15	0

Kicking	FG	PCT	LONG	XP	PTS
L. Tiffin	4/5	80	49	2/2	14

Note: Table data from "Alabama 34-24 Virginia Tech (Sep 5, 2009) Box Score" (50)

09/12/09 - Alabama (4) vs Florida International

Team	1	2	3	4	T		Passing	Rushing	Total
Florida International	7	7	0	0	14		213	1	214
Alabama (4)	10	10	6	14	40		241	275	516

The Golden Panthers of Florida International proved a tougher opponent than Alabama expected in the first half. However, the Tide pulled away with a 40-14 victory in the 2009 home opener. Alabama opened the scoring with a 23-yard Leigh Tiffin field goal on its opening 13-play, 55-yard drive that took the first 5:58 of the game. After forcing a punt, the Tide drove 80 yards in seven plays and extended their lead to 10-0 on a 24-yard Greg McElroy touchdown pass to Mike McCoy. FIU followed the McElroy touchdown with T. Y. Hilton returning the ensuing kickoff 96 yards, bringing the score to 10-7. Bama responded with a 50-yard drive and a 29-yard Tiffin field goal to extend the lead to 13-7 early in the second quarter. The following kickoff was booted out of bounds which set up the Golden Panthers at the 40-yard line. The ensuing 60-yard drive resulted in a 9-yard Paul McCall touchdown pass to Greg Ellingson that gave FIU a 14-13 lead. Bama responded with a 64-yard drive culminating with a 2-yard Mark Ingram II touchdown run. Three punts later, two by FIU, and Alabama was up 20-14 at the half.

The second half started with three punts, a 39-yard field goal miss by Bama, and another FIU punt. Then Trent Richardson continued the Alabama scoring in the third quarter with a 9-yard touchdown run to extend the lead to 26-14. Three more punts ensued, and on the third one, Javier Arenas returned it 46 yards to set up Richardson's second score on a 35-yard touchdown run on the first play of the fourth quarter. Alabama led 33-14. After stopping the Golden Panthers on 4th-and-2 at the Alabama 44-yard line, Terry Grant scored the Tide's final points with a 42-yard touchdown run to bring the final score to 40-14. Julio Jones suffered a knee sprain during this game, and it lingered throughout the season. Alabama outgained FIU 516-214 in total offense and 275-1 in rushing offense. Greg McElroy set an all-time Alabama record by completing 14 consecutive pass attempts and was 18-of-24 for 241 yards and a touchdown. For his 118-yard, two-touchdown rushing performance, Richardson was named the SEC Freshman of the Week.[48]

Passing	C/ATT	YDS	AVG	TD	INT	QBR
G. McElroy	18/24	241	10	1	0	59.1

Rushing	CAR	YDS	AVG	TD	LONG
T. Richardson	15	118	7.9	2	35
T. Grant	6	69	11.5	1	42
M. Ingram II	10	56	5.6	1	16
D. Goode	4	24	6	0	14
R. Upchurch	4	17	4.3	0	9
J. Jones	1	5	5	0	5
G. McElroy	2	-14	-7	0	1
Team	42	275	6.5	4	42

Interceptions	INT	YDS	TD
M.Barron	1	17	0

Kicking	FG	PCT	LONG	XP	PTS
L. Tiffin	2/3	66.7	29	4/4	10

Punting	NO	YDS	AVG	TB	IN 20	LONG
PJ Fitzgerald	3	129	43	0	0	45

Receiving	REC	YDS	AVG	TD	LONG
M. McCoy	5	100	20	1	35
M. Ingram II	4	47	11.8	0	31
T. Richardson	2	23	11.5	0	12
E. Alexander	2	20	10	0	11
P. Dial	1	19	19	0	19
C. Peek	1	13	13	0	13
D. Hanks	1	11	11	0	11
J. Jones	1	9	9	0	9
B. Smelley	1	-1	-1	0	-1
Team	18	241	13.4	1	35

Kick returns	NO	YDS	AVG	LONG	TD
J. Arenas	1	25	25	25	0
D. Square	1	5	5	5	0
Team	2	30	15	25	0

Punt returns	NO	YDS	AVG	LONG	TD
J. Arenas	6	101	16.8	46	0

Note: Table data from "Alabama 40-14 Florida Intl (Sep 12, 2009) Box Score" (51)

54

09/19/09 - Alabama (4) vs North Texas

Team	1	2	3	4	T		Passing	Rushing	Total
North Texas	0	0	7	0	7		126	61	187
Alabama (4)	14	16	14	9	53		263	260	523

Alabama's second consecutive matchup with a Sun Belt opponent on the season resulted in its second consecutive victory as the Tide defeated the North Texas Mean Green 53-7. Greg McElroy lost a fumble on the very first play of the game, then Alabama scored on its next six possessions in a row, including five in the first half. North Texas punted on every possession until a couple of minutes were left in the third quarter. Their first punt was downed at the Alabama 5-yard line, and the Tide drove all 95 yards in 5:52 and 13 plays when Greg McElroy opened the scoring with a 2-yard touchdown run. Marquis Maze capped a 6-play, 78-yard drive with a 34-yard touchdown reception to take a 14-0 first quarter lead.

The Tide continued the scoring in the second quarter with a 1-yard Trent Richardson touchdown run set up by his 38-yard run and a 20-yard reception by Darius Hanks. Mark Ingram II caught a 29-yard touchdown pass to cap 7-play, 68-yard drive, and Leigh Tiffin followed that with a 35-yard field goal. This gave Alabama a 30-0 lead at the half due to the missed PAT after the last touchdown.

In the third quarter, Alabama extended its lead to 44-0 following touchdown runs of five and one yard respectively from Ingram II and Terry Grant. After North Texas reached the end zone on a 34-yard Nathan Tune touchdown pass to Lance Dunbar, Alabama closed the game with ten fourth-quarter points on a 20-yard Tiffin field goal and 9-yard Grant touchdown run.

Alabama outgained the Mean Green 523-187 in yards of total offense. It was the most points for Alabama in a game since beating Texas-El Paso 56-7 in 2001 and the most scored at Bryant-Denny since defeating Tulane 62-0 in 1991. By completing of 13-of-15 passes, McElroy tied a school record with an overall completion percentage of 86.7. The game was notable for McElroy as the North Texas head coach, Todd Dodge, was his high school head coach when McElroy led Southlake Carroll to the 2005 Texas Class 5A high school football championship.[48]

Passing	C/ATT	YDS	AVG	TD	INT	QBR
G. McElroy	13/15	176	11.7	2	0	97.4
S. Jackson	9/13	87	6.7	0	0	67.2
Team	22/28	263	9.4	2	0	--

Rushing	CAR	YDS	AVG	TD	LONG
M. Ingram II	8	91	11.4	1	22
T. Richardson	11	87	7.9	1	38
T. Grant	19	79	4.2	2	9
G. McElroy	3	16	5.3	1	8
D.Goode	1	14	14	0	14
Team	3	-27	-9.0	0	0
Team	45	260	5.8	5	38

Kick returns	NO	YDS	AVG	LONG	TD
J. Arenas	1	61	61	61	0
B. Huber	1	10	10	10	0
Team	2	71	35.5	61	0

Punting	NO	YDS	AVG	TB	IN 20	LONG
PJ Fitzgerald	1	49	49	0	0	49

Receiving	REC	YDS	AVG	TD	LONG
M. Maze	4	49	12.3	1	34
M. Ingram II	3	38	12.7	1	29
M. McCoy	3	38	12.7	0	20
T. Grant	2	29	14.5	0	17
D. Hanks	2	28	14	0	20
C. Peek	2	26	13	0	19
B. Gibson	1	21	21	0	21
B. Smelley	2	13	6.5	0	7
E. Alexander	1	11	11	0	11
M. Bowman	1	7	7	0	7
T. Richardson	1	3	3	0	3
Team	22	263	12	2	34

Kicking	FG	PCT	LONG	XP	PTS
L. Tiffin	2/2	100	35	5/7	11

Punt returns	NO	YDS	AVG	LONG	TD
J. Arenas	6	90	15	36	0

Note: Table data from "Alabama 53-7 North Texas (Sep 19, 2009) Box Score" (52)

09/26/09 - Alabama (3) vs Arkansas

Team	1	2	3	4	T		Passing	Rushing	Total
Arkansas	0	0	7	0	7		191	63	254
Alabama (3)	0	14	14	7	35		291	134	425

In Bobby Petrino's first visit to Tuscaloosa as a head coach, Alabama opened conference play by defeating the Arkansas Razorbacks 35-7. After a scoreless first quarter which consisted of six punts, two big touchdown plays had the Tide up 14-0 at the half. The first was a 52-yard run by Trent Richardson capping a 6-play, 86-yard drive, and the second was a 50-yard pass from Greg McElroy to Julio Jones on the first play of Alabama's next possession. The Hogs punted on all seven of their possessions in the first half except for their last one where they ran a single play before time ran out.

Arkansas responded early in the third quarter and cut the lead to 14-7 after Ryan Mallett hit Greg Childs for an 18-yard touchdown reception; the Hogs would not reach the end zone again as the Tide responded with three unanswered touchdowns. Alabama scored first on an 80-yard touchdown pass from McElroy to Marquis Maze on the first play of that possession. This was followed with two touchdowns by Mark Ingram II, one on a 14-yard pass from McElroy and the other on a 2-yard run that capped an impressive 13-play, 99-yard drive which brought the final score to 35-7.

Alabama outgained the Razorbacks 425-254 in yards of total offense. McElroy threw for career highs of 291 yards and three touchdowns. For his 65-yard, nine-carry, one-touchdown performance, Richardson was named the SEC Freshman of the Week.[48]

Passing	C/ATT	YDS	AVG	TD	INT	QBR
G. McElroy	17/24	291	12.1	3	0	89.2

Rushing	CAR	YDS	AVG	TD	LONG
T. Richardson	9	65	7.2	1	52
M. Ingram II	17	50	2.9	1	14
T. Grant	13	16	1.2	0	10
G. McElroy	2	3	1.5	0	5
Team	41	134	3.3	2	52

Interceptions	INT	YDS	TD
J. Woodall	1	24	0

Kicking	FG	PCT	LONG	XP	PTS
L. Tiffin	0/0	0	0	5/5	5

Punting	NO	YDS	AVG	TB	IN 20	LONG
PJ Fitzgerald	7	288	41.1	0	0	51

Receiving	REC	YDS	AVG	TD	LONG
M. Maze	2	88	44	1	80
J. Jones	2	65	32.5	1	50
D. Hanks	1	32	32	0	32
R. Upchurch	3	30	10	0	13
M. Ingram II	3	21	7	1	14
C. Peek	2	19	9.5	0	14
T. Grant	1	18	18	0	18
T. Richardson	2	16	8	0	9
P. Dial	1	2	2	0	2
Team	17	291	17.1	3	80

Kick returns	NO	YDS	AVG	LONG	TD
T. Grant	2	33	16.5	20	0

Punt returns	NO	YDS	AVG	LONG	TD
J. Arenas	5	59	11.8	18	0
L. Washington	1	16	16	16	0
Team	6	75	12.5	18	0

Note: Table data from "Alabama 35-7 Arkansas (Sep 26, 2009) Box Score" (53)

10/03/09 - Alabama (3) at Kentucky

Team	1	2	3	4	T		Passing	Rushing	Total
Alabama (3)	7	14	17	0	38		148	204	352
Kentucky	6	0	7	7	20		168	133	301

In Alabama's first trip to Lexington since 2004, and its first road game of the 2009 season, the Tide defeated the Kentucky Wildcats 38-20. Alabama scored on its opening drive after Javier Arenas returned the opening kickoff 60 yards, which set up an 11-yard Mark Ingram II touchdown for an early 7-0 lead. Kentucky responded with a pair of 49-yard Lones Seiber field goals. The score was 7-6 at the end of the first quarter. The Tide extended their lead late in the second quarter following a nearly seven-minute, 13-play, 97-yard touchdown drive. Greg McElroy passes of 27 and 21 yards and a 13-yard run by Ingram II moved Bama down the field, culminating with a 3-yard touchdown pass from McElroy to Colin Peek to put the Tide up 14-6. With only 40 seconds remaining in the half, Kentucky tailback Derrick Locke fumbled the ball after catching a short pass. Courtney Upshaw returned 45 yards for an Alabama touchdown that put the Tide ahead 21-6 at halftime.

On the second play of the third quarter, Rolando McClain intercepted a Mike Hartline pass, giving Alabama possession at the Wildcat 38-yard line. Two plays later, Ingram II scored on a 32-yard run, making the score 28-6. Following an Eryk Anders interception that set up a 36-yard Leigh Tiffin field goal, the Wildcats reached the end zone for the first time on the ensuing drive. Hartline connected with Randall Cobb for a 45-yard touchdown reception bringing the score to 31-13. The Tide responded with a 7-yard Darius Hanks touchdown reception to complete a 13-play, 76-yard drive. Kentucky scored the afternoon's final points in the fourth quarter on a 2-yard Alfonso Smith touchdown run. The final score was 38-20. Kentucky's four turnovers sabotaged an effort that was better than any other of Alabama's previous opponents as the Wildcats gained 301 yards in total offense and held Alabama to 352. McElroy threw for two touchdowns, giving him nine on the season against only one interception, and Ingram II rushed for 140 yards on 22 carries. For his 12 tackles (eight solo), one interception, one forced fumble, and one pass break-up, McClain was named both the SEC Defensive Player of the Week and the Bronko Nagurski Award National Defensive Player of the Week.[48]

Passing	C/ATT	YDS	AVG	TD	INT	QBR
G. McElroy	15/26	148	5.7	2	0	77.5

Rushing	CAR	YDS	AVG	TD	LONG
M. Ingram II	22	140	6.4	2	32
T. Richardson	14	26	1.9	0	6
PJ Fitzgerald	1	17	17	0	17
R. Upchurch	1	13	13	0	13
G. McElroy	3	5	1.7	0	6
M. Maze	1	3	3	0	3
Team	42	204	4.9	2	32

Interceptions	INT	YDS	TD
R. McClain	1	21	0
M. Barron	1	6	0
E. Anders	1	0	0
Team	3	27	0

Punting	NO	YDS	AVG	TB	IN 20	LONG
PJ Fitzgerald	5	199	39.8	0	0	52

Receiving	REC	YDS	AVG	TD	LONG
C. Peek	6	65	10.8	1	21
D. Hanks	2	34	17	1	27
E. Alexander	1	21	21	0	21
J. Jones	2	13	6.5	0	9
T. Richardson	1	9	9	0	9
M. Ingram II	1	6	6	0	6
R. Upchurch	2	0	0	0	4
Team	15	148	9.9	2	27

Kick returns	NO	YDS	AVG	LONG	TD
J. Arenas	3	97	32.3	60	0
T. Grant	2	44	22	25	0
Team	5	141	28.2	60	0

Punt returns	NO	YDS	AVG	LONG	TD
J. Arenas	1	0	0	0	0

Kicking	FG	PCT	LONG	XP	PTS
L. Tiffin	1/1	100	36	5/5	8

Note: Table data from "Alabama 38-20 Kentucky (Oct 3, 2009) Box Score" (54)

10/10/09 - Alabama (3) at Ole Miss (20)

Team	1	2	3	4	T		Passing	Rushing	Total
Alabama (3)	3	13	3	3	22		154	200	354
Ole Miss (20)	0	0	3	0	3		140	57	197

Before the largest crowd to ever witness a game in Vaught-Hemingway Stadium, Alabama defeated its long-time rival, the Ole Miss Rebels, 22-3. Alabama struggled to put the ball in the end zone all afternoon with drives stalling at the Mississippi eight, four, four, four, and 13. Each of those drives resulted in field goals by Leigh Tiffin, who was 5-for-5 on the day. Other special teams contributions included a blocked punt in the second quarter and a recovered Dexter McCluster fumble on a punt return in the third quarter, both by Cory Reamer. Greg McElroy struggled, completing only 15-of-34 passes for 147 yards, but Mark Ingram II ran for a then career-high 172 yards and accounted for Alabama's only touchdown on a 36-yard run in the second quarter.

The Alabama defense had an excellent day, with Javier Arenas, Kareem Jackson, Rolando McClain, and Cory Reamer each intercepting a Jevan Snead pass. Overall, the Tide held the Rebels to 197 yards of total offense and a single Joshua Shene field goal in the third quarter. Center William Vlachos was named the SEC Offensive Lineman of the Week and Leigh Tiffin was named the Lou Groza Award "Star of Stars" for his five field goal performance. The victory was the team's sixth in a row over the Rebels.[48]

Passing	C/ATT	YDS	AVG	TD	INT	QBR
G. McElroy	15/34	147	4.3	0	0	37.6
PJ Fitzgerald	1/1	7	7	0	0	100
Team	16/35	154	4.4	0	0	--

Rushing	CAR	YDS	AVG	TD	LONG
M. Ingram II	28	172	6.1	1	36
T. Richardson	9	40	4.4	0	10
G. McElroy	4	-12	-3	0	5
Team	41	200	4.9	1	36

Interceptions	INT	YDS	TD
J. Arenas	1	0	0
J. Woodall	1	0	0
R. McClain	1	0	0
K. Jackson	1	-11	0
Team	4	-11	0

Punting	NO	YDS	AVG	TB	IN 20	LONG
PJ Fitzgerald	6	245	40.8	0	0	44

Receiving	REC	YDS	AVG	TD	LONG
M. Maze	4	48	12	0	16
J. Jones	4	42	10.5	0	14
C. Peek	3	32	10.7	0	14
M. Ingram II	3	16	5.3	0	13
T. Richardson	1	9	9	0	9
M. Barron	1	7	7	0	7
Team	16	154	9.6	0	16

Kick returns	NO	YDS	AVG	LONG	TD
J. Arenas	2	40	20	21	0

Punt returns	NO	YDS	AVG	LONG	TD
C. Reamer	1	3	3	3	0
J. Arenas	4	2	0.5	2	0
Team	5	5	1.7	3	0

Kicking	FG	PCT	LONG	XP	PTS
L. Tiffin	5/5	100	31	1/1	16

Note: Table data from "Alabama 22-3 Ole Miss (Oct 10, 2009) Box Score" (55)

58

10/17/09 - Alabama (2) vs South Carolina (22)

Team	1	2	3	4	T		Passing	Rushing	Total
South Carolina (22)	0	6	0	0	6		214	64	**278**
Alabama (2)	10	3	0	7	20		92	264	**356**

In South Carolina's first trip to Bryant-Denny since 2004, the Tide defeated the South Carolina Gamecocks 20-6 on Homecoming in Tuscaloosa. On the second play from the start of the game, Mark Barron intercepted a Stephen Garcia pass and returned it 77 yards for a touchdown and a 7-0 Alabama lead. Greg McElroy struggled as he threw a pair of first-quarter interceptions on Bama's first two offensive possessions. South Carolina's C.C. Whitlock fumbled the ball on the return of the second interception and possession was recovered by Darius Hanks. The Tide continued their drive to the Gamecock 8-yard line, and Leigh Tiffin kicked a 25-yard field goal to put Alabama ahead 10-0.

Following a failed 49-yard Leigh Tiffin field goal attempt in the second quarter, South Carolina answered by driving to the Alabama 5-yard line. However, the Bama defense held the Gamecock offense to three consecutive incompletions; the result was a 22-yard Spencer Lanning field goal to make the score 10-3. On the following possession, Mark Ingram II ran 54 yards to the South Carolina 28. The drive stalled at the 17, and Tiffin's field goal made it 13-3. South Carolina responded with a quick drive that ended with a 31-yard Lanning field goal as time expired in the first half with Bama up 13-6.

After a scoreless third quarter with 8:08 to go, Alabama took possession at its own 32-yard line following a Gamecock punt. Taking direct snaps out of the wildcat formation, Ingram II rushed for 64 yards on five carries, then took a pitch from Greg McElroy for the last four yards and the touchdown, sealing Alabama's 20-6 victory. The Alabama offense turned the ball over four times in this game after committing only two turnovers in the first six games. Mark Ingram II's 246 yards rushing marked his third consecutive career-high effort and the third highest single game total in Alabama history. For their performances, Ingram II was named the SEC Offensive Player of the Week and Rolando McClain was named the Lott Trophy IMPACT Player of the Week.[48]

Passing	C/ATT	YDS	AVG	TD	INT	QBR
G. McElroy	10/20	92	4.6	0	2	10.9

Rushing	CAR	YDS	AVG	TD	LONG
M. Ingram II	24	246	10.3	1	54
R. Upchurch	4	27	6.8	0	15
T. Richardson	5	13	2.6	0	14
G. McElroy	2	1	0.5	0	6
M. Maze	1	-2	-2	0	0
Team	36	264	7.3	1	54

Interceptions	INT	YDS	TD
M. Barron	1	77	1

Punting	NO	YDS	AVG	TB	IN 20	LONG
PJ Fitzgerald	3	136	45.3	0	0	49

Receiving	REC	YDS	AVG	TD	LONG
M. Ingram II	2	23	11.5	0	22
C. Peek	2	21	10.5	0	16
M. Maze	2	19	9.5	0	13
R. Upchurch	2	18	9	0	14
T. Richardson	2	11	5.5	0	9
Team	10	92	9.2	0	22

Kick returns	NO	YDS	AVG	LONG	TD
T. Grant	1	25	25	25	0
T. Richardson	1	20	20	20	0
Team	2	45	22.5	25	0

Punt returns	NO	YDS	AVG	LONG	TD
J. Jones	5	75	15	33	0

Kicking	FG	PCT	LONG	XP	PTS
L. Tiffin	2/3	66.7	35	2/2	8

Note: Table data from "Alabama 20-6 South Carolina (Oct 17, 2009) Box Score" (56)

10/24/09 - Alabama (2) vs Tennessee

Team	1	2	3	4	T		Passing	Rushing	Total
Tennessee	0	3	0	7	10		265	76	341
Alabama (2)	3	6	0	3	12		120	136	256

This edition of the Third Saturday in October was a defensive struggle with a surprise finish as the Crimson Tide defeated the Tennessee Volunteers 12-10. In a defensive struggle for both teams, Leigh Tiffin was 4-for-4 on field goals and accounted for all of Alabama's scoring.

With the Tennessee defense stopping the Tide on consecutive drives, Alabama's defense responded with Mark Barron intercepting a Jonathan Crompton pass at the Bama 19-yard line in the first quarter. The ensuing drive resulted in a 38-yard Leigh Tiffin field goal and a 3-0 lead. The Vols responded with a 24-yard Daniel Lincoln field goal that tied the game at 3-3. Tiffin hit field goals from 50 and 22 yards before Lincoln missed a 47-yard attempt just short at the end of the first half, leaving the score 9-3 at halftime. After a scoreless third quarter, Tennessee drove to the Alabama 27-yard line, but Terrence Cody blocked Lincoln's field goal. On the ensuing possession, Tiffin hit a 49-yard field goal to bring the score to 12-3.

Late in the fourth quarter, Mark Ingram II lost a fumble for the first time in his collegiate career, giving Tennessee possession at the Alabama 43-yard line with 3:29 remaining in the game. The Vols drove the ball 43 yards in 2:10, culminating with an 11-yard Crompton touchdown pass to Gerald Jones to cut the gap to 12-10. The Vols followed with a successful onside kick attempt and regained possession of the ball at their own 41-yard line. After Tennessee was penalized five yards for a false start, Crompton completed a pass to Luke Stocker for 23 yards to the Alabama 27-yard line. With the clock ticking off the final seconds and Tennessee out of timeouts, Crompton spiked the ball to stop the clock with four seconds left. This set up Lincoln for a 45-yard field goal attempt to win the game. However, Terrence Cody knocked his blocker over and broke through the line. He blocked Lincoln's field goal as time expired, preserving Alabama's 12-10 victory and perfect season. For their performances, Cody was named the SEC Defensive Lineman of the Week and Tiffin was named the SEC Special Teams Player of the Week.[48]

Passing	C/ATT	YDS	AVG	TD	INT	QBR
G. McElroy	18/29	120	4.1	0	0	64.7

Rushing	CAR	YDS	AVG	TD	LONG
M. Ingram II	18	99	5.5	0	25
G. McElroy	3	22	7.3	0	12
T. Richardson	8	18	2.3	0	5
R. Upchurch	1	-3	-3	0	0
Team	30	136	4.5	0	25

Interceptions	INT	YDS	TD
M. Barron	1	11	0

Kicking	FG	PCT	LONG	XP	PTS
L. Tiffin	4/4	100	50	0/0	12

Punting	NO	YDS	AVG	TB	IN 20	LONG
PJ Fitzgerald	3	132	44	0	0	49

Receiving	REC	YDS	AVG	TD	LONG
J. Jones	7	54	7.7	0	14
M. Maze	1	19	19	0	19
D. Hanks	3	17	5.7	0	8
B. Smelley	1	10	10	0	10
R. Upchurch	2	6	3	0	4
B. Huber	1	4	4	0	4
P. Dial	1	4	4	0	4
M. Williams	1	4	4	0	4
T. Richardson	1	2	2	0	2
Team	18	120	6.7	0	19

Kick returns	NO	YDS	AVG	LONG	TD
T. Grant	1	30	30	30	0

Punt returns	NO	YDS	AVG	LONG	TD
J. Arenas	3	33	11	24	0

Note: Table data from "Alabama 12-10 Tennessee (Oct 24, 2009) Box Score" (57)

11/07/09 - Alabama (3) vs LSU (9)

Team	1	2	3	4	T		Passing	Rushing	Total
LSU (9)	0	7	8	0	15		158	95	253
Alabama (3)	0	3	7	14	24		276	176	452

With the SEC West divisional championship on the line, Alabama defeated its long-time rival the LSU Tigers 24-15 to secure a spot in the SEC Championship Game. Following a scoreless first quarter, LSU took possession on its own 9-yard line on the last play of the first quarter and embarked on a 13-play, 91-yard drive that ended in a 12-yard touchdown pass from Jordan Jefferson to Deangelo Peterson and a 7-0 lead. Javier Arenas returned the ensuing punt 40 yards to the Alabama 49, and the Tide drove to the LSU 11-yard line before settling for a 28-yard Leigh Tiffin field goal that made the score 7-3. Neither team could mount a sustained drive for the rest of the half.

At the start of the second half, Alabama received the kickoff, took possession at its own 19-yard line, and started getting the ball to Mark Ingram II. On the drive, Ingram II was responsible for a 12-yard reception from Greg McElroy and rushes of four, 12, 12, and 18 yards that advanced the ball to the Tiger 23-yard line. Two plays later, McElroy hit Darius Hanks for his first touchdown pass since the Kentucky game, and Alabama was up 10-7. The ensuing LSU drive stalled at the Tide 46-yard line, and the LSU punt was downed at the Alabama 1-yard line. Two plays later, McElroy was sacked for a safety, making the score 10-9. LSU returned the free kick to its own 41-yard line and drove 59 yards for the touchdown, the big play coming on a 34-yard run by Charles Scott. The two-point conversion attempt failed, leaving the score 15-10 in favor of LSU.

Alabama received the kickoff and again relied on Ingram II - seven of his rushes for 48 yards accounted for most of the offense on a drive that ended with a 20-yard Tiffin field goal, making the score 15-13. Following an LSU three-and-out, Alabama took possession on its own 27-yard line. On first down, McElroy completed a screen pass to Julio Jones which he turned into a 73-yard touchdown. After a successful two-point conversion, Alabama led 21-15. LSU went three-and-out again. A methodical 11-play, 31-yard Alabama drive consumed 6:14 of game time and ended in a 40-yard Tiffin field goal with 3:04 left to seal a 24-15 Alabama victory. Alabama won the SEC Western Division championship and clinched a berth in the SEC Championship Game against Florida, which clinched the East that same day with a 27-3 victory over Vanderbilt. Ingram II rushed for 144 yards and Jones had 102 receiving yards.[48]

Passing	C/ATT	YDS	AVG	TD	INT	QBR
G. McElroy	19/34	276	8.1	2	1	66.7

Rushing	CAR	YDS	AVG	TD	LONG
M. Ingram II	22	144	6.5	0	25
T. Richardson	6	27	4.5	0	11
G. McElroy	6	21	3.5	0	11
Team	4	-16	-4	0	0
Team	38	176	4.6	0	25

Interceptions	INT	YDS	TD
R. Green	1	0	0

Punting	NO	YDS	AVG	TB	IN 20	LONG
PJ Fitzgerald	4	151	37.8	0	0	41

Receiving	REC	YDS	AVG	TD	LONG
J. Jones	4	102	25.5	1	73
M. Maze	6	88	14.7	0	37
M. Ingram II	5	30	6	0	12
M. Williams	2	25	12.5	0	14
D. Hanks	1	21	21	1	21
B. Smelley	1	10	10	0	10
Team	19	276	14.5	2	73

Kick returns	NO	YDS	AVG	LONG	TD
J. Arenas	3	78	26	40	0

Punt returns	NO	YDS	AVG	LONG	TD
J. Arenas	6	11	1.8	6	0

Kicking	FG	PCT	LONG	XP	PTS
L. Tiffin	3/3	100	40	1/1	10

Note: Table data from "Alabama 24-15 LSU (Nov 7, 2009) Box Score" (58)

11/14/09 - Alabama (2) at Mississippi State

Team	1	2	3	4	T		Passing	Rushing	Total
Alabama (2)	0	14	3	14	**31**		192	252	**444**
Mississippi State	0	0	0	3	**3**		99	114	**213**

Playing in front of the largest crowd to ever witness a game in Davis Wade Stadium, and with the Bulldogs wearing black jerseys for the first time in their history, Alabama cruised to a 31-3 victory over long-time rival Mississippi State. After a scoreless first quarter, Alabama scored a pair of touchdowns in the second to take a 14-0 lead. The first touchdown came on a 6-play, 80-yard drive finished off by a 45-yard Darius Hanks reception from Greg McElroy. Mark Ingram II scored the second one from a yard out, capping an 11-play, 72-yard drive.

After a 39-yard field goal by Leigh Tiffin extended the lead to 17-0 in the third quarter, the Bulldogs scored their only points of the night on a 34-yard Derek DePasquale field goal. On the ensuing kickoff, Javier Arenas returned the ball 46 yards and on the next play, McElroy hit Julio Jones for a 48-yard touchdown reception. This extended Alabama's lead to 24-3. Mark Barron intercepted a Tyson Lee pass at the Alabama 30-yard line on the next Bulldog offensive series. On the following play, Ingram II scored a touchdown on a 70-yard run to bring the final score to 31-3.

For the game, McElroy threw for 192 yards and two touchdowns on 13-of-18 passing, and Mark Ingram II rushed for 149 yards two touchdowns. Mississippi State was held to 213 total yards, with Barron intercepting two Tyson Lee passes and Marquis Johnson intercepting one Chris Relf pass. For his performance, left guard Mike Johnson was named the SEC Offensive Lineman of the Week.[48]

Passing	C/ATT	YDS	AVG	TD	INT	QBR
G. McElroy	13/18	192	10.7	2	0	87.8

Rushing	CAR	YDS	AVG	TD	LONG
M. Ingram II	19	149	7.8	2	70
T. Richardson	11	47	4.3	0	18
G. McElroy	4	30	7.5	0	16
R. Upchurch	5	19	3.8	0	5
M. Maze	1	7	7	0	7
Team	40	252	6.3	2	70

Interceptions	INT	YDS	TD
M. Barron	2	0	0
M. Johnson	1	0	0
Team	3	0	0

Punting	NO	YDS	AVG	TB	IN 20	LONG
PJ Fitzgerald	5	206	41.2	0	0	50

Receiving	REC	YDS	AVG	TD	LONG
J. Jones	4	66	16.5	1	48
D. Hanks	3	59	19.7	1	45
M. Maze	4	55	13.8	0	42
M. Ingram II	1	9	9	0	9
R. Upchurch	1	3	3	0	3
Team	13	192	14.8	2	48

Kick returns	NO	YDS	AVG	LONG	TD
J. Arenas	2	70	35	46	0

Punt returns	NO	YDS	AVG	LONG	TD
J. Arenas	4	0	0	0	0

Kicking	FG	PCT	LONG	XP	PTS
L. Tiffin	1/1	100	50	4/4	7

Note: Table data from "Alabama 31-3 Mississippi State (Nov 14, 2009) Box Score" (59)

11/21/09 - Alabama (2) vs Chattanooga

Team	1	2	3	4	T		Passing	Rushing	Total
Chattanooga	0	0	0	0	0		36	48	**84**
Alabama (2)	21	14	3	7	**45**		109	313	**422**

On senior day in Tuscaloosa, Alabama dipped down to college football's Football Championship Subdivision and defeated the Mocs of UT-Chattanooga 45-0. After being stopped on its first possession, Alabama reached the end zone on the next five consecutive possessions and ran up a 35-0 lead in the first half. In the first quarter, Trent Richardson capped off an 11-play, 51-yard drive with a 2-yard touchdown run. On Alabama's next possession, Julio Jones caught a 44-yard pass from Greg McElroy before Mark Ingram II took it to the house on a 25-yard run. 17 seconds later, Cory Reamer picked off a pass, returned it to the Chattanooga 31-yard line, then Julio Jones scored on a 19-yard touchdown reception.

In the second quarter, touchdowns were scored by Javier Arenas on a 66-yard punt return and on a 40-yard Ingram II run (capping a 5-play, 62-yard drive in 1:45). With the only third quarter points coming on a 41-yard Leigh Tiffin field goal, Alabama's final points of the afternoon came on a 21-yard Roy Upchurch touchdown run in the fourth quarter.

Javier Arenas set the all-time SEC record with his seventh punt return for a touchdown and was named the SEC Special Teams Player of the Week. Mark Ingram II led the offense with 102 yards and two touchdowns before being pulled early in the second quarter. Alabama outgained Chattanooga in total offense 422-84 and recorded its first defensive shutout since defeating Auburn 36-0 in 2008.[48]

Passing	C/ATT	YDS	AVG	TD	INT	QBR
G. McElroy	6/11	80	7.3	1	0	52.2
S. Jackson	4/5	29	5.8	0	0	2.5
Team	10/16	109	6.8	1	0	--

Rushing	CAR	YDS	AVG	TD	LONG
M. Ingram II	11	102	9.3	2	40
R. Upchurch	17	70	4.1	1	21
D. Goode	11	70	6.4	0	11
T. Richardson	9	60	6.7	1	15
G. McElroy	2	8	4	0	6
S. Jackson	6	3	0.5	0	10
Team	56	313	5.6	4	40

Interceptions	INT	YDS	TD
J. Arenas	1	22	0
J. Woodall	1	9	0
C. Reamer	1	8	0
Team	3	39	0

Punting	NO	YDS	AVG	TB	IN 20	LONG
PJ Fitzgerald	2	78	39	0	0	55

Receiving	REC	YDS	AVG	TD	LONG
J. Jones	3	65	21.7	1	44
B. Smelley	2	18	9	0	11
M. McCoy	2	11	5.5	0	6
C. Peek	1	8	8	0	8
B. Gibson	1	4	4	0	4
T. Richardson	1	3	3	0	3
Team	10	109	10.9	1	44

Kick returns	NO	YDS	AVG	LONG	TD
J. Jones	1	12	12	12	0

Punt returns	NO	YDS	AVG	LONG	TD
J. Arenas	2	68	34	66	1
K. Jackson	1	0	0	0	0
J. Jones	3	0	0	0	0
Team	6	68	11.3	66	1

Kicking	FG	PCT	LONG	XP	PTS
L. Tiffin	1/1	100	41	5/5	8
J. Shelley	0/1	0	0	1/1	1
Team	1/2	50	41	6/6	9

Note: Table data from "Alabama 45-0 Chattanooga (Nov 21, 2009) Box Score" (60)

11/27/09 - Alabama (2) at Auburn

Team	1	2	3	4	T		Passing	Rushing	Total
Alabama (2)	0	14	6	6	**26**		218	73	**291**
Auburn	14	0	7	0	**21**		181	151	**332**

A year after Alabama's 36-0 victory in Tuscaloosa, the 2009 Iron Bowl ended with a 26-21 Tide victory and a 12-0 regular season. The Tigers took the ball after Alabama's initial three-and-out and struck quickly. On their fourth play from scrimmage, Terrell Zachery raced 67 yards on a reverse for a touchdown and a 7-0 Auburn lead. The run was the longest allowed by the Tide since an Arkansas's Darren McFadden in 2005. Auburn then successfully executed an onside kick. Then they drove 58 yards in 12 plays, scoring on a 1-yard touchdown pass from Chris Todd to Eric Smith. The Crimson Tide, which had never trailed in a game by more than seven points all season, found themselves down 14-0 before the first quarter was over.

Early in the second quarter, Alabama completed a 10-play, 58-yard drive by scoring on a 2-yard run by backup tailback Trent Richardson. The key plays were a 15-yard pass from McElroy to Darius Hanks and a 13-yard pass to Richardson. After an exchange of punts gave Alabama good starting position at the Auburn 45-yard line, the Tide quickly struck again with McElroy hitting tight end Colin Peek on a 33-yard touchdown pass that left the game tied at 14-14 at halftime.

In the third quarter, Auburn took possession on its 24-yard line after an Alabama punt. Kodi Burns rushed for four yards, and then Chris Todd hit Darvin Adams on a 72-yard completion that put Auburn back in front 21-14. The completion marked the longest play from scrimmage allowed by the Bama defense all season and the longest pass play since 1999. Javier Arenas gave Alabama an opportunity by returning the ensuing kickoff 46 yards to the Auburn 45-yard line, but Mark Ingram II, who struggled the entire game, rushed for seven yards and two yards, and then was held for no gain on both 3rd-and-1 and 4th-and-1. Auburn went three-and-out and punted, and Arenas set the Tide up again, returning the punt 56 yards to the Auburn 33-yard line. Alabama drove to the Auburn 10-yard line before settling for a Leigh Tiffin 27-yard field goal that cut the deficit to 21-17. Alabama kicked off, and two plays later Auburn quarterback Todd threw an interception (Mark Barron) that gave Alabama possession at the Auburn 43-yard line. The Tide drove to the Tigers' 13-yard line before this drive also stalled, forcing another Leigh Tiffin field goal (this one from 31 yards) that made the score 21-20, Auburn on top.

Neither team could make progress with possessions early in the fourth quarter, and after an exchange of punts, Alabama got the ball on its own 21-yard line with 8:27 to go and began what would soon be known as "The Drive". Richardson opened with a 7-yard rush, and on 3rd-and-3, McElroy completed a 9-yard pass to Julio Jones for a first down. Three plays later, on 3rd-and-5, McElroy completed a 6-yard pass to Jones for another first down and advanced the ball to the Tide 48-yard line. Two plays later, on 2nd-and-8, a third pass from McElroy to Jones for 11 yards led to a third first down. Two plays after that, a fourth pass from McElroy to Jones and a fourth first down and got the ball to the Auburn 28-yard line. On 2nd-and-9 at the Auburn 27-yard line, McElroy chose a different target, hitting Richardson for a first down to the Auburn 11-yard line. After a 4-yard run by Richardson to the Auburn 7-yard line, the Tigers called timeout with 1:34 left. Richardson took the ball three more yards to the Auburn 4-yard line, leaving the Tide at 3rd-and-3. Each team called a timeout in succession with 1:29 left. Alabama's offensive coaches called for a running play, but Head Coach Nick Saban, unwilling to settle for a field goal, overruled this decision and demanded a pass. McElroy completed a 4-yard touchdown pass to third-string tailback Roy Upchurch, giving Alabama a 26-21 lead with 1:24 to go. McElroy had completed seven consecutive passes on The Drive after missing his first.

A two-point conversion attempt failed, and the lead was five points. Auburn took possession at the 25-yard line following the kickoff and took 1:14 to run four plays and advance the ball to its own 46-yard line with ten seconds left in the game. Todd completed a 17-yard pass to Darvin Adams at the Alabama 37-yard line, and after spiking the ball, Todd's last pass fell incomplete and the game was over. Alabama had survived, beating Auburn 26-21 despite being outgained 332 yards to 291 and being held to only 73 yards rushing.[48]

Passing	C/ATT	YDS	AVG	TD	INT	QBR
G. McElroy	21/31	218	7	2	0	79.9
M. Ingram II	0/1	0	0	0	0	3.1
Team	21/32	218	6.8	2	0	--

Rushing	CAR	YDS	AVG	TD	LONG
T. Richardson	15	51	3.4	1	7
M. Ingram II	16	30	1.9	0	8
G. McElroy	4	-8	-2	0	0
Team	35	73	2.1	1	8

Interceptions	INT	YDS	TD
M.Barron	1	14	0

Punting	NO	YDS	AVG	TB	IN 20	LONG
PJ Fitzgerald	5	226	45.2	0	0	55

Receiving	REC	YDS	AVG	TD	LONG
J. Jones	9	83	9.2	0	18
C. Peek	3	53	17.7	1	33
T. Richardson	3	31	10.3	0	17
M. Ingram II	3	21	7	0	9
R. Upchurch	2	15	7.5	1	11
D. Hanks	1	15	15	0	15
Team	21	218	10.4	2	33

Kick returns	NO	YDS	AVG	LONG	TD
J. Arenas	1	46	46	46	0

Punt returns	NO	YDS	AVG	LONG	TD
J. Arenas	4	67	16.8	56	0

Kicking	FG	PCT	LONG	XP	PTS
L. Tiffin	2/3	66.7	31	2/2	8

Note: Table data from "Alabama 26-21 Auburn (Nov 27, 2009) Box Score" (61)

12/05/09 - Alabama (2) vs Florida (1)

Team	1	2	3	4	T		Passing	Rushing	Total
Florida (1)	3	10	0	0	13		247	88	335
Alabama (2)	9	10	7	6	32		239	251	490

Alabama faced Florida in the SEC Championship Game in a rematch of the 2008 contest with the Tide capturing their 22nd conference championship following their 32-13 victory over the Gators. The Tide struck first, driving 47 yards with the opening possession before Leigh Tiffin kicked a 48-yard field goal giving Alabama a 3-0 lead. Following a Florida three-and-out on its first possession, Alabama responded with an 8-play, 76-yard touchdown drive. On the drive, Greg McElroy completed key passes to Colin Peek and Marquis Maze, and Mark Ingram II rushed for 37 yards and the touchdown in taking a 9-0 lead following a missed extra point. On the ensuing possession, Caleb Sturgis hit a 48-yard field goal that made the score 9-3 at the end of the first quarter.

Alabama scored first in the second quarter on a 34-yard Tiffin field goal to complete a 68-yard drive and extend the Bama lead to 12-3. Florida followed with what turned out to be their only touchdown drive of the game. Rushes of 23 yards and 15 yards from quarterback and former Heisman Trophy winner Tim Tebow were followed by a 23-yard touchdown pass to David Nelson, and Florida had cut the lead to two, 12-10. On the next offensive play, Ingram II took a short pass from McElroy and raced 69 yards to the Gator 3-yard line and ran it in for a touchdown on the next play. The Gators ended the first half with a 32-yard Sturgis field goal to make the halftime score 19-13, Bama on top.

Florida opened the third quarter with a three-and-out. On the Tide's first offensive series of the second half, McElroy completed a 28-yard pass to Marquis Maze that was followed with a 15-yard personal foul penalty that brought the ball into the red zone. On the next play, McElroy completed the drive with a 17-yard touchdown pass to tight end Colin Peek, giving Alabama a 26-13 lead. Florida got one first down on their next possession before punting the ball back to Alabama. Taking the ball at its own 12-yard line with 7:36 to go in the third quarter, Alabama held the ball for the rest of the quarter and into the fourth, using up 8:47 of game time on a 12-play, 88-yard drive. Ingram II, who rushed for 37 yards on the drive, scored on a 1-yard touchdown run early in the fourth quarter to increase Bama's lead to 32-13. Florida mounted a late drive that reached the Alabama 6-yard line before Tebow threw an interception to Javier Arenas in the end zone. On Florida's next possession, the Gators turned the ball over on downs at the Alabama 13-yard line, and the Tide was able to run out the clock to secure the 32-13 victory.

For his 239-yard, one touchdown passing performance, Greg McElroy was named the game's MVP. Ingram II rushed for 113 and Trent Richardson rushed for 80 yards. The victory gave Alabama its 22nd SEC title, its third since the inception of the Championship Game in 1992 and its first in ten years—the longest time the Crimson Tide program has ever gone without an SEC championship.[48]

Passing	C/ATT	YDS	AVG	TD	INT	QBR
G. McElroy	12/18	239	13.3	1	0	98.5

Rushing	CAR	YDS	AVG	TD	LONG
M. Ingram II	28	113	4	3	15
T. Richardson	11	80	7.3	0	25
R. Upchurch	7	57	8.1	0	29
G. McElroy	4	10	2.5	0	8
Team	2	-9	-2	0	0
Team	52	251	4.8	3	29

Interceptions	INT	YDS	TD
J. Arenas	1	0	0

Punting	NO	YDS	AVG	TB	IN 20	LONG
PJ Fitzgerald	2	83	41.5	0	0	43

Receiving	REC	YDS	AVG	TD	LONG
M. Maze	5	96	19.2	0	34
M. Ingram II	2	76	38	0	69
C. Peek	3	39	13	1	19
J. Jones	2	28	14	0	18
Team	12	239	19.9	1	69

Kick returns	NO	YDS	AVG	LONG	TD
J. Arenas	3	79	26.3	32	0

Punt returns	NO	YDS	AVG	LONG	TD
J. Arenas	2	8	4	8	0

Kicking	FG	PCT	LONG	XP	PTS
L. Tiffin	2/2	100	48	2/3	8

Note: Table data from "Alabama 32-13 Florida (Dec 5, 2009) Box Score" (62)

01/07/10 - Alabama (1) vs Texas (2)

Team	1	2	3	4	T		Passing	Rushing	Total
Texas (2)	6	0	7	8	21		195	81	276
Alabama (1)	0	24	0	13	37		58	205	263

Following victories in their respective conference championship games on December 6, the final Bowl Championship Series (BCS) standings were unveiled, pitting the No. 1 ranked Crimson Tide against the No. 2 ranked Texas Longhorns for the 2010 BCS National Championship. The game was held in the Rose Bowl, although it was not the actual Rose Bowl Game. Alabama came into the game having never beaten Texas, compiling an all-time 0-7-1 record against the Longhorns.

Alabama won the toss and elected to receive the opening kickoff. After losing thirteen yards on a sack and a penalty, Nick Saban called for a fake punt which resulted in a Texas interception by Blake Gideon at the Alabama 37-yard line. On the initial possession, Texas quarterback Colt McCoy suffered a hit from Marcell Dareus which forced him to leave the game. Suffering from a pinched nerve in his throwing shoulder, McCoy did not return. With McCoy out, freshman Garrett Gilbert replaced him at quarterback, and the Longhorns settled for a field goal and a 3-0 lead. The ensuing kickoff was an onside kick, and Texas retained possession of the ball when Alabama failed to field the kick. The Longhorns only advanced the ball five yards and Hunter Lawrence kicked another field goal to go ahead 6-0.

The Tide went ahead in the second quarter. Greg McElroy threw for only 58 yards on 6-of-11 passing for Alabama, but 23 of those yards came on a completion to Julio Jones that advanced the ball to the Texas 12-yard line. Three plays later, Mark Ingram II ran it in from two yards out, and Alabama went ahead 7-6. After an exchange of punts, Bama took possession on the Texas 49-yard line, and on the second play Trent Richardson burst through a hole in the middle and raced 49 yards untouched for the touchdown, extending the lead to 14-6. Texas continued to struggle for offense in McCoy's absence, and on the next possession a Texas drive ended when Javier Arenas intercepted a Gilbert pass at the Alabama 25-yard line. Following a short punt late in the quarter, Bama drove to the Texas 9-yard line and increased its lead to 17-6 following a successful 26-yard Leigh Tiffin field goal. It appeared that the Crimson Tide would go into the locker room leading 17-6. However, after gaining nine yards on a rush up the middle, Texas called timeout with 15 seconds left. With the ball at the Texas 37-yard line, Gilbert threw a shovel pass to D.J. Monroe who bobbled the ball and batted it into the arms of Alabama defensive lineman Marcell Dareus who lumbered 28 yards for a touchdown that made the halftime score 24-6.

Having been sacked four times in the first half but had considerable success rushing the ball, Alabama came out rushing after halftime, attempting only two passes in the third quarter. Meanwhile, Gilbert, who had struggled early in the game, started to find his rhythm, mostly due to the efforts of Jordan Shipley, one of only two Texas receivers to catch a pass thrown beyond the line of scrimmage in the game. A 44-yard touchdown pass from Gilbert to Shipley cut the lead to 24-13. Early in the fourth quarter, Leigh Tiffin missed a 52-yard field goal. On the ensuing possession, the Longhorns drove 65 yards and scored another touchdown on a 28-yard Shipley reception. A successful two-point conversion pulled the score to within three points, 24-21. Following an Alabama punt, Texas gained possession on its own 7-yard line with 3:14 to go. On the second play of the drive, Eryk Anders laid a hit on Gilbert that forced a fumble, and Alabama recovered at the Texas 3-yard line. Three plays later, Ingram II, who rushed for 116 yards in the game, ran it in for the score that gave Alabama a 31-21 lead. On the following drive, Gilbert threw a second interception to Arenas, and a Trent Richardson touchdown with 47 seconds left made the final score 37-21.

For their performances, Mark Ingram II was named the game's offensive MVP and Marcell Dareus was named defensive MVP. Alabama beat Texas for the first time in its history, won its first ever BCS championship game, and won its first national championship since 1992. It was Alabama's thirteenth national championship and ninth perfect season. Alabama became the third school in major college history to go 14-0, joining the 2002 Ohio State Buckeyes and the 2009 Boise State Broncos.[48]

Passing	C/ATT	YDS	AVG	TD	INT	QBR
G. McElroy	6/11	58	5.3	0	0	25.8
PJ Fitzgerald	0/1	0	0	0	1	3.6
Team	6/12	58	4.8	0	1	--

Rushing	CAR	YDS	AVG	TD	LONG
M. Ingram II	22	116	5.3	2	19
T. Richardson	19	109	5.7	2	49
R. Upchurch	2	9	4.5	0	5
G. McElroy	7	-27	-3.9	0	6
Team	1	-2	-2	0	0
Team	51	205	4.0	4	49

Kick returns	NO	YDS	AVG	LONG	TD
M. Williams	2	17	8.5	11	0

Punting	NO	YDS	AVG	TB	IN 20	LONG
PJ Fitzgerald	7	261	37.3	0	0	41

Receiving	REC	YDS	AVG	TD	LONG
J. Jones	1	23	23	0	23
T. Richardson	2	19	9.5	0	11
M. Ingram II	2	12	6	0	7
M. Maze	1	4	4	0	4
Team	6	58	9.7	0	23

Interceptions	INT	YDS	TD
J. Arenas	2	3	0
M. Dareus	1	28	1
T. King	1	0	0
Team	4	31	1

Punt returns	NO	YDS	AVG	LONG	TD
J. Arenas	4	19	4.8	12	0

Kicking	FG	PCT	LONG	XP	PTS
L. Tiffin	1/2	50	26	4/5	7

Note: Table data from "Alabama 37-21 Texas (Jan 7, 2010) Box Score" (63)

Season Stats

Record	14-0	1st of 120
SEC Record	9-0	
Rank	1	
Points for	449	
Points against	164	
Points/game	32.1	22nd of 120
Opp points/game	11.7	2nd of 120
SOS[3]	6.62	2nd of 120

Team stats (averages per game)

		Passing					Rushing				Total Offense		
Split	G	Cmp	Att	Pct	Yds	TD	Att	Yds	Avg	TD	Plays	Yds	Avg
Offense	14	15.1	24.7	61.3	187.9	1.2	42.9	215.1	5	2.2	67.6	403	6
Defense	14	15	32.1	46.8	166	0.8	28.2	78.1	2.8	0.4	60.3	244.1	4
Difference		0.1	-7.4	14.5	21.9	0.4	14.7	137	2.2	1.8	7.3	158.9	2

	First Downs				Penalties		Turnovers		
Split	Pass	Rush	Pen	Tot	No.	Yds	Fum	Int	Tot
Offense	8.4	10.9	1.3	20.6	4.9	42.7	0.5	0.4	0.9
Defense	7.5	4.7	1.2	13.4	6.1	52.1	0.5	1.7	2.2
Difference	0.9	6.2	0.1	7.2	-1.2	-9.4	0	-1.3	-1.3

Passing

			Passing								
Rk	Player	G	Cmp	Att	Pct	Yds	Y/A	AY/A	TD	Int	Rate
1	Greg McElroy	14	198	325	60.9	2508	7.7	8.2	17	4	140.5
2	Star Jackson	5	13	18	72.2	116	6.4	6.4	0	0	126.4
3	P.J. Fitzgerald	14	1	2	50	7	3.5	-19	0	1	-20.6
4	Mark Ingram II	14	0	1	0	0	0	0	0	0	0

Rushing and receiving

			Rushing				Receiving				Scrimmage			
Rk	Player	G	Att	Yds	Avg	TD	Rec	Yds	Avg	TD	Plays	Yds	Avg	TD
1	Mark Ingram II	14	271	1658	6.1	17	32	334	10.4	3	303	1992	6.6	20
2	Trent Richardson	14	145	751	5.2	8	16	126	7.9	0	161	877	5.4	8
3	Greg McElroy	14	54	83	1.5	1					54	83	1.5	1
4	Roy Upchurch	13	48	299	6.2	2	12	72	6	1	60	371	6.2	3
5	Terry Grant	8	40	166	4.2	3	3	47	15.7	0	43	213	5	3
6	Demetrius Goode	11	16	108	6.8	0					16	108	6.8	0
7	Star Jackson	5	6	3	0.5	0					6	3	0.5	0
8	Marquis Maze	14	4	7	1.8	0	31	523	16.9	2	35	530	15.1	2
9	Julio Jones	13	2	4	2	0	43	596	13.9	4	45	600	13.3	4
10	P.J. Fitzgerald	14	1	17	17	0					1	17	17	0
11	Colin Peek	14					26	313	12	3	26	313	12	3
12	Darius Hanks	14					17	272	16	3	17	272	16	3
13	Mike McCoy	13					10	149	14.9	1	10	149	14.9	1
14	Brad Smelley	13					7	50	7.1	0	7	50	7.1	0
15	Earl Alexander	14					4	52	13	0	4	52	13	0
16	Michael Williams	14					3	29	9.7	0	3	29	9.7	0
17	Preston Dial	14					3	25	8.3	0	3	25	8.3	0
18	Brandon Gibson	4					2	25	12.5	0	2	25	12.5	0
19	Michael Bowman	4					1	7	7	0	1	7	7	0
20	Mark Barron	14					1	7	7	0	1	7	7	0
21	Baron Huber	14					1	4	4	0	1	4	4	0

Defense and fumbles

Rk	Player	G	Tackles					Def Int					Fumbles			
			Solo	Ast	Tot	Loss	Sk	Int	Yds	Avg	TD	PD	FR	Yds	TD	FF
1	Rolando McClain	14	53	52	105	14.5	4	2	21	10.5	0					
2	Mark Barron	14	43	33	76	3.5	0.5	7	125	17.9	1					
3	Javier Arenas	13	47	24	71	12	5	5	25	5	0					
4	Eryk Anders	14	32	34	66	14.5	6	1	0	0	0					
5	Cory Reamer	14	28	22	50	7	2	1	8	8	0					
6	Kareem Jackson	14	30	19	49	3	0	1	79	79	0					
7	Justin Woodall	14	30	15	45	2.5	0	3	33	11	0					
8	Marcell Dareus	14	19	14	33	9	6.5	1	28	28	1					
9	Robby Green	14	22	11	33	0	0	1	0	0	0					
10	Marquis Johnson	14	24	5	29	1	0	1	0	0	0					
11	Nico Johnson	12	17	11	28	4.5	1					2				1
12	Terrence Cody	14	12	16	28	6	0					1				
13	Brandon Deaderick	14	10	13	23	4.5	1									
14	Ali Sharrief	14	11	10	21	0	0									
15	Lorenzo Washington	14	13	8	21	5	2									
16	Tyrone King	14	8	10	18	1.5	1.5	1	0	0	0					
17	Josh Chapman	13	6	11	17	2.5	0.5									
18	Dont'a Hightower	4	5	11	16	4	1					1				
19	Courtney Upshaw	14	7	8	15	1	1						1	45	1	0
20	Chris Jordan	14	10	2	12	0	0									
21	Chris Rogers	14	9	2	11	0	0					1				1
22	Luther Davis	14	3	8	11	1.5	0									
23	Dre Kirkpatrick	12	3	5	8	0	0									
24	Robert Lester	8	6	2	8	0	0									
25	Nick Gentry	4	0	7	7	0	0									
26	Rod Woodson	12	5	2	7	0	0									
27	Trent Richardson	14	4	2	6	0	0									
28	Jerrell Harris	6	1	2	3	0	0									
29	Kerry Murphy	6	0	3	3	0	0									
30	Roy Upchurch	13	1	2	3	0	0									
31	Chavis Williams	7	1	1	2	0	0									
32	P.J. Fitzgerald	14	2	0	2	0	0									
33	Terry Grant	8	1	1	2	0	0									
34	Leigh Tiffin	14	1	1	2	0	0									
35	James Carpenter	14	1	0	1	0	0									
36	Hampton Gray	1	1	0	1	0	0									
37	Colin Peek	14	1	0	1	0	0									
38	Brian Selman	14	0	1	1	0	0									
39	Milton Talbert	1	0	1	1	0	0									
40	Alex Watkins	4	0	1	1	0	0									
41	Julio Jones	13	1	0	1	0	0									
42	Marquis Maze	14	1	0	1	0	0									
43	Greg McElroy	14	0	1	1	0	0									
44	Damion Square	2	0	1	1	0.5	0									

Kick and punt returns

Rk	Player	G	Ret	Yds	Avg	TD	Ret	Yds	Avg	TD
				Kick Ret				Punt Ret		
1	Javier Arenas	13	19	551	29	0	32	493	15.4	1
2	Terry Grant	8	8	176	22	0				
3	Michael Williams	14	2	17	8.5	0				
4	Trent Richardson	14	1	20	20	0				
5	Julio Jones	13	1	12	12	0	5	75	15	0
6	Baron Huber	14	1	10	10	0				
7	Damion Square	2	1	5	5	0				
8	Lorenzo Washington	14					1	16	16	0
9	Cory Reamer	14					1	3	3	0

Kicking and punting

Rk	Player	G	XPM	XPA	XP%	FGM	FGA	FG%	Pts	Punts	Yds	Avg
					Kicking						Punting	
1	Leigh Tiffin	14	42	46	91.3	30	35	85.7	132			
2	Jeremy Shelley	1	1	1	100	0	1	0	1			
3	P.J. Fitzgerald	14								58	2407	41.5

Scoring

Rk	Player	G	Rush	Rec	Int	FR	PR	KR	Tot	XPM	FGM	2PM	Sfty	Pts
					Touchdowns						Kicking			
1	Leigh Tiffin	14								42	30			132
2	Mark Ingram II	14	17	3					20					120
3	Trent Richardson	14	8						8			1		50
4	Julio Jones	13		4					4					24
5	Colin Peek	14		3					3					18
6	Darius Hanks	14		3					3					18
7	Roy Upchurch	13	2	1					3					18
8	Terry Grant	8	3						3					18
9	Marquis Maze	14		2					2					12
10	Greg McElroy	14	1						1			1		8
11	Courtney Upshaw	14				1			1					6
12	Javier Arenas	13					1		1					6
13	Marcell Dareus	14			1				1					6
14	Mark Barron	14			1				1					6
15	Mike McCoy	13		1					1					6
16	Jeremy Shelley	1								1				1

Stats include bowl games
Note: Table data from "2009 Alabama Crimson Tide Stats" (3)

Awards and honors

Name	Award	Type
Javier Arenas	Permanent Team Captain	Team
Mike Johnson	Permanent Team Captain	Team
Rolando McClain	Permanent Team Captain	Team
Mark Ingram II	Co-MVP	Team
Rolando McClain	Co-MVP	Team
Mark Ingram II	Offensive Player of the Year	Team
Mike Johnson	Offensive Player of the Year	Team
Terrence Cody	Defensive Player of the Year	Team
Rolando McClain	Defensive Player of the Year	Team
Nick Saban	Coach of the Year	SEC
Mark Ingram II	Offensive Player of the Year	SEC
Rolando McClain	Defensive Player of the Year	SEC
Javier Arenas	AP All-SEC First Team	SEC
Terrence Cody	AP All-SEC First Team	SEC
Mark Ingram II	AP All-SEC First Team	SEC
Mike Johnson	AP All-SEC First Team	SEC
Rolando McClain	AP All-SEC First Team	SEC
Leigh Tiffin	AP All-SEC First Team	SEC
Javier Arenas	AP All-SEC Second Team	SEC
James Carpenter	AP All-SEC Second Team	SEC
Colin Peek	AP All-SEC Second Team	SEC
Javier Arenas	Coaches' All-SEC First Team	SEC
Mark Barron	Coaches' All-SEC First Team	SEC
Terrence Cody	Coaches' All-SEC First Team	SEC

Name	Award	Type
Mark Ingram II	Coaches' All-SEC First Team	SEC
Mike Johnson	Coaches' All-SEC First Team	SEC
Rolando McClain	Coaches' All-SEC First Team	SEC
Leigh Tiffin	Coaches' All-SEC First Team	SEC
Julio Jones	Coaches' All-SEC Second Team	SEC
Nico Johnson	Freshman All-SEC	SEC
Barrett Jones	Freshman All-SEC	SEC
Trent Richardson	Freshman All-SEC	SEC
Javier Arenas	AFCA Al-American Team	National
Mark Ingram II	AFCA Al-American Team	National
Mike Johnson	AFCA Al-American Team	National
Rolando McClain	AFCA Al-American Team	National
Javier Arenas	AP All-America First Team	National
Terrence Cody	AP All-America First Team	National
Mark Ingram II	AP All-America First Team	National
Mike Johnson	AP All-America First Team	National
Rolando McClain	AP All-America First Team	National
Leigh Tiffin	AP All-America First Team	National
Mark Barron	AP All-America Second Team	National
Kirby Smart	Broyles Award	National
Rolando McClain	Butkus Award	National
Terrence Cody	Chuck Bednarik Award Finalist	National
Javier Arenas	Consensus All-American	National
Terrence Cody	Consensus All-American	National
Mark Ingram II	Consensus All-American	National
Mike Johnson	Consensus All-American	National
Rolando McClain	Consensus All-American	National
Mark Ingram II	Doak Walker Award Finalist	National
Mark Ingram II	Heisman Trophy	National
Rolando McClain	Jack Lambert Award	National
Leigh Tiffin	Lou Groza Award Finalist	National
Mark Ingram II	Maxwell Award Finalist	National
Mark Ingram II	Unanimous All-American	National
Rolando McClain	Unanimous All-American	National
Terrence Cody	Walter Camp All-America First Team	National
Mike Johnson	Walter Camp All-America First Team	National
Rolando McClain	Walter Camp All-America First Team	National
Javier Arenas	Walter Camp All-America Second Team	National
Leigh Tiffin	Walter Camp All-America Second Team	National
Lorenzo Washington	All-Star Texas vs the Nation Game	All-Star Team
Justin Woodall	All-Star East-West Shrine Game	All-Star Team
Javier Arenas	Senior Bowl	All-Star Team
Terrence Cody	Senior Bowl	All-Star Team
Mike Johnson	Senior Bowl	All-Star Team
Colin Peek	Senior Bowl	All-Star Team
Leigh Tiffin	Senior Bowl	All-Star Team

NFL

Season	Year drafted	Round	Pick	Overall	Player	Position	Team
2009	2010	1	8	8	Rolando McClain	LB	Oakland Raiders
2009	2010	1	20	20	Kareem Jackson	CB	Houston Texans
2009	2010	2	18	50	Javier Arenas	DB	Kansas City Chiefs
2009	2010	2	25	57	Terrence Cody	DE	Baltimore Ravens
2009	2010	3	34	98	Mike Johnson	OG	Atlanta Falcons
2009	2010	7	4	211	Marquis Johnson	DB	Los Angeles Rams
2009	2010	7	40	247	Brandon Deaderick	DE	New England Patriots

Note: Table data from "2009 Alabama Crimson Tide football team" (48)

2010

Overall

Record	10-3
SEC Record	5-3
Rank	10
Points for	464
Points against	176
Points/game	35.7
Opp points/game	13.5
SOS[4]	4.69

Football's a tough game for tough people. I'm really not apologizing for anything I did, to be honest with you. A.J. doesn't have a problem with it. Nobody else should have a problem with it. I've been getting patted on the ass since I was nine years old playing Pee Wee football. If you don't like that, I guess you should watch the Golf Channel. -Nick Saban

Games

Date	Bama Rank		Opp Rank	Opponent	Bama	Opp	Result	SEC
09/04/10	1	vs		San Jose State	48	3	W	
09/11/10	1	vs	18	Penn State	24	3	W	
09/18/10	1	@		Duke	62	13	W	
09/25/10	1	@	10	Arkansas	24	20	W	W
10/02/10	1	vs	7	Florida	31	6	W	W
10/09/10	1	@	19	South Carolina	21	35	L	L
10/16/10	8	vs		Ole Miss	23	10	W	W
10/23/10	8	@		Tennessee	41	10	W	W
11/06/10	6	@	10	LSU	21	24	L	L
11/13/10	12	vs	19	Mississippi State	30	10	W	W
11/18/10	11	vs		Georgia State	63	7	W	
11/26/10	11	vs	2	Auburn	27	28	L	L
01/01/11	16	N	9	Michigan State	49	7	W	

Coaches

Name	Position	Year
Nick Saban	Head Coach	4
Burton Burns	Associate Head Coach / Running Backs	4
Curt Cignetti	Wide Receivers / Recruiting Coordinator	4
Scott Cochran	Strength and Conditioning	4
Bo Davis	Defensive Line	4
Jim McElwain	Offensive Coordinator / Quarterbacks	3
Joe Pendry	Offensive Line	4
Jeremy Pruitt	Secondary	1
Freddie Roach	Assistant Strength and Conditioning	3
Kirby Smart	Defensive Coordinator	4
Sal Sunseri	Assistant Head Coach / Linebackers	2
Bobby Williams	Tight Ends / Special Teams	3

Recruits

Name	Pos	Pos Rank	Scout	Rivals	247 Sports	ESPN	ESPN Grade	Hometown	High school / college	Height	Weight	Committed
Deion Belue	ATH	40	3	3	3	3	78	Tuscumbia, AL	Deshler HS	6-0	165	6/20/09
Ronald Carswell	WR	65	4	3	3	3	78	Macon, GA	Westside HS	6-0	171	4/7/09
Cade Foster	K	12	4	2	3	3	76	Southlake, TX	Carroll HS	6-1	215	11/29/08
Jalston Fowler	OLB		4	4	4	3	77	Prichard, AL	Vigor HS	6-0	245	2/14/09
John Fulton	CB	4		4	4	4	83	Manning, SC	Manning HS	6-1	180	1/2/10
Corey Grant	RB	23	4	4	N/A	3	79	Opelika, AL	Opelika HS	5-9	190	7/23/09
Adrian Hubbard	DE	5	3	3	4	4	82	Norcross, GA	Norcross HS	6-7	227	12/8/09
Brandon Ivory	DT	58	3	3	3	3	77	Memphis, TN	Memphis East HS	6-3	330	1/28/10
Harrison Jones	TE	9	3	3	3	4	80	Cordova, TN	Evangelical Christian School	6-4	225	8/25/09
Arie Kouandjio	OG	14	4	4	4	3	79	Hyattsville, MD	DeMatha Catholic HS	6-6	314	2/2/10
Brandon Lewis	DE		3	3	3	N/A	NR	Scooba, MS	E Mississippi Community College	6-3	280	2/5/09
Chad Lindsay	OG	1	3	3	3	4	81	Woodlands, TX	The Woodlands HS	6-3	310	4/6/09
Wilson Love	DT	34	3	3	3	3	79	Mountain Brook, AL	Mountain Brook HS	6-4	270	4/18/09
Keiwone Malone	WR	13	3	4	4	4	81	Memphis, TN	Mitchell HS	5-11	165	2/6/09
Darius McKeller	OT	58		3	3	3	78	Jonesboro, GA	Jonesboro High Sschool	6-6	319	4/24/08
DeQuan Menzie	CB		4	4	4	N/A	NR	Wesson, MS	Copiah-Lincoln Community College	5-11	200	1/31/10
Dee Milliner	CB	2	5	5	5	4	84	Millbrook, AL	Stanhope Elmore HS	6-1	185	6/4/09
C.J. Mosley	OLB	7	4	4	4	4	81	Theodore, AL	Theodore HS	6-2	212	1/9/10
Anthony Orr	OLB	7		3	3	3	76	Mobile, AL	Sparkman HS	6-4	270	7/29/08
Nick Perry	S	27	4	4	4	3	79	Prattville, AL	Prattville HS	6-2	190	4/1/09
Austin Shepherd	OT	46	3	3	3	3	77	Suwanee, GA	North Gwinnett HS	6-4	310	3/9/09
Blake Sims	ATH	64	4	4	4	3	78	Gainesville, GA	Gainesville HS	6-0	191	4/4/09
Phillip Sims	QB	1	5	4	5	4	83	Chesapeake, VA	Oscar F. Smith HS	6-2	215	4/15/09
Petey Smith	ILB	32		3	4	4	81	Seffner, FL	Armwood HS	6-1	245	1/28/09
Brian Vogler	TE	7	4	4	4	4	81	Columbus, GA	Brookstone School	6-7	246	7/22/09
DeAndrew White	WR	26	4	4	4	4	80	Galena Park, TX	North Shore HS	6-0	170	10/12/09
Jarrick Williams	S		4	4	4	4	79	Prichard, AL	Mattie T. Blount HS	6-2	205	6/26/09
Jay Williams	K	9	3	2	3	3	77	Thomasville, AL	Thomasville HS	6-4	220	6/20/09

	Scout	Rivals	247Sports	ESPN
5 Stars	2	1	2	0
4 Stars	12	13	13	12
3 Stars	10	12	12	14
2 Stars	0	2	0	0

Note: Table data from "2010 Alabama Crimson Tide football team" (64)

Roster

Num	Player	Pos	Class	Height	Weight	Hometown	Last School
82	Earl Alexander	WR	SR	6-4	207	Phenix City, AL	Central
19	Jonathan Atchison	LB	FR	6-2	228	Atlanta, GA	Douglass
31	John Baites	TE	JR	6-4	235	Hendersonville, TN	Beech
4	**Mark Barron**	**DB**	**JR**	**6-2**	**210**	**Mobile, AL**	**St. Paul's**
7	Kenny Bell	WR	FR	6-1	172	Rayville, LA	Rayville
86	Undra Billingsley	TE	SO	6-2	269	Birmingham, AL	Woodlawn
69	David Blalock	OL	JR	6-5	255	Charlotte, NC	Providence
93	Chris Bonds	DL	FR	6-4	263	Columbia, SC	Richland Northeast
67	John Michael Boswell	OL	JR	6-5	291	Northport, AL	Tuscaloosa County
88	Michael Bowman	WR	SO	6-4	225	Rossville, GA	Ridgeland
37	Hardie Buck	WR	SO	5-9	184	Birmingham, AL	Vestavia Hills
87	Drew Bullard	LB	JR	6-3	232	Florence, AL	Florence
34	Hunter Bush	DB	SO	5-11	181	Wetempka, AL	Wetumpka
20	Nate Carlson	RB	JR	6-4	230	Birmingham, AL	Air Force
77	**James Carpenter**	**OL**	**SR**	**6-5**	**300**	**Augusta, GA**	**Coffeyville CC**
33	Caleb Castille	DB	FR	5-11	163	Birmingham, AL	Briarwood Christian
99	**Josh Chapman**	**DL**	**JR**	**6-1**	**310**	**Hoover, AL**	**Hoover**
57	**Marcell Dareus**	**DL**	**JR**	**6-4**	**306**	**Huffman, AL**	**Huffman**
96	**Luther Davis**	**DL**	**SR**	**6-3**	**279**	**West Monroe, LA**	**West Monroe**
51	Michael DeJohn	LB	SR	6-1	237	Hoover, AL	Hoover
85	**Preston Dial**	**TE**	**SR**	**6-3**	**237**	**Mobile, AL**	**UMS-Wright**
40	DeMarcus DuBose	LB	JR	6-1	240	Montgomery, AL	Jefferson Davis
13	Rob Ezell	WR	SR	5-10	172	Athens, AL	Athens
76	**D.J. Fluker**	**OL**	**FR**	**6-6**	**340**	**Foley, AL**	**Foley**
43	**Cade Foster**	**PK**	**FR**	**6-1**	**221**	**Southlake, TX**	**Southlake Carroll**
45	Jalston Fowler	RB	FR	6-1	236	Mobile, AL	Vigor
10	John Fulton	DB	FR	6-0	179	Manning, SC	Manning
95	Colin Gallagher	PK	SR	5-10	194	Atlanta, GA	Marist
58	Nick Gentry	DL	JR	6-1	282	Prattville, AL	Prattville
11	Brandon Gibson	WR	JR	6-1	196	Mobile, AL	UMS-Wright
6	Demetrius Goode	RB	JR	5-10	190	LaGrange, GA	Hargrave
25	Corey Grant	RB	FR	5-9	186	Opelika, AL	Opelika
68	Austin Gray	OL	FR	6-0	309	Woodstock, GA	Alan C. Pope
23	Robby Green	DB	JR	6-0	181	New Orleans, LA	John Curtis Christian
15	**Darius Hanks**	**WR**	**JR**	**6-0**	**184**	**Norcross, GA**	**Norcross**
54	Glenn Harbin	DL	SO	6-5	260	Mobile, AL	McGill-Toolen
48	Rowdy Harrell	LB	SO	6-0	213	Moundville, AL	Hale County
5	**Jerrell Harris**	**LB**	**JR**	**6-3**	**231**	**Gadsden, AL**	**Gadsden City**
30	**Dont'a Hightower**	**LB**	**SO**	**6-4**	**260**	**Lewisburg, TN**	**Marshall County**
15	Mark Holt	DB	SR	6-1	172	Muscle Shoals, AL	Muscle Shoals
21	Ben Howell	RB	SO	5-9	193	Gordo, AL	Gordo
42	Adrian Hubbard	LB	FR	6-6	227	Lawrenceville, GA	Norcross
22	**Mark Ingram II**	**RB**	**JR**	**5-10**	**215**	**Flint, MI**	**Southwestern Academy**
62	Brandon Ivory	DL	FR	6-4	335	Memphis, TN	East
35	**Nico Johnson**	**LB**	**SO**	**6-3**	**238**	**Andalusia, AL**	**Andalusia**
57	Aaron Joiner	OL	SO	6-2	258	Florence, AL	Florence
75	**Barrett Jones**	**OL**	**SO**	**6-5**	**301**	**Memphis, TN**	**Evangelical Christian**
40	Harrison Jones	TE	FR	6-4	235	Germantown, TN	Evangelical Christian
8	**Julio Jones**	**WR**	**JR**	**6-4**	**220**	**Foley, AL**	**Foley**
9	Phelon Jones	DB	JR	5-11	199	Moblie, AL	LSU
36	Chris Jordan	LB	JR	6-3	232	Brentwood, TN	Brentwood Academy
43	Sam Kearns	DB	JR	5-6	156	Mobile, AL	McGill-Toolen
26	Kendall Kelly	WR	FR	6-3	214	Gadsden, AL	Gadsden City
10	J.B. Kern	LB	SR	6-1	232	Dove Canyon, CA	Mission Viejo
21	**Dre Kirkpatrick**	**DB**	**SO**	**6-3**	**190**	**Gadsden, AL**	**Gadsden City**
59	Arie Kouandjio	OL	FR	6-5	335	Beltsville, MD	DeMatha Catholic
42	Eddie Lacy	RB	FR	6-0	212	Geismar, LA	Dutchtown
37	**Robert Lester**	**DB**	**SO**	**6-2**	**206**	**Foley, AL**	**Foley**
95	Brandon Lewis	DL	JR	6-3	274	Pleasant Grove, AL	East Mississippi CC
78	Chad Lindsay	OL	FR	6-2	277	The Woodlands, TX	The Woodlands
72	Tyler Love	OL	SO	6-6	304	Mountain Brook, AL	Mountain Brook
29	Will Lowery	DB	JR	5-9	188	Hoover, AL	Hoover
7	Keiwone Malone	WR	FR	5-11	165	Memphis, TN	Mitchell
32	Cody Mandell	P	FR	6-4	201	Lafayette, LA	Acadiana
33	Mike Marrow	RB	FR	6-2	235	Holland, OH	Central Catholic
4	**Marquis Maze**	**WR**	**JR**	**5-10**	**182**	**Birmingham, AL**	**Tarrant**
24	Nathan McAlister	WR	FR	5-11	165	Russellville, AL	Russellville
10	A.J. McCarron	QB	FR	6-4	190	Mobile, AL	Saint Paul's Episcopal School
52	Alfred McCullough	OL	JR	6-2	309	Athens, AL	Athens
12	**Greg McElroy**	**QB**	**SR**	**6-3**	**225**	**Southlake, TX**	**Southlake Carroll**
24	DeQuan Menzie	DB	JR	6-0	195	Columbus, GA	Copiah-Lincoln CC
28	Dee Milliner	DB	FR	6-1	182	Millbrook, AL	Stanhope Elmore

Num	Player	Pos	Class	Height	Weight	Hometown	Last School
56	William Ming	DL	FR	6-3	263	Athens, AL	Athens
97	Brandon Moore	DL	FR	6-5	305	Montgomery, AL	Carver
32	C.J. Mosley	LB	FR	6-2	225	Theodore, AL	Theodore
66	Brian Motley	OL	SR	6-3	289	Autaugaville, AL	Autaugaville
64	Kerry Murphy	DL	SO	6-4	319	Hoover, AL	Hargrave/Hoover
46	Wesley Neighbors	DB	SO	6-1	205	Huntsville, AL	Huntsville
83	Kevin Norwood	WR	FR	6-2	187	D'Iberville, MS	D'Iberville
18	Morgan Ogilvie	QB	FR	6-0	198	Mountain Brook, AL	Mountain Brook
53	Anthony Orr	DL	FR	6-4	268	Madison, AL	Sparkman
2	Tana Patrick	LB	FR	6-3	231	Bridgeport, AL	North Jackson
39	Kyle Pennington	DB	JR	5-11	188	Chatom, AL	Washington County
27	Nick Perry	DB	FR	6-1	193	Prattville, AL	Prattville
3	Trent Richardson	RB	SO	5-11	220	Pensacola, FL	Escambia
74	David Ross	OL	SR	6-3	302	Homewood, AL	Homewood
1	**B.J. Scott**	**DB**	**SO**	**5-11**	**193**	**Prichard, AL**	**Vigor**
94	Darrington Sentimore	DL	FR	6-3	261	Norco, LA	Destrehan
90	Jeremy Shelley	PK	SO	5-10	165	Raleigh, NC	Broughton
79	Austin Shepherd	OL	FR	6-5	307	Buford, GA	North Gwinnett
18	Blake Sims	ATH	FR	6-0	195	Gainesville, GA	Gainesville
14	Phillip Sims	QB	FR	6-2	214	Chesapeake, VA	Oscar Smith
71	Allen Skelton	OL	SO	6-1	261	Coker, AL	Tuscaloosa County
17	Brad Smelley	TE	JR	6-3	227	Tuscaloosa, AL	American Christian
38	Petey Smith	LB	FR	6-1	250	Tampa, FL	Armwood
92	Damion Square	DL	SO	6-3	284	Houston, TX	Yates
61	Anthony Steen	OL	FR	6-3	292	Lambert, MS	Lee Academy
47	Ed Stinson	LB	FR	6-4	252	Homestead, FL	South Dade
46	William Strickland	WR	FR	6-0	188	Tuscaloosa, AL	Northridge
47	Logan Thomas	WR	SR	6-3	206	Houston, TX	Cyrpress Creek
51	Carson Tinker	LS	SO	6-1	220	Murfreesboro, TN	Riverdale
26	Nick Tinker	RB	FR	5-10	215	Ralph, AL	Tuscaloosa County
87	Chris Underwood	TE	SO	6-4	238	Vestavia Hills, AL	Vestavia Hills
41	**Courtney Upshaw**	**LB**	**JR**	**6-2**	**263**	**Eufaula, AL**	**Eufaula**
73	**William Vlachos**	**OL**	**JR**	**6-1**	**289**	**Birmingham, AL**	**Mountain Brook**
84	Brian Vogler	TE	FR	6-7	242	Columbus, GA	Brookstone
65	**Chance Warmack**	**OL**	**SO**	**6-3**	**300**	**Atlanta, GA**	**Westlake**
91	Alex Watkins	LB	JR	6-3	232	Brownsville, TN	Haywood
49	Ranzell Watkins	DB	FR	5-9	168	Charlotte, NC	Independence
2	DeAndrew White	WR	FR	6-0	180	Houston, TX	North Shore
55	Chavis Williams	LB	SR	6-4	223	Dora, AL	Dora
60	David Williams	OL	SO	6-3	267	Duncanville, AL	Hillcrest
20	Jarrick Williams	DB	FR	6-1	203	Mobile, AL	Blount
44	**Jay Williams**	**P**	**FR**	**6-3**	**208**	**Thomasville, AL**	**Thomasville**
63	Kellen Williams	OL	FR	6-3	307	Lawrenceville, GA	Brookwood
89	**Michael Williams**	**TE**	**SO**	**6-6**	**270**	**Reform, AL**	**Pickens County**
9	Nick Williams	WR	FR	5-10	179	Fort Lauderdale, FL	St. Thomas Aquinas

Note: Starters in bold
Note: Table data from "2010 Alabama Crimson Tide Roster" (65)

Games

09/04/10 - Alabama (1) vs San Jose State

Team	1	2	3	4	T	Passing	Rushing	Total
San Jose State	3	0	0	0	3	86	89	175
Alabama (1)	14	17	10	7	48	334	257	591

The Crimson Tide began their defense of their 2010 BCS championship at home against the San Jose State Spartans and before a record crowd in a newly expanded Bryant-Denny Stadium, Alabama was victorious 48-3. Alabama scored a touchdown on its first possession on a 1-yard Trent Richardson run to complete an 8-play, 71-yard drive. The Spartans responded on the next drive with their only points of the game on a 31-yard Harrison Waid field goal to make the score 7-3. On the ensuing drive, Alabama extended its lead to 14-3 with a 48-yard Greg McElroy touchdown pass to Marquis Maze, capping a 5-play, 77-yard drive in 2:24.

Alabama reached the end zone again early in the second quarter on a 39-yard Richardson run on a quick 3-play, 54-yard drive that only took 1:12 off the clock. After a San Jose State punt went out of bounds at the at the SJSU 40-yard line, A.J. McCarron threw two straight passes to Julio Jones. The first one went for 11 yards, and the second one was for a 29-yard touchdown just 33 seconds after starting the drive (28-3). Cade Foster scored the final points of the half on a 31-yard field goal as time expired to bring the halftime score to 31-3.

Alabama opened the second half by scoring on its first two possessions. Alabama drove 92 yards in six plays (including a 25-yard pass to Julio Jones) as Eddie Lacy scored on a 37-yard run. Then Foster hit a 24-yard field goal capping an 8-play, 67-yard drive to extend the Crimson Tide lead to 41-3. Lacy scored the final points of the game with a 10-yard run to make the final score 48-3. Both McElroy and McCarron combined to pass for 334 yards on 22 completions and a pair of touchdowns. For the game, the Alabama outgained San Jose in total offense by a margin of 591-175. The 101,821 in attendance marked the first crowd of over 100,000 to attend a football game in the state of Alabama.[64]

Passing	C/ATT	YDS	AVG	TD	INT	QBR
G. McElroy	13/16	218	13.6	1	0	94.1
AJ McCarron	9/14	116	8.3	1	0	91.8
Team	22/30	334	11.1	2	0	--

Rushing	CAR	YDS	AVG	TD	LONG
E. Lacy	13	111	8.5	2	37
T. Richardson	10	66	6.6	2	39
D. Goode	11	66	6	0	13
J. Jones	1	13	13	0	13
G. McElroy	3	7	2.3	0	6
AJ McCarron	1	-2	-2	0	0
Team	2	-4	-2	0	0
Team	41	257	6.3	4	39

Interceptions	INT	YDS	TD
R. Lester	1	15	0

Kicking	FG	PCT	LONG	XP	PTS
C. Foster	2/2	100	41	2/2	8
J. Shelley	0/0	0	0	4/4	4
Team	2/2	100	41	6/6	12

Punting	NO	YDS	AVG	TB	IN 20	LONG
C. Mandell	3	122	40.7	0	0	52

Receiving	REC	YDS	AVG	TD	LONG
J. Jones	6	93	15.5	1	29
M. Maze	3	68	22.7	1	48
D. Hanks	3	66	22	0	34
T. Richardson	3	46	15.3	0	19
B. Gibson	3	21	7	0	14
P. Dial	1	19	19	0	19
E. Alexander	1	9	9	0	9
B. Smelley	1	9	9	0	9
E. Lacy	1	3	3	0	3
Team	22	334	15.2	2	48

Kick returns	NO	YDS	AVG	LONG	TD
T. Richardson	1	34	34	34	0
M. Williams	1	9	9	9	0
Team	2	43	21.5	34	0

Punt returns	NO	YDS	AVG	LONG	TD
M. Maze	3	8	2.7	5	0
D. Hanks	1	1	1	1	0
J. Jones	1	0	0	0	0
Team	5	9	1.8	5	0

Note: Table data from "Alabama 48-3 San Jose State (Sep 4, 2010) Box Score" (66)

09/11/10 - Alabama (1) vs Penn State (18)

Team	1	2	3	4	T		Passing	Rushing	Total
Penn State (18)	0	0	0	3	3		156	127	**283**
Alabama (1)	7	10	0	7	**24**		229	180	**409**

With ESPN's College GameDay in town, Alabama defeated the Penn State Nittany Lions 24-3 in a renewal of their historic rivalry. After exchanging punts, Alabama scored first on a 36-yard touchdown pass from Greg McElroy to Kevin Norwood on a 5-play, 68-yard drive. After an interception by Will Lowery, the Crimson Tide added to their lead in the second quarter as they drove 97 yards in nine plays, capped by a 14-yard McElroy touchdown pass to Preston Dial. On Penn State's next possession, Robert Lester recovered a fumble and ran it back 89 yards before he fumbled it back to Penn State at their own 2-yard line. Bama forced a punt, drove to the PSU 9-yard line, and Jeremy Shelley kicked a 31-yard field goal. The Tide led 17-0 at the half after another Penn State punt and a missed 44-yard field goal attempt by Cade Foster.

To start the third quarter, Penn State drove to the Alabama 26-yard line before Robert Lester intercepted a pass at the 13-yard line. Both teams traded punts, then Alabama drove 71 yards into the fourth quarter when Trent Richardson scored on a 1-yard run. On the next possession, Penn State's Collin Wagner hit a 36-yard field goal to make the final score 24-3.

Richardson led the team in rushing with 144 yards on 22 carries and was also the first back to gain over 100 yards on the ground against Penn State since their 2008 game against Iowa. The defense also stood out with Mark Barron, Robert Lester, and Will Lowery each making an interception and Alabama only allowing 283 yards of total offense. After compiling 207 all-purpose yards and scoring a touchdown, Richardson was named Co-SEC Offensive Player of the Week with South Carolina's Marcus Lattimore.[64]

Passing	C/ATT	YDS	AVG	TD	INT	QBR
G. McElroy	16/24	229	9.5	2	0	80

Rushing	CAR	YDS	AVG	TD	LONG
T. Richardson	22	144	6.5	1	33
E. Lacy	6	21	3.5	0	7
G. McElroy	5	8	1.6	0	10
M. Maze	1	7	7	0	7
Team	34	180	5.3	1	33

Interceptions	INT	YDS	TD
M. Barron	1	2	0
R. Lester	1	0	0
W. Lowery	1	0	0
Team	3	2	0

Punting	NO	YDS	AVG	TB	IN 20	LONG
C. Mandell	3	111	37	0	0	44

Receiving	REC	YDS	AVG	TD	LONG
D. Hanks	3	52	17.3	0	31
J. Jones	4	49	12.3	0	21
T. Richardson	4	46	11.5	0	29
K. Norwood	1	36	36	1	36
M. Maze	2	28	14	0	20
P. Dial	2	18	9	1	14
Team	16	229	14.3	2	36

Kick returns	NO	YDS	AVG	LONG	TD
T. Richardson	1	17	17	17	0

Punt returns	NO	YDS	AVG	LONG	TD
J. Jones	2	0	0	0	0

Kicking	FG	PCT	LONG	XP	PTS
J. Shelley	1/1	100	31	3/3	6
C. Foster	0/1	0	0	0/0	0
Team	1/2	50	31	3/3	6

Note: Table data from "Penn State 3-24 Alabama (Sep 11, 2010) Box Score" (67)

09/18/10 - Alabama (1) at Duke

Team	1	2	3	4	T		Passing	Rushing	Total
Alabama (1)	28	17	10	7	62		311	315	626
Duke	3	10	0	0	13		156	146	302

In Alabama's first-ever trip to Duke, the Crimson Tide defeated the Blue Devils by a final score of 62-13 in front of the largest crowd at Wallace Wade Stadium since the 1994 season. Playing in his first game of the 2010 season following knee surgery, Mark Ingram II ran for a team-high 151 yards on nine carries with two touchdowns.

Alabama scored on all four of their first quarter possessions. The first one only took 1:19 and three plays as Greg McElroy hooked up with Darius Hanks for a 9-yard TD capping the 60-yard drive. The next one took 2:12 and six plays as the Tide drove 62 yards with Julio Jones catching the 18-yard TD. Mark Ingram II got in on the action rushing for two scores, the first being a 1-yard touchdown run capping a 6-play, 77-yard drive. The other 3-play, 48-yard drive (set up by a Dre Kirkpatrick interception and a nice 31-yard catch by Darius Hanks) ended with his 17-yard score. After a 22-yard field goal by Duke, Alabama was ahead 28-3 after one quarter of play.

After Greg McElroy threw an interception on Alabama's first possession of the second quarter, he threw a 15-yard touchdown pass to Preston Dial on the next. It was a 56-yard drive that took five plays and 1:50 and extended Alabama's lead to 35-3. Trent Richardson scored Alabama's first special teams touchdown of the season with a 96-yard kickoff return after Duke hit a 42-yard field goal (42-6). Duke responded with a 13-play, 68-yard touchdown drive, then Foster kicked a 44-yard field goal as time expired in the half. Alabama led 45-13 at the break.

Foster connected on a 21-yard field goal in between two Duke punts before Trent Richardson took the first play of Alabama's next possession to the house for a 45-yard score. The only score in the fourth quarter came on a 1-yard rush by Eddie Lacy which capped off a 7-play, 39-yard drive and brought the final to 62-13. After allowing 13 points in the first half, the Alabama defense shut out the Duke offense in the second half. The 62 points scored by the Tide was the most since a 62-0 victory over Tulane during the 1991 season, and the 45 points scored in the first half were the most scored in one half since scoring 45 in the second half of the 1973 victory over California. The 626 yards of total offense were the most amassed by an Alabama team since gaining 644 against LSU in 1989.[64]

Passing	C/ATT	YDS	AVG	TD	INT	QBR
G. McElroy	14/20	258	12.9	3	1	96.5
AJ McCarron	3/6	53	8.8	0	0	69.6
Team	17/26	311	12.0	3	1	--

Rushing	CAR	YDS	AVG	TD	LONG
M. Ingram II	9	151	16.8	2	50
T. Richardson	7	61	8.7	1	45
E. Lacy	7	52	7.4	1	31
J. Fowler	6	48	8	0	17
G. McElroy	3	7	2.3	0	8
D. Goode	2	4	2	0	3
AJ McCarron	1	-8	-8	0	0
Team	35	315	9.0	4	50

Kicking	FG	PCT	LONG	XP	PTS
C. Foster	2/2	100	44	2/2	8
J. Shelley	0/0	0	0	6/6	6
Team	2/2	100	44	8/8	14

Punting	NO	YDS	AVG	TB	IN 20	LONG
C. Mandell	2	81	40.5	0	0	47

Receiving	REC	YDS	AVG	TD	LONG
J. Jones	5	106	21.2	1	35
D. Hanks	3	52	17.3	1	31
P. Dial	3	39	13	1	20
E. Alexander	1	28	28	0	28
C. Underwood	1	28	28	0	28
B. Gibson	1	18	18	0	18
M. Maze	1	16	16	0	16
E. Lacy	1	15	15	0	15
T. Richardson	1	9	9	0	9
Team	17	311	18.3	3	35

Interceptions	INT	YDS	TD
D. Kirkpatrick	1	21	0

Kick returns	NO	YDS	AVG	LONG	TD
T. Richardson	3	114	38	91	1
J. Jones	1	36	36	36	0
Team	4	150	37.5	91	1

Punt returns	NO	YDS	AVG	LONG	TD
M. Maze	2	26	13	17	0
J. Jones	2	3	1.5	3	0
Team	4	29	7.3	17	0

Note: Table data from "Alabama 62-13 Duke (Sep 18, 2010) Box Score" (68)

09/25/10 - Alabama (1) at Arkansas (10)

Team	1	2	3	4	T		Passing	Rushing	Total
Alabama (1)	7	0	7	10	24		194	227	421
Arkansas (10)	10	7	3	0	20		357	64	421

In the first game played between two teams ranked in the top ten at Donald W. Reynolds Razorback Stadium since the 1979 season, Alabama was victorious with a 24-20 come-from-behind victory. On the first possession of the game, Ryan Mallett threw a 43-yard touchdown to take an early 7-0 lead. After both teams punted, Alabama responded with a 54-yard Mark Ingram II touchdown run to tie the game at 7-7, capping a 4-play, 80-yard drive that only took 1:54. Arkansas retook the lead with a 31-yard field goal. After an Alabama punt, both teams traded interceptions in both end zones (Robert Lester for Bama, and Andru Stewart for Arkansas). After holding the Hogs to another punt, Greg McElroy threw another interception. Arkansas capitalized, driving 66 yards and scoring on a 1-yard Mallett run to take a 17-7 lead at the half.

Midway through the third quarter, Arkansas extended its lead to 20-7 on a 48-yard field goal. Alabama brought the score to 20-14 late in the quarter after a 20-yard Trent Richardson touchdown reception from Greg McElroy. The Arkansas lead was then cut to three after a 36-yard Jeremy Shelley field goal with just over six minutes remaining in the fourth quarter. After Robert Lester intercepted a Mallett pass and returned it to the 12-yard line, Ingram II took the next three snaps that culminated in a 1-yard touchdown run to take a 24-20 lead. After a late Dre Kirkpatrick interception, McElroy gained a first down on a 4th-and-inches quarterback sneak to seal the victory for the Crimson Tide.

Ingram II led the team with 157 yards rushing on 24 carries and Trent Richardson finished with 85 yards on eight carries. Dre Kirkpatrick led the defense with nine tackles and an interception. For his five-tackle, two-interception performance, Robert Lester was recognized as both the FWAA/Bronko Nagurski National Defensive Player of the Week and the SEC Defensive Player of the Week.[64]

Passing	C/ATT	YDS	AVG	TD	INT	QBR
G. McElroy	18/26	194	7.5	1	2	57

Rushing	CAR	YDS	AVG	TD	LONG
M. Ingram II	24	157	6.5	2	54
T. Richardson	8	85	10.6	0	53
D. Hanks	1	1	1	0	1
J. Jones	1	1	1	0	1
G. McElroy	5	-15	-3	0	6
Team	1	-2	-2	0	0
Team	40	227	5.7	2	54

Punt returns	NO	YDS	AVG	LONG	TD
J. Jones	2	0	0	0	0

Kicking	FG	PCT	LONG	XP	PTS
J. Shelley	1/1	100	36	3/3	6

Punting	NO	YDS	AVG	TB	IN 20	LONG
C. Mandell	3	137	45.7	0	0	59

Receiving	REC	YDS	AVG	TD	LONG
J. Jones	5	55	11	0	19
M. Maze	3	33	11	0	18
D. Hanks	2	27	13.5	0	14
M. Ingram II	2	27	13.5	0	20
T. Richardson	2	25	12.5	1	20
P. Dial	2	18	9	0	12
M. Williams	2	9	4.5	0	7
Team	18	194	10.8	1	20

Kick returns	NO	YDS	AVG	LONG	TD
T. Richardson	4	117	29.3	39	0
M. Williams	1	6	6	6	0
Team	5	123	24.6	39	0

Interceptions	INT	YDS	TD
R. Lester	2	33	0
D. Kirkpatrick	1	0	0
Team	3	33	0

Note: Table data from "Alabama 24-20 Arkansas (Sep 25, 2010) Box Score" (69)

10/02/10 - Alabama (1) vs Florida (7)

Team	1	2	3	4	T		Passing	Rushing	Total
Florida (7)	0	3	3	0	6		202	79	281
Alabama (1)	3	21	7	0	31		103	170	273

In a rematch of the previous two SEC Championship Games, Alabama defeated the Florida Gators 31-6. There were only three possessions in the first quarter. After a 10-play, 68-yard drive, Alabama opened the scoring with a 28-yard Jeremy Shelley field goal. Florida drove 74 yards in 12 plays before being intercepted by Nico Johnson in the end zone on 4th-and-2 at the AL 2-yard line. Alabama was still driving when time ran out in the first quarter.

The Tide scored a trio of touchdowns in the second quarter. Mark Ingram II scored on runs of six and one yard sandwiching a Florida punt. On the Gators' next possession, Dre Kirkpatrick intercepted John Brantley at the Florida 27-yard line and returned it to the 18-yard line. Two plays later, Marquis Maze threw a 19-yard touchdown pass to Michael Williams on a wide receiver pass. After both teams punted, Florida got on the board late in the second quarter with a 39-yard Chas Henry field goal to bring the halftime score to 24-3.

After a second Henry field goal in the third quarter, C.J. Mosley returned an interception 35 yards for a touchdown to make the final score 31-6 as neither team scored in the fourth quarter.

Although Florida outgained the Crimson Tide in total offense 281 to 273 yards, its three turnovers resulted in 21 Alabama points. In addition to Mosley, Nico Johnson intercepted Trey Burton in the end zone, and Dre Kirkpatrick intercepted a John Brantley pass. The game marked the first time Florida had been held without a touchdown since its previous visit to Tuscaloosa in 2005 and resulted in Alabama leading the nation in scoring defense by allowing only 45 points through five games. Courtney Upshaw was named the SEC Defensive Player of the Week after making seven total tackles (four for losses), a fumble recovery, and two pass deflections. Chance Warmack was recognized as the SEC's Offensive Lineman of the Week for his performance.[64]

Passing	C/ATT	YDS	AVG	TD	INT	QBR
G. McElroy	11/17	84	4.9	0	0	83.4
M. Maze	1/1	19	19	1	0	100
Team	12/18	103	5.7	1	0	--

Rushing	CAR	YDS	AVG	TD	LONG
T. Richardson	10	63	6.3	0	30
M. Ingram II	12	47	3.9	2	9
G. McElroy	7	33	4.7	0	17
E. Lacy	4	20	5	0	8
J. Jones	0	5	0	0	5
AJ McCarron	1	2	2	0	2
Team	34	170	5.0	2	30

Kick returns	NO	YDS	AVG	LONG	TD
T. Richardson	3	58	19.3	23	0

Punting	NO	YDS	AVG	TB	IN 20	LONG
C. Mandell	4	161	40.3	0	0	53

Receiving	REC	YDS	AVG	TD	LONG
D. Hanks	3	33	11	0	14
M. Williams	1	19	19	1	19
M. Ingram II	3	19	6.3	0	9
J. Jones	4	19	4.8	0	15
M. Maze	1	13	13	0	13
Team	12	103	8.6	1	19

Interceptions	INT	YDS	TD
CJ Mosley	1	35	1
D. Kirkpatrick	1	9	0
N. Johnson	1	0	0
Team	3	44	1

Punt returns	NO	YDS	AVG	LONG	TD
J. Jones	1	41	41	41	0

Kicking	FG	PCT	LONG	XP	PTS
J. Shelley	1/1	100	28	4/4	7

Note: Table data from "Alabama 31-6 Florida (Oct 2, 2010) Box Score" (70)

10/09/10 - Alabama (1) at South Carolina (19)

Team	1	2	3	4	T		Passing	Rushing	Total
Alabama (1)	3	6	5	7	21		315	36	351
South Carolina (19)	14	7	7	7	35		201	110	311

With ESPN's College GameDay in town and in front of a sold-out Williams-Brice Stadium, Alabama was upset by the South Carolina Gamecocks 35-21. After Alabama scored on its opening drive with a 32-yard Jeremy Shelley field goal, South Carolina responded with three consecutive touchdowns. Stephen Garcia threw three touchdown passes, with the first to Marcus Lattimore for nine yards followed by strikes of 26 and 15 yards to Alshon Jeffery to give South Carolina a 21-3 lead in the second quarter. Alabama reached the end zone late in the second on a 9-yard Greg McElroy pass to Julio Jones to make the halftime score 21-9 after the extra point failed.

On the first play from scrimmage in the third quarter, Garcia threw the ball out of the end zone for a safety following a bad snap. After the free kick, Alabama scored on a 39-yard Shelley field goal to make the score 21-14. After a 1-yard Lattimore touchdown run, Alabama answered with a 51-yard Darius Hanks touchdown reception from McElroy to make the score 28-21. However, Lattimore scored on a 2-yard touchdown run late in the fourth to give the Gamecocks a 35-21 victory. The win marked South Carolina's first all-time victory over a team ranked number one in the AP poll.

For the game, McElroy set a career-high in passing for 315 yards on 27-of-34 passes, and Jones had a team-high 118 yards on eight catches. Marcell Dareus was recognized as an honorable mention SEC Defensive Player of the Week for his eight-tackle performance. The 35 points allowed by the Crimson Tide defense were the most allowed since giving up 41 to LSU in 2007. The loss also marked the end of a 29-game regular season win streak, an overall 19-game win streak, and an 18-game regular season conference winning streak. It was Alabama's first overall loss since being defeated by Utah in the 2009 Sugar Bowl and its first regular season and regular season conference loss since losing to Auburn in 2007.[64]

Passing	C/ATT	YDS	AVG	TD	INT	QBR
G. McElroy	27/34	315	9.3	2	0	64
AJ McCarron	0/1	0	0	0	0	0
Team	27/35	315	9	2	0	--

Rushing	CAR	YDS	AVG	TD	LONG
M. Ingram II	11	41	3.7	0	13
T. Richardson	6	23	3.8	0	8
G. McElroy	12	-28	-2.3	0	6
Team	29	36	1.2	0	13

Interceptions	INT	YDS	TD
W. Lowery	1	0	0

Kicking	FG	PCT	LONG	XP	PTS
J. Shelley	2/3	66.7	39	1/2	7

Punting	NO	YDS	AVG	TB	IN 20	LONG
C. Mandell	2	68	34	0	0	53

Receiving	REC	YDS	AVG	TD	LONG
J. Jones	8	118	14.8	1	26
D. Hanks	2	55	27.5	1	51
M. Maze	4	41	10.3	0	20
M. Williams	1	32	32	0	32
P. Dial	5	29	5.8	0	8
M. Ingram II	4	16	4	0	11
B. Smelley	1	12	12	0	12
T. Richardson	2	12	6	0	8
Team	27	315	11.7	2	51

Kick returns	NO	YDS	AVG	LONG	TD
T. Richardson	6	142	23.7	31	0
M. Maze	1	31	31	31	0
Team	7	173	24.7	31	0

Punt returns	NO	YDS	AVG	LONG	TD
M. Maze	1	28	28	28	0

Note: Table data from "South Carolina 35-21 Alabama (Oct 9, 2010) Box Score" (71)

83

10/16/10 - Alabama (8) vs Ole Miss

Team	1	2	3	4	T		Passing	Rushing	Total
Ole Miss	0	3	7	0	10		110	133	243
Alabama (8)	10	6	7	0	23		219	100	319

A week after its first regular season loss since the 2007 season, Alabama defeated its long-time rival, the Ole Miss Rebels on Homecoming in Tuscaloosa 23-10. The Rebels were stopped on their first possession and punted to Alabama. The Tide drove 51 yards in 11 plays and scored on a 7-yard Greg McElroy touchdown pass to Preston Dial. After three punts (two by Ole Miss), Cade Foster nailed a 49-yard field goal to take a 10-0 lead with less than a minute remaining in the first quarter.

Scoring continued in the second quarter with Alabama's Jeremy Shelley and Cade Foster connecting on field goals of 19 and 44 yards. Mississippi's Bryson Rose connected on a 22-yard field goal to make the halftime score 16-3.

In the second half, both teams traded punts then touchdowns. McElroy connected with Trent Richardson for an 85-yard touchdown reception. The catch was the fourth longest touchdown reception in school history. The Rebels responded when Jeremiah Masoli connected with Melvin Harris for a 15-yard touchdown reception to make the score 23-10. This ended up being the final as there was no scoring in the fourth quarter.

On special teams, Marquis Maze totaled 125 yards on seven punt returns and was named SEC Co-Special Teams Player of the Week for his performance.[64]

Passing	C/ATT	YDS	AVG	TD	INT	QBR
G. McElroy	17/25	219	8.8	2	0	40.5

Rushing	CAR	YDS	AVG	TD	LONG
M. Ingram II	15	60	4	0	11
T. Richardson	11	45	4.1	0	12
M. Maze	1	1	1	0	1
G. McElroy	7	-6	-0.9	0	9
Team	34	100	2.9	0	12

Interceptions	INT	YDS	TD
M. Barron	1	4	0

Kick returns	NO	YDS	AVG	LONG	TD
T. Richardson	3	74	24.7	27	0

Punting	NO	YDS	AVG	TB	IN 20	LONG
C. Mandell	5	191	38.2	0	0	50

Receiving	REC	YDS	AVG	TD	LONG
T. Richardson	5	101	20.2	1	85
M. Maze	3	42	14	0	20
E. Alexander	2	32	16	0	23
K. Bell	1	18	18	0	18
J. Jones	1	8	8	0	8
P. Dial	1	7	7	1	7
M. Ingram II	3	7	2.3	0	4
D. Hanks	1	4	4	0	4
Team	17	219	12.9	2	85

Punt returns	NO	YDS	AVG	LONG	TD
M. Maze	7	125	17.9	37	0

Kicking	FG	PCT	LONG	XP	PTS
C. Foster	2/2	100	49	0/0	6
J. Shelley	1/2	50	19	2/2	5
Team	3/4	75	49	2/2	11

Note: Table data from "Alabama 23-10 Ole Miss (Oct 16, 2010) Box Score" (72)

10/23/10 - Alabama (8) at Tennessee

Team	1	2	3	4	T		Passing	Rushing	Total
Alabama (8)	3	10	21	7	**41**		326	210	**536**
Tennessee	7	3	0	0	**10**		156	159	**315**

In the 93rd edition of the Third Saturday in October, the Crimson Tide defeated the Tennessee Volunteers 41-10. After both teams punted to start the game, Tennessee scored first on a 59-yard Tauren Poole touchdown run to take an early 7-0 lead. Alabama responded by scoring on a 36-yard Jeremy Shelley field goal before forcing the Vols to punt after a three-and-out. Alabama then drove 59 yards in nine plays, scoring on a 1-yard Greg McElroy touchdown run to take a 10-7 lead less than 20 seconds into the second quarter. The second quarter closed with a 42-yard Shelley field goal and a 33-yard field goal by Michael Palardy of Tennessee to make the halftime score 13-10, Bama.

Alabama opened the second half by driving 70 yards in four plays with Julio Jones having receptions of 38 and 19 yards, and Mark Ingram II punching in the touchdown from one yard out to extend its lead to 20-10. After Palardy missed a 52-yard field goal, Trent Richardson ran the ball 65 yards for a touchdown on the second play of the ensuing drive for a 27-10 Alabama lead. Later, Robert Lester intercepted a Matt Simms pass, and Alabama extended its lead to 34-10 after an 80-yard drive with Ingram II scoring from one yard out. Alabama scored the final points of the evening in the fourth quarter when A.J. McCarron hit Richardson for a 5-yard touchdown reception to make the final score 41-10. It was Alabama's most lopsided victory over Tennessee since defeating the Volunteers 35-0 in 1963.

For the game, Julio Jones set a school record with 221 receiving yards, eclipsing the previous mark of 217 yards set by David Palmer against Vanderbilt in 1993. Mark Ingram II and Trent Richardson finished with 88 and 119 yards on the ground respectively. For his performance, left tackle James Carpenter was selected as the SEC Offensive Lineman of the Week. With his 117 yards on 14 carries, Tauren Poole ended Alabama's 41-game streak of not allowing a 100-yard rusher dating back to BenJarvus Green-Ellis' 131-yard performance for Ole Miss in 2007. The game also marked the first between Nick Saban and Derek Dooley who previously worked for Saban as an assistant coach at LSU and with the Miami Dolphins.[64]

Passing	C/ATT	YDS	AVG	TD	INT	QBR
G. McElroy	21/32	264	8.3	0	0	82.5
AJ McCarron	3/3	62	20.7	1	0	100
Team	24/35	326	9.3	1	0	--

Rushing	CAR	YDS	AVG	TD	LONG
T. Richardson	12	119	9.9	1	65
M. Ingram II	14	88	6.3	2	42
AJ McCarron	1	4	4	0	4
D. Goode	2	4	2	0	2
J. Fowler	2	3	1.5	0	4
G. McElroy	2	-6	-3	1	1
Team	1	-2	-2	0	0
Team	34	210	6.2	4	65

Interceptions	INT	YDS	TD
R. Lester	1	20	0
B. Scott	1	0	0
Team	2	20	0

Punting	NO	YDS	AVG	TB	IN 20	LONG
C. Mandell	2	94	47	0	0	51

Receiving	REC	YDS	AVG	TD	LONG
J. Jones	12	221	18.4	0	47
M. Maze	4	73	18.3	0	36
P. Dial	1	11	11	0	11
D. Hanks	3	10	3.3	0	9
T. Richardson	1	5	5	1	5
M. Williams	1	4	4	0	4
E. Alexander	1	3	3	0	3
M. Ingram II	1	-1	-1	0	0
Team	24	326	13.6	1	47

Kick returns	NO	YDS	AVG	LONG	TD
T. Richardson	2	48	24	25	0

Punt returns	NO	YDS	AVG	LONG	TD
M. Maze	3	-4	-1.3	0	0

Kicking	FG	PCT	LONG	XP	PTS
J. Shelley	2/3	66.7	42	4/4	10
C. Foster	0/0	0	0	1/1	1
Team	2/3	66.7	42	5/5	11

Note: Table data from "Alabama 41-10 Tennessee (Oct 23, 2010) Box Score" (73)

11/06/10 - Alabama (6) at LSU (10)

Team	1	2	3	4	T		Passing	Rushing	Total
Alabama (6)	0	7	7	7	**21**		223	102	**325**
LSU (10)	3	0	7	14	**24**		208	225	**433**

Coming off its bye week and in what was dubbed by some as "Saban Bowl IV," Alabama was upset by its long-time rival, the LSU Tigers, 24-21. After both teams punted to start the game, LSU intercepted a pass from Greg McElroy and scored first on a 45-yard Josh Jasper field goal to take a 3-0 lead. After two more punts brought the game into the second quarter, Alabama drove 81 yards in 11 plays and scored its first points on a 1-yard Greg McElroy touchdown pass to Trent Richardson. Alabama had a 7-3 halftime lead after both teams punted two more times and then time ran out in the half before LSU could score again.

LSU drove down to the Alabama 28-yard line and missed a 45-yard field goal to start the third quarter. After an Alabama punt, both teams traded touchdowns. The Tigers scored first on a 75-yard Rueben Randle reception from Jordan Jefferson, capping a 2-play, 94-yard drive. The Crimson Tide responded with a 5-yard Mark Ingram II touchdown run capping a 10-play, 73-yard drive.

LSU scored 14 fourth quarter points to secure the victory with a pair of Jasper field goals, a 1-yard Stevan Ridley touchdown run, and a successful two-point conversion. Alabama fumbled twice then scored on a 9-yard Julio Jones touchdown reception but was unable to get a defensive stop late in the game preserving the 24-21 LSU victory. Turnovers proved costly for Alabama with LSU scoring field goals on drives after a McElroy interception in the first and fumble in the fourth.[64]

Passing	C/ATT	YDS	AVG	TD	INT	QBR
G. McElroy	21/34	223	6.6	2	1	75.6

Rushing	CAR	YDS	AVG	TD	LONG
M. Ingram II	21	97	4.6	1	13
T. Richardson	6	28	4.7	0	22
J. Jones	1	5	5	0	5
G. McElroy	3	-28	-9.3	0	0
Team	31	102	3.3	1	22

Kick returns	NO	YDS	AVG	LONG	TD
M. Maze	3	73	24.3	27	0
J. Jones	1	31	31	31	0
T. Richardson	1	12	12	12	0
Team	5	116	23.2	31	0

Punting	NO	YDS	AVG	TB	IN 20	LONG
C. Mandell	6	246	41	0	0	50

Receiving	REC	YDS	AVG	TD	LONG
J. Jones	10	89	8.9	1	19
D. Hanks	2	40	20	0	18
P. Dial	2	35	17.5	0	19
M. Maze	4	35	8.8	0	14
M. Williams	1	18	18	0	18
B. Smelley	1	5	5	0	5
T. Richardson	1	1	1	1	1
Team	21	223	10.6	2	19

Punt returns	NO	YDS	AVG	LONG	TD
M. Maze	2	3	1.5	3	0

Kicking	FG	PCT	LONG	XP	PTS
J. Shelley	0/0	0	0	3/3	3

Note: Table data from "LSU 24-21 Alabama (Nov 6, 2010) Box Score" (74)

11/13/10 - Alabama (12) vs Mississippi State (19)

Team	1	2	3	4	T	Passing	Rushing	Total
Mississippi State (19)	3	0	0	7	10	150	149	299
Alabama (12)	6	14	7	3	30	277	175	452

A week after being upset by LSU, Alabama returned to Bryant-Denny and began a three-game homestand to end the season by defeating long-time rival Mississippi State 30-10. The Crimson Tide took a 6-3 lead in the first quarter by trading field goals with the Bulldogs on a 36-yarder from Jeremy Shelley, a 24-yarder from Derek DePasquale, and a 45-yarder from Cade Foster. In the second quarter, Alabama reached the end zone for the first time of the evening after Greg McElroy hit Marquis Maze for a 45-yard touchdown reception capping a 5-play, 75-yard drive (13-3). After a punt on the next Bulldog series, an 80-yard Maze touchdown return was called back as a result of an illegal block on the play by Alex Watkins. On the next play, Mark Ingram II took a short bubble screen pass from McElroy 78 yards for a 20-3 lead at the half.

On its first offensive possession of the second half, and on the third consecutive offensive play, Alabama scored on a long touchdown play. This time Julio Jones ran the ball 56 yards for a touchdown to extend the Alabama lead to 27-3. After holding the Bulldogs to a punt, McElroy threw an interception on the very first play of the next possession. After three more punts, Shelley scored Alabama's final points in the fourth on a 28-yard field goal with State scoring its lone touchdown late on a 27-yard Chad Bumphis touchdown reception from Tyler Russell. The Alabama defense allowed only 149 rushing yards, registered five sacks, and recorded two interceptions.

In this game, the Crimson Tide wore Nike Pro Combat uniforms for the first time. These uniforms featured crimson jerseys with grey and white houndstooth numbers, a houndstooth stripe on the helmet, houndstooth gloves, and an American flag sewn into one of the sleeves in honor of Veterans Day. The houndstooth design was chosen as a tribute to former Alabama coach Bear Bryant who was known for wearing a houndstooth fedora during games.[64]

Passing	C/ATT	YDS	AVG	TD	INT	QBR
G. McElroy	12/18	227	12.6	2	1	88.5
AJ McCarron	2/5	50	10	0	0	66.9
Team	14/23	277	12	2	1	--

Rushing	CAR	YDS	AVG	TD	LONG
J. Jones	1	56	56	1	56
M. Ingram II	18	53	2.9	0	13
E. Lacy	8	35	4.4	0	15
G. McElroy	3	20	6.7	0	15
J. Fowler	3	15	5	0	6
D. Goode	2	6	3	0	4
AJ McCarron	1	-10	-10	0	0
Team	36	175	4.9	1	56

Interceptions	INT	YDS	TD
R. Lester	2	12	0

Punting	NO	YDS	AVG	TB	IN 20	LONG
C. Mandell	4	153	38.3	0	0	44

Receiving	REC	YDS	AVG	TD	LONG
M. Maze	5	89	17.8	1	45
M. Ingram II	2	77	38.5	1	78
D. Hanks	3	55	18.3	0	39
J. Jones	3	41	13.7	0	23
M. Williams	1	15	15	0	15
Team	14	277	19.8	2	78

Kick returns	NO	YDS	AVG	LONG	TD
M. Maze	2	41	20.5	28	0
M. Ingram II	1	19	19	19	0
Team	3	60	20	28	0

Punt returns	NO	YDS	AVG	LONG	TD
M. Maze	4	36	9	22	0

Kicking	FG	PCT	LONG	XP	PTS
J. Shelley	2/2	100	36	3/3	9
C. Foster	1/1	100	45	0/0	3
Team	3/3	100	45	3/3	12

Note: Table data from "Alabama 30-10 Mississippi State (Nov 13, 2010) Box Score" (75)

11/18/10 - Alabama (11) vs Georgia State

Team	1	2	3	4	T	Passing	Rushing	Total
Georgia State	0	7	0	0	**7**	74	91	**165**
Alabama (11)	14	28	14	7	**63**	216	262	**478**

In the first ever meeting against the Georgia State Panthers, the Crimson Tide was victorious 63-7. Alabama scored on its first possession as they drove 67 yards in eight plays, finishing with an 8-yard Greg McElroy pass to Julio Jones. After a Mark Barron interception ended the first Georgia State drive, Alabama responded with a 71-yard drive capped by a 1-yard Mark Ingram II touchdown run to take a 14-0 lead.

In the second quarter, Alabama scored on a defensive play when C.J. Mosley returned a Drew Little interception 41 yards for a touchdown. Alabama then extended its lead to 28-0 on a 10-yard Julio Jones touchdown reception from Greg McElroy, capping a 4-play, 72-yard drive in just 1:46. At the end of the Panthers next possession, Chavis Williams blocked a Bo Schlechter punt that was returned 22 yards for a touchdown by Brandon Gibson. On the following kickoff, an Albert Wilson fumble was recovered by Gibson to give the Tide possession deep in Panther territory. Four plays later, Alabama extended its lead to 42-0 on a 3-yard Eddie Lacy touchdown run. On the ensuing kickoff, the Panthers scored their only points on the evening when Albert Wilson returned the kickoff 97 yards for a touchdown and a halftime score of 42-7.

With the game in hand midway through the second quarter, Alabama played many of its reserve players in the second half. The Tide scored in the third quarter first on a 7-yard A.J. McCarron touchdown pass to Chris Underwood and again on a 1-yard Demetrius Goode touchdown run after a Chris Jordan interception to take a 56-7 lead into the final quarter. In the fourth, Jalston Fowler scored on a 36-yard touchdown run to make the final score 63-7.

After completing 12-of-13 passes, Greg McElroy set a new single-game Alabama record for completion percentage (92.3%) to break the previous record he set against North Texas in 2009. The game also marked the first time Alabama played on a Thursday night since defeating Southern Miss in 2001 and the return of both former Alabama HC Bill Curry as the Panthers' head coach and QB Star Jackson who transferred to Georgia State prior to the 2010 season. The 63 points were the most scored by Alabama since defeating Vanderbilt 63-3 in 1979.[64]

Passing	C/ATT	YDS	AVG	TD	INT	QBR
G. McElroy	12/13	159	12.2	2	0	76.7
AJ McCarron	7/9	57	6.3	1	0	72.5
Team	19/22	216	9.8	3	0	--

Rushing	CAR	YDS	AVG	TD	LONG
M. Ingram II	12	86	7.2	1	27
E. Lacy	13	81	6.2	1	18
J. Fowler	2	42	21	1	36
D. Goode	7	24	3.4	1	15
B. Howell	5	11	2.2	0	6
N. Tinker	4	9	2.3	0	3
J. Jones	1	7	7	0	7
G. McElroy	1	2	2	0	2
Team	45	262	5.8	4	36

Interceptions	INT	YDS	TD
CJ Mosley	1	41	1
C. Jordan	1	25	0
M. Barron	1	0	0
D. Milliner	1	0	0
Team	4	66	1

Punting	NO	YDS	AVG	TB	IN 20	LONG
C. Mandell	1	29	29	0	0	29

Receiving	REC	YDS	AVG	TD	LONG
J. Jones	7	86	12.3	2	33
M. Maze	2	29	14.5	0	20
D. Hanks	2	23	11.5	0	21
K. Norwood	2	20	10	0	15
M. Ingram II	1	16	16	0	16
E. Alexander	1	11	11	0	11
B. Smelley	1	9	9	0	9
K. Bell	1	8	8	0	8
C. Underwood	1	7	7	1	7
P. Dial	1	7	7	0	7
Team	19	216	11.4	3	33

Kick returns	NO	YDS	AVG	LONG	TD
M. Maze	2	44	22	22	0

Punt returns	NO	YDS	AVG	LONG	TD
M. Maze	2	23	11.5	23	0
B. Gibson	1	22	22	22	1
C. Williams	1	15	15	15	0
Team	4	60	15	23	1

Kicking	FG	PCT	LONG	XP	PTS
J. Shelley	0/1	0	0	7/7	7
C. Foster	0/1	0	0	2/2	2
Team	0/2	0	0	9/9	9

Note: Table data from "Alabama 63-7 Georgia State (Nov 18, 2010) Box Score" (76)

11/26/10 - Alabama (11) vs Auburn (2)

Team	1	2	3	4	T		Passing	Rushing	Total
Auburn (2)	0	7	14	7	28		216	108	324
Alabama (11)	21	3	3	0	27		377	69	446

In the 75th edition of the Iron Bowl, the Auburn Tigers overcame a 24-point deficit to defeat the Crimson Tide 28-27. Alabama opened a 21-0 lead after the first quarter with touchdown scores on its first three offensive possessions while holding Auburn to three punts. The first was on a 7-play, 71-yard drive, capped by a 9-yard Mark Ingram II run. The next score only took two plays as Greg McElroy hooked up with Julio Jones for a 68-yard touchdown. Then Darius Hanks capped a 10-play, 61-yard drive with this 12-yard reception for another score. The lead was pushed to 24-0 in the second quarter after a 20-yard Jeremy Shelley field goal before the Tigers began their comeback. Auburn scored its first points late in the second quarter on a 36-yard Cam Newton pass to Emory Blake to bring the score to 24-7 at the half.

With the only Alabama points in the third quarter scored on a 32-yard Jeremy Shelley field goal, Auburn brought the margin to 27-21 entering the fourth quarter on a 70-yard Cam Newton touchdown pass to Terrell Zachery and a 1-yard Newton run. The Tigers took a 28-27 lead on a 7-yard Philip Lutzenkirchen reception from Newton that held to the end of regulation.

With his ten-catch, 199-yard performance, Julio Jones set Alabama single-season records for both receptions and receiving yards in eclipsing the previous marks of 67 receptions by D.J. Hall in 2007 and 1,056 yards by Hall in 2006. The loss ended a 20-game home winning streak for the Tide dating back to the 2007 loss to Louisiana Monroe. The CBS telecast of this game earned a 7.5 rating, the highest for any game of the 2010 college football season through week 13.[64]

Passing	C/ATT	YDS	AVG	TD	INT	QBR
G. McElroy	27/37	377	10.2	2	0	76.5
AJ McCarron	0/4	0	0	0	0	1.3
Team	27/41	377	9.2	2	0	--

Rushing	CAR	YDS	AVG	TD	LONG
M. Ingram II	10	36	3.6	1	9
T. Richardson	10	24	2.4	0	7
J. Jones	1	12	12	0	12
M. Maze	1	7	7	0	7
G. McElroy	8	-10	-1.3	0	10
Team	30	69	2.3	1	12

Punting	NO	YDS	AVG	TB	IN 20	LONG
C. Mandell	4	135	33.8	0	0	47

Receiving	REC	YDS	AVG	TD	LONG
J. Jones	10	199	19.9	1	68
M. Ingram II	4	91	22.8	0	41
D. Hanks	5	39	7.8	1	12
P. Dial	3	26	8.7	0	13
M. Maze	2	13	6.5	0	9
T. Richardson	3	9	3	0	9
Team	27	377	14	2	68

Kick returns	NO	YDS	AVG	LONG	TD
J. Jones	3	62	20.7	25	0

Punt returns	NO	YDS	AVG	LONG	TD
M. Maze	4	0	0	0	0

Kicking	FG	PCT	LONG	XP	PTS
J. Shelley	2/2	100	32	3/3	9

Note: Table data from "Auburn 28-27 Alabama (Nov 26, 2010) Box Score" (77)

01/01/11 - Alabama (16) at Michigan State (9)

Team	1	2	3	4	T		Passing	Rushing	Total
Alabama (16)	7	21	14	7	49		271	275	546
Michigan State (9)	0	0	0	7	7		219	-48	171

On December 5th, Capital One Bowl officials announced Alabama would face the Big Ten co-champion Michigan State Spartans in the 2011 Capital One Bowl. In a strong defensive performance where the Spartans were held to a total of -48 yards rushing, Alabama was victorious 49-7. Alabama scored touchdowns on its first four offensive possessions. Mark Ingram II scored first on a 1-yard touchdown run to complete a 13-play, 79-yard drive. After a Robert Lester interception of a Kirk Cousins pass on the Spartans' opening drive, the Tide scored on an 8-yard Trent Richardson touchdown run. Alabama extended its lead to 28-0 at the half following touchdown runs of six and 35 yards by Ingram II and Julio Jones.

After holding Michigan State to a three-and-out to open the third quarter, Alabama scored its fifth touchdown in six offensive possessions when Marquis Maze scored on a 37-yard Greg McElroy pass. Up by 35 points late in the third quarter, the Crimson Tide pulled many of their starters that resulted in many players seeing action from deep in the depth chart. Eddie Lacy extended the lead to 49-0 with touchdown runs of 12 yards in the third quarter and 62 yards in the fourth quarter. Michigan State scored its only points late in the fourth quarter on a 49-yard Bennie Fowler touchdown reception from Keith Nichol to make the final score 49-7. The 42-point margin of victory was Alabama's largest in a bowl game since defeating Syracuse 61-6 in the 1953 Orange Bowl.

The -48 yards rushing allowed by the Alabama defense was the fewest ever allowed in a bowl game and the second fewest allowed all-time only eclipsed by a minus 49-yard performance against Houston in 1962. With his pair of touchdowns, Mark Ingram II established a new Alabama record for career rushing touchdowns with 42 to eclipse the previous mark of 41 set by Shaun Alexander. The contest also marked both Nick Saban's and Bobby Williams' first game against the Spartans since their respective terms as Michigan State's head coach between 1995-1999 and 2000-2002.[64]

Passing	C/ATT	YDS	AVG	TD	INT	QBR
G. McElroy	13/17	220	12.9	1	0	94.5
AJ McCarron	6/6	51	8.5	0	0	95.3
Team	19/23	271	11.8	1	0	--

Rushing	CAR	YDS	AVG	TD	LONG
E. Lacy	5	86	17.2	2	62
M. Ingram II	12	59	4.9	2	14
T. Richardson	10	42	4.2	1	9
J. Jones	2	36	18	1	35
D. Goode	10	36	3.6	0	8
D. Hanks	1	6	6	0	6
G. McElroy	1	4	4	0	4
AJ McCarron	1	4	4	0	4
J. Fowler	1	3	3	0	3
Team	1	-1	-1	0	0
Team	44	275	6.3	6	62

Interceptions	INT	YDS	TD
R. Lester	1	22	0

Punting	NO	YDS	AVG	TB	IN 20	LONG
C. Mandell	2	79	39.5	0	0	40

Receiving	REC	YDS	AVG	TD	LONG
M. Maze	4	77	19.3	1	37
P. Dial	4	55	13.8	0	24
J. Jones	3	49	16.3	0	28
M. Ingram II	1	30	30	0	30
B. Smelley	2	20	10	0	13
D. Goode	1	17	17	0	17
T. Richardson	1	12	12	0	12
E. Alexander	1	7	7	0	7
M. Williams	1	3	3	0	3
C. Underwood	1	1	1	0	1
Team	19	271	14.3	1	37

Kick returns	NO	YDS	AVG	LONG	TD
T. Richardson	1	18	18	18	0

Punt returns	NO	YDS	AVG	LONG	TD
M. Maze	5	22	4.4	17	0
T. Richardson	1	0	0	0	0
Team	6	22	3.7	17	0

Kicking	FG	PCT	LONG	XP	PTS
J. Shelley	0/0	0	0	7/7	7

Note: Table data from "Alabama 49-7 Michigan State (Jan 1, 2011) Box Score" (78)

Season Stats

Record	10-3	16th of 120
SEC Record	5-3	
Rank	10	
Points for	464	
Points against	176	
Points/game	35.7	18th of 120
Opp points/game	13.5	3rd of 120
SOS[4]	4.69	18th of 120

Team stats (averages per game)

Split		Passing					Rushing				Total Offense		
	G	Cmp	Att	Pct	Yds	TD	Att	Yds	Avg	TD	Plays	Yds	Avg
Offense	13	19.5	27.8	69.9	261.2	1.8	35.9	182.9	5.1	2.3	63.8	444.1	7
Defense	13	14.8	28.2	52.3	176.2	0.9	33.5	110.2	3.3	0.5	61.7	286.4	4.6
Difference		4.7	-0.4	17.6	85	0.9	2.4	72.7	1.8	1.8	2.1	157.7	2.4

Split	First Downs				Penalties		Turnovers		
	Pass	Rush	Pen	Tot	No.	Yds	Fum	Int	Tot
Offense	11.6	9.7	0.8	22.1	5.1	37.7	0.7	0.4	1.1
Defense	7.6	6.5	1.1	15.2	5.5	44.2	0.3	1.7	2
Difference	4	3.2	-0.3	6.9	-0.4	-6.5	0.4	-1.3	-0.9

Passing

Rk	Player	G	Passing								
			Cmp	Att	Pct	Yds	Y/A	AY/A	TD	Int	Rate
1	Greg McElroy	13	222	313	70.9	2987	9.5	10.1	20	5	169
2	A.J. McCarron	13	30	48	62.5	389	8.1	9.4	3	0	151.2
3	Marquis Maze	13	1	1	100	19	19	39	1	0	589.6

Rushing and receiving

Rk	Player	G	Rushing					Receiving				Scrimmage			
			Att	Yds	Avg	TD	Rec	Yds	Avg	TD	Plays	Yds	Avg	TD
1	Mark Ingram II	11	158	875	5.5	13	21	282	13.4	1	179	1157	6.5	14
2	Trent Richardson	11	112	700	6.3	6	23	266	11.6	4	135	966	7.2	10
3	Greg McElroy	13	60	-12	-0.2	1					60	-12	-0.2	1
4	Eddie Lacy	12	56	406	7.3	6	2	18	9	0	58	424	7.3	6
5	Demetrius Goode	6	34	140	4.1	1	1	17	17	0	35	157	4.5	1
6	Jalston Fowler	11	14	111	7.9	1					14	111	7.9	1
7	Julio Jones	13	8	135	16.9	2	78	1133	14.5	7	86	1268	14.7	9
8	A.J. McCarron	13	6	-10	-1.7	0					6	-10	-1.7	0
9	Ben Howell	1	5	11	2.2	0					5	11	2.2	0
10	Nick Tinker	1	4	9	2.3	0					4	9	2.3	0
11	Marquis Maze	13	3	15	5	0	38	557	14.7	3	41	572	14	3
12	Darius Hanks	13	2	7	3.5	0	32	456	14.3	3	34	463	13.6	3
13	Preston Dial	13					25	264	10.6	3	25	264	10.6	3
14	Michael Williams	13					8	100	12.5	1	8	100	12.5	1
15	Earl Alexander	13					7	90	12.9	0	7	90	12.9	0
16	Brad Smelley	13					6	55	9.2	0	6	55	9.2	0
17	Brandon Gibson	12					4	39	9.8	0	4	39	9.8	0
18	Kevin Norwood	13					3	56	18.7	1	3	56	18.7	1
19	Chris Underwood	13					3	36	12	1	3	36	12	1
20	Kenny Bell	10					2	26	13	0	2	26	13	0

Defense and fumbles

Rk	Player	G	Solo	Ast	Tot	Loss	Sk	Int	Yds	Avg	TD	PD	FR	FF
					Tackles				Def Int				Fumbles	
1	Mark Barron	12	54	21	75	3	2	3	6	2	0	6		1
2	Dont'a Hightower	13	30	39	69	3.5	0					3		
3	C.J. Mosley	13	30	37	67	1.5	0.5	2	76	38	2	10		
4	Dee Milliner	13	41	14	55	4	0	1	0	0	0	8		1
5	Dre Kirkpatrick	13	39	14	53	4	0	3	30	10	0	7	1	1
6	Robert Lester	13	29	23	52	1.5	1	8	102	12.8	0	4	1	0
7	Courtney Upshaw	13	32	20	52	14.5	7					2	1	4
8	Will Lowery	13	21	12	33	0	0	2	0	0	0	1		
9	Nico Johnson	13	22	11	33	3.5	0	1	0	0	0	1		
10	Marcell Dareus	11	20	13	33	11	4.5					4		
11	Dequan Menzie	12	26	7	33	5	2					4		
12	Josh Chapman	13	18	13	31	3.5	1					2		
13	Damion Square	13	20	7	27	7	3							
14	Jerrell Harris	9	17	7	24	1	0							
15	Luther Davis	13	11	10	21	3	0					1		
16	Phelon Jones	9	11	6	17	1	0					1		
17	Alex Watkins	12	9	7	16	2.5	2.5							
18	Chris Jordan	10	8	7	15	2	1	1	25	25	0	0		
19	Nick Gentry	13	4	10	14	1	1							
20	Ed Stinson	9	8	6	14	0	0							
21	Wesley Neighbors	11	6	6	12	0	0							
22	Chavis Williams	13	5	7	12	0.5	0							
23	Cade Foster	13	6	3	9	0	0							1
24	Darrington Sentimore	11	3	6	9	0.5	0							1
25	Hardie Buck	10	4	5	9	0	0							
26	Kerry Murphy	12	4	5	9	0	0							
27	B.J. Scott	6	3	3	6	0	0	1	0	0	0			
28	Brandon Moore	4	3	3	6	0	0							
29	Trent Richardson	11	5	1	6	0	0							
30	John Fulton	11	3	2	5	0.5	0.5					2		
31	Brandon Gibson	12	4	1	5	0	0						1	0
32	Jonathan Atchison	4	0	4	4	0	0							
33	Tana Patrick	5	3	1	4	0	0							
34	Eddie Lacy	12	0	4	4	0	0							
35	Michael Dejohn	1	1	2	3	0	0							
36	Undra Billingsley	12	2	0	2	0	0							
37	Jalston Fowler	11	2	0	2	0	0							
38	A.J. McCarron	13	1	1	2	0	0							
39	Kyle Pennington	2	1	1	2	0	0							
40	Nick Perry	6	1	0	1	0	0					1		
41	Carson Tinker	12	0	1	1	0	0							
42	Kenny Bell	10	1	0	1	0	0							
43	Drew Bullard	1	1	0	1	1	1							
44	Glenn Harbin	1	0	1	1	0	0							
45	Marquis Maze	13	0	1	1	0	0							
46	Brad Smelley	13	0	1	1	0	0							
47	Jarrick Williams	4	0	1	1	0	0							
48	Preston Dial	13	1	0	1	0	0							
49	Demetrius Goode	6	1	0	1	0	0							
50	Mark Ingram II	11	1	0	1	0	0							

Kick and punt returns

Rk	Player	G	Ret	Yds	Avg	TD	Ret	Yds	Avg	TD
				Kick Ret				Punt Ret		
1	Trent Richardson	11	24	634	26.4	1				
2	Marquis Maze	13	8	189	23.6	0	21	267	12.7	0
3	Julio Jones	13	5	129	25.8	0	5	44	8.8	0
4	Michael Williams	13	2	15	7.5	0				
5	Mark Ingram II	11	1	19	19	0				
6	Chavis Williams	13					1	15	15	0
7	Darius Hanks	13					1	1	1	0
8	Brandon Gibson	12						22		1

Kicking and punting

Rk	Player	G	Kicking							Punting		
			XPM	XPA	XP%	FGM	FGA	FG%	Pts	Punts	Yds	Avg
1	Jeremy Shelley	13	50	51	98	12	16	75	86			
2	Cade Foster	13	7	7	100	7	9	77.8	28			
3	Cody Mandell	13								41	1607	39.2

Scoring

Rk	Player	G	Touchdowns							Kicking				Pts
			Rush	Rec	Int	FR	PR	KR	Tot	XPM	FGM	2PM	Sfty	
1	Jeremy Shelley	13								50	12			86
2	Mark Ingram II	11	13	1					14					84
3	Trent Richardson	11	6	4			1		11					66
4	Julio Jones	13	2	7					9					54
5	Eddie Lacy	12	6						6					36
6	Cade Foster	13								7	7			28
7	Darius Hanks	13		3					3					18
8	Marquis Maze	13		3					3					18
9	Preston Dial	13		3					3					18
10	C.J. Mosley	13			2				2					12
11	Demetrius Goode	6	1						1					6
12	Greg McElroy	13	1						1					6
13	Jalston Fowler	11	1						1					6
14	Kevin Norwood	13		1					1					6
15	Chris Underwood	13		1					1					6
16	Michael Williams	13		1					1					6
17	Brandon Gibson	12					1		1					6

Stats include bowl games
Note: Table data from "2010 Alabama Crimson Tide Stats" (4)

Awards and honors

Name	Award	Type
Mark Barron	Permanent Team Captain	Team
Dont'a Hightower	Permanent Team Captain	Team
Greg McElroy	Permanent Team Captain	Team
Julio Jones	MVP	Team
Mark Ingram II	Offensive Player of the Year	Team
Greg McElroy	Offensive Player of the Year	Team
Mark Barron	Defensive Player of the Year	Team
Dont'a Hightower	Defensive Player of the Year	Team
Mark Barron	AP All-SEC First Team	SEC
Barrett Jones	AP All-SEC First Team	SEC
Julio Jones	AP All-SEC First Team	SEC
James Carpenter	AP All-SEC Second Team	SEC
Marcell Dareus	AP All-SEC Second Team	SEC
Dont'a Hightower	AP All-SEC Second Team	SEC
Mark Ingram II	AP All-SEC Second Team	SEC
Robert Lester	AP All-SEC Second Team	SEC
Greg McElroy	AP All-SEC Honorable Mention Team	SEC
William Vlachos	AP All-SEC Honorable Mention Team	SEC
Mark Barron	Coaches' All-SEC First Team	SEC
James Carpenter	Coaches' All-SEC First Team	SEC
Marcell Dareus	Coaches' All-SEC First Team	SEC
Julio Jones	Coaches' All-SEC First Team	SEC
Dont'a Hightower	Coaches' All-SEC Second Team	SEC
Mark Ingram II	Coaches' All-SEC Second Team	SEC
Barrett Jones	Coaches' All-SEC Second Team	SEC
Dre Kirkpatrick	Coaches' All-SEC Second Team	SEC
Robert Lester	Coaches' All-SEC Second Team	SEC
Trent Richardson	Coaches' All-SEC Second Team	SEC
William Vlachos	Coaches' All-SEC Second Team	SEC
D.J. Fluker	Freshman All-SEC	SEC
Cody Mandell	Freshman All-SEC	SEC
Dee Milliner	Freshman All-SEC	SEC
C.J. Mosley	Freshman All-SEC	SEC
Mark Barron	AP All-America Second Team	National

Name	Award	Type
Julio Jones	AP All-America Second Team	National
Marcell Dareus	AP All-America Third Team	National
Barrett Jones	AP All-America Third Team	National
Mark Barron	All-America First Team	National
James Carpenter	Senior Bowl	All-Star Team
Preston Dial	Senior Bowl	All-Star Team
Greg McElroy	Senior Bowl	All-Star Team

NFL

Season	Year drafted	Round	Pick	Overall	Player	Position	Team
2010	2011	1	3	3	Marcell Dareus	DT	Buffalo Bills
2010	2011	1	6	6	Julio Jones	WR	Atlanta Falcons
2010	2011	1	25	25	James Carpenter	OT	Seattle Seahawks
2010	2011	1	28	28	Mark Ingram II	RB	New Orleans Saints
2010	2011	7	5	208	Greg McElroy	QB	New York Jets

Note: Table data from "2010 Alabama Crimson Tide football team" (64)

2011

Overall

Record	12-1
SEC Record	8-1
Rank	1
Points for	453
Points against	106
Points/game	34.8
Opp points/game	8.2
SOS[5]	4.21

What makes you think you can just assume they (backups) are going to get to play? Because you're assuming the other team is not very good? Y'all don't remember the Georgia Southern game, do you? I don't think we had a guy on that field that didn't play in the NFL, and about four or five of them were first round draft picks. And I think that team won a national championship, but I'm not sure. And they ran through our ass like shit through a tinhorn, man, and we could not stop 'em. Could not stop 'em! Could not stop 'em! -Nick Saban

Games

Date	Bama Rank		Opp Rank	Opponent	Bama	Opp	Result	SEC
09/03/11	2	vs		Kent State	48	7	W	
09/10/11	3	@	23	Penn State	27	11	W	
09/17/11	2	vs		North Texas	41	0	W	
09/24/11	3	vs	14	Arkansas	38	14	W	W
10/01/11	3	@	12	Florida	38	10	W	W
10/08/11	2	vs		Vanderbilt	34	0	W	W
10/15/11	2	@		Ole Miss	52	7	W	W
10/22/11	2	vs		Tennessee	37	6	W	W
11/05/11	2	vs	1	LSU	6	9	L	L
11/12/11	3	@		Mississippi State	24	7	W	W
11/19/11	3	vs		Georgia Southern	45	21	W	
11/26/11	2	@	24	Auburn	42	14	W	W
01/09/12	2	N	1	LSU	21	0	W	W

Coaches

Name	Position	Year
Nick Saban	Head Coach	5
Burton Burns	Associate Head Coach / Running Backs	5
Scott Cochran	Strength and Conditioning	5
Mike Groh	Wide Receivers / Recruiting Coordinator	1
Jim McElwain	Offensive Coordinator / Quarterbacks	4
Jeremy Pruitt	Secondary	2
Chris Rumph	Defensive Line	1
Kirby Smart	Defensive Coordinator	5
Jeff Stoutland	Offensive Line	1
Sal Sunseri	Assistant Head Coach / Linebackers	3
Bobby Williams	Tight Ends / Special Teams	4

Recruits

Name	Pos	Pos Rank	Scout	Rivals	247 Sports	ESPN	ESPN Grade	Hometown	High school / college	Height	Weight	Committed
Brent Calloway	ATH		4	4	4	4	80	Russellville, AL	Russellville HS	6-1	210	2/2/11
Ronald Carswell	WR	71		3	3	3	78	Macon, GA	Westside HS	6-0	180	2/3/10
Ha Ha Clinton-Dix	S	23	5	5	5	4	84	Orlando, FL	Dr. Phillips HS	6-2	190	4/17/10
Trey DePriest	OLB	2	5	4	5	4	82	Springfield, OH	Springfield HS	6-2	230	7/30/10
Quinton Dial	DT		4	4	4	N/A	NR	Clay, AL	East Mississippi Community College	6-5	310	2/4/10
Xzavier Dickson	DE	4	4	4	4	4	83	Griffin, GA	Griffin HS	6-4	248	1/5/11
Aaron Douglas	OT		3	4	4	N/A	NR	Maryville, TN	Arizona Western College	6-6	290	12/16/10
Phillip Ely	QB	40	3	3	3	3	77	Tampa, FL	Plant HS	6-1	186	8/11/10
Malcolm Faciane	TE	4	3	4	4	4	81	Picayune, MS	Picayune Memorial HS	6-6	263	4/15/10
LaMichael Fanning	DE	14	4	4	4	4	80	Hamilton, GA	Harris County HS	6-7	270	4/17/10
Demetrius Hart	RB	8	4	5	4	4	81	Orlando, FL	Dr. Phillips HS	5-8	190	1/8/11
Christion Jones	CB	10	3	4	3	4	80	Adamsville, AL	Minor HS	5-10	175	9/30/10
Ryan Kelly	OC	4	4	3	4	3	79	West Chester Township, Butler County, OH	Lakota West HS	6-5	280	7/19/10
Cyrus Kouandjio	OT	1	5	5	5	5	87	Hyattsville, MD	DeMatha Catholic HS	6-7	325	2/5/11
Wilson Love	DT	42		3	N/A	3	79	Mountain Brook, AL	Mountain Brook HS	6-4	270	4/18/09
Isaac Luatua	OG	18	3	3	3	3	79	La Mirada, CA	La Mirada HS	6-3	298	6/8/10
Jeoffrey Pagan	DE	8	4	4	4	4	81	Asheville, NC	Asheville HS	6-4	272	2/2/11
D.J. Pettway	DE	21	3	4	4	4	80	Pensacola, FL	Pensacola Catholic HS	6-3	255	4/19/10
Marvin Shinn	WR	14	4	4	4	4	81	Prichard, AL	Vigor HS	6-4	195	4/18/09
Vinnie Sunseri	OLB	18	3	3	3	4	79	Tuscaloosa, AL	Northridge HS	6-0	205	6/12/10
Bradley Sylve	WR	5	4	4	4	4	82	Port Sulphur, LA	South Plaquemines HS	5-11	175	5/12/10
Jabriel Washington	ATH	29	4	3	4	4	79	Jackson, TN	Trinity Christian Academy	5-11	165	4/18/10
Jesse Williams	DT		4	4	4	N/A	NR	Brisbane, Australia	Arizona Western College	6-5	340	9/4/10
Danny Woodson Jr.	WR	22	4	4	4	4	80	Mobile, AL	Le Flore HS	6-2	198	3/13/10

	Scout	Rivals	247Sports	ESPN
5 Stars	3	3	3	1
4 Stars	12	14	15	15
3 Stars	7	7	5	5
2 Stars	0	0	0	0

Note: Table data from "2011 Alabama Crimson Tide football team" (78)

Roster

Num	Player	Pos	Class	Height	Weight	Hometown	Last School
19	Jonathan Atchison	LB	SO	6-2	240	Atlanta, GA	Douglass
31	John Baites	TE	SR	6-4	231	Hendersonville, TN	Beech
4	**Mark Barron**	**DB**	**SR**	**6-2**	**218**	**Mobile, AL**	**St. Paul's**
13	Diege Barry	DB	JR	5-10	180	Mobile, AL	St. Paul's
7	Kenny Bell	WR	SO	6-1	175	Rayville, LA	Rayville
31	Jerrod Bierbower	DB	FR	6-1	180	Dublin, OH	Coffman
86	Undra Billingsley	DL	JR	6-2	288	Birmingham, AL	Woodlawn
69	David Blalock	OL	SR	6-5	261	Charlotte, NC	Providence
93	Chris Bonds	DL	SO	6-4	269	Columbia, SC	Richland Northeast
67	John Michael Boswell	OL	SR	6-5	300	Northport, AL	Tuscaloosa County
88	Michael Bowman	WR	SO	6-4	225	Rossville, GA	Ridgeland
81	Hardie Buck	WR	JR	5-9	190	Birmingham, AL	Vestavia Hills
34	Hunter Bush	DB	JR	5-11	195	Wetempka, AL	Wetumpka
21	Brent Calloway	RB	FR	6-1	217	Russellville, AL	Russellville
20	Nate Carlson	TE	JR	6-4	236	Birmingham, AL	Air Force
5	Ronald Carswell	WR	FR	6-0	180	Macon, GA	Westside
8	Duron Carter	WR	JR	6-4	210	Fort Lauderdale, FL	Ohio State/Coffeyville CC
25	Caleb Castille	DB	FR	5-11	170	Birmingham, AL	Briarwood Christian
99	**Josh Chapman**	**DL**	**SR**	**6-1**	**310**	**Hoover, AL**	**Hoover**
6	Ha Ha Clinton-Dix	DB	FR	6-1	203	Orlando, FL	Dr. Phillips
43	Taylor Conant	WR	JR	6-0	195	Tuscaloosa, AL	Tuscaloosa Academy
18	Levi Cook	DB	JR	5-10	190	Decatur, AL	Decatur
50	Robert Cramer	DS	FR	6-0	240	Hoover, AL	Hoover
33	Trey DePriest	LB	FR	6-2	242	Springfield, OH	Springfield
90	Quinton Dial	DL	JR	6-6	294	Pinson, AL	East Mississippi CC
55	Josh Dickerson	LB	SO	6-1	235	Evans, GA	Lakeside
47	Xzavier Dickson	LB	FR	6-3	240	Griffin, GA	Griffin
40	DeMarcus DuBose	LB	SR	6-1	240	Montgomery, AL	Jefferson Davis
12	Phillip Ely	QB	FR	6-1	187	Tampa, FL	Plant
85	Malcolm Faciane	TE	FR	6-5	259	Picayune, MS	Picayune Memorial
44	LaMichael Fanning	DL	FR	6-7	275	Hamilton, GA	Harris County
76	**D.J. Fluker**	**OL**	**SO**	**6-6**	**335**	**Foley, AL**	**Foley**
43	**Cade Foster**	**PK**	**SO**	**6-1**	**216**	**Southlake, TX**	**Southlake Carroll**
45	Jalston Fowler	RB	SO	6-1	246	Mobile, AL	Vigor
10	John Fulton	DB	SO	6-0	187	Manning, SC	Manning
58	Nick Gentry	DL	SR	6-1	284	Prattville, AL	Prattville
11	**Brandon Gibson**	**WR**	**SR**	**6-2**	**194**	**Mobile, AL**	**UMS-Wright**
68	Austin Gray	OL	SO	6-0	309	Woodstock, GA	Alan C. Pope
15	**Darius Hanks**	**WR**	**SR**	**6-0**	**185**	**Norcross, GA**	**Norcross**
48	Rowdy Harrell	LB	SR	6-0	219	Moundville, AL	Hale County
5	**Jerrell Harris**	**LB**	**SR**	**6-3**	**242**	**Gadsden, AL**	**Gadsden City**
1	Dee Hart	RB	FR	5-9	187	Orlando, FL	Dr. Phillips
30	**Dont'a Hightower**	**LB**	**JR**	**6-4**	**260**	**Lewisburg, TN**	**Marshall County**
25	Ben Howell	RB	JR	5-9	202	Gordo, AL	Gordo
42	Adrian Hubbard	LB	FR	6-6	237	Lawrenceville, GA	Norcross
62	Brandon Ivory	DL	FR	6-4	308	Memphis, TN	East
19	Ronald James	WR	JR	5-8	166	Castro Valley, CA	Bishop O'Dowd
31	Kelly Johnson	DS	SR	6-3	230	Bluffton, SC	Providence Day
35	**Nico Johnson**	**LB**	**JR**	**6-3**	**245**	**Andalusia, AL**	**Andalusia**
57	Aaron Joiner	OL	JR	6-2	275	Florence, AL	Florence
75	**Barrett Jones**	**OL**	**JR**	**6-5**	**311**	**Memphis, TN**	**Evangelical Christian**
22	Christion Jones	DB	FR	5-11	175	Adamsville, AL	Minor
82	Harrison Jones	TE	FR	6-4	248	Memphis, TN	Evangelical Christian
9	Phelon Jones	DB	SR	5-11	194	Moblie, AL	LSU
36	Chris Jordan	LB	SR	6-3	240	Brentwood, TN	Brentwood Academy
43	Sam Kearns	DB	SR	5-6	155	Mobile, AL	McGill-Toolen
70	Ryan Kelly	OL	FR	6-5	281	West Chester, OH	Lakota West
48	Tommy Keys	FB	FR	6-2	230	West Point, MS	West Point
21	**Dre Kirkpatrick**	**DB**	**JR**	**6-3**	**192**	**Gadsden, AL**	**Gadsden City**
59	Arie Kouandjio	OL	FR	6-5	335	Beltsville, MD	DeMatha Catholic
71	Cyrus Kouandjio	OL	FR	6-6	322	Hyattsville, MD	DeMatha Catholic
42	Eddie Lacy	RB	SO	6-0	220	Geismar, LA	Dutchtown
37	**Robert Lester**	**DB**	**JR**	**6-2**	**210**	**Foley, AL**	**Foley**
95	Brandon Lewis	DL	JR	6-3	288	Pleasant Grove, AL	East Mississippi CC
78	Chad Lindsay	OL	FR	6-2	287	The Woodlands, TX	The Woodlands
72	Tyler Love	OL	JR	6-6	307	Mountain Brook, AL	Mountain Brook
51	Wilson Love	DL	FR	6-3	276	Mountain Brook, AL	Mountain Brook
29	Will Lowery	DB	JR	5-9	180	Hoover, AL	Hoover
68	Issac Luatua	OL	FR	6-2	299	La Mirada, CA	La Mirada
29	**Cody Mandell**	**P**	**SO**	**6-4**	**202**	**Lafayette, LA**	**Acadiana**
4	**Marquis Maze**	**WR**	**SR**	**5-10**	**180**	**Birmingham, AL**	**Tarrant**
24	Nathan McAlister	WR	FR	5-11	165	Russellville, AL	Russellville
10	**A.J. McCarron**	**QB**	**SO**	**6-4**	**205**	**Mobile, AL**	**Saint Paul's Episcopal School**

97

Num	Player	Pos	Class	Height	Weight	Hometown	Last School
52	**Alfred McCullough**	OL	SR	6-2	311	Athens, AL	Athens
24	DeQuan Menzie	DB	SR	6-0	198	Columbus, GA	Copiah-Lincoln CC
28	Dee Milliner	DB	SO	6-1	196	Millbrook, AL	Stanhope Elmore
56	William Ming	DL	SO	6-3	283	Athens, AL	Athens
32	**C.J. Mosley**	LB	SO	6-2	234	Theodore, AL	Theodore
83	Kevin Norwood	WR	SO	6-2	193	D'Iberville, MS	D'Iberville
18	Morgan Ogilvie	QB	FR	6-0	198	Mountain Brook, AL	Mountain Brook
53	Anthony Orr	DL	FR	6-4	258	Madison, AL	Sparkman
8	Jeoffrey Pagan	DL	FR	6-4	272	Asheville, NC	Asheville
2	Tana Patrick	LB	SO	6-3	236	Bridgeport, AL	North Jackson
27	Nick Perry	DB	SO	6-1	205	Prattville, AL	Prattville
57	D.J. Pettway	DL	FR	6-2	272	Pensacola, FL	Pensacola Catholic
54	Russell Raines	OL	SO	6-2	281	Satsuma, AL	Satsuma
3	**Trent Richardson**	RB	JR	5-11	224	Pensacola, FL	Escambia
90	**Jeremy Shelley**	PK	JR	5-10	165	Raleigh, NC	Broughton
79	Austin Shepherd	OL	FR	6-5	321	Buford, GA	North Gwinnett
80	Marvin Shinn	WR	FR	6-3	193	Prichard, AL	Vigor
6	Blake Sims	ATH	FR	6-0	212	Gainesville, GA	Gainesville
14	Phillip Sims	QB	FR	6-2	217	Chesapeake, VA	Oscar Smith
74	Allen Skelton	OL	JR	6-1	267	Coker, AL	Tuscaloosa County
17	**Brad Smelley**	TE	SR	6-3	229	Tuscaloosa, AL	American Christian
92	**Damion Square**	DL	JR	6-3	285	Houston, TX	Yates
61	Anthony Steen	OL	SO	6-3	303	Lambert, MS	Lee Academy
49	**Ed Stinson**	DL	SO	6-4	279	Homestead, FL	South Dade
46	William Strickland	WR	SR	6-0	191	Tuscaloosa, AL	Northridge
3	Vinnie Sunseri	DB	FR	6-0	217	Tuscaloosa, AL	Northridge
16	Bradley Sylve	WR	FR	5-11	170	Port Sulphur, LA	South Palquemines
49	M.K. Taylor	DS	SO	5-10	208	Anniston, AL	Oxford
51	**Carson Tinker**	LS	JR	6-1	220	Murfreesboro, TN	Riverdale
26	Nick Tinker	RB	SO	5-10	207	Ralph, AL	Tuscaloosa County
87	Chris Underwood	TE	SR	6-4	243	Vestavia Hills, AL	Vestavia Hills
41	**Courtney Upshaw**	LB	SR	6-2	265	Eufaula, AL	Eufaula
73	**William Vlachos**	OL	SR	6-1	294	Birmingham, AL	Mountain Brook
84	Brian Vogler	TE	FR	6-7	252	Columbus, GA	Brookstone
65	**Chance Warmack**	OL	JR	6-3	320	Atlanta, GA	Westlake
26	Jabriel Washington	DB	FR	5-11	165	Jackson, TN	Trinity Christian Academy
91	Alex Watkins	LB	SR	6-3	234	Brownsville, TN	Haywood
11	Ranzell Watkins	DB	SO	5-9	170	Charlotte, NC	Independence
2	DeAndrew White	WR	FR	6-0	181	Houston, TX	North Shore
20	Jarrick Williams	DB	SO	6-1	210	Mobile, AL	Blount
44	Jay Williams	P	FR	6-3	221	Thomasville, AL	Thomasville
54	Jesse Williams	DL	JR	6-4	319	Brisbane, Australia	Western Arizona CC
63	Kellen Williams	OL	SO	6-3	305	Lawrenceville, GA	Brookwood
89	**Michael Williams**	TE	JR	6-6	269	Reform, AL	Pickens County
9	Nick Williams	WR	SO	5-10	185	Fort Lauderdale, FL	St. Thomas Aquinas
25	Danny Woodson Jr.	WR	FR	6-1	205	Mobile, AL	LeFlore

Note: Starters in bold
Note: Table data from "2011 Alabama Crimson Tide Roster" (80)

Transfers

Player	School	Direction
Demetrius Goode	North Alabama	Outgoing
Corey Grant	Auburn	Outgoing
Robby Green	California University of Pennsylvania	Outgoing
Keiwone Malone	Memphis	Outgoing
Brandon Moore	East Mississippi Community College	Outgoing
B.J. Scott	South Alabama	Outgoing
Petey Smith	Holmes Community College	Outgoing

Note: Table data from "2011 Alabama Crimson Tide football team" (79)

Games

09/03/11 - Alabama (2) vs Kent State

Team	1	2	3	4	T		Passing	Rushing	Total
Kent State	0	0	7	0	**7**		99	-9	**90**
Alabama (2)	21	3	14	10	**48**		299	183	**482**

The Crimson Tide opened the 2011 season at home against Nick Saban's alma mater, the Kent State Golden Flashes of the Mid-American Conference. In the meeting that was the first all-time against the Golden Flashes, the Crimson Tide won 48-7. After holding the Golden Flashes to a three-and-out on the opening possession, Trent Richardson scored the Crimson Tide's first touchdown on a 1-yard run to give Alabama a 7-0 lead. After holding Kent State again to a three-and-out, Alabama responded with a 4-play, 74-yard touchdown drive that featured a 48-yard Eddie Lacy reception and a 24-yard Marquis Maze touchdown reception from A.J. McCarron to take a 14-0 lead. The Tide scored their final points of the first quarter on a 1-yard Richardson run to take a 21-0 lead into the second quarter. After only scoring on a 36-yard Jeremy Shelley field goal in the second quarter, Alabama led 24-0 at the half.

On the second Crimson Tide possession of the third quarter, Phillip Sims threw an interception to Norman Wolfe that was returned to the Alabama 3-yard line. Two plays later, Kent State scored its only points of the game when Spencer Keith connected with Justin Thompson for a 3-yard touchdown reception to cut the lead to 24-7. The Crimson Tide responded with touchdowns on the next two consecutive drives. Trent Richardson and Eddie Lacy both scored on 1-yard runs to extend Alabama's lead to 38-7 entering the fourth quarter. In the fourth, the Tide scored their final touchdown of the afternoon on a 49-yard Jalston Fowler run and their final points on a 32-yard Shelley field goal to make the final score 48-7. For the game, Alabama's defense was dominant in allowing -9 yards rushing and 90 yards of total offense against Kent State in the contest. On offense, the Crimson Tide had 482 total yards with three different running backs scoring touchdowns and Marquis Maze totaling 118 yards receiving on eight catches with one touchdown.[79]

Passing	C/ATT	YDS	AVG	TD	INT	QBR
AJ McCarron	14/23	226	9.8	1	2	82.2
P. Sims	7/14	73	5.2	0	2	--
Team	21/37	299	8.1	1	4	--

Rushing	CAR	YDS	AVG	TD	LONG
J. Fowler	4	69	17.3	1	49
E. Lacy	8	58	7.3	1	23
T. Richardson	13	37	2.8	3	10
B. Sims	6	16	2.7	0	6
P. Sims	3	3	1	0	15
AJ McCarron	1	0	0	0	0
Team	35	183	5.2	5	49

Interceptions	INT	YDS	TD
P. Jones	1	0	0

Kick returns	NO	YDS	AVG	LONG	TD
M. Maze	1	39	39	39	0
D. White	1	24	24	24	0
Team	2	63	31.5	39	0

Punting	NO	YDS	AVG	TB	IN 20	LONG
C. Mandell	3	127	42.3	0	0	47

Receiving	REC	YDS	AVG	TD	LONG
M. Maze	8	118	14.8	1	26
E. Lacy	3	76	25.3	0	48
D. White	4	44	11	0	16
B. Gibson	1	18	18	0	18
T. Richardson	1	16	16	0	16
B. Smelley	1	8	8	0	8
Ch. Jones	1	8	8	0	8
B. Vogler	1	6	6	0	6
K. Norwood	1	5	5	0	5
Team	21	299	14.2	1	48

Punt returns	NO	YDS	AVG	LONG	TD
M. Maze	9	96	10.7	27	0
D. White	2	34	17	23	0
Ch. Jones	1	18	18	18	0
Team	12	148	12.3	27	0

Kicking	FG	PCT	LONG	XP	PTS
J. Shelley	2/2	100	36	6/6	12
C. Foster	0/1	0	0	0/0	0
Team	2/3	66.7	36	6/6	12

Note: Table data from "Alabama 48-7 Kent State (Sep 3, 2011) Box Score" (81)

09/10/11 - Alabama (3) at Penn State (23)

Team	1	2	3	4	T		Passing	Rushing	Total
Alabama (3)	7	10	3	7	27		163	196	359
Penn State (23)	3	0	0	8	11		144	107	251

In what was the second consecutive meeting between the Crimson Tide and the Penn State Nittany Lions, and first at Happy Valley since 1989, Alabama won 27-11. Penn State took the opening possession down the field and recorded a 43-yard field goal by Evan Lewis to take an early 3-0 lead by using all three of their timeouts. Alabama took a 7-3 lead later in the first quarter after A.J. McCarron connected with Michael Williams for a 5-yard touchdown reception to cap an 11-play, 69-yard drive. A 22-yard Jeremy Shelley kick extended the Crimson Tide lead to 10-3 early in the second quarter. Then after trading punts, Dre Kirkpatrick forced Andrew Szczerba to fumble the ball that was recovered by Alabama's DeQuan Menzie. Ten plays later, the Crimson Tide led 17-3 after a 3-yard Trent Richardson touchdown run.

After each team punted twice to start the third quarter, Jeremy Shelley connected on an 18-yard field goal to extend Bama's lead to 20-3. Mark Barron intercepted a pass, three punts occurred, then Alabama recovered a fumble at its own 35-yard line. Trent Richardson then scored his second rushing touchdown of the game midway through the fourth quarter on a 13-yard run to give Alabama a 27-3 lead. The final points of the game came late in the fourth quarter when Silas Redd scored on a 1-yard touchdown for the Nittany Lions, and Rob Bolden converted the two-point conversion to bring the final score to 27-11.

Trent Richardson ran for 111 yards and two touchdowns while Eddie Lacy ran for 85 yards. A.J. McCarron threw for 163 yards and a touchdown. For his seven tackles, interception, and fumble recovery, Mark Barron was named SEC Defensive Player of the Week. The 107,846 fans in attendance were the most to ever see an Alabama squad compete on the gridiron. The outcome was also noted as the final career loss for Joe Paterno as the Nittany Lions' head coach.[79]

Passing	C/ATT	YDS	AVG	TD	INT	QBR
AJ McCarron	19/31	163	5.3	1	0	75.8

Rushing	CAR	YDS	AVG	TD	LONG
T. Richardson	26	111	4.3	2	22
E. Lacy	11	85	7.7	0	30
AJ McCarron	2	4	2	0	3
B. Smelley	1	1	1	0	1
M. Maze	1	-5	-5	0	0
Team	41	196	4.8	2	30

Interceptions	INT	YDS	TD
M. Barron	1	0	0

Punt returns	NO	YDS	AVG	LONG	TD
M. Maze	3	43	14.3	44	0

Punting	NO	YDS	AVG	TB	IN 20	LONG
C. Mandell	6	223	37.2	0	0	44

Receiving	REC	YDS	AVG	TD	LONG
M. Maze	4	42	10.5	0	29
M. Williams	3	34	11.3	1	24
K. Norwood	3	25	8.3	0	12
T. Richardson	4	19	4.8	0	7
B. Smelley	2	18	9	0	10
K. Bell	1	14	14	0	14
E. Lacy	1	6	6	0	6
B. Gibson	1	5	5	0	5
Team	19	163	8.6	1	29

Kick returns	NO	YDS	AVG	LONG	TD
D. Milliner	1	21	21	21	0
T. Richardson	1	19	19	19	0
Team	2	40	20	21	0

Kicking	FG	PCT	LONG	XP	PTS
J. Shelley	2/2	100	22	3/3	9

Note: Table data from "Alabama 27-11 Penn State (Sep 10, 2011) Box Score" (82)

09/17/11 - Alabama (2) vs North Texas

Team	1	2	3	4	T		Passing	Rushing	Total
North Texas	0	0	0	0	**0**		101	68	**169**
Alabama (2)	10	10	7	14	**41**		239	347	**586**

In its meeting against the North Texas Mean Green, Alabama outgained its opponent 586 to 169 yards of total offense in Alabama's 41-0 victory. After a 26-yard Jeremy Shelley field goal gave the Crimson Tide a 3-0 lead, Trent Richardson scored their first touchdown of the evening on Alabama's second offensive possession to give them a 10-0 lead at the end of the first quarter. It took them 3:16 and seven plays to complete the 58-yard scoring drive. The Tide extended their lead to 17-0 after a 43-yard Eddie Lacy touchdown run capping a 6-play, 76-yard drive that only took 2:32. Jeremy Shelley made the score 20-0 at halftime when he connected on a 37-yard field goal.

North Texas opened the second half with a 9-play, 54-yard drive to set up a 42-yard Zach Olen field goal attempt. However, the kick was blocked by Robert Lester to preserve the shutout. Alabama extended its lead to 27-0 in the third quarter after Richardson scored his second touchdown of the evening on a 58-yard run. After Shelley missed a 42-yard field goal on the first play of the fourth quarter, Trent Richardson scored again with a 71-yard touchdown run on Alabama's next offensive possession to extend the lead to 34-0. Eddie Lacy scored the final points of the game midway through the fourth quarter with his second touchdown of the evening on a 67-yard run to give Alabama the 41-0 victory.

Trent Richardson ran for a career-high 167 yards and three touchdowns and Eddie Lacy ran for 161 yards and two touchdowns and became the first pair of running backs to each run for 150 yards in a game. The shutout was the Crimson Tide's first since they defeated Chattanooga 45-0 in 2009.[79]

Passing	C/ATT	YDS	AVG	TD	INT	QBR
AJ McCarron	15/21	190	9	0	0	64.2
P. Sims	6/8	49	6.1	0	0	--
Team	21/29	239	8.5	0	0	--

Rushing	CAR	YDS	AVG	TD	LONG
T. Richardson	11	167	15.2	3	71
E. Lacy	9	161	17.9	2	67
J. Fowler	3	20	6.7	0	9
B. Sims	3	13	4.3	0	15
M. Maze	1	6	6	0	6
P. Sims	1	-5	-5	0	0
AJ McCarron	4	-14	-3.5	0	0
Team	1	-1	-1	0	0
Team	33	347	10.5	5	71

Kick returns	NO	YDS	AVG	LONG	TD
M. Maze	1	20	20	20	0

Punting	NO	YDS	AVG	TB	IN 20	LONG
C. Mandell	1	35	35	0	0	35

Receiving	REC	YDS	AVG	TD	LONG
K. Bell	4	55	13.8	0	25
B. Smelley	4	46	11.5	0	20
Ch. Jones	2	41	20.5	0	30
B. Gibson	3	35	11.7	0	19
M. Maze	3	26	8.7	0	16
D. Hanks	2	20	10	0	14
M. Williams	1	10	10	0	10
D. White	1	5	5	0	5
T. Richardson	1	1	1	0	1
Team	21	239	11.4	0	30

Punt returns	NO	YDS	AVG	LONG	TD
M. Maze	6	56	9.3	28	0
Ch. Jones	2	0	0	0	0
Team	8	56	7	28	0

Kicking	FG	PCT	LONG	XP	PTS
J. Shelley	2/4	50	37	5/5	11

Note: Table data from "Alabama 41-0 North Texas (Sep 17, 2011) Box Score" (83)

09/24/11 - Alabama (3) vs Arkansas (14)

Team	1	2	3	4	T		Passing	Rushing	Total
Arkansas (14)	7	0	7	0	**14**		209	17	**226**
Alabama (3)	7	10	21	0	**38**		200	197	**397**

After three consecutive victories to start the season, the Crimson Tide opened conference play against the Arkansas Razorbacks and defeated them 38-14 at Bryant-Denny Stadium. Alabama scored first with a trick play on its opening possession. After driving to the Arkansas 37-yard line, Cade Foster lined up for a 54-yard field goal attempt. Alabama quarterback A.J. McCarron received the snap as the holder and proceeded to throw a 37-yard touchdown pass to Michael Williams to give the Crimson Tide a 7-0 lead. The Razorbacks tied the game at 7-7 late in the first quarter when Tyler Wilson threw a 10-yard touchdown pass to Dennis Johnson. After an Arkansas goal-line stand, Jeremy Shelley connected on a 20-yard field goal to give Alabama a 10-7 lead. On the ensuing Arkansas possession, the Crimson Tide scored when DeQuan Menzie intercepted a Wilson pass and returned it 25 yards for a touchdown to give Alabama a 17-7 lead at the half.

After holding Arkansas scoreless on its first possession of the third quarter, Alabama's Marquis Maze returned a Dylan Breeding punt 83 yards for a touchdown and a 24-7 Crimson Tide lead. On Alabama's next possession, Trent Richardson caught a screen pass from McCarron and ran it 61 yards for a touchdown and extended the Alabama lead to 31-7. The Razorbacks scored on the following possession when Wilson threw his second touchdown pass of the afternoon after he connected on a 19-yard pass to Cobi Hamilton. Eddie Lacy then scored the final points of the game late in the third quarter on a 4-yard touchdown run to give the Crimson Tide the 38-14 victory. The Alabama defense only allowed 17 rushing and 226 of total offense to the Razorbacks in the victory. For his 235 all-purpose yards and touchdown reception, Trent Richardson was named the SEC Offensive Player of the Week.[79]

Passing	C/ATT	YDS	AVG	TD	INT	QBR
AJ McCarron	15/20	200	10	2	0	69.9

Rushing	CAR	YDS	AVG	TD	LONG
T. Richardson	17	126	7.4	0	31
E. Lacy	13	61	4.7	1	10
J. Fowler	4	11	2.8	0	4
AJ McCarron	5	-1	-0.2	0	4
Team	39	197	5.1	1	31

Kick returns	NO	YDS	AVG	LONG	TD
T. Richardson	1	24	24	24	0

Punt returns	NO	YDS	AVG	LONG	TD
M. Maze	8	125	15.6	83	1

Punting	NO	YDS	AVG	TB	IN 20	LONG
C. Mandell	6	225	37.5	0	0	44

Receiving	REC	YDS	AVG	TD	LONG
T. Richardson	3	85	28.3	1	61
M. Maze	5	40	8	0	17
M. Williams	1	37	37	1	37
B. Smelley	1	15	15	0	15
D. Hanks	2	13	6.5	0	8
K. Bell	1	8	8	0	8
E. Lacy	1	4	4	0	4
B. Gibson	1	-2	-2	0	-2
Team	15	200	13.3	2	61

Interceptions	INT	YDS	TD
D. Menzie	1	25	1
D. Milliner	1	0	0
Team	2	25	1

Kicking	FG	PCT	LONG	XP	PTS
J. Shelley	1/1	100	20	5/5	8

Note: Table data from "Alabama 38-14 Arkansas (Sep 24, 2011) Box Score" (84)

102

10/01/11 - Alabama (3) at Florida (12)

Team	1	2	3	4	T	Passing	Rushing	Total
Alabama (3)	10	14	0	14	38	140	226	366
Florida (12)	10	0	0	0	10	207	15	222

In what was the first meeting as opposing head coaches between Nick Saban and his former assistant coach from both LSU and the Miami Dolphins, Will Muschamp, the Crimson Tide defeated the Florida Gators, 38-10 at The Swamp. After receiving the opening kickoff, Florida scored its only touchdown of the game on its first offensive play from scrimmage. The Gators took an early 7-0 lead when John Brantley threw a 65-yard touchdown pass to Andre Debose. Alabama responded on the following drive of 52 yards with Jeremy Shelley connecting on a 32-yard field goal to cut the Florida lead to 7-3. The Gators responded with what turned out to be their final points of the game when Caleb Sturgis connected on a 21-yard field goal. Alabama's Marquis Maze then returned the ensuing kickoff 70 yards to the Florida 29-yard line, and Bama tied the game at 10-10 seven plays later on a 5-yard Trent Richardson touchdown run.

Alabama got the lead 24-10 at halftime with a pair of second-quarter touchdowns. Courtney Upshaw scored a defensive touchdown early in the second quarter after he intercepted a Brantley pass and returned it 45 yards for the score. A.J. McCarron scored later in the quarter on a 1-yard quarterback sneak to cap a 10-play, 61-yard drive. Late in the quarter, the Gators did have a scoring opportunity by driving to the Alabama 13-yard line. However, the Alabama defense sacked Brantley on consecutive snaps for a loss of 22 yards and knocked him out of the game with an injury. Sturgis then missed a 52-yard field goal attempt and Alabama led 24-10 at the half.

After a scoreless third quarter, a pair of fourth-quarter touchdowns gave Alabama the 38-10 victory. Trent Richardson scored his second touchdown of the game with 12:25 remaining on a 36-yard run capping an 11-play, 89-yard drive, and Eddie Lacy scored the final points of the game on a 20-yard run. For the game, Alabama's defense was dominant in only allowing 222 total yards of offense, with the 15 rushing yards being the fewest ever allowed against Florida in their all-time series. Trent Richardson established a new career high for rushing yards in game with his 181 yards on 29 attempts.[79]

Passing	C/ATT	YDS	AVG	TD	INT	QBR
AJ McCarron	12/25	140	5.6	0	0	71.6

Rushing	CAR	YDS	AVG	TD	LONG
T. Richardson	29	181	6.2	2	36
E. Lacy	5	32	6.4	1	20
J. Fowler	5	19	3.8	0	7
AJ McCarron	1	1	1	1	1
Team	3	-7	-2.3	0	0
Team	43	226	5.3	4	36

Interceptions	INT	YDS	TD
C. Upshaw	1	45	1

Punting	NO	YDS	AVG	TB	IN 20	LONG
C. Mandell	5	199	39.8	0	0	49

Receiving	REC	YDS	AVG	TD	LONG
M. Maze	2	36	18	0	18
M. Williams	3	32	10.7	0	22
T. Richardson	2	27	13.5	0	22
D. Hanks	2	19	9.5	0	13
B. Smelley	1	16	16	0	16
K. Bell	1	7	7	0	7
E. Lacy	1	3	3	0	3
Team	12	140	11.7	0	22

Kick returns	NO	YDS	AVG	LONG	TD
M. Maze	3	123	41	70	0

Punt returns	NO	YDS	AVG	LONG	TD
M. Maze	2	0	0	0	0

Kicking	FG	PCT	LONG	XP	PTS
J. Shelley	1/1	100	32	5/5	8

Note: Table data from "Alabama 38-10 Florida (Oct 1, 2011) Box Score" (85)

10/08/11 - Alabama (2) vs Vanderbilt

Team	1	2	3	4	T		Passing	Rushing	Total
Vanderbilt	0	0	0	0	0		149	41	190
Alabama (2)	7	7	13	7	34		266	153	419

For the 91st Homecoming football game in Alabama history, the Crimson Tide defeated the Vanderbilt Commodores 34-0 who made their first visit to Bryant-Denny Stadium since the 2006 season. After a three-and-out on its opening drive, Alabama scored its first touchdown of the evening on a 6-yard A.J. McCarron touchdown pass to Brad Smelley to complete a 10-play, 77-yard drive. On the following drive, Vanderbilt had an opportunity to cut into the lead, but Carey Spear missed a 47-yard field goal to keep the Alabama lead at 7-0. Spear missed a second field goal later in the second quarter from 38 yards, and the Crimson Tide responded with their second touchdown drive of the game. McCarron threw a 5-yard TD pass to DeAndrew White, capping a 13-play, 78-yard drive to give Alabama a 14-0 halftime lead.

In the second half, Alabama scored on its first three possessions. On their first drive, which consisted of 94 yards, Trent Richardson carried the ball on eight of the 12 plays, including big runs of 19 and 24 yards as well as his 1-yard touchdown run. This was followed by a 39-yard McCarron touchdown pass to DeAndrew White, capping another long drive (81 yards in nine plays). Following an unsuccessful extra point by Jeremy Shelley, Alabama led 27-0 entering the fourth quarter. Early in the fourth, Dee Milliner intercepted a Jordan Rodgers pass and returned it 37 yards to the Commodores' 20-yard line. Three plays later, McCarron threw a 17-yard touchdown pass, his fourth of the day, to Darius Hanks to make the final score 34-0.

For the game, Trent Richardson ran for 107 yards to extend his streak of consecutive games rushing for at least 100 yards to five games. The defense was dominant in completing its second shutout of the season and only allowing Vanderbilt 190 yards of total offense. The victory improved Alabama's all-time Homecoming record to 77-13-1 and its record against the Commodores to 61-18-4.[79]

Passing	C/ATT	YDS	AVG	TD	INT	QBR
AJ McCarron	23/30	237	7.9	4	0	96.5
P. Sims	3/3	29	9.7	0	0	--
Team	26/33	266	8.1	4	0	--

Rushing	CAR	YDS	AVG	TD	LONG
T. Richardson	19	107	5.6	1	24
J. Fowler	13	58	4.5	0	10
B. Sims	8	4	0.5	0	5
M. Maze	1	-1	-1	0	0
AJ McCarron	1	-7	-7	0	0
P. Sims	1	-8	-8	0	0
Team	43	153	3.6	1	24

Interceptions	INT	YDS	TD
D. Milliner	1	37	0
N. Johnson	1	2	0
Team	2	39	0

Punting	NO	YDS	AVG	TB	IN 20	LONG
C. Mandell	3	118	39.3	0	0	50

Receiving	REC	YDS	AVG	TD	LONG
M. Maze	9	93	10.3	0	29
D. Hanks	5	60	12	1	19
D. White	3	58	19.3	2	39
B. Smelley	3	19	6.3	1	8
B. Sims	2	18	9	0	10
B. Gibson	1	12	12	0	12
H. Jones	1	5	5	0	5
T. Richardson	2	1	0.5	0	2
Team	26	266	10.2	4	39

Kick returns	NO	YDS	AVG	LONG	TD
M. Williams	1	3	3	3	0

Punt returns	NO	YDS	AVG	LONG	TD
M. Maze	4	3	0.5	5	0

Kicking	FG	PCT	LONG	XP	PTS
J. Shelley	0/0	0	0	4/4	4

Note: Table data from "Alabama 34-0 Vanderbilt (Oct 8, 2011) Box Score" (86)

10/15/11 - Alabama (2) at Ole Miss

Team	1	2	3	4	T		Passing	Rushing	Total
Alabama (2)	7	10	28	7	**52**		226	389	**615**
Ole Miss	7	0	0	0	**7**		113	28	**141**

After Ole Miss took an early 7-0 lead, the Crimson Tide scored 52 unanswered points in their 52-7 victory over the Rebels at Vaught-Hemingway Stadium. The Rebels scored their only points of the game on their first possession. Jeff Scott scored on a 1-yard touchdown run to cap a 5-play, 72-yard drive to give Ole Miss their only lead of the game at 7-0. Alabama responded on the following drive with the first of four Trent Richardson touchdowns of the evening on an 8-yard run to tie the game at 7-7. The Crimson Tide added ten points in the second quarter to take a 17-7 halftime lead. Richardson scored on a 7-yard touchdown, and after Cade Foster missed a 53-yard field goal attempt, Jeremy Shelley connected for a 24-yard field goal.

In the third quarter, Alabama put the game away with four touchdowns. After five consecutive A.J. McCarron passes gained 65 yards, Richardson gained the final eight on his third touchdown of the evening. On the next Alabama possession, Richardson gained 16 yards and then scored a touchdown on a 76-yard run, the longest of his career, for a 31-7 lead. On the first play of the ensuing Rebels possession, Courtney Upshaw forced a Randall Mackey fumble that was recovered by Ed Stinson at the Ole Miss 15-yard line. Two plays later, the Crimson Tide led 38-7 after Jalston Fowler scored on an 8-yard touchdown run. The final points of the quarter came on a 10-yard McCarron touchdown pass to Brandon Gibson, and the final points of the game came in the fourth quarter on a 69-yard Fowler touchdown run to make the final score 52-7.

Alabama's defense again had a strong performance in only allowing the Rebels 141 total yards of offense (28 rushing, 113 passing). Richardson set a new career high with his 183 rushing yards and four rushing touchdowns. For his performance, Richardson was named the SEC Offensive Player of the Week. The 52 total points were the most Alabama had scored in a SEC game since defeating Vanderbilt 59-28 in 1990. The victory was the eighth straight over Ole Miss.[79]

Passing	C/ATT	YDS	AVG	TD	INT	QBR
AJ McCarron	19/24	224	9.3	1	0	76.4
P. Sims	1/1	2	2	0	0	--
Team	20/25	226	9	1	0	--

Rushing	CAR	YDS	AVG	TD	LONG
T. Richardson	17	183	10.8	4	76
J. Fowler	9	125	13.9	2	69
B. Sims	5	74	14.8	0	45
E. Lacy	5	22	4.4	0	15
AJ McCarron	3	-9	-3	0	4
Team	3	-6	-2	0	0
Team	42	389	9.3	6	76

Kicking	FG	PCT	LONG	XP	PTS
J. Shelley	1/1	100	24	7/7	10
C. Foster	0/1	0	0	0/0	0
Team	1/2	50	24	7/7	10

Punting	NO	YDS	AVG	TB	IN 20	LONG
C. Mandell	1	44	44	0	0	44

Receiving	REC	YDS	AVG	TD	LONG
D. Hanks	4	63	15.8	0	36
M. Williams	2	39	19.5	0	34
K. Bell	3	31	10.3	0	17
T. Richardson	2	30	15	0	15
D. White	3	23	7.7	0	15
M. Maze	3	21	7	0	10
B. Gibson	1	10	10	1	10
B. Smelley	2	9	4.5	0	6
Team	20	226	11.3	1	36

Kick returns	NO	YDS	AVG	LONG	TD
M. Maze	1	27	27	27	0
D. Hanks	1	16	16	16	0
Team	2	43	21.5	27	0

Punt returns	NO	YDS	AVG	LONG	TD
M. Maze	2	12	6	12	0
D. Hanks	1	4	4	4	0
Team	3	16	5.3	12	0

Interceptions	INT	YDS	TD
R. Lester	1	30	0

Note: Table data from "Alabama 52-7 Ole Miss (Oct 15, 2011) Box Score" (87)

10/22/11 - Alabama (2) vs Tennessee

Team	1	2	3	4	T		Passing	Rushing	Total
Tennessee	3	3	0	0	6		63	92	**155**
Alabama (2)	3	3	21	10	**37**		294	143	**437**

In the 2011 edition of the Third Saturday in October, Alabama entered the game as a 30-point favorite over the rival Tennessee Volunteers. At Bryant-Denny Stadium, the Volunteers were looking for the upset after tying the game at six at halftime. However, 31 unanswered points resulted in a 37-6 Crimson Tide victory to extend their overall record to 8-0. The first half was dominated by both defenses with each only allowing a pair of field goals. Mike Palardy connected from 40 and 52 yards for Tennessee, and Jeremy Shelley connected from 26 and 29 yards for Alabama.

After holding the Volunteers to a three-and-out to open the second half, the Alabama offense responded with their first of three third-quarter touchdowns with a 2-yard A.J. McCarron touchdown run. On the following Tennessee drive, the Alabama defense stopped quarterback Matt Simms on a 4th-and-1 to give the Crimson Tide offense the ball on the Volunteers' 39-yard line. On the next play, McCarron threw a 39-yard touchdown pass to Kenny Bell to extend the Alabama lead to 20-6. Trent Richardson then scored his first touchdown of the game on the following Alabama possession on a 12-yard run to cap a 6-play, 63-yard drive. Cade Foster scored early in the fourth quarter with his 45-yard field goal, and after a Dont'a Hightower interception, Richardson scored his second touchdown of the day on a 1-yard run to make the final score 37-6.

In the game, Marquis Maze had 106 yards receiving on five catches and A.J. McCarron set a new career high with 284 yards passing. For his defensive performance, Dont'a Hightower was named both the Lott IMPACT Player of the Week and the SEC Defensive Player of the Week. The victory was Alabama's fifth consecutive over Tennessee.[79]

Passing	C/ATT	YDS	AVG	TD	INT	QBR
AJ McCarron	17/26	284	10.9	1	1	82.5
P. Sims	1/2	10	5	0	0	--
Team	18/28	294	10.5	1	1	--

Receiving	REC	YDS	AVG	TD	LONG
M. Maze	5	106	21.2	0	69
D. Hanks	3	55	18.3	0	21
K. Bell	3	52	17.3	1	39
B. Smelley	2	34	17	0	17
T. Richardson	3	33	11	0	22
E. Lacy	2	14	7	0	9
Team	18	294	16.3	1	69

Rushing	CAR	YDS	AVG	TD	LONG
T. Richardson	17	77	4.5	2	16
E. Lacy	7	46	6.6	0	19
J. Fowler	9	27	3	0	12
M. Maze	1	-1	-1	0	0
AJ McCarron	2	-2	-1	1	2
Team	2	-4	-2	0	0
Team	38	143	3.8	3	19

Interceptions	INT	YDS	TD
D. Hightower	1	29	0

Punt returns	NO	YDS	AVG	LONG	TD
M. Maze	4	4	1	4	0

Kick returns	NO	YDS	AVG	LONG	TD
M. Maze	3	29	9.7	20	0
C. Underwood	1	7	7	7	0
Team	4	36	9	20	0

Kicking	FG	PCT	LONG	XP	PTS
J. Shelley	2/2	100	29	4/4	10
C. Foster	1/1	100	45	0/0	3
Team	3/3	100	45	4/4	13

Punting	NO	YDS	AVG	TB	IN 20	LONG
C. Mandell	2	81	40.5	0	0	41

Note: Table data from "Alabama 6-37 Tennessee (Oct 22, 2011) Box Score" (88)

106

11/05/11 - Alabama (2) vs LSU (1)

Team	1	2	3	4	OT	T		Passing	Rushing	Total
LSU (1)	0	3	0	3	3	9		91	148	**239**
Alabama (2)	0	3	3	0	0	6		199	96	**295**

Coming off their bye and in what was hyped as the latest "Game of the Century" in college football, the LSU Tigers defeated the Crimson Tide 9-6 in overtime. After a scoreless first quarter that saw the Crimson Tide miss two field goals and another blocked early in the second quarter, Alabama took a 3-0 lead midway through the second quarter on a 34-yard Jeremy Shelley field goal. LSU responded on its following possession by driving to the Alabama 2-yard line and kicking a 19-yard Drew Alleman field goal as time expired to tie the game at 3-3 at halftime.

Just as the first half was dominated by both defenses, the second was no different with both Alabama and LSU only managing a pair of field goals. Alabama's came in the third quarter on a 46-yard Cade Foster score, and LSU's came in the fourth quarter on a 30-yard Alleman score. In the overtime period, Foster missed a 52-yard field goal attempt, and Alleman connected on a 25-yard attempt to give the Tigers the 9-6 victory. Both defenses held each offense to less than 300 yards of total offense with each having a pair of interceptions. With the loss, Alabama dropped to 4-8 all-time in overtime games.[79]

Passing	C/ATT	YDS	AVG	TD	INT	QBR
AJ McCarron	16/28	199	7.1	0	1	48.5
M. Maze	0/1	0	0	0	1	0
Team	16/29	199	6.9	0	2	--

Rushing	CAR	YDS	AVG	TD	LONG
T. Richardson	23	89	3.9	0	24
E. Lacy	5	19	3.8	0	20
AJ McCarron	2	-6	-3	0	0
M. Maze	1	-6	-6	0	0
Team	31	96	3.1	0	24

Interceptions	INT	YDS	TD
M. Barron	1	14	0
R. Lester	1	0	0
Team	2	14	0

Punting	NO	YDS	AVG	TB	IN 20	LONG
C. Mandell	2	79	39.5	0	0	41

Receiving	REC	YDS	AVG	TD	LONG
T. Richardson	5	80	16	0	39
M. Maze	6	61	10.2	0	19
D. Hanks	2	38	19	0	19
E. Lacy	1	11	11	0	11
B. Smelley	1	8	8	0	8
M. Williams	1	1	1	0	1
Team	16	199	12.4	0	39

Kick returns	NO	YDS	AVG	LONG	TD
M. Maze	1	26	26	26	0
T. Richardson	1	23	23	23	0
Team	2	49	24.5	26	0

Punt returns	NO	YDS	AVG	LONG	TD
Ch. Jones	2	0	0	0	0

Kicking	FG	PCT	LONG	XP	PTS
J. Shelley	1/2	50	34	0/0	3
C. Foster	1/4	25	46	0/0	3
Team	2/6	33.3	46	0/0	6

Note: Table data from "LSU 9-6 Alabama (Nov 5, 2011) Box Score" (89)

11/12/11 - Alabama (3) at Mississippi State

Team	1	2	3	4	T		Passing	Rushing	Total
Alabama (3)	0	7	3	14	24		163	223	386
Mississippi State	0	0	0	7	7		119	12	131

A week after its loss to LSU, Alabama traveled to Starkville and defeated its long-time rival, the Mississippi State Bulldogs, 24-7. After a pair of missed field goals, one from 19 yards by Cade Foster and the second from 31 yards by Jeremy Shelley, Alabama scored its first points in the second quarter. Eddie Lacy capped a 5-play, 52-yard drive with a 2-yard touchdown run to give the Crimson Tide a 7-0 lead. Later in the quarter, Derek DePasquale missed a 41-yard field goal attempt for the Bulldogs, but on the ensuing Alabama possession, Cameron Lawrence intercepted an A.J. McCarron pass and returned it to the Alabama 4-yard line. However, the Alabama defense held the Bulldogs to only a field goal attempt which was then missed from 29 yards by Brian Egan to preserve a 7-0 halftime lead for the Crimson Tide.

Alabama extended its lead to 10-0 after Shelley connected on a 24-yard field goal early in the third quarter. Early in the fourth quarter, Trent Richardson scored on a 2-yard run for a 17-0 Crimson Tide lead. However, the ensuing kickoff was returned 68 yards to the Alabama 22-yard line by John Fulton, and four plays later the Bulldogs cut the score to 17-7 after Tyler Russell threw a 12-yard touchdown pass to Chris Smith. The Crimson Tide then closed the game with an 11-play, 73-yard drive, all on the ground, with Lacy scoring his second touchdown of the night from 32 yards out to give Alabama the 24-7 victory. The 127 rushing yards gained by Richardson was his seventh 100-yard rushing game of the season.[79]

Passing	C/ATT	YDS	AVG	TD	INT	QBR
AJ McCarron	14/24	163	6.8	0	1	37.3

Rushing	CAR	YDS	AVG	TD	LONG
T. Richardson	32	127	4	1	25
E. Lacy	11	96	8.7	2	32
AJ McCarron	1	0	0	0	0
Team	44	223	5.1	3	32

Kicking	FG	PCT	LONG	XP	PTS
J. Shelley	1/2	50	24	3/3	6
C. Foster	0/1	0	0	0/0	0
Team	1/3	33.3	24	3/3	6

Punting	NO	YDS	AVG	TB	IN 20	LONG
C. Mandell	4	149	37.3	0	0	44

Receiving	REC	YDS	AVG	TD	LONG
K. Norwood	2	60	30	0	38
T. Richardson	2	26	13	0	19
M. Maze	4	22	5.5	0	13
D. White	3	21	7	0	8
M. Williams	1	16	16	0	16
K. Bell	1	16	16	0	16
D. Hanks	1	2	2	0	?
Team	14	163	11.6	0	38

Kick returns	NO	YDS	AVG	LONG	TD
M. Maze	1	23	23	23	0

Punt returns	NO	YDS	AVG	LONG	TD
M. Maze	5	21	4.2	18	0

Note: Table data from "Alabama 24-7 Mississippi State (Nov 12, 2011) Box Score" (90)

11/19/11 - Alabama (3) vs Georgia Southern

Team	1	2	3	4	T		Passing	Rushing	Total
Georgia Southern	0	14	7	0	21		39	302	341
Alabama (3)	10	14	14	7	45		190	272	462

Against the triple option attack of the Georgia Southern Eagles, ranked No. 3 in the Football Championship Subdivision (FCS), the Alabama defense gave up the most total yards, rushing yards, and points of the season in their 45-21 victory at Bryant-Denny Stadium. After receiving the opening kickoff, the Crimson Tide drove to the Eagles' 14-yard line where Jeremy Shelley connected on a 32-yard field goal for a 3-0 lead. On its opening possession, Georgia Southern had a 9-play, 49-yard drive to set up a 42-yard field goal attempt. However, the Adrian Mora attempt was blocked by Dont'a Hightower and returned by Dre Kirkpatrick 55 yards for a touchdown and a 10-0 Crimson Tide lead. In the second quarter, A.J. McCarron threw a 4-yard touchdown pass to Trent Richardson to complete a 10-play, 71-yard drive for a 17-0 lead. However, the Eagles responded on their next offensive play when Dominique Swope scored on an 82-yard touchdown run to cut the Alabama lead to 17-7. Both teams then traded touchdowns when Richardson scored on a 1-yard run for Alabama, and Jaybo Shaw threw a 39-yard touchdown pass to Jonathan Bryant for Georgia Southern. After Cade Foster missed a 47-yard field goal attempt late, Alabama led 24-14 at halftime.

After forcing a punt to open the second half, Alabama scored a touchdown on its opening possession with a 34-yard touchdown reception by Brad Smelley from McCarron. However, on the ensuing kickoff, Laron Scott returned it 95 yards for a touchdown to cut the lead again to 31-21. Alabama responded on the following drive with Richardson accounting for 46 yards of it on seven carries with a 1-yard touchdown run for a 38-21 Alabama lead. In the fourth quarter, Alabama stopped the Eagles at the Crimson Tide 8-yard line after an incomplete Shaw pass on fourth down. From there, the Alabama offense achieved a 15-play, 92-yard drive that took 8:36 and finished with McCarron throwing a 4-yard touchdown pass to Smelley for the final points in their 45-21 win. For the game, Richardson had 175 yards on the ground with a pair of rushing touchdowns and one receiving. His 1-yard touchdown run in the third quarter gave him the Alabama single-season rushing touchdown record, breaking the previous mark of 19 set by Shaun Alexander in 1999.[79]

Passing	C/ATT	YDS	AVG	TD	INT	QBR
AJ McCarron	14/19	190	10	3	0	77.4

Rushing	CAR	YDS	AVG	TD	LONG
T. Richardson	32	175	5.5	2	20
E. Lacy	6	45	7.5	0	19
J. Fowler	8	41	5.1	0	22
AJ McCarron	3	11	3.7	0	6
Team	49	272	5.6	2	22

Kicking	FG	PCT	LONG	XP	PTS
J. Shelley	1/1	100	32	6/6	9
C. Foster	0/1	0	0	0/0	0
Team	1/2	50	32	6/6	9

Receiving	REC	YDS	AVG	TD	LONG
B. Smelley	4	58	14.5	2	34
B. Gibson	4	49	12.3	0	23
M. Maze	3	44	14.7	0	24
K. Norwood	1	22	22	0	22
E. Lacy	1	13	13	0	13
T. Richardson	1	4	4	1	4
Team	14	190	13.6	3	34

Kick returns	NO	YDS	AVG	LONG	TD
M. Maze	2	55	27.5	36	0
M. Williams	1	19	19	19	0
Team	3	74	24.7	36	0

Punt returns	NO	YDS	AVG	LONG	TD
M. Maze	2	4	2	4	0

Note: Table data from "Alabama 45-21 Georgia Southern (Nov 19, 2011) Box Score" (91)

109

11/26/11 - Alabama (2) at Auburn (24)

Team	1	2	3	4	T		Passing	Rushing	Total
Alabama (2)	14	10	3	15	42		184	213	397
Auburn (24)	7	0	7	0	14		62	78	140

After the loss against the Auburn Tigers the previous year in which the Crimson Tide surrendered a 24-point lead, for nearly a year, reminders of the defeat and the phrase "never again" were utilized by the team as even greater motivation to win in an already heated rivalry. With a potential berth in the 2012 BCS National Championship Game on the line, the Alabama defense did not allow an offensive touchdown in their 42-14 victory on The Plains. After trading a pair of three-and-outs to open the game, Alabama scored its first points of the game when A.J. McCarron threw a 41-yard touchdown pass to Kenny Bell for a 7-0 lead. Following a 10-yard Steven Clark punt on the ensuing Auburn possession, Alabama got the ball on the Tigers' 35-yard line. On the next play, McCarron threw a 35-yard touchdown pass to Brad Smelley for a 14-0 lead. On the first play of Alabama's fourth offensive possession, Corey Lemonier forced a McCarron fumble that was recovered for a touchdown by Kenneth Carter to cut the Crimson Tide lead to 14-7 at the end of the first quarter. A pair of long drives in the second quarter resulted in a 5-yard Trent Richardson touchdown reception and a 30-yard Jeremy Shelley field goal to give Alabama a 24-7 halftime lead.

On the opening kickoff of the second half, Onterio McCalebb scored a touchdown on an 83-yard return to cut the Alabama lead to 24-14. Alabama responded on its next possession with a 28-yard Shelley field goal for a 27-14 lead entering the fourth quarter. On the third play of the fourth quarter, Auburn's Clint Moseley threw an interception to Dee Milliner that was returned 35 yards for a touchdown, and after a successful two-point conversion, Alabama led 35-14. After getting the ball back on downs late in the quarter, Jalston Fowler scored on a 15-yard touchdown run to cap a drive that included a 57-yard Trent Richardson run and made the final score 42-14.

In the game, Trent Richardson set a new career high with his 203 rushing yards and tied Mark Ingram II for the most 100-yard rushing games in a season with nine. The defense held Auburn to 140 total yards of offense, with only 78 yards on the ground, and zero offensive touchdowns in the victory.[79]

Passing	C/ATT	YDS	AVG	TD	INT	QBR
AJ McCarron	18/23	184	8	3	0	87.2

Rushing	CAR	YDS	AVG	TD	LONG
T. Richardson	27	203	7.5	0	57
J. Fowler	1	15	15	1	15
E. Lacy	4	6	1.5	0	4
M. Maze	1	1	1	0	1
AJ McCarron	1	-10	-10	0	0
Team	1	-2	-2	0	0
Team	35	213	6.1	1	57

Interceptions	INT	YDS	TD
D. Milliner	1	35	1

Punting	NO	YDS	AVG	TB	IN 20	LONG
C. Mandell	3	121	40.3	0	0	44

Receiving	REC	YDS	AVG	TD	LONG
B. Smelley	6	86	14.3	1	35
K. Bell	2	46	23	1	41
M. Maze	4	18	4.5	0	7
B. Gibson	2	13	6.5	0	8
M. Williams	2	12	6	0	8
T. Richardson	1	5	5	1	5
E. Lacy	1	4	4	0	4
Team	18	184	10.2	3	41

Punt returns	NO	YDS	AVG	LONG	TD
M. Maze	3	21	7	16	0

Kicking	FG	PCT	LONG	XP	PTS
J. Shelley	2/2	100	30	4/4	10

Note: Table data from "Alabama 42-14 Auburn (Nov 26, 2011) Box Score" (92)

01/09/12 - Alabama (2) at LSU (1)

Team	1	2	3	4	T		Passing	Rushing	Total
Alabama (2)	3	6	6	6	21		234	150	384
LSU (1)	0	0	0	0	0		53	39	92

On December 4, 2011, the final Bowl Championship Series standings were unveiled with a rematch between No. 1 LSU and No. 2 Alabama in the BCS National Championship Game. In the game, the Crimson Tide defeated the Tigers 21-0 to clinch their second BCS Championship in three years. The first points of the game were set up after Marquis Maze returned a Brad Wing punt 49 yards to the LSU 26-yard line in the first quarter. Five plays later, Jeremy Shelley connected on a 23-yard field goal to give Alabama a 3-0 lead. After his first attempt in the second quarter was blocked by the Tigers' Michael Brockers, Shelley connected on field goals of 34 and 41 yards to give the Crimson Tide a 9-0 halftime lead.

Shelley extended the Crimson Tide lead to 12-0 after he converted a 35-yard field goal on Alabama's first possession of the second half. He then missed a 41-yard field goal attempt wide right before he connected on a 44-yard attempt to give the Crimson Tide a 15-0 lead at the end of the third quarter. Midway through the fourth quarter, the LSU offense crossed the 50-yard line for the first time of the game only to be pushed back to the 50 after Dont'a Hightower sacked Jordan Jefferson on a fourth down play to give possession back to Alabama. On that possession, the Crimson Tide scored the only touchdown of the game on a 34-yard Trent Richardson run to make the final score 21-0 after the missed extra point.

In the game, Alabama outgained LSU in total offense 384 to 92 yards, and the shutout was the first ever completed in a BCS game since the advent of the BCS in 1998. Jeremy Shelley established the all-time bowl record with seven field goal attempts and tied the all-time bowl record with five made. For their performances, Courtney Upshaw was named the defensive player of the game and A.J. McCarron was named the offensive player of the game. McCarron became the first sophomore quarterback to lead a team to a BCS National Title.[79]

Passing	C/ATT	YDS	AVG	TD	INT	QBR
AJ McCarron	23/34	234	6.9	0	0	91.4

Rushing	CAR	YDS	AVG	TD	LONG
T. Richardson	20	96	4.8	1	34
E. Lacy	11	43	3.9	0	11
AJ McCarron	4	11	2.8	0	13
Team	35	150	4.3	1	34

Interceptions	INT	YDS	TD
CJ Mosley	1	1	0

Kicking	FG	PCT	LONG	XP	PTS
J. Shelley	5/7	71.4	44	0/0	15

Punting	NO	YDS	AVG	TB	IN 20	LONG
C. Mandell	3	133	44.3	0	0	52

Receiving	REC	YDS	AVG	TD	LONG
K. Norwood	4	78	19.5	0	26
D. Hanks	5	58	11.6	0	19
B. Smelley	7	39	5.6	0	15
K. Bell	1	26	26	0	26
C. Underwood	2	12	6	0	8
T. Richardson	2	11	5.5	0	6
M. Williams	2	10	5	0	6
Team	23	234	10.2	0	26

Punt returns	NO	YDS	AVG	LONG	TD
Ch. Jones	1	32	32	32	0

Punt returns	NO	YDS	AVG	LONG	TD
M. Maze	2	52	26	49	0
Ch. Jones	4	15	3.8	15	0
Team	6	67	11.2	49	0

Note: Table data from "Alabama 21-0 LSU (Jan 9, 2012) Box Score" (93)

Season Stats

Record	12-1	3rd of 120
SEC Record	8-1	
Rank	1	
Points for	453	
Points against	106	
Points/game	34.8	20th of 120
Opp points/game	8.2	1st of 120
SOS[5]	4.21	17th of 120

Team stats (averages per game)

		Passing					Rushing				Total Offense		
Split	G	Cmp	Att	Pct	Yds	TD	Att	Yds	Avg	TD	Plays	Yds	Avg
Offense	13	18.2	27.5	66.4	215.2	1.2	39.1	214.5	5.5	2.6	66.5	429.6	6.5
Defense	13	12.6	25.7	49.1	111.5	0.5	29.7	72.2	2.4	0.2	55.4	183.6	3.3
Difference		5.6	1.8	17.3	103.7	0.7	9.4	142.3	3.1	2.4	11.1	246	3.2

	First Downs				Penalties		Turnovers		
Split	Pass	Rush	Pen	Tot	No.	Yds	Fum	Int	Tot
Offense	10.4	10.3	0.8	21.5	3.8	31.5	0.3	0.6	0.9
Defense	4.8	4.4	0.8	10.1	4.5	34.8	0.5	1	1.5
Difference	5.6	5.9	0	11.4	-0.7	-3.3	-0.2	-0.4	-0.6

Passing

							Passing				
Rk	Player	G	Cmp	Att	Pct	Yds	Y/A	AY/A	TD	Int	Rate
1	A.J. McCarron	13	219	328	66.8	2634	8	8.3	16	5	147.3
2	Phillip Sims	8	18	28	64.3	163	5.8	2.6	0	2	98.9
3	Marquis Maze	13	0	1	0	0	0	-45	0	1	-200

Rushing and receiving

			Rushing				Receiving				Scrimmage			
Rk	Player	G	Att	Yds	Avg	TD	Rec	Yds	Avg	TD	Plays	Yds	Avg	TD
1	Trent Richardson	13	283	1679	5.9	21	29	338	11.7	3	312	2017	6.5	24
2	Eddie Lacy	12	95	674	7.1	7	11	131	11.9	0	106	805	7.6	7
3	Jalston Fowler	13	56	385	6.9	4					56	385	6.9	4
4	A.J. McCarron	13	30	-22	-0.7	2					30	-22	-0.7	2
5	Blake Sims	5	22	107	4.9	0	2	18	9	0	24	125	5.2	0
6	Marquis Maze	13	6	-6	-1	0	56	627	11.2	1	62	621	10	1
7	Phillip Sims	8	5	-10	-2	0					5	-10	-2	0
8	Brad Smelley	13	1	1	1	0	34	356	10.5	4	35	357	10.2	4
9	Darius Hanks	10					26	328	12.6	1	26	328	12.6	1
10	Kenny Bell	13					17	255	15	2	17	255	15	2
11	Michael Williams	13					16	191	11.9	2	16	191	11.9	2
12	Deandrew White	12					14	151	10.8	2	14	151	10.8	2
13	Brandon Gibson	13					14	140	10	1	14	140	10	1
14	Kevin Norwood	11					11	190	17.3	0	11	190	17.3	0
15	Christion Jones	12					3	49	16.3	0	3	49	16.3	0
16	Chris Underwood	13					2	12	6	0	2	12	6	0
17	Brian Vogler	9					1	6	6	0	1	6	6	0
18	Harrison Jones	8					1	5	5	0	1	5	5	0

Defense and fumbles

Rk	Player	G	Tackles					Def Int					Fumbles		
			Solo	Ast	Tot	Loss	Sk	Int	Yds	Avg	TD	PD	FR	TD	FF
1	Dont'a Hightower	13	40	45	85	11	4	1	29	29	0	3			1
2	Mark Barron	13	43	25	68	5	1	2	14	7	0	5	1		0
3	Courtney Upshaw	13	37	15	52	18	9.5	1	45	45	1	0			2
4	Nico Johnson	13	25	22	47	6.5	1	1	2	2	0	2	1		0
5	Dequan Menzie	13	27	14	41	4	1.5	1	25	25	1	11	1		0
6	Robert Lester	13	22	17	39	1.5	0	2	30	15	0	3			1
7	C.J. Mosley	11	17	20	37	4.5	2	1	1	1	0	2			
8	Damion Square	13	13	19	32	7	1					1			
9	Vinnie Sunseri	13	18	13	31	0	0					1	1		0
10	Dre Kirkpatrick	13	24	6	30	4	0					9		1	2
11	Jerrell Harris	13	17	12	29	3.5	0								
12	Dee Milliner	13	14	13	27	1	0	3	72	24	1	11			
13	Trey DePriest	13	11	14	25	1.5	0								
14	Quinton Dial	12	10	14	24	3	1								
15	Jesse Williams	13	10	14	24	4	0.5					1			
16	Nick Gentry	12	11	12	23	6	4.5						1		0
17	Josh Chapman	12	10	13	23	3.5	1					2			
18	Will Lowery	11	14	6	20	0.5	0					2			
19	Ed Stinson	13	10	9	19	5	1					1	2		1
20	Alex Watkins	13	9	8	17	2	1								1
21	Ha Ha Clinton-Dix	13	5	6	11	0	0					2			
22	Hardie Buck	13	3	6	9	0	0								
23	Adrian Hubbard	9	3	6	9	1.5	0								
24	Tana Patrick	10	2	5	7	0	0								
25	Brandon Gibson	13	3	4	7	0	0								
26	Cade Foster	13	4	2	6	0	0								
27	John Fulton	12	2	3	5	0	0					1			
28	Brandon Ivory	4	0	5	5	0	0								
29	Kelly Johnson	9	3	2	5	0	0					1			
30	Jarrick Williams	7	4	1	5	0	0								
31	Phelon Jones	9	2	2	4	0	0	1	0	0	0	0			
32	Undra Billingsley	13	1	3	4	1	0.5								
33	Jeoffrey Pagan	6	0	4	4	0	0								
34	Chris Jordan	6	0	3	3	0.5	0								1
35	Xzavier Dickson	7	2	1	3	1.5	0.5								
36	Nick Perry	9	1	1	2	0	0								
37	Marquis Maze	13	0	2	2	0	0								
38	Brad Smelley	13	1	1	2	0	0								
39	Deandrew White	12	2	0	2	0	0								
40	D.J. Fluker	13	1	0	1	0	0								
41	Carson Tinker	13	1	0	1	0	0								
42	Ranzell Watkins	2	0	1	1	0	0								
43	Trent Richardson	13	1	0	1	0	0								1
44	Jalston Fowler	13	1	0	1	0	0								
45	Christion Jones	12	1	0	1	0	0								
46	Eddie Lacy	12	0	1	1	0	0								
47	A.J. McCarron	13	1	0	1	0	0								
48	Jeremy Shelley	13	1	0	1	0	0								
49	Blake Sims	5	1	0	1	0	0								
50	Phillip Sims	8	1	0	1	0	0								
51	Michael Williams	13	1	0	1	0	0								

Kick and punt returns

Rk	Player	G	Kick Ret				Punt Ret			
			Ret	Yds	Avg	TD	Ret	Yds	Avg	TD
1	Marquis Maze	13	12	342	28.5	0	33	436	13.2	1
2	Trent Richardson	13	3	66	22	0				
3	Michael Williams	13	2	22	11	0				
4	Christion Jones	12	1	32	32	0	3	33	11	0
5	Deandrew White	12	1	24	24	0	2	34	17	0
6	Dee Milliner	13	1	21	21	0				
7	Darius Hanks	10	1	16	16	0	1	4	4	0
8	Chris Underwood	13	1	7	7	0				

113

Kicking and punting

			Kicking							Punting		
Rk	Player	G	XPM	XPA	XP%	FGM	FGA	FG%	Pts	Punts	Yds	Avg
1	Jeremy Shelley	13	52	54	96.3	21	27	77.8	115			
2	Cade Foster	13				2	9	22.2				
3	Cody Mandell	12								39	1534	39.3

Scoring

			Touchdowns							Kicking				
Rk	Player	G	Rush	Rec	Int	FR	PR	KR	Tot	XPM	FGM	2PM	Sfty	Pts
1	Trent Richardson	13	21	3					24					144
2	Jeremy Shelley	13								52	21			115
3	Eddie Lacy	12	7						7					42
4	Brad Smelley	13		4					4					24
5	Jalston Fowler	13	4						4					24
6	A.J. McCarron	13	2						2			1		14
7	Deandrew White	12		2					2					12
8	Kenny Bell	13		2					2					12
9	Marquis Maze	13		1			1		2					12
10	Michael Williams	13		2					2					12
11	Darius Hanks	10		1					1					6
12	Dee Milliner	13			1				1					6
13	Dequan Menzie	13			1				1					6
14	Dre Kirkpatrick	13				1			1					6
15	Courtney Upshaw	13			1				1					6
16	Cade Foster	13										2		6
17	Brandon Gibson	13		1					1					6

Stats include bowl games
Note: Table data from "2011 Alabama Crimson Tide Stats" (5)

Awards and honors

Name	Award	Type
Mark Barron	Permanent Team Captain	Team
Dont'a Hightower	Permanent Team Captain	Team
Trent Richardson	Permanent Team Captain	Team
Trent Richardson	MVP	Team
Marquis Maze	Offensive Player of the Year	Team
A.J. McCarron	Offensive Player of the Year	Team
Mark Barron	Defensive Player of the Year	Team
Dont'a Hightower	Defensive Player of the Year	Team
Courtney Upshaw	Defensive Player of the Year	Team
Trent Richardson	AP Offensive Player of the Year	SEC
Mark Barron	AP All-SEC First Team	SEC
Barrett Jones	AP All-SEC First Team	SEC
Trent Richardson	AP All-SEC First Team	SEC
Courtney Upshaw	AP All-SEC First Team	SEC
William Vlachos	AP All-SEC First Team	SEC
Josh Chapman	AP All-SEC Second Team	SEC
Dont'a Hightower	AP All-SEC Second Team	SEC
Dre Kirkpatrick	AP All-SEC Second Team	SEC
Mark Barron	Coaches' All-SEC First Team	SEC
Dont'a Hightower	Coaches' All-SEC First Team	SEC
Barrett Jones	Coaches' All-SEC First Team	SEC
Trent Richardson	Coaches' All-SEC First Team	SEC
Courtney Upshaw	Coaches' All-SEC First Team	SEC
William Vlachos	Coaches' All-SEC First Team	SEC
Josh Chapman	Coaches' All-SEC Second Team	SEC
Dre Kirkpatrick	Coaches' All-SEC Second Team	SEC
Marquis Maze	Coaches' All-SEC Second Team	SEC
Chance Warmack	Coaches' All-SEC Second Team	SEC
Cyrus Kouandjio	Freshman All-SEC	SEC
Vinnie Sunseri	Freshman All-SEC	SEC
Barrett Jones	Jacobs Blocking Trophy	SEC
Trent Richardson	Offensive Player of the Year	SEC
Barrett Jones	Scholar-Athlete of the Year	SEC
Dont'a Hightower	AFCA All-America Team	National
DeQuan Menzie	AFCA All-America Team	National
Trent Richardson	AFCA All-America Team	National
Mark Barron	All-America First Team	National

Name	Award	Type
Mark Barron	AP All-America First Team	National
Barrett Jones	AP All-America First Team	National
Dont'a Hightower	AP All-America First Team	National
Trent Richardson	AP All-America First Team	National
Dont'a Hightower	AP All-America Second Team	National
Dre Kirkpatrick	AP All-America Second Team	National
Barrett Jones	ARA Sportsmanship Award	National
Mark Barron	Bronko Nagurski Trophy Finalist	National
Dont'a Hightower	Butkus Award Finalist	National
Courtney Upshaw	Butkus Award Finalist	National
Dont'a Hightower	Chuck Bednarik Award Finalist	National
Mark Barron	Consensus All-American	National
Dont'a Hightower	Consensus All-American	National
Barrett Jones	Consensus All-American	National
Trent Richardson	Consensus All-American	National
Whole team	Disney's Wide World of Sports Spirit Award	National
Trent Richardson	Doak Walker Award	National
Sal Sunseri	Frank Broyles Award Finalist	National
Mark Barron	FWAA All-America First Team	National
Barrett Jones	FWAA All-America First Team	National
Dre Kirkpatrick	FWAA All-America First Team	National
Trent Richardson	FWAA All-America First Team	National
Courtney Upshaw	FWAA All-America First Team	National
Trent Richardson	Heisman Trophy Finalist	National
Mark Barron	Jim Thorpe Award Finalist	National
Dont'a Hightower	Lombardi Award Finalist	National
Courtney Upshaw	Lombardi Award Finalist	National
Dont'a Hightower	Lott Trophy Finalist	National
Trent Richardson	Maxwell Award Finalist	National
Barrett Jones	Outland Trophy	National
William Vlachos	Rimington Trophy Finalisst	National
Mark Barron	Sporting News (TSN) All-America Team	National
Barrett Jones	Sporting News (TSN) All-America Team	National
Trent Richardson	Sporting News (TSN) All-America Team	National
Courtney Upshaw	Sporting News (TSN) All-America Team	National
Mark Barron	Unanimous All-American	National
Barrett Jones	Unanimous All-American	National
Trent Richardson	Unanimous All-American	National
Mark Barron	Walter Camp All-America First Team	National
Dont'a Hightower	Walter Camp All-America First Team	National
Barrett Jones	Walter Camp All-America First Team	National
Trent Richardson	Walter Camp All-America First Team	National
Courtney Upshaw	Walter Camp All-America Second Team	National
William Vlachos	Walter Camp All-America Second Team	National
Barrett Jones	Wuerffel Trophy	National
D.J. Fluker	Senior Bowl	All-Star Team
Nico Johnson	Senior Bowl	All-Star Team
Barrett Jones	Senior Bowl	All-Star Team
Robert Lester	Senior Bowl	All-Star Team
Carson Tinker	Senior Bowl	All-Star Team
Chance Warmack	Senior Bowl	All-Star Team
Jesse Williams	Senior Bowl	All-Star Team
Michael Williams	Senior Bowl	All-Star Team

NFL

Season	Year drafted	Round	Pick	Overall	Player	Position	Team
2011	2012	1	3	3	Trent Richardson	RB	Cleveland Browns
2011	2012	1	7	7	Mark Barron	S	Tampa Bay Buccaneers
2011	2012	1	17	17	Dre Kirkpatrick	CB	Cincinnati Bengals
2011	2012	1	25	25	Dont'a Hightower	LB	New England Patriots
2011	2012	2	3	35	Courtney Upshaw	LB	Baltimore Ravens
2011	2012	5	1	136	Josh Chapman	DT	Indianapolis Colts
2011	2012	5	11	146	Dequan Menzie	CB	Kansas City Chiefs
2011	2012	7	40	247	Brad Smelley	TE	Cleveland Browns

Note: Table data from "2011 Alabama Crimson Tide football team" (79)

2012

Overall

Record	13-1
SEC Record	8-1
Rank	1
Points for	542
Points against	153
Points/game	38.7
Opp points/game	10.9
SOS[6]	5.51

We try to pride ourselves always on people not scoring on our defense. We try to get zero and have no one score on us. That's a big accomplishment for us. -Nick Saban

Is this really what we want football to be? -Nick Saban

Games

Date	Bama Rank		Opp Rank	Opponent	Bama	Opp	Result	SEC
09/01/12	2	N	8	Michigan	41	14	W	
09/08/12	1	vs		Western Kentucky	35	0	W	
09/15/12	1	@		Arkansas	52	0	W	W
09/22/12	1	vs		Florida Atlantic	40	7	W	
09/29/12	1	vs		Ole Miss	33	14	W	W
10/13/12	1	@		Missouri	42	10	W	W
10/20/12	1	@		Tennessee	44	13	W	W
10/27/12	1	vs	11	Mississippi State	38	7	W	W
11/03/12	1	@	5	LSU	21	17	W	W
11/10/12	1	vs	15	Texas A&M	24	29	L	L
11/17/12	4	vs		Western Carolina	49	0	W	
11/24/12	2	vs		Auburn	49	0	W	W
12/01/12	2	N	3	Georgia	32	28	W	W
01/07/13	2	N	1	Notre Dame	42	14	W	

Coaches

Name	Position	Year
Nick Saban	Head Coach	6
Burton Burns	Associate Head Coach / Running Backs	6
Scott Cochran	Strength and Conditioning	6
Mike Groh	Wide Receivers / Recruiting Coordinator	2
Doug Nussmeier	Offensive Coordinator / Quarterbacks	1
Jeremy Pruitt	Secondary	3
Chris Rumph	Defensive Line	2
Kirby Smart	Defensive Coordinator	6
Jeff Stoutland	Offensive Line	2
Lance Thompson	Linebackers	1 (3rd overall)
Bobby Williams	Tight Ends / Special Teams	5

Recruits

Name	Pos	Pos Rank	Scout	Rivals	247 Sports	ESPN	ESPN Grade	Hometown	High school / college	Height	Weight	Committed
Ryan Anderson	OLB	7	4	4	4	4	80	Daphne, AL	Daphne HS	6-3	250	4/19/11
Dakota Ball	DT	27		3	3	4	80	Lindale, GA	Pepperell HS	6-2	290	10/14/10
Deion Belue	CB		3	3	3	N/A	NR	Tuscumbia, AL	Northeast Mississippi Community College	6-0	165	1/11/12
Chris Black	WR	2	4	4	4	4	83	Jacksonville, FL	First Coast HS	5-11	170	8/5/11
Landon Collins	S	1	5	5	5	5	85	Geismar, LA	Dutchtown HS	6-0	210	1/5/12
Amari Cooper	WR	7	4	4	4	4	82	Miami, FL	Miami Northwestern HS	6-1	175	9/22/11
Denzel Devall	DE	22	4	4	4	4	80	Bastrop, LA	Bastrop HS	6-2	240	12/7/11
Travell Dixon	CB		4	4	4	N/A	NR	Miami, FL	Eastern Arizona College	6-2	200	12/21/11
Kenyan Drake	RB	14	4	4	4	4	80	Powder Springs, GA	Hillgrove HS	6-0	195	2/14/11
Kurt Freitag	TE	13	3	3	3	4	79	Buford, GA	Buford HS	6-4	237	12/5/11
Brandon Greene	OT	6	4	4	4	4	83	Ellenwood, GA	Cedar Grove HS	6-6	295	3/5/11
Adam Griffith	K	7	3	3	3	3	78	Calhoun, GA	Calhoun HS	5-9	165	1/29/11
Caleb Gulledge	OG	69	3	3	3	3	76	Prattville, AL	Prattville HS	6-4	270	10/2/10
Tyler Hayes	OLB	10	4	4	4	4	80	Thomasville, AL	Thomasville HS	6-3	220	2/14/11
Brandon Hill	OT	77	3	3	3	3	77	Collierville, TN	St. George's Independent Schools	6-6	350	11/10/11
Cyrus Jones	ATH	4	5	4	4	4	83	Baltimore, MD	Gilman School	5-10	185	1/5/12
Korren Kirven	DT	8	4	4	4	4	80	Lynchburg, VA	Brookville HS	6-4	280	2/1/12
Darren Lake	DT	54	3	3	3	3	78	York, AL	Sumter County HS	6-3	328	3/18/11
Dillon Lee	OLB	6	4	4	4	4	81	Buford, GA	Buford HS	6-4	220	5/16/11
Alec Morris	QB	46	3	3	3	3	78	Allen, TX	Allen HS	6-4	235	8/5/11
Reggie Ragland	ILB	2	5	4	4	4	80	Madison, AL	Bob Jones HS	6-4	245	12/30/10
Geno Smith	CB	2	4	4	4	4	82	Atlanta, GA	St. Pius X Catholic HS	6-0	165	8/17/11
Alphonse Taylor	DT	15	4	3	4	4	80	Mobile, AL	Davidson HS	6-6	340	12/23/11
Dalvin Tomlinson	DT	42	4	4	4	3	78	McDonough, GA	Henry County HS	6-3	270	2/1/12
Eddie Williams	ATH	2	4	5	5	5	85	Panama City Beach, FL	Arnold HS	6-4	205	8/24/10
T.J. Yeldon	RB	4	4	5	5	4	81	Daphne, AL	Daphne HS	6-2	205	12/18/11

	Scout	Rivals	247Sports	ESPN
5 Stars	3	3	3	2
4 Stars	15	14	15	16
3 Stars	7	9	8	6
2 Stars	0	0	0	0

Note: Table data from "2012 Alabama Crimson Tide football team" (94)

Roster

Num	Player	Pos	Class	Height	Weight	Hometown	Last School
14	Edward Aldag	QB	FR	6-0	183	Birmingham, AL	Mountain Brook
7	Ryan Anderson	LB	FR	6-2	252	Daphne, AL	Daphne
19	Jonathan Atchison	LB	JR	6-3	236	Atlanta, GA	Douglass
94	Dakota Ball	DL	FR	6-2	295	Lindale, GA	Pepperell
87	Parker Barrineau	WR	SO	6-0	175	Northport, AL	American Christian Academy
7	Kenny Bell	WR	JR	6-1	180	Rayville, LA	Rayville
13	**Deion Belue**	**DB**	**JR**	**5-11**	**179**	**Tuscambia, AL**	**Northeast Mississippi CC**
31	Jerrod Bierbower	DB	SO	6-1	185	Dublin, OH	Coffman
5	Chris Black	WR	FR	5-11	178	Jacksonville, FL	First Coast
93	Chris Bonds	DL	JR	6-4	273	Columbia, SC	Richland Northeast
22	Hunter Bush	DB	SR	5-11	195	Wetumpka, AL	Wetumpka
21	Brent Calloway	LB	FR	6-1	217	Russellville, AL	Russellville
17	Caleb Castille	DB	SO	5-11	170	Birmingham, AL	Briarwood Christian
6	**Ha Ha Clinton-Dix**	**DB**	**SO**	**6-1**	**209**	**Orlando, FL**	**Dr. Phillips**
26	Landon Collins	DB	FR	6-0	202	Geismar, LA	Dutchtown
18	Levi Cook	DB	SR	5-10	190	Decatur, AL	Decatur
9	Amari Cooper	WR	FR	6-1	198	Miami, FL	Northwestern
33	**Trey DePriest**	**LB**	**SO**	**6-2**	**245**	**Springfield, OH**	**Springfield**
30	Denzel Devall	LB	FR	6-2	243	Bastrop, LA	Bastrop
90	Quinton Dial	DL	SR	6-6	304	Pinson, AL	East Mississippi CC
55	Josh Dickerson	LB	SO	6-1	238	Evans, GA	Lakeside
47	**Xzavier Dickson**	**LB**	**SO**	**6-3**	**262**	**Griffin, GA**	**Griffin**
98	Dillon Drake	K	SO	5-9	175	Fort Walton Beach, FL	Choctawhatchee
17	Kenyan Drake	RB	FR	6-1	204	Powder Spring, GA	Hillgrove
19	Dustin Ellison	QB	SO	6-0	180	Monroeville, AL	Monroe Academy
12	Phillip Ely	QB	FR	6-1	198	Tampa, FL	Plant
85	Malcolm Faciane	TE	FR	6-5	259	Picayune, MS	Picayune Memorial
44	LaMichael Fanning	DL	FR	6-7	298	Hamilton, GA	Harris County
76	**D.J. Fluker**	**OL**	**JR**	**6-6**	**335**	**Foley, AL**	**Foley**
43	Cade Foster	PK	JR	6-1	218	Southlake, TX	Southlake Carroll
45	Jalston Fowler	RB	JR	6-1	242	Mobile, AL	Vigor
41	Kurt Freitag	TE	FR	6-4	240	Buford, GA	Buford
10	John Fulton	DB	JR	6-0	187	Manning, SC	Manning
58	Brandon Greene	OL	FR	6-5	292	Ellenwood, GA	Cedar Grove
99	Adam Griffith	PK	FR	5-10	174	Calhoun, GA	Calhoun
74	Caleb Gulledge	OL	FR	6-4	280	Prattville, AL	Prattville
48	Rowdy Harrell	LB	SR	6-0	221	Moundville, AL	Hale County
1	Dee Hart	RB	FR	5-9	190	Orlando, FL	Dr. Phillips
36	Tyler Hayes	LB	FR	6-2	210	Thomasville, AL	Thomasville
34	Ben Howell	RB	SR	5-9	194	Gordo, AL	Gordo
42	**Adrian Hubbard**	**LB**	**SO**	**6-6**	**248**	**Lawrenceville, GA**	**Norcross**
62	Brandon Ivory	DL	SO	6-4	315	Memphis, TN	East
31	**Kelly Johnson**	**TE**	**SR**	**6-3**	**230**	**Bluffton, SC**	**Providence Day**
35	**Nico Johnson**	**LB**	**SR**	**6-3**	**245**	**Andalusia, AL**	**Andalusia**
57	Aaron Joiner	OL	SR	6-2	265	Florence, AL	Florence
75	**Barrett Jones**	**OL**	**SR**	**6-5**	**302**	**Germantown, TN**	**Evangelical Christian**
22	**Christion Jones**	**WR**	**SO**	**5-11**	**185**	**Adamsville, AL**	**Minor**
8	Cyrus Jones	ATH	FR	5-10	192	Baltimore, MD	Gilman
82	Harrison Jones	TE	SO	6-4	244	Germantown, TN	Evangelical Christian
70	Ryan Kelly	OL	FR	6-5	288	West Chester, OH	Lakota West
85	Korren Kirven	DL	FR	6-5	292	Lynchburg, VA	Brookville
77	Arie Kouandjio	OL	SO	6-5	310	Hyattsville, MD	DeMatha Catholic
71	**Cyrus Kouandjio**	**OL**	**SO**	**6-6**	**311**	**Hyattsville, MD**	**DeMatha Catholic**
42	**Eddie Lacy**	**RB**	**JR**	**6-0**	**220**	**Geismar, LA**	**Dutchtown**
95	Darren Lake	DL	FR	6-3	315	York, AL	Sumter County
25	Dillon Lee	LB	FR	6-4	240	Buford, GA	Buford
37	**Robert Lester**	**DB**	**SR**	**6-2**	**210**	**Foley, AL**	**Foley**
78	Chad Lindsay	OL	SO	6-2	290	The Woodlands, TX	The Woodlands
51	Wilson Love	DL	FR	6-3	281	Mountain Brook, AL	Mountain Brook
68	Isaac Luatua	OL	FR	6-2	313	La Mirada, CA	La Mirada
88	Josh Magee	WR	FR	6-0	170	Hoover, AL	Hoover
29	**Cody Mandell**	**P**	**JR**	**6-4**	**202**	**Lafayette, LA**	**Acadiana**
24	Nathan McAlister	WR	SR	5-11	165	Russellville, AL	Russellville
10	**A.J. McCarron**	**QB**	**JR**	**6-4**	**210**	**Mobile, AL**	**Saint Paul's Episcopal School**
47	Corey McCarron	TE	SO	6-2	240	Mobile, AL	Spanish Fort
28	**Dee Milliner**	**DB**	**JR**	**6-1**	**199**	**Millbrook, AL**	**Stanhope Elmore**
56	William Ming	DL	JR	6-3	283	Athens, AL	Athens
11	Alec Morris	QB	FR	6-3	225	Allen, TX	Allen
23	Taylor Morton	DB	SO	5-11	185	Centreville, AL	Bibb County
32	**C.J. Mosley**	**LB**	**JR**	**6-2**	**232**	**Theodore, AL**	**Theodore**
64	Michael Newsome	DL	SO	6-2	250	Cockeysville, MD	Boys' Latin
59	Harold Nicholson	OL	SO	6-5	292	Columbus, OH	St. Francis DeSales

Num	Player	Pos	Class	Height	Weight	Hometown	Last School
83	**Kevin Norwood**	**WR**	**JR**	**6-2**	**195**	**D'Iberville, MS**	**D'Iberville**
46	Michael Nysewander	TE	SO	6-1	230	Hoover, AL	Hoover
53	Anthony Orr	DL	SO	6-4	258	Madison, AL	Sparkman
34	Tyler Owens	LB	SO	6-0	220	Columbiana, AL	Clay-Chalkville
8	Jeoffrey Pagan	DL	SO	6-4	285	Asheville, NC	Asheville
11	Tana Patrick	LB	JR	6-3	236	Bridgeport, AL	North Jackson
27	Nick Perry	DB	JR	6-1	208	Prattville, AL	Prattville
57	D.J. Pettway	DL	FR	6-2	285	Pensacola, FL	Pensacola Catholic
17	Parker Philpot	DB	JR	5-10	180	Alpharetta, GA	Milton
33	Marcus Polk	WR	SO	5-8	180	Lithonia, GA	Woodward Academy
18	Reggie Ragland	LB	FR	6-2	247	Madison, AL	Bob Jones
54	Russell Raines	OL	JR	6-2	277	Satsuma, AL	Satsuma
13	Ty Reed	QB	JR	6-1	190	Rocky Hill, CT	Rocky Hill
32	Trey Roberts	RB	FR	6-0	189	Mobile, AL	McGill-Toolen
5	**Jeremy Shelley**	**PK**	**SR**	**5-10**	**165**	**Raleigh, NC**	**Broughton**
79	Austin Shepherd	OL	SO	6-5	312	Buford, GA	North Gwinnett
67	Alex Shine	OL	FR	6-3	300	Scottsdale, AZ	Chaparral
80	Marvin Shinn	WR	FR	6-3	198	Prichard, AL	Vigor
6	Blake Sims	RB	SO	6-0	212	Gainesville, GA	Gainesville
24	Geno Smith	DB	FR	6-0	182	Atlanta, GA	St. Pius X
92	**Damion Square**	**DL**	**SR**	**6-3**	**286**	**Houston, TX**	**Yates**
61	**Anthony Steen**	**OL**	**JR**	**6-3**	**303**	**Lambert, MS**	**Lee Academy**
49	**Ed Stinson**	**DL**	**JR**	**6-4**	**282**	**Homestead, FL**	**South Dade**
3	Vinnie Sunseri	DB	SO	6-0	215	Tuscaloosa, AL	Northridge
16	Bradley Sylve	DB	FR	5-11	178	Port Sulphur, LA	South Palquemines
50	Alphonse Taylor	DL	FR	6-5	340	Mobile, AL	Davidson
52	M.K. Taylor	LS	JR	5-10	210	Oxford, AL	Oxford
51	**Carson Tinker**	**LS**	**SR**	**6-1**	**220**	**Murfreesboro, TN**	**Riverdale**
52	Dalvin Tomlinson	DL	FR	6-2	266	McDonaugh, GA	Henry County
84	Brian Vogler	TE	SO	6-7	258	Columbus, GA	Brookstone
69	Paul Waldrop	OL	FR	6-4	267	Phenix City, AL	Central
65	**Chance Warmack**	**OL**	**SR**	**6-3**	**320**	**Atlanta, GA**	**Westlake**
23	Jabriel Washington	DB	FR	5-11	183	Jackson, TN	Trinity Christian Academy
11	Ranzell Watkins	DB	JR	5-9	172	Charlotte, NC	Independence
2	**DeAndrew White**	**WR**	**SO**	**6-0**	**185**	**Houston, TX**	**North Shore**
46	Wilson Whorton	P	SO	5-10	175	Leeds, AL	Briarwood Christian
15	Eddie Williams	WR	FR	6-3	204	Panama City Beach, FL	Arnold
20	Jarrick Williams	DB	JR	6-1	212	Mobile, AL	Blount
54	**Jesse Williams**	**DL**	**SR**	**6-4**	**320**	**Brisbane, Australia**	**Western Arizona CC**
63	Kellen Williams	OL	JR	6-3	303	Lawrenceville, GA	Brookwood
89	**Michael Williams**	**TE**	**SR**	**6-6**	**269**	**Reform, AL**	**Pickens County**
18	Nick Williams	WR	JR	5-10	185	Fort Lauderdale, FL	St. Thomas Aquinas
81	Danny Woodson Jr.	WR	FR	6-1	195	Mobile, AL	LeFlore
4	T.J. Yeldon	RB	FR	6-2	216	Daphne, AL	Daphne

Note: Starters in bold
Note: Table data from "2012 Alabama Crimson Tide Roster" (95)

119

Games

09/01/12 - Alabama (2) vs Michigan (8)

AT&T Stadium
Arlington, TX

Team	1	2	3	4	T		Passing	Rushing	Total
Michigan (8)	0	7	7	0	14		200	69	269
Alabama (2)	21	10	3	7	41		199	232	431

Alabama and the University of Michigan opened the 2012 season in the Cowboys Classic in Arlington, Texas. In the game, Alabama took a 21-0 first quarter lead and defeated the Wolverines 41-14 to open the season.

Michigan won the coin toss and elected to defer to the second half, and Alabama opened play with a three-and-out. Michigan was then held to only one first down before they punted on their first possession. On the drive that ensued, Alabama drove 61 yards with a mix of play-action passes and rushes that ended with a 2-yard touchdown reception by Michael Williams from A.J. McCarron for a 7-0 lead. After the Crimson Tide defense again forced a Wolverine punt, on Alabama's next drive, McCarron connected with DeAndrew White for a 51-yard touchdown reception and a 14-0 lead. That drive only took 45 seconds and three plays. Michigan stalled on its next drive after Denard Robinson threw an interception to Dee Milliner who returned it to Michigan's 17-yard line. On third down, Eddie Lacy rushed nine yards into the end zone for a touchdown and a 21-0 lead at the end of the first quarter.

On its first possession of the second quarter, Alabama drove 61 yards to the Michigan 5-yard line where Jeremy Shelly kicked a 22-yard field goal for a 24-0 lead. After each team traded punts on their next possessions, Robinson threw his second interception of the game. This time, C.J. Mosley returned the interception 16 yards for a touchdown and a 31-0 Crimson Tide lead. On the Wolverines' next drive, Robinson found a wide-open Jeremy Gallon for a 71-yard pass completion to the Alabama 1-yard line. Robinson then scored on a 1-yard run to make the score to 31-7. Alabama then ended the first half with a Lacy fumble that was recovered by Raymon Taylor as time expired with the Crimson Tide up 31-7.

Michigan received the ball to start the second half, and on its opening drive Robinson rushed for six yards and threw a 20-yard pass to Drew Dileo before Alabama's defense forced a punt. Alabama's next drive started strong with a 28-yard reception by Kevin Norwood and a pair of 14-yard runs by T.J. Yeldon. However, McCarron was sacked for a 16-yard loss, and as a result, Cade Foster later missed a 52-yard field goal wide left. On the Michigan drive that ensued, the Wolverines stalled at around midfield, but Michigan elected to go for it on 4th-and-3. Robinson then rushed for what was initially ruled a 3-yard first down but later was overturned by video evidence that turned the ball over on downs. Alabama then drove to the Michigan 33-yard-line where Foster connected on a 51-yard field goal that extended the Crimson Tide lead to 34-7. The Wolverines responded on their next possession with their final points of the game after Robinson connected with Devin Gardner for a 44-yard touchdown reception to make the score 34-14 at the end of the third quarter. After each team again traded punts, on their second possession of the fourth quarter, the Crimson Tide started at their own 43-yard-line. On the drive, Jalston Fowler rushed for 25 yards, McCarron passed to Kelly Johnson for 16 yards, and Michigan was called for a 15-yard pass interference penalty to set up a 1-yard touchdown run for Yeldon and a 41-14 Alabama lead. After this, Michigan and Alabama traded possessions without scoring, and on Michigan's last possession of the game, backup Michigan quarterback Russell Bellomy threw an interception to Alabama's Dillon Lee.

In the game, Yeldon became the first non-redshirted freshman to rush for 100 yards in his first game with the Crimson Tide. For their individual performances, Yeldon was named SEC Co-

Freshman of the Week and Milliner was named both SEC and Walter Camp Foundation Defensive Player of the Week.[94]

Passing	C/ATT	YDS	AVG	TD	INT	QBR
AJ McCarron	11/21	199	9.5	2	0	77.5

Rushing	CAR	YDS	AVG	TD	LONG
TJ Yeldon	11	111	10.1	1	40
J. Fowler	8	67	8.4	0	18
E. Lacy	9	35	3.9	1	9
D. Hart	9	19	2.1	0	7
K. Drake	1	2	2	0	2
AJ McCarron	4	-2	-0.5	0	15
Team	42	232	5.5	2	40

Interceptions	INT	YDS	TD
CJ Mosley	1	16	1
D. Milliner	1	35	0
D. Lee	1	0	0
Team	3	51	1

Punting	NO	YDS	AVG	TB	IN 20	LONG
C. Mandell	4	188	47	0	0	59

Receiving	REC	YDS	AVG	TD	LONG
K. Norwood	3	53	17.7	0	28
D. White	1	51	51	1	51
TJ Yeldon	1	26	26	0	26
K. Bell	2	26	13	0	19
K. Johnson	1	16	16	0	16
A. Cooper	1	15	15	0	15
E. Lacy	1	10	10	0	10
M. Williams	1	2	2	1	2
Team	11	199	18.1	2	51

Punt returns	NO	YDS	AVG	LONG	TD
Ch. Jones	4	56	14	19	0

Kicking	FG	PCT	LONG	XP	PTS
J. Shelley	1/1	100	22	5/5	8
C. Foster	1/2	50	51	0/0	3
Team	2/3	66.7	51	5/5	11

Note: Table data from "Alabama 41-14 Michigan (Sep 1, 2012) Box Score" (96)

09/08/12 - Alabama (1) vs Western Kentucky

Team	1	2	3	4	T	Passing	Rushing	Total
Western Kentucky	0	0	0	0	0	178	46	224
Alabama (1)	14	7	7	7	35	225	103	328

In the home opener for the 2012 season, Alabama shut out the Hilltoppers of Western Kentucky University (WKU) 35-0. To open the game, Alabama scored on a 14-yard A.J. McCarron touchdown pass to Christion Jones that capped a 4-play, 72-yard drive. On the WKU drive that ensued, Nico Johnson forced a Marquis Sumler fumble that was recovered by Damion Square at the WKU 49-yard line. However, the Crimson Tide was unable to capitalize on the turnover after McCarron was sacked twice and they were forced to punt. The defense responded on the next drive with their second recovered fumble of the game. This time, Adrian Hubbard caused the Antonio Andrews fumble that was recovered by Brandon Ivory at the WKU 33-yard line. On the next play, McCarron threw a 33-yard touchdown pass to Kevin Norwood for a 14-0 Crimson Tide lead.

Early in the second quarter, Xzavier Dickson sacked Kawaun Jakes and forced the third WKU fumble of the game; this time it was recovered by Vinnie Sunseri and returned to the Alabama 32-yard line. Seven plays later, Alabama took a 21-0 lead when Christion Jones caught a 22-yard McCarron touchdown pass. Each team then traded punts until halftime.

WKU opened the third quarter on offense, and three plays later Jakes threw an interception to Deion Belue that was returned to the Hilltoppers' 25-yard line. Two plays after a facemask penalty brought the ball to the 12-yard line, McCarron connected with Norwood for a 12-yard touchdown reception and a 28-0 lead. The teams again traded punts late into the fourth quarter, then Kenyan Drake scored on a 32-yard run to cap a 12-play, 81-yard drive that made the final score 35-0.

Jones and Norwood became the first pair of Alabama receivers to each score a pair of touchdowns in the same game since three were caught by Al Lary and two by Ed Lary in the 1950 season. Late in the game, backup running back Jalston Fowler suffered a knee injury that sidelined him for the remainder of the season.[94]

Passing	C/ATT	YDS	AVG	TD	INT	QBR
AJ McCarron	14/19	219	11.5	4	0	90.8
B. Sims	1/1	6	6	0	0	99.5
Team	15/20	225	11.3	4	0	--

Rushing	CAR	YDS	AVG	TD	LONG
E. Lacy	9	36	4	0	18
K. Drake	1	32	32	1	32
TJ Yeldon	6	25	4.2	0	8
C. Mandell	1	18	18	0	18
J. Fowler	3	18	6	0	8
D. Hart	3	12	4	0	5
AJ McCarron	8	-38	-4.8	0	7
Team	31	103	3.3	1	32

Interceptions	INT	YDS	TD
D. Belue	1	15	0

Punting	NO	YDS	AVG	TB	IN 20	LONG
C. Mandell	5	224	44.8	0	0	48

Receiving	REC	YDS	AVG	TD	LONG
K. Norwood	3	92	30.7	2	47
Ch. Jones	3	47	15.7	2	22
TJ Yeldon	4	47	11.8	0	15
D. White	1	15	15	0	15
A. Cooper	2	12	6	0	7
J. Fowler	1	6	6	0	6
D. Hart	1	6	6	0	6
Team	15	225	15	4	47

Punt returns	NO	YDS	AVG	LONG	TD
Ch. Jones	3	21	7	13	0

Kicking	FG	PCT	LONG	XP	PTS
J. Shelley	0/0	0	0	5/5	5

Kick returns	NO	YDS	AVG	LONG	TD
K. Norwood	1	22	22	22	0

Note: Table data from "Alabama 35-0 Western Kentucky (Sep 8, 2012) Box Score" (97)

09/15/12 - Alabama (1) at Arkansas

Team	1	2	3	4	T		Passing	Rushing	Total
Alabama (1)	7	17	14	14	52		213	225	438
Arkansas	0	0	0	0	0		79	58	137

Redshirt freshman Brandon Allen made his first start at QB (due to Wilson's injury), and the Crimson Tide had their second consecutive shutout in their 52-0 victory over Arkansas.

Each team traded punts on their first possessions. The Arkansas long snapper snapped the ball over the head of the punter that gave Alabama possession at the Razorbacks' 6-yard line. On the next play, Eddie Lacy scored on a 6-yard run for a 7-0 Crimson Tide lead. The Razorbacks responded with an 8-play, 51-yard drive, but failed to score any points after a 41-yard Zach Hocker field goal hit the left upright. Each team again traded punts before the Crimson Tide extended their lead to 10-0 early in the second quarter on a 51-yard Cade Foster field goal.

Next, Vinnie Sunseri intercepted a Brandon Allen pass. Six plays later, A.J. McCarron threw a 20-yard touchdown pass to Amari Cooper for a 17-0 lead. Later in the quarter, Ha Ha Clinton-Dix intercepted another Allen pass and returned it to the 3-yard line. Three plays later, Lacy had his second touchdown on a 1-yard run and the Crimson Tide led at halftime 24-0.

Alabama opened the third quarter with a 6-play, 75-yard drive that ended with a 10-yard Lacy touchdown run. On the kickoff, Demetrius Hart forced a fumble that was recovered by Foster at the Razorbacks' 27-yard line. Two plays later, T.J. Yeldon scored on a 1-yard run (38-0). Arkansas responded with its longest drive of the game; however, it ended when Deion Belue forced a fumble that was recovered by Nick Perry at the Alabama 20-yard line. With most starters pulled, the Tide reserves led Bama on a 15-play, 80-yard drive that ended with a 12-yard Kenyan Drake touchdown run early in the fourth quarter. The final touchdown of the game occurred on a Jeoffrey Pagan tackle that caused a fumble that was recovered by Denzel Devall. Two plays later, backup quarterback Blake Sims made the final score 52-0 with his 27-yard quarterback sneak for a touchdown.

The shutout was the first for Arkansas since its 28-0 loss to LSU in 1995 and was its first in Fayetteville since a 7-0 loss to Baylor in 1966. It also marked the first time Alabama had shut out opponents in consecutive weeks since the 1980 season. For his performance, Chance Warmack was named the SEC Offensive Lineman of the Week.[94]

Passing	C/ATT	YDS	AVG	TD	INT	QBR
AJ McCarron	11/16	189	11.8	1	0	76.7
P. Ely	2/3	15	5	0	0	97.7
B. Sims	1/1	9	9	0	0	99.6
Team	14/20	213	10.7	1	0	--

Receiving	REC	YDS	AVG	TD	LONG
Ch. Jones	3	74	24.7	0	34
A. Cooper	2	46	23	1	26
M. Williams	2	20	10	0	12
TJ Yeldon	1	18	18	0	18
K. Norwood	1	14	14	0	14
D. White	1	13	13	0	13
K. Bell	2	12	6	0	9
D. Woodson Jr.	1	9	9	0	9
M. Shinn	1	7	7	0	7
Team	14	213	15.2	1	34

Rushing	CAR	YDS	AVG	TD	LONG
K. Drake	6	57	9.5	1	21
E. Lacy	12	55	4.6	3	11
TJ Yeldon	13	55	4.2	1	14
B. Sims	2	25	12.5	1	27
D. Hart	4	21	5.3	0	11
B. Howell	6	18	3	0	8
AJ McCarron	1	-2	-2	0	0
Team	1	-4	-4	0	0
Team	45	225	5	6	27

Interceptions	INT	YDS	TD
H. Clinton-Dix	1	46	0
V. Sunseri	1	13	0
Team	2	59	0

Punt returns	NO	YDS	AVG	LONG	TD
Ch. Jones	2	4	2	6	0

Kicking	FG	PCT	LONG	XP	PTS
J. Shelley	0/0	0	0	7/7	7
C. Foster	1/2	50	51	0/0	3
Team	1/2	50	51	7/7	10

Punting	NO	YDS	AVG	TB	IN 20	LONG
C. Mandell	2	70	35	0	0	36

Note: Table data from "Alabama 52-0 Arkansas (Sep 15, 2012) Box Score" (98)

09/22/12 - Alabama (1) vs Florida Atlantic

Team	1	2	3	4	T		Passing	Rushing	Total
Florida Atlantic	0	0	0	7	**7**		34	76	**110**
Alabama (1)	14	16	3	7	**40**		247	256	**503**

In its fourth game of the 2012 season, Alabama defeated the Florida Atlantic Owls in their first all-time meeting by a final score of 40-7. The Crimson Tide scored on the third play of their first offensive possession when A.J. McCarron connected with Kenny Bell for an 85-yard touchdown pass and an early 7-0 lead. After the Alabama defense held the Owls to a three-and-out on their first possession, the Crimson Tide took a 14-0 lead on the drive that ensued when McCarron threw a 4-yard touchdown pass to DeAndrew White. After the defense again held FAU to a three-and-out, Christion Jones fumbled the punt that was recovered by the Owls' Tim Raber at the Alabama 25-yard line. After another defensive hold, Jesse Williams blocked the Vinny Zaccario field goal attempt to keep the score 14-0.

In the second quarter, the Crimson Tide scored on a 52-yard Cade Foster field goal and on field goals of 26 and 30 yards by Jeremy Shelley before McCarron threw a 4-yard touchdown pass to Christion Jones to make the halftime score 30-0. The defense also dominated the quarter and did not allow FAU a single third down conversion during the quarter.

In the third quarter, Foster connected on a 46-yard field goal and early in the fourth quarter Kenyan Drake scored on an 8-yard touchdown run for a 40-0 lead. With the game in hand, Alabama played many of its backups in the second half. As such, late in the fourth quarter the Crimson Tide shutout streak that stretched back to the third quarter of their week one victory over Michigan ended when the Owls' Graham Wilbert threw a 6-yard touchdown pass to Alex Deleon that made the final score 40-7.

In the game, Eddie Lacy rushed for 106 yards on 15 carries for his first 100-yard rushing game of the season. The late FAU touchdown ended the Alabama shutout streak at 192:25 minutes that stretched back to the 0:14 mark of the third quarter in its game against Michigan.[94]

Passing	C/ATT	YDS	AVG	TD	INT	QBR
AJ McCarron	15/25	212	8.5	3	0	64.4
B. Sims	1/1	35	35	0	0	46.2
Team	16/26	247	9.5	3	0	--

Rushing	CAR	YDS	AVG	TD	LONG
E. Lacy	15	106	7.1	0	15
TJ Yeldon	10	63	6.3	0	15
K. Drake	5	35	7	1	15
D. Hart	4	29	7.3	0	11
B. Howell	4	20	5	0	7
AJ McCarron	2	3	1.5	0	15
B. Sims	6	2	0.3	0	9
P. Ely	1	-2	-2	0	0
Team	47	256	5.4	1	15

Kick returns	NO	YDS	AVG	LONG	TD
Ch. Jones	2	25	12.5	15	0

Punting	NO	YDS	AVG	TB	IN 20	LONG
C. Mandell	1	29	29	0	0	29

Receiving	REC	YDS	AVG	TD	LONG
K. Bell	1	85	85	1	85
A. Cooper	4	65	16.3	0	23
Cy. Jones	1	35	35	0	35
M. Williams	4	25	6.3	0	14
D. White	4	17	4.3	1	5
B. Vogler	1	16	16	0	16
Ch. Jones	1	4	4	1	4
Team	16	247	15.4	3	85

Punt returns	NO	YDS	AVG	LONG	TD
Ch. Jones	4	61	15.3	31	0
D. Hart	2	28	14	15	0
Team	6	89	14.8	31	0

Kicking	FG	PCT	LONG	XP	PTS
J. Shelley	2/2	100	30	4/4	10
C. Foster	2/2	100	52	0/0	6
Team	4/4	100	52	4/4	16

Note: Table data from "Alabama 40-7 Florida Atlantic (Sep 22, 2012) Box Score" (99)

09/29/12 - Alabama (1) vs Ole Miss

Team	1	2	3	4	T		Passing	Rushing	Total
Ole Miss	0	7	7	0	14		138	80	218
Alabama (1)	6	21	0	6	33		180	125	305

Alabama played its first home conference game in its annual rivalry game against the Ole Miss Rebels in Tuscaloosa. In the game, 21 second quarter points after the Rebels briefly held a lead resulted in the 33-14 Crimson Tide victory. After each team traded punts on their first possessions, Jeremy Shelley connected from 38 yards on the first of four field goals to give the Crimson Tide an early 3-0 lead. After Shelley made his second 38-yard field goal to extend the Alabama lead to 6-0, Ole Miss responded with a 13-play, 75-yard drive that culminated with a 1-yard Jeff Scott touchdown run that gave the Rebels a 7-6 lead early in the second quarter. At the time the Rebels took the lead, it marked the first time Alabama trailed in regulation since its 2011 game against Tennessee.

The Ole Miss lead only lasted for fifteen seconds as Christion Jones scored a touchdown on the kickoff that ensued with his 99-yard return that gave the Crimson Tide a 13-7 lead. On the Rebels' next possession, Bo Wallace threw an interception to Dee Milliner, and four plays later A.J. McCarron threw a 16-yard touchdown pass to Amari Cooper that extended the Alabama lead to 20-7. On their next drive, Ole Miss was intercepted by the Crimson Tide on two separate occasions. First, Robert Lester intercepted a Bo Wallace pass that he subsequently fumbled and was recovered by Jeff Scott, and then two plays later, Randall Mackey threw an interception to Deion Belue at the Alabama 32-yard line. The Crimson Tide then drove 68 yards and took a 27-7 halftime lead after McCarron threw a 12-yard touchdown pass to Amari Cooper.

Ole Miss scored the only points of the third quarter on a 12-yard Randall Mackey touchdown run that capped a 70-yard drive that saw the Rebels convert a pair of fourth downs. The final margin of 33-14 was provided by a pair of Shelley field goals from 26 and 24 yards in the fourth quarter.

In the game, A.J. McCarron eclipsed Brody Croyle's team record of 190 consecutive pass attempts without throwing an interception. Starting wide receiver DeAndrew White and backup running back Demetrius Hart both suffered knee injuries during the game that sidelined both of them for the remainder of the season.[94]

Passing	C/ATT	YDS	AVG	TD	INT	QBR
AJ McCarron	22/30	180	6	2	0	86.9

Rushing	CAR	YDS	AVG	TD	LONG
E. Lacy	19	82	4.3	0	23
TJ Yeldon	10	38	3.8	0	10
D. Hart	1	7	7	0	7
AJ McCarron	4	-2	-0.5	0	7
Team	34	125	3.7	0	23

Interceptions	INT	YDS	TD
R. Lester	1	20	0
D. Milliner	1	0	0
D. Belue	1	0	0
Team	3	20	0

Punting	NO	YDS	AVG	TB	IN 20	LONG
C. Mandell	3	123	41	0	0	42

Receiving	REC	YDS	AVG	TD	LONG
A. Cooper	8	84	10.5	2	16
K. Norwood	2	20	10	0	17
Ch. Jones	2	19	9.5	0	16
K. Bell	2	15	7.5	0	8
E. Lacy	3	15	5	0	7
D. Hart	1	12	12	0	12
D. White	1	9	9	0	9
B. Vogler	1	5	5	0	5
TJ Yeldon	1	3	3	0	3
B. Calloway	1	-2	-2	0	0
Team	22	180	8.2	2	17

Kick returns	NO	YDS	AVG	LONG	TD
Ch. Jones	3	142	47.3	99	1

Punt returns	NO	YDS	AVG	LONG	TD
D. Hart	2	22	11	22	0

Kicking	FG	PCT	LONG	XP	PTS
J. Shelley	4/4	100	38	3/3	15

Note: Table data from "Alabama 33-14 Ole Miss (Sep 29, 2012) Box Score" (100)

125

10/13/12 - Alabama (1) at Missouri

Team	1	2	3	4	T		Passing	Rushing	Total
Alabama (1)	21	7	0	14	**42**		171	348	**519**
Missouri	0	7	3	0	**10**		126	3	**129**

In what was its first meeting since Alabama defeated the Tigers 38-28 during the 1978 season, and its first as conference foes, Alabama won 42-10 at Missouri on a stormy afternoon. The Crimson Tide opened the scoring on their second offensive play when Eddie Lacy had a 73-yard touchdown run for an early 7-0 Alabama lead. After each team traded punts, Vinnie Sunseri intercepted a Corbin Berkstresser pass that set up Alabama's second scoring drive from the 50-yard line. A.J. McCarron threw a 44-yard completion to Kenny Bell, then Lacy scored his second touchdown of the afternoon two plays later on a 3-yard run for a 14-0 lead. The third Crimson Tide touchdown of the first quarter was set up after Landon Collins blocked a Trey Barrow punt that was recovered at the Missouri 17-yard line. Three T.J. Yeldon runs later, Alabama led 21-0.

After a pair of Tiger possessions that ended with punts and an Alabama possession that ended with a lost fumble by McCarron, the Crimson Tide started their fourth scoring drive of the afternoon. The drive began with a 22-yard McCarron pass to Christion Jones and finished with a 15-yard Yeldon touchdown run. Immediately after Yeldon scored, the referees stopped the game temporarily and cleared the field due to lightning strikes in the immediate vicinity of the stadium. After a 40-minute stoppage, the game resumed with a Jeremy Shelley extra point and a Crimson Tide lead of 28-0. Missouri responded on the kickoff with its only touchdown of the afternoon on a 98-yard Marcus Murphy return that made the halftime score 28-7.

The Tigers opened the third quarter with a 41-yard Andrew Baggett field goal that cut the Crimson Tide lead to 28-10. Each team then traded punts through the fourth quarter after Lacy scored his third touchdown of the afternoon on a 1-yard run that extended the Alabama lead to 35-10. The Crimson Tide defense then got their third turnover of the game on the next Tigers possession when a Berkstresser pass was intercepted by Ha Ha Clinton-Dix and returned to the Alabama 46-yard line. With the second string in the game, the final points were scored by Kenyan Drake on a 3-yard run that made the final score 42-10. In the game, Lacy ran for 177 yards and Yeldon ran for 144 yards with a combined five touchdowns.[94]

Passing	C/ATT	YDS	AVG	TD	INT	QBR
AJ McCarron	16/21	171	8.1	0	0	85.9

Rushing	CAR	YDS	AVG	TD	LONG
E. Lacy	18	177	9.8	3	73
TJ Yeldon	18	144	8	2	27
B. Sims	1	36	36	0	36
K. Drake	4	11	2.8	1	10
Ch. Jones	1	2	2	0	2
AJ McCarron	4	-5	-1.3	0	6
C. Mandell	1	-17	-17	0	0
Team	47	348	7.4	6	73

Interceptions	INT	YDS	TD
H. Clinton-Dix	1	10	0
V. Sunseri	1	0	0
Team	2	10	0

Kicking	FG	PCT	LONG	XP	PTS
J. Shelley	0/0	0	0	6/6	6

Punting	NO	YDS	AVG	TB	IN 20	LONG
C. Mandell	4	152	38	0	0	53

Receiving	REC	YDS	AVG	TD	LONG
K. Bell	2	46	23	0	44
A. Cooper	4	41	10.3	0	27
K. Norwood	3	25	8.3	0	15
Ch. Jones	2	19	9.5	0	22
M. Williams	1	17	17	0	17
E. Lacy	2	17	8.5	0	9
Cy. Jones	1	4	4	0	4
K. Johnson	1	2	2	0	2
Team	16	171	10.7	0	44

Kick returns	NO	YDS	AVG	LONG	TD
Cy. Jones	1	23	23	23	0
Ch. Jones	1	15	15	15	0
Team	2	38	19	23	0

Punt returns	NO	YDS	AVG	LONG	TD
Ch. Jones	2	33	16.5	30	0
L. Collins	1	13	13	13	0
Cy. Jones	1	2	2	2	0
Team	4	48	12	30	0

Note: Table data from "Alabama 42-10 Missouri (Oct 13, 2012) Box Score" (101)

10/20/12 - Alabama (1) at Tennessee

Team	1	2	3	4	T		Passing	Rushing	Total
Alabama (1)	7	16	7	14	**44**		306	233	**539**
Tennessee	3	7	0	3	**13**		203	79	**282**

In its annual rivalry game, Alabama defeated the Tennessee Volunteers at Knoxville 44-13 for its sixth consecutive victory in the series. After the teams traded punts to open the game, Alabama scored its first touchdown on its second possession on a 23-yard A.J. McCarron pass to Amari Cooper. The Volunteers responded on the drive that ensued with a 32-yard Michael Palardy field goal that cut the Crimson Tide lead to 7-3. After the next Alabama drive ended with a missed Cade Foster field goal from 44 yards, the Crimson Tide defense responded with their first turnover of the game when C.J. Mosley intercepted a Tyler Bray pass at the Tennessee 32-yard line. Four T.J. Yeldon runs and 32 yards later, Alabama led 13-3 after he scored on a 1-yard touchdown run. The Crimson Tide extended their lead further to 20-3 on their next possession when Michael Williams scored on a 1-yard McCarron pass that completed a drive that included a 54-yard Cooper reception. Tennessee responded on its next possession with its only touchdown of the evening on a 2-yard A.J. Johnson run. Alabama then closed the half with a 34-yard Jeremy Shelley field goal for a 23-10 halftime lead.

The Crimson Tide opened the second half with a second missed Cade Foster field goal followed by each team again trading punts before the next Alabama points. The fourth Crimson Tide touchdown of the game came on a 42-yard McCarron pass to Cooper that extended the Alabama lead to 30-10. Tennessee advanced the ball to the Crimson Tide 21-yard line on its next possession before Robert Lester intercepted the second Bray pass of the evening for a touchback. Early in the fourth quarter, Alabama extended its lead to 37-10 on a 39-yard McCarron pass to Kenny Bell. The Alabama defense then held the Volunteers on a fourth down to give the Crimson Tide possession at their 42-yard line. Three plays later, Yeldon scored on a 43-yard run for the final Alabama points and a 44-10 lead. Tennessee then scored the final points of the game on a 21-yard Palardy field goal that was set up after a Blake Sims fumble gave the Volunteers possession at the Alabama 24-yard line that made the final score 44-13.

Several Alabama players had career days with the performance on the field. McCarron had both career highs in passing yards and touchdowns with 306 and four; Cooper established an Alabama freshman record for receiving yards with his 162 in the game. Yeldon also had his third 100-yard rushing game of the season with his 129 yards on 15 carries and two touchdowns.[94]

Passing	C/ATT	YDS	AVG	TD	INT	QBR
AJ McCarron	17/22	306	13.9	4	0	95.6

Rushing	CAR	YDS	AVG	TD	LONG
TJ Yeldon	15	129	8.6	2	43
E. Lacy	17	79	4.6	0	14
K. Drake	4	22	5.5	0	10
B. Sims	4	10	2.5	0	4
B. Calloway	2	6	3	0	5
AJ McCarron	3	-13	-4.3	0	2
Team	45	233	5.2	2	43

Interceptions	INT	YDS	TD
R. Lester	1	0	0
CJ Mosley	1	0	0
Team	2	0	0

Punting	NO	YDS	AVG	TB	IN 20	LONG
C. Mandell	2	88	44	0	0	49

Receiving	REC	YDS	AVG	TD	LONG
A. Cooper	7	162	23.1	2	54
K. Bell	2	68	34	1	39
K. Norwood	2	43	21.5	0	35
E. Lacy	3	18	6	0	7
Ch. Jones	1	9	9	0	9
M. Williams	2	6	3	1	5
Team	17	306	18	4	54

Kick returns	NO	YDS	AVG	LONG	TD
Cy. Jones	1	27	27	27	0
H. Jones	1	9	9	9	0
Team	2	36	18	27	0

Punt returns	NO	YDS	AVG	LONG	TD
Cy. Jones	4	59	14.8	32	0

Kicking	FG	PCT	LONG	XP	PTS
J. Shelley	1/1	100	34	5/5	8
C. Foster	0/2	0		0/0	0
Team	1/3	33.3	34	5/5	8

Note: Table data from "Alabama 44-13 Tennessee (Oct 20, 2012) Box Score" (102)

10/27/12 - Alabama (1) vs Mississippi State (11)

Team	1	2	3	4	T		Passing	Rushing	Total
Mississippi State (11)	0	0	0	7	7		209	47	**256**
Alabama (1)	14	10	0	14	**38**		235	179	**414**

In its annual rivalry game, Alabama defeated the Mississippi State Bulldogs in Tuscaloosa on Homecoming 38-7. The Crimson Tide led 21-0 early in the second quarter after they scored touchdowns on their first three offensive possessions. They opened the game with a 41-yard Cyrus Jones kickoff return that set up a 59-yard drive that ended with an 11-yard T.J. Yeldon touchdown run. After Dee Milliner blocked a Devon Bell field goal attempt, the Crimson Tide took possession and six plays later led 14-0 on a 57-yard A.J. McCarron touchdown pass to Kenny Bell. The Alabama defense then forced their first punt of the game, and for the third time in three possessions, the Crimson Tide scored a touchdown on a 9-yard McCarron pass to Michael Williams for a 21-0 lead. Each team then traded three-and-outs until nearly the end of the second quarter when Alabama was able to convert a 34-yard Jeremy Shelley field goal for a 24-0 halftime lead.

After each team traded punts to open the third quarter, the Bulldogs sustained their longest drive of the game. They drove 97 yards in 16 plays, but Tyler Russell threw a pass that was intercepted by Robert Lester in the end zone for a touchback that halted the drive. On the Alabama drive that ensued, State managed to force a punt, however, it was fumbled by Deontae Skinner that gave the Crimson Tide possession at the Bulldogs' 28-yard line early in the fourth quarter. Three plays later, Phillip Ely threw his first career touchdown pass to Eddie Lacy from 27 yards for a 31-0 Alabama lead. On the kickoff that ensued, Christion Jones forced a Jameon Lewis fumble that was recovered by Landon Collins at the State 43-yard line, and eight plays later Alabama led 38-0 on a 3-yard Kenyan Drake touchdown run. With the Crimson Tide reserves in on defense, the Bulldogs did manage to break up the shutout bid late in the fourth quarter when State scored its lone points on a 2-yard Dak Prescott touchdown pass to Robert Johnson and made the final score 38-7.[94]

Passing	C/ATT	YDS	AVG	TD	INT	QBR
AJ McCarron	16/23	208	9	2	0	82.3
P. Ely	1/1	27	27	1	0	99.1
Team	17/24	235	9.8	3	0	--

Rushing	CAR	YDS	AVG	TD	LONG
TJ Yeldon	10	84	8.4	1	30
K. Drake	8	47	5.9	1	13
E. Lacy	10	26	2.6	0	6
B. Sims	3	19	6.3	0	10
B. Calloway	1	5	5	0	5
Ch. Jones	1	4	4	0	4
Cy. Jones	1	2	2	0	2
AJ McCarron	5	-6	-1.2	0	7
Team	1	-2	-2	0	0
Team	40	179	4.5	2	30

Punting	NO	YDS	AVG	TB	IN 20	LONG
C. Mandell	5	211	42.2	0	0	61

Receiving	REC	YDS	AVG	TD	LONG
K. Bell	1	57	57	1	57
E. Lacy	4	51	12.8	1	27
A. Cooper	4	47	11.8	0	25
M. Williams	5	38	7.6	1	9
Ch. Jones	1	22	22	0	22
K. Norwood	1	14	14	0	14
K. Johnson	1	6	6	0	6
Team	17	235	13.8	3	57

Kick returns	NO	YDS	AVG	LONG	TD
Cy. Jones	2	76	38	41	0

Punt returns	NO	YDS	AVG	LONG	TD
Cy. Jones	1	4	4	4	0

Kicking	FG	PCT	LONG	XP	PTS
J. Shelley	1/1	100	34	5/5	8

Interceptions	INT	YDS	TD
R. Lester	1	0	0

Note: Table data from "Alabama 38-7 Mississippi State (Oct 27, 2012) Box Score" (103)

11/03/12 - Alabama (1) at LSU (5)

Team	1	2	3	4	T		Passing	Rushing	Total
Alabama (1)	0	14	0	7	21		165	166	331
LSU (5)	3	0	7	7	17		296	139	435

In its annual rivalry game, Alabama trailed the LSU Tigers 17-14 with only 1:34 remaining in the game. They went on a 5-play, 72-yard drive capped by a 28-yard A.J. McCarron touchdown pass to T.J. Yeldon with only 51 seconds left and defeated LSU 21-17 in Baton Rouge.

After each team traded punts on their first possessions, LSU took a 3-0 first quarter lead when Drew Alleman connected on a 38-yard field goal. After each team again traded punts, Alabama scored the first touchdown of the game early in the second quarter. A 7-yard Eddie Lacy touchdown run completed an 11-play, 92-yard drive and gave the Crimson Tide a 7-3 lead. On the LSU possession that ensued, the Alabama defense held the Tigers to a three-and-out. However, Cyrus Jones fumbled the Brad Wing punt that was recovered by LSU at the Crimson Tide 36-yard line. LSU then failed to capitalize on the turnover as Alleman was tackled for a 2-yard loss on a fake field goal attempt and gave Alabama possession at its 33-yard-line. After another Alabama punt and a missed 54-yard Alleman field goal, the Crimson Tide took a 14-3 halftime lead on a 9-yard McCarron touchdown run with only 11 seconds left in the half.

After a series of punts to open the third quarter, LSU scored its first touchdown on a 1-yard Jeremy Hill run that cut the Alabama lead to 14-10. On the kickoff that ensued, a failed onside kick gave the Crimson Tide possession at the Tigers' 44-yard line. The drive stalled at the 10-yard line when a Yeldon fumble was recovered by Sam Montgomery. LSU responded with a 7-play, 90-yard drive and took a 17-14 lead when Jarvis Landry caught a 14-yard touchdown pass from Zach Mettenberger early in the fourth quarter. The next four possessions included a pair of three-and-outs for Alabama and LSU drives that stalled on a failed fourth down conversion and a missed 45-yard Alleman field goal before the Tide went on their game-winning drive. With only 1:34 left in the game, Alabama took possession at its own 28-yard line. McCarron then completed three consecutive passes to Kevin Norwood and moved the ball to the LSU 28-yard line. After an incompletion to Norwood, the game-winning touchdown was scored when McCarron threw a short screen pass to Yeldon that he took 28 yards to score and create a 21-17 lead. After a pair of short passes, the game ended when Mettenberger was sacked by Damion Square as time expired.

For his 12-tackle performance in the game, Adrian Hubbard was named the SEC Defensive Player of the Week.[94]

Passing	C/ATT	YDS	AVG	TD	INT	QBR
AJ McCarron	14/27	165	6.1	1	0	76.8

Rushing	CAR	YDS	AVG	TD	LONG
E. Lacy	11	83	7.5	1	28
TJ Yeldon	11	76	6.9	0	23
AJ McCarron	3	7	2.3	1	9
Team	25	166	6.6	2	28

Kick returns	NO	YDS	AVG	LONG	TD
X. Dickson	1	9	9	9	0

Punting	NO	YDS	AVG	TB	IN 20	LONG
C. Mandell	7	316	45.1	0	0	56

Receiving	REC	YDS	AVG	TD	LONG
K. Norwood	5	62	12.4	0	18
Ch. Jones	4	40	10	0	16
TJ Yeldon	1	28	28	1	28
E. Lacy	1	19	19	0	19
K. Johnson	1	10	10	0	10
M. Williams	1	6	6	0	6
M. Shinn	1	0	0	0	0
Team	14	165	11.8	1	28

Punt returns	NO	YDS	AVG	LONG	TD
Cy. Jones	1	-4	-4	-4	0

Kicking	FG	PCT	LONG	XP	PTS
J. Shelley	0/0	0	0	3/3	3

Note: Table data from "Alabama 21-17 LSU (Nov 3, 2012) Box Score" (104)

129

11/10/12 - Alabama (1) vs Texas A&M (15)

Team	1	2	3	4	T		Passing	Rushing	Total
Texas A&M (15)	20	0	0	9	29		253	165	418
Alabama (1)	0	14	3	7	24		309	122	431

In its first meeting as conference foes, Alabama was upset by the Texas A&M Aggies in Tuscaloosa 29-24. After the Crimson Tide opened with a three-and-out, A&M scored on its first possession, aided by a 29-yard run by quarterback Johnny Manziel, on a 1-yard Christine Michael touchdown run for a 7-0 lead. On their next possession, the Tide reached their own 48-yard line, but A.J. McCarron threw his first interception of the season to Sean Porter. Four plays later, the Aggies led 14-0 after Manziel nearly fumbled, rolled out, and found Ryan Swope wide open for a 10-yard touchdown pass. The A&M defense then held Alabama to its second three-and-out. The Aggies increased their lead to 20-0 (missed PAT) late in the first when Michael scored on his second 1-yard touchdown run that completed a 14-play, 73-yard drive. Once again, Manziel broke containment, this time with a 32-yard run to the Alabama- 27 on 3rd-and-6. The Crimson Tide finally responded with a 13-play, 75-yard drive, including a 4th-and-4 conversion with a 4-yard catch by Eddie Lacy, and scored on a 2-yard touchdown run by T.J. Yeldon. A&M appeared primed to continue its scoring barrage but turned the ball over on downs at the Alabama 32-yard line. An 18-yard completion from McCarron to Christion Jones and an 18-yard run by Lacy moved the ball to the A&M 31. Six plays later, Lacy scored on a 2-yard touchdown run, trimming the deficit to 20-14 at halftime.

On its second possession of the second half, Alabama stormed all the way to the A&M 11-yard line but had to settle for a 28-yard Jeremy Shelley field goal that made the score 20-17 as the teams entered the fourth quarter. Finishing the drive following Shelley's field goal, Taylor Bertolet connected on a 29-yard field goal, extending its slim lead to 23-17. Following an Alabama three-and-out, A&M had a chance to put the game away, but Bertolet missed a field goal from 37 yards out. On the drive that ensued, McCarron connected with Amari Cooper for a 50-yard gain into A&M territory, but on the very next play Yeldon lost a fumble. Manziel completed a 42-yard pass to Swope and then a 24-yard touchdown pass to Malcome Kennedy for a 29-17 lead following a missed two-point conversion. The Tide responded on their next possession - starting at their own 6-yard line, they reached their own 46-yard line, then a 54-yard McCarron touchdown pass to Cooper cut the Aggies lead to 29-24. After the defense forced a punt, McCarron hit Kenny Bell for a 54-yard gain to the A&M 6-yard line. On 3rd-and-goal from the 5-yard line, a broken play turned into a 3-yard gain after a crazy McCarron scramble. However, on 4th-and-goal, McCarron threw an interception that gave A&M possession at the Aggies' 4-yard line. On the possession that ensued, the Alabama defense forced an Aggies punt with 40 seconds left in the game, but an offside call on Alabama gave the Aggies a first down and sealed their 29-24 victory.[94]

Passing	C/ATT	YDS	AVG	TD	INT	QBR
AJ McCarron	21/34	309	9.1	1	2	67.7

Rushing	CAR	YDS	AVG	TD	LONG
E. Lacy	16	92	5.8	1	18
TJ Yeldon	10	29	2.9	1	9
AJ McCarron	5	1	0.2	0	3
Team	31	122	3.9	2	18

Kick returns	NO	YDS	AVG	LONG	TD
Cy. Jones	2	35	17.5	23	0

Punting	NO	YDS	AVG	TB	IN 20	LONG
C. Mandell	4	226	56.5	0	0	60

Receiving	REC	YDS	AVG	TD	LONG
A. Cooper	6	136	22.7	1	54
K. Bell	3	73	24.3	0	54
E. Lacy	4	35	8.8	0	21
Ch. Jones	3	21	7	0	18
M. Williams	1	20	20	0	20
TJ Yeldon	2	9	4.5	0	5
M. Shinn	1	8	8	0	8
K. Norwood	1	7	7	0	7
Team	21	309	14.7	1	54

Punt returns	NO	YDS	AVG	LONG	TD
Ch. Jones	1	5	5	5	0

Kicking	FG	PCT	LONG	XP	PTS
J. Shelley	1/1	100	28	3/3	6

Note: Table data from "Alabama 24-19 Texas A&M (Nov 10, 2012) Box Score" (105)

11/17/12 - Alabama (4) vs Western Carolina

Team	1	2	3	4	T		Passing	Rushing	Total
Western Carolina	0	0	0	0	**0**		93	70	**163**
Alabama (4)	21	21	7	0	**49**		160	300	**460**

In the final non-conference game of the 2012 season, Alabama shut out the Western Carolina Catamounts 49-0 in Tuscaloosa. The Crimson Tide scored three touchdowns in each of the first two quarters and took a 42-0 halftime lead. Alabama took the opening possession 62 yards in six plays and Eddie Lacy scored the first touchdown on a 7-yard run for a 7-0 lead. After the defense held the Catamounts to a three-and-out, T.J. Yeldon scored the second Crimson Tide touchdown on a 3-yard run, capping a 44-yard drive on four plays in only 1:56 for a 14-0 lead. After a second three-and-out, Alabama scored its third touchdown in three possessions on Lacy's second 7-yard touchdown run for a 21-0 lead at the end of the first quarter.

To open the second quarter, the Crimson Tide went 4-for-4 on touchdowns. Alabama drove 99 yards in eight plays as A.J. McCarron connected on a 29-yard pass to Christion Jones for a 28-0 lead. Up by four touchdowns, backup quarterback Blake Sims took over for McCarron and led Alabama 71 yards to their fifth touchdown in as many possessions as Eddie Lacy scored on a 3-yard run, his third touchdown of the afternoon. After the defense again held Carolina to another three-and-out, Christion Jones fumbled the Catamounts' punt to give them possession at the Alabama 29-yard line. However, Western Carolina was unable to capitalize on the turnover as a Troy Mitchell fumble was recovered by Deion Belue and returned 57 yards for a touchdown and a 42-0 halftime lead. With reserves playing on both offense and defense for the Crimson Tide in the second half, the final touchdown came in the third quarter when Blake Sims scored on a 5-yard run to make the final score 49-0. This was the first time that Bryant-Denny Stadium was not sold out for an Alabama game since 2002.[94]

Passing	C/ATT	YDS	AVG	TD	INT	QBR
AJ McCarron	6/6	133	22.2	1	0	97.3
B. Sims	2/6	27	4.5	0	0	91.3
Team	8/12	160	13.3	1	0	--

Rushing	CAR	YDS	AVG	TD	LONG
E. Lacy	10	99	9.9	3	21
B. Sims	8	70	8.8	1	23
TJ Yeldon	7	55	7.9	1	15
B. Calloway	7	52	7.4	0	11
AJ McCarron	2	18	9	0	24
B. Howell	5	9	1.8	0	7
Team	1	-3	-3	0	0
Team	40	300	7.5	5	24

Punting	NO	YDS	AVG	TB	IN 20	LONG
C. Mandell	2	84	42	0	0	46

Receiving	REC	YDS	AVG	TD	LONG
A. Cooper	2	50	25	0	36
K. Bell	1	34	34	0	34
Ch. Jones	1	29	29	1	29
M. Williams	1	22	22	0	22
M. Shinn	1	13	13	0	13
Cy. Jones	2	12	6	0	14
Team	8	160	20	1	36

Punt returns	NO	YDS	AVG	LONG	TD
Ch. Jones	3	24	8	28	0
Cy. Jones	1	0	0	0	0
Team	4	24	6	28	0

Kicking	FG	PCT	LONG	XP	PTS
J. Shelley	0/0	0	0	7/7	7

Note: Table data from "Alabama 49-0 Western Carolina (Nov 17, 2012) Box Score" (106)

11/24/12 - Alabama (2) vs Auburn

Team	1	2	3	4	T		Passing	Rushing	Total
Auburn	0	0	0	0	**0**		71	92	**163**
Alabama (2)	14	28	7	0	**49**		216	267	**483**

In the 2012 edition of the Iron Bowl, Alabama shut out the Auburn Tigers 49-0 in Tuscaloosa. The Crimson Tide opened the game with a 10-play, 75-yard drive that culminated in a 2-yard Eddie Lacy touchdown run and a 7-0 lead. After the Alabama defense held Auburn to a three-and-out on its first possession, its offense responded with its second touchdown of the afternoon on a 2-yard T.J. Yeldon touchdown run which capped a 10-play, 61-yard drive and gave them a 14-0 lead. The Crimson Tide forced a Tigers' punt on their second possession and then scored their third touchdown in as many possessions when A.J. McCarron threw a 37-yard pass to Amari Cooper for a 21-0 lead early in the second quarter. Eddie Lacy contributed a nice 32-yard run on that that 6-play, 88-yard drive.

On the Auburn possession that ensued, the Alabama defense collected their first turnover of the game when Robert Lester intercepted a Jonathan Wallace pass at the Tigers' 29-yard line. Five plays later, the Crimson Tide led 28-0 after McCarron threw a 7-yard touchdown pass to Kevin Norwood. The Alabama defense held Auburn to their second three-and-out of the game, and then the Crimson Tide scored their fifth touchdown of the game on a 1-yard Lacy run for a 35-0 lead. Auburn then committed its second turnover of the game when Nico Johnson forced a Tre Mason fumble that Dee Milliner recovered and returned to the Tigers' 35-yard line. Alabama then took a 42-0 halftime lead when McCarron threw a 29-yard touchdown pass to Cooper.

With the Alabama starters in the game for the first possession of the second half, the defense again held the Tigers to a three-and-out and forced a punt. The offense then made it 7-for-7 on offense when McCarron threw a 38-yard touchdown pass to Norwood for a 49-0 lead. The Alabama defense then did not allow Auburn to get past its own 41-yard line for the duration of the game and secured their fourth shutout of the season. The victory was the second largest in the history of the Iron Bowl after the 55-0 Alabama win in 1948.[94]

Passing	C/ATT	YDS	AVG	TD	INT	QBR
AJ McCarron	15/21	216	10.3	4	0	97.6
B. Sims	0/1	0	0	0	0	41.8
Team	15/22	216	9.8	4	0	--

Rushing	CAR	YDS	AVG	TD	LONG
E. Lacy	18	131	7.3	2	32
K. Drake	10	67	6.7	0	38
TJ Yeldon	8	38	4.8	1	19
B. Sims	6	25	4.2	0	10
B. Howell	3	5	1.7	0	6
AJ McCarron	1	4	4	0	4
Team	1	-3	-3	0	0
Team	47	267	5.7	3	38

Punting	NO	YDS	AVG	TB	IN 20	LONG
C. Mandell	2	97	48.5	0	0	50

Receiving	REC	YDS	AVG	TD	LONG
A. Cooper	5	109	21.8	2	37
K. Norwood	5	65	13	2	38
Ch. Jones	3	22	7.3	0	10
K. Bell	1	15	15	0	15
M. Williams	1	5	5	0	5
Team	15	216	14.4	4	38

Kicking	FG	PCT	LONG	XP	PTS
J. Shelley	0/0	0	0	7/7	7

Interceptions	INT	YDS	TD
R. Lester	1	31	0
H. Clinton-Dix	1	0	0
Team	2	31	0

Note: Table data from "Alabama 49-0 Auburn (Nov 24, 2012) Box Score" (107)

12/01/12 - Alabama (2) at Georgia (3)

Team	1	2	3	4	T		Passing	Rushing	Total
Alabama (2)	0	10	8	14	32		162	350	512
Georgia (3)	0	7	14	7	28		281	113	394

With its victory over Auburn in the Iron Bowl, Alabama clinched the SEC Western Division championship and qualified to play Georgia in the 2012 SEC Championship Game where they defeated the Bulldogs 32-28. After each team traded punts on their opening possessions, Christian Robinson recovered an A.J. McCarron fumble for the Bulldogs and gave Georgia possession at the Alabama 40-yard line. The Crimson Tide defense then held the Bulldogs to a 50-yard field goal attempt that was missed by Marshall Morgan that kept the game scoreless.

After the first quarter ended in a scoreless tie, Georgia scored its first touchdown early in the second quarter. The 19-yard touchdown pass from Aaron Murray to Jay Rome was set up by a fake punt earlier in the drive that gave the Bulldogs a 7-0 lead. After each team again traded punts, Alabama drove the ball 77 yards, aided by a 44-yard catch by Amari Cooper, to the Bulldogs' 1-yard line. However, Eddie Lacy fumbled on second down and then McCarron threw an interception in the end zone to Sanders Commings to end the drive. The Crimson Tide forced another punt on the next Bulldogs possession, and Alabama responded on the drive that ensued by going 70 yards to get its first touchdown of the game on a 41-yard Lacy run that tied the game at 7-7. On the next drive, Ha Ha Clinton-Dix intercepted a Murray pass and returned it to the Georgia 47-yard line with just over a minute left in the half. Five plays later, Jeremy Shelley connected on a 22-yard field goal as time expired and gave the Crimson Tide a 10-7 halftime lead.

Down by three to start the second half, Georgia responded with a pair of touchdowns and took a 21-10 lead early in the third quarter. The first was scored on a 3-yard Todd Gurley run that completed a 75-yard drive that opened the quarter. The second came on a special teams play on the drive that ensued when Cornelius Washington blocked a 49-yard Cade Foster field goal attempt. It was recovered by Alec Ogletree and returned 55 yards for a touchdown and a 21-10 lead. Alabama responded on its next possession with a 4-play, 77-yard drive that was capped by a 10-yard T.J. Yeldon touchdown run followed with Yeldon converting the two-point conversion on a 2-yard run that made the score 21-18. After a Georgia three-and-out, Alabama took a 25-21 lead on the first play of the fourth quarter on a 1-yard Lacy touchdown run behind the blocking of Jesse Williams. He carried the ball on five of the seven plays of the 74-yard drive for 60 yards in total.

Georgia responded with a 10-yard Gurley touchdown run on the next drive and took a 28-25 lead. Each team then traded punts again before Alabama scored what proved to be the game-winning touchdown on a 44-yard McCarron pass to Amari Cooper for a 32-28 lead. Each team then forced three-and-outs, and with just over one minute left in the game, Georgia drove to the Alabama 8-yard line on a drive that saw several long Murray completions and an overturned interception by Dee Milliner. The final play of the game was a Murray pass tipped by C.J. Mosley and caught by Chris Conley at the Alabama 5-yard line, but Georgia did not have any timeouts remaining and the clock ran out to give Alabama the 32-28 victory. In the game Lacy, rushed for 181 yards and Yeldon rushed for 153 yards, and Lacy was named the SEC Championship Game MVP for his performance.[94]

Passing	C/ATT	YDS	AVG	TD	INT	QBR
AJ McCarron	13/21	162	7.7	1	1	59.3

Rushing	CAR	YDS	AVG	TD	LONG
E. Lacy	20	181	9.1	2	41
TJ Yeldon	25	153	6.1	1	31
AJ McCarron	6	16	2.7	0	22
Team	51	350	6.9	3	41

Interceptions	INT	YDS	TD
H. Clinton-Dix	1	35	0

Punting	NO	YDS	AVG	TB	IN 20	LONG
C. Mandell	5	209	41.8	0	0	48

Receiving	REC	YDS	AVG	TD	LONG
A. Cooper	8	128	16	1	45
Ch. Jones	1	22	22	0	22
E. Lacy	2	7	3.5	0	6
M. Williams	2	5	2.5	0	3
Team	13	162	12.5	1	45

Kick returns	NO	YDS	AVG	LONG	TD
Cy. Jones	4	89	22.3	25	0

Punt returns	NO	YDS	AVG	LONG	TD
Ch. Jones	1	8	8	8	0

Kicking	FG	PCT	LONG	XP	PTS
J. Shelley	1/1	100	22	3/3	6
C. Foster	0/1	0	0	0/0	0
Team	1/2	50	22	3/3	6

Note: Table data from "Alabama 32-28 Georgia (Dec 1, 2012) Box Score" (108)

01/07/13 - Alabama (2) vs Notre Dame (1)

BCS Championship
Sun Life Stadium
Miami, FL

Team	1	2	3	4	T		Passing	Rushing	Total
Notre Dame (1)	0	0	7	7	14		270	32	302
Alabama (2)	14	14	7	7	42		264	265	529

With its victory over Georgia in the SEC Championship Game, Alabama qualified for the 2013 BCS National Championship Game, and against Notre Dame the Crimson Tide captured their third BCS Championship in four years with a 42-14 victory over the Fighting Irish. After Notre Dame won the coin toss and elected to defer until the second half, Alabama took its opening possession 82 yards in five plays and Eddie Lacy gave the Crimson Tide an early 7-0 lead with his 20-yard touchdown run. On the first Irish possession that followed, the Crimson Tide held them to a three-and-out and forced a punt. The kick was subsequently fumbled by Christion Jones and recovered by Notre Dame; however, a kick catching interference penalty was called against the Irish and gave possession back to Alabama. On the drive that ensued, the Crimson Tide took a 14-0 lead when A.J. McCarron threw a 3-yard touchdown pass to Michael Williams that capped a 10-play, 61-yard drive. After the Alabama defense forced their second punt of the game, the Crimson Tide responded with their third touchdown of the game. Alabama stormed 80 yards in eight plays and T.J. Yeldon extended the Alabama lead to 21-0 with his 1-yard run on the first play of the second quarter. Notre Dame then responded with its longest play from scrimmage of the game on a 31-yard Everett Golson pass to DaVaris Daniels. However, the Irish then surrendered the ball on downs when they failed to convert on 4th-and-5 four plays later. Each team then traded punts over the next four possessions before the Crimson Tide scored their final points of the first half after driving 71 yards in nine plays. With just 31 seconds left in the quarter, McCarron threw an 11-yard touchdown pass to Lacy that made the halftime score 28-0.

Notre Dame opened the third quarter on offense, but Ha Ha Clinton-Dix intercepted a Golson pass that gave Alabama possession at the Irish 3-yard line. The Crimson Tide then drove 97 yards in ten plays that ended with a 34-yard McCarron touchdown pass to Amari Cooper that extended their lead to 35-0. Notre Dame then responded with its first points of the game on the drive that ensued with a 2-yard Golson touchdown run that made the score 35-7. Alabama then began its final scoring drive of the night. The final Crimson Tide touchdown came early in the fourth quarter on a 19-yard McCarron touchdown pass to Cooper that capped a 14-play, 86-yard drive that took 7:41 off the clock and made the score 42-7. The Irish then made the final score 42-14 when Golson threw a 6-yard touchdown pass to Theo Riddick. The teams then traded punts with the final play of the game being a short Notre Dame run as time expired.

For their performances on the field, Eddie Lacy was named the game's offensive MVP and C.J. Mosley was named defensive MVP. In the game, Lacy rushed for 140 and T.J. Yeldon for 108 yards, and each scored a touchdown in the win. A.J. McCarron became Alabama's all-time leader in touchdown passes when he surpassed the previous record of 47 set by John Parker Wilson. Amari Cooper also set the record for touchdown receptions in a season after he caught a pair to give him 11 for the season as he surpassed the previous record of ten caught by Al Lary in 1955.[94]

Passing	C/ATT	YDS	AVG	TD	INT	QBR
AJ McCarron	20/28	264	9.4	4	0	97.5

Rushing	CAR	YDS	AVG	TD	LONG
E. Lacy	20	140	7	1	20
TJ Yeldon	21	108	5.1	1	10
AJ McCarron	1	9	9	0	9
K. Drake	3	8	2.7	0	6
Team	45	265	5.9	2	20

Interceptions	INT	YDS	TD
H. Clinton-Dix	1	35	0

Kick returns	NO	YDS	AVG	LONG	TD
Ch. Jones	2	31	15.5	17	0

Punting	NO	YDS	AVG	TB	IN 20	LONG
C. Mandell	4	197	49.3	0	0	55

Receiving	REC	YDS	AVG	TD	LONG
A. Cooper	6	105	17.5	2	34
K. Norwood	3	66	22	0	29
Ch. Jones	2	40	20	0	27
E. Lacy	2	17	8.5	1	11
M. Williams	3	17	5.7	1	8
M. Shinn	2	14	7	0	7
K. Johnson	1	5	5	0	5
TJ Yeldon	1	0	0	0	0
Team	20	264	13.2	4	34

Punt returns	NO	YDS	AVG	LONG	TD
Ch. Jones	1	1	1	1	0

Kicking	FG	PCT	LONG	XP	PTS
J. Shelley	0/0	0	0	6/6	6

Note: Table data from "Alabama 42-14 Notre Dame (Jan 7, 2013) Box Score" (109)

Season Stats

Record	13-1	2nd of 124
SEC Record	8-1	
Rank	1	
Points for	542	
Points against	153	
Points/game	38.7	12th of 124
Opp points/game	10.9	1st of 124
SOS[6]	5.51	14th of 124

Team stats (averages per game)

Split	G	Passing					Rushing				Total Offense		
		Cmp	Att	Pct	Yds	TD	Att	Yds	Avg	TD	Plays	Yds	Avg
Offense	14	15.6	23.4	66.8	218	2.2	40.7	227.5	5.6	2.6	64.1	445.5	6.9
Defense	14	15.5	28.4	54.7	173.6	0.6	31.4	76.4	2.4	0.7	59.8	250	4.2
Difference		0.1	-5	12.1	44.4	1.6	9.3	151.1	3.2	1.9	4.3	195.5	2.7

Split	First Downs				Penalties		Turnovers		
	Pass	Rush	Pen	Tot	No.	Yds	Fum	Int	Tot
Offense	9.4	11.4	0.9	21.6	3.9	33.4	0.9	0.2	1.1
Defense	8.2	4.5	1	13.7	4.8	40.4	0.8	1.3	2.1
Difference	1.2	6.9	-0.1	7.9	-0.9	-7	0.1	-1.1	-1

Passing

Rk	Player	G	Passing								
			Cmp	Att	Pct	Yds	Y/A	AY/A	TD	Int	Rate
1	A.J. McCarron	14	211	314	67.2	2933	9.3	10.8	30	3	175.3
2	Blake Sims	10	5	10	50	77	7.7	7.7	0	0	114.7
3	Phillip Ely	6	3	4	75	42	10.5	15.5	1	0	245.7

Rushing and receiving

Rk	Player	G	Rushing				Receiving				Scrimmage			
			Att	Yds	Avg	TD	Rec	Yds	Avg	TD	Plays	Yds	Avg	TD
1	Eddie Lacy	14	204	1322	6.5	17	22	189	8.6	2	226	1511	6.7	19
2	T.J. Yeldon	14	175	1108	6.3	12	11	131	11.9	1	186	1239	6.7	13
3	A.J. McCarron	14	49	4	0.1	1					49	4	0.1	1
4	Kenyan Drake	12	42	281	6.7	5					42	281	6.7	5
5	Blake Sims	10	30	187	6.2	2					30	187	6.2	2
6	Dee Hart	5	21	88	4.2	0	2	18	9	0	23	106	4.6	0
7	Ben Howell	7	18	52	2.9	0					18	52	2.9	0
8	Jalston Fowler	2	11	85	7.7	0	1	6	6	0	12	91	7.6	0
9	Brent Calloway	13	10	63	6.3	0	1	-2	-2	0	11	61	5.5	0
10	Christion Jones	14	2	6	3	0	27	368	13.6	4	29	374	12.9	4
11	Cody Mandell	14	2	1	0.5	0					2	1	0.5	0
12	Cyrus Jones	11	1	2	2	0	4	51	12.8	0	5	53	10.6	0
13	Phillip Ely	6	1	-2	-2	0					1	-2	-2	0
14	Danny Woodson Jr.	5					1	9	9	0	1	9	9	0
15	Amari Cooper	14					59	1000	16.9	11	59	1000	16.9	11
16	Kevin Norwood	13					29	461	15.9	4	29	461	15.9	4
17	Michael Williams	14					24	183	7.6	4	24	183	7.6	4
18	Kenny Bell	12					17	431	25.4	3	17	431	25.4	3
19	Deandrew White	5					8	105	13.1	2	8	105	13.1	2
20	Marvin Shinn	14					6	42	7	0	6	42	7	0
21	Kelly Johnson	14					5	39	7.8	0	5	39	7.8	0
22	Brian Vogler	14					2	21	10.5	0	2	21	10.5	0

Defense and fumbles

Rk	Player	G	Solo	Ast	Tot	Loss	Sk	Int	Yds	Avg	TD	PD	FR	Yds	TD	FF
					Tackles					Def Int					Fumbles	
1	C.J. Mosley	14	66	41	107	8	4	2	16	8	1					
2	Trey DePriest		30	29	59	4	0					2				
3	Nico Johnson		23	32	55	2	0					1				2
4	Dee Milliner		34	20	54	4	1.5	2	35	17.5		22	1	17	0	1
5	Vinnie Sunseri	14	35	19	54	6	1.5	2	13	6.5	0					
6	Robert Lester	14	24	24	48	3.5	1.5	4	51	12.8	0					
7	Adrian Hubbard		24	17	41	11	7					1				3
8	Deion Belue	14	28	12	40	6.5	0	2	15	7.5	0			57	1	
9	Nick Perry		18	20	38	2	1					2				
10	Ha Ha Clinton-Dix	14	23	14	37	0.5	0	5	91	18.2	0	9				1
11	Jesse Williams		7	30	37	2.5	1					2				
12	Damion Square		11	22	33	4	3.5					1				
13	Xzavier Dickson	14	12	21	33	5	3.5									
14	Ed Stinson		20	10	30	8.5	3									
15	Jeoffrey Pagan		10	13	23	4	1.5									1
16	Quinton Dial		10	12	22	5	1.5									
17	Brandon Ivory		7	15	22	1	0									
18	Denzel Devall		7	11	18	3	2									
19	Landon Collins	14	8	9	17	0	0									
20	Tana Patrick		6	10	16	0	0									
21	John Fulton		12	3	15	0	0					5				
22	Tyler Hayes		10	4	14	0	0									
23	Geno Smith		4	5	9	0.5	0					2				
24	Reggie Ragland		5	3	8	0	0									1
25	D.J. Pettway		3	5	8	4	2.5									
26	Brent Calloway	13	5	3	8	0	0									
27	Bradley Sylve		4	2	6	0	0					2				
28	Christion Jones	14	4	2	6	0	0									
29	Lamichael Fanning		3	1	4	0	0									
30	Darren Lake		1	2	3	1	0									
31	Jonathan Atchison		0	2	2	0	0									
32	Jabriel Washington		0	2	2	0	0									
33	Cade Foster	14	0	2	2	0	0									
34	Dee Hart	5	2	0	2	0	0									
35	Deandrew White	5	2	0	2	0	0									
36	Dillon Lee	8	1	0	1	0	0	1	0	0	0					
37	Chris Bonds		0	1	1	0	0									
38	Anthony Steen		1	0	1	0	0									
39	Ranzell Watkins		1	0	1	0	0									
40	Amari Cooper	14	1	0	1	0	0									
41	Kenyan Drake	12	0	1	1	0	0									
42	Kelly Johnson	14	0	1	1	0	0									
43	Dee Milliner	13						2	35	17.5	0					
44	Blake Sims	10						1	10	10						

Kick and punt returns

Rk	Player	G	Ret	Yds	Avg	TD	Ret	Yds	Avg	TD
				Kick Ret				Punt Ret		
1	Cyrus Jones	11	10	250	25	0	8	61	7.6	0
2	Christion Jones	14	8	213	26.6	1	21	213	10.1	0
3	Kevin Norwood	13	1	22	22	0				
4	Harrison Jones	10	1	9	9	0				
5	Xzavier Dickson	14	1	9	9	0				
6	Dee Hart	5					4	50	12.5	0
7	Landon Collins	14					1	13	13	0

138

Kicking and punting

Rk	Player	G	Kicking							Punting		
			XPM	XPA	XP%	FGM	FGA	FG%	Pts	Punts	Yds	Avg
1	Jeremy Shelley	14	69	69	100	11	11	100	102			
2	Cade Foster	14				4	9	44.4				
3	Cody Mandell	14								50	2214	44.3

Scoring

Rk	Player	G	Touchdowns							Kicking				Pts
			Rush	Rec	Int	FR	PR	KR	Tot	XPM	FGM	2PM	Sfty	
1	Eddie Lacy	14	17	2					19					114
2	Jeremy Shelley	14								69	11			102
3	T.J. Yeldon	14	12	1					13			1		80
4	Amari Cooper	14		11					11					66
5	Christion Jones	14		4				1	5					30
6	Kenyan Drake	12	5						5					30
7	Kevin Norwood	13		4					4					24
8	Michael Williams	14		4					4					24
9	Kenny Bell	12		3					3					18
10	Blake Sims	10	2						2					12
11	Cade Foster	14									4			12
12	Deandrew White	5		2					2					12
13	A.J. McCarron	14	1						1					6
14	C.J. Mosley	14			1				1					6
15	Deion Belue	14				1			1					6

Stats include bowl games
Note: Table data from "2012 Alabama Crimson Tide Stats" (6)

Awards and honors

Name	Award	Type
Barrett Jones	Permanent Team Captain	Team
Damian Square	Permanent Team Captain	Team
Chance Warmack	Permanent Team Captain	Team
C.J. Mosley	MVP	Team
A.J. McCarron	Offensive Player of the Year	Team
Nico Johnson	Defensive Player of the Year	Team
Dee Milliner	Defensive Player of the Year	Team
Barrett Jones	AP All-SEC First Team	SEC
Dee Milliner	AP All-SEC First Team	SEC
C.J. Mosley	AP All-SEC First Team	SEC
Chance Warmack	AP All-SEC First Team	SEC
Ha Ha Clinton-Dix	AP All-SEC Honorable Mention Team	SEC
Robert Lester	AP All-SEC Honorable Mention Team	SEC
D.J. Fluker	AP All-SEC Second Team	SEC
Eddie Lacy	AP All-SEC Second Team	SEC
A.J. McCarron	AP All-SEC Second Team	SEC
Jesse Williams	AP All-SEC Second Team	SEC
D.J. Fluker	Coaches' All-SEC First Team	SEC
Barrett Jones	Coaches' All-SEC First Team	SEC
Eddie Lacy	Coaches' All-SEC First Team	SEC
Dee Milliner	Coaches' All-SEC First Team	SEC
C.J. Mosley	Coaches' All-SEC First Team	SEC
Chance Warmack	Coaches' All-SEC First Team	SEC
Robert Lester	Coaches' All-SEC Second Team	SEC
A.J. McCarron	Coaches' All-SEC Second Team	SEC
Amari Cooper	Freshman All SEC Team	SEC
Ryan Kelly	Freshman All SEC Team	SEC
D.J. Pettway	Freshman All SEC Team	SEC
T.J. Yeldon	Freshman All SEC Team	SEC
Barrett Jones	Scholar-Athlete of the Year	SEC
Barrett Jones	Academic All-America of the Year	National
Dee Milliner	AFCA All-America Team	National
C.J. Mosley	AFCA All-America Team	National
Chance Warmack	AFCA All-America Team	National
Kirby Smart	AFCA FBS Assistant Coach of the Year	National
Barrett Jones	AP All-America First Team	National
Dee Milliner	AP All-America First Team	National

Name	Award	Type
C.J. Mosley	AP All-America First Team	National
Chance Warmack	AP All-America First Team	National
D.J. Fluker	AP All-America Second Team	National
A.J. McCarron	AP All-America Third Team	National
Dee Milliner	Bronko Nagurski Trophy Finalist	National
C.J. Mosley	Butkus Award Finalist	National
Barrett Jones	Consensus All-American	National
Dee Milliner	Consensus All-American	National
C.J. Mosley	Consensus All-American	National
Chance Warmack	Consensus All-American	National
Barrett Jones	FWAA All-America First Team	National
Dee Milliner	FWAA All-America First Team	National
Chance Warmack	FWAA All-America First Team	National
Dee Milliner	Jim Thorpe Award Finalist	National
A.J. McCarron	Johnny Unitas Golden Arm Award Finalist	National
Barrett Jones	Lombardi Award Finalist	National
A.J. McCarron	Manning Award Finalist	National
Barrett Jones	Outland Trophy	National
Barrett Jones	Rimington Trophy	National
Barrett Jones	Sporting News (TSN) All-America Team	National
Dee Milliner	Sporting News (TSN) All-America Team	National
C.J. Mosley	Sporting News (TSN) All-America Team	National
Chance Warmack	Sporting News (TSN) All-America Team	National
Amari Cooper	TSN Freshman All-America Team	National
Denzell Devall	TSN Freshman All-America Team	National
T.J. Yeldon	TSN Freshman All-America Team	National
Dee Milliner	Unanimous All-American	National
Chance Warmack	Unanimous All-American	National
Barrett Jones	Walter Camp All-America First Team	National
Dee Milliner	Walter Camp All-America First Team	National
C.J. Mosley	Walter Camp All-America First Team	National
Chance Warmack	Walter Camp All-America First Team	National
D.J. Fluker	Walter Camp All-America Second Team	National
Barrett Jones	William V. Campbell Trophy	National
Deion Belue	Senior Bowl	All-Star Team
Adrian Hubbard	Senior Bowl	All-Star Team
Cody Mandell	Senior Bowl	All-Star Team
A.J. McCarron	Senior Bowl	All-Star Team
C.J. Mosley	Senior Bowl	All-Star Team
Kevin Norwood	Senior Bowl	All-Star Team
Ed Stinson	Senior Bowl	All-Star Team
Quinton Dial	Raycom College Football All-Star Classic	All-Star Team
Kelly Johnson	Raycom College Football All-Star Classic	All-Star Team
Jeremy Shelley	Raycom College Football All-Star Classic	All-Star Team
Damian Square	Raycom College Football All-Star Classic	All-Star Team
Carson Tinker	Raycom College Football All-Star Classic	All-Star Team

NFL

Season	Year drafted	Round	Pick	Overall	Player	Position	Team
2012	2013	1	9	9	Dee Milliner	CB	New York Jets
2012	2013	1	10	10	Chance Warmack	G	Tennessee Titans
2012	2013	1	11	11	D.J. Fluker	OT	Los Angeles Chargers
2012	2013	2	29	61	Eddie Lacy	RB	Green Bay Packers
2012	2013	4	2	99	Nico Johnson	LB	Kansas City Chiefs
2012	2013	4	16	113	Barrett Jones	C	Los Angeles Rams
2012	2013	5	4	137	Jesse Williams	DT	Seattle Seahawks
2012	2013	5	24	157	Quinton Dial	DE	San Francisco 49ers
2012	2013	7	5	211	Michael Williams	TE	Detroit Lions

Note: Table data from "2012 Alabama Crimson Tide football team" (94)

2013

Overall

Record	11-2
SEC Record	7-1
Rank	7
Points for	496
Points against	181
Points/game	38.2
Opp points/game	13.9
SOS[7]	3.76

Mediocre people don't like high achievers, and high achievers don't like mediocre people. -Nick Saban

If I had a barometer up your ass to say whether you were giving effort or not, it was about 50 percent. -Nick Saban

Games

Date	Bama Rank		Opp Rank	Opponent	Bama	Opp	Result	SEC
08/31/13	1	N		Virginia Tech	35	10	W	
09/14/13	1	@	6	Texas A&M	49	42	W	W
09/21/13	1	vs		Colorado State	31	6	W	
09/28/13	1	vs	21	Ole Miss	25	0	W	W
10/05/13	1	vs		Georgia State	45	3	W	
10/12/13	1	@		Kentucky	48	7	W	W
10/19/13	1	vs		Arkansas	52	0	W	W
10/26/13	1	vs		Tennessee	45	10	W	W
11/09/13	1	vs	13	LSU	38	17	W	W
11/16/13	1	@		Mississippi State	20	7	W	W
11/23/13	1	vs		Chattanooga	49	0	W	
11/30/13	1	@	4	Auburn	28	34	L	L
01/02/14	3	N	11	Oklahoma	31	45	L	

Coaches

Name	Position	Year
Nick Saban	Head Coach	7
Greg Brown	Secondary	1
Burton Burns	Associate Head Coach / Running Backs	7
Scott Cochran	Strength and Conditioning	7
Mario Cristobal	Offensive Line / Recruiting Coordinator	1
Billy Napier	Wide Receivers	1
Doug Nussmeier	Offensive Coordinator / Quarterbacks	2
Chris Rumph	Defensive Line	3
Kirby Smart	Defensive Coordinator	7
Lance Thompson	Outside Linebackers	2 (4th overall)
Bobby Williams	Tight ends / Special Teams	6

Recruits

Name	Pos	Pos Rank	Scout	Rivals	247 Sports	ESPN	ESPN Grade	Hometown	High school / college	Height	Weight	Committed
Jonathan Allen	DE	3	5	5	5	4	88	Ashburn, VA	Stone Bridge HS	6-3	255	5/21/12
Anthony Averett	ATH	22	4	3	4	4	83	Glassboro, NJ	Woodbury Junior-Senior HS	6-1	178	4/14/12
Cooper Bateman	QB	3	4	4	4	4	87	Salt Lake City, UT	Cottonwood HS	6-3	190	5/16/12
Leon Brown	OT	2	4	3	4	4	83	Riverdale Park, MD	ASA College	6-6	315	6/10/12
Jonathan Cook	CB	73	3	3	3	3	75	Spanish Fort, AL	Spanish Fort HS	6-0	185	12/15/12
Raheem Falkins	WR	41	3	4	3	4	82	New Orleans, LA	G. W. Carver HS	6-4	192	1/28/12
Robert Foster	WR	2	3	4	5	4	88	Monaca, PN	Central Valley HS	6-2	180	12/21/12
Reuben Foster	ILB	1	5	5	5	4	88	Auburn, AL	Auburn HS	6-1	240	2/4/13
Derrick Henry	ATH	1	5	4	5	5	90	Yulee, FL	Yulee HS	6-3	243	9/28/12
Brandon Hill	OT		3	3	3	3	74	Collierville, TN	Hargrave Military Academy	6-6	350	12/25/12
Grant Hill	OG	1	4	4	4	4	84	Huntsville, AL	Huntsville HS	6-6	315	2/22/12
O.J. Howard	TE	2	5	5	5	4	87	Prattville, AL	Autauga Academy	6-6	220	7/18/11
Eddie Jackson	WR	54	3	3	3	4	81	Lauderdale Lakes, FL	Boyd H. Anderson HS	6-1	180	1/30/13
Tyren Jones	RB	8	4	4	4	4	85	Marietta, GA	George Walton Comprehensive HS	5-9	197	2/21/12
Walker Jones	ILB	26	3	3	3	3	79	Cordova, TN	Evangelical Christian School	6-2	225	7/23/12
Alvin Kamara	RB	4	4	4	4	4	88	Norcross, GA	Norcross HS	5-10	191	2/6/13
Dee Liner	DT	4	4	4	4	4	88	Muscle Shoals, AL	Muscle Shoals HS	6-4	294	2/6/13
Cole Mazza	LS	3	2	3	3	2	68	Bakersfield, CA	Liberty HS	6-3	190	6/14/12
Parker McLeod	QB	31	3	3	3	3	78	Marietta, GA	George Walton Comprehensive HS	6-2	189	6/8/12
Darius Paige	DT	21	4	4	4	4	83	Foley, AL	Foley HS	6-4	292	5/19/12
A'Shawn Robinson	DT	11	5	5	5	4	84	Fort Worth, TX	Arlington Heights HS	6-4	305	2/6/13
Maurice Smith	CB	12	4	4	4	4	84	Sugar Land, TX	Dulles HS	5-11	174	6/7/12
ArDarius Stewart	ATH	18	4	4	4	4	83	Fultondale, AL	Fultondale HS	6-1	185	1/28/12
Altee Tenpenny	RB	10	4	4	4	4	84	North Little Rock, AR	North Little Rock HS	6-0	203	1/28/12
Tim Williams	DE	5	4	4	4	4	87	Baton Rouge, LA	Louisiana State University Laboratory School	6-4	230	1/12/13

	Scout	Rivals	247Sports	ESPN
5 Stars	5	4	6	1
4 Stars	12	13	12	19
3 Stars	7	8	7	4
2 Stars	1	0	0	1

Note: Table data from "2013 Alabama Crimson Tide football team" (110)

142

Roster

Num	Player	Pos	Class	Height	Weight	Hometown	Last School
93	Jonathan Allen	LB	FR	6-3	264	Leesburg, VA	Stone Bridge
7	Ryan Anderson	LB	FR	6-2	255	Daphne, AL	Daphne
28	Anthony Averett	DB	FR	6-0	170	Woodbury, NJ	Woodbury
94	Dakota Ball	DL	FR	6-2	270	Lindale, GA	Pepperell
87	Parker Barrineau	WR	SO	6-0	183	Northport, AL	American Christian Academy
35	Tyler Bass	WR	SR	5-10	175	Birmingham, AL	Vestavia Hills
18	Cooper Bateman	QB	FR	6-3	208	Murray, UT	Cottonwood
7	Kenny Bell	WR	SR	6-1	180	Rayville, LA	Rayville
13	**Deion Belue**	**DB**	**SR**	**5-11**	**183**	**Tuscumbia, AL**	**Northeast Mississippi CC**
31	Jerrod Bierbower	DB	JR	6-1	190	Dublin, OH	Coffman
5	Chris Black	WR	FR	5-11	182	Jacksonville, FL	First Coast
72	Leon Brown	OL	JR	6-6	313	Riverdale, MD	ASA College
6	**Ha Ha Clinton-Dix**	**DB**	**JR**	**6-1**	**208**	**Orlando, FL**	**Dr. Phillips**
26	Landon Collins	DB	SO	6-0	215	Geismar, LA	Dutchtown
15	Jonathan Cook	DB	FR	6-0	186	Daphne, AL	Spanish Fort
9	**Amari Cooper**	**WR**	**SO**	**6-1**	**202**	**Miami, FL**	**Northwestern**
39	Paden Crowder	LB	SO	6-4	200	Vestavia, AL	Vestavia Hills
33	**Trey DePriest**	**LB**	**SO**	**6-2**	**245**	**Springfield, OH**	**Springfield**
14	Luke Del Rio	QB	FR	6-2	203	Highlands Ranch, CO	Valor Christian
30	Denzel Devall	LB	SO	6-2	250	Bastrop, LA	Bastrop
55	Josh Dickerson	LB	JR	6-1	244	Evans, GA	Lakeside
47	**Xzavier Dickson**	**LB**	**JR**	**6-3**	**265**	**Griffin, GA**	**Griffin**
36	Dustin Ellison	WR	JR	6-0	170	Monroeville, AL	Monroe Academy
17	Kenyan Drake	RB	SO	6-1	201	Powder Spring, GA	Hillgrove
85	Malcolm Faciane	TE	SO	6-5	267	Picayune, MS	Picayune Memorial
80	Raheem Falkins	WR	FR	6-4	203	New Orleans, LA	G.W. Carver
44	LaMichael Fanning	DL	SO	6-7	270	Hamilton, GA	Harris County
43	**Cade Foster**	**PK**	**SR**	**6-1**	**224**	**Southlake, TX**	**Southlake Carroll**
2	Reuben Foster	LB	FR	6-1	244	Auburn, AL	Auburn
8	Robert Foster	WR	FR	6-3	187	Monaca, PA	Central Valley
45	**Jalston Fowler**	**RB**	**JR**	**6-1**	**250**	**Mobile, AL**	**Vigor**
41	Kurt Freitag	TE	FR	6-4	235	Buford, GA	Buford
10	**John Fulton**	**DB**	**SR**	**6-0**	**186**	**Manning, SC**	**Manning**
41	Daniel Geddes	DB	JR	5-6	170	Northport, AL	Tuscaloosa County
89	Brandon Greene	OL	FR	6-5	307	Ellenwood, GA	Cedar Grove
99	Adam Griffith	PK	FR	5-10	187	Calhoun, GA	Calhoun
74	Caleb Gulledge	OL	FR	6-4	286	Prattville, AL	Prattville
58	Alex Harrelson	LS	SO	6-0	220	Vestavia, AL	Vestavia Hills
86	Truett Harris	TE	SO	6-3	210	Bentwood, TN	Brentwood
1	Dee Hart	RB	SO	5-9	187	Orlando, FL	Dr. Phillips
21	Derrick Henry	RB	FR	6-3	238	Yulee, FL	Yulee
73	Brandon Hill	OL	FR	6-6	385	Collierville, TN	St. George's/Hargrave
64	Grant Hill	OL	FR	6-6	301	Huntsville, AL	Huntsville
37	Zach Houston	DB	SO	6-1	183	Daphne, AL	Daphne
88	O.J. Howard	TE	FR	6-6	237	Prattville, AL	Autauga Academy
42	**Adrian Hubbard**	**LB**	**JR**	**6-6**	**252**	**Lawrenceville, GA**	**Norcross**
99	**Brandon Ivory**	**DL**	**JR**	**6-4**	**310**	**Memphis, TN**	**East**
4	Eddie Jackson	DB	FR	6-0	175	Lauderdale Lakes, FL	Boyd Anderson
90	Bernel Jones	DL	JR	6-3	240	Montgomery, AL	Jefferson Davis
22	**Christion Jones**	**WR**	**JR**	**5-11**	**185**	**Adamsville, AL**	**Minor**
5	Cyrus Jones	WR	SO	5-10	196	Baltimore, MD	Gilman
82	Harrison Jones	TE	JR	6-4	241	Germantown, TN	Evangelical Christian
20	Tyren Jones	RB	FR	5-9	215	Marietta, GA	Walton
35	Walker Jones	LB	FR	6-2	234	Germantown, TN	Evangelical Christian
26	Alvin Kamara	RB	FR	5-10	195	Norcross, GA	Norcross
39	Kyle Kazakevicius	WR	JR	6-0	185	Ocala, FL	Trinity Catholic
70	**Ryan Kelly**	**OL**	**SO**	**6-5**	**290**	**West Chester, OH**	**Lakota West**
85	Korren Kirven	DL	FR	6-5	281	Lynchburg, VA	Brookville
77	**Arie Kouandjio**	**OL**	**JR**	**6-5**	**315**	**Hyattsville, MD**	**DeMatha Catholic**
71	**Cyrus Kouandjio**	**OL**	**JR**	**6-6**	**310**	**Hyattsville, MD**	**DeMatha Catholic**
95	Darren Lake	DL	SO	6-3	324	York, AL	Sumter County
25	Dillon Lee	LB	SO	6-4	242	Buford, GA	Buford
40	Issac Leon	TE	FR	6-6	214	Boynton Beach, FL	American Heritage
78	Chad Lindsay	OL	JR	6-2	302	The Woodlands, TX	The Woodlands
52	Dee Liner	DL	FR	6-3	281	Muscle Shoals, AL	Muscle Shoals
51	Wilson Love	DL	SO	6-3	286	Mountain Brook, AL	Mountain Brook
68	Isaac Luatua	OL	SO	6-2	313	La Mirada, CA	La Mirada
29	**Cody Mandell**	**P**	**SR**	**6-4**	**213**	**Lafayette, LA**	**Acadiana**
55	Cole Mazza	LS	FR	6-1	246	Bakersfield, CA	Liberty
10	**A.J. McCarron**	**QB**	**SR**	**6-4**	**214**	**Mobile, AL**	**Saint Paul's Episcopal School**
47	Corey McCarron	TE	SO	6-2	238	Mobile, AL	Spanish Fort
15	Parker McLeod	QB	FR	6-3	193	Marietta, GA	Walton
19	Jai Miller	DB	FR	6-3	213	Valley Grande, AL	Selma

143

Num	Player	Pos	Class	Height	Weight	Hometown	Last School
60	Brandon Moore	OL	SO	6-0	313	Cincinnati, OH	Cincinnati Hills Christian Academy
11	Alec Morris	QB	FR	6-3	230	Allen, TX	Allen
12	Taylor Morton	DB	JR	5-11	186	Centerville, AL	Bibb County
32	**C.J. Mosley**	**LB**	**SR**	**6-2**	**232**	**Theodore, AL**	**Theodore**
64	Michael Newsome	DL	JR	6-2	250	Cockeysville, MD	Boys' Latin
59	Harold Nicholson	OL	JR	6-5	283	Columbus, OH	St. Francis DeSales
83	**Kevin Norwood**	**WR**	**SR**	**6-2**	**195**	**D'Iberville, MS**	**D'Iberville**
46	Michael Nysewander	TE	JR	6-1	235	Hoover, AL	Hoover
53	Anthony Orr	DL	JR	6-4	282	Madison, AL	Sparkman
34	Tyler Owens	LB	JR	6-0	220	Columbiana, AL	Clay-Chalkville
8	**Jeoffrey Pagan**	**DL**	**JR**	**6-4**	**290**	**Asheville, NC**	**Asheville**
91	Darius Paige	DL	FR	6-4	314	Foley, AL	Foley
11	Tana Patrick	LB	SR	6-3	238	Bridgeport, AL	North Jackson
67	Austin Peavler	OL	FR	6-3	290	Weldington, FL	Wellington Community
27	Nick Perry	DB	SR	6-1	212	Prattville, AL	Prattville
18	Reggie Ragland	LB	SO	6-2	259	Madison, AL	Bob Jones
81	Ty Reed	WR/QB	SR	6-1	190	Rocky Hill, CT	Rocky Hill
32	Trey Roberts	RB	SO	6-0	180	Mobile, AL	McGill-Toolen
86	A'Shawn Robinson	DL	FR	6-4	320	Fort Worth, TX	Arlington Heights
44	Matt Sandlin	QB	JR	6-3	207	Tuscaloosa, AL	Tuscaloosa County
79	**Austin Shepherd**	**OL**	**JR**	**6-5**	**315**	**Buford, GA**	**North Gwinnett**
6	Blake Sims	QB	JR	6-0	202	Gainesville, GA	Gainesville
29	Caleb Sims	WR	FR	5-9	181	Hoover, AL	Hoover
24	Geno Smith	DB	SO	6-0	186	Atlanta, GA	St. Pius X
21	Maurice Smith	DB	FR	6-0	180	Sugar Land, TX	Fort Bend Dulles
61	**Anthony Steen**	**OL**	**SR**	**6-3**	**309**	**Clarksdale, MS**	**Lee Academy**
13	ArDarius Stewart	ATH	FR	6-0	190	Fultondale, AL	Fultondale
49	**Ed Stinson**	**DL**	**SR**	**6-4**	**292**	**Homestead, FL**	**South Dade**
3	**Vinnie Sunseri**	**DB**	**JR**	**6-0**	**210**	**Tuscaloosa, AL**	**Northridge**
16	Bradley Sylve	DB	SO	5-11	180	Port Sulphur, LA	South Palquemines
50	Alphonse Taylor	OL	FR	6-5	335	Mobile, AL	Davidson
50	M.K. Taylor	SN	JR	5-10	230	Oxford, AL	Oxford
23	Altee Tenpenny	RB	FR	6-0	207	North Little Rock, AR	North Little Rock
43	Matt Tinney	LB	SR	6-1	247	Hoover, AL	Spain Park
54	Dalvin Tomlinson	DL	FR	6-2	287	McDonaugh, GA	Henry County
84	**Brian Vogler**	**TE**	**JR**	**6-7**	**260**	**Columbus, GA**	**Brookstone**
69	Paul Waldrop	OL	SO	6-4	276	Phenix City, AL	Central
23	Jabriel Washington	DB	SO	5-11	185	Jackson, TN	Trinity Christian Academy
38	Jared Watson	WR	SR	6-0	170	Northport, AL	Tuscaloosa County
33	Jeremy Watson	WR	SR	6-1	184	Northport, AL	Tuscaloosa County
2	DeAndrew White	WR	JR	6-0	190	Houston, TX	North Shore
20	Jarrick Williams	DB	JR	6-1	210	Mobile, AL	Blount
63	Kellen Williams	OL	SR	6-3	302	Lawrenceville, GA	Brookwood
89	Kieran Williams	TE	FR	6-4	236	Lawrenceville, GA	Archer
56	Tim Williams	LB	FR	6-3	235	Baton Rouge, LA	University Lab
36	Brandon Wilson	DB	FR	5-10	203	Elmore, AL	Stanhope Elmore
97	Jay Woods	DL	SO	6-2	275	Frisco, TX	Wakeland
4	**T.J. Yeldon**	**RB**	**SO**	**6-2**	**218**	**Daphne, AL**	**Daphne**

Note: Starters in bold
Note: Table data from "2013 Alabama Crimson Tide Roster" (111)

144

Games

08/31/13 - Alabama (1) at Virginia Tech

Chick-fil-A College Kickoff
Georgia Dome
Atlanta, GA

Team	1	2	3	4	T		Passing	Rushing	Total
Alabama (1)	14	14	7	0	35		110	96	206
Virginia Tech	7	3	0	0	10		59	153	212

On July 7, 2011, officials from both Alabama and Virginia Tech announced the Crimson Tide and the Hokies would meet to open the 2013 season in the Chick-fil-A Kickoff Game at Atlanta. In the game, the offense struggled, but Christion Jones became the first Alabama player to score two non-offensive touchdowns in a single game and led the Crimson Tide to a 35-10 victory at the Georgia Dome. After the Hokies were held to a three-and-out on the first possession of the game, Christion Jones gave Alabama a 7-0 lead with his first touchdown on a 72-yard punt return. After three punts (two by Virginia Tech), T.J. Yeldon extended the Alabama lead to 14-0 with his 2-yard touchdown run that capped an 11-play, 49-yard drive. Virginia Tech responded on the possession that ensued with its only touchdown of the game on a 77-yard Trey Edmunds touchdown run that cut the lead to 14-7.

Early in the second quarter after forcing Alabama to punt, Vinnie Sunseri intercepted a Logan Thomas pass and returned it 38 yards for a touchdown and a 21-7 lead. The teams then again traded punts (two by Virginia Tech) before Kyle Fuller intercepted an A.J. McCarron pass that set up an eventual 29-yard Cody Journell field goal. On the kickoff that ensued, Jones scored his second non-offensive touchdown of the game on a 94-yard return that made the halftime score 28-10.

Neither team scored again until late in the third quarter when McCarron connected with Christion Jones on a 38-yard touchdown pass that made the final score 35-10 as the fourth quarter consisted of all punts (22 total punts in the game). For his three touchdown and 256 all-purpose yardage performance, Christion Jones was recognized as the Walter Camp National Player of the Week.[110]

Passing	C/ATT	YDS	AVG	TD	INT	QBR
AJ McCarron	10/23	110	4.8	1	1	54.5
B. Sims	0/1	0	0	0	0	4.6
Team	10/24	110	4.6	1	1	--

Rushing	CAR	YDS	AVG	TD	LONG
TJ Yeldon	17	75	4.4	1	27
A. Tenpenny	6	24	4	0	20
D. Hart	5	15	3	0	5
B. Sims	2	7	3.5	0	8
J. Fowler	2	1	0.5	0	6
D. Henry	2	-3	-1.5	0	0
AJ McCarron	4	-23	-5.8	0	0
Team	38	96	2.5	1	27

Interceptions	INT	YDS	TD
V. Sunseri	1	38	1

Punting	NO	YDS	AVG	TB	IN 20	LONG
C. Mandell	9	418	46.4	0	0	61

Receiving	REC	YDS	AVG	TD	LONG
Ch. Jones	2	47	23.5	1	38
A. Cooper	4	38	9.5	0	18
D. White	2	14	7	0	12
K. Norwood	1	11	11	0	11
J. Fowler	1	0	0	0	0
Team	10	110	11	1	38

Kick returns	NO	YDS	AVG	LONG	TD
Ch. Jones	2	109	54.5	94	1

Punt returns	NO	YDS	AVG	LONG	TD
Ch. Jones	4	100	25	72	1
D. Hart	2	18	9	18	0
Team	6	118	19.7	72	1

Kicking	FG	PCT	LONG	XP	PTS
C. Foster	0/0	0	0	5/5	5

Note: Table data from "Alabama 35-10 Virginia Tech (Aug 31, 2013) Box Score" (112)

145

09/14/13 - Alabama (1) at Texas A&M (6)

Team	1	2	3	4	T		Passing	Rushing	Total
Alabama (1)	7	21	14	7	**49**		334	234	**568**
Texas A&M (6)	14	0	7	21	**42**		464	164	**628**

Alabama defeated Texas A&M at College Station, 49-42. A&M opened the game with a pair of touchdowns on its first two offensive possessions and took a 14-0 lead. After they received the opening kickoff, they scored on their first possession when Johnny Manziel threw a 1-yard TD pass to Cameron Clear and on their second possession with a 1-yard Malena touchdown run. Bama responded with its first of five consecutive TDs on its next possession and cut the A&M lead to 14-7 when A.J. McCarron threw a 22-yard touchdown pass to Kevin Norwood.

After the Tide defense held the Aggies to a punt, McCarron threw his second touchdown pass of the afternoon on the drive that ensued early in the second quarter on a 44-yard flea flicker pass to DeAndrew White that tied the game at 14-14. On the next drive, Cyrus Jones intercepted a Manziel pass in the end zone for a touchback and an Alabama possession. McCarron then threw his third touchdown pass of the game from 51 yards to Kenny Bell and gave the Crimson Tide their first lead of the game, 21-14. Alabama then closed the first half with an 11-play, 93-yard drive capped with a 4-yard T.J. Yeldon touchdown run for a 28-14 halftime lead.

After the A&M defense forced a punt on the opening possession of the third quarter, Vinnie Sunseri intercepted the first Manziel pass of the second half and returned it 73 yards for a TD and extended the Alabama lead to 35-14. The Aggies responded on the drive that followed with a 14-yard Manziel TD pass to Malcome Kennedy which was followed with a 3-yard Kenyan Drake TD run that made the score 42-21 in favor of the Crimson Tide at the end of the third quarter. In the fourth, the Aggies scored first on a 12-yard Kennedy touchdown reception, and Alabama looked like they were about to respond with a touchdown as well, but Yeldon fumbled at the 2-yard line and it was recovered by A&M. Three plays later, Manziel threw a 95-yard touchdown pass to Mike Evans that cut the Crimson Tide lead to 42-35. Alabama rebounded on their next drive that was capped with a 5-yard McCarron touchdown pass to Jalston Fowler that extended its lead to 49-35. A 4-yard touchdown pass from Manziel to Kennedy in the last 20 seconds made the final score 49-42. Alabama recovered the ensuing onside kick to seal the win.

The 628 yards of total offense by A&M were the most ever surrendered by an Alabama defense in the history of the program. For his career-high 334 yards on 20-of-29 passing and four touchdowns, A.J. McCarron was recognized as the SEC Offensive Player of the Week.[110]

Passing	C/ATT	YDS	AVG	TD	INT	QBR
AJ McCarron	20/29	334	11.5	4	0	96.5

Rushing	CAR	YDS	AVG	TD	LONG
TJ Yeldon	25	149	6	1	14
K. Drake	7	50	7.1	1	16
J. Fowler	4	37	9.3	0	15
Team	1	-2	-2	0	0
Team	37	234	6.3	2	16

Interceptions	INT	YDS	TD
V. Sunseri	1	73	1
Cy. Jones	1	0	0
Team	2	73	1

Kick returns	NO	YDS	AVG	LONG	TD
Ch. Jones	4	83	20.8	35	0

Punting	NO	YDS	AVG	TB	IN 20	LONG
C. Mandell	3	159	53	0	0	60

Receiving	REC	YDS	AVG	TD	LONG
D. White	4	82	20.5	1	44
OJ Howard	3	68	22.7	0	27
K. Norwood	3	52	17.3	1	22
K. Bell	1	51	51	1	51
A. Cooper	2	34	17	0	21
B. Vogler	3	24	8	0	12
Ch. Jones	1	12	12	0	12
J. Fowler	1	5	5	1	5
TJ Yeldon	1	4	4	0	4
K. Drake	1	2	2	0	2
Team	20	334	16.7	4	51

Punt returns	NO	YDS	AVG	LONG	TD
Ch. Jones	1	5	5	5	0

Kicking	FG	PCT	LONG	XP	PTS
C. Foster	0/0	0	0	7/7	7

Note: Table data from "Alabama 49-42 Texas A&M (Sep 14, 2013) Box Score" (113)

09/21/13 - Alabama (1) vs Colorado State

Team	1	2	3	4	T		Passing	Rushing	Total
Colorado State	0	0	6	0	**6**		228	51	**279**
Alabama (1)	7	10	0	14	**31**		272	66	**338**

Although Alabama was a 40-point favorite as they entered the game, the Rams played the Crimson Tide close through the fourth quarter when a pair of late touchdowns gave Alabama a 31-6 victory.

Cade Foster missed a 46-yard field goal to start the game, then three punts followed. Drake was able to score the first touchdown as he was the starting running back in the game due to T.J. Yeldon being suspended for the first quarter by Nick Saban for his unsportsmanlike conduct penalty against A&M the week before. He capped an 8-play, 84-yard drive that that included long reception gains from DeAndrew White (35 yards) and Christion Jones (28 yards) before his 3-yard touchdown run to put Alabama up 7-0. The Tide extended their lead to 14-0 early in the second quarter when Drake blocked a Rams punt that was returned 15 yards by Dillon Lee for a touchdown, and then to 17-0 at halftime when Cade Foster connected on a 46-yard field goal late in the quarter.

After Bernard Blake intercepted an A.J. McCarron pass on Alabama's first possession of the second half, Jared Roberts kicked a 45-yard field goal on the drive that ensured that made the score 17-3. Roberts then scored the Rams' only other points on their next possession with his 31-yard field goal. Early in the fourth quarter, Trey DePriest both forced and recovered a Garrett Grayson fumble. On the next play, Alabama scored on a 30-yard McCarron touchdown pass to DeAndrew White for a 24-6 lead. The Crimson Tide then made the final score 31-6 with a 15-yard Blake Sims touchdown pass to Chris Black. In the game, the Rams were led by former Crimson Tide offensive coordinator Jim McElwain and received $1.5 million to play the game at Bryant-Denny Stadium.[110]

Passing	C/ATT	YDS	AVG	TD	INT	QBR
AJ McCarron	20/26	258	9.9	1	1	62.6
B. Sims	1/1	14	14	1	0	99.9
Team	21/27	272	10.1	2	1	--

Rushing	CAR	YDS	AVG	TD	LONG
TJ Yeldon	7	49	7	0	38
J. Fowler	5	10	2	0	3
A. Tenpenny	2	7	3.5	0	5
D. Henry	1	4	4	0	4
K. Drake	3	3	1	1	3
AJ McCarron	3	-7	-2.3	0	8
Team	21	66	3.1	1	38

Kick returns	NO	YDS	AVG	LONG	TD
Ch. Jones	2	46	23	24	0
D. White	1	14	14	14	0
Team	3	60	20	24	0

Punting	NO	YDS	AVG	TB	IN 20	LONG
C. Mandell	5	225	45	0	0	53

Receiving	REC	YDS	AVG	TD	LONG
Ch. Jones	9	90	10	0	28
D. White	2	65	32.5	1	35
OJ Howard	3	38	12.7	0	23
K. Drake	1	22	22	0	22
K. Bell	2	21	10.5	0	16
C. Black	1	14	14	1	14
B. Vogler	2	13	6.5	0	8
TJ Yeldon	1	9	9	0	9
Team	21	272	13	2	35

Punt returns	NO	YDS	AVG	LONG	TD
Ch. Jones	4	26	6.5	14	0
K. Drake	1	19	19	19	0
D. Lee	1	15	15	15	1
Team	6	60	10	19	1

Kicking	FG	PCT	LONG	XP	PTS
C. Foster	1/2	50	46	3/3	6
A. Griffith	0/0	0	0	1/1	1
Team	1/2	50	46	4/4	7

Note: Table data from "Alabama 31-6 Colorado State (Sep 21, 2013) Box Score" (114)

09/28/13 - Alabama (1) vs Ole Miss (21)

Team	1	2	3	4	T		Passing	Rushing	Total
Ole Miss (21)	0	0	0	0	0		159	46	205
Alabama (1)	3	6	7	9	25		180	254	434

In its first home conference game of the 2013 season, Alabama shut out the Ole Miss Rebels 25-0 in Tuscaloosa. After the Crimson Tide defense forced a punt on the Rebels' first possession, A.J. McCarron led the Alabama offense on an 11-play, 61-yard drive that ended with a 3-0 lead after a 28-yard Cade Foster field goal. Each team played strong defense for the remainder of the quarter with an Eddie Jackson interception of a Laquon Treadwell sideline pass for Alabama being the major play. Alabama then extended its lead in the second quarter to 9-0 at halftime after Foster connected on field goals of 53 and 42 yards.

On the second play of the third quarter, Alabama scored its first touchdown of the game. It came on a 68-yard T.J. Yeldon run and gave the Crimson Tide a 16-0 lead. Each team again traded punts before the Alabama defense stopped an Ole Miss scoring opportunity on a 4th-and-2 play from their own 7-yard line that kept the score 16-0. In the fourth quarter, Cody Mandell had a punt downed at the Rebels' 1-yard line, and on the next play, C.J. Mosley sacked Ole Miss quarterback Bo Wallace for a safety and an 18-0 lead. On the next offensive play for Alabama after they received the safety kick, Kenyan Drake scored on a 50-yard touchdown run that made the final score 25-0. The shutout was the first for the Rebels since their loss against Arkansas in 1998.[110]

Passing	C/ATT	YDS	AVG	TD	INT	QBR
AJ McCarron	25/32	180	5.6	0	1	71.7

Rushing	CAR	YDS	AVG	TD	LONG
TJ Yeldon	17	121	7.1	1	68
K. Drake	12	99	8.3	1	50
D. Henry	2	18	9	0	12
J. Fowler	2	9	4.5	0	5
B. Sims	2	5	2.5	0	6
A. Tenpenny	1	4	4	0	4
AJ McCarron	3	1	0.3	0	4
Team	1	-3	-3	0	0
Team	40	254	6.4	2	68

Interceptions	INT	YDS	TD
E. Jackson	1	0	0

Punting	NO	YDS	AVG	TB	IN 20	LONG
C. Mandell	5	231	46.2	0	0	56

Receiving	REC	YDS	AVG	TD	LONG
Ch. Jones	5	61	12.2	0	17
K. Norwood	5	40	8	0	10
A. Cooper	3	28	9.3	0	12
K. Bell	4	23	5.8	0	7
TJ Yeldon	3	16	5.3	0	13
B. Vogler	1	7	7	0	7
D. White	3	6	2	0	3
K. Drake	1	-1	-1	0	0
Team	25	180	7.2	0	17

Punt returns	NO	YDS	AVG	LONG	TD
Ch. Jones	3	4	1.3	3	0

Kicking	FG	PCT	LONG	XP	PTS
C. Foster	3/3	100	53	2/2	11

Note: Table data from "Alabama 25-0 Ole Miss (Sep 28, 2013) Box Score" (115)

148

10/05/13 - Alabama (1) vs Georgia State

Team	1	2	3	4	T		Passing	Rushing	Total
Georgia State	0	0	3	0	3		160	15	175
Alabama (1)	21	17	7	0	45		296	181	477

In its fifth game of the 2013 season and its second home game, Alabama defeated the Georgia State Panthers 45-3. To begin the game, A.J. McCarron led a 71-yard drive capped off with an 8-yard touchdown pass to Christion Jones for a 7-0 lead. On its first possession, Georgia State gained one first down but was quickly driven back by Alabama's defense who forced a punt. Alabama's next drive saw it lean more on the running game, and T.J. Yeldon scored on a 4-yard touchdown run for a 14-0 Crimson Tide lead. On the kickoff that ensued, Dee Hart forced a fumble that Crimson Tide linebacker Dillon Lee recovered and returned to the Panthers' 10-yard line. On the next play, McCarron completed a touchdown pass to DeAndrew White that increased Alabama's lead to 21-0.

The Crimson Tide scored on their next two possessions as well with McCarron completing touchdown passes to running backs Kenyan Drake and Jalston Fowler. Drake capped a 5-play, 62-yard drive with his 23-yard touchdown catch, and Fowler scored on a 1-yard catch to cap the 8-play, 80-yard drive. With the lead at 35-0 late in the second quarter, Alabama played its reserves for much of the remainder of the game. After the Crimson Tide defense forced another punt from the Panthers, McCarron was replaced by backup quarterback Blake Sims. On his first possession at the helm of Alabama's offense, Sims led the team to the Georgia State 1-yard line, but a pair of false starts forced Alabama to settle for a field goal that increased the lead to 38-0 at halftime.

Georgia State opened the second half with a drive to the Alabama 36-yard line to set up a school record 53-yard field goal by Wil Lutz. Alabama responded with a 10-play, 68-yard march that ended with a 10-yard touchdown pass from Blake Sims to Chris Black for a 45-3 lead. Neither team scored again. After a Panthers punt, Alabama's next drive ended with Crimson Tide's backup kicker Adam Griffith missing a 30-yard field goal. After three punts, Alabama ran the final 1:48 off the clock to seal the 45-3 victory. Before his exit late in the second quarter, McCarron set the Alabama record for passing accuracy at 93.75%, going 15-for-16, and surpassed the previous record of 84.2% held by Ken Stabler.[110]

Passing	C/ATT	YDS	AVG	TD	INT	QBR
AJ McCarron	15/16	166	10.4	4	0	91.4
B. Sims	14/18	130	7.2	1	0	52
Team	29/34	296	8.7	5	0	--

Rushing	CAR	YDS	AVG	TD	LONG
TJ Yeldon	6	51	8.5	1	28
D. Henry	5	50	10	0	17
K. Drake	5	40	8	0	22
J. Fowler	3	23	7.7	0	13
B. Sims	2	10	5	0	6
A. Tenpenny	4	10	2.5	0	5
D. Hart	4	0	0	0	6
Team	1	-3	-3	0	0
Team	29	181	6.2	1	28

Kick returns	NO	YDS	AVG	LONG	TD
H. Jones	2	17	8.5	9	0

Punt returns	NO	YDS	AVG	LONG	TD
D. Hart	1	37	37	37	0

Punting	NO	YDS	AVG	TB	IN 20	LONG
C. Mandell	1	42	42	0	0	42

Receiving	REC	YDS	AVG	TD	LONG
C. Black	6	54	9	1	16
D. White	4	45	11.3	1	13
K. Norwood	3	42	14	0	26
K. Bell	2	37	18.5	0	19
K. Drake	1	23	23	1	23
Ch. Jones	3	22	7.3	1	12
M. Faciane	2	14	7	0	8
OJ Howard	1	13	13	0	13
H. Jones	1	12	12	0	12
K. Freitag	1	11	11	0	11
B. Vogler	1	9	9	0	9
P. Barrineau	1	6	6	0	6
A. Tenpenny	1	4	4	0	4
T. Reed	1	3	3	0	3
J. Fowler	1	1	1	1	1
Team	29	296	10.2	5	26

Kicking	FG	PCT	LONG	XP	PTS
C. Foster	1/1	100	27	5/5	8
A. Griffith	0/1	0	0	1/1	1
Team	1/2	50	27	6/6	9

Note: Table data from "Alabama 45-3 Georgia State (Oct 5, 2013) Box Score" (116)

10/12/13 - Alabama (1) at Kentucky

Team	1	2	3	4	T	Passing	Rushing	Total
Alabama (1)	0	24	10	14	48	369	299	668
Kentucky	0	0	7	0	7	76	94	170

For the first time since 2009, Alabama played Kentucky in Lexington, and Alabama defeated the Wildcats 48-7. Although the Crimson Tide defense opened the game strong and forced Kentucky to punt after they held the Wildcats to a series of three-and-outs on their initial possessions, the Alabama offense did not see the same on-field success. After they were held to a punt on their first possession, fumbles by Kenyan Drake and T.J. Yeldon on the next two Crimson Tide possessions inside the Wildcats' 15-yard line kept the game scoreless in the first quarter.

Alabama took a 3-0 lead early in the second quarter on a 25-yard Cade Foster field goal. On their next possession, the Crimson Tide scored their first touchdown on a 2-play drive that saw a 42-yard Kevin Norwood reception and a 1-yard Drake touchdown run for a 10-0 lead. Alabama then extended its lead to 24-0 at halftime after touchdown runs of 24 yards from Yeldon and one yard from Drake on its final two possessions of the half. Yeldon's capped a 12-play, 88-yard drive, and Drake's capped a 6-play, 70-yard drive that also saw him rush twice for 11 yards each and catch pass for a 24-yard gain.

On their first possession of the second half, the Crimson Tide extended their lead further to 31-0 after Yeldon scored on a 3-yard run that capped a drive that featured a 34-yard Yeldon run and 42-yard Amari Cooper reception. On the Kentucky possession that ensued, the Wildcats scored their only points of the game on a 30-yard Maxwell Smith touchdown pass to Javess Blue that made the score 31-7. The touchdown was the first allowed by the Alabama defense since the Texas A&M game and ended a 14-quarter touchdown-free streak for the Crimson Tide. A 20-yard field goal by Cade Foster then made the score 34-7 as they entered the fourth quarter.

In the fourth quarter, the Crimson Tide scored touchdowns on both of their offensive possessions and made the final score 48-7. The first capped an 80-yard drive and came on a 20-yard A.J. McCarron pass to Kevin Norwood, and the second was a 57-yard drive that ended on a 7-yard Altee Tenpenny touchdown run. Offensively, McCarron threw for 359 yards, and Drake and Yeldon ran for 106 yards and 124 respectively. This marked the first time in team history that Alabama had a 300-yard passer and two 100-yard runners in a single game. For his performance, right guard Anthony Steen was recognized as SEC Offensive Linemen of the Week.[110]

Passing	C/ATT	YDS	AVG	TD	INT	QBR
AJ McCarron	21/35	359	10.3	1	0	80.1
B. Sims	1/1	10	10	0	0	9.8
Team	22/36	369	10.3	1	0	--

Rushing	CAR	YDS	AVG	TD	LONG
TJ Yeldon	16	124	7.8	2	34
K. Drake	14	106	7.6	2	19
A. Tenpenny	5	21	4.2	1	7
D. Henry	3	16	5.3	0	11
Ch. Jones	1	14	14	0	14
D. Hart	2	9	4.5	0	5
AJ McCarron	2	8	4	0	6
B. Sims	1	1	1	0	1
Team	44	299	6.8	5	34

Punting	NO	YDS	AVG	TB	IN 20	LONG
C. Mandell	1	47	47	0	0	47

Receiving	REC	YDS	AVG	TD	LONG
K. Norwood	4	81	20.3	1	42
D. White	4	80	20	0	31
A. Cooper	3	64	21.3	0	42
K. Drake	3	44	14.7	0	24
OJ Howard	2	37	18.5	0	25
TJ Yeldon	2	30	15	0	21
Ch. Jones	3	23	7.7	0	10
P. Barrineau	1	10	10	0	10
Team	22	369	16.8	1	42

Kick returns	NO	YDS	AVG	LONG	TD
Ch. Jones	2	29	24.5	28	0

Punt returns	NO	YDS	AVG	LONG	TD
Ch. Jones	3	52	17.3	30	0

Kicking	FG	PCT	LONG	XP	PTS
C. Foster	2/2	100	25	6'6	12

Note: Table data from "Alabama 48-7 Kentucky (Oct 12, 2013) Box Score" (117)

150

10/19/13 - Alabama (1) vs Arkansas

Team	1	2	3	4	T		Passing	Rushing	Total
Arkansas	0	0	0	0	**0**		91	165	**256**
Alabama (1)	14	14	17	7	**52**		180	352	**532**

In what was the first Bret Bielema coached team to play against the Crimson Tide, Alabama shut out the Arkansas Razorbacks 52-0 at Bryant-Denny Stadium. Alabama took a 7-0 lead on its first possession with a 4-yard A.J. McCarron touchdown pass to Jalston Fowler capping a 12-play, 68-yard drive. The Tide extended their lead to 14-0 on their second possession with a 1-yard Kenyan Drake touchdown run. Later in the first, Ha Ha Clinton-Dix intercepted a Brandon Allen pass in what was his return to the team after he served a two-game suspension for a violation of NCAA rules.

After both teams punted to start the second quarter, Alabama drove 84 yards in five plays highlighted by T.J. Yeldon's 27-yard run and Drake's 46-yard touchdown run to extend Alabama's lead to 21-0. Arkansas responded on its next possession with its longest drive of the game (67 yards). However, they were unable to score any points as Deion Belue blocked a 41-yard Zach Hocker field goal that preserved the shutout. On the next possession, Alabama closed the first half with a 30-yard McCarron touchdown pass to Amari Cooper that made the halftime score 28-0.

On the opening kickoff of the second half, Derrick Henry forced a Keon Hatcher fumble that was recovered by Eddie Jackson for the Crimson Tide. Three plays later, Alabama led 35-0 after McCarron threw a 17-yard touchdown pass to O.J. Howard. After holding the Hogs to another punt, Alabama took the ball 72 yards in eight plays with T.J. Yeldon scoring on a 24-yard touchdown run that extended the Crimson Tide lead to 42-0. The Alabama defense then had their second Allen interception of the evening on the Razorbacks possession that ensued with Cyrus Jones' play at the 47-yard line. With the offensive reserves in the game, Blake Sims led the team to a 45-0 lead after Cade Foster connected on a 48-yard field goal. Henry then made the final score 52-0 in the final minute of play with his 80-yard touchdown run.[110]

Passing	C/ATT	YDS	AVG	TD	INT	QBR
AJ McCarron	15/21	180	8.6	3	0	95.7
B. Sims	0/3	0	0	0	0	2.5
Team	15/24	180	7.5	3	0	--

Rushing	CAR	YDS	AVG	TD	LONG
D. Henry	6	111	18.5	1	80
K. Drake	8	104	13	2	46
TJ Yeldon	12	88	7.3	1	27
D. Hart	4	24	6	0	13
B. Sims	4	17	4.3	0	10
J. Fowler	3	8	2.7	0	5
Team	37	352	9.5	4	80

Kick returns	NO	YDS	AVG	LONG	TD
Ch. Jones	1	32	32	32	0

Punting	NO	YDS	AVG	TB	IN 20	LONG
C. Mandell	1	51	51	0	0	51

Receiving	REC	YDS	AVG	TD	LONG
A. Cooper	3	65	21.7	1	30
TJ Yeldon	4	45	11.3	0	17
Ch. Jones	3	20	6.7	0	9
OJ Howard	1	17	17	1	17
K. Drake	1	11	11	0	11
K. Norwood	1	10	10	0	10
D. White	1	8	8	0	8
J. Fowler	1	4	4	1	4
Team	15	180	12	3	30

Interceptions	INT	YDS	TD
H. Clinton-Dix	1	8	0
Cy. Jones	1	1	0
Team	2	9	0

Kicking	FG	PCT	LONG	XP	PTS
C. Foster	1/1	100	48	6/6	9
A. Griffith	0/0	0	0	1/1	1
Team	1/1	100	48	7/7	10

Note: Table data from "Alabama 52-0 Arkansas (Oct 19, 2013) Box Score" (118)

10/26/13 - Alabama (1) vs Tennessee

Team	1	2	3	4	T		Passing	Rushing	Total
Tennessee	0	0	3	7	10		195	127	322
Alabama (1)	21	14	7	3	45		275	204	479

In its annual rivalry game, Alabama defeated the Tennessee Volunteers 45-10 in Tuscaloosa. The Crimson Tide took a 21-0 lead after they scored touchdowns on all three of their first quarter possessions. The first score only took three plays and came on a 54-yard A.J. McCarron pass to Amari Cooper. Next, T.J. Yeldon then capped a 7-play, 66-yard drive with his touchdown run from a yard out. And then the Tide drove 66 yards in 12 plays as McCarron hit Kevin Norwood for a 22-yard TD strike.

After Alabama extended its lead to 28-0 early in the second quarter on Yeldon's second 1-yard touchdown run of the game, the defense made their first turnover when Deion Belue intercepted a Justin Worley pass. However, the Crimson Tide was unable to capitalize on the drive that ensued after Kenyan Drake fumbled the ball at the goal line which was recovered by the Vols' Cameron Sutton. Looking to score before halftime, Tennessee drove from its 1-yard line to the Alabama 24-yard line before Worley threw his second interception of the game. This time Landon Collins made the play at the 11-yard line and returned it 89 yards for a touchdown and a 35-0 halftime lead.

Tennessee opened the second half with its first points of the game on a 37-yard Michael Palardy field goal that made the score 35-3. The Crimson Tide responded later in the third quarter with an incredible 98-yard drive and Yeldon's third 1-yard touchdown run of the game and extended their lead to 42-3.

In the fourth quarter, the Vols scored their only touchdown on a 3-yard Rajion Neal run and Adam Griffith then kicked his first field goal for the Crimson Tide and made the final score 45-10. For his six-tackle performance and long interception return, Landon Collins was recognized as the SEC Defensive Player of the Week.[110]

Passing	C/ATT	YDS	AVG	TD	INT	QBR
AJ McCarron	19/27	275	10.2	2	0	94
B. Sims	0/1	0	0	0	0	0.6
Team	19/28	275	9.8	2	0	--

Rushing	CAR	YDS	AVG	TD	LONG
K. Drake	14	89	6.4	0	11
TJ Yeldon	15	72	4.8	3	24
Ch. Jones	1	20	20	0	20
D. Henry	3	20	6.7	0	23
D. Hart	2	5	2.5	0	3
AJ McCarron	1	1	1	0	1
Team	1	-3	-3	0	0
Team	37	204	5.5	3	24

Interceptions	INT	YDS	TD
L. Collins	1	89	1
D. Belue	1	28	0
Team	2	117	1

Punting	NO	YDS	AVG	TB	IN 20	LONG
C. Mandell	2	80	40	0	0	42

Receiving	REC	YDS	AVG	TD	LONG
K. Norwood	6	112	18.7	1	34
A. Cooper	5	75	15	1	54
D. White	2	29	14.5	0	18
TJ Yeldon	3	29	9.7	0	23
K. Drake	1	15	15	0	15
K. Bell	1	9	9	0	9
Ch. Jones	1	6	6	0	6
Team	19	275	14.5	2	54

Kick returns	NO	YDS	AVG	LONG	TD
Ch. Jones	2	106	53	57	0
B. Vogler	1	7	7	7	0
Team	3	113	37.7	57	0

Punt returns	NO	YDS	AVG	LONG	TD
Ch. Jones	2	19	9.5	17	0

Kicking	FG	PCT	LONG	XP	PTS
C. Foster	0/0	0	0	5/5	5
A. Griffith	1/1	100	20	1/1	4
Team	1/1	100	48	7/7	9

Note: Table data from "Alabama 45-10 Tennessee (Oct 26, 2013) Box Score" (119)

152

11/09/13 - Alabama (1) vs LSU (13)

Team	1	2	3	4	T		Passing	Rushing	Total
LSU (13)	0	14	3	0	17		241	43	284
Alabama (1)	3	14	7	14	38		179	193	372

In its annual rivalry game, Alabama defeated the LSU Tigers in Tuscaloosa 38-17. After LSU forced an Alabama punt on its first possession, they proceeded to drive 79 yards to the Crimson Tide 3-yard line. On the next play, Tana Patrick forced a J.C. Copeland fumble at the 1-yard line that prevented a Tigers' score. The ball was recovered by Landon Collins and gave the Crimson Tide possession at their 10-yard line. After the LSU defense forced a second punt, their offense had their second turnover of the game when a Zach Mettenberger fumble was recovered by Trey DePriest at the Tigers' 27-yard line. Four plays later, Alabama took a 3-0 lead on a 41-yard Cade Foster field goal.

Early in the second quarter, LSU responded with its first touchdown and a 7-3 lead on a 3-yard Jeremy Hill run. Alabama then retook a 10-7 lead on the next possession when O.J. Howard took a short slant pass from A.J. McCarron 52 yards for a touchdown. After the Crimson Tide defense forced a punt, their offense extended their lead to 17-7 on a 9-yard McCarron pass to Kevin Norwood. LSU then made the halftime score 17-14 after Mettenberger threw a 6-yard touchdown pass to Travin Dural.

After the Tigers tied the game at 17-17 on a 41-yard Colby Delahoussaye field goal to open the second half, the Crimson Tide went on their first of three consecutive touchdown drives. Their first touchdown came on a 4-yard T.J. Yeldon run that capped a 14-play, 79-yard drive that included a successful fake punt. On their next possession, Yeldon scored on a 1-yard touchdown run that extended Alabama's lead to 31-17. Odell Beckham Jr. then returned the kickoff that ensued 82 yards to the Crimson Tide 18-yard line. However, the offense was unable to capitalize on the good field position as the Alabama defense forced a turnover on downs. The Crimson Tide then drove 78 yards in eight plays, capping the drive with a 3-yard McCarron touchdown pass to Jalston Fowler that made the score 38-17. The Alabama defense then closed the game with three consecutive sacks of Mettenberger, winning 38-17. For his 12-tackle performance, C.J. Mosley was recognized as both the SEC Defensive Player of the Week and as the Lott IMPACT National Player of the Week.[110]

Passing	C/ATT	YDS	AVG	TD	INT	QBR
AJ McCarron	14/20	179	9	3	0	90

Rushing	CAR	YDS	AVG	TD	LONG
TJ Yeldon	25	133	5.3	2	22
K. Drake	10	65	6.5	0	16
J. Williams	1	6	6	0	6
AJ McCarron	3	-2	-0.7	0	4
Team	3	-9	-3	0	0
Team	42	193	4.6	2	22

Kicking	FG	PCT	LONG	XP	PTS
C. Foster	1/1	100	41	5/5	8

Punting	NO	YDS	AVG	TB	IN 20	LONG
C. Mandell	2	87	43.5	0	0	44

Receiving	REC	YDS	AVG	TD	LONG
OJ Howard	1	52	52	1	52
A. Cooper	3	46	15.3	0	21
K. Norwood	4	38	9.5	1	12
D. White	2	17	8.5	0	13
TJ Yeldon	1	13	13	0	13
K. Drake	1	10	10	0	10
J. Fowler	1	3	3	1	3
Ch. Jones	1	0	0	0	0
Team	14	179	12.8	3	52

Kick returns	NO	YDS	AVG	LONG	TD
. D. White	2	42	21	22	0
Ch. Jones	2	41	20.5	21	0
Team	4	83	20.8	22	0

Note: Table data from "Alabama 38-17 LSU (Nov 9, 2013) Box Score" (120)

153

11/16/13 - Alabama (1) at Mississippi State

Team	1	2	3	4	T		Passing	Rushing	Total
Alabama (1)	3	7	7	3	**20**		187	196	**383**
Mississippi State	0	0	7	0	**7**		144	53	**197**

In its annual rivalry game, Alabama defeated the Mississippi State Bulldogs 20-7 in Starkville despite having four turnovers. Alabama won the coin toss and elected to receive the ball to start the game. They scored on a 33-yard Cade Foster field goal for an early 3-0 lead. Both teams then traded punts for the next six combined possessions before the Bulldogs missed a 23-yard field goal midway through the second quarter. On the Alabama drive that ensued, the Crimson Tide had their first of four turnovers on a Taveze Calhoun interception of an A.J. McCarron pass. Alabama rebounded on its next possession going 78 yards in six plays ending with an 18-yard touchdown pass from McCarron to Brian Vogler that made the halftime score 10-0.

After the Crimson Tide defense forced a Mississippi State punt to open the third quarter, Kendrick Market forced a T.J. Yeldon fumble that was recovered by Beniquez Brown at the State 49-yard line. The Bulldogs scored on their drive that ensued after Charles Siddoway recovered a Tyler Russell fumble (caused by C.J. Mosley) in the end zone that made the score 10-7. Alabama responded on its next possession with an 11-yard McCarron touchdown pass to Kevin Norwood capping a 9-play, 77-yard drive that extended its lead to 17-7. After the Mississippi State possession that followed, Ha Ha Clinton-Dix intercepted a Tyler Russell pass. Cade Foster then made the score 20-7 with his 35-yard field goal early in the fourth quarter. The Crimson Tide then had a difficult time closing the game as turnovers occurred on consecutive possessions on a McCarron interception and a Kenyan Drake fumble. The Bulldogs went for it on fourth down on all three of their final possessions, and Alabama stopped them each time bringing the final to 20-7.[110]

Passing	C/ATT	YDS	AVG	TD	INT	QBR
AJ McCarron	18/32	187	5.8	2	2	70

Rushing	CAR	YDS	AVG	TD	LONG
TJ Yeldon	24	160	6.7	0	50
K. Drake	4	28	7	0	21
AJ McCarron	3	12	4	0	10
Team	2	-4	-2	0	0
Team	33	196	5.9	0	50

Interceptions	INT	YDS	TD
H. Clinton-Dix	1	16	0

Kicking	FG	PCT	LONG	XP	PTS
C. Foster	2/2	100	35	2/2	8

Punting	NO	YDS	AVG	TB	IN 20	LONG
C. Mandell	4	220	55	0	0	63

Receiving	REC	YDS	AVG	TD	LONG
A. Cooper	4	45	11.3	0	19
Ch. Jones	5	37	7.4	0	26
D. White	2	28	14	0	15
K. Norwood	2	23	11.5	1	12
OJ Howard	1	21	21	0	21
B. Vogler	1	18	18	1	18
K. Drake	2	9	4.5	0	8
TJ Yeldon	1	6	6	0	6
Team	18	187	10.4	2	26

Punt returns	NO	YDS	AVG	LONG	TD
Ch. Jones	1	18	18	18	0

Punt returns	NO	YDS	AVG	LONG	TD
Ch. Jones	1	3	3	3	0

Note: Table data from "Alabama 20-7 Mississippi State (Nov 16, 2013) Box Score" (121)

11/23/13 - Alabama (1) vs Chattanooga

Team	1	2	3	4	T		Passing	Rushing	Total
Chattanooga	0	0	0	0	**0**		82	93	**175**
Alabama (1)	7	21	14	7	**49**		184	251	**435**

In the final non-conference game the 2013 season, Alabama shut out the Chattanooga Mocs of the Southern Conference 49-0 on senior day at Bryant-Denny Stadium. After the Alabama defense forced a Mocs three-and-out on the first possession of the game, Christion Jones fumbled the punt that ensued with Sema'je Kendall for Chattanooga making the recovery at the Alabama 34-yard line. The Alabama defense once again held strong, and Trey DePriest ended the possession with his interception at the 17-yard line on fourth down. The Crimson Tide offense then took the ball 83 yards on their first possession with Kenyan Drake making the score 7-0 on his 13-yard touchdown run.

Derrick Henry scored Alabama's next touchdown early in the second quarter on a 5-yard run that extended their lead to 14-0. On the next Chattanooga possession, Alabama again forced a punt, but this time Jones returned it 75 yards for a touchdown and a 21-0 lead. The Mocs responded with their best drive of the game, however, A'Shawn Robinson blocked a 48-yard Nick Pollard field goal attempt that kept Chattanooga scoreless. The Crimson Tide then closed the half with a 28-yard A.J. McCarron touchdown pass to Kevin Norwood that made the halftime score 28-0.

Alabama continued its scoring into the third quarter with touchdowns on its first two possessions of the half. The first came on a 38-yard McCarron pass to Amari Cooper on a drive that also saw McCarron complete a pass to his brother, Corey McCarron. The second came on a 31-yard Chris Black run that made the score 42-0. With the Crimson Tide significantly up, mostly backup players completed the fourth quarter. After a long drive stalled at the Mocs' 23-yard line, Eddie Jackson returned a C.J. Board fumble caused by Jonathan Allen to the Chattanooga 6-yard line. On the next play, Dee Hart made the final score 49-0 with his 6-yard touchdown run.[110]

Passing	C/ATT	YDS	AVG	TD	INT	QBR
AJ McCarron	13/16	171	10.7	2	0	90.6
B. Sims	2/4	13	3.3	0	0	12.8
Team	**15/20**	**184**	**9.2**	**2**	**0**	--

Rushing	CAR	YDS	AVG	TD	LONG
K. Drake	11	77	7	1	19
D. Henry	6	66	11	1	27
C. Black	1	31	31	1	31
D. Hart	5	25	5	1	6
B. Sims	4	21	5.3	0	11
A. Tenpenny	4	16	4	0	7
AJ McCarron	1	15	15	0	15
Team	**32**	**251**	**7.8**	**4**	**31**

Interceptions	INT	YDS	TD
T. DePriest	1	0	0

Kick returns	NO	YDS	AVG	LONG	TD
X. Dickson	1	14	14	14	0

Receiving	REC	YDS	AVG	TD	LONG
K. Norwood	4	84	21	1	50
A. Cooper	3	42	14	1	38
Ch. Jones	2	24	12	0	15
K. Bell	2	13	6.5	0	11
C. Black	1	11	11	0	11
D. White	1	8	8	0	8
C. McCarron	1	3	3	0	3
J. Fowler	1	-1	-1	0	-1
Team	**15**	**184**	**12.3**	**2**	**50**

Punt returns	NO	YDS	AVG	LONG	TD
Ch. Jones	2	75	37.5	75	1
D. Hart	1	3	3	3	0
K. Bell	1	0	0	0	0
Team	**4**	**78**	**19.5**	**75**	**1**

Kicking	FG	PCT	LONG	XP	PTS
C. Foster	0/0	0	0	6/6	6
A. Griffith	0/0	0	0	1/1	1
Team	**0/0**	**0**	**0**	**7/7**	**7**

Note: Table data from "Alabama 49-0 Chattanooga (Nov 23, 2013) Box Score" (122)

11/30/13 - Alabama (1) at Auburn (4)

Team	1	2	3	4	T	Passing	Rushing	Total
Alabama (1)	0	21	0	7	28	277	218	495
Auburn (4)	7	7	7	13	34	97	296	393

In the final regular season game in the 2013 season, Alabama lost 34-28 to the Auburn Tigers after Chris Davis returned a missed Adam Griffith field goal 109 yards for the game-winning score with no time left on the clock in a game since dubbed the "Kick Six". Going into the game, Alabama had been ranked atop the polls all season while Auburn was fourth in all major polls, making this the highest combined ranking ever in the Iron Bowl. With the victory, Auburn won the SEC West division title and prevented Alabama from potentially playing for its third consecutive national championship.

After Alabama failed to score on the first drive when Cade Foster missed a 44-yard field goal attempt, Auburn took a 7-0 lead on its second offensive possession on a 45-yard Nick Marshall touchdown run. The Crimson Tide responded early in the second quarter and tied the game at 7-7 on a 3-yard A.J. McCarron touchdown pass to Jalston Fowler. Alabama's Landon Collins both forced and recovered a Tre Mason fumble on the Tigers' possession that ensued. Four plays later, Alabama took a 14-7 lead on a 20-yard McCarron pass to Kevin Norwood. The Crimson Tide then went ahead 21-7 on a 1-yard T.J. Yeldon touchdown run, but Auburn responded with a late Mason touchdown run that made the halftime score 21-14, Bama on top.

The Tigers tied the score at 21-21 on their first possession of the third quarter when Marshall threw a 13-yard touchdown pass to C.J. Uzomah. Early in the fourth quarter, Foster missed a 33-yard field goal attempt, but on their next possession, McCarron connected with Amari Cooper for a 99-yard touchdown reception and a 28-21 lead. Late in the game, Ryan Smith blocked a 44-yard Foster field goal attempt, and on the Auburn possession that ensued, Marshall threw a 39-yard touchdown pass to Sammie Coates that tied the game at 28-28.

With seven seconds left in regulation and the score tied, Yeldon made a long run as time expired. The play was reviewed from the replay booth, and one second was put back on the clock after the referees determined Yeldon had stepped out of bounds just before time expired. Alabama then opted to attempt a game-winning 57-yard field goal but chose freshman kicker Adam Griffith over Foster due to Foster's woes that day. Alabama failed its fourth field goal of the day with Griffith's attempt falling short, but Auburn's Chris Davis fielded it nine yards deep in his own end zone, and with no Crimson Tide skill players in his path (the field goal unit was made up almost entirely of offensive linemen), sprinted for a 109-yard touchdown return and a 34-28 Auburn win. Under NCAA scoring rules, Davis was only credited for 100 yards on the play.[110]

Passing	C/ATT	YDS	AVG	TD	INT	QBR
AJ McCarron	17/29	277	9.6	3	0	91.2

Rushing	CAR	YDS	AVG	TD	LONG
TJ Yeldon	26	141	5.4	1	31
K. Drake	4	33	8.3	0	11
A. Cooper	1	28	28	0	28
AJ McCarron	4	16	4	0	10
Team	35	218	6.2	1	31

Kicking	FG	PCT	LONG	XP	PTS
C. Foster	0/3	0	0	4/4	4

Punting	NO	YDS	AVG	TB	IN 20	LONG
C. Mandell	4	220	55	0	0	63

Receiving	REC	YDS	AVG	TD	LONG
A. Cooper	6	178	29.7	1	99
K. Norwood	3	45	15	1	20
OJ Howard	2	23	11.5	0	12
D. White	2	13	6.5	0	9
TJ Yeldon	2	8	4	0	9
Ch. Jones	1	7	7	0	7
J. Fowler	1	3	3	1	3
Team	17	277	16.3	3	99

Kick returns	NO	YDS	AVG	LONG	TD
Ch. Jones	2	43	21.5	24	0
K. Bell	1	11	11	11	0
Team	3	54	18	24	0

Punt returns	NO	YDS	AVG	LONG	TD
Ch. Jones	1	19	19	19	0

Note: Table data from "Alabama 28-34 Auburn (Nov 30, 2013) Box Score" (123)

156

01/02/14 - Alabama (3) vs Oklahoma (11)

Team	1	2	3	4	T		Passing	Rushing	Total
Oklahoma (11)	14	17	0	14	45		348	81	429
Alabama (3)	10	7	7	7	31		387	129	516

On December 9th, Alabama was selected as an at-large BCS participant to play in the Sugar Bowl against Oklahoma. Against the Sooners, the Crimson Tide was upset 45-31 against an upstart Oklahoma squad. Alabama opened the game with a 4- play, 75-yard touchdown drive that saw A.J. McCarron complete a 53-yard pass to Amari Cooper and T.J. Yeldon score on a 1-yard run for a 7-0 lead. On the first Oklahoma possession of the game, Landon Collins intercepted a Trevor Knight pass that halted the Sooners' drive. However, on the Alabama play that ensued, McCarron threw an interception to Gabe Lynn and Oklahoma responded on its next play with a 45-yard Knight pass to Lacoltan Bester that tied the game at 7-7. Alabama retook a 10-7 lead on a 27-yard Cade Foster field goal, but the Sooners again responded and took a 14-10 lead at the end of the first quarter when Knight threw an 8-yard touchdown pass to Jalen Saunders.

Early in the second quarter, McCarron threw a 67-yard touchdown pass to DeAndrew White for a 17-14 lead. However, this would be the last time the Crimson Tide led in the game as a pair of turnovers by the Crimson Tide later in the quarter directly resulted in a pair of Oklahoma touchdowns. After the Sooners tied the game with a 47-yard Michael Hunnicutt field goal, Geneo Grissom recovered a Yeldon fumble at their 8-yard line and returned it to the 34. Seven plays later, Knight threw a 43-yard touchdown pass to Saunders for a 24-17 Oklahoma lead. On the next offensive series, McCarron threw his second interception of the game to Zack Sanchez who returned it to the Alabama 13-yard line. On the next play, Sterling Shepard extended the Sooners' lead to 31-17 with his 13-yard touchdown run. The Crimson Tide was able to get into field goal range late, but Foster missed an attempt from 32 yards as time expired in the first half.

After the teams traded punts to open the second half, Derrick Henry made the score 31-24 with his 43-yard touchdown run for the only points scored in the third quarter. Oklahoma scored on its opening possession of the fourth quarter on a 9-yard Knight touchdown pass to Shepard that capped an 8-play drive. Later in the quarter, Henry scored his second long touchdown of the game for Alabama on a 61-yard reception from McCarron that cut the Oklahoma lead to 38-31. However, the Sooners closed the game with a long drive that ran down the clock and in the final minute, an Eric Striker sack of McCarron caused a fumble that Grissom recovered and returned eight yards for a touchdown and made the final score 45-31.[110]

Passing	C/ATT	YDS	AVG	TD	INT	QBR
AJ McCarron	19/30	387	12.9	2	2	55.7

Rushing	CAR	YDS	AVG	TD	LONG
D. Henry	8	100	12.5	1	43
TJ Yeldon	17	72	4.2	1	16
AJ McCarron	10	-43	-4.3	0	4
Team	35	129	3.7	2	43

Interceptions	INT	YDS	TD
L. Collins	1	0	0

Punting	NO	YDS	AVG	TB	IN 20	LONG
C. Mandell	4	174	43.5	0	0	48

Receiving	REC	YDS	AVG	TD	LONG
D. White	3	139	46.3	1	67
A. Cooper	9	121	13.4	0	53
D. Henry	1	61	61	1	61
K. Norwood	2	30	15	0	21
TJ Yeldon	2	23	11.5	0	19
K. Bell	2	13	6.5	0	7
Team	19	387	20.4	2	67

Kick returns	NO	YDS	AVG	LONG	TD
Ch. Jones	4	104	26	35	0

Punt returns	NO	YDS	AVG	LONG	TD
Ch. Jones	2	18	9	9	0

Kicking	FG	PCT	LONG	XP	PTS
C. Foster	1/2	50	27	4/4	7

Note: Table data from "Alabama 45-31 Oklahoma (Jan 2, 2014) Box Score" (124)

Season Stats

Record	11-2	9th of 125
SEC Record	7-1	
Rank	7	
Points for	496	
Points against	181	
Points/game	38.2	17th of 125
Opp points/game	13.9	4th of 125
SOS[7]	3.76	35th of 125

Team stats (averages per game)

Split	G	Passing						Rushing				Total Offense		
		Cmp	Att	Pct	Yds	TD	Att	Yds	Avg	TD	Plays	Yds	Avg
Offense	13	18.8	28.1	66.8	248.5	2.3	35.5	205.6	5.8	2.2	63.5	454.1	7.1
Defense	13	15.2	27.3	55.5	180.3	1	32	106.2	3.3	0.6	59.3	286.5	4.8
Difference		3.6	0.8	11.3	68.2	1.3	3.5	99.4	2.5	1.6	4.2	167.6	2.3

Split	First Downs				Penalties		Turnovers		
	Pass	Rush	Pen	Tot	No.	Yds	Fum	Int	Tot
Offense	10.8	10.9	1.5	23.2	4.8	40	0.8	0.5	1.3
Defense	7.8	6	1.2	14.9	5.5	43.1	0.6	0.8	1.5
Difference	3	4.9	0.3	8.3	-0.7	-3.1	0.2	-0.3	-0.2

Passing

Rk	Player	G	Passing								
			Cmp	Att	Pct	Yds	Y/A	AY/A	TD	Int	Rate
1	A.J. McCarron	13	226	336	67.3	3063	9.1	9.8	28	7	167.2
2	Blake Sims	8	18	29	62.1	167	5.8	7.1	2	0	133.2

Rushing and receiving

Rk	Player	G	Rushing					Receiving				Scrimmage			
			Att	Yds	Avg	TD	Rec	Yds	Avg	TD	Plays	Yds	Avg	TD
1	T.J. Yeldon	12	207	1235	6	14	20	183	9.2	0	227	1418	6.2	14
2	Kenyan Drake	11	92	694	7.5	8	12	135	11.3	1	104	829	8	9
3	Derrick Henry	10	35	382	10.9	3	1	61	61	1	36	443	12.3	4
4	A.J. McCarron	13	34	-22	-0.6	0					34	-22	-0.6	0
5	Altee Tenpenny	6	22	82	3.7	1	1	4	4	0	23	86	3.7	1
6	Dee Hart	9	22	78	3.5	1					22	78	3.5	1
7	Jalston Fowler	9	20	88	4.4	0	7	15	2.1	5	27	103	3.8	5
8	Blake Sims	8	15	61	4.1	0					15	61	4.1	0
9	Christion Jones	13	2	34	17	0	36	349	9.7	2	38	383	10.1	2
10	Chris Black	3	1	31	31	1	8	79	9.9	2	9	110	12.2	3
11	Amari Cooper	11	1	28	28	0	45	736	16.4	4	46	764	16.6	4
12	Jarrick Williams	12	1	6	6	0					1	6	6	0
13	Kevin Norwood	12					38	568	14.9	7	38	568	14.9	7
14	Deandrew White	13					32	534	16.7	4	32	534	16.7	4
15	O.J. Howard	10					14	269	19.2	2	14	269	19.2	2
16	Kenny Bell	8					14	167	11.9	1	14	167	11.9	1
17	Brian Vogler	6					8	71	8.9	1	8	71	8.9	1
18	Parker Barrineau	2					2	16	8	0	2	16	8	0
19	Malcolm Faciane	2					2	14	7	0	2	14	7	0
20	Harrison Jones	1					1	12	12	0	1	12	12	0
21	Kurt Freitag	1					1	11	11	0	1	11	11	0
22	Corey McCarron	1					1	3	3	0	1	3	3	0
23	Ty Reed	1					1	3	3	0	1	3	3	0

Defense and fumbles

Rk	Player	G	Solo	Ast	Tot	Loss	Sk	Int	Yds	Avg	TD	PD	FR	FF
			Tackles					**Def Int**					**Fumbles**	
1	C.J. Mosley	13	62	44	106	9	0					5		1
2	Landon Collins	13	54	14	68	4	0	2	89	44.5	1	6	2	2
3	Trey DePriest	12	30	31	61	7.5	2	1	0	0	0	1	2	2
4	Ha Ha Clinton-Dix	11	30	20	50	3.5	0	2	24	12	0	4		
5	Ed Stinson	13	19	22	41	2	1.5					1	1	0
6	Jarrick Williams	12	26	14	40	2	1					2		
7	A'Shawn Robinson	12	17	21	38	8	5.5							
8	Adrian Hubbard	13	20	13	33	5.5	3					3		
9	Jeoffrey Pagan	12	17	16	33	3.5	2							
10	Denzel Devall	13	14	15	29	5	3					1		2
11	Cyrus Jones	9	18	7	25	1.5	1	2	1	0.5	0	5		
12	Brandon Ivory	12	9	15	24	1.5	0					1		
13	Vinnie Sunseri	6	14	6	20	1	0	2	111	55.5	2	4		
14	Deion Belue	8	17	3	20	1	0	1	28	28	0	3		
15	Eddie Jackson	6	16	3	19	1	0	1	0	0	0	2	1	0
16	John Fulton	8	10	9	19	2	0					1		
17	Reggie Ragland	10	6	11	17	0.5	0							
18	Dillon Lee	10	7	9	16	0	0						1	0
19	Jonathan Allen	7	10	5	15	3	0.5							1
20	Darren Lake	7	9	6	15	0	0							
21	Xzavier Dickson	10	6	7	13	2	1							
22	Maurice Smith	6	5	8	13	0.5	0					3		
23	Tana Patrick	7	2	10	12	0	0					1		1
24	Reuben Foster	6	4	8	12	1	0							
25	Geno Smith	7	7	3	10	1	0					3		
26	Bradley Sylve	5	8	2	10	0	0					2		
27	Dee Hart	9	7	2	9	0	0							1
28	Christion Jones	13	7	2	9	0	0							1
29	Ryan Anderson	3	4	1	5	1.5	1.5							
30	Altee Tenpenny	6	2	3	5	0	0							
31	Kenyan Drake	11	3	1	4	0	0							
32	Korren Kirven	3	2	2	4	0	0							
33	Anthony Orr	3	1	3	4	0.5	0							
34	Dalvin Tomlinson	1	2	2	4	0	0							
35	Deandrew White	13	4	0	4	0	0							
36	Derrick Henry	10	2	1	3	0	0							1
37	Luke Del Rio	1	1	2	3	0	0							
38	Lamichael Fanning	3	0	3	3	0	0							
39	Tim Williams	3	2	1	3	1	0							
40	O.J. Howard	10	2	0	2	0	0							
41	Dee Liner	1	1	1	2	0	0							
42	Kenny Bell	8	1	0	1	0	0							
43	Amari Cooper	11	1	0	1	0	0							
44	Cody Mandell	12	1	0	1	0	0							
45	Jabriel Washington	1	0	1	1	0	0							

Kick and punt returns

Rk	Player	G	Kick Ret				Punt Ret			
			Ret	Yds	Avg	TD	Ret	Yds	Avg	TD
1	Christion Jones	13	22	631	28.7	1	23	321	14	2
2	Deandrew White	13	3	56	18.7	0				
3	Harrison Jones	1	2	17	8.5	0				
4	Xzavier Dickson	10	1	14	14	0				
5	Kenny Bell	8	1	11	11	0	1	0	0	0
6	Brian Vogler	6	1	7	7	0				
7	Dee Hart	9					4	58	14.5	0
8	Kenyan Drake	11					1	19	19	0
9	Dillon Lee	10						15		1

Kicking and punting

Rk	Player	G	Kicking							Punting		
			XPM	XPA	XP%	FGM	FGA	FG%	Pts	Punts	Yds	Avg
1	Cade Foster	13	60	60	100	12	17	70.6	96			
2	Adam Griffith	6	5	5	100	1	3	33.3	8			
3	Cody Mandell	12								39	1836	47.1

Scoring

Rk	Player	G	Touchdowns							Kicking				Pts
			Rush	Rec	Int	FR	PR	KR	Tot	XPM	FGM	2PM	Sfty	
1	Cade Foster	13								60	12			96
2	T.J. Yeldon	12	14						14					84
3	Kenyan Drake	11	8	1					9					54
4	Kevin Norwood	12		7					7					42
5	Christion Jones	13		2			2	1	5					30
6	Jalston Fowler	9		5					5					30
7	Amari Cooper	11		4					4					24
8	Deandrew White	13		4					4					24
9	Derrick Henry	10	3	1					4					24
10	Chris Black	3	1	2					3					18
11	Vinnie Sunseri	6			2				2					12
12	O.J. Howard	10		2					2					12
13	Adam Griffith	6								5	1			8
14	Kenny Bell	8		1					1					6
15	Dillon Lee	10					1		1					6
16	Dee Hart	9	1						1					6
17	Landon Collins	13			1				1					6
18	Brian Vogler	6		1					1					6
19	Altee Tenpenny	6	1						1					6

Stats include bowl games
Note: Table data from "2013 Alabama Crimson Tide Stats" (7)

Awards and honors

Name	Award	Type
A.J. McCarron	Permanent Team Captain	Team
C.J. Mosley	Permanent Team Captain	Team
Kevin Norwood	Permanent Team Captain	Team
C.J. Mosley	MVP	Team
A.J. McCarron	Offensive Player of the Year	Team
T.J. Yeldon	Offensive Player of the Year	Team
Ha Ha Clinton-Dix	Defensive Player of the Year	Team
C.J. Mosley	Defensive Player of the Year	Team
C.J. Mosley	Co-Defensive Player of the Year	SEC
Christion Jones	Special Teams Player of the Year	SEC
Cyrus Kouandjio	AP All-SEC First Team	SEC
Cody Mandell	AP All-SEC First Team	SEC
C.J. Mosley	AP All-SEC First Team	SEC
Anthony Steen	AP All-SEC First Team	SEC
Ha Ha Clinton-Dix	AP All-SEC Second Team	SEC
Landon Collins	AP All-SEC Second Team	SEC
Trey DePriest	AP All-SEC Second Team	SEC
Christion Jones	AP All-SEC Second Team	SEC
T.J. Yeldon	AP All-SEC Second Team	SEC
Brandon Ivory	AP All-SEC Honorable Mention Team	SEC
A.J. McCarron	AP All-SEC Honorable Mention Team	SEC
Vinnie Sunseri	AP All-SEC Honorable Mention Team	SEC
Ha Ha Clinton-Dix	Coaches' All-SEC First Team	SEC
Barrett Jones	Coaches' All-SEC First Team	SEC
Cyrus Kouandjio	Coaches' All-SEC First Team	SEC
C.J. Mosley	Coaches' All-SEC First Team	SEC
T.J. Yeldon	Coaches' All-SEC First Team	SEC
Cody Mandell	Coaches' All-SEC Second Team	SEC
A.J. McCarron	Coaches' All-SEC Second Team	SEC
Anthony Steen	Coaches' All-SEC Second Team	SEC
Ed Stinson	Coaches' All-SEC Second Team	SEC
A'Shawn Robinson	Freshman All SEC Team	SEC
Ha Ha Clinton-Dix	AFCA All-America Team	National
Cyrus Kouandjio	AFCA All-America Team	National

Name	Award	Type
A.J. McCarron	AFCA All-America Team	National
C.J. Mosley	AFCA All-America Team	National
Ha Ha Clinton-Dix	AP All-America Second Team	National
Cyrus Kouandjio	AP All-America First Team	National
C.J. Mosley	AP All-America First Team	National
A.J. McCarron	AP All-America Second Team	National
C.J. Mosley	Bronko Nagurski Trophy Finalist	National
C.J. Mosley	Butkus Award	National
C.J. Mosley	Chuck Bednarik Award Finalist	National
Ha Ha Clinton-Dix	Consensus All-American	National
Cyrus Kouandjio	Consensus All-American	National
C.J. Mosley	Consensus All-American	National
A.J. McCarron	Davey O'Brien Award Finalist	National
Ha Ha Clinton-Dix	FWAA All-America First Team	National
Cyrus Kouandjio	FWAA All-America First Team	National
C.J. Mosley	FWAA All-America First Team	National
A.J. McCarron	Heisman Trophy Finalist	National
A.J McCarron	Johnny Unitas Golden Arm Award	National
C.J. Mosley	Lombardi Award Finalist	National
A.J. McCarron	Maxwell Award	National
Ha Ha Clinton-Dix	Sporting News (TSN) All-America Team	National
C.J. Mosley	Sporting News (TSN) All-America Team	National
C.J. Mosley	Unanimous All-American	National
Cyrus Kouandjio	Walter Camp All-America First Team	National
A.J. McCarron	Walter Camp All-America First Team	National
C.J. Mosley	Walter Camp All-America First Team	National
Kenny Bell	College All-Star Bowl	All-Star Team
John Fulton	College All-Star Bowl	All-Star Team
Adrian Hubbard	Senior Bowl	All-Star Team
Cody Mandell	Senior Bowl	All-Star Team
Kevin Norwood	Senior Bowl	All-Star Team
Ed Stinson	Senior Bowl	All-Star Team

NFL

Season	Year drafted	Round	Pick	Overall	Player	Position	Team
2013	2014	1	17	17	C.J. Mosley	LB	Baltimore Ravens
2013	2014	1	21	21	Ha Ha Clinton-Dix	S	Green Bay Packers
2013	2014	2	12	44	Cyrus Kouandjio	OT	Buffalo Bills
2013	2014	4	23	123	Kevin Norwood	WR	Seattle Seahawks
2013	2014	5	20	160	Ed Stinson	DE	Arizona Cardinals
2013	2014	5	24	164	A.J. McCarron	QB	Cincinnati Bengals
2013	2014	5	27	167	Vinnie Sunseri	S	New Orleans Saints
2013	2014	6	1	177	Jeoffrey Pagan	DE	Houston Texans

Note: Table data from "2013 Alabama Crimson Tide football team" (110)

2014

Overall

Record	12-2
SEC Record	8-1
Rank	4
Points for	517
Points against	258
Points/game	36.9
Opp points/game	18.4
SOS[8]	7.26

Everybody's got such a high expectation of what our team should be. I was just happy to see our players be happy about playing the game and winning. It really, sort of, if you want to know the truth about it, pisses me off when I talk to people that have this expectation like they are disappointed that we only won the game 14-13 and in the way we played. Really, that's frustrating. You want to talk about something that's frustrating, that's frustrating, to me, for our players, who play with a lot of heart in the game. -Nick Saban

Games

Date	Bama Rank		Opp Rank	Opponent	Bama	Opp	Result	SEC
08/30/14	2	N		West Virginia	33	23	W	
09/06/14	2	vs		Florida Atlantic	41	0	W	
09/13/14	3	vs		Southern Mississippi	52	12	W	
09/20/14	3	vs		Florida	42	21	W	W
10/04/14	3	@	11	Ole Miss	17	23	L	L
10/11/14	7	@		Arkansas	14	13	W	W
10/18/14	7	vs	21	Texas A&M	59	0	W	W
10/25/14	4	@		Tennessee	34	20	W	W
11/08/14	5	@	16	LSU	20	13	W	W
11/15/14	5	vs	1	Mississippi State	25	20	W	W
11/22/14	1	vs		Western Carolina	48	14	W	
11/29/14	1	vs	15	Auburn	55	44	W	W
12/06/14	1	N	16	Missouri	42	13	W	W
01/01/15	1	N	4	Ohio State	35	42	L	

Coaches

Name	Position	Year
Nick Saban	Head Coach	8
Burton Burns	Associate Head Coach / Running Backs	8
Scott Cochran	Strength and Conditioning	8
Mario Cristobal	Offensive Line / Recruiting Coordinator	2
Bo Davis	Defensive Line	1 (5th overall)
Lane Kiffin	Offensive Coordinator / Quarterbacks	1
Billy Napier	Wide Receivers	2
Kirby Smart	Defensive Coordinator	8
Kevin Steele	Linebackers	1 (3rd overall)
Lance Thompson	Outside Linebackers	3 (5th overall)
Bobby Williams	Tight Ends / Special Teams	7

Recruits

Name	Pos	Pos Rank	Scout	Rivals	247 Sports	ESPN	ESPN Grade	Hometown	High school / college	Height	Weight	Committed
Tony Brown	CB	2	5	5	5	5	92	Beaumont, TX	Ozen HS	6-0	182	1/2/14
Joshua Casher	OC	1	3	4	4	4	83	Mobile, AL	St. Paul's Episcopal	6-1	280	10/29/13
Ronnie Clark	ATH	7	4	4	4	4	84	Calera, AL	Calera HS	6-3	205	10/4/13
Jake Coker	QB	18		3	3			Mobile, AL	Florida State University	6-4	230	6/21/10
David Cornwell	QB	4	4	4	4	4	84	Norman, OK	Norman North HS	6-5	235	6/14/13
Johnny Dwight	DT	33	4	3	3	4	80	Rochelle, GA	Wilcox County HS	6-3	298	6/4/13
Rashaan Evans	OLB	2	5	5	5	4	84	Auburn, AL	Auburn HS	6-3	218	2/5/14
Ty Flournoy-Smith	TE	6	3	2	3	3	76	Moultrie, GA	Georgia Military College	6-3	245	2/3/14
Joshua Frazier	DT	10	4	4	4	4	83	Springdale, AR	Har-Ber HS	6-3	334	11/23/13
Shaun Dion Hamilton	ILB	6	3	4	4	4	83	Montgomery, AL	G. W. Carver HS	6-0	241	4/17/13
Da'Shawn Hand	DE	2	5	5	5	5	94	Woodbridge, VA	Woodbridge HS	6-4	260	11/14/13
J. C. Hassenauer	OC	2	4	4	4	4	83	Woodbury, MN	East Ridge HS	6-3	295	6/17/13
Keith Holcombe	OLB	21	3	3	4	4	82	Tuscaloosa, AL	Hillcrest HS	6-4	209	6/30/13
Marlon Humphrey	CB	5	5	5	5	5	90	Hoover, AL	Hoover HS	6-0	174	1/29/14
Dominick Jackson	OT	1	4	4	4	4	82	Cupertino, CA	College of San Mateo	6-7	312	6/26/13
Hootie Jones	S	3	4	4	4	4	86	Monroe, LA	Neville HS	6-2	210	1/2/14
Derek Kief	WR	26	4	4	4	4	82	Cincinnati, OH	La Salle HS	6-4	199	6/16/13
Montel McBride	OG	28	3	3	3	3	79	Plant City, FL	Plant City HS	6-4	332	7/2/13
Christian Miller	OLB	1	4	4	4	4	84	Columbia, SC	Spring Valley HS	6-4	215	7/25/13
D.J. Pettway	DE	2	4	4	4	4	80	Pensacola, FL	East Mississippi Community College	6-3	255	12/18/13
Ross Pierschbacher	OG	3	4	4	4	4	84	Cedar Falls, IA	Cedar Falls HS	6-4	295	8/11/13
Jarran Reed	DT	7	4	3	4	3	79	Goldsboro, NC	East Mississippi Community College	6-4	305	12/19/13
Cameron Robinson	OT	1	5	5	5	5	95	West Monroe, LA	West Monroe HS	6-6	320	9/4/13
Bo Scarbrough	ATH	2	5	5	5	5	90	Northport, AL	IMG Academy	6-2	222	9/7/12
JK Scott	K	5	3	3	3	3	78	Denver, CO	Mullen HS	6-5	185	6/9/13
Cam Sims	WR	8	4	4	4	4	84	Monroe, LA	Ouachita Parish HS	6-4	208	8/24/13
O.J. Smith	DT	18	3	3	3	4	82	Bossier City, LA	Airline HS	6-2	330	5/24/13

	Scout	Rivals	247Sports	ESPN
5 Stars	6	6	6	5
4 Stars	13	13	15	17
3 Stars	7	7	6	4
2 Stars	0	1	0	0

Note: Table data from "2014 Alabama Crimson Tide football team" (125)

Roster

Num	Player	Pos	Class	Height	Weight	Hometown	Last School
93	Jonathan Allen	DL	SO	6-3	272	Leesburg, VA	Stone Bridge
7	Ryan Anderson	LB	SO	6-2	258	Daphne, AL	Daphne
28	Anthony Averett	DB	FR	6-0	180	Woodbury, NJ	Woodbury
94	Dakota Ball	DL	SO	6-2	280	Lindale, GA	Pepperell
87	Parker Barrineau	WR	JR	6-0	184	Northport, AL	American Christian Academy
18	Cooper Bateman	QB	FR	6-3	215	Murray, UT	Cottonwood
31	Jerrod Bierbower	DB	SR	6-1	198	Dublin, OH	Coffman
1	Chris Black	WR	SO	5-11	186	Jacksonville, FL	First Coast
75	Bradley Bozeman	OL	FR	6-5	325	Roanoke, AL	Handley
72	Leon Brown	OL	SR	6-6	320	Riverdale, MD	ASA College
2	Tony Brown	DB	FR	6-0	198	Beaumont, TX	Ozen
43	Gussie Busch	LB	FR	6-0	210	St. Louis, MO	Priory
67	Joshua Casher	OL	FR	6-1	295	Mobile, AL	St. Paul's
1	Ronnie Clark	DB	FR	6-3	215	Calera, AL	Calera
14	Jake Coker	QB	JR	6-5	230	Mobile, AL	Florida State
26	Landon Collins	DB	JR	6-0	222	New Orleans, LA	Dutchtown
12	Jonathan Cook	DB	FR	6-0	190	Daphne, AL	Spanish Fort
9	Amari Cooper	WR	JR	6-1	210	Miami, FL	Northwestern
12	David Cornwell	QB	FR	6-5	234	Norman, OK	Norman North
39	Paden Crowder	LB	JR	6-4	235	Vestavia Hills, AL	Vestavia Hills
48	David D'Amico	TE	SO	6-0	213	Birmingham, AL	Vestavia Hills
62	Will Davis	OL	SO	6-5	316	Letohatchee, AL	Fort Dale Academy
33	Trey DePriest	LB	SR	6-2	250	Springfield, OH	Springfield
30	Denzel Devall	LB	JR	6-2	254	Bastrop, LA	Bastrop
55	Josh Dickerson	LB	SR	6-1	228	Evans, GA	Lakeside
47	Xzavier Dickson	LB	SR	6-3	268	Griffin, GA	Griffin
17	Kenyan Drake	RB	JR	6-1	202	Powder Spring, GA	Hillgrove
36	Johnny Dwight	DL	FR	6-3	300	Rochelle, GA	Wilcox County
32	Rashaan Evans	LB	FR	6-3	225	Auburn, AL	Auburn
85	Malcolm Faciane	TE	JR	6-5	265	Picayune, MS	Picayune Memorial
80	Raheem Falkins	WR	SO	6-4	210	New Orleans, LA	G.W. Carver
83	Ty Flournoy-Smith	TE	JR	6-3	245	Moultrie, GA	Georgia Military
10	Reuben Foster	LB	SO	6-1	244	Auburn, AL	Auburn
8	Robert Foster	WR	FR	6-3	191	Monaca, PA	Central Valley
45	Jalston Fowler	RB	SR	6-1	248	Mobile, AL	Vigor
69	Joshua Frazier	DL	FR	6-3	335	Springdale, AR	Har-Ber
41	Kurt Freitag	TE	SO	6-4	255	Buford, GA	Buford
37	Daniel Geddes	DB	SR	5-6	170	Northport, AL	Tuscaloosa County
48	Bo Grant	DB	SO	6-3	198	Valley, AL	Valley
58	Brandon Greene	OL	SO	6-5	304	Ellenwood, GA	Cedar Grove
99	Adam Griffith	PK	SO	5-10	188	Calhoun, GA	Calhoun
11	Shaun Dion Hamilton	LB	FR	6-0	233	Montgomery, AL	Carver
9	Da'Shawn Hand	DL	FR	6-4	273	Woodbridge, VA	Woodbridge
58	Alex Harrelson	SN	JR	6-0	226	Vestavia Hills, AL	Vestavia Hills
86	Truett Harris	TE	JR	6-3	210	Brentwood, TN	Brentwood
63	J.C. Hassenauer	OL	FR	6-3	290	Woodbury, MN	East Ridge
27	Derrick Henry	RB	SO	6-3	241	Yulee, FL	Yulee
64	Grant Hill	OL	SO	6-6	322	Huntsville, AL	Huntsville
96	Stephen Hodge	DL	JR	6-1	257	Akron, AL	Hale County
42	Keith Holcombe	LB	FR	6-3	215	Tuscaloosa, AL	Hillcrest
37	Zach Houston	DB	JR	6-1	192	Daphne, AL	Daphne
88	O.J. Howard	TE	SO	6-6	240	Prattville, AL	Autauga Academy
29	Marlon Humphrey	DB	FR	6-1	186	Hoover, AL	Hoover
99	Brandon Ivory	DL	SR	6-4	308	Memphis, TN	East
76	Dominick Jackson	OL	JR	6-7	320	Cupertino, CA	College of San Mateo
4	Eddie Jackson	DB	SO	6-0	188	Lauderdale Lakes, FL	Boyd Anderson
89	Bernel Jones	DL	SR	6-3	253	Montgomery, AL	Jefferson Davis
22	Christion Jones	WR	SR	5-11	187	Adamsville, AL	Minor
5	Cyrus Jones	DB	JR	5-10	194	Baltimore, MD	Gilman
6	Hootie Jones	DB	FR	6-2	221	Monroe, LA	Neville
20	Tyren Jones	RB	FR	5-9	212	Marietta, GA	Walton
35	Walker Jones	LB	FR	6-2	238	Germantown, TN	Evangelical Christian
39	Kyle Kazakevicius	WR	SO	6-0	184	Ocala, FL	Trinity Catholic
70	Ryan Kelly	OL	JR	6-5	296	West Chester, OH	Lakota West
81	Derek Kief	WR	FR	6-5	200	Cincinnati, OH	La Salle
85	Korren Kirven	DL	SO	6-5	297	Lynchburg, VA	Brookville
77	Arie Kouandjio	OL	SR	6-5	315	Hyattsville, MD	DeMatha Catholic
95	Darren Lake	DL	JR	6-3	323	York, AL	Sumter County
98	Adrian Lamothe	P	SO	5-9	190	Monterrey, Mexico	Prepa Tec
25	Dillon Lee	LB	JR	6-4	243	Buford, GA	Buford
40	Isaac Leon	TE	SO	6-6	215	Boynton Beach, FL	American Heritage
52	Dee Liner	DL	SO	6-3	295	Muscle Shoals, AL	Muscle Shoals
51	Jake Long	DL	SO	5-10	229	Vestavia Hilla, AL	Vestavia Hills
68	Isaac Luatua	OL	JR	6-2	315	La Mirada, CA	La Mirada
55	Cole Mazza	SN	SO	6-1	251	Bakersfield, CA	Liberty
65	Montel McBride	OL	FR	6-4	330	Plant City, FL	Plant City
47	Corey McCarron	TE	JR	6-2	245	Mobile, AL	Spanish Fort
34	Christian Miller	LB	FR	6-4	215	Columbia, SC	Spring Valley
60	Brandon Moore	OL	JR	6-0	277	Cincinnati, OH	Cincinnati Hills Christian Academy
11	Alec Morris	QB	SO	6-3	230	Allen, TX	Allen

164

Num	Player	Pos	Class	Height	Weight	Hometown	Last School
16	Jamey Mosley	LB	FR	6-5	210	Mobile, AL	Theodore
46	Michael Nysewander	TE	SR	6-1	238	Hoover, AL	Hoover
53	Anthony Orr	DL	SR	6-4	289	Madison, AL	Sparkman
38	Tyler Owens	LB	SR	6-0	225	Columbiana, AL	Clay-Chalkville
61	Austin Peavler	OL	SO	6-3	317	Weldington, FL	Wellington Community
25	Buddy Pell	RB	FR	6-0	200	Mountain Brook, AL	Mountain Brook
27	**Nick Perry**	**DB**	**SR**	**6-1**	**211**	**Prattville, AL**	**Prattville**
57	*D.J. Pettway*	*LB*	*JR*	*6-2*	*265*	*Pensacola, FL*	*East Mississippi CC*
71	Ross Pierschbacher	OL	FR	6-4	295	Cedar Falls, IA	Cedar Falls
97	John Pizzitola	P	SO	5-11	175	Birmingham, AL	Spain Park
66	Chris Posa	OL	SO	6-3	269	Commerce, MI	St Mary's Prep
96	Gunnar Raborn	PK	FR	5-9	187	Lafayette, LA	St. Thomas More
19	**Reggie Ragland**	**LB**	**JR**	**6-2**	**254**	**Madison, AL**	**Bob Jones**
90	*Jarran Reed*	*DL*	*JR*	*6-4*	*315*	*Goldsboro, NC*	*East Mississippi CC*
86	**A'Shawn Robinson**	**DL**	**SO**	**6-4**	**320**	**Fort Worth, TX**	**Arlington Heights**
74	**Cam Robinson**	**OL**	**FR**	**6-6**	**323**	**Monroe, LA**	**West Monroe**
15	**JK Scott**	**P**	**FR**	**6-4**	**185**	**Denver, CO**	**Mullen**
79	**Austin Shepherd**	**OL**	**SR**	**6-5**	**320**	**Buford, GA**	**North Gwinnett**
6	**Blake Sims**	**QB**	**SR**	**6-0**	**208**	**Gainesville, GA**	**Gainesville**
7	Cam Sims	WR	FR	6-4	208	Monroe, LA	Ouachita Parish
24	Geno Smith	DB	JR	6-0	186	Atlanta, GA	St. Pius X
21	Maurice Smith	DB	SO	6-0	195	Sugar Land, TX	Fort Bend Dulles
91	O.J. Smith	DL	FR	6-2	330	Bossier City, LA	Airline
22	Nate Staskelunas	DB	SO	6-3	206	Grenville, NC	Arendell Parrott Academy
13	ArDarius Stewart	WR	FR	6-0	193	Fultondale, AL	Fultondale
3	**Bradley Sylve**	**DB**	**JR**	**5-11**	**180**	**Port Sulphur, LA**	**South Palquemines**
50	**Alphonse Taylor**	**OL**	**SO**	**6-5**	**325**	**Mobile, AL**	**Davidson**
59	M.K. Taylor	SN	SR	5-10	230	Oxford, AL	Oxford
28	Altee Tenpenny	RB	SO	6-0	218	North Little Rock, AR	North Little Rock
54	Dalvin Tomlinson	DL	SO	6-2	290	McDonaugh, GA	Henry County
84	**Brian Vogler**	**TE**	**SR**	**6-7**	**263**	**Columbus, GA**	**Brookstone**
69	Paul Waldrop	OL	JR	6-4	285	Phenix City, AL	Central
44	Levi Wallace	DB	FR	6-1	172	Tucson, AZ	Tucson
23	Jabriel Washington	DB	JR	5-11	183	Jackson, TN	Trinity Christian Academy
2	**DeAndrew White**	**WR**	**SR**	**6-0**	**192**	**Houston, TX**	**North Shore**
20	**Jarrick Williams**	**DB**	**SR**	**6-1**	**215**	**Mobile, AL**	**Blount**
49	Kieran Williams	TE	FR	6-4	243	Lawrenceville, GA	Archer
56	Tim Williams	LB	SO	6-3	242	Baton Rouge, LA	University Lab
4	**T.J. Yeldon**	**RB**	**JR**	**6-2**	**221**	**Daphne, AL**	**Daphne**

Note: Starters in bold
Note: Table data from "2014 Alabama Crimson Tide Roster" (126)

Transfers

Player	School	Direction
Jake Coker	Florida State	Incoming
D.J. Pettway	East Mississippi Community College	Incoming
Jarren Reed	East Mississippi Community College	Incoming
Luke Del Rio	Oregon State	Outgoing
Dee Hart	Colorado State	Outgoing
Chad Lindsay	Ohio State	Outgoing

Note: Table data from "2014 Alabama Crimson Tide football team" (125)

Games

08/30/14 - Alabama (2) vs West Virginia

Team	1	2	3	4	T	Passing	Rushing	Total
West Virginia	3	14	3	3	**23**	365	28	**393**
Alabama (2)	3	17	10	3	**33**	250	288	**538**

On May 17, 2012, officials from both Alabama and West Virginia announced the Crimson Tide and the Mountaineers would meet for the first time to open the 2014 season at the Chick-fil-A College Kickoff in Atlanta. As they entered their game week preparations, Alabama Head Coach Nick Saban announced starting linebacker Trey DePriest would be suspended for the game due to an NCAA violation. Although Alabama entered the game as a heavy favorite over the Mountaineers, the Crimson Tide only defeated West Virginia by a score of 33-23 in Blake Sims' first start at quarterback. After Alabama won the coin toss and deferred until the second half, West Virginia had a 14-play drive that took them as far as the Crimson Tide 3-yard line. It was from there that Josh Lambert gave the Mountaineers a 3-0 lead with his 20-yard field goal. Alabama responded on the next possession when Adam Griffith connected on a 47-yard field goal that tied the game at 3-3. After the Crimson Tide defense forced a punt on the Mountaineers possession that followed, Alabama scored its first touchdown on the 14-play, 95-yard drive that ensued. Behind a strong running attack, T.J. Yeldon gave the Crimson Tide a 10-3 lead with his 15-yard touchdown run early in the second quarter.

West Virginia responded on its next possession with a long touchdown drive of its own. Led by quarterback Clint Trickett, the Mountaineers went 75 yards in nine plays with Trickett throwing a 19-yard touchdown pass to Kevin White that tied the game at 10-10. Late in the quarter, Alabama retook a 17-10 lead on a 1-yard Yeldon touchdown run. However, on the kickoff that ensued, Mario Alford dodged several Crimson Tide tackles en route to a 100-yard touchdown return that tied the game at 17-17. Alabama responded with a quick 50-yard drive that ended with a 41-yard Adam Griffith field goal that gave the Crimson Tide a 20-17 halftime lead.

After Alabama was stopped on a fourth down conversion and the Mountaineers missed a 47-yard field goal on their opening possessions of the second half, the Crimson Tide took a 27-17 lead behind a 19-yard Derrick Henry touchdown run. Both teams then traded field goals on the next two possessions and made the score 30-20 in favor of the Crimson Tide as they entered the fourth quarter. Although only a pair of field goals were scored in the fourth quarter that made the final score 33-23, the Alabama defense played their best quarter of the game and forced the Mountaineers into several three-and-out possessions late in the game. For his four field goal performance, Adam Griffith was recognized as both the SEC Special Teams Player of the Week and as a Lou Groza Award National Star of the Week.[125]

Passing	C/ATT	YDS	AVG	TD	INT	QBR
B. Sims	24/33	250	7.6	0	1	87.9

Rushing	CAR	YDS	AVG	TD	LONG
TJ Yeldon	23	126	5.5	2	26
D. Henry	17	113	6.6	1	19
B. Sims	6	42	7	0	21
K. Drake	3	7	2.3	0	6
Team	49	288	5.9	3	26

Kicking	FG	PCT	LONG	XP	PTS
A. Griffith	4/4	100	47	3/3	15

Punting	NO	YDS	AVG	TB	IN 20	LONG
JK Scott	2	101	50.5	0	1	62

Receiving	REC	YDS	AVG	TD	LONG
A. Cooper	12	130	10.8	0	24
D. White	6	73	12.2	0	38
Ch. Jones	3	31	10.3	0	22
C. Black	1	8	8	0	8
J. Fowler	1	7	7	0	7
TJ Yeldon	1	1	1	0	1
Team	24	250	10.4	0	38

Kick returns	NO	YDS	AVG	LONG	TD
Ch. Jones	4	99	24.8	26	0

Punt returns	NO	YDS	AVG	LONG	TD
Ch. Jones	1	-1	-1	0	0

Note: Table data from "Alabama 33-23 West Virginia (Aug 30, 2014) Box Score" (127)

09/06/14 - Alabama (2) vs Florida Atlantic

Team	1	2	3	4	T		Passing	Rushing	Total
Florida Atlantic	0	0	0	0	**0**		88	57	**145**
Alabama (2)	21	10	7	3	**41**		430	190	**620**

To open its 2014 home schedule, Alabama defeated the Florida Atlantic Owls 41-0 in a game that was called midway through the fourth quarter due to lightning strikes within eight miles of Bryant-Denny Stadium. The Crimson Tide elected to receive the ball to open the game and then went on a 7-play, 74-yard drive that culminated in a 7-yard Blake Sims touchdown run. After the Alabama defense forced a punt on the Owls' first possession, Sims connected with Amari Cooper on a 52-yard touchdown pass for a 14-0 lead. The Crimson Tide extended their lead further to 21-0 on their next possession when Sims threw a 39-yard touchdown pass to Kenyan Drake. On the first defensive play that followed, Eddie Jackson forced a Kamrin Solomon fumble that was recovered by Reggie Ragland at the Owls' 42-yard line.

It was on this possession that backup quarterback Jake Coker entered the game. He led the Crimson Tide on a 37-yard drive that resulted in a 24-0 lead after Adam Griffith connected on a 22-yard field goal early in the second quarter. The Alabama defense continued their strong performance and forced a three-and-out before the offense started their fourth touchdown drive of the game. Coker led the Crimson Tide on a 12-play, 87-yard drive that ended with a 3-yard Coker touchdown pass to Jalston Fowler for a 31-0 lead. FAU responded with its longest drive of the game only to have to punt again. Alabama then had its final drive of the first half stall at the Owls' 9-yard line; that made the halftime score 31-0.

On the first Alabama possession of the third quarter, Eugene Fau recovered a Sims fumble at the FAU 1-yard line and prevented another Crimson Tide touchdown. They scored their fifth touchdown on a 3-yard Kenyan Drake touchdown run later in the third that extended their lead to 38-0. With many of Alabama's backups in the game, Adam Griffith scored the final points of the game with his 28-yard field goal. After Cyrus Jones set up a late Crimson Tide scoring opportunity with his 70-yard punt return, officials delayed the game due to lightning strikes in the vicinity of the stadium with Alabama in a 4th-and-goal situation. Within fifteen minutes of the delay, both schools agreed to call the game with 7:53 to play in the fourth quarter. The game marked the first in Alabama history where two quarterbacks had over 200 yards passing, and Cooper's 13 receptions also tied a Crimson Tide single-game record set by D.J. Hall in 2007.[125]

Passing	C/ATT	YDS	AVG	TD	INT	QBR
B. Sims	12/14	228	16.3	2	0	97.3
J. Coker	15/24	202	8.4	1	0	72.8
Team	27/38	430	11.3	3	0	--

Rushing	CAR	YDS	AVG	TD	LONG
TJ Yeldon	7	43	6.1	0	14
T. Jones	4	33	8.3	0	20
K. Drake	6	31	5.2	1	11
J. Coker	4	23	5.8	0	15
D. Henry	5	23	4.6	0	6
A. Cooper	1	20	20	0	20
B. Sims	3	14	4.7	1	9
A. Tenpenny	2	3	1.5	0	4
Team	32	190	5.9	2	20

Kicking	FG	PCT	LONG	XP	PTS
A. Griffith	2/2	100	28	5/5	11

Receiving	REC	YDS	AVG	TD	LONG
A. Cooper	13	189	14.5	1	52
A. Stewart	3	63	21	0	40
K. Drake	2	53	26.5	1	39
Ch. Jones	2	52	26	0	41
C. Black	3	45	15	0	19
TJ Yeldon	1	18	18	0	18
T. Flournoy-Smith	1	4	4	0	4
J. Fowler	1	3	3	1	3
R. Foster	1	3	3	0	3
Team	27	430	15.9	3	52

Kick returns	NO	YDS	AVG	LONG	TD
Ch. Jones	1	26	26	26	0

Punt returns	NO	YDS	AVG	LONG	TD
Cy. Jones	1	70	70	70	0
Ch. Jones	2	7	3.5	5	0
Team	3	77	25.7	70	0

Note: Table data from "Alabama 41-0 Florida Atlantic (Sep 6, 2014) Box Score" (128)

09/13/14 - Alabama (3) vs Southern Mississippi

Team	1	2	3	4	T		Passing	Rushing	Total
Southern Mississippi	3	3	3	3	12		207	56	263
Alabama (3)	7	14	14	17	52		214	333	547

In its third game of the 2014 season and second consecutive home non-conference game, Alabama defeated the Southern Miss Golden Eagles 52-12. Behind their passing game led by Nick Mullins, the Golden Eagles took a 3-0 lead behind a 33-yard Corey Acosta field goal on their opening possession. Alabama responded on the next possession with a 22-yard Blake Sims touchdown pass to Amari Cooper capping a 7-play, 70-yard drive for a 7-3 lead. After three punts, the Crimson Tide extended their lead to 14-3 early in the second quarter by driving 80 yards in 13 plays that concluded with a 4-yard Sims touchdown run. After forcing another punt that gave Alabama the ball at the Southern Miss 38-yard line, they scored in six plays with Kenyan Drake's 1-yard touchdown run. Acosta then made the score 21-6 with his 43-yard field goal just prior to halftime.

To open the second half, Blake Sims led the Crimson Tide 75 yards in eight plays with Kenyan Drake scoring his second touchdown for a 28-6 lead. Acosta connected on his third field goal on the drive that ensued for Southern Miss, but Alabama would go on and score on each of its final four offensive possessions. In the third quarter, Alabama drove 68 yards in seven plays, and Sims completed a 5-yard touchdown pass to Brian Vogler. Then Jake Coker entered the game on the following possession and led the Crimson Tide on three scoring drives in the fourth quarter. The first was a whopping 99-yard drive capped by Drake on a 29-yard touchdown run. After USM scored on a 30-yard field goal, Bama drove 46 yards in nine plays before Adam Griffith kicked a 30-yarder of his own. Tyren Jones scored the final points of the game with his 2-yard touchdown run for the 52-12 victory.[125]

Passing	C/ATT	YDS	AVG	TD	INT	QBR
B. Sims	12/17	168	9.9	2	0	93.4
J. Coker	5/7	46	6.6	0	0	29.8
Team	17/24	214	8.6	2	0	--

Rushing	CAR	YDS	AVG	TD	LONG
D. Henry	11	73	6.6	0	21
K. Drake	9	59	6.6	3	29
T. Jones	7	57	8.1	1	22
TJ Yeldon	9	56	6.2	0	15
B. Sims	5	46	9.2	1	20
A. Tenpenny	5	39	7.8	0	13
A. Cooper	1	9	9	0	9
J. Coker	2	-6	-3	0	5
Team	49	333	6.8	5	29

Punting	NO	YDS	AVG	TB	IN 20	LONG
JK Scott	1	34	34	0	1	34

Receiving	REC	YDS	AVG	TD	LONG
A. Cooper	8	135	16.9	1	27
Ch. Jones	4	50	12.5	0	22
M. Nysewander	1	9	9	0	9
K. Drake	1	9	9	0	9
B. Vogler	1	5	5	1	5
C. Black	1	5	5	0	5
R. Foster	1	1	1	0	1
Team	17	214	12.6	2	27

Kick returns	NO	YDS	AVG	LONG	TD
Ch. Jones	4	111	27.8	37	0

Punt returns	NO	YDS	AVG	LONG	TD
Ch. Jones	1	14	14	14	0
T. Jones	1	0	0	0	0
Team	2	14	7	14	0

Kicking	FG	PCT	LONG	XP	PTS
A. Griffith	1/1	100	30	7/7	10

Note: Table data from "Alabama 52-12 Southern Mississippi (Sep 13, 2014) Box Score" (129)

09/20/14 - Alabama (3) vs Florida

Team	1	2	3	4	T		Passing	Rushing	Total
Florida	14	0	7	0	21		93	107	200
Alabama (3)	14	7	14	7	42		449	223	672

Florida surrendered a school-record 672 yards of total offense to Alabama in this 42-21 Bama victory. Florida got the ball first. After they held Florida to a three-and-out, Alabama scored on its first play from scrimmage on an 87-yard touchdown pass from Blake Sims to Kenyan Drake. Drake lost a fumble on their next possession at the Alabama 31-yard line. A 28-yard touchdown pass from Jeff Driskel to Valdez Showers tied the game at 7-7. Alabama's next possession also ended in a lost fumble which was returned by Florida for a touchdown (14-7 Florida). On the next possession that ensued, Alabama drove 52 yards to set up an Adam Griffith field goal, but he missed the 45-yarder. The Crimson Tide forced another Florida three-and-out and punt, and the Alabama offense immediately tied the game at 14-14 on a 79-yard touchdown pass to Amari Cooper. On Florida's next possession, Alabama recorded its first interception of the season when Jabriel Washington picked off a Driskel pass at the Alabama 13-yard line. The ensuing Tide possession ended in yet another fumble, this time by Sims, but the Tide defense held as Florida and Alabama exchanged punts. Alabama forced a fumble from Florida running back Matt Jones to set up a 56-yard drive that ended in a touchdown pass from Sims to Jalston Fowler to regain the lead, and Alabama led by a touchdown at halftime, 21-14.

Alabama turned the ball over again on the opening possession of the second half when a Blake Sims pass was batted into the air and intercepted. Two plays later, Driskel ran 14 yards for a TD and tied the game at 21-21. Alabama used more than seven minutes and converted five third downs on its next possession and regained the lead on a 3-yard Henry TD run. Florida punted again, and on Bama's next possession, Sims injured his shoulder on a 24-yard run. Backup Jake Coker entered the game, but Alabama relied mostly on runs from Henry and T.J. Yeldon to move the ball to the Florida 4-yard line. Coker threw a 4-yard touchdown pass to Cooper and extended Alabama's lead to 35-21. Florida's next possession ended with Driskel's second interception of the day, this time to Landon Collins. After the interception, Sims reentered the game and led a 60-yard drive that ended with a TD pass to Cooper that made the score 42-21.

Blake Sims' 445 passing yards were the second highest single-game passing total in Alabama history behind Scott Hunter's 1969 record, and his 484 yards of total offense (including 39 total yards rushing) broke Hunter's single-game total offense record. Amari Cooper became Bama's all-time leader in TD receptions after he eclipsed the previous record of 18 (Dennis Homan).[125]

Passing	C/ATT	YDS	AVG	TD	INT	QBR
B. Sims	23/33	445	13.5	4	1	94.3
J. Coker	1/2	4	2	1	0	99.9
Team	24/35	449	12.8	5	1	--

Rushing	CAR	YDS	AVG	TD	LONG
D. Henry	20	111	5.6	1	25
TJ Yeldon	18	59	3.3	0	10
B. Sims	8	39	4.9	0	24
K. Drake	4	15	3.8	0	11
T. Jones	2	-1	-0.5	0	2
Team	52	223	4.3	1	25

Interceptions	INT	YDS	TD
L. Collins	1	12	0
J. Washington	1	0	0
Team	2	12	0

Punting	NO	YDS	AVG	TB	IN 20	LONG
JK Scott	2	87	43.5	1	0	57

Receiving	REC	YDS	AVG	TD	LONG
A. Cooper	10	201	20.1	3	79
K. Drake	1	87	87	1	87
D. White	6	48	8	0	17
TJ Yeldon	1	37	37	0	37
D. Henry	1	29	29	0	29
OJ Howard	2	22	11	0	12
J. Fowler	2	21	10.5	1	19
Ch. Jones	1	4	4	0	4
Team	24	449	18.7	5	87

Kick returns	NO	YDS	AVG	LONG	TD
Ch. Jones	3	70	23.3	28	0

Punt returns	NO	YDS	AVG	LONG	TD
Ch. Jones	2	17	8.5	17	0

Kicking	FG	PCT	LONG	XP	PTS
A. Griffith	0/1	0	0	6/6	6

Note: Table data from "Alabama 42-21 Florida (Sep 20, 2014) Box Score" (130)

169

10/04/14 - Alabama (3) at Ole Miss (11)

Team	1	2	3	4	T	Passing	Rushing	Total
Alabama (3)	0	14	3	0	17	228	168	396
Ole Miss (11)	3	0	7	13	23	251	76	327

In what was its first true road game of the season, Alabama was upset by the Ole Miss Rebels 23-17 in Oxford. After the Rebels elected to start the game on offense, Mark Dodson returned the opening kickoff 54 yards to the Alabama 39-yard line. After a first down run by Bo Wallace, Ole Miss didn't gain a single yard and settled for a Gary Wunderlich 46-yard field goal to give Ole Miss an early 3-0 lead. Alabama responded by driving deep into Ole Miss territory, but Adam Griffith missed a 46-yard field goal. Ole Miss moved the ball easily before the drive stalled at the Alabama 15-yard line, but Andrew Fletcher missed a chip shot 33-yard field goal. From there until 6:59 remaining in the second quarter, both teams traded punts. Finally, Alabama managed to march 68 yards in 12 plays as Blake Sims gave them a 7-3 lead with his touchdown run from one yard out on 4th-and-goal. The Crimson Tide then extended their lead to 14-3 at halftime after Cyrus Jones forced a fumble by I'Tavius Mathers and returned it 17 yards for a touchdown.

Alabama opened the second half with a 14-play drive only to have Adam Griffith miss on a 51-yard field goal attempt. Ole Miss responded on the possession that ensued with Wallace connecting on a 50-yard pass to tight end Evan Engram and on a 14-yard touchdown pass to Laquon Treadwell two plays later that made the score 14-10. Alabama then drove to the Ole Miss 15-yard line, but two penalties moved them back to the 29-yard line. However, Griffith did connect on a 44-yard field goal and extended the Alabama lead to 17-10 as they entered the fourth quarter.

Alabama punted from its own 5-yard line, and Ole Miss returned it nine yards to the Rebels' 44-yard line. After a 6-yard run by Jaylen Walton, Wallace connected with Engram for a 16-yard gain to the Alabama 34-yard line. Finally, the Rebels tied the game on the next play when Wallace connected with Vince Sanders on a 34-yard touchdown reception. The extra point tied the game at 17-17. On the kickoff that ensued, Channing Ward forced a Christion Jones fumble that was recovered by Kailo Moore at the Alabama 31-yard line. Five plays later, the Rebels took a 23-17 lead after Wallace threw a 10-yard touchdown pass to Jaylen Walton, but Fletcher missed the extra point. Ole Miss then secured the win late in the quarter after Senquez Golson intercepted a Sims pass in the end zone to effectively end the game.[125]

Passing	C/ATT	YDS	AVG	TD	INT	QBR
B. Sims	19/31	228	7.4	0	1	88.7

Rushing	CAR	YDS	AVG	TD	LONG
TJ Yeldon	20	123	6.2	0	22
D. Henry	17	37	2.2	0	8
B. Sims	7	8	1.1	1	8
Team	44	168	3.8	1	22

Kick returns	NO	YDS	AVG	LONG	TD
Ch. Jones	3	72	24	38	0
Cy. Jones	1	20	20	20	0
Team	4	92	23	38	0

Punting	NO	YDS	AVG	TB	IN 20	LONG
JK Scott	6	311	51.8	2	3	64

Receiving	REC	YDS	AVG	TD	LONG
A. Cooper	9	91	10.1	0	30
OJ Howard	3	81	27	0	53
C. Black	2	19	9.5	0	10
Ch. Jones	1	17	17	0	17
K. Drake	1	10	10	0	10
TJ Yeldon	2	7	3.5	0	7
B. Vogler	1	3	3	0	3
Team	19	228	12	0	53

Punt returns	NO	YDS	AVG	LONG	TD
Ch. Jones	1	3	3	3	0

Kicking	FG	PCT	LONG	XP	PTS
A. Griffith	1/3	33	44	2/2	5

Note: Table data from "Alabama 23-17 Ole Miss (Oct 4, 2014) Box Score" (131)

10/11/14 - Alabama (7) at Arkansas

Team	1	2	3	4	T		Passing	Rushing	Total
Alabama (7)	0	7	0	7	**14**		161	66	**227**
Arkansas	0	6	7	0	**13**		246	89	**335**

In the 2014 edition of its game against Arkansas, Alabama traveled to Fayetteville and defeated the Razorbacks 14-13 with a missed PAT providing for the winning margin. Each team committed a turnover to start the game. After the Alabama defense forced a three-and-out to open the game, Christion Jones fumbled the punt that followed, and Arkansas recovered it at the 31-yard line. On the Razorbacks' possession that ensued, Trey DePriest forced a Kody Walker fumble out of the end zone for a touchback. Neither team had another scoring opportunity in the quarter, and the score was tied at 0-0 at the end of the first.

On their first possession of the second quarter, Adam Griffith missed a 30-yard field goal attempt. However, on the next play A'Shawn Robinson forced an Alex Collins fumble that was recovered by Ryan Anderson at the Razorbacks' 23-yard line. Three plays later, Blake Sims threw a 22-yard touchdown pass to T.J. Yeldon for a 7-0 Crimson Tide lead. Arkansas responded on the next possession with an 81-yard drive that was capped with a 3-yard Jonathan Williams touchdown run. Down by a single point, the John Henson PAT was blocked by Jonathan Allen and Alabama held a 7-6 lead into halftime.

Alabama retained its lead until midway through the third quarter when Brandon Allen connected with AJ Derby on a 54-yard touchdown pass to give Arkansas a 13-7 lead. The Crimson Tide retook a 14-13 lead early in the fourth quarter after Sims connected with DeAndrew White on a 6-yard touchdown pass. Both defenses then controlled the remainder of the game with Landon Collins sealing the Crimson Tide victory late in the quarter after he intercepted an Allen pass. For his performance, JK Scott was named SEC Special Teams Player of the Week.[125]

Passing	C/ATT	YDS	AVG	TD	INT	QBR
B. Sims	11/21	161	7.7	2	0	44.2

Rushing	CAR	YDS	AVG	TD	LONG
TJ Yeldon	16	45	2.8	0	12
D. Henry	7	25	3.6	0	8
B. Sims	7	5	0.7	0	7
D. White	1	-3	-3	0	0
A. Cooper	1	-6	-6	0	0
Team	32	66	2.1	0	12

Interceptions	INT	YDS	TD
L. Collins	1	0	0

Kicking	FG	PCT	LONG	XP	PTS
A. Griffith	0/1	0	0	2/2	2

Punting	NO	YDS	AVG	TB	IN 20	LONG
JK Scott	8	354	44.3	0	7	58

Receiving	REC	YDS	AVG	TD	LONG
OJ Howard	1	47	47	0	47
TJ Yeldon	2	35	17.5	1	22
D. White	4	33	8.3	1	21
A. Cooper	2	22	11	0	12
C. Sims	1	15	15	0	15
J. Fowler	1	9	9	0	9
Team	11	161	14.6	2	47

Kick returns	NO	YDS	AVG	LONG	TD
Ch. Jones	2	48	24	26	0
L. Collins	1	9	9	9	0
R. Anderson	1	5	5	5	0
Team	4	62	15.5	26	0

Punt returns	NO	YDS	AVG	LONG	TD
Cy. Jones	2	7	3.5	6	0
M. Smith	1	0	0	0	0
Ch. Jones	1	-3	-3	0	0
Team	4	4	1	6	0

Note: Table data from "Alabama 14-13 Arkansas (Oct 11, 2014) Box Score" (132)

10/18/14 - Alabama (7) vs Texas A&M (21)

Team	1	2	3	4	T		Passing	Rushing	Total
Texas A&M (21)	0	0	0	0	**0**		141	31	**172**
Alabama (7)	10	35	7	7	**59**		304	298	**602**

In the second home conference game of the 2014 season, Alabama shellacked the Texas A&M Aggies 59-0 in Tuscaloosa behind a 35-point second quarter. The Crimson Tide scored on every possession of the first half en route to a 45-0 halftime lead while holding A&M to six punts. After Adam Griffith scored the first points of the game with his 21-yard field goal capping a 10-play, 71-yard drive, T.J. Yeldon capped an 11-play, 72-yard drive as he scored the first Alabama touchdown on a 9-yard run for a 10-0 lead at the end of the first quarter.

Yeldon then opened the second quarter with a 1-yard touchdown run that finished off an 84-yard drive for the first of 35 second-quarter points. Blake Sims and Derrick Henry then extended the Crimson Tide lead to 31-0 behind respective runs of 43 and eight yards on consecutive possessions. The next Alabama touchdown was set up after a 47-yard Christion Jones punt return gave the Crimson Tide possession at the A&M 24-yard line. On the next play, Sims threw a 24-yard touchdown pass to Amari Cooper, his first of three touchdown passes in the game. Sims then made the halftime score 45-0 after he connected with Henry on a 41-yard touchdown pass in the final minute of the half.

The Crimson Tide then scored on their eighth consecutive possession to start the third quarter on a 45-yard Sims touchdown pass to Cooper. Alabama scored its final points late in the game when Jake Coker threw a 14-yard touchdown pass to Ty Flournoy-Smith for the 59-0 victory.[125]

Passing	C/ATT	YDS	AVG	TD	INT	QBR
B. Sims	16/27	268	9.9	3	0	87.2
J. Coker	5/8	36	4.5	1	0	44.1
Team	21/35	304	8.7	4	0	--

Rushing	CAR	YDS	AVG	TD	LONG
TJ Yeldon	13	114	8.8	2	31
D. Henry	10	70	7	1	13
B. Sims	4	54	13.5	1	43
T. Jones	9	34	3.8	0	12
A. Tenpenny	8	30	3.8	0	13
J. Coker	1	-4	-4	0	0
Team	45	298	6.6	4	43

Interceptions	INT	YDS	TD
R. Ragland	1	1	0

Punting	NO	YDS	AVG	TB	IN 20	LONG
JK Scott	4	200	50	0	1	56

Receiving	REC	YDS	AVG	TD	LONG
A. Cooper	8	140	17.5	2	45
TJ Yeldon	3	45	15	0	17
D. Henry	1	41	41	1	41
D. White	3	30	10	0	17
T. Flournoy-Smith	1	14	14	1	14
C. Sims	3	14	4.7	0	8
J. Fowler	1	12	12	0	12
A. Stewart	1	8	8	0	8
Team	21	304	14.5	4	45

Punt returns	NO	YDS	AVG	LONG	TD
Ch. Jones	3	53	17.7	47	0

Kicking	FG	PCT	LONG	XP	PTS
A. Griffith	1/1	100	21	7/7	10
JK Scott	0/0	0	0	1/1	1
Team	1/1	100	21	8/8	11

Note: Table data from "Alabama 59-0 Texas A&M (Oct 18, 2014) Box Score" (133)

10/25/14 - Alabama (4) at Tennessee

Team	1	2	3	4	T		Passing	Rushing	Total
Alabama (4)	20	7	7	0	**34**		286	183	**469**
Tennessee	0	10	7	3	**20**		202	181	**383**

In their annual rivalry game, Amari Cooper set the single game receiving yardage record as Alabama defeated Tennessee 34-20 for its eighth consecutive win over the Volunteers. The Crimson Tide opened the game with a pair of long Cooper touchdown receptions as they took a 13-0 lead. On Alabama's first offensive play, Blake Sims connected with him on an 80-yard scoring pass and again on their second drive from 41 yards out (PAT failed) capping a 7-play, 79-yard drive. They extended their lead to 20-0 on their third offensive possession going 90 yards in nine plays ending on a 1-yard T.J. Yeldon touchdown run.

Early in the second quarter, Reggie Ragland forced a Joshua Dobbs fumble that was recovered by Eddie Jackson and returned to the Vols' 19-yard line. Three plays after a Jarran Reed personal foul penalty pushed the ball back to the 34-yard line, Sims scored on a 28-yard touchdown run for a 27-0 lead. Tennessee responded on its next two offensive possessions to close the half and cut the Alabama lead to 27-10. First, Dobbs led Tennessee on an 84-yard scoring drive capped with his 9-yard touchdown pass to Josh Malone. He then led them on a 59-yard drive, and Aaron Medley connected on a 27-yard field goal as time expired.

After its defense forced an Alabama punt to open the third quarter, Tennessee scored on its third consecutive possession on a 9-yard Dobbs touchdown pass to Von Pearson that made the score 27-17. The Crimson Tide responded on the possession that ensued with a 28-yard Derrick Henry touchdown run capping a 13-play, 76-yard drive that extended their lead to 34-17.

In the final quarter, Cyrus Jones intercepted a Dobbs pass and returned it to the Alabama 30-yard line. However, on the play that ensued, Sims fumbled and the Vols regained possession at the Crimson Tide 23-yard line. Six plays later, Medley connected on a 24-yard field goal that made the score 34-20. Alabama responded with a long 78-yard drive but did not score as Cameron Sutton forced a Jalston Fowler fumble that was recovered by the Vols' Jalen Reeves-Maybin at their 1-yard line. This resulted in the final score of 34-20. The 224 yards receiving in the game established a new Crimson Tide record, and for his performance, Amari Cooper was recognized as the SEC Co-Offensive Player of the Week alongside Mississippi State's Josh Robinson.[125]

Passing	C/ATT	YDS	AVG	TD	INT	QBR
B. Sims	14/24	286	11.9	2	0	98.5

Rushing	CAR	YDS	AVG	TD	LONG
D. Henry	16	78	4.9	1	28
TJ Yeldon	14	52	3.7	1	15
B. Sims	6	42	7	1	28
J. Fowler	2	24	12	0	21
D. White	1	-1	-1	0	0
A. Cooper	1	-9	-9	0	0
Team	1	-3	-3	0	0
Team	41	183	4.5	3	28

Punting	NO	YDS	AVG	TB	IN 20	LONG
JK Scott	4	171	42.8	0	3	60

Receiving	REC	YDS	AVG	TD	LONG
A. Cooper	9	224	24.9	2	80
D. White	4	59	14.8	0	18
TJ Yeldon	1	3	3	0	3
Team	14	286	20.4	2	80

Kick returns	NO	YDS	AVG	LONG	TD
Cy. Jones	3	57	19	20	0
L. Collins	1	16	16	16	0
Team	4	73	18.3	20	0

Interceptions	INT	YDS	TD
Cy. Jones	1	-5	0

Kicking	FG	PCT	LONG	XP	PTS
A. Griffith	0/0	0	0	4/5	4

Note: Table data from "Alabama 34-20 Tennessee (Oct 25, 2014) Box Score" (134)

11/08/14 - Alabama (5) at LSU (16)

Team	1	2	3	4	OT	T		Passing	Rushing	Total
Alabama (5)	0	10	0	3	7	20		209	106	315
LSU (16)	7	0	3	3	0	13		76	183	259

In its annual rivalry game, Alabama defeated the LSU Tigers in overtime at Baton Rouge by a final score of 20-13. After each defense forced punts on the opening five possessions, LSU took advantage of a very short field, marching 41 yards, taking a 7-0 lead behind a 14-yard Anthony Jennings touchdown pass to Malachi Dupre. Late in the first quarter, after both teams punted, Alabama drove all the way to the 10-yard line where the drive stalled and Griffith missed a 27-yard field goal attempt. After LSU punted on its next drive, the Crimson Tide tied the game at 7-7 when Blake Sims threw a 23-yard touchdown pass to Amari Cooper in the second quarter. With just under a minute left in the half, Eddie Jackson intercepted a Jennings pass and returned it 18 yards back to the Tigers' 29-yard line. Although he missed one earlier from 27-yards out, Adam Griffith then gave the Crimson Tide a 10-7 halftime lead with his 39-yard field goal.

LSU took the second-half kickoff and reached the 18-yard line where Colby Delahoussaye tied the game at 10-10 with his 35-yard field goal. The next seven possessions ended in punts which took the game late in the fourth quarter. With just over one minute remaining in the game, Lamar Louis forced a T.J. Yeldon fumble that was recovered by Kendell Beckwith at the Alabama 6-yard line. After a very critical unsportsmanlike conduct penalty and two short runs, Delahoussaye gave the Tigers a 13-10 lead with just under a minute remaining in regulation with his 39-yard field goal. Alabama got a break when the kickoff went out of bounds, giving them the ball at its own 35-yard line. Sims then proceeded to drive the Crimson Tide 55 yards in nine plays, converting two third downs with his legs, where Griffith tied the game at 13-13 with his 27-yard field goal and sent the game into overtime.

Alabama took a 20-13 lead in the first overtime period when Sims connected with DeAndrew White on a 6-yard touchdown reception. The Tigers were unable to respond on their overtime possession as four straight incompletions gave the Crimson Tide the 20-13 win.[125]

Passing	C/ATT	YDS	AVG	TD	INT	QBR
B. Sims	20/45	209	4.6	2	0	66.2

Rushing	CAR	YDS	AVG	TD	LONG
TJ Yeldon	15	68	4.5	0	18
D. Henry	8	24	3	0	8
B. Sims	5	12	2.4	0	13
J. Fowler	1	2	2	0	2
Team	29	106	3.7	0	18

Interceptions	INT	YDS	TD
E. Jackson	1	18	0

Punting	NO	YDS	AVG	TB	IN 20	LONG
JK Scott	9	437	48.6	1	2	66

Receiving	REC	YDS	AVG	TD	LONG
A. Cooper	8	83	10.4	1	23
Ch. Jones	3	38	12.7	0	22
D. White	3	36	12	1	16
B. Greene	1	24	24	0	24
OJ Howard	3	21	7	0	9
TJ Yeldon	1	5	5	0	5
A. Stewart	1	2	2	0	2
Team	20	209	10.5	2	24

Kick returns	NO	YDS	AVG	LONG	TD
Ch. Jones	3	83	27.7	34	0

Kicking	FG	PCT	LONG	XP	PTS
A. Griffith	2/3	66.7	39	2/2	8

Note: Table data from "Alabama 20-13 LSU (Nov 8, 2014) Box Score" (135)

11/15/14 - Alabama (5) vs Mississippi State (1)

Team	1	2	3	4	T		Passing	Rushing	Total
Mississippi State (1)	0	3	3	14	20		290	138	428
Alabama (5)	5	14	0	6	25		211	124	335

In its annual rivalry game, Alabama defeated the No. 1 ranked Mississippi State Bulldogs 25-20 in Tuscaloosa. After the teams traded punts on the first three possessions of the game, Trey DePriest gave the Crimson Tide a 2-0 lead when he tackled Josh Robinson in the end zone for a safety. On the possession that followed the free kick, Adam Griffith extended Alabama's lead to 5-0 with his 36-yard field goal. After trading punts, Nick Perry picked off a Dak Prescott pass at the Alabama 22-yard line. However, Bama was not able to capitalize, and the two teams traded punts once again.

The Crimson Tide then scored their first touchdown midway through the second quarter when Blake Sims hit Amari Cooper for a 4-yard touchdown pass. The 61-yard drive only took 1:51 and five plays, and it and extended Alabama's lead to 12-0. On their next offensive series, Sims threw a 50-yard completion to Amari Cooper, then Derrick Henry scored from one yard out that extended the Crimson Tide lead to 19-0. The Bulldogs responded with a 14-play, 70-yard drive that was capped with a 23-yard Evan Sobiesk field goal that made the halftime score 19-3.

State opened the third quarter with another long drive, but again were held to only a Sobiesk field goal. Later in the quarter, with the Bulldogs in scoring position, Cyrus Jones intercepted a Dak Prescott pass for a touchback and ended the scoring threat. Early in the fourth quarter, Prescott threw a 4-yard touchdown pass to Fred Ross that brought the score to 19-13. Alabama responded on its possession that followed with a 15-play, 76-yard drive that was capped with a 7-yard T.J. Yeldon touchdown run for a 25-13 Crimson Tide lead after the failed two-point conversion attempt. The Bulldogs did score once more late in the final minute on a 4-yard Jameon Lewis touchdown reception from Prescott, but they were unable to recover the onside kick and Alabama won 25-20.[125]

Passing	C/ATT	YDS	AVG	TD	INT	QBR
B. Sims	19/31	211	6.8	1	0	83.4

Rushing	CAR	YDS	AVG	TD	LONG
TJ Yeldon	16	72	4.5	1	11
D. Henry	11	36	3.3	1	9
B. Sims	4	18	4.5	0	11
Team	1	-2	-2	0	0
Team	32	124	3.9	2	11

Interceptions	INT	YDS	TD
L. Collins	1	2	0
N. Perry	1	1	0
Cy. Jones	1	0	0
Team	3	3	0

Punting	NO	YDS	AVG	TB	IN 20	LONG
JK Scott	7	319	45.6	0	5	56

Receiving	REC	YDS	AVG	TD	LONG
A. Cooper	8	88	11	1	50
D. White	4	40	10	0	17
J. Fowler	1	35	35	0	35
A. Stewart	2	25	12.5	0	17
TJ Yeldon	2	16	8	0	8
B. Vogler	1	5	5	0	5
OJ Howard	1	2	2	0	2
Team	19	211	11.1	1	50

Kick returns	NO	YDS	AVG	LONG	TD
Ch. Jones	4	92	23	26	0
OJ Howard	1	5	5	5	0
D. White	1	1	1	1	0
Team	6	98	16.3	26	0

Kicking	FG	PCT	LONG	XP	PTS
A. Griffith	1/2	50	36	2/2	5

Note: Table data from "Alabama 25-20 Mississippi State (Nov 15, 2014) Box Score" (136)

11/22/14 - Alabama (1) vs Western Carolina

Team	1	2	3	4	T		Passing	Rushing	Total
Western Carolina	7	7	0	0	14		221	-8	213
Alabama (1)	10	28	10	0	48		337	275	612

The Alabama defense limited Western Carolina to -8 rushing yards while the Crimson Tide offense set a single-game record for first downs as top-ranked Alabama overcame a sluggish start to roll to a 48-14 win over Western Carolina. The win was Alabama's 15th straight at Bryant-Denny Stadium, the nation's longest active home winning streak.

Alabama's offense tallied 612 total yards and a school-record 36 first downs while holding the Catamounts to 213 total yards and dominating play after WCU took the opening kickoff and drove for a touchdown to an early 7-0 lead over the Tide, the first time in 23 games that an Alabama opponent has opened the game with a touchdown drive. Western Carolina scored one more touchdown in the second quarter, and that would be it for the rest of the game. Meanwhile, Alabama scored six times in the first half, starting with a 4-yard touchdown pass from Blake Sims to Cam Sims. After Gunnar Raborn kicked a 20-yard field goal, Derrick Henry scored from ten yards out. Then after a 7-yard rushing score by Tyren Jones, Derrick Henry scored on a 23-yard run and a 9-yard catch, giving Alabama a 38-14 lead at the half.

With the reserves in for the remainder of the game, Alabama scored another field goal and touchdown in the third quarter before a scoreless fourth quarter. Amari Cooper tied the Alabama career receptions mark in the game, catching three passes in the early going before leaving with a minor injury. The catches moved Cooper's career total to 194, matching the record set by DJ Hall. Henry became the 55th player in Alabama history to eclipse 1,000 career rushing yards as he now has 1,064 career yards for his career. Reserve backs Tyren Jones and Altee Tenpenny combined for 139 rushing yards for the Tide with Jones gaining 75 and a touchdown on 11 carries while Tenpenny rushed for 64 yards on 11 carries.

The Crimson Tide defense was led by safety Landon Collins' seven tackles. Linebacker Trey DePriest had five stops. Alabama's defense had two quarterback sacks in the game, five tackles for loss, and three quarterback hurries. The Tide never punted in the game. Freshman kicker Gunnar Raborn made his debut for Alabama as placekicker Adam Griffith did not play in the game. Raborn's opener was a successful one as he made all six extra-point kicks and was 2-for-3 on field goals. Raborn was good from 20 and 28 yards before missing on a 31-yard attempt.[125]

Passing	C/ATT	YDS	AVG	TD	INT	QBR
B. Sims	17/25	222	8.9	2	1	36
J. Coker	12/18	115	6.4	1	0	58.7
Team	29/43	337	7.8	3	1	--

Rushing	CAR	YDS	AVG	TD	LONG
D. Henry	12	92	7.7	2	23
T. Jones	11	75	6.8	1	13
A. Tenpenny	11	64	5.8	0	23
J. Fowler	5	30	6	0	12
B. Pell	2	15	7.5	0	8
B. Sims	4	-1	-0.3	0	7
Team	45	275	6.1	3	23

Kick returns	NO	YDS	AVG	LONG	TD
L. Collins	1	30	30	30	0
X. Dickson	1	7	7	7	0
OJ Howard	1	5	5	5	0
Team	3	42	14	30	0

Receiving	REC	YDS	AVG	TD	LONG
C. Black	6	101	16.8	0	26
A. Stewart	5	51	10.2	0	18
A. Cooper	3	46	15.3	0	27
R. Foster	4	40	10	0	14
C. Sims	3	33	11	1	22
OJ Howard	2	33	16.5	0	26
M. Nysewander	1	12	12	1	12
Ch. Jones	1	11	11	0	11
D. Henry	1	9	9	1	9
M. Faciane	2	2	1	0	3
T. Jones	1	-1	-1	0	0
Team	29	337	11.6	3	27

Punt returns	NO	YDS	AVG	LONG	TD
Ch. Jones	3	27	9	22	0
Cy. Jones	1	5	5	5	0
Team	4	32	8	22	0

Kicking	FG	PCT	LONG	XP	PTS
G. Raborn	2/3	66.7	28	6/6	12

Note: Table data from "Alabama 48-14 Western Carolina (Nov 22, 2014) Box Score" (137)

11/29/14 - Alabama (1) vs Auburn (15)

Team	1	2	3	4	T		Passing	Rushing	Total
Auburn (15)	6	20	10	8	**44**		456	174	**630**
Alabama (1)	14	7	13	21	**55**		312	227	**539**

In the 2014 edition of the Iron Bowl, Alabama defeated the Auburn Tigers 55-44 in Tuscaloosa in what was the highest scoring game between the rivals. On the opening kickoff, the Crimson Tide failed to recover an onside kick and gave Auburn good field position to start the game. On the next play, the Tigers turned the ball over on a failed lateral pass from Nick Marshall to Roc Thomas. Five plays later, the Crimson Tide took a 7-0 lead behind an 8-yard T.J. Yeldon touchdown run. Alabama scored its second touchdown on a 17-yard Amari Cooper reception from Blake Sims after Daniel Carlson converted a 20-yard field goal that made the score 14-3. Auburn then took a 16-14 lead behind a pair of 24-yard Carlson field goals and a 34-yard Nick Marshall touchdown pass to Sammie Coates. The Crimson Tide then briefly took a 21-16 lead behind a 1-yard Yeldon touchdown run before Auburn scored ten points en route to a 26-21 halftime lead. First, Marshall threw a 68-yard touchdown pass to Coates, and after Sims threw a late interception, Carlson connected on a 20-yard field goal as time expired in the second quarter.

On the second play of the second half, Sims threw his third interception of the game, and on the Auburn drive that ensued, the Tigers took a 33-21 lead behind a 5-yard Marshall TD pass to Bray. The Tide responded on their next possession with a 39-yard Sims TD pass to Cooper (PAT blocked) and the Tigers followed with a 33-yard Carlson field goal for a 36-27 Tigers lead. After this, the Crimson Tide scored touchdowns on their next four possessions and took a 55-36 lead into the final minutes of the game. After Cooper scored on a 75-yard touchdown reception, Nick Perry intercepted a Marshall pass for the Alabama defense. Five plays later, Sims scored on a 5-yard touchdown run and completed the two-point conversion pass to DeAndrew White.

On the Auburn possession that followed, Marshall was unable to make a third down conversion, and the ball was punted back to Alabama. The Crimson Tide then extended their lead further when Sims connected with DeAndrew White on a 6-yard touchdown pass. The Crimson Tide defense then forced a turnover on downs on the next Tigers possession. On the drive that ensued, Derrick Henry had a 49-yard run and followed it two plays later with a 25-yard touchdown run for a 55-36 Crimson Tide lead. A 5-yard Corey Grant touchdown run for Auburn in the final minute made the final score 55-44 in favor of Alabama. With his 13 receptions, 224 yards receiving and three touchdown receptions, Cooper tied the Alabama single-game record in all three categories.[125]

Passing	C/ATT	YDS	AVG	TD	INT	QBR
B. Sims	20/27	312	11.6	4	3	94.2

Rushing	CAR	YDS	AVG	TD	LONG
TJ Yeldon	19	127	6.7	2	25
D. Henry	5	72	14.4	1	49
B. Sims	5	23	4.6	1	11
J. Fowler	3	11	3.7	0	8
Ch. Jones	1	-4	-4	0	0
Team	1	-2	-2	0	0
Team	34	227	6.7	4	49

Interceptions	INT	YDS	TD
N. Perry	1	23	0

Punt returns	NO	YDS	AVG	LONG	TD
Ch. Jones	2	24	12	29	0

Punting	NO	YDS	AVG	TB	IN 20	LONG
JK Scott	2	111	55.5	1	1	70

Receiving	REC	YDS	AVG	TD	LONG
A. Cooper	13	224	17.2	3	75
Ch. Jones	1	21	21	0	21
OJ Howard	1	20	20	0	20
D. White	3	19	6.3	1	10
J. Fowler	1	15	15	0	15
TJ Yeldon	1	13	13	0	13
Team	20	312	15.6	4	75

Kick returns	NO	YDS	AVG	LONG	TD
Ch. Jones	3	63	21	37	0
X. Dickson	1	0	0	0	0
Team	4	63	15.8	37	0

Kicking	FG	PCT	LONG	XP	PTS
G. Raborn	0/0	0	0	3/4	3
A. Griffith	0/0	0	0	2/2	2
Team	0/0	0	0	5/6	5

Note: Table data from "Alabama 55-44 Auburn (Nov 29, 2014) Box Score" (138)

177

12/06/14 - Alabama (1) at Missouri (16)

Team	1	2	3	4	T		Passing	Rushing	Total
Alabama (1)	7	14	0	21	**42**		262	242	**504**
Missouri (16)	0	3	10	0	**13**		272	41	**313**

Blake Sims completed 23-of-27 passes for 262 yards and two TDs on the way to earning MVP honors, and Amari Cooper had a game-record 12 catches for 83 yards to lead the top-ranked Tide to a 42-13 victory over 16th-ranked Missouri in the SEC Championship Game. Alabama held Missouri to three points in the first half while forcing five punts. T.J. Yeldon scored touchdowns from one and two yards out, and DeAndrew White scored on a 58-yard catch to put the Tide up 21-3 at the half. Missouri made a push in the third quarter that narrowed the margin to 21-13, but the Tide scored three more touchdowns in the fourth quarter to put the game away. Christion Jones scored on a 6-yard pass, then Derrick Henry scored on runs from 26 and one yard out.

The Crimson Tide set new SEC title game records for first downs (28), points scored (42), offensive plays (76), rushing touchdowns (4), and pass completions (23). The Alabama defense limited Missouri to 313 yards (272 passing, 41 rushing) and ten first downs. A'Shawn Robinson led the Tide's effort with nine tackles (five solo), including three for loss and a QB hurry. Landon Collins had seven stops (six solo), a tackle for a loss, forced a fumble, and recovered a fumble. The Tide defense had a season-high 11 QB hurries in the game, six tackles for loss, broke up four passes, and made numerous negative plays in the running game.

Four Tide players set individual highs for an SEC title game as Blake Sims set overall game records for total offense (281 yards) and completion percentage (85.1 percent) without an interception; Amari Cooper set the mark for catches (12); Christion Jones set a game record for average yards per kickoff return (28.3 yards per return on three returns); and A'Shawn Robinson set a Tide record for tackles for loss in an SEC title game (3). Derrick Henry set career single-game highs for rushes, rushing yards, and rushing touchdowns with 141 yards and two scores on 20 carries. In addition to Cooper's 12 catches, DeAndrew White had a team-leading 101 receiving yards and a touchdown on four catches.

The Alabama defense was led in tackles by Trey DePriest with 14 while safety Nick Perry had 13 stops, and Geno Smith had ten tackles (two for loss). Perry also had two tackles for loss, a key interception, and broke up another pass. Reggie Ragland had three tackles, including a crucial fumble recovery. The Tide defense ended the game with two QB sacks, nine tackles for loss, six pass breakups, and eight QB hurries. JK Scott averaged 43.3 yards on his punts, including a 52-yarder and two punts that were downed inside the 20. The win gave Alabama a league-leading 24th SEC championship, and its victory marks the eighth time in Alabama's history with 12 wins in a season, including the fifth time in eight seasons under Nick Saban. The Tide moved to 31-10 against nationally ranked opponents since 2008.[125]

Passing	C/ATT	YDS	AVG	TD	INT	QBR
B. Sims	23/27	262	9.7	2	0	87.5

Rushing	CAR	YDS	AVG	TD	LONG
D. Henry	20	141	7.1	2	45
TJ Yeldon	14	47	3.4	2	12
T. Jones	3	26	8.7	0	14
B. Sims	9	19	2.1	0	17
A. Cooper	1	9	9	0	9
J. Fowler	1	2	2	0	2
Team	1	-2	-2	0	0
Team	49	242	4.9	4	45

Punting	NO	YDS	AVG	TB	IN 20	LONG
JK Scott	3	130	43.3	0	2	52

Receiving	REC	YDS	AVG	TD	LONG
D. White	4	101	25.3	1	58
A. Cooper	12	83	6.9	0	17
Ch. Jones	3	40	13.3	1	17
OJ Howard	2	20	10	0	17
J. Fowler	1	13	13	0	13
B. Vogler	1	5	5	0	5
Team	23	262	11.4	2	58

Kick returns	NO	YDS	AVG	LONG	TD
Ch. Jones	3	85	28.3	36	0

Punt returns	NO	YDS	AVG	LONG	TD
Ch. Jones	1	1	1	1	0

Kicking	FG	PCT	LONG	XP	PTS
A. Griffith	0/1	0	0	6/6	6

Note: Table data from "Alabama 42-13 Missouri (Dec 6, 2014) Box Score" (139)

01/01/15 - Alabama (1) at Ohio State (4)

Team	1	2	3	4	T		Passing	Rushing	Total
Alabama (1)	14	7	7	7	35		237	170	407
Ohio State (4)	6	14	14	8	42		256	281	537

The opening kickoff to Alabama resulted in a touchback that came out to the 20-yard line. Alabama was forced to punt on its first drive, going three-and-out. The Buckeyes began its first drive of the night from its own 15-yard line. They drove down the field into the red zone, but failed to get a touchdown and were forced to kick a field goal, giving them a 3-0 lead. The drive involved a 54-yard run by Ezekiel Elliott in which it saw him break tackles and hurdle another tackler. Alabama was forced to punt on its next drive. However, on the first play of Ohio State's next drive, Elliott lost the first fumble of his career, which was recovered by Landon Collins at the Ohio State 32-yard line. Two plays into Alabama's next drive, Derrick Henry ran 25 yards untouched into the end zone for a touchdown, giving the Crimson Tide their first lead of the game, 7-3. Ohio State drove into the Alabama red zone, but once again had to settle for a field goal, cutting the Alabama lead to 7-6. However, the Crimson Tide responded with a 15-yard touchdown pass from Blake Sims to Amari Cooper, increasing the Tide's lead to 14-6.

After back-to-back punts by each team, Cardale Jones threw an interception to Cyrus Jones that was returned to the Ohio State 15-yard line. From there, Alabama cashed in with a 2-yard touchdown run by T.J. Yeldon to make the score 21-6 Crimson Tide. The next drive for the Buckeyes started with an unsportsmanlike conduct penalty by Alabama on the ensuing kickoff, giving them the ball at their own 29-yard line. With several big plays during the drive, Ohio State scored a touchdown with Elliott taking it in from three yards out to cut the Tide lead to 21-13. After Alabama punted on its next possession, Ohio State took over with 1:32 remaining in the half. With several big plays, including a big run by Jones which set up the Buckeyes in the red zone, Ohio State scored right before the half on an end around touchdown completed with wide receiver Evan Spencer throwing to wide receiver Michael Thomas in the end zone. Replays showed Thomas making an unbelievable catch along the sidelines by keeping his foot in bounds while maintaining possession of the ball. The touchdown was reviewed and upheld on replay, and Alabama's lead was cut to 21-20 at halftime.

Despite trailing by one at the half, Ohio State dominated the stat sheet, outgaining Alabama 348-139 and being 7-of-10 on third downs and Alabama being only 1-of-7. Out of Ohio State's seven 3rd down conversions in the first half, six of them were conversions of 8+ yards, the most allowed by Alabama in a decade.

In the second half, Ohio State got the ball first to begin the third quarter. The drive was completed with Cardale Jones throwing a 47-yard touchdown pass to Devin Smith to give Ohio State a 27-21 lead. After back-to-back punts by each team, Blake Sims threw an interception that was returned by Steve Miller 36 yards for a touchdown, increasing the Buckeyes lead to 34-21. Sims' pick-six was the first pick-six thrown by an Alabama quarterback since 2007. The Crimson Tide, however, were able to go down the field and score a touchdown of their own, cutting the lead to 34-28, which was the score heading into the final quarter.

After a long scoring hiatus that saw the two teams punt back and forth to each other, Ohio State managed to increase its lead with an 85-yard touchdown run by Ezekiel Elliott, the longest play from scrimmage Alabama had allowed all season. This play earned the game the nickname "85 Yards Through the Heart of the South." and the "Zeke Streak". The two-point conversion was successful, giving the Buckeyes a 42-28 lead. However, the Crimson Tide scored quickly, going 65 yards in 1:25 to cut the lead to 42-35. After Ohio State was forced to punt on its next drive, the Tide got the ball back with no timeouts, needing to score a touchdown to force overtime. However, it was not to be, as Blake Sims' last second Hail Mary pass was intercepted in the end

179

zone by Tyvis Powell, ending the game and sending Ohio State to the national championship game for the first time since 2008. Sims finished with a career-high three interceptions.[125]

Passing	C/ATT	YDS	AVG	TD	INT	QBR
B. Sims	22/36	237	6.6	2	3	47.8

Rushing	CAR	YDS	AVG	TD	LONG
D. Henry	13	95	7.3	1	25
TJ Yeldon	10	47	4.7	1	10
B. Sims	10	29	2.9	1	18
Team	1	-1	-1	0	0
Team	34	170	5.0	3	25

Interceptions	INT	YDS	TD
Cy. Jones	1	32	0

Kicking	FG	PCT	LONG	XP	PTS
A. Griffith	0/0	0	0	5/5	5

Punting	NO	YDS	AVG	TB	IN 20	LONG
JK Scott	7	385	55	0	5	73

Receiving	REC	YDS	AVG	TD	LONG
A. Cooper	9	71	7.9	2	15
D. White	3	65	21.7	0	51
D. Henry	2	54	27	0	52
J. Fowler	2	14	7	0	10
OJ Howard	2	14	7	0	8
C. Black	2	10	5	0	8
B. Vogler	2	9	4.5	0	5
Team	22	237	10.8	2	52

Kick returns	NO	YDS	AVG	LONG	TD
Ch. Jones	7	102	14.6	34	0

Punt returns	NO	YDS	AVG	LONG	TD
Ch. Jones	2	10	5	10	0

Note: Table data from "Alabama 35-42 Ohio State (Jan 1, 2015) Box Score" (140)

Season Stats

Record	12-2	6th of 128
SEC Record	8-1	
Rank	4	
Points for	517	
Points against	258	
Points/game	36.9	16th of 128
Opp points/game	18.4	6th of 128
SOS[8]	7.26	5th of 128

Team stats (averages per game)

Split	G	Passing					Rushing				Total Offense		
		Cmp	Att	Pct	Yds	TD	Att	Yds	Avg	TD	Plays	Yds	Avg
Offense	14	20.7	32.2	64.3	277.9	2.3	40.5	206.6	5.1	2.5	72.7	484.5	6.7
Defense	14	19.1	35.2	54.4	226	1.4	32.3	102.4	3.2	0.4	67.5	328.4	4.9
Difference		1.6	-3	9.9	51.9	0.9	8.2	104.2	1.9	2.1	5.2	156.1	1.8

Split	First Downs				Penalties		Turnovers		
	Pass	Rush	Pen	Tot	No.	Yds	Fum	Int	Tot
Offense	12.1	11	1.1	24.3	4.9	40.1	0.9	0.7	1.6
Defense	10.1	5.8	0.9	16.7	4.4	36.9	0.6	0.8	1.4
Difference	2	5.2	0.2	7.6	0.5	3.2	0.3	-0.1	0.2

Passing

Rk	Player	G	Passing								
			Cmp	Att	Pct	Yds	Y/A	AY/A	TD	Int	Rate
1	Blake Sims	14	252	391	64.5	3487	8.9	9.2	28	10	157.9
2	Jake Coker	5	38	59	64.4	403	6.8	8.2	4	0	144.2

Rushing and receiving

Rk	Player	G	Rushing					Receiving				Scrimmage			
			Att	Yds	Avg	TD	Rec	Yds	Avg	TD	Plays	Yds	Avg	TD	
1	T.J. Yeldon	13	194	979	5	11	15	180	12	1	209	1159	5.5	12
2	Derrick Henry	14	172	990	5.8	11	5	133	26.6	2	177	1123	6.3	13
3	Blake Sims	14	83	350	4.2	7					83	350	4.2	7
4	Tyren Jones	6	36	224	6.2	2	1	-1	-1	0	37	223	6	2
5	Altee Tenpenny	4	26	136	5.2	0					26	136	5.2	0
6	Kenyan Drake	5	22	112	5.1	4	5	159	31.8	2	27	271	10	6
7	Jalston Fowler	12	12	69	5.8	0	11	129	11.7	2	23	198	8.6	2
8	Jake Coker	5	7	13	1.9	0					7	13	1.9	0
9	Amari Cooper	14	5	23	4.6	0	124	1727	13.9	16	129	1750	13.6	16
10	Buddy Pell	1	2	15	7.5	0					2	15	7.5	0
11	Deandrew White	10	2	-4	-2	0	40	504	12.6	4	42	500	11.9	4
12	Christion Jones	13	1	-4	-4	0	19	264	13.9	1	20	260	13	1
13	O.J. Howard	9					17	260	15.3	0	17	260	15.3	0
14	Chris Black	6					15	188	12.5	0	15	188	12.5	0
15	Ardarius Stewart	6					12	149	12.4	0	12	149	12.4	0
16	Cam Sims	4					7	62	8.9	1	7	62	8.9	1
17	Robert Foster	3					6	44	7.3	0	6	44	7.3	0
18	Brian Vogler	5					6	27	4.5	1	6	27	4.5	1
19	Michael Nysewander	3					2	21	10.5	1	2	21	10.5	1
20	Ty Flournoy-Smith	2					2	18	9	1	2	18	9	1
21	Malcolm Faciane	1					2	2	1	0	2	2	1	0
22	Brandon Greene	1					1	24	24	0	1	24	24	0

181

Defense and fumbles

Rk	Player	G	Tackles					Def Int					Fumbles			
			Solo	Ast	Tot	Loss	Sk	Int	Yds	Avg	TD	PD	FR	Yds	TD	FF
1	Landon Collins	14	60	39	99	4.5	0	3	14	4.7	0	7	2			1
2	Reggie Ragland	13	46	47	93	10.5	1.5	1	1	1	0	3	3			1
3	Trey DePriest	13	43	44	87	5	0					2				
4	Nick Perry	13	52	26	78	4.5	0	2	24	12	0	5				
5	Geno Smith	14	33	21	54	3	0					1				1
6	Jarran Reed	13	22	32	54	6.5	1					5				
7	A'Shawn Robinson	12	16	33	49	6.5	0					3				1
8	Cyrus Jones	14	36	8	44	2	0	3	27	9	0	13	1	13	1	2
9	Xzavier Dickson	13	32	10	42	12.5	9					2				
10	Eddie Jackson	9	29	8	37	1	1	1	18	18	0	6	1			1
11	Jonathan Allen	14	16	16	32	11	5					1				
12	Ryan Anderson	13	12	13	25	8	3						1			0
13	Reuben Foster	9	12	11	23	2	1									
14	Dillon Lee	9	11	12	23	0	0									
15	D.J. Pettway	12	14	8	22	3.5	2.5					3				
16	Dalvin Tomlinson	8	8	14	22	4.5	1									
17	Jabriel Washington	12	12	5	17	0	0	1	0	0	0	2				
18	Rashaan Evans	9	11	3	14	2	1									
19	Brandon Ivory	5	1	12	13	0.5	0									
20	Jarrick Williams	7	9	4	13	0.5	0					3				
21	Denzel Devall	7	3	8	11	1	0									
22	Maurice Smith	8	7	3	10	0.5	0.5					1				
23	Tony Brown	5	6	3	9	0	0					1				
24	Bradley Sylve	2	7	1	8	0	0					2				
25	Da'Shawn Hand	6	4	3	7	2	2									
26	Christion Jones	13	5	0	5	0	0									
27	Darren Lake	4	2	3	5	0	0									
28	Tim Williams	6	2	3	5	1.5	1.5									
29	Dominick Jackson	1	3	1	4	1	0									1
30	Cole Mazza	2	1	3	4	0	0									
31	Kenyan Drake	5	3	0	3	0	0									
32	Shaun Dion Hamilton	2	0	3	3	0	0									
33	Derrick Henry	14	2	1	3	0	0									
34	O.J. Howard	9	3	0	3	0	0									
35	Jalston Fowler	12	2	0	2	0	0									
36	Ardarius Stewart	6	1	1	2	0	0									
37	Altee Tenpenny	4	2	0	2	0	0									
38	Parker Barrineau	1	1	0	1	0	0									
39	Leon Brown	1	1	0	1	0	0									
40	Robert Foster	3	1	0	1	0	0									
41	Joshua Frazier	1	1	0	1	1	1									
42	Hootie Jones	1	0	1	1	0	0									
43	Tyren Jones	6	0	1	1	0	0									
44	Korren Kirven	1	0	1	1	0	0									
45	Dee Liner	1	1	0	1	0	0									
46	Michael Nysewander	3	1	0	1	0	0									
47	Cam Robinson	1	1	0	1	0	0									
48	Cam Sims	4	1	0	1	0	0									
49	Deandrew White	10	1	0	1	1	0									

Kick and punt returns

Rk	Player	G	Kick Ret				Punt Ret			
			Ret	Yds	Avg	TD	Ret	Yds	Avg	TD
1	Christion Jones	13	37	851	23	0	19	152	8	1
2	Cyrus Jones	14	4	77	19.3	0	4	82	20.5	0
3	Landon Collins	14	3	55	18.3	0				
4	O.J. Howard	9	2	10	5	0				
5	Xzavier Dickson	13	2	7	3.5	0				
6	Deandrew White	10	1	1	1	0				
7	Ryan Anderson	13		5						
8	Maurice Smith	8					1	0	0	0
9	Tyren Jones	6					1	0	0	0

Kicking and punting

Rk	Player	G	Kicking								Punting		
			XPM	XPA	XP%	FGM	FGA	FG%	Pts	Punts	Yds	Avg
1	Adam Griffith	13	53	54	98.1	12	19	63.2	89			
2	Gunnar Raborn	2	9	10	90	2	3	66.7	15			
3	JK Scott	12	1	1	100	0	0		1	55	2640	48

Scoring

Rk	Player	G	Touchdowns							Kicking				Pts
			Rush	Rec	Int	FR	PR	KR	Tot	XPM	FGM	2PM	Sfty	
1	Amari Cooper	14		16					16					96
2	Adam Griffith	13								53	12			89
3	Derrick Henry	14	11	2					13					78
4	T.J. Yeldon	13	11	1					12					72
5	Blake Sims	14	7						7					42
6	Kenyan Drake	5	4	2					6					36
7	Deandrew White	10		4					4			1		26
8	Gunnar Raborn	2								9	2			15
9	Christion Jones	13		1			1		2					12
10	Jalston Fowler	12		2					2					12
11	Tyren Jones	6	2						2					12
12	Brian Vogler	5		1					1					6
13	Cam Sims	4		1					1					6
14	Cyrus Jones	14				1			1					6
15	Michael Nysewander	3		1					1					6
16	Ty Flournoy-Smith	2		1					1					6
17	JK Scott	12								1				1

Stats include bowl games
Note: Table data from "2014 Alabama Crimson Tide Stats" (8)

Awards and honors

Name	Award	Type
Landon Collins	Permanent Team Captain	Team
Amari Cooper	Permanent Team Captain	Team
Jalston Fowler	Permanent Team Captain	Team
Blake Sims	Permanent Team Captain	Team
Amari Cooper	MVP	Team
Amari Cooper	Offensive Player of the Year	Team
Blake Sims	Offensive Player of the Year	Team
Landon Collins	Defensive Player of the Year	Team
Trey DePriest	Defensive Player of the Year	Team
Amari Cooper	AP Player of the Year	SEC
Jonathan Allen	AP All-SEC First Team	SEC
Landon Collins	AP All-SEC First Team	SEC
Amari Cooper	AP All-SEC First Team	SEC
Arie Kouandjio	AP All-SEC First Team	SEC
Reggie Ragland	AP All-SEC First Team	SEC
JK Scott	AP All-SEC First Team	SEC
Cyrus Jones	AP All-SEC Second Team	SEC
Austin Shepherd	AP All-SEC Second Team	SEC
Blake Sims	AP All-SEC Second Team	SEC
Trey DePriest	AP All-SEC Honorable Mention Team	SEC
Ryan Kelly	AP All-SEC Honorable Mention Team	SEC
Jarran Reed	AP All-SEC Honorable Mention Team	SEC
A'Shawn Robinson	AP All-SEC Honorable Mention Team	SEC
Landon Collins	Coaches' All-SEC First Team	SEC
Amari Cooper	Coaches' All-SEC First Team	SEC
Trey DePriest	Coaches' All-SEC First Team	SEC
Arie Kouandjio	Coaches' All-SEC First Team	SEC
JK Scott	Coaches' All-SEC First Team	SEC
Blake Sims	Coaches' All-SEC Second Team	SEC
T.J. Yeldon	Coaches' All-SEC Second Team	SEC
Landon Collins	AFCA All-America Team	National
Amari Cooper	AFCA All-America Team	National
Trey DePriest	AFCA All-America Team	National
Arie Kouandjio	AFCA All-America Team	National
Landon Collins	AP All-America First Team	National
Amari Cooper	AP All-America First Team	National
Arie Kouandjio	AP All-America Second Team	National

Name	Award	Type
JK Scott	AP All-America Second Team	National
Landon Collins	Bronko Nagurski Trophy Finalist	National
Amari Cooper	FWAA All-America First Team	National
Landon Collins	Consensus All-American	National
Amari Cooper	Consensus All-American	National
Amari Cooper	Biletnikoff Award	National
Landon Collins	FWAA All-America First Team	National
Amari Cooper	Heisman Trophy Finalist	National
Landon Collins	Jim Thorpe Award Finalist	National
JK Scott	Ray Guy Award Finalist	National
Landon Collins	Sporting News (TSN) All-America Team	National
Amari Cooper	Sporting News (TSN) All-America Team	National
JK Scott	Sporting News (TSN) All-America Team	National
Landon Collins	Unanimous All-American	National
Amari Cooper	Unanimous All-American	National
Landon Collins	Walter Camp All-America First Team	National
Amari Cooper	Walter Camp All-America First Team	National
Amari Cooper	Walter Camp Award Finalist	National
Jalston Fowler	Senior Bowl	All-Star Team
Arie Kouandjio	Senior Bowl	All-Star Team
Austin Shepherd	Senior Bowl	All-Star Team
Blake Sims	Senior Bowl	All-Star Team

Note: Table data from "2014 Alabama Crimson Tide football team" (125)

NFL

Season	Year drafted	Round	Pick	Overall	Player	Position	Team
2014	2015	1	4	4	Amari Cooper	WR	Las Vegas Raiders
2014	2015	2	1	33	Landon Collins	S	New York Giants
2014	2015	2	4	36	T.J. Yeldon	RB	Jacksonville Jaguars
2014	2015	4	9	108	Jalston Fowler	FB	Tennessee Titans
2014	2015	4	13	112	Arie Kouandjio	OG	Washington Commanders
2014	2015	7	11	228	Austin Shepherd	OT	Minnesota Vikings
2014	2015	7	36	253	Xzavier Dickson	LB	New England Patriots

Note: Table data from "2015 NFL Draft" (141)

2015

Overall

Record	14-1
SEC Record	8-1
Rank	1
Points for	526
Points against	227
Points/game	35.1
Opp points/game	15.1
SOS[9]	7.46

I said before, I believe in our team. I do believe in our team, and we're going to work hard to make our team better, and I hope the players respond the right way. And it's not going to be for you! The fans, yes. Because if it was up to you, we were six foot under already. We're dead and buried and gone. Gone! So if that was the case, we'd have to get some respirators out or something there to put the life back in people.
-Nick Saban

Games

Date	Bama Rank		Opp Rank	Opponent	Bama	Opp	Result	SEC
09/05/15	3	N	20	Wisconsin	35	17	W	
09/12/15	2	vs		Middle Tennessee State	37	10	W	
09/19/15	2	vs	15	Ole Miss	37	43	L	L
09/26/15	12	vs		Louisiana Monroe	34	0	W	
10/03/15	13	@	8	Georgia	38	10	W	W
10/10/15	8	vs		Arkansas	27	14	W	W
10/17/15	10	@	9	Texas A&M	41	23	W	W
10/24/15	8	vs		Tennessee	19	14	W	W
11/07/15	2	vs	4	LSU	30	16	W	W
11/14/15	2	@	17	Mississippi State	31	6	W	W
11/21/15	2	vs		Charleston Southern	56	6	W	
11/28/15	2	@		Auburn	29	13	W	W
12/05/15	2	N	18	Florida	29	15	W	W
12/31/15	2	N	3	Michigan State	38	0	W	
01/11/16	2	N	1	Clemson	45	40	W	

Coaches

Name	Position	Year
Nick Saban	Head Coach	9
Burton Burns	Associate Head Coach / Running Backs	9
Scott Cochran	Strength and Conditioning	9
Mario Cristobal	Offensive Line / Recruiting Coordinator	3
Bo Davis	Defensive Line	2 (6th overall)
Lane Kiffin	Offensive Coordinator / Quarterbacks	2
Tosh Lupoi	Outside Linebackers	1
Billy Napier	Wide Receivers	3
Freddie Roach	Director of Player Development	1 (4th overall)
Kirby Smart	Defensive Coordinator	9
Mel Tucker	Defensive Backs	1
Bobby Williams	Tight ends / Special Teams	8

Recruits

Name	Pos	Pos Rank	Scout	Rivals	247 Sports	ESPN	ESPN Grade	Hometown	High school / college	Height	Weight	Committed
Keaton Anderson	OLB	29	3	3	3	3	79	Florence, AL	Florence HS	6-1	215	5/29/14
Blake Barnett	QB	1	5	5	5	5	90	Corona, CA	Santiago HS	6-5	200	6/18/15
Mekhi Brown	OLB	10	4	4	4	4	83	Columbus, GA	Carver HS	6-5	218	4/8/13
Shawn Burgess-Becker	S	7	4	4	4	4	83	Coconut Creek, FL	Monarch HS	6-0	200	4/19/14
Daylon Charlot	WR	8	4	4	4	4	85	Patterson, LA	Patterson HS	6-0	177	2/4/15
Lester Cotton Sr.	OG	7	4	4	4	4	83	Tuscaloosa, AL	Tuscaloosa Central HS	6-4	328	2/1/14
Minkah Fitzpatrick	CB	4	4	4	4	4	88	Jersey City, NJ	Saint Peters Prep	6-1	194	4/19/15
DeSherrius Flowers	RB	10	4	4	4	4	83	Prichard, AL	Vigor HS	6-0	210	4/15/13
Damien Harris	RB	2	4	4	4	4	88	Berea, KY	Madison Southern HS	5-10	208	1/9/15
Ronnie Harrison Jr.	S	25	4	4	4	4	80	Tallahassee, FL	Florida HS	6-2	192	7/29/14
Hale Hentges	TE	3	4	4	4	4	83	Jefferson City, MO	Helias HS	6-4	230	5/25/14
Anfernee Jennings	DE	28	4	4	4	4	80	Dadeville, AL	Dadeville HS	6-3	245	3/6/14
Brandon Kennedy	OG	5	4	4	4	4	83	Wetumpka, AL	Wetumpka HS	6-3	285	7/18/14
Joshua McMillon	ILB	5	4	4	4	4	82	Memphis, TN	Whitehaven HS	6-3	249	8/22/14
Da'Ron Payne	DT	9	4	4	4	4	86	Birmingham, AL	Shades Valley HS	6-3	348	1/2/15
Richie Petitbon	OG	10	4	4	4	4	82	Washington, D.C.	Gonzaga College HS	6-4	313	4/4/14
Calvin Ridley	WR	1	4	4	5	5	89	Coconut Creek, FL	Monarch HS	6-1	169	4/19/14
Bo Scarbrough	ATH	2		5	5	5	90	Northport, AL	Tuscaloosa County HS	6-2	215	9/8/12
Kendall Sheffield	CB	3	5	5	5	5	90	Missouri City, TX	Thurgood Marshall HS	6-0	180	1/2/15
Jonathan Taylor	DT	2		3	3	4	81	Millen, GA	Copiah-Lincoln Community College	6-3	335	1/7/15
Adonis Thomas	OLB	5	4	4	4	4	85	Lawrenceville, GA	Central Gwinnett HS	6-4	219	12/8/14
Deionte Thompson	S	3	4	4	4	4	84	Orange, TX	West Orange-Stark HS	6-1	175	2/23/13
Dallas Warmack	OG	19	4	4	4	4	81	Atlanta, GA	Benjamin E. Mays HS	6-2	306	7/22/13
Matt Womack	OT	59	3	3	3	3	78	Senatobia, MS	Magnolia Heights School	6-6	325	12/14/14

	Scout	Rivals	247Sports	ESPN
5 Stars	2	3	4	4
4 Stars	18	18	17	18
3 Stars	2	3	3	2
2 Stars	0	0	0	0

Note: Table data from "2015 Alabama Crimson Tide football team" (142)

Roster

Num	Player	Pos	Class	Height	Weight	Hometown	Last School
93	Jonathan Allen	DL	JR	6-3	283	Leesburg, VA	Stone Bridge
41	Blaine Anderson	DB	JR	5-10	170	Charlotte, NC	Myers Park
18	Keaton Anderson	LB	FR	6-1	220	Florence, AL	Florence
22	Ryan Anderson	LB	JR	6-2	249	Daphne, AL	Daphne
28	Anthony Averett	DB	SO	6-0	180	Woodbury, NJ	Woodbury
94	Dakota Ball	TE	JR	6-3	254	Lindale, GA	Pepperell
6	Blake Barnett	QB	FR	6-5	200	Corona, CA	Santiago
87	Parker Barrineau	WR	SR	6-0	184	Northport, AL	American Christian Academy
18	Cooper Bateman	QB	SO	6-3	220	Murray, UT	Cottonwood
1	Chris Black	WR	JR	6-0	192	Jacksonville, FL	First Coast
61	Nolan Boatner	OL	FR	6-2	272	Gadsden, AL	Gadsden City
75	Bradley Bozeman	OL	SO	6-5	320	Roanoke, AL	Handley
48	Mekhi Brown	LB	FR	6-5	240	Columbus, GA	Carver
7	Tony Brown	DB	SO	6-0	195	Beaumont, TX	Ozen
45	Hunter Bryant	TE	SO	6-5	222	Roswell, GA	Fellowship Christian School
27	Shawn Burgess-Becker	DB	FR	6-1	205	Coconut Creek, FL	Monarch
43	Gussie Busch	LB	FR	5-11	205	St. Louis, MO	Priory
67	Joshua Casher	OL	SO	6-1	294	Mobile, AL	St. Paul's
4	Daylon Charlot	WR	FR	6-0	195	Patterson, LA	Patterson
5	Ronnie Clark	RB	FR	6-2	228	Calera, AL	Calera
14	Jake Coker	QB	SR	6-5	232	Mobile, AL	Florida State
12	David Cornwell	QB	FR	6-5	221	Norman, OK	Norman North
66	Lester Cotton Sr.	OL	FR	6-4	315	Tuscaloosa, AL	Central
39	Paden Crowder	LB	SR	6-3	208	Vestavia Hils, AL	Vestavia Hills
48	David D'Amico	TE	JR	6-0	211	Birmingham, AL	Vestavia Hills
62	Will Davis	OL	JR	6-5	315	Letohatchee, AL	Fort Dale Academy
30	Denzel Devall	LB	SR	6-2	252	Bastrop, LA	Bastrop
17	Kenyan Drake	RB	SR	6-1	210	Powder Spring, GA	Hillgrove
36	Johnny Dwight	DL	FR	6-3	300	Rochelle, GA	Wilcox County
43	Lawrence Erekosima	RB	SO	5-7	175	Simpsonville, SC	Clinton
32	Rashaan Evans	LB	SO	6-3	225	Auburn, AL	Auburn
80	Raheem Falkins	WR	JR	6-4	210	New Orleans, LA	G.W. Carver
29	Minkah Fitzpatrick	DB	FR	6-1	195	Old Bridge, NJ	St. Peter's Prep
83	Ty Flournoy-Smith	TE	SR	6-3	247	Moultrie, GA	Georgia Military
10	Reuben Foster	LB	JR	6-1	240	Auburn, AL	Auburn
8	Robert Foster	WR	SO	6-2	194	Monaca, PA	Central Valley
69	Joshua Frazier	DL	SO	6-4	315	Springdale, AR	Har-Ber
46	Derrick Garnett	LB	SO	6-1	250	Tuscaloosa, AL	Holy Spirit
33	Derrick Gore	RB	SO	5-11	210	Syracuse, NY	Coffeyville CC
47	Bo Grant	DB	JR	6-2	195	Valley, AL	Valley
58	Brandon Greene	TE	JR	6-5	300	Ellenwood, GA	Cedar Grove
99	Adam Griffith	PK	JR	5-10	192	Calhoun, GA	Calhoun
20	Shaun Dion Hamilton	LB	SO	6-0	229	Montgomery, AL	Carver
9	Da'Shawn Hand	DL	SO	6-4	273	Woodbridge, VA	Woodbridge
58	Alex Harrelson	SN	SR	6-0	234	Vestavia Hills, AL	Vestavia Hills
34	Damien Harris	RB	FR	5-11	205	Berea, KY	Madison Southern
86	Truett Harris	TE	SR	6-3	220	Brentwood, TN	Brentwood
15	Ronnie Harrison Jr.	DB	FR	6-3	218	Tallahassee, FL	FSU University School
63	J.C. Hassenauer	OL	SO	6-2	295	Woodbury, MN	East Ridge
2	Derrick Henry	RB	JR	6-3	242	Yulee, FL	Yulee
84	Hale Hentges	TE	FR	6-5	235	Jefferson City, MO	Helias
96	Stephen Hodge	DL	SR	6-2	254	Akron, AL	Hale County
42	Keith Holcombe	LB	FR	6-4	223	Tuscaloosa, AL	Hillcrest
88	O.J. Howard	TE	JR	6-6	242	Prattville, AL	Autauga Academy
26	Marlon Humphrey	DB	FR	6-1	192	Hoover, AL	Hoover
39	Tevin Isom	WR	JR	6-1	185	Atlanta, GA	Lakeside
76	Dominick Jackson	OL	SR	6-6	315	Cupertino, CA	College of San Mateo
4	Eddie Jackson	DB	JR	6-0	194	Lauderdale Lakes, FL	Boyd Anderson
33	Anfernee Jennings	LB	FR	6-3	255	Dadeville, AL	Dadeville
38	Austin Johnson	WR	FR	6-2	190	Elba, AL	Elba
89	Bernel Jones	LB	SR	6-2	248	Montgomery, AL	Jefferson Davis
5	Cyrus Jones	DB	SR	5-10	196	Baltimore, MD	Gilman
6	Hootie Jones	DB	SO	6-2	219	Monroe, LA	Neville
35	Walker Jones	LB	SO	6-2	240	Germantown, TN	Evangelical Christian
70	Ryan Kelly	OL	SR	6-5	297	West Chester, OH	Lakota West
56	Brandon Kennedy	OL	FR	6-3	290	Wetumpka, AL	Wetumpka
81	Derek Kief	WR	FR	6-4	198	Cincinnati, OH	La Salle
78	Korren Kirven	OL	JR	6-4	300	Lynchburg, VA	Brookville
95	Darren Lake	DL	SR	6-3	315	York, AL	Sumter County
25	Dillon Lee	LB	SR	6-4	242	Buford, GA	Buford
51	Jake Long	DL	JR	5-9	226	Vestavia Hills, AL	Vestavia Hills
68	Isaac Luatua	OL	SR	6-2	315	La Mirada, CA	La Mirada
36	Torin Marks	WR	FR	5-11	170	Rosenberg, TX	George Ranch

187

Num	Player	Pos	Class	Height	Weight	Hometown	Last School
31	Xavian Marks	RB	FR	5-8	160	Rosenberg, TX	George Ranch
24	Geno Matias-Smith	DB	SR	6-0	196	Atlanta, GA	St. Pius X
55	Cole Mazza	SN	JR	6-2	240	Bakersfield, CA	Liberty
40	Joshua McMillon	LB	FR	6-3	240	Memphis, TN	Whitehaven
34	Christian Miller	LB	FR	6-4	213	Columbia, SC	Spring Valley
60	Brandon Moore	TE	SR	6-0	251	Cincinnati, OH	Cincinnati Hills Christian Academy
11	Alec Morris	QB	JR	6-3	233	Allen, TX	Allen
16	Jamey Mosley	LB	FR	6-5	221	Mobile, AL	Theodore
16	*Richard Mullaney*	*WR*	*SR*	*6-3*	*208*	*Thousand Oaks, CA*	*Oregon State*
46	Michael Nysewander	TE	SR	6-1	237	Hoover, AL	Hoover
94	Da'Ron Payne	DL	FR	6-2	315	Birmingham, AL	Shades Valley
72	Richie Petitbon	OL	R-FR	6-4	315	Annapolis, MD	Gonzaga
57	D.J. Pettway	DL	SR	6-2	270	Pensacola, FL	East Mississippi CC
71	**Ross Pierschbacher**	**OL**	**SO**	**6-4**	**298**	**Cedar Falls, IA**	**Cedar Falls**
65	Chris Posa	OL	JR	6-4	281	Commerce, MI	St. Mary's Prep
45	Cedric Powell	DB	SO	5-11	185	Birmingham, AL	G.W. Carver
89	Armani Purifoye	WR	SO	6-0	195	Kingsland, GA	Camden County
96	Gunnar Raborn	PK	SO	5-9	187	Lafayette, LA	St. Thomas More
19	**Reggie Ragland**	**LB**	**SR**	**6-2**	**252**	**Madison, AL**	**Bob Jones**
90	**Jarran Reed**	**DL**	**SR**	**6-4**	**313**	**Goldsboro, NC**	**East Mississippi CC**
37	Jonathan Rice	WR	FR	6-4	207	Madison, AL	Bob Jones
3	Calvin Ridley	WR	FR	6-1	188	Coconut Creek, FL	Monarch
86	**A'Shawn Robinson**	**DL**	**JR**	**6-4**	**312**	**Fort Worth, TX**	**Arlington Heights**
74	**Cam Robinson**	**OL**	**SO**	**6-6**	**326**	**Monroe, LA**	**West Monroe**
9	Bo Scarbrough	RB	FR	6-2	240	Tuscaloosa, AL	Tuscaloosa County
15	**JK Scott**	**P**	**SO**	**6-5**	**195**	**Denver, CO**	**Mullen**
11	Kendall Sheffield	DB	FR	6-0	185	Missouri City, TX	Fort Bend Marshall
7	Cam Sims	WR	SO	6-5	209	Monroe, LA	Ouachita Parish
24	**Geno Smith**	**DB**	**SR**	**6-0**	**196**	**Atlanta, GA**	**St.Pius X**
21	Maurice Smith	DB	JR	6-0	199	Sugar Land, TX	Fort Bend Dulles
91	O.J. Smith	DL	FR	6-2	308	Bossier City, LA	Airline
31	Nate Staskelunas	DB	JR	6-3	210	Greenville, NC	Arendell Parrott Academy
13	**ArDarius Stewart**	**WR**	**SO**	**6-1**	**204**	**Fultondale, AL**	**Fultondale**
3	Bradley Sylve	DB	SR	6-0	180	Port Sulphur, LA	South Palquemines
50	**Alphonse Taylor**	**OL**	**JR**	**6-5**	**325**	**Mobile, AL**	**Davidson**
17	Adonis Thomas	LB	FR	6-2	228	Lawrenceville, GA	Central Gwinnett
23	Deionte Thompson	DB	FR	6-2	183	Orange, TX	West Orange-Stark
54	Dalvin Tomlinson	DL	JR	6-3	294	McDonaugh, GA	Henry County
29	Brandon Turner	RB	SO	5-9	171	Birmingham, AL	John Carroll Catholic
44	Levi Wallace	DB	SO	6-0	172	Tucson, AZ	Tucson
59	Dallas Warmack	OL	FR	6-2	297	Atlanta, GA	Mays
23	Jabriel Washington	DB	SR	5-11	182	Jackson, TN	Trinity Christian Academy
82	Thayer Weaver	WR	SO	5-11	180	St. Louis, MO	DeSmet
56	Tim Williams	LB	JR	6-4	230	Baton Rouge, LA	University Lab
82	JaMichael Willis	WR	JR	6-0	180	Gardendale, AL	Southern Miss.
77	Matt Womack	OL	FR	6-7	315	Hernando, MS	Magnolia Heights
35	Thomas Woods	WR	SO	5-6	165	Birmingham, AL	Vestavia Hills

Note: Starters in bold
Note: Table data from "2015 Alabama Crimson Tide Roster" (143)

Transfers

Player	School	Direction
Richard Mullaney	Oregon State	Incoming

Note: Table data from "Richard Mullaney" (144)

188

Games

09/05/15 - Alabama (3) vs Wisconsin (20)

AT&T Stadium
Arlington, TX

Team	1	2	3	4	T	Passing	Rushing	Total
Wisconsin (20)	0	7	3	7	17	228	40	268
Alabama (3)	7	7	14	7	35	264	238	502

The University of Alabama's junior running back Derrick Henry had a career day, rushing 13 times for 147 yards and three touchdowns to lead the No. 3 Crimson Tide past No. 20 Wisconsin 35-17 in the Advocare Classic inside AT&T Stadium in Arlington, Texas on Saturday night.

Henry opened up the game's scoring, breaking off a 37-yard run in the first quarter to put Alabama ahead 7-0. After a punt by each team, the Badgers evened the score at seven on a 6-yard TD reception ending a 9-play, 63-yard drive. Alabama responded on its next possession with an 8-play, 88-yard drive finished off with a 17-yard TD reception from Foster (14-7).

Henry put up two more scores in the third quarter, including a 56-yard touchdown rush that put him over 100 yards for the night, the sixth time in his career he has eclipsed the century mark in a game. The other was a 2-yard run capping off a 7-play, 67-yard drive. Wisconsin scored on a 43-yard field goal (Bama up 28-10). Both teams scored in the fourth (43-yard run by Kenyan Drake and 3-yard reception for the Badgers). Alabama won 35-17.

Senior quarterback Jake Coker, making his debut as the Crimson Tide's starting quarterback, was an efficient 15-of-21 for 213 yards and one touchdown to go along with no turnovers. Sophomore Cooper Bateman also saw action in the second half, finishing 7-for-8 with 51 yards. Defensively, Alabama was dominant at the line of scrimmage, holding the Badgers to just 40 yards rushing on 21 attempts, an average of 1.9 yards per rush. Senior linebacker Reggie Ragland recorded 12 total tackles, including five solo. Additionally, Jonathan Allen had two sacks and the team broke up seven passes on the night.

Overall, the Tide gained 502 yards (264 passing and 238 rushing), picked up 28 first downs, and averaged 7.6 yards per play. Wisconsin totaled 268 yards (228 passing and 40 rushing), along with converting 17 first downs and averaging 4.5 yards per play. The Tide also did not commit a turnover on the night. Alabama won its season opener for the 97th time in 121 season opening games with the victory. The Tide also moved to 6-0 in neutral-site season opening games.[142]

Passing	C/ATT	YDS	AVG	TD	INT	QBR
J. Coker	15/21	213	10.1	1	0	65.6
C. Bateman	7/8	51	6.4	0	0	65.6
Team	22/29	264	9.1	1	0	--

Rushing	CAR	YDS	AVG	TD	LONG
D. Henry	13	147	11.3	3	56
K. Drake	10	77	7.7	1	43
D. Harris	9	23	2.6	0	10
C. Bateman	2	4	2	0	6
J. Coker	3	-13	-4.3	0	11
Team	37	238	6.4	4	56

Interceptions	INT	YDS	TD
E. Jackson	1	41	0

Punt returns	NO	YDS	AVG	LONG	TD
Cy. Jones	4	25	6.3	18	0

Punting	NO	YDS	AVG	TB	IN 20	LONG
JK Scott	4	147	36.8	0	0	46

Receiving	REC	YDS	AVG	TD	LONG
R. Foster	4	50	12.5	1	22
K. Drake	2	48	24	0	33
A. Stewart	4	44	11	0	16
R. Mullaney	2	38	19	0	22
OJ Howard	3	37	12.3	0	21
C. Ridley	3	22	7.3	0	13
T. Flournoy-Smith	1	17	17	0	17
D. Henry	2	12	6	0	11
D. Harris	1	-4	-4	0	0
Team	22	264	12	1	33

Kick returns	NO	YDS	AVG	LONG	TD
K. Drake	2	28	14	16	0
C. Black	1	7	7	7	0
Team	3	35	11.7	16	0

Kicking	FG	PCT	LONG	XP	PTS
A. Griffith	0/2	0	0	5/5	5

Note: Table data from "Alabama 35-17 Wisconsin (Sep 5, 2015) Box Score" (145)

189

09/12/15 - Alabama (2) vs Middle Tennessee State

Team	1	2	3	4	T		Passing	Rushing	Total
Middle Tennessee State	0	3	0	7	10		189	86	275
Alabama (2)	7	16	14	0	37		312	220	532

The No. 2-ranked Alabama Crimson Tide opened their 2015 home slate in impressive fashion, forcing four turnovers en route to a 37-10 victory over visiting Middle Tennessee in front of 98,568 fans at Bryant-Denny Stadium on Saturday afternoon.

Alabama got off to a slow start going three-and-out on its first drive. Marlon Humphrey recovered a fumble on MTSU's very first play of their first drive, and senior quarterback Jake Coker, who had another solid game, took advantage of the short field. He hit Robert Foster for a 19-yard touchdown to open the scoring, capping a 4-play, 32-yard drive. In the second quarter, Derrick Henry added touchdown runs of one and two yards, Middle Tennessee State missed a 46-yard field goal and connected on a 31-yarder, and Ronnie Harrison picked up a safety. Each team also threw interceptions, and Alabama led 23-3 at halftime.

Alabama scored two more touchdowns in the third quarter. Sophomore quarterback Cooper Bateman recorded his first touchdown pass of his career, connecting with Kenyan Drake on a shovel pass for a 14-yard score, and Derrick Henry reached the end zone a third time thanks to a 28-yard burst. MTSU scored their only touchdown of the game late in the fourth quarter, bringing the final to 37-10.

Defensively, Alabama recovered all three fumbles it forced while also getting one interception, the most turnovers an Alabama defense has forced since September 8, 2012 against Western Kentucky. Senior linebacker Reggie Ragland led the team in tackles once again, recording a total of 7.5, including six solo stops. The secondary also broke up six passes.

For the game, Alabama totaled 532 yards (312 passing and 220 rushing), notched 28 first downs, and averaged 6.5 yards per play. Middle Tennessee gained 275 yards (189 passing and 86 rushing), along with collecting 15 first downs and averaging 3.7 yards per play. The Tide limited their penalties on the day, being flagged only five times for 40 yards.[142]

Passing	C/ATT	YDS	AVG	TD	INT	QBR
J. Coker	15/26	214	8.2	1	1	60.5
C. Bateman	11/17	98	5.8	1	1	14.4
Team	26/43	312	7.3	2	2	--

Rushing	CAR	YDS	AVG	TD	LONG
D. Henry	18	96	5.3	3	28
D. Harris	8	55	6.9	0	41
K. Drake	6	40	6.7	0	13
R. Clark	2	9	4.5	0	5
D. Gore	2	9	4.5	0	8
C. Bateman	2	6	3	0	6
J. Coker	1	5	5	0	5
Team	39	220	5.6	3	41

Interceptions	INT	YDS	TD
Cy. Jones	1	0	0

Kicking	FG	PCT	LONG	XP	PTS
A. Griffith	0/2	0	0	5/5	5

Punting	NO	YDS	AVG	TB	IN 20	LONG
JK Scott	5	201	40.2	0	0	44

Receiving	REC	YDS	AVG	TD	LONG
K. Drake	5	91	18.2	1	69
OJ Howard	4	68	17	0	42
R. Foster	4	49	12.3	1	19
C. Ridley	4	37	9.3	0	16
T. Flournoy-Smith	1	31	31	0	31
A. Stewart	6	21	3.5	0	8
D. Harris	1	8	8	0	8
R. Mullaney	1	7	7	0	7
Team	26	312	12	2	69

Kick returns	NO	YDS	AVG	LONG	TD
K. Drake	3	71	23.7	40	0
R. Mullaney	1	16	16	16	0
Team	4	87	21.8	40	0

Punt returns	NO	YDS	AVG	LONG	TD
R. Mullaney	1	22	22	22	0
R. Harrison Jr.	1	8	8	8	0
Cy. Jones	1	5	5	5	0
Team	3	35	11.7	22	0

Note: Table data from "Alabama 37-10 Middle Tennessee" (146)

09/19/15 - Alabama (2) vs Ole Miss (15)

Team	1	2	3	4	T		Passing	Rushing	Total
Ole Miss (15)	3	14	13	13	**43**		341	92	**433**
Alabama (2)	0	10	7	20	**37**		288	215	**503**

The No. 2 ranked Alabama Crimson Tide could not overcome five turnovers in their SEC opener, falling by a final score of 43-37 to the No. 15 Ole Miss Rebels in a back-and-forth contest in front of a sellout crowd of 101,821 on Saturday night at Bryant-Denny Stadium in Tuscaloosa.

The opening kickoff of the game would set the tone for Alabama, as a fumble by sophomore receiver ArDarius Stewart on the return was recovered by Ole Miss. The Rebels were able to turn that into three points, the only points of the quarter. The Tide evened the score early in the second quarter on an Adam Griffith 20-yard field goal after going 69 yards in 13 plays, but two more turnovers (interception thrown by Bateman and a fumbled kickoff by Drake) in the quarter allowed the Rebels to take advantage of short fields to reach the end zone twice. Alabama was playing from behind for the rest of the game, twice getting within six points, but unable to complete the comeback. They were down 17-10 at the half after a Mullaney 9-yard touchdown reception that capped a 16-play, 75-yard drive.

In the third quarter, Ole Miss scored a touchdown and two field goals before Alabama scored a touchdown from three yards out on a Coker run (Ole Miss up 30-17). Derrick Henry had a 31-yard gain on that 9-play, 69-yard drive. Both teams traded touchdowns early in the fourth quarter (8-yard reception by Stewart and a 73-yard reception for Ole Miss), putting the Rebels up 36-24 after a failed two-point attempt. Then Coker threw another pick that led to another Ole Miss touchdown (43-24). Alabama responded with a 14-play, 75-yard touchdown drive as Henry took it in two yards for the score. After failing to convert the two-point attempt, the Tide recovered their onside kick and quickly scored again, this time a 2-yard reception by Mullaney, bringing the score to 43-37. After holding Ole Miss to a punt, Bama had the ball with 2:54 left on its own 33-yard line, but another Coker interception sealed the victory for Ole Miss.

For the game, the Tide offense totaled 503 yards (288 passing and 215 rushing), picked up 29 first downs, and averaged an even 5.0 yards per play. Ole Miss gained 433 yards (341 passing and 92 rushing), along with converting 16 first downs and averaging 6.7 yards per play. Alabama limited its penalties again, getting flagged just four times for 36 yards, but lost the turnover battle by a 5-0 margin.[142]

Passing	C/ATT	YDS	AVG	TD	INT	QBR
J. Coker	21/45	201	4.5	3	2	79.8
C. Bateman	11/14	87	6.2	0	1	63
Team	32/59	288	4.9	3	3	--

Rushing	CAR	YDS	AVG	TD	LONG
D. Henry	23	127	5.5	1	31
J. Coker	7	58	8.3	1	26
K. Drake	11	33	3	0	8
A. Stewart	1	-3	-3	0	0
Team	42	215	5.1	2	31

Kicking	FG	PCT	LONG	XP	PTS
A. Griffith	1/1	100	20	4/4	7

Punting	NO	YDS	AVG	TB	IN 20	LONG
JK Scott	2	84	42	0	0	49

Receiving	REC	YDS	AVG	TD	LONG
A. Stewart	8	73	9.1	1	19
OJ Howard	4	70	17.5	0	30
R. Mullaney	7	61	8.7	2	14
D. Henry	5	39	7.8	0	16
C. Ridley	6	28	4.7	0	23
R. Foster	2	17	8.5	0	16
Team	32	288	9	3	30

Kick returns	NO	YDS	AVG	LONG	TD
K. Drake	4	71	17.8	29	0
A. Stewart	2	17	8.5	16	0
Team	6	88	22	29	0

Punt returns	NO	YDS	AVG	LONG	TD
Cy. Jones	2	-4	-2	-1	0

Note: Table data from "Ole Miss 43-37 Alabama (Sep 19, 2015) Box Score" (147)

191

09/26/15 - Alabama (12) vs Louisiana Monroe

Team	1	2	3	4	T		Passing	Rushing	Total
Louisiana Monroe	0	0	0	0	**0**		83	9	**92**
Alabama (12)	7	7	10	10	**34**		166	137	**303**

The 12th-ranked Alabama Crimson Tide shut out the visiting ULM Warhawks with a final score of 34-0 in front of 101,323 fans at Bryant-Denny Stadium on Saturday afternoon. The Tide got off to another slow start offensively as both teams traded punts to start the game. Alabama got on the board with 2:38 remaining in the first quarter, thanks to a 3-yard run by junior running back Derrick Henry that capped an 11-play, 55-yard drive. Each team punted again to close out the first quarter.

Early in the second quarter, a bad snap on a Louisiana Monroe punt gave Alabama the ball at the ULM 15-yard line. Senior quarterback Jake Coker found freshman wide receiver Calvin Ridley for a touchdown on the very next play, the first of the rookie's career. There was no more scoring in the first half as ULM punted four times and threw an interception after the ball was batted into the air. Alabama also threw an interception, they punted twice, and they did not convert on a 4th-and-4 attempt. Bama led 14-0 at the half.

In the second half, Alabama was able to put the game away by scoring ten more points in each quarter. Junior placekicker Adam Griffith made field goals of 35 and 40 yards, and Coker tossed two more touchdowns. The first was to Nysewander, who took a pass 19 yards for the score making a man miss at the 5-yard line. Then, after an interception by Ronnie Harrison, Coker hit ArDarius Stewart for a 16-yard touchdown reception, bringing the final score to 34-0.

Defensively, the Tide dominated ULM. For the game, the Alabama defense allowed a total of 92 yards from scrimmage, the fewest yards given up by an Alabama defense since the 2012 BCS Championship Game against LSU when the Tigers also gained 92 yards of offense. The defense also recorded six quarterback sacks and 12 tackles for loss.

Alabama gained 303 yards total yards (166 passing and 137 rushing) and converted 17 first downs. The Warhawks picked up 83 yards through the air and nine on the ground, along with gaining ten first downs.[142]

Passing	C/ATT	YDS	AVG	TD	INT	QBR
J. Coker	17/31	158	5.1	3	1	22.6
C. Bateman	1/1	8	8	0	0	98.2
Team	18/32	166	5.2	3	1	--

Rushing	CAR	YDS	AVG	TD	LONG
K. Drake	10	65	6.5	0	15
D. Henry	13	52	4	1	10
D. Harris	4	23	5.8	0	14
D. Gore	3	2	0.7	0	4
R. Clark	1	0	0	0	0
J. Coker	4	-5	-1.3	0	6
Team	35	137	3.9	1	15

Interceptions	INT	YDS	TD
G. Matias-Smith	1	16	0
R. Harrison Jr.	1	12	0
Team	2	28	0

Punting	NO	YDS	AVG	TB	IN 20	LONG
JK Scott	6	227	37.8	0	0	52

Receiving	REC	YDS	AVG	TD	LONG
A. Stewart	3	39	13	1	16
C. Ridley	4	38	9.5	1	15
C. Black	2	23	11.5	0	19
C. Sims	3	21	7	0	11
M. Nysewander	1	19	19	1	19
R. Mullaney	2	10	5	0	6
D. Charlot	1	8	8	0	8
OJ Howard	2	8	4	0	6
Team	18	166	9.2	3	19

Kick returns	NO	YDS	AVG	LONG	TD
A. Stewart	1	13	13	13	0

Punt returns	NO	YDS	AVG	LONG	TD
Cy. Jones	5	43	8.6	22	0

Kicking	FG	PCT	LONG	XP	PTS
A. Griffith	2/2	100	40	4/4	10

Note: Table data from "Alabama 34-0 Louisiana Monroe (Sep 26, 2015) Box Score" (148)

192

10/03/15 - Alabama (13) at Georgia (8)

Team	1	2	3	4	T	Passing	Rushing	Total
Alabama (13)	3	21	14	0	**38**	190	189	**379**
Georgia (8)	0	3	7	0	**10**	106	193	**299**

The No. 13 Alabama Crimson Tide put together a dominating performance on the road to beat No. 8 Georgia 38-10 Saturday afternoon at Sanford Stadium in Athens, GA.

In a game played mostly in a steady rain, senior quarterback Jake Coker and the Alabama offense were efficient while the defense had both Bulldogs quarterbacks under duress all game long. The only score in the first quarter was a 29-yard field goal by Adam Griffith. Georgia tied it with a field goal of its own midway through the second quarter, then Alabama scored three touchdowns. The first was a 30-yard run from Derrick Henry capping off an 8-play, 75-yard drive. Next, freshman Minkah Fitzpatrick blocked a punt and scored. Then after forcing Georgia to a three-and-out, Coker threw a 45-yard strike to Ridley on the first play of their next possession to put Bama up 24-3.

After Alabama punted to start the second half, Eddie Jackson got a pick-six taking it 50 yards to the house. The Bama defense then held the Bulldogs to a punt that gave the ball back to Alabama on the UGA 38-yard line. On the fourth play of the drive, Coker ran it into the end zone from two yards out making the score 38-3. With five seconds left in the third quarter, UGA's Nick Chubb ran it 83 yards for a touchdown. Neither team scored in the fourth quarter which made the final score 38-10 in favor of Alabama.

Freshman receiver Calvin Ridley caught five passes for 120 yards, his first game over the century mark, and one touchdown while Derrick Henry set a new career-high in attempts (26) and rushing yards (148). The Alabama defense was a disruptive force in the wet conditions all day, forcing a total of four turnovers including three interceptions by three different members of the secondary. Georgia's two quarterbacks completed only 11-of-31 pass attempts and averaged 3.2 yards per pass. The Tide gained 379 yards of offense (190 passing and 189 rushing) and converted 15 first downs. The Bulldogs picked up 299 yards for the game (106 passing and 193 rushing) along with converting 12 first downs.[142]

Passing	C/ATT	YDS	AVG	TD	INT	QBR
J. Coker	11/16	190	11.9	1	0	94

Rushing	CAR	YDS	AVG	TD	LONG
D. Henry	26	148	5.7	1	30
J. Coker	6	28	4.7	1	10
D. Harris	7	8	1.1	0	4
B. Scarbrough	2	5	2.5	0	3
K. Drake	6	0	0	0	7
Team	47	189	4	2	30

Interceptions	INT	YDS	TD
E. Jackson	1	50	1
R. Harrison Jr.	1	29	0
M. Humphrey	1	0	0
Team	3	79	1

Punting	NO	YDS	AVG	TB	IN 20	LONG
JK Scott	7	287	41	1	1	54

Receiving	REC	YDS	AVG	TD	LONG
C. Ridley	5	120	24	1	50
R. Mullaney	3	44	14.7	0	24
A. Stewart	2	24	12	0	23
K. Drake	1	2	2	0	2
Team	11	190	17.3	1	50

Kick returns	NO	YDS	AVG	LONG	TD
D. Harris	3	61	20.3	24	0

Punt returns	NO	YDS	AVG	LONG	TD
Cy. Jones	5	53	10.6	23	0
M. Fitzpatrick	1	16	16	1	1
Team	6	69	11.5	23	1

Kicking	FG	PCT	LONG	XP	PTS
A. Griffith	1/1	100	29	5/5	8

Note: Table data from "Alabama 38-10 Georgia (Oct 3, 2015) Box Score" (149)

10/10/15 - Alabama (8) vs Arkansas

Team	1	2	3	4	T		Passing	Rushing	Total
Arkansas	0	7	0	7	14		176	44	220
Alabama (8)	3	0	7	17	27		262	134	396

In a gritty performance on Saturday night, the University of Alabama defeated the Arkansas Razorbacks 27-14 in the 2015 Homecoming game before a capacity crowd of 101,821 at Bryant-Denny Stadium. In the first quarter, Alabama connected on a field goal from 24 yards and missed one from 25. They also punted once, and Jake Coker threw two interceptions. The second one led to an Arkansas touchdown on a 4-yard pass by quarterback Brandon Allen to wide receiver Drew Morgan with 1:29 left in the half. Alabama missed a 48-yard field goal attempt to close out the half with the Hogs up 7-3.

After the second half started with three punts each, Alabama erased the 7-3 deficit late in the third quarter on an 81-yard pass from quarterback Jake Coker to wide receiver Calvin Ridley, a play that ignited an offense that had struggled to finish drives most of the game to that point. That score, with 1:39 left in the third quarter, turned the game in Alabama's favor as the Crimson Tide stopped an Arkansas drive at the Hogs' 43-yard line on the ensuing possession. Alabama then marched 43 yards to a touchdown on a 3-yard pass from Coker to wideout Richard Mullaney for a 17-7 lead. After an Eddie Jackson interception for the Tide a few plays later, Alabama tacked on a 35-yard Adam Griffith field goal for a 20-7 edge with 10:07 left in the fourth quarter. After three more punts (two by Arkansas), both teams scored touchdowns before time expired. Derrick Henry added a 1-yard touchdown run with 2:44 left, marking the 11th consecutive game in which he has scored on the ground. Arkansas responded with a 54-yard touchdown pass on a drive that only took 1:07 off the clock, but they failed to recover the onside kick, giving Bama the final 27-14 victory.

Led by linebacker Reggie Ragland's eight tackles (seven solo), Alabama's defense was unyielding, allowing only 220 total yards to the Razorbacks (176 passing, 44 rushing) while allowing just 1.8 yards per rush. Ragland also had one quarterback sack, broke up a pass, had two quarterback hurries, and forced a fumble.

The Tide offense gained 396 total yards, including 134 on the ground against one of the nation's top rushing defenses. Jake Coker completed 24-of-33 passes for 262 yards and two touchdowns with two interceptions. Calvin Ridley caught nine passes for 140 yards and a touchdown. Derrick Henry rushed for 95 yards and a touchdown on 27 carries. Alabama punter JK Scott averaged 50 yards per punt on four attempts, placing two inside the Arkansas 20-yard line.[142]

Passing	C/ATT	YDS	AVG	TD	INT	QBR
J. Coker	24/33	262	7.9	2	2	42.7

Rushing	CAR	YDS	AVG	TD	LONG
D. Henry	27	95	3.5	1	15
K. Drake	7	29	4.1	0	7
J. Coker	7	17	2.4	0	15
D. Harris	3	-4	-1.3	0	1
Team	2	-3	-1.5	0	0
Team	46	134	2.9	1	15

Interceptions	INT	YDS	TD
E. Jackson	1	20	0

Kicking	FG	PCT	LONG	XP	PTS
A. Griffith	2/4	50	35	3/3	9

Punting	NO	YDS	AVG	TB	IN 20	LONG
JK Scott	4	200	50	0	2	58

Receiving	REC	YDS	AVG	TD	LONG
C. Ridley	9	140	15.6	1	81
A. Stewart	2	38	19	0	37
K. Drake	5	37	7.4	0	18
R. Mullaney	4	25	6.3	1	9
OJ Howard	3	17	5.7	0	7
H. Hentges	1	5	5	0	5
Team	24	262	10.9	2	81

Kick returns	NO	YDS	AVG	LONG	TD
D. Harris	1	22	22	22	0
M. Nysewander	1	16	16	16	0
Team	2	38	19	22	0

Punt returns	NO	YDS	AVG	LONG	TD
Cy. Jones	3	39	13	27	0

Note: Table data from "Arkansas 14-27 Alabama (Oct 10, 2015) Box Score" (150)

10/17/15 - Alabama (10) at Texas A&M (9)

Team	1	2	3	4	T		Passing	Rushing	Total
Alabama (10)	14	14	3	10	41		138	258	396
Texas A&M (9)	3	10	7	3	23		284	32	316

The 10th-ranked University of Alabama football team used a punishing rushing offense and big plays from its defense to defeat No. 9 Texas A&M 41-23 on Saturday before a crowd of 105,733 at Kyle Field. Alabama intercepted four passes, returning three for touchdowns, to knock off the previously unbeaten Aggies.

Alabama built a 28-6 lead midway through the second quarter with Henry rushing 15 times for 178 yards and two scores in the first half and the Tide defense holding the explosive A&M offense to 189 total yards. After Fitzpatrick's 33-yard interception return for a touchdown, Derrick Henry rumbled 55 yards to paydirt with 5:26 left in the opening quarter. The Aggies managed to score on a 54-yard field goal with 1:14 left in the first quarter (14-3).

Henry tacked on a 6-yard scoring run on the first play of the second quarter capping a 5-play, 68-yard drive in 1:23. A&M responded with another long field goal on their next possession, this one from 52 yards. Eddie Jackson's 93-yard pick-six extended the lead to 28-6 before A&M struck back on a 68-yard punt return touchdown by Christian Kirk with 3:03 left in the first half. Alabama led 28-13 at halftime.

A&M narrowed the Alabama lead to 28-20 early in the third quarter on a 3-yard pass from quarterback Kyle Allen to wide receiver Ricky Seals-Jones after Cyrus Jones fumbled a punt around midfield. The Tide extended their lead to 34-20 on a pair of Adam Griffith field goals before A&M's Taylor Bertolet hit a 36-yard field goal with 7:57 left in the fourth quarter, Bertolet's third counter of the game. Fitzpatrick stopped an Aggie drive with his second interception of the day which he returned 55 yards for his second score of the game. It set a Crimson Tide single-game record for interceptions returned for touchdowns, both for the team and an individual, and the Tide won 41-23.

Derrick Henry rushed for 236 yards and two touchdowns while cornerback Minkah Fitzpatrick and strong safety Eddie Jackson nabbed two interceptions each. Jackson returned one for a 93-yard touchdown as the Tide defense scored three times - a first in Alabama history. Fitzpatrick scored two touchdowns via interception returns, first on a 33-yard return in the first quarter, and later on a game-clinching 55-yarder. Alabama quarterback Jake Coker passed for 138 yards while completing 19-of-25 passes.[142]

Passing	C/ATT	YDS	AVG	TD	INT	QBR
J. Coker	19/25	138	5.5	0	0	70.6

Rushing	CAR	YDS	AVG	TD	LONG
D. Henry	32	236	7.4	2	55
J. Coker	7	13	1.9	0	16
K. Drake	5	11	2.2	0	11
Team	1	-2	-2.0	0	0
Team	45	258	5.7	2	55

Kick returns	NO	YDS	AVG	LONG	TD
D. Harris	4	61	15.3	20	0

Punt returns	NO	YDS	AVG	LONG	TD
Cy. Jones	3	35	11.7	23	0

Punting	NO	YDS	AVG	TB	IN 20	LONG
JK Scott	8	386	48.3	0	0	56

Receiving	REC	YDS	AVG	TD	LONG
C. Ridley	7	52	7.4	0	28
OJ Howard	3	35	11.7	0	24
R. Mullaney	4	32	8	0	11
D. Henry	1	18	18	0	18
A. Stewart	1	4	4	0	4
K. Drake	2	0	0	0	6
D. Kief	1	-3	-3	0	-3
Team	19	138	7.3	0	28

Interceptions	INT	YDS	TD
M. Fitzpatrick	2	88	2
E. Jackson	2	119	1
Team	4	207	3

Kicking	FG	PCT	LONG	XP	PTS
A. Griffith	2/2	100	32	5/5	11

Note: Table data from "Alabama 41-23 Texas A&M (Oct 17, 2015) Box Score" (151)

10/24/15 - Alabama (8) vs Tennessee

Team	1	2	3	4	T		Passing	Rushing	Total
Tennessee	7	0	0	7	14		171	132	303
Alabama (8)	7	0	3	9	19		247	117	364

In a tight, hard-hitting struggle that lived up to the legacy of one of college football's most history-rich rivalries, Alabama used a clutch touchdown drive by its offense and a staunch outing from its defense to overcome a late deficit in a 19-14 win over Tennessee before a capacity crowd of 101,821 at Bryant-Denny Stadium.

After Tennessee tailback Jalen Hurd ran 12 yards for a touchdown with 5:49 left, the Tide offense responded with a decisive 71-yard march to the end zone. Tide quarterback Jake Coker completed key passes of 29 yards to wide receiver ArDarius Stewart and 15 yards to wide receiver Calvin Ridley on the drive that was punctuated by running back Derrick Henry's tough running. Henry carried five times for 35 yards on the winning drive, including the game-winning 14-yard touchdown run with 2:24 left.

Henry rushed for 143 yards and two touchdowns, Stewart had five catches for 88 yards, and Coker passed for 247 yards while completing 21-of-27 passes. Linebacker Reggie Ragland led the Tide defense with a game-high 12 tackles (eight solo), including a tackle for loss, and punter JK Scott averaged 49.8 yards on four punts, including a 56-yarder.

Alabama broke on top early on a 20-yard touchdown run by Henry with 7:14 left in the first quarter. The score marked the 13th consecutive game in which Henry has scored a rushing touchdown. Tennessee struck back to tie it at 7-7 on an 11-yard pass from quarterback Joshua Dobbs to wide receiver Josh Smith with three minutes left in the opening quarter.

Tied at 7-7 at halftime, Alabama broke on top on the first possession of the second half by driving 73 yards in 12 plays to a 19-yard field goal by Adam Griffith for a 10-7 lead with nine minutes left in the third quarter. Three Tennessee scoring opportunities ended in missed field goals, a 43-yarder in the first quarter on the game's first series, a 51-yarder on the final play of the first half, and another 51-yarder with 14:06 left in the fourth quarter.

Taking the ball at the Tide 33-yard line with 14:06 left in the fourth quarter, Alabama moved 56 yards in 12 plays while eating 6:58 of game time. A key sequence on the drive began with a 3rd-and-11 play at the UT 46-yard line with 10:19 left. Coker completed a 15-yard pass to Stewart for a first down at the UT 31-yard line. After a 10-yard penalty created a 1st-and-20 at the UT 41-yard line, a pass to receiver Calvin Ridley gained 26 yards to the UT 15-yard line. Ridley adjusted back to the pass after being covered on the play, grabbing the ball at the sideline and gaining several more yards after the catch. Henry gained five yards on a rush at right tackle to the Vols 10-yard line on first down then was dropped for a loss of a yard on second down. On 3rd-and-6 at the UT 11-yard line, Coker's fade pass to receiver Richard Mullaney was incomplete in the end zone. That set up a 28-yard field goal attempt by Griffith with 7:13 on the clock. Griffith kicked it true to give the Tide a 13-7 lead with 7:08 left in the fourth quarter.

Tennessee stormed back with authority to take a 14-13 lead, blazing 75 yards in just four plays to take the lead on a 12-yard run by tailback Jalen Hurd with 5:49 left on the clock. Dobbs connected with Smith for 27 yards on a crossing pattern to start the drive, reaching the Tide 48-yard line. Two plays later, Dobbs hit a slant pass to receiver Josh Malone for 34 yards to the Tide 12-yard line. Hurd raced around left end into the end zone on the next play.

Alabama responded on the ensuing possession. Facing 2nd-and-11 at the Tide 27-yard line, Coker completed a 27-yard pass to Stewart at the UT 44-yard line with 4:29 left on the clock.

Stewart made an acrobatic catch despite tight coverage. Henry gained two yards at left guard to the UT 42-yard line on first down, then carried for two more yards to the Vols 40-yard line. Facing 3rd-and-6 at the 40-yard line, Coker lobbed a pass to Ridley at the left sideline, and Ridley made a leaping catch over a Tennessee defender for a 15-yard gain to the Tennessee 25-yard line. Henry gained six yards at right guard on first down to the UT 19-yard line. Tennessee called its first timeout with 3:02 left. On 2nd-and-4, Henry muscled up the middle for five yards to a first down at the UT 14-yard line. With the clock running under 2:30, Henry took a handoff at left end and ran behind good blocking for 14 yards and a touchdown with 2:24 left. Leading by five points, Alabama went for a two-point conversion. A pass to Ridley was incomplete, broken up by Tennessee cornerback Justin Martin, and the Tide held a 19-14 lead with 2:24 left in the game.

Tennessee took possession at its 25-yard line following a touchback on the kickoff. On the third play of the possession, Alabama defensive end Jonathan Allen sacked Dobbs for a 9-yard loss at the UT 26-yard line. Facing a 2nd-and-24 at the UT 21-yard line following a false start penalty, Dobbs was sacked by Tide linebacker Ryan Anderson for a loss of ten more yards at the UT 11-yard line. Dobbs fumbled on the play, and Alabama's A'Shawn Robinson recovered at the UT 13-yard line. Robinson returned the fumble nine yards to the UT 4-yard line with 1:18 left in the game. Coker took a knee on three consecutive snaps to end the game.[142]

Passing	C/ATT	YDS	AVG	TD	INT	QBR
J. Coker	21/27	247	9.1	0	1	71.9

Rushing	CAR	YDS	AVG	TD	LONG
D. Henry	28	143	5.1	2	20
K. Drake	3	10	3.3	0	7
A. Stewart	1	-3	-3	0	0
J. Coker	7	-26	-3.7	0	1
Team	3	-7	-2.3	0	0
Team	42	117	2.8	2	20

Punting	NO	YDS	AVG	TB	IN 20	LONG
JK Scott	4	199	49.8	0	0	56

Receiving	REC	YDS	AVG	TD	LONG
A. Stewart	5	88	17.6	0	29
C. Ridley	7	88	12.6	0	26
OJ Howard	7	55	7.9	0	18
R. Mullaney	1	13	13	0	13
K. Drake	1	3	3	0	3
Team	21	247	11.8	0	29

Kicking	FG	PCT	LONG	XP	PTS
A. Griffith	2/2	100	28	1/1	7

Kick returns	NO	YDS	AVG	LONG	TD
K. Drake	2	62	31	33	0

Note: Table data from "Alabama 19-14 Tennessee (Oct 24, 2015) Box Score" (152)

11/07/15 - Alabama (2) vs LSU (4)

Team	1	2	3	4	T		Passing	Rushing	Total
LSU (4)	0	10	0	6	16		128	54	182
Alabama (2)	0	13	14	3	30		184	250	434

The Alabama defense limited LSU running back Leonard Fournette to 31 rushing yards while the Crimson Tide offense rode a 210-yard, three-touchdown rushing performance by running back Derrick Henry to a 30-16 victory. Fournette, who entered the game as the nation's leading rusher averaging 193.1 yards rushing per game, could not get going against the Crimson Tide defense. But Henry rushed for touchdowns of two yards, one yard, and seven yards while carrying the ball 38 times, the third-most carries by one player in a single game in Alabama football history. Fournette had an 18-yard run at the 11-minute mark in the fourth quarter after a Henry fumble set up the Tigers at the Tide 22-yard line. But by that time the Tide had built a 30-10 lead, and the outcome was already decided.

Alabama was dominant early, breaking out to a 10-0 lead in the second quarter on a 22-yard Adam Griffith field goal and Henry's 2-yard scoring rush that came after a 40-yard run. But the Tigers struck back to tie it at 10-10 with an explosive passing game. Quarterback Brandon Harris hit wide receiver Travin Dural for a 40-yard touchdown pass, and Trent Domingue followed with a 39-yard field goal to tie it. But Alabama took a 13-10 lead at halftime on a career-long 55-yard field goal by Griffith with 14 seconds left in the half.

After Tide linebacker Dillon Lee intercepted a Harris pass on the first play of the third quarter to set Alabama up at the LSU 28-yard line, Henry capped a touchdown drive with a 1-yard run to stake the Tide to a 20-10 lead with 13 minutes left in the quarter. Henry extended the lead with a 7-yard scoring run with 2:47 left in the third quarter, and Griffith added a 29-yard field goal with 12:45 left in the game for a 30-10 Alabama lead.

LSU showed life late after Henry lost a fumble at the Tide 22-yard line. The Tigers marched 22 yards in four plays with Fournette scoring on a 1-yard run with 9:18 left on the clock. The extra point was blocked by the Tide's A'Shawn Robinson as the Tide held a 30-16 lead.

The Alabama defense created seven plays of negative yardage by the LSU offense in the game, including seven tackles for loss and two sacks. LSU was limited to 182 total yards in the game (54 rushing, 128 passing). The Alabama offense gained 434 total yards, including 250 rushing, and had the ball for 39:27 of game time. Tide safety Geno Matias-Smith led the Tide defense with six tackles. Alabama punter JK Scott averaged 45 yards on three punts with a long of 50 yards, including one punt downed inside the LSU 20-yard line. Adam Griffith made all three field goal attempts, running his streak of successful attempts to seven straight.[142]

Passing	C/ATT	YDS	AVG	TD	INT	QBR
J. Coker	18/24	184	7.7	0	0	52

Rushing	CAR	YDS	AVG	TD	LONG
D. Henry	38	210	5.5	3	40
K. Drake	10	68	6.8	0	24
J. Coker	6	-26	-4.3	0	3
Team	1	-2	-2.0	0	0
Team	55	250	4.5	3	40

Interceptions	INT	YDS	TD
D. Lee	1	4	0

Punting	NO	YDS	AVG	TB	IN 20	LONG
JK Scott	3	135	45	0	1	50

Receiving	REC	YDS	AVG	TD	LONG
C. Ridley	7	51	7.3	0	15
A. Stewart	3	47	15.7	0	19
K. Drake	3	40	13.3	0	25
R. Mullaney	3	28	9.3	0	11
OJ Howard	2	18	9	0	15
Team	18	184	10.2	0	25

Kick returns	NO	YDS	AVG	LONG	TD
K. Drake	3	55	18.3	33	0

Punt returns	NO	YDS	AVG	LONG	TD
Cy. Jones	2	23	11.5	12	0

Kicking	FG	PCT	LONG	XP	PTS
A. Griffith	3/3	100	55	3/3	12

Note: Table data from "Alabama 30-16 LSU (Nov 7, 2015) Box Score" (153)

198

11/14/15 - Alabama (2) at Mississippi State (17)

Team	1	2	3	4	T		Passing	Rushing	Total
Alabama (2)	0	21	3	7	31		144	235	379
Mississippi State (17)	0	3	3	0	6		304	89	393

The Alabama defense sacked Mississippi State quarterback Dak Prescott nine times, and Bama's RB Derrick Henry rushed for 204 yards and two touchdowns in a 31-6 victory over the Bulldogs before an overflow crowd of 62,435 at Davis Wade Stadium at Scott Field on Saturday.

Alabama broke on top, 7-0, early in the second quarter on a 69-yard punt return by Cyrus Jones. On Alabama's next possession, WR Calvin Ridley took a pass from Jake Coker at the Tide 49-yard line in the middle of the field, cut back and juked a defender, then raced to the end zone to complete a 60-yard scoring play, extending the Tide lead to 14-0. State responded on the next possession with a 31-yard field goal by Westin Graves that narrowed the lead to 14-3 before Henry raced 74 yards for a touchdown to give the Tide a 21-3 lead at the half.

A 42-yard field goal by Adam Griffith gave Alabama a 24-3 lead early in the third quarter. The Bulldogs added a 39-yard field goal by Graves late in the third quarter before Henry sealed the verdict with a 65-yard touchdown run with 7:53 left in the game.

Alabama's defense produced 12 plays for losses against a high-powered Mississippi State offense, limiting the explosive Prescott to 14 rushing yards on 26 attempts and holding the Bulldogs out of the end zone for the first time in 36 games dating back to MSU's 2013 season opener. It also marked the end of a 32-game streak by Prescott in which he had scored a touchdown in a game, the longest streak in the FBS. The nine sacks by the Tide defense are the most by an Alabama defense since 1998 when it also tallied nine against Vanderbilt.

Henry scored on runs of 74 and 65 yards as the Crimson Tide offense overcame a slow start with a methodical ground game while the Tide defense held off several State scoring threats. Henry turned in over 200 yards rushing in a game for the third time in 2015, becoming the second Alabama back to do that three times in a single season, following Bobby Humphrey who rushed for 200+ yards in three games during the 1986 season.

Tide LB Reuben Foster led Alabama with ten tackles (six solo). DE Jonathan Allen had three sacks among his seven tackles. DE A'Shawn Robinson had 2.5 sacks among his five tackles, LB Ryan Anderson had two sacks among his five tackles, and LB Tim Williams added two sacks in his five stops. Da'Ron Payne had 1.5 sacks in his three stops while LB Denzel Devall had one sack on his only tackle of the day. Bama racked up 12 tackles for losses totaling 58 yards, forced three fumbles (recovering one), broke up seven passes, and had four QB hurries on the day.[142]

Passing	C/ATT	YDS	AVG	TD	INT	QBR
J. Coker	15/25	144	5.8	1	1	34.3

Rushing	CAR	YDS	AVG	TD	LONG
D. Henry	22	204	9.3	2	74
B. Scarbrough	3	13	4.3	0	8
A. Stewart	1	8	8	0	8
J. Coker	1	6	6	0	6
D. Harris	3	4	1.3	0	2
Team	30	235	7.8	2	74

Interceptions	INT	YDS	TD
M. Humphrey	1	29	0

Punting	NO	YDS	AVG	TB	IN 20	LONG
JK Scott	5	200	40	0	0	47

Receiving	REC	YDS	AVG	TD	LONG
C. Ridley	5	76	15.2	1	60
A. Stewart	4	32	8	0	19
OJ Howard	1	15	15	0	15
K. Drake	2	13	6.5	0	8
D. Harris	1	5	5	0	5
R. Mullaney	1	3	3	0	3
D. Henry	1	0	0	0	0
Team	15	144	9.6	1	60

Punt returns	NO	YDS	AVG	LONG	TD
Cy. Jones	1	69	69	69	1

Kicking	FG	PCT	LONG	XP	PTS
A. Griffith	1/2	50	42	4/4	7

Note: Table data from "Alabama 31-6 Mississippi State (Nov 14, 2015) Box Score" (154)

11/21/15 - Alabama (2) vs Charleston Southern

Team	1	2	3	4	T		Passing	Rushing	Total
Charleston Southern	0	0	0	6	6		49	85	134
Alabama (2)	28	21	0	7	56		208	195	403

Alabama raced to a 28-0 lead after the first quarter on the way to a 49-0 halftime advantage, scoring touchdowns on its first five offensive possessions and adding scores on a pair of punt returns.

Henry started the scoring with a 17-yard touchdown run with 11:36 left in the first quarter, capping the game's first possession of the 9-play, 64-yard drive. It was Henry's 16th consecutive game with a touchdown. Henry ended the Tide's next 10-play, 55-yard possession with a 2-yard scoring run to give Alabama a 14-0 lead with 5:50 left in the opening quarter. That gave him 21 rushing touchdowns in 2015, tying the school record set by Trent Richardson in 2011, and it also gave Henry 35 career rushing scores to tie Richardson for fourth on the Tide's career rushing touchdowns list. After the Tide forced another CSU punt, they capped their third possession with their third touchdown of the game, this one a 21-yard pass from Coker to wide receiver Richard Mullaney with 2:28 left in the opening quarter. Cyrus Jones closed the quarter with a 43-yard punt return for a touchdown on the final play of the quarter for a 28-0 Alabama lead, marking the second consecutive game in which Jones has taken a punt the distance.

A 30-yard pass from Coker to wide receiver Calvin Ridley gave the Tide a 35-0 lead at the 7:07 mark of the second quarter, capping an 86-yard drive and giving Alabama four touchdowns in four offensive possessions. Three minutes later, following CSU's next possession, Jones took another punt for a touchdown, this one going 72 yards for a 42-0 lead. It marked the first time in Crimson Tide history that an Alabama player has returned two punts for touchdowns in the same game. Alabama led 49-0 via Bo Scarborough's 1-yard touchdown run with 1:53 left in the half. The 49 points scored by the Tide was the most in a half by an Alabama team since scoring 52 points against Vanderbilt 1990.

After both teams failed to score in the third quarter, CSU quarterback Kyle Copeland's 3-yard run early in the fourth quarter prevented a shutout. Alabama running back Damien Harris ending the scoring on a 6-yard run to give the Tide a 56-6 victory.

Playing only the first quarter, Derrick Henry rushed for 68 yards and two touchdowns on only nine carries. He also caught a pass for 28 yards. Henry's two rushing touchdowns opened the scoring and Cyrus Jones' punt returns highlighted the opening half. Bama's defense was dominant throughout, allowing only 31 total yards and three first downs in the opening half.

Alabama's starters sat out the second half. In two quarters of play, QB Jake Coker completed 11-of-13 pass attempts for 155 yards and two touchdowns without throwing an interception. WR Calvin Ridley had four catches for 49 yards, WR ArDarius Stewart had four catches for 45 yards, and WR Richard Mullaney had one catch for a 21-yard touchdown. The offensive starters yielded to the Tide's second-team offense late in the second quarter. Reserve running back Bo Scarborough had a game-high 69 rushing yards and a touchdown on ten carries.

The Alabama defense limited CSU to 134 total yards (85 rushing, 49 passing) and eight first downs in the game, holding the Buccaneers to 1-of-10 on third downs while causing two turnovers (one fumble and one interception). Cornerback Bradley Sylve and defensive end Dalvin Tomlinson both had four tackles each to lead the Tide.[142]

Passing	C/ATT	YDS	AVG	TD	INT	QBR
J. Coker	11/13	155	11.9	2	0	88.6
C. Bateman	7/11	47	4.3	0	0	29
A. Morris	1/1	6	6	0	0	21.7
Team	19/25	208	8.3	2	0	--

Rushing	CAR	YDS	AVG	TD	LONG
B. Scarbrough	10	69	6.9	1	24
D. Henry	9	68	7.6	2	17
D. Harris	10	44	4.4	1	8
R. Clark	2	11	5.5	0	11
D. Gore	1	4	4	0	4
J. Coker	1	1	1	0	1
X. Marks	1	0	0	0	0
C. Bateman	1	-2	-2	0	0
Team	35	195	5.6	4	24

Interceptions	INT	YDS	TD
J. Washington	1	34	0

Kicking	FG	PCT	LONG	XP	PTS
A. Griffith	0/0	0	0	7/7	7
JK Scott	0/1	0	0	1/1	1
Team	0/1	0	0	8/8	8

Receiving	REC	YDS	AVG	TD	LONG
C. Ridley	4	49	12.3	1	30
A. Stewart	4	45	11.3	0	21
D. Henry	1	28	28	0	28
C. Sims	3	25	8.3	0	16
R. Mullaney	1	21	21	1	21
X. Marks	2	19	9.5	0	13
OJ Howard	1	12	12	0	12
D. Ball	1	8	8	0	8
D. Charlot	1	1	1	0	1
T. Flournoy-Smith	1	0	0	0	0
Team	19	208	10.9	2	30

Kick returns	NO	YDS	AVG	LONG	TD
T. Flournoy-Smith	1	19	19	19	0
H. Hentges	1	2	2	2	0
Team	2	21	10.5	19	0

Punt returns	NO	YDS	AVG	LONG	TD
Cy. Jones	2	115	57.5	72	2
R. Mullaney	1	8	8	8	0
Team	3	123	41	72	2

Note: Table data from "Alabama 56-6 Charleston Southern (Nov 21, 2015) Box Score" (155)

11/28/15 - Alabama (2) at Auburn

Team	1	2	3	4	T		Passing	Rushing	Total
Alabama (2)	3	9	7	10	29		179	286	465
Auburn	6	0	7	0	13		170	91	261

University of Alabama running back Derrick Henry rushed for 271 yards and a touchdown on a school-record 46 carries to lead the Crimson Tide to a 29-13 victory over the Auburn Tigers. With the game on the line in the final quarter, Henry rushed 19 times for 114 yards in the fourth quarter alone to lead the Tide out of a tense situation in which they were clinging to a 19-13 lead midway through the quarter. After Alabama took a 22-13 lead on Adam Griffith's fifth field goal of the game with 10:04 left, Henry carried on every Crimson Tide snap the rest of the way, carrying the ball on 14 consecutive plays to close out the game. Henry's totals stand as the third-most rushing yards in a game by any Alabama back, and his yardage is the most ever gained by an Auburn opponent.

Alabama broke on top early with a field goal to cap its first offensive possession of the game. The Tide marched 48 yards in eight plays to the Auburn 9-yard line where Adam Griffith entered to kick a 26-yard field goal, giving Alabama a 3-0 lead with 11:28 left in the first quarter. Henry carried four times for 36 yards on the march, keying the drive with a 30-yard run to the Auburn 14-yard line. ArDarius Stewart caught three passes for 12 yards on the opening drive. Auburn struck right back, moving 68 yards in nine plays to a 24-yard field goal by Daniel Carlson that tied the game at 3-3 with 7:35 on the clock. Auburn took the lead on its next series, a 7-play, 22-yard drive that stalled at the Tide 27-yard line. From there, Carlson entered to kick a 44-yard field goal that gave Auburn a 6-3 lead with 1:49 left in the first. The Tide came right back with a field goal to tie it at 6-6, this one a 41-yarder by Griffith with 11:47 left in the second quarter. Henry carried seven times for 51 yards on the 14-play drive that covered 67 yards.

The Tide moved 55 yards in five plays to take the lead early in the second quarter, highlighted by a 46-yard pass from Jake Coker to Calvin Ridley, who made an outstanding catch in double coverage at the Tiger 5-yard line. Alabama settled for a third field goal, this one a 26-yarder by Griffith, for a 9-6 lead with 6:58 left in the half. After an Auburn drive ended in a missed 48-yard field goal with 1:24 left, Alabama moved quickly. Stewart made a spectacular leaping catch for a 17-yard gain on the first play, then Derrick Henry took a handoff around the right tackle for 15 yards to the Auburn 36-yard line. After Henry gained three on a rush up the middle, two incompletions forced a 50-yard field goal try by Griffith. Griffith nailed it for his fourth of the half to give the Tide a 12-6 lead with 24 seconds left until halftime.

Alabama lengthened its lead late in the third quarter, moving 85 yards in nine plays to a touchdown on an impressive 34-yard pass from Coker to Stewart. Under a heavy rush, Coker left the pocket and evaded two rushers before firing a dart on the run to Stewart in the end zone. Griffith's kick gave Alabama a 19-6 lead with 5:14 left in the third quarter. But Auburn retaliated quickly, as quarterback Jeremy Johnson hit wide receiver Jason Smith on a 77-yard touchdown pass on a 3rd-and-long play in which Smith bobbled the ball twice into the air before hauling it in and racing untouched to the end zone. With the point-after kick by Carlson, Alabama's lead was trimmed to 19-13 with 4:27 left in the third quarter.

On a first down at the Tide 35-yard line, Coker was flushed from the pocket and rushed to the sideline for a 1-yard gain. A 15-yard personal foul was called on Auburn safety Johnathan Ford for a late hit on Coker as he exited the field. Another 15-yard penalty was assessed to Auburn for unsportsmanlike conduct after that play, moving the ball to the Auburn 34-yard line. Three plays later, Griffith kicked a 47-yard field goal to give the Tide a 22-13 lead with 10:04 left in the fourth quarter. This drive is infamous for the commentary by the Auburn radio announcers who showed extreme bias in complaining about the officiating and attacking Coach Nick Saban in their deflection of Auburn's sideline penalty.

After forcing an Auburn punt, Alabama took over possession with 7:49 left at its own 18-yard line. Henry and the Tide offensive line took over from there, beginning with a 16-yard gain on the first play and giving the ball to Henry 14 consecutive times. The first ten of those plays ended when Henry was stopped on a 4th-and-1 play at the Auburn 31-yard line with 2:46 left. After Auburn was stuffed on the next possession, Alabama took over again at the Tiger 34-yard line. Henry carried the next four plays, closing it out with a 25-yard burst around right end for the clinching touchdown with 26 seconds left in the game, giving Alabama the 29-13 victory.

In addition to Henry's heroics, Alabama's offense was keyed by an accurate passing performance by quarterback Jake Coker, who completed 17-of-26 attempts for 179 yards and a touchdown. Wide receiver ArDarius Stewart caught a game-high eight catches for 81 yards and a score while wideout Calvin Ridley had 90 yards receiving on six catches. Griffith made good on all five field goal attempts in the game, the most by a Tide kicker in four seasons. The Alabama defense permitted only one big play in the game while limiting the explosive Tigers offense to 261 total yards (170 passing, 91 rushing).

Alabama outgained Auburn 465 to 261 while the Tide rushed for 286 yards and passed for 179. The Tide notched 24 first downs to Auburn's 12, limited the Tigers to 3-of-15 on third downs, and had the ball for 35:23 compared to Auburn's 24:37. Safety Geno Matias-Smith led the Tide with eight tackles and a forced fumble. Linebacker Reuben Foster had six stops, a pass breakup, and a quarterback hurry, while Tide cornerback Marlon Humphrey had six tackles on the night. Linebacker Reggie Ragland had five stops while directing the Tide defense on the field.[142]

Passing	C/ATT	YDS	AVG	TD	INT	QBR
J. Coker	17/26	179	6.9	1	0	62.5

Rushing	CAR	YDS	AVG	TD	LONG
D. Henry	46	271	5.9	1	30
J. Coker	3	13	4.3	0	7
D. Harris	1	2	2	0	2
Team	50	286	5.7	1	30

Kicking	FG	PCT	LONG	XP	PTS
A. Griffith	5/5	100	50	2/2	17

Punting	NO	YDS	AVG	TB	IN 20	LONG
JK Scott	3	145	48.3	0	0	50

Receiving	REC	YDS	AVG	TD	LONG
C. Ridley	6	90	15	0	46
A. Stewart	8	81	10.1	1	34
D. Harris	1	4	4	0	4
R. Mullaney	2	4	2	0	5
Team	17	179	10.5	1	46

Kick returns	NO	YDS	AVG	LONG	TD
D. Harris	1	30	30	30	0
R. Mullaney	1	10	10	10	0
Team	2	40	20	30	0

Punt returns	NO	YDS	AVG	LONG	TD
Cy. Jones	1	3	3	3	0

Note: Table data from "Alabama 29-13 Auburn (Nov 28, 2015) Box Score" (156)

12/05/15 - Alabama (2) vs Florida (18)

Team	1	2	3	4	T		Passing	Rushing	Total
Florida (18)	0	7	0	8	15		165	15	180
Alabama (2)	2	10	10	7	29		204	233	437

The Alabama defense stifled Florida for much of the game, holding them to 180 total yards (only 15 rushing). From the end of the first quarter until 13:16 left in the game, the Alabama defense held the Gators to only three yards of total offense. During that time frame, the Tide erased an early 7-2 deficit while running off 27 unanswered points to secure the victory.

Alabama opened the scoring with a safety on a blocked punt by LB Keith Holcombe to give the Tide a 2-0 lead in the first quarter. Early in the second quarter, Florida took a 7-2 lead on an 85-yard punt return by Antonio Calloway, the longest in SEC Championship Game history. Later in the quarter after Alabama blocked a FG then fumbled three possessions later, the Tide responded with a 28-yard field goal by Adam Griffith, narrowing the Gator lead to 7-5. Late in the first half, a 55-yard bomb from Coker to receiver Calvin Ridley took the ball to the Gator 3-yard line, setting up a 2-yard touchdown run by Henry to put the Tide in the lead 12-7 at halftime.

Alabama extended its lead to 15-7 midway through the third quarter on a 30-yard field goal by Griffith. The lead moved to 22-7 later in the third on a leaping 32-yard touchdown grab of a Coker pass amidst three Florida defenders by receiver ArDarius Stewart. Alabama's lead grew to 29-7 on a 9-yard pass from Coker to receiver Richard Mullaney capping a 9-play, 58-yard drive midway in the fourth. Florida's offense reached paydirt in the fourth quarter on a 46-yard pass from Treon Harris to receiver C.J. Worton. Harris ran for two points, and the Alabama lead had narrowed to 29-15 with 5:02 left in the game. Even though Alabama was forced to punt on its next possession, its defense held by sacking Harris on a fourth down attempt.

Henry rushed for 189 yards and a touchdown on 44 carries, increasing his 2015 season rushing total to 1,986 yards. He broke the SEC single-season rushing yards record previously held by Herschel Walker of Georgia (1,891 yards in 1981). Henry earned MVP honors for his performance. Tide quarterback Jake Coker completed 18-of-26 passes for 204 yards and two touchdowns without throwing an interception. Wide receiver Calvin Ridley had 102 yards on a game-high eight catches, and receiver ArDarius Stewart had four catches for 64 yards.

Alabama registered five sacks, posted nine tackles for loss, intercepted a pass, and forced a fumble. Florida's offense managed only seven first downs and had the ball for 16:31 (Bama had it for 43:29). Linebacker Ryan Anderson led Alabama with four tackles and three quarterback hurries while cornerback Marlon Humphrey had three stops and an interception.[142]

Passing	C/ATT	YDS	AVG	TD	INT	QBR
J. Coker	18/26	204	7.8	2	0	90.9

Rushing	CAR	YDS	AVG	TD	LONG
D. Henry	44	189	4.3	1	21
J. Coker	8	23	2.9	0	17
K. Drake	4	14	3.5	0	7
A. Stewart	1	5	5	0	5
C. Ridley	1	2	2	0	2
Team	58	233	4	1	21

Punt returns	NO	YDS	AVG	LONG	TD
Cy. Jones	7	32	4.6	15	0
K. Holcombe	1	13	13	0	0
Team	8	45	5.6	15	0

Punting	NO	YDS	AVG	TB	IN 20	LONG
JK Scott	6	307	51.2	0	5	59

Receiving	REC	YDS	AVG	TD	LONG
C. Ridley	8	102	12.8	0	55
A. Stewart	4	64	16	1	32
R. Mullaney	3	22	7.3	1	9
K. Drake	3	16	5.3	0	9
Team	18	204	11.3	2	55

Interceptions	INT	YDS	TD
M. Humphrey	1	-1	0

Kick returns	NO	YDS	AVG	LONG	TD
Cy. Jones	1	24	24	24	0
K. Drake	1	22	22	22	0
Team	2	46	23	24	0

Kicking	FG	PCT	LONG	XP	PTS
A. Griffith	2/3	67	30	3/3	9

Note: Table data from "Alabama 29-15 Florida (Dec 5, 2015) Box Score" (157)

12/31/15 - Alabama (2) vs Michigan State (3)

Team	1	2	3	4	T		Passing	Rushing	Total
Michigan State (3)	0	0	0	0	0		210	29	239
Alabama (2)	0	10	21	7	38		286	154	440

The Alabama defense produced another excellent performance, shutting down the Spartans' offense for much of the game, holding the Spartans to only 29 rushing yards and 239 total yards. Meanwhile, Tide CB Cyrus Jones produced game-changing plays with an interception to stop an MSU scoring threat and a punt return for a touchdown that sealed the verdict.

After a scoreless first quarter, the teams continued in a standoff well into the second quarter until the Tide moved 80 yards in six plays to a touchdown to break on top, 7-0, on a 1-yard run by Henry with 5:36 left in the first half. Clutch plays in the passing game keyed the drive that was highlighted by a 50-yard pass from Jake Coker to Calvin Ridley that reached the MSU 1-yard line. Henry's touchdown run was his 24th, breaking the SEC record for rushing TDs in a season. PK Adam Griffith connected on a 47-yard field goal to give the Tide a 10-0 lead with 1:25 left in the half. Tide CB Cyrus Jones made a huge play at the end of the first half. The Spartans had marched to the Tide 12-yard line in the final minute of the half before Jones leaped high to intercept a Connor Cook pass at the Tide 2-yard line in the waning seconds of the half, ending a scoring threat and protecting the Tide's 10-0 lead heading into halftime.

Alabama extended the lead to 17-0 on the opening drive of the second half, moving 75 yards in nine plays to paydirt on a 6-yard pass to Ridley along the sideline in the end zone. Later in the third, Jones returned an MSU punt 57 yards for a touchdown (24-0 Tide). Just 1:04 later, Coker and Ridley connected on a 50-yard touchdown bomb to move the Tide to a 31-0 lead with 2:20 left in the third. Henry closed the scoring with an 11-yard run with 7:52 left in the game.

The Tide defense registered four QB sacks, posted six tackles for loss, and intercepted two passes. LB Reggie Ragland led Alabama with seven tackles while LB Dillon Lee had six stops and intercepted a pass. LB Ryan Anderson had four tackles, including a sack and two tackles for losses. LB Reuben Foster and safety Geno Matias-Smith also had four tackles in the game.

Alabama's offense produced 440 yards led by QB Jake Coker's career-best 286 passing yards and two TDs. Coker was deadly accurate, completing 25-of-30 pass attempts. Freshman WR Calvin Ridley had 138 receiving yards on eight catches for two TDs, setting a new Alabama freshman record for single season receiving yards (1,031). Heisman Trophy winning running back Derrick Henry rushed for 75 yards and two touchdowns on 20 carries, becoming only the 25th running back in NCAA history (encompassing all divisions) to rush for 2,000 yards in a season.[142]

Passing	C/ATT	YDS	AVG	TD	INT	QBR
J. Coker	25/30	286	9.5	2	0	89.8
C. Bateman	0/1	0	0	0	0	1.4
Team	25/31	286	9.2	2	0	--

Receiving	REC	YDS	AVG	TD	LONG
C. Ridley	8	138	17.3	2	50
OJ Howard	3	59	19.7	0	41
R. Mullaney	3	53	17.7	0	26
A. Stewart	7	37	5.3	0	12
K. Drake	3	5	1.7	0	9
D. Henry	1	-6	-6	0	0
Team	25	286	11.4	2	50

Rushing	CAR	YDS	AVG	TD	LONG
D. Henry	20	75	3.8	2	14
K. Drake	4	60	15	0	58
B. Scarbrough	3	17	5.7	0	9
A. Stewart	1	7	7	0	7
D. Harris	1	2	2	0	2
Team	1	-1	-1	0	0
J. Coker	5	-6	-1.2	0	4
Team	35	154	4.4	2	58

Interceptions	INT	YDS	TD
Cy. Jones	1	21	0
D. Lee	1	0	0
Team	2	21	0

Punt returns	NO	YDS	AVG	LONG	TD
Cy. Jones	5	80	16	57	1

Kicking	FG	PCT	LONG	XP	PTS
A. Griffith	1/1	100	47	5/5	8

Note: Table data from "Alabama 38-0 Michigan State (Dec 31, 2015) Box Score" (158)

01/11/16 - Alabama (2) at Clemson (1)

Team	1	2	3	4	T		Passing	Rushing	Total
Alabama (2)	7	7	7	24	45		335	138	473
Clemson (1)	14	0	10	16	40		405	145	550

Alabama came off a stellar defensive performance in the semifinal game and was looking to contain Clemson's QB Deshaun Watson, but the Alabama defense was quickly forced into conceding most of the field and stopping Clemson in the red zone. Alabama's offense was stressed at the line of scrimmage by Clemson's defensive line led by Shaq Lawson. Despite being statistically outplayed by Clemson offensively (550 Clemson offensive yards to 473 Alabama) and statistically tied in other areas, Alabama was able to capitalize on three key plays: an interception of Deshaun Watson's pass early in the second quarter, a surprise Alabama onside kick early in the fourth quarter, and an Alabama kickoff return for a touchdown in the middle of the fourth quarter. These plays accounted for 21 points, and Alabama won the game 45-40.

Having won the coin toss to start the game, Clemson elected to defer to the second half. Characteristic of Alabama, the offensive opening drive was slow and cautious but notable for utilizing Derrick Henry four times, a schematic change of pace from that of the Semifinal game against Michigan State. Alabama and Clemson traded punts, then on the next Alabama possession, Derrick Henry was utilized three times. On the third run, Henry found an opening for a 50-yard touchdown run (7-0). However, on the next two Clemson possessions, Deshaun Watson used his characteristic speed, agility, and elusiveness to sustain drives with a mixture of quarterback runs and fade routes against Alabama's top-ranked defense. These two drives both culminated in touchdown passes to Hunter Renfrow, the latter of which ended the first quarter with Clemson up 14-7.

On Alabama's next possession to start the second quarter, despite a promising start in a 29-yard pass to Richard Mullaney, Alabama's offensive line conceded a sack by Kevin Dodd and a tackle for loss on Derrick Henry. Characteristic of Alabama, facing third and long, offensive coordinator Lane Kiffin enacted for extra field position on a punt with a short throw to Ridley rather than attempting a first down pass. Despite the seemingly dire situation, on the ensuing Clemson drive, Deshaun Watson was intercepted by Eddie Jackson at the Clemson 42-yard line. The resulting Alabama possession culminated in a 1-yard TD run by Derrick Henry (14-14). After this flurry, both Clemson and Alabama played more cautiously as each of the three following possessions by both teams went no further than 40 yards. Clemson's last possession of the half resulted in a blocked field goal.

Going into the third quarter, Clemson opted to receive the ball but was forced into a quick three-and-out. On Alabama's next possession, TE OJ Howard found himself open in space for a 53-yard touchdown (21-14). Clemson responded with a mixture of quarterback runs, pass plays by Deshaun Watson, and key run plays by running back Wayne Gallman on its next two drives to get a 37-yard field goal by Greg Hugel and a 1-yard touchdown run by Wayne Gallman. Both teams were then stalled for three-and-outs or near three-and-outs on their next two possessions to close the third quarter. Clemson led 24-21.

On Alabama's first possession of the fourth quarter, Jake Coker found ArDarius Stewart in single man coverage for 38 yards. This gain, however, did not translate into a touchdown as the offense was stalled by good secondary play from Clemson. Alabama settled for a field goal from 33 yards to tie the game at 24-24. On the ensuing kickoff, Alabama gambled on a surprise onside kick, executed to perfection by Adam Griffith and caught by Marlon Humphrey. Alabama capitalized almost immediately with another 50+ touchdown pass to a wide open OJ Howard (31-24, Bama). Clemson then drove to the Alabama 14-yard line, however, Alabama's defense held in the red zone and forced a field goal to get them within four (31-27, Bama). On

206

the ensuing kickoff, Alabama running back Kenyan Drake stunned Clemson by taking the ball 95 yards for an Alabama touchdown (38-27).

Deshaun Watson quickly answered with an 8-play, 75-yard touchdown drive which culminated in a 15-yard touchdown pass to wide receiver Artavius Scott. In attempt to pull within three points of Alabama (and thus within a field goal of tying the game), Clemson attempted a two-point conversion that morphed into a naked bootleg quarterback run by Deshaun Watson which was stopped short (38-33). On Alabama's next possession, Jake Coker passed the ball in a checkdown screen to OJ Howard who, getting good blocking, ran for 63 yards. With less than three minutes left in the game, Alabama ran the ball up the middle to convert downs. After a key third down scramble for a first down by Jake Coker, Derrick Henry, on third down, broke the touchdown plane with the nose of the ball over the top of the goal line pile of players for a 1-yard touchdown (45-33). A stellar performance by Deshaun Watson on a 55-second drive culminated in a 24-yard touchdown pass to Jordan Leggett with 12 seconds left on the clock (45-40). Clemson attempted an onside kick, but the ball was recovered by Alabama, sealing the victory and the national championship for the Crimson Tide. This was the fourth Alabama national championship win in seven years, first of the CFP era, and Head Coach Nick Saban's fifth overall.[142]

Passing	C/ATT	YDS	AVG	TD	INT	QBR
J. Coker	16/25	335	13.4	2	0	85.9

Rushing	CAR	YDS	AVG	TD	LONG
D. Henry	36	158	4.4	3	50
K. Drake	1	1	1	0	1
J. Coker	8	-20	-2.5	0	8
Team	1	-1	-1	0	0
Team	45	138	3.1	3	50

Interceptions	INT	YDS	TD
E. Jackson	1	0	0

Punting	NO	YDS	AVG	TB	IN 20	LONG
JK Scott	7	297	42.4	0	3	52

Receiving	REC	YDS	AVG	TD	LONG
OJ Howard	5	208	41.6	2	63
A. Stewart	2	63	31.5	0	38
R. Mullaney	1	29	29	0	29
K. Drake	2	21	10.5	0	7
C. Ridley	6	14	2.3	0	9
Team	16	335	20.9	2	63

Kick returns	NO	YDS	AVG	LONG	TD
K. Drake	5	196	39.2	95	1

Punt returns	NO	YDS	AVG	LONG	TD
Cy. Jones	1	12	12	12	0

Kicking	FG	PCT	LONG	XP	PTS
A. Griffith	1/2	50	33	6/6	9

Note: Table data from "Alabama 45-40 Clemson (Jan 11, 2016) Box Score" (159)

Season Stats

Record	14-1	1st of 128
SEC Record	8-1	
Rank	1	
Points for	526	
Points against	227	
Points/game	35.1	20th of 128
Opp points/game	15.1	3rd of 128
SOS[9]	7.46	1st of 128

Team stats (averages per game)

		Passing					Rushing				Total Offense		
Split	G	Cmp	Att	Pct	Yds	TD	Att	Yds	Avg	TD	Plays	Yds	Avg
Offense	15	20.1	29.7	67.5	227.1	1.5	42.8	199.9	4.7	2.2	72.5	427.1	5.9
Defense	15	16.7	33	50.5	200.5	1.1	31.2	75.7	2.4	0.5	64.2	276.3	4.3
Difference		3.4	-3.3	17	26.6	0.4	11.6	124.2	2.3	1.7	8.3	150.8	1.6

	First Downs				Penalties		Turnovers		
Split	Pass	Rush	Pen	Tot	No.	Yds	Fum	Int	Tot
Offense	9.8	10.5	1.7	22	5.9	55.7	0.5	0.7	1.1
Defense	8.6	4.5	1.8	14.9	6	46.4	0.5	1.3	1.8
Difference	1.2	6	-0.1	7.1	-0.1	9.3	0	-0.6	-0.7

Passing

			Passing								
Rk	Player	G	Cmp	Att	Pct	Yds	Y/A	AY/A	TD	Int	Rate
1	Jake Coker	15	263	393	66.9	3110	7.9	8.1	21	8	147
2	Cooper Bateman	6	37	52	71.2	291	5.6	4.3	1	2	116.8
3	Alec Morris	1	1	1	100	6	6	6	0	0	150.4

Rushing and receiving

			Rushing				Receiving				Scrimmage			
Rk	Player	G	Att	Yds	Avg	TD	Rec	Yds	Avg	TD	Plays	Yds	Avg	TD
1	Derrick Henry	15	395	2219	5.6	28	11	91	8.3	0	406	2310	5.7	28
2	Kenyan Drake	13	77	408	5.3	1	29	276	9.5	1	106	684	6.5	2
3	Jake Coker	15	74	68	0.9	2					74	68	0.9	2
4	Damien Harris	10	46	157	3.4	1	4	13	3.3	0	50	170	3.4	1
5	Bo Scarbrough	4	18	104	5.8	1					18	104	5.8	1
6	Derrick Gore	4	6	15	2.5	0					6	15	2.5	0
7	Ronnie Clark	3	5	20	4	0					5	20	4	0
8	Ardarius Stewart	15	5	14	2.8	0	63	700	11.1	4	68	714	10.5	4
9	Cooper Bateman	6	5	8	1.6	0					5	8	1.6	0
10	Calvin Ridley	15	1	2	2	0	89	1045	11.7	7	90	1047	11.6	7
11	Xavian Marks	1	1	0	0	0	2	19	9.5	0	3	19	6.3	0
12	O.J. Howard	12					38	602	15.8	2	38	602	15.8	2
13	Richard Mullaney	15					38	390	10.3	5	38	390	10.3	5
14	Robert Foster	3					10	116	11.6	2	10	116	11.6	2
15	Cam Sims	2					6	46	7.7	0	6	46	7.7	0
16	Ty Flournoy-Smith	3					3	48	16	0	3	48	16	0
17	Chris Black	2					2	23	11.5	0	2	23	11.5	0
18	Daylon Charlot	2					2	9	4.5	0	2	9	4.5	0
19	Michael Nysewander	7					1	19	19	1	1	19	19	1
20	Dakota Ball	2					1	8	8	0	1	8	8	0
21	Hale Hentges	2					1	5	5	0	1	5	5	0
22	Derek Kief	1					1	-3	-3	0	1	-3	-3	0

Defense and fumbles

Rk	Player	G	Solo	Ast	Tot	Loss	Sk	Int	Yds	Avg	TD	PD	FR	FF
					Tackles					Def Int			Fumbles	
1	Reggie Ragland	15	60	42	102	6.5	2.5					7		2
2	Reuben Foster	15	48	25	73	8	1					7		
3	Geno Smith	15	51	21	72	1	0	1	16	16	0	1	1	1
4	Jarran Reed	15	17	40	57	4.5	1					2	1	0
5	Eddie Jackson	15	34	12	46	3	0	6	230	38.3	2	2	1	1
6	A'Shawn Robinson	15	18	28	46	7.5	3.5					2	1	0
7	Marlon Humphrey	15	35	10	45	3.5	0	3	28	9.3	0	8		2
8	Minkah Fitzpatrick	14	30	15	45	3	2	2	88	44	2	10		
9	Cyrus Jones	15	29	8	37	4	0	2	21	10.5	0	7	1	2
10	Ryan Anderson	13	21	16	37	11.5	6						2	2
11	Jonathan Allen	14	19	17	36	14.5	12					3		2
12	Dalvin Tomlinson	14	12	22	34	0.5	0					5		
13	Dillon Lee	11	16	11	27	1.5	1	2	4	2	0	0		
14	Shaun Dion Hamilton	10	14	13	27	1.5	0					1		
15	Denzel Devall	13	11	14	25	5	1					2		
16	D.J. Pettway	11	11	7	18	5	2					2		
17	Tim Williams	11	12	6	18	11.5	9.5					1		
18	Ronnie Harrison Jr.	14	11	6	17	1	1	2	41	20.5	0	6		1
19	Tony Brown	11	12	4	16	1	0					2		1
20	Da'Shawn Hand	8	7	9	16	6.5	3							
21	Bradley Sylve	8	9	7	16	1	0					1		
22	Maurice Smith	8	7	8	15	1	1					1	1	1
23	Da'Ron Payne	8	6	7	13	0.5	0.5					1		1
24	Rashaan Evans	8	7	3	10	4	4							
25	Keith Holcombe	8	6	3	9	0	0					1		
26	Jabriel Washington	4	4	2	6	0	0	1	34	34	0	0		
27	Michael Nysewander	7	3	3	6	0	0							
28	Joshua Frazier	4	1	3	4	0	0							
29	Shawn Burgess-Becker	3	3	0	3	0	0							
30	Darren Lake	5	1	2	3	0	0					2		
31	Cole Mazza	3	1	2	3	0	0							
32	Anthony Averett	2	1	1	2	0	0							
33	Damien Harris	10	2	0	2	0	0							
34	O.J. Howard	12	2	0	2	0	0							
35	Hootie Jones	1	0	2	2	0	0							
36	Dakota Ball	2	0	1	1	0	0							
37	Robert Foster	3	1	0	1	0	0							
38	Derrick Gore	4	1	0	1	0	0							
39	Adam Griffith	15	1	0	1	0	0							
40	Derrick Henry	15	1	0	1	0	0							
41	Dominick Jackson	1	1	0	1	0	0							
42	Walker Jones	1	1	0	1	0	0							
43	Ryan Kelly	1	1	0	1	0	0							
44	Calvin Ridley	15	1	0	1	0	0							
45	O.J. Smith	1	0	1	1	0	0							
46	Adonis Thomas	1	1	0	1	0	0							

Kick and punt returns

Rk	Player	G	Kick Ret				Punt Ret			
			Ret	Yds	Avg	TD	Ret	Yds	Avg	TD
1	Kenyan Drake	13	19	505	26.6	1				
2	Damien Harris	10	9	174	19.3	0				
3	Ardarius Stewart	15	2	30	15	0				
4	Richard Mullaney	15	2	26	13	0	2	30	15	0
5	Cyrus Jones	15	1	24	24	0	42	530	12.6	4
6	Ty Flournoy-Smith	3	1	19	19	0				
7	Michael Nysewander	7	1	16	16	0				
8	Chris Black	2	1	7	7	0				
9	Hale Hentges	2	1	2	2	0				
10	Minkah Fitzpatrick	14					1	16	16	1
11	Keith Holcombe	8					1	13	13	0
12	Ronnie Harrison Jr.	14					1	8	8	0

Kicking and punting

Rk	Player	G	Kicking							Punting		
			XPM	XPA	XP%	FGM	FGA	FG%	Pts	Punts	Yds	Avg
1	Adam Griffith	15	62	62	100	23	32	71.9	131			
2	JK Scott	15	1	1	100	0	1	0	1	70	3094	44.2

Scoring

Rk	Player	G	Touchdowns								Kicking				Pts
			Rush	Rec	Int	FR	PR	KR	Tot	XPM	FGM	2PM	Sfty	
1	Derrick Henry	15	28						28					168
2	Adam Griffith	15								62	23			131
3	Calvin Ridley	15		7					7					42
4	Richard Mullaney	15		5					5					30
5	Ardarius Stewart	15		4					4					24
6	Cyrus Jones	15					4		4					24
7	Kenyan Drake	13	1	1				1	3					18
8	Minkah Fitzpatrick	14			2		1		3					18
9	Eddie Jackson	15			2				2					12
10	Jake Coker	15	2						2					12
11	O.J. Howard	12		2					2					12
12	Robert Foster	3		2					2					12
13	Bo Scarbrough	4	1						1					6
14	Damien Harris	10	1						1					6
15	Michael Nysewander	7		1					1					6
16	JK Scott	15								1				1

Stats include bowl games
Note: Table data from "2015 Alabama Crimson Tide Stats" (9)

Awards and honors

Name	Award	Type
Jake Coker	Permanent Team Captain	Team
Derrick Henry	Permanent Team Captain	Team
Ryan Kelly	Permanent Team Captain	Team
Reggie Ragland	Permanent Team Captain	Team
Derrick Henry	MVP	Team
Derrick Henry	Offensive Player of the Year	Team
Ryan Kelly	Offensive Player of the Year	Team
Reggie Ragland	Defensive Player of the Year	Team
Jarran Reed	Defensive Player of the Year	Team
A'Shawn Robinson	Defensive Player of the Year	Team
Derrick Henry	Offensive Player of the Year	SEC
Reggie Ragland	Defensive Player of the Year	SEC
Jonathan Allen	AP All-SEC First Team	SEC
Derrick Henry	AP All-SEC First Team	SEC
Eddie Jackson	AP All-SEC First Team	SEC
Ryan Kelly	AP All-SEC First Team	SEC
Reggie Ragland	AP All-SEC First Team	SEC
A'Shawn Robinson	AP All-SEC First Team	SEC
Cam Robinson	AP All-SEC First Team	SEC
Jarran Reed	AP All-SEC Second Team	SEC
Calvin Ridley	AP All-SEC Second Team	SEC
Jonathan Allen	Coaches' All-SEC First Team	SEC
Derrick Henry	Coaches' All-SEC First Team	SEC
Eddie Jackson	Coaches' All-SEC First Team	SEC
Ryan Kelly	Coaches' All-SEC First Team	SEC
Reggie Ragland	Coaches' All-SEC First Team	SEC
A'Shawn Robinson	Coaches' All-SEC First Team	SEC
Cam Robinson	Coaches' All-SEC First Team	SEC
Adam Griffith	Coaches' All-SEC Second Team	SEC
Dominick Jackson	Coaches' All-SEC Second Team	SEC
Calvin Ridley	Coaches' All-SEC Second Team	SEC
Ryan Kelly	Jacobs Blocking Trophy	SEC
Ryan Kelly	Scholar-Athlete of the Year	SEC
Ryan Kelly	William V. Campbell Trophy Finalist	SEC
Derrick Henry	AFCA All-America Team	National
Ryan Kelly	AFCA All-America Team	National
Reggie Ragland	AFCA All-America Team	National

Name	Award	Type
A'Shawn Robinson	AFCA All-America Team	National
Derrick Henry	AP All-America First Team	National
Ryan Kelly	AP All-America First Team	National
Reggie Ragland	AP All-America First Team	National
A'Shawn Robinson	AP All-America First Team	National
Ryan Kelly	AP All-America Second Team	National
Eddie Jackson	AP All-America Third Team	National
Reggie Ragland	Bronko Nagurski Trophy Finalist	National
Reggie Ragland	Chuck Bednarik Award Finalist	National
Derrick Henry	Consensus All-American	National
Ryan Kelly	Consensus All-American	National
Reggie Ragland	Consensus All-American	National
A'Shawn Robinson	Consensus All-American	National
Derrick Henry	Doak Walker Award	National
Derrick Henry	FWAA All-America First Team	National
Ryan Kelly	FWAA All-America First Team	National
Reggie Ragland	FWAA All-America First Team	National
A'Shawn Robinson	FWAA All-America First Team	National
Derrick Henry	Heisman Trophy	National
Derrick Henry	Maxwell Award	National
A'Shawn Robinson	Outland Trophy Finalist	National
Ryan Kelly	Rimington Trophy	National
Derrick Henry	Sporting News (TSN) All-America Team	National
Ryan Kelly	Sporting News (TSN) All-America Team	National
Reggie Ragland	Sporting News (TSN) All-America Team	National
A'Shawn Robinson	Sporting News (TSN) All-America Team	National
Derrick Henry	Unanimous All-American	National
Reggie Ragland	Unanimous All-American	National
Derrick Henry	Walter Camp Award	National
Jake Coker	Senior Bowl	All-Star Team
Kenyan Drake	Senior Bowl	All-Star Team
Cyrus Jones	Senior Bowl	All-Star Team
Reggie Ragland	Senior Bowl	All-Star Team
Jarran Reed	Senior Bowl	All-Star Team

NFL

Season	Year drafted	Round	Pick	Overall	Player	Position	Team
2015	2016	1	18	18	Ryan Kelly	C	Indianapolis Colts
2015	2016	2	10	41	Reggie Ragland	LB	Buffalo Bills
2015	2016	2	14	45	Derrick Henry	RB	Tennessee Titans
2015	2016	2	15	46	A'Shawn Robinson	DT	Detroit Lions
2015	2016	2	18	49	Jarran Reed	DT	Seattle Seahawks
2015	2016	2	29	60	Cyrus Jones	CB	New England Patriots
2015	2016	3	10	73	Kenyan Drake	RB	Miami Dolphins

Note: Table data from "2015 Alabama Crimson Tide football team" (142)

2016

Overall

Record	14-1
SEC Record	9-0
Rank	2
Points for	582
Points against	195
Points/game	38.8
Opp points/game	13
SOS[10]	7.29

There's no arguments; those are called ass-chewings. -Nick Saban

Games

Date	Bama Rank		Opp Rank	Opponent	Bama	Opp	Result	SEC
09/03/16	1	N	20	USC	52	6	W	
09/10/16	1	vs		Western Kentucky	38	10	W	
09/17/16	1	@	19	Ole Miss	48	43	W	W
09/24/16	1	vs		Kent State	48	0	W	
10/01/16	1	vs		Kentucky	34	6	W	W
10/08/16	1	@	16	Arkansas	49	30	W	W
10/15/16	1	@	9	Tennessee	49	10	W	W
10/22/16	1	vs	6	Texas A&M	33	14	W	W
11/05/16	1	@	13	LSU	10	0	W	W
11/12/16	1	vs		Mississippi State	51	3	W	W
11/19/16	1	vs		Chattanooga	31	3	W	
11/26/16	1	vs	13	Auburn	30	12	W	W
12/03/16	1	N	15	Florida	54	16	W	W
12/31/16	1	N	4	Washington	24	7	W	
01/09/17	1	N	2	Clemson	31	35	L	

Coaches

Name	Position	Year
Nick Saban	Head Coach	10
Derrick Ansley	Defensive Backs	1
Burton Burns	Associate Head Coach / Running Backs	10
Scott Cochran	Strength and Conditioning	10
Mario Cristobal	Offensive Line / Recruiting Coordinator	4
Karl Dunbar	Defensive Line	1
Brent Key	Offensive Line	1
Lane Kiffin	Offensive Coordinator / Quarterbacks	3
Mike Locksley	Offensive Analyst	1
Tosh Lupoi	Outside Linebackers	2
Billy Napier	Wide Receivers	4
Jeremy Pruitt	Defensive Coordinator / Inside Linebackers	1
Freddie Roach	Director of Player Development	2 (5th overall)
Steve Sarkisian	Analyst	1

Recruits

Name	Pos	Pos Rank	Scout	Rivals	247 Sports	ESPN	ESPN Grade	Hometown	High school / college	Height	Weight	Committed
Charles Baldwin	OT	1	5	5	4	4	83	Windsor, CT	ASA College	6-5	300	6/6/15
Christian Bell	DE		3	3	3	4	81	Birmingham, AL	Hoover HS	6-4	225	4/24/14
Deonte Brown	OG	7	4	3	4	4	83	Decatur, AL	Austin HS	6-3	340	4/30/16
Shyheim Carter	CB	6	4	4	4	4	86	Kentwood, LA	Kentwood HS	6-0	177	2/3/16
Ben Davis	ILB	1	5	5	5	4	87	Gordo, AL	Gordo HS	6-4	237	2/3/16
Raekwon Davis	DT	18	4	4	4	4	82	Meridian, MS	Meridian HS	6-8	318	1/18/16
Trevon Diggs	ATH	6	4	4	4	4	83	Gaithersburg, MD	The Avalon School	6-2	182	11/7/15
B.J. Emmons	RB	1	4	4	4	4	86	Morganton, NC	Freedom HS	5-11	220	7/20/15
Miller Forristall	TE	11	4	3	3	3	79	Cartersville, GA	Cartersville HS	6-6	210	6/13/15
Terrell Hall	DE	6	4	5	4	4	85	Washington, DC	Saint John's College HS	6-6	254	2/3/16
Jalen Hurts	QB	13	4	4	4	4	80	Channelview, TX	Channelview HS	6-2	208	6/6/15
Josh Jacobs	RB	36	3	3	3	3	79	Tulsa, OK	McLean HS	5-10	200	2/3/16
Shawn Jennings	S	44	3	3	3	3	78	Dadeville, AL	Dadeville HS	6-1	215	7/29/15
Kendell Jones	DT	15	5	4	4	4	83	Killeen, TX	Shoemaker HS	6-5	361	5/23/15
Jamar King	DE	8	3	3	3	3	79	Detroit, MI	Mendocino College	6-4	270	2/3/16
Nigel Knott	CB	5	4	4	4	4	86	Madison, MS	Germantown HS	5-11	174	2/1/16
Scott Lashley	OT	15	4	3	4	4	83	West Point, MS	West Point HS	6-6	305	2/2/16
Jared Mayden	CB	17	4	4	4	4	82	Sachse, TX	Sachse HS	6-1	198	2/3/16
Chris Owens	OG	3	4	3	4	4	84	Arlington, TX	Lamar HS	6-3	312	4/22/15
Aaron Robinson	ATH	18	3	3	3	4	80	Deerfield Beach, FL	Deerfield Beach HS	6-1	175	2/3/16
T.J. Simmons	WR	110	4	4	3	3	78	Pinson, AL	Clay-Chalkville HS	6-2	189	2/19/15
Irv Smith Jr.	TE	6	3	3	3	4	80	New Orleans, LA	Brother Martin HS	6-4	230	2/3/16
Jonah Williams	OT	3	4	5	5	4	87	Folsom, CA	Folsom HS	6-5	280	4/4/15
Quinnen Williams	DE	31	4	4	4	4	81	Birmingham, AL	Wenonah HS	6-4	265	6/30/15
Mack Wilson	OLB	5	4	5	5	4	86	Montgomery, AL	Carver HS	6-2	236	2/3/16

	Scout	Rivals	247Sports	ESPN
5 Stars	3	5	3	0
4 Stars	16	10	14	20
3 Stars	6	10	8	5
2 Stars	0	0	0	0

Note: Table data from "2016 Alabama Crimson Tide football team" (160)

Roster

Num	Player	Pos	Class	Height	Weight	Hometown	Last School
93	Jonathan Allen	DL	SR	6-3	291	Leesburg, VA	Stone Bridge
41	Blaine Anderson	DB	SR	5-10	187	Charlotte, NC	Myers Park
31	Keaton Anderson	LB	R-FR	6-1	215	Florence, AL	Florence
22	Ryan Anderson	LB	R-SR	6-2	253	Daphne, AL	Daphne
28	Anthony Averett	DB	R-JR	6-0	183	Woodbury, NJ	Woodbury
44	Dakota Ball	DL	R-SR	6-3	268	Lindale, GA	Pepperell
8	Blake Barnett	QB	FR	6-5	211	Corona, CA	Santiago
18	Cooper Bateman	QB	R-JR	6-3	220	Murray, UT	Cottonwood
41	Parker Bearden	WR	SO	6-1	201	Bessemer, AL	Bessemer Academy
75	Bradley Bozeman	OL	R-JR	6-5	319	Roanoke, AL	Handley
65	Deonte Brown	OL	FR	6-4	350	Decatur, AL	Austin
48	Mekhi Brown	LB	R-FR	6-5	246	Columbus, GA	Carver
2	Tony Brown	DB	JR	6-0	198	Beaumont, TX	Ozen
45	Hunter Bryant	TE	JR	6-5	226	Roswell, GA	Fellowship Christian School
5	Shyheim Carter	DB	FR	6-0	190	Kentwood, LA	Kentwood
67	Joshua Casher	OL	R-SO	6-1	287	Mobile, AL	St. Paul's
5	Ronnie Clark	RB	R-SO	6-2	215	Calera, AL	Calera
12	David Cornwell	QB	R-SO	6-5	228	Norman, OK	Norman North
66	Lester Cotton Sr.	OL	SO	6-4	319	Tuscaloosa, AL	Central
1	Ben Davis	LB	FR	6-4	234	Gordo, AL	Gordo
99	Raekwon Davis	DL	FR	6-7	315	Meridian, MS	Meridian
62	Will Davis	OL	SR	6-5	315	Letohatchee, AL	Fort Dale Academy
11	*Gehrig Dieter*	*WR*	*SR*	*6-3*	*207*	*South Bend, IN*	*Washington/Bowling Green*
7	Trevon Diggs	WR/DB	FR	6-2	195	Gaithersburg, MD	Avalon School
36	Johnny Dwight	DL	R-SO	6-3	306	Rochelle, GA	Wilcox County
21	B.J. Emmons	RB	FR	6-0	206	Morganton, NC	Freedom
43	Lawrence Erekosima	RB	JR	5-7	180	Simpsonville, SC	Clinton
32	Rashaan Evans	LB	JR	6-3	231	Auburn, AL	Auburn
80	Raheem Falkins	WR	R-JR	6-4	200	New Orleans, LA	G.W. Carver
29	Minkah Fitzpatrick	DB	SO	6-1	203	Old Bridge, NJ	St. Peter's Prep
87	Miller Forristall	TE	FR	6-5	225	Cartersville, GA	Cartersville
10	Reuben Foster	LB	SR	6-1	228	Auburn, AL	Auburn
1	Robert Foster	WR	R-JR	6-2	191	Monaca, PA	Central Valley
69	Joshua Frazier	DL	JR	6-4	315	Springdale, AR	Har-Ber
46	Derrick Garnett	LB	SR	6-1	240	Tuscaloosa, AL	Holy Spirit
27	Derrick Gore	RB	R-SO	5-11	210	Syracuse, NY	Coffeyville C.C./Milford Academy
45	Bo Grant	DB	SR	6-2	195	Valley, AL	Valley
89	Brandon Greene	TE	R-SR	6-5	295	Ellenwood, GA	Cedar Grove
99	Adam Griffith	PK	R-SR	5-10	191	Calhoun, GA	Calhoun
24	Terrell Hall	LB	FR	6-5	247	Washington, DC	St. John's
20	Shaun Dion Hamilton	LB	JR	6-0	232	Montgomery, AL	Carver
9	Da'Shawn Hand	DL	JR	6-4	280	Woodbridge, VA	Woodbridge
34	Damien Harris	RB	SO	5-11	214	Richmond, KY	Madison Southern
86	Truett Harris	TE	SR	6-3	235	Brentwood, TN	Brentwood
15	Ronnie Harrison Jr.	DB	SO	6-3	216	Tallahassee, FL	FSU University School
63	J.C. Hassenauer	OL	JR	6-2	299	Woodbury, MN	East Ridge
84	Hale Hentges	TE	SO	6-5	256	Jefferson City, MO	Helias
42	Keith Holcombe	LB	R-SO	6-4	227	Tuscaloosa, AL	Hillcrest
88	O.J. Howard	TE	SR	6-6	251	Prattville, AL	Autauga Academy
26	Marlon Humphrey	DB	R-SO	6-1	196	Hoover, AL	Hoover
2	Jalen Hurts	QB	FR	6-2	209	Channelview, TX	Channelview
4	Eddie Jackson	DB	SR	6-0	194	Lauderdale Lakes, FL	Boyd Anderson
25	Josh Jacobs	RB	FR	5-10	204	Tulsa, OK	McLain
33	Anfernee Jennings	LB	R-FR	6-3	264	Dadeville, AL	Dadeville
19	Shawn Jennings	LB	FR	6-1	220	Dadeville, AL	Dadeville
38	Austin Johnson	WR	SO	6-2	200	Elba, AL	Elba
6	Hootie Jones	DB	JR	6-2	215	Monroe, LA	Neville
50	Vohn Keith	DL	JR	6-2	221	Mobile, AL	Faith Academy
56	Brandon Kennedy	OL	R-FR	6-3	301	Wetumpka, AL	Wetumpka
81	Derek Kief	WR	R-SO	6-4	200	Cincinnati, OH	La Salle
90	*Jamar King*	*DL*	*JR*	*6-4*	*290*	*Detroit, MI*	*Denby/Mendocino C.C./Denby*
78	Korren Kirven	OL	SR	6-4	311	Lynchburg, VA	Brookville
13	Nigel Knott	DB	FR	5-11	175	Madison, MS	Germantown
76	Scott Lashley	OL	FR	6-7	313	West Point, MS	West Point
85	Donnie Lee Jr.	WR	JR	6-0	180	Northport, AL	Tuscaloosa County
21	D.J. Lewis	DB	JR	5-11	196	Birmingham, AL	Gardendale
24	Terrell Lewis	LB	FR	6-5	247	Washington, DC	St. John's
51	Jake Long	DL	SR	5-9	228	Vestavia Hills, AL	Vestavia Hills
35	Torin Marks	DB	R-FR	5-11	175	Rosenberg, TX	George Ranch
19	Xavian Marks	WR	SO	5-8	166	Rosenberg, TX	George Ranch
60	Malik Martin	OL	SO	6-3	370	Tuscaloosa, AL	Hillcrest
8	Jared Mayden	DB	FR	6-0	200	Sachse, TX	Sachse

Num	Player	Pos	Class	Height	Weight	Hometown	Last School
55	**Cole Mazza**	**SN**	**SR**	**6-2**	**235**	**Bakersfield, CA**	**Liberty**
40	Joshua McMillon	LB	R-FR	6-3	237	Memphis, TN	Whitehaven
52	Scott Meyer	SN	FR	6-2	222	Alpharetta, GA	Blessed Trinity Catholic
47	Christian Miller	LB	R-SO	6-4	230	Columbia, SC	Spring Valley
64	Brandon Moore	OL	SR	6-0	248	Cincinnati, OH	Hills Christian Academy
37	Donavan Mosley	DB	SO	5-10	180	San Antonio, TX	James Madison
16	Jamey Mosley	LB	R-SO	6-5	228	Mobile, AL	Theodore
19	Montana Murphy	QB	FR	6-3	201	Southlake, TX	Carroll Senior
79	Chris Owens	OL	FR	6-3	307	Arlington, TX	Lamar
92	Andy Pappanastos	PK	R-JR	5-11	198	Montgomery, AL	Trinity Presbyterian/Ole Miss
42	Jacob Parker	TE	JR	6-1	222	Meridianville, AL	Westminster Christian
53	Ryan Parris	SN	SO	6-0	209	Madison, AL	James Clemons
94	**Da'Ron Payne**	**DL**	**SO**	**6-2**	**319**	**Birmingham, AL**	**Shades Valley**
72	Richie Petitbon	OL	SR-FR	6-4	302	Annapolis, MD	Gonzaga
71	**Ross Pierschbacher**	**OL**	**R-SO**	**6-4**	**304**	**Cedar Falls, IA**	**Cedar Falls**
58	Daniel Powell	DL	FR	5-11	238	Aliceville, AL	Pickens Academy
61	Jacob Probasco	OL	FR	6-3	317	Plainsboro, NJ	West Windsor-Plainsboro
47	Josh Pugh	WR	SO	6-1	208	Chelsea, AL	Chelsea
89	Armani Purifoye	WR	JR	6-0	193	Kingsland, GA	Camden County
44	Avery Reid	RB	SO	6-0	192	Oneonta, AL	Oneonta
37	Jonathan Rice	WR	SO	6-4	207	Madison, AL	Bob Jones
3	**Calvin Ridley**	**WR**	**SO**	**6-1**	**188**	**Coconut Creek, FL**	**Monarch**
23	Aaron Robinson	DB	FR	6-1	181	Deerfield Beach, FL	Deerfield Beach
74	**Cam Robinson**	**OL**	**JR**	**6-6**	**310**	**Monroe, LA**	**West Monroe**
98	Brannon Satterfield	P	SO	6-2	210	Austin, TX	Lake Travis
9	**Bo Scarbrough**	**RB**	**SO**	**6-2**	**228**	**Tuscaloosa, AL**	**Tuscaloosa County**
15	**JK Scott**	**P**	**JR**	**6-6**	**202**	**Denver, CO**	**Mullen**
16	T.J. Simmons	WR	FR	6-2	201	Pinson, AL	Clay-Chalkville
17	Cam Sims	WR	JR	6-5	203	Monroe, LA	Ouachita Parish
91	O.J. Smith	DL	R-SO	6-2	309	Bossier City, LA	Airline
82	Irv Smith Jr.	TE	FR	6-4	235	New Orleans, LA	Brother Martin
34	Nate Staskelunas	DB	SR	6-3	207	Greenville, NC	Arendell Parrott Academy
13	**ArDarius Stewart**	**WR**	**R-JR**	**6-1**	**204**	**Fultondale, AL**	**Fultondale**
83	Cam Stewart	TE	FR	6-8	254	San Jose, CA	Valley Christian
50	**Alphonse Taylor**	**OL**	**R-SR**	**6-5**	**345**	**Mobile, AL**	**Davidson**
14	Deionte Thompson	DB	R-FR	6-2	190	Orange, TX	West Orange-Stark
54	Dalvin Tomlinson	DL	R-SR	6-3	305	McDonaugh, GA	Henry County
39	Levi Wallace	DB	JR	6-0	170	Tucson, AZ	Tucson
59	Dallas Warmack	OL	SO	6-2	299	Atlanta, GA	Mays
73	**Jonah Williams**	**OL**	**FR**	**6-5**	**296**	**Folsom, CA**	**Folsom**
92	Quinnen Williams	DL	FR	6-4	284	Birmingham, AL	Wenonah
56	**Tim Williams**	**LB**	**SR**	**6-4**	**252**	**Baton Rouge, LA**	**University Lab**
30	Mack Wilson	LB	FR	6-2	244	Montgomery, AL	Carver
77	Matt Womack	OL	R-FR	6-7	316	Hernando, MS	Magnolia Heights
35	Thomas Woods	WR	JR	5-6	165	Birmingham, AL	Vestavia Hills

Note: Starters in bold
Note: Table data from "2016 Alabama Crimson Tide Roster" (161)

Transfers

Player	School	Direction
Gehrig Dieter	Oregon State	Incoming
Jamar King	Mendocino Community College	Incoming
Alec Morris	North Texas	Outgoing

Note: Table data from "Position-by-Position Preview of Alabama's 2016 Roster" (162)

Games

09/03/16 - Alabama (1) vs USC (20)

AT&T Stadium
Arlington, TX

Team	1	2	3	4	T	Passing	Rushing	Total
USC (20)	3	0	3	0	6	130	64	194
Alabama (1)	0	17	21	14	52	223	242	465

The game started with USC taking an early 3-0 lead. On its second offensive play, USC quarterback Max Browne went deep and connected with wide receiver Darreus Rogers for a 36-yard gain to the Tide 33-yard line. Three plays later, kicker Matt Boermeester nailed a 47-yard field goal. Alabama's true freshman quarterback Jalen Hurts made his college debut in the first quarter on the Tide's third possession, replacing starter Blake Barnett. USC dominated the first quarter, outgaining Alabama 78-12 in total yards.

In the second quarter, Alabama capitalized on excellent field position at the USC 36-yard line after a punt and personal foul penalty. On 3rd-and-13 at the Trojan 39, Hurts hit ArDarius Stewart for a 39-yard touchdown, giving Alabama a 7-3 lead. The Tide kept rolling, with Damien Harris breaking off big runs of 11 and 46 yards, setting up an Adam Griffith field goal from 11 yards out to make it 10-3. After a USC kickoff blunder led to an ejection of Ruffin for kicking Minkah Fitzpatrick, Marlon Humphrey returned an interception 18 yards for a touchdown, extending Alabama's lead to 17-3 at halftime.

Alabama took complete control in the third quarter. Hurts connected with Stewart again for a 71-yard score (24-3). The play marked the longest reception of Stewart's Alabama career and gave him a career-high 113 receiving yards in the game. USC fell on the ball on its own 13-yard line after a botched snap on a punt attempt. After a few plays, Hurts kept on a zone read and ran for seven yards and the touchdown (31-3).

Alabama's offensive juggernaut showed no signs of slowing down. Two possessions later, they embarked on an 85-yard, 3-play scoring drive that further extended their commanding lead. The highlight of the march was a blistering 73-yard run by Harris, which left the Trojans grasping at air as he galloped down to the USC 6-yard line. Seizing the opportunity, quarterback Jalen Hurts capped off the drive with a nifty 6-yard touchdown run on a quarterback sweep around the right end. The Crimson Tide's relentless assault had pushed the score to a 38-3 advantage. Not to be outdone, the Trojans mustered their most sustained offensive push since the opening quarter. They methodically moved 56 yards down the field, but their efforts only yielded a 41-yard field goal. As the third quarter wound down with 2:34 remaining, the score stood at 38-6, with Alabama firmly in control.

The third quarter saw a resurgence from the Alabama offense, ignited by the return of quarterback Blake Barnett. His presence under center immediately paid dividends as he engineered a 65-yard scoring drive over nine plays. The highlight was a 40-yard strike to tight end O.J. Howard, setting up 1st-and-goal at the USC 8-yard line as the quarter expired. On the first play of the fourth quarter, running back Bo Scarborough barreled into the end zone from two yards out on fourth down, extending Alabama's lead to 45-6. The Crimson Tide wasted no time getting back on the scoreboard. Barnett guided the offense 67 yards in just four plays, capping the lightning-quick drive with a 45-yard touchdown strike to receiver Gehrig Dieter. Adam Griffith's extra point made it 52-6 with 9:25 remaining, putting the game firmly out of reach.

Alabama's 52-6 demolition of No. 20 USC etched its name into the record books in resounding fashion. The 46-point margin of victory stands as the second largest ever for the Crimson Tide against a top 20 opponent. Only one game exceeds it - a 55-point thrashing of Syracuse (61-6) in the 1953 Orange Bowl after the 1952 season. The largest Alabama victory margin over a ranked foe came more recently in 2014 when they annihilated No. 21 Texas A&M by a staggering 59-0 score.

The Alabama defense smothered USC, with several players having standout performances. Redshirt freshman cornerback Anthony Averett led the way with a team-high eight total tackles, including seven solo stops. Cornerback Minkah Fitzpatrick added six tackles and two pass breakups. Defensive end Jonathan Allen terrorized the Trojans' backfield with two sacks. Overall, the Tide racked up seven pass breakups, nine tackles for loss, and three sacks in a suffocating defensive effort. While the defense shut down USC, Alabama's offense methodically moved the ball. The Tide picked up 15 first downs and averaged an impressive 7.4 yards per play. In contrast, the Trojans managed just 11 first downs while averaging a paltry 2.9 yards per play against the stifling Crimson Tide defense.[163]

Passing	C/ATT	YDS	AVG	TD	INT	QBR
J. Hurts	6/11	118	10.7	2	1	71.7
B. Barnett	5/6	100	16.7	1	0	18.5
C. Bateman	1/1	5	5	0	0	1
Team	12/18	223	12.4	3	1	--

Rushing	CAR	YDS	AVG	TD	LONG
D. Harris	9	138	15.3	0	73
B. Scarbrough	11	36	3.3	1	9
J. Hurts	9	32	3.6	2	9
J. Jacobs	4	20	5	0	8
BJ Emmons	6	18	3	0	6
A. Stewart	1	17	17	0	17
C. Bateman	1	-9	-9	0	0
B. Barnett	4	-10	-2.5	0	2
Team	45	242	5.4	3	73

Interceptions	INT	YDS	TD
M. Humphrey	1	18	1

Punting	NO	YDS	AVG	TB	IN 20	LONG
JK Scott	5	235	47	0	0	54

Receiving	REC	YDS	AVG	TD	LONG
A. Stewart	4	113	28.3	2	71
G. Dieter	1	45	45	1	45
OJ Howard	3	39	13	0	40
C. Sims	1	12	12	0	12
C. Ridley	2	9	4.5	0	10
B. Greene	1	5	5	0	5
Team	12	223	18.6	3	71

Kick returns	NO	YDS	AVG	LONG	TD
T. Diggs	1	24	24	24	0

Punt returns	NO	YDS	AVG	LONG	TD
C. Ridley	3	4	1.3	6	0

Kicking	FG	PCT	LONG	XP	PTS
A. Griffith	1/1	100	29	7/7	10

Note: Table data from "Alabama 52-6 USC (Sep 3, 2016) Box Score" (164)

09/10/16 - Alabama (1) vs Western Kentucky

Team	1	2	3	4	T		Passing	Rushing	Total
Western Kentucky	3	0	0	7	10		216	23	239
Alabama (1)	10	7	7	14	38		351	124	475

In his first career start, true freshman quarterback Jalen Hurts passed for 287 yards and two touchdowns to lead No. 1 Alabama to a convincing 38-10 victory over Western Kentucky. He also had two likely touchdown passes dropped. His impressive 23-of-36 passing performance likely cemented his role as the Crimson Tide's starting signal-caller, making him the first true freshman quarterback to start for Alabama since Vince Sutton in 1984.

The game started slowly as Alabama and Western Kentucky traded field goals from 36 and 25 yards, respectively. However, the Tide defense provided the catalyst for an offensive outburst. Ronnie Harrison Jr. intercepted a pass, and nine plays later, Jalen Hurts found Calvin Ridley for a 4-yard touchdown strike, giving Bama a 10-3 lead. The defensive onslaught continued when Eddie Jackson picked off a pass and took it to the house, returning the interception 55 yards for a pick-six touchdown. Jackson's electrifying play extended Bama's advantage to 17-3 as the defense's big plays ignited the offense and swung the momentum firmly in Alabama's favor.

After both teams punted to start the second half, Bama scored three touchdowns. The first two were from eight yards out (Hurts to Stewart, then a Bo Scarbrough run). The third was by B.J. Emmons from six yards out. Western Kentucky scored a TD in garbage time, making the final 38-10. Alabama's stifling defense, which had surrendered a mere 16 points through the first two games, smothered WKU, outgaining them 475-239 in total yards. Calvin Ridley torched the secondary with nine catches for 129 yards, while ArDarius Stewart added 90 yards on five receptions (both receivers logged carries as well). The Tide's defensive prowess forced Western Kentucky QB Mike White from the game late in the third quarter. White, coming off a 517-yard performance against Rice, managed just 10-of-24 passing for 135 yards and a pick before his early exit. The Hilltoppers salvaged a touchdown by converting a turnover in the final minute.

While not a spectacular showing, Bama got the job done behind another robust defensive effort complemented by a series of explosive plays. Stewart, Ridley, and Gehrig Dieter ignited the offense with catches of 52, 51, and 40 yards. The relentless Tide defense recorded four sacks and limited WKU to a paltry 23 rushing yards. Eddie Jackson's 55-yard pick-six provided breathing room in a 10-3 game and was his third such touchdown over the past two seasons.[165]

Passing	C/ATT	YDS	AVG	TD	INT	QBR
J. Hurts	23/36	287	8	2	0	47.5
B. Barnett	2/6	64	10.7	0	0	43.4
Team	25/42	351	8.4	2	0	--

Rushing	CAR	YDS	AVG	TD	LONG
D. Harris	11	45	4.1	0	11
BJ Emmons	6	41	6.8	1	14
B. Scarbrough	5	19	3.8	1	8
J. Hurts	11	19	1.7	0	6
A. Stewart	2	12	6	0	11
C. Ridley	1	6	6	0	6
D. Gore	1	1	1	0	1
R. Foster	1	-5	-5	0	0
Team	1	-14	-14	0	0
Team	39	124	3.2	2	14

Kicking	FG	PCT	LONG	XP	PTS
A. Griffith	1/2	50	36	5/5	8

Punting	NO	YDS	AVG	TB	IN 20	LONG
JK Scott	5	232	46.4	0	0	58

Receiving	REC	YDS	AVG	TD	LONG
C. Ridley	9	129	14.3	1	51
A. Stewart	5	90	18	1	52
G. Dieter	2	56	28	0	40
OJ Howard	2	29	14.5	0	20
T. Diggs	1	14	14	0	14
D. Harris	2	14	7	0	9
R. Foster	3	13	4.3	0	6
H. Hentges	1	6	6	0	6
Team	25	351	14	2	52

Interceptions	INT	YDS	TD
E. Jackson	1	55	1
R. Harrison Jr.	1	6	0
Team	2	61	1

Kick returns	NO	YDS	AVG	LONG	TD
T. Diggs	3	63	21	24	0

Punt returns	NO	YDS	AVG	LONG	TD
T. Diggs	2	15	7.5	13	0

Note: Table data from "Western Kentucky 10-38 Alabama (Sep 10, 2016) Box Score" (166)

09/17/16 - Alabama (1) at Ole Miss (19)

Team	1	2	3	4	T		Passing	Rushing	Total
Alabama (1)	3	14	17	14	**48**		158	334	**492**
Ole Miss (19)	7	17	3	16	**43**		421	101	**522**

The Rebels opened the game by driving 75 yards in seven plays (1:53) and scored a touchdown. The Tide responded by gaining 61 yards on 17 plays ending in an Adam Griffith field goal to make it 7-3. Bama forced a punt, drove down to the 29-yard line, and Griffith missed a 47-yard field goal. After a few punts (including a 63-yarder by Scott), he shanked one that only went eight yards to the Ole Miss 44-yard line with 9:20 left in the half. The Rebels drove down and scored a field goal to go up 10-3.

Bama punted, and Chad Kelly faked a pitchout and found a wide-open Evan Engram for a 63-yard touchdown to go up 17-3. On the next Alabama possession, Hurts fumbled, and Ole Miss returned it 44 yards for a touchdown (24-3). The 24 points surrendered represented the most points Alabama had ever allowed in a single half under Saban's leadership, and it also tied his largest deficit. In a blistering 65 second span, Alabama struck back with fury. First, it was Calvin Ridley who took a direct snap on a motion play 66 yards untouched into the end zone. Then Eddie Jackson returned a punt for a touchdown (Bama down 24-17 at the half).

Alabama scored on a sack fumble (Ryan Anderson) as Da'Ron Payne scooped and scored to tie it at 24-24. With 11:47 left in the third quarter, Alabama had scored three touchdowns in all three facets - offense, defense, and special teams. Both teams scored field goals, and the game was tied at 27-27. Bo Scarborough scored on a 1-yard touchdown run, and Ole Miss scored a field goal giving Alabama a 34-30 lead with 13:17 left in the fourth quarter. On a 2nd-and-goal, Damien Harris scored a 1-yard touchdown. Alabama led 41-30 with 7:33 remaining in the game. Jonathan Allen recorded an interception and returned it 75 yards for a touchdown (Tide up 48-30 with 5:28 left in the game).

Ole Miss drove 78 yards in 12 plays to score on a 5-yard pass with 2:59 left (Bama up 48-37). Ole Miss recovered an onside kick then scored on the next play on a 37-yard pass from Kelly to WR A.J. Brown with 2:51 on the clock. A two-point pass play was incomplete, leaving the Tide with a 48-43 lead that held up. The 21 points was the largest deficit overcome in the program's history. Jalen Hurts became the first Tide quarterback to rush for more than 100 yards since Tyler Watts in 2001. Damien Harris rushed for a career-best 144 yards giving Bama two 100-yard rushers in the same game for the 18th time in Tide history. Reuben Foster recorded a team-best 12 tackles, including four solo. The Tide defense had two quarterback sacks, four tackles for loss, intercepted one pass, broke up six passes, forced one fumble, and was credited with two quarterback hurries.[167]

Passing	C/ATT	YDS	AVG	TD	INT	QBR
J. Hurts	19/31	158	5.1	0	0	70.9

Rushing	CAR	YDS	AVG	TD	LONG
J. Hurts	18	146	8.1	0	41
D. Harris	16	144	9	1	67
J. Jacobs	3	33	11	0	25
B. Scarbrough	7	13	1.9	1	5
C. Ridley	2	2	1	1	6
Team	2	-4	-2	0	0
Team	48	334	7.0	3	67

Kick returns	NO	YDS	AVG	LONG	TD
T. Diggs	3	79	26.3	41	0

Punting	NO	YDS	AVG	TB	IN 20	LONG
JK Scott	5	194	38.8	0	0	63

Receiving	REC	YDS	AVG	TD	LONG
C. Ridley	8	81	10.1	0	45
G. Dieter	2	47	23.5	0	30
OJ Howard	2	24	12	0	18
H. Hentges	1	3	3	0	3
A. Stewart	4	2	0.5	0	5
D. Harris	2	1	0.5	0	8
Team	19	158	8.3	0	45

Punt returns	NO	YDS	AVG	LONG	TD
E. Jackson	2	95	47.5	85	1

Kicking	FG	PCT	LONG	XP	PTS
A. Griffith	2/3	66.7	32	6/6	12

Note: Table data from "Alabama 48-43 Ole Miss (Sep 17, 2016) Box Score" (168)

09/24/16 - Alabama (1) vs Kent State

Team	1	2	3	4	T	Passing	Rushing	Total
Kent State	0	0	0	0	0	84	82	166
Alabama (1)	21	20	7	0	48	217	285	502

Alabama wasted no time demonstrating its prowess, marching 70 yards in just eight plays on the opening drive. Quarterback Jalen Hurts capped it off with a 20-yard touchdown run around the right end, giving the Tide an early 7-0 lead less than three minutes into the game. Kent State showed a spark on its first possession with a 47-yard run but missed a 37-yard field goal attempt.

Starting at their own 21, the Tide moved 79 yards in ten plays to a score (1-yard run by Josh Jacobs). Bama got a third touchdown in its first three drives following another KSU punt. The Tide moved 55 yards in four plays with Jacobs scoring on a 24-yard run to go up 21-0 with 3:39 left in the first. After another KSU punt, Bama drove 75 yards and scored a 28-yard FG (24-0).

Anthony Averett forced a fumble recovered by Ronnie Harrison Jr. setting up a 48-yard field goal by Adam Griffith (27-0). With Blake Barnett in at quarterback, Alabama moved 61 yards including a 34-yard touchdown pass to O.J. Howard. Xavian Marks returned a punt 75 yards for another touchdown (41-0 with 2:14 left in the half). The return marked the sixth consecutive game that Alabama has scored a non-offensive touchdown (a school record).

Alabama scored again in the second half (Hurts to Mack Wilson) making it 48-0. Kent State then mounted its best drive, moving 73 yards in 11 plays to the Tide 1-yard line. But Christian Miller stuffed them on fourth down to preserve the shutout - Alabama's 17th shutout victory for the Tide in the Saban era and Alabama's 95th shutout win since 1958.

The Crimson Tide racked up 26 first downs and averaged 6.3 yards per play, while holding Kent State to just 3.6 yards per play. Reuben Foster led the way defensively with seven total tackles, while the unit combined for three sacks, five tackles for loss, a forced fumble, and six quarterback hurries.[169]

Passing	C/ATT	YDS	AVG	TD	INT	QBR
J. Hurts	16/24	164	6.8	1	0	90.9
B. Barnett	4/7	55	7.9	1	0	20.2
C. Bateman	2/3	-2	-0.7	0	0	3
Team	22/34	217	6.4	2	0	--

Rushing	CAR	YDS	AVG	TD	LONG
J. Jacobs	11	97	8.8	2	24
J. Hurts	7	54	7.7	1	20
BJ Emmons	8	51	6.4	0	17
D. Gore	6	45	7.5	0	20
B. Scarbrough	3	19	6.3	0	14
D. Harris	4	18	4.5	0	9
C. Ridley	1	7	7	0	7
A. Reid	2	4	2	0	2
Team	1	-3	-3	0	0
B. Barnett	3	-7	-2.3	0	0
Team	46	285	6.2	3	24

Punting	NO	YDS	AVG	TB	IN 20	LONG
JK Scott	2	98	49	0	0	53

Receiving	REC	YDS	AVG	TD	LONG
OJ Howard	3	60	20	1	34
C. Sims	4	54	13.5	0	31
J. Jacobs	2	23	11.5	0	15
T. Diggs	3	23	7.7	0	17
BJ Emmons	1	17	17	0	17
D. Kief	3	17	5.7	0	8
G. Dieter	1	10	10	0	10
B. Scarbrough	1	6	6	0	6
C. Ridley	1	5	5	0	5
M. Wilson	1	1	1	1	1
H. Hentges	1	1	1	0	1
D. Gore	1	0	0	0	0
Team	22	217	9.9	2	34

Punt returns	NO	YDS	AVG	LONG	TD
X. Marks	4	90	22.5	75	1

Kicking	FG	PCT	LONG	XP	PTS
A. Griffith	2/2	100	48	4/4	10
A. Pappanastos	0/0	0	0	2/2	2
Team	2/2	100	48	6/6	12

Note: Table data from "Alabama 48-0 Kent State (Sep 24, 2016) Box Score" (170)

10/01/16 - Alabama (1) vs Kentucky

Team	1	2	3	4	T		Passing	Rushing	Total
Kentucky	3	0	0	3	6		89	72	161
Alabama (1)	3	14	14	3	34		315	173	488

Cam Sims dropped a 4th down pass on the opening drive. Kentucky marched down 36 yards and scored on a 45-yard field goal. Bo Scarborough ran into Jalen Hurts' arm as he was passing causing a fumble on the Tide 49-yard line that was recovered by Kentucky. The Cats moved into scoring position, but Miller and Anderson sacked Johnson, and Anderson recovered on the Tide 31-yard line. Bama drove 35 yards and tied the game at 3-3 with a 44-yard field goal.

Early in the second quarter, Josh Jacobs ran six straight times accounting for 57 of the 61 yards on the drive and scoring on a 1-yard rush to take a 10-3 lead. On Kentucky's next possession, Rashaan Evans recorded a sack that caused a fumble. Ronnie Harrison Jr. picked it up at the Alabama 45-yard line and returned it 55 yards for a touchdown (17-3). The Crimson Tide's defensive prowess continued to shine as they extended an impressive streak of scoring non-offensive touchdowns to seven consecutive games, leading the nation in this remarkable feat. Following another stalled drive by the Wildcats, resulting in a punt, Alabama methodically marched down the field, orchestrating a 14-play, 62-yard drive. However, their efforts were thwarted as Adam Griffith's 35-yard field goal attempt sailed wide left with just 44 seconds remaining in the first half. Alabama was ahead 17-3 at the break.

Alabama added to its lead in the second half by driving 78 yards in eight plays ending in a 10-yard touchdown pass to Calvin Ridley (24-3). Kentucky punted again, then Bama drove 76 yards with some sharp passes by Hurts that concluded with a 19-yard touchdown pass to Ridley (31-3). On their next possession after a UK punt, Griffith connected on a 24-yard field goal to give the Tide a 34-3 lead with 14:51 left in the game. The Cats moved 63 yards down the field and scored on a 30-yard field goal making it 34-6, which ending up being the final score.

Calvin Ridley was unstoppable, hauling in a career-high 11 receptions for 174 yards and two touchdowns. Josh Jacobs also had a standout game, rushing for 100 yards on 16 carries while adding 54 receiving yards on three catches. This marked Jacobs' first 100-yard rushing game in the Crimson Tide uniform. The defense was equally impressive, led by Shaun Dion Hamilton's eight total tackles, four of them solo efforts. As a unit, they relentlessly pressured the quarterback, recording four sacks, nine tackles for loss, forcing three fumbles, and tallying six quarterback hurries.[171]

Passing	C/ATT	YDS	AVG	TD	INT	QBR
J. Hurts	20/33	262	7.9	2	0	56
C. Bateman	5/5	53	10.6	0	0	61.7
Team	25/38	315	8.3	2	0	--

Rushing	CAR	YDS	AVG	TD	LONG
J. Jacobs	16	100	6.3	1	28
J. Hurts	9	25	2.8	0	11
B. Scarbrough	5	21	4.2	0	14
BJ Emmons	3	16	5.3	0	8
D. Harris	2	11	5.5	0	7
C. Ridley	1	6	6	0	6
Team	1	-6	-6	0	0
Team	37	173	4.7	1	28

Kicking	FG	PCT	LONG	XP	PTS
A. Griffith	2/3	66.7	44	4/4	10

Punting	NO	YDS	AVG	TB	IN 20	LONG
JK Scott	1	58	58	0	0	58

Receiving	REC	YDS	AVG	TD	LONG
C. Ridley	11	174	15.8	2	46
J. Jacobs	3	54	18	0	24
R. Foster	2	32	16	0	17
T. Diggs	2	14	7	0	8
OJ Howard	2	13	6.5	0	12
G. Dieter	1	11	11	0	11
B. Scarbrough	1	9	9	0	9
D. Harris	1	6	6	0	6
BJ Emmons	1	3	3	0	3
C. Sims	1	-1	-1	0	0
Team	25	315	12.6	2	46

Kick returns	NO	YDS	AVG	LONG	TD
X. Marks	2	33	16.5	22	0

Punt returns	NO	YDS	AVG	LONG	TD
E. Jackson	1	17	17	17	0
X. Marks	1	15	15	15	0
Team	2	32	16	17	0

Note: Table data from "Alabama 34-6 Kentucky (Oct 1, 2016) Box Score" (172)

10/08/16 - Alabama (1) at Arkansas (16)

Team	1	2	3	4	T		Passing	Rushing	Total
Alabama (1)	14	21	7	7	49		253	264	517
Arkansas (16)	7	10	7	6	30		400	73	473

Alabama drove 80 yards on its first possession dominating with their ground attack, but a fumble prevented them from scoring. After forcing a punt, the Tide struck quickly, needing just three plays to cover 73 yards, highlighted by a 57-yard run from Harris and a Hurts quarterback keeper for the touchdown. Just two minutes later, Alabama's defense struck again. Hootie Jones jarred the ball loose on the kickoff, and Mack Wilson pounced on it. The Tide offense didn't let the gift go to waste as Hurts called his own number again, plunging in from six yards out on a QB keeper which extended the lead to 14-0. Arkansas refused to go away quietly, mounting a 75-yard touchdown drive in nine plays, converting two long crucial third downs along the way (3rd-and-19 and 3rd-and-9). The TD was a 24-yard pass (Bama up 14-7). The Tide defense swiftly responded as Da'Shawn Hand's relentless pressure forced Arkansas' QB to cough up the ball. Tim Williams pounced on it and rumbled 23 yards for a touchdown to extend the lead to 21-7.

The offensive onslaught continued as Hurts threw a screen pass to Harris where he broke through a defender and turned it into a 56-yard touchdown (28-7). Arkansas answered with a 25-yard field goal, then Bo Scarbrough bounced to the outside and ran down the sideline for a 21-yard touchdown to extend Alabama's lead to 35-10 with 1:25 left in the half. The Razorbacks kept battling and gained 57 yards on a pass to Cornelius after Eddie Jackson fell on what appeared to be a jump ball situation. Minkah Fitzpatrick ran him down and tackled him at the Alabama 16. They scored on the next play with a 16-yard pass to Hatcher (35-17 going into the half).

ArDarius Stewart fumbled at the end of a 67-yard pass play, but Fitzpatrick got the ball back on a diving interception three plays later. The Tide scored in four plays as Hurts hit Calvin Ridley for a 4-yard catch (42-17). Hurts' first interception in 139 attempts (second-longest streak in Alabama history) gave Arkansas excellent field position at the Tide 36. The Razorbacks found the end zone six plays later on a 10-yard pass, making the score 42-24. Bama punted, Arkansas moved the ball 62 yards in 15 plays, then Fitzpatrick recorded another interception, this time in the end zone. He took it the distance for a 100-yard TD. It was the longest interception return in Alabama history and was Fitzpatrick's third career interception return for a touchdown, tying an Alabama record. The score was now 49-24 with 10:18 left in the game. The Razorbacks added a late touchdown going 94 yards in seven plays, but the Tide was too much. It was 49-30 after a failed two-point conversion attempt. Hamilton and Anderson led the Tide with a game-high nine tackles. The Tide defense got three picks, forced three fumbles, had six sacks, nine tackles for loss, broke up five passes, and were credited with 12 quarterback hurries on the night.[173]

Passing	C/ATT	YDS	AVG	TD	INT	QBR
J. Hurts	13/17	253	14.9	2	1	88.5

Rushing	CAR	YDS	AVG	TD	LONG
D. Harris	13	122	9.4	0	57
J. Jacobs	3	57	19	0	56
B. Scarbrough	7	56	8	1	21
J. Hurts	8	20	2.5	2	6
BJ Emmons	3	9	3	0	5
Team	34	264	7.8	3	57

Interceptions	INT	YDS	TD
M. Fitzpatrick	3	114	1

Punting	NO	YDS	AVG	TB	IN 20	LONG
JK Scott	4	206	51.5	0	0	63

Receiving	REC	YDS	AVG	TD	LONG
A. Stewart	5	120	24	0	67
D. Harris	2	60	30	1	56
M. Forristall	1	32	32	0	32
OJ Howard	1	21	21	0	21
C. Ridley	3	14	4.7	1	9
G. Dieter	1	6	6	0	6
Team	13	253	19.5	2	67

Kick returns	NO	YDS	AVG	LONG	TD
X. Marks	5	90	18	25	0

Punt returns	NO	YDS	AVG	LONG	TD
E. Jackson	2	12	6	9	0

Kicking	FG	PCT	LONG	XP	PTS
A. Griffith	0/0	0	0	7/7	7

Note: Table data from "Alabama 49-30 Arkansas (Oct 8, 2016) Box Score" (174)

10/15/16 - Alabama (1) at Tennessee (9)

Team	1	2	3	4	T		Passing	Rushing	Total
Alabama (1)	14	7	14	14	49		185	409	594
Tennessee (9)	0	7	3	0	10		131	32	163

After starting the game with three punts (two by TN), Alabama had the ball on their own nine. Hurts led a 91-yard TD drive, capped by a 29-yard score on a reverse (shovel pass to Ridley then handoff to ArDarius Stewart) to put Alabama up 7-0. With time winding down in the first quarter, Ronnie Harrison stepped in front of a Josh Dobbs pass, intercepted it at the Tide 42-yard line, and raced untouched into the end zone for a 58-yard pick-six (14-0). This was Alabama's eighth defensive touchdown of the season (leading the nation) and their 10th non-offensive TD.

Hurts was sacked for a loss of 14 at the Tide 11 on a third-down play, fumbled, and TN recovered. It only took Kamara two rushes to score (14-7). But Alabama answered with a quick scoring march, advancing 65 yards in just six plays. On the scoring play, Hurts faked a handoff to Jacobs and kept running right. He broke free from the defense and sprinted the final 45 yards untouched into the end zone to complete the scoring drive (21-7). Alabama's next drive, sparked by a 37-yard scamper by Hurts, advanced them to the UT 12-yard line. But they failed to increase their lead when Hurts was pressured, and his deflected pass was intercepted at Alabama's 25-yard line. Griffith missed a 37-yard FG with two seconds remaining in the half.

On the first possession of the second half, Hurts became the first Alabama QB since Tyler Watts (2001) to rush for over 100 yards twice in a season, but the possession ended in a punt. After holding TN to a punt, Alabama drove down the field ending with Hurts scoring on a 2-yard run (28-7). Tennessee responded by driving 49 yards to the Alabama 19-yard line in ten plays, culminating in a 37-yard field goal. Dobbs completed all five of his pass attempts on the drive, accounting for 43 of the 49 total yards. Bama was now up 28-10. Hurts scored again at the end of Bama's next drive (of 75 yards) on a run-pass option where he opted to keep the ball and scamper to the right side, ultimately scoring from a yard out to extended Bama's lead to 35-10.

On the first play of the fourth quarter, Eddie Jackson returned a punt 79 yards for a touchdown (42-10). This was his third TD of the season (two punt returns and one interception return) and the fifth of his career (three interception returns and two punt returns). Bama held TN to a punt, then Scarbrough took a handoff, turned the corner around the left tackle, and sprinted 85 yards for a TD (49-10). The 39-point victory is the second-highest margin by either team in the series, eclipsed only by a 51-0 Alabama win in 1906. Alabama's defense produced ten tackles for loss, three QB sacks, broke up six passes, intercepted a pass, and had numerous QB hurries.[175]

Passing	C/ATT	YDS	AVG	TD	INT	QBR
J. Hurts	17/27	172	6.4	1	1	82.7
C. Bateman	1/1	13	13	0	0	28.8
Team	18/28	185	6.6	1	1	--

Rushing	CAR	YDS	AVG	TD	LONG
J. Hurts	12	132	11	3	45
B. Scarbrough	5	109	21.8	1	85
D. Harris	14	94	6.7	0	18
J. Jacobs	6	38	6.3	0	22
BJ Emmons	9	38	4.2	0	14
C. Bateman	2	-2	-1	0	4
Team	48	409	8.5	4	85

Interceptions	INT	YDS	TD
R. Harrison Jr.	1	58	1

Punting	NO	YDS	AVG	TB	IN 20	LONG
JK Scott	4	200	50	0	0	62

Receiving	REC	YDS	AVG	TD	LONG
A. Stewart	8	90	11.3	1	36
C. Ridley	6	58	9.7	0	31
OJ Howard	1	23	23	0	23
T. Diggs	1	13	13	0	13
J. Jacobs	1	8	8	0	8
D. Harris	1	-7	-7	0	0
Team	18	185	10.3	1	36

Kick returns	NO	YDS	AVG	LONG	TD
BJ Emmons	1	26	26	26	0

Punt returns	NO	YDS	AVG	LONG	TD
E. Jackson	4	108	27	79	1

Kicking	FG	PCT	LONG	XP	PTS
A. Griffith	0/1	0	0	7/7	7

Note: Table data from "Alabama 49-10 Tennessee (Oct 15, 2016) Box Score" (176)

10/22/16 - Alabama (1) vs Texas A&M (6)

Team	1	2	3	4	T		Passing	Rushing	Total
Texas A&M (6)	0	7	7	0	14		164	114	278
Alabama (1)	6	7	13	7	33		164	287	451

After a completing a pass to Howard to open the game, Alabama went to its ground game for the next five plays. The drive ended with a 32-yard FG. The Aggies punted on their first possession, then Alabama scored another FG from 28 yards out. On the kickoff, Mack Wilson hit return man Speedy Noil so hard that he knocked his tooth out. The Aggies were forced to punt once again. Alabama moved the ball in the second quarter, including a nice 30-yard run by Harris, and scored its first TD with a 5-yard pass to Howard (13-0). A&M punted again, then they forced Alabama to punt for the first time (59 yards). A&M went three-and-out, intercepted Hurts' pass, got a targeting penalty, then threw its own interception (Humphrey) at the Bama 25. Stewart caught a 46-yard pass on the drive which ended in a missed 29-yard field goal attempt. A&M scored a 9-yard TD pass on its next drive making the score 13-7, Bama. With five seconds left in the half, Hurts threw deep and was intercepted in the end zone by Justin Evans.

The Aggies came out running in the second half and ended the drive with a 25-yard TD pass to Kirk, going ahead by one (14-13). Alabama regained the lead on the next possession. During the drive, a fourth down would have come up had there not been a roughing the passer penalty. Hurts hit Ridley for the 4-yard touchdown (20-14). The two teams traded punts, giving A&M the ball back. During the drive, Ryan Anderson caused a fumble that Jonathan Allen recovered and returned 30 yards for a touchdown. Alabama's two-point conversion attempt failed, and the Tide led 26-14. It was Alabama's fourth consecutive game with a defensive touchdown and its 10th with a non-offensive TD.

Knight was sacked for a 12-yard loss to start the fourth quarter, and the Aggies punted two plays later. It only took Bama three plays to score another TD, the last a 37-yard run by Hurts into the end zone (33-14). The battle for field position intensified as neither squad could capitalize on their offensive drives. Three consecutive possessions ended with a turnover on downs, and with time ticking away, Bo Scarbrough ran out the rest of the clock with his five final rushes.

Reuben Foster's stat line read like a symphony of disruption, with 12 tackles, eight of which were unassisted, solo stops. The Tide defense sacked the QB five times behind the line of scrimmage, resulting in a staggering 50 yards lost. Furthermore, the defense amassed 11 tackles for loss, setting the opposition back by a whopping 74 yards. Tim Williams and Ryan Anderson were particularly disruptive forces. Williams recorded two sacks, accounting for 27 yards of lost ground, while Anderson's three tackles for loss cost the opposing offense 12 precious yards.[177]

Passing	C/ATT	YDS	AVG	TD	INT	QBR
J. Hurts	15/25	164	6.6	2	2	68.5

Rushing	CAR	YDS	AVG	TD	LONG
D. Harris	17	128	7.5	0	30
J. Hurts	21	93	4.4	1	37
B. Scarbrough	8	33	4.1	0	16
J. Jacobs	11	33	3	0	8
Team	57	287	5	1	37

Kick returns	NO	YDS	AVG	LONG	TD
A. Stewart	1	23	23	23	0
D. Ball	1	13	13	13	0
Team	2	36	18	23	0

Punting	NO	YDS	AVG	TB	IN 20	LONG
JK Scott	2	107	53.5	0	0	60

Receiving	REC	YDS	AVG	TD	LONG
OJ Howard	8	69	8.6	1	21
A. Stewart	2	57	28.5	0	45
C. Ridley	4	27	6.8	1	9
J. Jacobs	1	11	11	0	11
Team	15	164	10.9	2	45

Interceptions	INT	YDS	TD
M. Humphrey	1	0	0

Punt returns	NO	YDS	AVG	LONG	TD
E. Jackson	2	21	10.5	17	0

Kicking	FG	PCT	LONG	XP	PTS
A. Griffith	2/3	66.7	32	3/3	9

Note: Table data from "Alabama 33-14 Texas A&M (Oct 22, 2016) Box Score" (178)

11/05/16 - Alabama (1) at LSU (13)

Team	1	2	3	4	T		Passing	Rushing	Total
Alabama (1)	0	0	0	10	10		107	216	323
LSU (13)	0	0	0	0	0		92	33	125

The game began with a defensive struggle. Alabama's opening drive stalled when LSU's Jamal Adams intercepted Jalen Hurts at the Alabama 33-yard line. However, LSU couldn't capitalize, missing a long field goal attempt that was deflected by Ronnie Harrison Jr. Alabama went three-and-out on its next possession, then they stopped Fournette and sacked Etling twice, forcing them to punt as well. Both teams then traded three more punts each (Bama's Scott booted one of them 66 yards) and failed to move the ball. Adam Griffith missed a 42-yard field goal attempt wide left in between the punt fest. There was no score at the half. The Crimson Tide offense found themselves consistently pinned deep in their own territory during the opening half, with their average starting field position at their own 17-yard line.

After another LSU three-and-out to start the second half, Alabama struck quickly. Hurts connected with ArDarius Stewart for a 52-yard pass on their first play, setting up 1st-and-goal at the 8-yard line. Three rushes later (two by Harris and one by Hurts) set them up with 1st-and-goal from the 1-yard line, but they turned it over on downs after Hurts was stopped short on fourth down.

LSU punt, Bama punt, LSU punt, Hurts sacked - fumble recovered by LSU on the UA 42-yard line. That drive ended in a sack by Tomlinson where LSU lost 11 yards and was forced to punt again. Early in the fourth quarter, Alabama finally broke through. Hurts capped an impressive 90-yard drive with a third down 21-yard touchdown run dodging would-be tacklers along the way. These first points of the game gave the Tide a 7-0 lead. On the very next play after the ensuing kickoff, Minkah Fitzpatrick logged an interception on the Tide 43-yard line. Alabama proceeded to milk 9:51 off the clock before extending the lead to 10-0 on a field goal by Griffith from 25 yards out. LSU went three-and-out on its final possession, and Alabama ran out the clock on the final drive of the game.

Alabama's defense was outstanding, limiting LSU to just 125 total yards and six first downs while registering five sacks and nine tackles for loss. Reuben Foster led the way with 11 tackles, including two solo stops. Marlon Humphrey had six solo stops and eight overall. Alabama freshman quarterback Jalen Hurts scored his tenth rushing touchdown of the season and 22nd overall. The Tide held Leonard Fournette, who had rushed for a school-record 284 yards the week before, to only 35 yards on 17 carries.[179]

Passing	C/ATT	YDS	AVG	TD	INT	QBR
J. Hurts	10/19	107	5.6	0	1	89.1

Rushing	CAR	YDS	AVG	TD	LONG
J. Hurts	20	114	5.7	1	28
D. Harris	12	53	4.4	0	13
B. Scarbrough	11	52	4.7	0	11
A. Stewart	1	4	4	0	4
J. Jacobs	5	-3	-0.6	0	3
Team	2	-4	-2	0	0
Team	51	216	4.2	1	28

Interceptions	INT	YDS	TD
M. Fitzpatrick	1	0	0

Punting	NO	YDS	AVG	TB	IN 20	LONG
JK Scott	5	258	51.6	0	0	66

Receiving	REC	YDS	AVG	TD	LONG
A. Stewart	3	55	18.3	0	52
C. Ridley	2	23	11.5	0	21
M. Forristall	1	22	22	0	22
T. Diggs	1	9	9	0	9
J. Jacobs	1	3	3	0	3
D. Harris	1	-2	-2	0	0
OJ Howard	1	-3	-3	0	0
Team	10	107	10.7	0	52

Kick returns	NO	YDS	AVG	LONG	TD
A. Stewart	1	14	14	14	0

Punt returns	NO	YDS	AVG	LONG	TD
T. Diggs	2	1	0.5	1	0

Kicking	FG	PCT	LONG	XP	PTS
A. Griffith	1/2	50	25	1/1	4

Note: Table data from "Alabama 10-0 LSU (Nov 5, 2016) Box Score" (180)

11/12/16 - Alabama (1) vs Mississippi State

Team	1	2	3	4	T		Passing	Rushing	Total
Mississippi State	0	0	3	0	3		180	94	**274**
Alabama (1)	10	20	14	7	51		397	218	**615**

Alabama took control from the opening kickoff. After receiving the ball, they marched down the field to the MSU 12-yard line where Adam Griffith split the uprights from 30 yards out for an early 3-0 lead. Tim Williams' sack for a loss of 11 yards forced an MSU punt, and it only went 17 yards giving Alabama good field position at the MSU 32-yard line. Calvin Ridley caught a touchdown pass making the score 10-0 less than halfway through the first quarter. MSU missed a field goal on its next possession, Alabama threw a pick, then there were three punts (MSU, Bama, MSU).

It only took Alabama two plays score on its next possession. The first was an incomplete pass, and the second was a shovel pass to ArDarius Stewart who took it 61 yards to the house (17-0). After State returned the kickoff 50 yards to the Bama 45-yard line, they threw four incomplete passes in a row and turned the ball over on downs. Jalen Hurts added a rushing TD to go up 24-0 from four yards out capping off a 4-play, 66-yard drive. After Alabama forced a punt, Hurts had a nice 60-yard run to the MSU 16. Griffith finished the drive by hitting a 28-yard field goal (27-0). Alabama closed out the half with another field goal (39 yards) making the score 30-0.

MSU started the second half with its first score of the game, a 47-yard field goal (30-3). Hurts fumbled on the next possession, then Bama forced another punt. On Alabama's next two possessions, Hurts hit Stewart for TDs of 15 and 20 yards (his third of the day) making it 44-3. State and Alabama traded punts on their next two possessions. Tony Brown got a pick, but Bama had to punt during that drive. Both teams then brought in their backup quarterbacks. Cooper Bateman hit Trevon Diggs for a 5-yard touchdown making the final score 51-3.

Hurts became the first player in Alabama football's history to throw for 300 yards (347) and rush for 100 yards (100) in the same game. His primary passing target on Saturday afternoon, wide receiver ArDarius Stewart, became the sixth player in UA history to catch three receiving touchdowns in the same game. Defensively, 27 different players notched at least one tackle, including six each from Reuben Foster, Minkah Fitzpatrick, Rashaan Evans, and Dalvin Tomlinson. Ryan Anderson, Tim Williams, and Raekwon Davis all had sacks for -29 yards. [181]

Passing	C/ATT	YDS	AVG	TD	INT	QBR
J. Hurts	28/37	347	9.4	4	1	79.2
C. Bateman	3/4	50	12.5	1	0	72.1
Team	31/41	397	9.7	5	1	--

Receiving	REC	YDS	AVG	TD	LONG
A. Stewart	8	156	19.5	3	67
OJ Howard	6	77	12.8	0	30
C. Sims	3	45	15	0	31
J. Jacobs	3	34	11.3	0	26
C. Ridley	4	26	6.5	1	20
M. Forristall	3	19	6.3	0	8
D. Kief	1	14	14	0	14
D. Harris	1	11	11	0	11
G. Dieter	1	10	10	0	10
T. Diggs	1	5	5	1	5
Team	31	397	12.8	5	67

Rushing	CAR	YDS	AVG	TD	LONG
J. Hurts	11	100	9.1	1	60
J. Jacobs	9	89	9.9	0	43
R. Clark	4	14	3.5	0	7
D. Harris	3	9	3	0	4
D. Gore	4	6	1.5	0	3
Team	31	218	7	1	60

Interceptions	INT	YDS	TD
T. Brown	1	9	0

Punt returns	NO	YDS	AVG	LONG	TD
T. Diggs	1	1	1	1	0

Punting	NO	YDS	AVG	TB	IN 20	LONG
JK Scott	3	154	51.3	0	0	62

Kicking	FG	PCT	LONG	XP	PTS
A. Griffith	3/3	100	39	5/5	14
A. Pappanastos	0/0	0	0	1/1	1
Team	3/3	100	39	6/6	15

Note: Table data from "Alabama 51-3 Mississippi State (Nov 12, 2016) Box Score" (182)

11/19/16 - Alabama (1) vs Chattanooga

Team	1	2	3	4	T		Passing	Rushing	Total
Chattanooga	3	0	0	0	3		114	70	184
Alabama (1)	0	14	7	10	31		136	196	332

Alabama received the opening kickoff and ended its first possession with a punt. The Mocs drove down and scored their only points of the game on a 47-yard field goal. Both teams punted on their next possessions. Jalen Hurts showcased his dual-threat abilities as he initiated the drive with a crafty 4-yard quarterback draw, keeping the defense honest. However, it was through the air where he truly made his mark. He unleashed a 47-yard strike, finding Calvin Ridley for Alabama's first touchdown of the evening (7-3). Chattanooga and Alabama both punted, but Alabama's was fumbled by Board when his own blocker backed into him, and UA linebacker Keaton Anderson recovered on the Mocs' 9-yard line. On 4th-and-goal at the 1-yard line, Hurts passed to Gehrig Dieter for a touchdown (14-3).

The second half started with punts by both teams, and the Mocs went three-and-out on their next drive. The Tide started their drive with three Harris rushes in the first four plays, capped by a 25-yard touchdown rush by Harris with 4:07 left in the quarter (21-3). Andy Pappanastos hit a 33-yard field goal early in the fourth quarter putting Alabama up 24-3. Chattanooga went three-and-out on its first possession of the fourth quarter, then they forced and recovered a fumble at the UTC 31-yard line.

Both teams then went three-and-out, but Rashaan Evans recovered a fumble at the UTC 20-yard line. In just four plays Alabama marched the 20 yards where the drive culminated in a familiar sight – Hurts connecting with Dieter for a 1-yard touchdown strike, the duo's second such scoring collaboration of the game. With the clock ticking down to 3:45 remaining, Alabama had established a formidable 31-3 advantage. Chattanooga's offense sputtered on their final drive, going three-and-out.

Ronnie Harrison Jr. had a game-high 11 tackles, with eight of them solo stops. The victory etched another milestone in Alabama head coach Nick Saban's illustrious career. It marked his 41st win while leading the nation's top-ranked team, a testament to his ability to maintain excellence at the pinnacle of college football. Saban's Tide teams have now won an impressive 41-of-46 games when holding the coveted No. 1 ranking. Furthermore, Saban's 46 games coaching the nation's top-ranked squad ties him with Ohio State legend Woody Hayes for the most games at the helm of the No. 1 team.[183]

Passing	C/ATT	YDS	AVG	TD	INT	QBR
J. Hurts	15/21	136	6.5	3	0	28.9

Rushing	CAR	YDS	AVG	TD	LONG
D. Harris	13	91	7	1	25
J. Hurts	16	68	4.3	0	34
D. Gore	3	20	6.7	0	9
J. Jacobs	5	17	3.4	0	7
Team	37	196	5.3	1	34

Punt returns	NO	YDS	AVG	LONG	TD
T. Diggs	3	20	6.7	14	0

Punting	NO	YDS	AVG	TB	IN 20	LONG
JK Scott	6	293	48.8	0	0	56

Receiving	REC	YDS	AVG	TD	LONG
C. Ridley	7	94	13.4	1	47
C. Sims	4	34	8.5	0	13
OJ Howard	1	7	7	0	7
G. Dieter	3	1	0.3	2	1
Team	15	136	9.1	3	47

Kick returns	NO	YDS	AVG	LONG	TD
G. Dieter	1	11	11	11	0
H. Hentges	1	7	7	7	0
Team	2	18	9	11	0

Kicking	FG	PCT	LONG	XP	PTS
A. Pappanastos	1/1	100	33	2/2	5
A. Griffith	0/0	0	0	2/2	2
Team	1/1	100	33	4/4	7

Note: Table data from "Alabama 31-3 Chattanooga (Nov 19, 2016) Box Score" (184)

11/26/16 - Alabama (1) vs Auburn (13)

Team	1	2	3	4	T	Passing	Rushing	Total
Auburn (13)	3	6	3	0	12	116	66	182
Alabama (1)	10	3	14	3	30	298	203	501

Alabama received the opening kickoff and was forced to punt. It was returned 58 yards to the Bama 21-yard line, ending with Scott shoving Roberts out of bounds saving a touchdown. Auburn took at 3-0 lead by kicking a 42-yard field goal. Alabama drove down the field and kicked a field goal of its own (from 29 yards). Auburn only mustered to gain a single yard before being forced to punt after a quick three-and-out series. Jalen Hurts hit Damien Harris for a 17-yard touchdown on their drive to go up 10-3. Auburn punted again after gaining a mere three yards in three plays. As Trevon Diggs fielded the kick, he fumbled the ball momentarily before regaining possession. However, the mishap cost Alabama eight yards back to its 26-yard line. To compound matters, during the return Tony Brown committed a targeting penalty resulting in his ejection from the game.

Hurts was intercepted on the first play of the second quarter which set up the Tigers on the Alabama 41-yard line. Bama's lead was cut to 10-6 after a 52-yard field goal from Carlson. The Tide offense ignited with a pair of explosive gains. First, wide receiver ArDarius Stewart found O.J. Howard for a 12-yard strike, then on the very next snap, Damien Harris burst through the line gaining 20 yards to the AU 37-yard line. The drive ended when Hurts was intercepted. Auburn drove down and scored another field goal, then Alabama did the same (from 25 yards out). Alabama was up at the half by a score of 13-9.

Auburn started the second half with a three-and-out. Alabama drove down and had a 1st-and-goal from the 6-yard line. After gaining two yards on the previous play, Hurts ran just inside the right pylon for a 4-yard score (20-9). This marked his 12th rushing touchdown of the year. On the opening play of its second possession after the half, Auburn finally moved the chains for just the second time in the contest. Carlson's 52-yard attempt was wide left. Hurts rolled right and found Stewart for a short pass that he took down the sideline 38 yards to paydirt, staying in bounds as he dodged a tackler at the 5-yard line (27-9). Auburn brought in John Franklin at quarterback, and he led them on a 9-play, 65-yard drive that ended with a 27-yard field goal from Carlson (27-12). Alabama responded with a 34-yard field goal, then Shaun Dion Hamilton snagged an interception at Bama's 5-yard line to stop Auburn's most productive drive of the half. The Tide asserted their dominance, consuming the final nine minutes of the game. Reuben Foster and Shaun Dion Hamilton were the defensive anchors, each tallying eight tackles.[185]

Passing	C/ATT	YDS	AVG	TD	INT	QBR
J. Hurts	27/36	286	7.9	2	2	69.7
A. Stewart	1/1	12	12	0	0	98.9
Team	28/37	298	8.1	2	2	--

Rushing	CAR	YDS	AVG	TD	LONG
B. Scarbrough	17	90	5.3	0	20
D. Harris	9	47	5.2	0	20
J. Hurts	12	37	3.1	1	17
J. Jacobs	5	32	6.4	0	26
Team	1	-3	-3	0	0
Team	44	203	4.6	1	26

Kick returns	NO	YDS	AVG	LONG	TD
A. Stewart	2	37	18.5	21	0
G. Dieter	1	25	25	25	0
Team	3	62	20.7	25	0

Punting	NO	YDS	AVG	TB	IN 20	LONG
JK Scott	2	79	39.5	0	0	43

Receiving	REC	YDS	AVG	TD	LONG
A. Stewart	10	127	12.7	1	39
OJ Howard	5	45	9	0	14
C. Ridley	5	44	8.8	0	25
J. Jacobs	1	30	30	0	30
D. Harris	3	22	7.3	1	17
G. Dieter	1	12	12	0	12
T. Diggs	2	10	5	0	7
C. Sims	1	8	8	0	8
Team	28	298	10.6	2	39

Interceptions	INT	YDS	TD
S. Hamilton	1	0	0

Kicking	FG	PCT	LONG	XP	PTS
A. Griffith	3/3	100	34	3/3	12

Punt returns	NO	YDS	AVG	LONG	TD
T. Diggs	2	0	0	8	0

Note: Table data from "Alabama 30-12 Auburn (Nov 26, 2016) Box Score" (186)

12/03/16 - Alabama (1) at Florida (15)

Team	1	2	3	4	T		Passing	Rushing	Total
Alabama (1)	16	17	7	14	54		138	234	372
Florida (15)	9	7	0	0	16		261	0	261

The game began with Florida converting three consecutive third downs, sustaining an impressive opening drive. Callaway capped it off by making a fingertip grab in the end zone for the first score. This touchdown ended Alabama's incredible streak of not allowing an offensive score since October 22nd, a span of over four full games. It was also the first time an opposing team had even reached inside the Alabama 10-yard line since that time. However, Alabama quickly responded. After going three-and-out on offense, defensive back Shaun Dion Hamilton intercepted a pass and returned it to the Florida 12-yard line. Unable to punch it in for a touchdown, they settled for a 31-yard field goal, narrowing Florida's lead to 7-3. The Tide defense then made a big play of their own as Minkah Fitzpatrick intercepted a pass and took it 44 yards to the house for a touchdown. It was Alabama's 13th non-offensive score of the season, giving them their first lead at 10-7. The momentum continued to shift on special teams, with back-to-back blocked kicks resulting in a touchdown for Alabama (scored by Josh Jacobs) and a defensive extra point for Florida. This wild sequence left Alabama leading 16-9 heading into the second quarter.

The second quarter began with Florida's punt traveling 62 yards after another three-and-out. Trevon Diggs received the punt at Alabama's 10-yard line and returned it an impressive 47 yards to Florida's 43-yard line. From there, the Crimson Tide offense took control. Alabama methodically moved the ball down the field, with Bo Scarbrough gaining 30 yards on three powerful rushes. ArDarius Stewart added six more yards on a pass from Hurts, setting up Adam Griffith's 25-yard field goal to extend the lead to 26-9. On Florida's next possession, Alabama's defense struck again, picking off the Gators for the third time in the first half. Tony Brown intercepted the pass at the Tide's 38-yard line, then Bama capitalized on the turnover as Josh Jacobs capped off the drive with a 6-yard touchdown run which made the score 33-9 in Alabama's favor. The Gators drove 92 yards ending with a 25-yard touchdown pass making the score 33-16.

The Crimson Tide defense came up huge to start the second half. After going three-and-out on their opening possession, Alabama's defense stiffened in the red zone. Florida had marched down to the 2-yard line, but the Tide held strong, stuffing the Gators on fourth down. Taking over at their own 2-yard line, Alabama's offense then engineered an impressive 98-yard scoring drive. Big plays fueled the march, with ArDarius Stewart hauling in a 34-yard reception and Damien Harris ripping off a 34-yard run. Capping the drive was Bo Scarbrough, who punched it in from two yards out to extend Alabama's lead to 40-16 with 3:25 remaining in the third quarter. The fourth quarter opened with Alabama's offense pounding the rock. Seven straight running plays moved the chains, with Harris ripping off a 21-yard gain to reach the Florida 20. Hurts hit Stewart for a 5-yard screen pass, then they set up 1st-and-goal from the 7-yard line after a couple of rushes and a personal foul on the Gators. Scarbrough rushed twice, punching it in with a powerful 1-yard plunge up the gut, extending the lead to 47-16.

Back-to-back sacks killed Florida's next drive before it could get started. Diggs gave Alabama great field position, returning a 42-yard punt 36 yards to the Florida 21-yard line. Derrick Gore took it from there, carrying it four straight times including a 10-yard touchdown burst to make it 54-16. The Gators' final drive fizzled out after picking up just 20 yards as time expired on Alabama's third consecutive SEC championship.

Alabama put on a defensive masterclass against Florida. Their swarming defense completely shut down the Gators' rushing attack, holding them to an astonishing zero yards on 30 attempts -

the fewest rushing yards Florida has ever had against Alabama. But the Tide's dominance went beyond just stifling the run game. They scored from every phase, including an interception return and a blocked punt return for touchdowns. Their 54 points were the most Alabama has ever scored against Florida in the storied history of this rivalry. Leading the way for Alabama's defensive onslaught was linebacker Reuben Foster, who earned MVP honors with a stat-stuffing performance of 11 tackles, nine solo stops, two sacks, and two tackles for loss. He had plenty of help too, as Minkah Fitzpatrick, Tony Brown, and Shaun Dion Hamilton all hauled in interceptions, with Fitzpatrick taking his to the house.

This game marked a historic achievement, the third time the storied Crimson Tide program has finished 13-0. Their victory over Florida in the SEC Championship Game secured their third consecutive conference title for the third time in history, a feat they last accomplished during their dynastic run from 1977-1979. The Tide's winning streak against ranked opponents now stands at an impressive 15 games, dating back to their 2015 loss against Ole Miss. Alabama's all-time record versus ranked foes is a formidable 153-124-7 (.551), rising to an even more dominant 124-75-3 (.621) when ranked themselves. Overall, the Crimson Tide now holds a 26-14 (.650) edge in the all-time series against Florida and 12-8 (.600) when the Gators are nationally ranked. This SEC title was the 26th in Alabama's illustrious history and their seventh SEC Championship Game victory since the inaugural event in 1992. Incredibly, Alabama has now won their last five consecutive appearances in the SEC title game, cementing their status as the premier program in the nation's toughest conference.[187]

Passing	C/ATT	YDS	AVG	TD	INT	QBR
J. Hurts	11/20	138	6.9	1	0	63.1

Rushing	CAR	YDS	AVG	TD	LONG
B. Scarbrough	11	91	8.3	2	34
D. Harris	8	86	10.8	0	23
J. Jacobs	6	35	5.8	1	12
D. Gore	4	21	5.3	1	11
J. Hurts	8	1	0.1	0	12
A. Stewart	1	0	0	0	0
Team	38	234	6.2	4	34

Interceptions	INT	YDS	TD
M. Fitzpatrick	1	44	1
S. Hamilton	1	40	0
T. Brown	1	0	0
Team	3	84	1

Punting	NO	YDS	AVG	TB	IN 20	LONG
JK Scott	2	81	40.5	0	0	41

Receiving	REC	YDS	AVG	TD	LONG
C. Ridley	4	43	10.8	0	52
A. Stewart	3	42	14	0	31
OJ Howard	2	41	20.5	0	32
G. Dieter	1	6	6	1	6
J. Jacobs	1	6	6	0	6
Team	11	138	12.5	1	52

Punt returns	NO	YDS	AVG	LONG	TD
T. Diggs	3	90	30	47	0
J. Jacobs	0	27	0	27	1
D. Gore	1	0	0	0	0
Team	4	117	29.3	47	1

Kicking	FG	PCT	LONG	XP	PTS
A. Griffith	2/3	67	31	5/6	11
A. Pappanastos	0/0	0	0	1/1	1
Team	2/3	66.7	31	6/7	12

Note: Table data from "Alabama 54-16 Florida (Dec 3, 2016) Box Score" (188)

12/31/16 - Alabama (1) vs Washington (4)

Team	1	2	3	4	T		Passing	Rushing	Total
Washington (4)	7	0	0	0	7		150	44	194
Alabama (1)	7	10	0	7	24		57	269	326

The coin toss favored Alabama, but they deferred, allowing Washington to receive first. Both teams came out firing blanks, trading three-and-outs. But the Huskies soon found their rhythm, marching 64 yards downfield in a crisp 8-play drive capped by a 16-yard touchdown strike through the air. Alabama refused to be outdone, answering with a touchdown drive of its own. The relentless Bo Scarbrough punched it in from 18 yards out, tying the game at 7-7. The Huskies were on the move again, then Anthony Averett stripped the ball from the receiver's grasp, and Jonathan Allen pounced on the loose ball at midfield. The Crimson Tide capitalized, driving down for a 47-yard field goal as the second quarter began, edging ahead 10-7. Washington's offense sputtered, with Tony Brown and Jonathan Allen each making thunderous plays for losses. A three-and-out and punt followed. The two teams then traded punts and three-and-outs over the next four possessions in a defensive slugfest. Just when it looked like a low-scoring affair, Ryan Anderson made the game's defining play – a 26-yard pick-six that stunned the Huskies and extended Alabama's lead to 17-7 just before halftime. It was the Alabama defense's 11th touchdown (by eight different players) of a truly remarkable 2016 season.

The second half began with ArDarius Stewart returning the kickoff 25 yards then Alabama immediately establishing their ground game. Hurts ripped off a 33-yard run, but two penalties stalled the drive which led to a punt. Both teams then traded punts twice more before the fourth quarter (one from Scott pinned Washington inside the 10-yard line). After three-and-outs by both teams, Washington booted a 50-yard punt to the Alabama 2-yard line ten seconds into the fourth quarter. Alabama then embarked on an epic 98-yard scoring drive, punctuated by Scarbrough's 68-yard tackle-breaking touchdown jaunt to make it 24-7. Possessions went back and forth, and the Huskies' final desperate heave was picked off by Minkah Fitzpatrick who returned it 28 yards with just 24 seconds left on the clock, sealing the victory.

When the dust settled, Alabama had set a bowl record with 180 rushing yards from the unstoppable Scarbrough (Offensives MVP), extended its win streak to 26 games (longest active streak in CFB), and earned it 36th all-time bowl victory (most in CFB history). Anderson was named Defensive MVP after his game-changing pick-six. The Crimson Tide defense was utterly dominant, racking up five sacks for losses (-38 yards), seven tackles for loss (-48 yards), two interceptions (returned for 54 yards and one touchdown), and a forced fumble. Averett led the way with six solo tackles, a 13-yard sack, and that crucial forced fumble. In another stellar performance, Reuben Foster chipped in with nine total tackles and six assists (team-high).[189]

Passing	C/ATT	YDS	AVG	TD	INT	QBR
J. Hurts	7/14	57	4.1	0	0	31.5

Rushing	CAR	YDS	AVG	TD	LONG
B. Scarbrough	19	180	9.5	2	68
J. Hurts	19	50	2.6	0	33
D. Harris	9	30	3.3	0	8
A. Stewart	2	10	5	0	9
Team	1	-1	-1	0	0
Team	50	269	5.4	2	68

Interceptions	INT	YDS	TD
R. Anderson	1	26	1
M. Fitzpatrick	1	28	0
Team	2	54	1

Punting	NO	YDS	AVG	TB	IN 20	LONG
JK Scott	8	367	45.9	3	3	55

Receiving	REC	YDS	AVG	TD	LONG
OJ Howard	4	44	11	0	16
G. Dieter	1	10	10	0	10
C. Ridley	1	6	6	0	6
J. Jacobs	1	-3	-3	0	0
Team	7	57	8.1	0	16

Kick returns	NO	YDS	AVG	LONG	TD
A. Stewart	2	45	22.5	25	0

Punt returns	NO	YDS	AVG	LONG	TD
T. Diggs	1	3	3	3	0

Kicking	FG	PCT	LONG	XP	PTS
A. Griffith	1/1	100	41	3/3	6

Note: Table data from "Alabama 54-16 Florida (Dec 3, 2016) Box Score" (190)

231

01/09/17 - Alabama (1) vs Clemson (2)

Team	1	2	3	4	T		Passing	Rushing	Total
Clemson (2)	0	7	7	21	35		420	91	511
Alabama (1)	7	7	10	7	31		155	221	376

The College Football Playoff National Championship game between Alabama and Clemson started with Alabama receiving the opening kickoff, but the drive quickly stalled after only gaining two yards in three plays. This led to a booming 55-yard punt by JK Scott that Wayne Gallman returned to the Clemson 22-yard line. Clemson's first possession featured a mix of plays, including a 12-yard run by Gallman, a sack on Deshaun Watson by Alabama's defensive linemen Da'Ron Payne and Jonathan Allen, an unnecessary roughness penalty on Alabama, and a crucial 4th-and-1 stop at the Bama 41-yard line. The Tide then marched down the field, highlighted by a 20-yard run from Hurts, and scored on a 25-yard touchdown pass to O.J. Howard, who powered his way into the end zone carrying Clemson players with him (Alabama up 7-0).

After trading punts, including a partially blocked kick by Alabama that traveled 25 yards to the Tiger 37-yard line, Clemson faced a 3rd-and-5 situation. An errant snap bounced off Watson's knee, and Ryan Anderson pounced on the loose ball for Alabama. However, the Tide failed to capitalize, going three-and-out and pinning Clemson at their own 1-yard line with JK Scott's punt. After holding Clemson to another punt, Alabama got the ball back on its own 26-yard line. On this drive, Bo Scarbrough broke free for a 37-yard touchdown run, aided by a great block from Cam Robinson (14-0). Both teams punted on their next possessions. Clemson finally got on the board before halftime with Watson's 8-yard rushing touchdown, capping off a 7-play, 87-yard drive. The drive included passes of 43 and 26 yards and made the score 14-7 in favor of Alabama at the break.

The second half started with a bang, as Ryan Anderson stripped the ball from Watson and returned it 12 yards to the Clemson 16-yard line. Alabama settled for a 27-yard field goal by Adam Griffith, extending its lead to 17-7. On a gutsy fourth down call, Clemson's quarterback Watson executed a pooch kick that pinned Alabama at its own 5-yard line. The Tide went three-and-out and punted to Clemson's 42-yard line. The Tigers capitalized in four plays with a 24-yard touchdown pass to Hunter Renfrow, cutting the deficit to 17-14. After trading punts, Hurts connected with O.J. Howard for a 68-yard touchdown, giving Alabama a 24-14 lead. Clemson responded by driving to the Alabama 8-yard line as the third quarter ended.

The fourth quarter began with Watson rushing for four yards followed by a 4-yard touchdown pass to Williams, getting Clemson back within three (24-21). Alabama punted, both teams went three-and-out, Clemson punted, then Bama went three-and-out again. On the next drive, Watson mixed three complete passes for 52 yards with 20 yards rushing before handing the ball off to Gallman, who plunged in from one yard out for a touchdown and a 28-24 Clemson lead. Alabama answered quickly, with Hurts leading a crucial drive that included a 15-yard pass to ArDarius Stewart on 3rd-and-16 and a 4th-and-1 conversion by Damien Harris. Stewart then threw a 24-yard lateral pass to Howard, setting up Hurts' 30-yard touchdown run that put Alabama back on top, 31-28, with 2:01 remaining.

Facing immense pressure, Clemson's offense came through in the clutch. Watson orchestrated a masterful drive, completing three straight passes for 25 yards to the Alabama 43-yard line before finding Renfrow for six yards and Leggett for 17. These crucial gains gave the Tigers the ball on the AL 9-yard line. A pass interference penalty on Alabama gave Clemson 1st-and-goal at the 2-yard line with nine seconds left. Watson then hit Renfrow for the game-winning 2-yard touchdown pass with just one second remaining. Clemson recovered the onside kick and secured a 35-31 victory, ending Alabama's 26-game winning streak.

The Alabama defense was spearheaded by a pair of senior linebackers who made their presence felt all over the field. Reuben Foster was a disruptive force, racking up an impressive 12 tackles, with six of those being solo stops. He also brought down the quarterback for a sack, causing havoc in the backfield. Not to be outdone, Ryan Anderson was a menace to the opposition's ball carriers. He not only caused a fumble, but also recovered two loose balls and tallied seven tackles. Freshman quarterback Jalen Hurts was 13-of-31 for 131 yards and a touchdown through the air, adding 63 rushing yards and a 30-yard rushing touchdown with 2:07 left in the game. Sophomore running back Bo Scarbrough rushed for 93 yards and two touchdowns on 16 carries before exiting with an injury midway through the third quarter. Senior tight end O.J. Howard led all receivers with 106 yards and a touchdown on four receptions.[191]

Passing	C/ATT	YDS	AVG	TD	INT	QBR
J. Hurts	13/31	131	4.2	1	0	60.5
A. Stewart	1/1	24	24	0	0	100
Team	14/32	155	4.8	1	0	--

Rushing	CAR	YDS	AVG	TD	LONG
B. Scarbrough	16	93	5.8	2	37
J. Hurts	10	63	6.3	1	30
A. Stewart	1	25	25	0	25
D. Harris	5	24	4.8	0	13
J. Jacobs	2	16	8	0	13
Team	34	221	6.5	3	37

Punting	NO	YDS	AVG	TB	IN 20	LONG
JK Scott	10	458	45.8	2	5	57

Receiving	REC	YDS	AVG	TD	LONG
OJ Howard	4	106	26.5	1	68
C. Ridley	5	36	7.2	0	15
A. Stewart	2	12	6	0	15
B. Scarbrough	2	7	3.5	0	7
D. Harris	1	-6	-6	0	0
Team	14	155	11.1	1	68

Kick returns	NO	YDS	AVG	LONG	TD
A. Stewart	2	42	21	30	0
H. Hentges	1	15	15	15	0
Team	3	57	19	30	0

Punt returns	NO	YDS	AVG	LONG	TD
G. Dieter	1	9	9	9	0

Kicking	FG	PCT	LONG	XP	PTS
A. Griffith	1/1	100	27	4/4	7

Note: Table data from "Clemson 35-31 Alabama (Jan 9, 2017) Box Score" (192)

Season Stats

Record	14-1	1st of 128
SEC Record	9-0	
Rank	2	
Points for	582	
Points against	195	
Points/game	38.8	16th of 128
Opp points/game	13	1st of 128
SOS[10]	7.29	1st of 128

Team stats (averages per game)

Split	G	Passing					Rushing				Total Offense		
		Cmp	Att	Pct	Yds	TD	Att	Yds	Avg	TD	Plays	Yds	Avg
Offense	15	17.7	27.8	63.5	210.3	1.7	42.6	245	5.8	2.2	70.4	455.3	6.5
Defense	15	18.2	33.8	53.8	197.9	1	31.7	63.9	2	0.3	65.5	261.8	4
Difference		-0.5	-6	9.7	12.4	0.7	10.9	181.1	3.8	1.9	4.9	193.5	2.5

Split	First Downs				Penalties		Turnovers		
	Pass	Rush	Pen	Tot	No.	Yds	Fum	Int	Tot
Offense	8.1	12.1	0.8	21	5.7	44	0.7	0.6	1.3
Defense	8.3	4.7	1.4	14.5	3.9	31.4	0.9	1.1	1.9
Difference	-0.2	7.4	-0.6	6.5	1.8	12.6	-0.2	-0.5	-0.6

Passing

Rk	Player	G	Passing								
			Cmp	Att	Pct	Yds	Y/A	AY/A	TD	Int	Rate
1	Jalen Hurts	15	240	382	62.8	2780	7.3	7.4	23	9	139.1
2	Blake Barnett	3	11	19	57.9	219	11.5	13.6	2	0	189.5
3	Cooper Bateman	5	12	14	85.7	119	8.5	9.9	1	0	180.7
4	Ardarius Stewart	12	2	2	100	36	18	18	0	0	251.2

Rushing and receiving

Rk	Player	G	Rushing				Receiving				Scrimmage			
			Att	Yds	Avg	TD	Rec	Yds	Avg	TD	Plays	Yds	Avg	TD
1	Jalen Hurts	15	191	954	5	13					191	954	5	13
2	Damien Harris	15	146	1037	7.1	2	14	99	7.1	2	160	1136	7.1	4
3	Bo Scarbrough	13	125	812	6.5	11	4	22	5.5	0	129	834	6.5	11
4	Joshua Jacobs	14	85	567	6.7	4	14	156	11.1	0	99	723	7.3	4
5	B.J. Emmons	6	35	173	4.9	1	2	20	10	0	37	193	5.2	1
6	Derrick Gore	5	18	93	5.2	1	1	0	0	0	19	93	4.9	1
7	Ardarius Stewart	12	8	68	8.5	0	54	864	16	8	62	932	15	8
8	Blake Barnett	3	7	-17	-2.4	0					7	-17	-2.4	0
9	Calvin Ridley	15	5	21	4.2	1	72	769	10.7	7	77	790	10.3	8
10	Ronnie Clark	1	4	14	3.5	0					4	14	3.5	0
11	Cooper Bateman	5	3	-11	-3.7	0					3	-11	-3.7	0
12	Avery Reid	1	2	4	2	0					2	4	2	0
13	Robert Foster	3	1	-5	-5	0	5	55	11	0	6	50	8.3	0
14	O.J. Howard	15					45	595	13.2	3	45	595	13.2	3
15	Gehrig Dieter	13					15	214	14.3	4	15	214	14.3	4
16	Cam Sims	6					14	152	10.9	0	14	152	10.9	0
17	Trevon Diggs	14					11	88	8	1	11	88	8	1
18	Miller Forristall	3					5	73	14.6	0	5	73	14.6	0
19	Derek Kief	4					4	31	7.8	0	4	31	7.8	0
20	Hale Hentges	5					3	10	3.3	0	3	10	3.3	0
21	Brandon Greene	1					1	5	5	0	1	5	5	0
22	Mack Wilson	8					1	1	1	1	1	1	1	1

Defense and fumbles

Rk	Player	G	Tackles					Def Int					Fumbles		
			Solo	Ast	Tot	Loss	Sk	Int	Yds	Avg	TD	PD	FR	TD	FF
1	Reuben Foster	15	60	55	115	13	5					2			
2	Ronnie Harrison Jr.	14	56	27	83	1.5	0	2	64	32	1	7	2	1	0
3	Jonathan Allen	15	33	36	69	16	10.5		75		1	2	3	1	0
4	Minkah Fitzpatrick	15	42	24	66	5.5	1.5	6	186	31	2	7			1
5	Shaun Dion Hamilton	12	31	33	64	9	2	2	40	20	0	1			1
6	Dalvin Tomlinson	15	17	45	62	5.5	3					4			1
7	Ryan Anderson	15	31	30	61	18.5	8.5	1	26	26	1	3	3		4
8	Rashaan Evans	13	31	21	52	4.5	4					2	1		1
9	Anthony Averett	15	39	9	48	3	1					8			2
10	Marlon Humphrey	14	26	10	36	3	0	2	18	9	1	5			1
11	Da'Ron Payne	13	12	24	36	3.5	1.5					1	1	1	0
12	Tony Brown	10	21	11	32	2.5	0.5	2	9	4.5	0	0			
13	Tim Williams	14	22	9	31	16	9					2	1	1	2
14	Eddie Jackson	8	15	9	24	2.5	0	1	55	55	1	2			
15	Keith Holcombe	9	13	11	24	1	0					1			
16	Da'Shawn Hand	10	10	11	21	2.5	1								1
17	Hootie Jones	11	16	4	20	0	0					4			1
18	Anfernee Jennings	10	7	12	19	2	0								
19	Christian Miller	9	5	11	16	2.5	2								
20	Dakota Ball	8	6	6	12	1	0.5								
21	Terrell Hall	6	7	4	11	1	1								
22	Levi Wallace	6	7	4	11	0	0					2			
23	Deionte Thompson	6	4	5	9	0	0								
24	Mack Wilson	8	5	3	8	0	0						1		0
25	Joshua Frazier	7	1	7	8	1	1								
26	Shyheim Carter	3	4	3	7	0	0								
27	Trevon Diggs	14	2	3	5	0	0								1
28	Aaron Robinson	4	3	2	5	1	0								
29	Raekwon Davis	4	1	3	4	1	1								1
30	Keaton Anderson	4	2	2	4	0	0						1		0
31	JK Scott	15	1	3	4	0	0								
32	Gehrig Dieter	13	2	1	3	0	0								
33	Damien Harris	15	2	1	3	0	0								
34	Derek Kief	4	2	1	3	0	0								
35	B.J. Emmons	6	0	2	2	0	0								
36	Jamar King	1	0	2	2	0	0								
37	Robert Foster	3	1	0	1	0	0								
38	O.J. Howard	15	1	0	1	0	0								
39	Jalen Hurts	15	1	0	1	0	0								
40	Joshua Jacobs	14	1	0	1	0	0								
41	Rogria Lewis	1	1	0	1	0	0								
42	Jared Mayden	2	1	0	1	0	0					1			
43	Calvin Ridley	15	1	0	1	0	0								
44	T.J. Simmons	1	1	0	1	0	0								
45	O.J. Smith	1	1	0	1	0	0								

Kick and punt returns

Rk	Player	G	Kick Ret				Punt Ret			
			Ret	Yds	Avg	TD	Ret	Yds	Avg	TD
1	Ardarius Stewart	12	8	161	20.1	0				
2	Trevon Diggs	14	7	166	23.7	0	13	130	10	0
3	Xavian Marks	3	7	123	17.6	0	5	105	21	1
4	Gehrig Dieter	13	2	36	18	0	1	9	9	0
5	Hale Hentges	5	2	22	11	0				
6	B.J. Emmons	6	1	26	26	0				
7	Dakota Ball	8	1	13	13	0				
8	Eddie Jackson	8					11	253	23	2
9	Calvin Ridley	15					2	4	2	0
10	Derrick Gore	5					1	0	0	0
11	Joshua Jacobs	14					27			1

235

Kicking and punting

Rk	Player	G	Kicking							Punting		
			XPM	XPA	XP%	FGM	FGA	FG%	Pts	Punts	Yds	Avg
1	Adam Griffith	15	66	67	98.5	21	28	75	129			
2	Andy Pappanastos	4	6	6	100	1	1	100	9			
3	JK Scott	15								64	3020	47.2

Scoring

Rk	Player	G	Touchdowns							Kicking				Pts
			Rush	Rec	Int	FR	PR	KR	Tot	XPM	FGM	2PM	Sfty	
1	Adam Griffith	15								66	21			129
2	Jalen Hurts	15	13						13					78
3	Bo Scarbrough	13	11						11					66
4	Ardarius Stewart	12		8					8					48
5	Calvin Ridley	15	1	7					8					48
6	Joshua Jacobs	14	4				1		5					30
7	Damien Harris	15	2	2					4					24
8	Gehrig Dieter	13		4					4					24
9	O.J. Howard	15		3					3					18
10	Eddie Jackson	8			1		2		3					18
11	Ronnie Harrison Jr.	14			1	1			2					12
12	Minkah Fitzpatrick	15			2				2					12
13	Jonathan Allen	15			1	1			2					12
14	Andy Pappanastos	4								6	1			9
15	Mack Wilson	8		1					1					6
16	Marlon Humphrey	14			1				1					6
17	Derrick Gore	5	1						1					6
18	Da'Ron Payne	13				1			1					6
19	B.J. Emmons	6	1						1					6
20	Ryan Anderson	15			1				1					6
21	Tim Williams	14				1			1					6
22	Trevon Diggs	14		1					1					6
23	Xavian Marks	3					1		1					6

Stats include bowl games
Note: Table data from "2016 Alabama Crimson Tide Stats" (10)

Awards and honors

Name	Award	Type
Jonathan Allen	Permanent Team Captain	Team
Reuben Foster	Permanent Team Captain	Team
Eddie Jackson	Permanent Team Captain	Team
Cam Robinson	Permanent Team Captain	Team
Reuben Foster	MVP	Team
Cam Robinson	Offensive Player of the Year	Team
ArDarius Stewart	Offensive Player of the Year	Team
Jonathan Allen	Defensive Player of the Year	Team
Ryan Anderson	Defensive Player of the Year	Team
Reuben Foster	Defensive Player of the Year	Team
Nick Saban	Coach of the Year	SEC
Lane Kiffin	Offensive Coordinator of the Year	SEC
Jeremy Pruitt	Defensive Coordinator of the Year	SEC
Jalen Hurts	Offensive Player of the Year	SEC
Jonathan Allen	Defensive Player of the Year	SEC
Jalen Hurts	Freshman of the Year	SEC
Jonah Williams	Freshman of the Year Runner Up	SEC
Jonathan Allen	AP All-SEC First Team	SEC
Minkah Fitzpatrick	AP All-SEC First Team	SEC
Reuben Foster	AP All-SEC First Team	SEC
Cam Robinson	AP All-SEC First Team	SEC
JK Scott	AP All-SEC First Team	SEC
ArDarius Stewart	AP All-SEC First Team	SEC
Jonah Williams	AP All-SEC First Team	SEC
Tim Williams	AP All-SEC First Team	SEC
Ryan Anderson	AP All-SEC Second Team	SEC
Bradley Bozeman	AP All-SEC Second Team	SEC
O.J. Howard	AP All-SEC Second Team	SEC
Jalen Hurts	AP All-SEC Second Team	SEC
Eddie Jackson	AP All-SEC Second Team	SEC
Marlon Humphrey	AP All-SEC Third Team	SEC

Name	Award	Type
Eddie Jackson	AP All-SEC Third Team	SEC
Calvin Ridley	AP All-SEC Third Team	SEC
Dalvin Tomlinson	AP All-SEC Third Team	SEC
Jonathan Allen	Coaches' All-SEC First Team	SEC
Minkah Fitzpatrick	Coaches' All-SEC First Team	SEC
Reuben Foster	Coaches' All-SEC First Team	SEC
Jalen Hurts	Coaches' All-SEC First Team	SEC
Cam Robinson	Coaches' All-SEC First Team	SEC
JK Scott	Coaches' All-SEC First Team	SEC
ArDarius Stewart	Coaches' All-SEC First Team	SEC
O.J. Howard	Coaches' All-SEC Second Team	SEC
Eddie Jackson	Coaches' All-SEC Second Team	SEC
Calvin Ridley	Coaches' All-SEC Second Team	SEC
Tim Williams	Coaches' All-SEC Second Team	SEC
Cam Robinson	Jacobs Blocking Trophy	SEC
Jonathan Allen	AFCA All-America Team	National
Minkah Fitzpatrick	AFCA All-America Team	National
Reuben Foster	AFCA All-America Team	National
Cam Robinson	AFCA All-America Team	National
Jonathan Allen	AP All-America First Team	National
Minkah Fitzpatrick	AP All-America First Team	National
Reuben Foster	AP All-America First Team	National
Cam Robinson	AP All-America First Team	National
Tim Williams	AP All-America Second Team	National
O.J. Howard	AP All-America Third Team	National
Jonathan Allen	Bednarik Award	National
Reuben Foster	Butkus Award	National
Jonathan Allen	Consensus All-American	National
Minkah Fitzpatrick	Consensus All-American	National
Reuben Foster	Consensus All-American	National
Cam Robinson	Consensus All-American	National
Jonathan Allen	FWAA All-America First Team	National
Reuben Foster	FWAA All-America First Team	National
Marlon Humphrey	FWAA All-America First Team	National
Cam Robinson	FWAA All-America First Team	National
Jonathan Allen	Nagurski Trophy	National
Cam Robinson	Outland Trophy	National
Jonathan Allen	Sporting News (TSN) All-America Team	National
Reuben Foster	Sporting News (TSN) All-America Team	National
Cam Robinson	Sporting News (TSN) All-America Team	National
Minkah Fitzpatrick	Sporting News (TSN) All-America Second Team	National
Jonathan Allen	Unanimous All-American	National
Reuben Foster	Unanimous All-American	National
Cam Robinson	Unanimous All-American	National
Ryan Anderson	Senior Bowl	All-Star Team
O.J. Howard	Senior Bowl	All-Star Team
Cole Mazza	Senior Bowl	All-Star Team
Dalvin Tomlinson	Senior Bowl	All-Star Team

Note: Table data from "Alabama football holds awards banquet" (193), SEC 2016 Season Awards and All-Conference Team (194), Alabama Football: Crimson Tide dominates national player awards (195)

NFL

Season	Year drafted	Round	Pick	Overall	Player	Position	Team
2016	2017	1	16	16	Marlon Humphrey	CB	Baltimore Ravens
2016	2017	1	17	17	Jonathan Allen	DE	Washington Commanders
2016	2017	1	19	19	O.J. Howard	TE	Tampa Bay Buccaneers
2016	2017	1	31	31	Reuben Foster	LB	San Francisco 49ers
2016	2017	2	2	34	Cam Robinson	OT	Jacksonville Jaguars
2016	2017	2	17	49	Ryan Anderson	OLB	Washington Commanders
2016	2017	2	23	55	Dalvin Tomlinson	DT	New York Giants
2016	2017	3	14	78	Tim Williams	DE	Baltimore Ravens
2016	2017	3	15	79	ArDarius Stewart	WR	New York Jets
2016	2017	4	5	112	Eddie Jackson	S	Chicago Bears

Note: Table data from "2016 Alabama Crimson Tide football team" (160)

2017

Overall

Record	13-1
SEC Record	8-1
Rank	1
Points for	519
Points against	167
Points/game	37.1
Opp points/game	11.9
SOS[11]	5.46

I'm trying to get our players to listen to me instead of listen to you guys. All that stuff you write about how good we are and all that stuff they hear on ESPN, it's like poison, you know what I mean? It's like taking poison, like rat poison. I'm asking them 'are you going to listen to me, or are you going to listen to these guys about how good you are?' -Nick Saban

Games

Date	Bama Rank		Opp Rank	Opponent	Bama	Opp	Result	SEC
09/02/17	1	N	3	Florida State	24	7	W	
09/09/17	1	vs		Fresno State	41	10	W	
09/16/17	1	vs		Colorado State	41	23	W	
09/23/17	1	@		Vanderbilt	59	0	W	W
09/30/17	1	vs		Ole Miss	66	3	W	W
10/07/17	1	@		Texas A&M	27	19	W	W
10/14/17	1	vs		Arkansas	41	9	W	W
10/21/17	1	vs		Tennessee	45	7	W	W
11/04/17	2	vs	19	LSU	24	10	W	W
11/11/17	2	@	16	Mississippi State	31	24	W	W
11/18/17	1	vs		Mercer	56	0	W	
11/25/17	1	@	6	Auburn	14	26	L	L
01/01/18	4	N	1	Clemson	24	6	W	
01/08/18	4	N	3	Georgia	26	23	W	W

Coaches

Name	Position	Year
Nick Saban	Head Coach	11
Derrick Ansley	Defensive Backs	2
Burton Burns	Associate Head Coach / Running Backs	11
Scott Cochran	Strength and Conditioning	11
Brian Daboll	Offensive Coordinator / Quarterbacks	1
Karl Dunbar	Defensive Line	2
Brent Key	Offensive Line	2
Mike Locksley	Co-Offensive Coordinator / Wide Receivers	2
Tosh Lupoi	Co-Defensive Coordinator / Outside Linebackers	3
Joe Pannunzio	Tight Ends / Special Teams	1
Jeremy Pruitt	Defensive Coordinator / Inside Linebackers	2

Recruits

Name	Pos	Pos Rank	Scout	Rivals	247 Sports	ESPN	ESPN Grade	Hometown	High school / college	Height	Weight	Committed
Chris Allen	OLB	4	4	4	4	4	82	Baton Rouge, LA	Southern University Lab School	6-4	234	11/27/16
Elliot Baker	OT	1	4	5	4	4	84	San Francisco, CA	City College of San Francisco	6-7	295	6/6/16
Markail Benton	OLB	7	4	4	4	4	85	Phenix City, AL	Central HS	6-2	237	6/10/16
Isaiah Buggs	DE	1	4	5	4	4	83	Gilbert, LA	Mississippi Gulf Coast CC	6-4	280	12/13/16
Joseph Bulovas	K	6	3	3	3	3	76	Mandeville, LA	Mandeville HS	6-0	205	1/25/17
VanDarius Cowan	OLB	4	5	4	4	4	81	Palm Beach Gardens, FL	Palm Beach Gardens HS	6-4	226	4/9/16
Thomas Fletcher	LS	3	2	2	2	2	69	Bradenton, FL	IMG Academy	6-4	220	6/23/16
Najee Harris	RB	1	5	5	5	5	90	Antioch, CA	Antioch HS	6-3	226	4/18/15
Kedrick James	TE	12	4	4	4	4	80	Waco, TX	La Vega HS	6-5	245	2/3/16
Jerry Jeudy	WR	3	4	5	4	4	88	Deerfield Beach, FL	Deerfield Beach HS	6-1	180	7/28/16
Mac Jones	QB	18	4	4	4	4	80	Jacksonville, FL	The Bolles School	6-3	180	6/7/16
Alex Leatherwood	OT	1	5	5	5	5	90	Pensacola, FL	Booker T. Washington HS	6-6	327	6/2/15
Phidarian Mathis	DT	7	4	4	4	4	86	Monroe, LA	Neville HS	6-4	287	2/1/17
Kyriq McDonald	CB	45	3	4	3	3	77	Madison, AL	James Clemens HS	5-10	190	7/31/16
Xavier McKinney	S	6	4	4	4	4	84	Roswell, GA	Roswell HS	6-1	196	1/1/17
Dylan Moses	ATH	1	5	5	5	5	92	Bradenton, FL	IMG Academy	6-2	235	10/2/16
Kendall Randolph	OT	12	4	4	4	4	82	Madison, AL	Bob Jones HS	6-5	285	7/31/16
LaBryan Ray	DT	2	4	4	5	4	89	Madison, AL	James Clemens HS	6-5	270	2/1/17
Brian Robinson Jr.	RB	8	4	4	4	4	82	Tuscaloosa, AL	Hillcrest HS	6-2	216	11/9/15
Henry Ruggs III	WR	11	4	4	4	4	82	Montgomery, AL	Robert E. Lee HS	6-0	175	2/1/17
Tyrell Shavers	WR	12	4	4	4	4	83	Lewisville, TX	Lewisville HS	6-4	220	6/13/16
DeVonta Smith	WR	9	4	4	4	4	81	Amite, LA	Amite HS	6-1	157	2/1/17
Tua Tagovailoa	QB	1	4	4	5	4	85	Honolulu, HI	St. Louis School	6-1	215	5/2/16
Major Tennison	TE	9	4	4	4	4	81	Bullard, TX	Bullard HS	6-5	245	10/23/16
Chadarius Townsend	ATH	5	4	4	4	4	82	Tanner, AL	Tanner HS	6-0	180	7/29/15
Jedrick Wills	OG	7	4	4	4	4	86	Lexington, KY	Lafayette HS	6-5	315	11/15/16
Daniel Wright	S	16	4	4	4	4	85	Fort Lauderdale, FL	Boyd Anderson HS	6-0	168	12/9/16

	Scout	Rivals	247Sports	ESPN
5 Stars	4	6	5	3
4 Stars	20	19	19	21
3 Stars	2	1	2	2
2 Stars	1	1	1	1

Note: Table data from "2017 Alabama Crimson Tide football team" (196)

Roster

Num	Player	Pos	Class	Height	Weight	Hometown	Last School
4	Christopher Allen	LB	FR	6-4	239	Baton Rouge, LA	Southern Lab School
40	Giles Amos	TE	SO	6-4	242	Perry, GA	Westfield
31	Keaton Anderson	DB	R-SO	6-1	201	Florence, AL	Florence
28	Anthony Averett	DB	R-SR	6-0	185	Woodbury, NJ	Woodbury
78 .	Elliot Baker	OL	JR	6-7	302	San Francisco, CA	Archbishop Riordan/City College of San Francisco
43	Parker Bearden	DB	SO	6-1	218	Bessemer, AL	Bessemer Academy
36	Markail Benton	LB	FR	6-2	237	Phenix City, AL	Central
97	Mike Bernier	P	JR	6-2	217	Madison, AL	Bob Jones/Eastern Illinois
75	Bradley Bozeman	OL	R-SR	6-5	314	Roanoke, AL	Handley
50	Hunter Brannon	OL	FR	6-4	290	Cullman, AL	Cullman
65	Deonte Brown	OL	R-FR	6-4	350	Decatur, AL	Austin
48	Mekhi Brown	LB	SO	6-5	241	Columbus, GA	Carver
2	Tony Brown	DB	SR	6-0	198	Beaumont, TX	Ozen
45	Hunter Bryant	TE	SR	6-5	226	Roswell, GA	Fellowship Christian School
49	Isaiah Buggs	DL	JR	6-5	293	Ruston, LA	Ruston/Mississippi Gulf Coast Community College
97	Joseph Bulovas	PK	FR	6-0	212	Mandeville, LA	Mandeville
57	Ryan Burns	LB	SO	6-0	214	Dallas, GA	Hillgrove
5	Shyheim Carter	DB	SO	6-0	195	Kentwood, LA	Kentwood
67	Joshua Casher	OL	R-JR	6-1	291	Mobile, AL	St. Paul's
5	Ronnie Clark	RB	JR	6-2	224	Calera, AL	Calera
66	Lester Cotton Sr.	OL	JR	6-4	324	Tuscaloosa, AL	Central
43	VanDarius Cowan	LB	FR	6-4	236	Palm Beach Gardens, FL	Palm Beach Gardens
1	Ben Davis	LB	R-FR	6-4	237	Gordo, AL	Gordo
99	Raekwon Davis	DL	SO	6-7	306	Meridian, MS	Meridian
7	Trevon Diggs	DB	SO	6-2	195	Gaithersburg, MD	Avalon School
95	Johnny Dwight	DL	R-JR	6-3	301	Rochelle, GA	Wilcox County
16	Kyle Edwards	QB	SO	6-1	216	Springfield, VA	Lake Braddock Secondary School
32	Rashaan Evans	LB	SR	6-3	234	Auburn, AL	Auburn
29	Minkah Fitzpatrick	DB	JR	6-1	202	Old Bridge, NJ	St. Peter's Prep
45	Thomas Fletcher	LS	FR	6-2	220	Georgetown, TX	IMG Academy
87	Miller Forristall	TE	SO	6-5	238	Cartersville, GA	Cartersville
1	Robert Foster	WR	R-SR	6-2	194	Monaca, PA	Central Valley
69	Joshua Frazier	DL	SR	6-4	315	Springdale, AR	Har-Ber
48	Sean Goodman	TE	SO	6-1	243	Madison, AL	Bob Jones
45	Bo Grant	DB	SR	6-2	201	Valley, AL	Valley
20	Shaun Dion Hamilton	LB	SR	6-0	235	Montgomery, AL	Carver
9	Da'Shawn Hand	DL	SR	6-4	288	Woodbridge, VA	Woodbridge
34	Damien Harris	RB	JR	5-11	221	Richmond, KY	Madison Southern
22	Najee Harris	RB	FR	6-2	227	Antioch, CA	Antioch
18	Wheeler Harris	QB	FR	6-3	198	Scottsdale, AZ	Mountain View
15	Ronnie Harrison Jr.	DB	JR	6-3	214	Tallahassee, FL	FSU University School
46	Joseph Harvey	TE	SR	5-9	211	Tyrone, GA	Sandy Creek
63	J.C. Hassenauer	OL	SR	6-2	295	Woodbury, MN	East Ridge
84	Hale Hentges	TE	JR	6-5	249	Jefferson City, MO	Helias
36	Mac Hereford	WR	SO	6-2	215	Birmingham, AL	Woodberry Forest
41	Chris Herring	WR	SO	6-4	170	Tampa, FL	Robinson
42	Keith Holcombe	LB	R-JR	6-4	236	Tuscaloosa, AL	Hillcrest
2	Jalen Hurts	QB	SO	6-2	218	Houston, TX	Channelview
32	Swade Hutchinson	WR	SR	6-3	190	Atlanta, GA	Arlington Christian
8	Josh Jacobs	RB	SO	5-10	212	Tulsa, OK	McLain
44	Kedrick James	TE	FR	6-5	272	Waco, TX	La Vega
33	Anfernee Jennings	LB	R-RO	6-3	262	Dadeville, AL	Dadeville
4	Jerry Jeudy	WR	FR	6-1	187	Deerfield Beach, FL	Deerfield Beach
27	Austin Johnson	WR	SR	6-2	202	Elba, AL	Elba
6	Hootie Jones	DB	SR	6-2	215	Monroe, LA	Neville
10	Mac Jones	QB	FR	6-2	190	Jacksonville, FL	The Bolles School
50	Keith Vohn Jr.	DL	SR	6-2	248	Mobile, AL	Faith Academy
56	Brandon Kennedy	OL	R-SO	6-3	305	Wetumpka, AL	Wetumpka
81	Derek Kief	WR	R-JR	6-4	204	Cincinnati, OH	La Salle
90	Jamar King	DL	SR	6-4	290	Detroit, MI	Denby
98	Preston Knight	P	SO	6-5	212	Prattville, AL	Prattville
13	Nigel Knott	DB	R-FR	5-11	183	Madison, MS	Germantown
76	Scott Lashley	OL	R-FR	6-7	310	West Point, MS	West Point
70	Alex Leatherwood	OL	FR	6-6	322	Pensacola, FL	Booker T. Washington
23	D.J. Lewis	DB	SR	5-11	196	Birmingham, AL	Gardendale
24	Terrell Lewis	LB	SO	6-5	254	Washington, DC	St. John's
38	Zavier Mapp	RB	R-JR	5-9	206	Thomasville, AL	Thomasville
19	Xavian Marks	WR	JR	5-8	174	Rosenberg, TX	George Ranch
93	Phidarian Mathis	DL	FR	6-4	306	Monroe, LA	Neville
21	Jared Mayden	DB	SO	6-0	197	Sachse, TX	Sachse

240

Num	Player	Pos	Class	Height	Weight	Hometown	Last School
26	Kyriq McDonald	DB	FR	5-11	195	Madison, AL	James Clemens
25	Xavier McKinney	DB	FR	6-1	197	Roswell, GA	Roswell
40	Joshua McMillon	LB	R-SSO	6-3	241	Memphis, TN	Whitehaven
52	**Scott Meyer**	**SN**	**R-FR**	**6-2**	**233**	**Alpharetta, GA**	**Blessed Trinity Catholic**
47	**Christian Miller**	**LB**	**R-JR**	**6-4**	**240**	**Columbia, SC**	**Spring Valley**
18	Dylan Moses	LB	FR	6-3	232	Baton Rouge, LA	IMG Academy
37	Donavan Mosley	DB	JR	5-10	188	San Antonio, TX	James Madison
16	Jamey Mosley	LB	R-JR	6-5	248	Mobile, AL	Theodore
18	Montana Murphy	QB	SO	6-3	205	Southlake, TX	Carroll Senior
79	Chris Owens	OL	R-FR	6-3	307	Arlington, TX	Lamar
12	*Andy Pappanastos*	*PK*	*R-SR*	*5-11*	*190*	*Montgomery, AL*	*Trinity Presbyterian*
42	Jacob Parker	TE	SR	6-1	226	Meridianville, AL	Westminster Christian
53	Ryan Parris	SN	JR	6-0	228	Madison, AL	James Clemens
94	**Da'Ron Payne**	**DL**	**JR**	**6-2**	**308**	**Birmingham, AL**	**Shades Valley**
72	Richie Petitbon	OL	R-SO	6-4	308	Annapolis, MD	Gonzaga
71	**Ross Pierschbacher**	**OL**	**R-JR**	**6-4**	**303**	**Cedar Falls, IA**	**Cedar Falls**
58	Daniel Powell	DL	SO	5-11	246	Aliceville, AL	Pickens Academy
60	Kendall Randolph	OL	FR	6-4	309	Madison, AL	Bob Jones
89	LaBryan Ray	DL	FR	6-5	272	Madison, AL	James Clemens
37	Jonathan Rice	WR	JR	6-4	215	Madison, AL	Bob Jones
51	Tucker Riddick	LB	R-SO	6-3	218	Alcoa, TN	Webb School of Knoxville
3	**Calvin Ridley**	**WR**	**JR**	**6-1**	**190**	**Fort Lauderdale, FL**	**Monarch**
24	Brian Robinson Jr.	RB	FR	6-1	218	Tuscaloosa, AL	Hillcrest
11	Henry Ruggs III	WR	FR	6-0	175	Montgomery, AL	Lee
96	Brannon Satterfield	P	JR	6-2	223	Austin, TX	Lake Travis
9	**Bo Scarbrough**	**RB**	**JR**	**6-2**	**235**	**Northport, AL**	**Tuscaloosa County/IMG Academy**
10	**JK Scott**	**P**	**SR**	**6-6**	**204**	**Denver, CO**	**Mullen**
14	Tyrell Shavers	WR	FR	6-6	209	Lewisville, TX	Lewisville
17	**Cam Sims**	**WR**	**SR**	**6-5**	**214**	**Monroe, LA**	**Ouachita Parish**
30	Daniel Skehan	WR	SR	6-0	205	Lancaster, PA	Catholic
6	DeVonta Smith	WR	FR	6-1	165	Amite, LA	Amite
82	**Irv Smith Jr.**	**TE**	**SO**	**6-4**	**246**	**New Orleans, LA**	**Brother Martin**
38	Jerffrey Stacy Jr.	DB	JR	6-2	190	Linden, AL	Linden
83	Cam Stewart	TE	SO	6-8	266	San Jose, CA	Valley Christian
13	Tua Tagovailoa	QB	FR	6-1	219	Ewa Beach, HI	St. Louis
88	Major Tennison	TE	FR	6-5	245	Flint, TX	Bullard
14	Deionte Thompson	DB	R-SO	6-2	194	Orange, TX	West Orange-Stark
12	Chadarius Townsend	WR	FR	6-0	191	Tanner, AL	Tanner
39	Levi Wallace	DB	SR	6-0	183	Tucson, AZ	Tucson
59	Dallas Warmack	OL	JR	6-2	308	Atlanta, GA	Mays
73	**Jonah Williams**	**OL**	**SO**	**6-5**	**301**	**Folsom, CA**	**Folsom**
92	Quinnen Williams	DL	R-FR	6-4	285	Birmingham, AL	Wenonah
74	Jedrick Wills Jr.	OL	FR	6-5	314	Lexington, KY	Lafayette
30	Mack Wilson	LB	SO	6-2	236	Montgomery, AL	Carver
68	Taylor Wilson	DL	SO	6-0	276	Huntington Beach, CA	Mater Dei
77	**Matt Womack**	**OL**	**R-SO**	**6-7**	**324**	**Hernando, MS**	**Magnolia Heights**
3	Daniel Wright	DB	FR	6-1	185	Fort Lauderdale, FL	Boyd Anderson

Note: Starters in bold

Transfers

Player	School	Direction
Andy Pappanastos	Ole Miss	Incoming
Blake Barnett	Arizona State	Outgoing
Cooper Bateman	Utah	Outgoing
David Cornwell	Nevada	Outgoing
Derrick Gore	Louisiana Monroe	Outgoing
B.J. Emmons	Hutchinson Community College	Outgoing
Aaron Robinson	UCF	Outgoing

Note: Table data from "2017 Alabama Crimson Tide Roster" (197) and "Alabama adds Ole Miss kicker transfer" (470)

241

Games

09/02/17 - Alabama (1) vs FSU (3)

Chick-fil-A College Kickoff
Mercedes-Benz Stadium
Atlanta, GA

Team	1	2	3	4	T		Passing	Rushing	Total
FSU (3)	0	7	0	0	7		210	40	250
Alabama (1)	3	7	11	3	24		96	173	269

The Tide opened the season in the brand-new Mercedes-Benz Stadium in Atlanta, Georgia against No. 3-ranked Florida State. Alabama came into the game with the mantra "Don't waste a failure", a reference to the disappointing loss to Clemson in the previous season's 2017 CFP National Championship Game. Although having a competitive first half, the game was considered by some to fall short of preseason expectations. The game for Alabama proved somewhat of a costly victory as linebackers Terrell Lewis and Christian Miller would be out with significant injuries, a theme that would continue to haunt the Alabama defense for the entirety of the regular season.

The first half was characterized largely as a defensive struggle for both teams. After a turnover on downs stop by the Alabama defense on 4th-and-2, the offense marched down the field for a 36-yard Andy Pappanastos field goal (3-0) late in the first quarter. FSU responded with a drive of its own culminating in a 3-yard pass to Auden Tate (FSU up 7-3) which was matched by a 53-yard bomb from Alabama's Jalen Hurts to Calvin Ridley for a touchdown on Alabama's next drive (AL up 10-7). Both teams held the other's offense to minimal production for the rest of the half, including a blocked field goal attempt by FSU from Alabama's Minkah Fitzpatrick.

Florida State opened the second half with a promising drive that stalled at midfield after an Alabama sack. After a few possession exchanges, Alabama found themselves in prime position to score after a punt attempt by Florida State was blocked and recovered by Alabama deep in FSU territory. This culminated in an Andy Pappanastos field goal for 25 yards (13-7 Bama). On the ensuing kick return, Dylan Moses forced a fumble that was recovered by Alabama, and on the first play of Bama's drive, Damien Harris scored on a rushing touchdown from 11 yards out. Alabama came away with a successful two-point conversion after the touchdown to go up by two touchdowns (21-7). For the rest of the game, the Alabama defense dominated FSU, including picking off two passes by Deondre Francois. Alabama kicked one more field goal late in the game from 33 yards out to seal the Alabama victory (24-7). The Alabama defense held the Seminoles to 40 yards rushing.[196]

Passing	C/ATT	YDS	AVG	TD	INT	QBR
J. Hurts	10/18	96	5.3	1	0	54.5

Rushing	CAR	YDS	AVG	TD	LONG
D. Harris	9	73	8.1	1	34
J. Hurts	15	55	3.7	0	20
B. Scarbrough	15	40	2.7	0	8
N. Harris	3	5	1.7	0	3
Team	42	173	4.1	1	34

Interceptions	INT	YDS	TD
L. Wallace	1	0	0
M. Wilson	1	0	0
Team	2	0	0

Punting	NO	YDS	AVG	TB	IN 20	LONG
JK Scott	6	211	35.2	0	0	53

Receiving	REC	YDS	AVG	TD	LONG
C. Ridley	7	82	11.7	1	53
D. Harris	1	11	11	0	11
B. Scarbrough	1	4	4	0	4
J. Hurts	1	-1	-1	0	0
Team	10	96	9.6	1	53

Kick returns	NO	YDS	AVG	LONG	TD
H. Ruggs III	1	15	15	15	0

Punt returns	NO	YDS	AVG	LONG	TD
D. Harris	1	19	19	19	0

Kicking	FG	PCT	LONG	XP	PTS
A. Pappanastos	3/5	60	35	1/1	10

Note: Table data from "Alabama 24-7 Florida State (Sep 2, 2017) Box Score" (198)

242

09/09/17 - Alabama (1) vs Fresno State

Team	1	2	3	4	T		Passing	Rushing	Total
Fresno State	3	0	0	7	10		216	57	273
Alabama (1)	14	14	3	10	41		192	305	497

The Tide welcomed Fresno State to Bryant-Denny Stadium for their first home game of the season in what would be a predictable blowout of the talented but outmatched Bulldogs, a team that would go on to play in the Mountain West Championship Game.

Alabama started the game on offense to begin the first quarter. On the second play of Alabama's opening drive, quarterback Jalen Hurts ran for a 55-yard touchdown. Alabama also scored a touchdown on its next possession on a 23-yard Jalen Hurts pass to Hale Hentges (10-play, 62-yard drive), and again on the drive after that on a 4-yard Bo Scarbrough run less than a minute into the second quarter (11-play, 75-yard drive). During this time, Fresno State put together a respectable 70-yard drive for a field goal (21-3). Late in the second quarter, Alabama saw a Damien Harris touchdown run from five yards out capping a 6-play, 77-yard drive that included a 28-yard run by Hurts. Fresno State stalled on its last possession of the half making it 28-3 in favor of the Tide.

In the second half, Alabama put together a drive which culminated in an Andy Pappanastos field goal from 24 yards out in the third quarter before pulling starting quarterback Jalen Hurts for the backup quarterback and future CFP National Championship Game offensive MVP, Tua Tagovailoa (31-3). In the fourth quarter, Tua engineered a drive that ended in a 22-yard field goal from Pappanastos. He also conducted a 75-yard touchdown drive ending with a 16-yard pass to Henry Ruggs III while Fresno State found the end zone after a 63-yard punt return and 26-yard touchdown pass from quarterback Chason Virgil to Derrion Grim (41-10). The Alabama defense held the Bulldogs to 57 yards rushing while the Tide amassed 305 yards on the ground.[196]

Passing	C/ATT	YDS	AVG	TD	INT	QBR
J. Hurts	14/18	128	7.1	1	0	98.9
Tu. Tagovailoa	6/9	64	7.1	1	0	23.5
Team	20/27	192	7.1	2	0	--

Rushing	CAR	YDS	AVG	TD	LONG
J. Hurts	10	154	15.4	2	55
N. Harris	13	70	5.4	0	25
B. Scarbrough	6	36	6	0	9
D. Harris	6	32	5.3	1	9
C. Ridley	1	13	13	0	13
Tu. Tagovailoa	3	0	0	0	8
Team	39	305	7.8	3	55

Interceptions	INT	YDS	TD
A. Averett	1	30	0

Punting	NO	YDS	AVG	TB	IN 20	LONG
JK Scott	3	125	41.7	0	0	49

Receiving	REC	YDS	AVG	TD	LONG
C. Ridley	5	45	9	0	16
C. Sims	3	28	9.3	0	18
X. Marks	1	24	24	0	24
H. Hentges	1	23	23	1	23
R. Foster	2	23	11.5	0	14
H. Ruggs III	1	16	16	1	16
B. Scarbrough	2	15	7.5	0	8
N. Harris	1	10	10	0	10
J. Jeudy	1	8	8	0	8
I. Smith Jr.	2	7	3.5	0	8
D. Harris	1	-7	-7	0	0
Team	20	192	9.6	2	24

Kick returns	NO	YDS	AVG	LONG	TD
T. Diggs	1	19	19	19	0

Punt returns	NO	YDS	AVG	LONG	TD
T. Diggs	2	12	6	8	0

Kicking	FG	PCT	LONG	XP	PTS
A. Pappanastos	2/2	100	24	5/5	11

Note: Table data from "Alabama 41-10 Fresno State (Sep 9, 2017) Box Score" (199)

09/16/17 - Alabama (1) vs Colorado State

Team	1	2	3	4	T	Passing	Rushing	Total
Colorado State	0	10	0	13	**23**	247	144	**391**
Alabama (1)	17	7	14	3	**41**	248	239	**487**

Alabama welcomed the Colorado State Rams for the second home game of the season. Although Alabama won convincingly, this game was marked by several momentum shifts which benefited Colorado State against the Alabama defense (lacking several key starters due to injury) early in the game and at the end of the game during garbage time. Offensively, Alabama posted a strong 487 yards, including passing and rushing touchdowns from Alabama quarterback Jalen Hurts. Colorado State went on to post a winning record (7-6) on the year and finish second in its division within the Mountain West Conference.

Alabama received the ball to start the game and scored on its first three drives. The first one consisted of six plays and 75 yards culminating in a Jalen Hurts 27-yard run for a score. The second only took 1:28 as Hurts threw a 78-yard touchdown pass to Calvin Ridley on the fourth play of the drive. And the third was an Andy Pappanastos field goal from 46 yards out (17-0). Although the Alabama defense held CSU to zero points in the first quarter, they engineered two lengthy drives in the second quarter, comprising of a field goal and touchdown off strong passing proficiency from CSU quarterback Nick Stevens (Bama up 17-10). The Alabama offense rallied though late in the second quarter wherein Jalen Hurts found Robert Foster for a 52-yard passing touchdown to effectively end the first half with Bama on top 24-10.

In the second half, Nick Stevens was picked off two times in the third quarter (by Ronnie Harrison Jr. and Hootie Jones), and Alabama capitalized on both situations for touchdowns. The first one was a long 14-play, 88-yard drive ending with a Bo Scarbrough touchdown run from nine yards out, and the second was a much shorter 2-play, 11-yard drive ending with a 5-yard touchdown run by Damien Harris. This virtually guaranteed the Alabama win as the score was now 38-10. In the fourth quarter, the Alabama defense gave up two touchdown drives while the Alabama offense, under the control of backup quarterback Tua Tagovailoa, posted a 43-yard field goal to end the game (41-23).[196]

Passing	C/ATT	YDS	AVG	TD	INT	QBR
J. Hurts	12/17	248	14.6	2	0	96.9
Tu. Tagovailoa	1/4	0	0	0	0	0.5
Team	13/21	248	11.8	2	0	--

Rushing	CAR	YDS	AVG	TD	LONG
J. Hurts	11	103	9.4	1	27
B. Scarbrough	12	66	5.5	1	17
D. Harris	11	53	4.8	1	10
N. Harris	4	11	2.8	0	7
J. Jacobs	1	6	6	0	6
Team	39	239	6.1	3	27

Interceptions	INT	YDS	TD
H. Jones	1	65	0
R. Harrison Jr.	1	0	0
Team	2	65	0

Punting	NO	YDS	AVG	TB	IN 20	LONG
JK Scott	2	100	50	0	0	59

Receiving	REC	YDS	AVG	TD	LONG
C. Ridley	3	92	30.7	1	78
R. Foster	1	52	52	1	52
B. Scarbrough	3	36	12	0	13
D. Harris	2	25	12.5	0	17
D. Smith	1	24	24	0	24
M. Forristall	1	12	12	0	12
C. Sims	1	7	7	0	7
N. Harris	1	0	0	0	0
Team	13	248	19.1	2	78

Kick returns	NO	YDS	AVG	LONG	TD
H. Ruggs III	2	42	21	22	0

Punt returns	NO	YDS	AVG	LONG	TD
T. Diggs	1	9	9	9	0

Kicking	FG	PCT	LONG	XP	PTS
A. Pappanastos	2/2	100	46	5/5	11
JK Scott	0/1	0	0	0/0	0
Team	2/3	66.7	46	5/5	11

Note: Table data from "Alabama 41-23 Colorado State (Sep 16, 2017) Box Score" (200)

09/23/17 - Alabama (1) at Vanderbilt

Team	1	2	3	4	T		Passing	Rushing	Total
Alabama (1)	21	10	21	7	59		181	496	**677**
Vanderbilt	0	0	0	0	0		38	40	**78**

Vanderbilt posted a top 20 defense and had a team return 16 starters from last season. At the end of the Kansas State game, Vanderbilt Stadium erupted in chants of "We want Bama!", a running gag of sorts within college football at the time. Vanderbilt defensive lineman Nifae Lealao was also interviewed after the Kansas State game, stating "When you come to our house, we show you how to play some SEC ball. It don't matter where you from…Alabama, you're next" which was republished throughout the week by various outlets in the lead up to the game. Alabama won the game 59-0, posted a school record 38 first downs and a school record margin of total offense of 599 yards (677 yards Alabama to Vanderbilt's 78).

Vanderbilt had the first possession of the game which was intercepted four plays into the drive by Alabama's Ronnie Harrison Jr. Although the Tide would not capitalize on this turnover, they found the end zone for four rushing touchdowns on their next four possessions. The first came off a run by Bo Scarbrough from six yards out, the second a 61-yard Damien Harris run, the third (off a fumble recovery forced by Anfernee Jennings) a methodical rushing drive culminating in a 2-yard Damien Harris touchdown, and the fourth drive which ended with a 2-yard touchdown from Bo Scarbrough (28-0). Bama tacked on one more field goal in the second quarter, and Vanderbilt was held to very minimal offensive production (31-0).

Alabama opened the second half with a drive consisting largely of the run ending in a 2-yard TD by Damien Harris. After a Vanderbilt three-and-out, Alabama backup QB Tua Tagovailoa played for the remainder of the game and accounted for two passing TDs, one to Jerry Jeudy from 34 yards out and one to DeVonta Smith from 27 yards out. Bama tacked on one more TD with the help of a long passing play to set up a 17-yard run from Brian Robinson Jr. (59- 0).

The shift between Hurts and Tua was marked by a dramatic shift in play calling and offensive scheme which was representative of the strengths of each QB. Drives orchestrated by Hurts tended to use an offensive scheme developed by former OC Lane Kiffin - a hybrid between an option offense for running schemes and a west-coast offense characterized by running veers and horizontal passing attacks. The offensive scheme under Tua resembled a traditional pro-style offense, a scheme that then OC Brian Daboll favored, which emphasized pocket presence, multiple downfield reads, play-action, vertical passing, and between-the-tackles-running.[196]

Passing	C/ATT	YDS	AVG	TD	INT	QBR
Tu. Tagovailoa	8/10	103	10.3	2	0	99.3
J. Hurts	9/17	78	4.6	0	0	35.9
Team	**17/27**	**181**	**6.7**	**2**	**0**	--

Rushing	CAR	YDS	AVG	TD	LONG
D. Harris	12	151	12.6	3	61
B. Scarbrough	11	79	7.2	2	19
N. Harris	10	70	7	0	14
B. Robinson Jr.	5	51	10.2	1	17
J. Hurts	9	48	5.3	0	22
R. Clark	10	48	4.8	0	19
J. Jacobs	4	28	7	0	13
Tu. Tagovailoa	1	22	22	0	22
C. Ridley	1	4	4	0	4
Team	3	-5	-1.7	0	0
Team	**66**	**496**	**7.5**	**6**	**61**

Interceptions	INT	YDS	TD
R. Harrison Jr.	1	1	0

Punting	NO	YDS	AVG	TB	IN 20	LONG
JK Scott	2	64	32	0	0	36

Receiving	REC	YDS	AVG	TD	LONG
J. Jeudy	3	68	22.7	1	34
C. Ridley	5	43	8.6	0	12
D. Smith	1	27	27	1	27
I. Smith Jr.	2	14	7	0	11
C. Sims	1	11	11	0	11
D. Harris	1	9	9	0	9
M. Tennison	1	9	9	0	9
N. Harris	1	3	3	0	3
B. Scarbrough	1	2	2	0	2
R. Foster	1	-5	-5	0	0
Team	**17**	**181**	**10.6**	**2**	**34**

Punt returns	NO	YDS	AVG	LONG	TD
T. Diggs	2	17	8.5	11	0
H. Ruggs III	1	16	16	16	0
Team	**3**	**33**	**11**	**16**	**0**

Kicking	FG	PCT	LONG	XP	PTS
A. Pappanastos	1/1	100	22	8/8	11

Note: Table data from "Alabama 59-0 Vanderbilt (Sep 23, 2017) Box Score" (201)

09/30/17 - Alabama (1) vs Ole Miss

Team	1	2	3	4	T		Passing	Rushing	Total
Ole Miss	3	0	0	0	3		165	88	253
Alabama (1)	21	14	24	7	66		248	365	613

Although Alabama was heavily favored going into this game, the recent history of this meeting was a tumultuous one for Alabama, having lost to Ole Miss in 2014 and 2015, and narrowly avoiding losing to them in 2016 (Alabama at one point trailed 24-3 and required a come-from-behind victory in the fourth quarter). However, 2017 Ole Miss was coached by interim coach Matt Luke and not previous head coach Hugh Freeze. This was a result of a sudden departure of Hugh Freeze during the off-season who was all but forced to resign when it came to light that a "concerning pattern" of behavior came to light wherein Ole Miss was made aware of several call logs between Hugh Freeze and a female escort service. As such, Ole Miss was in less of a position (due to off-the-field distractions) to cause Alabama trouble as it had in the past.

In the first quarter, Alabama found the end zone three times. Two of these scores were on offense, the first being the result of favorable starting position that culminated in a 6-yard Bo Scarbrough rushing touchdown (7-0), and the second a long 85-yard drive comprising a spectacular 60-yard reception from Cam Sims that culminated in a 3-yard Hale Hentges' touchdown reception. These two scores bookended an interception for a touchdown from Levi Wallace. Ole Miss found the scoreboard off a field goal late in the first quarter from 26 yards out (21-3). The second quarter included an 18-yard Hurts touchdown pass to Josh Jacobs, and after a fumble recovery gave Bama a short field, Hurts ran twice including a 10-yard TD (35-3).

Alabama received the ball to start the second half which culminated in a beautiful 48-yard field goal from JK Scott (38-3). By this point, Ole Miss could not generate any form of offense or defense, allowing Alabama to simply pile on drive after drive. Najee Harris ran for a 4-yard touchdown (45-3), then after a quarterback exchange and off the back of a 45-yard Josh Jacobs rush, backup QB Tua Tagovailoa scored from three yards out (52-3). Then off another Levi Wallace interception, Tua threw an 8-yard TD pass to Henry Ruggs III (59-3), and finally, Bama put together a 91-yard drive lasting over eight in-game minutes that culminated in a Ronnie Clark 9-yard touchdown run (66-3). This was Alabama's largest margin-of-victory since 1979. However, in line with the rest of the season, Alabama linebacker Da'Shawn Hand was injured in the third quarter, further depleting Alabama's already sparse defensive backfield.[196]

Passing	C/ATT	YDS	AVG	TD	INT	QBR
J. Hurts	12/19	197	10.4	2	0	97.4
Tu. Tagovailoa	3/5	51	10.2	1	0	99
Team	15/24	248	10.3	3	0	--

Rushing	CAR	YDS	AVG	TD	LONG
J. Hurts	10	101	10.1	1	29
D. Harris	7	67	9.6	0	46
J. Jacobs	2	51	25.5	0	45
N. Harris	7	43	6.1	1	12
Tu. Tagovailoa	4	37	9.3	1	16
B. Robinson Jr.	7	34	4.9	0	11
R. Clark	5	22	4.4	1	9
B. Scarbrough	6	18	3	1	6
Team	48	365	7.6	5	46

Kicking	FG	PCT	LONG	XP	PTS
A. Pappanastos	0/1	0	0	9/9	9
JK Scott	1/1	100	48	0/0	3
Team	2/2	50	48	9/9	12

Punting	NO	YDS	AVG	TB	IN 20	LONG
JK Scott	2	85	42.5	0	0	55

Receiving	REC	YDS	AVG	TD	LONG
C. Sims	1	60	60	0	60
C. Ridley	4	60	15	0	22
J. Jacobs	2	36	18	1	18
J. Jeudy	2	31	15.5	0	26
R. Foster	2	25	12.5	0	25
D. Kief	1	21	21	0	21
H. Ruggs III	1	8	8	1	8
I. Smith Jr.	1	4	4	0	4
H. Hentges	1	3	3	1	3
Team	15	248	16.5	3	60

Kick returns	NO	YDS	AVG	LONG	TD
H. Ruggs III	2	42	21	22	0

Punt returns	NO	YDS	AVG	LONG	TD
T. Diggs	2	37	18.5	23	0
H. Ruggs III	2	21	10.5	16	0
Team	4	58	14.5	23	0

Interceptions	INT	YDS	TD
L. Wallace	2	66	1

Note: Table data from "Alabama 66-3 Ole Miss (Sep 30, 2017) Box Score" (202)

10/07/17 - Alabama (1) at Texas A&M

Team	1	2	3	4	T		Passing	Rushing	Total
Alabama (1)	7	10	7	3	27		123	232	355
Texas A&M	3	0	7	9	19		237	71	308

Alabama next traveled to SEC West foe Texas A&M and were 26.5-point favorites in the game. The game ended up being closer than expected, as Alabama pulled out a 27-19 victory.

Texas A&M took an early lead with a 52-yard field goal by Daniel LaCamera in the first quarter. On the very next offensive play for Alabama, running back Damien Harris broke off a 75-yard touchdown run. The Crimson Tide added a 34-yard field goal by Andy Pappanastos (JK Scott missed a 50-yard attempt earlier) and a 1-yard touchdown run by Jalen Hurts (capping off a 4-play 43-yard drive taking only 1:49) in the second quarter to make the score 17-3 at the half.

Alabama's opening drive of the second half was a 9-play, 75-yard drive that ended with an 8-yard touchdown pass from Hurts to Henry Ruggs III. On their next drive, Robert Foster fumbled the ball which the Aggies recovered on the Alabama 36-yard line. Texas A&M took advantage of the opportunity and scored via a 2-yard touchdown pass from Kellen Mond to Christian Kirk. Texas A&M's next drive ended with an interception by Minkah Fitzpatrick near Alabama's goal line. Four plays later, Alabama was forced to punt out of its own end zone, and the kick was blocked for a safety, after which the score was 24-12, Alabama. Alabama kicked a 44-yard field goal with 2:09 left to play, and then Texas A&M led a touchdown drive in the final minutes that ended with a 1-yard Kellen Mond touchdown run to make the score 27-19 with 17 seconds remaining. The Aggies failed to convert an onside kick, and Alabama ran out the clock to end the game. Damien Harris finished with 124 yards and a touchdown in the game.[196]

Passing	C/ATT	YDS	AVG	TD	INT	QBR
J. Hurts	13/22	123	5.6	1	0	58.8

Rushing	CAR	YDS	AVG	TD	LONG
D. Harris	14	124	8.9	1	75
J. Hurts	14	56	4	1	38
B. Scarbrough	15	55	3.7	0	9
Team	1	-3	-3	0	0
Team	44	232	5.3	2	75

Interceptions	INT	YDS	TD
M. Fitzpatrick	1	0	0

Kick returns	NO	YDS	AVG	LONG	TD
M. Fitzpatrick	1	39	39	39	0

Punting	NO	YDS	AVG	TB	IN 20	LONG
J. Scott	4	146	36.5	0	0	46

Receiving	REC	YDS	AVG	TD	LONG
C. Ridley	5	68	13.6	0	30
J. Jeudy	2	24	12	0	17
B. Scarbrough	3	21	7	0	11
H. Ruggs III	1	8	8	1	8
R. Foster	1	1	1	0	1
I. Smith Jr.	1	1	1	0	1
Team	13	123	9.5	1	30

Punt returns	NO	YDS	AVG	LONG	TD
H. Ruggs III	3	10	3.3	12	0

Kicking	FG	PCT	LONG	XP	PTS
A. Pappanastos	2/2	100	44	3/3	9
J. Scott	0/1	0	0	0/0	0
Team	2/3	66.7	44	3/3	9

Note: Table data from "Alabama 27-19 Texas A&M (Oct 7, 2017) Box Score" (203)

10/14/17 - Alabama (1) vs Arkansas

Team	1	2	3	4	T		Passing	Rushing	Total
Arkansas	0	0	3	6	9		200	27	227
Alabama (1)	17	7	7	10	41		188	308	496

Alabama next hosted SEC West foe Arkansas. The Crimson Tide won in a blowout, 41-9. On the very first offensive play of the game, Alabama's Damien Harris ran for a 75-yard touchdown. Arkansas's first drive resulted in a three-and-out followed by a fumbled snap by the punter, resulting in a turnover on downs at the Arkansas 25-yard line. Alabama was unable to gain a first down and settled with a 39-yard field goal. After another Arkansas three-and-out, Alabama completed a 65-yard drive that ended with a 4-yard score by Damien Harris, after which the score was 17-0 midway through the first quarter. Alabama struggled to move the ball on its next few drives but scored again in the final two minutes of the half via an 11-yard touchdown run by Jalen Hurts. This capped a 9-play, 75-yard drive and the score was 24-0 at the break.

Alabama's first drive in the second half ended with a Jalen Hurts interception to Arkansas's Kevin Richardson II, after which Arkansas scored its first points of the day via a 30-yard field goal (24-3). Hurts responded with a 20-yard touchdown pass to Henry Ruggs III on the next 6-play, 78-yard drive. Alabama's first drive of the fourth quarter ended with a 4-yard touchdown run by freshman Najee Harris. After Shaun Dion Hamilton got a sack, Mack Wilson intercepted Cole Kelley which led to a 21-yard field goal by Andy Pappanastos (41-3). Arkansas's first touchdown came with 3:03 left to go via a 3-yard touchdown pass from Cole Kelley to Jordan Jones (missed the PAT), after which Alabama ran out with the clock with a final score of 41-9. Damien Harris finished with 125 yards and two touchdowns on just nine carries in the game.[196]

Passing	C/ATT	YDS	AVG	TD	INT	QBR
J. Hurts	12/19	155	8.2	1	1	60.7
Tu. Tagovailoa	1/2	33	16.5	0	0	23.8
Team	13/21	188	9	1	1	--

Rushing	CAR	YDS	AVG	TD	LONG
D. Harris	9	125	13.9	2	75
B. Scarbrough	7	65	9.3	0	21
J. Hurts	10	41	4.1	0	18
J. Jacobs	9	39	4.3	0	10
N. Harris	5	33	6.6	1	16
B. Robinson Jr.	2	7	3.5	0	5
Team	1	-2	-2	0	0
Team	43	308	7.2	4	75

Interceptions	INT	YDS	TD
M. Wilson	1	0	0

Punting	NO	YDS	AVG	TB	IN 20	LONG
JK Scott	3	131	43.7	0	0	55

Receiving	REC	YDS	AVG	TD	LONG
C. Ridley	4	51	12.8	0	27
J. Jacobs	2	36	18	0	33
J. Jeudy	1	29	29	0	29
H. Ruggs III	1	20	20	1	20
C. Sims	2	20	10	0	14
D. Smith	1	16	16	0	16
B. Scarbrough	1	8	8	0	8
D. Harris	1	8	8	0	8
Team	13	188	14.5	1	33

Kick returns	NO	YDS	AVG	LONG	TD
H. Ruggs III	2	40	20	23	0

Punt returns	NO	YDS	AVG	LONG	TD
T. Diggs	3	11	3.7	10	0
H. Ruggs III	2	-1	-0.5	0	0
Team	5	10	2	10	0

Kicking	FG	PCT	LONG	XP	PTS
A. Pappanastos	2/2	100	39	5/5	11

Note: Table data from "Alabama 41-9 Arkansas (Oct 14, 2017) Box Score" (204)

248

10/21/17 - Alabama (1) vs Tennessee

Team	1	2	3	4	T		Passing	Rushing	Total
Tennessee	0	0	7	0	**7**		44	64	**108**
Alabama (1)	7	14	10	14	**45**		332	272	**604**

Alabama next hosted its East Division rival Tennessee. Alabama won in a blowout, 45-7, its 11th straight win in the series. Tennessee received the opening kickoff but was forced to punt after three plays. Alabama's first drive was a 12-play, 63-yard drive that ended in a 1-yard touchdown run by Bo Scarbrough. In the second quarter, an 85-yard drive ended in another 1-yard score by Scarbrough, and with 1:18 remaining in the half, Damien Harris capped a 77-yard drive with an 11-yard touchdown run. The score was 21-0 at halftime.

Alabama's opening drive of the second half only took 2:21 and consisted of 75 yards in eight plays, ending with a 14-yard touchdown pass from Jalen Hurts to Irv Smith Jr. Tua Tagovailoa came in at quarterback and led a drive down to the Tennessee 5-yard line, but Tennessee's Daniel Bituli intercepted a pass and returned it for a 97-yard score for Tennessee's only points on the day. Andy Pappanastos hit a 25-yard field goal on the Tide's next possession. Tua added a 23-yard rushing touchdown and a 60-yard passing touchdown to Henry Ruggs III (both drives were 77 yards) before the end of the game to make the score 45-7 at the final horn. Alabama out-gained Tennessee 604 to 108 in total yards on the day.[196]

Passing	C/ATT	YDS	AVG	TD	INT	QBR
J. Hurts	13/21	198	9.4	1	0	62
Tu. Tagovailoa	9/12	134	11.2	1	1	80.6
Team	22/33	332	10.1	2	1	--

Rushing	CAR	YDS	AVG	TD	LONG
D. Harris	13	72	5.5	1	11
N. Harris	7	50	7.1	0	18
J. Jacobs	8	47	5.9	0	22
Tu. Tagovailoa	4	36	9	1	23
B. Robinson Jr.	3	23	7.7	0	13
B. Scarbrough	9	18	2	2	5
R. Clark	2	16	8	0	12
J. Hurts	5	14	2.8	0	7
Team	2	-4	-2	0	0
Team	53	272	5.1	4	23

Interceptions	INT	YDS	TD
M. Wilson	1	21	0

Punting	NO	YDS	AVG	TB	IN 20	LONG
JK Scott	2	84	42	0	0	50

Receiving	REC	YDS	AVG	TD	LONG
C. Ridley	8	82	10.3	0	26
H. Ruggs III	1	60	60	1	60
I. Smith Jr.	3	60	20	1	34
J. Jeudy	3	48	16	0	19
H. Hentges	2	34	17	0	19
J. Jacobs	2	24	12	0	21
C. Sims	1	14	14	0	14
N. Harris	2	10	5	0	8
Team	22	332	15.1	2	60

Kick returns	NO	YDS	AVG	LONG	TD
H. Ruggs III	2	36	18	21	0

Punt returns	NO	YDS	AVG	LONG	TD
X. Marks	6	25	4.2	12	0

Kicking	FG	PCT	LONG	XP	PTS
A. Pappanastos	1/1	100	25	6/6	9

Note: Table data from "Alabama 45-7 Tennessee (Oct 21, 2017) Box Score" (205)

249

11/04/17 - Alabama (2) vs LSU (19)

Team	1	2	3	4	T		Passing	Rushing	Total
LSU (19)	0	3	7	0	10		155	151	306
Alabama (2)	7	7	7	3	24		183	116	299

Alabama next faced its second ranked opponent of the year in a home game against SEC West foe No. 19 LSU. In a low-scoring game for the Tide, Alabama led by two scores for most of the game and won by a score of 24-10.

Alabama got on the board first after a 9-play, 90-yard drive ended with a 4-yard touchdown pass from Jalen Hurts to Irv Smith Jr. Late in the first quarter, Alabama safety Ronnie Harrison Jr. intercepted a pass from LSU's Danny Etling at the LSU 37-yard line, after which Bo Scarbrough ran for a 9-yard touchdown run to make the score 14-0. LSU's next drive moved the ball to the Alabama 4-yard line, but the Tigers were stopped and had to settle for a 21-yard field goal. Alabama led 14-3 at halftime.

Both teams struggled to move the ball at the start of the second half until Jalen Hurts capped a 7-play, 56-yard drive with a 3-yard touchdown run late in the third quarter. LSU responded with its own touchdown drive in which Darrel Williams ran for 54 yards to the Alabama 2-yard line and then ran it in for the score two plays later. Alabama's Andy Pappanastos kicked a 40-yard field goal to make the score 24-10 with 13:25 left to play. The Alabama defense was the story for the rest of the game as LSU accumulated only 24 yards on three drives in the final 13 minutes while the Alabama offense did not score.[196]

Passing	C/ATT	YDS	AVG	TD	INT	QBR
J. Hurts	11/24	183	7.6	1	0	80.8

Rushing	CAR	YDS	AVG	TD	LONG
J. Hurts	14	44	3.1	1	19
B. Scarbrough	11	39	3.5	1	11
D. Harris	9	33	3.7	0	8
J. Jacobs	1	3	3	0	3
Team	1	-3	-3	0	0
Team	36	116	3.2	2	19

Interceptions	INT	YDS	TD
R. Harrison Jr.	1	6	0

Punting	NO	YDS	AVG	TB	IN 20	LONG
JK Scott	8	413	51.6	0	0	58

Receiving	REC	YDS	AVG	TD	LONG
C. Ridley	3	61	20.3	0	24
H. Ruggs III	1	47	47	0	47
I. Smith Jr.	2	25	12.5	1	21
R. Foster	2	23	11.5	0	14
C. Sims	1	15	15	0	15
D. Smith	1	12	12	0	12
B. Scarbrough	1	0	0	0	0
Team	11	183	16.6	1	47

Kick returns	NO	YDS	AVG	LONG	TD
H. Ruggs III	1	18	18	18	0

Punt returns	NO	YDS	AVG	LONG	TD
X. Marks	3	11	3.7	7	0

Kicking	FG	PCT	LONG	XP	PTS
A. Pappanastos	1/1	100	40	3/3	6

Note: Table data from "Alabama 24-10 LSU (Nov 4, 2017) Box Score" (206)

250

11/11/17 - Alabama (2) at Mississippi State (16)

Team	1	2	3	4	T	Passing	Rushing	Total
Alabama (2)	7	7	3	14	31	242	202	444
Mississippi State (16)	7	7	7	3	24	158	172	330

After defeating LSU, Alabama traveled to play No. 16 Mississippi State. Alabama pulled ahead late to secure a 31-24 victory.

Mississippi State opened the scoring with an 11-yard touchdown run from Aeris Williams on its second drive. Alabama responded with a 65-yard drive that included a 63-yard pass from Jalen Hurts to Calvin Ridley and ended with a 1-yard touchdown run from Hurts. Mississippi State's next drive again ended with an Aeris Williams touchdown run, this time from five yards out. Once again, Alabama responded with a touchdown drive as Hurts connected with Ridley again for a 61-yard pass and Josh Jacobs ended the drive with a 1-yard run. Both teams failed to score for the last nine minutes of the half, and the 14-14 score carried into halftime.

Alabama received the second half kickoff and advanced to the Mississippi State 12-yard line but settled for a 30-yard field goal from Andy Pappanastos. The Bulldogs then went on a 13-play, 69-yard drive that ended with a 2-yard touchdown run by quarterback Nick Fitzgerald to take a 21-17 lead. Mississippie State extended its lead to seven points early in the fourth quarter with a 25-yard field goal (24-17). Alabama drove 82 yards in ten plays to tie the game at 24-24 with a 14-yard touchdown run by Damien Harris with 9:49 left to go. A would-be go-ahead 41-yard field goal from Pappanastos missed with 2:03 left in the game, but Alabama forced a Mississippi State three-and-out and got the ball back with 1:01 left on the clock. Jalen Hurts marched the team 68 yards down the field and scored the go-ahead touchdown via a 26-yard pass to DeVonta Smith with 25 seconds left in the game. Mississippi State attempted a Hail Mary pass as time expired, but the pass sailed out of the end zone and the game ended with Bama on top, 31-24.[196]

Passing	C/ATT	YDS	AVG	TD	INT	QBR
J. Hurts	10/18	242	13.4	1	0	91.7

Rushing	CAR	YDS	AVG	TD	LONG
D. Harris	8	93	11.6	1	48
J. Hurts	19	40	2.1	1	14
J. Jacobs	6	36	6	1	13
B. Scarbrough	5	33	6.6	0	13
Team	38	202	5.3	3	48

Kick returns	NO	YDS	AVG	LONG	TD
H. Ruggs III	1	18	18	18	0

Punting	NO	YDS	AVG	TB	IN 20	LONG
JK Scott	4	174	43.5	0	0	52

Receiving	REC	YDS	AVG	TD	LONG
C. Ridley	5	171	34.2	0	63
D. Smith	1	26	26	1	26
C. Sims	1	18	18	0	18
J. Jacobs	2	18	9	0	12
H. Hentges	1	9	9	0	9
Team	10	242	24.2	1	63

Punt returns	NO	YDS	AVG	LONG	TD
X. Marks	1	-6	-6	-6	0

Kicking	FG	PCT	LONG	XP	PTS
A. Pappanastos	1/2	50	30	4/4	7

Note: Table data from "Alabama 31-24 Mississippi State (Nov 11, 2017) Box Score" (207)

11/18/17 - Alabama (1) vs Mercer

Team	1	2	3	4	T		Passing	Rushing	Total
Mercer	0	0	0	0	**0**		54	107	**161**
Alabama (1)	14	21	14	7	**56**		265	265	**530**

Alabama next returned home for its final non-conference game against FCS opponent Mercer. Alabama won in a predictable blowout, 56-0.

Alabama's first five possessions of the first half all ended with touchdowns. The first came in 3:33 from an 8-yard pass from Jalen Hurts to Irv Smith Jr. that capped a 10-play, 75-yard drive. After Mercer missed a 52-yard field goal attempt, Alabama drove 65 yards in five plays taking only 1:41 as Najee Harris rushed three yards for the score. After a Mercer punt, Alabama took over at its own 2-yard line. Four plays later, Hurts threw a 66-yard touchdown pass to Calvin Ridley. Hootie Jones intercepted the very next Mercer pass, and Alabama scored three plays later via a 7-yard pass to Josh Jacobs. Tua Tagovailoa took over at quarterback and after Scarbrough ran twice, one for a nice 44-yard gain, Tua hit Hale Hentges for a 4-yard touchdown in the second quarter.

In the second half, Alabama was forced to punt once before rattling off three more touchdown drives with mostly backups on the field. All drives were extremely short starting with a 6-play, 58-yard drive that took 2:33. After an interception gave Alabama the ball on the Mercer 6-yard line, it only took the Tide two plays to score in nine seconds. Xavian Marks then returned a punt 26 yards to the Mercer 17-yard line. 47 seconds and two plays later, Tua hit Derek Kief for a 13-yard touchdown. This brought the final score to 56-0.[196]

Passing	C/ATT	YDS	AVG	TD	INT	QBR
J. Hurts	7/7	180	25.7	3	0	100
Tu. Tagovailoa	7/11	85	7.7	3	0	75.8
Team	**14/18**	**265**	**14.7**	**6**	**0**	--

Rushing	CAR	YDS	AVG	TD	LONG
B. Scarbrough	5	54	10.8	0	44
B. Robinson Jr.	7	50	7.1	1	15
J. Jacobs	6	41	6.8	0	13
D. Harris	6	32	5.3	0	9
J. Hurts	2	30	15	0	26
N. Harris	6	24	4	1	10
R. Clark	4	21	5.3	0	7
Tu. Tagovailoa	3	11	3.7	0	9
A. Johnson	2	8	4	0	6
Team	1	-6	-6	0	0
Team	**42**	**265**	**6.3**	**2**	**44**

Punt returns	NO	YDS	AVG	LONG	TD
X. Marks	2	52	26	26	0

Punting	NO	YDS	AVG	TB	IN 20	LONG
JK Scott	2	105	52.5	0	0	54

Receiving	REC	YDS	AVG	TD	LONG
C. Ridley	3	103	34.3	1	66
J. Jacobs	2	45	22.5	1	38
R. Foster	1	24	24	0	24
C. Sims	2	21	10.5	1	13
M. Tennison	1	21	21	0	21
H. Ruggs III	1	16	16	0	16
D. Kief	1	13	13	1	13
D. Smith	1	10	10	0	10
I. Smith Jr.	1	8	8	1	8
H. Hentges	1	4	4	1	4
Team	**14**	**265**	**18.9**	**6**	**66**

Interceptions	INT	YDS	TD
D. Thompson	1	21	0
D. Moses	1	11	0
H. Jones	1	0	0
Team	**3**	**32**	**0**

Kicking	FG	PCT	LONG	XP	PTS
JK Scott	0/0	0	0	8/8	8

Note: Table data from "Alabama 56-0 Mercer (Nov 18, 2017) Box Score" (208)

11/25/17 - Alabama (1) at Auburn (6)

Team	1	2	3	4	T		Passing	Rushing	Total
Alabama (1)	0	7	7	0	**14**		103	211	**314**
Auburn (6)	7	3	10	6	**26**		240	168	**408**

In the final game of the regular season, Alabama traveled to play in-state rival No. 6 Auburn in the 82nd Iron Bowl. Two weeks earlier, Auburn had defeated then-No. 2 Georgia at home and could claim the West Division title with another home win against the top-ranked Crimson Tide. Auburn did just that, pulling off the 26-14 victory. It was Auburn's first win in the rivalry since upsetting top-ranked Alabama in 2013 in a game known as the Kick Six.

After each team punted to start the game, the Tigers led a 12-play, 95-yard drive that ended with a 3-yard touchdown pass from running back Kerryon Johnson to Nate Craig-Myers. Alabama's next drive ended with a fumble by Jalen Hurts. After Auburn drove to the Bama 4-yard line, Alabama got the ball back when Jarrett Stidham fumbled as well. After each team punted again, Alabama drove 60 yards in seven plays and tied the game with a 36-yard pass from Jalen Hurts to Jerry Jeudy. Auburn kicked a 33-yard field goal as time expired in the second quarter to go up 10-7 at halftime.

Alabama received the second half kickoff and took a 14-10 lead with a 21-yard touchdown run by Bo Scarbrough. The drive only took 1:38 for the Tide to drive 79 yards in five plays including a 31-yard run by Damien Harris. Auburn was able to score on its next two drives via a 44-yard field goal and then a 1-yard touchdown run by Kerryon Johnson, taking a 20-14 lead. Alabama's next drive ended with a botched field goal snap and a turnover on downs. Auburn then extended its lead early in the fourth quarter with a 16-yard touchdown run by Jarrett Stidham. Auburn failed on the two-point attempt, and the score was 26-14. Alabama's next two drives were both lengthy but ended with failed fourth down attempts and turnovers on downs. Auburn got the ball with 2:21 left to go and was able to wind down the clock to win the game.[196]

Passing	C/ATT	YDS	AVG	TD	INT	QBR
J. Hurts	1/22	112	5.1	1	0	78.6
JK Scott	1/1	-9	-9	0	0	--
Team	13/23	103	4.5	1	0	--

Rushing	CAR	YDS	AVG	TD	LONG
J. Hurts	18	82	4.6	0	17
D. Harris	6	51	8.5	0	31
B. Scarbrough	6	46	7.7	1	21
J. Jacobs	6	25	4.2	0	6
R. Foster	1	12	12	0	12
Team	1	-5	-5	0	0
Team	38	211	5.6	1	31

Punting	NO	YDS	AVG	TB	IN 20	LONG
JK Scott	4	184	46	0	0	64

Receiving	REC	YDS	AVG	TD	LONG
C. Ridley	3	38	12.7	0	26
J. Jeudy	1	36	36	1	36
D. Harris	2	20	10	0	12
B. Scarbrough	2	6	3	0	4
J. Jacobs	2	6	3	0	6
R. Foster	1	3	3	0	3
I. Smith Jr.	1	3	3	0	3
A. Pappanastos	1	-9	-9	0	-9
Team	13	103	7.9	1	36

Kick returns	NO	YDS	AVG	LONG	TD
T. Diggs	1	55	55	55	0
J. Jacobs	2	44	22	23	0
Team	3	99	33	55	0

Kicking	FG	PCT	LONG	XP	PTS
A. Pappanastos	0/0	0	0	2/2	2

Note: Table data from "Alabama 14-26 Auburn (Nov 25, 2017) Box Score" (209)

253

01/01/18 - Alabama (4) at Clemson (1)

Team	1	2	3	4	T		Passing	Rushing	Total
Alabama (4)	10	0	14	0	24		120	141	261
Clemson (1)	0	3	3	0	6		124	64	188

During the Final Selection Day by the College Football Playoff committee held on December 3, 2017, Alabama was selected over the only other serious contenders, the Ohio State Buckeyes and the Wisconsin Badgers, for inclusion in the CFP at number four. This decision was controversial for some media outlets and commentators. Wisconsin was 12-0 heading into the Big Ten Championship and had a Playoff spot locked up if they were to win, but they lost 27-21 to Ohio State, who was 10-2. Neither the Buckeyes nor the Badgers would receive the fourth Playoff spot as Ohio State had two losses (including a 55-24 drubbing by Iowa) and Wisconsin had a weak strength of schedule compared to other Playoff contenders.

Going into the game, Alabama was looking to avenge losing on the last play of the game during the 2016 College Football National Championship Game against Clemson and to prove they belonged in the CFP after its controversial inclusion. The game was marked throughout the game by strong defensive performances by both Clemson and a healthy, rejuvenated Alabama defense. During the middle of the first quarter, Alabama had an opportunity in the red zone but stalled and settled for a 24-yard field goal (3-0). After another three-and-out by Clemson, Alabama drove 46 yards down the field which culminated in a 12-yard pass from Hurts to Ridley (10-0). Clemson responded in the second quarter with a drive which ended with a 44-yard field goal making it 10-3. Defensive performances by both teams kept this score the same going into the half.

In the second half, Alabama received the ball but fumbled deep in its own territory on a muffed handoff between Hurts and Harris. A strong Alabama defensive response limited this turnover to a 42-yard field goal (10-6 Bama). After a Bama three and out, a promising Clemson drive was cut short when QB Kelly Bryant was tackled as he threw the ball causing it to wobble into the arms of Alabama defensive tackle Da'Ron Payne for an interception. Alabama capitalized on this momentum with a drive into the Clemson red zone, where, on 2nd-and-goal, Alabama brought in its goal line set which included Payne as a downhill blocker fullback. However, instead of running Payne up the middle, he rolled out for a 1-yard reception from Jalen Hurts (17-6) in what is affectionately known as a "big man touchdown". On the first play of Clemson's next drive, Bryant's intended pass to Deon Cain was deflected by Alabama's Levi Wallace into the arms of Mack Wilson for an interception returned for a touchdown (24-6). The Alabama defense controlled Clemson for the remainder of the game, ending with the score 24-6.[196]

Passing	C/ATT	YDS	AVG	TD	INT	QBR
J. Hurts	16/24	120	5	2	0	86.7

Rushing	CAR	YDS	AVG	TD	LONG
D. Harris	19	77	4.1	0	11
J. Hurts	11	40	3.6	0	19
B. Scarbrough	12	24	2	0	6
Team	42	141	3.4	0	19

Interceptions	INT	YDS	TD
M. Wilson	1	18	1
D. Payne	1	21	0
Team	2	39	1

Kick returns	NO	YDS	AVG	LONG	TD
H. Ruggs III	3	48	16	22	0

Punting	NO	YDS	AVG	TB	IN 20	LONG
JK Scott	6	213	35.5	1	3	41

Receiving	REC	YDS	AVG	TD	LONG
C. Ridley	4	39	9.8	1	13
H. Ruggs III	2	25	12.5	0	15
N. Harris	1	22	22	0	22
B. Scarbrough	2	16	8	0	15
I. Smith Jr.	1	6	6	0	6
D. Smith	1	4	4	0	4
D. Harris	2	4	2	0	9
J. Jacobs	2	3	1.5	0	3
D. Payne	1	1	1	1	1
Team	16	120	7.5	2	22

Punt returns	NO	YDS	AVG	LONG	TD
T. Diggs	3	30	10	14	0

Kicking	FG	PCT	LONG	XP	PTS
A. Pappanastos	1/2	50	24	3/3	6

Note: Table data from "Alabama 24-6 Clemson (Jan 1, 2018) Box Score" (210)

01/08/18 - Alabama (4) at Georgia (3)

Team	1	2	3	4	OT	T		Passing	Rushing	Total
Alabama (4)	0	0	10	10	6	**26**		187	184	**371**
Georgia (3)	0	13	7	0	3	**23**		232	133	**365**

After Alabama's win in the CFP Semifinal in the Sugar Bowl over Clemson and Georgia's overtime win over Oklahoma in the Rose Bowl, Alabama and Georgia, who did not play during SEC play, were slated to play in the Mercedes-Benz Dome in Atlanta, Georgia for the 2018 College Football National Championship Game. This game marked the first time ex-Defensive Coordinator for Alabama Kirby Smart, head coach of Georgia, faced off against his mentor, Nick Saban.

Alabama won the coin toss and elected to defer. On Georgia's opening drive, Alabama's Tony Brown intercepted a pass intended for Georgia's Riley Ridley, the younger brother of Alabama's Calvin Ridley. Alabama used this momentum to get Andy Pappanastos in a position for a 40-yard field goal, but he shanked it badly to the left. This was Alabama's only meaningful offensive production for the entire half. On the Georgia side, Georgia quarterback Jake Fromm utilized a very effective balanced offensive to stress an increasingly exhausted Alabama defense (due to a combination of abysmal offensive production by Alabama and excellent, extraordinary play from the Georgia offense). During the middle of the first quarter, on 3rd-and-20, the Alabama defense was gashed by Georgia's Sony Michel for 26 yards to get within field goal range. The Alabama defense tightened up and held Georgia to a completed 41-yard field goal from Georgia's Rodrigo Blankenship (3-0 UGA). After another Alabama three-and-out, Georgia again marched down the field to the Alabama red zone. Again, Alabama held Georgia to a field goal, this time from 27 yards (6-0 UGA). Alabama and Georgia traded minimal drives until Georgia gained possession of the ball with 1:12 left in the half. On this drive, which included a strong QB run from Jake Fromm, Georgia ultimately capitalized on a tired and frustrated Alabama defense with a 1-yard touchdown run by Georgia Mecole Hardman. Alabama took a knee to end the half with Georgia up 13-0.

Alabama received the ball to start the second half with one significant modification of personnel - benching two-year starting quarterback Jalen Hurts for true freshman Hawaiian phenom Tua Tagovailoa. Though Alabama did not see an immediate benefit, its first drive going for a three-and-out, Tua almost single-handedly resurrected a rudderless Alabama offense.

After holding Georgia to a three-and-out, a reinvigorated Alabama offense faced a 3rd-and-7 near midfield. Tua eluded four unblocked defenders in the backfield and ran for an Alabama first down. Capturing the momentum, Alabama sealed the drive with a 6-yard strike from Tua to Henry Ruggs III (13-7 UGA). Four plays into Georgia's next drive, on 3rd-and-long, Fromm threw an 80-yard pass to Mecole Hardman for a touchdown (20-7 UGA), negating Alabama's gain. Worse yet for Alabama, on its next possession Tua was picked off deep in Alabama territory on an ill-advised pass. At the brink of collapse, Alabama received a godsend on the very next play in a deflected Jake Fromm pass for an Alabama interception by Raekwon Davis. Using this sudden turnover, Alabama drove into field goal range where Andy Pappanastos kicked a 43-yarder (20-10 UGA). Alabama and Georgia traded minimal drives to end the third quarter. On Georgia's first drive of the fourth quarter, the beleaguered Alabama defense once more stood tall and allowed Alabama to get the ball back. During Alabama's first drive of the fourth quarter, another freshman phenom, running back Najee Harris, put the Alabama offense in position for another completed field goal, this time from 30 yards (20-13 UGA). After stopping Georgia on its next possession, Alabama again drove down the field. On 4th-and-4, deep in Georgia territory, Alabama elected to go for the touchdown instead of kicking another field goal. Tua's pass was completed into triple coverage to Calvin Ridley for a 7-yard touchdown (20-20). The exhausted Alabama defense proved once again their mettle and held Georgia to a three-and-out. In prime position with 2:50 left in the game, Alabama drove down the field and set up a potentially game-winning field goal with three seconds left on the clock. However, reminiscent of his first kick of the game, Andy Pappanastos missed wide left from 36 yards out, sending the game into overtime.

In overtime, Alabama again won the coin toss and elected to play defense. For the last time, the Alabama defense stood tall with a Terrell Lewis sack of Jake Fromm for a 13-yard loss. Despite the distance, a stellar 51-yard kick for from Rodrigo Blankenship put Georgia up 23-20. On Alabama's first play of its drive, Tua, showing his inexperience, attempted to outmaneuver two unblocked defenders in the backfield instead of throwing the ball away, putting Alabama back 16 yards. With everything on the line, instead of trying to get some of the yards back, Alabama elected to run what it calls "Seattle", a play designed for long passes. Tua, recognizing Cover 2 in the back, shifted the safety as far to the middle of the field as he could with his eyes and then immediately threw a pass to freshman DeVonta Smith for 41 yards and the game-winning touchdown, and Alabama won 26-23 in overtime. This was Alabama's 17th National Championship and fifth in nine years for head coach Nick Saban.[196]

Passing	C/ATT	YDS	AVG	TD	INT	QBR
Tu. Tagovailoa	14/24	166	6.9	3	1	90.4
J. Hurts	3/8	21	2.6	0	0	49.2
Team	17/32	187	5.8	3	1	--

Rushing	CAR	YDS	AVG	TD	LONG
N. Harris	6	64	10.7	0	35
J. Hurts	6	47	7.8	0	31
Tu. Tagovailoa	12	27	2.3	0	9
B. Scarbrough	4	23	5.8	0	16
D. Harris	6	17	2.8	0	6
J. Jacobs	3	8	2.7	0	5
Team	2	-2	-1	0	0
Team	39	184	4.7	0	35

Interceptions	INT	YDS	TD
R. Davis	1	19	0
T. Brown	1	0	0
Team	2	19	0

Punting	NO	YDS	AVG	TB	IN 20	LONG
JK Scott	6	285	47.5	0	2	56

Receiving	REC	YDS	AVG	TD	LONG
D. Smith	1	41	41	1	41
C. Ridley	4	32	8	1	9
H. Ruggs III	3	29	9.7	1	14
R. Foster	3	28	9.3	0	15
D. Harris	2	21	10.5	0	17
J. Jeudy	1	20	20	0	20
C. Sims	1	13	13	0	13
H. Hentges	1	2	2	0	2
B. Scarbrough	1	1	1	0	1
Team	17	187	11	3	41

Kick returns	NO	YDS	AVG	LONG	TD
J. Jacobs	2	42	21	22	0

Punt returns	NO	YDS	AVG	LONG	TD
T. Diggs	5	38	7.6	14	0

Kicking	FG	PCT	LONG	XP	PTS
A. Pappanastos	2/4	50	43	2/2	8

Note: Table data from "Alabama 26-23 Georgia (Jan 8, 2018) Box Score" (211)

Season Stats

Record	13-1	2nd of 130
SEC Record	8-1	
Rank	1	
Points for	519	
Points against	167	
Points/game	37.1	15th of 130
Opp points/game	11.9	1st of 130
SOS[11]	5.46	22 of 130

Team stats (averages per game)

Split	G	Passing					Rushing				Total Offense		
		Cmp	Att	Pct	Yds	TD	Att	Yds	Avg	TD	Plays	Yds	Avg
Offense	14	14.6	23.8	61.3	193.4	2	43.7	250.6	5.7	2.6	67.5	444.1	6.6
Defense	14	16.4	30.4	53.8	165.7	0.6	34.7	95.7	2.8	0.6	65.1	261.4	4
Difference		-1.8	-6.6	7.5	27.7	1.4	9	154.9	2.9	2	2.4	182.7	2.6

Split	First Downs				Penalties		Turnovers		
	Pass	Rush	Pen	Tot	No.	Yds	Fum	Int	Tot
Offense	8.6	12.4	1.4	22.2	4.9	40.6	0.5	0.2	0.7
Defense	8.1	5.4	1.8	15.4	4.4	32.5	0.4	1.4	1.7
Difference	0.5	7	-0.4	6.8	0.5	8.1	0.1	-1.2	-1

Passing

Rk	Player	G	Passing								
			Cmp	Att	Pct	Yds	Y/A	AY/A	TD	Int	Rate
1	Jalen Hurts	14	154	255	60.4	2081	8.2	9.3	17	1	150.2
2	Tua Tagovailoa	8	49	77	63.6	636	8.3	9.9	11	2	175
3	JK Scott	14	1	1	100	-9	-9	-9	0	0	24.4

Rushing and receiving

Rk	Player	G	Rushing				Receiving				Scrimmage			
			Att	Yds	Avg	TD	Rec	Yds	Avg	TD	Plays	Yds	Avg	TD
1	Jalen Hurts	14	154	855	5.6	8	1	-1	-1	0	155	854	5.5	8
2	Damien Harris	14	135	1000	7.4	11	12	91	7.6	0	147	1091	7.4	11
3	Bo Scarbrough	14	124	596	4.8	8	17	109	6.4	0	141	705	5	8
4	Najee Harris	10	61	370	6.1	3	6	45	7.5	0	67	415	6.2	3
5	Joshua Jacobs	11	46	284	6.2	1	14	168	12	2	60	452	7.5	3
6	Tua Tagovailoa	8	27	133	4.9	2					27	133	4.9	2
7	B. Robinson Jr.	6	24	165	6.9	2					24	165	6.9	2
8	Ronnie Clark	4	21	107	5.1	1					21	107	5.1	1
9	DeVonta Smith	10	6	15	2.5	0	8	160	20	3	14	175	12.5	3
10	Calvin Ridley	14	2	17	8.5	0	63	967	15.3	5	65	984	15.1	5
11	Austin Johnson	1	2	8	4	0					2	8	4	0
12	Robert Foster	10	1	12	12	0	14	174	12.4	1	15	186	12.4	1
13	Jerry Jeudy	8					14	264	18.9	2	14	264	18.9	2
14	Cam Sims	11					14	207	14.8	1	14	207	14.8	1
15	Irv Smith Jr	9					14	128	9.1	3	14	128	9.1	3
16	Henry Ruggs III	14					12	229	19.1	6	12	229	19.1	6
17	Hale Hentges	6					7	75	10.7	3	7	75	10.7	3
18	Derek Kief	4					2	34	17	1	2	34	17	1
19	Major Tennison	2					2	30	15	0	2	30	15	0
20	Xavian Marks	5					1	24	24	0	1	24	24	0
21	Miller Forristall	1					1	12	12	0	1	12	12	0
22	Da'Ron Payne	14					1	1	1	1	1	1	1	1
23	Andy Pappanastos	13					1	-9	-9	0	1	-9	-9	0

Defense and fumbles

| Rk | Player | G | Tackles | | | | | Def Int | | | | | Fumbles | |
			Solo	Ast	Tot	Loss	Sk	Int	Yds	Avg	TD	PD	FR	FF
1	Ronnie Harrison Jr.	14	43	31	74	4.5	2.5	3	7	2.3	0	4		
2	Rashaan Evans	12	35	39	74	13	6					3	1	1
3	Raekwon Davis	13	24	45	69	10	8.5	1	19	19	0	0	1	0
4	Minkah Fitzpatrick	13	38	22	60	8	1.5	1	0	0	0	7		1
5	Hootie Jones	12	31	22	53	1	0	2	65	32.5	0	2		
6	Da'Ron Payne	14	21	32	53	1	1	1	21	21	0	3	1	0
7	Isaiah Buggs	13	20	31	51	4	1.5							
8	Levi Wallace	14	31	17	48	4.5	2	3	66	22	1	15		
9	Anthony Averett	14	31	17	48	4	1	1	30	30	0	8		
10	Anfernee Jennings	10	20	21	41	6	1					2		2
11	Mack Wilson	11	21	19	40	2.5	0	4	39	9.8	1	2		
12	Shaun Dion Hamilton	9	20	20	40	5.5	2.5					2		1
13	Keith Holcombe	10	15	23	38	2	1					3	1	0
14	Dylan Moses	8	19	11	30	5.5	1.5	1	11	11	0	0		1
15	Tony Brown	13	17	12	29	1	0	1	0	0	0	2		
16	Da'Shawn Hand	10	9	18	27	3.5	3					1		
17	Deionte Thompson	9	18	7	25	1	0	1	21	21	0	1		
18	Quinnen Williams	9	11	9	20	6.5	2							
19	Terrell Lewis	4	10	6	16	2	1					1		
20	Joshua Frazier	11	8	7	15	2.5	0					3		1
21	Jamey Mosley	6	2	8	10	0.5	0					1		
22	Johnny Dwight	4	6	3	9	3.5	1							
23	Daniel Wright	5	4	5	9	0	0							
24	Mekhi Brown	5	3	4	7	0	0							
25	Shyheim Carter	7	2	5	7	0	0					1		
26	Christopher Allen	3	4	2	6	1	0							1
27	Trevon Diggs	12	3	3	6	0	0					3		
28	Xavier McKinney	4	4	2	6	1.5	0							
29	Christian Miller	4	4	2	6	2	1							
30	Joshua McMillon	4	3	2	5	0	0							
31	Labryan Ray	4	2	3	5	2.5	1							
32	Jamar King	4	0	4	4	0	0					1		
33	Jared Mayden	2	4	0	4	1	0							
34	Keaton Anderson	3	2	1	3	0	0							
35	Vandarius Cowan	2	1	1	2	0	0							
36	Derek Kief	4	1	1	2	0	0							
37	Brian Robinson Jr.	6	2	0	2	0	0							
38	Cam Sims	11	1	1	2	0	0							
39	Robert Foster	10	0	1	1	0	0							
40	Joshua Jacobs	11	1	0	1	0	0							
41	Henry Ruggs III	14	1	0	1	0	0							
42	DeVonta Smith	10	1	0	1	0	0							
43	Bo Scarbrough	14				0	0						1	0

Kick and punt returns

| Rk | Player | G | Kick Ret | | | | Punt Ret | | | |
			Ret	Yds	Avg	TD	Ret	Yds	Avg	TD
1	Henry Ruggs III	14	13	239	18.4	0	8	46	5.8	0
2	Joshua Jacobs	11	4	86	21.5	0				
3	Trevon Diggs	12	2	74	37	0	18	154	8.6	0
4	Minkah Fitzpatrick	13	1	39	39	0				
5	Xavian Marks	5					11	82	7.5	0
6	Damien Harris	14					1	19	19	0

Kicking and punting

| Rk | Player | G | Kicking | | | | | | | Punting | | |
			XPM	XPA	XP%	FGM	FGA	FG%	Pts	Punts	Yds	Avg
1	Andy Pappanastos	13	56	56	100	18	25	72	110			
2	JK Scott	14	8	8	100	1	3	33.3	11	54	2320	43

258

Scoring

Rk	Player	G	Rush	Rec	Int	FR	PR	KR	Tot	XPM	FGM	Pts
					Touchdowns					Kicking		
1	Adam Griffith	15								66	21	129
2	Jalen Hurts	15	13						13			78
3	Bo Scarbrough	13	11						11			66
4	Ardarius Stewart	12		8					8			48
5	Calvin Ridley	15	1	7					8			48
6	Joshua Jacobs	14	4				1		5			30
7	Damien Harris	15	2	2					4			24
8	Gehrig Dieter	13		4					4			24
9	O.J. Howard	15		3					3			18
10	Eddie Jackson	8			1		2		3			18
11	Ronnie Harrison Jr.	14			1	1			2			12
12	Minkah Fitzpatrick	15			2				2			12
13	Jonathan Allen	15			1	1			2			12
14	Andy Pappanastos	4								6	1	9
15	Mack Wilson	8		1					1			6
16	Marlon Humphrey	14			1				1			6
17	Derrick Gore	5	1						1			6
18	Da'Ron Payne	13				1			1			6
19	B.J. Emmons	6	1						1			6
20	Ryan Anderson	15			1				1			6
21	Tim Williams	14				1			1			6
22	Trevon Diggs	14		1					1			6
23	Xavian Marks	3					1		1			6

Stats include bowl games
Note: Table data from "2017 Alabama Crimson Tide Stats" (11)

Awards and honors

Name	Award	Type
Bradley Bozeman	Permanent Team Captain	Team
Rashaan Evans	Permanent Team Captain	Team
Minkah Fitzpatrick	Permanent Team Captain	Team
Shaun Dion Hamilton	Permanent Team Captain	Team
Minkah Fitzpatrick	MVP	Team
Damien Harris	Offensive Player of the Year	Team
Jalen Hurts	Offensive Player of the Year	Team
Calvin Ridley	Offensive Player of the Year	Team
Rashaan Evans	Defensive Player of the Year	Team
Ronnie Harrison Jr.	Defensive Player of the Year	Team
Da'Ron Payne	Defensive Player of the Year	Team
Bradley Bozeman	AP All-SEC First Team	SEC
Raekwon Davis	AP All-SEC First Team	SEC
Rashaan Evans	AP All-SEC First Team	SEC
Minkah Fitzpatrick	AP All-SEC First Team	SEC
Calvin Ridley	AP All-SEC First Team	SEC
JK Scott	AP All-SEC First Team	SEC
Jonah Williams	AP All-SEC First Team	SEC
Ronnie Harrison Jr.	AP All-SEC Second Team	SEC
Da'Ron Payne	AP All-SEC Second Team	SEC
Ross Pierschbacher	AP All-SEC Second Team	SEC
Levi Wallace	AP All-SEC Second Team	SEC
Damien Harris	AP All-SEC Third Team	SEC
Jalen Hurts	AP All-SEC Third Team	SEC
Raekwon Davis	Coaches' All-SEC First Team	SEC
Minkah Fitzpatrick	Coaches' All-SEC First Team	SEC
Calvin Ridley	Coaches' All-SEC First Team	SEC
JK Scott	Coaches' All-SEC First Team	SEC
Jonah Williams	Coaches' All-SEC First Team	SEC
Bradley Bozeman	Coaches' All-SEC Second Team	SEC
Rashaan Evans	Coaches' All-SEC Second Team	SEC
Da'Shawn Hand	Coaches' All-SEC Second Team	SEC
Ronnie Harrison Jr.	Coaches' All-SEC Second Team	SEC
Da'Ron Payne	Coaches' All-SEC Second Team	SEC
Rashaan Evans	AFCA All-America Team	National
Minkah Fitzpatrick	AFCA All-America Team	National

Name	Award	Type
Minkah Fitzpatrick	AP All-America First Team	National
Bradley Bozeman	AP All-America Second Team	National
Jonah Williams	AP All-America Third Team	National
Minkah Fitzpatrick	Bednarik Award	National
Minkah Fitzpatrick	Consensus All-American	National
Minkah Fitzpatrick	FWAA All-America First Team	National
Bradley Bozeman	FWAA All-America Second Team	National
Nick Saban	George Munger Award	National
Minkah Fitzpatrick	Jim Thorpe Award	National
Minkah Fitzpatrick	Sporting News (TSN) All-America Team	National
Bradley Bozeman	Sporting News (TSN) All-America Second Team	National
Minkah Fitzpatrick	Unanimous All-American	National
Bradley Bozeman	Senior Bowl	All-Star Team
Da'Shawn Hand	Senior Bowl	All-Star Team
JK Scott	Senior Bowl	All-Star Team
Levi Wallace	Senior Bowl	All-Star Team

NFL

Season	Year drafted	Round	Pick	Overall	Player	Position	Team
2017	2018	1	11	11	Minkah Fitzpatrick	S	Miami Dolphins
2017	2018	1	13	13	Da'Ron Payne	NT	Washington Commanders
2017	2018	1	22	22	Rashaan Evans	LB	Tennessee Titans
2017	2018	1	26	26	Calvin Ridley	WR	Atlanta Falcons
2017	2018	3	29	93	Ronnie Harrison Jr.	S	Jacksonville Jaguars
2017	2018	4	14	114	Da'Shawn Hand	DE	Detroit Lions
2017	2018	4	18	118	Anthony Averett	CB	Baltimore Ravens
2017	2018	5	35	172	JK Scott	P	Green Bay Packers
2017	2018	6	23	197	Shaun Dion Hamilton	LB	Washington Commanders
2017	2018	6	41	215	Bradley Bozeman	C	Baltimore Ravens
2017	2018	7	18	236	Bo Scarbrough	RB	Dallas Cowboys
2017	2018	7	28	246	Joshua Frazier	DT	Pittsburgh Steelers

Note: Table data from "2017 Alabama Crimson Tide football team" (196)

2018

Overall

Record	14-1
SEC Record	9-0
Rank	2
Points for	684
Points against	271
Points/game	45.6
Opp points/game	18.1
SOS[12]	6.63

I still like both guys. I think both guys are good players. I think both guys can help our team. So why do you continually try to get me to say something that doesn't respect one of them? I'm not going to, so quit asking. -Nick Saban

I hope we elect to kick ass. -Nick Saban

Games

Date	Bama Rank		Opp Rank	Opponent	Bama	Opp	Result	SEC
09/01/18	1	N		Louisville	51	14	W	
09/08/18	1	vs		Arkansas State	57	7	W	
09/15/18	1	@		Ole Miss	62	7	W	W
09/22/18	1	vs	22	Texas A&M	45	23	W	W
09/29/18	1	vs		Louisiana	56	14	W	
10/06/18	1	@		Arkansas	65	31	W	W
10/13/18	1	vs		Missouri	39	10	W	W
10/20/18	1	@		Tennessee	58	21	W	W
11/03/18	1	@	3	LSU	29	0	W	W
11/10/18	1	vs	16	Mississippi State	24	0	W	W
11/17/18	1	vs		Citadel	50	17	W	
11/24/18	1	vs		Auburn	52	21	W	W
12/01/18	1	N	4	Georgia	35	28	W	W
12/29/18	1	N	4	Oklahoma	45	34	W	
01/07/19	1	N	2	Clemson	16	44	L	

Coaches

Name	Position	Year
Nick Saban	Head Coach	12
Jeff Banks	Special Teams Coordinator / Tight Ends	1
Scott Cochran	Strength and Conditioning	12
Dan Enos	Quarterbacks	1
Josh Gattis	Co-Offensive Coordinator / Wide Receivers	1
Pete Golding	Co-Defensive Coordinator / Inside Linebackers	1
Brent Key	Offensive Line	3
Craig Kuligowski	Defensive Line	1
Mike Locksley	Offensive Coordinator	3
Tosh Lupoi	Defensive Coordinator / Outside Linebackers	4
Joe Pannunzio	Running Backs	2
Karl Scott	Defensive Backs	1

Recruits

Name	Pos	Pos Rank	Scout	Rivals	247 Sports	ESPN	ESPN Grade	Hometown	High school / college	Height	Weight	Committed
Eyabi Anoma	DE	2	5	5	5	5	94	Baltimore, MD	St. Frances Academy	6-6	223	12/20/17
Jalyn Armour-Davis	CB	28	4	4	4	4	82	Mobile, AL	St. Paul's Episcopal	6-0	165	6/23/17
Christian Barmore	DT	4	4	4	4	4	85	Philadelphia, PA	Neumann-Goretti HS	6-5	290	12/20/17
Slade Bolden	ATH	64	3	3	3	3	77	West Monroe, LA	West Monroe HS	5-11	195	8/3/17
Tommy Brown	OT	10	4	4	4	4	85	Santa Ana, CA	Mater Dei HS	6-7	315	7/21/17
Jordan Davis	DE	12	4	4	4	4	84	Memphis, TN	Southwind HS	6-5	238	12/10/16
Skyler DeLong	K	6	3	3	3	3	77	Fort Mill, SC	Nation Ford HS	6-2	180	6/15/17
Emil Ekiyor Jr.	OG	3	4	4	4	4	85	Indianapolis, IN	Cathedral HS	6-3	339	10/29/17
Jerome Ford	RB		3	3	4	4	81	Seffner, FL	Armwood HS	5-10	195	12/17/17
Josh Jobe	CB	15	4	4	4	4	84	Cheshire, CT	Cheshire Academy	6-0	178	12/16/17
Brandon Kaho	OLB		4	4	5	3	78	Reno, NV	Reno	6-1	218	12/16/17
Cameron Latu	DE	16	4	4	4	4	83	Salt Lake City, UT	Olympus HS	6-5	236	8/4/17
Jaylen Moody	ILB	33	3	2	3	3	75	Conway, SC	Conway HS	6-1	225	2/7/18
Michael Parker	TE	26	3	3	3	3	76	Huntsville, AL	Westminster Christian Academy (AL)	6-6	230	12/6/17
Jarez Parks	DE	8		4	4	4	83	Sebastian River, FL	Sebastian River HS	6-4	245	2/16/17
Eddie Smith	CB	62	3	3	3	3	78	Slidell, LA	Salmen HS	6-0	172	2/7/18
Saivion Smith	CB	1	4	4	4	4	84	St. Petersburg, FL	Mississippi Gulf Coast CC (JC)	6-1	185	12/6/17
Patrick Surtain II	CB	1	5	5	5	5	93	Plantation, FL	American Heritage HS	6-2	192	2/7/18
Jaylen Waddle	WR	12	4	5	4	4	85	Bellaire, TX	Episcopal HS	5-10	169	2/7/18
Xavier Williams	ATH	3	4	4	4	4	87	Hollywood, FL	Chaminade-Madonna College Preparatory School	6-1	190	1/17/17
Stephon Wynn	DE	9	4	4	4	4	84	Bradenton, FL	IMG Academy	6-4	279	7/1/17

	Scout	Rivals	247Sports	ESPN
5 Stars	2	3	3	2
4 Stars	12	12	13	13
3 Stars	6	5	5	6
2 Stars	0	1	0	0

Note: Table data from "2018 Alabama Crimson Tide football team" (212)

Roster

Num	Player	Pos	Class	Height	Weight	Hometown	Last School
86	Connor Adams	WR	JR	6-1	194	Sugar Land, TX	Austin
37	Dalton Adkison	WR	FR	6-0	180	New Brockton, AL	New Brockton
4	Christopher Allen	LB	SO	6-4	242	Baton Rouge, LA	Southern Lab School
40	Giles Amos	TE	JR	6-4	245	Perry, GA	Westfield
31	Keaton Anderson	DB	R-JR	6-1	196	Florence, AL	Florence
9	Eyabi Anoma	LB	FR	6-5	245	Baltimore, MD	St. Frances Academy
22	Jalyn Armour-Davis	DB	FR	6-1	181	Mobile, AL	St. Paul's
78	Elliot Baker	OL	R-JR	6-7	307	San Francisco, CA	Riordan/City College of San Francisco
7	Braxton Barker	QB	FR	6-1	195	Birmingham, AL	Spain Park
58	Christian Barmore	DL	FR	6-5	292	Philadelphia, PA	Neumann Goretti
51	Wes Baumhower	LB	FR	6-0	220	Fairhope, AL	Fairhope
36	Markail Benton	LB	R-FR	6-2	231	Phenix City, AL	Central
98	Mike Bernier	P	SR	6-2	219	Madison, AL	Bob Jones/Eastern Illinois
34	Brandon Bishop	DB	FR	6-0	187	Tuscaloosa, AL	Hillcrest
18	Slade Bolden	WR	R-FR	5-11	200	West Monroe, LA	West Monroe
50	Hunter Brannon	OL	R-FR	6-4	296	Cullman, AL	Cullman
65	Deonte Brown	OL	R-SO	6-4	344	Decatur, AL	Austin
75	Tommy Brown	OL	FR	6-7	309	Santa Ana, CA	Mater Dei
49	**Isaiah Buggs**	**DL**	**SR**	**6-5**	**286**	**Ruston, LA**	**Ruston/MS Gulf Coast Community College**
97	Joseph Bulovas	PK	R-FR	6-0	206	Mandeville, LA	Mandeville
5	Shyheim Carter	DB	JR	6-0	195	Kentwood, LA	Kentwood
67	Joshua Casher	OL	R-SR	6-1	290	Mobile, AL	St. Paul's
5	Ronnie Clark	RB	R-SR	6-2	230	Calera, AL	Calera
55	William Cooper	LB	SO	6-2	234	Huntsville, AL	Huntsville
66	**Lester Cotton Sr.**	**OL**	**SR**	**6-4**	**325**	**Tuscaloosa, AL**	**Central**
1	Ben Davis	LB	R-SO	6-4	236	Gordo, AL	Gordo
99	**Raekwon Davis**	**DL**	**JR**	**6-7**	**316**	**Meridian, MS**	**Meridian**
12	**Skyler DeLong**	**P**	**FR**	**6-4**	**189**	**Fort Mill, SC**	**Nation Ford**
7	**Trevon Diggs**	**DB**	**JR**	**6-2**	**199**	**Gaithersburg, MD**	**Avalon School**
57	Joe Donald	LB	JR	6-3	216	Mountain Brook, AL	Mountain Brook
54	Trae Drake	LB	SO	5-10	221	Roanoke, AL	Handley
95	Johnny Dwight	DL	R-SR	6-3	301	Rochelle, GA	Wilcox County
16	Kyle Edwards	QB	JR	6-2	194	Springfield, VA	Lake Braddock Secondary School
55	Emil Ekiyor Jr.	OL	R-FR	6-3	342	Indianapolis, IN	Cathedral
45	**Thomas Fletcher**	**SN**	**SO**	**6-2**	**221**	**Georgetown, TX**	**IMG Academy**
27	Jerome Ford	RB	R-FR	5-11	206	Seffner, FL	Armwood
87	Miller Forristall	TE	R-SO	6-5	240	Cartersville, GA	Cartersville
85	Chris Golden	WR	SO	6-5	197	Germantown, MD	Northwest
34	**Damien Harris**	**RB**	**SR**	**5-11**	**215**	**Richmond, KY**	**Madison Southern**
22	Najee Harris	RB	SO	6-2	230	Antioch, CA	Antioch
18	Layne Hatcher	QB	FR	6-0	196	Little Rock, AR	Pulaski Academy
84	**Hale Hentges**	**TE**	**SR**	**6-5**	**254**	**Jefferson City, MO**	**Helias**
36	Mac Hereford	WR	JR	6-2	213	Birmingham, AL	Woodberry Forest
30	Chris Herring	WR	JR	6-4	178	Tampa, FL	Robinson
2	**Jalen Hurts**	**QB**	**JR**	**6-2**	**218**	**Houston, TX**	**Channelview**
32	Jalen Jackson	WR	SR	6-3	184	Waldorf, MD	Thomas Stone
8	Josh Jacobs	RB	JR	5-10	216	Tulsa, OK	McLain
44	Kedrick James	TE	SO	6-5	263	Waco, TX	La Vega
33	**Anfernee Jennings**	**LB**	**R-JR**	**6-3**	**266**	**Dadeville, AL**	**Dadeville**
4	**Jerry Jeudy**	**WR**	**SO**	**6-1**	**192**	**Deerfield Beach, FL**	**Deerfield Beach**
28	Josh Jobe	DB	FR	6-1	191	Miami, FL	Cheshire Academy (Conn.)
29	*Austin Jones*	*PK*	*SR*	*5-10*	*215*	*Orlando, FL*	*Boone/Temple*
10	Mac Jones	QB	R-FR	6-2	205	Jacksonville, FL	The Bolles School
10	Ale Kaho	LB	FR	6-1	218	Reno, NV	Reno
38	Sean Kelly	DB	JR	5-11	191	Cary, NC	Green Hope
81	Derek Kief	WR	R-SR	6-4	204	Cincinnati, OH	La Salle
98	Preston Knight	P	JR	6-5	212	Prattville, AL	Prattville
13	Nigel Knott	DB	R-SO	5-11	182	Madison, MS	Germantown
76	Scott Lashley	OL	R-SO	6-7	313	West Point, MS	West Point
20	Cameron Latu	LB	FR	6-5	246	Salt Lake City, UT	Olympus
70	**Alex Leatherwood**	**OL**	**SO**	**6-6**	**304**	**Pensacola, FL**	**Booker T. Washington**
35	D.J. Lewis	DB	SR	5-11	196	Birmingham, AL	Gardendale
24	**Terrell Lewis**	**LB**	**JR**	**6-5**	**256**	**Washington, DC**	**St. John's**
35	De'Marquise Lockridge	RB	SR	5-11	196	Columbia, TN	Lawrence County
56	Preston Malone	LB	SO	5-11	226	Northport, AL	Northside
19	Xavian Marks	WR	SR	5-8	174	Rosenberg, TX	George Ranch
48	Phidarian Mathis	DL	R-FR	6-4	310	Monroe, LA	Neville
21	Jared Mayden	DB	JR	6-0	197	Sachse, TX	Sachse
26	Kyriq McDonald	DB	R-FR	5-11	197	Madison, AL	James Clemens
15	**Xavier McKinney**	**DB**	**SO**	**6-1**	**198**	**Roswell, GA**	**Roswell**
40	Joshua McMillon	LB	R-JR	6-3	238	Memphis, TN	Whitehaven
52	Scott Meyer	SN	R-SO	6-2	234	Alpharetta, GA	Blessed Trinity Catholic

263

Num	Player	Pos	Class	Height	Weight	Hometown	Last School
47	Christian Miller	LB	R-SR	6-4	244	Columbia, SC	Spring Valley
42	Jaylen Moody	LB	FR	6-2	227	Conway, SC	Conway
32	**Dylan Moses**	**LB**	**SO**	**6-3**	**233**	**Baton Rouge, LA**	**IMG Academy**
37	Donavan Mosley	DB	SR	5-10	186	San Antonio, TX	James Madison
16	Jamey Mosley	LB	R-SR	6-5	239	Mobile, AL	Theodore
91	Tevita Musika	DL	JR	6-1	338	Milpitas, CA	Milpitas/San Mateo Junior College
31	Bryce Musso	WR	SO	5-9	168	New Orleans, LA	Jesuit
33	Kendall Norris	RB	SR	5-10	213	Centreville, AL	Tuscaloosa County
79	Chris Owens	OL	R-SO	6-3	310	Arlington, TX	Lamar
83	John Parker	WR	JR	6-0	187	Huntsville, AL	Westminster Christian
80	Michael Parker	TE	FR	6-6	224	Huntsville, AL	Westminster Christian
23	Jarez Parks	LB	FR	6-4	251	Fellsmere, FL	Sebastian River
53	Ryan Parris	SN	SR	6-0	231	Madison, AL	James Clemens
61	Alex Pearman	OL	FR	6-1	258	Alabaster, AL	Thompson
72	Richie Petitbon	OL	R-JR	6-4	316	Annapolis, MD	Gonzaga
71	**Ross Pierschbacher**	**OL**	**R-SR**	**6-4**	**309**	**Cedar Falls, IA**	**Cedar Falls**
43	Daniel Powell	TE	JR	5-11	246	Aliceville, AL	Pickens Academy
60	Kendall Randolph	OL	R-FR	6-4	298	Madison, AL	Bob Jones
89	LaBryan Ray	DL	SO	6-5	294	Madison, AL	James Clemens
68	Galen Richardson	DL	SO	6-3	296	Marietta, GA	Walton
24	Brian Robinson Jr.	RB	SO	6-1	221	Tuscaloosa, AL	Hillcrest
62	Jackson Roby	OL	FR	6-5	267	Huntsville, AL	Huntsville
11	**Henry Ruggs III**	**WR**	**SO**	**6-0**	**183**	**Montgomery, AL**	**Lee**
14	Tyrell Shavers	WR	R-FR	6-6	216	Lewisville, TX	Lewisville
6	**DeVonta Smith**	**WR**	**SO**	**6-1**	**173**	**Amite, LA**	**Amite**
25	Eddie Smith	DB	FR	6-0	184	Slidell, LA	Salmen
4	*Saivion Smith*	*DB*	*JR*	*6-1*	*200*	*Tampa, FL*	*IMG Academy/Mississippi Gulf Coast C.C.*
82	Irv Smith Jr.	TE	JR	6-4	241	New Orleans, LA	Brother Martin
2	Patrick Surtain II	DB	FR	6-2	202	Plantation, FL	American Heritage
13	**Tua Tagovailoa**	**QB**	**SO**	**6-1**	**218**	**Ewa Beach, HI**	**St. Louis**
88	Major Tennison	TE	R-SO	6-5	246	Flint, TX	Bullard
14	**Deionte Thompson**	**DB**	**R-JR**	**6-2**	**196**	**Orange, TX**	**West Orange-Stark**
12	Chadarius Townsend	WR	R-FR	6-0	194	Tanner, AL	Tanner
17	Jaylen Waddle	WR	FR	5-10	177	Houston, TX	Episcopal
98	Quindarius Watkins	DL	SO	6-4	229	Hinesville, GA	Bradwell Institute
44	Cole Weaver	LB	SO	5-9	214	Lacey's Spring, AL	Brewer
73	**Jonah Williams**	**OL**	**JR**	**6-5**	**301**	**Folsom, CA**	**Folsom**
92	**Quinnen Williams**	**DL**	**R-SO**	**6-4**	**295**	**Birmingham, AL**	**Wenonah**
9	Xavier Williams	WR	R-FR	6-1	182	Hollywood, FL	Chaminade-Madonna Prep
74	**Jedrick Wills Jr.**	**OL**	**SO**	**6-5**	**309**	**Lexington, KY**	**Lafayette**
30	Mack Wilson	LB	JR	6-2	239	Montgomery, AL	Carver
96	Taylor Wilson	DL	JR	6-0	231	Huntington Beach, CA	Mater Dei
77	Matt Womack	OL	R-JR	6-7	325	Hernando, MS	Magnolia Heights
3	Daniel Wright	DB	R-SO	6-1	185	Fort Lauderdale, FL	Boyd Anderson
90	Stephon Wynn Jr.	DL	R-FR	6-4	299	Anderson, SC	IMG Academy

Note: Starters in bold
Note: Table data from "2018 Alabama Crimson Tide Roster" (213)

Transfers

Player	School	Direction
Austin Jones	Temple	Incoming
Mekhi Brown	Tennessee State	Outgoing
Dallas Warmack	Oregon	Outgoing

Note: Table data from "2018 Alabama Crimson Tide football team" (212)

Games

09/01/18 - Alabama (1) vs Louisville

Camping World Kickoff
Camping World Stadium
Orlando, FL

Team	1	2	3	4	T	Passing	Rushing	Total
Louisville	0	0	7	7	**14**	252	16	**268**
Alabama (1)	14	14	16	7	**51**	297	222	**519**

Alabama kicked off their season in dominant fashion, steamrolling the Cardinals 51-14 at Camping World Stadium in Orlando. QB Tua marched the Tide 65 yards down the field on the opening drive in seven plays, culminating in an 11-yard TD strike to Jerry Jeudy. Alabama's offense kept rolling, fueled by the powerful legs of Damien Harris. He burst through the line, churning out a 32-yard gain that planted the Tide at the Louisville 23-yard line. After a 5-play drive, Tua evaded the Cardinals' defense with his elusive footwork, running untouched into the end zone on a 9-yard scoring scamper. The touchdown extended Alabama's lead to 14-0.

In the second quarter, Thompson intercepted a pass in the end zone and returned it 25 yards to set up another Bama scoring drive. On the third play of the drive, Tua found Jaylen Waddle for a 49-yard bomb to the Louisville nine. Four plays later, Najee Harris dove in for the score from a yard out to extend the lead to 21-0. This scoring drive consisted of 75 yards in six plays. With just 41 seconds left in the half, Waddle's 31-yard punt return set up Tua's 25-yard touchdown pass to Jeudy, giving Alabama a commanding 28-0 advantage with nine seconds left in the half.

Tua showed no signs of slowing down in the second half. He connected with Irv Smith Jr. for a 32-yard gain to the UL 27-yard line. Jacobs then had back-to-back runs, the latter an 18-yard TD scamper around the edge. A missed extra point left the score at 34-0. After Louisville finally got on the board with a 12-yard catch to make it 34-7, Jacobs answered for the Tide. A personal foul forced the Cardinals to kickoff from their own 20-yard line, and Jacobs returned it 77 yards for a touchdown - his second TD of the day and the first kickoff return TD of his career (41-7). After a Louisville punt, the Tide marched 37 yards in six plays, with Austin Jones capping the drive with a 39-yard field goal as the fourth quarter began (44-7). Midway through the fourth, Shyheim Carter returned an interception 45 yards for a score (51-7). The Cardinals managed a consolation TD with 1:55 remaining, but it was too late, as Alabama cruised to a 51-14 victory. Quinnen Williams was a disruptive force, racking up six tackles including a team-high 3.5 tackles for loss, a quarterback hurry, and a pass breakup. Deionte Thompson tallied five tackles (1.5 for loss), and he broke up three passes and snagged an interception.[214]

Passing	C/ATT	YDS	AVG	TD	INT	QBR
Tu. Tagovailoa	12/16	227	14.2	2	0	98.8
J. Hurts	5/9	70	7.8	0	0	31.1
M. Jones	0/1	0	0	0	0	0.3
Team	17/26	297	11.4	2	0	--

Rushing	CAR	YDS	AVG	TD	LONG
D. Harris	7	55	7.9	0	32
J. Jacobs	6	45	7.5	1	18
B. Robinson Jr.	7	42	6	0	10
N. Harris	8	30	3.8	1	12
Tu. Tagovailoa	5	26	5.2	1	9
R. Clark	3	10	3.3	0	4
J. Hurts	3	9	3	0	3
J. Ford	2	4	2	0	3
M. Jones	1	1	1	0	1
Team	42	222	5.3	3	32

Kick returns	NO	YDS	AVG	LONG	TD
J. Jacobs	1	77	77	77	1

Punting	NO	YDS	AVG	TB	IN 20	LONG
S. DeLong	3	109	36.3	0	0	39

Receiving	REC	YDS	AVG	TD	LONG
D. Smith	4	99	24.8	0	28
J. Waddle	3	66	22	0	49
J. Jeudy	4	64	16	2	25
I. Smith Jr.	2	39	19.5	0	32
H. Ruggs III	2	15	7.5	0	9
D. Harris	1	14	14	0	14
N. Harris	1	0	0	0	0
Team	17	297	17.5	2	49

Interceptions	INT	YDS	TD
S. Carter	1	45	1
D. Thompson	1	25	0
Team	2	70	1

Punt returns	NO	YDS	AVG	LONG	TD
J. Waddle	4	80	20	31	0

Kicking	FG	PCT	LONG	XP	PTS
A. Jones	1/2	50	39	6/7	9

Note: Table data from "Alabama 51-14 Louisville (Sep 1, 2018) Box Score" (215)

09/08/18 - Alabama (1) vs Arkansas State

Team	1	2	3	4	T		Passing	Rushing	Total
Arkansas State	0	0	7	0	7		218	173	**391**
Alabama (1)	19	21	10	7	57		321	278	**599**

In under two minutes of play, Tua unleashed a 58-yard touchdown strike over the middle to Jerry Jeudy, putting the Tide on the board. Moments later, Tua's arm struck again, this time finding Henry Ruggs III for a 31-yard scoring connection, extending Alabama's lead to 13-0 after a missed extra point. Tua continued his aerial assault, completing his third TD pass of the game with a 41-yard dart to a wide-open DeVonta Smith. This trio of passing scores marked the most by an Alabama quarterback in a single quarter since A.J. McCarron's three-touchdown outburst against Auburn in 2012. Despite another missed PAT, the Tide held a commanding 19-0 lead.

In the second quarter, it was Jalen Hurts' turn to orchestrate Alabama's offensive onslaught. The dual-threat quarterback engineered a 7-play, 63-yard drive, capping it off with a 10-yard pass to tight end Irv Smith Jr. for another Crimson Tide touchdown. Just over a minute later, Hurts and Jeudy connected again, this time for a 7-yard scoring strike, extending Alabama's lead to 33-0. The Tide's defensive unit joined the scoring party when Saivion Smith intercepted a pass and returned it 38 yards for a touchdown, further widening the gap to 40-0.

Arkansas State opened the second half with a spirited 8-play, 75-yard drive, culminating in a 23-yard touchdown pass to trim Alabama's lead to 40-7. However, the Tide responded quickly, marching 23 yards down the field to set up Joseph Bulovas' first career field goal, a 39-yard effort (43-7). With 1:30 remaining in the third quarter, Alabama put up 50 when Tua delivered a strike, threading the needle through the defense's tightest seams. Derek Kief hauled in the 14-yard dart, executing a ballet-like toe-tap along the sideline before waltzing into the end zone untouched (50-7). In the fourth quarter, the Tide continued to pile it on with Najee Harris punching in a 1-yard touchdown to cap a 9-play, 75-yard drive with 12:06 remaining in the game. This put the Tide up 57-7, which was the eventual final.

Alabama's six scoring tosses equaled the second-most in a single game in Alabama school history, while Tua's four touchdown passes ranked second on the individual single-game list. Najee Harris eclipsed the 100-yard rushing mark for the first time in his career, amassing 135 yards and a touchdown on 13 carries. Defensively, Xavier McKinney led the Tide with a career-high seven tackles, while Saivion Smith's 38-yard interception return for a touchdown marked Alabama's third non-offensive score of the season.[216]

Passing	C/ATT	YDS	AVG	TD	INT	QBR
Tu. Tagovailoa	13/19	228	12	4	0	98.6
J. Hurts	7/9	93	10.3	2	0	31.9
M. Jones	0/1	0	0	0	0	0.3
Team	**20/29**	**321**	**11.1**	**6**	**0**	**--**

Rushing	CAR	YDS	AVG	TD	LONG
N. Harris	13	135	10.4	1	26
D. Harris	12	61	5.1	0	17
J. Hurts	5	32	6.4	0	15
Tu. Tagovailoa	4	20	5	0	15
B. Robinson Jr.	5	16	3.2	0	8
J. Jacobs	5	14	2.8	0	10
Team	**44**	**278**	**6.3**	**1**	**2**

Interceptions	INT	YDS	TD
S. Smith	1	38	1

Punting	NO	YDS	AVG	TB	IN 20	LONG
S. DeLong	4	140	35	0	0	39

Receiving	REC	YDS	AVG	TD	LONG
J. Jeudy	4	87	21.8	2	58
D. Smith	3	77	25.7	1	41
H. Ruggs III	3	56	18.7	1	31
I. Smith Jr.	4	41	10.3	1	22
J. Jacobs	3	23	7.7	0	10
D. Kief	1	14	14	1	14
D. Harris	1	14	14	0	14
J. Waddle	1	9	9	0	9
Team	**20**	**321**	**16.1**	**6**	**58**

Kick returns	NO	YDS	AVG	LONG	TD
M. Forristall	1	0	0	0	0

Punt returns	NO	YDS	AVG	LONG	TD
J. Waddle	3	-6	-2	0	0

Kicking	FG	PCT	LONG	XP	PTS
J. Bulovas	1/1	100	39	5/5	8
A. Jones	0/0	0	0	1/3	1
Team	**1/1**	**100**	**39**	**6/8**	**9**

Note: Table data from "Alabama 57-7 Arkansas State (Sep 8, 2018) Box Score" (217)

09/15/18 - Alabama (1) at Ole Miss

Team	1	2	3	4	T		Passing	Rushing	Total
Alabama (1)	28	21	10	3	62		306	210	516
Ole Miss	7	0	0	0	7		133	115	248

The game started with a bang as Ole Miss struck first, hitting a 75-yard touchdown pass just 11 seconds into the game to take a 7-0 lead. But Alabama wasn't fazed. The Crimson Tide responded with a lightning-quick 3-play, 72-yard drive, punctuated by running back Damien Harris rumbling for a 43-yard score to tie it up. Tua found his rhythm, orchestrating a blistering scoring drive by hitting Jerry Jeudy streaking down the middle for a 79-yard touchdown strike. The Tide kept pouring it on after an Ole Miss fumble, marching 62 yards in six plays, with Najee Harris punching it in untouched from ten yards out to make it 21-7. The onslaught continued as Thompson intercepted the ball and returned it 40 yards, setting Alabama up at the Rebels' 15-yard line. Three plays later, Tua unleashed a precise strike to Irv Smith Jr. for a 12-yard touchdown, extending the lead to 28-7. Midway through the second quarter, Alabama took over at its own 48-yard line after Ole Miss failed to convert on fourth down. Four plays later, Josh Jacobs barreled his way into the end zone for a 4-yard score (35-7).

After an Ole Miss three-and-out, Waddle's 30-yard punt return set up Alabama at the Ole Miss 30-yard line. Three plays was all it took for Jalen Hurts to find Jeudy again for his second TD catch of the half, this time from 22 yards out (42-7). Hurts capped off a 7-play, 50-yard drive just before halftime by hitting Henry Ruggs III with a 13-yard touchdown screen pass. Alabama took a staggering 49-7 lead into the locker room, the most points by an SEC team in a conference game since 2005.

The second half brought no relief for the beleaguered Ole Miss defense. Jacobs ripped off a 74-yard kickoff return to set up a field goal from 20 that made it 52-7. Xavier McKinney's 30-yard pick-six extended the lead to 59-7. With the game firmly in hand, redshirt freshman Mac Jones took over at QB in the fourth quarter. He methodically guided Alabama on a 13-play, 46-yard drive that ended with Joseph Bulovas' career-long 44-yard field goal, pushing the final score to an eye-popping 62-7. When the dust settled, Alabama had scored an incredible 62 unanswered points, becoming the first SEC team to score 50+ in their first three games of a season. Quinnen Williams led the defensive charge with six tackles, while Christian Miller added five tackles and 2.5 sacks.[218]

Passing	C/ATT	YDS	AVG	TD	INT	QBR
Tu. Tagovailoa	11/15	191	12.7	2	0	98.5
J. Hurts	7/10	85	8.5	2	1	90.3
M. Jones	1/3	30	10	0	0	38.8
Team	19/28	306	10.9	4	1	--

Rushing	CAR	YDS	AVG	TD	LONG
D. Harris	5	62	12.4	1	43
Tu. Tagovailoa	5	47	9.4	0	15
N. Harris	9	38	4.2	1	10
B. Robinson Jr.	10	32	3.2	0	13
J. Hurts	4	20	5	0	11
J. Jacobs	6	18	3	1	10
R. Clark	1	1	1	0	1
J. Ford	2	0	0	0	1
Team	1	-1	-1	0	0
M. Jones	1	-7	-7	0	0
Team	44	210	4.8	3	43

Kick returns	NO	YDS	AVG	LONG	TD
J. Jacobs	2	101	50.5	74	0

Punting	NO	YDS	AVG	TB	IN 20	LONG
S. DeLong	2	74	37	0	0	39

Receiving	REC	YDS	AVG	TD	LONG
J. Jeudy	3	136	45.3	2	79
I. Smith Jr.	3	42	14	1	17
J. Waddle	1	30	30	0	30
D. Smith	3	28	9.3	0	17
H. Ruggs III	3	25	8.3	0	13
D. Harris	4	23	5.8	0	12
J. Jacobs	1	18	18	0	18
H. Hentges	1	4	4	0	4
Team	19	306	16.1	4	79

Interceptions	INT	YDS	TD
X. McKinney	1	30	1
D. Thompson	1	40	0
Team	2	70	1

Punt returns	NO	YDS	AVG	LONG	TD
J. Waddle	1	37	37	37	0

Kicking	FG	PCT	LONG	XP	PTS
J. Bulovas	2/3	66.7	44	8/8	14

Note: Table data from "Alabama 62-7 Ole Miss (Sep 15, 2018) Box Score" (219)

09/22/18 - Alabama (1) vs Texas A&M (22)

Team	1	2	3	4	T		Passing	Rushing	Total
Texas A&M (22)	7	6	3	7	23		263	130	393
Alabama (1)	14	17	14	0	45		415	109	524

The game between Alabama and Texas A&M turned into an offensive showcase, with both teams trading blows. It began with a diving interception by Mack Wilson on the second play of the game, setting up Bama at the A&M 30. On the very next play, DeVonta Smith dove for an amazing 30-yard TD catch to put Bama on the board first 7-0. The Aggies responded with an 8-play, 99-yard drive finished off with a 15-yard TD pass to tie the game at 7-7.

The Tide took the lead again as Tua orchestrated a 9-play, 75-yard drive capped by his 1-yard rushing touchdown before Texas A&M responded with a 52-yard field goal from Seth Small to trim the deficit to 14-10 in the second quarter. Alabama answered once again when Tua found Hentges for a 23-yard catch to complete the 6-play, 75-yard drive (21-10). Despite falling behind, Texas A&M refused to go away quietly. They marched 60 yards and kicked another FG (from 32) to make it 21-13. However, Tua's fourth TD pass of the game and second to Hentges (this one from six yards out), kept the Tide comfortably ahead 28-13. With under a minute remaining in the half, Patrick Surtain II got his first career interception, picking off the Aggies' pass at the 40-yard line and returning it 20 yards. A personal foul penalty on Texas A&M tacked on additional yards, giving Bama excellent field position. Three players later, Bulovas connected on 47-yard field goal as time expired and gave Alabama the 31-13 lead at the break.

The second half was more of the same, with Tua engineering a 7-play, 80-yard drive capped by Josh Jacobs' untouched 3-yard TD run (38-13). On A&M's next drive, they marched 67 yards in ten plays, settling for a 25-yard field goal to make it 38-16. Alabama quickly responded with a 92-yard scoring drive in just two plays - Harris rumbled for 35 yards, then Ruggs III took a shovel pass 57 yards to the house (45-16). The Aggies closed the gap with an 11-play, 88-yard drive scoring a touchdown with 7:36 left, but Alabama held on for a 45-23 victory.

Tua accounted for a career-high five touchdowns (four passing and one rushing). He unleashed a career-best 387 passing yards, completing an impressive 22 of his 30 attempts. Both his completion and attempt totals set new personal records. His four touchdown passes equaled his previous career-high mark. Moreover, his remarkable passing yardage performance tied for the fifth-best in school history. On defense, Isaiah Buggs dominated with three sacks and seven tackles, while Dylan Moses racked up nine total tackles (five solo).[220]

Passing	C/ATT	YDS	AVG	TD	INT	QBR
Tu. Tagovailoa	22/30	387	12.9	4	0	95.5
J. Hurts	3/3	28	9.3	0	0	7.9
Team	25/33	415	12.6	4	0	--

Rushing	CAR	YDS	AVG	TD	LONG
D. Harris	7	52	7.4	0	35
N. Harris	8	43	5.4	0	19
J. Jacobs	6	11	1.8	1	3
Tu. Tagovailoa	4	10	2.5	1	5
J. Hurts	3	-7	-2.3	0	3
Team	28	109	3.9	2	35

Interceptions	INT	YDS	TD
P. Surtain II	1	20	0
M. Wilson	1	0	0
Team	2	20	0

Punting	NO	YDS	AVG	TB	IN 20	LONG
S. DeLong	6	216	36	0	0	51

Receiving	REC	YDS	AVG	TD	LONG
H. Ruggs III	3	84	28	1	57
J. Jeudy	6	78	13	0	21
I. Smith Jr.	4	74	18.5	0	42
D. Smith	4	56	14	1	30
D. Harris	2	48	24	0	52
H. Hentges	2	29	14.5	2	23
J. Jacobs	1	25	25	0	25
J. Waddle	3	21	7	0	14
Team	25	415	16.6	4	57

Punt returns	NO	YDS	AVG	LONG	TD
J. Waddle	2	25	12.5	15	0

Kicking	FG	PCT	LONG	XP	PTS
J. Bulovas	1/1	100	47	6/6	9

Note: Table data from "Texas A&M 23-45 Alabama (Sep 22, 2018) Box Score" (221)

09/29/18 - Alabama (1) vs Louisiana

Team	1	2	3	4	T		Passing	Rushing	Total
Louisiana	0	0	0	14	14		88	200	288
Alabama (1)	28	21	7	0	56		340	268	608

The Alabama Crimson Tide started the game on an explosive note, marching down the field for a touchdown on their opening drive for the fifth consecutive game. Josh Jacobs capped off the 8-play, 72-yard drive with an untouched 9-yard scoring run. Louisiana's first offensive possession was short-lived, resulting in a three-and-out. On Louisiana's punt attempt, Derek Kief burst through the line, blocked the kick, and recovered the ball at the 14-yard line. Two plays later, Tua unleashed a 13-yard pass that found Henry Ruggs III streaking into the back of the end zone (14-0). After another Louisiana three-and out, Jaylen Waddle seized the opportunity on the ensuing punt, showcasing his game-breaking speed and elusiveness by weaving through defenders for an electrifying 63-yard punt return touchdown. The Tide's offensive onslaught continued, needing just five plays to go 69 yards, culminating in Jacobs' second rushing touchdown of the day from one yard out, making the score 28-0 with 2:28 left in the first quarter.

Three plays into the second quarter, Jalen Hurts connected with Henry Ruggs III for a 54-yard touchdown strike. Later in the quarter, Bama embarked on a methodical 10-play, 70-yard drive ending with Damien Harris bulldozing his way into the end zone for the last five yards and the score. Just before halftime, Tua found Jaylen Waddle for his first career receiving touchdown - a 20-yard scoring strike that extended the lead to 49-0 with 1:28 left in the half.

Late in the third, Mac Jones etched his name in Alabama's record books, finding Waddle on a 94-yard scoring strike, tying the second-longest passing touchdown in school history (56-0). The Ragin' Cajuns finally got on the board in the fourth quarter, scoring on a 1-yard touchdown run to cap a 78-yard drive in six plays. They added another score with 3:58 remaining, an 18-yard touchdown pass capping an 11-play, 80-yard drive, accounting for the final 56-14 margin.

Tua completed all eight of his pass attempts for 128 yards and two touchdowns. Josh Jacobs matched his career-best with a pair of rushing scores. Alabama amassed a staggering 608 total yards which marked the fifth game in which the Crimson Tide surpassed the 500-yard threshold this season. This was the first time in school history a Tide team has reached that milestone in five consecutive games. The 56 points accumulated by Alabama extended its streak to five consecutive games with 45 or more points scored, also a school record. On the defensive side, Deionte Thompson spearheaded the Tide's efforts, leading the team with seven tackles.[222]

Passing	C/ATT	YDS	AVG	TD	INT	QBR
Tu. Tagovailoa	8/8	128	16	2	0	98.3
J. Hurts	4/6	118	19.7	1	0	99.1
M. Jones	1/2	94	47	1	0	95.6
Team	13/16	340	21.3	4	0	--

Rushing	CAR	YDS	AVG	TD	LONG
N. Harris	11	73	6.6	1	30
B. Robinson Jr.	12	65	5.4	0	12
J. Jacobs	6	49	8.2	2	11
J. Ford	3	33	11	0	15
D. Harris	5	20	4	0	7
Tu. Tagovailoa	2	12	6	0	10
R. Clark	3	8	2.7	0	5
J. Hurts	4	8	2	0	7
Team	46	268	5.8	3	30

Interceptions	INT	YDS	TD
T. Diggs	1	0	0
X. McKinney	1	-7	0
Team	2	-7	0

Receiving	REC	YDS	AVG	TD	LONG
J. Waddle	3	138	46	2	94
H. Ruggs III	5	116	23.2	2	54
J. Jeudy	2	58	29	0	34
I. Smith Jr.	1	13	13	0	13
D. Smith	1	9	9	0	9
D. Harris	1	6	6	0	6
Team	13	340	26.2	4	94

Kick returns	NO	YDS	AVG	LONG	TD
B. Robinson Jr.	1	30	30	30	0
M. Forristall	1	4	4	4	0
Team	2	34	17	30	0

Punt returns	NO	YDS	AVG	LONG	TD
J. Waddle	1	63	63	63	1
D. Kief	1	17	17	17	0
Team	2	80	40	63	1

Kicking	FG	PCT	LONG	XP	PTS
J. Bulovas	0/2	0	0	8/8	8

Note: Table data from "Alabama 56-14 Louisiana (Sep 29, 2018) Box Score" (223)

269

10/06/18 - Alabama (1) at Arkansas

Team	1	2	3	4	T		Passing	Rushing	Total
Alabama (1)	21	20	7	17	**65**		393	246	**639**
Arkansas	7	7	3	14	**31**		233	172	**405**

It only took Alabama one play and 21 seconds to get on the board. On the first play of the game, Tua connected with Irv Smith Jr. who streaked up the sideline for a 76-yard touchdown, extending Alabama's streak of scoring on the opening drive to six games. The Tide quickly made it 14-0 when Tua found Smith again, this time on a 47-yard reception, but a forward fumble allowed Henry Ruggs III to pick it up and score from 12 yards out. After Arkansas went three-and-out, Alabama orchestrated a calculated 76-yard touchdown march. Junior running back Josh Jacobs capped the 8-play drive with a 1-yard plunge. The Razorbacks countered with a long drive of their own, marching 75 yards on 11 plays, culminating in an 8-yard scoring grab. Bama was on top 21-7 with 24 seconds left in the first quarter.

In the second quarter, a forced fumble by Dylan Moses at the Bama 1-yard line set up a 5-play, 99-yard scoring drive finished off with a 42-yard touchdown pass from Tua to Jeudy. Arkansas answered in seven plays with another 75-yard touchdown drive to cut the deficit to 28-14, but Alabama pulled away before halftime. Damien Harris carried the ball five times on the 8-play, 75-yard drive, with his last carry a 2-yard touchdown run. After the missed extra point, Alabama led 34-14. After forcing an Arkansas punt, Tua only needed a single play to hit Jeudy on a slant for a 60-yard score (their second hookup of the day) to make it 41-14 at the break.

Alabama stopped the Hogs on 4th-and-1 to start the second half, gaining possession at their own 44-yard line. Damien Harris ran six times and picked up all 44 yards on his own and scored on his final 1-yard carry, stretching the ball over the goal line. Arkansas trimmed the deficit to 48-17 with a 41-yard field goal on their next possession, then quarterback Jalen Hurts entered the game for the Tide. He put together a 10-play, 58-yard drive that ended with a 27-yard field goal from Bulovas. With 13:37 left in the game, Bama was in control 51-17. The Razorbacks' ensuing drive was cut short when Shyheim Carter snagged a deflected pass and raced for his second pick-six touchdown of the season. Arkansas responded with a touchdown to make it 58-24. Brian Robinson Jr. capped off an 11-play, 72-yard drive with a powerful 5-yard touchdown run late in the game. Not to be outdone, the Razorbacks found the end zone with 14 seconds left in the game on a 1-yard score, making the final tally 65-31 in Alabama's favor.

Dylan Moses was a force on defense, racking up ten tackles, including two for loss, while also forcing a fumble and applying QB pressure. Junior defensive back Deionte Thompson contributed with nine tackles and a pass breakup, solidifying the Tide's defensive dominance.[224]

Passing	C/ATT	YDS	AVG	TD	INT	QBR
Tu. Tagovailoa	10/13	334	25.7	4	0	99.7
J. Hurts	4/5	59	11.8	0	0	99.9
Team	14/18	393	21.8	4	0	--

Rushing	CAR	YDS	AVG	TD	LONG
D. Harris	15	111	7.4	2	19
N. Harris	7	63	9	0	23
J. Hurts	4	35	8.8	0	27
B. Robinson Jr.	6	23	3.8	1	7
J. Jacobs	5	10	2	1	9
Tu. Tagovailoa	3	7	2.3	0	3
Team	1	-3	-3	0	0
Team	41	246	6.0	4	27

Interceptions	INT	YDS	TD
S. Carter	1	44	1

Receiving	REC	YDS	AVG	TD	LONG
J. Jeudy	4	135	33.8	2	60
I. Smith Jr.	2	123	61.5	1	76
J. Waddle	4	49	12.3	0	17
D. Smith	2	40	20	0	26
H. Ruggs III	1	33	33	1	21
D. Harris	1	13	13	0	13
Team	14	393	28.1	4	76

Kick returns	NO	YDS	AVG	LONG	TD
J. Jacobs	3	42	14	20	0
B. Robinson Jr.	2	19	9.5	11	0
I. Smith Jr.	1	6	6	6	0
Team	6	67	11.2	37	0

Kicking	FG	PCT	LONG	XP	PTS
J. Bulovas	1/1	100	27	8/9	11

Note: Table data from "Alabama 65-31 Arkansas (Oct 6, 2018) Box Score" (225)

270

10/13/18 - Alabama (1) vs Missouri

Team	1	2	3	4	T	Passing	Rushing	Total
Missouri	10	0	0	0	10	142	70	212
Alabama (1)	13	17	2	7	39	380	184	564

Continuing their impressive streak, Tua connected with Jeudy for an 81-yard touchdown strike a mere 23 seconds into the game, marking the seventh straight contest in which the Crimson Tide found the end zone on their opening drive. Missouri's second offensive play resulted in a costly turnover, with Saivion Smith intercepting the pass at the Tigers' 47-yard line and returning it 33 yards, setting up Alabama's offense at the Missouri 14-yard line. Three plays later, Joseph Bulovas converted a 30-yard field goal, extending the Tide's lead to 10-0. Capitalizing on an Alabama fumble later in the quarter, the Tigers marched 37 yards in seven plays, settling for a 43-yard field goal to break the scoring drought. Not to be outdone, the Crimson Tide answered quickly with a 9-play, 67-yard drive, culminating in a 28-yard field goal to make it 13-3. Missouri wasted no time scoring again. In a 6-play, 73-yard sequence, the Tigers found the end zone on a 20-yard touchdown reception, cutting Bama's lead to 13-10.

The second quarter witnessed Alabama stretching their lead with back-to-back touchdowns in under two minutes. First, capping a 9-play, 75-yard drive, Tua found Irv Smith Jr. in the back of the end zone for a 2-yard score. Then, after Isaiah Buggs forced a fumble on his 14-yard sack that Anfernee Jennings pounced on at the MU 13-yard line, the Tide scored again. Tua hit DeVonta Smith for a 13-yard score, extending their lead to 27-10. As the second quarter progressed, Tua connected with DeVonta Smith once again, this time on a breathtaking 57-yard bomb, positioning the offense at the MU 17-yard line. Five plays later, Bulovas calmly split the uprights with a 20-yard field goal, stretching the advantage to 30-10 as the teams headed into halftime.

The only score in the third quarter came on the very last play when Quinnen Williams sacked Drew Lock for a 7-yard loss in the end zone for a safety. On the ensuing kickoff, Josh Jacobs returned the kick 50 yards to the Missouri 40-yard line. Hurts led Bama to a score in five plays and 1:28 with Damien Harris taking it in from two yards out (39-10). The Tigers drove down the field, and Saivion Smith snagged his second interception of the game, this time hauling it in at the back of the end zone to thwart the Tigers' late offensive threat.

Jerry Jeudy and DeVonta Smith each eclipsed 100 yards for the third straight game. Mack Wilson spearheaded the defensive effort with a team-best 11 tackles and a sack, complemented by Quinnen Williams' seven tackles and Alabama's first safety in three years.[226]

Passing	C/ATT	YDS	AVG	TD	INT	QBR
Tu. Tagovailoa	12/22	265	12	3	0	88.3
J. Hurts	7/8	115	14.4	0	0	86.8
Team	19/30	380	12.7	3	0	--

Rushing	CAR	YDS	AVG	TD	LONG
D. Harris	14	62	4.4	1	20
N. Harris	13	57	4.4	0	14
J. Jacobs	9	52	5.8	0	18
J. Hurts	3	15	5	0	9
B. Robinson Jr.	4	3	0.8	0	3
Tu. Tagovailoa	2	-5	-2.5	0	9
Team	45	184	4.1	1	20

Interceptions	INT	YDS	TD
S. Smith	2	33	0

Punting	NO	YDS	AVG	TB	IN 20	LONG
S. DeLong	1	12	12	0	0	12

Receiving	REC	YDS	AVG	TD	LONG
J. Jeudy	3	147	49	1	81
D. Smith	4	100	25	1	57
H. Ruggs III	4	50	12.5	0	29
D. Harris	2	31	15.5	0	20
J. Waddle	2	27	13.5	0	14
D. Kief	2	16	8	0	17
J. Hurts	1	7	7	0	7
I. Smith Jr.	1	2	2	1	2
Team	19	380	20	3	81

Punt returns	NO	YDS	AVG	LONG	TD
J. Waddle	1	1	1	1	0

Kicking	FG	PCT	LONG	XP	PTS
J. Bulovas	3/4	75	30	4/4	13

Note: Table data from "Alabama 39-10 Missouri (Oct 13, 2018) Box Score" (227)

271

10/20/18 - Alabama (1) at Tennessee

Team	1	2	3	4	T		Passing	Rushing	Total
Alabama (1)	28	14	16	0	58		327	218	545
Tennessee	0	14	7	0	21		227	31	258

Alabama wasted no time asserting its dominance, scoring on its opening drive for the eighth consecutive game. Tua connected with Jerry Jeudy for an 11-yard touchdown, capping a 9-play, 58-yard march. A 22-yard sack by Xavier McKinney that caused a fumble recovered by Christian Miller on Tennessee's third play set up a quick 3-yard scoring run by Josh Jacobs. After forcing a three-and-out, Tua only needed one play to score the third TD of the quarter. He hit Waddle in stride for a 77-yard touchdown strike. Their fourth scoring drive took a little longer than the first two. In 2:44, it was a methodical 9-play, 93-yard affair that saw Damien Harris punch it in from three yards out, making it 28-0 after the first quarter. Alabama's 28-point first quarter was only the fifth time an SEC team has scored that many points in the opening frame against a conference foe in the last 15 seasons. Remarkably, it was the second time the Tide accomplished the feat this year.

Tennessee finally got on the board with a 10-yard touchdown pass, but Alabama responded with an 8-play, 43-yard scoring drive after recovering the Tennessee onside kick. Jacobs scored his second touchdown from two yards out, making it 35-7. The Vols struck again on a 20-yard TD pass, but the Tide answered with an 85-yard touchdown drive in 2:01. It featured six straight Tua completions, including a 9-yard scoring strike to Irv Smith Jr., making it 42-14 at halftime.

The second half began with a safety on Tennessee's first snap, extending Alabama's lead to 44-14 just eight seconds into the third quarter. It was Alabama's second safety in as many games. Alabama extended its lead after the free kick, with Tua connecting with Henry Ruggs III for a 41-yard scoring strike. Tennessee managed to put points on the board through a defensive score. An interception was returned for a touchdown, resulting in a pick-six that made the score 51-21, still heavily in Alabama's favor. Hurts then broke the school QB rushing touchdown record with his 22nd career score from 21 yards out, part of an 8-play, 70-yard drive. A scoreless fourth quarter resulted in a 58-21 Alabama victory, its highest point total ever against Tennessee.

The Tide racked up over 500 yards of offense for the 8th straight game, a program first. Defensively, Deionte Thompson led with seven tackles and a forced fumble, while Xavier McKinney had five stops and a sack. Senior defensive lineman Isaiah Buggs and senior linebacker Christian Miller also registered sacks against the Vols.[228]

Passing	C/ATT	YDS	AVG	TD	INT	QBR
Tu. Tagovailoa	19/29	306	10.6	4	0	95.5
J. Hurts	2/3	21	7	0	1	93.3
Team	21/32	327	10.2	4	1	--

Rushing	CAR	YDS	AVG	TD	LONG
J. Jacobs	12	68	5.7	2	16
B. Robinson Jr.	13	60	4.6	0	20
N. Harris	9	50	5.6	0	14
J. Hurts	2	24	12	1	21
D. Harris	3	12	4	1	5
Tu. Tagovailoa	1	6	6	0	6
Team	2	-2	-1	0	0
Team	42	218	5.2	4	21

Kicking	FG	PCT	LONG	XP	PTS
J. Bulovas	0/0	0	0	8/8	8

Punting	NO	YDS	AVG	TB	IN 20	LONG
M. Bernier	2	82	41	0	0	41

Receiving	REC	YDS	AVG	TD	LONG
J. Waddle	4	117	29.3	1	77
J. Jeudy	5	72	14.4	1	31
H. Ruggs III	3	65	21.7	1	41
I. Smith Jr.	5	50	10	1	25
D. Harris	1	11	11	0	11
D. Kief	1	9	9	0	9
J. Jacobs	1	2	2	0	2
N. Harris	1	1	1	0	1
Team	21	327	15.6	4	77

Kick returns	NO	YDS	AVG	LONG	TD
J. Jacobs	3	63	21	42	0
B. Robinson Jr.	1	23	23	23	0
Team	4	86	21.5	42	0

Punt returns	NO	YDS	AVG	LONG	TD
J. Waddle	1	-7	-7	-7	0

Note: Table data from "Alabama 58-21 Tennessee (Oct 20, 2018) Box Score" (229)

11/03/18 - Alabama (1) at LSU (3)

Team	1	2	3	4	T		Passing	Rushing	Total
Alabama (1)	6	10	6	7	29		295	281	576
LSU (3)	0	0	0	0	0		184	12	196

Alabama's offense did not score on their opening possession for the first time this season, but they quickly made amends. On their second drive, they drove 78 yards in five plays and scored when Tua hit Henry Ruggs III for a 15-yard touchdown. The extra point was missed which made the score 6-0. The teams then traded punts for the rest of the quarter.

Alabama took 7:15 off the clock on a 15-play, 75-yard drive in the second quarter that ended with a 22-yard field goal by Joseph Bulovas. The Tide led 9-0 with 6:59 left in the second quarter. After getting the ball back near midfield with 1:42 left in the half, Tua struck again in just two plays. He connected with Jerry Jeudy for 29 yards, then he hit Irv Smith Jr. for a 25-yard score. Alabama took a 16-0 advantage into halftime, marking the ninth straight game Tua had multiple first-half touchdown passes.

Following an exchange of punts to start the second half, Alabama took over at its own 28-yard line with 8:11 left in the third quarter. Facing a daunting 3rd-and-15 situation, the Tide produced a well-executed 16-yard screen pass to Smith Jr. that provided the much-needed first down, allowing the drive to continue its momentum. Four plays later, the stage was set for Tua's heroics. On a 3rd-and-8, the elusive quarterback took matters into his own hands on a 44-yard touchdown scamper. This career-long run extended the Tide's lead to 22-0 with 5:14 remaining in the quarter after the extra point attempt was blocked.

In the fourth quarter, the Tide capped the scoring with an 8-play, 80-yard drive culminating in a 1-yard Najee Harris plunge. The 29-0 final score saw Alabama limit LSU to just 12 rushing yards while clinching the SEC West.

Quinnen Williams had a monster game, recording a career-high ten tackles, including 3.5 for loss, and 2.5 sacks. Savion Smith and Dylan Moses each made six stops, while Mack Wilson nabbed an interception in the dominant defensive effort.[230]

Passing	C/ATT	YDS	AVG	TD	INT	QBR
Tu. Tagovailoa	25/42	295	7	2	1	94

Rushing	CAR	YDS	AVG	TD	LONG
D. Harris	19	107	5.6	1	21
N. Harris	6	83	13.8	0	29
Tu. Tagovailoa	3	49	16.3	1	44
B. Robinson Jr.	4	27	6.8	0	16
J. Jacobs	4	17	4.3	0	7
Team	1	-2	-2	0	0
Team	37	281	7.6	2	44

Interceptions	INT	YDS	TD
M. Wilson	1	0	0

Punting	NO	YDS	AVG	TB	IN 20	LONG
M. Bernier	4	131	32.8	0	0	36

Receiving	REC	YDS	AVG	TD	LONG
J. Jeudy	8	103	12.9	0	30
I. Smith Jr.	4	64	16	1	25
H. Ruggs III	4	55	13.8	1	15
J. Waddle	4	44	11	0	28
J. Jacobs	2	23	11.5	0	17
D. Harris	3	6	2	0	5
Team	25	295	11.8	2	30

Punt returns	NO	YDS	AVG	LONG	TD
J. Waddle	1	-3	-3	-3	0

Kicking	FG	PCT	LONG	XP	PTS
J. Bulovas	1/1	100	23	2/4	5

Note: Table data from "Alabama 29-0 LSU (Nov 3, 2018) Box Score" (231)

273

11/10/18 - Alabama (1) vs Mississippi State (16)

Team	1	2	3	4	T		Passing	Rushing	Total
Mississippi State (16)	0	0	0	0	**0**		125	44	**169**
Alabama (1)	14	7	0	3	**24**		163	142	**305**

The Alabama Crimson Tide asserted their dominance over the Mississippi State Bulldogs right out of the gate. Their opening drive consisted of a balanced attack of rushing and passing going 73 yards in nine plays capped off by a 1-yard touchdown plunge by Damien Harris. It was the ninth time they have scored on their opening drive this season. After forcing a three-and-out, Alabama's offense took over at their own 17-yard line and embarked on another impressive drive. This time, it was Josh Jacobs who capped off the 13-play, 83-yard journey with a 1-yard touchdown run, extending the Tide's lead to 14-0.

The second quarter saw both teams trade punts, but a muffed punt by the Bulldogs gave Alabama a golden opportunity. Tua capitalized on the short field, only taking three plays to find Jacobs out of the backfield for a 14-yard touchdown pass, making the score 21-0 with 3:26 left before halftime.

The third quarter was a defensive stalemate, with neither team able to dent the scoreboard. However, midway through the fourth quarter, the Alabama defense stepped up once again, stopping the Bulldogs on fourth down and giving the offense excellent field position at the Mississippi State 42-yard line. Six plays later, Joseph Bulovas drilled a career-long 49-yard field goal, extending the Tide's lead to 24-0, which would ultimately be the final score.

Alabama's defense was relentless throughout the game, recording five sacks and limiting the Bulldogs to a mere 44 rushing yards. Dylan Moses and Quinnen Williams led the way with six tackles each. This was Alabama's 11th consecutive season and the 38th time in program history that the team has reached the impressive 10-win mark. The victory also extended its home winning streak to 24 consecutive games, tying the school record set from 1971-74. The Alabama defense recorded back-to-back shutouts for the first time since consecutive 49-0 victories over Western Carolina and Auburn in 2012.[232]

Passing	C/ATT	YDS	AVG	TD	INT	QBR
Tu. Tagovailoa	14/21	164	7.8	1	1	63.7
M. Jones	3/6	-1	-0.2	0	0	10.5
Team	17/27	163	6	1	1	--

Rushing	CAR	YDS	AVG	TD	LONG
J. Jacobs	20	97	4.9	1	17
D. Harris	14	53	3.8	1	12
N. Harris	3	16	5.3	0	8
Tu. Tagovailoa	8	-24	-3	0	10
Team	45	142	3.2	2	17

Punting	NO	YDS	AVG	TB	IN 20	LONG
M. Bernier	5	183	36.6	0	0	43

Receiving	REC	YDS	AVG	TD	LONG
I. Smith Jr.	5	70	14	0	25
J. Jeudy	6	45	7.5	0	13
J. Waddle	3	26	8.7	0	12
J. Jacobs	2	12	6	1	14
D. Smith	1	10	10	0	10
Team	17	163	9.6	1	25

Kick returns	NO	YDS	AVG	LONG	TD
J. Jacobs	1	27	27	27	0

Kicking	FG	PCT	LONG	XP	PTS
J. Bulovas	1/1	100	49	3/3	6

Note: Table data from "Alabama 24-0 Mississippi State (Nov 10, 2018) Box Score" (233)

11/17/18 - Alabama (1) vs Citadel

Team	1	2	3	4	T		Passing	Rushing	Total
Citadel	0	10	0	7	17		0	275	275
Alabama (1)	7	3	27	13	50		371	190	561

Alabama cruised to a 50-17 victory over The Citadel, showcasing their offensive firepower and defensive prowess. The win marked Alabama's 22nd season with at least 11 victories in school history and their tenth under Nick Saban. After forcing a punt, Alabama scored on its opening possession for the tenth time in 11 games this season, capping an 8-play, 80-yard drive with a 21-yard touchdown pass from Tua to Jaylen Waddle. The Citadel tied the game at 7-7 in the second quarter with a 45-yard touchdown run. Alabama responded with a 9-play, 86-yard drive, ending with a 23-yard field goal by Joseph Bulovas to take a 10-7 lead with 4:59 left in the half. The Bulldogs tied the game at 10-10 just before halftime with a 48-yard field goal.

After Alabama lost possession due to a fumble and The Citadel missed a field goal attempt to begin the third quarter, Tua completed three consecutive passes to Henry Ruggs III. The longest of these was a 54-yard play, which advanced the Crimson Tide to the Bulldogs' 3-yard line. Two plays later, Tua threw a 5-yard pass to Waddle for the duo's second touchdown of the day (17-10). Just 12 seconds later, Alabama found the end zone again. Deionte Thompson forced a fumble, and Anfernee Jennings scooped up the loose ball and raced 18 yards for a touchdown. This defensive score made it 24-10 in favor of the Crimson Tide.

In the third quarter, Alabama's offense continued to roll as Tua connected with Irv Smith Jr. for a big play. He found him wide open in the middle of the field, and he rumbled 68 yards to the end zone untouched, extending Alabama's lead to 30-10 after the missed PAT. With his touchdown pass, Tua broke the single-season school record of 30 set by A.J. McCarron in 2013, bringing his total for the year to 31. Later in the quarter, Tua added to his impressive stat line with his legs by scoring his fourth TD of the day. He capped off a 6-play, 63-yard drive with a 1-yard touchdown plunge, giving Alabama a commanding 37-10 lead heading into the fourth quarter.

Jalen Hurts entered the game at QB, and after a Damien Harris 73-yard run, Hurts threw a 7-yard touchdown pass to DeVonta Smith, making it 43-10 after the PAT was blocked. The Citadel managed to find the end zone for the second time that afternoon, this time on a 44-yard scamper along the sideline. However, Alabama was quick to respond as Brian Robinson Jr. powered his way into the promised land from just one yard away, capping off the scoring for the Crimson Tide at 50-17. Jennings led the Alabama defense with 11 tackles and an 18-yard fumble return for a touchdown in the third quarter scoring barrage. The Crimson Tide extended their streak of winning 11 games or more to eight consecutive seasons, the longest in SEC history.[234]

Passing	C/ATT	YDS	AVG	TD	INT	QBR
Tu. Tagovailoa	18/22	340	15.5	3	0	95.1
J. Hurts	3/4	31	7.8	1	0	91
Team	21/26	371	14.3	4	0	--

Rushing	CAR	YDS	AVG	TD	LONG
D. Harris	7	83	11.9	0	73
N. Harris	4	51	12.8	0	32
Tu. Tagovailoa	4	37	9.3	1	16
R. Clark	3	14	4.7	0	7
B. Robinson Jr.	2	4	2	1	2
J. Jacobs	2	3	1.5	0	4
Team	1	-2	-2	0	0
Team	23	190	8.3	2	73

Punting	NO	YDS	AVG	TB	IN 20	LONG
M. Bernier	1	34	34	0	0	34

Receiving	REC	YDS	AVG	TD	LONG
H. Ruggs III	6	114	19	0	54
J. Waddle	6	90	15	2	29
J. Jeudy	6	77	12.8	0	22
I. Smith Jr.	1	68	68	1	68
J. Jacobs	1	15	15	0	15
D. Smith	1	7	7	1	7
Team	21	371	17.7	4	68

Kick returns	NO	YDS	AVG	LONG	TD
B. Robinson Jr.	1	12	12	12	0
M. Forristall	1	1	1	1	0
Team	2	13	6.5	12	0

Kicking	FG	PCT	LONG	XP	PTS
J. Bulovas	1/1	100	23	4/6	7
A. Jones	0/0	0	0	1/1	1
Team	1/1	100	23	5/7	8

Note: Table data from "Alabama 50-17 The Citadel (Nov 17, 2018) Box Score" (235)

11/24/18 - Alabama (1) vs Auburn

Team	1	2	3	4	T		Passing	Rushing	Total
Auburn	7	7	7	0	21		153	130	283
Alabama (1)	7	10	21	14	52		377	123	500

The Iron Bowl between Alabama and Auburn began with both teams exchanging punts. However, on their second possession, the Crimson Tide found the scoreboard. After an Auburn penalty gave Alabama a short field, Tua capped a 5-play drive with a 7-yard rushing touchdown to put the Tide up 7-0. The Tigers quickly responded, marching 73 yards in ten plays and scoring on a 9-yard rushing touchdown to tie the game at 7-7. Alabama answered on its next drive, highlighted by a critical 21-yard scramble by Tua on 3rd down to keep the chains moving. This set them up at the Auburn 39-yard line, and five plays later, Tua threw a 4-yard screen pass to Henry Ruggs III to regain the lead at 14-7. Later in the quarter, Joseph Bulovas hit a 30-yard field goal to cap a 10-play, 57-yard drive and extend Alabama's advantage to 17-7. However, a blocked punt set up the Tigers with great field position at their own 23-yard line, and they scored on a 23-yard trick play wide receiver pass to cut their deficit to 17-14 at the end of the first half.

Alabama's offense exploded in the third quarter, with Tua leading a series of impressive drives. On the first possession, he delivered a pinpoint pass to Jerry Jeudy who raced 46 yards into the end zone, capping a 5-play, 75-yard drive and extending Alabama's lead to 24-14. The Crimson Tide struck again just three minutes later as Tua found Josh Jacobs for a 33-yard touchdown. Jacobs made an acrobatic over-the-shoulder catch to make the score 31-14. However, Auburn refused to go away quietly. The Tigers responded with a 52-yard touchdown pass of their own, cutting Alabama's advantage to 31-21. Tua and the Tide offense wasted no time in answering. In just over a minute, Tua connected with DeVonta Smith for a 40-yard touchdown, his fourth passing score of the game. The 3-play, 60-yard drive extended Alabama's lead to 38-21.

The scoring onslaught continued in the fourth quarter with Tua throwing a 22-yard touchdown pass to Ruggs III who made a beautiful leaping catch to make it 45-21. After Anfernee Jennings picked off Jarrett Stidham's pass, Jalen Hurts entered the game and threw a 53-yard touchdown pass to Jaylen Waddle on his first snap to provide the final margin of 52-21.

Defensively, Anfernee Jennings led Alabama with eight tackles, one sack, and an interception. Dylan Moses and LaBryan Ray paced the defense with nine tackles each. Ray also contributed to one of the Tide's three sacks during the game. Tua accounted for six total touchdowns (five through the air and one on the ground), setting a single-game school record. As a result, he went from fifth to a second-place tie on Alabama's career passing touchdowns list at 47. The win completed a perfect 12-0 (8-0 in the SEC) regular season for Alabama.[236]

Passing	C/ATT	YDS	AVG	TD	INT	QBR
Tu. Tagovailoa	25/32	324	10.1	5	0	97.6
J. Hurts	1/1	53	53	1	0	99.9
Team	26/33	377	11.4	6	0	--

Rushing	CAR	YDS	AVG	TD	LONG
D. Harris	9	41	4.6	0	8
J. Jacobs	5	28	5.6	0	13
Tu. Tagovailoa	4	26	6.5	1	21
N. Harris	7	25	3.6	0	15
J. Hurts	1	3	3	0	3
Team	26	123	4.7	1	21

Interceptions	INT	YDS	TD
A. Jennings	1	8	0

Punting	NO	YDS	AVG	TB	IN 20	LONG
M. Bernier	4	164	41	0	0	48

Receiving	REC	YDS	AVG	TD	LONG
J. Jeudy	5	77	15.4	1	46
J. Waddle	3	73	24.3	1	53
D. Smith	4	72	18	1	40
H. Ruggs III	5	62	12.4	2	22
J. Jacobs	4	53	13.3	1	33
I. Smith Jr.	3	27	9	0	11
D. Harris	1	11	11	0	11
N. Harris	1	2	2	0	2
Team	26	377	14.5	6	53

Punt returns	NO	YDS	AVG	LONG	TD
J. Waddle	1	0	0	0	0

Kicking	FG	PCT	LONG	XP	PTS
J. Bulovas	1/1	100	30	7'7	10

Note: Table data from "Auburn 21-52 Alabama (Nov 24, 2018) Box Score" (237)

276

12/01/18 - Alabama (1) at Georgia (4)

Team	1	2	3	4	T		Passing	Rushing	Total
Alabama (1)	0	14	7	14	35		246	157	403
Georgia (4)	7	14	7	0	28		301	153	454

Neither team scored on their first two drives. The Bulldogs broke the deadlock late in the first quarter with a 20-yard TD pass. Alabama responded quickly as Jacobs rushed for a 1-yard touchdown on the first play of the second quarter, capping an 8-play, 75-yard drive that was highlighted by a 23-yard pass from Tua to Ruggs III that put Alabama inside UGA territory. In the second quarter, Georgia found its rhythm, finding the end zone twice. The first score came on a 9-yard rushing TD that capped a 13-play, 74-yard drive. On their next possession after forcing Alabama to punt, they ran four straight times before Fromm threw an 11-yard TD. This 6-play, 51-yard drive extended their lead to 21-7. Alabama struck back immediately as Jacobs ran 59 yards on the first play of the ensuing drive. Two plays later, on 1st-and-goal from the one, he took the handoff, fumbled it into the end zone, and recovered it for the touchdown (21-14, UGA). The Alabama defense then forced a Georgia punt as time expired in the first half.

After an Alabama three-and-out to start the second half, Georgia scored in three plays going 51 yards (28-14). The Tide responded when Tua connected with Waddle on a 51-yard scoring strike after Georgia missed a 30-yard FG attempt. The quick 4-play, 72-yard TD drive consumed just 1:29 off the clock and reduced the deficit to 28-21. Alabama tied the score with a 16-play, 80-yard TD drive. Hurts entered the game early in the drive after Tua sustained an injury and proceeded to lead Bama down the field. On a crucial 3rd-and-10 play, he scrambled out of the pocket and found Jeudy in the end zone for the TD, tying the game at 28-28.

The Georgia fake punt attempt fell short, failing to pick up the necessary yardage for a first down. Undeterred, Hurts led the Crimson Tide offense back onto the field, starting from their own 48-yard line. Two impressive completions, each gaining over 15 yards, moved the ball into the red zone. With the game on the line, Hurts took matters into his own hands, sprinting 15 yards into the end zone for the touchdown (35-28). With just 57 seconds remaining on the clock, Alabama's defense stepped up to seal the victory. Batting down a pair of passes in the end zone, they thwarted Georgia's last-ditch efforts to tie the game.

Josh Jacobs earned MVP honors as he scored the team's first two TDs and led them in rushing with an impressive 83 yards on just eight carries. Alabama's defense, which allowed 21 points in the first half, made a remarkable comeback in the second half. They limited the Bulldogs to a single touchdown early in the third. Saivion Smith emerged as the game's top tackler, setting a new career-best record with 11 tackles, including eight solo stops. It was the second-most tackles by a Bama player in an SEC Championship Game. Deionte Thompson and Quinnen Williams each recorded eight tackles, with Williams adding a sack and two tackles for loss.[238]

Passing	C/ATT	YDS	AVG	TD	INT	QBR
Tu. Tagovailoa	10/25	164	6.6	1	2	29.2
J. Hurts	7/9	82	9.1	1	0	99.4
Team	17/34	246	7.2	2	2	--

Rushing	CAR	YDS	AVG	TD	LONG
J. Jacobs	8	83	10.4	2	59
D. Harris	9	52	5.8	0	14
J. Hurts	5	28	5.6	1	15
N. Harris	4	15	3.8	0	17
Tu. Tagovailoa	3	-21	-7	0	0
Team	29	157	5.4	3	59

Punting	NO	YDS	AVG	TB	IN 20	LONG
M. Bernier	5	201	40.2	0	0	46

Receiving	REC	YDS	AVG	TD	LONG
J. Waddle	4	113	28.3	1	51
H. Ruggs III	3	49	16.3	0	23
I. Smith Jr.	3	35	11.7	0	19
D. Smith	3	26	8.7	0	13
J. Jeudy	3	24	8	1	12
D. Harris	1	-1	-1	0	0
Team	17	246	14.5	2	51

Punt returns	NO	YDS	AVG	LONG	TD
J. Waddle	1	36	36	36	0

Kicking	FG	PCT	LONG	XP	PTS
J. Bulovas	0/0	0	0	5/5	5

Note: Table data from "Alabama 35-28 Georgia (Dec 1, 2018) Box Score" (239)

277

12/29/18 - Alabama (1) vs Oklahoma (4)

Team	1	2	3	4	T		Passing	Rushing	Total
Oklahoma (4)	0	10	10	14	34		308	163	471
Alabama (1)	21	10	0	14	45		328	200	528

Alabama's offense exploded in the opening minutes, with Tua connecting with DeVonta Smith for a 50-yard gain on the first play. Six plays later, Damien Harris punched it in from the 1-yard line, putting the Tide on the scoreboard. After Oklahoma's offense stalled, Tua found Ruggs III in the back of the end zone for a toe-tapping 10-yard touchdown. Alabama's third drive ended with Harris' second 1-yard touchdown run, capping a 5-play, 61-yard drive and giving the Crimson Tide a 21-0 lead in the first quarter of play.

The onslaught continued in the second quarter with Tua finding Josh Jacobs out of the backfield, and Jacobs scampering 27 yards for Alabama's fourth score (28-0). Oklahoma finally got on the board with a touchdown and a field goal to make it 28-10, but Alabama responded as Bulovas booted a 37-yard field goal just before halftime to give the Tide a 31-10 advantage at the break.

Oklahoma scored a 26-yard field goal and a 49-yard receiving touchdown in the third quarter, narrowing Alabama's lead to 31-20 before the final quarter. Alabama failed to score any points in the third as they only got the ball twice. They punted once and were driving when the third quarter expired.

In the fourth quarter, Smith caught another quick slant, this one going for a 10-yard touchdown. This completed the 9-play, 87-yard drive and extended Alabama's lead to 38-20. Oklahoma responded with its second touchdown of the half, cutting their deficit to 38-27, but the Tide came right back and scored again. Tua found Jeudy for a 13-yard score, ending a 5-play, 46-yard drive and putting Alabama up 45-27. The Sooners scored again with 4:23 remaining, cutting the deficit to 45-34, but Alabama secured the onside kick and ran out the clock for the win.

Dylan Moses spearheaded the defensive effort with six tackles, while Xavier McKinney contributed five tackles and a game-high four pass breakups.[240]

Passing	C/ATT	YDS	AVG	TD	INT	QBR
Tu. Tagovailoa	24/27	318	11.8	4	0	95.3
J. Hurts	1/1	10	10	0	0	82.9
Team	25/28	328	11.7	4	0	--

Rushing	CAR	YDS	AVG	TD	LONG
J. Jacobs	15	98	6.5	0	19
D. Harris	13	48	3.7	2	11
N. Harris	6	45	7.5	0	16
Tu. Tagovailoa	5	9	1.8	0	9
J. Hurts	1	4	4	0	4
Team	2	-4	-2	0	0
Team	42	200	4.8	2	19

Punting	NO	YDS	AVG	TB	IN 20	LONG
M. Bernier	2	56	28	0	0	34

Receiving	REC	YDS	AVG	TD	LONG
D. Smith	6	104	17.3	1	50
J. Jeudy	4	73	18.3	1	40
J. Jacobs	4	60	15	1	27
D. Harris	2	25	12.5	0	15
J. Waddle	2	20	10	0	11
I. Smith Jr.	2	19	9.5	0	13
H. Ruggs III	3	14	4.7	1	10
J. Hurts	1	9	9	0	9
N. Harris	1	4	4	0	4
Team	25	328	13.1	4	50

Kicking	FG	PCT	LONG	XP	PTS
J. Bulovas	1/1	100	38	6/6	9

Note: Table data from "Alabama 45-34 Oklahoma (Dec 29, 2018) Box Score" (241)

01/07/19 - Alabama (1) vs Clemson (2)

Team	1	2	3	4	T		Passing	Rushing	Total
Clemson (2)	14	17	13	0	44		347	135	482
Alabama (1)	13	3	0	0	16		295	148	443

The Alabama Crimson Tide opened the game on defense, forcing the Clemson Tigers into a quick three-and-out possession. However, on the Tide's third offensive play, Tua threw an ill-advised pass that was intercepted by Clemson cornerback A.J. Terrell who returned it 44 yards for a touchdown to give the Tigers an early 7-0 lead. Tua quickly shook off the mistake and led Alabama on a lightning-quick 3-play, 75-yard touchdown drive, capped by a 62-yard scoring strike to wide receiver Jerry Jeudy to tie the game at 7-7. But the Tigers answered in 90 seconds when Trevor Lawrence connected with Tee Higgins for a 62-yard gain. Two plays later, running back Travis Etienne punched it in from 17 yards out to put Clemson back on top 14-7. The Tide offense kept battling, going on a methodical 10-play, 75-yard touchdown drive. Tua found TE Hale Hentges wide open in the back of the end zone for a 1-yard score. However, the extra point was missed, leaving Clemson clinging to a 14-13 lead.

After another Clemson three-and-out, Alabama took its first lead of the game on a field goal after driving 45 yards in 11 plays. Joseph Bulovas converted a 25-yard field goal to make it 16-14. But the Tigers answered right back, going 65 yards in 11 plays, capped by another Etienne 1-yard touchdown run to go up 21-16. Tua's second interception, this one returned 46 yards to the Alabama 47-yard line, set up Clemson's next scoring drive. Eight plays later, Lawrence found Etienne for a 5-yard touchdown pass to extend the lead to 28-16. The Tigers added a 36-yard field goal with only 45 seconds remaining in the half to take a 31-16 lead into the locker room.

Alabama's opening second-half drive stalled after a failed fake field goal, while Clemson's subsequent possession resulted in a 74-yard touchdown pass, extending their lead to 37-16. Later, a Clemson 12-play, 89-yard drive ended with a 5-yard touchdown pass, extending its lead to 44-16. The game remained scoreless in the fourth quarter. Defensively, McKinney had seven tackles and a pass breakup, while Mack Wilson and Isaiah Buggs each had six tackles.[242]

Passing	C/ATT	YDS	AVG	TD	INT	QBR
Tu. Tagovailoa	22/34	295	8.7	2	2	58.8
J. Hurts	0/2	0	0	0	0	2.8
Team	22/36	295	8.2	2	2	--

Rushing	CAR	YDS	AVG	TD	LONG
N. Harris	9	59	6.6	0	13
D. Harris	11	57	5.2	0	15
J. Jacobs	11	47	4.3	0	11
M. Jones	1	-2	-2	0	0
J. Hurts	1	-4	-4	0	0
Tu. Tagovailoa	4	-9	-2.3	0	0
Team	37	148	4	0	15

Punting	NO	YDS	AVG	TB	IN 20	LONG
M. Bernier	2	100	50	0	1	55

Receiving	REC	YDS	AVG	TD	LONG
J. Jeudy	5	139	27.8	1	62
D. Smith	6	65	10.8	0	23
I. Smith Jr.	4	43	10.8	0	21
J. Waddle	2	25	12.5	0	19
J. Jacobs	1	16	16	0	16
H. Ruggs III	1	3	3	0	3
D. Harris	2	3	1.5	0	7
H. Hentges	1	1	1	1	1
Team	22	295	13.4	2	62

Kick returns	NO	YDS	AVG	LONG	TD
J. Jacobs	1	30	30	30	0

Punt returns	NO	YDS	AVG	LONG	TD
J. Waddle	1	7	7	7	0

Kicking	FG	PCT	LONG	XP	PTS
J. Bulovas	1/1	100	25	1/2	4

Note: Table data from "Clemson 44-16 Alabama (Jan 7, 2019) Box Score" (243)

Season Stats

Record	14-1	2nd of 130
SEC Record	9-0	
Rank	2	
Points for	684	
Points against	271	
Points/game	45.6	3rd of 130
Opp points/game	18.1	12th of 130
SOS[12]	6.63	3rd of 130

Team stats (averages per game)

		Passing					Rushing				Total Offense		
Split	G	Cmp	Att	Pct	Yds	TD	Att	Yds	Avg	TD	Plays	Yds	Avg
Offense	15	20.1	29.2	68.7	323.6	3.5	38.1	198.4	5.2	2.2	67.3	522	7.8
Defense	15	16.3	31	52.5	198.3	1.5	34.3	122	3.6	0.7	65.3	320.3	4.9
Difference		3.8	-1.8	16.2	125.3	2	3.8	76.4	1.6	1.5	2	201.7	2.9

	First Downs				Penalties		Turnovers		
Split	Pass	Rush	Pen	Tot	No.	Yds	Fum	Int	Tot
Offense	13	10.3	1.4	24.7	5.8	53.1	0.5	0.5	1
Defense	8.7	6.2	1.9	16.9	6.1	51.7	0.5	0.9	1.4
Difference	4.3	4.1	-0.5	7.8	-0.3	1.4	0	-0.4	-0.4

Passing

							Passing				
Rk	Player	G	Cmp	Att	Pct	Yds	Y/A	AY/A	TD	Int	Rate
1	Tua Tagovailoa	15	245	355	69	3966	11.2	12.8	43	6	199.4
2	Jalen Hurts	13	51	70	72.9	765	10.9	11.9	8	2	196.7
3	Mac Jones	6	5	13	38.5	123	9.5	11	1	0	143.3

Rushing and receiving

			Rushing				Receiving				Scrimmage			
Rk	Player	G	Att	Yds	Avg	TD	Rec	Yds	Avg	TD	Plays	Yds	Avg	TD
1	Damien Harris	15	150	876	5.8	9	22	204	9.3	0	172	1080	6.3	9
2	Joshua Jacobs	15	120	640	5.3	11	20	247	12.4	3	140	887	6.3	14
3	Najee Harris	15	117	783	6.7	4	4	7	1.8	0	121	790	6.5	4
4	Brian Robinson Jr.	15	63	272	4.3	2					63	272	4.3	2
5	Tua Tagovailoa	15	57	190	3.3	5					57	190	3.3	5
6	Jalen Hurts	13	36	167	4.6	2	2	16	8	0	38	183	4.8	2
7	Ronnie Clark	4	10	33	3.3	0					10	33	3.3	0
8	Jerome Ford	4	7	37	5.3	0					7	37	5.3	0
9	Mac Jones	6	3	-8	-2.7	0					3	-8	-2.7	0
10	Jerry Jeudy	15					68	1315	19.3	14	68	1315	19.3	14
11	Henry Ruggs III	15					46	741	16.1	11	46	741	16.1	11
12	Jaylen Waddle	15					45	848	18.8	7	45	848	18.8	7
13	Irv Smith Jr	15					44	710	16.1	7	44	710	16.1	7
14	DeVonta Smith	13					42	693	16.5	6	42	693	16.5	6
15	Derek Kief	15					4	39	9.8	1	4	39	9.8	1
16	Hale Hentges	3					4	34	8.5	3	4	34	8.5	3

Defense and fumbles

Rk	Player	G	Tackles					Def Int					Fumbles		
			Solo	Ast	Tot	Loss	Sk	Int	Yds	Avg	TD	PD	FR	TD	FF
1	Dylan Moses	15	45	41	86	10	3.5					1			1
2	Deionte Thompson	14	47	31	78	3.5	0	2	65	32.5	0	6	1		3
3	Xavier McKinney	15	45	29	74	6	3	2	23	11.5	1	10			2
4	Quinnen Williams	15	45	26	71	19.5	8					1			
5	Mack Wilson	15	33	32	65	4.5	1	2	0	0	0	5			
6	Saivion Smith	14	36	24	60	0.5	0	3	71	23.7	1	5			1
7	Raekwon Davis	14	24	31	55	5.5	1.5								
8	Isaiah Buggs	15	23	29	52	13.5	9.5					3	1		2
9	Anfernee Jennings	15	26	24	50	13	5.5	1	8	8	0	11	2	1	0
10	Shyheim Carter	12	26	17	43	3.5	0	2	89	44.5	2	10			1
11	Labryan Ray	13	19	20	39	6	2.5					2			
12	Patrick Surtain II	15	28	9	37	1.5	0	1	20	20	0	7			1
13	Christian Miller	14	16	18	34	11	8					1	1		0
14	Trevon Diggs	6	18	2	20	0	0	1	0	0	0	6			1
15	Phidarian Mathis	11	4	14	18	0	0						1		0
16	Jared Mayden	10	8	9	17	1	1					2			
17	Markail Benton	8	4	10	14	0	0								
18	Joshua McMillon	5	11	3	14	1	0								
19	Keaton Anderson	5	8	4	12	0	0								
20	Ale Kaho	9	5	5	10	0	0						1		0
21	Eyabi Okie	6	6	3	9	2	0								
22	Josh Jobe	4	7	1	8	0	0					1			
23	Jamey Mosley	6	4	4	8	3	1					1			
24	Daniel Wright	2	5	3	8	0	0					2			
25	Johnny Dwight	6	3	4	7	1.5	0.5					1			
26	Kyriq McDonald	5	4	3	7	0	0								
27	Henry Ruggs III	15	6	1	7	0	0								
28	D.J. Lewis	5	2	4	6	0	0								
29	Preston Malone	1	3	3	6	0.5	0								
30	Jaylen Moody	4	2	3	5	0	0								
31	Stephon Wynn Jr.	3	1	2	3	0	0								
32	Tevita Musika	2	0	2	2	0	0								
33	Thomas Fletcher	1	0	1	1	0	0								
34	Jerome Ford	4	0	1	1	0	0								
35	Joshua Jacobs	15	0	1	1	0	0							1	
36	Derek Kief	15	1	0	1	0	0								
37	Nigel Knott	1	1	0	1	0	0								
38	Cameron Latu	1	0	1	1	0	0								
39	Ross Pierschbacher	1	1	0	1	0	0								
40	Irv Smith Jr	15	0	1	1	0	0								
41	Tua Tagovailoa	15	1	0	1	0	0								

Kick and punt returns

Rk	Player	G	Kick Ret				Punt Ret			
			Ret	Yds	Avg	TD	Ret	Yds	Avg	TD
1	Joshua Jacobs	15	14	428	30.6	1				
2	Brian Robinson Jr.	15	5	84	16.8	0				
3	Miller Forristall	2	2	5	2.5	0				
4	Irv Smith Jr	15	1	6	6	0				
5	Jaylen Waddle	15					16	233	14.6	1
6	Derek Kief	15					1	17	17	0

281

Kicking and punting

			Kicking							Punting		
Rk	Player	G	XPM	XPA	XP%	FGM	FGA	FG%	Pts	Punts	Yds	Avg
1	Joseph Bulovas	14	75	81	92.6	14	18	77.8	117			
2	Austin Jones	3	8	11	72.7	1	2	50	11			
3	Mike Bernier	8								25	951	38
4	Skyler Delong	5								16	551	34.4

Scoring

			Touchdowns							Kicking				
Rk	Player	G	Rush	Rec	Int	FR	PR	KR	Tot	XPM	FGM	2PM	Sfty	Pts
1	Joseph Bulovas	14								75	14			117
2	Joshua Jacobs	15	11	3		1		1	16					96
3	Jerry Jeudy	15		14					14					84
4	Henry Ruggs III	15		11					11					66
5	Damien Harris	15	9						9					54
6	Jaylen Waddle	15		7			1		8					48
7	Irv Smith Jr	15		7					7					42
8	DeVonta Smith	13		6					6					36
9	Tua Tagovailoa	15	5						5					30
10	Najee Harris	15	4						4					24
11	Hale Hentges	3		3					3					18
12	Brian Robinson Jr.	15	2						2					12
13	Shyheim Carter	12			2				2					12
14	Jalen Hurts	13	2						2					12
15	Austin Jones	3								8	1			11
16	Saivion Smith	14			1				1					6
17	Derek Kief	15		1					1					6
18	Anfernee Jennings	15				1			1					6
19	Xavier McKinney	15			1				1					6

Stats include bowl games
Note: Table data from "2018 Alabama Crimson Tide Stats" (12)

Awards and honors

Name	Award	Type
Damien Harris	Permanent Team Captain	Team
Hale Hentges	Permanent Team Captain	Team
Christian Miller	Permanent Team Captain	Team
Ross Piersbacher	Permanent Team Captain	Team
Tua Tagovailoa	MVP	Team
Jerry Jeudy	Offensive Player of the Year	Team
Ross Piersbacher	Offensive Player of the Year	Team
Tua Tagovailoa	Offensive Player of the Year	Team
Isaiah Buggs	Defensive Player of the Year	Team
Xavier McKinney	Defensive Player of the Year	Team
Quinnen Williams	Defensive Player of the Year	Team
Mike Locksley	Offensive Coordinator of the Year	SEC
Tua Tagovailoa	Offensive Player of the Year	SEC
Jaylen Waddle	Freshman of the Year (Offense)	SEC
Patrick Surtain II	Freshman of the Year (Defense)	SEC
Jerry Jeudy	AP All-SEC First Team	SEC
Tua Tagovailoa	AP All-SEC First Team	SEC
Deionte Thompson	AP All-SEC First Team	SEC
Jonah Williams	AP All-SEC First Team	SEC
Quinnen Williams	AP All-SEC First Team	SEC
Isaiah Buggs	AP All-SEC Second Team	SEC
Irv Smith	AP All-SEC Second Team	SEC
Josh Jacobs	AP All-SEC Second Team	SEC
Ross Piersbacher	AP All-SEC Second Team	SEC
Jaylen Waddle	AP All-SEC Second Team	SEC
Raekwon Davis	AP All-SEC Third Team	SEC
Damien Harris	AP All-SEC Third Team	SEC
Jerry Jeudy	Coaches' All-SEC First Team	SEC
Tua Tagovailoa	Coaches' All-SEC First Team	SEC
Deionte Thompson	Coaches' All-SEC First Team	SEC
Jonah Williams	Coaches' All-SEC First Team	SEC
Quinnen Williams	Coaches' All-SEC First Team	SEC

Name	Award	Type
Isaiah Buggs	Coaches' All-SEC Second Team	SEC
Damien Harris	Coaches' All-SEC Second Team	SEC
Alex Leatherwood	Coaches' All-SEC Second Team	SEC
Dylan Moses	Coaches' All-SEC Second Team	SEC
Ross Piersbacher	Coaches' All-SEC Second Team	SEC
Irv Smith	Coaches' All-SEC Second Team	SEC
Mack Wilson	Coaches' All-SEC Second Team	SEC
Jonah Williams	Jacobs Blocking Trophy	SEC
Hale Hentges	Scholar-Athlete of the Year	SEC
Jerry Jeudy	AFCA All-America Team	National
Tua Tagovailoa	AFCA All-America Team	National
Deionte Thompson	AFCA All-America Team	National
Jonah Williams	AFCA All-America Team	National
Quinnen Williams	AFCA All-America Team	National
Isaiah Buggs	AFCA All-America Second Team	National
Irv Smith	AFCA All-America Second Team	National
Mack Wilson	AFCA All-America Second Team	National
Jerry Jeudy	AP All-America First Team	National
Deionte Thompson	AP All-America First Team	National
Jonah Williams	AP All-America First Team	National
Quinnen Williams	AP All-America First Team	National
Ross Piersbacher	AP All-America Second Team	National
Tua Tagovailoa	AP All-America Second Team	National
Jerry Jeudy	Biletnikoff Award	National
Mike Locksley	Broyles Award	National
Deionte Thompson	Consensus All-American	National
Tua Tagovailoa	Consensus All-American	National
Deionte Thompson	Consensus All-American	National
Jonah Williams	Consensus All-American	National
Quinnen Williams	Consensus All-American	National
Jonah Williams	FWAA All-America First Team	National
Quinnen Williams	FWAA All-America First Team	National
Tua Tagovailoa	FWAA All-America Second Team	National
Deionte Thompson	FWAA All-America Second Team	National
Tua Tagovailoa	Heisman Trophy Finalist	National
Tua Tagovailoa	Maxwell Award	National
Quinnen Williams	Outland Trophy	National
Jerry Jeudy	Sporting News (TSN) All-America Team	National
Ross Piersbacher	Sporting News (TSN) All-America Team	National
Tua Tagovailoa	Sporting News (TSN) All-America Team	National
Deionte Thompson	Sporting News (TSN) All-America Team	National
Jonah Williams	Sporting News (TSN) All-America Team	National
Quinnen Williams	Sporting News (TSN) All-America Team	National
Jonah Williams	Unanimous All-American	National
Quinnen Williams	Unanimous All-American	National
Tua Tagovailoa	Walter Camp Award	National
Isaiah Buggs	Senior Bowl	All-Star Team
Ross Piersbacher	Senior Bowl	All-Star Team

NFL

Season	Year drafted	Round	Pick	Overall	Player	Position	Team
2018	2019	1	3	3	Quinnen Williams	DT	New York Jets
2018	2019	1	11	11	Jonah Williams	OT	Cincinnati Bengals
2018	2019	1	24	24	Josh Jacobs	RB	Las Vegas Raiders
2018	2019	2	18	50	Irv Smith Jr.	TE	Minnesota Vikings
2018	2019	3	24	87	Damien Harris	RB	New England Patriots
2018	2019	4	13	115	Christian Miller	LB	Carolina Panthers
2018	2019	5	1	139	Deionte Thompson	S	Arizona Cardinals
2018	2019	5	15	153	Ross Pierschbacher	OG	Washington Commanders
2018	2019	5	17	155	Mack Wilson	LB	Cleveland Browns
2018	2019	6	20	192	Isaiah Buggs	DT	Pittsburgh Steelers

Note: Table data from "2018 Alabama Crimson Tide football team" (212)

283

2019

Overall

Record	11-2
SEC Record	6-2
Rank	8
Points for	614
Points against	242
Points/game	47.2
Opp points/game	18.6
SOS[13]	2.81

If it's my philosophy that we should play 12 power five schools, I'd say the answer to that would be "yes". But that's a philosophical answer, a'ight. And that's not the way it is. A'ight, so, I don't know why you would ask me that question. As if I could do something about it. When I can't do anything about it. So we're playing the best teams we can get to play us. Why don't you start calling around and see if you can get somebody else to play us, and we'll play 'em. We'll play anybody you can get to play us. -Nick Saban

Games

Date	Bama Rank		Opp Rank	Opponent	Bama	Opp	Result	SEC
08/31/19	2	N		Duke	42	3	W	
09/07/19	2	vs		New Mexico State	62	10	W	
09/14/19	2	@		South Carolina	47	23	W	W
09/21/19	2	vs		Southern Mississippi	49	7	W	
09/28/19	2	vs		Ole Miss	59	31	W	W
10/12/19	1	@	24	Texas A&M	47	28	W	W
10/19/19	1	vs		Tennessee	35	13	W	W
10/26/19	1	vs		Arkansas	48	7	W	W
11/09/19	3	vs	2	LSU	41	46	L	L
11/16/19	5	@		Mississippi State	38	7	W	W
11/23/19	5	vs		Western Carolina	66	3	W	
11/30/19	5	@	15	Auburn	45	48	L	L
01/01/20	13	N	14	Michigan	35	16	W	

Coaches

Name	Position	Year
Nick Saban	Head Coach	13
Brian Baker	Associate Head Coach / Defensive Line	1
Jeff Banks	Special Teams Coordinator / Tight Ends	2
Scott Cochran	Strength and Conditioning	13
Kyle Flood	Offensive Line	1
Pete Golding	Defensive Coordinator / Inside Linebackers	2
Charles Huff	Associate Head Coach / Running Backs	1
Charles Kelly	Associate Defensive Coordinator / Safeties	1
Steve Sarkisian	Offensive Coordinator / Quarterbacks	1
Karl Scott	Cornerbacks	2
Sal Sunseri	Outside Linebackers	1 (4th overall)
Holmon Wiggins	Wide Receivers	1

Recruits

Name	Pos	Pos Rank	Rivals	247 Sports	ESPN	ESPN Grade	Hometown	High school / college	Height	Weight	Committed
Antonio Alfano	DT	1	5	5	4	86	Colonia, NJ	Colonia HS	6-4	275	5/18/18
Marcus Banks	CB	23	4	4	4	81	Houston, TX	Andy Dekaney HS	6-0	166	1/5/19
Jordan Battle	S	4	4	4	4	84	Fort Lauderdale, FL	Saint Thomas Aquinas HS	6-1	187	12/19/18
Jahleel Billingsley	TE	11	4	4	4	80	Chicago, IL	Wendell Phillips Academy	6-4	216	7/7/18
Tanner Bowles	OT	23	3	4	4	82	Glasgow, KY	Glasgow HS	6-5	273	4/22/18
Jeffery Carter	CB	4	4	5	4	86	Mansfield, TX	Mansfield Legacy HS	6-0	182	4/16/18
Darrian Dalcourt	OC	3	4	4	4	84	Baltimore, MD	St. Frances Academy	6-3	299	8/9/18
DJ Dale	DT	14	3	4	4	83	Pinson, AL	Clay-Chalkville HS	6-4	323	5/2/18
Justin Eboigbe	DE	5	4	4	4	86	Forest Park, GA	Forest Park HS	6-5	263	6/16/18
Christian Harris	ATH	6	4	4	4	84	Baton Rouge, LA	LSU Laboratory School	6-1	225	11/28/18
Kevin Harris	DE	10	4	4	4	84	Loganville, GA	Grayson HS	6-4	217	5/1/18
DeMarcco Hellams	ATH	10	4	4	4	84	Hyattsville, MD	DeMatha Catholic HS	6-1	203	6/11/18
Braylen Ingraham	DE	12	4	4	4	84	Fort Lauderdale, FL	Saint Thomas Aquinas HS	6-4	270	10/23/18
Amari Kight	OT	8	4	4	4	86	Alabaster, AL	Thompson HS	6-7	307	4/29/18
Shane Lee	ILB	1	4	4	4	84	Baltimore, MD	St Frances Academy	6-0	243	4/17/18
John Metchie III	WR	52	4	4	4	80	Hightstown, NJ	The Peddie School	6-0	195	7/7/18
King Mwikuta	DE	19	4	4	4	83	LaGrange, GA	Troup County HS	6-5	222	12/15/17
Evan Neal	OT	2	5	5	5	91	Bradenton, FL	IMG Academy	6-7	360	12/19/18
Pierce Quick	OT	4	4	4	5	91	Trussville, AL	Hewitt-Trussville HS	6-5	287	4/22/17
Will Reichard	K	1	3	3	3	79	Hoover, AL	Hoover HS	6-1	185	5/23/18
Keilan Robinson	RB	12	4	3	4	82	Washington, D.C.	St. John's College HS	5-10	186	6/27/18
Trey Sanders	RB	2	5	5	4	88	Bradenton, FL	IMG Academy	6-0	216	12/19/18
Ishmael Sopsher	DT	2	4	4	4	86	Amite, LA	Amite HS	6-4	330	2/6/19
Taulia Tagovailoa	QB	5	4	4	4	83	Alabaster, AL	Thompson HS	6-0	204	4/22/18
Brandon Turnage	CB	6	4	4	4	84	Oxford, MS	Lafayette HS	6-0	180	12/22/17
Paul Tyson	QB	14	4	3	4	80	Trussville, AL	Hewitt-Trussville HS	6-4	217	4/5/18
Byron Young	DE	11	4	4	4	84	Laurel, MS	West Jones HS	6-4	255	7/3/18

	Rivals	247Sports	ESPN
5 Stars	3	4	2
4 Stars	21	20	24
3 Stars	3	3	1
2 Stars	0	0	0

Note: Table data from "2019 Alabama Crimson Tide football team" (244)

Roster

Num	Player	Pos	Class	Height	Weight	Hometown	Last School
86	Connor Adams	DB	SR	6-1	194	Sugar Land, TX	Austin
4	Christopher Allen	LB	R-SO	6-4	250	Baton Rouge, LA	Southern Lab School
40	Giles Amos	TE	SR	6-4	245	Perry, GA	Westfield
22	Jalyn Armour-Davis	DB	R-FR	6-1	182	Mobile, AL	St. Paul's
26	Marcus Banks	DB	FR	6-0	170	Houston, TX	Dekaney
7	Braxton Barker	QB	R-FR	6-1	202	Birmingham, AL	Spain Park
58	Christian Barmore	DL	R-FR	6-5	310	Philadelphia, PA	Neumann Goretti
9	Jordan Battle	DB	FR	6-1	201	Fort Lauderdale, FL	St. Thomas Aquinas
51	Wes Baumhower	LB	R-FR	6-0	220	Fairhope, AL	Fairhope
36	Markail Benton	LB	R-SO	6-2	235	Phenix City, AL	Central
98	Mike Bernier	P	R-SR	6-2	219	Madison, AL	Bob Jones/Eastern Illinois
19	Jahleel Billingsley	TE	FR	6-4	228	Chicago, IL	Phillips Academy
46	Melvin Billingsley	TE	SO	6-3	230	Opelika, AL	Opelika
20	Cooper Bishop	RB	FR	6-0	195	Vestavia Hills, AL	Vestavia Hills
18	Slade Bolden	WR	R-FR	5-11	191	West Monroe, LA	West Monroe
93	Landon Bothwell	DL	SO	5-11	220	Oneonta, AL	Oneonta
51	Tanner Bowles	OL	FR	6-5	280	Glasgow, KY	Glasgow
50	Hunter Brannon	OL	R-SO	6-4	307	Cullman, AL	Cullman
65	Deonte Brown	OL	R-JR	6-4	338	Decatur, AL	Austin
75	Tommy Brown	OL	R-FR	6-7	317	Santa Ana, CA	Mater Dei
97	**Joseph Bulovas**	**PK**	**R-SO**	**6-0**	**203**	**Mandeville, LA**	**Mandeville**
11	Scooby Carter	DB	FR	6-0	186	Mansfield, TX	Mansfield Legacy
5	**Shyheim Carter**	**DB**	**SR**	**6-0**	**191**	**Kentwood, LA**	**Kentwood**
31	Michael Collins	DB	R-JR	5-10	173	Montgomery, AL	Montgomery Catholic
55	William Cooper	LB	JR	6-2	229	Huntsville, AL	Huntsville
71	Darrian Dalcourt	OL	FR	6-3	292	Havre de Grace, MD	St. Frances Academy
94	**DJ Dale**	**DL**	**FR**	**6-3**	**308**	**Birmingham, AL**	**Clay-Chalkville**
1	Ben Davis	LB	R-JR	6-4	243	Gordo, AL	Gordo
99	**Raekwon Davis**	**DL**	**SR**	**6-7**	**312**	**Meridian, MS**	**Meridian**
12	Skyler DeLong	P	SO	6-4	188	Fort Mill, SC	Nation Ford
69	*Landon Dickerson*	*OL*	*R-JR*	*6-6*	*308*	*Hickory, NC*	*South Caldwell*
7	**Trevon Diggs**	**DB**	**SR**	**6-2**	**207**	**Gaithersburg, MD**	**Avalon School**
57	Joe Donald	LB	SR	6-3	216	Mountain Brook, AL	Mountain Brook
20	DJ Douglas	DB	FR	6-0	202	Montgomery, AL	Thompson
92	Justin Eboigbe	DL	FR	6-5	294	Forest Park, GA	Forest Park
55	**Emil Ekiyor Jr.**	**OL**	**R-FR**	**6-3**	**327**	**Indianapolis, IN**	**Cathedral**
45	**Thomas Fletcher**	**SN**	**JR**	**6-2**	**220**	**Georgetown, TX**	**IMG Academy**
27	Jerome Ford	RB	R-FR	5-11	212	Seffner, FL	Armwood
87	**Miller Forristall**	**TE**	**R-JR**	**6-5**	**242**	**Cartersville, GA**	**Cartersville**
63	Rowdy Garza	OL	FR	6-4	312	Trussville, AL	Hewitt-Trussville
31	A.J. Gates	RB	FR	5-7	170	Mountain Brook, AL	Mountain Brook
16	Jayden George	QB	FR	6-3	192	Indianapolis, IN	Warren Central
59	Jake Hall	SN	R-FR	6-3	207	Saraland, AL	Saraland
8	**Christian Harris**	**LB**	**FR**	**6-2**	**244**	**Baton Rouge, LA**	**University Lab**
22	**Najee Harris**	**RB**	**JR**	**6-2**	**230**	**Antioch, CA**	**Antioch**
44	Kevin Harris II	LB	FR	6-4	222	Loganville, GA	Grayson
29	DeMarcco Hellams	DB	FR	6-1	213	Washington, DC	DeMatha Catholic
36	Mac Hereford	WR	SR	6-2	215	Birmingham, AL	Woodberry Forest
19	Stone Hollenbach	QB	FR	6-3	208	Catawissa, PA	Southern Columbia
82	Richard Hunt	TE	FR	6-7	235	Memphis, TN	Briarcrest Christian
52	Braylen Ingraham	DL	FR	6-4	291	Fort Lauderdale, FL	St. Thomas Aquinas
32	Jalen Jackson	WR	R-SR	6-3	186	Waldorf, MD	Thomas Stone/Troy
33	**Anfernee Jennings**	**LB**	**R-SR**	**6-3**	**259**	**Dadeville, AL**	**Dadeville**
4	**Jerry Jeudy**	**WR**	**JR**	**6-1**	**192**	**Deerfield Beach, FL**	**Deerfield Beach**
28	Josh Jobe	DB	SO	6-1	189	Miami, FL	Cheshire Academy (Conn.)
10	Mac Jones	QB	R-SO	6-2	205	Jacksonville, FL	The Bolles School
10	Ale Kaho	LB	SO	6-1	228	Reno, NV	Reno
38	Sean Kelly	DB	SR	5-11	190	Cary, NC	Green Hope
78	Amari Kight	OL	FR	6-7	302	Alabaster, AL	Thompson
85	Drew Kobayashi	WR	R-JR	6-2	200	Honolulu, HI	St. Louis
89	Grant Krieger	WR	FR	6-2	192	Pittsburgh, PA	Pine-Richland
84	Joshua Lanier	WR	SR	5-11	160	Tuscaloosa, AL	Tuscaloosa Academy
76	Scott Lashley	OL	R-JR	6-7	307	West Point, MS	West Point
81	Cameron Latu	TE	R-FR	6-5	247	Salt Lake City, UT	Olympus
70	**Alex Leatherwood**	**OL**	**JR**	**6-6**	**310**	**Pensacola, FL**	**Booker T. Washington**
35	Shane Lee	LB	FR	6-0	246	Burtonsville, MD	St. Frances Academy
24	**Terrell Lewis**	**LB**	**R-JR**	**6-5**	**252**	**Washington, DC**	**St. John's**
35	De'Marquise Lockridge	RB	R-SR	5-11	216	Columbia, TN	Lawrence County
54	Julian Lowenstein	LB	FR	6-0	201	Sarasota, FL	Riverview
52	Preston Malone	LB	JR	5-11	222	Northport, AL	Northside
95	Jack Martin	P	FR	6-0	206	Mobile, AL	McGill-Toolen
48	Phidarian Mathis	DL	R-SO	6-4	312	Wisner, LA	Neville

Num	Player	Pos	Class	Height	Weight	Hometown	Last School
21	Jared Mayden	DB	SR	6-0	205	Sachse, TX	Sachse
15	**Xavier McKinney**	**DB**	**JR**	**6-1**	**200**	**Roswell, GA**	**Roswell**
40	Joshua McMillon	LB	R-SR	6-3	237	Memphis, TN	Whitehaven
8	John Metchie III	WR	FR	6-0	195	Brampton, Canada	St. James School (Md.)
42	Jaylen Moody	LB	SO	6-2	228	Conway, SC	Conway
32	**Dylan Moses**	**LB**	**JR**	**6-3**	**235**	**Baton Rouge, LA**	**IMG Academy**
91	Tevita Musika	DL	SR	6-1	338	Milpitas, CA	Milpitas/San Mateo J.C.
30	King Mwikuta	LB	FR	6-5	243	West Point, GA	Troup County
73	Evan Neal	OL	FR	6-7	360	Okeechobee, FL	IMG Academy
84	**Chris Owens**	**OL**	**R-JR**	**6-3**	**315**	**Arlington, TX**	**Lamar**
83	John Parker	WR	SR	6-0	190	Huntsville, AL	Westminster Christian
80	Michael Parker	TE	R-FR	6-6	216	Huntsville, AL	Westminster Christian
23	Jarez Parks	LB	R-FR	6-4	239	Fellsmere, FL	Sebastian River
99	Ty Perine	PK	FR	6-1	190	Prattville, AL	Prattville
38	Eric Poellnitz	WR	FR	5-11	170	Mobile, AL	Mobile Christian
43	Daniel Powell	TE	SR	5-11	213	Aliceville, AL	Pickens Academy
50	Gabe Pugh	SN	FR	6-5	273	Tuscaloosa, AL	Northridge
72	Pierce Quick	OL	FR	6-5	291	Trussville, AL	Hewitt-Trussville
85	Kendall Randolph	TE/OL	R-SO	6-4	296	Madison, AL	Bob Jones
89	**LaBryan Ray**	**DL**	**JR**	**6-5**	**292**	**Madison, AL**	**James Clemens**
42	Sam Reed	WR	FR	6-1	165	Mountain Brook, AL	John Carroll
16	**Will Reichard**	**PK**	**FR**	**6-1**	**180**	**Hoover, AL**	**Hoover**
27	Joshua Robinson	DB	JR	5-9	180	Hoover, AL	Hoover
2	Keilan Robinson	RB	FR	5-9	190	Washington, DC	St. John's
24	Brian Robinson Jr.	RB	JR	6-0	226	Tuscaloosa, AL	Hillcrest
62	Jackson Roby	OL	SO	6-5	285	Huntsville, AL	Huntsville
11	**Henry Ruggs III**	**WR**	**JR**	**6-0**	**190**	**Montgomery, AL**	**Lee**
26	Trey Sanders	RB	FR	6-0	214	Port Saint Joe, FL	IMG Academy
14	Tyrell Shavers	WR	R-SO	6-6	205	Lewisville, TX	Lewisville
93	Tripp Slyman	PK/P	R-FR	6-1	180	Huntsville, AL	Randolph
6	**DeVonta Smith**	**WR**	**JR**	**6-1**	**175**	**Amite, LA**	**Amite**
25	Eddie Smith	DB	SO	6-0	196	Slidell, LA	Salmen
41	Kyle Smoak	WR	FR	5-8	160	Alabaster, AL	Thompson
95	Ishmael Sopsher	DL	FR	6-4	334	Amite, LA	Amite
2	**Patrick Surtain II**	**DB**	**SO**	**6-2**	**203**	**Plantation, FL**	**American Heritage**
5	Taulia Tagovailoa	QB	FR	5-11	208	Ewa Beach, HI	Thompson
13	**Tua Tagovailoa**	**QB**	**JR**	**6-1**	**218**	**Ewa Beach, HI**	**St. Louis**
88	Major Tennison	TE	R-SO	6-5	248	Flint, TX	Bullard
12	Chadarius Townsend	RB/WR	R-SO	6-0	194	Tanner, AL	Tanner
14	Brandon Turnage	DB	FR	6-1	185	Oxford, MS	Lafayette
15	Paul Tyson	QB	FR	6-5	220	Trussville, AL	Hewitt-Trussville
39	Loren Ugheoke	DB	SR	5-10	183	Huntsville, AL	Randolph
17	**Jaylen Waddle**	**WR**	**SO**	**5-10**	**182**	**Houston, TX**	**Episcopal**
41	Carson Ware	DB	FR	6-1	190	Muscle Shoals, AL	Muscle Shoals
86	Quindarius Watkins	TE	JR	6-4	230	Fort Stewart, GA	Bradwell Institute
9	Xavier Williams	WR	R-FR	6-1	195	Hollywood, FL	Chaminade-Madonna Prep
74	**Jedrick Wills Jr.**	**OL**	**JR**	**6-5**	**320**	**Lexington, KY**	**Lafayette**
96	Taylor Wilson	DL	SR	6-0	232	Huntington Beach, CA	Mater Dei
77	Matt Womack	OL	R-SR	6-7	325	Hernando, MS	Magnolia Heights
3	Daniel Wright	DB	R-SO	6-1	190	Fort Lauderdale, FL	Boyd Anderson
90	Stephon Wynn Jr.	DL	R-FR	6-4	311	Anderson, SC	IMG Academy
47	Byron Young	DL	FR	6-3	295	Laurel, MS	West Jones

Note: Starters in bold
Note: Table data from "2019 Alabama Crimson Tide Roster" (245)

Transfers

Player	School	Direction
Landon Dickerson	FSU	Incoming
Eyabi Anoma	Houston	Outgoing
Layne Hatcher	Arkansas State	Outgoing
Jalen Hurts	Oklahoma	Outgoing
Kedrick James	SMU	Outgoing
Kyriq McDonald	Cincinnati	Outgoing
Scott Meyer	Vanderbilt	Outgoing
Richie Petitbon	Illinois	Outgoing

Note: Table data from "2019 Alabama Crimson Tide football team" (244)

Games

08/31/19 - Alabama (2) vs Duke

Chick-fil-A College Kickoff
Mercedes-Benz Stadium
Atlanta, GA

Team	1	2	3	4	T	Passing	Rushing	Total
Duke	0	3	0	0	3	97	107	204
Alabama (2)	0	14	21	7	42	367	145	512

The Alabama offense sputtered out of the gate, failing to score in the first quarter. They punted, fumbled (Jerome Ford), and missed a field goal (Reichard from 49). But Tua and company soon found their rhythm, marching 80 yards in 12 plays to draw first blood. Tua connected with TE Miller Forristall for a 27-yard touchdown, the first of Forristall's career, to put Alabama up 7-0. On their next drive, the Tide struck again. RB Brian Robinson Jr. capped a 7-play, 76-yard possession with a 1-yard plunge into the end zone, extending the lead to 14-0 with 5:13 left in the half. Duke managed a 30-yard field goal just before halftime to make it 14-3 at the break.

Alabama's defense set up the next score, stopping Duke on fourth down to give the offense the ball at their own 35. Tua led a 9-play, 65-yard TD drive, finding TE Major Tennison for a 1-yard score, Tennison's first career TD catch (21-3). Alabama's stifling defense struck again on the very next play. CB Patrick Surtain II ripped the ball out of the Duke receiver's grasp, and Trevon Diggs was there to scoop it up at the Duke 28-yard line. The Tide quickly capitalized as Tua needed just three snaps to find the end zone for the third time. He zipped an 8-yard TD pass to DeVonta Smith. The score extended Alabama's lead to 28-3 over the Blue Devils.

Alabama's offense was unstoppable, marching down the field on their next drive for another touchdown. Tua connected with Jerry Jeudy on a 21-yard scoring strike to cap off the 90-yard, 9-play possession, making the score 35-3. As the fourth quarter began, Alabama's backups got in on the action. Redshirt freshman RB Jerome Ford broke free for a 37-yard TD run, the first of his career. The Tide now led 42-3 with under five minutes remaining. With the game well in hand, Alabama's defense sealed the victory with an interception by DB Jordan Battle in the final minute of play. The Crimson Tide cruised to a lopsided win over their overmatched opponent.

Tua had a career day in completions, completing 26-of-31 passes for 336 yards and four touchdowns. He finished with an outstanding QBR of 96.3. Jerry Jeudy also had a career day in receptions with his ten catches for 137 yards and a score. Trevon Diggs stepped up with a pair of big plays, first by recovering a fumble, then by recording the second interception of his career. Xavier McKinney topped all Crimson Tide defenders with a career-high eight tackles.[246]

Passing	C/ATT	YDS	AVG	TD	INT	QBR
Tu. Tagovailoa	26/31	336	10.8	4	0	96.3
M. Jones	4/5	31	6.2	0	0	90.9
Team	30/36	367	10.2	4	0	--

Rushing	CAR	YDS	AVG	TD	LONG
J. Ford	10	64	6.4	1	37
N. Harris	12	52	4.3	0	15
Tu. Tagovailoa	5	15	3	0	10
B. Robinson Jr.	9	9	1	1	5
K. Robinson	2	5	2.5	0	4
M. Jones	2	4	2	0	4
Team	2	-4	-2	0	0
Team	42	145	3.5	2	37

Kicking	FG	PCT	LONG	XP	PTS
W. Reichard	0/2	0	0	6/6	6

Punting	NO	YDS	AVG	TB	IN 20	LONG
W. Reichard	2	80	40	0	1	41

Receiving	REC	YDS	AVG	TD	LONG
J. Jeudy	10	137	13.7	1	21
J. Waddle	5	90	18	0	39
D. Smith	5	54	10.8	1	24
M. Forristall	2	33	16.5	1	27
B. Robinson Jr.	1	14	14	0	14
H. Ruggs III	2	14	7	0	9
J. Ford	2	11	5.5	0	9
M. Tennison	2	9	4.5	1	8
J. Metchie III	1	5	5	0	5
Team	30	367	12.2	4	39

Kick returns	NO	YDS	AVG	LONG	TD
H. Ruggs III	1	22	22	22	0

Interceptions	INT	YDS	TD
T. Diggs	1	0	0
J. Battle	1	0	0
Team	2	0	0

Note: Table data from "Alabama 42-3 Duke (Aug 31, 2019) Box Score" (247)

288

09/07/19 - Alabama (2) vs New Mexico State

Team	1	2	3	4	T		Passing	Rushing	Total
New Mexico State	0	0	7	3	10		161	101	262
Alabama (2)	21	17	24	0	62		285	318	603

Alabama's offense exploded in the first quarter, scoring three touchdowns in quick succession. On the first play from scrimmage, wide receiver Henry Ruggs III rushed for a 75-yard touchdown just 13 seconds into the game. On their next possession, the Tide marched 89 yards in 10 plays, capped by a 21-yard touchdown catch by Jerry Jeudy. Tua then found Jeudy again for a 23-yard score as time expired in the quarter, putting Alabama up 21-0.

The onslaught continued in the second quarter. Tua connected with Ruggs for a 10-yard touchdown to finish a 7-play, 72-yard drive (28-0). On the ensuing possession, cornerback Patrick Surtain II intercepted a pass at the Alabama 16-yard line. The Tide offense needed just five plays to go 84 yards, with Tua scoring on a 25-yard run. Just before halftime, kicker Will Reichard connected on a 48-yard field goal, the first of his career, to give Alabama a 38-0 lead at the break.

The second half was more of the same. Running back Najee Harris scored on an 8-yard run to cap a 9-play, 55-yard drive to go up 45-0. New Mexico State finally got on the board midway through the third quarter with a 4-yard touchdown catch, but Alabama answered immediately. Junior QB Mac Jones found Jeudy for his third score of the day, a 19-yard strike (52-7). Reichard added a 49-yard field goal later in the quarter (55-7). Freshman Keilan Robinson then broke free for a 74-yard touchdown run, the first of his career, to close the third quarter. New Mexico State kicked a field goal in the fourth quarter to make the final score 62-10.

Tua found the end zone four times for the second game in a row. Jerry Jeudy racked up over 100 receiving yards for the third straight game, dating back to the end of last season. He also set a new personal best with three touchdown catches. Xavier McKinney and Raekwon Davis were the team's top tacklers with six each. Five of McKinney's were solo stops, the most on the squad. He also forced a fumble and hurried the quarterback. Patrick Surtain II recorded his first interception of the season and forced a fumble in addition to breaking up a pass to lock down his part of the defense. The Alabama defense was stifling, with seven tackles for loss and three sacks. The Crimson Tide won the turnover battle 3-0 after forcing two fumbles and picking off one pass.[248]

Passing	C/ATT	YDS	AVG	TD	INT	QBR
Tu. Tagovailoa	16/24	227	9.5	3	0	91.5
M. Jones	5/9	58	6.4	1	0	37
Team	21/33	285	8.6	4	0	--

Rushing	CAR	YDS	AVG	TD	LONG
K. Robinson	5	80	16	1	74
H. Ruggs III	1	75	75	1	75
N. Harris	12	68	5.7	1	19
B. Robinson Jr.	11	57	5.2	0	16
Tu. Tagovailoa	2	33	16.5	1	25
J. Ford	1	5	5	0	5
Team	32	318	9.9	4	75

Punting	NO	YDS	AVG	TB	IN 20	LONG
S. DeLong	3	123	41	0	0	44
W. Reichard	1	39	39	0	0	39
Team	4	162	40.5	0	0	44

Receiving	REC	YDS	AVG	TD	LONG
J. Jeudy	8	103	12.9	3	23
H. Ruggs III	4	66	16.5	1	39
J. Waddle	2	52	26	0	29
D. Smith	5	47	9.4	0	22
N. Harris	1	12	12	0	12
G. Amos	1	5	5	0	5
Team	21	285	13.6	4	39

Kick returns	NO	YDS	AVG	LONG	TD
H. Ruggs III	1	19	19	19	0

Punt returns	NO	YDS	AVG	LONG	TD
J. Waddle	3	28	9.3	23	0

Kicking	FG	PCT	LONG	XP	PTS
W. Reichard	2/2	100	49	8/8	14

Interceptions	INT	YDS	TD
P. Surtain II	1	0	0

Note: Table data from "New Mexico State 10-62 Alabama (Sep 7, 2019) Box Score" (249)

09/14/19 - Alabama (2) at South Carolina

Team	1	2	3	4	T		Passing	Rushing	Total
Alabama (2)	14	10	10	13	47		495	76	571
South Carolina	10	0	3	10	23		324	135	459

Alabama scored in under two minutes on its opening possession when RB Najee Harris caught a pass from Tua and raced 24 yards into the end zone for a TD. After a 44-yard field goal made it 7-3, both teams traded punts and touchdowns. Ruggs III caught Alabama's second touchdown, a drive that also took less than two minutes, taking Tua's pass and sprinting 81 yards for the score (14-3). South Carolina's TD came from a 31-yard pass after they drove 75 yards in six plays. Alabama started the second quarter with a 23-yard FG to make the score 17-10. The Alabama defense stopped the Gamecocks the rest of the half forcing a punt and stopping two fourth down attempts. Meanwhile, Najee Harris broke two tacklers and hurdled a defender to score on a 42-yard pass from Tua. After Reichard missed a 37-yard field goal, Bama led 24-10 at the half.

South Carolina scored a 28-yard field goal to start the second half, and Alabama immediately responded with a 5-play, 75-yard touchdown drive that only took 1:34 off the clock. Tua hooked up with DeVonta Smith for the 42-yard score, making it 31-13. After Anfernee Jennings forced a fumble that was recovered by DJ Dale, both teams traded field goals. Bama scored two more TDs sandwiching a pick from McKinney in the end zone. The first only took 1:08 when Tua hit DeVonta Smith again from 11 yards out. After Reichard missed the PAT, the score was 40-16. The other was from backup QB Mac Jones with a 1-yard quarterback sneak up the middle. SC scored a meaningless touchdown with 11 seconds left in the game, bringing the final to 47-23.

Tua had a career-best five touchdown passes, with two each to Najee Harris and DeVonta Smith, in a standout performance that saw him throw for a personal-high 444 yards. This marked the third consecutive game in which he had 4+ TD passes. Alabama's receiving duo of Smith (136) and Ruggs III (122) both exceeded 100 receiving yards, a feat accomplished only nine times in school history and for the first time this season. Najee Harris scored his first two career receiving touchdowns and had five catches after only catching 11 all last season. He also rushed for 36 yards on seven attempts, contributing to his overall all-purpose yardage of 123 yards.

In the defensive effort, 22 players made tackles with safety Xavier McKinney leading the way with nine, five of which were solo. He also intercepted a pass and logged a tackle for loss. Outside linebacker Anfernee Jennings sacked the quarterback and forced a fumble, while freshman defensive lineman DJ Dale and defensive back Jordan Battle each recorded a sack.[250]

Passing	C/ATT	YDS	AVG	TD	INT	QBR
Tu. Tagovailoa	28/36	444	12.3	5	0	97.9
M. Jones	3/3	51	17	0	0	100
Team	31/39	495	12.7	5	0	--

Rushing	CAR	YDS	AVG	TD	LONG
N. Harris	7	36	5.1	0	12
B. Robinson Jr.	8	33	4.1	0	11
K. Robinson	4	12	3	0	4
J. Waddle	1	5	5	0	5
S. Bolden	1	2	2	0	2
M. Jones	1	1	1	1	1
Team	1	-1	-1	0	0
Tu. Tagovailoa	2	-12	-6	0	0
Team	25	76	3.0	1	12

Punting	NO	YDS	AVG	TB	IN 20	LONG
S. DeLong	1	14	14	0	0	14

Receiving	REC	YDS	AVG	TD	LONG
D. Smith	8	136	17	2	42
H. Ruggs III	6	122	20.3	1	81
N. Harris	5	87	17.4	2	42
J. Jeudy	6	68	11.3	0	30
B. Robinson Jr.	2	37	18.5	0	34
S. Bolden	1	14	14	0	14
M. Tennison	1	12	12	0	12
J. Waddle	1	12	12	0	12
M. Forristall	1	7	7	0	7
Team	31	495	16.0	5	81

Punt returns	NO	YDS	AVG	LONG	TD
J. Waddle	1	18	18	18	0

Kicking	FG	PCT	LONG	XP	PTS
W. Reichard	2/3	66.7	23	5/6	11

Interceptions	INT	YDS	TD
X. McKinney	1	0	0

Note: Table data from "Alabama 47-23 South Carolina (Sep 14, 2019) Box Score" (251)

09/21/19 - Alabama (2) vs Southern Mississippi

Team	1	2	3	4	T		Passing	Rushing	Total
Southern Mississippi	0	7	0	0	7		174	52	226
Alabama (2)	14	14	14	7	49		338	176	514

The game started with a bang as Tua unleashed his aerial assault. He connected with Henry Ruggs III on two deep strikes, one from 74 yards out and another from 45 yards, both resulting in touchdowns. These explosive plays propelled the Tide to a commanding 14-0 lead by the end of the first quarter. In the second quarter, Tua continued his masterful performance, finding Najee Harris for a 5-yard touchdown pass, his third scoring strike of the game. Later in the same quarter, he spotted a wide-open Jerry Jeudy and delivered a precise 17-yard pass for yet another touchdown, extending the Tide's lead to a formidable 28-0. Just before halftime, Southern Miss managed to get on the scoreboard, adding a touchdown to narrow the deficit to 28-7 as the teams headed into the break.

Tua's aerial assault continued in the third quarter as he unleashed his fifth touchdown strike of the day, finding Jeudy for the second time from 20 yards out, further padding their point tally (35-7). Brian Robinson Jr. joined the party, scampering into the end zone for a 6-yard touchdown romp with 5:43 remaining in the third quarter, extending the Tide's lead to a commanding 42-7. As the game drew to a close, the Tide showed no signs of slowing down. Jerome Ford rumbled his way into the end zone for a 5-yard scoring plunge, putting an exclamation point on the dominant performance with a final score of 49-7.

Tua tossed five touchdown passes in just three quarters of play. This remarkable feat marked the second consecutive week and third time in his illustrious career that he achieved this milestone, making Alabama history. Wide receiver Henry Ruggs III had a night to remember, setting a new personal best with 148 receiving yards on a mere four catches, averaging a staggering 37 yards per reception. Running back Najee Harris joined the party, eclipsing the 100-yard rushing mark for the second time in his career and the first time this season.

Safety Jared Mayden led the defensive charge, posting a career-high eight tackles, while linebacker Christian Harris was close behind with six tackles, including 1.5 tackles for loss. Cornerback Trevon Diggs showcased his ball-hawking skills, snagging his second interception of the season and adding three tackles to his stat line. Defensive lineman Phidarian Mathis made his presence felt, forcing a fumble that was recovered by freshman defensive back Jordan Battle.[252]

Passing	C/ATT	YDS	AVG	TD	INT	QBR
Tu. Tagovailoa	17/21	293	14	5	0	99.2
M. Jones	2/3	25	8.3	0	1	18.8
Ta. Tagovailoa	1/1	20	20	0	0	100
Team	20/25	338	13.5	5	1	--

Rushing	CAR	YDS	AVG	TD	LONG
N. Harris	14	110	7.9	0	17
B. Robinson Jr.	8	39	4.9	1	14
J. Ford	8	21	2.6	1	7
Tu. Tagovailoa	3	8	2.7	0	8
C. Townsend	2	-2	-1	0	1
Team	35	176	5	2	17

Kicking	FG	PCT	LONG	XP	PTS
J. Bulovas	0/0	0	0	5/5	5
W. Reichard	0/0	0	0	2/2	2
Team	0/0	0	0	7/7	7

Punting	NO	YDS	AVG	TB	IN 20	LONG
S. DeLong	2	74	37	0	0	38

Receiving	REC	YDS	AVG	TD	LONG
H. Ruggs III	4	148	37	2	74
J. Jeudy	6	96	16	2	36
J. Waddle	3	43	14.3	0	25
D. Smith	2	26	13	0	17
S. Bolden	1	20	20	0	20
N. Harris	1	5	5	1	5
B. Robinson Jr.	1	3	3	0	3
M. Forristall	1	1	1	0	1
J. Metchie III	1	-4	-4	0	0
Team	20	338	16.9	5	74

Interceptions	INT	YDS	TD
T. Diggs	1	-5	0

Kick returns	NO	YDS	AVG	LONG	TD
B. Robinson Jr.	1	1	1	1	0

Punt returns	NO	YDS	AVG	LONG	TD
J. Waddle	1	41	41	41	0

Note: Table data from "Alabama 49-7 Southern Mississippi (Sep 21, 2019) Box Score" (253)

09/28/19 - Alabama (2) vs Ole Miss

Team	1	2	3	4	T	Passing	Rushing	Total
Ole Miss	10	0	7	14	**31**	197	279	**476**
Alabama (2)	7	31	14	7	**59**	418	155	**573**

Tua wasted no time, finding Smith for a 74-yard touchdown strike to take a 7-0 lead in just four plays and 1:10 into the game. Ole Miss capitalized on an Alabama muffed punt deep in their territory, with QB Plumlee punching it in from a yard out to knot the score at 7-7. The Rebels added a FG to snatch a 10-7 advantage after one quarter. From that point on, it was all Alabama. Tua sparked a 31-point unanswered onslaught, starting with a 5-yard rushing TD to put the Tide back on top 14-10. Bulovas tacked on a field goal, and the defense held firm, setting the stage for Tua's aerial assault. He connected with Smith for three touchdowns (25, 23, and 33 yards) in a blistering five-minute span, propelling Alabama to a commanding 38-10 halftime lead.

The dynamic duo of Tua and Smith continued their performance in the second half. As the third quarter began, Smith soared high to snag a 27-yard pass from Tua, his fifth TD reception of the game (45-10). Ole Miss responded with a 9-yard TD to make it 45-17. After Bulovas missed a 28-yard FG, Ole Miss went three-and-out and punted. Ale Kaho blocked the punt and pounced on the loose ball in the end zone for a touchdown, stretching the lead to a daunting 52-17. Tua and the potent Alabama offense remained in high gear, as he found TE Miller Forristall for a 19-yard scoring strike, pushing the score to 59-17. While the Rebels managed to add two late touchdowns in the fourth quarter, including one with mere seconds remaining, it was too little, too late. The final scoreline of 59-31 reflected Alabama's utter dominance over their SEC rivals.

DeVonta Smith etched his name in the record books with a career-defining performance. He hauled in 11 receptions for a staggering 274 yards, including five TDs - all career highs. He caught 11 of his 12 targets and averaged an impressive 24.9 yards per catch. His first-half numbers were particularly noteworthy, with eight catches, four touchdowns, and 221 yards. His five TDs tied the SEC receiving touchdowns mark. Tua was equally unstoppable, setting new career and school records with six passing touchdowns and seven total touchdowns. His QBR of 95.2 reflected his dominance over the opposition's defense. While the offense stole the show, the defense had its share of standout performers. Safety Xavier McKinney led the charge with a career-high 13 tackles, accompanied by a quarterback hurry. Linebacker Anfernee Jennings was close behind with nine tackles, including one for a loss. Senior Jared Mayden etched his name in the stat sheet with his first career interception and a 36-yard return in the fourth quarter.[254]

Passing	C/ATT	YDS	AVG	TD	INT	QBR
Tu. Tagovailoa	26/36	418	11.6	6	0	95.2
M. Jones	0/1	0	0	0	0	0
Team	26/37	418	11.3	6	0	--

Rushing	CAR	YDS	AVG	TD	LONG
N. Harris	9	71	7.9	0	13
B. Robinson Jr.	10	60	6	0	12
K. Robinson	5	20	4	0	8
S. Bolden	1	5	5	0	5
Tu. Tagovailoa	4	1	0.3	1	7
Team	1	-2	-2	0	0
Team	30	155	5.2	1	13

Interceptions	INT	YDS	TD
J. Mayden	1	36	0

Kicking	FG	PCT	LONG	XP	PTS
J. Bulovas	1/2	50	36	8/8	11

Punting	NO	YDS	AVG	TB	IN 20	LONG
S. DeLong	2	60	30	0	2	37

Receiving	REC	YDS	AVG	TD	LONG
D. Smith	11	274	24.9	5	74
J. Jeudy	8	84	10.5	0	25
M. Forristall	2	40	20	1	21
H. Ruggs III	1	11	11	0	11
B. Robinson Jr.	1	9	9	0	9
N. Harris	2	0	0	0	2
J. Waddle	1	0	0	0	0
Team	26	418	16.1	6	74

Kick returns	NO	YDS	AVG	LONG	TD
T. Diggs	2	44	22	36	0
B. Robinson Jr.	1	13	13	13	0
Team	3	57	19	36	0

Punt returns	NO	YDS	AVG	LONG	TD
J. Waddle	3	52	17.3	29	0
A. Kaho	1	20	20	0	1
Team	4	72	18	29	1

Note: Table data from "Alabama 59-31 Ole Miss (Sep 28, 2019) Box Score" (255)

10/12/19 - Alabama (1) at Texas A&M (24)

Team	1	2	3	4	T	Passing	Rushing	Total
Alabama (1)	14	10	10	13	47	293	155	**448**
Texas A&M (24)	7	6	7	8	28	264	125	**389**

The Aggies took the opening possession and methodically marched down the field. Their 15-play, 75-yard drive culminated in an early 7-0 lead. Undeterred, the Crimson Tide responded with a calculated 10-play, 73-yard scoring drive of their own. Tua connected with Jaylen Waddle for a 31-yard touchdown pass, tying the game. After forcing a three-and-out from the Aggies, Alabama's offense struck again. Tua found DeVonta Smith on a slant pattern, and Smith turned the short pass into a 47-yard touchdown, giving the Tide a 14-7 lead at the end of the first quarter. In the second quarter, both teams traded field goals, however, Tua wasn't done. He threw his third touchdown of the half, finding Najee Harris from 16 yards out, extending Alabama's lead to 24-10. The Aggies managed to add a field goal before halftime, cutting the Tide's lead to 24-13 as the teams headed to the locker rooms.

Alabama took control from the start of the second half. They marched 51 yards in nine plays, capped by Bulovas' 27-yard FG to extend their lead to 27-13. The Tide's onslaught continued as Ruggs III hauled in a 33-yard TD pass, making it 34-13. Texas A&M tried to stay in the game, scoring through the air on a 25-yard strike to cut the deficit to 34-20. In the fourth quarter, Waddle returned a punt 42 yards to give his team excellent field position. Five plays later, Brian Robinson Jr. punched it in from two yards out, pushing the lead to 40-20 after a blocked extra point. Ale Kaho blocked an Aggies punt deep in their territory, and Tyrell Shavers scooped and scored from two yards out, extending Alabama's lead to 47-20. Texas A&M added a late touchdown and two-point conversion, but it was not enough as the Tide rolled to a 47-28 victory.

Tua's four-touchdown performance brought his season total to 27 in just six games. He has now surpassed A.J. McCarron's previous career touchdown mark of 77 with 81 scoring strikes. Ruggs III hauled in a 33-yard touchdown catch and averaged an impressive 33 yards on four kickoff returns. Sophomore sensation Jaylen Waddle amassed 128 yards on four punt returns, including a long of 43 yards, consistently giving Alabama excellent field position. His impact extended beyond the return game. He totaled 176 all-purpose yards, catching three passes for 48 yards and his first receiving touchdown of the season, complementing his punt return yards.

The Crimson Tide defense relentlessly pressured Texas A&M quarterback Kellen Mond, recording five sacks and allowing just one score on offense. Linebackers Anfernee Jennings and Shane Lee led the charge with eight tackles each. Jennings added a sack, two tackles for loss, and a pass breakup, while Shyheim Carter anchored the secondary with seven tackles, two pass breakups, and a forced fumble.[256]

Passing	C/ATT	YDS	AVG	TD	INT	QBR
Tu. Tagovailoa	21/34	293	8.6	4	1	93.8

Rushing	CAR	YDS	AVG	TD	LONG
N. Harris	20	114	5.7	0	25
B. Robinson Jr.	10	51	5.1	1	15
Tu. Tagovailoa	1	-10	-10	0	0
Team	31	155	5	1	25

Punt returns	NO	YDS	AVG	LONG	TD
J. Waddle	4	128	32	43	0
A. Kaho	1	22	22	0	0
T. Shavers	0	2	0	2	1
Team	5	152	30.4	43	1

Punting	NO	YDS	AVG	TB	IN 20	LONG
S. DeLong	2	59	29.5	0	1	36

Receiving	REC	YDS	AVG	TD	LONG
D. Smith	7	99	14.1	1	47
J. Jeudy	4	50	12.5	0	26
J. Waddle	3	48	16	1	31
H. Ruggs III	1	33	33	1	33
B. Robinson Jr.	2	33	16.5	0	23
N. Harris	3	19	6.3	1	16
M. Forristall	1	11	11	0	11
Team	21	293	14	4	47

Kick returns	NO	YDS	AVG	LONG	TD
H. Ruggs III	4	131	32.8	40	0
T. Diggs	1	28	28	28	0
Team	5	159	31.8	40	0

Kicking	FG	PCT	LONG	XP	PTS
J. Bulovas	2/2	100	35	5/6	11

Note: Table data from "Alabama 47-28 Texas A&M (Oct 12, 2019) Box Score" (257)

10/19/19 - Alabama (1) vs Tennessee

Team	1	2	3	4	T		Passing	Rushing	Total
Tennessee	7	3	3	0	13		117	114	231
Alabama (1)	14	7	7	7	35		233	140	373

The Alabama Crimson Tide came out swinging against the Tennessee Volunteers, forcing a quick three-and-out on defense. The offense wasted no time, with Jaylen Waddle's 13-yard punt return setting them up at the Vols' 35-yard line. Four plays later, Najee Harris barreled into the end zone from a yard out, drawing first blood for the Tide. After exchanging interceptions, Tennessee knotted the score at 7-7 with a 41-yard scoring drive. Alabama quickly regained the lead, orchestrating a 6-play, 65-yard touchdown drive, punctuated by RB Robinson Jr.'s 8-yard scamper into the end zone (14-7). Undeterred, the Vols chipped away at the deficit in the second quarter, adding a field goal to trim the margin to 14-10. The Tide, however, refused to relinquish control, mounting another touchdown drive highlighted by a 40-yard aerial strike to Ruggs III, positioning them deep in Tennessee territory. Najee Harris then ran untouched from a yard out for his second score of the day, propelling Alabama to a 21-10 advantage. Mac Jones replaced the injured Tua for the rest of the game.

Tennessee made it a one-possession game early in the third quarter by kicking a 32-yard field goal (21-13), but the Tide had an answer. After Jones and Harris drove to the UT 6-yard line, Slade Bolden took a direct snap and found a wide-open Miller Forristall for a 6-yard touchdown, stretching the lead to 28-13. The game's pivotal moment came in the fourth quarter when Tennessee, going for it on 4th-and-goal from the 1-yard line, saw Jarrett Guarantano fumble into the end zone. Trevon Diggs scooped up the loose ball and raced 100 yards the other way for a backbreaking touchdown, effectively sealing Alabama's 35-13 victory.

Tua was efficient before exiting with an injury late in the second quarter, completing 11-of-12 passes for 155 yards. Mac Jones capably filled in, going 6-of-11 for 72 yards. Najee Harris was the workhorse, rumbling for 105 yards and a career-high two scores on 21 carries while adding 48 receiving yards. This was his third 100-yard rushing game of the season.

The Tide defense dominated, led by Christian Harris' career-best eight tackles (one for a loss). Terrell Lewis had seven tackles, a game-high two sacks, and a career-high three tackles for loss. Shane Lee forced a fumble for the first time in his career, notched six tackles, and had a sack. Jared Mayden intercepted a pass (second of his career) and broke up two others, while Trevon Diggs' 100-yard fumble return TD put an exclamation point on the win.[258]

Passing	C/ATT	YDS	AVG	TD	INT	QBR
Tu. Tagovailoa	11/12	155	12.9	0	1	86.7
M. Jones	6/11	72	6.5	0	0	58.5
S. Bolden	1/1	6	6	1	0	99.4
Team	18/24	233	9.7	1	1	--

Rushing	CAR	YDS	AVG	TD	LONG
N. Harris	21	105	5	2	15
B. Robinson Jr.	7	40	5.7	1	11
K. Robinson	3	6	2	0	4
Tu. Tagovailoa	1	-5	-5	0	0
M. Jones	2	-6	-3	0	4
Team	34	140	4.1	3	15

Interceptions	INT	YDS	TD
J. Mayden	1	4	0

Punting	NO	YDS	AVG	TB	IN 20	LONG
T. Perine	2	93	46.5	0	0	51
W. Reichard	1	33	33	0	0	33
Team	3	126	42	0	0	51

Receiving	REC	YDS	AVG	TD	LONG
H. Ruggs III	4	72	18	0	48
N. Harris	4	48	12	0	21
J. Jeudy	3	41	13.7	0	19
M. Forristall	3	28	9.3	1	14
D. Smith	1	18	18	0	18
J. Waddle	1	13	13	0	13
B. Robinson Jr.	2	13	6.5	0	8
Team	18	233	12.9	1	48

Kick returns	NO	YDS	AVG	LONG	TD
H. Ruggs III	2	43	21.5	24	0

Punt returns	NO	YDS	AVG	LONG	TD
J. Waddle	2	35	17.5	22	0

Kicking	FG	PCT	LONG	XP	PTS
J. Bulovas	0/1	0	0	5/5	5

Note: Table data from "Alabama 35-13 Tennessee (Oct 19, 2019) Box Score" (259)

10/26/19 - Alabama (1) vs Arkansas

Team	1	2	3	4	T	Passing	Rushing	Total
Arkansas	0	0	0	7	**7**	107	106	**213**
Alabama (1)	17	24	7	0	**48**	280	179	**459**

After holding Arkansas to a punt, the Crimson Tide drew first blood with a 31-yard field goal, courtesy of Joseph Bulovas' trusty foot on their first drive of the game. On Arkansas' next possession, Christian Harris recovered a fumble and returned it 37 yards to the Arkansas 14-yard line. It only took one play for Mac Jones to connect with Henry Ruggs III in the end zone for a score (10-0). The Tide converted another turnover on the Hogs' next possession - a diving interception by Anfernee Jennings at the Arkansas 48-yard line. The Tide capitalized by turning that into six points when Jeudy hauled in a 14-yard touchdown from Mac Jones with 34 ticks remaining in the first quarter (17-0). Alabama kicked off the second quarter with a pair of 1-yard plunges into the promised land by Najee Harris, ballooning the scoreline to 31-0. Bulovas added three more from his 30-yard kick. After capitalizing on 17 points off turnovers in the first quarter, Trevon Diggs joined the party with a pick-six, taking the pigskin 84 yards to the house to close out the second quarter, making the score 41-0 at the half.

On Alabama's opening drive of the third quarter, Mac Jones threw a 40-yard bomb to Jerry Jeudy, extending Alabama's lead to 48-0. The Razorbacks managed to avoid a shutout, scoring a touchdown midway through the fourth quarter to make the final score 48-7. Alabama ran the clock for out the rest of the game (one drive consisted of 15 plays and took a whopping 9:20 off the clock).

Redshirt sophomore quarterback Mac Jones got his first career start in place of the injured Tua Tagolvailoa. He completed an impressive 18-of-22 passes for a staggering 235 yards and three touchdowns – all in just over two quarters of play. Jerry Jeudy had his third 100+ yard receiving game of the season.

Alabama's stifling defense wreaked havoc, capitalizing on four turnovers. Senior DB Trevon Diggs ignited the onslaught with an 84-yard pick-six. Two fumble recoveries and another interception resulted in 17 additional points off turnovers. Linebacker Shane Lee spearheaded the defensive charge with six tackles including five solo, two for loss, and a sack. Christian Harris matched Lee's six tackles, including four solo stops and a 37-yard fumble return for a touchdown in the opening quarter.[260]

Passing	C/ATT	YDS	AVG	TD	INT	QBR
M. Jones	18/22	235	10.7	3	0	91.9
Ta. Tagovailoa	6/8	45	5.6	0	0	38.2
Team	24/30	280	9.3	3	0	--

Rushing	CAR	YDS	AVG	TD	LONG
N. Harris	13	86	6.6	2	20
B. Robinson Jr.	13	67	5.2	0	37
K. Robinson	9	29	3.2	0	5
M. Jones	1	1	1	0	1
Ta. Tagovailoa	1	-2	-2	0	0
Team	1	-2	-2	0	0
Team	38	179	4.7	2	37

Kicking	FG	PCT	LONG	XP	PTS
J. Bulovas	2/2	100	31	6/6	12

Punting	NO	YDS	AVG	TB	IN 20	LONG
T. Perine	2	95	47.5	0	1	49

Receiving	REC	YDS	AVG	TD	LONG
J. Jeudy	7	103	14.7	2	40
D. Smith	4	67	16.8	0	47
H. Ruggs III	4	47	11.8	1	18
J. Waddle	5	39	7.8	0	15
M. Forristall	2	11	5.5	0	11
B. Robinson Jr.	1	8	8	0	8
J. Metchie III	1	5	5	0	5
Team	24	280	11.7	3	47

Kick returns	NO	YDS	AVG	LONG	TD
M. Forristall	1	3	3	0	0
H. Ruggs III	1	0	0	0	0
Team	2	3	1.5	0	0

Interceptions	INT	YDS	TD
T. Diggs	1	84	1
P. Surtain II	1	24	0
A. Jennings	1	0	0
Team	3	108	1

Note: Table data from "Alabama 48-7 Arkansas (Oct 26, 2019) Box Score" (261)

11/09/19 - Alabama (3) vs LSU (2)

Team	1	2	3	4	T		Passing	Rushing	Total
LSU (2)	10	23	0	13	46		393	166	559
Alabama (3)	7	6	7	21	41		418	123	541

LSU jumped out to an early 10-0 lead in the first ten minutes of the game thanks to two fumbles (one by Tua and a bad snap on a punt attempt). Jaylen Waddle ignited the Crimson Tide's offense with an electrifying 77-yard punt return touchdown on LSU's first punt of the game. It was the second of his career and first of the season. The Tigers responded early in the second quarter with Burrow connecting on a 29-yard touchdown pass. Xavier McKinney blocked the PAT, so LSU led 16-7. Tua struck back, finding a wide-open DeVonta Smith for a 64-yard scoring strike (16-13). However, LSU exploded for 17 points in the final five minutes of the half, turning a close game into a rout. They scored a 45-yard field goal and two touchdowns, one after an interception by Patrick Queen. LSU took a commanding 33-13 lead into halftime.

The second half was a showcase of offensive firepower, with both teams trading touchdowns. Alabama's Najee Harris scored twice, cutting LSU's lead to 33-27 at the end of three. One was a 15-yard leaping catch at the goal line capping a 10-play, 95-yard drive. He leapt into the end zone from one yard out for his other one, finishing a 9-play, 78-yard drive. The Tigers answered with a touchdown of their own but failed on the two-point conversion attempt (39-27). Alabama refused to go away as they put together a 14-play, 75-yard drive that included two fourth-down conversions. Tua hit Jeudy for a touchdown on 4th-and-2 from the LSU 5-yard line to make it 39-34 with 5:32 remaining in the game. LSU extended its lead to 46-34 with 97 ticks left, but Tua and Smith connected for an 85-yard touchdown strike on the first play after the kickoff to keep Alabama within striking distance. But LSU managed to pick up a crucial first down on its final drive, sealing a 46-41 victory in this offensive slugfest.

DeVonta Smith had a standout performance against the Tigers, racking up 213 receiving yards. This marked his second 200+ yard game of the season, making him the first Alabama player to achieve multiple 200-yard receiving games in a single season since Amari Cooper in 2014. Xavier McKinney had an impressive all-around game, tying his career high with 13 tackles. He also set a new personal best with two sacks, forced a fumble, and blocked an extra point attempt. Jared Mayden and Trevon Diggs both recorded career highs in tackles. Mayden finished the game with 11 tackles, while Diggs totaled ten. Anfernee Jennings contributed with eight tackles and a career-high two sacks.[262]

Passing	C/ATT	YDS	AVG	TD	INT	QBR
Tu. Tagovailoa	21/40	418	10.5	4	1	72.8

Rushing	CAR	YDS	AVG	TD	LONG
N. Harris	19	146	7.7	1	31
B. Robinson Jr.	3	3	1	0	7
S. Bolden	1	0	0	0	0
Team	1	-2	-2	0	0
Tu. Tagovailoa	3	-5	-1.7	0	4
T. Perine	1	-19	-19	0	0
Team	28	123	4.4	1	31

Kicking	FG	PCT	LONG	XP	PTS
J. Bulovas	0/0	0	0	5/6	5

Punting	NO	YDS	AVG	TB	IN 20	LONG
T. Perine	3	146	48.7	1	0	51

Receiving	REC	YDS	AVG	TD	LONG
D. Smith	7	213	30.4	2	85
J. Jeudy	5	71	14.2	1	26
H. Ruggs III	3	68	22.7	0	26
N. Harris	3	44	14.7	1	23
J. Waddle	3	22	7.3	0	9
Team	21	418	19.9	4	85

Kick returns	NO	YDS	AVG	LONG	TD
H. Ruggs III	3	71	23.7	29	0
B. Robinson Jr.	1	12	12	12	0
M. Tennison	1	8	8	8	0
Team	5	91	18.2	29	0

Punt returns	NO	YDS	AVG	LONG	TD
J. Waddle	1	77	77	77	1

Note: Table data from "LSU 46-41 Alabama (Nov 9, 2019) Box Score" (263)

11/16/19 - Alabama (5) at Mississippi State

Team	1	2	3	4	T	Passing	Rushing	Total
Alabama (5)	21	14	3	0	38	350	160	510
Mississippi State	7	0	0	0	7	82	188	270

Alabama got off to a fast start in the game, scoring on its opening drive. Running back Najee Harris capped off a 5-play, 55-yard drive with a 10-yard touchdown run in less than two minutes. The Tide defense got the ball back nine seconds later as linebacker Shane Lee intercepted Mississippi State's first pass attempt on their first possession. Lee's pick set Alabama up at the MSU 19-yard line. On the very next play, five seconds later, Tua connected with Harris for a 19-yard touchdown pass, giving Alabama a 14-0 lead. Mississippi State answered with a touchdown of its own, but Harris quickly responded with his third score of the opening quarter. The junior running back rumbled in from five yards out to extend Alabama's lead to 21-7.

Early in the second quarter, Tua hooked up with Jaylen Waddle for a 35-yard touchdown. Harris then added his career-best fourth touchdown of the half, scoring on another 5-yard run to cap a 13-play, 70-yard drive. Alabama took a commanding 35-7 lead into halftime. The defenses took over in the second half, with the only points coming on a 22-yard field goal by Alabama's Joseph Bulovas. The 38-7 score held up as the final.

Alabama was flawless in the red zone, converting all five of its opportunities into points. They found the end zone four times and added a field goal for good measure. Najee Harris had a career day, setting the Alabama single season record for receiving touchdowns by a running back with his sixth of the year. He also became the first Tide player since Mark Ingram II in 2009 to record rushing and receiving scores in back-to-back games. He found the end zone a total of four times, all before halftime. Three of them came in the first quarter alone, making him the first Alabama running back to accomplish that feat.

Defensively, Shane Lee delivered a standout performance by recording a career-best ten tackles and getting his first interception of the season on Mississippi State's first pass of the game. Anfernee Jennings, another key contributor to Alabama's stifling defense, followed closely behind with eight tackles, one of which resulted in a loss of yardage.[264]

Passing	C/ATT	YDS	AVG	TD	INT	QBR
Tu. Tagovailoa	14/18	256	14.2	2	0	99.1
M. Jones	7/11	94	8.5	0	0	70.7
Team	21/29	350	12.1	2	0	--

Rushing	CAR	YDS	AVG	TD	LONG
N. Harris	17	88	5.2	3	20
B. Robinson Jr.	8	56	7	0	20
T. Shavers	1	14	14	0	14
K. Robinson	3	10	3.3	0	9
Tu. Tagovailoa	2	-8	-4	0	0
Team	31	160	5.2	3	20

Punting	NO	YDS	AVG	TB	IN 20	LONG
T. Perine	2	79	39.5	0	1	42

Receiving	REC	YDS	AVG	TD	LONG
J. Jeudy	7	114	16.3	0	37
D. Smith	6	92	15.3	0	34
N. Harris	3	51	17	1	23
H. Ruggs III	3	39	13	0	26
J. Waddle	1	35	35	1	35
J. Billingsley	1	19	19	0	19
Team	21	350	16.7	2	37

Interceptions	INT	YDS	TD
S. Lee	1	10	0

Punt returns	NO	YDS	AVG	LONG	TD
J. Waddle	2	28	14	26	0

Kicking	FG	PCT	LONG	XP	PTS
J. Bulovas	1/1	100	22	5/5	8

Note: Table data from "Alabama 38-7 Mississippi State (Nov 16, 2019) Box Score" (265)

11/23/19 - Alabama (5) vs Western Carolina

Team	1	2	3	4	T		Passing	Rushing	Total
Western Carolina	0	0	0	3	3		112	67	179
Alabama (5)	17	21	21	7	66		310	231	541

Alabama opened the scoring against Western Carolina with a 29-yard field goal by Joseph Bulovas, capping off their first drive of 46 yards in eight plays. However, the real story of the first half was Alabama's defense, which forced three turnovers that all resulted in touchdowns. After Xavier McKinney's first interception, Mac Jones threw a short pass to DeVonta Smith. Smith caught the ball and turned upfield, sprinting 57 yards to the end zone. Later in the half, McKinney struck again. He snagged a pass that had been tipped twice then raced 81 yards down the sideline for a pick-six. McKinney also forced a fumble that was recovered by Patrick Surtain II. This turnover set up the offense with excellent field position, and Brian Robinson Jr. capitalized, rushing five yards for a touchdown to conclude a 6-play, 63-yard scoring drive. Alabama was on top 24-0 less than five minutes into the second quarter. Najee Harris caught a pass from Mac Jones and sprinted 12 yards into the end zone, scoring the Crimson Tide's fifth touchdown of the game. This extended their lead to 31-0. On the very first play of their next drive, Jaylen Waddle hauled in a pass from Mac Jones and blazed past the defense for a 54-yard score. This capped off a dominant first half performance, with the Tide heading into the locker room with a commanding 38-0 advantage.

In the third quarter, Alabama's defense continued to dominate, forcing more turnovers that led to two additional touchdowns. Najee Harris punched it in from three yards out, while QB Taulia Tagovailoa found DeVonta Smith for a 15-yard TD pass, the first of Taulia's young career. Later in the period, Brian Robinson Jr. broke free for a 46-yard touchdown run, Bama's third score of the quarter. Western Carolina finally got on the board early in the fourth with a 38-yard FG, making it 59-3. However, Alabama's offensive onslaught was not quite over. On their next possession, the Tide marched down the field and Jerome Ford capped the drive with a 6-yard touchdown run. It was Alabama's ninth touchdown of the game and its tenth score of the day.

Alabama's 66-3 margin of victory was the largest since they won by the same score against Ole Miss in 2017. Najee Harris made history by becoming the first SEC player in the last two decades to rush for a touchdown and catch a TD pass in three consecutive games. Alabama has outscored its opponents 121-31 in points off turnovers this season. McKinney was a playmaker, recording two interceptions, a forced fumble, and three tackles (one for a loss). Lee led the team with seven tackles, while Barmore, Young, Eboigbe and Jennings combined for four sacks.[266]

Passing	C/ATT	YDS	AVG	TD	INT	QBR
M. Jones	10/12	275	22.9	3	0	98.2
Ta. Tagovailoa	2/3	35	11.7	1	0	99.7
Team	12/15	310	20.7	4	0	--

Rushing	CAR	YDS	AVG	TD	LONG
K. Robinson	8	92	11.5	1	46
N. Harris	14	66	4.7	1	22
J. Ford	5	24	4.8	1	8
C. Townsend	6	24	4	0	9
D. Lockridge	2	12	6	0	8
B. Robinson Jr.	4	11	2.8	1	5
M. Jones	1	4	4	0	4
Team	2	-2	-1	0	0
Team	42	231	5.5	4	46

Kicking	FG	PCT	LONG	XP	PTS
J. Bulovas	1/1	100	29	9/9	12

Punting	NO	YDS	AVG	TB	IN 20	LONG
T. Perine	1	33	33	0	0	33

Receiving	REC	YDS	AVG	TD	LONG
J. Waddle	3	101	33.7	1	54
D. Smith	4	94	23.5	2	57
J. Jeudy	2	66	33	0	44
T. Shavers	1	20	20	0	20
J. Metchie III	1	17	17	0	17
N. Harris	1	12	12	1	12
Team	12	310	25.8	4	57

Kick returns	NO	YDS	AVG	LONG	TD
K. Robinson	1	22	22	22	0
J. Waddle	1	20	20	20	0
Team	2	42	21	22	0

Punt returns	NO	YDS	AVG	LONG	TD
J. Waddle	2	67	33.5	49	0

Interceptions	INT	YDS	TD
X. McKinney	2	78	1
J. Mayden	2	14	0
Team	4	92	1

Note: Table data from "Alabama 66-3 Western Carolina (Nov 23, 2019) Box Score" (267)

11/30/19 - Alabama (5) at Auburn (15)

Team	1	2	3	4	T		Passing	Rushing	Total
Alabama (5)	3	28	7	7	45		335	180	515
Auburn (15)	7	20	13	8	48		173	181	354

Auburn got the ball first and was forced to punt. Alabama scored on its opening drive when Joseph Bulovas kicked a season-long 43-yard field goal, capping off a 10-play, 55-yard drive. After both teams traded punts, Auburn put together a scoring drive that resulted in a touchdown. The Tigers took a 7-3 lead, but it didn't last long as Alabama answered by putting together an impressive 75-yard drive of its own. Najee Harris scored from six yards out, reclaiming the lead (10-7). Auburn tied the game on its next possession with a 43-yard field goal (10-10). Following an Auburn pick-six, Jaylen Waddle took the ensuing kickoff 98 yards for a touchdown to tie the game at 17-17.

On the second play of Auburn's next drive, Xavier McKinney forced a fumble, and Christian Harris recovered it at the AU 37-yard line. The Tide seized the opportunity as Mac Jones connected with DeVonta Smith for a 33-yard gain, bringing the ball to the Auburn 4-yard line. Just two plays later, Jones found Henry Ruggs III in the end zone for a 3-yard touchdown, putting Alabama ahead 24-17. Auburn scored another touchdown with 1:06 left in the half. But Alabama didn't even need that long to go 62 yards in two plays as Jones finding Waddle for a 58-yard score to give the Crimson Tide a 31-24 lead with 33 seconds left in the half. With one second in the half, Auburn added a 52-yard field goal as time expired, making it 31-27, Bama.

The second half started off with Alabama punting on its first drive. Auburn capitalized on its first possession, nailing a 43-yard field goal to cut Alabama's lead to one point, 31-30. After a second pick-six by the Tigers (a lucky bounce off the back of Najee Harris), Waddle answered with his third touchdown of the day, taking Jones' pass 12 yards to the end zone and putting Alabama back on top, 38-37. After both teams punted, Auburn re-gained the lead (40-38) with a 44-yard field goal. Jones and Waddle connected once again, this time from 28 yards out, to give Alabama a 45-40 lead with time winding down. Auburn mounted one final drive and punched in a touchdown with just over eight minutes remaining. The Tigers converted the two-point try to take a 48-45 lead which would hold up as the final score.

Jaylen Waddle found the end zone an impressive four times, including three touchdown receptions and an electrifying 98-yard kickoff return. He amassed an astounding 230 all-purpose yards, including 98 yards receiving on only four catches. Three of his four catches went for touchdowns (from 58, 12, and 28 yards). On the defensive side of the ball, two standouts emerged for the Crimson Tide, Xavier McKinney and Raekwon Davis. Both players recorded eight tackles on the day, including seven solo stops each. McKinney also forced a fumble in the second quarter.[268]

Passing	C/ATT	YDS	AVG	TD	INT	QBR
M. Jones	26/39	335	8.6	4	2	89.8

Rushing	CAR	YDS	AVG	TD	LONG
N. Harris	27	146	5.4	1	23
M. Jones	8	32	4	0	18
S. Bolden	1	3	3	0	3
B. Robinson Jr.	2	-1	-0.5	0	2
Team	38	180	4.7	1	23

Kicking	FG	PCT	LONG	XP	PTS
J. Bulovas	1/2	50	43	6/6	9

Punting	NO	YDS	AVG	TB	IN 20	LONG
T. Perine	3	135	45	0	0	47

Receiving	REC	YDS	AVG	TD	LONG
H. Ruggs III	6	99	16.5	1	33
J. Waddle	4	98	24.5	3	58
D. Smith	5	80	16	0	33
N. Harris	4	26	6.5	0	13
J. Jeudy	5	26	5.2	0	10
B. Robinson Jr.	1	7	7	0	7
M. Jones	1	-1	-1	0	0
Team	26	335	12.9	4	58

Kick returns	NO	YDS	AVG	LONG	TD
J. Waddle	3	132	44	98	1
T. Diggs	3	45	15	24	0
C. Latu	1	0	0	0	0
Team	7	177	25.3	98	1

Note: Table data from "Auburn 48-45 Alabama (Nov 30, 2019) Box Score" (269)

01/01/20 - Alabama (13) vs Michigan (14)

Team	1	2	3	4	T		Passing	Rushing	Total
Michigan (14)	10	6	0	0	**16**		233	162	**395**
Alabama (13)	7	7	7	14	**35**		327	153	**480**

Michigan went three-and-out to start the game. Alabama wasted no time making its mark in the Citrus Bowl. On the very first play from scrimmage, Mac Jones found Jerry Jeudy streaking down the sideline for an electrifying 85-yard touchdown. It was the second-longest pass play in Citrus Bowl history. After both teams traded punts, Michigan tied the game at 7-7 on a 7-yard touchdown pass. Bama punted on its next two possessions while Michigan scored field goals on theirs (from 36 and 42 yards) to take a 13-7 lead. Alabama got on the board again when Najee Harris leapt into the end zone for a 9-yard touchdown, giving him a rushing TD for the seventh game in a row. But Michigan regained the lead as time expired in the first half when Quinnn Nordin kicked an incredibly long 57-yard field goal. The Wolverines led 16-14 at the half.

Alabama started the second half much like the first. Mac Jones hit DeVonta Smith for a 42-yard touchdown on the opening drive to go ahead 21-16. Alabama scored in the fourth quarter after five consecutive punts (three by Michigan and two by Bama). Jones found Forristall for a 20-yard touchdown strike, marking his triumphant return to the gridiron after a four-game absence late in the regular season. After two more punts, one by each team, Shyheim Carter picked off a pass at the Alabama 25-yard line. This led to a 2-yard TD plunge by Najee Harris to ice the game with just 24 seconds left. That brought the final to 35-16.

Jerry Jeudy (Citrus Bowl MVP) finished the day with a career-high 204 receiving yards on six catches, putting him over 1,000 yards for the season (and second time in his career). He totaled 1,163 yards in 2019. His 34-yard average per reception is simply absurd. His 85-yard reception was the second longest completion in Citrus Bowl history.

The Alabama defense was led by a trio of standout performers. Xavier McKinney and Anfernee Jennings tied for the team lead with ten tackles each. Shane Lee made his presence felt with a game-high seven solo stops and nine overall tackles. McKinney and Lee also each recorded a sack. Jennings and Tevita Musika combined forces to bring down the QB for another sack. The secondary also stepped up with Shyheim Carter and Josh Jobe both hauling in interceptions in the second half, providing crucial momentum shifts. Alabama's appearance in this bowl game marked the program's NCAA-best 67th bowl trip. The Tide also secured their 39th bowl/postseason victory – the most in college football history. Alabama has now won 10+ games for the 12th consecutive year. Even more impressive, the Crimson Tide has tallied 11+ wins in each of the last nine seasons.[270]

Passing	C/ATT	YDS	AVG	TD	INT	QBR
M. Jones	16/25	327	13.1	3	0	95.3

Rushing	CAR	YDS	AVG	TD	LONG
N. Harris	24	136	5.7	2	25
B. Robinson Jr.	3	16	5.3	0	18
J. Jeudy	1	1	1	0	1
M. Jones	1	0	0	0	0
H. Ruggs III	1	0	0	0	0
Team	30	153	5.1	2	25

Interceptions	INT	YDS	TD
S. Carter	1	0	0
J. Jobe	1	0	0
Team	2	0	0

Punting	NO	YDS	AVG	TB	IN 20	LONG
M. Bernier	6	254	42.3	1	4	52

Receiving	REC	YDS	AVG	TD	LONG
J. Jeudy	6	204	34	1	85
D. Smith	3	56	18.7	1	42
M. Forristall	3	36	12	1	20
H. Ruggs III	2	27	13.5	0	25
J. Waddle	1	7	7	0	7
J. Billingsley	1	-3	-3	0	0
Team	16	327	20.4	3	85

Kick returns	NO	YDS	AVG	LONG	TD
J. Waddle	1	23	23	23	0

Punt returns	NO	YDS	AVG	LONG	TD
J. Waddle	1	13	13	13	0

Kicking	FG	PCT	LONG	XP	PTS
J. Bulovas	0/0	0	0	5/5	5

Note: Table data from "Michigan 16-35 Alabama (Jan 1, 2020) Box Score" (271)

Season Stats

Record	11-2	10th of 130
SEC Record	6-2	
Rank	8	
Points for	614	
Points against	242	
Points/game	47.2	2nd of 130
Opp points/game	18.6	13th of 130
SOS[13]	2.81	39th of 130

Team stats (averages per game)

		Passing					Rushing			
Split	G	Cmp	Att	Pct	Yds	TD	Att	Yds	Avg	TD
Offense	13	22.1	31.2	70.7	342.2	3.8	33.5	168.7	5	2.1
Defense	13	17.7	31.5	56.1	187.2	1.2	35.8	137.4	3.8	0.7
Difference		4.4	-0.3	14.6	155	2.6	-2.3	31.3	1.2	1.4

	Total Offense			First Downs				Penalties		Turnovers		
Split	Plays	Yds	Avg	Pass	Rush	Pen	Tot	No.	Yds	Fum	Int	Tot
Offense	64.7	510.9	7.9	13	9.7	1.8	24.5	7.3	65.8	0.3	0.5	0.8
Defense	67.3	324.6	4.8	9.3	7.3	2.3	19	5.8	48.3	0.8	1.3	2.2
Difference	-2.6	186.3	3.1	3.7	2.4	-0.5	5.5	1.5	17.5	-0.5	-0.8	-1.4

Passing

			Passing								
Rk	Player	G	Cmp	Att	Pct	Yds	Y/A	AY/A	TD	Int	Rate
1	Tua Tagovailoa	9	180	252	71.4	2840	11.3	13.4	33	3	206.9
2	Mac Jones	12	97	141	68.8	1503	10.7	11.7	14	3	186.8
3	Taulia Tagovailoa	5	9	12	75	100	8.3	10	1	0	172.5
4	Slade Bolden	12	1	1	100	6	6	26	1	0	480.4

Rushing and receiving

			Rushing					Receiving				Scrimmage			
Rk	Player	G	Att	Yds	Avg	TD	Rec	Yds	Avg	TD	Plays	Yds	Avg	TD
1	Najee Harris	13	209	1224	5.9	13	27	304	11.3	7	236	1528	6.5	20
2	Brian Robinson Jr.	13	96	441	4.6	5	11	124	11.3	0	107	565	5.3	5
3	Keilan Robinson	8	39	254	6.5	2					39	254	6.5	2
4	Jerome Ford	4	24	114	4.8	3	2	11	5.5	0	26	125	4.8	3
5	Tua Tagovailoa	9	23	17	0.7	2					23	17	0.7	2
6	Mac Jones	12	16	36	2.3	1	1	-1	-1	0	17	35	2.1	1
7	Chadarius Townsend	5	8	22	2.8	0					8	22	2.8	0
8	Slade Bolden	12	4	10	2.5	0	2	34	17	0	6	44	7.3	0
9	Henry Ruggs III	12	2	75	37.5	1	40	746	18.7	7	42	821	19.5	8
10	De'marquise Lockridge	1	2	12	6	0					2	12	6	0
11	Tyrell Shavers	12	1	14	14	0	1	20	20	0	2	34	17	0
12	Jaylen Waddle	13	1	5	5	0	33	560	17	6	34	565	16.6	6
13	Jerry Jeudy	13	1	1	1	0	77	1163	15.1	10	78	1164	14.9	10
14	Taulia Tagovailoa	5	1	-2	-2	0					1	-2	-2	0
15	Ty Perine	6	1	-19	-19	0					1	-19	-19	0
16	DeVonta Smith	13					68	1256	18.5	14	68	1256	18.5	14
17	Miller Forristall	9					15	167	11.1	4	15	167	11.1	4
18	John Metchie III	12					4	23	5.8	0	4	23	5.8	0
19	Major Tennison	12					3	21	7	1	3	21	7	1
20	Jahleel Billingsley	9					2	16	8	0	2	16	8	0
21	Giles Amos	9					1	5	5	0	1	5	5	0

301

Defense and fumbles

Rk	Player	G	Solo	Ast	Tot	Loss	Sk	Int	Yds	Avg	TD	PD	FR	TD	FF
1	Xavier McKinney	13	59	36	95	5.5	3	3	78	26	1	5	1		4
2	Shane Lee	13	47	39	86	6.5	4.5	1	10	10	0	0	1		2
3	Anfernee Jennings	13	45	38	83	12.5	8	1	0	0	0	5			1
4	Christian Harris	12	27	34	61	7.5	0					1	1		0
5	Jared Mayden	12	31	28	59	1	0	4	54	13.5	0	3			
6	Raekwon Davis	12	18	29	47	3	0.5								
7	Shyheim Carter	13	24	19	43	2.5	0	1	0	0	0	7			1
8	Patrick Surtain II	13	32	10	42	1	0	2	24	12	0	8	1		3
9	Trevon Diggs	12	20	17	37	0.5	0	3	79	26.3	1	8	2	1	0
10	Terrell Lewis	10	21	10	31	11.5	6					2	1		0
11	Jordan Battle	13	18	12	30	2	1	1	0	0	0	1	1		0
12	Josh Jobe	12	21	7	28	0	0	1	0	0	0	3	1		0
13	Phidarian Mathis	11	13	14	27	0.5	0								1
14	Christian Barmore	11	12	14	26	6	2					2			
15	Byron Young	9	6	17	23	1.5	1					1			
16	Markail Benton	7	11	8	19	1	0					1			
17	Ale Kaho	13	6	13	19	1	0								
18	DJ Dale	8	6	11	17	3	1						1		0
19	Tevita Musika	8	4	12	16	1	0.5								
20	Christopher Allen	5	6	5	11	4.5	0.5								
21	Justin Eboigbe	4	6	4	10	3	1.5								
22	Jaylen Moody	6	4	6	10	0	0								
23	Labryan Ray	3	4	5	9	1.5	1								1
24	Daniel Wright	5	3	5	8	0	0								
25	Stephon Wynn Jr.	4	1	6	7	0	0								
26	Henry Ruggs III	12	3	3	6	0	0								
27	Slade Bolden	12	3	2	5	0	0								
28	Ben Davis	5	3	1	4	1	1					1			
29	Demarcco Hellams	2	2	2	4	0.5	0.5								
30	Braylen Ingraham	2	2	2	4	0	0								
31	King Mwikuta	2	1	3	4	0	0								
32	Kevin Harris II	1	2	0	2	0	0						1		1
33	Najee Harris	13	1	1	2	0	0								
34	DeVonta Smith	13	2	0	2	0	0								
35	Jahleel Billingsley	9	1	0	1	0	0								1
36	Jalyn Armour-Davis	2	0	1	1	0	0					2			
37	Scooby Carter	1	1	0	1	0	0								
38	DJ Douglas	1	0	1	1	0	0								
39	Thomas Fletcher	1	1	0	1	0	0								
40	Jerry Jeudy	13	0	1	1	0	0								
41	Cameron Latu	10	1	0	1	0	0								
42	John Metchie III	12	1	0	1	0	0								
43	Ty Perine	6	0	1	1	0	0								
44	Brian Robinson Jr.	13	1	0	1	0	0								
45	Joshua Robinson	1	0	1	1	0	0								

Kick and punt returns

| | | | Kick Ret | | | | Punt Ret | | | |
Rk	Player	G	Ret	Yds	Avg	TD	Ret	Yds	Avg	TD
1	Henry Ruggs III	12	12	286	23.8	0				
2	Trevon Diggs	12	6	117	19.5	0				
3	Jaylen Waddle	13	5	175	35	1	20	487	24.4	1
4	Brian Robinson Jr.	13	3	26	8.7	0				
5	Keilan Robinson	8	1	22	22	0				
6	Major Tennison	12	1	8	8	0				
7	Miller Forristall	9	1	3	3	0				
8	Cameron Latu	10	1	0	0	0				
9	Ale Kaho	13					2	42	21	1
10	Tyrell Shavers	12					1	2	2	1

Kicking and punting

Rk	Player	G	XPM	XPA	XP%	FGM	FGA	FG%	Pts	Punts	Yds	Avg
					Kicking						Punting	
1	Joseph Bulovas	11	59	61	96.7	8	11	72.7	83			
2	Will Reichard	5	21	22	95.5	4	7	57.1	33	4	152	38
3	Ty Perine	6								13	581	44.7
4	Skyler Delong	5								10	330	33
5	Mike Bernier	1								6	254	42.3

Scoring

Rk	Player	G	Rush	Rec	Int	FR	PR	KR	Tot	XPM	FGM	2PM	Sfty	Pts
					Touchdowns					Kicking				
1	Najee Harris	13	13	7					20					120
2	DeVonta Smith	13		14					14					84
3	Joseph Bulovas	11								59	8			83
4	Jerry Jeudy	13		10					10					60
5	Henry Ruggs III	12	1	7					8					48
6	Jaylen Waddle	13		6			1	1	8					48
7	Will Reichard	5								21	4			33
8	Brian Robinson Jr.	13	5						5					30
9	Miller Forristall	9		4					4					24
10	Jerome Ford	4	3						3					18
11	Keilan Robinson	8	2						2					12
12	Trevon Diggs	12			1	1			2					12
13	Tua Tagovailoa	9	2						2					12
14	Xavier McKinney	13			1				1					6
15	Ale Kaho	13					1		1					6
16	Tyrell Shavers	12					1		1					6
17	Major Tennison	12		1					1					6
18	Mac Jones	12	1						1					6

Stats include bowl games
Note: Table data from "2019 Alabama Crimson Tide Stats" (13)

Awards and honors

Name	Award	Type
Anfernee Jennings	Permanent Team Captain	Team
Xavier McKinney	Permanent Team Captain	Team
DeVonta Smith	Permanent Team Captain	Team
Tua Tagovailoa	Permanent Team Captain	Team
Tua Tagovailoa	MVP	Team
Jerry Jeudy	Offensive Player of the Year	Team
Tua Tagovailoa	Offensive Player of the Year	Team
Jedrick Wills	Offensive Player of the Year	Team
Anfernee Jennings	Defensive Player of the Year	Team
Xavier McKinney	Defensive Player of the Year	Team
Jaylen Waddle	Special Teams Player of the Year	SEC
Trevon Diggs	AP All-SEC First Team	SEC
Anfernee Jennings	AP All-SEC First Team	SEC
Xavier McKinney	AP All-SEC First Team	SEC
DeVonta Smith	AP All-SEC First Team	SEC
Jedrick Wills	AP All-SEC First Team	SEC
Landon Dickerson	AP All-SEC Second Team	SEC
Najee Harris	AP All-SEC Second Team	SEC
Jerry Jeudy	AP All-SEC Second Team	SEC
Alex Leatherwood	AP All-SEC Second Team	SEC
Tua Tagovailoa	AP All-SEC Second Team	SEC
Anfernee Jennings	Coaches' All-SEC First Team	SEC
Jerry Jeudy	Coaches' All-SEC First Team	SEC
Xavier McKinney	Coaches' All-SEC First Team	SEC
Jaylen Waddle	Coaches' All-SEC First Team	SEC
Jedrick Wills	Coaches' All-SEC First Team	SEC
Raekwon Davis	Coaches' All-SEC Second Team	SEC
Landon Dickerson	Coaches' All-SEC Second Team	SEC
Trevon Diggs	Coaches' All-SEC Second Team	SEC
Najee Harris	Coaches' All-SEC Second Team	SEC
Terrell Lewis	Coaches' All-SEC Second Team	SEC
DeVonta Smith	Coaches' All-SEC Second Team	SEC

Name	Award	Type
Tua Tagovailoa	Coaches' All-SEC Second Team	SEC
Jaylen Waddle	Coaches' All-SEC Second Team	SEC
DeVonta Smith	AP All-America Second Team	National
Jaylen Waddle	AP All-America Second Team	National
Jedrick Wills	AP All-America Second Team	National
Trevon Diggs	AP All-America Third Team	National
Xavier McKinney	AP All-America Third Team	National
Jaylen Waddle	Sporting News (TSN) All-America Team	National
Trevon Diggs	Sporting News (TSN) All-America Second Team	National
Xavier McKinney	Sporting News (TSN) All-America Second Team	National
DeVonta Smith	Sporting News (TSN) All-America Second Team	National
Jedrick Wills	Sporting News (TSN) All-America Second Team	National
Jaylen Waddle	FWAA All-America First Team	National
Jerry Jeudy	AFCA All-America Team	National
Alex Leatherwood	AFCA All-America Team	National
Anfernee Jennings	Senior Bowl	All-Star Team
Terrell Lewis	Senior Bowl	All-Star Team
Jared Mayden	Senior Bowl	All-Star Team

NFL

Season	Year drafted	Round	Pick	Overall	Player	Position	Team
2019	2020	1	5	5	Tua Tagovailoa	QB	Miami Dolphins
2019	2020	1	10	10	Jedrick Wills	T	Cleveland Browns
2019	2020	1	12	12	Henry Ruggs III	WR	Las Vegas Raiders
2019	2020	1	15	15	Jerry Jeudy	WR	Denver Broncos
2019	2020	2	4	36	Xavier McKinney	S	New York Giants
2019	2020	2	19	51	Trevon Diggs	CB	Dallas Cowboys
2019	2020	2	24	56	Raekwon Davis	DT	Miami Dolphins
2019	2020	3	20	84	Terrell Lewis	LB	Los Angeles Rams
2019	2020	3	23	87	Anfernee Jennings	LB	New England Patriots

Note: Table data from "2019 Alabama Crimson Tide football team" (244)

Note: Jalen Hurts received a degree from the University of Alabama, but he transferred to the University of Oklahoma before he was drafted into the NFL. The NFL uses the last school in which a player attended for the official NFL Draft.

2020

Overall

Record	13-0
SEC Record	11-0
Rank	1
Points for	630
Points against	252
Points/game	48.5
Opp points/game	19.4
SOS[14]	9.64

This is just the most together, committed group I think we've ever had the opportunity to be associated with. I think that's special. I think all these guys on this team will remember being part of this team for the rest of their life because it's a really, really exceptionally special experience to bring a group of people together, have them all buy into the principles and values that it takes to be successful, and make the sacrifices, have the work ethic, especially in a year like this where you had to overcome so much adversity, and then accomplish what they were able to accomplish. -Nick Saban

Games

Date	Bama Rank		Opp Rank	Opponent	Bama	Opp	Result	SEC
09/26/20	2	@		Missouri	38	19	W	W
10/03/20	2	vs	13	Texas A&M	52	24	W	W
10/10/20	2	@		Ole Miss	63	48	W	W
10/17/20	2	vs	3	Georgia	41	24	W	W
10/24/20	2	@		Tennessee	48	17	W	W
10/31/20	2	vs		Mississippi State	41	0	W	W
11/21/20	1	vs		Kentucky	63	3	W	W
11/28/20	1	vs	22	Auburn	42	13	W	W
12/05/20	1	@		LSU	55	17	W	W
12/12/20	1	@		Arkansas	52	3	W	W
12/19/20	1	N	7	Florida	52	46	W	W
01/01/21	1	N	4	Notre Dame	31	14	W	
01/11/21	1	N	3	Ohio State	52	24	W	

Coaches

Name	Position	Year
Nick Saban	Head Coach	14
David Ballou	Strength and Conditioning	1
Jeff Banks	Special Teams Coordinator / Tight Ends	3
Kyle Flood	Offensive Line	2
Pete Golding	Defensive Coordinator / Inside Linebackers	3
Charles Huff	Associate Head Coach / Running Backs	2
Charles Kelly	Associate Defensive Coordinator / Safeties	2
Freddie Roach	Defensive Line	1 (6th overall)
Steve Sarkisian	Offensive Coordinator / Quarterbacks	2
Karl Scott	Cornerbacks	3
Sal Sunseri	Outside Linebackers	2 (5th overall)
Holmon Wiggins	Wide Receivers	2

Recruits

Name	Pos	Pos Rank	Rivals	247 Sports	ESPN	ESPN Grade	Hometown	High school / college	Height	Weight	Committed
William Anderson	DE	6	5	5	4	85	Hampton, GA	Dutchtown HS	6-3	229	6/17/19
Javon Baker	WR	45	4	4	4	80	Powder Springs, GA	McEachern HS	6-0	180	11/25/18
Brian Branch	S	3	4	4	4	84	Tyrone, GA	Sandy Creek HS	6-0	175	4/19/19
Chris Braswell	DE	3	5	5	5	91	Baltimore, MD	St. Frances Academy	6-3	220	11/25/18
Jackson Bratton	ILB	5	4	4	4	83	Muscle Shoals, AL	Muscle Shoals HS	6-3	220	3/24/18
Jamil Burroughs	DT	22	4	4	4	80	Powder Springs, GA	McEachern HS	6-4	322	10/16/19
Caden Clark	TE	6	3	3	4	80	Akron, OH	Archbishop Hoban HS	6-4	257	7/31/18
Javion Cohen	OT	56	4	4	3	79	Phenix City, AL	Central HS	6-5	275	12/11/19
Kyle Edwards	RB	42	4	3	3	79	Destrehan, LA	Destrehan HS	6-0	200	8/23/19
Damieon George Jr.	OT	30	3	3	4	80	Houston, TX	North Shore HS	6-6	315	6/15/19
Traeshon Holden	WR	41	4	4	4	81	Harbor City, CA	Narbonne HS	6-3	185	3/2/19
Thaiu Jones-Bell	WR	9	3	4	4	84	Miami, FL	Miami Carol City Senior HS	5-11	185	5/20/19
Demouy Kennedy	OLB	7	5	4	4	84	Theodore, A	Theodore HS	6-2	205	6/9/19
Jah-Marien Latham	DT	9	4	4	4	84	Reform, AL	Pickens County HS	6-3	270	11/19/18
Jase McClellan	RB	6	4	4	4	86	Aledo, TX	Aledo HS	5-11	200	12/18/19
Seth McLaughlin	OC	4	3	3	4	80	Buford, GA	Buford HS	6-4	270	3/24/19
Malachi Moore	CB	23	4	4	4	81	Trussville, AL	Hewitt-Trussville HS	5-11	171	8/13/18
Jahquez Robinson	CB	33	4	4	3	79	Jacksonville, FL	Sandalwood HS	6-2	175	2/18/19
Quandarrius Robinson	OLB	8	4	4	4	84	Birmingham, AL	P.D. Jackson-Olin HS	6-5	215	6/11/19
Drew Sanders	ATH	4	4	5	4	86	Denton, TX	Billy Ryan HS	6-5	220	4/29/19
Timothy Smith	DT	13	4	4	4	83	Sebastian, FL	Sebastian River HS	6-4	324	7/17/19
Kristian Story	ATH	15	4	4	4	81	Lanett, AL	Lanett HS	6-1	206	7/18/19
Ronald Williams	S	3	4	4	3	79	Ferriday, LA	Hutchinson Community College (JC)	6-2	190	12/14/19
Roydell Williams	RB	10	4	4	4	84	Hueytown, AL	Hueytown HS	5-11	200	11/24/18
Bryce Young	QB	1	5	5	5	91	Philadelphia, PA	Mater Dei HS (CA)	6-0	180	9/22/19

	Rivals	247Sports	ESPN
5 Stars	4	4	2
4 Stars	17	17	19
3 Stars	4	4	4
2 Stars	0	0	0

Note: Table data from "2020 Alabama Crimson Tide football team" (272)

Roster

Num	Player	Pos	Class	Height	Weight	Hometown	Last School
82	Chase Allen	PK	FR	6-2	188	Colleyville, TX	Colleyville Heritage
4	Christopher Allen	LB	R-JR	6-4	250	Baton Rouge, LA	Southern Lab School
31	Will Anderson Jr.	LB	FR	6-4	235	Hampton, GA	Dutchtown
5	Jalyn Armour-Davis	DB	R-SO	6-1	192	Mobile, AL	St. Paul's
5	Javon Baker	WR	FR	6-2	195	Powder Springs, GA	McEachern
26	Marcus Banks	DB	SO	6-0	180	Houston, TX	Dekaney
7	Braxton Barker	QB	R-SO	6-1	202	Birmingham, AL	Spain Park
58	Christian Barmore	DL	R-SO	6-5	310	Philadelphia, PA	Neumann Goretti
53	Matthew Barnhill	LB	SO	6-1	209	Woodway, TX	Midway
9	Jordan Battle	DB	SO	6-1	210	Fort Lauderdale, FL	St. Thomas Aquinas
25	Jonathan Bennett	WR	FR	5-8	178	Birmingham, AL	Oak Mountain
19	Jahleel Billingsley	TE	SO	6-4	230	Chicago, IL	Phillips Academy
46	Melvin Billingsley	TE	JR	6-3	230	Opelika, AL	Opelika
35	Cooper Bishop	RB	R-FR	6-0	195	Vestavia Hills, AL	Vestavia Hills
18	Slade Bolden	WR	R-SO	5-11	191	West Monroe, LA	West Monroe
36	Bret Bolin	WR	R-JR	6-0	176	Lemont, IL	Lemont/Indiana
96	Landon Bothwell	DL	R-SO	5-11	220	Oneonta, AL	Oneonta/Culver-Stockton
51	Tanner Bowles	OL	R-FR	6-5	293	Glasgow, KY	Glasgow
14	Brian Branch	DB	FR	6-0	190	Tyrone, GA	Sandy Creek
41	Chris Braswell	LB	FR	6-3	220	Baltimore, MD	St. Frances Academy
33	Jackson Bratton	LB	FR	6-3	225	Muscle Shoals, AL	Muscle Shoals
65	Deonte Brown	OL	R-SR	6-4	350	Decatur, AL	Austin
75	Tommy Brown	OL	R-SO	6-7	320	Santa Ana, CA	Mater Dei
97	Joseph Bulovas	PK	R-JR	6-0	215	Mandeville, LA	Mandeville
12	Logan Burnett	QB	SR	6-2	200	Pelham, AL	Bessemer Academy / TCU / Miss State
98	Jamil Burroughs	DL	FR	6-3	326	Powder Springs, GA	McEachern
66	Brandon Cade	OL	FR	6-2	264	Birmingham, AL	Minor
57	Javion Cohen	OL	FR	6-4	325	Phenix City, AL	Central
71	Darrian Dalcourt	OL	SO	6-3	300	Havre de Grace, MD	St. Frances Academy
94	DJ Dale	DL	SO	6-3	307	Birmingham, AL	Clay-Chalkville
1	Ben Davis	LB	R-SR	6-4	250	Gordo, AL	Gordo
12	Skyler DeLong	P	JR	6-4	188	Fort Mill, SC	Nation Ford
69	Landon Dickerson	OL	R-SR	6-6	325	Hickory, NC	South Caldwell/Florida State
57	Joe Donald	LB	R-SR	6-3	216	Mountain Brook, AL	Mountain Brook
20	DJ Douglas	DB	R-FR	6-0	202	Montgomery, AL	Thompson
92	Justin Eboigbe	DL	SO	6-5	285	Forest Park, GA	Forest Park
38	Jalen Edwards	DB	R-FR	6-0	177	Columbus, MS	Eufaula
27	Kyle Edwards	RB	FR	6-0	209	Destrehan, LA	Destrehan
55	Emil Ekiyor Jr.	OL	R-SO	6-3	324	Indianapolis, IN	Cathedral
51	Robert Ellis	LB	FR	6-0	220	Enterprise, AL	Enterprise
45	Thomas Fletcher	SN	SR	6-2	231	Georgetown, TX	IMG Academy
54	Kyle Flood Jr.	LB	FR	6-0	209	Middlesex, NJ	St. Joseph
87	Miller Forristall	TE	R-SR	6-5	244	Cartersville, GA	Cartersville
16	Jayden George	QB	R-FR	6-3	192	Indianapolis, IN	Warren Central
74	Damieon George Jr.	OL	FR	6-6	345	Houston, TX	North Shore
24	Clark Griffin	LB	FR	5-9	195	Mountain Brook, AL	Mountain Brook
59	Jake Hall	SN	R-SO	6-3	238	Saraland, AL	Saraland
67	Donovan Hardin	OL	FR	6-3	285	Dublin, OH	Dublin Scioto
8	Christian Harris	LB	SO	6-2	232	Baton Rouge, LA	University Lab
22	Najee Harris	RB	SR	6-2	230	Antioch, CA	Antioch
44	Kevin Harris II	LB	FR	6-4	228	Loganville, GA	Grayson
29	DeMarcco Hellams	DB	SO	6-1	208	Washington, DC	DeMatha Catholic
11	Traeshon Holden	WR	FR	6-3	208	Kissimmee, FL	Narbonne
19	Stone Hollenbach	QB	R-FR	6-3	208	Catawissa, PA	Southern Columbia
83	Richard Hunt	TE	R-FR	6-7	235	Memphis, TN	Briarcrest Christian
97	LT Ikner	DL	JR	6-4	261	Daphne, AL	Daphne/Hutchinson C.C.
52	Braylen Ingraham	DL	R-FR	6-4	289	Fort Lauderdale, FL	St. Thomas Aquinas
28	Josh Jobe	DB	JR	6-1	192	Miami, FL	Cheshire Academy (Conn.)
98	Sam Johnson	P	FR	6-3	215	Birmingham, AL	Oak Mountain
10	Mac Jones	QB	R-JR	6-3	214	Jacksonville, FL	The Bolles School
14	Thaiu Jones-Bell	WR	FR	6-0	190	Hallandale, FL	Miami Carol City
10	Ale Kaho	LB	JR	6-1	235	Reno, NV	Reno
37	Demouy Kennedy	LB	FR	6-3	215	Theodore, AL	Theodore
78	Amari Kight	OL	R-FR	6-7	318	Alabaster, AL	Thompson
85	Drew Kobayashi	WR	R-SR	6-2	200	Honolulu, HI	St. Louis/Cal/Riverside C.C./Wash State
89	Grant Krieger	WR	SO	6-2	192	Pittsburgh, PA	Pine-Richland
84	Joshua Lanier	WR	R-SR	5-11	160	Tuscaloosa, AL	Tuscaloosa Academy/North Alabama
93	Jah-Marien Latham	DL	FR	6-3	285	Reform, AL	Pickens County
81	Cameron Latu	TE	R-SO	6-5	250	Salt Lake City, UT	Olympus
70	Alex Leatherwood	OL	SR	6-6	312	Pensacola, FL	Booker T. Washington
35	Shane Lee	LB	SO	6-0	240	Burtonsville, MD	St. Frances Academy
49	Julian Lowenstein	LB	R-FR	6-0	201	Sarasota, FL	Riverview
89	Kyle Mann	DL	FR	6-0	270	Powder Springs, GA	McEachern

307

Num	Player	Pos	Class	Height	Weight	Hometown	Last School
95	Jack Martin	P	SO	v	206	Mobile, AL	McGill-Toolen
48	Phidarian Mathis	DL	JR	6-4	312	Wisner, LA	Neville
25	Jacobi McBride	DB	FR	6-1	143	Madison, AL	Madison Academy
21	Jase McClellan	RB	FR	5-11	212	Aledo, TX	Aledo
56	Seth McLaughlin	OL	FR	6-4	280	Buford, GA	Buford
40	Joshua McMillon	LB	SR	6-3	240	Memphis, TN	Whitehaven
8	**John Metchie III**	**WR**	**SO**	**6-0**	**195**	**Brampton, Canada**	**St. James School (Md.)**
42	Jaylen Moody	LB	JR	6-2	225	Conway, SC	Conway
13	**Malachi Moore**	**DB**	**FR**	**6-0**	**182**	**Trussville, AL**	**Hewitt-Trussville**
32	**Dylan Moses**	**LB**	**SR**	**6-3**	**240**	**Alexandria, LA**	**IMG Academy**
30	King Mwikuta	LB	SO	6-5	238	West Point, GA	Troup County
73	**Evan Neal**	**OL**	**SO**	**6-7**	**360**	**Okeechobee, FL**	**IMG Academy**
79	Chris Owens	OL	R-SR	6-3	315	Arlington, TX	Lamar
80	Michael Parker	TE	R-SO	6-6	232	Huntsville, AL	Westminster Christian
23	Jarez Parks	LB	R-SO	6-4	240	Fellsmere, FL	Sebastian River
99	**Ty Perine**	**P/PK**	**SO**	**6-1**	**218**	**Prattville, AL**	**Prattville**
50	Gabe Pugh	SN	R-FR	6-5	273	Tuscaloosa, AL	Northridge
72	Pierce Quick	OL	R-FR	6-5	280	Trussville, AL	Hewitt-Trussville
85	Kendall Randolph	TE/OL	R-JR	6-4	298	Madison, AL	Bob Jones
18	**LaBryan Ray**	**DL**	**R-JR**	**6-5**	**295**	**Madison, AL**	**James Clemens**
42	Sam Reed	WR	SO	6-1	165	Mountain Brook, AL	John Carroll
91	Gavin Reeder	DL	R-FR	6-0	292	Charlotte, NC	Providence
16	**Will Reichard**	**PK**	**SO**	**6-1**	**190**	**Hoover, AL**	**Hoover**
21	Jahquez Robinson	DB	FR	6-2	190	Jacksonville, FL	Sandalwood
27	Joshua Robinson	DB	R-JR	5-9	180	Hoover, AL	Hoover
2	Keilan Robinson	RB	SO	5-9	190	Washington, DC	St. John's
34	Quandarrius Robinson	LB	FR	6-5	220	Birmingham, AL	Jackson-Olin
4	Brian Robinson Jr.	RB	SR	6-0	228	Tuscaloosa, AL	Hillcrest
62	Jackson Roby	OL	JR	6-5	285	Huntsville, AL	Huntsville
16	Drew Sanders	LB	FR	6-5	230	Denton, TX	Ryan
24	Trey Sanders	RB	R-FR	6-0	214	Port Saint Joe, FL	IMG Academy
85	*Charlie Scott*	*P*	*SR*	*6-1*	*195*	*Greenwood Village, CO*	*Cherry Creek/Air Force*
56	Charlie Skehan	LB	FR	6-1	232	Columbia, SC	Cardinal Newman
93	Tripp Slyman	PK/P	R-SO	6-1	180	Huntsville, AL	Randolph
6	**DeVonta Smith**	**WR**	**SR**	**6-1**	**175**	**Amite, LA**	**Amite**
15	Eddie Smith	DB	R-SO	6-0	196	Slidell, LA	Salmen
43	Jordan Smith	LB	FR	5-10	210	Chelsea, AL	Chelsea
50	Tim Smith	DL	FR	6-4	320	Sebastian, FL	Sebastian River
95	Ishmael Sopsher	DL	FR	6-4	310	Amite, LA	Amite
68	Alajujuan Sparks Jr.	OL	FR	6-4	345	Hoover, AL	Hoover
11	Kristian Story	DB	FR	6-1	215	Lanett, AL	Lanett
2	**Patrick Surtain II**	**DB**	**JR**	**6-2**	**202**	**Plantation, FL**	**American Heritage**
46	Christian Swann	DB	SR	5-9	179	Mableton, GA	Pebblebrook
88	Major Tennison	TE	R-JR	6-5	252	Flint, TX	Bullard
86	*Carl Tucker*	*TE*	*SR*	*6-2*	*248*	*Concord, NC*	*Hough/North Carolina*
7	Brandon Turnage	DB	R-FR	6-1	186	Oxford, MS	Lafayette
15	Paul Tyson	QB	R-FR	6-5	228	Trussville, AL	Hewitt-Trussville
17	**Jaylen Waddle**	**WR**	**JR**	**5-10**	**182**	**Houston, TX**	**Episcopal**
39	Carson Ware	DB	R-FR	6-1	190	Muscle Shoals, AL	Muscle Shoals
59	Bennett Whisenhunt	LB	FR	6-1	222	Vestavia Hills, AL	Vestavia Hills
32	C.J. Williams	WR	FR	5-10	159	Gallion, AL	Demopolis
23	Roydell Williams	RB	FR	5-10	210	Hueytown, AL	Hueytown
31	Shatarius Williams	WR	FR	6-3	187	Demopolis, AL	Demopolis
3	Xavier Williams	WR	R-SO	6-1	190	Hollywood, FL	Chaminade-Madonna Prep
22	Ronald Williams Jr.	DB	JR	6-2	190	Ferriday, LA	Ferriday/Hutchinson C.C.
37	Sam Willoughby	DB	FR	5-10	165	Vestavia Hills, AL	Vestavia Hills
3	**Daniel Wright**	**DB**	**R-JR**	**6-1**	**195**	**Fort Lauderdale, FL**	**Boyd Anderson**
90	Stephon Wynn Jr.	DL	R-SO	6-4	310	Anderson, SC	IMG Academy
9	Bryce Young	QB	FR	6-0	194	Pasadena, CA	Mater Dei
47	Byron Young	DL	SO	6-3	292	Laurel, MS	West Jones

Note: Starters in bold
Note: Table data from "2020 Alabama Crimson Tide Roster" (273)

308

Transfers

Player	School	Direction
Charlie Scott	Air Force	Incoming
Carl Tucker	North Carolina	Incoming
Giles Amos	Arkansas State	Outgoing
Jerome Ford	Cincinnati	Outgoing
Mac Hereford	Vanderbilt	Outgoing
Scott Lashley	Mississippi State	Outgoing
Tyrell Shavers	Mississippi State	Outgoing
Taulia Tagovailoa	Maryland	Outgoing

Note: Table data from "2020 Alabama Crimson Tide football team" (272)

Games

09/26/20 - Alabama (2) at Missouri

Team	1	2	3	4	T		Passing	Rushing	Total
Alabama (2)	14	14	7	3	38		303	111	414
Missouri	0	3	3	13	19		253	69	322

The Alabama defense held Missouri to a single field goal in the first half, forcing them to punt three times and stopping them on 4th-and-2. Meanwhile, Alabama scored four touchdowns while only punting twice. Najee Harris drew first blood for Alabama, punching in a 1-yard touchdown run that capped off a methodical 12-play, 66-yard march that drained 4:47 off the clock. Later in the opening quarter, Mac Jones went over the top, hitting Jaylen Waddle in the end zone's front porch for an 18-yard scoring strike. The dynamic duo accounted for 64 of the 66 yards on the drive, highlighted by Waddle's 48-yard catch to ignite the possession. Less than a minute into the second quarter, Harris etched his name on the scoreboard once more, plunging across the goal line from a mere yard out. This play was the culmination of a meticulously orchestrated 8-play drive that spanned a staggering 91 yards, leaving defenders in its wake. As the first half drew to a close, Waddle hauled in a 23-yard touchdown strike from the ever-precise Jones. This dynamic duo's second connection of the half extended Alabama's lead to a commanding 28-3.

In the third quarter, Najee Harris punched it in from eight yards out for his third touchdown of the night. That scoring drive covered 37 yards in just five plays. Missouri managed to get a field goal on the board from 37 yards out that capped an 18-play, 55-yard grind of a drive (35-6). The Tigers finally found the end zone in the fourth quarter after Bryce Young was sacked and lost a fumble on the Mizzou 43-yard line. QB Shawn Robinson hit Tyler Badie for a 54-yard scoring strike to make it 35-13. Alabama answered with a 34-yard field goal from Will Reichard. As time expired, Missouri's Connor Bazelak scored on a 7-yard quarterback keeper, but it was too late as Alabama prevailed 38-19 behind Harris' monster game.

Alabama kicked off their season with a resounding victory, extending their remarkable streak of opening season wins to 14 consecutive years. The offense was spearheaded by Najee Harris, who etched his name in the record books by matching his career-high with three rushing touchdowns. On the defensive side, Daniel Wright emerged as the standout performer, amassing a career-high 11 tackles, including a tackle for loss. Wright's tenacious play was part of a collective defensive effort that saw the Bama defense rack up an impressive eight tackles for loss, resulting in a staggering -37 yards. This was the most tackles for loss an Alabama defense has recorded since they posted ten against Mississippi State in 2018. Christian Harris, LaBryan Ray, and Josh Jobe each recorded a sack.[274]

Passing	C/ATT	YDS	AVG	TD	INT	QBR
M. Jones	18/24	249	10.4	2	0	95.1
B. Young	5/8	54	6.8	0	0	83.3
Team	23/32	303	9.5	2	0	--

Rushing	CAR	YDS	AVG	TD	LONG
N. Harris	17	98	5.8	3	18
B. Robinson Jr.	4	18	4.5	0	9
M. Jones	1	4	4	0	4
B. Young	4	2	0.5	0	12
T. Sanders	9	1	0.1	0	2
D. Smith	1	-12	-12	0	0
Team	36	111	3.1	3	18

Punting	NO	YDS	AVG	TB	IN 20	LONG
S. Johnson	3	117	39	0	1	45

Receiving	REC	YDS	AVG	TD	LONG
J. Waddle	8	134	16.8	2	46
D. Smith	8	89	11.1	0	23
J. Metchie III	2	42	21	0	22
M. Forristall	1	34	34	0	34
N. Harris	2	8	4	0	5
T. Sanders	1	-2	-2	0	0
B. Robinson Jr.	1	-2	-2	0	0
Team	23	303	13.2	2	46

Kicking	FG	PCT	LONG	XP	PTS
W. Reichard	1/1	100	34	5/5	8

Note: Table data from "Alabama 38-19 Missouri (Sep 26, 2020) Box Score" (275)

310

10/03/20 - Alabama (2) vs Texas A&M (13)

Team	1	2	3	4	T	Passing	Rushing	Total
Texas A&M (13)	7	7	3	7	24	335	115	450
Alabama (2)	14	21	7	10	52	435	109	544

The Crimson Tide struck first when Mac Jones unleashed a deep bomb, finding John Metchie III streaking downfield for a 78-yard touchdown strike. The lightning-quick drive, spanning just three plays in 1:18, covered 80 yards and followed a missed field goal attempt by Texas A&M. Alabama kept the pressure on as workhorse Najee Harris capped off a methodical 7-play, 66-yard drive with a 6-yard bulldozing run into the end zone, giving the Tide a 14-0 cushion. Not to be outdone, the Aggies responded late in the opening quarter. Kellen Mond aired it out, hitting Ainias Smith in stride for a 47-yard touchdown connection. The 5-play, 75-yard drive trimmed Alabama's lead to 14-7.

The second quarter saw Texas A&M draw level, with Kellen Mond connecting with Ryan Renick for a 17-yard touchdown reception. This scoring play came immediately after Leal's 23-yard interception return. However, Alabama quickly regained the lead when Najee Harris punched it in from two yards out, capping a 7-play, 66-yard drive that took 2:34 off the clock (21-14 Alabama). The Crimson Tide defense then made a statement as Daniel Wright picked off Mond and raced 47 yards to the end zone for Alabama's first non-offensive touchdown of the season. The Tide scored again after holding A&M to a three-and-out when Mac Jones hit DeVonta Smith for a 2-yard scoring strike. This crisp 8-play, 64-yard march lasted just 59 seconds, extending Alabama's lead to 35-14 heading into the half.

The Aggies opened the scoring in the second half as Small's 29-yard FG capped off a 12-play, 40-yard drive. Alabama responded with Jones finding Jaylen Waddle for an 87-yard touchdown reception, the Tide's third receiving score of the day. The drive lasted just 1:39 and covered 75 yards in three plays, extending Alabama's lead to 42-17. In the final quarter, Reichard's 27-yard field goal finished off a 10-play, 68-yard drive that consumed 5:32 off the clock. Mond then connected with Smith for a 14-yard TD, culminating a 7-play, 75-yard drive that narrowed the gap to 45-24. However, Jones and Metchie III combined for a 63-yard scoring strike, sealing the 52-24 victory for Alabama. This final drive lasted 1:52 and covered 75 yards in four plays.

Alabama extended its home opener winning streak to 19 games. John Metchie III caught a career-high five receptions for a staggering 181 yards and two touchdowns. Bama's defense forced two crucial turnovers - Daniel Wright's 47-yard interception return for a touchdown and Malachi Moore's end zone interception. Christian Harris racked up ten tackles and a quarterback hurry, while Jordan Battle had nine tackles and a pass breakup.[276]

Passing	C/ATT	YDS	AVG	TD	INT	QBR
M. Jones	20/27	435	16.1	4	1	95.7

Rushing	CAR	YDS	AVG	TD	LONG
B. Robinson Jr.	10	60	6	0	16
N. Harris	12	43	3.6	2	6
T. Sanders	2	14	7	0	9
J. Waddle	1	3	3	0	3
M. Jones	2	-2	-1	0	2
Team	1	-9	-9	0	0
Team	28	109	3.9	2	16

Kicking	FG	PCT	LONG	XP	PTS
W. Reichard	1/1	100	27	7/7	10

Punting	NO	YDS	AVG	TB	IN 20	LONG
S. Johnson	2	66	33	0	0	40

Receiving	REC	YDS	AVG	TD	LONG
J. Metchie III	5	181	36.2	2	78
J. Waddle	5	142	28.4	1	87
D. Smith	6	63	10.5	1	20
N. Harris	2	26	13	0	16
M. Forristall	2	23	11.5	0	12
Team	20	435	21.8	4	87

Punt returns	NO	YDS	AVG	LONG	TD
J. Waddle	1	11	11	11	0

Interceptions	INT	YDS	TD
D. Wright	1	47	1
M. Moore	1	0	0
Team	2	47	1

Note: Table data from "Alabama 52-24 Texas A&M (Oct 3, 2020) Box Score" (277)

10/10/20 - Alabama (2) at Ole Miss

Team	1	2	3	4	T		Passing	Rushing	Total
Alabama (2)	7	14	21	21	63		417	306	723
Ole Miss	7	14	14	13	48		379	268	647

The clash between Ole Miss and Alabama turned into an electrifying offensive duel. The Rebels drew first blood when Matt Corral connected with Kenny Yeboah for a 6-yard touchdown strike. However, the Crimson Tide responded quickly as Mac Jones found DeVonta Smith for a 14-yard scoring play, capping a 10-play, 85-yard drive. In the second quarter, Ole Miss regained the advantage with a methodical 93-yard march, culminating in Jerrion Ealy's 3-yard touchdown run (14-7). Alabama's Brian Robinson Jr. then took center stage, accounting for 36 of the Tide's 72 yards on the ensuing drive, including a 1-yard plunge into the end zone for his first score of the season (14-14). The Rebels wasted no time answering, orchestrating an 11-play, 75-yard drive that consumed 3:36 off the clock. Snoop Conner's 2-yard rush put Ole Miss back in front 21-14. Not to be outdone, Alabama's Najee Harris tied the score at 21-21 just before halftime with a 5-yard touchdown run, set up by Mac Jones' clutch passing and scrambling. He completed three passes for 50 total yards and converted a crucial 3rd-down with a 5-yard rush.

The second half was a seesaw battle between Alabama and Ole Miss, with the lead changing hands multiple times. The Crimson Tide struck first, taking their initial lead of the game with a blistering 85-yard drive capped by a 33-yard touchdown run from Harris. However, Ole Miss quickly answered. Less than a minute later, Corral connected with Kenny Yeboah for a 68-yard scoring strike, evening the score at 28-28. Just over two minutes after falling behind, the Crimson Tide reclaimed the advantage when Jones connected with Miller Forristall on a 3-yard touchdown strike. However, the Rebels refused to stay down. They methodically marched 75 yards over 10 plays, bleeding four minutes off the clock. Running back Ealy capped the marathon drive with his second touchdown of the night, a 9-yard scoring run that knotted the game at 35-35. In a display of resilience, the Crimson Tide answered with another Harris touchdown run, this time from three yards out. His career-high tying third score of the night gave Alabama a 42-35 lead after a 72-yard drive lasting over three and a half minutes.

The fourth quarter was a breathtaking offensive showcase. Ole Miss struck first as sophomore running back Conner punched it in from inches out, knotting the score at 42-42 after his rushing touchdown. Alabama came right back when Harris found the end zone from 16 yards out for his career-high fourth touchdown, regaining the lead for the Tide. The Rebels kept battling, with Luke Logan capping off an 8-play, 54-yard drive by splitting the uprights from 39 yards to make it 49-45, Alabama on top. The scoring frenzy continued as Jones connected with DeVonta Smith for a 14-yard touchdown, pushing the Tide's lead to double digits at 56-45. Logan added another field goal from 29 yards to chip away at the deficit. However, Harris delivered the dagger with a 39-yard rushing touchdown, his fifth of the night, essentially putting the game away. When the dust settled, Alabama emerged victorious in this fourth quarter shootout, winning 63-48 in an absolute offensive explosion.

The gridiron witnessed a stellar display of running prowess as Najee Harris etched his name in the annals of Alabama football history. The senior tailback orchestrated a ground assault amassing a career-high 206 yards on 23 carries. He crossed the goal line an astonishing five times, matching the program's single-game touchdown record. His 200-yard masterpiece etched his name among the elite, becoming the 19th Crimson Tide rusher to achieve such a feat. While Harris commanded the spotlight, quarterback Mac Jones connected with his favorite target, DeVonta Smith, on 13 occasions for 164 yards and a touchdown. Smith's exceptional outing tied the all-time mark for receptions in a single game.

The Crimson Tide's defensive unit was spearheaded by Dylan Moses' career-best performance. He tallied an impressive 13 tackles, including a half-tackle for loss. Jordan Battle contributed 11 tackles, a half-tackle for loss, and a pass breakup. Alabama's relentless pass rush proved too much for the Ole Miss quarterback, as Christopher Allen and Christian Barmore each recorded a sack.

The victory marked another milestone for Alabama's head coach, Nick Saban, as he extended his remarkable unbeaten streak against his former assistants to 21-0 during his tenure with the Crimson Tide.[278]

Passing	C/ATT	YDS	AVG	TD	INT	QBR
M. Jones	28/32	417	13	2	0	97.2

Rushing	CAR	YDS	AVG	TD	LONG
N. Harris	23	206	9	5	39
B. Robinson Jr.	10	76	7.6	1	18
D. Smith	1	14	14	1	14
J. Waddle	1	11	11	0	11
M. Jones	3	1	0.3	0	5
Team	1	-2	-2	0	0
Team	39	306	7.8	7	39

Punting	NO	YDS	AVG	TB	IN 20	LONG
S. Johnson	1	40	40	1	0	40

Receiving	REC	YDS	AVG	TD	LONG
D. Smith	13	164	12.6	1	36
J. Waddle	6	120	20	0	45
J. Metchie III	4	75	18.8	0	32
N. Harris	3	42	14	0	24
M. Forristall	2	16	8	1	13
Team	28	417	14.9	2	45

Kick returns	NO	YDS	AVG	LONG	TD
D. Smith	2	42	21	22	0
C. Tucker	1	23	23	23	0
J. Waddle	2	2	1	2	0
Team	5	67	13.4	23	0

Kicking	FG	PCT	LONG	XP	PTS
W. Reichard	0/0	0	0	9/9	9

Note: Table data from "Alabama 63-48 Ole Miss (Oct 10, 2020) Box Score" (279)

10/17/20 - Alabama (2) vs Georgia (3)

Team	1	2	3	4	T	Passing	Rushing	Total
Georgia (3)	7	17	0	0	24	269	145	414
Alabama (2)	7	13	14	7	41	417	147	564

After Mac Jones was intercepted on the first play of the game, Justin Eboigbe got the ball back three plays later when he picked off Stetson Bennett. Three plays after that, Mac Jones threw a deep bomb to John Metchie III who raced 40 yards into the end zone to put the Tide on the board first. After two punts each, Georgia RB Zamir White evened things up, bursting through the line and sprinting ten yards to tie the game at 7-7 as the first quarter ended. Just 11 seconds into the second quarter, James Cook took a pass 82 yards for a touchdown and the Bulldogs' first lead of the night (14-7). After each team traded field goals (Bama from 33 and UGA from 50), they traded touchdowns. For Bama, DeVonta Smith caught a 17-yard TD pass to finish a 6-play, 75-yard drive. Waddle had a nice 38-yard catch along the way. For Georgia, it was Jermaine Burton who caught the 5-yard TD pass to cap off a 12-play, 66-yard drive. As the first half came to a close, Reichard drilled a career-best 52-yard field goal, cutting Alabama's deficit to 24-20.

The second half opened with three punts. With Alabama starting at their own 9-yard line, Brian Robinson Jr. only gained one yard. Then Mac Jones hit Waddle for the other 90 yards and the touchdown, the scoring drive only lasting 49 seconds. Alabama led 27-24, and they never looked back. Georgia's last three possessions of the game resulted in two interceptions and a missed field goal from 35. Meanwhile, Alabama scored two more touchdowns. Harris' rushing TD streak reached 11 games after he powered his way into the end zone from two yards out. Then DeVonta Smith drug his toes along the back of the end zone, hauling in a 13-yard touchdown pass. This score extended Alabama's lead to 41-24, which held up as the final score.

Mac Jones completed 24-of-32 passes for 417 yards, throwing for 400+ yards now three games in a row. He threw four touchdowns with one interception. Jaylen Waddle hauled in six catches for a career-high 161 yards, and he has surpassed the 100-yard receiving mark in all four games this season. DeVonta Smith's 167-yard performance extended a streak where he and Waddle have both eclipsed 100 receiving yards in back-to-back games. Najee Harris had a career-best 152 rushing yards on 31 carries. He extended his streak of games with at least one rushing score to 11. Defensively, Malachi Moore, Daniel Wright, and Justin Eboigbe each came away with an interception, with two of those coming on back-to-back drives. DeMarcco Hellams (11) and Dylan Moses (10) led the way in tackles. Moses and Christian Barmore also contributed with a sack each. This victory marked Nick Saban's third win in the last four games against a former assistant, and he improved to 22-0 when facing off against them.[280]

Passing	C/ATT	YDS	AVG	TD	INT	QBR
M. Jones	24/32	417	13	4	1	96.9

Rushing	CAR	YDS	AVG	TD	LONG
N. Harris	31	152	4.9	1	17
B. Robinson Jr.	7	20	2.9	0	5
J. Waddle	1	-2	-2	0	0
M. Jones	3	-20	-6.7	0	0
Team	1	-3	-3	0	0
Team	43	147	3.4	1	17

Interceptions	INT	YDS	TD
M. Moore	1	42	0
D. Wright	1	18	0
J. Eboigbe	1	4	0
Team	3	64	0

Punting	NO	YDS	AVG	TB	IN 20	LONG
S. Johnson	4	131	32.8	0	3	36

Receiving	REC	YDS	AVG	TD	LONG
D. Smith	11	167	15.2	2	34
J. Waddle	6	161	26.8	1	90
J. Metchie III	3	50	16.7	1	40
M. Forristall	3	29	9.7	0	14
N. Harris	1	10	10	0	10
Team	24	417	17.4	4	90

Kick returns	NO	YDS	AVG	LONG	TD
J. Waddle	1	22	22	22	0

Punt returns	NO	YDS	AVG	LONG	TD
J. Waddle	1	2	2	2	0

Kicking	FG	PCT	LONG	XP	PTS
W. Reichard	2/2	100	52	5/5	11

Note: Table data from "Alabama 41-24 Georgia (Oct 17, 2020) Box Score" (281)

10/24/20 - Alabama (2) at Tennessee

Team	1	2	3	4	T	Passing	Rushing	Total
Alabama (2)	14	14	14	6	48	417	170	587
Tennessee	0	10	7	0	17	163	139	302

After each team punted, Alabama opened the scoring with a 1-yard rushing touchdown by Najee Harris, capping off a 6-play, 70-yard drive that took 2:50 off the clock. This gave the Crimson Tide an early 7-0 lead. After holding TN to another punt, Mac Jones punched it in from one yard out to complete a 7-play, 76-yard scoring drive that consumed 3:35, extending Alabama's advantage. In the second quarter, Tennessee finally got on the board with a 33-yard field goal at the end of a 13-play possession, making it 14-3. Robinson Jr. then rumbled up the middle for a 7-yard touchdown run for Alabama's third rushing score of the day. That capped off a 9-play, 75-yard drive. Tennessee responded when Guarantano connected with Hyatt for a 38-yard TD pass, as Tennessee drove 75 yards in 1:59 to cut the deficit to 21-10. Alabama answered right back with a touchdown of its own in just over two minutes. Metchie III made a spectacular 45-yard grab as he out-battled two defenders to secure the ball. This set up Harris' third TD of the game as he walked into the end zone untouched from two yards out to bring the score to 28-10.

As Tennessee started the second half, Moore forced, recovered, and returned a fumble 28 yards into the end zone. Harris scored his third rushing TD of the day as he punched it in from the one-yard line after an 80-yard drive, extending the lead to 42-10. Tennessee refused to go down without a fight as Josh Palmer caught a 27-yard touchdown pass in the corner of the end zone to close out the third quarter (42-17). Will Reichard added six more points to Alabama's lead with a couple of field goals in the fourth (from 39 and 24 yards out), bringing the final to 48-17.

Sophomore linebacker Christian Harris was a defensive standout for Alabama, recording a team-high ten tackles in the game. Meanwhile, defensive back Malachi Moore continued his impressive start to the season, forcing a fumble and returning it 28 yards for a touchdown early in the third quarter. This was Moore's third takeaway in just his first five collegiate games.

Alabama has now won 14 straight games against Tennessee, 29 straight against opponents from the SEC East, and 94 straight against unranked opponents. This was Nick Saban's fourth victory over a former assistant coach this season, bringing his overall record against former assistants to 23-0. With their 48-point performance against Tennessee, the Crimson Tide have now scored 35+ points in 18 consecutive games, the longest streak in major college football history. Quarterback Mac Jones set an Alabama record by completing 19 passes in a row. He achieved this feat by closing out the previous game against Georgia with eight straight completions and starting the Tennessee game with 11 consecutive successful passes.[282]

Passing	C/ATT	YDS	AVG	TD	INT	QBR
M. Jones	25/31	387	12.5	0	0	95.5
B. Young	3/5	30	6	0	0	86.5
Team	28/36	417	11.6	0	0	--

Rushing	CAR	YDS	AVG	TD	LONG
N. Harris	20	96	4.8	3	16
T. Sanders	7	39	5.6	0	20
B. Robinson Jr.	4	29	7.3	1	13
M. Jones	5	4	0.8	1	7
R. Williams	2	3	1.5	0	4
S. Bolden	1	1	1	0	1
B. Young	1	-2	-2	0	0
Team	40	170	4.3	5	20

Receiving	REC	YDS	AVG	TD	LONG
J. Metchie III	7	151	21.6	0	45
S. Bolden	6	94	15.7	0	30
D. Smith	7	73	10.4	0	16
N. Harris	6	61	10.2	0	14
M. Forristall	1	25	25	0	25
J. Billingsley	1	13	13	0	13
Team	28	417	14.9	0	45

Kick returns	NO	YDS	AVG	LONG	TD
J. Waddle	1	15	15	15	0

Punt returns	NO	YDS	AVG	LONG	TD
S. Bolden	1	4	4	4	0

Punting	NO	YDS	AVG	TB	IN 20	LONG
C. Scott	2	69	34.5	0	2	41

Kicking	FG	PCT	LONG	XP	PTS
W. Reichard	2/2	100	39	6/6	12

Note: Table data from "Alabama 48-17 Tennessee (Oct 24, 2020) Box Score" (283)

315

10/31/20 - Alabama (2) vs Mississippi State

Team	1	2	3	4	T	Passing	Rushing	Total
Mississippi State	0	0	0	0	0	163	37	200
Alabama (2)	17	10	0	14	41	291	208	499

The Alabama defense forced Mississippi State to punt on all seven of their possessions in the first half, while they scored five times. Kicker Will Reichard got the scoring started with a 40-yard field goal on Alabama's opening drive. Mac Jones then connected with wide receiver DeVonta Smith for a pair of touchdown passes, the first from 35 yards capping 6-play, 61-yard drive that lasted just under two minutes, and the second from 53 yards away, to give the Tide a 17-0 lead after the first quarter. In the second quarter, Reichard added another field goal from 24 yards before Jones and Smith hooked up again for an 11-yard touchdown, capping off an 88-yard drive that took nearly six minutes off the clock. Alabama took a commanding 27-0 lead into halftime.

After both teams failed to score in the third quarter, Dylan Moses picked off a pass in the end zone and took it out to the 1-yard line before he was tackled. Alabama had a long field ahead of them, and they mustered an impressive 99-yard drive in nine plays finished off when Mac Jones found his favorite target, DeVonta Smith, for the 10-yard touchdown that extended Alabama's lead to 34-0. Both teams punted and lost fumbles on the next four possessions. With the game still in hand, the Crimson Tide defense went to work. Cornerback Patrick Surtain II jumped a route and picked off Will Rogers' pass at the MSU 25-yard line. Surtain raced to the end zone untouched for the pick-six, putting the exclamation point on a dominant 41-0 victory for the Tide. This was his first interception of the season, fourth of his career, his first pick-six, and Alabama's third defensive touchdown of the season.

Defensively, Alabama was led by Malachi Moore's eight tackles, while Brian Branch and Dylan Moses each had seven stops. Moses also had an interception in the end zone. Christopher Allen and Phidarian Mathis also recorded sacks for the Tide. This was Alabama's first shutout of the season (and first since 2018 when they blanked Mississippi State 24-0), and they have now scored 35+ points in 19 consecutive games, the longest streak in major college football history.[284]

Passing	C/ATT	YDS	AVG	TD	INT	QBR
M. Jones	24/31	291	9.4	4	0	80.8
B. Young	0/2	0	0	0	0	0
Team	24/33	291	8.8	4	0	--

Rushing	CAR	YDS	AVG	TD	LONG
N. Harris	21	119	5.7	0	14
T. Sanders	12	80	6.7	0	25
B. Robinson Jr.	2	5	2.5	0	5
M. Jones	4	4	1	0	14
B. Young	1	0	0	0	0
Team	40	208	5.2	0	25

Interceptions	INT	YDS	TD
P. Surtain II	1	25	1
D. Moses	1	1	0
Team	2	26	1

Punting	NO	YDS	AVG	TB	IN 20	LONG
C. Scott	4	152	38	0	1	46

Receiving	REC	YDS	AVG	TD	LONG
D. Smith	11	203	18.5	4	53
N. Harris	6	36	6	0	11
S. Bolden	3	20	6.7	0	13
J. Metchie III	3	18	6	0	9
M. Forristall	1	14	14	0	14
Team	24	291	12.1	4	53

Kick returns	NO	YDS	AVG	LONG	TD
T. Sanders	1	17	17	17	0

Punt returns	NO	YDS	AVG	LONG	TD
S. Bolden	4	26	6.5	14	0

Kicking	FG	PCT	LONG	XP	PTS
W. Reichard	2/2	100	40	5/5	12

Note: Table data from "Alabama 41-0 Mississippi State (Oct 31, 2020) Box Score" (285)

11/21/20 - Alabama (1) vs Kentucky

Team	1	2	3	4	T		Passing	Rushing	Total
Kentucky	3	0	0	0	3		120	59	179
Alabama (1)	7	21	21	14	63		283	226	509

Alabama's running back Najee Harris punched it in from a yard out for the Crimson Tide's first touchdown of the day. The score capped off a 55-yard drive that took six plays. Kentucky managed to get their only points of the day with a 33-yard field goal by Matt Ruffolo. In the second quarter, Mac Jones connected with DeVonta Smith on a pinpoint 10-yard strike in the back of the end zone, capping off a 4-play, 58-yard drive that took only 1:52. After Kentucky missed a 42-yard field goal attempt, Najee Harris broke loose for a 42-yard touchdown scamper, his second of the game, extending Bama's lead to 21-3. John Metchie III capped the scoring onslaught with an 18-yard catch-and-run, sending the Tide into the locker room at halftime with a commanding 28-3 lead.

Alabama scored three more touchdowns in the third quarter to blow the game wide open. Linebacker Jordan Battle intercepted a Kentucky pass and returned it 45 yards for a touchdown. Robinson Jr. capped off a 29-yard drive with a 1-yard touchdown plunge, his first of the day. And sophomore quarterback Bryce Young threw his first career touchdown when he connected with DeVonta Smith for an 18-yard score (49-3). In the fourth quarter, freshman Roydell Williams scored his first career touchdown, powering in from two yards out. With 1:35 remaining, Jase McClellan broke free for a 19-yard touchdown run, the first of his career. This brought the final score to an emphatic 63-3 in favor of the Crimson Tide.

With DeVonta Smith's 10-yard TD catch early in the third quarter from Mac Jones, he broke the SEC and Alabama records for career receiving touchdowns (32), surpassing the previous mark of 31. But Smith wasn't done there. Late in the third quarter, he hauled in an 18-yard touchdown pass from QB Bryce Young that extended his record to 33 career receiving TDs. He finished the night with 144 receiving yards, marking the fourth time this season he has eclipsed the 100-yard receiving mark. Najee Harris has scored two or more rushing touchdowns in a game on five occasions this season. Christian Harris spearheaded the defensive effort by recording 11 tackles, including eight solo stops and a sack, limiting Kentucky to a single field goal. Jordan Battle secured his first interception of the season and second of his career, returning it 45 yards for a pick-six. The Alabama defense has maintained a remarkable streak, holding opposing teams without a touchdown for the last nine quarters of play, dating back to the third quarter of the Tennessee game. Furthermore, the Tide has kept their opponents scoreless for eight of the last nine quarters. Alabama matched their highest point total of the season, after beating Ole Miss 63-48. This also marked the team's largest scoring differential of the season at 60 points.[286]

Passing	C/ATT	YDS	AVG	TD	INT	QBR
M. Jones	16/24	230	9.6	2	1	96.4
B. Young	2/2	53	26.5	1	0	94.5
Team	18/26	283	10.9	3	1	--

Rushing	CAR	YDS	AVG	TD	LONG
J. McClellan	10	99	9.9	1	23
N. Harris	13	83	6.4	2	42
R. Williams	10	30	3	1	11
B. Robinson Jr.	6	22	3.7	1	11
B. Young	1	-8	-8	0	0
Team	40	226	5.7	5	42

Interceptions	INT	YDS	TD
J. Battle	1	45	1

Punting	NO	YDS	AVG	TB	IN 20	LONG
C. Scott	2	92	46	1	0	51

Receiving	REC	YDS	AVG	TD	LONG
D. Smith	9	144	16	2	35
J. Billingsley	3	78	26	0	34
N. Harris	2	27	13.5	0	24
J. Metchie III	1	18	18	1	18
S. Bolden	3	16	5.3	0	9
Team	18	283	15.7	3	35

Kick returns	NO	YDS	AVG	LONG	TD
B. Robinson Jr.	1	25	25	25	0

Punt returns	NO	YDS	AVG	LONG	TD
D. Smith	2	50	25	41	0
S. Bolden	2	19	9.5	16	0
Team	4	69	17.3	41	0

Kicking	FG	PCT	LONG	XP	PTS
W. Reichard	0/0	0	0	9/9	9

Note: Table data from "Alabama 63-3 Kentucky (Nov 21, 2020) Box Score" (287)

11/28/20 - Alabama (1) vs Auburn (22)

Team	1	2	3	4	T		Passing	Rushing	Total
Auburn (22)	0	3	3	7	13		227	120	347
Alabama (1)	7	14	14	7	42		302	143	445

For the only score in the first quarter, Mac Jones found DeVonta Smith wide open for a 66-yard touchdown strike. Jones continued his aerial assault in the second quarter, tossing two more touchdowns, sandwiching a 47-yard field goal by Auburn. First, he delivered a pinpoint pass, finding John Metchie III in the back of end zone behind the Auburn defense. The 7-yard TD strike capped off an impressive 7-play, 66-yard drive. Next, he connected with Jahleel Billingsley for a 24-yard touchdown, capping an attack that covered 75 yards in just five plays, consuming a mere 2:27 off the clock. Alabama held a commanding 21-3 lead at the half.

The third quarter saw Carlson drill a 45-yard field goal, his second of the day. Smith then snagged a short pass and outran the Auburn defense for a 58-yard touchdown score. That lightning-quick drive lasted a mere 1:28. After Auburn missed a 56-yard field goal attempt, Najee Harris found a gaping hole on the right side and exploded through it for a 39-yard touchdown jaunt. This 5-play, 61-yard drive only took 2:07 off the clock. Bama led 35-6 after three quarters of play. In the fourth quarter, Metchie III hauled in his second TD grab of the contest, a 24-yard strike from Jones to extend the lead. Auburn's Bo Nix managed a 1-yard scoring plunge, but it was too little, too late as Alabama prevailed 42-13.

DeVonta Smith amassed a staggering 171 receiving yards on seven catches, including a pair of touchdowns. This performance marked the fifth time this season that he has surpassed the 140-yard receiving mark. His exploits also propelled him past the coveted 1,000-yard threshold for the season, a milestone he has now achieved twice in his career (1,074 receiving yards on 72 catches this season and 1,256 yards in 2019). He now holds two of the program's eleven 1,000-yard seasons. Moreover, Smith's touchdown receptions further extended his SEC and Alabama career receiving touchdown record, which now stands at an impressive 35.

Mac Jones tied the Iron Bowl passing touchdown record with a career-high five scoring strikes. He racked up 302 yards through the air, completing 18-of-26 attempts. Najee Harris found the end zone for the seventh time in eight games this season, bringing his rushing touchdown tally to an impressive 17. Josh Jobe led the defense with a career-high ten tackles, including five solo stops. Malachi Moore and Brian Branch each snagged an interception, with Branch returning his first pick for 30 yards. Christopher Allen, Christian Barmore, and Will Anderson Jr. each recorded a sack against the Tigers.[288]

Passing	C/ATT	YDS	AVG	TD	INT	QBR
M. Jones	18/26	302	11.6	5	0	96

Rushing	CAR	YDS	AVG	TD	LONG
N. Harris	11	96	8.7	1	39
B. Robinson Jr.	7	39	5.6	0	15
D. Smith	1	9	9	0	9
M. Jones	4	6	1.5	0	4
J. McClellan	2	3	1.5	0	2
Team	1	-2	-8	0	0
B. Young	1	-8	-8	0	0
Team	26	143	5.3	1	39

Kicking	FG	PCT	LONG	XP	PTS
W. Reichard	0/0	0	0	6/6	6

Punting	NO	YDS	AVG	TB	IN 20	LONG
C. Scott	4	151	37.8	0	2	44

Receiving	REC	YDS	AVG	TD	LONG
D. Smith	7	171	24.4	2	66
J. Metchie III	6	55	9.2	2	24
N. Harris	2	34	17	0	25
J. Billingsley	2	33	16.5	1	24
M. Forristall	1	9	9	0	9
Team	18	302	16.8	5	66

Kick returns	NO	YDS	AVG	LONG	TD
B. Robinson Jr.	1	21	21	21	0

Punt returns	NO	YDS	AVG	LONG	TD
D. Smith	2	18	9	11	0

Interceptions	INT	YDS	TD
B. Branch	1	30	0
M. Moore	1	0	0
Team	2	30	0

Note: Table data from "Alabama 42-13 Auburn (Nov 28, 2020) Box Score" (289)

12/05/20 - Alabama (1) at LSU

Team	1	2	3	4	T		Passing	Rushing	Total
Alabama (1)	21	24	7	3	55		385	265	650
LSU	0	14	3	0	17		254	98	352

From the opening whistle, Alabama seized control, scoring touchdowns on its first five possessions (every possession in the first half) leaving the Tigers gasping for air. LSU only scored two touchdowns and one field goal the entire game. Najee Harris set the tone early, weaving through the LSU defense for a 14-yard touchdown on the opening drive. He found paydirt again ten minutes later, punching it in from a yard out to cap a lightning-quick 2:02 drive spanning five plays and 85 yards. Jones then found a wide-open Jahleel Billingsley in the corner of the end zone for a 24-yard touchdown, Alabama's third of the opening quarter (21-0).

Seven seconds into the second quarter, TJ Finley threw a pass to Kayshon Boutte who took it 44 yards, but he fumbled it at the goal line. Luckily for LSU, Jontre Kirklan picked it up in the end zone for the score (21-7). Less than a minute and a half later, DeVonta Smith added another touchdown (his 13th of the season) as he got past the LSU defense and caught a 65-yard bomb to bring the score to 28-7. About a minute later, John Emery Jr. found a gap in the defense for a 54-yard rushing touchdown (28-14). However, Alabama quickly responded with a blistering 3-play, 75-yard drive, consuming a mere 1:18 off the clock. The drive culminated in a 61-yard aerial connection between Jones and Smith. As the half drew to a close, Will Reichard split the uprights with a 30-yard field goal. In a display of remarkable athleticism, Smith then hauled in a 20-yard touchdown reception with a jaw-dropping one-handed grab in the corner of the end zone. This scoring flurry propelled Alabama to a commanding 45-14 advantage at the half.

Late in the third quarter, Najee Harris added his third touchdown of the game with an 11-yard scamper that extended Alabama's lead 52-14. The only other scores of the game were field goals from each team (a 52-yarder by LSU in the third quarter, and a 34-yarder by Bama in the fourth). Alabama cruised to a convincing 55-17 victory.

The Tide's defense, led by Will Anderson Jr. and DeMarcco Hellams who each tallied eight tackles, stifled the Tigers' rushing attack, holding them to a mere 98 yards on the ground. Anderson Jr. also recorded two of Bama's five sacks. Meanwhile, Christopher Allen created and recovered a fumble. Alabama's offense amassed 650 total yards, including 385 passing yards and 265 rushing yards. DeVonta Smith's three scores extended his SEC and school record for career receiving touchdowns to 38.[290]

Passing	C/ATT	YDS	AVG	TD	INT	QBR
M. Jones	20/28	385	13.8	4	0	99.7
B. Young	0/1	0	0	0	0	0.2
Team	20/29	385	13.3	4	0	--

Rushing	CAR	YDS	AVG	TD	LONG
N. Harris	21	145	6.9	3	28
B. Robinson Jr.	11	62	5.6	0	11
J. McClellan	5	48	9.6	0	25
R. Williams	3	19	6.3	0	9
Team	2	-2	-1	0	0
B. Young	1	-7	-7	0	0
Team	43	265	6.2	3	28

Punting	NO	YDS	AVG	TB	IN 20	LONG
C. Scott	1	33	33	0	0	33

Receiving	REC	YDS	AVG	TD	LONG
D. Smith	8	231	28.9	3	65
J. Billingsley	4	68	17	1	27
J. Metchie III	4	58	14.5	0	24
S. Bolden	1	19	19	0	13
B. Robinson Jr.	1	6	6	0	6
N. Harris	2	3	1.5	0	8
Team	20	385	19.3	4	65

Kicking	FG	PCT	LONG	XP	PTS
W. Reichard	2/2	100	34	7/7	13

Note: Table data from "Alabama 55-17 LSU (Dec 5, 2020) Box Score" (291)

12/12/20 - Alabama (1) at Arkansas

Team	1	2	3	4	T		Passing	Rushing	Total
Alabama (1)	10	28	7	7	52		227	216	443
Arkansas	3	0	0	0	3		108	80	188

Will Reichard's 45-yard field goal drew first blood for Alabama. The Razorbacks responded on their next drive with a 26-yard field goal, but it was a mere speed bump on the Tide's path to destruction as they never scored again. DeVonta Smith's 84-yard punt return touchdown (first of his career) opened the floodgates, and there was no turning back for the Crimson Tide as they racked up 35 unanswered points before halftime.

The second quarter witnessed an offensive avalanche from the Crimson Tide as they relentlessly pounded their way into the end zone. Najee Harris kickstarted the scoring spree with a gritty 1-yard touchdown plunge, capping off an 8-play drive that set the tone for the quarter (17-3). Before Arkansas could catch their breath, Christopher Allen's thunderous sack jarred the ball loose, and DJ Dale recovered it to give Alabama prime field position. Seizing the opportunity, Najee Harris wasted no time, powering his way across the goal line from five yards out extending the Tide's lead to 24-3. The onslaught continued as Robinson Jr. joined the party, muscling his way across the line of scrimmage for a 1-yard touchdown (31-3). With 33 seconds left in the first half, Robinson Jr. delivered a 4-yard touchdown run giving Alabama a commanding 35-point advantage as they headed into the locker room up 38-3.

In the third quarter, Robinson Jr. punched in his third consecutive rushing touchdown. This scoring drive spanned a mammoth 7:36, showcasing the Tide's ability to control the clock and wear down the Hogs. The only other score of the game came one play after Branch's interception in the end zone that resulted in a touchback - McClellan raced 80 yards for a touchdown to push the final score to 52-3.

The Alabama defense recorded a season-high eight sacks in the game. Will Anderson Jr. and Christian Barmore combined for half of these, with two each. The Tide defense also forced four turnovers, including three fumbles and an interception. Jaylen Moody and Byron Young each tallied seven tackles to lead the charge. Brian Branch logged an interception to set up the Tide's final score in the fourth quarter. The win extended Alabama's record for the most consecutive 10-win seasons in SEC history to 13, and its streak of scoring 35+ points to 23 games, a college football record. Additionally, the Tide became the only team in SEC history to win ten conference games in a season.[292]

Passing	C/ATT	YDS	AVG	TD	INT	QBR
M. Jones	24/29	208	7.2	0	0	91.1
B. Young	3/4	19	4.8	0	0	56.6
Team	27/33	227	6.9	0	0	--

Rushing	CAR	YDS	AVG	TD	LONG
J. McClellan	6	95	15.8	1	80
B. Robinson Jr.	13	54	4.2	3	8
N. Harris	14	46	3.3	2	17
R. Williams	4	19	4.8	0	7
M. Jones	1	2	2	0	2
Team	38	216	5.7	6	80

Interceptions	INT	YDS	TD
B. Branch	1	0	0

Punting	NO	YDS	AVG	TB	IN 20	LONG
C. Scott	2	75	37.5	0	0	39

Receiving	REC	YDS	AVG	TD	LONG
J. Metchie III	5	72	14.4	0	23
M. Forristall	6	52	8.7	0	13
S. Bolden	4	43	10.8	0	17
D. Smith	3	22	7.3	0	10
B. Robinson Jr.	4	22	5.5	0	7
J. Baker	2	15	7.5	0	15
N. Harris	1	2	2	0	2
J. McClellan	1	1	1	0	1
T. Jones-Bell	1	-2	-2	0	0
Team	27	227	8.4	0	23

Kick returns	NO	YDS	AVG	LONG	TD
B. Robinson Jr.	1	10	10	10	0

Punt returns	NO	YDS	AVG	LONG	TD
D. Smith	3	111	37	84	1

Kicking	FG	PCT	LONG	XP	PTS
W. Reichard	1/1	100	45	7/7	10

Note: Table data from "Alabama 52-3 Arkansas (Dec 12, 2020) Box Score" (293)

12/19/20 - Alabama (1) at Florida (7)

Team	1	2	3	4	T	Passing	Rushing	Total
Alabama (1)	14	21	0	17	52	418	187	605
Florida (7)	10	7	14	15	46	408	54	462

The SEC Championship game between Alabama and Florida turned into an offensive showcase, with both teams trading blows throughout the night. Najee Harris kickstarted the scoring frenzy, weaving through the Gators' defense for an 8-yard touchdown run. Florida quickly responded when Kyle Trask connected with Kadarius Toney on a 51-yard scoring strike, evening the score at 7-7. Mac Jones was intercepted by Dean III on Alabama's next drive, and John Metchie III absolutely leveled him. His hit knocked the ball loose, and DeVonta Smith recovered it. On the very next play, Mac Jones found DeVonta Smith wide open for a 31-yard touchdown strike. After Florida drove 56 yards and kicked a 40-yard field goal, Alabama led 14-10 after one quarter of play. Najee Harris scored three receiving touchdowns in the second quarter from seven, 23, and 17 yards (the last with six seconds left until halftime). In between his last two, Florida scored when QB Trask took it in from one yard out. Alabama led 35-17 at the half.

The Gators refused to go down without a fight. In the third quarter, they held Alabama scoreless while mounting a comeback. Trask tossed a 50-yard touchdown to Grimes, and Evan McPherson scored on a 3-yard rush, cutting the deficit to 35-31. In the fourth quarter, Najee Harris stretched the ball across the goal line for one yard and his fifth touchdown of the game. Alabama extended its lead to 45-31 after a 20-yard field goal from Reichard with just under ten minutes left in the game. Florida's Dameon Pierce scored on a 1-yard rush, but the Tide countered with a 15-yard touchdown reception by Smith, making it 52-38. In the game's final moments, Trask hit Kyle Pitts with a 22-yard touchdown pass and converted the two-point conversion, but it was too little, too late. Alabama emerged victorious, 52-46, in an offensive showcase for the ages.

Najee Harris matched his career-high with a remarkable five touchdowns, three through the air and two on the ground. His all-purpose yardage totaled an impressive 245 yards, including 178 rushing and 67 receiving, cementing his status as the game's MVP. DeVonta Smith scored two touchdowns and put on a receiving clinic, setting a career-best and SEC Championship Game record with 15 catches. He tallied over 200 all-purpose yards including 184 receiving. The Tide defense was led by Will Anderson Jr. who tallied six tackles, including five solo stops and two sacks. Christian Harris had two sacks, the second of which sealed the victory on the final play of the game. Dylan Moses, Jordan Battle, and Daniel Wright each contributed six tackles, while Christopher Allen added another sack. This win gave Alabama its 28th SEC championship and seventh in a row.[294]

Passing	C/ATT	YDS	AVG	TD	INT	QBR
M. Jones	33/43	418	9.7	5	1	92.3

Rushing	CAR	YDS	AVG	TD	LONG
N. Harris	31	178	5.7	2	29
B. Robinson Jr.	4	19	4.8	0	8
M. Forristall	1	1	1	0	1
J. Billingsley	1	-3	-3	0	0
M. Jones	3	-8	-2.7	0	1
Team	40	187	4.7	2	29

Punt returns	NO	YDS	AVG	LONG	TD
D. Smith	1	20	20	20	0

Punting	NO	YDS	AVG	TB	IN 20	LONG
C. Scott	2	87	43.5	1	1	44

Receiving	REC	YDS	AVG	TD	LONG
D. Smith	15	184	12.3	2	31
N. Harris	5	67	13.4	3	23
J. Metchie III	4	62	15.5	0	26
S. Bolden	2	40	20	0	25
J. Billingsley	2	29	14.5	0	15
M. Forristall	3	20	6.7	0	11
X. Williams	1	12	12	0	12
M. Tennison	1	4	4	0	4
Team	33	418	12.7	5	31

Kick returns	NO	YDS	AVG	LONG	TD
J. Billingsley	3	66	22	27	0
D. Smith	1	4	4	4	0
Team	4	70	17.5	27	0

Kicking	FG	PCT	LONG	XP	PTS
W. Reichard	1/1	100	20	7/7	10

Note: Table data from "Alabama 52-46 Florida (Dec 19, 2020) Box Score" (295)

01/01/21 - Alabama (1) vs Notre Dame (4)

Team	1	2	3	4	T	Passing	Rushing	Total
Notre Dame (4)	0	7	0	7	14	236	139	375
Alabama (1)	14	7	7	3	31	297	140	437

Due to COVID, this College Football Playoff Semifinal at the Rose Bowl was actually played in AT&T Stadium in Arlington, TX. Alabama shut out Notre Dame in the first quarter while scoring two touchdowns of its own. On their first possession, Mac Jones hit DeVonta Smith for 26 yards, capping off a 7-play, 79-yard drive that saw Jones complete 5-of-6 passes. After holding Notre Dame to a punt to the AL 3-yard line, Alabama was driving when Najee Harris got the ball and looked like he was going to lose yardage on the play. Instead, he bounced outside and ran for 53 yards, hurdling a defender along the way. This set up a touchdown catch by Jahleel Billingsley as Mac Jones found him wide open in the end zone from 12 yards out. Alabama led 14-0 after one quarter of play.

Notre Dame got on the board in the second quarter after a 15-play, 75-yard drive that took a whopping 8:03 off the clock. Kyren Williams capped it off with a 1-yard run cutting their deficit in half, 14-7. Alabama answered on its next possession as Jones unleashed a 34-yard strike, finding Smith in the end zone for his second touchdown of the day. Notre Dame missed a 51-yard field goal attempt with seconds left in the half which left Alabama with a 21-7 lead going into the locker room.

The only score in the third quarter came on the drive after Christian Harris intercepted Ian Book. During the drive, Mac Jones hit John Metchie III in stride over the middle, and he took it 40 yards to the ND 22. Five plays later, Jones rolled to the right and hit DeVonta Smith at the front corner of the end zone giving Alabama a commanding 28-7 lead. The fourth quarter saw Will Reichard maintain his perfect record this season. His 13th field goal sailed through the uprights, extending Alabama's lead by three. Notre Dame orchestrated an impressive 14-play, 80-yard drive and scored a TD with 56 seconds left in the game. They recovered the onside kick, but it was too late as Alabama won 31-14 and advanced to the CFP National Championship Game.

DeVonta Smith, the Offensive Player of the Game, tied a Rose Bowl record and Alabama Bowl record with his three receiving touchdowns on his seven catches for 130 yards. Patrick Surtain II was the Defensive Player of the Game as he tallied five tackles, including a tackle for loss and a pass breakup. DeMarcco Hellams led the Tide with a game-high 12 tackles, six of which were solo stops, and he also recorded a sack. Christian Harris logged an interception, and Christian Barmore registered a sack to complement his five tackles.[296]

Passing	C/ATT	YDS	AVG	TD	INT	QBR
M. Jones	25/30	297	9.9	4	0	94.3

Rushing	CAR	YDS	AVG	TD	LONG
N. Harris	15	125	8.3	0	53
M. Jones	5	12	2.4	0	9
B. Robinson Jr.	3	10	3.3	0	6
Team	1	-2	-2	0	0
D. Smith	1	-5	-5	0	0
Team	25	140	5.6	0	53

Receiving	REC	YDS	AVG	TD	LONG
D. Smith	7	130	18.6	3	34
J. Metchie III	3	53	17.7	0	40
J. Billingsley	4	39	9.8	1	15
M. Forristall	3	31	10.3	0	15
N. Harris	4	30	7.5	0	14
S. Bolden	2	22	11	0	14
X. Williams	1	0	0	0	0
M. Jones	1	-8	-8	0	0
Team	25	297	11.9	4	40

Interceptions	INT	YDS	TD
C. Harris	1	0	0

Kick returns	NO	YDS	AVG	LONG	TD
J. Billingsley	1	16	16	16	0

Kicking	FG	PCT	LONG	XP	PTS
W. Reichard	1/1	100	41	4/4	7

Punt returns	NO	YDS	AVG	LONG	TD
D. Smith	1	20	20	20	0

Punting	NO	YDS	AVG	TB	IN 20	LONG
C. Scott	3	127	42.3	0	2	46

Note: Table data from "Alabama 31-14 Notre Dame (Jan 1, 2021) Box Score" (297)

01/11/21 - Alabama (1) vs Ohio State (3)

Team	1	2	3	4	T		Passing	Rushing	Total
Ohio State (3)	7	10	7	0	24		194	147	341
Alabama (1)	7	28	10	7	52		464	157	621

Alabama wasted no time getting on the scoreboard as Najee Harris punched it in from one yard out. Ohio State responded quickly, as Master Teague III scampered eight yards to the end zone on the Buckeyes' second possession, knotting the game at 7-7. In the second quarter, Mac Jones found Heisman Trophy winner DeVonta Smith for a 5-yard touchdown, capping a 75-yard drive and putting Alabama back on top 14-7. After Alabama forced a punt, Mac Jones was sacked and fumbled the ball. Ohio State recovered it on the AL 19-yard line, and two plays later Teague III scored his second rushing touchdown of the evening, tying the game at 14-14.

Najee Harris set the SEC single-season touchdown record with his 29th score on Alabama's next possession, taking a Jones pass 26 yards to the house. Ohio State managed a FG on its next possession to make it 21-17. It had been a back-and-forth game up until that point, but Alabama scored two more TDs before the half, both passes to DeVonta Smith. He hauled in a short 5-yard toss from Jones, then sprinted into the end zone for his second touchdown of the contest. The speedy wideout later added a third score, this time on a perfectly thrown 42-yard bomb from Jones. The long TD strike gave the Crimson Tide an 18-point cushion at intermission as they headed to the locker room with a commanding 35-17 lead. Smith was unstoppable in the first half, catching 12 passes for 215 yards and three touchdowns, all CFP Championship Game records. He was named Offensive MVP despite missing most of the second half with an injury.

Will Reichard extended the lead to 38-17 with a 20-yard field goal to open the third quarter. Justin Fields found Garrett Wilson for a 20-yard touchdown pass, but Alabama answered with another Jones-to-Smith scoring strike and a Slade Bolden touchdown catch to make it 45-24 after three quarters. He was the third different receiver to catch a touchdown pass from Mac Jones in the game. The only score in the fourth quarter was when Harris carried for one yard for his second rushing touchdown and third overall in the game, bringing the final score to 52-24.

DeVonta Smith set Championship Game records with 12 receptions and three receiving TDs, racking up 215 yards which amounted to over 46% of their 464 total receiving yards. Christian Barmore (Defensive MVP) logged five tackles, including two for loss and a sack. Mac Jones etched his name in the CFP record books by throwing for an astounding 464 yards on 36-of-45 passing. His performance included a CFP title game record-tying five touchdown passes. Najee Harris became the fifth player to score both rushing and receiving touchdown in a BCS/CFP title game. He totaled 158 yards of total offense, rushing for 79 yards on 22 attempts catching seven passes for 79 yards. Christian Harris and Dylan Moses led the defense with six tackles each.[298]

Passing	C/ATT	YDS	AVG	TD	INT	QBR
M. Jones	36/45	464	10.3	5	0	98

Receiving	REC	YDS	AVG	TD	LONG
D. Smith	12	215	17.9	3	44
J. Metchie III	8	81	10.1	0	27
N. Harris	7	79	11.3	1	26
J. Waddle	3	34	11.3	0	15
J. Billingsley	2	27	13.5	0	22
S. Bolden	3	16	5.3	1	7
X. Williams	1	12	12	0	12
Team	36	464	12.9	5	44

Rushing	CAR	YDS	AVG	TD	LONG
N. Harris	22	79	3.6	2	13
B. Robinson Jr.	10	69	6.9	0	21
M. Jones	4	11	2.8	0	10
Team	2	-2	-1	0	0
Team	38	157	4.1	2	21

Kick returns	NO	YDS	AVG	LONG	TD
J. Billingsley	1	7	7	7	0
D. Smith	1	6	6	6	0
Team	2	13	6.5	7	0

Kicking	FG	PCT	LONG	XP	PTS
W. Reichard	1/1	100	20	7/7	10

Punt returns	NO	YDS	AVG	LONG	TD
D. Smith	2	18	9	19	0

Punting	NO	YDS	AVG	TB	IN 20	LONG
C. Scott	2	76	38	0	1	40

Note: Table data from "Alabama 52-24 Ohio State (Jan 11, 2021) Box Score" (299)

Season Stats

Record	13-0	1st of 127
SEC Record	11-0	
Rank	1	
Points for	630	
Points against	252	
Points/game	48.5	2nd of 127
Opp points/game	19.4	13th of 127
SOS[14]	9.64	3rd of 127

Team stats (averages per game)

Split	G	Passing					Rushing				Total Offense		
		Cmp	Att	Pct	Yds	TD	Att	Yds	Avg	TD	Plays	Yds	Avg
Offense	13	24.9	32.7	76.2	358.2	3.2	36.6	183.6	5	2.8	69.3	541.8	7.8
Defense	13	20.9	36	58.1	239.2	1.2	33.9	113.1	3.3	1.2	69.9	352.2	5
Difference		4	-3.3	18.1	119	2	2.7	70.5	1.7	1.6	-0.6	189.6	2.8

Split	First Downs				Penalties		Turnovers		
	Pass	Rush	Pen	Tot	No.	Yds	Fum	Int	Tot
Offense	16.2	10.2	1.8	28.1	6	48.1	0.6	0.3	0.9
Defense	11	6.8	2.1	19.9	5.8	45.5	0.8	0.9	1.7
Difference	5.2	3.4	-0.3	8.2	0.2	2.6	-0.2	-0.6	-0.8

Passing

Rk	Player	G	Passing								
			Cmp	Att	Pct	Yds	Y/A	AY/A	TD	Int	Rate
1	Mac Jones	13	311	402	77.4	4500	11.2	12.8	41	4	203.1
2	Bryce Young	9	13	22	59.1	156	7.1	8	1	0	133.7

Rushing and receiving

Rk	Player	G	Rushing					Receiving				Scrimmage			
			Att	Yds	Avg	TD	Rec	Yds	Avg	TD	Plays	Yds	Avg	TD
1	Najee Harris	13	251	1466	5.8	26	43	425	9.9	4	294	1891	6.4	30
2	Brian Robinson Jr.	13	91	483	5.3	7	6	26	4.3	0	97	509	5.2	7
3	Mac Jones	13	35	14	0.4	1	1	-8	-8	0	36	6	0.2	1
4	Trey Sanders	4	30	134	4.5	0	1	-2	-2	0	31	132	4.3	0
5	Jase McClellan	12	23	245	10.7	2	1	1	1	0	24	246	10.3	2
6	Roydell Williams	8	19	71	3.7	1					19	71	3.7	1
7	Bryce Young	9	9	-23	-2.6	0					9	-23	-2.6	0
8	DeVonta Smith	13	4	6	1.5	1	117	1856	15.9	23	121	1862	15.4	24
9	Jaylen Waddle	6	3	12	4	0	28	591	21.1	4	31	603	19.5	4
10	Slade Bolden	13	1	1	1	0	24	270	11.3	1	25	271	10.8	1
11	Miller Forristall	12	1	1	1	0	23	253	11	1	24	254	10.6	1
12	Jahleel Billingsley	12	1	-3	-3	0	18	287	15.9	3	19	284	14.9	3
13	John Metchie III	13					55	916	16.7	6	55	916	16.7	6
14	Xavier Williams	6					3	24	8	0	3	24	8	0
15	Javon Baker	8					2	15	7.5	0	2	15	7.5	0
16	Major Tennison	12					1	4	4	0	1	4	4	0
17	Thaiu Jones-Bell	3					1	-2	-2	0	1	-2	-2	0

Defense and fumbles

Rk	Player	G	Tackles					Def Int					Fumbles		
			Solo	Ast	Tot	Loss	Sk	Int	Yds	Avg	TD	PD	FR	TD	FF
1	Christian Harris	13	52	27	79	7	4.5	1	0	0	0	2			
2	Dylan Moses	13	40	36	76	6	1	1	1	1	0	3			1
3	Jordan Battle	13	41	25	66	3	0	1	45	45	1	4			
4	Daniel Wright	13	44	16	60	1	0	2	65	32.5	1	3			
5	Demarcco Hellams	11	32	24	56	1.5	1					3			
6	Josh Jobe	13	39	16	55	2.5	2					11			2
7	Will Anderson Jr.	13	34	18	52	10.5	7								1
8	Malachi Moore	12	28	16	44	4	0	3	42	14	0	6	1	1	1
9	Patrick Surtain II	13	22	15	37	3.5	0	1	25	25	1	9			
10	Christian Barmore	11	22	15	37	9.5	8					3			3
11	Christopher Allen	11	24	13	37	13	6						1		2
12	Phidarian Mathis	10	16	15	31	5	1.5					3			1
13	Brian Branch	12	19	8	27	0.5	0	2	30	15	0	7			
14	Byron Young	9	11	15	26	5.5	0.5						1		0
15	DJ Dale	8	8	13	21	1	0					2	1		0
16	Justin Eboigbe	13	10	9	19	0.5	0	1	4	4	0	0			
17	Jaylen Moody	6	12	7	19	0.5	0						1		1
18	Tim Smith	8	8	6	14	2.5	1						2		1
19	Labryan Ray	5	8	4	12	1	1								
20	Joshua McMillon	4	4	5	9	1	0					1			
21	Drew Sanders	8	4	5	9	0	0								
22	Jamil Burroughs	3	1	4	5	0	0								
23	Najee Harris	13	3	1	4	0	0								
24	Shane Lee	2	2	1	3	1	1								1
25	Ben Davis	3	2	1	3	0	0								
26	Bryce Young	9	0	3	3	1	0.5								
27	Chase Allen	1	0	2	2	0	0								
28	Jalyn Armour-Davis	2	0	2	2	0	0								
29	Marcus Banks	2	1	1	2	0	0								
30	Ale Kaho	2	2	0	2	0	0								
31	John Metchie III	13	1	0	1	0	0								1
32	DeVonta Smith	13	1	0	1	0	0						1		0
33	Landon Dickerson	1	1	0	1	0	0								
34	Miller Forristall	12	0	1	1	0	0								
35	Braylen Ingraham	1	0	1	1	0	0								
36	King Mwikuta	1	0	1	1	0	0								
37	Kendall Randolph	1	1	0	1	0	0								
38	Brian Robinson Jr.	13	1	0	1	0	0								
39	Trey Sanders	4	1	0	1	0	0								
40	Jaylen Waddle	6	1	0	1	0	0								
41	Ronald Williams Jr.	2	1	0	1	0	0								
42	Stephon Wynn Jr.	1	0	1	1	0	0								
43	Thomas Fletcher	1				0	0						1		0

Kick and punt returns

Rk	Player	G	Kick Ret				Punt Ret			
			Ret	Yds	Avg	TD	Ret	Yds	Avg	TD
1	Jahleel Billingsley	12	5	89	17.8	0				
2	DeVonta Smith	13	4	52	13	0	11	237	21.5	1
3	Jaylen Waddle	6	4	39	9.8	0	2	13	6.5	0
4	Brian Robinson Jr.	13	3	56	18.7	0				
5	Carl Tucker	7	1	23	23	0				
6	Trey Sanders	4	1	17	17	0				
7	Slade Bolden	13					7	49	7	0

Kicking and punting

Rk	Player	G	Kicking							Punting		
			XPM	XPA	XP%	FGM	FGA	FG%	Pts	Punts	Yds	Avg
1	Will Reichard	13	84	84	100	14	14	100	126			
2	Charlie Scott	9								22	862	39.2
3	Sam Johnson	4								10	354	35.4

Scoring

Rk	Player	G	Touchdowns								Kicking				
			Rush	Rec	Int	FR	PR	KR	Tot	XPM	FGM	2PM	Sfty	Pts
1	Najee Harris	13	26	4					30					180
2	DeVonta Smith	13	1	23			1		25					150
3	Will Reichard	13								84	14			126
4	Brian Robinson Jr.	13	7						6					42
5	John Metchie III	13		6					6					36
6	Jaylen Waddle	6		4					4					24
7	Jahleel Billingsley	12		3					3					18
8	Jase McClellan	12	2						2					12
9	Daniel Wright	13			1				1					6
10	Jordan Battle	13			1				1					6
11	Mac Jones	13	1						1					6
12	Malachi Moore	12				1			1					6
13	Miller Forristall	12		1					1					6
14	Patrick Surtain II	13			1				1					6
15	Roydell Williams	8	1						1					6
16	Slade Bolden	13		1					1					6

Stats include bowl games
Note: Table data from "2020 Alabama Crimson Tide Stats" (14)

Awards and honors

Name	Award	Type
Landon Dickerson	Permanent Team Captain	Team
Mac Jones	Permanent Team Captain	Team
Alex Leatherwood	Permanent Team Captain	Team
DeVonta Smith	Permanent Team Captain	Team
DeVonta Smith	MVP	Team
Najee Harris	Offensive Player of the Year	Team
Mac Jones	Offensive Player of the Year	Team
DeVonta Smith	Offensive Player of the Year	Team
Will Anderson Jr.	Defensive Player of the Year	Team
Christian Harris	Defensive Player of the Year	Team
Patrick Surtain II	Defensive Player of the Year	Team
Nick Saban	Coach of the Year	SEC
DeVonta Smith	Offensive Player of the Year	SEC
Patrick Surtain II	Defensive Player of the Year	SEC
Will Anderson Jr.	Freshman All SEC Team	SEC
Javion Cohen	Freshman All SEC Team	SEC
Malachi Moore	Freshman All SEC Team	SEC
Christian Barmore	AP All-SEC First Team	SEC
Deonte Brown	AP All-SEC First Team	SEC
Landon Dickerson	AP All-SEC First Team	SEC
Najee Harris	AP All-SEC First Team	SEC
Mac Jones	AP All-SEC First Team	SEC
Alex Leatherwood	AP All-SEC First Team	SEC
Dylan Moses	AP All-SEC First Team	SEC
DeVonta Smith	AP All-SEC First Team	SEC
Patrick Surtain II	AP All-SEC First Team	SEC
Christopher Allen	AP All-SEC Second Team	SEC
Malachi Moore	AP All-SEC Second Team	SEC
Jaylen Waddle	AP All-SEC Second Team	SEC
Christian Barmore	Coaches' All-SEC First Team	SEC
Deonte Brown	Coaches' All-SEC First Team	SEC
Landon Dickerson	Coaches' All-SEC First Team	SEC
Najee Harris	Coaches' All-SEC First Team	SEC
Mac Jones	Coaches' All-SEC First Team	SEC
Alex Leatherwood	Coaches' All-SEC First Team	SEC
Dylan Moses	Coaches' All-SEC First Team	SEC

Name	Award	Type
DeVonta Smith	Coaches' All-SEC First Team	SEC
Patrick Surtain II	Coaches' All-SEC First Team	SEC
Christopher Allen	Coaches' All-SEC Second Team	SEC
Malachi Moore	Coaches' All-SEC Second Team	SEC
Jaylen Waddle	Coaches' All-SEC Second Team	SEC
Landon Dickerson	Jacobs Blocking Trophy	SEC
Alex Leatherwood	Jacobs Blocking Trophy	SEC
Mac Jones	Scholar-Athlete of the Year	SEC
Landon Dickerson	AFCA All-America Team	National
Najee Harris	AFCA All-America Team	National
Mac Jones	AFCA All-America Team	National
Alex Leatherwood	AFCA All-America Team	National
Dylan Moses	AFCA All-America Team	National
DeVonta Smith	AFCA All-America Team	National
Patrick Surtain II	AFCA All-America Team	National
Christian Barmore	AP All-America Third Team	National
Landon Dickerson	AP All-America First Team	National
Najee Harris	AP All-America First Team	National
Mac Jones	AP All-America First Team	National
Alex Leatherwood	AP All-America First Team	National
Dylan Moses	AP All-America Third Team	National
DeVonta Smith	AP All-America First Team	National
Patrick Surtain II	AP All-America First Team	National
DeVonta Smith	Biletnikoff Award	National
Steve Sarkisian	Broyles Award	National
Landon Dickerson	Consensus All-American	National
Najee Harris	Consensus All-American	National
Mac Jones	Consensus All-American	National
Alex Leatherwood	Consensus All-American	National
DeVonta Smith	Consensus All-American	National
Patrick Surtain II	Consensus All-American	National
Mac Jones	Davey O'Brien Award	National
Najee Harris	Doak Walker Award	National
Landon Dickerson	FWAA All-America First Team	National
Najee Harris	FWAA All-America First Team	National
Alex Leatherwood	FWAA All-America First Team	National
DeVonta Smith	FWAA All-America First Team	National
Patrick Surtain II	FWAA All-America First Team	National
DeVonta Smith	Heisman Trophy	National
Najee Harris	Heisman Trophy Finalist	National
Mac Jones	Heisman Trophy Finalist	National
DeVonta Smith	Maxwell Award	National
Alex Leatherwood	Outland Trophy	National
Landon Dickerson	Rimington Award	National
Landon Dickerson	Sporting News (TSN) All-America Team	National
Najee Harris	Sporting News (TSN) All-America Team	National
Mac Jones	Sporting News (TSN) All-America Team	National
Alex Leatherwood	Sporting News (TSN) All-America Team	National
DeVonta Smith	Sporting News (TSN) All-America Team	National
Patrick Surtain II	Sporting News (TSN) All-America Team	National
Will Reichard	Sporting News (TSN) All-America Second Team	National
Landon Dickerson	Unanimous All-American	National
Najee Harris	Unanimous All-American	National
Alex Leatherwood	Unanimous All-American	National
DeVonta Smith	Unanimous All-American	National
Patrick Surtain II	Unanimous All-American	National
DeVonta Smith	Walter Camp Award	National
Deonte Brown	Senior Bowl	All-Star Team
Landon Dickerson	Senior Bowl	All-Star Team
Thomas Fletcher	Senior Bowl	All-Star Team
Najee Harris	Senior Bowl	All-Star Team
Mac Jones	Senior Bowl	All-Star Team
Alex Leatherwood	Senior Bowl	All-Star Team
DeVonta Smith	Senior Bowl	All-Star Team

NFL

Season	Year drafted	Round	Pick	Overall	Player	Position	Team
2020	2021	1	6	6	Jaylen Waddle	WR	Miami Dolphins
2020	2021	1	9	9	Patrick Surtain II	CB	Denver Broncos
2020	2021	1	10	10	DeVonta Smith	WR	Philadelphia Eagles
2020	2021	1	15	15	Mac Jones	QB	New England Patriots
2020	2021	1	17	17	Alex Leatherwood	OT	Las Vegas Raiders
2020	2021	1	24	24	Najee Harris	RB	Pittsburgh Steelers
2020	2021	2	5	37	Landon Dickerson	C	Philadelphia Eagles
2020	2021	2	6	38	Christian Barmore	DT	New England Patriots
2020	2021	6	9	193	Deonte Brown	OG	Carolina Panthers
2020	2021	6	38	222	Thomas Fletcher	LS	Carolina Panthers

Note: Table data from "2020 Alabama Crimson Tide football team" (272)

2021

Overall

Record	13-2
SEC Record	8-2
Rank	2
Points for	598
Points against	302
Points/game	39.9
Opp points/game	20.1
SOS[15]	5.69

You guys gave us a lot of really positive rat poison. The rat poison that you usually give us is usually fatal. But the rat poison that you put out there this week was yummy. -Nick Saban

Games

Date	Bama Rank		Opp Rank	Opponent	Bama	Opp	Result	SEC
09/04/21	1	N	14	Miami	44	13	W	
09/11/21	1	vs		Mercer	48	14	W	
09/18/21	1	@	11	Florida	31	29	W	W
09/25/21	1	vs		Southern Miss	63	14	W	
10/02/21	1	vs	12	Ole Miss	42	21	W	W
10/09/21	1	@		Texas A&M	38	41	L	L
10/16/21	5	@		Mississippi State	49	9	W	W
10/23/21	4	vs		Tennessee	52	24	W	W
11/06/21	2	vs		LSU	20	14	W	W
11/13/21	2	vs		New Mexico State	59	3	W	
11/20/21	2	vs	21	Arkansas	42	35	W	W
11/27/21	3	@		Auburn	24	22	W	W
12/04/21	3	N	1	Georgia	41	24	W	W
12/31/21	1	N	4	Cincinnati	27	6	W	
01/10/22	1	N	3	Georgia	18	33	L	L

Coaches

Name	Position	Year
Nick Saban	Head Coach	15
David Ballou	Strength and Conditioning	2
Robert Gillespie	Running Backs	1
Pete Golding	Defensive Coordinator / Inside Linebackers	4
Charles Kelly	Associate Defensive Coordinator / Safeties	3
Doug Marrone	Offensive Line	1
Bill O'Brien	Offensive Coordinator / Quarterbacks	1
Freddie Roach	Defensive Line	2 (7th overall)
Sal Sunseri	Outside Linebackers	3 (6th overall)
Jay Valai	Cornerbacks	1
Holmon Wiggins	Wide Receivers	3

Recruits

Name	Pos	Pos Rank	Rivals	247 Sports	ESPN	ESPN Grade	Hometown	High school / college	Height	Weight	Committed
Terrion Arnold	S	3	4	4	4	83	Tallahassee, FL	John Paul II Catholic Academy	6-0	180	2/3/21
Anquin Barnes	DT	25	3	3	4	80	Montgomery, AL	Robert E. Lee HS	6-5	300	4/17/20
Kendrick Blackshire	ILB	7	4	4	4	83	Duncanville, TX	Duncanville HS	6-1	250	7/14/20
James Brockermeyer	OC	1	4	4	4	84	Fort Worth, TX	All Saints Episcopal School	6-3	255	7/17/20
Tommy Brockermeyer	OT	1	5	5	5	91	Fort Worth, TX	All Saints Episcopal School	6-6	280	7/17/20
Jacorey Brooks	WR		4	5	4	86	Miami, FL	Booker T. Washington HS	6-2	185	5/8/20
Kadarius Calloway	S	16	3	4	4	81	Philadelphia, MS	Philadelphia HS	6-0	195	7/8/20
JoJo Earle	WR	10	4	4	4	86	Aledo, TX	Aledo HS	5-9	170	12/25/20
Terrance Ferguson	OT	8	4	4	4	85	Fort Valley, GA	Peach County HS	6-4	300	7/19/20
Monkell Goodwine	DE	19	4	4	4	83	Fort Washington, MD	National Christian Academy	6-4	265	8/15/20
Agiye Hall	WR	3	4	4	4	86	Valrico, FL	Bloomingdale HS	6-3	190	4/18/20
Ian Jackson	OLB	28	4	4	4	81	Prattville, AL	Prattville HS	6-3	215	5/28/20
Khyree Jackson	CB	1	4	3	4	82	Upper Marlboro, MD	East Mississippi Community College (JC)	6-4	265	8/15/20
Tim Keenan	DT	24	4	3	4	80	Birmingham, AL	Ramsay HS	6-2	340	8/29/20
Keanu Koht	DE	15	4	4	4	81	Vero Beach, FL	Vero Beach HS	6-4	225	12/16/20
JC Latham	OT	2	5	5	5	90	Bradenton, FL	IMG Academy	6-6	310	6/12/20
Deontae Lawson	OLB	14	4	4	4	84	Mobile, AL	Mobile Christian HS	6-3	210	12/27/19
Christian Leary	ATH	7	4	4	4	85	Orlando, FL	Edgewater HS	5-9	180	6/16/20
Kool-Aid McKinstry	ATH	4	4	5	4	87	Pinson, AL	Pinson Valley HS	6-0	175	10/25/20
Jalen Milroe	QB	16	4	4	4	84	Katy, TX	Obra D. Tompkins HS	6-2	195	8/17/20
Robbie Ouzts	TE	11	3	3	3	79	Rock Hill, SC	Rock Hill HS	6-4	240	9/6/20
Damon Payne	DT	3	4	5	4	88	Belleville, MI	Belleville HS	6-4	295	7/26/20
Jaeden Roberts	OG	3	3	4	4	84	Houston, TX	North Shore HS	6-5	345	12/25/20
DeVonta Smith	CB	41	3	4	3	78	Cincinnati, OH	La Salle HS	5-11	180	6/29/20
Dallas Turner	OLB	3	5	5	5	90	Fort Lauderdale, FL	St. Thomas Aquinas HS	6-4	230	7/1/20
Camar Wheaton	RB	3	5	5	4	86	Garland, TX	Lakeview Centennial HS	5-11	195	12/23/20
Kaine Williams	S	7	4	4	4	83	Marrero, LA	John Ehret HS	6-1	195	5/15/20

	Rivals	247Sports	ESPN
5 Stars	4	7	3
4 Stars	18	16	22
3 Stars	5	4	2
2 Stars	0	0	0

Note: Table data from "2021 Alabama Crimson Tide football team" (300)

330

Roster

Num	Player	Pos	Class	Height	Weight	Hometown	Last School
82	Chase Allen	PK	SO	6-2	188	Colleyville, TX	Colleyville Heritage
4	Christopher Allen	LB	R-SR	6-4	252	Baton Rouge, LA	Southern Lab School
31	Will Anderson Jr.	LB	SO	6-4	235	Hampton, GA	Dutchtown
5	Jalyn Armour-Davis	DB	R-JR	6-1	192	Mobile, AL	St. Paul's
12	Terrion Arnold	DB	FR	6-0	188	Tallahassee, FL	John Paul II Catholic
5	Javon Baker	WR	SO	6-2	195	Powder Springs, GA	McEachern
26	Marcus Banks	DB	JR	6-0	180	Houston, TX	Dekaney
7	Braxton Barker	QB	R-JR	6-1	202	Birmingham, AL	Spain Park
59	Anquin Barnest Jr.	DL	FR	6-5	305	Montgomery, AL	Robert E. Lee
9	Jordan Battle	DB	JR	6-1	210	Fort Lauderdale, FL	St. Thomas Aquinas
25	Jonathan Bennett	WR	SO	5-8	178	Birmingham, AL	Oak Mountain
19	Jahleel Billingsley	TE	JR	6-4	230	Chicago, IL	Phillips Academy
46	Melvin Billingsley	TE	SR	6-3	230	Opelika, AL	Opelika
40	Kendrick Blackshire	LB	FR	6-2	232	Duncanville, TX	Duncanville
18	Slade Bolden	WR	R-JR	5-11	191	West Monroe, LA	West Monroe
36	Bret Bolin	WR	R-SR	6-0	176	Lemont, IL	Lemont
51	Tanner Bowles	OL	R-SO	6-5	293	Glasgow, KY	Glasgow
84	Jacoby Boykins	WR	FR	5-11	182	Houston, TX	Lamar
14	Brian Branch	DB	SO	6-0	190	Tyrone, GA	Sandy Creek
41	Chris Braswell	LB	SO	6-3	220	Baltimore, MD	St. Frances Academy
33	Jackson Bratton	LB	SO	6-3	225	Muscle Shoals, AL	Muscle Shoals
58	James Brockermeyer	OL	FR	6-3	270	Fort Worth, TX	All Saints Episcopal
76	Tommy Brockermeyer	OL	FR	6-5	292	Fort Worth, TX	All Saints Episcopal
7	Ja'Corey Brooks	WR	FR	6-2	190	Miami, FL	IMG Academy
75	Tommy Brown	OL	R-JR	6-7	320	Santa Ana, CA	Mater Dei
56	Colin Bryant	LB	FR	6-3	218	Mount Pleasant, SC	Wando
86	James Burnip	P	FR	6-6	216	Mount Macedon, AUS	Victoria University, Melbourne
98	Jamil Burroughs	DL	SO	6-3	326	Powder Springs, GA	McEachern
86	Greg Carroll Jr.	WR	SO	6-0	171	Mobile, AL	Mattie Blount
87	Caden Clark	TE	FR	6-4	258	Akron, OH	Archbishop Hoban
70	Javion Cohen	OL	SO	6-4	325	Phenix City, AL	Central
97	Keelan Cox	DL	SO	6-5	240	Missouri City, TX	Manel / Tyler J.C.
29	Elijah Crockett	RB	FR	5-11	210	Chino Hills, CA	Ruben S. Ayala
71	Darrian Dalcourt	OL	JR	6-3	300	Havre de Grace, MD	St. Frances Academy
94	DJ Dale	DL	JR	6-3	307	Birmingham, AL	Clay-Chalkville
10	JoJo Earle	WR	FR	5-10	170	Aledo, TX	Aledo
92	Justin Eboigbe	DL	JR	6-5	285	Forest Park, GA	Forest Park
38	Jalen Edwards	DB	R-SO	6-0	177	Columbus, MS	Eufaula
27	Kyle Edwards	RB	SO	6-0	209	Destrehan, LA	Destrehan
55	Emil Ekiyor Jr.	OL	R-JR	6-3	324	Indianapolis, IN	Cathedral
43	Robert Ellis	TE	SO	6-0	220	Enterprise, AL	Enterprise
69	Terrence Ferguson II	OL	FR	6-4	290	Fort Valley, GA	Peach
54	Kyle Flood Jr.	LB	SO	6-0	209	Middlesex, NJ	St. Joseph
74	Damieon George Jr.	OL	SO	6-6	345	Houston, TX	North Shore
95	Monkell Goodwine	DL	FR	6-4	278	Upper Marlboro, MD	Rock Creek Christian Academy
24	Clark Griffin	DB	SO	5-9	195	Mountain Brook, AL	Mountain Brook
84	Agiye Hall	WR	FR	6-3	195	Valrico, FL	Bloomingdale
59	Jake Hall	SN	R-JR	6-3	238	Saraland, AL	Saraland
67	Donovan Hardin	OL	SO	6-3	285	Dublin, OH	Dublin Scioto
8	Christian Harris	LB	JR	6-2	232	Baton Rouge, LA	University Lab
2	DeMarco Hellams	DB	JR	6-1	208	Washington, DC	DeMatha Catholic
22	Chris Herren Jr.	WR	SR	6-3	175	Portsmouth, RI	Tabor Academy / Boston College/San Diego
51	Kneeland Hibbett	SN	FR	6-2	235	Florence, AL	Florence
11	Traeshon Holden	WR	SO	6-3	208	Kissimmee, FL	Narbonne
19	Stone Hollenbach	QB	R-SO	6-3	208	Catawissa, PA	Southern Columbia
83	Richard Hunt	TE	R-SO	6-7	235	Memphis, TN	Briarcrest Christian
97	LT Ikner	DL	SR	6-4	261	Daphne, AL	Daphne
52	Braylen Ingraham	DL	R-SO	6-4	289	Fort Lauderdale, FL	St. Thomas Aquinas
36	Ian Jackson	LB	FR	6-1	225	Prattville, AL	Prattville
6	Khyree Jackson	DB	JR	6-3	197	Upper Marlboro, MD	Wise / East Mississippi C.C.
28	Josh Jobe	DB	SR	6-1	192	Miami, FL	Cheshire Academy (Conn.)
58	Christian Johnson	LB	FR	6-5	230	Flowery Branch, GA	IMG Academy
98	Sam Johnson	P	SO	6-3	215	Birmingham, AL	Oak Mountain
14	Thaiu Jones-Bell	WR	SO	6-0	190	Hallandale, FL	Miami Carol City
96	Tim Keenan III	DL	FR	6-2	335	Birmingham, AL	Ramsay
37	Demouy Kennedy	LB	SO	6-3	215	Theodore, AL	Theodore
78	Amari Kight	OL	R-SO	6-7	318	Alabaster, AL	Thompson
19	Keanu Koht	LB	FR	6-4	215	Vero Beach, FL	Vero Beach
89	Grant Krieger	WR	JR	6-2	192	Pittsburgh, PA	Pine-Richland
21	Brylan Lanier	DB	FR	6-1	170	Tuscaloosa, AL	Paul W. Bryant
65	JC Latham	OL	FR	6-6	325	Oak Creek, WI	IMG Academy
93	Jah-Marien Latham	DL	SO	6-3	278	Reform, AL	Pickens County

331

Num	Player	Pos	Class	Height	Weight	Hometown	Last School
81	Cameron Latu	TE	R-JR	6-5	250	Salt Lake City, UT	Olympus
32	Deontae Lawson	LB	FR	6-2	217	Mobile, AL	Mobile Christian
12	Christian Leary	WR	FR	5-10	185	Orlando, FL	Edgewater
35	Shane Lee	LB	JR	6-0	240	Burtonsville, MD	St. Frances Academy
46	Julian Lowenstein	DB	R-SO	6-0	201	Sarasota, FL	Riverview
89	Kyle Mann	DL	SO	6-0	270	Powder Springs, GA	McEachern
95	*Jack Martin*	*P*	*JR*	*6-0*	*206*	*Mobile, AL*	*McGill-Toolen*
48	**Phidarian Mathis**	**DL**	**R-SR**	**6-4**	**312**	**Wisner, LA**	**Neville**
47	Jacobi McBride	DB	SO	6-1	143	Madison, AL	Madison Academy
21	Jase McClellan	RB	SO	5-11	212	Aledo, TX	Aledo
1	Kool-Aid McKinstry	DB	FR	6-1	180	Birmingham, AL	Pinson Valley
56	Seth McLaughlin	OL	SO	6-4	280	Buford, GA	Buford
8	**John Metchie III**	**WR**	**JR**	**6-0**	**195**	**Brampton, Canada**	**St. James School (Md.)**
2	Jalen Milroe	QB	FR	6-2	201	Katy, TX	Tompkins
42	Jaylen Moody	LB	SR	6-2	225	Conway, SC	Conway
13	**Malachi Moore**	**DB**	**SO**	**6-0**	**182**	**Trussville, AL**	**Hewitt-Trussville**
30	King Mwikuta	LB	JR	6-5	238	West Point, GA	Troup County
73	**Evan Neal**	**OL**	**JR**	**6-7**	**360**	**Okeechobee, FL**	**IMG Academy**
45	Robbie Ouzts	TE	FR	6-4	260	Rock Hill, SC	Rock Hill
35	Austin Owens	RB	FR	6-1	175	Double Springs, AL	Winston County
79	**Chris Owens**	**OL**	**R-SR**	**6-3**	**315**	**Arlington, TX**	**Lamar**
22	Jarelis Owens	DB	JR	6-0	157	Muscle Shoals, AL	Muscle Shoals
44	Damon Payne Jr.	DL	FR	6-4	297	Belleville, MI	Belleville
99	Ty Perine	P/PK	JR	6-1	218	Prattville, AL	Prattville
29	Blake Pugh	DB	FR	6-0	175	Birmingham, AL	Mountain Brook
50	Gabe Pugh	SN	R-SO	6-5	273	Tuscaloosa, AL	Northridge
72	Pierce Quick	OL	R-SO	6-5	280	Trussville, AL	Hewitt-Trussville
57	Chase Quigley	DL	FR	6-1	236	Libertyville, IL	Libertyville
85	**Kendall Randolph**	**TE**	**SR**	**6-4**	**298**	**Madison, AL**	**Bob Jones**
18	**LaBryan Ray**	**DL**	**R-SR**	**6-5**	**295**	**Madison, AL**	**James Clemens**
42	Sam Reed	WR	JR	6-1	165	Mountain Brook, AL	Mountain Brook
16	**Will Reichard**	**PK**	**JR**	**6-1**	**190**	**Hoover, AL**	**Hoover**
30	D.J. Rias	WR	SO	5-9	186	Phenix City, AL	Central
77	Jaeden Roberts	OL	FR	6-5	328	Houston, TX	North Shore
23	Jahquez Robinson	DB	SO	6-2	197	Jacksonville, FL	Sandalwood
45	Joshua Robinson	DB	SR	5-9	180	Hoover, AL	Hoover
34	Quandarrius Robinson	LB	SO	6-5	220	Birmingham, AL	Jackson-Olin
4	**Brian Robinson Jr.**	**RB**	**SR**	**6-1**	**228**	**Tuscaloosa, AL**	**Hillcrest**
62	Jackson Roby	OL	SR	6-5	285	Huntsville, AL	Huntsville
61	Graham Roten	OL	FR	6-3	285	Fairview, TN	Christ Presbyterian Academy
20	**Drew Sanders**	**LB**	**SO**	**6-5**	**230**	**Denton, TX**	**Ryan**
6	Trey Sanders	RB	R-SO	6-0	214	Port Saint Joe, FL	IMG Academy
97	Reid Schuback	PK	FR	6-0	185	Poway, CA	Poway
52	Carter Short	SN	FR	5-10	190	Hoover, AL	Hoover
44	Charlie Skehan	TE	SO	6-1	232	Columbia, SC	Cardinal Newman
27	DeVonta Smith	DB	FR	6-0	185	Cincinnati, OH	La Salle
43	Jordan Smith	LB	SO	5-10	210	Chelsea, AL	Chelsea
50	Tim Smith	DL	SO	6-4	320	Sebastian, FL	Sebastian River
68	Alajujuan Sparks Jr.	OL	SO	6-4	345	Hoover, AL	Hoover
11	Kristian Story	DB	SO	6-1	215	Lanett, AL	Lanett
25	Jordan Tate-Parker	DB	JR	6-2	199	Phenix City, AL	Hardaway
88	Major Tennison	TE	R-SR	6-5	252	Flint, TX	Bullard
80	Adam Thorsland	TE	FR	6-5	232	Walhalla, SC	Walhalla
10	*Henry To'oTo'o*	*LB*	*JR-TR*	*6-2*	*235*	*Sacramento, CA*	*De La Salle*
15	Dallas Turner	LB	FR	6-4	245	Fort Lauderdale, FL	St. Thomas Aquinas
17	Paul Tyson	QB	R-SO	6-5	228	Trussville, AL	Hewitt-Trussville
39	Carson Ware	DB	R-SO	6-1	190	Muscle Shoals, AL	Muscle Shoals
53	Kade Wehby	SN	FR	5-9	185	Plantation, FL	St. Thomas Aquinas
25	Camar Wheaton	RB	FR	5-11	190	Garland, TX	Lakeview Centennial
55	Bennett Whisenhunt	LB	SO	6-1	222	Vestavia Hills, AL	Vestavia Hills
1	*Jameson Williams*	*WR*	*JR-TR*	*6-2*	*189*	*St. Louis, MI*	*Cardinal Ritter College Prep*
49	Kaine Williams	DB	FR	6-2	203	Marrero, LA	John Ehert
23	Roydell Williams	RB	SO	5-10	210	Hueytown, AL	Hueytown
31	Shatarius Williams	WR	SO	6-3	187	Demopolis, AL	Demopolis
3	Xavier Williams	WR	R-JR	6-1	190	Hollywood, FL	Chaminade-Madonna Prep
37	Sam Willoughby	WR	SO	5-10	165	Vestavia Hills, AL	Vestavia Hills
3	**Daniel Wright**	**DB**	**R-SR**	**6-1**	**195**	**Fort Lauderdale, FL**	**Boyd Anderson**
90	Stephon Wynn Jr.	DL	R-JR	6-4	310	Anderson, SC	IMG Academy
9	**Bryce Young**	**QB**	**SO**	**6-0**	**194**	**Pasadena, CA**	**Mater Dei**
47	**Byron Young**	**DL**	**JR**	**6-3**	**292**	**Laurel, MS**	**West Jones**

Note: Starters in bold
Note: Table data from "2021 Alabama Crimson Tide Roster" (301)

332

Transfers

Player	School	Direction
Jack Martin	Troy	Incoming
Henry To'oTo'o	Tennessee	Incoming
Jameson Williams	Ohio State	Incoming
Joseph Bulovas	Vanderbilt	Outgoing
Ben Davis	Texas	Outgoing
Kevin Harris	Georgia Tech	Outgoing
Ale Kaho	UCLA	Outgoing
Joshua Lanier	Jackson State	Outgoing
Keilan Robinson	Texas	Outgoing
Eddie Smith	Illinois	Outgoing
Ishmael Sopsher	USC	Outgoing
Brandon Turnage	Tennessee	Outgoing
Ronald Williams Jr.	Michigan State	Outgoing

Note: Table data from "2021 Alabama Crimson Tide football team" (300)

Games

09/04/21 - Alabama (1) at Miami (14)

Chick-fil-A College Kickoff
Mercedes-Benz Stadium
Atlanta, GA

Team	1	2	3	4	T		Passing	Rushing	Total
Alabama (1)	10	17	14	3	44		354	147	501
Miami (14)	0	3	10	0	13		178	88	266

Alabama wasted no time making its mark in the season opener. Bryce Young, making his first career start, connected with John Metchie III for a 37-yard touchdown pass on the Tide's opening drive which capped off a 7-play, 75-yard drive. After forcing Miami to punt, Will Reichard extended his streak of made field goals to 17 by splitting the uprights from 38 yards out. Bama led 10-0 at the end of the first quarter. Alabama's defense continued to stifle Miami in the second quarter. TE Cameron Latu caught a 9-yard touchdown pass to cap a 10-play, 80-yard drive, stretching the lead to 17-0. Christopher Allen then forced a fumble that was recovered by Phidarian Mathis, setting up Reichard for a 51-yard field goal and a 20-0 advantage. Young and Latu connected again for a 25-yard touchdown pass, but the Hurricanes avoided a shutout with a 37-yard field goal as time expired in the half, making the score 27-3 in favor of the Tide.

To start the second half, Miami drove the ball down to set up 1st-and-goal from the eight. Bama held, and they went for it on 4th-and-goal from the 1-yard line. Bama held again and forced a turnover on downs. Young tied the Chick-fil-A Kickoff Game record with his fourth touchdown pass on a 94-yard haul from Jameson Williams. Malachi Moore picked off a pass on Miami's next drive, and Trey Sanders scored his first career touchdown of 20 yards to end a 5-play, 45-yard drive (41-3). On the following drive, Miami tossed a 29-yarder to give the Canes their first TD of the game (41-10). After a fumble by Young, Alabama held Miami to a 28-yard field goal (41-13). The only score in the fourth quarter was from Reichard's 40-yard field goal (44-13).

Alabama scored on its first five possessions, winning its 15th consecutive season opener under Nick Saban. Bryce Young, making his first start, completed 27-of-38 passes for 344 yards and four touchdowns. This tied him with former Alabama QB Tua Tagovailoa and former Ole Miss quarterback Bo Wallace for the most touchdown passes in a Chick-fil-A Kickoff Game. Defensively, Will Anderson Jr. led the team with nine tackles, including two solo stops and a sack. Malachi Moore and Jaylen Moody each recorded an interception. Will Reichard extended his streak of made field goals to 18. He successfully converted attempts from 38, 51, and 40 yards out, while also making all five of his extra point attempts.[302]

Passing	C/ATT	YDS	AVG	TD	INT	QBR
B. Young	27/38	344	9.1	4	0	94.5
P. Tyson	1/1	10	10	0	0	100
Team	28/39	354	9.1	4	0	--

Rushing	CAR	YDS	AVG	TD	LONG
B. Robinson Jr.	12	60	5	0	19
T. Sanders	8	41	5.1	1	20
J. McClellan	9	36	4	0	15
R. Williams	6	18	3	0	8
B. Young	2	-1	-0.5	0	8
J. Milroe	1	-7	-7	0	0
Team	38	147	3.9	1	20

Interceptions	INT	YDS	TD
J. Moody	1	13	0
M. Moore	1	-1	0
Team	2	12	0

Punting	NO	YDS	AVG	TB	IN 20	LONG
J. Burnip	2	62	31	0	0	36

Receiving	REC	YDS	AVG	TD	LONG
J. Williams	4	126	31.5	1	94
J. Metchie III	6	76	12.7	1	37
C. Latu	3	43	14.3	2	25
S. Bolden	3	26	8.7	0	11
J. Earle	2	25	12.5	0	16
J. Baker	3	21	7	0	10
J. McClellan	3	15	5	0	6
T. Holden	1	12	12	0	12
A. Hall	1	10	10	0	10
B. Robinson Jr.	2	0	0	0	4
Team	28	354	12.6	4	94

Kick returns	NO	YDS	AVG	LONG	TD
J. Billingsley	1	17	17	17	0

Punt returns	NO	YDS	AVG	LONG	TD
S. Bolden	3	20	6.7	10	0

Kicking	FG	PCT	LONG	XP	PTS
W. Reichard	3/3	100	51	5/5	14

Note: Table data from "Alabama 44-13 Miami (Sep 4, 2021) Box Score" (303)

09/11/21 - Alabama (1) vs Mercer

Team	1	2	3	4	T		Passing	Rushing	Total
Mercer	0	0	7	7	**14**		168	48	**216**
Alabama (1)	14	17	14	3	**48**		266	158	**424**

The scoring began when Chris Braswell blocked a Mercer punt, and Jase McClellan scooped it up and raced 33 yards into the end zone. On Mercer's next possession, Kool-Aid McKinstry intercepted a pass at the Alabama 46-yard line. Bryce Young, making just his second career start, orchestrated a 54-yard drive, capped off by a 4-yard touchdown run from Brian Robinson Jr., his first of the season. Mercer punted for the rest of the half. Less than ten seconds into the second quarter, Young connected with Slade Bolden for an 18-yard scoring strike, capping a 7-play, 65-yard drive in 2:15. Three punts later (two by Mercer), McClellan rushed five yards for his second TD of the game (28-0). After another Mercer punt, Will Reichard continued his streak of made field goals with a 30-yarder to conclude Alabama's last drive of the half (31-0).

The second half opened with Young finding Jameson Williams for an 8-yard touchdown strike, culminating a 5-play, 81-yard drive. Mercer managed to avoid a shutout when they connected on a 60-yard pass, capping a 5-play, 85-yard drive to cut it 38-7. McClellan scored his third TD of the day on the next possession as he hauled in a 21-yard pass to punctuate a 5-play, 64-yard drive (45-7). In the fourth quarter, Ty James caught a 22-yard TD pass ending a 10-play, 80-yard drive. Reichard connected on a 40-yard FG for the last score of the game to make it 48-14.

Christian Harris racked up eight tackles, four of them solo, and also had a tackle for loss. Kool-Aid McKinstry and Marcus Banks both logged interceptions. The Tide's pass rush was relentless, with Young, Mathis, and Dale all recording sacks. Bryce Young became the first player to throw seven touchdown passes in his first two starts. Jase McClellan stole the show, finding the end zone three times in three different ways. After his blocked punt return (Alabama's 81st non-offensive touchdown of the Saban era), he added a 5-yard rushing touchdown and a 21-yard receiving score. This game marked the 20th consecutive home opener win and Alabama's 15th straight under Nick Saban, and they have now won 55 of the last 57 home games. Since 1929, Alabama has established a home winning percentage of 83.4%, with a record of 278-54-3 (best all-time in the FBS). They extended their school record as they have now scored in 270 straight games. Alabama currently leads the FBS in consecutive games scoring 30+ points (with 28 games), which is the second-longest in major college football history. Only UCF has achieved a longer streak, with 31 from 2017 to 2019.[304]

Passing	C/ATT	YDS	AVG	TD	INT	QBR
B. Young	19/27	227	8.4	3	0	34.1
P. Tyson	1/3	39	13	0	0	22
J. Milroe	0/1	0	0	0	0	91.2
Team	**20/31**	**266**	**8.6**	**3**	**0**	--

Rushing	CAR	YDS	AVG	TD	LONG
B. Robinson Jr.	10	70	7	1	14
J. Milroe	7	33	4.7	0	14
T. Sanders	7	30	4.3	0	16
J. McClellan	4	13	3.3	1	5
R. Williams	4	11	2.8	0	4
B. Young	2	1	0.5	0	8
Team	**34**	**158**	**4.6**	**2**	**16**

Interceptions	INT	YDS	TD
K. McKinstry	1	0	0
M. Banks	1	0	0
Team	**2**	**0**	**0**

Punting	NO	YDS	AVG	TB	IN 20	LONG
J. Burnip	3	130	43.3	0	1	44

Receiving	REC	YDS	AVG	TD	LONG
J. Earle	7	85	12.1	0	39
J. Metchie III	5	70	14	0	41
J. Williams	3	31	10.3	1	18
T. Holden	2	31	15.5	0	17
J. McClellan	1	21	21	1	21
S. Bolden	1	18	18	1	18
B. Robinson Jr.	1	10	10	0	10
Team	**20**	**266**	**13.3**	**3**	**41**

Kick returns	NO	YDS	AVG	LONG	TD
S. Bolden	1	24	24	24	0
C. Latu	2	7	3.5	7	0
Team	**3**	**31**	**10.3**	**24**	**0**

Punt returns	NO	YDS	AVG	LONG	TD
J. Earle	2	45	22.5	29	0
J. McClellan	0	33	0	33	1
S. Bolden	3	29	9.7	25	0
C. Braswell	1	11	11	11	0
Team	**6**	**118**	**19.7**	**33**	**1**

Kicking	FG	PCT	LONG	XP	PTS
W. Reichard	2/3	67	40	6/6	12

Note: Table data from "Alabama 48-14 Mercer (Sep 11, 2021) Box Score" (305)

09/18/21 - Alabama (1) at Florida (11)

Team	1	2	3	4	T		Passing	Rushing	Total
Alabama (1)	21	0	7	3	31		240	91	331
Florida (11)	3	6	14	6	29		195	245	440

Bryce Young and the Tide offense came out firing, marching 75 yards on the opening drive capped by a Jase McClellan 7-yard touchdown catch. The Gators responded with a field goal, but Young struck again, hitting Jahleel Billingsley for a 26-yard score to complete a 7-play, 75-yard drive, his first of the season (14-3). Jalyn Armour-Davis picked off a Florida pass on their next drive, setting up a Young-to-Robinson Jr. touchdown, this one from seven yards out capping a 6-play, 38-yard drive (21-3). In the second quarter, Florida went for it on 4th-and-3 at the Alabama 37-yard line, but the Tide stopped them. After three punts (two by Bama), Malik Davis rushed for 26 yards to record Florida's first touchdown of the game. The extra point was missed, making it 21-9 which ended up being the score at the end of the half after both teams punted to close it out.

The second half was a back-and-forth affair, with both teams trading scores on five consecutive possessions. The offensive onslaught began with Dameon Pierce's 3-yard rushing touchdown, capping off a 10-play, 75-yard drive that cut their deficit to 21-16. Not to be outdone, Brian Robinson Jr. muscled his way into the end zone on 4th-and-inches, completing a 13-play, 75-yard march to give the Crimson Tide a 28-16 lead. Florida capped off an impressive 99-yard drive when quarterback Emory Jones punched it in from five yards out, getting within five once again (28-23). Will Reichard split the uprights with a 24-yard field goal, extending the Crimson Tide's lead to 31-23. In the final scoring play of the night, Florida's Pierce found the end zone on a 17-yard rushing touchdown. However, the Gators' attempt at a two-point conversion failed, leaving them just short at 31-29.

DeMarcco Hellams led the team with 11 tackles, including an impressive six solo stops, the highest tally in the game. Alabama extended its winning streak against Florida, securing its eighth consecutive victory over the Gators. This run matches Alabama's own record for the second-longest streak by any team against Florida, a feat they previously achieved from 1964 to 1986. Further, Alabama has been victorious in 38 out of their last 42 away games dating back to 2011. This was Nick Saban's 50th SEC road victory at Alabama. Since his arrival in 2007, Saban has a record of 14-1 in SEC road openers. Moreover, when Alabama's first SEC game of the season takes place on the road, Saban is a perfect 11-0. Additionally, he has established an incredible 42-3 record against the SEC East. Saban has also amassed an impressive 69 wins at Alabama against teams ranked in the Top 25, and this places him third in all-time road wins against ranked opponents with 25 victories.[306]

Passing	C/ATT	YDS	AVG	TD	INT	QBR
B. Young	22/35	240	6.9	3	0	86.8

Rushing	CAR	YDS	AVG	TD	LONG
B. Robinson Jr.	15	78	5.2	1	23
J. McClellan	9	17	1.9	0	5
B. Young	4	-4	-1	0	7
Team	28	91	3.3	1	23

Interceptions	INT	YDS	TD
J. Armour-Davis	1	4	0

Punting	NO	YDS	AVG	TB	IN 20	LONG
J. Burnip	4	170	42.5	0	0	48

Receiving	REC	YDS	AVG	TD	LONG
J. Williams	4	61	15.3	0	29
J. Metchie III	6	49	8.2	0	12
J. McClellan	4	41	10.3	1	18
J. Billingsley	1	26	26	1	26
C. Latu	2	19	9.5	0	10
S. Bolden	3	19	6.3	0	15
J. Earle	1	18	18	0	18
B. Robinson Jr.	1	7	7	1	7
Team	22	240	10.9	3	29

Kick returns	NO	YDS	AVG	LONG	TD
J. Williams	2	51	25.5	30	0

Kicking	FG	PCT	LONG	XP	PTS
W. Reichard	1/1	100	24	4/4	7

Note: Table data from "Alabama 31-29 Florida (Sep 18, 2021) Box Score" (307)

09/25/21 - Alabama (1) vs Southern Miss

Team	1	2	3	4	T		Passing	Rushing	Total
Southern Miss	0	7	0	7	14		131	82	213
Alabama (1)	21	21	7	14	63		395	211	606

Jameson Williams returned Southern Miss' opening kickoff for a touchdown. After a USM punt, Jahleel Billingsley caught a 16-yard touchdown pass to cap a 7-play, 45-yard drive. After DeMarcco Hellams picked off a pass, Bryce Young connected with John Metchie III for a 22-yard gain, Metchie III fumbled it, then TE Cameron Latu picked it up and took it across the goal line for a touchdown (21-0). Alabama forced another punt, then Roydell Williams scored his first touchdown of the season from a yard out to conclude a 4-play, 60-yard drive less than a minute into the second quarter. The Bama defense held again, forcing another punt before Jameson Williams recorded his second-longest receiving touchdown of his career (81 yards). After both teams traded punts, they traded touchdowns. Ty Keyes orchestrated a crisp 5-play, 46-yard drive, capping it off with a 14-yard touchdown strike to Chandler Pittman. Then Bryce Young engineered an impressive 10-play, 97-yard march down the field. The drive culminated with Young finding Jase McClellan for a 9-yard touchdown connection. As the teams headed to the locker room, Alabama had established a commanding 42-7 lead.

The only score in the third quarter was an 11-yard touchdown pass from Young to Latu (his second of the game), capping a 4-play, 68-yard drive (49-7). Early in the fourth quarter, Keyes threw an 11-yard touchdown pass to Demarcus Jones, capping off an 84-yard drive (49-14). On the ensuing kickoff, Jameson Williams scored his second touchdown of the night by returning it 83 yards to paydirt (56-14). The rest of the game consisted of punts by both teams except for one Bama score when rookie quarterback Jalen Milroe hit Javon Baker for a 24-yard touchdown strike, giving both their first Crimson Tide touchdowns. This made the final 63-14.

Jordan Battle led the way for Alabama's defense, racking up seven total tackles. DeMarcco Hellams, Christian Harris, and Will Anderson Jr. were close behind, each contributing five solo tackles. Hellams also had a memorable moment, snagging his first interception while donning the Crimson Tide uniform. Roydell Williams etched his name in the record books, becoming the first Alabama player to surpass the 100-yard rushing mark this season. He accomplished this feat by gaining an impressive 110 yards on the ground.

Bryce Young connected on a remarkable 20-of-22 pass attempts (90.9% completion rate), setting a school record for the best completion percentage in a single game (with a minimum of 20 completions). He threw for 313 yards and tossed five touchdowns in the game, tying him for the second-highest single-game touchdown pass mark in program history. His five touchdown passes ties Gary Hollingsworth (once at Ole Miss in 1989), Tua Tagovailoa (three times, most recent vs. Southern Miss in 2019), and Mac Jones (three times, most recent vs. Ohio State in 2021).

Jameson Williams became the first player in the program's history to return two kickoffs for touchdowns in a single game. His first kickoff return for a touchdown covered an electrifying 100 yards, marking the eighth time a Crimson Tide player has achieved this feat, and the first since Tyrone Prothro's 100-yard return against Kentucky in 2004. Gary Martin was the last Alabama player to record a 100-yard kickoff return for a touchdown on the opening drive (at Miami in 1963).

Alabama secured its 100th consecutive victory against an unranked opponent under Nick Saban. His record in games played at Bryant-Denny Stadium stands at an impressive 90-8. This dominance is further highlighted by the fact that the Crimson Tide has emerged victorious in 60 of their last 63 home contests. Since Saban's arrival, the Crimson Tide has amassed an impressive 83 non-offensive touchdowns. This season alone, Alabama has already recorded three such scores. Tonight's game saw the seventh and eighth kickoff return touchdowns in the Saban Era.

Alabama's offense amassed a staggering 606 total yards. This marked the 12th time in the program's history that the 600+ yard barrier was eclipsed in a single game. The Crimson Tide's offensive onslaught has been relentless, as they have now accumulated over 400 yards of total offense in an astonishing 43 out of their last 45 games. Alabama is the nation's top team in terms of home winning percentage as their impressive record now stands at an astounding 279-54-3, translating to a remarkable 83.4 winning percentage. They have now scored 30+ points in 30 straight games.[308]

Passing	C/ATT	YDS	AVG	TD	INT	QBR
B. Young	20/22	313	14.2	5	1	99.1
P. Tyson	2/3	58	19.3	0	0	98.1
J. Milroe	1/1	24	24	1	0	98.3
Team	23/26	395	15.2	6	1	--

Rushing	CAR	YDS	AVG	TD	LONG
R. Williams	11	110	10	1	55
J. McClellan	12	97	8.1	0	27
T. Sanders	5	12	2.4	0	4
J. Milroe	2	5	2.5	0	3
B. Young	2	-11	-5.5	0	0
Team	1	-2	-2	0	0
Team	33	211	6.4	1	55

Interceptions	INT	YDS	TD
D. Hellams	1	6	0

Punting	NO	YDS	AVG	TB	IN 20	LONG
J. Burnip	2	78	39	0	0	40

Receiving	REC	YDS	AVG	TD	LONG
J. Billingsley	5	105	21	1	33
J. Williams	1	81	81	1	81
J. Baker	2	59	29.5	1	35
C. Latu	3	57	19	2	23
J. Metchie III	7	45	6.4	0	21
S. Bolden	2	27	13.5	0	20
J. McClellan	1	9	9	1	9
T. Holden	1	9	9	0	9
T. Sanders	1	3	3	0	3
Team	23	395	17.2	6	81

Kick returns	NO	YDS	AVG	LONG	TD
J. Williams	3	177	59	100	2

Punt returns	NO	YDS	AVG	LONG	TD
J. Earle	3	-2	-0.7	0	0

Kicking	FG	PCT	LONG	XP	PTS
W. Reichard	0/0	0	0	9/9	9

Note: Table data from "Alabama 63-14 Southern Miss (Sep 25, 2021) Box Score" (309)

10/02/21 - Alabama (1) vs Ole Miss (12)

Team	1	2	3	4	T		Passing	Rushing	Total
Ole Miss (12)	0	0	7	14	21		213	78	291
Alabama (1)	7	21	7	7	42		241	210	451

In the pre-game interview just before kickoff, Lane Kiffin was asked by the reporter what notes he had to give Nick Saban's defense fits. He replied by saying, "Get your popcorn ready!" before taking off his headset, tossing it down, then jogging back to the sideline while the reporter was still asking more questions.

Ole Miss got the ball first and drove all the way down to the Alabama 6-yard line. Alabama stopped them on a 4th-and-1 run, then had a 14-play, 94-yard opening drive that concluded with a Bryce Young to John Metchie III pass for a 16-yard touchdown. On the Rebels' next drive, they were stopped again on 4th-and-2 at their own 47-yard line. Alabama then drove 46 yards in ten plays to the Ole Miss 1-yard line. Facing a crucial 4th-and-goal situation, the Tide turned to Brian Robinson Jr., and without hesitation, he powered his way into the end zone. The touchdown extended Alabama's lead to 14-0 with 12:14 remaining in the second quarter.

Both teams traded punts, then Ole Miss once again turned the ball over on downs neglecting to gain a yard on 4th-and-1 from their own 31-yard line (the play actually lost four yards). On the ensuing Alabama drive, Bryce Young hit Cameron Latu from three yards out after driving 27 yards in six plays to make it 21-0. On the first play after the kickoff, Phidarian Mathis sacked Matt Corral for a loss of nine yards which caused a fumble that was recovered by Justin Oboigbe. The Tide extended their lead over the Rebels with a short but efficient 4-play, 14-yard drive. Brian Robinson Jr. punched it in from a yard out for his second touchdown of the half. The score put an exclamation point on Alabama's commanding 28-0 advantage heading into the locker room for halftime.

On the opening drive of the second half, Brian Robinson Jr. wasted no time getting into the end zone for this third score of the night as he ran it in from a yard out again after a 6-play, 77-yard drive. However, the Rebels refused to go down without a fight. Quarterback Matt Corral orchestrated an 11-play, 75-yard drive, showcasing his dual-threat abilities as he ran for a 10-yard touchdown (Bama on top 35-7). Alabama drove all the way down the field, but Young threw an interception into the end zone which was returned to the Ole Miss 1-yard line. Alabama forced another punt, then drove down the field into the fourth quarter.

Brian Robinson Jr. scored his career-best fourth touchdown of the game from two yards out, finishing a 9-play, 66-yard drive. Alabama turned the ball over on downs in between two Ole Miss touchdowns. Snoop Connor scored a one-yard touchdown run to end a 7-play, 70-yard drive, then Corral threw a 2-yard pass to Chase Rogers for the final points of the game. Alabama won with a final of 42-21.

DeMarcco Hellams (11) and Henry To'oTo'o (10) spearheaded the defensive effort, each racking up double-digit tackles. Jordan Battle led the way with seven solo stops. The Crimson Tide's pass rush was relentless, with Will Anderson Jr. and Phidarian Mathis each recording a sack against the Rebels' offense. Anderson Jr. continued his disruptive season, tallying 2.5 tackles for loss, bringing his season total to an impressive 11. Bryce Young completed all seven of his passing attempts in the first quarter. Brian Robinson Jr. had a career day on the ground, gashing the Rebels' defense for 171 rushing yards and an incredible four touchdowns.

The victory not only extended Alabama's winning streak against Nick Saban's former assistants to 24-0 (2-0 against Lane Kiffin and 3-0 against Kiffin all-time including his stint at Tennessee), but it also marked the 23rd time Saban has defeated a ranked opponent by 25+ points. The

Tide's 30-point scoring streak now stands at 31 games, tying the record held by UCF from 2017-2019. Keeping the Rebels scoreless in the first half marked the first time since 2018 that the Crimson Tide had shut out a ranked opponent in the opening half when they blanked then-No. 16 Mississippi State. Additionally, Alabama has a remarkable 45-game winning streak when scoring a touchdown on its opening offensive drive, and they have racked up 400+ yards of total offense in a staggering 44 of their last 46 contests. This marked the second consecutive season an Alabama quarterback achieved perfection against Ole Miss in the opening frame, following Mac Jones' 10-for-10 performance in 2020.[310]

Passing	C/ATT	YDS	AVG	TD	INT	QBR
B. Young	20/26	241	9.3	2	1	94.3

Rushing	CAR	YDS	AVG	TD	LONG
B. Robinson Jr.	36	171	4.8	4	21
J. McClellan	6	28	4.7	0	10
R. Williams	3	15	5	0	6
B. Young	5	-4	-0.8	0	4
Team	50	210	4.2	4	21

Kick returns	NO	YDS	AVG	LONG	TD
J. Williams	1	22	22	22	0
S. Bolden	1	18	18	18	0
Team	2	40	20	22	0

Punting	NO	YDS	AVG	TB	IN 20	LONG
J. Burnip	1	37	37	0	0	37

Receiving	REC	YDS	AVG	TD	LONG
J. Williams	5	65	13	0	26
S. Bolden	4	58	14.5	0	29
J. Billingsley	4	47	11.8	0	19
J. Metchie III	3	35	11.7	1	16
T. Holden	1	21	21	0	21
J. McClellan	1	11	11	0	11
C. Latu	1	3	3	1	3
J. Earle	1	1	1	0	1
Team	20	241	12.1	2	29

Punt returns	NO	YDS	AVG	LONG	TD
J. Earle	1	2	2	2	0

Kicking	FG	PCT	LONG	XP	PTS
W. Reichard	0/0	0	0	6/6	6

Note: Table data from "Alabama 42-21 Ole Miss (Oct 2, 2021) Box Score" (311)

340

10/09/21 - Alabama (1) at Texas A&M

Team	1	2	3	4	T	Passing	Rushing	Total
Alabama (1)	7	3	14	14	**38**	369	153	**522**
Texas A&M	17	7	7	10	**41**	285	94	**379**

Texas A&M drew first blood with a 38-yard field goal, but Alabama responded with a 20-yard touchdown strike from Bryce Young to Roydell Williams, capping a 10-play, 65-yard drive (7-3). Three plays later, the Aggies scored a touchdown of their own with passes of 14, 34, and 27 yards to go up 10-7. Brian Robinson Jr. fumbled on Alabama's next drive which set up A&M the Bama 41-yard line. Texas A&M capitalized with a touchdown pass to Ainias Smith from six yards out putting them up 17-7. On Alabama's next possession, Young was intercepted in the end zone, then both teams traded punts. On A&M's next play, DeMarcco Hellams got a pick that led to a 38-yard field goal. Before the half ended, running back Isaiah Spiller capped off a 75-yard drive with a 15-yard touchdown run into the end zone. The 7-play march downfield allowed the Aggies to extend their lead to 24-10 at halftime.

Both teams punted on their first possessions of the second half, however, Ja'Corey Brooks blocked Texas A&M's punt and King Mwikuta recovered it in the end zone for a touchdown (first of his career). This brought Bama within seven (A&M up 24-17). On Alabama's kickoff right after this score, Devon Achane returned it 96 yards for an immediate answer to extend their lead to 31-17. Alabama responded with a 6-play, 75-yard drive that ended with a 29-yard touchdown pass from Bryce Young to Jameson Williams, cutting Texas A&M's lead to 31-24. The Aggies punted, then Alabama kicked a 26-yard field goal to make the score 31-27, A&M on top. Reichard connected on another filed goal (from 22 yards) in between two more A&M punts making it a one-point game with A&M up 31-30. As the clock ticked down, Bryce Young threw a 7-yard touchdown pass to Jameson Williams, then he hit Williams again for the two-point conversion. Alabama took a 38-31 lead with five minutes left in the game. Texas A&M tied it up two minutes later as Calzada found Smith for a 25-yard touchdown. Alabama punted with two minutes left, but Texas A&M drove down and kicked a 28-yard field goal to win the game 41-38 as time expired.

Defensively, Brian Branch racked up a team-leading and career-high 11 tackles, a game and career-best eight solo stops, and a career-high two tackles for loss. DeMarcco Hellams logged seven tackles, four solo stops, and an interception. On offense, Brian Robinson Jr. ran for 147 yards, going over the 100-yard mark for the second game in a row. Alabama extended its streak of scoring 30+ points to 32 consecutive games, setting a new major college football record. Alabama also recorded its 84th non-offensive touchdown (fourth this season) in the Nick Saban era.[312]

Passing	C/ATT	YDS	AVG	TD	INT	QBR
B. Young	28/48	369	7.7	3	1	81.9

Rushing	CAR	YDS	AVG	TD	LONG
B. Robinson Jr.	24	147	6.1	0	24
J. Williams	1	4	4	0	4
R. Williams	2	3	1.5	0	3
B. Young	7	-1	-0.1	0	15
Team	34	153	4.5	0	24

Interceptions	INT	YDS	TD
J. Armour-Davis	1	0	0

Kicking	FG	PCT	LONG	XP	PTS
W. Reichard	3/3	100	38	3/3	12

Punting	NO	YDS	AVG	TB	IN 20	LONG
J. Burnip	4	140	35	0	2	43

Receiving	REC	YDS	AVG	TD	LONG
J. Williams	10	146	14.6	2	32
J. Metchie III	7	88	12.6	0	40
B. Robinson Jr.	4	60	15	0	29
R. Williams	2	28	14	1	20
J. Earle	1	19	19	0	19
S. Bolden	2	16	8	0	9
C. Latu	1	10	10	0	10
T. Holden	1	2	2	0	2
Team	28	369	13.2	3	40

Punt returns	NO	YDS	AVG	LONG	TD
J. Brooks	1	19	19	19	0
J. Earle	2	17	8.5	20	0
K. Mwikuta	0	0	0	0	1
Team	3	36	12	20	1

Note: Table data from "Alabama 41-38 Texas A&M (Oct 9, 2021) Box Score" (313)

10/16/21 - Alabama (5) at Mississippi State

Team	1	2	3	4	T		Passing	Rushing	Total
Alabama (5)	14	7	14	14	49		348	195	543
Mississippi State	3	3	3	0	9		300	-1	299

The game kicked off with a bang as Bryce Young connected with John Metchie III for a 46-yard touchdown, capping a 65-yard drive set up by Josh Jobe's interception. Mississippi State responded with a 44-yard field goal. Four plays after Alabama was forced to punt, Jordan Battle scored on a 40-yard pick-six (Bama up 14-3). Three punts later, and the game was in the second quarter with 10:32 left. Both teams scored before the half. First, Brian Robinson Jr. bulldozed his way into the end zone from a yard out, culminating a 16-play, 93-yard drive. Then MSU kicked a 37-yard field goal, and Alabama led 21-6 at the half.

The onslaught continued in the second half as Jameson Williams scored on a 75-yard bomb from Young on the opening play. On the next possession, State kicked a 37-yard field goal (28-9). Both teams traded punts, then Robinson Jr. scored his second touchdown (his first receiving) on a 51-yard pass from Young, concluding a 7-play, 84-yard series. After another punt by MSU, Alabama drove 60 yards in ten plays, capped by a 3-yard rushing touchdown by Robinson Jr., his third of the day (42-9). Bama held once again, forcing another punt. Traeshon Holden added the dagger by scoring the last points of the game on a 29-yard TD catch to make the final 49-9.

Alabama's defense put on a show in Starkville, led by the remarkable performance of Will Anderson Jr. He became just the third player in program history to record at least four sacks in a single game, and the first since 1988. He also recorded four tackles for loss, bringing his total to 15, which leads the nation. Henry To'oTo'o logged a season-high 13 total tackles, including a game-high seven solo stops, and he added 1.5 tackles for loss. Jordan Battle also made his presence felt, snagging two interceptions, one of which he returned for a 40-yard pick-six (second of his career) in the first quarter, while also contributing seven tackles, five of them solo. On the offensive side, wide receiver John Metchie III had a night to remember. He eclipsed the 100-yard receiving mark for the first time this season, hauling in seven catches for 117 yards and a touchdown.

This game marked the 95th time Alabama has held an opponent to less than ten points under Nick Saban. Since 2015, their defense has limited opponents to ten or fewer points 38 times (out of 91 games). The Crimson Tide extended their streak of scoring 30+ points to 33 games, a major college football record. They also recorded their 85th non-offensive touchdown of the Saban era, tying last season's total.[314]

Passing	C/ATT	YDS	AVG	TD	INT	QBR
B. Young	20/28	348	12.4	4	0	96.1

Rushing	CAR	YDS	AVG	TD	LONG
R. Williams	11	78	7.1	0	29
B. Robinson Jr.	19	73	3.8	2	11
T. Sanders	4	27	6.8	0	20
B. Young	6	18	3	0	13
Team	1	-1	-1	0	0
Team	41	195	4.8	2	29

Interceptions	INT	YDS	TD
J. Battle	2	69	1
J. Jobe	1	6	0
Team	3	75	1

Punting	NO	YDS	AVG	TB	IN 20	LONG
J. Burnip	3	112	37.3	0	2	45

Receiving	REC	YDS	AVG	TD	LONG
J. Metchie III	7	117	16.7	1	46
J. Williams	2	77	38.5	1	75
T. Holden	3	70	23.3	1	29
B. Robinson Jr.	5	68	13.6	1	51
S. Bolden	2	9	4.5	0	5
R. Williams	1	7	7	0	7
Team	20	348	17.4	4	75

Kick returns	NO	YDS	AVG	LONG	TD
J. Williams	2	65	32.5	45	0

Punt returns	NO	YDS	AVG	LONG	TD
J. Earle	1	2	2	2	0

Kicking	FG	PCT	LONG	XP	PTS
W. Reichard	0/0	0	0	7/7	7

Note: Table data from "Alabama 49-9 Mississippi State (Oct 16, 2021) Box Score" (315)

10/23/21 - Alabama (4) vs Tennessee

Team	1	2	3	4	T		Passing	Rushing	Total
Tennessee	14	0	3	7	24		282	65	347
Alabama (4)	7	14	3	28	52		371	203	574

After a Tennessee punt, both teams scored touchdowns. After a 19-yard pickup from Bryce Young to Jameson Williams, a personal foul penalty on Tennessee moved the ball to the TN 22-yard line. Three plays later, Brian Robinson Jr. scored from eight yards out. This concluded a 12-play, 85-yard drive (7-0). Tennessee responded in 1:50, driving 75 yards and scoring on an 8-yard pass from Hendon Hooker (7-7). After Alabama missed a 54-yard field goal attempt, Tennessee regained the lead in 2:18 when Hooker found Payton for a 57-yard bomb. Less than a minute into the second quarter, Jameson Williams caught a pass and fumbled it. Tennessee recovered on its own 15-yard line, gained nine yards in two plays, lost nine yards on two penalties, then were forced to punt after an incomplete pass. Alabama tied the game at 14-14 when Young took it in himself from five yards out, capping a 7-play, 44-yard drive. Bama forced Tennessee to a three-and-out, then drove 79 yards in 12 plays, scoring on a 6-yard pass to Metchie III. After both teams punted, Alabama led 21-14 at the break.

After three punts, both teams scored FGs (TN from 32, and Bama from 45). After another punt by the Vols, Alabama drove down to the TN 14 as the third quarter ended. The fourth quarter saw lots of action, starting with Young plunging into the end zone from six yards out, capping an 11-play, 80-yard drive (31-17). Both teams scored TDs on their next possessions. Hooker unleashed a 70-yard scoring strike in a quick 2-play, 75-yard drive. Robinson Jr. responded with a 15-yard rushing TD, punctuating a 4-play, 75-yard series (38-24). On TN's next drive, Armour-Davis returned a pick 47 yards to the TN 18. Robinson Jr. capitalized, plunging in from a yard out to cap a 4-play, 18-yard drive. Bama stopped the Vols, then Bryce Young connected with John Metchie III for a 19-yard touchdown pass. This scoring play brought Alabama's point total in the fourth quarter to 28, and the final score was Alabama 52, Tennessee 24.

Anderson Jr. led the defense by racking up eight tackles (five solo stops and 1.5 sacks). Metchie III (11-121-2) and Jameson Williams (6-123-0) both eclipsed the 100-yard receiving mark. Robinson Jr. ran for 107 yards and scored three TDs on 26 carries. Young rushed ten times for a career-high 42 yards, recording five first downs and two rushing TDs. This was Alabama's 18th straight Homecoming victory and 15th consecutive win over Tennessee. The Tide amassed 574 yards of total offense, marking the 45th time in the last 93 games they have surpassed the 500-yard mark and the fourth instance this season. Alabama has scored a touchdown on its opening drive in seven out of their eight games this season (six straight). Alabama has now scored 30+ points in 34 straight games, the longest streak in major college football history.[316]

Passing	C/ATT	YDS	AVG	TD	INT	QBR
B. Young	31/43	371	8.6	2	0	90.6

Rushing	CAR	YDS	AVG	TD	LONG
B. Robinson Jr.	26	107	4.1	3	15
B. Young	10	42	4.2	2	16
R. Williams	8	29	3.6	0	9
T. Sanders	3	19	6.3	0	11
J. Metchie III	1	8	8	0	8
Team	1	-2	-2	0	0
Team	49	203	4.1	5	16

Interceptions	INT	YDS	TD
J. Armour-Davis	1	47	0

Punting	NO	YDS	AVG	TB	IN 20	LONG
J. Burnip	2	85	42.5	0	0	46

Receiving	REC	YDS	AVG	TD	LONG
J. Williams	6	123	20.5	0	65
J. Metchie III	11	121	11	2	28
C. Latu	3	55	18.3	0	27
T. Holden	2	34	17	0	26
S. Bolden	3	16	5.3	0	7
B. Robinson Jr.	4	16	4	0	17
J. Billingsley	1	8	8	0	8
R. Williams	1	-2	-2	0	0
Team	31	371	12	2	65

Kick returns	NO	YDS	AVG	LONG	TD
S. Bolden	1	10	10	10	0

Kicking	FG	PCT	LONG	XP	PTS
W. Reichard	1/2	50	45	7/7	10

Note: Table data from "Alabama 52-24 Tennessee (Oct 23, 2021) Box Score" (317)

343

11/06/21 - Alabama (2) vs LSU

Team	1	2	3	4	T		Passing	Rushing	Total
LSU	7	0	7	0	14		186	109	295
Alabama (2)	0	14	6	0	20		302	6	308

Alabama missed a 49-yard field goal on its opening possession, and LSU scored a touchdown on theirs with an 8-play drive of 68 yards capped by an 8-yard touchdown pass. Those were the only points of the first quarter as both teams traded punts over the next four possessions. Alabama failed to convert on 4th-and-2 in the second quarter, then LSU punted again. Bama evened the score when Brian Robinson Jr. scored on a 2-yard rushing touchdown, capping a 12-play, 77-yard drive. On LSU's next possession, Jaylen Armour-Davis intercepted a pass on the LSU 39-yard line. The Tide capitalized with a 5-play, 39-yard drive ending with an 8-yard touchdown pass from Bryce Young to John Metchie III. Alabama led 14-7 at the half.

The second half belonged to the Crimson Tide defense. Henry To'oTo'o caused a fumble, Phidarian Mathis recovered it, and two plays later Bryce Young threw a 58-yard touchdown pass to Jameson Williams. Despite a missed extra point, Alabama extended its lead to 20-7. After both teams punted, LSU managed to score on an 8-yard touchdown pass from Johnson to Bech, capping a 14-play, 89-yard drive. Three punts later, LSU failed to convert on 4th-and-goal from the 7-yard line. Young got sacked and fumbled, LSU turned it over on downs, Bama punted, LSU drove to the Alabama 30-yard line, but time ran out before they could score. Alabama won 20-14.

Will Anderson Jr. led the Tide's defensive charge with an impressive performance recording 12 tackles (including eight solo stops), four tackles for loss (tying his career high), 1.5 sacks, and a pass breakup. He continues to lead the nation with 21 tackles for loss (-88 yards). Henry To'oTo'o logged nine tackles and forced a fumble. Will Anderson Jr. (1.5), Christian Harris (.5), Dallas Tuner (2), and Phidarian Mathis (1) combined for five sacks (-29 yards) on the night. Jameson Williams recorded his seventh reception of at least 55 yards or more (all seven lead the team's longest plays of the season), with six of those seven leading to touchdowns. Jalyn Armour-Davis snagged his third interception of the season, and the Alabama defense has now forced 103 interceptions in the last 94 games, returning 36 of those for touchdowns.[318]

Passing	C/ATT	YDS	AVG	TD	INT	QBR
B. Young	24/37	302	8.2	2	0	61.9

Rushing	CAR	YDS	AVG	TD	LONG
B. Robinson Jr.	13	18	1.4	1	5
R. Williams	2	9	4.5	0	7
J. Williams	1	1	1	0	1
S. Bolden	1	0	0	0	0
B. Young	9	-22	-2.4	0	15
Team	26	6	0.2	1	15

Interceptions	INT	YDS	TD
J. Armour-Davis	1	0	0

Punting	NO	YDS	AVG	TB	IN 20	LONG
J. Burnip	6	238	39.7	0	3	47

Receiving	REC	YDS	AVG	TD	LONG
J. Williams	10	160	16	1	58
J. Metchie III	9	73	8.1	1	22
R. Williams	1	24	24	0	24
S. Bolden	2	22	11	0	15
C. Latu	1	15	15	0	15
B. Robinson Jr.	1	8	8	0	8
Team	24	302	12.6	2	58

Kick returns	NO	YDS	AVG	LONG	TD
J. Williams	1	22	22	22	0

Punt returns	NO	YDS	AVG	LONG	TD
J. Earle	3	31	10.3	17	0

Kicking	FG	PCT	LONG	XP	PTS
W. Reichard	0/1	0	0	2/3	2

Note: Table data from "Alabama 20-14 LSU (Nov 6, 2021) Box Score" (319)

11/13/21 - Alabama (2) vs New Mexico State

Team	1	2	3	4	T		Passing	Rushing	Total
New Mexico State	3	0	0	0	3		129	9	138
Alabama (2)	14	35	0	10	59		340	247	587

After both teams punted to start the game, New Mexico State drew first blood with a 50-yard field goal. The Tide responded by scoring touchdowns on their next seven consecutive drives in the first half while forcing four punts and recovering a fumble (forced by Christian Harris, recovered by Justin Eboigbe). The offense struck with lightning quickness as Jameson Williams hauled in a 50-yard scoring strike, capping off a blink-and-you-missed-it 71-yard drive that took just two plays. Next, Cameron Latu got in on the act, snagging a 12-yard touchdown reception that punctuated a methodical 7-play, 86-yard march downfield.

After Christian Leary blocked a punt to start the second quarter, Brian Robinson Jr. rushed one yard into the end zone capping a 3-play, 4-yard drive. It only took Alabama two plays to score on its next drive as Williams caught a 32-yard touchdown pass (his second touchdown of the game) on a drive totaling 34 yards. After that, Robinson Jr. ran it in for a 63-yard touchdown (his second of the day), capping off the 76-yard drive. Bryce Young then found Jameson Williams for a third time, this one for a 9-yard scoring strike. This touchdown capped off a methodical 6-play, 22-yard drive. And finally, Jahleel Billingsley added an exclamation point with a 5-yard touchdown reception. This score punctuated an 8-play, 92-yard drive which brought Alabama's lead to 49-3 at the half behind Young's five touchdown passes.

It was a scoreless third quarter, but in the fourth Paul Tyson orchestrated an 11-play, 80-yard drive and found Trey Sanders in the end zone for a 5-yard touchdown strike. Following a punt by New Mexico State, freshman kicker Jack Martin split the uprights from 29 yards out for his first career field goal. That capped off an emphatic 59-3 victory for the University of Alabama.

Jalyn Armour-Davis was the defensive leader for Alabama, recording six solo tackles and deflecting a pass. Will Anderson Jr. recorded two sacks, contributing to Alabama's total of seven in the game. With his two sacks, Anderson Jr. now has 12.5 sacks this season, ranking third in Alabama's history behind the legendary Derrick Thomas, who had 18 sacks in 1987 and an astonishing 27 sacks in 1988. In addition to his sack production, Anderson Jr. also had two tackles for loss, bringing his season total to 23. This total of 23 tackles for loss ranks third in Alabama's history, trailing only Derrick Thomas' remarkable 39 tackles for loss in 1988 and Wallace Gilberry's 27 tackles for loss in 2007.

Bryce Young put on a clinic against New Mexico State, etching his name in the Crimson Tide's record books with an outstanding performance. In just over two quarters of play, he showcased his precision and efficiency, completing an impressive 21-of-23 passes for 270 yards and five touchdowns. His five touchdown passes (all in the first half) tied his own record from earlier in the season for the second-most in a single game. He set a new school record for the best completion percentage (with a minimum of 20 completions) in a single game, connecting on an astonishing 91.3% of his passes (21-of-23). This performance marked the second time Young has broken this record this season, having previously completed 90.9% of his passes (20-of-22) against Southern Miss on September 25th. Young completed an impressive 13 consecutive passes for 183 yards. This streak of 13 straight completions tied for the sixth-longest in Alabama history and marked the most consecutive completions to start a game in his career. In addition to his record-breaking accuracy, he also eclipsed the 3,000-yard passing mark for the season, becoming just the sixth quarterback in Alabama history to achieve this feat. With 3,025 yards, Young currently ranks sixth on the Crimson Tide's all-time single season passing yards list, trailing only A.J. McCarron (3,063), Jake Coker (3,110), Blake Sims (3,487), Tua Tagovailoa (3,966), and Mac Jones, who set the record last year with 4,500 yards.

345

In the first quarter, Jameson Williams hauled in a 50-yard touchdown strike from quarterback Bryce Young. This explosive play marked his eighth reception of 50+ yards this season. Remarkably, seven of those eight catches spanning half the length of the field have resulted in touchdowns. With his 158 receiving yards against New Mexico State, he eclipsed the 1,000-yard receiving mark for the season. His current tally of 1,028 receiving yards places him ninth on Alabama's all-time single season receiving yards list.

Brian Robinson Jr. rushed for 99 yards, bringing his career total to 2,184. This moved him up to the 17th spot on the Alabama all-time career rushing yards list. In the second quarter, he rushed for a 63-yard touchdown, the longest of his career.

Alabama's relentless pursuit and impenetrable wall limited the Aggies to a mere three points. This remarkable feat marked the second occasion this season that Nick Saban's squad has held an opponent to ten points or fewer. This dominant performance extended their streak to 40 times in the last 94 games where they have achieved this impressive defensive milestone.[320]

Passing	C/ATT	YDS	AVG	TD	INT	QBR
B. Young	21/23	270	11.7	5	0	94.5
P. Tyson	6/8	43	5.4	0	0	54.8
J. Milroe	2/5	17	3.4	0	0	40.6
B. Barker	1/1	10	10	0	0	100
Team	30/37	340	9.2	5	0	--

Rushing	CAR	YDS	AVG	TD	LONG
B. Robinson Jr.	9	99	11	2	63
T. Sanders	12	66	5.5	1	12
J. Milroe	5	26	5.2	0	15
C. Leary	3	22	7.3	0	12
D. Kennedy	7	16	2.3	0	7
R. Williams	1	11	11	0	11
B. Young	4	7	1.8	0	12
Team	41	247	6.0	3	63

Kicking	FG	PCT	LONG	XP	PTS
W. Reichard	0/0	0	0	8/8	8
J. Martin	1/1	100	29	0/0	3
Team	1/1	100	29	8/8	11

Punting	NO	YDS	AVG	TB	IN 20	LONG
J. Burnip	2	76	38	0	1	39

Receiving	REC	YDS	AVG	TD	LONG
J. Williams	6	158	26.3	3	50
J. Metchie III	6	48	8	0	26
B. Robinson Jr.	5	36	7.2	0	21
J. Baker	2	21	10.5	0	16
T. Jones-Bell	2	16	8	0	8
S. Bolden	1	13	13	0	13
C. Latu	1	12	12	1	12
T. Holden	2	11	5.5	0	13
A. Hall	1	10	10	0	10
J. Brooks	1	9	9	0	9
R. Ouzts	1	8	8	0	8
J. Billingsley	1	5	5	1	5
C. Leary	1	-7	-7	0	0
Team	30	340	11.3	5	50

Kick returns	NO	YDS	AVG	LONG	TD
S. Bolden	1	15	15	15	0

Punt returns	NO	YDS	AVG	LONG	TD
S. Bolden	2	37	18.5	24	0
J. Moody	0	20	0	20	0
C. Leary	1	2	2	2	0
J. Earle	1	0	0	0	0
Team	4	59	14.8	24	0

Note: Table data from "Alabama 59-3 New Mexico State (Nov 13, 2021) Box Score" (321)

11/20/21 - Alabama (2) vs Arkansas (21)

Team	1	2	3	4	T	Passing	Rushing	Total
Arkansas (21)	0	14	7	14	35	358	110	468
Alabama (2)	3	21	10	8	42	559	112	671

Alabama held Arkansas to a punt on their first possession then drove down the field to the Hogs' 30. Brian Robinson Jr. lost a yard on 4th-and-1, then Dallas Turner recovered a fumble on the very next play. Four plays later, Will Reichard hit a 48-yard FG to put Alabama on the board first. Arkansas punted again, and Alabama got the ball back on the 2-yard line. The Tide drove the full 98 yards in nine plays with the score coming from a Bryce Young pass to John Metchie III for a 20-yard touchdown. The score came on the first play of the second quarter to make it 10-0. After both teams traded punts, the Razorbacks answered with a 96-yard touchdown drive, culminating in a 15-yard K.J. Jefferson to Treylon Burks scoring strike (10-7 Bama). However, the Tide quickly regained control on their next drive as Young hit Jameson Williams for a 79-yard bomb. Arkansas closed the gap again on Dominique Johnson's 1-yard plunge, but another Young-to-Williams touchdown, this time for 32 yards, gave Alabama a 24-14 halftime lead.

Christian Leary's 11-yard touchdown catch (first of his career and Bama's fourth passing TD of the game) extended Alabama's advantage on the first possession of the third quarter. Arkansas countered with a 66-yard Jefferson-to-Burks TD to make it 31-21, Bama on top. After Bama missed a 47-yard field goal and an Arkansas punt, Reichard hit a 30-yard field goal to finish off a 9-play, 63-yard drive (34-21). Less than five minutes into the fourth quarter, Arkansas scored on a 32-yard fake field goal jump pass to trim the deficit to 34-28. Latu fumbled, Bama held the Hogs to a punt, then Williams recorded his third touchdown of the game, tying his career high, on a 40-yard catch. The Tide made a successful two-point conversion to pull in front 42-28. Jefferson found Raheim Sanders for a late 17-yard score, bringing the final to 42-35.

Alabama's defense was relentless, with three players recording 11+ tackles. Henry To'oTo'o led the way with 13, while Will Anderson Jr. and DeMarcco Hellams each contributed 11. The Tide's defense racked up ten tackles for loss, with Anderson Jr. accounting for 3.5 of them and To'oTo'o adding three more. Bryce Young broke the single-game school record for passing yards with 559. He became the first Bama player to surpass the 500-yard passing barrier. The previous record was held by Scott Hunter, who had thrown for 484 yards on November 29, 1969. Jameson Williams and John Metchie III both eclipsed the 100-yard mark in the same game for the second time this season. Williams had a career-best 190 yards, while Metchie racked up 173 yards, both reaching the century mark in the first half. Running back Brian Robinson Jr. rushed for 122 yards and surpassed the 100-yard mark for the fourth time this year. Alabama's 671 yards of total offense ranks as the fifth-highest single-game total in program history. The Crimson Tide extended their SEC record for most consecutive 10-win seasons to 14 and have now won 61 of their last 63 games at Bryant-Denny Stadium, including the last 13 straight.[322]

Passing	C/ATT	YDS	AVG	TD	INT	QBR
B. Young	31/40	559	14	5	0	96.5

Rushing	CAR	YDS	AVG	TD	LONG
B. Robinson Jr.	27	122	4.5	0	15
T. Sanders	1	3	3	0	3
B. Young	6	-11	-1.8	0	16
Team	2	-2	-1	0	0
Team	36	112	3.1	0	16

Kicking	FG	PCT	LONG	XP	PTS
W. Reichard	2/3	67	48	4/4	10

Punting	NO	YDS	AVG	TB	IN 20	LONG
J. Burnip	1	32	32	0	1	32

Receiving	REC	YDS	AVG	TD	LONG
J. Williams	8	190	23.8	3	79
J. Metchie III	10	173	17.3	1	33
C. Latu	3	58	19.3	0	28
S. Bolden	3	49	16.3	0	27
T. Sanders	1	36	36	0	36
B. Robinson Jr.	3	18	6	0	8
J. Brooks	1	12	12	0	12
J. Billingsley	1	12	12	0	12
C. Leary	1	11	11	1	11
Team	31	559	18	5	79

Punt returns	NO	YDS	AVG	LONG	TD
S. Bolden	2	-2	-1	1	0

Note: Table data from "Arkansas 35-42 Alabama (Nov 20, 2021) Box Score" (323)

11/27/21 - Alabama (3) at Auburn

Team	1	2	3	4	OT	T		Passing	Rushing	Total
Alabama (3)	0	0	0	10	14	24		317	71	388
Auburn	0	7	3	0	12	22		137	22	159

The game started with a defensive slugfest, as both teams punted the ball away on their first five possessions each. The stalemate was broken when Jameson Williams was ejected for targeting which gave Auburn the ball on the AL 39-yard line. The Tigers scored four plays later with a 15-yard touchdown pass from TJ Finley to Kobe Hudson. Auburn was up 7-0 with 6:50 left in the first half. The offenses continued to sputter as each team traded punts to end the first half, and Auburn maintained the 7-0 lead at the break.

Alabama punted again to start the second half, but Auburn managed to put together a 4-play, 5-yard series, resulting in a 33-yard field goal to extend their lead to 10-0. Alabama's offense finally showed signs of life when Bryce Young was intercepted on his own 45-yard line. However, Auburn punted the ball back, and Alabama drove down to the Auburn 19-yard line. On 4th-and-11, a bad snap led to an incomplete pass and a turnover on downs. After another Auburn punt, Alabama couldn't convert on a 4th-and-2 from the Auburn 39-yard line. Josh Jobe intercepted the next Auburn pass, and Alabama drove 46 yards in seven plays to score their first points of the game with a field goal by Will Reichard from 30 yards out. The defensive battle continued as Auburn punted two more times, sandwiching an Alabama 4th-and-1 conversion attempt that they failed to convert, leaving the score at 10-3 as the game progressed.

With the clock ticking down and Auburn nursing a 10-3 lead, the Tigers seemed to have the Iron Bowl well in hand. They were up 10-3 and had the ball with 1:56 left on the clock. They chewed up the clock with three straight running plays forcing Alabama to burn their last two timeouts. They would have burned more clock had Tank Bigsby not run out of bounds on one of the plays. This forced an Auburn punt, and when the Crimson Tide finally got the ball back, they were pinned at their own 3-yard line with just 1:32 remaining in the game.

The odds were stacked against them. Alabama had struggled mightily on offense all game, barely crossing midfield. They were out of timeouts. After two incomplete passes setting up 3rd-and-3, Young fired a strike to John Metchie III for 22 yards to spark the comeback attempt. Two plays later, they had a fresh set of downs at the Auburn 45-yard line with 53 ticks left on the clock. Young then used his legs to pick up a few crucial yards before his next two passes fell incomplete, setting up a dire 4th-and-7 from the AU 42-yard line with just 38 seconds left in the game. With the season on the line, Young calmly delivered a 14-yard pass to Jaheel Billingsly to move the chains again. After two incompletions, it was 3rd-and-10 from the AU 28-yard line with 24 seconds left on the clock. Bryce Young dropped a perfectly placed touchdown pass into the arms of Ja'Corey Brooks to cap an improbable 12-play, 97-yard scoring drive in 1:11. Will Reichard's extra point knotted the score at 10-10, sending the game to overtime and silencing the Jordan-Hare crowd.

It was Bryce Young who struck first in OT, hitting Slade Bolden with a 6-yard touchdown pass to put Alabama on the board. Auburn responded as T.J. Finley found Landen King for a 5-yard pass to even the score. The back-and-forth continued in the second overtime. Auburn took the lead with a 49-yard field goal, but Alabama's Will Reichard answered with a 38-yarder of his own, sending the game into a third OT. After two overtimes, the rules dictated that both teams had to go for two-point conversions for the remainder of the game. Young connected with John Metchie III to give Alabama the advantage in the third OT. Undeterred, Finley hit John Samuel Shenker to force a fourth overtime. Auburn failed to convert their two-point try in the fourth OT as Finley's pass was almost picked off by Kool-Aid McKinstry and fell incomplete. With the game on the line, Young once again found his trusted target, Metchie III, for the decisive two-point score, sealing a 24-22 victory for the Crimson Tide. This epic Iron Bowl clash marked the first time in the 86-game history of the rivalry that the game went into overtime.

Henry To'oTo'o led the Alabama defense with nine total tackles, including six solo stops. Will Anderson Jr. logged seven total tackles (six solo), three tackles for loss, and a sack. Phidarian Mathis and Dallas Turner led the Crimson Tide with 1.5 sacks and 1.5 tackles for loss respectively. Anderson Jr. further solidified his status as one of the nation's best defensive players, leading the country with 30.5 tackles for loss (-128 yards) and ranking second with 14.5 sacks (-90 yards). Kool-Aid McKinstry recorded his first career sack (-13 yards) in the third quarter, while Josh Jobe snagged his third career interception and second of the season.[324]

Passing	C/ATT	YDS	AVG	TD	INT	QBR
B. Young	25/51	317	6.2	2	1	66.4
P. Tyson	0/1	0	0	0	0	0
Team	25/52	317	6.1	2	1	--

Rushing	CAR	YDS	AVG	TD	LONG
B. Robinson Jr.	16	71	4.4	0	37
T. Sanders	10	23	2.3	0	7
B. Young	11	-23	-2.1	0	9
Team	37	71	1.9	0	37

Interceptions	INT	YDS	TD
J. Jobe	1	0	0

Punting	NO	YDS	AVG	TB	IN 20	LONG
J. Burnip	7	263	37.6	0	2	46

Receiving	REC	YDS	AVG	TD	LONG
J. Metchie III	13	150	11.5	0	27
J. Brooks	2	49	24.5	1	28
J. Williams	2	43	21.5	0	34
B. Robinson Jr.	3	29	9.7	0	17
C. Latu	1	14	14	0	14
J. Billingsley	1	14	14	0	14
T. Sanders	2	12	6	0	11
S. Bolden	1	6	6	1	6
Team	25	317	12.7	2	34

Kick returns	NO	YDS	AVG	LONG	TD
J. Metchie III	1	13	13	13	0

Punt returns	NO	YDS	AVG	LONG	TD
S. Bolden	1	6	6	6	0

Kicking	FG	PCT	LONG	XP	PTS
W. Reichard	2/2	100	38	2/2	8

Note: Table data from "Alabama 24-22 Auburn (Nov 27, 2021) Box Score" (325)

349

12/04/21 - Alabama (3) vs Georgia (1)

Team	1	2	3	4	T	Passing	Rushing	Total
Georgia (1)	3	14	0	7	24	340	109	449
Alabama (3)	0	24	7	10	41	421	115	536

After both teams punted on their first possessions, Georgia scored first with a 38-yard field goal to conclude a 11-play, 52-yard drive. Those were the only points scored in the first quarter. On the first play of the second quarter, Stetson Bennett found Darnell Washington for a 5-yard touchdown, culminating a lengthy 97-yard drive to go up 10-0. However, Bryce Young responded in just 44 seconds, going 75 yards in only three plays, hitting Jameson Williams for a 67-yard scoring strike. After they held Georgia to a punt, the Crimson Tide seized momentum as Young connected with John Metchie III for a 13-yard touchdown, capping a 6-play, 80-yard march to go on top 14-10. After Georgia went three-and-out, there were three consecutive scores before the half. First, Alabama extended its lead with a 33-yard field goal by Will Reichard, the result of a methodical 12-play, 79-yard drive. Then Bennett found Ladd McConkey for a 32-yard touchdown pass, capping a 3-play, 75-yard drive. And finally, Young capped a 3-play, 75-yard drive with an 11-yard touchdown run, giving Alabama a 24-17 halftime lead.

The second half opened with a bang as Bryce Young unleashed a 55-yard bomb, finding Jameson Williams streaking down the field for a touchdown. This explosive play capped off a quick 5-play, 75-yard drive in less than two minutes, extending Alabama's lead to 31-17. Georgia drove down to the Alabama 9-yard line, then DeMarcco Hellams intercepted Bennett's pass. After a Bama punt, the Bulldogs drove down to the 19-yard line and went for it on 4th-and-9. Alabama came up with a stop to end the third quarter, drove to its own 41-yard line, then punted to the UGA 20-yard line. Three plays later, Jordan Battle picked off Stetson Bennett's pass and returned it 42 yards for the score, extending Bama's lead to 38-17. Georgia refused to wave the white flag as Bennett connected with Brock Bowers for an 18-yard touchdown, trimming the deficit to 38-24. But it was too late. After both teams punted, Will Reichard's 41-yard field goal sealed the 41-24 victory for the Crimson Tide.

The Alabama defense was led by DeMarcco Hellams, who racked up nine total tackles against Georgia in the SEC Championship Game. Hellams, Henry To'oTo'o, and Josh Jobe each tallied six solo stops, leading the Crimson Tide's defensive effort. Will Anderson Jr. continued his dominant season recording six tackles, including two tackles for loss and a sack. Hellams added to his impressive season by grabbing his third interception, tying the team high. Jordan Battle's 42-yard pick-six marked his second interception return for a touchdown this season. The play also etched its place in SEC Championship Game history, becoming the 12th interception return for a touchdown in the game's history, with the last instance occurring in 2016 when Alabama achieved the same feat against Florida. This interception marked Alabama's 15th of the season.

Bryce Young was awarded the MVP as he amassed an incredible 421 yards through the air, setting an SEC Championship Game record. Young's dual-threat abilities were on full display as he added 40 rushing yards on just three attempts, including a touchdown run. Young's total offensive output of 461 yards (421 passing, 40 rushing) set a new championship game record. In the first half alone, he torched the Georgia defense for 286 passing yards, completing 17 of his 27 attempts and finding the end zone twice. Remarkably, Young's first half passing yardage eclipsed the total passing yards allowed by Georgia in entire games against all but one of their opponents this season (11-of-12 opponents). His 286 yards in the opening two quarters established a new SEC Championship Game record for most passing yards in a single half.

Jameson Williams had 112 receiving yards in the first half. This feat marked the sixth time a player has amassed 100+ receiving yards in a single half. Moreover, Williams' performance extended Alabama's streak of having a 100-yard receiver in the championship game to three consecutive years, following DeVonta Smith's 184 yards in 2020 and Jaylen Waddle's 113 yards in 2018. He has hauled in 11 catches of 50 yards or more, with an astonishing ten of those resulting in touchdowns. He has also caught eight passes of 65+ yards with seven of those finding the end zone, and all seven of his catches of 67+ yards have resulted in touchdowns. His 67-yard touchdown catch in the first half stands as the longest in the history of the SEC Championship Game. Moreover, his 184 receiving yards in the game tied for the second-highest total in the championship game, matching the outstanding performance of Alabama's DeVonta Smith in 2020.

After punting on their first two drives in the game, Alabama scored on its next five consecutive possessions. They reached the end zone three times through the air, added another touchdown on the ground, and tacked on a field goal for good measure. Saturday's victory propelled the Crimson Tide to the top of the record books for most wins against teams ranked No. 1 in the nation. With their tenth victory, they surpassed the previous mark they had shared with the Miami Hurricanes. The win also marked their 29th SEC Championship overall (eight under Nick Saban).[326]

Passing	C/ATT	YDS	AVG	TD	INT	QBR
B. Young	26/44	421	9.6	3	0	98.1

Rushing	CAR	YDS	AVG	TD	LONG
B. Robinson Jr.	16	55	3.4	0	15
B. Young	3	40	13.3	1	15
Team	1	-1	-1	0	0
T. Sanders	6	21	3.5	0	14
Team	26	115	4.4	1	15

Kicking	FG	PCT	LONG	XP	PTS
W. Reichard	2/2	100	41	5/5	11

Punting	NO	YDS	AVG	TB	IN 20	LONG
J. Burnip	5	219	43.8	0	1	50

Receiving	REC	YDS	AVG	TD	LONG
J. Williams	7	184	26.3	2	67
J. Metchie III	6	97	16.2	1	40
S. Bolden	5	54	10.8	0	24
J. Billingsley	2	27	13.5	0	22
T. Holden	2	21	10.5	0	15
B. Robinson Jr.	2	16	8	0	8
C. Latu	1	13	13	0	13
J. Brooks	1	9	9	0	9
Team	26	421	16.2	3	67

Interceptions	INT	YDS	TD
J. Battle	1	42	1
D. Hellams	1	3	0
Team	2	45	1

Note: Table data from "Alabama 41-24 Georgia (Dec 4, 2021) Box Score" (327)

12/31/21 - Alabama (1) vs Cincinnati (4)

Team	1	2	3	4	T		Passing	Rushing	Total
Cincinnati (4)	3	0	3	0	6		144	74	218
Alabama (1)	7	10	0	10	27		181	301	482

Alabama set the tone right from the opening drive, marching 75 yards in 11 plays, scoring on an 8-yard touchdown pass from Bryce Young to Slade Bolden. The two teams then traded field goals (CIN from 33 after a 13-play, 60-yard series, and Bama from 26 concluding a 13-play, 67-yard drive). Alabama missed a 44-yard field goal attempt after three punts (two by the Bearcats and one by the Tide). With less than two minutes before the end of the first half, the Tide increased their lead to 17-3 on a 44-yard reception from Young to Ja-Corey Brooks, capping an 8-play, 94-yard drive that only took 2:03 off the clock.

The Bearcats scored on their first possession of the second half when Cole Smith split the uprights from 37 yards out cutting their deficit to 17-6. After trading punts, Bryce Young was intercepted around midfield. Alabama scored less than a minute and a half into the fourth quarter on a pass from Young to Cameron Latu for nine yards. This third passing touchdown of the game capped off a 9-play, 70-yard drive and put Bama up 24-6. Cincinnati drove down to the Bama 22-yard line but failed to convert on 4th-and-3. The final points of the game came from Will Reichard's 43-yard field goal, making the final 27-6.

Alabama's defense limited Cincinnati to a mere 218 total yards and tied their season-high with six pass breakups, matching their performance against LSU earlier in the year. Will Anderson Jr. earned the game's defensive MVP honors as he racked up six tackles, including a team-high two sacks. Brian Branch, who led the Tide with eight tackles (six of them solo), added a sack and two pass breakups to his impressive stat line.

Heisman Trophy winner Bryce Young amassed an impressive 181 yards through the air, completing 17 of his 28 pass attempts, and found the end zone three times. He achieved the Alabama single season passing yards record with 4,503 yards through 14 games. This surpassed Mac Jones who set the record the year before with 4,500. Young also set a new record for the most passing touchdowns in a single season at Alabama with 46. In the first half alone, Brian Robinson Jr. amassed 134 rushing yards, marking the second time this season he has surpassed the 100-yard mark in a single half. He earned the game's offensive MVP award recording a bowl record and a career-high 204 rushing yards on 26 carries, surpassing Bo Scarbrough's previous mark of 180 yards against Washington in 2016. Alabama won its 41st bowl game in the College Football Playoff Semifinal at the 2021 Goodyear Cotton Bowl Classic at AT&T Stadium in Arlington, Texas, the most in college football history. They gained 172 rushing yards in the first half alone, the most they have had in a single half all season long.[328]

Passing	C/ATT	YDS	AVG	TD	INT	QBR
B. Young	17/28	181	6.5	3	1	72.4

Rushing	CAR	YDS	AVG	TD	LONG
B. Robinson Jr.	26	204	7.8	0	23
T. Sanders	14	67	4.8	0	18
J. Williams	1	18	18	0	18
B. Young	6	12	2	0	12
Team	47	301	6.4	0	23

Kicking	FG	PCT	LONG	XP	PTS
W. Reichard	2/3	67	43	3/3	9

Punting	NO	YDS	AVG	TB	IN 20	LONG
J. Burnip	2	88	44	0	0	47

Receiving	REC	YDS	AVG	TD	LONG
J. Brooks	4	66	16.5	1	44
J. Williams	7	62	8.9	0	20
S. Bolden	3	31	10.3	1	16
J. Billingsley	1	12	12	0	12
C. Latu	1	9	9	1	9
T. Sanders	1	1	1	0	1
Team	17	181	10.6	3	44

Kick returns	NO	YDS	AVG	LONG	TD
J. Williams	1	15	15	15	0

Punt returns	NO	YDS	AVG	LONG	TD
S. Bolden	2	-1	-0.5	0	0
J. Earle	2	-7	-3.5	2	0
Team	4	-8	-2	2	0

Note: Table data from "Alabama 27-6 Cincinnati (Dec 31, 2021) Box Score" (329)

01/10/22 - Alabama (1) vs Georgia (3)

Team	1	2	3	4	T		Passing	Rushing	Total
Georgia (3)	0	6	7	20	33		224	140	**364**
Alabama (1)	3	6	0	9	18		369	30	**399**

The only score in the first quarter was Will Reichard's 37-yard field goal capping a 4-play, 56-yard drive. The rest of the quarter consisted of four punts. Both teams scored a pair of field goals in the second quarter. Georgia tied the game on its 24-yarder after an 11-play, 87-yard drive. Reichard connected from 45 and 37 yards, and each of those drives saw big passing plays. The first was a 40-yard pass to Jameson Williams, and the second included a 61-yarder to Latu. Georgia cut its deficit with another one from 49. Alabama led 9-6 at the half, but they suffered a huge loss as star receiver Jameson Williams went down with a devastating torn ACL.

After holding the Bulldogs to a punt to start the second half, Georgia intercepted Bryce Young on the Tide's second play. Bama held and got the ball back on their own 2-yard line after Georgia's punt. They took 7:45 off the clock and drove 68 yards in 17 plays to the UGA 30-yard line. Reichard's FG attempt was blocked, and Georgia was able to score the first TD of the game on its next drive. It started with a huge 67-yard run by Cook on their first play, then Zamir White capped it off with his 1-yard run into the end zone. The Bulldogs took the lead, 13-9. In the fourth quarter, Reichard kicked a 21-yard field goal (his fourth of the game) capping a 10-play, 72-yard drive to come within a point (13-12, UGA). On the third play of Georgia's possession, Bennett was sacked by Harris for a loss of 11 which resulted in a fumble that was recovered by Branch. Five plays later, Cameron Latu scored a 3-yard touchdown pass. Bama was back on top, 18-13 after an unsuccessful two-point conversion attempt. On Georgia's next possession, Adonia Mitchell caught a 40-yard touchdown pass. After a failed two-point conversion attempt, Georgia led 19-18 with 8:09 left in the game. The Bulldogs scored again after forcing an Alabama punt, this time on a 15-yard pass to Brock Bowers (26-18). With 54 seconds left in the game, Ringo returned an interception 79 yards to seal the Georgia win, 33-18.

Bryce Young completed 33-of-57 passes for 369 yards and a touchdown. Brian Robinson Jr. amassed 68 yards on 22 carries while also contributing 28 yards on four receptions. Tight end Cameron Latu stepped up in the absence of John Metchie III and the injured Jameson Williams, leading the Crimson Tide's receiving corps by hauling in five catches for 102 yards, including a career-long 61-yard reception, and he also found the end zone for a touchdown. DeMarco Hellams led the defensive charge with seven tackles, while Christian Harris and Henry To'oTo'o each recorded six. Christian Harris and Dallas Turner led the team with two sacks apiece, and Harris also logged three tackles for loss. This matchup marked Alabama's 13th appearance in the College Football Playoff since its inception in 2014. The Crimson Tide boasts an impressive 9-4 record in CFP games, and they are the only team to participate in seven of the eight Playoffs. They hold the records for the most CFP wins (9) and the most games played (13).[330]

Passing	C/ATT	YDS	AVG	TD	INT	QBR
B. Young	35/57	369	6.5	1	2	82.3

Rushing	CAR	YDS	AVG	TD	LONG
B. Robinson Jr.	22	68	3.1	0	16
T. Sanders	2	5	2.5	0	4
B. Young	4	-43	-10.8	0	0
Team	28	30	1.1	0	16

Kicking	FG	PCT	LONG	XP	PTS
W. Reichard	4/5	80	45	0/0	12

Punting	NO	YDS	AVG	TB	IN 20	LONG
J. Burnip	4	148	37	0	2	43

Receiving	REC	YDS	AVG	TD	LONG
C. Latu	5	102	20.4	1	61
J. Williams	4	65	16.3	0	40
A. Hall	2	52	26	0	28
J. Brooks	6	47	7.8	0	20
S. Bolden	7	44	6.3	0	11
B. Robinson Jr.	4	28	7	0	12
T. Holden	6	28	4.7	0	10
T. Sanders	1	3	3	0	3
Team	35	369	10.5	1	61

Punt returns	NO	YDS	AVG	LONG	TD
S. Bolden	1	-2	-2	-2	0

Note: Table data from "Georgia 33-18 Alabama (Jan 10, 2022) Box Score" (331)

Season Stats

Record	13-2	4th of 130
SEC Record	8-2	
Rank	2	
Points for	598	
Points against	302	
Points/game	39.9	6th of 130
Opp points/game	20.1	18th of 130
SOS[15]	5.69	7th of 130

Team stats (averages per game)

Split	G	Passing					Rushing				Total Offense		
		Cmp	Att	Pct	Yds	TD	Att	Yds	Avg	TD	Plays	Yds	Avg
Offense	15	25.3	38.1	66.5	338.2	3.2	36.5	150.1	4.1	1.4	74.5	488.3	6.6
Defense	15	19.8	31.4	63.1	218.1	1.7	32.3	84.9	2.6	0.6	63.7	302.9	4.8
Difference		5.5	6.7	3.4	120.1	1.5	4.2	65.2	1.5	0.8	10.8	185.4	1.8

Split	First Downs				Penalties		Turnovers		
	Pass	Rush	Pen	Tot	No.	Yds	Fum	Int	Tot
Offense	14.3	8.7	1.5	24.4	7.1	65.9	0.5	0.5	0.9
Defense	9.3	5.7	2.6	17.7	6.8	49.4	0.3	1	1.3
Difference	5	3	-1.1	6.7	0.3	16.5	0.2	-0.5	-0.4

Passing

Rk	Player	G	Passing								
			Cmp	Att	Pct	Yds	Y/A	AY/A	TD	Int	Rate
1	Bryce Young	15	366	547	66.9	4872	8.9	10	47	7	167.5
2	Paul Tyson	12	10	16	62.5	150	9.4	9.4	0	0	141.3
3	Jalen Milroe	4	3	7	42.9	41	5.9	8.7	1	0	139.2
4	Braxton Barker	1	1	1	100	10	10	10	0	0	184

Rushing and receiving

Rk	Player	G	Rushing					Receiving				Scrimmage		
			Att	Yds	Avg	TD	Rec	Yds	Avg	TD	Plays	Yds	Avg	TD
1	Brian Robinson Jr.	14	271	1343	5	14	35	296	8.5	2	306	1639	5.4	16
2	Bryce Young	15	81	0	0	3					81	0	0	3
3	Trey Sanders	13	72	314	4.4	2	6	55	9.2	0	78	369	4.7	2
4	Roydell Williams	10	48	284	5.9	1	5	57	11.4	1	53	341	6.4	2
5	Jase McClellan	5	40	191	4.8	1	10	97	9.7	3	50	288	5.8	4
6	Jalen Milroe	4	15	57	3.8	0					15	57	3.8	0
7	Demouy Kennedy	14	7	16	2.3	0					7	16	2.3	0
8	Jameson Williams	15	3	23	7.7	0	79	1572	19.9	15	82	1595	19.5	15
9	Christian Leary	8	3	22	7.3	0	2	4	2	1	5	26	5.2	1
10	John Metchie III	13	1	8	8	0	96	1142	11.9	8	97	1150	11.9	8
11	Slade Bolden	15	1	0	0	0	42	408	9.7	3	43	408	9.5	3
12	Cameron Latu	15					26	410	15.8	8	26	410	15.8	8
13	Traeshon Holden	15					21	239	11.4	1	21	239	11.4	1
14	Jahleel Billingsley	15					17	256	15.1	3	17	256	15.1	3
15	Ja'Corey Brooks	15					15	192	12.8	2	15	192	12.8	2
16	Jojo Earle	12					12	148	12.3	0	12	148	12.3	0
17	Javon Baker	11					7	101	14.4	1	7	101	14.4	1
18	Agiye Hall	7					4	72	18	0	4	72	18	0
19	Thaiu Jones-Bell	4					2	16	8	0	2	16	8	0
20	Robbie Ouzts	11					1	8	8	0	1	8	8	0

354

Defense and fumbles

Rk	Player	G	Tackles					Def Int					Fumbles	
			Solo	Ast	Tot	Loss	Sk	Int	Yds	Avg	TD	PD	FR	FF
1	Henry To'oto'o	15	52	59	111	7.5	4					1		1
2	Will Anderson Jr.	15	56	45	101	31	17.5					3		
3	Demarcco Hellams	15	54	33	87	2.5	0	2	6	3	0	3		
4	Jordan Battle	15	50	35	85	1	0	3	111	37	2	3		
5	Christian Harris	15	45	35	80	11.5	5.5					3		2
6	Brian Branch	13	34	21	55	5	1					9	1	0
7	Phidarian Mathis	14	20	33	53	10.5	9					2	2	1
8	Josh Jobe	12	28	10	38	1	0	2	6	3	0	4		
9	Byron Young	14	18	15	33	7.5	2							
10	Jalyn Armour-Davis	11	22	10	32	1	0	3	51	17	0	4		
11	Dallas Turner	11	14	16	30	10	8.5						1	0
12	Daniel Wright	13	16	13	29	2	1					3		
13	Kool-Aid McKinstry	15	9	17	26	1	1	1	0	0	0	1		
14	Tim Smith	11	11	14	25	5	0.5					1		
15	Drew Sanders	7	12	12	24	2.5	1					2		
16	Justin Eboigbe	13	8	11	19	0.5	0.5					2	2	0
17	DJ Dale	11	12	6	18	3	2							
18	Malachi Moore	15	10	6	16	2	0	1	-1	-1	0	1		
19	Chris Braswell	14	7	6	13	1	0							
20	Jaylen Moody	15	3	8	11	0	0	1	13	13	0	0		
21	Labryan Ray	11	5	6	11	3	1							
22	Khyree Jackson	4	5	2	7	0	0					2		
23	Demouy Kennedy	14	3	4	7	0	0							
24	Bryce Young	15	1	6	7	0	0							
25	Marcus Banks	8	4	2	6	0	0	1	0	0	0	0		
26	Shane Lee	3	1	5	6	0.5	0.5							
27	Stephon Wynn Jr.	4	1	4	5	0	0							
28	Jase McClellan	5	1	3	4	0	0							
29	Chase Allen	1	2	1	3	1	1							1
30	Kendrick Blackshire	3	2	1	3	0	0							
31	Jameson Williams	15	2	1	3	0	0							
32	Jamil Burroughs	1	2	0	2	1	1							
33	Devonta Smith	2	1	1	2	0	0							
34	Kristian Story	2	1	1	2	0	0							
35	Slade Bolden	15	1	0	1	0	0							
36	Darrian Dalcourt	1	1	0	1	0	0							
37	Jojo Earle	12	0	1	1	0	0							
38	Traeshon Holden	15	0	1	1	0	0							
39	Jah-Marien Latham	1	1	0	1	0	0							
40	King Mwikuta	13	1	0	1	0	0							
41	Trey Sanders	13	1	0	1	0	0							
42	Roydell Williams	10	1	0	1	0	0							

Kick and punt returns

Rk	Player	G	Kick Ret				Punt Ret			
			Ret	Yds	Avg	TD	Ret	Yds	Avg	TD
1	Jameson Williams	15	10	352	35.2	2				
2	Slade Bolden	15	5	67	13.4	0	15	99	6.6	0
3	Cameron Latu	15	2	7	3.5	0				
4	Jahleel Billingsley	15	1	17	17	0				
5	John Metchie III	13	1	13	13	0				
6	Jojo Earle	12					16	88	5.5	0
7	Ja'Corey Brooks	15					1	19	19	0
8	Chris Braswell	14					1	11	11	0
9	Christian Leary	8					1	2	2	0
10	Jase McClellan	5						33		1
11	Jaylen Moody	15						20		

355

Kicking and punting

Rk	Player	G	Kicking							Punting		
			XPM	XPA	XP%	FGM	FGA	FG%	Pts	Punts	Yds	Avg
1	Will Reichard	15	71	72	98.6	22	28	78.6	137			
2	Jack Martin	4	0	0		1	1	100	3			
3	James Burnip	15								48	1878	39.1

Scoring

Rk	Player	G	Touchdowns							Kicking				Pts
			Rush	Rec	Int	FR	PR	KR	Tot	XPM	FGM	2PM	Sfty	
1	Will Reichard	15								71	22			137
2	Jameson Williams	15		15				2	17					102
3	Brian Robinson Jr.	14	14	2					16					96
4	Cameron Latu	15		8					8					48
5	John Metchie III	13		8					8					48
6	Jase McClellan	5	1	3		1			5					30
7	Bryce Young	15	3						3					18
8	Slade Bolden	15		3					3					18
9	Jahleel Billingsley	15		3					3					18
10	Ja'Corey Brooks	15		2					2					12
11	Jordan Battle	15			2				2					12
12	Roydell Williams	10	1	1					2					12
13	Trey Sanders	13	2						2					12
14	Javon Baker	11		1					1					6
15	King Mwikuta	13					1		1					6
16	Traeshon Holden	15		1					1					6
17	Christian Leary	8		1					1					6
18	Jack Martin	4									1			3

Stats include bowl games
Note: Table data from "2021 Alabama Crimson Tide Stats" (15)

Awards and honors

Name	Award	Type
Will Anderson Jr.	Permanent Team Captain	Team
Phidarian Mathis	Permanent Team Captain	Team
Evan Neal	Permanent Team Captain	Team
Bryce Young	Permanent Team Captain	Team
Bryce Young	MVP	Team
John Metchie III	Offensive Player of the Year	Team
Jameson Williams	Offensive Player of the Year	Team
Bryce Young	Offensive Player of the Year	Team
Will Anderson Jr.	Defensive Player of the Year	Team
Phidarian Mathis	Defensive Player of the Year	Team
Bryce Young	Offensive Player of the Year	SEC
Will Anderson Jr.	Defensive Player of the Year	SEC
Jameson Williams	Co-Special Teams Player of the Year	SEC
Will Anderson Jr.	AP All-SEC First Team	SEC
Jordan Battle	AP All-SEC First Team	SEC
Evan Neal	AP All-SEC First Team	SEC
Brian Robinson Jr.	AP All-SEC First Team	SEC
Jameson Williams	AP All-SEC First Team	SEC
Bryce Young	AP All-SEC First Team	SEC
Jalyn Armour-Davis	AP All-SEC Second Team	SEC
Phidarian Mathis	AP All-SEC Second Team	SEC
John Metchie III	AP All-SEC Second Team	SEC
Henry To'oTo'o	AP All-SEC Second Team	SEC
Jameson Williams	AP All-SEC Second Team	SEC
Will Anderson Jr.	Coaches' All-SEC First Team	SEC
Jordan Battle	Coaches' All-SEC First Team	SEC
Evan Neal	Coaches' All-SEC First Team	SEC
Brian Robinson Jr.	Coaches' All-SEC First Team	SEC
Jameson Williams	Coaches' All-SEC First Team	SEC
Bryce Young	Coaches' All-SEC First Team	SEC
Jalyn Armour-Davis	Coaches' All-SEC Second Team	SEC
Phidarian Mathis	Coaches' All-SEC Second Team	SEC
John Metchie III	Coaches' All-SEC Second Team	SEC
Henry To'oTo'o	Coaches' All-SEC Second Team	SEC
Jameson Williams	Coaches' All-SEC Second Team	SEC
JoJo Earle	Freshman All SEC Team	SEC

Name	Award	Type
Kool-aid McKinstry	Freshman All SEC Team	SEC
Dallas Turner	Freshman All SEC Team	SEC
Will Anderson Jr.	AFCA All-American First Team	National
Evan Neal	AFCA All-American First Team	National
Jordan Battle	AFCA All-American Second Team	National
Phidarian Mathis	AFCA All-American Second Team	National
Jameson Williams	AFCA All-American Second Team	National
Bryce Young	AFCA All-American Second Team	National
Will Anderson Jr.	AP All-America First Team	National
Jameson Williams	AP All-America First Team	National
Bryce Young	AP All-America First Team	National
Jordan Battle	AP All-America Second Team	National
Evan Neal	AP All-America Third Team	National
Bryce Young	AP College Football Player of the Year	National
Will Anderson Jr.	Bednarik Award Finalist	National
Jameson Williams	Biletnikoff Award Finalist	National
Will Anderson Jr.	Bronko Nagurski Trophy	National
Will Anderson Jr.	Consensus All-American	National
Evan Neal	Consensus All-American	National
Bryce Young	Consensus All-American	National
Bryce Young	Davey O'Brien Award	National
Will Anderson Jr.	FWAA All-America First Team	National
Evan Neal	FWAA All-America First Team	National
Jameson Williams	FWAA All-America First Team	National
Bryce Young	FWAA All-America Second Team	National
Bryce Young	Heisman Trophy	National
Will Anderson Jr.	Heisman Trophy Finalist	National
Bryce Young	Manning Award	National
Bryce Young	Maxwell Award	National
Will Anderson Jr.	Sporting News (TSN) All-America Team	National
Evan Neal	Sporting News (TSN) All-America Team	National
Jameson Williams	Sporting News (TSN) All-America Team	National
Bryce Young	Sporting News (TSN) All-America Team	National
Bryce Young	Sporting News College Football Player of the Year	National
Will Anderson Jr.	Unanimous All-American	National
Will Anderson Jr.	Walter Camp All-America First Team	National
Evan Neal	Walter Camp All-America First Team	National
Jameson Williams	Walter Camp All-America Second Team	National
Bryce Young	Walter Camp All-America Second Team	National
Phidarian Mathis	Senior Bowl	All-Star Team
Brian Robinson Jr.	Senior Bowl	All-Star Team

Note: Table data from "2021 Alabama Crimson Tide football team" (300) and "Alabama football team awards: Who did Crimson Tide players vote as their MVP?" (332)

NFL

Season	Year drafted	Round	Pick	Overall	Player	Position	Team
2021	2022	1	7	7	Evan Neal	OL	New York Giants
2021	2022	1	12	12	Jameson Williams	WR	Detroit Lions
2021	2022	2	12	44	John Metchie III	WR	Houston Texans
2021	2022	2	15	47	Phidarian Mathis	DT	Washington Commanders
2021	2022	3	11	75	Christian Harris	LB	Houston Texans
2021	2022	3	34	98	Brian Robinson	RB	Washington Commanders
2021	2022	4	14	119	Jalyn Armour-Davis	DB	Baltimore Ravens

Note: Table data from "2022 Alabama Crimson Tide football team" (333)

2022

Overall

Record	11-2
SEC Record	6-2
Rank	5
Points for	537
Points against	233
Points/game	41.3
Opp points/game	17.9
SOS[16]	4.58

I've told you guys more than once: when I was in the NFL, I watched players. I didn't know who they were playing against - I was just evaluating them. So that means when we play a team that's not as good as somebody else, you don't play as good? So you let the opponent determine how you play? You let the score determine how you play? Where you're playing, that determines how you play?
-Nick Saban

Games

Date	Bama Rank		Opp Rank	Opponent	Bama	Opp	Result	SEC
09/03/22	1	vs		Utah State	55	0	W	
09/10/22	1	@		Texas	20	19	W	
09/17/22	2	vs		Louisiana Monroe	63	7	W	
09/24/22	2	vs		Vanderbilt	55	3	W	W
10/01/22	2	@	20	Arkansas	49	26	W	W
10/08/22	1	vs		Texas A&M	24	20	W	W
10/15/22	3	@	6	Tennessee	49	52	L	L
10/22/22	6	vs	24	Mississippi State	30	6	W	W
11/05/22	6	@	10	LSU	31	32	L	L
11/12/22	9	@	11	Ole Miss	30	24	W	W
11/19/22	8	vs		Austin Peay	34	0	W	
11/26/22	7	vs		Auburn	49	27	W	W
12/31/22	5	N	9	Kansas State	45	20	W	

Coaches

Name	Position	Year
Nick Saban	Head Coach	16
David Ballou	Strength and Conditioning	3
Joe Cox	Tight Ends	1
Robert Gillespie	Running Backs	2
Pete Golding	Defensive Coordinator / Inside Linebackers	5
Coleman Hutzler	Special Teams Coordinator / Outside Linebackers	1
Charles Kelly	Associate Defensive Coordinator / Safeties	4
Bill O'Brien	Offensive Coordinator / Quarterbacks	2
Freddie Roach	Defensive Line	3 (8th overall)
Travaris Robinson	Cornerbacks	1
Holmon Wiggins	Wide Receivers	4
Eric Wolford	Offensive Line	1

Recruits

Name	Pos	Rivals	247 Sports	ESPN	ESPN Grade	Hometown	High school / college	Height	Weight	Committed
Jeremiah Alexander	DE	5	5	5	90	Alabaster, AL	Thompson HS	6-2	230	7/8/21
Aaron Anderson	WR	4	4	4	84	New Orleans, LA	Louisiana Edna Karr School	5-10	180	10/29/21
Isaiah Bond	WR	4	4	4	84	Buford, GA	Buford HS	6-0	190	12/7/21
Tyler Booker	OT	4	4	5	91	Bradenton, FL	IMG Academy	6-5	325	7/16/21
Elijah Brown	TE	4	4	4	80	Dayton, OH	Wayne HS	6-5	225	2/12/21
Jihaad Campbell	LB	4	4	4	83	Bradenton, FL	IMG Academy	6-3	215	12/15/21
Trequon Fegans	CB	4	4	4	85	Alabaster, AL	Thompson HS	6-1	185	10/18/21
Isaiah Hastings	DT	3	3	4	80	Toronto, Canada	Clearwater Academy (FL)	6-5	260	11/9/21
Emmanuel Henderson	RB	4	5	4	89	Hartford, AL	Geneva County HS	6-1	185	3/13/21
Antonio Kite	ATH	4	4	4	85	Anniston, AL	Anniston HS	6-2	180	7/4/21
Kendrick Law	ATH	4	4	4	83	Shreveport, LA	Captain Shreve HS	5-11	185	12/17/21
Danny Lewis	TE	3	3	4	97	New Iberia, LA	Westgate HS	6-4	230	2/2/22
Earl Little Jr	CB	4	4	4	82	Plantation, FL	Florida American Heritage School	6-0	165	12/15/21
Jam Miller	RB	4	4	4	83	Tyler, TX	Tyler Legacy HS	5-9	185	12/15/21
Shawn Murphy	LB	4	4	4	87	Manassas, VA	Unity Reed HS	6-2	215	7/25/21
Amari Niblack	TE	3	3	4	80	Saint Petersburg, FL	Florida Lakewood HS	6-3	215	6/24/21
Jaheim Oatis	DT	4	4	4	87	Columbia, MS	Columbia HS	6-4	350	4/14/21
Khurtiss Perry	DT	4	4	4	86	Montgomery, AL	Park Crossing HS	6-3	265	12/15/21
Jake Pope	S	3	3	4	80	Buford, GA	Buford HS	6-0	190	8/16/21
Kobe Prentice	**WR**	3	3	4	80	**Calera, AL**	**Calera HS**	5-10	175	7/27/21
Shazz Preston	WR	4	4	5	90	St. James, LA	Louisiana Saint James HS	5-11	180	12/15/21
Elijah Pritchett	OT	4	4	4	84	Columbus, GA	Carver HS	6-6	280	9/28/21
Ty Simpson	QB	4	5	4	87	Martin, TN	Westview HS	6-2	200	2/26/21

	Rivals	247Sports	ESPN
5 Stars	1	3	3
4 Stars	17	15	20
3 Stars	5	5	0
2 Stars	0	0	0

Note: Table data from "2022 Alabama Crimson Tide football team" (333)

359

Roster

Num	Player	Pos	Class	Height	Weight	Hometown	Last School
82	Chase Allen	PK	SO	6-2	188	Colleyville, TX	Colleyville Heritage
4	Christopher Allen	LB	SR	6-4	242	Baton Rouge, LA	Southern Lab School
31	**Will Anderson Jr.**	**LB**	**SO**	**6-4**	**243**	**Hampton, GA**	**Dutchtown**
5	Jalyn Armour-Davis	DB	JR	6-1	192	Mobile, AL	St. Paul's
12	**Terrion Arnold**	**DB**	**RS-FR**	**6-0**	**188**	**Tallahassee, FL**	**John Paul II Catholic**
5	Javon Baker	WR	SO	6-2	206	Atlanta, GA	McEachern
26	Marcus Banks	DB	JR	6-0	186	Houston, TX	Dekaney
7	Braxton Barker	QB	JR	6-1	202	Birmingham, AL	Spain Park
59	Anquin Barnes Jr.	DL	RS-FR	6-5	305	Montgomery, AL	Robert E. Lee
9	**Jordan Battle**	**DB**	**JR**	**6-1**	**210**	**Fort Lauderdale, FL**	**St. Thomas Aquinas**
26	Jonathan Bennett	RB	SO	5-8	178	Birmingham, AL	Oak Mountain
19	Jahleel Billingsley	TE	JR	6-4	230	Chicago, IL	Phillips Academy
46	Melvin Billingsley	TE	SR	6-3	230	Opelika, AL	Opelika
40	Kendrick Blackshire	LB	FR	6-2	232	Duncanville, TX	Duncanville
18	Slade Bolden	WR	JR	5-11	194	West Monroe, LA	West Monroe
36	Bret Bolin	WR	RS-SR	6-0	176	Lemont, IL	Lemont / Indiana
51	Tanner Bowles	OL	RS-JR	6-5	293	Glasgow, KY	Glasgow
84	Jacoby Boykins	WR	FR	5-11	182	Houston, TX	Lamar
14	**Brian Branch**	**DB**	**SO**	**6-0**	**190**	**Tyrone, GA**	**Sandy Creek**
41	Chris Braswell	LB	SO	6-3	240	Baltimore, MD	St. Frances Academy
33	Jackson Bratton	LB	SO	6-3	225	Muscle Shoals, AL	Muscle Shoals
58	James Brockermeyer	OL	RS-FR	6-3	281	Fort Worth, TX	All Saints Episcopal
76	Tommy Brockermeyer	OL	RS-FR	6-5	305	Fort Worth, TX	All Saints Episcopal
7	Ja'Corey Brooks	WR	FR	6-2	190	Miami, FL	IMG Academy
75	Tommy Brown	OL	JR	6-7	320	Santa Ana, CA	Mater Dei
56	Colin Bryant	LB	FR	6-3	218	Mount Pleasant, SC	Wando
86	**James Burnip**	**P**	**RS-SO**	**6-6**	**216**	**Mount Macedon, AUS**	**Victoria University, Melbourne**
3	*Jermaine Burton*	*WR*	*SO*	*6-0*	*200*	*Calabasas, CA*	*Georgia*
98	Jamil Burroughs	DL	SO	6-3	312	Powder Springs, GA	McEachern
86	Greg Carroll Jr.	WR	SO	6-0	171	Mobile, AL	Mattie Blount
87	Caden Clark	TE	FR	6-4	258	Akron, OH	Archbishop Hoban
70	**Javion Cohen**	**OL**	**SO**	**6-4**	**305**	**Phenix City, AL**	**Central**
97	Keelan Cox	DL	SO	6-5	240	Missouri City, TX	Manvel / Tyler J.C.
29	Elijah Crockett	RB	FR	5-11	210	Chino Hills, CA	Ruben S. Ayala
71	**Darrian Dalcourt**	**OL**	**JR**	**6-3**	**300**	**Havre de Grace, MD**	**St. Frances Academy**
94	**DJ Dale**	**DL**	**JR**	**6-3**	**300**	**Birmingham, AL**	**Clay-Chalkville**
10	JoJo Earle	WR	FR	5-10	170	Aledo, TX	Aledo
92	Justin Eboigbe	DL	JR	6-5	285	Forest Park, GA	Forest Park
38	Jalen Edwards	DB	SO	6-0	177	Columbus, MS	Eufaula
27	Kyle Edwards	RB	SO	6-0	209	Destrehan, LA	Destrehan
55	**Emil Ekiyor Jr.**	**OL**	**RS-SR**	**6-3**	**324**	**Indianapolis, IN**	**Cathedral**
43	Robert Ellis	TE	SO	6-0	220	Enterprise, AL	Enterprise
69	Terrence Ferguson II	OL	RS-FR	6-4	290	Fort Valley, GA	Peach
54	Kyle Flood Jr.	LB	SO	6-0	209	Middlesex, NJ	St. Joseph
74	Damieon George Jr.	OL	SO	6-6	339	Houston, TX	North Shore
1	*Jahmyr Gibbs*	*RB*	*SO*	*5-11*	*200*	*Dalton, GA*	*Georgia Tech*
95	Monkell Goodwine	DL	RS-FR	6-4	291	Upper Marlboro, MD	Rock Creek Christian Academy
24	Clark Griffin	DB	SO	'5-9	195	Mountain Brook, AL	Mountain Brook
84	Agiye Hall	WR	FR	6-3	195	Valrico, FL	Bloomingdale
59	Jake Hall	SN	JR	6-3	238	Saraland, AL	Saraland
67	Donovan Hardin	OL	SO	6-3	285	Dublin, OH	Dublin Scioto
8	Christian Harris	LB	JR	6-2	232	Baton Rouge, LA	University Lab
8	*Tyler Harrell*	*WR*	*RS-JR*	*6-0*	*197*	*Miami, FL*	*Louisville*
2	**DeMarcco Hellams**	**DB**	**JR**	**6-1**	**208**	**Washington, DC**	**DeMatha Catholic**
22	Chris Herren Jr.	WR	SR	6-3	175	Portsmouth, RI	Tabor Academy / Boston College/San Diego
51	Kneeland Hibbett	SN	FR	6-2	235	Florence, AL	Florence
11	**Traeshon Holden**	**WR**	**SO**	**6-3**	**208**	**Kissimmee, FL**	**Narbonne**
19	Stone Hollenbach	QB	SO	6-3	208	Catawissa, PA	Southern Columbia
83	Richard Hunt	TE	SO	6-7	235	Memphis, TN	Briarcrest Christian
52	Braylen Ingraham	DL	SO	6-4	298	Fort Lauderdale, FL	St. Thomas Aquinas
36	Ian Jackson	LB	RS-FR	6-1	235	Prattville, AL	Prattville
6	Khyree Jackson	DB	JR	6-3	197	Upper Marlboro, MD	Wise / East Mississippi C.C.
28	Josh Jobe	DB	SR	6-1	194	Miami, FL	Cheshire Academy (Conn.)
58	Christian Johnson	LB	FR	6-5	230	Flowery Branch, GA	IMG Academy
98	Sam Johnson	P	SO	6-3	215	Birmingham, AL	Oak Mountain
14	Thaiu Jones-Bell	WR	SO	6-0	190	Hallandale, FL	Miami Carol City
96	Tim Keenan III	DL	RS-FR	6-2	335	Birmingham, AL	Ramsay
37	Demouy Kennedy	LB	SO	6-3	220	Theodore, AL	Theodore
78	Amari Kight	OL	RS-JR	6-7	318	Alabaster, AL	Thompson
19	Keanu Koht	LB	RS-FR	6-4	220	Vero Beach, FL	Vero Beach
89	Grant Krieger	WR	JR	6-2	192	Pittsburgh, PA	Pine-Richland
21	Brylan Lanier	DB	FR	6-1	170	Tuscaloosa, AL	Paul W. Bryant
65	**JC Latham**	**OL**	**FR**	**6-6**	**325**	**Oak Creek, WI**	**IMG Academy**

Num	Player	Pos	Class	Height	Weight	Hometown	Last School
93	Jah-Marien Latham	DL	RS-SO	6-3	278	Reform, AL	Pickens County
81	**Cameron Latu**	**TE**	**RS-SR**	**6-5**	**250**	**Salt Lake City, UT**	**Olympus**
32	Deontae Lawson	LB	RS-FR	6-2	226	Mobile, AL	Mobile Christian
12	Christian Leary	WR	FR	5-10	175	Orlando, FL	Edgewater
35	Shane Lee	LB	6-0	240	Burtonsville, MD	St. Frances Academy
46	Julian Lowenstein	DB	SO	6-0	201	Sarasota, FL	Riverview
89	Kyle Mann	DL	SO	6-0	270	Powder Springs, GA	McEachern
95	Jack Martin	P	JR	6-2	222	Dothan, AL	Northview / Troy
48	Phidarian Mathis	DL	SR	6-4	312	Wisner, LA	Neville
47	Jacobi McBride	DB	SO	6-1	143	Madison, AL	Madison Academy
21	Jase McClellan	RB	SO	5-11	212	Aledo, TX	Aledo
1	**Kool-Aid McKinstry**	**DB**	**FR**	**6-1**	**190**	**Birmingham, AL**	**Pinson Valley**
56	**Seth McLaughlin**	**OL**	**RS-SO**	**6-4**	**295**	**Buford, GA**	**Buford**
8	John Metchie III	WR	JR	6-0	195	Brampton, Canada	St. James School (Md.)
2	Jalen Milroe	QB	RS-FR	6-2	212	Katy, TX	Tompkins
42	**Jaylen Moody**	**LB**	**RS-SR**	**6-2**	**225**	**Conway, SC**	**Conway**
13	**Malachi Moore**	**DB**	**SO**	**6-0**	**190**	**Trussville, AL**	**Hewitt-Trussville**
30	King Mwikuta	LB	JR	6-5	238	West Point, GA	Troup County
33	*Joseph Narcisse II*	*DB*	*JR*	*6-1*	*190*	*Miami, FL*	*Alabama A&M*
73	Evan Neal	OL	JR	6-7	350	Okeechobee, FL	IMG Academy
45	Robbie Ouzts	TE	FR	6-4	260	Rock Hill, SC	Rock Hill
35	Austin Owens	RB	FR	6-1	175	Double Springs, AL	Winston County
22	Jarelis Owens	DB	JR	6-0	157	Muscle Shoals, AL	Muscle Shoals
44	Damon Payne Jr.	DL	RS-FR	6-4	297	Belleville, MI	Belleville
99	Ty Perine	P	JR	6-1	218	Prattville, AL	Prattville
29	Blake Pugh	DB	FR	6-0	175	Birmingham, AL	Mountain Brook
50	Gabe Pugh	SN	RS-JR	6-5	273	Tuscaloosa, AL	Northridge
72	Pierce Quick	OL	SO	6-5	306	Trussville, AL	Hewitt-Trussville
57	Chase Quigley	DL	FR	6-1	236	Libertyville, IL	Libertyville
85	Kendall Randolph	TE	RS-GR	6-4	298	Madison, AL	Bob Jones
18	LaBryan Ray	DL	SR	6-5	285	Madison, AL	James Clemens
42	Sam Reed	DB	JR	6-1	165	Mountain Brook, AL	Mountain Brook
16	**Will Reichard**	**PK**	**JR**	**6-1**	**197**	**Hoover, AL**	**Hoover**
30	D.J. Rias	WR	SO	5-9	186	Phenix City, AL	Central
7	*Elias Ricks*	*CB*	*SO*	*6-2*	*196*	*Rancho Cucamonga, CA*	*LSU*
77	Jaeden Roberts	OL	RS-FR	6-5	328	Houston, TX	North Shore
23	Jahquez Robinson	DB	SO	6-2	197	Jacksonville, FL	Sandalwood
45	Joshua Robinson	DB	SR	5-9	180	Hoover, AL	Hoover
34	Quandarrius Robinson	LB	RS-SO	6-5	220	Birmingham, AL	Jackson-Olin
4	Brian Robinson Jr.	RB	SR	6-1	225	Tuscaloosa, AL	Hillcrest
62	Jackson Roby	OL	RS-SR	6-5	285	Huntsville, AL	Huntsville
61	Graham Roten	OL	FR	6-3	285	Fairview, TN	Christ Presbyterian Academy
20	Drew Sanders	LB	SO	6-5	244	Denton, TX	Ryan
6	Trey Sanders	RB	RS-JR	6-0	214	Port Saint Joe, FL	IMG Academy
97	Reid Schuback	PK	FR	6-0	185	Poway, CA	Poway
52	Carter Short	SN	FR	5-10	190	Hoover, AL	Hoover
44	Charlie Skehan	TE	SO	6-1	232	Columbia, SC	Cardinal Newman
27	DeVonta Smith	DB	FR	6-0	185	Cincinnati, OH	La Salle
43	Jordan Smith	LB	SO	5-10	210	Chelsea, AL	Chelsea
50	**Tim Smith**	**DL**	**SO**	**6-4**	**308**	**Gifford, FL**	**Sebastian River**
68	Alajujuan Sparks Jr.	OL	SO	6-4	345	Hoover, AL	Hoover
11	Kristian Story	DB	RS-SO	6-1	209	Lanett, AL	Lanett
54	*Tyler Steen*	*OL*	*SR*	*6-5*	*315*	*Miami, FL*	*Vanderbilt*
25	Jordan Tate-Parker	DB	JR	6-2	199	Phenix City, AL	Hardaway
88	Major Tennison	TE	SR	6-5	252	Flint, TX	Bullard
80	Adam Thorsland	TE	FR	6-5	232	Walhalla, SC	Walhalla
10	**Henry To'oTo'o**	**LB**	**JR**	**6-2**	**228**	**Sacramento, CA**	**De La Salle / Tennessee**
15	**Dallas Turner**	**LB**	**FR**	**6-4**	**245**	**Fort Lauderdale, FL**	**St. Thomas Aquinas**
17	Paul Tyson	QB	SO	6-5	228	Trussville, AL	Hewitt-Trussville
39	Carson Ware	DB	SO	6-1	190	Muscle Shoals, AL	Muscle Shoals
53	Kade Wehby	SN	FR	5-9	185	Plantation, FL	St. Thomas Aquinas
25	Camar Wheaton	RB	FR	5-11	190	Garland, TX	Lakeview Centennial
55	Bennett Whisenhunt	LB	SO	6-1	222	Vestavia Hills, AL	Vestavia Hills
1	Jameson Williams	WR	JR	6-2	189	St. Louis, MO	Cardinal Ritter College Prep / Ohio St.
49	Kaine Williams	DB	FR	6-2	203	Marrero, LA	John Ehret
23	Roydell Williams	RB	SO	5-10	208	Hueytown, AL	Hueytown
31	Shatarius Williams	WR	SO	6-3	187	Demopolis, AL	Demopolis
3	Xavier Williams	WR	JR	6-1	190	Hollywood, FL	Chaminade-Madonna Prep
37	Sam Willoughby	WR	SO	5-10	165	Vestavia Hills, AL	Vestavia Hills
3	Daniel Wright	DB	SR	6-1	195	Fort Lauderdale, FL	Boyd Anderson
90	Stephon Wynn Jr.	DL	JR	6-4	310	Anderson, SC	IMG Academy
9	**Bryce Young**	**QB**	**SO**	**6-0**	**194**	**Pasadena, CA**	**Mater Dei**
47	**Byron Young**	**DL**	**JR**	**6-3**	**292**	**Laurel, MS**	**West Jones**

Note: Starters in bold
Note: Table data from "2022 Alabama Crimson Tide Roster" (334)

Transfers

Player	School	Direction
Jermaine Burton	Georgia	Incoming
Jahmyr Gibbs	Georgia Tech	Incoming
Tyler Harrell	Louisville	Incoming
Joseph Narcisse II	Alabama A&M	Incoming
Elias Ricks	LSU	Incoming
Tyler Steen	Vanderbilt	Incoming
Javon Baker	UCF	Outgoing
Marcus Banks	Mississippi State	Outgoing
Jahleel Billingsley	Texas	Outgoing
Jackson Bratton	UAB	Outgoing
Tommy Brown	Colorado	Outgoing
Caden Clark	Akron	Outgoing
Keelan Cox	Wyoming	Outgoing
Kyle Edwards	SE Louisiana	Outgoing
Agiye Hall	Texas	Outgoing
Donovan Hardin	LIU	Outgoing
Stone Hollenbach	Western Michigan	Outgoing
Brylan Lanier	Indiana	Outgoing
Shane Lee	USC	Outgoing
Kyle Mann	Alabama A&M	Outgoing
King Mwikuta	Arkansas State	Outgoing
Pierce Quick	Georgia Tech	Outgoing
DJ Rias	Samford	Outgoing
Drew Sanders	Arkansas	Outgoing
Dayne Shor	Uconn	Outgoing
Paul Tyson	Arizona State	Outgoing
Camar Wheaton	SMU	Outgoing
Kaine Williams	Nebraska	Outgoing
Xavier Williams	Utah State	Outgoing
Stephon Wynn Jr.	Nebraska	Outgoing

Note: Table data from "2022 Alabama Crimson Tide football team" (333)

Games

09/03/22 - Alabama (1) vs Utah State

Team	1	2	3	4	T	Passing	Rushing	Total
Utah State	0	0	0	0	0	57	79	136
Alabama (1)	17	24	14	0	55	281	278	559

Every one of Utah State's possessions was either a punt or turnover on downs. Alabama scored on every possession in the first half, starting with a 45-yard field goal to cap off a 7-play, 44-yard drive. Bryce Young then took over, tossing five touchdown passes before halftime. His first scoring strike went to Jermaine Burton after a 7-play, 60-yard march. Young then found Traeshon Holden for a 9-yard touchdown to cap a lightning-quick 3-play, 34-yard drive lasting just 1:01. Burton hauled in his second touchdown on a 2-yard pass to finish an 11-play, 82-yard drive. Holden's second score came on a 14-yard catch, highlighting a 4-play, 77-yard, 55 second drive that included Young's 63-yard run. Reichard added a 33-yarder after an 11-play, 51-yard drive before Jase McClellan grabbed an 8-yard touchdown pass as time expired. With his five touchdown passes in the first half, Bryce Young matched his single-game career high. Alabama led 41-0 at the break.

The onslaught continued after halftime as Young rushed for a 4-yard score to complete a 3-play, 65-yard drive in 1:19 as he achieved his career-best sixth TD of the game. Backup QB Jalen Milroe then threw his first career TD pass, hitting McClellan from 17 yards out to cap another short drive consisting of four plays and 44 yards that only lasted 1:54. He also threw his first interception in the game. Burnip attempted two punts in the second half; one traveled 51 yards, and the other was blocked. With no scoring in the fourth quarter, Alabama was victorious 55-0.

The Alabama defense accounted for five tackles for loss, four quarterback hurries, and a forced fumble. Jaylen Moody led the way with five tackles (one for loss) and a QB hurry. Bryce Young threw for 195 yards on 18-of-28 passes matching his career high with five touchdown passes (fourth time he has achieved that feat), and he added a team-leading and career-high 100 yards rushing (five rushes) with another touchdown on the ground (for a total of six). Jahmyr Gibbs debuted with 93 rushing yards on nine carries. Traeshon Holden (5 catches, 70 yards, 2 TDs) and Jermaine Burton (5 catches, 35 yards, 2 TDs) combined for 10 receptions, 105 yards and four touchdowns to lead the aerial attack. This was Alabama's 16th straight season opening victory as well as the largest margin of victory (55 points) for an opener in the Saban era. This game also marked the Tide's first shutout in a season opener in the last 34 years.[335]

Passing	C/ATT	YDS	AVG	TD	INT	QBR
B. Young	18/28	195	7	5	0	96.8
J. Milroe	8/10	76	7.6	1	1	62.7
T. Simpson	1/2	10	5	0	0	3.8
Team	27/40	281	7	6	1	--

Rushing	CAR	YDS	AVG	TD	LONG
B. Young	5	100	20	1	63
J. Gibbs	9	93	10.3	0	58
J. Miller	7	32	4.6	0	23
J. McClellan	5	23	4.6	0	11
R. Williams	3	15	5	0	12
J. Milroe	2	10	5	0	7
T. Sanders	1	5	5	0	5
Team	32	278	8.7	1	63

Kicking	FG	PCT	LONG	XP	PTS
W. Reichard	2/2	100	45	7/7	13

Punting	NO	YDS	AVG	TB	IN 20	LONG
J. Burnip	1	51	51	0	0	51

Receiving	REC	YDS	AVG	TD	LONG
T. Holden	5	70	14	2	17
K. Prentice	5	60	12	0	25
J. Burton	5	35	7	2	12
J. McClellan	2	25	12.5	2	17
I. Bond	2	23	11.5	0	13
K. Law	2	22	11	0	18
M. Kitselman	2	18	9	0	13
T. Sanders	1	10	10	0	10
R. Williams	1	7	7	0	7
C. Leary	1	6	6	0	6
J. Gibbs	1	5	5	0	5
Team	27	281	10.4	6	25

Kick returns	NO	YDS	AVG	LONG	TD
J. Brooks	1	18	18	18	0

Punt returns	NO	YDS	AVG	LONG	TD
K. McKinstry	3	20	6.7	9	0

Note: Table data from "Alabama 55-0 Utah State (Sep 3, 2022) Box Score" (336)

363

09/10/22 - Alabama (1) at Texas

Team	1	2	3	4	T		Passing	Rushing	Total
Alabama (1)	10	0	0	10	20		213	161	374
Texas	3	7	3	6	19		292	79	371

Alabama and Texas traded field goals to start the game. Will Reichard struck first, matching his career long from 52 yards that capped a 7-play, 44-yard drive. Texas then drove 67 yards in 15 plays and connected from 26 yards out to even the score. Next, both teams traded touchdowns, starting with Jase McClellan taking the first play of the drive 81 yards to the house. Texas responded as Bijan Robinson capped a 6-play, 75-yard drive with his one-yard touchdown run on the first play of the second quarter to even the score at 10-10. There was no more scoring in the first half as the teams traded a total of five punts, and Texas missed a 20-yard field goal as time expired in the half, closing it at a 10-10 tie.

After both teams each punted twice, Texas scored the only points of the third quarter on a 33-yard field goal capping off a 6-play, 25-yard drive. Alabama punted again, then Texas was driving as the third quarter ended with the Longhorns leading 13-10. They finished the drive early in the fourth, capping the 12-play, 65-yard drive with another field goal, this time from 24 yards to extend their lead to 16-10. Refusing to go down without a fight, Alabama responded with an 11-play, 75-yard drive capped by Bryce Young's 7-yard touchdown pass to Jahmyr Gibbs giving the Tide a 17-16 lead. After forcing Texas to punt, Alabama drove down to the TX 25-yard line. They went for it on 4th-and-1, but the Longhorns held. Texas took the lead back (19-17) with a 49-yard field goal, finishing off an 8-play, 44-yard drive, leaving only 1:29 to go in the game. Undeterred, Young led the Tide 61 yards down the field in 1:19, and with ten seconds left, Will Reichard drilled a 33-yard field goal to clinch a 20-19 victory for Alabama. Reichard's kick marked the first game-winning field goal in the final 30 seconds for the Tide during the Nick Saban era.

DeMarcco Hellams spearheaded Alabama's defensive efforts, racking up ten tackles, with eight of them unassisted. Jaylen Moody, Kool-Aid McKinstry, and Will Anderson Jr. each contributed a sack. Jase McClellan's 81-yard TD run in the opening quarter was the Tide's longest run since his 80-yard touchdown against Arkansas in 2020. Discipline was an issue for Alabama as they were flagged 15 times for 100 yards, the most penalties they've accumulated since tying the school record with 16 against Middle Tennessee State in 2002.[337]

Passing	C/ATT	YDS	AVG	TD	INT	QBR
B. Young	27/39	213	5.5	1	0	75.9

Receiving	REC	YDS	AVG	TD	LONG
J. Gibbs	9	74	8.2	1	23
T. Holden	4	39	9.8	0	21
J. Brooks	3	33	11	0	16
C. Latu	4	28	7	0	14
K. Prentice	4	27	6.8	0	13
J. Burton	2	10	5	0	8
J. McClellan	1	2	2	0	2
Team	27	213	7.9	1	23

Rushing	CAR	YDS	AVG	TD	LONG
J. McClellan	6	97	16.2	1	81
B. Young	7	38	5.4	0	20
J. Gibbs	9	22	2.4	0	7
R. Williams	2	4	2	0	4
Team	24	161	6.7	1	81

Kicking	FG	PCT	LONG	XP	PTS
W. Reichard	2/2	100	52	2/2	8

Kick returns	NO	YDS	AVG	LONG	TD
J. Gibbs	2	36	18	19	0

Punting	NO	YDS	AVG	TB	IN 20	LONG
J. Burnip	6	249	41.5	0	3	50

Punt returns	NO	YDS	AVG	LONG	TD
K. McKinstry	2	-3	-1.5	0	0

Note: Table data from "Alabama 20-19 Texas (Sep 10, 2022) Box Score" (338)

09/17/22 - Alabama (2) vs Louisiana Monroe

Team	1	2	3	4	T		Passing	Rushing	Total
Louisiana Monroe	0	7	0	0	**7**		91	78	**169**
Alabama (2)	28	7	14	14	**63**		236	273	**509**

The Crimson Tide wasted no time asserting their dominance, marching 75 yards in just four plays on the opening drive. Quarterback Bryce Young connected with Traeshon Holdenon a 33-yard touchdown strike that took a mere 1:48 off the clock. ULM punted, then Young threw an interception. Will Anderson Jr. picked off a deflected pass and returned it 25 yards for a defensive touchdown, the Tide's first of the season. The onslaught continued as Ja'Corey Brooks blocked a punt at the 4-yard line that was scooped up by Malachi Moore and returned for another non-offensive score, extending the lead to 21-0 in the first quarter. Following another ULM punt, Young orchestrated a 4-play, 41-yard drive that only took 1:45 off the clock, capping it off with a 7-yard rushing touchdown – the fourth score of the opening quarter.

The Warhawks got on the board in the second quarter with an 11-yard rushing touchdown capping an 8-play, 57-yard drive (28-7). After trading punts, Alabama traveled 93 yards in just six plays and 1:05, including a 38-yard reception from Latu that set up Amari Niblack for a 15-yard touchdown reception. Bama led 35-7 at halftime.

ULM punted for the rest of the game while Bama scored four more touchdowns. Gibbs caught a pass from Young and ran 37 yards for a touchdown, capping off a 4-play, 53-yard drive that lasted 1:23. Then Roydell Williams got his first touchdown of the year with a 10-yard run on the 5-play, 57-yard drive that lasted 1:56. The special teams unit joined in when Brian Branch returned a punt 68 yards for the third non-offensive touchdown of the game. Trey Sanders put an exclamation point on Alabama's dominant performance, capping a 10-play, 49-yard drive that consumed 3:17 with a 6-yard touchdown run. This final score cemented the Crimson Tide's resounding 63-7 victory over the overmatched ULM squad.

DeMarcco Hellams spearheaded Alabama's defensive onslaught, racking up a game-high nine tackles. Henry To'oTo'o contributed eight tackles, two tackles for loss, and a sack. Will Anderson Jr. logged five tackles, 1.5 tackles for loss, one sack, and his first career interception returned for a touchdown.

Bryce Young's aerial assault yielded 236 yards, propelling him past Jalen Hurts (5,626) to claim the ninth spot on Alabama's all-time passing yards leaderboard with 5,672 career yards. Additionally, Young leapt Mac Jones, securing the third position on the school's all-time passing touchdown list with 57 touchdowns, trailing only the legendary Tua Tagovailoa (87) and A.J. McCarron (77).

Kool-Aid McKinstry amassed a staggering 136 yards on five returns, averaging an impressive 27.2 yards per return. With this, he secured the third-highest single-game punt return yardage, trailing only the legendary Javier Arenas who holds the second spot with 147 yards.

Will Reichard converted all nine of his extra point attempts and now stands at an astonishing 194-for-196, setting a new school record for extra points made in a career, surpassing the previous mark held by Adam Griffith who had 186. His nine successful PATs today tied for the third-most in a single game in Alabama's history, following Harold "Red" Lutz (9/21/51 vs. Delta State) and Bill Davis (10/27/73 vs. Virginia Tech), who share the school record with 11 PATs in a game.

Alabama's first three scores of the day came in spectacular fashion – a touchdown on offense, followed by a defensive touchdown, and capped off by a special teams touchdown. Alabama scored three non-offensive touchdowns and shattered a 75-year-old school record by amassing an incredible 262 punt return yards.[339]

Passing	C/ATT	YDS	AVG	TD	INT	QBR
B. Young	13/18	236	13.1	3	2	79.2
J. Milroe	0/2	0	0	0	0	93.1
Team	13/20	236	11.8	3	2	--

Rushing	CAR	YDS	AVG	TD	LONG
R. Williams	8	58	7.3	1	16
J. Miller	4	51	12.8	0	25
J. McClellan	7	47	6.7	0	20
J. Milroe	2	42	21	0	25
J. Gibbs	4	36	9	0	17
T. Sanders	4	35	8.8	1	11
J. Bennett	2	12	6	0	10
B. Young	3	6	2	1	7
Team	5	-14	-2.8	0	0
Team	39	273	7.0	3	25

Interceptions	INT	YDS	TD
W. Anderson Jr.	1	25	1

Punting	NO	YDS	AVG	TB	IN 20	LONG
J. Burnip	2	84	42	1	1	47

Receiving	REC	YDS	AVG	TD	LONG
J. Gibbs	4	65	16.3	1	37
T. Holden	3	60	20	1	33
C. Latu	3	51	17	0	38
J. Brooks	1	29	29	0	29
J. Burton	1	16	16	0	16
A. Niblack	1	15	15	1	15
Team	13	236	18.2	3	38

Kick returns	NO	YDS	AVG	LONG	TD
J. Gibbs	1	57	57	57	0

Punt returns	NO	YDS	AVG	LONG	TD
K. McKinstry	5	136	27.2	44	0
B. Branch	1	68	68	68	1
I. Bond	1	34	34	34	0
J. Brooks	1	21	21	21	0
M. Moore	1	3	3	3	1
Team	9	262	32.8	68	2

Kicking	FG	PCT	LONG	XP	PTS
W. Reichard	0/0	0	0	9/9	9

Note: Table data from "Alabama 63-7 UL Monroe (Sep 17, 2022) Box Score" (340)

09/24/22 - Alabama (2) vs Vanderbilt

Team	1	2	3	4	T	Passing	Rushing	Total
Vanderbilt	3	0	0	0	3	115	14	129
Alabama (2)	14	17	10	14	55	400	228	628

After both teams traded punts, Bryce Young orchestrated a 68-yard drive that unfolded in a mere 1:16. He connected with Ja'Corey Brooks on four consecutive passes with the last a 21-yard touchdown strike. Vanderbilt responded with a 40-yard field goal before Young threw his second TD of the quarter – this one to Traeshon Holden for eight yards, capping a 10-play, 75-yard drive. Bama led 14-3 after one quarter of play. Bama stopped Vanderbilt on 4th-and-1, and they only needed one play and seven seconds to score again on a 34-yard pass from Young to Brooks, their second TD hookup of the day. The Commodores punted for the rest of the game (McKinstry fumbled one) while Bama scored five more times. Young passed to Gibbs for a 7-yard touchdown capping a 9-play, 77-yard drive. Thanks to a 48-yard gain on a pass to Jermaine Burton on a drive that only took 33 seconds to cover 58 yards in four plays, Will Reichard was able to split the uprights from 34 yards as time expired in the first half (Bama up 31-3).

The second half began with a 21-yard field goal from Reichard, culminating a 12-play, 84-yard drive. McClellan then took a handoff 12 yards to the end zone, capping a 6-play, 55-yard drive for Alabama's first rushing touchdown of the game. Jam Miller scored twice in the fourth quarter. First, he scored on a 1-yard rushing ending a season-best 15-play, 87-yard drive. Next, he scored on a 40-yard touchdown run, concluding a 5-play, 53-yard drive. Bama won 55-3.

Will Anderson Jr. led the defense by racking up five tackles (three for loss) and 2.5 sacks. Henry To'oTo'o totaled six tackles (one for loss) as the Tide amassed eight total tackles for loss. Bryce Young set a season high with 385 passing yards, and he was 25-of-36 through the air with four touchdowns. He amassed 316 passing yards in the first half - a career-best for Young and the highest by an Alabama QB since Mac Jones' 342-yard opening half against Ohio State in 2021. Ja'Corey Brooks led all receivers as he recorded his first career 100-yard receiving game, hauling in six catches for a personal-best 117 yards and two touchdowns, all coming in the first half. Alabama amassed 628 yards of total offense, including 400 through the air. Alabama's defense held Vandy to a mere 129 total yards (only 14 rushing) – the lowest allowed by the Crimson Tide this season and the third time in four games that they have held their opponent under 200 yards of total offense. The 499-yard differential in total offense was the fifth largest in Alabama history. The victory extended Alabama's winning streak over Vanderbilt to 23 games, dating back to 1985. Additionally, Nick Saban improved his record in SEC home openers to 15-1.[341]

Passing	C/ATT	YDS	AVG	TD	INT	QBR
B. Young	25/36	385	10.7	4	0	87.5
J. Milroe	4/6	10	1.7	0	0	71.8
T. Simpson	1/1	5	5	0	0	99.5
Team	30/43	400	9.3	4	0	--

Receiving	REC	YDS	AVG	TD	LONG
J. Brooks	6	117	19.5	2	34
J. Burton	4	94	23.5	0	48
T. Holden	3	45	15	1	24
J. Gibbs	3	43	14.3	1	26
K. Prentice	3	32	10.7	0	19
C. Latu	3	27	9	0	12
J. McClellan	2	19	9.5	0	15
I. Bond	2	13	6.5	0	8
T. Jones-Bell	1	5	5	0	5
T. Sanders	1	3	3	0	3
R. Ouzts	1	3	3	0	3
J. Miller	1	-1	-1	0	0
Team	30	400	13.3	4	48

Rushing	CAR	YDS	AVG	TD	LONG
J. McClellan	11	78	7.1	1	26
J. Miller	9	63	7	2	40
R. Williams	4	27	6.8	0	13
J. Gibbs	3	21	7	0	17
J. Milroe	2	20	10	0	28
T. Sanders	4	13	3.3	0	8
B. Young	1	6	6	0	6
Team	34	228	6.7	3	40

Kicking	FG	PCT	LONG	XP	PTS
W. Reichard	2/2	100	40	7/7	13

Punt returns	NO	YDS	AVG	LONG	TD
K. McKinstry	5	91	18.2	40	0
B. Branch	1	-3	-3	3	0
Team	6	88	17.6	40	0

Punting	NO	YDS	AVG	TB	IN 20	LONG
J. Burnip	2	87	43.5	0	1	47

Note: Table data from "Alabama 55-3 Vanderbilt (Sep 24, 2022) Box Score" (342)

10/01/22 - Alabama (2) at Arkansas (20)

Team	1	2	3	4	T	Passing	Rushing	Total
Alabama (2)	14	14	0	21	49	238	317	555
Arkansas (20)	0	7	16	3	26	190	187	377

After driving to the ARK 19, Bryce Young threw an interception inside the five. Arkansas punted, then Bama scored on a 47-yard pass to Kobe Prentice (first career TD), capping a 6-play, 65-yard drive that lasted 2:09. After holding the Hogs to another punt, Alabama scored on a 7-play, 80-yard drive ending with Young's third rushing touchdown of the season from eight yards out (14-0). Arkansas punted, then Reichard missed a 53-yard FG attempt. Hellams forced and recovered a fumble on Arkansas's next drive. Both teams traded punts, and McKinstry returned his 45 yards to the ARK 17. Jalen Milroe entered the game (due to a Bryce Young shoulder injury) and took only 45 seconds to score the first rushing touchdown of his career. After Gibbs ran twice for seven yards each, Milroe took the last three himself into the end zone for the score. Bama forced another punt, then both teams scored to close out the half. Milroe orchestrated a 10-play, 59-yard drive, capping it off with an 18-yard touchdown strike to JoJo Earle, then Jefferson engineered a 9-play, 75-yard drive and tossed a 6-yard TD. Bama led 28-7 at the half.

After both teams punted, Arkansas scored a 13-yard TD run, capping a 7-play, 78-yard drive. They followed it up with an onside kick recovery then drove 50 yards in 12 plays, scoring a 22-yard FG which cut Alabama's lead to 28-17. A botched Alabama punt gave the Hogs the ball at the AL 3-yard line. Sanders capitalized with a TD run on the very next play, which brought the score to 28-23 after the failed two-point conversion attempt. The Crimson Tide's offense then took over. Milroe's 77-yard run set up McClellan's 3-yard touchdown, capping a 5-play, 75-yard drive that only took 1:10. Bama held the Hogs to a punt, then Gibbs then joined the party with a 72-yard touchdown run on the first snap of the next possession. He became the sixth different Alabama player to score in the game, extending the score to 42-23. Arkansas managed a field goal, but Gibbs wasn't done. He added a 76-yard touchdown run, bringing the final to 49-26.

Henry To'oTo'o led the defense with a team-high ten total tackles. Jaylen Moody and Jaheim Oatis each recorded a sack while McKinstry tallied six solo stops. Hellams forced and recovered a fumble, marking the Tide's first turnover of the season. On the offensive side, Jahmyr Gibbs ran for a career-best 206 rushing yards and two TDs, the most yards since Brian Robinson Jr.'s 204-yard outing against Cincinnati in the 2021 CFP Semifinal. Alabama's offensive line paved the way for a staggering 317 rushing yards, the first time they've rushed for 300+ since gaining 301 against Cincinnati. The Razorbacks managed to put up 26 points, the most the Tide defense has surrendered this season. In three games at Bryant-Denny Stadium, they've allowed a mere ten points, a stark contrast to the 45 points conceded in their two road contests.[343]

Passing	C/ATT	YDS	AVG	TD	INT	QBR
B. Young	7/13	173	13.3	1	1	83.4
J. Milroe	4/9	65	7.2	1	0	98.7
Team	11/22	238	10.8	2	1	--

Rushing	CAR	YDS	AVG	TD	LONG
J. Gibbs	18	206	11.4	2	76
J. Milroe	6	91	15.2	1	77
R. Williams	5	17	3.4	0	6
T. Sanders	3	13	4.3	0	7
J. McClellan	6	11	1.8	1	6
B. Young	2	4	2	1	8
Team	2	-25	-12.5	0	0
Team	42	317	7.5	5	77

Punting	NO	YDS	AVG	TB	IN 20	LONG
J. Burnip	3	137	45.7	0	1	49

Receiving	REC	YDS	AVG	TD	LONG
K. Prentice	3	92	30.7	1	47
I. Bond	2	76	38	0	53
J. Earle	1	22	22	1	22
J. Gibbs	2	20	10	0	17
J. Burton	1	14	14	0	14
T. Holden	2	14	7	0	9
Team	11	238	21.6	2	53

Punt returns	NO	YDS	AVG	LONG	TD
K. McKinstry	3	77	25.7	45	0

Kicking	FG	PCT	LONG	XP	PTS
W. Reichard	0/1	0	0	7/7	7

Note: Table data from "Alabama 49-26 Arkansas (Oct 1, 2022) Box Score" (344)

368

10/08/22 - Alabama (1) vs Texas A&M

Team	1	2	3	4	T	Passing	Rushing	Total
Texas A&M	0	14	3	3	20	253	70	323
Alabama (1)	0	17	7	0	24	111	286	397

The first quarter was a defensive slugfest, with both teams trading punts and struggling to gain any momentum. But the game burst into life early in the second quarter when Alabama's Jalen Milroe found Cameron Latu for a 10-yard touchdown strike, capping off an impressive 74-yard drive. A&M punted, Milroe was sacked, he fumbled, and the Aggies recovered. Moose Muhammed III hauled in a 5-yard pass to even the score after a 30-yard drive. The lead was short-lived as Jermaine Burton caught a 35-yard bomb from Milroe just a minute later, putting Alabama back in front 14-7 after a lightning-quick 75-yard drive in just three plays. After an A&M punt, the Aggies capitalized on Milroe's second fumble of the quarter, evening the score at 14-14 after a 4-play, 49-yard drive. Both QBs then threw picks on consecutive possessions before Will Reichard drilled a 50-yard field goal to give the Tide a 17-14 halftime lead.

Alabama came out firing in the second half, with Ja'Corey Brooks catching a 29-yard touchdown pass to cap a 75-yard drive that only took 1:57. But the Aggies refused to go away, kicking a 41-yard field goal after Alabama's third fumble of the game (McClellan). Reichard missed his next two field goal attempts from 47 and 35 yards. The Aggies closed the gap to 24-20 with a 46-yard field goal after a lengthy 11-play, 53-yard drive. They forced an Alabama punt, then drove down to the Alabama 27-yard line where they had 1st-and-10 with 39 seconds left. They moved the ball and had another 1st-and-10, this time from the 15-yard line with 17 seconds left. They spiked the ball then threw two incomplete passes, but there was a holding penalty on Alabama. This gave A&M the ball on the 2-yard line with three seconds left in the game. Bama's defense made a goal-line stand on the final play to hold on to a 24-20 victory.

The Alabama defense was led by Branch's nine tackles, including two for loss, and two pass breakups. Terrion Arnold contributed eight tackles and an interception, while DeMarcco Hellams finished with seven tackles. Will Anderson Jr. tallied two tackles, one for loss, and an impressive eight quarterback hurries – a career-best and the second-highest single-game total in program history. Only the legendary Derrick Thomas has surpassed Anderson's quarterback pressure in a single game for Alabama. Making his first career start, Jalen Milroe showcased his dual-threat abilities, rushing for 81 yards on 17 carries while also throwing for 111 yards and three touchdowns on 12-of-19 passing. This was Nick Saban's 100th victory inside Bryant-Denny Stadium (100-8, 92.6%). This remarkable feat tops the legendary Paul "Bear" Bryant's record of 72 home wins and includes 69 wins in his last 72 home games. For the second consecutive game, Gibbs rushed for over 100 yards as he gained 154 yards on 21 carries.[345]

Passing	C/ATT	YDS	AVG	TD	INT	QBR
J. Milroe	12/19	111	5.8	3	1	60.8

Rushing	CAR	YDS	AVG	TD	LONG
J. Gibbs	21	154	7.3	0	37
J. Milroe	17	81	4.8	0	33
J. McClellan	10	32	3.2	0	8
R. Williams	3	19	6.3	0	11
Team	51	286	5.6	0	37

Interceptions	INT	YDS	TD
T. Arnold	1	21	0

Punting	NO	YDS	AVG	TB	IN 20	LONG
J. Burnip	4	167	41.8	0	2	48

Receiving	REC	YDS	AVG	TD	LONG
J. Burton	3	48	16	1	35
J. Brooks	2	44	22	1	29
J. Gibbs	3	13	4.3	0	6
C. Latu	1	10	10	1	10
K. Prentice	2	1	0.5	0	3
T. Holden	1	-5	-5	0	-5
Team	12	111	9.3	3	35

Kick returns	NO	YDS	AVG	LONG	TD
J. Gibbs	1	19	19	19	0

Punt returns	NO	YDS	AVG	LONG	TD
K. McKinstry	1	-2	-2	-2	0

Kicking	FG	PCT	LONG	XP	PTS
W. Reichard	1/3	33.3	50	3/3	6

Note: Table data from "Alabama 24-20 Texas A&M (Oct 8, 2022) Box Score" (346)

10/15/22 - Alabama (3) at Tennessee (6)

Team	1	2	3	4	T		Passing	Rushing	Total
Alabama (3)	7	13	15	14	49		455	114	569
Tennessee (6)	21	7	6	18	52		385	182	567

After Alabama punted on its opening drive, the Volunteers wasted no time, marching 56 yards in just 1:58 to find the end zone. Bryce Young and the Crimson Tide responded swiftly, with the quarterback connecting on 4-of-5 passes for 67 yards, setting up Jahmyr Gibbs' 8-yard touchdown run to cap an 8-play, 71-yard drive lasting 2:12. In a mere 1:16, Hendon Hooker orchestrated a 75-yard, 5-play scoring drive, finding Jalin Hyatt for a 36-yard touchdown strike to give Tennesse a 14-7 lead. After another Alabama punt, the Vols continued their onslaught by scoring their third consecutive touchdown, with Hyatt (again) hauling in an 11-yard touchdown pass to cap a lightning-quick 4-play, 35-yard drive that took just 1:02 off the clock, extending Tennessee's lead to 21-7. Alabama managed to get on the board again with a 21-yard field goal from Reichard, capping a 12-play, 73-yard drive. However, the Volunteers capitalized on a fumbled punt by Quandarrius Robinson, scoring from two yards out to finish a 3-play, 40-yard drive, pushing their advantage to 28-10. Young refused to go quietly, leading the Crimson Tide on a 12-play, 83-yard, march, culminating in a 7-yard touchdown pass to Ja'Corey Brooks. After Alabama's defense held firm on 4th-and-6, Reichard nailed his second field goal of the quarter to cap a 7-play, 39-yard drive, trimming Tennessee's lead to 28-20 at the half.

To start the second half, Alabama stalled Tennessee's opening drive by holding them on 4th-and-2 from the AL 42-yard line. It only took Alabama three plays to score as Jahmyr Gibbs took a handoff for a 26-yard touchdown. Young found Brooks in the back of the end zone for a successful two-point conversion, knotting the score at 28-28. Hendon Hooker struck back 55 seconds later, connecting with Jalin Hyatt for a 60-yard scoring strike ending a 3-play, 75-yard drive, but the Volunteers missed the extra point. Gibbs powered his way into the end zone again (from two yards out), capping a 12-play, 75-yard drive to give the Crimson Tide their first lead of the day, 35-34. DeMarcco Hellams got an interception, but the Tide could not capitalize and had to punt. Hooker and Hyatt torched the defense once more, this time for a 78-yard touchdown and a successful two-point conversion, handing Tennessee a 42-35 advantage. Bryce Young orchestrated a 10-play, 75-yard drive, finding Cameron Latu for a 1-yard score to tie the game at 42-42. Moments later, Dallas Turner scooped up a fumble and rumbled 11 yards for a defensive touchdown, swinging the lead back to Alabama, 49-42 with 7:49 left in the game. In a remarkable display, Hyatt hauled in his fifth touchdown reception of the game on a 13-yard pass from Hooker, tying the contest at 49-49. With 15 seconds remaining, Will Reichard's 50-yard field goal attempt fell short. Tennessee used their timeouts and advanced with completions of 18 and 27 yards to get to the Alabama 23-yard line with two seconds left in the game. Chase McGrath converted a game-winning 40-yard field goal as time expired, securing a 52-49 victory for the Volunteers.

The Alabama defense shined brightly, with several players making significant contributions. DeMarcco Hellams led the team with ten tackles (five solo) and logged an interception. Brian Branch tallied nine tackles, including four solo stops, while Henry To'oTo'o amassed nine total tackles with five solo. Dallas Turner logged Alabama's fourth defensive touchdown of the season and their first fumble return for a score since 2020 when he scooped up a Tennessee fumble and returned it 11 yards for the touchdown.

After recovering from a shoulder injury sustained two weeks ago at Arkansas, Bryce Young put on a remarkable display against Tennessee. He had a season-best performance, throwing for 455 yards on 35-of-52 passing, including two touchdowns. Nine different Alabama receivers caught passes during the game. Tight end Cameron Latu led the way, hauling in six receptions for 90 yards and a touchdown. Jahmyr Gibbs showcased his versatility, amassing 203 all-purpose yards. He rushed for 103 yards on 24 carries, caught five passes for 48 yards, and added 52 yards on kickoff returns, making him a constant threat on the field.

With his two field goals against Tennessee, kicker Will Reichard has now accumulated 363 career points (49 field goals, 216 extra points). This impressive tally moved him past Adam Griffith (357 points) into second place in Alabama's program history for scoring. Reichard now trails only Leigh Tiffin (385 points on 83 field goals and 136 extra points) on the all-time scoring list. Alabama was flagged for a school record 17 penalties for 130 yards. Tennessee's victory snapped a 15-game losing streak to the Crimson Tide in the series.[347]

Passing	C/ATT	YDS	AVG	TD	INT	QBR
B. Young	35/52	455	8.8	2	0	87.9

Rushing	CAR	YDS	AVG	TD	LONG
J. Gibbs	24	103	4.3	3	26
J. McClellan	3	15	5	0	11
B. Young	4	-4	-1	0	6
Team	31	114	3.7	3	26

Interceptions	INT	YDS	TD
D. Hellams	1	0	0

Kicking	FG	PCT	LONG	XP	PTS
W. Reichard	2/3	66.7	43	5/5	11

Punting	NO	YDS	AVG	TB	IN 20	LONG
J. Burnip	3	115	38.3	0	1	48

Receiving	REC	YDS	AVG	TD	LONG
C. Latu	6	90	15	1	27
J. Brooks	6	79	13.2	1	27
K. Prentice	9	66	7.3	0	14
J. Burton	2	49	24.5	0	36
J. Gibbs	5	48	9.6	0	30
J. Earle	1	42	42	0	42
I. Bond	2	39	19.5	0	33
J. McClellan	3	22	7.3	0	18
T. Holden	1	20	20	0	20
Team	35	455	13	2	42

Kick returns	NO	YDS	AVG	LONG	TD
J. Gibbs	3	52	17.3	28	0
J. Brooks	1	4	4	4	0
Team	4	56	14	28	0

Punt returns	NO	YDS	AVG	LONG	TD
Q. Robinson	1	3	3	3	0

Note: Table data from "Alabama 52-49 Tennessee (Oct 15, 2022) Box Score" (348)

10/22/22 - Alabama (6) vs Mississippi State (24)

Team	1	2	3	4	T		Passing	Rushing	Total
Mississippi State (24)	0	0	0	6	**6**		231	62	**293**
Alabama (6)	7	17	0	6	**30**		261	29	**290**

From the opening whistle, it was a one-sided affair with the Tide asserting their dominance on both sides of the ball. After both teams punted on their first possessions, State drove down to the AL 15-yard line, but Bama held when they went for it on 4th-and-4. Alabama opened the scoring when Bryce Young, facing intense pressure from the defense and the play seemingly breaking down, kept his composure and delivered a pinpoint strike to JoJo Earle, who hauled in the 31-yard touchdown reception in the back of the end zone. The scoring drive went 85 yards in six plays, taking only 2:18 off the clock. MSU moved the ball again but missed a 43-yard field goal. The Tide only needed 1:43 and three plays to score on their next possession. Jahmyr Gibbs capped off the 74-yard drive when he found a hole and took it in from 19 yards out (Bama up 14-0). The Bulldogs went for it on 4th-and-1 from their own 29-yard line, but Bama stifled them. 1:44 later, Traeshon Holden got in on the action, hauling in a 6-yard touchdown pass from Young, capping a 4-play, 29-yard drive. After forcing State to punt, Will Reichard contributed with a 50-yard field goal, his fifth career kick from 50+, finishing a 10-play, 56-yard drive, making it 24-0. Both teams punted before the half ended.

After Alabama punted to start the second half, Mississippi State drove down to the AL 31-yard line but failed to convert once again. Bama punted, State punted, then Bama punted again, but this time it was fumbled and recovered by Alabama's Jaylen Moody. In the fourth quarter, Reichard scored field goals from 33 and 38 yards. The other possessions ended in punts except for the very last play of the game when State scored as time expired to make the final 30-6.

The Crimson Tide defense tallied 15 pass breakups, six tackles for loss, and four sacks. Henry To'oTo'o led the team with a game-high 13 tackles while DeMarcco Hellams tallied 12 tackles and two pass breakups. KoolAid McKinstry and Eli Ricks were lockdown artists, each recording four pass breakups to tie for the team lead. Kicker Will Reichard continued his impressive season by drilling a 50-yard field goal, the fifth of his Alabama career and third of the season, from 50+ yards out.

With the 30-6 victory, Alabama extended its winning streak against Mississippi State to 15 games in a row. The Crimson Tide has outscored the Bulldogs 146-9 in the last four meetings in Tuscaloosa. Alabama also improved its record to 9-0 in games played following a regular-season loss dating back to 2008. Additionally, Saban remains unbeaten at home during the month of October while at Alabama, improving to 31-0 in all-time October games in Tuscaloosa.[349]

Passing	C/ATT	YDS	AVG	TD	INT	QBR
B. Young	21/35	249	7.1	2	0	91.3
J. Milroe	1/2	12	6	0	0	96
Team	22/37	261	7.1	2	0	--

Rushing	CAR	YDS	AVG	TD	LONG
J. Gibbs	10	37	3.7	1	19
J. McClellan	6	9	1.5	0	5
R. Williams	6	7	1.2	0	3
B. Young	4	-13	-3.3	0	2
Team	1	-11	-11	0	0
Team	27	29	1.1	1	19

Punting	NO	YDS	AVG	TB	IN 20	LONG
J. Burnip	6	222	37	0	3	50

Receiving	REC	YDS	AVG	TD	LONG
J. Brooks	3	74	24.7	0	40
J. Burton	2	40	20	0	23
J. Earle	3	38	12.7	1	31
J. Gibbs	4	33	8.3	0	13
T. Holden	2	23	11.5	1	17
T. Harrell	1	12	12	0	12
C. Latu	1	11	11	0	11
J. McClellan	1	11	11	0	11
R. Williams	2	10	5	0	6
I. Bond	1	8	8	0	8
K. Prentice	2	1	0.5	0	3
Team	22	261	11.9	2	40

Kicking	FG	PCT	LONG	XP	PTS
W. Reichard	3/3	100	50	3/3	12

Note: Table data from "Alabama 30-6 Mississippi State (Oct 22, 2022) Box Score" (350)

11/05/22 - Alabama (6) at LSU (10)

Team	1	2	3	4	OT	T	Passing	Rushing	Total
Alabama (6)	0	6	3	15	7	31	328	137	465
LSU (10)	0	7	7	10	8	32	182	185	367

After LSU opened with a punt, Alabama drove down to the LSU 4-yard line where Bryce Young was intercepted in the end zone. Both teams traded punts for the rest of the first quarter. Both teams started with punts in the second quarter as well, but on LSU's second possession, Jayden Daniels threw a 30-yard touchdown pass to John Emery Jr. that capped a 4-play, 49-yard drive and took 1:57 off the clock. Alabama responded with a pair of field goals from Will Reichard, surrounding a punt by LSU. The first was from 29 yards capping a 7-play, 63-yard drive, and the second was from 35 yards on a 12-play, 63-yard drive (the longest drive in the game so far). LSU maintained a slim 7-6 lead at halftime.

After receiving the second-half kickoff, Alabama orchestrated a 15-play, 55-yard drive that consumed a staggering 6:49 off the clock. Will Reichard split the uprights from 38 yards out, allowing Alabama to regain the lead at 9-7. LSU answered with a 2-yard touchdown run by Josh Williams, capping an 11-play, 75-yard drive that took 4:41 off the clock. Both teams then punted to bring it to the fourth quarter (14-9, LSU).

Roydell Williams powered through the defense for a 2-yard touchdown run, the Tide's first TD of the game. This capped an impressive 8-play, 76-yard drive, and Alabama took the lead 15-14 as the two-point conversion attempt failed. On the next Tiger possession, they went 69 yards in 11 plays and kicked a 32-yard field goal to seize a narrow 17-15 lead. Young responded by connecting with Ja'Corey Brooks for a 41-yard touchdown, capping a 65-yard drive. After the failed two-point conversion attempt, Bama led 21-17 with 4:44 remaining in the game. Not to be outdone, Jayden Daniels put together a 75-yard drive, finding Mason Taylor for a 7-yard score to regain the lead 24-21 with 1:47 remaining. Alabama responded quickly, needing just 1:26 to go 47 yards and set up Reichard's third field goal (this one from 46), forcing overtime at 24-24.

Alabama struck first in OT with a 1-yard touchdown run by Roydell Williams, but LSU responded with a 25-yard touchdown run by Daniels. In a bold move, LSU decided to go for the win with a two-point conversion attempt, and Daniels delivered, connecting with Mason Taylor to seal the 32-31 victory.

DeMarcco Hellams led the Alabama defense with 12 tackles (nine solo), while Brian Branch added nine stops, a QB hurry, and a pass breakup. This was Alabama's first overtime game since defeating Auburn a year ago, 24-22, in four overtimes. The last time Bama lost a game in OT was 11 years ago to the day when they lost 9-6 against LSU at home in 2011. The loss marked Alabama's second of the season, with both losses coming on the game's final play (field goal at Tennessee). It was also the first time Alabama failed to score in the first quarter this season.[351]

Passing	C/ATT	YDS	AVG	TD	INT	QBR
B. Young	25/51	328	6.4	1	1	69.9

Rushing	CAR	YDS	AVG	TD	LONG
J. Gibbs	15	99	6.6	0	34
J. McClellan	4	17	4.3	0	7
R. Williams	7	11	1.6	2	2
B. Young	4	10	2.5	0	11
Team	30	137	4.6	2	34

Punting	NO	YDS	AVG	TB	IN 20	LONG
J. Burnip	4	199	49.8	0	3	58

Receiving	REC	YDS	AVG	TD	LONG
J. Brooks	7	97	13.9	1	41
J. McClellan	2	74	37	0	65
J. Gibbs	8	64	8	0	14
C. Latu	3	50	16.7	0	21
J. Burton	2	19	9.5	0	15
J. Earle	1	15	15	0	15
R. Williams	1	5	5	0	5
K. Prentice	1	4	4	0	4
Team	25	328	13.1	1	65

Kicking	FG	PCT	LONG	XP	PTS
W. Reichard	4/4	100	46	1/1	13

Note: Table data from "LSU 32-31 Alabama (Nov 5, 2022) Box Score" (352)

11/12/22 - Alabama (9) at Ole Miss (11)

Team	1	2	3	4	T		Passing	Rushing	Total
Alabama (9)	0	14	10	6	**30**		209	108	**317**
Ole Miss (11)	7	10	7	0	**24**		212	191	**403**

On the Ole Miss opening possession, they drove the ball all the way to down to the AL 12-yard line, but Alabama denied them on 4th-and-2. Three punts later (two by Alabama), the Rebels scored a touchdown from a yard out, capping an 11-play, 68-yard drive. Alabama failed to convert on 4th-and-1 from its own 36-yard line to end the quarter. The Rebels took advantage of the short field and scored on a 22-yard field goal to go up 10-0. The Tide refused to back down as Bryce Young orchestrated a 7-play, 80-yard drive to get Alabama on the board with a 19-yard pass to Jermaine Burton. After forcing another punt, Young completed a 10-yard pass to JoJo Earl, but he fumbled, and Ole Miss recovered on the AL 49-yard line. They took advantage and scored in seven plays with Judkins powering his way into the end zone from a yard out, his second rushing touchdown of the half (17-7 Rebels). Bama punted again, then the Rebels fumbled on their first play and Terrion Arnold recovered it for the Tide. In a methodical 6-play march spanning 23 yards, with just seconds remaining before halftime, Young connected with Cameron Latu for an 8-yard touchdown strike. This cut the Ole Miss lead to 17-14 heading into the break.

Alabama tied the game at 17-17 with a 39-yard field goal on its opening drive of the second half, capping a 7-play, 54-yard drive. Both teams then had 75-yard scoring drives. Ole Miss did it in 11 plays on a 3-yard pass play to Jonathan Mingo, and Alabama answered in 14 plays with a 5-yard pass to Ja'Corey Brooks to even the score at 24-24. After an Ole Miss punt to start the fourth quarter, Alabama drove 44 yards in eight plays where Reichard booted a 23-yarder to take their first lead of the game, 27-24. There were a couple more punts, an Ole Miss turnover on downs, then Reichard added another field goal late in the game, extending Alabama's lead to 30-24. Bama stopped Ole Miss on 4th-and-16 from the AL 20-yard line to win the game.

Alabama's defense was led by Byron Young's 11 tackles (including two sacks), two quarterback hurries, and a pass breakup. DeMarcco Hellams (11) and Terrion Arnold (10) combined for 21 tackles. Nine of Arnold's were solo tackles, and he also logged a pair of pass breakups. Jase McClellan had a career-high 84 rushing yards on 19 carries. Bryce Young passed for 209 yards which brought his career total to 7,471, passing Tua Tagovailoa (7,442) for third place on the school's all-time passing yardage list. He now trails only John Parker Wilson (7,924) and A.J. McCarron (9,019). Nick Saban improved his record against former assistants to an impressive 28-2, including a perfect 4-0 mark against Lane Kiffin. Additionally, the win marked Saban's 27th road victory over a Top-25 team, tying him with Joe Paterno for second place all-time, with former Florida State head coach Bobby Bowden standing as the all-time leader with 33.[353]

Passing	C/ATT	YDS	AVG	TD	INT	QBR
B. Young	21/33	209	6.3	3	0	77.4

Rushing	CAR	YDS	AVG	TD	LONG
J. McClellan	19	84	4.4	0	12
R. Williams	2	13	6.5	0	8
B. Young	7	10	1.4	0	14
J. Gibbs	6	3	0.5	0	3
Team	2	-2	-1	0	0
Team	36	108	3.0	0	14

Kicking	FG	PCT	LONG	XP	PTS
W. Reichard	3/3	100	49	3/3	12

Punting	NO	YDS	AVG	TB	IN 20	LONG
J. Burnip	4	176	44	0	1	51

Receiving	REC	YDS	AVG	TD	LONG
J. Brooks	4	61	15.3	1	35
J. Burton	5	50	10	1	19
C. Latu	3	38	12.7	1	15
K. Law	3	26	8.7	0	10
J. Earle	3	21	7	0	10
K. Prentice	1	7	7	0	7
J. Gibbs	1	5	5	0	5
J. McClellan	1	1	1	0	1
Team	21	209	10	3	35

Kick returns	NO	YDS	AVG	LONG	TD
J. Brooks	2	27	13.5	14	0
J. Gibbs	1	4	4	4	0
Team	3	31	10.3	14	0

Note: Table data from "Alabama 30-24 Ole Miss (Nov 12, 2022) Box Score" (354)

374

11/19/22 - Alabama (8) vs Austin Peay

Team	1	2	3	4	T	Passing	Rushing	Total
Austin Peay	0	0	0	0	0	147	59	206
Alabama (8)	7	10	10	7	34	264	263	527

Alabama started the game with a commanding 92-yard drive, spanning 13 plays and lasting 6:28, culminating in Jase McClellan's 1-yard plunge into the end zone to open the scoring. After forcing an Austin Peay punt, Alabama fumbled and gave the ball right back to them. AP drove down to the 3-yard line where Bama's defense stopped them on 4th-and-goal. Bama fumbled at the AP 49 on its next series which led to an Austin Peay field goal attempt that they missed from 25 yards. However, the defense stopped Austin Peay's drive at the 3-yard line on 4th-and-goal. The Tide then marched 80 yards in eight plays with Jermaine Burton hauling in a 4-yard TD pass from Bryce Young midway through the second quarter. McKinstry logged an interception that led to a 29-yard FG by Reichard ending an 8-play, 34-yard drive. Bama led 17-0 at the half.

The second half began with three consecutive punts, but Alabama quickly regained momentum, needing just three plays to cover 65 yards in 58 seconds, with Jase McClellan racing in from nine yards out for his second score. Damon Payne recovered a fumble that led to another field goal, this time from 30 yards (27-0). After forcing another punt, Burton caught his second touchdown of the day, a 10-yard strike from Young, concluding an 8-play, 66-yard drive. The score stood at 34-0 after both teams threw picks (third career interception by Branch) to close things out.

Defensively, Henry To'oTo'o and Brian Branch led the way with eight tackles each, with Branch adding an interception and a tackle for loss. DeMarcco Hellams contributed seven tackles, including four solo stops. Jase McClellan spearheaded the ground attack, rushing for a career-high 156 yards on 17 carries (9.2 yards per carry) and two touchdowns.

Saturday's shutout victory marked Alabama's second of the season (55-0 over Utah State) and the 26th since Nick Saban's arrival in 2007. The Tide scored 34 points, marking the 58th time in the last 67 games (dating back to 2018) that they have scored 30+ points in a game. Bama's offense amassed 527 total yards which marked the 54th occasion out of the past 111 games where they have surpassed the 500-yard threshold in a game. The Crimson Tide found the end zone on their very first offensive drive of the game, and they have now emerged victorious in an astonishing 50 out of their last 51 games when scoring a touchdown on their opening possession.[355]

Passing	C/ATT	YDS	AVG	TD	INT	QBR
B. Young	18/24	221	9.2	2	0	36.6
J. Milroe	2/4	23	5.8	0	1	36.2
T. Simpson	2/2	20	10	0	0	94.8
Team	22/30	264	8.8	2	1	--

Rushing	CAR	YDS	AVG	TD	LONG
J. McClellan	17	156	9.2	2	35
R. Williams	10	51	5.1	0	13
J. Miller	10	33	3.3	0	9
J. Milroe	2	19	9.5	0	16
T. Sanders	2	14	7	0	8
B. Young	4	-10	-2.5	0	7
Team	45	263	5.8	2	35

Interceptions	INT	YDS	TD
K. McKinstry	1	26	0
B. Branch	1	0	0
Team	2	26	0

Punting	NO	YDS	AVG	TB	IN 20	LONG
J. Burnip	1	46	46	0	0	46

Receiving	REC	YDS	AVG	TD	LONG
J. Burton	7	128	18.3	2	50
T. Holden	3	38	12.7	0	18
I. Bond	3	19	6.3	0	11
J. Earle	3	17	5.7	0	8
R. Williams	1	15	15	0	15
E. Henderson Jr.	1	14	14	0	14
J. Brooks	1	13	13	0	13
R. Ouzts	1	11	11	0	11
T. Harrell	1	6	6	0	6
K. Law	1	3	3	0	3
Team	22	264	12	2	50

Kick returns	NO	YDS	AVG	LONG	TD
E. Henderson Jr.	1	8	8	8	0

Punt returns	NO	YDS	AVG	LONG	TD
K. McKinstry	1	10	10	10	0
K. Law	1	-2	-2	-2	0
Team	2	8	4	10	0

Kicking	FG	PCT	LONG	XP	PTS
W. Reichard	2/2	100	30	4/4	10

Note: Table data from "Alabama 34-0 Austin Peay (Nov 19, 2022) Box Score" (356)

11/26/22 - Alabama (7) vs Auburn

Team	1	2	3	4	T	Passing	Rushing	Total
Auburn	7	7	7	6	27	77	318	395
Alabama (7)	14	21	7	7	49	343	173	516

Both teams punted to start the game. Auburn drew first blood with Robby Ashford capping off a 6-play, 80-yard drive with a 24-yard touchdown run. Alabama responded on its next possession as Bryce Young orchestrated a 5-play, 62-yard drive, culminating in his own 5-yard rushing score to even the score in just 2:01. Bama held Auburn to a punt, then scored again in less than three minutes. Jase McClellan hauled in a 10-yard touchdown pass from Young, capping an 8-play, 65-yard drive (14-7). Four seconds into the second quarter, Roydell Williams punched in a 5-yard score after an Auburn turnover (DJ Dale recovered a fumble). This was Alabama's third consecutive scoring drive and only took one minute to go 48 yards in four plays (21-7). Auburn cut the deficit to 21-14 with Ashford's 20-yard scoring strike on their 10-play, 75-yard drive, but Young continued his aerial assault, finding Ja'Corey Brooks for a 32-yard touchdown to finish a 92-yard drive. Alabama held the Tigers to a punt, then punted themselves, but Auburn fumbled it, and Hibbett recovered it for the Tide. Alabama capitalized when Traeshon Holden took a short pass from Bryce Young 27 yards to paydirt to close out a 4-play, 37-yard drive. Alabama was on top 35-14 at the half.

As the second half kicked off, the offenses for both teams came out firing. Alabama struck first with a methodical 9-play, 72-yard march down the field. McClellan capped off the impressive drive by muscling his way into the end zone from two yards out for his second touchdown of the game. However, Auburn refused to go away quietly. The Tigers responded with a blistering 7-play, 75-yard scoring drive of their own. Ashford showcased his dual-threat abilities, scampering 14 yards to paydirt for his second rushing touchdown, trimming Alabama's lead to 42-21.

In the fourth quarter, after holding Alabama to a punt, Auburn drove 64 yards in 15 plays and scored a 32-yard field goal. Alabama drove to the AU 27-yard line before Young was picked off. Auburn took the ball down the field and kicked a 39-yard field goal to finish a 10-play, 60-yard drive, bringing the score to 42-27. Auburn attempted an onside kick, and Ja'Corey Brooks returned it 24 yards to the AU 27-yard line. Jahmyr Gibbs scored on the very next play, bringing the final score to 49-27.

With nine tackles including seven solo stops, Deontae Lawson led Alabama's defense in both categories. Henry To'oTo'o and Brian Branch chipped in with eight tackles each. Will Anderson Jr. continued his relentless pursuit, recording a sack and five tackles, including three for loss. His career total of 61 tackles for loss propelled him past the legendary Wallace Gilberry, securing the second spot in the Crimson Tide's illustrious history. Only the incomparable Derrick Thomas, with his awe-inspiring 68 tackles for loss, stands ahead of Anderson Jr. in this category.

Bryce Young amassed 391 total yards and accounted for four touchdowns, showcasing his dual-threat abilities. Young's precision through the air was particularly impressive, as he completed 20 of his 30 pass attempts for a staggering 343 yards. This outstanding display propelled him past John Parker Wilson's career passing yards mark of 7,924 yards, solidifying Young's position as the second-highest passer in Alabama's illustrious history with 8,035 career yards. The only name that now stands ahead of Bryce Young in the Crimson Tide's record books is the legendary A.J. McCarron, who set the program's career passing yards record with an impressive 9,019 yards during his tenure. With his remarkable talent and consistent performances, Young has joined an exclusive club, becoming only the second quarterback in Alabama's storied history to surpass the 8,000-yard mark in career passing yards.

With its third consecutive Iron Bowl win, Alabama extended its dominance over Auburn, winning 11 of the last 15 meetings. Nick Saban improved his record to 11-5 in Iron Bowl games as the Crimson Tide's head coach. Alabama's 10-win season marked the 44th such campaign in program history and the 15th consecutive under Saban's leadership.[357]

Passing	C/ATT	YDS	AVG	TD	INT	QBR
B. Young	20/30	343	11.4	3	1	98.2

Rushing	CAR	YDS	AVG	TD	LONG
J. Gibbs	17	76	4.5	1	23
B. Young	5	48	9.6	1	21
J. McClellan	11	44	4	1	8
R. Williams	1	5	5	1	5
Team	34	173	5.1	4	23

Kick returns	NO	YDS	AVG	LONG	TD
J. Gibbs	3	59	19.7	25	0
J. Brooks	3	57	19	24	0
Team	6	116	19.3	25	0

Punting	NO	YDS	AVG	TB	IN 20	LONG
J. Burnip	3	136	45.3	1	0	47

Receiving	REC	YDS	AVG	TD	LONG
J. Burton	3	87	29	0	52
J. Brooks	4	76	19	1	32
K. Law	2	52	26	0	39
I. Bond	4	36	9	0	13
R. Ouzts	2	29	14.5	0	17
T. Holden	1	27	27	1	27
C. Latu	1	18	18	0	18
J. McClellan	1	10	10	1	10
J. Gibbs	2	8	4	0	7
Team	20	343	17.2	3	52

Punt returns	NO	YDS	AVG	LONG	TD
K. McKinstry	2	-12	-6	-1	0

Kicking	FG	PCT	LONG	XP	PTS
W. Reichard	0/0	0	0	7/7	7

Note: Table data from "Alabama 49-27 Auburn (Nov 26, 2022) Box Score" (358)

12/31/22 - Alabama (5) at Kansas State (9)

Team	1	2	3	4	T	Passing	Rushing	Total
Alabama (5)	7	14	21	3	45	321	175	496
Kansas State (9)	10	0	3	7	20	210	191	401

The Mercedes-Benz Superdome in New Orleans was the stage for an epic clash between the Alabama Crimson Tide and the Kansas State Wildcats in the Sugar Bowl. The game started with a bang as Jordan Battle intercepted a pass on Kansas State's first possession, setting the tone for Alabama's defensive prowess. However, the Crimson Tide's offense sputtered initially, going three-and-out on their first drive. Undeterred, Kansas State marched down the field, 38 yards in 11 plays, and converted a 41-yard field goal to take an early 3-0 lead. After holding Alabama to another punt, the Wildcats were gaining momentum as Deuce Vaughn unleashed an 88-yard touchdown run on the first play of their ensuing drive, staking Kansas State to a 10-0 lead. Alabama responded with a 6-play, 69-yard drive, including a nice 60-yard pass from Bryce Young to Jahmyr Gibbs, ending with a 6-yard touchdown catch by Isaiah Bond. The Crimson Tide's offense was just getting started. After forcing a K-State punt, Young hit Jermaine Burton for a big 47-yard gain to the Kansas State 2-yard line. After Jase McClellan picked up one, Young hit Cameron Latu for the score, finishing off their 6-play, 63-yard that gave them a 14-10 lead. Kansas State took the ball to the Alabama 4-yard line, converting two fourth downs along the way. They had it 3rd-and-goal from the 2-yard line, but the Bama defense held them twice. Alabama then delivered a knockout blow, embarking on a 98-yard drive that took just seven plays and 58 seconds, culminating in a 12-yard touchdown catch by Jermaine Burton to extend its lead to 21-10 at halftime.

The second half was a showcase of Alabama's dominance. Roydell Williams recovered an onside kick attempt by Kansas State, and Alabama capitalized with a perfectly placed 32-yard touchdown pass from Young to Ja'Corey Brooks in the back corner of the end zone. It only took six plays and 1:05 for the Tide to extend their lead to 28-10. Brian Branch's interception at the Kansas State 17-yard line set up another score as Jase McClellan scored on Alabama's fifth consecutive touchdown drive (35-10). After both teams punted, the Wildcats scored on a 28-yard field goal after going 54 yards in eight plays (35-13). After trading punts again, the Crimson Tide's offensive onslaught continued when Kobe Prentice caught a 30-yard pass, broke tackles, then took it to the house for a 47-yard touchdown. That capped a 3-play, 51-yard drive and extended Bama's lead to 42-13. K-State punted on its next two possessions while Reichard converted a 49-yard field goal in between. This finished off a 6-play, 14-yard drive four minutes into the fourth quarter. Kansas State managed to score once more, but it was too little, too late as Alabama cruised to a 45-20 victory.

Alabama's stifling defense put the clamps on Kansas State's aerial attack. The Crimson Tide secondary snagged two interceptions and limited the Wildcats to a mere 210 passing yards. Jordan Battle hauled in the first pick and racked up an impressive nine total tackles, including half a tackle for loss. Brian Branch joined the turnover party with Alabama's second interception, complementing it with 12 tackles, a sack, and a game-high four tackles for loss. DeMarcco Hellams led all defenders with 13 stops.

Quarterback Bryce Young etched his name in Alabama's bowl history with a five-touchdown masterpiece, earning him the game's MVP honors. He has thrown for a career-high five touchdowns in a single game four times now. The junior signal-caller was a model of efficiency, completing 15-of-21 passes for 321 yards and the quintet of scores. Young's five touchdown tosses set an Alabama bowl record and matched Mac Jones' feat against Ohio State in the 2021 College Football Playoff National Championship Game for the most by a Crimson Tide quarterback in a postseason contest (bowls and College Football Playoffs). With 80 career passing touchdowns, Young leapfrogged A.J. McCarron (77) into second place on the school's all-time list, trailing only Tua Tagovailoa's 87. Remarkably, Young has thrown at least one touchdown pass in all 27 games he has started for Alabama.

Running back Jahmyr Gibbs continued his stellar campaign, finishing second among Crimson Tide running backs with 44 receptions in a single season. This impressive tally surpassed Najee Harris' 43 catches and fell just shy of Kevin Turner's program record of 48.

This game marked the Crimson Tide's 17th in the Sugar Bowl - the most by Alabama in any bowl and eight better than the Cotton, which holds second place at nine. Head coach Nick Saban secured his 23rd career victory by 25+ points against a top-25 team and his 25th win by 20+ points against a top-15 opponent. Saban stands alone as the NCAA's all-time record holder in both categories.[359]

Passing	C/ATT	YDS	AVG	TD	INT	QBR
B. Young	15/21	321	15.3	5	0	98.7
J. Milroe	0/1	0	0	0	0	0.3
Team	15/22	321	14.6	5	0	--

Rushing	CAR	YDS	AVG	TD	LONG
J. Gibbs	15	76	5.1	0	22
J. Miller	3	44	14.7	0	38
J. McClellan	7	42	6	1	17
R. Williams	5	23	4.6	0	12
B. Young	3	-10	-3.3	0	5
Team	33	175	5.3	1	38

Interceptions	INT	YDS	TD
B. Branch	1	2	0
J. Battle	1	0	0
Team	2	2	0

Punting	NO	YDS	AVG	TB	IN 20	LONG
J. Burnip	5	192	38.4	0	1	40

Receiving	REC	YDS	AVG	TD	LONG
J. Burton	3	87	29	1	47
J. Gibbs	2	66	33	0	60
C. Latu	5	54	10.8	1	23
J. Brooks	2	51	25.5	1	32
K. Prentice	1	47	47	1	47
J. McClellan	1	10	10	0	10
I. Bond	1	6	6	1	6
Team	15	321	21.4	5	60

Kick returns	NO	YDS	AVG	LONG	TD
J. Gibbs	2	31	15.5	30	0

Punt returns	NO	YDS	AVG	LONG	TD
K. McKinstry	1	15	15	15	0

Kicking	FG	PCT	LONG	XP	PTS
W. Reichard	1/1	100	49	6/6	9

Note: Table data from "Alabama 45-20 Kansas State (Dec 31, 2022) Box Score" (360)

Season Stats

Record	11-2	6th of 131
SEC Record	6-2	
Rank	5	
Points for	537	
Points against	233	
Points/game	41.3	4th of 131
Opp points/game	17.9	9th of 131
SOS[16]	4.58	26th of 131

Team stats (averages per game)

Split	G	Passing					Rushing				Total Offense		
		Cmp	Att	Pct	Yds	TD	Att	Yds	Avg	TD	Plays	Yds	Avg
Offense	13	21.5	33.7	63.9	281.5	2.8	35.2	195.5	5.6	2	68.9	477.1	6.9
Defense	13	18.3	33.4	54.8	187.8	0.9	35.9	130.4	3.6	1.2	69.3	318.2	4.6
Difference		3.2	0.3	9.1	93.7	1.9	-0.7	65.1	2	0.8	-0.4	158.9	2.3

Split	First Downs				Penalties		Turnovers		
	Pass	Rush	Pen	Tot	No.	Yds	Fum	Int	Tot
Offense	12.6	9.3	1.9	23.8	7.9	68.7	0.6	0.6	1.2
Defense	8.8	7.2	2.6	18.5	6.7	51	0.5	0.5	1.1
Difference	3.8	2.1	-0.7	5.3	1.2	17.7	0.1	0.1	0.1

Passing

Rk	Player	G	Passing								
			Cmp	Att	Pct	Yds	Y/A	AY/A	TD	Int	Rate
1	Bryce Young	12	245	380	64.5	3328	8.8	9.9	32	5	163.2
2	Jalen Milroe	8	31	53	58.5	297	5.6	4.9	5	3	125.4
3	Ty Simpson	4	4	5	80	35	7	7	0	0	138.8

Rushing and receiving

Rk	Player	G	Rushing					Receiving				Scrimmage			
			Att	Yds	Avg	TD	Rec	Yds	Avg	TD	Plays	Yds	Avg	TD
1	Jahmyr Gibbs	12	151	926	6.1	7	44	444	10.1	3	195	1370	7	10
2	Jase McClellan	13	112	655	5.8	7	14	174	12.4	3	126	829	6.6	10
3	Roydell Williams	13	56	250	4.5	4	5	37	7.4	0	61	287	4.7	4
4	Bryce Young	12	49	185	3.8	4					49	185	3.8	4
5	Jam Miller	13	33	223	6.8	2	1	-1	-1	0	34	222	6.5	2
6	Jalen Milroe	8	31	263	8.5	1					31	263	8.5	1
7	Trey Sanders	10	14	80	5.7	1	2	13	6.5	0	16	93	5.8	1
8	Jonathan Bennett	1	2	12	6	0					2	12	6	0
9	Jermaine Burton	13					40	677	16.9	7	40	677	16.9	7
10	Ja'Corey Brooks	13					39	674	17.3	8	39	674	17.3	8
11	Kobe Prentice	13					31	337	10.9	2	31	337	10.9	2
12	Cameron Latu	11					30	377	12.6	4	30	377	12.6	4
13	Traeshon Holden	10					25	331	13.2	6	25	331	13.2	6
14	Isaiah Bond	13					17	220	12.9	1	17	220	12.9	1
15	Jojo Earle	8					12	155	12.9	2	12	155	12.9	2
16	Kendrick Law	11					8	103	12.9	0	8	103	12.9	0
17	Robbie Ouzts	13					4	43	10.8	0	4	43	10.8	0
18	Miles Kitselman	6					2	18	9	0	2	18	9	0
19	Tyler Harrell	6					2	18	9	0	2	18	9	0
20	Amari Niblack	10					1	15	15	1	1	15	15	1
21	Emmanuel Henderson	12					1	14	14	0	1	14	14	0
22	Christian Leary	10					1	6	6	0	1	6	6	0
23	Thaiu Jones-Bell	4					1	5	5	0	1	5	5	0

Defense and fumbles

Rk	Player	G	Tackles					Def Int					Fumbles		
			Solo	Ast	Tot	Loss	Sk	Int	Yds	Avg	TD	PD	FR	TD	FF
1	Demarcco Hellams	13	67	41	108	3	1	1	0	0	0	7	1	0	1
2	Henry To'oto'o	13	45	49	94	8	2.5								
3	Brian Branch	13	58	32	90	14	3	2	2	1	0	7			
4	Jordan Battle	13	34	37	71	0.5	0	1	0	0	0	2			
5	Will Anderson Jr.	13	24	27	51	17	10	1	25	25	1	1			
6	Deontae Lawson	11	24	27	51	2.5	0					4			
7	Jaylen Moody	10	24	26	50	8	2						1	0	0
8	Byron Young	13	20	28	48	5.5	4					2			1
9	Terrion Arnold	11	34	11	45	1	0	1	21	21	0	8	1	0	0
10	Dallas Turner	13	16	21	37	8	4						1	1	0
11	Kool-Aid McKinstry	13	29	6	35	2	1	1	26	26	0	15			
12	Malachi Moore	13	19	12	31	1.5	1.5					5			
13	Jaheim Oatis	12	10	19	29	2	1					2			
14	Chris Braswell	13	8	12	20	4	2.5								1
15	Tim Smith	13	8	12	20	2	1								
16	DJ Dale	12	7	10	17	3.5	2.5					1	1	0	0
17	Eli Ricks	9	8	5	13	1	0					4			
18	Justin Eboigbe	4	5	6	11	0.5	0								
19	Jamil Burroughs	11	4	4	8	2	1								
20	Damon Payne Jr.	5	4	3	7	0.5	0						1	0	0
21	Khyree Jackson	9	6	1	7	1	0								
22	Quandarrius Robinson	13	3	4	7	0.5	0.5								
23	Kendrick Blackshire	8	2	4	6	1	0								
24	Roydell Williams	13	4	2	6	0	0								
25	Kendrick Law	11	3	2	5	0	0								
26	Kristian Story	13	5	0	5	0	0								
27	Jah-Marien Latham	12	1	3	4	0	0								
28	Emmanuel Henderson	12	1	2	3	0	0								
29	Shawn Murphy	5	2	0	2	0	0					1			
30	Jahquez Robinson	6	1	1	2	0.5	0.5								
31	Jeremiah Alexander	4	0	1	1	0	0								
32	Jihaad Campbell	9	0	1	1	0	0								
33	Isaiah Hastings	1	0	1	1	0	0								
34	Ian Jackson	3	1	0	1	0	0								
35	Tim Keenan III	2	0	1	1	0.5	0								
36	Demouy Kennedy	5	0	1	1	0	0								
37	Christian Leary	10	1	0	1	0	0								
38	Will Reichard	13	1	0	1	0	0								
39	Kneeland Hibbett	13				0	0						1	0	0

Kick and punt returns

Rk	Player	G	Kick Ret				Punt Ret			
			Ret	Yds	Avg	TD	Ret	Yds	Avg	TD
1	Jahmyr Gibbs	12	13	258	19.8	0				
2	Ja'Corey Brooks	13	7	106	15.1	0				
3	Emmanuel Henderson	12	1	8	8	0				
4	Kool-Aid McKinstry	13					21	332	15.8	0
5	Brian Branch	13					2	65	32.5	1
6	Isaiah Bond	13					1	34	34	0
7	Quandarrius Robinson	13					1	3	3	0
8	Kendrick Law	11					1	-2	-2	0
9	Malachi Moore	13						3		1

Kicking and punting

Rk	Player	G	Kicking							Punting		
			XPM	XPA	XP%	FGM	FGA	FG%	Pts	Punts	Yds	Avg
1	Will Reichard	13	64	64	100	22	26	84.6	130			
2	James Burnip	13								44	1861	42.3

Scoring

Rk	Player	G	Touchdowns							Kicking				Pts
			Rush	Rec	Int	FR	PR	KR	Tot	XPM	FGM	2PM	Sfty	
1	Will Reichard	13								64	22			130
2	Jase McClellan	13	7	3					10					60
3	Jahmyr Gibbs	12	7	3					10					60
4	Ja'Corey Brooks	13		8					8			1		50
5	Jermaine Burton	13		7					7					42
6	Traeshon Holden	10		6					6					36
7	Cameron Latu	11		4					4					24
8	Bryce Young	12	4						4					24
9	Roydell Williams	13	4						4					24
10	Jam Miller	13	2						2					12
11	Jojo Earle	8		2					2					12
12	Kobe Prentice	13		2					2					12
13	Brian Branch	13				1			1					6
14	Will Anderson Jr.	13			1				1					6
15	Trey Sanders	10	1						1					6
16	Malachi Moore	13				1			1					6
17	Amari Niblack	10		1					1					6
18	Jalen Milroe	8	1						1					6
19	Isaiah Bond	13		1					1					6
20	Dallas Turner	13				1			1					6

Stats include bowl games
Note: Table data from "2022 Alabama Crimson Tide Stats" (16)

Awards and honors

Name	Award	Type
Will Anderson Jr.	Permanent Team Captain	Team
Jordan Battle	Permanent Team Captain	Team
Bryce Young	Permanent Team Captain	Team
Bryce Young	MVP	Team
Ja'Corey Brooks	Offensive Player of the Year	Team
Jahmyr Gibbs	Offensive Player of the Year	Team
Bryce Young	Offensive Player of the Year	Team
Will Anderson Jr.	Defensive Player of the Year	Team
Brian Branch	Defensive Player of the Year	Team
Will Anderson Jr.	Defensive Player of the Year	SEC
Will Anderson Jr.	AP All-SEC First Team	SEC
Jordan Battle	AP All-SEC First Team	SEC
Emil Ekiyor Jr.	AP All-SEC First Team	SEC
Kool-Aid McKinstry	AP All-SEC First Team	SEC
Henry To'oTo'o	AP All-SEC First Team	SEC
Javion Cohen	AP All-SEC Second Team	SEC
Jahmyr Gibbs	AP All-SEC Second Team	SEC
Will Reichard	AP All-SEC Second Team	SEC
Tyler Steen	AP All-SEC Second Team	SEC
Will Anderson Jr.	Coaches' All-SEC First Team	SEC
Jordan Battle	Coaches' All-SEC First Team	SEC
Emil Ekiyor Jr.	Coaches' All-SEC First Team	SEC
Kool-Aid McKinstry	Coaches' All-SEC First Team	SEC
Henry To'oTo'o	Coaches' All-SEC First Team	SEC
Javion Cohen	Coaches' All-SEC Second Team	SEC
Jahmyr Gibbs	Coaches' All-SEC Second Team	SEC
Kool-Aid McKinstry	Coaches' All-SEC Second Team	SEC
Will Reichard	Coaches' All-SEC Second Team	SEC
Tyler Steen	Coaches' All-SEC Second Team	SEC
Terrion Arnold	Freshman All SEC Team	SEC
Tyler Booker	Freshman All SEC Team	SEC
Jaheim Oatis	Freshman All SEC Team	SEC
Will Anderson Jr.	AFCA All-American First Team	National
Kool-Aid McKinstry	AFCA All-American First Team	National
Brian Branch	AFCA All-American Second Team	National

Name	Award	Type
Kool-Aid McKinstry	AFCA All-American Second Team	National
Will Anderson Jr.	AP All-America First Team	National
Brian Branch	AP All-America Second Team	National
Jordan Battle	AP All-America Third Team	National
Jahmyr Gibbs	AP All-America Third Team	National
Kool-Aid McKinstry	AP All-America Third Team	National
Will Anderson Jr.	Bednarik Award	National
Will Anderson Jr.	Bronko Nagurski Trophy	National
Will Anderson Jr.	Consensus All-American	National
Will Anderson Jr.	FWAA All-America First Team	National
Kool-Aid McKinstry	FWAA All-America Second Team	National
Will Anderson Jr.	Lombardi Award	National
Will Anderson Jr.	Lott IMPACT Trophy	National
Will Anderson Jr.	Sporting News (TSN) All-America Team	National
Jordan Battle	Sporting News (TSN) All-America Second Team	National
Kool-Aid McKinstry	Sporting News (TSN) All-America Second Team	National
Will Anderson Jr.	Unanimous All-American	National
Will Anderson Jr.	Walter Camp All-America First Team	National
Jordan Battle	Senior Bowl	All-Star Team
DJ Dale	Senior Bowl	All-Star Team
Emil Ekiyor Jr.	Senior Bowl	All-Star Team
DeMarcco Hellams	Senior Bowl	All-Star Team
Cameron Latu	Senior Bowl	All-Star Team
Will Reichard	Senior Bowl	All-Star Team
Tyler Steen	Senior Bowl	All-Star Team
Henry To'oTo'o	Senior Bowl	All-Star Team
Byron Young	Senior Bowl	All-Star Team

Note: Table data from "2022 Alabama Crimson Tide football team" (333) and "Alabama football team awards: Here are permanent captains, team MVP" (361)

NFL

Season	Year drafted	Round	Pick	Overall	Player	Position	Team
2022	2023	1	1	1	Bryce Young	QB	Carolina Panthers
2022	2023	1	3	3	Will Anderson Jr.	LB	Houston Texans
2022	2023	1	12	12	Jahmyr Gibbs	RB	Detroit Lions
2022	2023	2	14	45	Brian Branch	CB	Detroit Lions
2022	2023	3	2	65	Tyler Steen	OT	Philadelphia Eagles
2022	2023	3	7	70	Byron Young	DT	Las Vegas Raiders
2022	2023	3	32	95	Jordan Battle	S	Cincinnati Bengals
2022	2023	3	38	101	Cameron Latu	TE	San Francisco 49ers
2022	2023	5	32	167	Henry To'oTo'o	LB	Houston Texans
2022	2023	7	7	224	DeMarcco Hellams	S	Atlanta Falcons

Note: Table data from "2023 NFL Draft" (362)

2023

Overall

Record	12-2
SEC Record	9-0
Rank	5
Points for	479
Points against	269
Points/game	34.2
Opp points/game	19.2
SOS[17]	6.58

It's not my position to confirm any of this stuff, and I really can't confirm it. Don't ask me anymore questions about that because that's all I have to say about it. I don't have anything else to say about it, so don't ask. There is no more. I know you would like to some kind of way extract something out of this bottle that's not there. It's not there. You all speculate and create things, and then you want people to respond to it. Get this bottle to respond to it because I don't know anything more than that. I told you everything I know. So you can ask the bottle, but don't ask me. -Nick Saban

Games

Date	Bama Rank		Opp Rank	Opponent	Bama	Opp	Result	SEC
09/02/23	4	vs		Middle Tennessee St	56	7	W	
09/09/23	3	vs	11	Texas	24	34	L	
09/16/23	10	@		South Florida	17	3	W	
09/23/23	13	vs	15	Ole Miss	24	10	W	W
09/30/23	12	@		Mississippi State	40	17	W	W
10/07/23	11	@		Texas A&M	26	20	W	W
10/14/23	11	vs		Arkansas	24	21	W	W
10/21/23	11	vs	17	Tennessee	34	20	W	W
11/04/23	8	vs	14	LSU	42	28	W	W
11/11/23	8	@		Kentucky	49	21	W	W
11/18/23	8	vs		Chattanooga	66	10	W	
11/25/23	8	@		Auburn	27	24	W	W
12/02/23	8	N	1	Georgia	27	24	W	W
01/01/24	4	N	1	Michigan	20	27	L	

Coaches

Name	Position	Year
Nick Saban	Head Coach	17
Robert Bala	Safeties / Inside Linebackers	1
David Ballou	Strength and Conditioning	4
Joe Cox	Tight Ends	2
Robert Gillespie	Running Backs	3
Coleman Hutzler	Special Teams Coordinator / Outside Linebackers	2
Tommy Rees	Offensive Coordinator / Quarterbacks	1
Freddie Roach	Defensive Line	4 (9th overall)
Travaris Robinson	Cornerbacks	2
Kevin Steele	Defensive Coordinator	1 (4th overall)
Holmon Wiggins	Wide Receivers	5
Eric Wolford	Offensive Line	2

Recruits

Name	Pos	Rivals	247 Sports	ESPN	ESPN Grade	Hometown	High school / college	Height	Weight	Committed
Cole Adams	WR	4	4	4	81	Owasso, OK	Owasso HS	5-10	190	6/29/22
Olaus Alinen	OT	4	4	4	84	Pori, Finland	Loomis Chaffee School (CT)	6-6	310	7/22/22
Malik Benson	WR	4	4	4	83	Lansing, KS	Hutchinson Comm. College (JC)	6-1	185	7/5/22
Caleb Downs	S	5	5	5	90	Hoschton, GA	Mill Creek HS	6-0	190	7/27/22
Wilkin Formby	OT	4	4	4	84	Tuscaloosa, AL	Northridge HS	6-7	300	6/20/22
Jalen Hale	WR	4	4	4	86	Longview, TX	Longview HS	6-2	185	9/21/22
Jaren Hamilton	WR	3	4	3	79	Gainesville, FL	Buchholz HS	6-1	190	11/28/22
Justice Haynes	RB	4	5	4	88	Buford, GA	Buford HS	6-2	170	7/17/22
Edric Hill	DT	4	4	4	80	N. Kansas City, MO	North Kansas City HS	6-3	285	8/22/22
Eli Holstein	QB	4	4	4	88	Zachary, LA	Zachary HS	6-4	225	5/24/22
Brayson Hubbard	ATH	3	3	4	80	Ocean Springs, MS	Ocean Springs HS	6-2	190	6/26/22
Jahlili Hurley	CB	4	4	4	87	Florence, AL	Florence HS	6-2	170	2/22/22
Justin Jefferson	LB	4	4	3	79	Memphis, TN	Pearl River Community College (JC)	6-2	215	6/28/22
Keon Keeley	DE	5	5	4	89	Tampa, FL	Berkeley Prep	6-5	245	12/12/22
Ty Lockwood	TE	4	4	4	83	Thompson's Station, TN	Independence HS	6-5	225	8/2/22
Dylan Lonergan	QB	4	4	4	87	Snellville, GA	Brookwood HS	6-2	210	7/11/22
RyQueze McElderry	OL	4	3	3	79	Anniston, AL	Anniston HS	6-3	340	7/4/22
Miles McVay	OT	4	4	4	83	East St. Louis, IL	East St. Louis HS	6-7	355	8/11/22
Tony Mitchell	CB	4	4	4	87	Alabaster, AL	Thompson HS	6-2	190	6/26/22
Hunter Osborne	DE	4	4	4	82	Trussville, AL	Hewitt-Trussville HS	6-4	255	8/1/22
Yhonzae Pierre	DE	4	4	4	82	Eufaula, AL	Eufaula HS	6-3	220	4/14/22
Kadyn Proctor	OL	5	5	5	90	Runnells, IA	Southeast Polk HS	6-6	315	12/20/22
Jordan Renaud	DT	4	4	4	86	Tyler, TX	Tyler Legacy HS	6-4	245	9/19/22
Desmond Ricks	CB	5	5	5	90	Bradenton, FL	IMG Academy	6-2	185	12/22/22
Jaquavious Russaw	LB	5	5	5	91	Montgomery, AL	Carver HS	6-3	220	12/21/22
James Smith	DT	5	5	5	90	Montgomery, AL	Carver HS	6-3	300	12/21/22
Conor Talty	PK	2	3	3	75	Chicago, IL	St. Rita of Cascia HS	6-2	170	7/20/22
Richard Young	RB	4	4	4	89	Lehigh Acres, FL	Lehigh Senior HS	5-11	195	7/29/22

	Rivals	247Sports	ESPN
5 Stars	6	7	5
4 Stars	19	18	19
3 Stars	2	3	4
2 Stars	1	0	0

Note: Table data from "2023 Alabama Crimson Tide football team" (363)

Roster

Num	Player	Pos	Class	Height	Weight	Hometown	Last School
13	Cole Adams	WR	FR	5-10	186	Owasso, OK	Owasso
35	Jeremiah Alexander	LB	RS-FR	6-2	249	Alabaster, AL	Thompson
73	Olaus Alinen	OL	FR	6-6	326	Pori, Finland	The Loomis Chaffee School (Conn.)
9	*Trey Amos*	DB	SR	6-1	197	*New Iberia, LA*	*Catholic-New Iberia / Louisiana*
3	**Terrion Arnold**	**DB**	**RS-SO**	**6-1**	**196**	**Tallahassee, FL**	**John Paul II Catholic**
51	Noland Asberry	LB	SO	6-1	190	Mobile, AL	Davidson
56	JD Baird	LB	SO	5-8	190	Tuscaloosa, AL	American Christian Academy
59	Anquin Barnes Jr.	DL	RS-SO	6-5	314	Montgomery, AL	Robert E. Lee
98	Upton Bellenfant	PK	SO	6-2	175	Murfreesboro, TN	Stewarts Creek
27	Jonathan Bennett	RB	SR	5-10	180	Birmingham, AL	Oak Mountain
11	**Malik Benson**	**WR**	**JR**	**6-1**	**195**	**Lansing, KS**	**Lansing / Hutchinson C.C.**
40	Kendrick Blackshire	LB	JR	6-2	233	Duncanville, TX	Duncanville
17	**Isaiah Bond**	**WR**	**SO**	**5-11**	**182**	**Buford, GA**	**Buford**
52	**Tyler Booker**	**OL**	**SO**	**6-5**	**352**	**New Haven, CT**	**IMG Academy**
41	**Chris Braswell**	**LB**	**SR**	**6-3**	**255**	**Baltimore, MD**	**Saint Frances Academy**
58	James Brockermeyer	OL	RS-SO	6-3	285	Fort Worth, TX	All Saints Episcopal
7	Ja'Corey Brooks	WR	JR	6-2	195	Miami, FL	IMG Academy
8	*Tyler Buchner*	QB	RS-SO	6-1	215	*San Diego, CA*	*The Bishop's School / Notre Dame*
86	**James Burnip**	**P**	**RS-JR**	**6-6**	**220**	**Mount Macedon, Australia**	**Victoria University, Melbourne**
3	**Jermaine Burton**	**WR**	**SR**	**6-1**	**194**	**Calabasas, CA**	**Calabasas / Georgia**
48	Prince Butler	DB	SO	6-1	200	Alexandria, VA	Hayfield
19	Miguel Camboia	QB	FR	6-1	190	Woodstock, Canada	Mobile Christian School
30	Jihaad Campbell	LB	SO	6-3	230	Erial, NJ	IMG Academy
16	Cade Carruth	QB	SO	6-1	195	Trussville, AL	Hewitt-Trussville
52	Braylon Chatman	LB	FR	6-1	200	Trussville, AL	Hewitt-Trussville
42	MJ Chirgwin	WR	SO	6-1	195	Huntington Beach, CA	Huntington Beach
35	Zarian Courtney	WR	SR	6-1	183	Arlington, TX	Timberview / Texas Col./Kilgore Col./Oklahoma Baptist
71	**Darrian Dalcourt**	**OL**	**SR**	**6-1**	**320**	**Havre de Grace, MD**	**Saint Frances Academy**
46	Chase Davis	DB	SO	6-1	182	Tuscaloosa, AL	Paul W. Bryant
36	Sawyer Deerman	WR	FR	5-10	175	Northport, AL	Tuscaloosa County
81	*CJ Dippre*	*TE*	*JR*	*6-5*	*257*	*Scranton, PA*	*Lakeland / Maryland*
2	**Caleb Downs**	**DB**	**FR**	**6-1**	**203**	**Hoschton, GA**	**Mill Creek**
92	**Justin Eboigbe**	**DL**	**RS-SR**	**6-5**	**292**	**Forest Park, GA**	**Forest Park**
43	Robert Ellis	TE	SR	6-1	220	Enterprise, AL	Enterprise
69	Terrence Ferguson II	OL	RS-SO	6-4	322	Fort Valley, GA	Peach
39	Kaleb Fleming	WR	SO	6-1	205	Macomb Township, MI	Spain Park
54	Kyle Flood Jr.	LB	SR	6-1	212	Middlesex, NJ	Saint Joseph
75	Wilkin Formby	OL	FR	6-7	320	Tuscaloosa, AL	Northridge
46	Peyton Fox	TE	SO	6-4	225	Pelham, AL	Briarwood Christian
41	JR Gardner	RB	FR	5-11	185	Gulf Shores, AL	Gulf Shores
95	Monkell Goodwine	DL	RS-SO	6-4	290	Upper Marlboro, MD	Rock Creek Christian Academy
14	Jalen Hale	WR	FR	6-1	189	Longview, TX	Longview
23	Jaren Hamilton	WR	FR	6-1	200	Gainesville, FL	F.W. Buchholz
96	Reed Harradine	PK	FR	6-3	185	Birmingham, AL	Mountain Brook
99	Isaiah Hastings	DL	RS-FR	6-4	290	Toronto, Canada	Clearwater Academy International (Fla.)
22	Justice Haynes	RB	FR	5-11	205	Buford, GA	Buford
24	Emmanuel Henderson Jr.	WR	SO	6-1	185	Hartford, AL	Geneva County
48	Kneeland Hibbett	SN	JR	6-2	245	Florence, AL	Florence
66	Baker Hickman	OL	FR	6-3	315	Tuscaloosa, AL	Northridge
94	Edric Hill	DL	FR	6-3	294	Kansas City, MO	North Kansas City
63	Wilder Hines	OL	SO	6-2	240	Birmingham, AL	Mountain Brook
10	Eli Holstein	QB	FR	6-4	237	Zachary, LA	Zachary
34	Terrance Howard	DB	FR	5-11	180	Missouri City, TX	Ridge Point
18	Bray Hubbard	DB	FR	6-2	195	Ocean Springs, MS	Ocean Springs
25	Jahlil Hurley	DB	FR	6-2	170	Florence, AL	Florence
39	Jake Ivie	DB	FR	6-1	205	Alabaster, AL	Thompson
36	Ian Jackson	LB	RS-SO	6-1	235	Prattville, AL	Prattville
28	Justin Jefferson	LB	JR	6-1	225	Memphis, TN	Bartlett / Pearl River C.C.
14	Thaiu Jones-Bell	WR	JR	6-1	198	Hallandale, FL	Miami Carol City
31	Keon Keeley	LB	FR	6-5	242	Tampa, FL	Berkeley Prep
96	**Tim Keenan III**	**DL**	**RS-SO**	**6-2**	**315**	**Birmingham, AL**	**Ramsay**
6	*Jaylen Key*	*DB*	*RS-SR*	*6-2*	*210*	*Quincy, FL*	*Amos P. Godby / UAB*
12	Antonio Kite	DB	RS-FR	6-1	182	Anniston, AL	Anniston
88	Miles Kitselman	TE	JR	6-5	250	Lyndon, KS	Lyndon / Hutchinson C.C.
19	Keanu Koht	LB	RS-SO	6-4	232	Vero Beach, FL	Vero Beach
65	JC Latham	OL	JR	6-6	360	Oak Creek, WI	IMG Academy
93	**Jah-Marien Latham**	**DL**	**RS-JR**	**6-3**	**275**	**Reform, AL**	**Pickens County**
19	Kendrick Law	WR	SO	5-11	201	Shreveport, LA	Captain Shreve
32	**Deontae Lawson**	**LB**	**RS-SO**	**6-2**	**230**	**Mobile, AL**	**Mobile Christian**
87	Danny Lewis Jr.	TE	RS-FR	6-5	255	New Iberia, LA	Westgate
20	Earl Little II	DB	RS-FR	6-1	186	Fort Lauderdale, FL	American Heritage

Num	Player	Pos	Class	Height	Weight	Hometown	Last School
89	Ty Lockwood	TE	FR	6-5	234	Thompson's Station, TN	Independence
12	Dylan Lonergan	QB	FR	6-2	212	Snellville, GA	Brookwood
32	Jay Loper Jr.	WR	SO	5-11	180	Daphne, AL	Bayside Academy
28	Michael Lorino III	RB	SO	6-1	185	Birmingham, AL	Mountain Brook
17	*Trezmen Marshall*	*LB*	*RS-SR*	*6-1*	*236*	*Homerville, GA*	*Clinch County / Georgia*
38	Alijah May	DB	JR	5-11	195	Pinson, AL	Pinson Valley
2	**Jase McClellan**	**RB**	**SR**	**5-11**	**212**	**Aledo, TX**	**Aledo**
45	Caleb McDougle	DB	SR	5-11	207	Muscle Shoals, AL	Muscle Shoals
-	RyQueze McElderry	OG	FR	6-3	334	Anniston, AL	Anniston
1	**Kool-Aid McKinstry**	**DB**	**JR**	**6-1**	**195**	**Birmingham, AL**	**Pinson Valley**
56	**Seth McLaughlin**	**OL**	**SR**	**6-4**	**305**	**Buford, GA**	**Buford**
34	Coby McNeal	TE	RS-SO	6-5	250	Dothan, AL	Ashford / Colorado State
54	Miles McVay	OL	FR	6-6	350	East Saint Louis, IL	East Saint Louis
26	Jam Miller	RB	SO	5-10	211	Tyler, TX	Tyler Legacy
4	**Jalen Milroe**	**QB**	**RS-SO**	**6-2**	**220**	**Katy, TX**	**Tompkins**
27	Tony Mitchell	DB	FR	6-2	205	Alabaster, AL	Thompson
55	Roq Montgomery	OL	FR	6-3	332	Anniston, AL	Anniston
13	**Malachi Moore**	**DB**	**SR**	**6-1**	**198**	**Trussville, AL**	**Hewitt-Trussville**
43	Shawn Murphy	LB	RS-FR	6-2	225	Manassas, VA	Unity Reed
48	Hayden Neighbors	WR	JR	6-3	185	Huntsville, AL	Huntsville
84	Amari Niblack	TE	SO	6-4	233	Saint Petersburg, FL	Lakewood
50	Brock O'Quinn	SN	FR	6-1	210	Southlake, TX	Southlake Carroll
91	**Jaheim Oatis**	**DL**	**SO**	**6-5**	**320**	**Columbia, MS**	**Columbia**
33	Hunter Osborne	DL	FR	6-4	275	Trussville, AL	Hewitt-Trussville
45	Robbie Ouzts	TE	JR	6-4	265	Rock Hill, SC	Rock Hill
44	Damon Payne Jr.	DL	RS-SO	6-4	303	Belleville, MI	Belleville
47	Kolby Peavy	DB	FR	6-1	180	Monroeville, AL	Excel
53	Vito Perri	LB	RS-FR	6-1	205	Alpharetta, GA	Alpharetta
97	Khurtiss Perry	DL	RS-FR	6-2	265	Pike Road, AL	Pike Road
62	Davis Peterson	OL	FR	6-1	235	Birmingham, AL	Mountain Brook
42	Yhonzae Pierre	LB	FR	6-3	223	Eufaula, AL	Eufaula
21	Jake Pope	DB	RS-FR	6-1	192	Buford, GA	Buford
49	Jax Porter	TE	RS-FR	6-6	232	Dallas, TX	IMG Academy
6	Kobe Prentice	WR	SO	5-10	182	Calera, AL	Calera
18	Shazz Preston	WR	RS-FR	6-1	202	Saint James, LA	Saint James
57	Elijah Pritchett	OL	RS-FR	6-6	312	Columbus, GA	Carver
74	**Kadyn Proctor**	**OL**	**FR**	**6-7**	**360**	**Des Moines, IA**	**Southeast Polk**
57	Chase Quigley	DL	JR	6-1	236	Libertyville, IL	Libertyville
R	**Will Reichard**	**PK**	**SR**	**6-1**	**194**	**Hoover, AL**	**Hoover**
90	Jordan Renaud	DL	FR	6-4	261	Sarasota, FL	Tyler Legacy
29	Dezz Ricks	DB	FR	6-1	182	Norfolk, VA	IMG Academy
77	Jaeden Roberts	OL	RS-SO	6-5	316	Houston, TX	North Shore
34	Quandarrius Robinson	LB	SR	6-5	231	Birmingham, AL	Jackson-Olin
68	Billy Roper	OL	FR	5-11	245	Huntsville, AL	Huntsville
37	Ty Roper	DB	SO	5-8	189	Foley, AL	Foley
44	Tonio Ross	DB	FR	6-2	180	Alexandria, AL	Alexandria
61	Graham Roten	OL	JR	6-3	285	Fairview, TN	Christ Presbyterian Academy
52	Alex Rozier	SN	SO	6-4	220	Hattiesburg, MS	Oak Grove
49	Qua Russaw	LB	FR	6-2	242	Montgomery, AL	Carver
33	Walter Sansing	DB	FR	5-10	160	Homewood, AL	Homewood
97	Reid Schuback	PK	JR	6-1	185	Poway, CA	Poway
99	Nick Serpa	P	SO	6-4	215	Foothill Ranch, CA	Trabuco Hills
15	Ty Simpson	QB	RS-FR	6-2	203	Martin, TN	Westview
44	Charlie Skehan	TE	SR	6-1	232	Columbia, SC	Cardinal Newman
8	DeVonta Smith	DB	JR	6-1	194	Cincinnati, OH	La Salle
47	James Smith	DL	FR	6-3	296	Montgomery, AL	Carver
58	Jordan Smith	LB	SR	5-10	210	Chelsea, AL	Chelsea
64	Mac Smith	OL	FR	6-3	270	Birmingham, AL	Mountain Brook
50	Tim Smith	DL	SR	6-4	302	Gifford, FL	Sebastian River
33	Jack Standeffer	WR	SO	5-10	160	Tuscaloosa, AL	Tuscaloosa Academy
4	Kristian Story	DB	SR	6-1	211	Lanett, AL	Lanett
31	Conor Talty	PK	FR	6-1	195	Chicago, IL	Saint Rita
57	John Thornton II	LB	FR	6-1	205	Columbus, GA	Pacelli
47	Adam Thorsland	TE	JR	6-5	232	Walhalla, SC	Walhalla
15	**Dallas Turner**	**LB**	**JR**	**6-4**	**252**	**Fort Lauderdale, FL**	**Saint Thomas Aquinas**
49	Conner Warhurst	DB	FR	6-2	190	Russellville, AL	Russellville
53	Kade Wehby	SN	JR	5-9	185	Plantation, FL	Saint Thomas Aquinas
55	Bennett Whisenhunt	LB	SR	6-1	222	Vestavia Hills, AL	Vestavia Hills
85	Lane Whisenhunt	LB	FR	6-2	285	Vestavia Hills, AL	Vestavia Hills
5	Roydell Williams	RB	SR	5-10	214	Hueytown, AL	Hueytown
37	Sam Willoughby	WR	SR	5 10	165	Vestavia Hills, AL	Vestavia Hills
39	Peyton Yates	DB	SO	5-10	180	Eads, TN	Briarcrest Christian
25	Richard Young	RB	FR	5-11	200	Lehigh Acres, FL	Lehigh Senior

Note: Starters in bold
Note: Table data from "2023 Alabama Crimson Tide Roster" (364)

Transfers

Player	School	Direction
Trey Amos	Louisiana	Incoming
Tyler Buchner	Notre Dame	Incoming
CJ Dippre	Maryland	Incoming
Jaylen Key	UAB	Incoming
Trezmen Marshall	Georgia	Incoming
Colby McNeal	Colorado State	Incoming
Aaron Anderson	LSU	Outgoing
Tanner Bowles	Kentucky	Outgoing
Jacoby Boykins	Abilene Christian	Outgoing
Tommy Brockermeyer	TCU	Outgoing
Jamil Burroughs	Miami	Outgoing
Elijah Brown	Florida Atlantic	Outgoing
Javion Cohen	Miami	Outgoing
Elijah Crockett	Cerritos College	Outgoing
JoJo Earle	TCU	Outgoing
Trequon Fegans	USC	Outgoing
Damieon George Jr.	Florida	Outgoing
Tyler Harrell	Miami	Outgoing
Traeshon Holden	Oregon	Outgoing
Braylen Ingraham	Syracuse	Outgoing
Khyree Jackson	Oregon	Outgoing
Rodney Johnson	Southern College	Outgoing
Demouy Kennedy	Colorado	Outgoing
Amari Kight	UCF	Outgoing
Christian Leary	Georgia Tech	Outgoing
Jack Martin	Houston	Outgoing
Gabe Pugh	Louisiana Tech	Outgoing
Jahquez Robinson	Colorado	Outgoing
Trey Sanders	TCU	Outgoing

Note: Table data from "2023 Alabama Crimson Tide football team" (363)

Games

09/02/23 - Alabama (4) vs Middle Tennessee State

Team	1	2	3	4	T		Passing	Rushing	Total
Middle Tennessee State	0	0	7	0	**7**		133	78	**211**
Alabama (4)	14	14	14	14	**56**		226	205	**431**

Alabama held MTSU to punts on their first three possessions. QB Jalen Milroe scored Bama's first TD of the season with a 21-yard scamper, capping off a 6-play, 63-yard drive. RB Jase McClellan followed, diving into the end zone from a yard out to finish an 11-play, 47-yard drive. After both teams punted, MTSU missed a 32-yard FG midway through the second. Alabama punted again before logging an interception (Key). Milroe found the end zone again with a 13-yard rushing touchdown, punctuating a quick, two-play, 42-yard drive in just 35 seconds (21-0). In between two more MTSU punts and just before halftime, Milroe connected with Isaiah Bond for a 47-yard touchdown strike on the first play of the drive that only took seven seconds (28-0).

Jermaine Burton kicked things off in the second half with a 48-yard touchdown reception, capping a 6-play, 75-yard drive in just 2:06. Alabama forced another punt, and Kool-Aid McKinstry returned it 33 yards to the MTSU 34-yard line. It only took Alabama two plays and 41 seconds to score again. This time, Amari Niblack hauled in a 29-yard TD pass (42-0). Both teams punted before MTSU managed to score a consolation TD, a 7-yard score which finished off an 11-play, 68-yard drive (42-7). In the fourth quarter, QBs Tyler Buchner and Ty Simpson added rushing touchdowns. Buchner scored from nine yards to finish off a 10-play, 77-yard drive to make it 49-7. Then after Blackshire recovered a fumble for the Tide, Simpson finished off a 6-play, 33-yard drive with his 1-yard run into the end zone to make the final 56-7.

Caleb Downs led the defense with eight tackles (six solo), while Deonte Lawson added seven tackles (two for loss) and a sack. The defense logged three sacks, seven tackles for loss, six QB hurries, and two turnovers. Milroe tied for the third-most total TDs (three passing, two rushing) in a single game. The Tide's trio of QBs accounted for eight of the nine TDs (three rushing and five passing). The victory extended Alabama's home winning streak to 21 games, the fourth-longest in program history. Saban remained undefeated in home openers, improving to 17-0. The Tide displayed remarkable discipline, committing just two penalties for 19 yards – a stark contrast to their average of 7.9 penalties and 68.7 penalty yards per game last season.[365]

Passing	C/ATT	YDS	AVG	TD	INT	QBR
J. Milroe	13/18	194	10.8	3	0	94
T. Buchner	3/5	27	5.4	0	0	82.9
T. Simpson	1/1	5	5	0	0	99.9
Team	17/24	226	9.4	3	0	--

Rushing	CAR	YDS	AVG	TD	LONG
J. Milroe	7	48	6.9	2	25
J. McClellan	10	39	3.9	1	20
R. Williams	7	36	5.1	0	11
J. Haynes	4	29	7.3	0	16
R. Young	5	18	3.6	0	11
J. Miller	4	14	3.5	0	6
T. Simpson	2	12	6	1	11
T. Buchner	1	9	9	1	9
Team	40	205	5.1	5	25

Interceptions	INT	YDS	TD
J. Key	1	13	0

Punting	NO	YDS	AVG	TB	IN 20	LONG
J. Burnip	3	139	46.3	0	1	53

Receiving	REC	YDS	AVG	TD	LONG
I. Bond	5	76	15.2	1	47
J. Burton	3	62	20.7	1	48
A. Niblack	2	49	24.5	1	29
K. Prentice	3	20	6.7	0	9
CJ Dippre	1	5	5	0	5
J. Hale	1	5	5	0	5
M. Benson	1	5	5	0	5
R. Williams	1	4	4	0	4
Team	17	226	13.3	3	48

Kick returns	NO	YDS	AVG	LONG	TD
K. Law	1	23	23	23	0

Punt returns	NO	YDS	AVG	LONG	TD
K. McKinstry	5	66	13.2	33	0
I. Bond	1	1	1	1	0
Team	6	67	11.2	33	0

Kicking	FG	PCT	LONG	XP	PTS
W. Reichard	0/0	0	0	7/7	7
C. Talty	0/0	0	0	1/1	1
Team	0/0	0	0	8/8	8

Note: Table data from "Alabama 56-7 Middle Tennessee (Sep 2, 2023) Box Score" (366)

09/09/23 - Alabama (3) vs Texas (11)

Team	1	2	3	4	T		Passing	Rushing	Total
Texas (11)	3	10	0	21	**34**		349	105	**454**
Alabama (3)	0	6	10	8	**24**		255	107	**362**

Texas started with a punt, then they intercepted Jalen Milroe at the Alabama 30-yard line. Texas struck first with a 32-yard field goal, but after a 12-play, 51-yard drive, Alabama's Will Reichard answered with a 42-yarder to tie the game five seconds into the second quarter. The Longhorns then took the lead when Quinn Ewers connected with Xavier Worthy for a 44-yard touchdown strike, capping a quick 4-play, 75-yard drive that only took 1:29. Alabama punted on its next possession, then Texas extended its lead to 13-3 with another field goal, this one from 29 yards closing out a 14-play, 82-yard drive. But Reichard closed the gap to 13-6 with a 30-yard kick as time expired in the half after taking eight plays to go 54 yards in 1:34.

Alabama opened the second half with a 51-yard field goal following a 7-play drive that covered 42 yards (Bama down 13-9). After trading punts, Texas missed a 42-yard field goal attempt. Alabama punted on its next possession before stopping the Longhorns on a 4th-and-2 from the Alabama 42-yard line. The Tide finally took their first lead of the game when Jalen Milroe found Jermaine Burton for a 49-yard touchdown, ending a 5-play, 59-yard drive (16-13).

Trailing by three entering the fourth quarter, the Longhorns exploded with three touchdowns in under six minutes to seal the victory. The first was a touchdown pass from Ewers for 7 yards, capping a 7-play, 75-yard drive to regain the lead 20-16. Then after an interception, they added a 5-yard rushing score just 15 seconds later (27-16). Milroe brought Alabama within three with a 39-yard touchdown strike to Amari Niblack ending a 6-play, 75-yard drive plus a successful two-point conversion (27-24). But the Longhorns answered with a 7-play, 75-yard drive, scoring on a 39-yard pass, bringing the final score to 34-24.

For Alabama, Caleb Downs and Trezman Marshall led the defense with ten tackles each, while Deontae Lawson added eight. Will Reichard's 51-yard field goal was his sixth career kick of 50+ yards, moving him to second on Alabama's all-time list behind Van Tiffin (7). He now has 442 career points, placing him 23rd on the NCAA's all-time scoring list. The loss was Alabama's first at home since November 9, 2019, their first non-conference home defeat since 2007, and just Nick Saban's third regular-season loss to a non-conference opponent during his tenure. It also snapped a 57-game winning streak against non-conference foes in the regular season and ended the Tide's 21-game home winning streak, the fourth-longest in Bryant-Denny Stadium history. Saban is now 28-3 when facing one of his former assistants.[367]

Passing	C/ATT	YDS	AVG	TD	INT	QBR
J. Milroe	14/27	255	9.4	2	2	63.8

Rushing	CAR	YDS	AVG	TD	LONG
J. McClellan	12	45	3.8	0	15
J. Milroe	15	44	2.9	0	20
R. Williams	6	12	2	0	5
J. Miller	2	6	3	0	5
Team	35	107	3.1	0	20

Kicking	FG	PCT	LONG	XP	PTS
W. Reichard	3/3	100	51	1/1	10

Punting	NO	YDS	AVG	TB	IN 20	LONG
J. Burnip	5	263	52.6	0	3	61

Receiving	REC	YDS	AVG	TD	LONG
K. Prentice	5	68	13.6	0	28
J. Burton	2	58	29	1	49
A. Niblack	2	45	22.5	1	39
I. Bond	1	34	34	0	34
M. Benson	2	33	16.5	0	27
J. McClellan	1	12	12	0	12
R. Williams	1	5	5	0	5
Team	14	255	18.2	2	49

Kick returns	NO	YDS	AVG	LONG	TD
K. Law	1	18	18	18	0

Punt returns	NO	YDS	AVG	LONG	TD
K. McKinstry	1	-6	-6	-6	0

Note: Table data from "Texas 34-24 Alabama (Sep 9, 2023) Box Score" (368)

09/16/23 - Alabama (10) at South Florida

Team	1	2	3	4	T		Passing	Rushing	Total
Alabama (10)	0	3	7	7	**17**		107	203	**310**
South Florida	3	0	0	0	**3**		87	177	**264**

The Alabama Crimson Tide bounced back from a disappointing performance in their previous game, securing a 17-3 victory over the South Florida Bulls. The game was marked by a strong defensive effort from the Tide, who limited the Bulls to just a single field goal and forced multiple turnovers. Jalen Milroe was benched and did not play in this game. Tyler Buchner started, but he was benched soon after, and Ty Simpson finished the game. The first half was a defensive battle, with both teams struggling to find their offensive rhythm. After trading punts on their opening possessions, Alabama fumbled deep in its own territory, allowing South Florida to take an early 3-0 lead with a 44-yard field goal. The rest of the half consisted of three punts by Bama and USF punting once and turning it over on downs twice. Alabama capitalized on a turnover, evening the score at 3-3 with a 30-yard field goal from Will Reichard. The game was delayed for 54 minutes at the 12:44 mark of the second quarter due to a lightning delay.

South Florida turned it over on downs to start the second half, then both teams traded punts. Next, Ty Simpson orchestrated a 6-play, 84-yard scoring drive capped by a 1-yard touchdown run from Roydell Williams to give the Tide a 10-3 lead. This drive took 2:19 off the clock and the score occurred with 4:35 left in the third quarter. South Florida threatened to tie the game, but the Alabama defense held firm, stopping the Bulls on 4th-and-2 at the Tide's 21-yard line. After three more punts (two by Alabama), Malachi Moore intercepted a pass in the end zone. Simpson continued to lead the offense, engineering another 80-yard touchdown drive late in the game, culminating in his own 1-yard scoring run to make the final score 17-3.

The Alabama defense allowed just 264 total yards and a first quarter field goal after a muffed punt deep in Alabama's territory. They also recorded four sacks and ten tackles for loss. Deontae Lawson led the way with ten total tackles, including one sack and 1.5 tackles for loss, while Dallas Turner had a monster game with 2.5 sacks and seven total tackles, including five solo stops.

Roydell Williams had a career day, rushing for 129 yards and a touchdown on 17 carries (7.6 yards per carry). The Tide's ground game was dominant, amassing 203 yards on 42 carries (4.8 yards per rush). Placekicker Will Reichard continued his ascent up the NCAA All-Time Career Points List, adding five points to his total (now 448) and moving to No. 18 on the list. The Crimson Tide has not lost consecutive regular season games since 2007.[369]

Passing	C/ATT	YDS	AVG	TD	INT	QBR
T. Simpson	5/9	73	8.1	0	0	15.2
T. Buchner	5/14	34	2.4	0	0	10.5
Team	10/23	107	4.7	0	0	--

Rushing	CAR	YDS	AVG	TD	LONG
R. Williams	17	129	7.6	1	48
J. McClellan	13	74	5.7	0	19
T. Buchner	2	11	5.5	0	8
J. Miller	1	1	1	0	1
T. Simpson	9	-12	-1.3	1	10
Team	42	203	4.8	2	48

Interceptions	INT	YDS	TD
M. Moore	1	0	0

Punting	NO	YDS	AVG	TB	IN 20	LONG
J. Burnip	8	369	46.1	3	4	60

Receiving	REC	YDS	AVG	TD	LONG
CJ Dippre	1	45	45	0	45
I. Bond	4	42	10.5	0	14
J. Burton	1	7	7	0	7
J. McClellan	1	6	6	0	6
R. Ouzts	1	5	5	0	5
R. Williams	1	2	2	0	2
M. Benson	1	0	0	0	0
Team	10	107	10.7	0	45

Kick returns	NO	YDS	AVG	LONG	TD
T. Arnold	1	22	22	22	0

Punt returns	NO	YDS	AVG	LONG	TD
K. McKinstry	1	-1	-1	-1	0

Kicking	FG	PCT	LONG	XP	PTS
W. Reichard	1/1	100	30	2/2	5

Note: Table data from "Alabama 17-3 South Florida (Sep 16, 2023) Box Score" (370)

09/23/23 - Alabama (13) vs Ole Miss (15)

Team	1	2	3	4	T		Passing	Rushing	Total
Ole Miss (15)	7	0	3	0	10		245	56	301
Alabama (13)	3	3	11	7	24		225	131	356

After holding Ole Miss to a punt, Alabama used 6:02 to take its first possession 61 yards in 11 plays as Will Reichard connected on a 48-yard field goal. Ole Miss responded in 3:02 with Jaxson Dart orchestrating a 7-play, 75-yard drive, capped by his 10-yard rushing touchdown to put the Rebels ahead 7-3. After trading punts, Jalen Milroe was intercepted in the end zone for a touchback. The Tide responded by blocking the Ole Miss punt (Ja'Corey Brooks) and Reichard connecting on his second field goal, this one from 40 yards out (Ole Miss up 7-6). The half closed after two more punts then a missed 34-yard field goal attempt by the Rebels.

The second half kicked off with Alabama marching down the field on a 9-play, 70-yard drive. Reichard kicked a 23-yard field goal giving the Tide their first lead of the game (9-7). Terrion Arnold then picked off a pass from Dart and returned it 27 yards to the AL 41. Seizing the opportunity, Milroe connected with Jalen Hale for a 33-yard touchdown strike, capping off a 6-play, 59-yard scoring drive. Ty Simpson converted the two-point attempt, extending the Tide's advantage to 17-7. Ole Miss trimmed the deficit to 17-10 when they converted a 35-yard FG. However, the momentum swung back to Bama as Jase McClellan capped a 6-play, 75-yard drive with his 8-yard rushing touchdown making the score 24-10, which ended up being the final.

Alabama's defense held Ole Miss to just ten points. Terrion Arnold recorded eight tackles (six solo), an interception, and two QB hurries. Dallas Turner wreaked havoc with two sacks and 3.5 tackles for loss, while Chris Braswell and Tim Smith added 1.5 sacks each. Jalen Milroe made a strong comeback as the starting QB, completing 17-of-21 pass attempts for a staggering 225 yards and a TD through the air. The receiving corps was led by the dynamic duo of Jalen Hale (who scored the first touchdown of his career) and Jermaine Burton. Both wideouts finished with a pair of catches, amassing 63 and 62 yards, respectively. Just a week after RB Roydell Williams eclipsed the 100-yard mark, McClellan followed suit, racking up an impressive 105 yards on 17 carries, averaging an impressive 6.2 yards per attempt. Kicker Will Reichard moved into a tie for 13th on the NCAA's all-time scoring list with a remarkable 454 career points.

Over the last eight quarters, Alabama has allowed a mere 13 points to be scored against them during this remarkable stretch. The Tide also secured their eighth consecutive victory over Ole Miss. During this stretch, the Crimson Tide has outscored the Rebels 394-187, averaging a staggering 49.3 points per game while only giving up an average of 23.4. Nick Saban improved his record to 29-3 when facing former assistants at Alabama (6-0 against Lane Kiffin).[371]

Passing	C/ATT	YDS	AVG	TD	INT	QBR
J. Milroe	17/21	225	10.7	1	1	62.8

Rushing	CAR	YDS	AVG	TD	LONG
J. McClellan	17	105	6.2	1	22
J. Milroe	16	28	1.8	0	20
R. Williams	8	21	2.6	0	6
J. Miller	1	-6	-6	0	0
Team	3	-17	-5.7	0	0
Team	45	131	2.9	1	22

Interceptions	INT	YDS	TD
T. Arnold	1	37	0

Punting	NO	YDS	AVG	TB	IN 20	LONG
J. Burnip	3	145	48.3	0	0	56

Receiving	REC	YDS	AVG	TD	LONG
J. Hale	2	63	31.5	1	33
J. Burton	2	62	31	0	54
CJ Dippre	2	28	14	0	22
R. Ouzts	1	21	21	0	21
R. Williams	3	13	4.3	0	7
J. McClellan	2	12	6	0	11
K. Law	2	11	5.5	0	11
I. Bond	1	10	10	0	10
A. Niblack	1	3	3	0	3
J. Brooks	1	2	2	0	2
Team	17	225	13.2	1	54

Punt returns	NO	YDS	AVG	LONG	TD
J. Brooks	1	4	4	4	0

Kicking	FG	PCT	LONG	XP	PTS
W. Reichard	3/3	100	48	1/1	10

Note: Table data from "Alabama 24-10 Ole Miss (Sep 23, 2023) Box Score" (372)

09/30/23 - Alabama (12) at Mississippi State

Team	1	2	3	4	T		Passing	Rushing	Total
Alabama (12)	14	17	3	6	40		164	193	357
Mississippi State	0	10	7	0	17		107	154	261

The game opened with a defensive stalemate, as both teams traded punts on their first two possessions. Alabama's offense finally found its rhythm when quarterback Jalen Milroe broke free for an electrifying 53-yard touchdown run, capping a lightning-quick 3-play, 70-yard drive in just 1:21. On Mississippi State's next possession, Chris Braswell intercepted a pass and raced 28 yards to the end zone for the first defensive touchdown of the season. The scoring continued as both teams traded field goals, with Mississippi State connecting from 31 yards out and Alabama answering from 48 yards. Alabama led 17-3 with 10:07 left in the half. The Bulldogs responded with 64-yard march in nine plays and scored their first touchdown of the game on a 15-yard quarterback keeper by Mike Wright to trim the deficit to 17-10. Alabama quickly regained control as running back Jase McClellan punched it in from two yards out to cap a methodical 12-play, 75-yard scoring drive, extending the Tide's lead to 24-10. The Crimson Tide defense then made a game-changing play, as Jihaad Campbell intercepted a pass to set up another Alabama scoring opportunity. Milroe capitalized, scampering ten yards for his second rushing touchdown of the half. As the teams headed to the locker room for halftime, Alabama held a commanding 31-10 advantage.

The second half kicked off with Mississippi State striking first, as quarterback Will Rogers found Lee for a 1-yard touchdown reception. This capped an 11-play, 75-yard opening drive for the Bulldogs. Alabama responded with Reichard drilling a 38-yard field goal to conclude a 12-play, 54-yard march, extending the Crimson Tide's lead to 34-17. Both teams then traded punts, carrying the action into the fourth quarter. Alabama's defense stepped up, stopping Mississippi State on fourth down. Capitalizing on the opportunity, Reichard split the uprights from 34 yards out, finishing a 6-play, 18-yard drive with his third field goal of the game. The Tide's momentum continued as Caleb Downs intercepted Will Rogers on the ensuing possession. Reichard remained automatic, knocking through his third consecutive field goal of the half and fourth of the game, this time from 48 yards, stretching Alabama's advantage to 40-17.

Alabama's defense logged three interceptions, eight tackles for loss, a defensive touchdown, and limited the Bulldogs to a mere 261 yards of total offense. Jihad Campbell had a career-high 14 tackles, complemented by an interception, a tackle for loss, and a half sack. Caleb Downs contributed 13 tackles, including five solo stops, and snagged an interception. Trezman Marshall added nine tackles, two tackles for loss, and 1.5 sacks. With his pick-six, Chris Braswell recorded the Tide's first defensive score of the season and the Tide's 91st non-offensive touchdown under Nick Saban. The Alabama defense's performance extended an impressive streak, marking the ninth consecutive year in which they have recorded at least one pick-six.

Jalen Milroe threw for an incredible 83.3% completion rate (10-for-12), tying for the eighth-best completion percentage in a single game (minimum of ten completions). Over his last two games as the starting quarterback, Milroe has maintained an impressive 81.8% completion percentage, connecting on 27 of his 33 passing attempts. Milroe strung together 14 consecutive completions, beginning with his final six completions against Ole Miss last week and going through his first eight passes in this game. This remarkable feat ties him for the third-longest streak of consecutive completions in Alabama's record books.

Will Reichard nailed field goals from distances of 48, 38, 34, and 48 yards, and accounted for a staggering 16 points which ties him for the third-highest single-game scoring output by a kicker in Alabama history. He also ascended to the seventh spot on the NCAA's all-time scoring list, amassing an impressive 484 career points.

Alabama's victory extended its remarkable winning streak against Mississippi State to 16 consecutive games, and it was Nick Saban's 150th SEC game victory (all-time).[373]

Passing	C/ATT	YDS	AVG	TD	INT	QBR
J. Milroe	10/12	164	13.7	0	0	97
T. Simpson	0/1	0	0	0	0	3.6
Team	10/13	164	12.6	0	0	--

Rushing	CAR	YDS	AVG	TD	LONG
J. Milroe	11	69	6.3	2	53
J. McClellan	15	63	4.2	1	12
R. Williams	10	44	4.4	0	11
J. Haynes	4	22	5.5	0	15
J. Miller	1	0	0	0	0
T. Simpson	1	-1	-1	0	0
Team	1	-4	-4	0	0
Team	43	193	4.5	3	53

Kick returns	NO	YDS	AVG	LONG	TD
K. Law	2	54	27	30	0
J. Brooks	1	19	19	19	0
Team	3	73	24.3	30	0

Punting	NO	YDS	AVG	TB	IN 20	LONG
J. Burnip	3	160	53.3	1	1	67

Receiving	REC	YDS	AVG	TD	LONG
A. Niblack	3	61	20.3	0	23
M. Benson	1	27	27	0	27
CJ Dippre	1	26	26	0	26
J. McClellan	2	25	12.5	0	19
I. Bond	1	17	17	0	17
K. Law	1	5	5	0	5
J. Brooks	1	3	3	0	3
Team	10	164	16.4	0	27

Interceptions	INT	YDS	TD
C. Braswell	1	28	1
C. Downs	1	11	0
J. Campbell	1	2	0
Team	3	3	3

Punt returns	NO	YDS	AVG	LONG	TD
K. McKinstry	1	-4	-4	-4	0

Kicking	FG	PCT	LONG	XP	PTS
W. Reichard	4/4	100	48	4/4	16

Note: Table data from "Alabama 40-17 Mississippi State (Sep 30, 2023) Box Score" (374)

394

10/07/23 - Alabama (11) at Texas A&M

Team	1	2	3	4	T	Passing	Rushing	Total
Alabama (11)	3	7	14	2	26	321	23	344
Texas A&M	3	14	0	3	20	239	67	306

Texas A&M received the kickoff and drove down to the AL 19 where the Tide stopped them on 4th-and-1. After an Alabama punt, Texas A&M put together a 7-play, 39-yard drive to score a 22-yard FG. Alabama answered with one of their own from 39 yards, capping a 6-play, 49-yard drive. After holding the Aggies to a punt, Bama scored the first TD of the game nine seconds into the second quarter. The drive only took 2:06 to go 66 yards in five plays, ending with Jalen Milroe connecting with Isaiah Bond for a 52-yard TD strike (10-3). The two teams traded punts, and Ainias Smith returned Bama's punt 46 yards to the Bama 22. They scored on the next play to tie the game at 10-10. After an Alabama punt, Moss scored on a 1-yard rushing touchdown to end an 11-play, 53-yard drive. Bama punted again and were down 17-10 at the half.

Milroe threw an interception on the opening drive of the second half, but the Tide's defense answered with a pick of their own, courtesy of Caleb Downs. Milroe then found Jermaine Burton for a 15-yard TD capping a 6-play, 39-yard drive, tying the game at 17-17. After forcing another Aggie punt, Milroe connected with Burton for another touchdown, this time on a 19-yard reception finishing a 6-play, 80-yard drive (Bama up 24-17). In the fourth quarter, after an Aggie punt, Burton fumbled giving A&M the ball on the AL 29-yard line. They went three-and-out and missed a field goal. After an Alabama punt, the defense scored two points with a sack for a safety, putting them up 26-17. Bama punted again, then the Aggies scored for the last time - a field goal to complete a 5-play, 62-yard drive. Alabama won, 26-20.

In the second half, the Alabama defense limited the Aggies to three points and 103 total yards of offense. Keenan III led the team with eight tackles and a sack. Caleb Downs added seven tackles and an interception. This was the fifth time in the last six games that the defense has intercepted a pass, bringing their total to seven on the year which matches its 2022 season total (13 games). With only 67 yards allowed on the ground, Alabama has now held 20 out of its last 34 opponents (dating back to 2021) to under 100 rushing yards. During the last 19 games, they have limited ten opponents to 80 rushing yards or fewer.

Milroe amassed a career-high 321 yards passing (21-of-33) and tossed three TDs. Burton finished with nine catches for 197 yards and two scores. Bond had 96 yards receiving on seven catches and TD. Reichard extended his consecutive FG streak to 25, dating back to last year. Nick Saban improved his record against former assistants to 30-3, with a 6-1 mark specifically against Jimbo Fisher. He now boasts an impressive 199-28 record over his 17 seasons.[375]

Passing	C/ATT	YDS	AVG	TD	INT	QBR
J. Milroe	21/33	321	9.7	3	1	75.1

Rushing	CAR	YDS	AVG	TD	LONG
J. McClellan	12	45	3.8	0	15
R. Williams	6	9	1.5	0	4
J. Milroe	8	-31	-3.9	0	12
Team	26	23	0.9	0	15

Interceptions	INT	YDS	TD
C. Downs	1	0	0

Punting	NO	YDS	AVG	TB	IN 20	LONG
W. Reichard	4	165	41.3	1	1	45
J. Burnip	2	92	46	0	0	63
Team	6	257	42.8	1	1	63

Receiving	REC	YDS	AVG	TD	LONG
J. Burton	9	197	21.9	2	46
I. Bond	7	96	13.7	1	52
A. Niblack	1	12	12	0	12
J. McClellan	2	6	3	0	8
K. Prentice	1	5	5	0	5
M. Benson	1	5	5	0	5
Team	21	321	15.3	3	52

Kick returns	NO	YDS	AVG	LONG	TD
K. Law	3	80	26.7	30	0

Punt returns	NO	YDS	AVG	LONG	TD
K. McKinstry	1	-1	-1	-1	0

Kicking	FG	PCT	LONG	XP	PTS
W. Reichard	1/1	100	39	3/3	6

Note: Table data from "Alabama 26-20 Texas A&M (Oct 7, 2023) Box Score" (376)

10/14/23 - Alabama (11) vs Arkansas

Team	1	2	3	4	T		Passing	Rushing	Total
Arkansas	6	0	7	8	21		150	100	250
Alabama (11)	7	14	3	0	24		238	177	415

The game started with a defensive stalemate as both teams punted on their opening possessions. Arkansas scored first on a 7-play, 27-yard drive with a 55-yard field goal. They extended their lead with another 49-yard field goal after Alabama's subsequent punt. However, the Crimson Tide responded when Jalen Milroe connected with Kobe Prentice for a 79-yard touchdown strike, capping off a lightning-quick 3-play, 75-yard drive that lasted just 1:07. Arkansas punted on its next three possessions while Alabama scored two touchdowns between them. Milroe showcased his dual-threat abilities, scoring on a 1-yard rushing touchdown to cap a 10-play, 83-yard drive. He then found Amari Niblack for a 29-yard receiving touchdown, finishing off a 5-play, 64-yard drive. Alabama took a commanding 21-6 lead into halftime.

The second half began with each team trading punts, then Alabama extended its lead on a Will Reichard 30-yard field goal after a 7-play, 77-yard drive. After trading punts again, Arkansas scored a 5-yard touchdown pass from KJ Jefferson to Sategna, capping a 10-play, 77-yard drive. The Razorbacks continued their comeback, scoring again after an Alabama punt. Jefferson threw a 14-yard touchdown pass followed by a successful two-point conversion ending a 9-play, 69-yard drive, narrowing the score to 24-21 with almost 11 minutes remaining. Both teams punted one more time, and Alabama was up by three with the ball with 5:05 left in the game. They milked the clock taking the ball down to the Arkansas 30-yard line where they were able to kneel it to secure the victory.

The Alabama Crimson Tide's defense limited the Arkansas Razorbacks to a mere 250 yards of total offense. Jaylen Key led the charge with a commanding performance, racking up seven tackles, including 1.5 tackles for loss. Caleb Downs complemented Key's efforts, contributing seven tackles of his own, with six solo stops. Jalen Milroe's 79-yard touchdown pass to Kobe Prentice not only represented the longest scoring connection of Milroe's young career, but also marked the 29th time in the storied history of the Crimson Tide that they have unleashed a scoring play of 79+ yards. The last time Alabama fans witnessed such an explosive scoring play was two years ago when Bryce Young and Jameson Williams connected for a 94-yard touchdown against Miami in 2021.

Will Reichard broke the SEC all-time career points record with his 481st point. He now has 485 career points, ranking seventh on the NCAA all-time scoring list, and has made an impressive 26 consecutive field goals. This victory was Nick Saban's 200th at Alabama, and his remarkable record now stands at an outstanding 200-28, translating to a staggering 87.7% winning percentage. He has now beaten Arkansas every year since his arrival 17 years ago.[377]

Passing	C/ATT	YDS	AVG	TD	INT	QBR
J. Milroe	10/21	238	11.3	2	0	67.7

Rushing	CAR	YDS	AVG	TD	LONG
J. McClellan	16	83	5.2	0	18
R. Williams	7	68	9.7	0	35
J. Miller	4	40	10	0	19
J. Haynes	2	11	5.5	0	10
J. Milroe	11	-19	-1.7	1	7
Team	2	-6	-3	0	0
Team	42	177	4.2	1	35

Punting	NO	YDS	AVG	TB	IN 20	LONG
J. Burnip	7	349	49.9	1	2	59

Receiving	REC	YDS	AVG	TD	LONG
K. Prentice	2	93	46.5	1	79
J. Burton	2	60	30	0	44
A. Niblack	2	43	21.5	1	29
J. Brooks	1	25	25	0	25
I. Bond	1	8	8	0	8
J. McClellan	1	5	5	0	5
M. Benson	1	4	4	0	4
Team	10	238	23.8	2	79

Punt returns	NO	YDS	AVG	LONG	TD
K. McKinstry	1	11	11	11	0

Kicking	FG	PCT	LONG	XP	PTS
W. Reichard	1/1	100	30	3/3	6

Note: Table data from "Alabama 24-21 Arkansas (Oct 14, 2023) Box Score" (378)

10/21/23 - Alabama (11) vs Tennessee (17)

Team	1	2	3	4	T		Passing	Rushing	Total
Tennessee (17)	13	7	0	0	**20**		271	133	**404**
Alabama (11)	0	7	17	10	**34**		220	138	**358**

Tennessee took the opening kickoff and quickly scored when quarterback Joe Milton III threw a 39-yard touchdown pass, culminating an 8-play, 75-yard drive that lasted 2:21. After three punts, including two by Alabama, the Volunteers extended their lead with a 24-yard field goal, the result of a 15-play, 79-yard drive. Deep in his own territory, Jalen Milroe was sacked, he fumbled, and Tennessee recovered. Five plays later, Tennessee added to its lead with a second field goal, giving them a 13-0 advantage with just 11 seconds remaining in the first quarter.

After both teams exchanged punts, Alabama scored its first touchdown when Milroe connected with Jermaine Burton for a 10-yard reception, ending a 9-play, 59-yard drive. The Tide defense then stopped Tennessee on a 4th-and-1 attempt from their own 34-yard line. However, Alabama failed to capitalize as Milroe was intercepted in the end zone with 3:10 left in the half. Tennessee finished the half strong, scoring a 6-yard receiving touchdown when Milton III found Castles, the result of a 10-play, 80-yard drive lasting 2:58. At halftime, Tennessee led 20-7.

Alabama wasted no time in the second half as they scored in just 41 seconds on two plays when Milroe hit Isaiah Bond for a 45-yard touchdown strike. After holding TN to a punt, Will Reichard kicked a 42-yard field goal to end a 6-play, 46-yard drive to bring the Tide within three (20-17). After another 4th-and-1 stop at the TN 47, Jase McClellan scored five plays later (from five yards out), giving Bama its first lead (24-20). Following another Vols punt, the Tide entered the fourth quarter with a 56-yard, 7:51 drive capped by Reichard's second field goal, increasing their lead to 27-20. On Tennessee's next possession, Jihaad Campbell capitalized on a fumble resulting from a quarterback sack, taking it 24 yards to the end zone. There was no more scoring, and Alabama came out on top 34-20 with a dominate second half comeback, outscoring Tennessee 27-0 in the final 30 minutes.

Deontae Lawson led the defense with 12 tackles, while Jihaad Campbell contributed ten tackles and a fumble recovery that he returned for a TD. Bama's defense recorded eight tackles for loss, four sacks, and four pass breakups. This marked their 92nd non-offensive TD under Saban and the second of the season. Jalen Milroe had a strong outing, completing 14-of-21 passes for 220 yards and two TDs, marking the fifth time in seven starts this season that he has reached at least 220 yards and two TDs. Jase McClellan led the ground attack, accounting for 115 of the Tide's 138 total rushing yards. Will Reichard extended his streak to 28 consecutive field goals and climbed to No. 5 on the NCAA all-time career points list with 495. Coach Saban improved his record to 16-1 against Tennessee as Alabama's head coach and 21-2 when avenging a previous loss. This season, Alabama has dominated the third quarter, outscoring opponents 79-24.[379]

Passing	C/ATT	YDS	AVG	TD	INT	QBR
J. Milroe	14/21	220	10.5	2	1	72.6

Rushing	CAR	YDS	AVG	TD	LONG
J. McClellan	27	115	4.3	1	29
R. Williams	6	20	3.3	0	5
J. Milroe	9	3	0.3	0	15
Team	42	138	3.3	1	29

Kicking	FG	PCT	LONG	XP	PTS
W. Reichard	2/2	100	50	4/4	10

Punting	NO	YDS	AVG	TB	IN 20	LONG
J. Burnip	5	218	43.6	1	2	52

Receiving	REC	YDS	AVG	TD	LONG
I. Bond	3	77	25.7	1	46
J. Burton	4	62	15.5	1	22
K. Law	2	38	19	0	34
M. Benson	1	17	17	0	17
CJ Dippre	1	15	15	0	15
J. McClellan	1	6	6	0	6
A. Niblack	1	5	5	0	5
R. Williams	1	0	0	0	0
Team	14	220	15.7	2	46

Kick returns	NO	YDS	AVG	LONG	TD
K. Law	1	21	21	21	0

Punt returns	NO	YDS	AVG	LONG	TD
K. McKinstry	1	-7	-7	-7	0

Note: Table data from "Alabama 34-20 Tennessee (Oct 21, 2023) Box Score" (380)

397

11/04/23 - Alabama (8) vs LSU (14)

Team	1	2	3	4	T		Passing	Rushing	Total
LSU (14)	7	14	7	0	28		272	206	478
Alabama (8)	14	7	14	7	42		219	288	507

Following Alabama's punt on their initial possession, both teams exchanged touchdowns. LSU took the lead when Jayden Daniels connected with Malik Nabers for a 46-yard touchdown reception, culminating a 5-play, 85-yard drive that took 2:42. Jalen Milroe responded with a 23-yard rushing touchdown, capping a 5-play, 76-yard drive that lasted 2:28. LSU attempted a 4th-and-1 conversion from Alabama's 42-yard line, but the Alabama defense stopped them. Milroe scored his second rushing touchdown, ending a 9-play, 58-yard drive, giving Alabama a 14-7 lead at the end of the first quarter. Both teams missed field goals (LSU from 46 and Bama from 47). Daniels then scored on a 9-yard rushing touchdown, concluding an 8-play, 71-yard drive, tying the game at 14-14. Milroe secured his third score of the half with a 21-yard rushing touchdown, finishing a 9-play, 74-yard drive. LSU countered as Lacy caught a 26-yard touchdown pass, closing out a 5-play, 75-yard drive that took just 56 seconds. The score was tied at 21-21 at halftime.

LSU began the second half with a strong push, as Josh Williams scored a 2-yard rushing touchdown, culminating a 9-play, 75-yard drive. Alabama answered as Roydell Williams crossed the goal line from 16 yards out, completing a 9-play, 70-yard drive to tie the game at 28-28. After forcing an LSU punt, Milroe added his fourth touchdown of the game, scoring an 11-yard rush to cap a 6-play, 68-yard drive, giving Alabama a 35-28 lead. On LSU's subsequent drive and less than a minute into the fourth quarter, Alabama intercepted Daniels at the LSU 27-yard line. Jase McClellan then extended the Tide's lead with a 10-yard rushing touchdown, their sixth of the night, increasing the lead to 42-28. LSU punted on its next drive, Alabama missed another field goal (from 43 yards out), then Bama held LSU scoreless for the final 4:21 of the game.

Caleb Downs led the defensive charge with a game-high 13 tackles, nine of which were solo stops. The Alabama defense demonstrated remarkable resilience in the second half, limiting LSU to just seven points. This impressive feat marked the seventh occasion this season, out of nine games, where the Tide has restricted their opponents to seven or fewer points in the second half.

Jalen Milroe led Alabama to victory over LSU with an impressive performance, amassing 374 total yards and four rushing touchdowns. Notably, his 155 rushing yards rank fifth among Alabama quarterbacks in a single game, while his four rushing touchdowns set a new record for Bama QBs. The Tide's ground attack was further bolstered by Jase McClellan (14 carries for 63 yards) and Roydell Williams (six carries for 56 yards), both of whom scored touchdowns. The team averaged 6.3 yards per carry, with 46 attempts, and finished with a season-high 288 yards and six touchdowns on the ground.

The 507 yards of total offense marks the 63rd time in the last 78 games that Alabama has gained 400 or more yards of total offense and the 50th time they have scored 40+ points during that span. Will Reichard made history by becoming the fourth collegiate football player to break the 500-point barrier in a career, accumulating an impressive 502 points and climbing to third place on the NCAA's all-time scoring leaders list.

Saban's victory marked a significant milestone as he improved his record to 22-2 in games where he avenged a previous loss (last season's 32-31 overtime defeat in Baton Rouge). Additionally, he surpassed Vince Dooley, the former head coach of Georgia, for the second-most wins at a single school, reaching a total of 202 victories. Saban now trails only the legendary Paul "Bear"

Bryant, who holds the record with 232 wins (also at Alabama). This season, Saban also achieved a perfect 4-0 record in SEC home games, marking the 10th time he has led Alabama to an unbeaten home record in conference play.[381]

Passing	C/ATT	YDS	AVG	TD	INT	QBR
J. Milroe	15/23	219	9.5	0	0	96.2

Rushing	CAR	YDS	AVG	TD	LONG
J. Milroe	20	155	7.8	4	23
J. McClellan	14	63	4.5	1	10
R. Williams	6	56	9.3	1	16
J. Miller	4	17	4.3	0	10
Team	2	-3	-1.5	0	0
Team	46	288	6.3	6	23

Kick returns	NO	YDS	AVG	LONG	TD
K. Law	3	77	25.7	30	0
R. Ouzts	1	11	11	11	0
Team	4	88	22	30	0

Punting	NO	YDS	AVG	TB	IN 20	LONG
J. Burnip	1	50	50	50	1	50

Receiving	REC	YDS	AVG	TD	LONG
I. Bond	5	60	12	0	21
J. McClellan	1	42	42	0	42
J. Miller	1	35	35	0	35
J. Burton	3	29	9.7	0	12
K. Law	2	25	12.5	0	16
K. Prentice	1	22	22	0	22
CJ Dippre	1	11	11	0	11
R. Williams	1	-5	-5	0	0
Team	15	219	14.6	0	42

Interceptions	INT	YDS	TD
T. Arnold	1	10	0

Kicking	FG	PCT	LONG	XP	PTS
W. Reichard	0/2	0	0	6/6	6

Note: Table data from "Alabama 42-28 LSU (Nov 4, 2023) Box Score" (382)

11/11/23 - Alabama (8) at Kentucky

Team	1	2	3	4	T		Passing	Rushing	Total
Alabama (8)	21	7	7	14	49		285	159	444
Kentucky	7	0	7	7	21		158	95	253

Alabama got on the board first when Jalen Milroe connected with Amari Niblack for a 26-yard touchdown, capping off a 10-play, 80-yard drive. After forcing Kentucky to punt, Milroe only needed 1:51 to score again when he linked up with Kobe Prentice for a 40-yard touchdown, concluding a 4-play, 55-yard drive. On the first play of Kentucky's next possession, Terrion Arnold forced a fumble that Caleb Downs recovered and returned to the 1-yard line. Milroe rushed it in for the score (21-0). He came off the field limping in what looked like a significant injury, but he somehow ended up being ok. Kool-Aid McKinstry muffed Kentucky's next punt, and the Cats recovered the ball on the Alabama 32-yard line. They capitalized on the mistake with Devin Leary finding Tayvion Robinson for a 6-yard touchdown, ending a 6-play, 32-yard drive. That brought the score to 21-7, which was the score after one quarter of play when Alabama punted to end the quarter. Kentucky punted to start the second quarter, then Milroe extended a play to find Roydell Williams for a 27-yard touchdown, completing a 5-play, 62-yard drive (28-7). The Wildcats drove down to the Alabama 9-yard line but failed to convert on 4th-and-2. Both teams punted after they both threw interceptions to end the half.

Kentucky began the second half with a strong push, driving 75 yards in ten plays scoring on a 2-yard rushing touchdown by Ray Davis. The Tide answered with a 65-yard drive in nine plays with Milroe capping it off from three yards out to score his second rushing touchdown of the game, extending their lead to 35-14. Bama scored again in between two Kentucky punts as Milroe scored his third rushing touchdown just 12 seconds into the fourth quarter. He ran it in from a yard out, capping an 8-play, 38-yard drive that increased Bama's lead to 42-14. Both teams scored touchdowns again after another Kentucky punt. Jam Miller scored from three yards out, capping off a 7-play, 66-yard drive that included a nice 51-yard pass from Ty Simpson to Jalen Hale as well as a 9-yard first-down run by Simpson on 3rd-and-8. Then Davis scored his second touchdown of the game, which came on a one-yard rush that concluded a 4-play, 75-yard drive that included a Ramon Jefferson run for 74 yards (Caleb Downs ran him down and tackled him at the 1-yard line). The Crimson Tide secured a decisive 49-21 victory.

Caleb Downs spearheaded the defensive effort, amassing 12 total tackles, which included five solo tackles and a half-sack. Jihaad Campbell contributed significantly with seven tackles, including one tackle for loss, and he also secured a fumble recovery that led to a 1-yard touchdown. Additionally, Campbell recorded a pass breakup and a quarterback hurry.

Jalen Milroe continued his impressive performance, leading the team to victory. Following his outstanding display against LSU the week before, where he accumulated 374 total yards and four touchdowns, he achieved a remarkable six total touchdowns, consisting of three rushing and three passing, tying for the second-most by any Alabama player in a single game in program history. In the game, Milroe threw for 234 yards and three touchdowns while rushing eight times for 36 yards and three additional scores. His six touchdowns matched the achievements of Bryce Young against Utah State in 2022 and Tua Tagovailoa against Auburn in 2018 for the second-most by any Alabama player in program history. In his last two outings, Milroe has amassed a remarkable 644 total yards and ten touchdowns, with seven of those coming via the ground and three through the air.

Meanwhile, Nick Saban remains undefeated against Kentucky while coaching at Alabama, boasting a flawless 5-0 record.[383]

Passing	C/ATT	YDS	AVG	TD	INT	QBR
J. Milroe	15/22	234	10.6	3	1	93.8
T. Simpson	1/3	51	17	0	0	99.4
Team	16/25	285	11.4	3	1	--

Rushing	CAR	YDS	AVG	TD	LONG
J. McClellan	9	43	4.8	0	17
J. Milroe	8	36	4.5	3	16
J. Haynes	6	33	5.5	0	14
R. Williams	6	20	3.3	0	8
J. Miller	6	11	1.8	1	6
T. Simpson	1	9	9	0	9
R. Young	2	4	2	0	3
I. Bond	1	3	3	0	3
Team	39	159	4.1	4	17

Kicking	FG	PCT	LONG	XP	PTS
W. Reichard	0/0	0	0	7/7	7

Punting	NO	YDS	AVG	TB	IN 20	LONG
W. Reichard	2	96	48	0	2	55
J. Burnip	1	40	40	0	0	40
Team	3	136	45.3	0	2	55

Receiving	REC	YDS	AVG	TD	LONG
K. Prentice	4	74	18.5	1	40
J. Hale	1	51	51	0	51
A. Niblack	2	38	19	1	26
R. Williams	2	30	15	1	26
CJ Dippre	1	30	30	0	30
I. Bond	2	24	12	0	17
M. Benson	1	15	15	0	15
K. Law	1	11	11	0	11
J. Miller	1	8	8	0	8
J. McClellan	1	4	4	0	4
Team	16	285	17.8	3	51

Kick returns	NO	YDS	AVG	LONG	TD
K. Law	2	52	26	26	0
R. Williams	2	51	25.5	34	0
Team	4	103	25.8	34	0

Interceptions	INT	YDS	TD
T. Arnold	1	0	0

Punt returns	NO	YDS	AVG	LONG	TD
K. McKinstry	2	22	11	27	0

Note: Table data from "Alabama 49-21 Kentucky (Nov 11, 2023) Box Score" (384)

11/18/23 - Alabama (8) vs Chattanooga

Team	1	2	3	4	T		Passing	Rushing	Total
Chattanooga	0	7	3	0	10		107	126	233
Alabama (8)	21	17	14	14	66		259	315	574

Alabama scored TDs on their first three possessions while the Mocs were forced to punt on theirs. Jermaine Burton bookended the first drive starting with a 56-yard catch and finishing with a 5-yarder. The 4-play, 67-yard drive only took Alabama 1:47. Jase McClellan scored a 2-yard rushing TD ending a 5-play, 70-yard drive in 2:37. And Roydell Williams followed with an 11-yard score ending an 11-play, 90-yard drive (21-0). Chattanooga punted to close out the first quarter. Both teams punted to start the second, then Milroe found Robbie Ouzts for a 7-yard TD on a 3-play, 55-yard drive that only took 1:15. Kristian Story intercepted the Mocs on their next possession which led to a Will Reichard a 50-yard field goal (31-0). Both teams scored TDs to end the half. Appleberry scored the Mocs' first points of the game when he ripped off a 40-yard rushing TD capping off a 6-play, 75-yard drive. Then Milroe connected with Malik Benson for a 20-yard touchdown finishing off a 5-play, 60-yard drive. Alabama led 38-7 at halftime.

The Mocs scored a 23-yard field goal on their opening possession of the second half, culminating a 9-play, 69-yard drive. Ty Simpson entered the game at QB, and Alabama responded in just two minutes with a TD of its own when Justice Haynes scored from a yard out, concluding a 6-play, 55-yard drive (45-10). After forcing a punt, Caleb Downs took it 85 yards for a TD (52-10). The Mocs punted the rest of the game, and Alabama scored two more times. In the fourth, it only took 1:12 for Bama to go 80 yards as Richard Young reached the end zone from a yard out. Finally, Justice Haynes took one in from 33 yards to make the final 66-10.

Downs logged an 85-yard punt return for a TD (Bama's sixth in the last seven years), seven tackles, and a pass breakup. Jihaad Campbell led with ten tackles (six solo), and a pass breakup. This was Bama's 93rd non-offensive TD under Saban. Milroe tied for fifth on the school's all-time list with 13 consecutive completed passes before being pulled early in the third. Reichard set a new school record with his eighth field goal of 50+ this season. Alabama extended its NCAA record of consecutive 10-win seasons to 16 straight. They amassed 574 yards of offense, including a season-high 315 yards on the ground. Their 66 points were the highest in a single game since 2019. Saban improved his record at Bryant-Denny Stadium to 108-9 (92.3%).[385]

Passing	C/ATT	YDS	AVG	TD	INT	QBR
J. Milroe	13/16	197	12.3	3	0	88.3
T. Simpson	4/6	50	8.3	0	0	99.4
D. Lonergan	2/2	12	6	0	0	94.3
Team	19/24	259	10.8	3	0	--

Receiving	REC	YDS	AVG	TD	LONG
J. Burton	3	105	35	1	56
K. Law	2	32	16	0	31
J. Hale	1	29	29	0	29
A. Niblack	2	24	12	0	19
M. Benson	3	23	7.7	1	20
I. Bond	4	23	5.8	0	10
C. Adams	2	11	5.5	0	7
R. Ouzts	1	7	7	1	7
D. Lewis Jr.	1	5	5	0	5
Team	19	259	13.6	3	56

Rushing	CAR	YDS	AVG	TD	LONG
T. Simpson	1	78	78	0	78
J. Miller	6	77	12.8	0	45
J. McClellan	6	62	10.3	1	28
R. Williams	7	52	7.4	1	15
J. Haynes	5	42	8.4	2	33
D. Lonergan	1	5	5	0	5
R. Young	2	2	1	1	1
J. Milroe	3	-1	-0.3	0	5
Team	2	-2	-1	0	0
Team	33	315	9.5	5	78

Kick returns	NO	YDS	AVG	LONG	TD
K. Law	1	33	33	33	0
D. Lewis Jr.	1	14	14	14	0
R. Ouzts	1	11	11	11	0
Team	3	58	19.3	33	0

Punt returns	NO	YDS	AVG	LONG	TD
C. Downs	2	90	45	85	1
K. McKinstry	1	6	6	6	0
Team	3	96	32	85	1

Interceptions	INT	YDS	TD
K. Story	1	2	0

Kicking	FG	PCT	LONG	XP	PTS
W. Reichard	1/1	100	50	9/9	12

Punting	NO	YDS	AVG	TB	IN 20	LONG
J. Burnip	2	89	44.5	1	0	47

Note: Table data from "Alabama 66-10 Chattanooga (Nov 18, 2023) Box Score" (386)

11/25/23 - Alabama (8) at Auburn

Team	1	2	3	4	T		Passing	Rushing	Total
Alabama (8)	7	10	3	7	27		259	192	451
Auburn	7	7	7	3	24		93	244	337

The Crimson Tide drew first blood following an Auburn punt as Roydell Williams scored from two yards out, culminating an 8-play, 69-yard drive. The Tigers responded after both teams exchanged punts when Damari Alston scored from four yards out, concluding a 5-play, 68-yard drive. Will Reichard converted a 32-yard field goal within the first minute of the second quarter to finish off a 12-play, 56-yard drive to put Bama up 10-7. Both teams traded punts, then touchdowns. Auburn capped off a 3-play, 88-yard drive with a 12-yard score. Immediately following, Jalen Milroe linked up with Jermaine Burton for a 68-yard touchdown reception, concluding a 3-play, 81-yard drive in just 44 seconds. Both teams exchanged punts before Auburn attempted a Hail Mary pass which was intercepted by Terrion Arnold as the first half came to a close with Alabama leading 17-14.

Alabama began the second half by scoring a 22-yard field goal from Reichard, marking his second successful kick of the day. This capped off a 12-play, 71-yard drive. Auburn quickly countered with a 27-yard touchdown pass, capping off a 5-play, 75-yard drive. The score gave Auburn a 21-20 advantage with 6:36 left in the third quarter. Alabama drove down to the Auburn 24-yard line but missed its field goal attempt before Auburn drove 72 yards and scored a 21-yard field goal giving them a 24-20 lead. Both teams punted, and Alabama had the ball on its own 18-yard line with 6:19 left in the game. After a three-and-out, they punted with 4:48 left on the clock, Auburn muffed it, and Alabama recovered. During their final drive, Milroe ran for 19 yards on 3rd-and-20 bringing up 4th-and-1 from the Auburn 10-yard line. They lined up for a quarterback sneak, but instead tossed it to Roydell Williams who picked up the first down which brought up 1st-and-goal from the 7-yard line with 1:43 left in the game. After a loss of one on the first play, a bad snap lost them 18 more. On third down, Alabama was penalized for an illegal forward pass. This brought up 4th-and-31 with 32 seconds left on the clock. Milroe dropped back, Auburn only rushed two, he had plenty of time, then he fired it to the back corner of the end zone where Isiah Bond got his foot down for the 31-yard game winning score. There were 32 seconds left on the clock, but everything ended when Alabama picked off the final pass of the game. Alabama won in dramatic fashion by a score of 27-24.

On the defensive front, Jalen Key made a strong return to the lineup, leading the University of Alabama with seven tackles. Deontae Lawson, also back in action after an absence, secured five total tackles, including a sack. Dallas Turner added to the defensive effort with four tackles, two of which were for loss, a sack, and a quarterback hurry. The combined efforts of Lawson and Turner helped the Crimson Tide finish the day with six tackles for loss and four sacks.

Isaiah Bond led the team in receptions, securing five catches for 75 yards and a touchdown, while Jermaine Burton tallied four catches for a team-high 107 yards and a score. Will Reichard has now tied the NCAA career points record with Keenan Reynolds (Navy) at 530 points. Additionally, he has moved into second place on Alabama's all-time field goals list with 80, trailing only Leigh Tiffin's record of 83.

Under the leadership of head coach Nick Saban, Alabama secured its 19th fourth-quarter comeback victory. This win also marked Saban's 15th time to record an 11-win season (and 13th straight, the longest streak of its kind in SEC history). The team concluded the season with a flawless 8-0 record in SEC play, marking the sixth time they have achieved a perfect conference finish during Saban's tenure.[387]

Passing	C/ATT	YDS	AVG	TD	INT	QBR
J. Milroe	16/24	259	10.8	2	0	89.6

Rushing	CAR	YDS	AVG	TD	LONG
J. Milroe	18	107	5.9	0	37
J. McClellan	15	66	4.4	0	11
R. Williams	8	30	3.8	1	11
J. Miller	2	7	3.5	0	5
Team	1	-18	-18	0	0
Team	44	192	4.4	1	37

Interceptions	INT	YDS	TD
T. Arnold	2	22	0

Punting	NO	YDS	AVG	TB	IN 20	LONG
J. Burnip	5	211	42.2	0	0	58

Receiving	REC	YDS	AVG	TD	LONG
J. Burton	4	107	26.8	1	68
I. Bond	5	75	15	1	31
M. Benson	1	33	33	0	33
A. Niblack	2	24	12	0	18
K. Law	3	12	4	0	6
J. McClellan	1	8	8	0	8
Team	16	259	16.2	2	68

Kick returns	NO	YDS	AVG	LONG	TD
K. Law	1	17	17	17	0

Punt returns	NO	YDS	AVG	LONG	TD
C. Downs	2	-3	-1.5	0	0

Kicking	FG	PCT	LONG	XP	PTS
W. Reichard	2/3	66.7	32	3/3	9

Note: Table data from "Alabama 27-24 Auburn (Nov 25, 2023) Box Score" (388)

12/02/23 - Alabama (8) vs Georgia (1)

Team	1	2	3	4	T		Passing	Rushing	Total
Georgia (1)	7	0	3	14	24		243	78	321
Alabama (8)	3	14	3	7	27		192	114	306

After an Alabama punt, Georgia opened the scoring when Milton rushed for a 17-yard touchdown, culminating an 8-play, 83-yard drive. After trading punts, Alabama responded with a 43-yard field goal, concluding an 8-play drive. After holding the Bulldogs to another punt, Jalen Milroe orchestrated a 10-play, 92-yard drive, ending in an 18-yard touchdown pass to Jam Miller. This put Alabama ahead 10-3 early in the second quarter. After driving down to the Alabama 31-yard line with a 13-play drive, Georgia missed a 50-yard field goal attempt. On Alabama's next possession, Milroe connected with Jermaine Burton for a 15-yard touchdown, concluding a 9-play, 69-yard drive. This extended Alabama's lead to 17-7 at the half.

After both teams punted to start the second half, Georgia hit a 34-yard field goal finishing off a 5-play, 54-yard drive that lasted 1:45. Alabama was forced to punt again, and then Trezmen Marshall recovered a Carson Beck fumble on the Georgia 11-yard line. After going three-and-out, Reichard connected on a 28-yard field goal to make it 20-10. Both teams punted to start the fourth quarter. The Bulldogs scored first in the fourth on a 1-yard rushing touchdown by Carson Beck, capping a 4-play, 35-yard drive. Alabama responded with a 1-yard rushing touchdown by Roydell Williams, concluding a 9-play, 75-yard drive to extend its lead to 27-17. Georgia countered with a 1-yard touchdown run by Milton up the middle, finishing a 10-play, 75-yard drive to narrow the deficit to 27-24. Alabama then managed the clock effectively to secure its 30th SEC Championship, marking Nick Saban's ninth title in the conference and his fourth undefeated record against Georgia in SEC Championship games.

Terrion Arnold stood out on defense for Alabama, recording six total tackles, including half a tackle for loss, and a pass breakup. Malachi Moore and Trezmen Marshall also made significant contributions, each with five tackles and one tackle for loss. Marshall also added a crucial fumble recovery to his stats. Jalen Milroe was named the game's MVP after guiding the team to its 11th consecutive win. He had an impressive performance, amassing 221 total yards, including 192 passing yards on 13-of-23 attempts and two touchdowns. Will Reichard made history by becoming the NCAA's all-time career leader in points with 539, surpassing the previous record of 530 set by Keenan Reynolds. Under Coach Saban, Alabama has enjoyed remarkable success in Atlanta, boasting an 18-1 record and an impressive 17-game winning streak. Notably, nine of his first year starting quarterbacks have maintained their starting position for at least ten games in a season. Furthermore, all but one of those quarterbacks have secured SEC Championships in their inaugural season, with A.J. McCarron being the only exception. While at Alabama, Saban has beaten eight No. 1 teams (NCAA record).[389]

Passing	C/ATT	YDS	AVG	TD	INT	QBR
J. Milroe	13/23	192	8.3	2	0	75.4

Rushing	CAR	YDS	AVG	TD	LONG
R. Williams	16	64	4	1	12
J. Milroe	14	29	2.1	0	30
J. Miller	9	23	2.6	0	8
Team	2	-2	-1	0	0
Team	41	114	2.8	1	30

Kicking	FG	PCT	LONG	XP	PTS
W. Reichard	2/2	100	43	3/3	9

Punting	NO	YDS	AVG	TB	IN 20	LONG
J. Burnip	5	233	46.6	0	3	60

Receiving	REC	YDS	AVG	TD	LONG
I. Bond	5	79	15.8	0	22
J. Miller	1	28	28	1	28
J. Burton	2	28	14	1	15
K. Prentice	1	19	19	0	19
A. Niblack	1	17	17	0	17
CJ Dippre	1	12	12	0	12
R. Williams	1	9	9	0	9
K. Law	1	0	0	0	0
Team	13	192	14.8	2	28

Kick returns	NO	YDS	AVG	LONG	TD
K. Law	1	0	0	0	0

Note: Table data from "Alabama 27-24 Georgia (Dec 2, 2023) Box Score" (390)

01/01/24 - Alabama (4) at Michigan (1)

Team	1	2	3	4	OT	T		Passing	Rushing	Total
Alabama (4)	7	3	0	10	0	20		116	172	**288**
Michigan (1)	7	6	0	7	7	27		221	130	**351**

On the first play of the game, Caleb Downs intercepted the pass by Michigan, however, it was reviewed and determined that his foot was out of bounds. Both teams punted on their first possessions, and Quandarrius Robinson recovered the muffed punt by Michigan. This led to a Jase McClellan score on a 34-yard run, capping a 4-play, 44-yard drive. Michigan responded with a 10-play, 75-yard drive, culminating in an 8-yard touchdown pass from J.J. McCarthy. The next five possessions were all punts (three by Alabama). Michigan took the lead for the first time when McCarthy connected with Tyler Morris for a 38-yard touchdown, finishing an 8-play, 83-yard drive. The extra point attempt was missed, leaving the score at 13-7 with 3:49 remaining in the half. Alabama's Will Reichard kicked a 50-yard field goal to end the first half, with Michigan leading 13-10.

The third quarter consisted of all punts, then Alabama regained the lead when McClellan scored on a 3-yard run, concluding an 8-play, 55-yard drive (17-13). After forcing a Michigan punt, Milroe fumbled on the second play of the next drive, and Michigan recovered. However, they missed a 49-yard FG. Reichard extended Alabama's lead to 20-13 with a 52-yard field goal, capping a 9-play, 35-yard drive with only 4:41 remaining in the game. Michigan drove 75 yards in eight plays and scored on a 4-yard passing play to even the score with less than two minutes remaining. Alabama punted with 54 seconds left on the clock, and Michigan fumbled it around the 10-yard line. The Wolverines recovered it near the goal line and were tackled for what appeared to be a safety. However, it was ruled down at the 1-yard line, and they kept possession. With 35 seconds left in regulation, Michigan just ran the clock out to send the game to overtime. Michigan scored on the second play in its overtime possession. Alabama had 4th-and-goal on the 3-yard line, but a bad snap didn't give Milroe much of a chance, and he was stopped short.

Caleb Downs led the defense with an impressive 14 tackles and a pass breakup. Kool-Aid McKinstry also made an impact, racking up ten tackles, while Deontae Lawson contributed six tackles and two crucial pass breakups. Meanwhile, Will Reichard surpassed Leigh Tiffin to become the all-time leader in career field goals. Reichard now boasts an impressive 84 career field goals, one more than Tiffin's 83. He concluded his career as the NCAA's all-time scoring leader with 547 points. Michigan finished the season undefeated and as National Champions, with Alabama being the only team able to take them to overtime. This marked Alabama's eighth Rose Bowl appearance where they hold a 5-2-1 record. The loss was Nick Saban's first in a CFP Semifinal since 2014, ending a streak of six consecutive Semifinal wins.[391]

Passing	C/ATT	YDS	AVG	TD	INT	QBR
J. Milroe	16/23	116	5	0	0	45.1

Rushing	CAR	YDS	AVG	TD	LONG
J. McClellan	14	87	6.2	2	34
J. Milroe	21	63	3	0	18
J. Haynes	4	31	7.8	0	11
J. Miller	1	11	11	0	11
R. Williams	1	-1	-1	0	0
Team	2	-19	-9.5	0	0
Team	43	172	4.0	2	34

Kicking	FG	PCT	LONG	XP	PTS
W. Reichard	2/2	100	52	2/2	8

Punting	NO	YDS	AVG	TB	IN 20	LONG
J. Burnip	7	352	50.3	0	5	62

Receiving	REC	YDS	AVG	TD	LONG
I. Bond	4	47	11.8	0	29
J. Burton	4	21	5.3	0	11
CJ Dippre	2	15	7.5	0	11
K. Prentice	1	13	13	0	13
J. McClellan	2	11	5.5	0	6
A. Niblack	1	6	6	0	6
J. Miller	1	2	2	0	2
K. Law	1	1	1	0	1
Team	16	116	7.3	0	29

Kick returns	NO	YDS	AVG	LONG	TD
K. Law	2	30	15	16	0

Punt returns	NO	YDS	AVG	LONG	TD
A. Kite	1	0	0	0	0

Note: Table data from "Michigan 27-20 Alabama (Jan 1, 2024) Box Score" (392)

Season Stats

Record	12-2	6th of 133
SEC Record	9-0	
Rank	5	
Points for	479	
Points against	269	
Points/game	34.2	24th of 133
Opp points/game	19.2	16th of 133
SOS[17]	6.58	3rd of 133

Team stats (averages per game)

Split	G	Passing					Rushing				Total Offense		
		Cmp	Att	Pct	Yds	TD	Att	Yds	Avg	TD	Plays	Yds	Avg
Offense	14	14.9	23.2	64	220.4	1.6	40.1	172.6	4.3	2.3	63.3	393.1	6.2
Defense	14	17.5	29.5	59.3	191.1	1.2	33.6	124.9	3.7	1.1	63.1	316	5
Difference		-2.6	-6.3	4.7	29.3	0.4	6.5	47.7	0.6	1.2	0.2	77.1	1.2

Split	First Downs				Penalties		Turnovers		
	Pass	Rush	Pen	Tot	No.	Yds	Fum	Int	Tot
Offense	8.9	9.9	1.3	20	5.6	46.8	0.4	0.4	0.8
Defense	8.1	6.8	1.4	16.3	5.1	39.2	0.5	0.9	1.4
Difference	0.8	3.1	-0.1	3.7	0.5	7.6	-0.1	-0.5	-0.6

Passing

Rk	Player	G	Passing								
			Cmp	Att	Pct	Yds	Y/A	AY/A	TD	Int	Rate
1	Jalen Milroe	13	187	284	65.8	2834	10	10.6	23	6	172.2
2	Ty Simpson	6	11	20	55	179	9	9	0	0	130.2
3	Tyler Buchner	2	8	19	42.1	61	3.2	3.2	0	0	69.1
4	Dylan Lonergan	1	2	2	100	12	6	6	0	0	150.4

Rushing and receiving

Rk	Player	G	Rushing					Receiving				Scrimmage			
			Att	Yds	Avg	TD	Rec	Yds	Avg	TD	Plays	Yds	Avg	TD
1	Jase McClellan	13	180	890	4.9	8	15	137	9.1	0	195	1027	5.3	8
2	Jalen Milroe	13	161	531	3.3	12					161	531	3.3	12
3	Roydell Williams	14	111	560	5	5	11	58	5.3	1	122	618	5.1	6
4	Jam Miller	14	41	201	4.9	1	4	73	18.3	1	45	274	6.1	2
5	Justice Haynes	13	25	168	6.7	2					25	168	6.7	2
6	Ty Simpson	6	14	86	6.1	2					14	86	6.1	2
7	Richard Young	3	9	24	2.7	1					9	24	2.7	1
8	Tyler Buchner	2	3	20	6.7	1					3	20	6.7	1
9	Dylan Lonergan	1	1	5	5	0					1	5	5	0
10	Isaiah Bond	14	1	3	3	0	48	668	13.9	4	49	671	13.7	4
11	Jermaine Burton	13					39	798	20.5	8	39	798	20.5	8
12	Amari Niblack	14					20	327	16.4	4	20	327	16.4	4
13	Kobe Prentice	13					18	314	17.4	2	18	314	17.4	2
14	Kendrick Law	13					15	135	9	0	15	135	9	0
15	Malik Benson	14					13	162	12.5	1	13	162	12.5	1
16	CJ Dippre	14					11	187	17	0	11	187	17	0
17	Jalen Hale	13					5	148	29.6	1	5	148	29.6	1
18	Robbie Ouzts	14					3	33	11	1	3	33	11	1
19	Ja'Corey Brooks	9					3	30	10	0	3	30	10	0
20	Cole Adams	2					2	11	5.5	0	2	11	5.5	0
21	Danny Lewis	14					1	5	5	0	1	5	5	0

Defense and fumbles

Rk	Player	G	Tackles					Def Int					Fumbles		
			Solo	Ast	Tot	Loss	Sk	Int	Yds	Avg	TD	PD	FR	TD	FF
1	Caleb Downs	14	70	37	107	3.5	0	2	11	5.5	0	4	1	0	1
2	Deontae Lawson	11	32	35	67	5.5	3					4			
3	Jihaad Campbell	13	34	32	66	4	0.5	1	2	2	0	3	2	1	0
4	Justin Eboigbe	14	29	35	64	11.5	7					1			
5	Terrion Arnold	14	40	23	63	6.5	1	5	69	13.8	0	12			1
6	Jaylen Key	12	35	25	60	1.5	0	1	13	13	0	1			
7	Trezmen Marshall	13	27	29	56	4.5	2.5						1	0	0
8	Dallas Turner	14	28	25	53	14.5	10					1			2
9	Malachi Moore	13	30	22	52	5	0	1	0	0	0	5			
10	Chris Braswell	14	16	26	42	10.5	8	1	28	28	1	1			3
11	Tim Keenan III	14	17	21	38	1.5	1					1			
12	Kool-Aid McKinstry	14	24	8	32	2	0					7			
13	Tim Smith	14	15	16	31	2	2								
14	Jaheim Oatis	13	9	17	26	1	0.5					2			
15	Quandarrius Robinson	14	16	8	24	2.5	1.5						1	0	0
16	Kendrick Blackshire	8	9	7	16	1	0						1	0	1
17	Kristian Story	13	9	6	15	1	0	1	2	2	0	2			
18	Trey Amos	14	6	6	12	0.5	0					5			
19	Damon Payne Jr.	14	1	8	9	1	0.5								
20	Jah-Marien Latham	14	2	6	8	1.5	1.5					1			
21	Justin Jefferson	14	3	1	4	0	0								1
22	Keanu Koht	3	2	2	4	1.5	0								
23	Jam Miller	14	3	1	4	0	0								
24	Devonta Smith	4	3	1	4	0	0								
25	Roydell Williams	14	3	1	4	0	0								
26	Jeremiah Alexander	14	1	2	3	0	0								
27	Shawn Murphy	13	2	1	3	0	0								
28	Jordan Renaud	2	0	3	3	0.5	0								
29	James Smith	9	1	1	2	0	0						1	0	0
30	CJ Dippre	14	2	0	2	0	0								
31	Emmanuel Henderson	9	1	1	2	0	0								
32	Kendrick Law	13	1	1	2	0	0								
33	Earl Little	8	1	1	2	0	0								
34	Malik Benson	14	1	0	1	0	0								
35	Ja'Corey Brooks	9	1	0	1	0	0								
36	Justice Haynes	13	1	0	1	0	0								
37	Kneeland Hibbett	14	0	1	1	0	0								
38	Edric Hill	2	1	0	1	0	0								
39	Bray Hubbard	9	1	0	1	0	0								
40	Jalen Milroe	13	1	0	1	0	0								
41	Tony Mitchell	7	0	1	1	0	0								
42	Conor Talty	3	1	0	1	0	0								

Kick and punt returns

Rk	Player	G	Kick Ret				Punt Ret			
			Ret	Yds	Avg	TD	Ret	Yds	Avg	TD
1	Kendrick Law	13	17	405	23.8	0				
2	Roydell Williams	14	2	51	25.5	0				
3	Robbie Ouzts	14	2	22	11	0				
4	Terrion Arnold	14	1	22	22	0				
5	Ja'Corey Brooks	9	1	19	19	0				
6	Danny Lewis	14	1	14	14	0				
7	Kool-Aid McKinstry	14					14	86	6.1	0
8	Caleb Downs	14					4	87	21.8	1
9	Isaiah Bond	14					1	1	1	0
10	Antonio Kite	7					1	0	0	0

Kicking and punting

Rk	Player	G	Kicking							Punting		
			XPM	XPA	XP%	FGM	FGA	FG%	Pts	Punts	Yds	Avg
1	Will Reichard	14	55	55	100	22	25	88	121	4	165	41.3
2	Conor Talty	3	1	1	100	0	0		1			
3	James Burnip	14								59	2806	47.6

Scoring

Rk	Player	G	Touchdowns							Kicking				Pts
			Rush	Rec	Int	FR	PR	KR	Tot	XPM	FGM	2PM	Sfty	
1	Will Reichard	14								55	22			121
2	Jalen Milroe	13	12						12					72
3	Jase McClellan	13	8						8					48
4	Jermaine Burton	13		8					8					48
5	Roydell Williams	14	5	1					6					36
6	Isaiah Bond	14		4					4			1		26
7	Amari Niblack	14		4					4					24
8	Ty Simpson	6	2						2			1		14
9	Jam Miller	14	1	1					2					12
10	Justice Haynes	13	2						2					12
11	Kobe Prentice	13		2					2					12
12	Jihaad Campbell	13			1				1					6
13	Tyler Buchner	2	1						1					6
14	Robbie Ouzts	14		1					1					6
15	Richard Young	3	1						1					6
16	Malik Benson	14		1					1					6
17	Jalen Hale	13		1					1					6
18	Chris Braswell	14				1			1					6
19	Caleb Downs	14					1		1					6
20	Conor Talty	3								1				1

Stats include bowl games
Note: Table data from "2023 Alabama Crimson Tide Stats" (17)

Awards and honors

Name	Award	Type
Jalen Milroe	Permanent Team Captain	Team
Malachi Moore	Permanent Team Captain	Team
Dallas Turner	Permanent Team Captain	Team
Jalen Milroe	MVP	Team
Jermaine Burton	Offensive Player of the Year	Team
Jase McClellan	Offensive Player of the Year	Team
Jalen Milroe	Offensive Player of the Year	Team
Kool-Aid McKinstry	Defensive Player of the Year	Team
Dallas Turner	Defensive Player of the Year	Team
Dallas Turner	Defensive Player of the Year	SEC
Will Reichard	Special Teams Player of the Year	SEC
Caleb Downs	Freshman of the Year	SEC
Tyler Booker	AP All-SEC First Team	SEC
JC Latham	AP All-SEC First Team	SEC
Kool-Aid McKinstry	AP All-SEC First Team	SEC
Will Reichard	AP All-SEC First Team	SEC
Dallas Turner	AP All-SEC First Team	SEC
Terrion Arnold	AP All-SEC Second Team	SEC
Chris Braswell	AP All-SEC Second Team	SEC
Caleb Downs	AP All-SEC Second Team	SEC
Justin Eboigbe	AP All-SEC Second Team	SEC
Jalen Milroe	AP All-SEC Second Team	SEC
Terrion Arnold	Coaches' All-SEC First Team	SEC
Caleb Downs	Coaches' All-SEC First Team	SEC
Justin Eboigbe	Coaches' All-SEC First Team	SEC
Kneeland Hibbett	Coaches' All-SEC First Team	SEC
JC Latham	Coaches' All-SEC First Team	SEC
Kool-Aid McKinstry	Coaches' All-SEC First Team	SEC
Will Reichard	Coaches' All-SEC First Team	SEC
Dallas Turner	Coaches' All-SEC First Team	SEC
Tyler Booker	Coaches' All-SEC Second Team	SEC
James Burnip	Coaches' All-SEC Second Team	SEC
Will Reichard	Coaches' All-SEC Second Team	SEC
Caleb Downs	Freshman All SEC Team	SEC

Name	Award	Type
Kadyn Proctor	Freshman All SEC Team	SEC
Dallas Turner	AFCA All-American First Team	National
Terrion Arnold	AFCA All-American Second Team	National
Kool-Aid McKinstry	AFCA All-American Second Team	National
Terrion Arnold	AP All-America First Team	National
Kool-Aid McKinstry	AP All-America First Team	National
Dallas Turner	AP All-America First Team	National
Caleb Downs	AP All-America Second Team	National
JC Latham	AP All-America Second Team	National
Will Reichard	AP All-America Second Team	National
Dallas Turner	Consensus All-American	National
Dallas Turner	FWAA All-America First Team	National
JC Latham	FWAA All-America Second Team	National
Kool-Aid McKinstry	Sporting News (TSN) All-America Team	National
Dallas Turner	Sporting News (TSN) All-America Team	National
Terrion Arnold	Sporting News (TSN) All-America Second Team	National
Caleb Downs	Sporting News (TSN) All-America Second Team	National
JC Latham	Sporting News (TSN) All-America Second Team	National
Will Reichard	Sporting News (TSN) All-America Second Team	National
JC Latham	Walter Camp All-America Second Team	National
Kool-Aid McKinstry	Walter Camp All-America Second Team	National
Dallas Turner	Walter Camp All-America Second Team	National
Chris Braswell	Senior Bowl	All-Star Team
Justin Eboigbe	Senior Bowl	All-Star Team
Will Reichard	Senior Bowl	All-Star Team

Note: Table data from "2023 Alabama Crimson Tide football team" (363), "Jumbo Package: Alabama names permanent captains" (393), "2024 Senior Bowl Roster" (394)

NFL

Season	Year drafted	Round	Pick	Overall	Player	Position	Team
2023	2024	1	7	7	JC Latham	OT	Tennessee Titans
2023	2024	1	17	17	Dallas Turner	DE	Minnesota Vikings
2023	2024	1	24	24	Terrion Arnold	CB	Detroit Lions
2023	2024	2	9	41	Kool-Aid McKinstry	CB	New Orleans Saints
2023	2024	2	25	57	Chris Braswell	LB	Tampa Bay Buccaneers
2023	2024	3	16	80	Jermaine Burton	WR	Cincinnati Bengals
2023	2024	4	5	105	Justin Eboigbe	DT	Los Angeles Chargers
2023	2024	6	10	186	Jase McClellan	RB	Atlanta Falcons
2023	2024	6	27	203	Will Reichard	K	Minnesota Vikings
2023	2024	7	37	257	Jaylen Key	S	New York Jets

Note: Table data from "2024 NFL Draft" (395)

Player Career Stats

Passing

Player	G	Passing							
		Cmp	Att	Pct	Yds	Y/A	AY/A	TD	Int
Jake Coker[396]	20	301	452	66.6	3513	7.8	8.1	25	8
Jalen Hurts[397]	42	445	707	62.9	5626	8.0	8.6	48	12
Mac Jones[398]	31	413	556	74.3	6126	11.0	12.5	56	7
A.J. McCarron[399]	53	686	1026	66.9	9019	8.8	9.6	77	15
Greg McElroy[400]	35	436	658	66.3	5691	8.6	9.2	39	10
Jalen Milroe[401]	25	221	344	64.2	3172	9.2	9.7	29	9
Blake Sims[402]	37	275	430	64.0	3731	8.7	9.0	30	10
Tua Tagovailoa[403]	32	474	684	69.3	7442	10.9	12.7	87	11
John Parker Wilson[404]	45	665	1175	56.6	7924	6.7	6.4	47	30
Bryce Young[405]	36	624	949	65.8	8356	8.8	9.9	80	12

Rushing and Receiving

Running Backs and Quarterbacks

Player	Rushing				Receiving				Scrimmage			
	Att	Yds	Avg	TD	Rec	Yds	Avg	TD	Plays	Yds	Avg	TD
Glen Coffee[406]	410	2107	5.1	14	42	351	8.4	2	452	2458	5.4	16
Jake Coker[396]	81	81	1	2	0	0	0	0	81	81	1	2
Kenyan Drake[407]	233	1495	6.4	18	46	570	12	4	279	2065	7.4	22
Jalston Fowler[408]	113	738	6.5	5	19	150	7.9	7	132	888	6.7	12
Jahmyr Gibbs[409]	151	926	6.1	7	44	444	10	3	195	1370	7	10
Terry Grant[410]	257	1167	4.5	12	33	259	7.8	1	290	1426	4.9	13
Damien Harris[411]	477	3070	6.4	23	52	407	7.8	2	529	3477	6.6	25
Najee Harris[412]	638	3843	6	46	80	781	9.8	11	718	4624	6.4	57
Derrick Henry[413]	602	3591	6	42	17	285	17	3	619	3876	6.3	45
Jalen Hurts[397]	381	1976	5.2	23	3	15	5	0	384	1991	5.2	23
Mark Ingram II[414]	572	3261	5.7	42	60	670	11	4	632	3931	6.2	46
Joshua Jacobs[415]	251	1491	5.9	16	48	571	12	5	299	2062	6.9	21
Jimmy Johns[416]	121	564	4.7	2	4	57	14	0	125	621	5	2
Mac Jones[398]	54	42	0.8	2	2	-9	-4.5	0	56	33	0.6	2
Eddie Lacy[417]	355	2402	6.8	30	35	338	9.7	2	390	2740	7	32
A.J. McCarron[399]	119	-50	-0.4	3	0	0	0	0	119	-50	-0.4	3
Jase McClellan[418]	355	1981	5.6	18	40	409	10	6	395	2390	6.1	24
Greg McElroy[400]	114	71	0.6	2	0	0	0	0	114	71	0.6	2
Jalen Milroe[401]	207	851	4.1	13	0	0	0	0	207	851	4.1	13
Trent Richardson[419]	540	3130	5.8	35	68	730	11	7	608	3860	6.3	42
Brian Robinson Jr.[420]	545	2704	5	30	52	446	8.6	2	597	3150	5.3	32
Bo Scarbrough[421]	267	1512	5.7	20	21	131	6.2	0	288	1643	5.7	20
Blake Sims[402]	150	705	4.7	9	2	18	9	0	152	723	4.8	9
Tua Tagovailoa[403]	107	340	3.2	9	0	0	0	0	107	340	3.2	9
Roy Upchurch[422]	168	923	5.5	9	28	224	8	1	196	1147	5.9	10
Roydell Williams[423]	234	1165	5	11	21	152	7.2	2	255	1317	5.2	13
John Parker Wilson[404]	238	175	0.7	11	1	-4	-4	0	239	171	0.7	11
T.J. Yeldon[424]	576	3322	5.8	37	46	494	11	2	622	3816	6.1	39
Bryce Young[405]	139	162	1.2	7	0	0	0	0	139	162	1.2	7

411

Wide Receivers

Player	Receiving				Rushing				Scrimmage			
	Rec	Yds	Avg	TD	Att	Yds	Avg	TD	Plays	Yds	Avg	TD
Kenny Bell[425]	50	879	17.6	6	0	0	0	0	50	879	17.6	6
Jahleel Billingsley[426]	37	559	15.1	6	1	-3	-3	0	38	556	14.6	6
Chris Black[427]	25	290	11.6	2	1	31	31	1	26	321	12.3	3
Slade Bolden[428]	68	712	10.5	4	6	11	1.8	0	74	723	9.8	4
Isaiah Bond[429]	65	888	13.7	5	1	3	3	0	66	891	13.5	5
Ja'Corey Brooks[430]	57	896	15.7	10	0	0	0	0	57	896	15.7	10
Jermaine Burton[431]	79	1475	18.7	15	0	0	0	0	79	1475	18.7	15
Amari Cooper[432]	228	3463	15.2	31	6	51	8.5	0	234	3514	15	31
Preston Dial[433]	30	318	10.6	3	0	0	0	0	30	318	10.6	3
Gehrig Dieter[434]	15	214	14.3	4	0	0	0	0	15	214	14.3	4
Miller Forristall[435]	44	505	11.5	5	1	1	1	0	45	506	11.2	5
Robert Foster[436]	35	389	11.1	3	2	7	3.5	0	37	396	10.7	3
D.J. Hall[437]	194	2923	15.1	17	9	59	6.6	0	203	2982	14.7	17
Darius Hanks[438]	84	1150	13.7	7	2	7	3.5	0	86	1157	13.5	7
Hale Hentges[439]	15	124	8.3	6	0	0	0	0	15	124	8.3	6
Traeshon Holden[440]	46	570	12.4	7	0	0	0	0	46	570	12.4	7
O.J. Howard[441]	114	1726	15.1	7	0	0	0	0	114	1726	15.1	7
Jerry Jeudy[442]	159	2742	17.2	26	1	1	1	0	160	2743	17.1	26
Christion Jones[443]	85	1030	12.1	7	5	36	7.2	0	90	1066	11.8	7
Julio Jones[444]	179	2653	14.8	15	10	139	14	2	189	2792	14.8	17
Cameron Latu[445]	56	787	14.1	12	0	0	0	0	56	787	14.1	12
Kendrick Law[446]	23	238	10.3	0	0	0	0	0	23	238	10.3	0
Marquis Maze[447]	136	1844	13.6	8	14	17	1.2	0	150	1861	12.4	8
John Metchie III[448]	155	2081	13.4	14	1	8	8	0	156	2089	13.4	14
Richard Mullaney[449]	38	390	10.3	5	0	0	0	0	38	390	10.3	5
Amari Niblack[450]	21	342	16.3	5	0	0	0	0	21	342	16.3	5
Kevin Norwood[451]	81	1275	15.7	12	0	0	0	0	81	1275	15.7	12
Colin Peek[452]	26	313	12	3	0	0	0	0	26	313	12	3
Kobe Prentice[453]	49	651	13.3	4	0	0	0	0	49	651	13.3	4
Calvin Ridley[454]	224	2781	12.4	19	8	40	5	1	232	2821	12.2	20
Henry Ruggs III[455]	98	1716	17.5	24	2	75	38	1	100	1791	17.9	25
Cam Sims[456]	41	467	11.4	2	0	0	0	0	41	467	11.4	2
Brad Smelley[457]	54	559	10.4	4	1	1	1	0	55	560	10.2	4
DeVonta Smith[458]	235	3965	16.9	46	10	21	2.1	1	245	3986	16.3	47
Irv Smith Jr.[459]	58	838	14.4	10	0	0	0	0	58	838	14.4	10
Ardarius Stewart[460]	129	1713	13.3	12	13	82	6.3	0	142	1795	12.6	12
Jaylen Waddle[461]	106	1999	18.9	17	4	17	4.3	0	110	2016	18.3	17
Deandrew White[462]	139	162	1.2	7	0	0	0	0	139	162	1.2	7
Jameson Williams[463]	79	1572	19.9	15	3	23	7.7	0	82	1595	19.5	15
Michael Williams[464]	51	503	9.9	7	0	0	0	0	51	503	9.9	7

Defense

Player	Pos	G	Tackles					Def Int					Fumbles			
			Solo	Ast	Tot	Loss	Sk	Int	Yds	Avg	TD	PD	FR	Yds	TD	FF
Christopher Allen[475]	LB	19	34	20	54	18.5	6.5	0	0	0	0	0	1	0	0	3
Jonathan Allen[476]	LB/DL	50	78	74	152	44.5	28	0	75	0	1	6	3	30	1	3
Eryk Anders[477]	LB	45	52	46	98	19	8.5	1	0	0	0	1	0	0	0	2
Ryan Anderson[478]	LB	44	68	60	128	39.5	19	1	26	26	1	3	6	0	0	6
Will Anderson Jr.[479]	LB	41	114	90	204	58.5	35	1	25	25	1	4	0	0	0	1
Javier Arenas[480]	DB	42	104	50	154	17.5	7	6	88	15	1	0	0	0	0	0
Jalyn Armour-Davis[481]	DB	15	22	13	35	1	0	3	51	17	0	6	0	0	0	0
Terrion Arnold[482]	DB	25	74	34	108	7.5	1	6	90	15	0	20	1	0	0	1
Anthony Averett[483]	DB	31	71	27	98	7	2	1	30	30	0	16	0	0	0	2
Christian Barmore[484]	DL	22	34	29	63	15.5	10	0	0	0	0	5	0	0	0	3
Mark Barron[485]	DB	42	149	86	235	13	5	12	145	12	1	11	1	0	0	1
Jordan Battle[486]	DB	54	143	109	252	6.5	1	6	156	26	3	10	1	0	0	0
Deion Belue[487]	DB	22	45	15	60	7.5	0	3	43	14	0	3	0	57	1	0
Brian Branch[488]	DB	38	111	61	172	19.5	4	4	32	8	0	23	1	0	0	0
Chris Braswell[489]	LB	41	31	44	75	15.5	11	1	28	28	1	1	0	0	0	4
Tony Brown[490]	DB	39	56	30	86	4.5	0.5	3	9	3	0	5	0	0	0	1
Isaiah Buggs[491]	DL	28	43	60	103	17.5	11	0	0	0	0	3	1	0	0	2
Jihaad Campbell[492]	LB	22	34	33	67	4	0.5	1	2	2	0	3	2	24	1	0
Shyheim Carter[493]	DB	35	56	44	100	6	0	3	89	30	2	18	0	0	0	2
Simeon Castille[494]	DB	48	103	59	162	14	4.5	12	105	8.8	1	0	0	0	0	0
Josh Chapman[495]	DL	49	44	44	88	13.5	2.5	0	0	0	0	4	0	0	0	0
Ha Ha Clinton-Dix[496]	DB	38	58	40	98	4	0	7	115	16	0	15	0	0	0	1
Terrence Cody[497]	DL	26	19	33	52	10.5	0.5	0	0	0	0	1	0	0	0	1
Landon Collins[498]	DB	41	122	62	184	8.5	0	5	103	21	1	13	4	0	0	3
DJ Dale[499]	DL	39	33	40	73	10.5	5.5	0	0	0	0	3	3	0	0	0
Marcell Dareus[500]	DL	25	39	27	66	20	11	1	28	28	1	4	0	0	0	0
Raekwon Davis[501]	DL	43	67	108	175	19.5	12	1	19	19	0	0	1	0	0	1
Brandon Deaderick[502]	DL	41	34	47	81	13	7	0	0	0	0	0	0	0	0	0
Trey DePriest[503]	LB	38	114	118	232	18	2	0	0	0	0	5	2	0	0	2
Denzel Devall[504]	LB	33	35	48	83	14	6	0	0	0	0	3	0	0	0	2
Quinton Dial[505]	DL	12	20	26	46	8	2.5	0	0	0	0	0	0	0	0	0
Xzavier Dickson[506]	DL/LB	44	52	39	91	21	14	0	0	0	0	2	0	0	0	0
Trevon Diggs[507]	WR/DB	34	43	25	68	0.5	0	4	79	20	1	17	2	0	1	2
Caleb Downs[508]	DB	14	70	37	107	3.5	0	2	11	5.5	0	4	1	12	0	1
Justin Eboigbe[509]	DL	48	58	65	123	16	9	1	4	4	0	3	2	0	0	0
Rashaan Evans[510]	LB	42	84	66	150	23.5	15	0	0	0	0	5	2	0	0	2
Brandon Fanney[511]	DL	23	28	45	73	9	1	0	0	0	0	1	0	0	0	0
Minkah Fitzpatrick[512]	DB	42	110	61	171	16.5	5	9	274	30	4	24	0	0	0	2
Reuben Foster[513]	LB	45	124	99	223	24	7	0	0	0	0	9	0	0	0	0
Nick Gentry[514]	DL	29	15	29	44	7	5.5	0	0	0	0	0	0	0	0	0
Wallace Gilberry[515]	DL	38	87	73	160	46	15	0	0	0	0	4	0	0	0	3
Robby Green[516]	DB	25	26	13	39	0	0	1	0	0	0	0	0	0	0	0
Bobby Greenwood[517]	DL	39	38	49	87	16.5	8.5	0	0	0	0	1	1	5	0	1
Prince Hall[518]	LB	35	85	67	152	13.5	3	1	10	10	0	2	1	50	1	1
Da'Shawn Hand[519]	DL	34	30	41	71	14.5	9	0	0	0	0	1	0	0	0	0
Shaun Dion Hamilton[520]	LB	33	65	69	134	16	4.5	2	40	20	0	4	0	0	0	2
Christian Harris[521]	LB	40	124	96	220	26	10	1	0	0	0	6	1	0	0	2
Jerrell Harris[522]	DB/LB	38	36	23	59	4.5	0	0	0	0	0	0	0	0	0	0
Ronnie Harrison Jr.[523]	DB	42	110	64	174	7	3.5	7	112	16	1	17	2	0	1	1
DeMarcco Hellams[524]	DB	41	155	100	255	7.5	2.5	3	6	2	0	13	1	0	0	1
Dont'a Hightower[525]	LB	44	101	133	234	21	5	1	29	29	0	7	1	8	0	2
Keith Holcombe[526]	LB	27	34	37	71	3	1	0	0	0	0	5	1	0	0	0
Adrian Hubbard[527]	LB	22	47	36	83	18	10	0	0	0	0	4	0	0	0	3
Marlon Humphrey[528]	DB	29	61	20	81	6.5	0	5	46	9.2	1	13	0	0	0	3
Brandon Ivory[529]	DL	21	17	47	64	3	0	0	0	0	0	1	0	0	0	0
Eddie Jackson[530]	DB	38	94	32	126	7.5	1	9	303	34	3	12	3	0	0	2
Kareem Jackson[531]	DB	40	106	53	159	8	0	5	164	33	0	0	0	0	0	0
Anfernee Jennings[532]	OL/LB	48	98	95	193	33.5	15	2	8	4	0	18	2	0	1	3
Josh Jobe[533]	DB	41	95	34	129	3.5	2	3	6	2	0	19	1	0	0	2
Marquis Johnson[534]	DB	49	62	27	89	2	0	3	7	2.3	0	1	1	1	0	0
Nico Johnson[535]	LB	38	87	76	163	16.5	2	2	2	1	0	6	1	0	0	3
Rashad Johnson[536]	DB	38	139	77	216	12	2	11	189	17	2	0	0	0	0	0
Cyrus Jones[537]	WR/DB	49	83	23	106	7.5	1	7	49	7	0	25	2	13	1	4
Hootie Jones[538]	DB	25	47	29	76	1	0	2	65	33	0	6	0	0	0	1
Jaylen Key[539]	DB	12	35	25	60	1.5	0	1	13	13	0	1	0	0	0	0
Dre Kirkpatrick[540]	DB	38	66	25	91	8	0	3	30	10	0	16	0	0	1	3
Ezekial Knight[541]	WR/DL	41	40	32	72	12	3	2	28	14	0	0	0	0	0	1
Deontae Lawson[542]	LB	22	56	62	118	8	3	0	0	0	0	8	0	0	0	0
Dillon Lee[543]	LB	38	35	32	67	1.5	1	3	4	1.3	0	1	0	0	0	0
Shane Lee[544]	LB	18	50	45	95	8	6	1	10	10	0	0	1	0	0	3
Robert Lester[545]	DB	48	81	66	147	6.5	2.5	14	183	13	0	7	1	0	0	1
Terrell Lewis[546]	LB	14	31	16	47	13.5	7	0	0	0	0	3	0	0	0	0
Will Lowery[547]	DB	14	35	18	53	0.5	0	2	0	0	0	3	0	0	0	0
Trezmen Marshall[548]	LB	13	27	29	56	4.5	2.5	1	0	0	0	1	1	0	0	0
Phidarian Mathis[549]	DL	46	53	76	129	16	11	0	0	0	0	5	3	0	0	3
Jared Mayden[550]	DB	26	44	37	81	3	1	4	54	14	0	6	0	0	0	0
Rolando McClain[551]	LB	##	135	274	32	8	5	73	15	0	0	0	4	1	0	0
Xavier McKinney[552]	DB	32	108	67	175	13	6	5	101	20	2	15	1	0	0	6
Kool-Aid McKinstry[553]	DB	42	62	31	93	5	2	2	26	13	0	23	0	0	0	0

413

Player	Pos	G	Tackles					Def Int					Fumbles			
			Solo	Ast	Tot	Loss	Sk	Int	Yds	Avg	TD	PD	FR	Yds	TD	FF
Dequan Menzie[554]	DB	25	53	21	74	9	3.5	1	25	25	1	15	1	0	0	0
Christian Miller[555]	LB	28	25	31	56	15.5	11	0	0	0	0	2	1	0	0	0
Dee Milliner[556]	DB	39	55	26	81	5	0	6	107	18	1	17	0	0	0	1
Jaylen Moody[557]	LB	41	45	50	95	8.5	2	1	13	13	0	0	2	0	0	1
Malachi Moore[558]	DB	53	87	56	143	12.5	1.5	5	41	8.2	0	17	1	0	1	1
Dylan Moses[559]	LB	36	104	88	192	21.5	6	2	12	6	0	4	0	0	0	3
C.J. Mosley[560]	LB	52	175	142	317	23	6.5	5	93	19	3	17	0	0	0	1
Darren Mustin[561]	LB	21	55	32	87	8.5	1	2	6	3	0	0	0	0	0	0
Jaheim Oatis[562]	DL	25	19	36	55	3	1.5	0	0	0	0	4	0	0	0	0
Jeoffrey Pagan[563]	DL	18	27	33	60	7.5	3.5	0	0	0	0	0	0	0	0	1
Da'Ron Payne[564]	DL	35	39	63	102	5	3	1	21	21	0	5	2	0	1	1
Nick Perry[565]	DB	29	72	47	119	6.5	1	2	24	12	0	9	0	0	0	0
D.J. Pettway[566]	DL/LB	23	28	20	48	12.5	7	0	0	0	0	5	0	0	0	0
Reggie Ragland[567]	LB	38	117	103	220	17.5	4	1	1	1	0	10	3	0	0	4
Labryan Ray[568]	DL	36	38	38	76	14	6.5	0	0	0	0	2	0	0	0	1
Cory Reamer[569]	DB	42	47	41	88	13	3	1	8	8	0	0	0	0	0	1
Jarren Reed[570]	DL	28	39	72	111	11	2	0	0	0	0	7	1	0	0	0
Eli Ricks[571]	CB	9	8	5	13	1	0	0	0	0	0	4	0	0	0	0
A'Shawn Robinson[572]	DL	39	51	82	133	22	9	0	0	0	0	5	1	0	0	1
Drew Sanders[573]	LB	15	16	17	33	2.5	1	0	0	0	0	2	0	0	0	0
Ali Sharrief[574]	RB/DB	54	48	25	73	3.5	0	0	0	0	0	6	0	0	0	0
Geno Smith[575]	DB	36	95	50	145	5.5	0	1	16	16	0	7	1	0	0	2
Saivion Smith[576]	DB	14	6	24	60	0.5	0	3	71	24	1	5	0	0	0	1
Tim Smith[577]	DL	46	42	48	90	11.5	4.5	0	0	0	0	1	2	0	0	1
Damion Square[578]	DL	42	44	49	93	18.5	7.5	0	0	0	0	2	0	0	0	0
Ed Stinson[579]	LB/DL	48	57	47	104	15.5	5.5	0	0	0	0	2	3	0	0	1
Vinnie Sunseri[580]	DB	33	67	38	105	7	1.5	4	124	31	2	5	1	0	0	0
Patrick Surtain II[581]	DB	41	82	34	116	6	0	4	69	17	1	24	1	0	0	4
Deionte Thompson[582]	DB	29	69	43	112	4.5	0	3	86	29	0	7	1	0	0	3
Henry To'oto'o[583]	LB	28	97	108	205	15.5	6.5	0	0	0	0	1	0	0	0	1
Dalvin Tomlinson[584]	DL	38	39	83	122	10.5	4	0	0	0	0	9	0	0	0	1
Dallas Turner[585]	LB	38	58	62	120	32.5	23	0	0	0	0	1	2	11	1	2
Courtney Upshaw[586]	LB	53	88	53	141	36.5	18	1	45	45	1	4	2	45	1	6
Levi Wallace[587]	DB	20	38	21	59	4.5	2	3	66	22	1	17	0	0	0	0
Lorenzo Washington[588]	DL	40	32	37	69	12	6	0	0	0	0	0	0	0	0	0
Jarrick Williams[589]	DB	30	39	20	59	2.5	1	0	0	0	0	5	0	0	0	0
Jesse Williams[590]	DL	26	17	44	61	6.5	1.5	0	0	0	0	3	0	0	0	0
Quinnen Williams[591]	DL	24	56	35	91	26	10	0	0	0	0	1	0	0	0	0
Tim Williams[592]	LB	34	38	19	57	30	20	0	0	0	0	3	1	0	1	2
Mack Wilson[593]	LB	34	59	54	113	7	1	6	39	6.5	1	7	1	0	0	0
Justin Woodall[594]	DB	40	69	29	98	4	0	7	132	19	1	1	0	0	0	0
Daniel Wright[595]	DB	38	72	42	114	3	1	2	65	33	1	8	0	0	0	0
Byron Young[596]	DL	45	55	75	130	20	7.5	0	0	0	0	3	1	0	0	1

All-Time Stats Leaders

The following stats show the all-time leaders for Alabama, and the players in bold and italic are from the Nick Saban era. If a player played for Saban at any time, they are included as a player from the Saban era (for example, if they played from 2004-2007).

Passing

Passing Yards

Career

Rank	Player	Yards	Years
1	*A.J. McCarron*	*9,019*	*2010-2013*
2	*Bryce Young*	*8,356*	*2020-2022*
3	*John Parker Wilson*	*7,924*	*2005-2008*
4	*Tua Tagovailoa*	*7,442*	*2017-2019*
5	Brodie Croyle	6,382	2002-2005
6	*Mac Jones*	*6,126*	*2018-2020*
7	Andrew Zow	5,983	1998-2001
8	*Greg McElroy*	*5,691*	*2007-2010*
9	Jay Barker	5,689	1991-1994
10	*Jalen Hurts*	*5,626*	*2016-2018*

Single Season

Rank	Player	Yards	Year
1	*Bryce Young*	*4,872*	*2021*
2	*Mac Jones*	*4,500*	*2020*
3	*Tua Tagovailoa*	*3,966*	*2018*
4	*Blake Sims*	*3,487*	*2014*
5	*Bryce Young*	*3,328*	*2022*
6	*Jake Coker*	*3,110*	*2015*
7	*A.J. McCarron*	*3,063*	*2013*
8	*Greg McElroy*	*2,987*	*2010*
9	*A.J. McCarron*	*2,933*	*2012*
10	*John Parker Wilson*	*2,846*	*2007*

Single Game

Rank	Player	Yards	Year	Opponent
1	*Bryce Young*	*559*	*2021*	*Arkansas*
2	Scott Hunter	484	1969	Auburn
3	*Mac Jones*	*464*	*2020*	*Ohio State (CFP National Championship)*
4	*Bryce Young*	*455*	*2022*	*Tennessee*
5	*Blake Sims*	*445*	*2014*	*Florida*
6	*Tua Tagovailoa*	*444*	*2019*	*South Carolina*
7	*Mac Jones*	*435*	*2020*	*Texas A&M*
8	*Bryce Young*	*421*	*2021*	*Georgia (SEC Championship Game)*
9	*Tua Tagovailoa*	*418*	*2019*	*Ole Miss*
9	*Tua Tagovailoa*	*418*	*2019*	*LSU*

Passing Touchdowns

Career

Rank	Player	TDs	Years
1	Tua Tagovailoa	87	2017-2019
2	Bryce Young	80	2020-2022
3	A.J. McCarron	77	2010-2013
4	Mac Jones	56	2018-2020
5	Jalen Hurts	48	2016-2018
6	John Parker Wilson	47	2005-2008
7	Brodie Croyle	41	2002-2005
8	Greg McElroy	39	2007-2010
9	Mike Shula	35	1983-1986
9	Andrew Zow	35	1998-2001

Single Season

Rank	Player	TDs	Year
1	Bryce Young	47	2021
2	Tua Tagovailoa	43	2018
3	Mac Jones	41	2020
4	Tua Tagovailoa	33	2019
5	Bryce Young	32	2022
6	A.J. McCarron	30	2012
7	A.J. McCarron	28	2013
7	Blake Sims	28	2014
9	Jalen Hurts	23	2016
9	Jalen Milroe	23	2023

Single Game

Rank	Player	TDs	Year	Opponent
1	Tua Tagovailoa	6	2019	Ole Miss
2	Gary Hollingsworth	5	1989	Ole Miss
2	Tua Tagovailoa	5	2018	Auburn
2	Tua Tagovailoa	5	2019	South Carolina
2	Tua Tagovailoa	5	2019	Southern Miss
2	Mac Jones	5	2020	Auburn
2	Mac Jones	5	2020	Florida (SEC Championship Game)
2	Mac Jones	5	2020	Ohio State (CFP National Championship)
2	Bryce Young	5	2021	Southern Miss
2	Bryce Young	5	2021	New Mexico State
2	Bryce Young	5	2022	Utah State
2	Bryce Young	5	2022	Kansas State (Sugar Bowl)

Rushing

Rushing Yards

Career

Rank	Player	Yards	Years
1	*Najee Harris*	*3,843*	*2017-2020*
2	*Derrick Henry*	*3,591*	*2013-2015*
3	Shaun Alexander	3,565	1996-1999
4	Bobby Humphrey	3,420	1985-1988
5	Kenneth Darby	3,324	2003-2006
6	*T.J. Yeldon*	*3,322*	*2012-2014*
7	*Mark Ingram II*	*3,261*	*2008-2010*
8	*Trent Richardson*	*3,130*	*2009-2011*
9	*Damien Harris*	*3,073*	*2015-2018*
10	Johnny Musso	2,741	1969-1971

Single Season

Rank	Player	Yards	Year
1	*Derrick Henry*	*2,219*	*2015*
2	*Trent Richardson*	*1,679*	*2011*
3	*Mark Ingram II*	*1,658*	*2009*
4	Bobby Humphrey	1,471	1986
5	*Najee Harris*	*1,466*	*2020*
6	Shaun Alexander	1,383	1999
6	*Glen Coffee*	*1,383*	*2008*
8	Shaud Williams	1,367	2003
9	*Brian Robinson Jr.*	*1,343*	*2021*
10	Sherman Williams	1,341	1994

Single Game

Rank	Player	Yards	Year	Opponent
1	Shaun Alexander	291	1996	LSU
2	Bobby Humphrey	284	1986	Mississippi State
3	*Derrick Henry*	*271*	*2015*	*Auburn*
4	*Mark Ingram II*	*246*	*2009*	*South Carolina*
5	*Derrick Henry*	*236*	*2015*	*Texas A&M*
6	Bobby Marlow	233	1951	Auburn
7	Johnny Musso	221	1970	Auburn
8	Bobby Humphrey	220	1987	Penn State
9	*Glen Coffee*	*218*	*2008*	*Kentucky*
10	Bobby Humphrey	217	1986	Tennessee

417

Rushing Touchdowns

Career

Rank	Player	TDs	Years
1	*Najee Harris*	*46*	*2017-2020*
2	*Mark Ingram II*	*42*	*2008-2010*
2	*Derrick Henry*	*42*	*2013-2015*
4	Shaun Alexander	41	1996-1999
5	*T.J. Yeldon*	*37*	*2012-2014*
6	*Trent Richardson*	*35*	*2009-2011*
7	Johnny Musso	34	1969-1972
8	Bobby Humphrey	33	1985-1988
9	*Eddie Lacy*	*30*	*2010-2012*
10	Tony Nathan	29	1975-1978
10	*Brian Robinson Jr.*	*29*	*2017-2021*

Single Season

Rank	Player	TDs	Year
1	*Derrick Henry*	*28*	*2015*
2	*Najee Harris*	*26*	*2020*
3	*Trent Richardson*	*21*	*2011*
4	Shaun Alexander	19	1999
5	Siran Stacy	17	1989
5	*Mark Ingram II*	*17*	*2009*
5	*Eddie Lacy*	*17*	*2012*
8	Johnny Musso	16	1971
9	Cotton Clark	15	1962
9	Tony Nathan	15	1977
9	Bobby Humphrey	15	1986

Single Game

Rank	Player	TDs	Year	Opponent
1	Shaun Alexander	5	1998	BYU
1	Santonio Beard	5	2002	Ole Miss
1	*Najee Harris*	*5*	*2020*	*Ole Miss*
4	Johnny Musso	4	1971	Florida
4	David Casteal	4	1988	Mississippi State
4	Siran Stacy	4	1989	Memphis State
4	Shaun Alexander	4	1996	LSU
4	*Trent Richardson*	*4*	*2011*	*Ole Miss*
4	*Brian Robinson Jr.*	*4*	*2021*	*Ole Miss*
4	*Jalen Milroe*	*4*	*2023*	*LSU*

Receiving

Receptions

Career

Rank	Player	Rec	Years
1	DeVonta Smith	235	2017-2020
2	Amari Cooper	228	2012-2014
3	Calvin Ridley	224	2015-2017
4	D.J. Hall	194	2004-2007
5	Julio Jones	179	2008-2010
6	Jerry Jeudy	159	2017-2019
7	John Metchie III	155	2019-2021
8	Freddie Milons	152	1998-2001
9	Marquis Maze	136	2008-2011
10	David Bailey	132	1969-1971

Single Season

Rank	Player	Rec	Year
1	Amari Cooper	124	2014
2	DeVonta Smith	117	2020
3	John Metchie III	96	2021
4	Calvin Ridley	89	2015
5	Jameson Williams	79	2021
6	Julio Jones	78	2010
7	Jerry Jeudy	77	2019
8	Calvin Ridley	72	2016
9	Jerry Jeudy	68	2018
9	DeVonta Smith	68	2019

Single Game

Rank	Player	Rec	Year	Opponent
1	DeVonta Smith	15	2020	Florida (SEC Championship Game)
2	D.J. Hall	13	2007	Tennessee
2	Amari Cooper	13	2014	Florida Atlantic
2	Amari Cooper	13	2014	Auburn
2	DeVonta Smith	13	2020	Ole Miss
2	John Metchie III	13	2021	Auburn
7	David Bailey	12	1969	Tennessee
7	David Bailey	12	1970	Tennessee
7	Julio Jones	12	2010	Tennessee
7	Amari Cooper	12	2014	West Virginia
7	Amari Cooper	12	2014	Missouri (SEC Championship Game)
7	DeVonta Smith	12	2020	Ohio State (CFP National Championship)

Receiving Yards

Career

Rank	Player	Yards	Years
1	DeVonta Smith	3,965	2017-2020
2	Amari Cooper	3,463	2012-2014
3	D.J. Hall	2,923	2004-2007
4	Calvin Ridley	2,781	2015-2017
5	Jerry Jeudy	2,742	2017-2019
6	Julio Jones	2,653	2008-2010
7	John Metchie III	2,081	2019-2021
8	Ozzie Newsome	2,070	1974-1977
9	Jaylen Waddle	1,999	2018-2020
10	Freddie Milons	1,859	1998-2001

Single Season

Rank	Player	Yards	Year
1	DeVonta Smith	1856	2020
2	Amari Cooper	1727	2014
3	Jameson Williams	1572	2021
4	Jerry Jeudy	1315	2018
5	DeVonta Smith	1256	2019
6	Jerry Jeudy	1163	2019
7	John Metchie III	1142	2021
8	Julio Jones	1133	2010
9	D.J. Hall	1056	2006
10	Calvin Ridley	1045	2015

Single Game

Rank	Player	Yards	Year	Opponent
1	DeVonta Smith	274	2019	Ole Miss
2	DeVonta Smith	231	2020	LSU
3	Amari Cooper	224	2014	Tennessee
3	Amari Cooper	224	2014	Auburn
5	Julio Jones	221	2010	Tennessee
6	David Palmer	217	1993	Vanderbilt
7	DeVonta Smith	215	2020	Ohio State (CFP National Championship)
8	DeVonta Smith	213	2019	LSU
9	O.J. Howard	208	2015	Clemson (CFP National Championship)
10	Jerry Jeudy	204	2019	Michigan (Citrus Bowl)

Receiving Touchdowns

Career

Rank	Player	TDs	Years
1	*DeVonta Smith*	*46*	*2017-2020*
2	*Amari Cooper*	*31*	*2012-2014*
3	*Jerry Jeudy*	*26*	*2017-2019*
4	*Henry Ruggs III*	*24*	*2017-2019*
5	*Calvin Ridley*	*19*	*2015-2017*
6	Dennis Homan	18	1965-1967
7	*D.J. Hall*	*17*	*2004-2007*
7	*Jaylen Waddle*	*17*	*2018-2020*
9	Ozzie Newsome	16	1974-1977
10	Joey Jones	15	1980-1983
10	*Julio Jones*	*15*	*2008-2010*
10	*Jameson Williams*	*15*	*2021*
10	*Jermaine Burton*	*15*	*2022-2023*

Single Season

Rank	Player	TDs	Year
1	*DeVonta Smith*	*23*	*2020*
2	*Amari Cooper*	*16*	*2014*
3	*Jameson Williams*	*15*	*2021*
4	*Jerry Jeudy*	*14*	*2018*
5	*DeVonta Smith*	*13*	*2019*
6	*Amari Cooper*	*11*	*2012*
6	*Henry Ruggs III*	*11*	*2018*
8	Al Lary	10	1950
8	*Jerry Jeudy*	*10*	*2019*
10	Dennis Homan	9	1967

Single Game

Rank	Player	TDs	Year	Opponent
1	*DeVonta Smith*	*5*	*2019*	*Ole Miss*
2	*DeVonta Smith*	*4*	*2020*	*Mississippi State*
3	Al Lary	3	1950	Tulane
3	Al Lary	3	1950	Southern Miss
3	Dennis Homan	3	1968	Southern Miss
3	Michael Vaughn	3	1998	Southern Miss
3	*Amari Cooper*	*3*	*2014*	*Florida*
3	*Amari Cooper*	*3*	*2014*	*Auburn*
3	*ArDarius Stewart*	*3*	*2016*	*Mississippi State*
3	*Jerry Jeudy*	*3*	*2019*	*New Mexico State*
3	*Jaylen Waddle*	*3*	*2019*	*Auburn*
3	*DeVonta Smith*	*3*	*2020*	*LSU*
3	*Najee Harris*	*3*	*2020*	*Florida (SEC Championship Game)*
3	*DeVonta Smith*	*3*	*2020*	*Notre Dame (Rose Bowl)*
3	*DeVonta Smith*	*3*	*2020*	*Ohio State (CFP National Championship)*
3	*Jameson Williams*	*3*	*2021*	*New Mexico State*
3	*Jameson Williams*	*3*	*2021*	*Arkansas*

Total Offense

These stats are combined passing/rushing.

Combined Yards

Career

Rank	Player	Yards	Years
1	A.J. McCarron	8,969	2010-2013
2	Bryce Young	8,518	2020-2022
3	John Parker Wilson	8,099	2005-2008
4	Tua Tagovailoa	7,782	2017-2019
5	Jalen Hurts	7,606	2016-2018
6	Brodie Croyle	6,205	2002-2005
7	Mac Jones	6,168	2018-2020
8	Andrew Zow	5,958	1998-2001
9	Greg McElroy	5,762	2007-2010
10	Walter Lewis	5,699	1980-1983

Single Season

Rank	Player	Yards	Year
1	Bryce Young	4872	2021
2	Mac Jones	4514	2020
3	Tua Tagovailoa	4156	2018
4	Blake Sims	3837	2014
5	Jalen Hurts	3734	2016
6	Bryce Young	3513	2022
7	Jalen Milroe	3365	2023
8	Jake Coker	3178	2015
9	A.J. McCarron	3041	2013
10	Greg McElroy	2975	2010

Single Game

Rank	Player	Yards	Year	Opponent
1	Bryce Young	548	2021	Arkansas
2	Blake Sims	484	2014	Florida
3	Mac Jones	475	2020	Ohio State (CFP National Championship)
4	Bryce Young	461	2021	Georgia (SEC Championship Game)
5	Scott Hunter	457	1969	Auburn
6	Bryce Young	451	2022	Tennessee
7	Jalen Hurts	447	2016	Mississippi State
8	Mac Jones	433	2020	Texas A&M
9	Tua Tagovailoa	432	2019	South Carolina
10	Tua Tagovailoa	419	2019	Ole Miss

TDs Responsible For

"Touchdowns responsible for" is the NCAA's official term for combined passing and rushing touchdowns.

Career

Rank	Player	TDs	Years
1	Tua Tagovailoa	96	2017-2019
2	Bryce Young	87	2020-2022
3	A.J. McCarron	80	2010-2013
4	Jalen Hurts	71	2016-2018
5	John Parker Wilson	58	2005-2008
5	Mac Jones	58	2018-2020
7	Najee Harris	57	2017-2020
8	Shaun Alexander	49	1996-1999
9	Harry Gilmer	48	1944-1947
10	Mark Ingram II	46	2008-2020

Single Season

Rank	Player	TDs	Year
1	Bryce Young	50	2021
2	Tua Tagovailoa	48	2018
3	Mac Jones	42	2020
4	Jalen Hurts	36	2016
4	Bryce Young	36	2022
6	Blake Sims	35	2014
6	Tua Tagovailoa	35	2019
6	Jalen Milroe	35	2023
9	A.J. McCarron	31	2012
10	Najee Harris	30	2020

Single Game

Rank	Player	TDs	Year	Opponent
1	Tua Tagovailoa	7	2019	Ole Miss
2	Tua Tagovailoa	6	2018	Auburn
2	Bryce Young	6	2022	Utah State
2	Jalen Milroe	6	2023	Kentucky
5	Gary Hollingsworth	5	1989	Ole Miss
5	Shaun Alexander	5	1998	BYU
5	Santonio Beard	5	2002	Ole Miss
5	Blake Sims	5	2014	Auburn
5	Jalen Hurts	5	2016	Mississippi State
5	Tua Tagovailoa	5	2018	Texas A&M
5	Tua Tagovailoa	5	2019	South Carolina
5	Tua Tagovailoa	5	2019	Southern Miss
5	Najee Harris	5	2020	Ole Miss
5	Mac Jones	5	2020	Auburn
5	Mac Jones	5	2020	Florida (SEC Championship)
5	Mac Jones	5	2020	Ohio St. (CFP National Championship)
5	Bryce Young	5	2021	Southern Miss
5	Bryce Young	5	2021	New Mexico State
5	Bryce Young	5	2022	Kansas State (Sugar Bowl)
5	Jalen Milroe	5	2023	Middle Tennessee

Defense

Interceptions

Career

Rank	Player	Ints	Years
1	Antonio Langham	19	1980-1983
2	Harry Gilmer	16	1944-1947
2	Jeremiah Castille	16	1979-1982
2	John Mangum	16	1986-1989
5	Steve Higginbotham	14	1969-1971
5	Kermit Kendrick	14	1985-1988
5	George Teague	14	1989-1992
5	*Robert Lester*	*14*	*2009-2012*
9	Tommy Johnson	12	1991-1994
9	Kevin Jackson	12	1995-1996
9	*Simeon Castille*	*12*	*2004-2007*
9	*Mark Barron*	*12*	*2008-2011*

Single Season

Rank	Player	Ints	Year
1	Hootie Ingram	10	1952
2	Harry Gilmer	8	1946
2	*Robert Lester*	*8*	*2010*
4	Steve Higginbotham	7	1971
4	Jeremiah Castille	7	1982
4	Antonio Langham	7	1993
4	Kevin Jackson	7	1996
4	*Mark Barron*	*7*	*2009*

Single Game

Rank	Player	Ints	Year	Opponent
1	Dicky Thompson	3	1966	Ole Miss
1	Jeremiah Castille	3	1982	Tennessee
1	Kevin Jackson	3	1995	Georgia
1	*Rashad Johnson*	*3*	*2008*	*LSU*
1	*Minkah Fitzpatrick*	*3*	*2016*	*Arkansas*

Tackles

Career

Rank	Player	Tackles	Years
1	Wayne Davis	327	1983-1986
2	Tom Boyd	324	1979-1982
3	*C.J. Mosley*	*319*	*2010-2013*
4	Woodrow Lowe	315	1972-1975
5	DeMeco Ryans	309	2002-2005
6	Roman Harper	307	2002-2005
7	Marcus Spencer	303	1997-2000
8	Cornelius Bennett	287	1983-1986
9	Robbie Jones	284	1979-1982
10	Saleem Rasheed	280	1999-2001

Single Season

Rank	Player	Tackles	Year
1	Woodrow Lowe	134	1973
2	DeMeco Ryans	126	2003
3	Wayne Davis	125	1985
4	Mike Hall	120	1968
4	Tom Boyd	120	1980
6	Marty Lyons	119	1978
6	Keith McCants	119	1989
8	Saleem Rasheed	115	2001
8	*Reuben Foster*	*115*	*2016*
10	Barry Krauss	112	1978

Single Game

Rank	Player	Tackles	Year	Opponent
1	Lee Roy Jordan	31	1962	Oklahoma
2	DeMeco Ryans	25	2003	Arkansas
3	Mike Hall	24	1968	Clemson
3	Wayne Davis	24	1985	Texas A&M
5	Leroy Cook	22	1975	Mississippi State

Sacks

Career

Rank	Player	Sacks	Years
1	Derrick Thomas	52	1985-1988
2	*Will Anderson Jr.*	*35*	*2020-2022*
3	*Jonathan Allen*	*28*	*2013-2016*
4	Kindal Moorehead	25	1998-2002
5	Jarret Johnson	23	1989-2002
5	Eric Curry	23	1990-1992
5	*Dallas Turner*	*23*	*2021-2023*
8	*Wallace Gilberry*	*22*	*2004-2007*
9	*Tim Williams*	*21*	*2013-2016*
9	Antwan Odom	21	2000-2003

Single Season

Rank	Player	Sacks	Year
1	Derrick Thomas	27	1988
2	Derrick Thomas	18	1987
2	*Will Anderson Jr.*	*18*	*2021*
4	*Jonathan Allen*	*12*	*2015*
5	Emanuel King	11	1983
5	John Copeland	11	1992
5	Eric Curry	11	1992
5	*Tim Williams*	*11*	*2015*
5	*Jonathan Allen*	*11*	*2016*
10	Cornelius Bennett	10	1986
10	Darrell Blackburn	10	1995
10	Damien Jeffries	10	1994
10	Jeremy Nunley	10	1993
10	*Wallace Gilberry*	*10*	*2007*
10	*Will Anderson Jr.*	*10*	*2022*
10	*Dallas Turner*	*10*	*2023*

Single Game

Rank	Player	Sacks	Year	Opponent
1	Derrick Thomas	5	1988	Texas A&M
2	Leroy Cook	4	1975	Tennessee
2	Derrick Thomas	4	1988	Kentucky
2	*Will Anderson Jr.*	*4*	*2021*	*Mississippi State*

Kicking

Field Goals

Career

Rank	Player	FGs	Years
1	*Will Reichard*	*84*	*2019-2023*
2	*Leigh Tiffin*	*83*	*2006-2009*
3	Philip Doyle	78	1987-1990
4	Michael Proctor	65	1992-1995
5	Van Tiffin	59	1983-1986
6	*Adam Griffith*	*57*	*2013-2016*
7	*Jeremy Shelley*	*44*	*2009-2012*
8	Brian Bostick	38	2002-2004
9	Peter Kim	37	1980-1982
10	Jamie Christensen	29	2005-2006

Single Season

Rank	Player	FGs	Year
1	*Leigh Tiffin*	*30*	*2009*
2	*Leigh Tiffin*	*25*	*2007*
3	Philip Doyle	24	1990
4	*Adam Griffith*	*23*	*2015*
5	Philip Doyle	22	1989
5	Michael Proctor	22	1993
5	*Will Reichard*	*22*	*2021*
5	*Will Reichard*	*22*	*2022*
5	*Will Reichard*	*22*	*2023*
10	*Jeremy Shelley*	*21*	*2011*
10	*Adam Griffith*	*21*	*2016*

Single Game

Rank	Player	FGs	Year	Opponent
1	Philip Doyle	6	1990	Southwestern Louisiana
2	*Leigh Tiffin*	*5*	*2009*	*Ole Miss*
2	*Jeremy Shelley*	*5*	*2012*	*LSU*
2	*Adam Griffith*	*5*	*2015*	*Auburn*

427

Field Goal Percentages

Career

Rank	Player	FG%	FGs	Years
1	*Will Reichard*	*84.0%*	*84*	*2019-2023*
2	*Jeremy Shelley*	*80.00%*	*44*	*2009-2012*
3	*Joseph Bulovas*	*75.90%*	*22*	*2018-2019*
4	*Leigh Tiffin*	*74.80%*	*83*	*2006-2009*
5	Philip Doyle	74.30%	78	1987-1990
6	Brian Bostick	73.10%	38	2002-2004
6	*Andy Pappanastos*	*73.10%*	*19*	*2016-2017*
8	Michael Proctor	71.40%	65	1992-1995
9	Neal Thomas	70.60%	24	2000-2001
10	Peter Kim	69.80%	37	1980-1982

Single Season

Rank	Player	FG%	FGs	Year
1	*Will Reichard*	*100.00%*	*14*	*2020*
1	*Jeremy Shelley*	*100.00%*	*11*	*2012*
3	Philip Doyle	88.00%	22	1989
3	*Will Reichard*	*88.00%*	*22*	*2023*
5	*Leigh Tiffin*	*85.70%*	*30*	*2009*
6	*Will Reichard*	*84.60%*	*22*	*2022*
7	Brian Bostick	84.20%	16	2004
8	Philip Doyle	82.80%	24	1990
9	Michael Proctor	81.30%	13	1994
10	*Will Reichard*	*78.60%*	*22*	*2021*

Longest Field Goals

Single Game

Rank	Player	Yards	Year	Opponent
1	Van Tiffin	57	1985	Texas A&M
2	Ryan Pflugner	55	1998	Arkansas
2	*Adam Griffith*	*55*	*2015*	*LSU*
4	*Leigh Tiffin*	*54*	*2008*	*Clemson*
5	Van Tiffin	53	1984	Penn State
5	Philip Doyle	53	1988	Temple
5	Michael Proctor	53	1993	Ole Miss
5	*Cade Foster*	*53*	*2013*	*Ole Miss*
9	Van Tiffin	52	1985	Auburn
9	*Cade Foster*	*52*	*2012*	*Florida Atlantic*
9	*Will Reichard*	*52*	*2020*	*Georgia*
9	*Will Reichard*	*52*	*2022*	*Texas*
9	*Will Reichard*	*52*	*2023*	*Michigan (Rose Bowl)*

Note: Table data from "Alabama Crimson Tide football statistical leaders" (465)

Other Stats and Streaks

- 206-29 overall (87.66%)
- 131-20 vs SEC opponents (86.75%)
  - Highest of any coach in SEC[467]
- Six National Championships (nine appearances)
- Nine SEC Championships (ten appearances, won nine straight)
- Six CFP victories (eight appearances)
- 16-7 in Bowl games (4-2 in non-CFP Bowls)
- 108-9 home game record
  - 52-1 in home games from 9/26/19 - 9/2/23
- 123-5 vs unranked opponents
- Two undefeated seasons (14-0 in 2009, 13-0 in 2020)
- 30-3 against his former assistant coaches

- Season wins:
  - 16x 10-win seasons (16 straight from 2008-2023)
    - Longest streak by any program in the AP Poll era (since 1936)[467]
  - 15x 10-win regular seasons
  - 15x 11-win seasons (13 straight from 2011-2023, longest streak in SEC history)
  - 12x 12-win seasons
  - 8x 13-win seasons
  - 4x 14-win seasons

- Ranks:[1-17]
  - 6 Number 1 finishes
  - 12 top 5 finishes (5-season streak between 2014-2018)
  - 16 top 10 finishes (16 years in a row starting in 2008, so all but 2007)
  - 15-year streak of being ranked Number 1 in the AP Top 25
    - At least once each season from 2008-2022
  - Times ranked Number 1:
    - 7x ranked number 1 during the pre-season[466]
    - 97x ranked number 1 during the season
    - 6x ranked number 1 after the season[466]
  - Longest streak of weeks being ranked number 1 = 23
    - 9/3/16 - 10/21/17

- Records vs ranked teams:
  - 83-24 vs top 25 teams
  - 38-16 vs top 10 teams
  - 24-11 vs top 5 teams
  - 8-2 vs number 1 teams (more than any other team)

- Winning streaks:
  - 26-game winning streak
    - 9/26/15 - 12/31/16
  - 31-game home winning streak
    - 9/26/15 - 10/26/19
    - 3 home-game winning streaks of 20+ games
  - 24-game SEC winning streak
    - 10/3/15 - 11/11/17
    - 22 not including SEC Championship Games

- o 16-game SEC West winning streak
  - 10/10/15 - 11/11/17
- o 34-game SEC East winning streak
  - 10/23/10 - 9/24/22
  - 27 not including SEC Championship Games
- o 9-game SEC Championship Game winning streak
- o 57-game regular-season winning streak against non-conference teams
  - 11/30/07 - 9/2/23
- o Longest consecutive winning streaks over SEC teams (Note: *italics* indicates that Alabama never lost to that team):
  - *Arkansas - 17 (2007-2023)*
  - Auburn - 4 (2020-2023)
  - Florida - 8 (2009-2021)
  - Georgia - 7 (2008-2021)
  - *Kentucky - 6 (2008-2023)*
  - LSU - 8 (2011-2018)
  - Mississippi State - 16 (2008-2023)
  - *Missouri - 4 (2012-2020)*
  - Ole Miss - 8 (2016-2023)
  - South Carolina - 1 (2009 and 2019)
  - Tennessee - 15 (2007-2021)
  - Texas A&M - 8 (2013-2020)
  - *Vanderbilt - 4 (2007-2022)*
- o Alabama won at least its most recent game against every other member of the SEC:
  - Arkansas (2023)
  - Auburn (2023)
  - Florida (2021)
  - Georgia (2023)
  - Kentucky (2023)
  - LSU (2023)
  - Mississippi State (2023)
  - Ole Miss (2023)
  - Missouri (2020)
  - South Carolina (2019)
  - Tennessee (2023)
  - Texas A&M (2023)
  - Vanderbilt (2022)
- o 10x 10-game winning streaks
- o 16 consecutive seasons with 10+ victories
  - Major college football record
- o No SEC team had a winning streak against Nick Saban
- o Undefeated at home in the month of October (34-0)

- Scoring streaks:
  - o 40-game streak of scoring 20+ points (8/31/19 - 21/31/21)
    - SEC record
  - o 34-game streak of scoring 25+ points (8/31/19 - 10/23/21)
  - o 34-game streak of scoring 30+ points (8/31/19 - 10/23/21)
  - o 24-game streak of scoring 35+ points (8/31/19 - 12/19/20)
    - Longest streak in college football history
  - o 10-game streak of scoring 40+ points (10/3/20 - 12/19/20)

- Largest margin of victory vs each SEC Opponents:
  - Arkansas - 52 (twice)
  - Auburn - 49
  - Florida - 38
  - UGA - 28
  - Kentucky - 60
  - LSU - 38
  - Miss State - 48
  - Missouri - 32
  - Ole Miss - 63
  - S Carolina - 24
  - Texas A&M - 59
  - Tennessee - 39
  - Vanderbilt - 59

- Undefeated in all 17 season-openers
- 190 straight regular-season games without back-to-back losses
- Scored in every single game
- Held opponents to zero points 26 times
- Outscored opponents by 5182 points
  - 8864 points scored (Average/season = 521.41)
  - 3682 points against (Average/season = 216.59)
- Never lost to 43 different teams
  - Beat every team they played at least once except for one (Utah, 2008)

- 151-15 (.910) from 2009-2020
  - Best success rate over 12 seasons for any major college football team since 1900[473]
- In ten years (2011-2020), Alabama posted a 127-12 record with five national championships and seven SEC Titles
- In ten years (2012 to 2021), Alabama won 128 games (13 losses)
  - Best of any major college school over a 10-year span since Bud Wilkinson at Oklahoma in the late 1940s through the late 1950s
- From the 4th quarter of 2016 vs Washington through the 11th game of the 2017 season, Alabama scored points in 49 consecutive quarters
  - Largest streak by any FBS team on record (since 1950) [474]

- Nick Saban never had a losing season
- He is the fastest coach to ever win six National Championships
  - Six in 12 years[472]
- He is the only coach to win a national title in three different decades
- His teams have lost by two or more touchdowns only five times
- He has the second-most wins at a single school in SEC history: [467]
  1. Bear Bryant – 232
  2. Nick Saban – 206
- He had the number 1 recruiting class in ten of the last 13 years[469]
- Every single player who played for four years over the 17-year stretch won at least one National Championship
- 35 men who were either assistant coaches to Nick Saban or played for him became coaches in college or the NFL
- During his 17 years at Alabama, no other SEC team had just one coach
  - The other 13 SEC teams went through 59 coaches (65 counting interims)

- He is the only coach in SEC history with multiple Heisman Trophy winners[468]
- Four Heisman Trophy winners at three different positions:
  - Mark Ingram II - RB (2009)
  - Derrick Henry - RB (2015)
  - DeVonta Smith - WR (2020)
  - Bryce Young - QB (2021)
- 26 Unanimous All-Americans
- 46 Consensus All-Americans

- NFL stats:
  - 133 NFL draft picks
  - 47 first round picks (most of any school)
  - Six first-round NFL draft picks in 2021
    - Tied an NCAA record with Miami (2004)
  - 16 consecutive years of first round draft picks
  - 13 consecutive years of at least seven players drafted
  - Six years with ten players drafted
  - Three years in a row with 10+ players drafted (2017-2019)
  - Most players drafted in a year = 12 (2018, school record)
  - At least one player drafted on every NFL team
  - At least one player drafted at every position
  - Most NFL draft picks from a single college football team
    - 39 players from the 2017 team
  - Saban had more NFL first-round picks than losses

Appendix

Box Scores

2007

Team	1	2	3	4	T
Western Carolina	0	3	0	3	6
Alabama	14	10	14	14	52

Team	1	2	3	4	T
Alabama	10	6	0	8	24
Vanderbilt	3	0	0	7	10

Team	1	2	3	4	T
Arkansas (16)	0	10	7	21	38
Alabama	21	0	10	10	41

Team	1	2	3	4	OT	T
Georgia (22)	7	3	7	3	6	26
Alabama (16)	0	3	7	10	3	23

Team	1	2	3	4	T
Alabama (22)	0	0	0	14	14
Florida State	0	0	7	14	21

Team	1	2	3	4	T
Houston	0	7	3	14	24
Alabama	23	0	7	0	30

Team	1	2	3	4	T
Alabama	3	14	0	10	27
Ole Miss	7	3	14	0	24

Team	1	2	3	4	T
Tennessee (21)	7	10	0	0	17
Alabama	10	14	6	11	41

Team	1	2	3	4	T
LSU (3)	10	7	7	17	41
Alabama (17)	3	17	7	7	34

Team	1	2	3	4	T
Alabama (22)	6	3	0	3	12
Mississippi St.	0	10	7	0	17

Team	1	2	3	4	T
Louisiana Monroe	0	14	7	0	21
Alabama	7	7	0	0	14

Team	1	2	3	4	T
Alabama	0	7	0	3	10
Auburn	10	0	0	7	17

Team	1	2	3	4	T
Alabama	20	7	0	3	30
Colorado	0	14	3	7	24

2008

Team	1	2	3	4	T
Alabama (24)	13	10	8	3	34
Clemson (9)	0	3	7	0	10

Team	1	2	3	4	T
Tulane	0	3	0	3	6
Alabama (13)	13	0	7	0	20

Team	1	2	3	4	T
Western Kentucky	0	7	0	0	7
Alabama (11)	17	14	10	0	41

Team	1	2	3	4	T
Alabama (9)	21	14	7	7	49
Arkansas	0	7	0	7	14

Team	1	2	3	4	T
Alabama (8)	10	21	0	10	41
Georgia (3)	0	0	10	20	30

Team	1	2	3	4	T
Kentucky	0	0	7	7	14
Alabama (2)	14	0	0	3	17

Team	1	2	3	4	T
Ole Miss	3	0	7	10	20
Alabama (2)	7	17	0	0	24

Team	1	2	3	4	T
Alabama (2)	6	7	9	7	29
Tennessee	3	0	0	6	9

Team	1	2	3	4	T
Arkansas State	0	0	0	0	0
Alabama (2)	7	7	14	7	35

Team	1	2	3	4	OT	T
Alabama (1)	7	7	7	0	6	27
LSU (16)	14	0	0	7	0	21

Team	1	2	3	4	T
Mississippi State	0	7	0	0	7
Alabama (1)	5	7	10	10	32

Team	1	2	3	4	T
Auburn	0	0	0	0	0
Alabama (1)	3	7	19	7	36

Team	1	2	3	4	T
Alabama (1)	10	0	10	0	20
Florida (4)	7	10	0	14	31

Team	1	2	3	4	T
Utah (6)	21	0	7	3	31
Alabama (4)	0	10	7	0	17

2009

Team	1	2	3	4	T
Alabama (5)	9	7	0	18	34
Virginia Tech (7)	7	10	0	7	24

Team	1	2	3	4	T
Florida International	7	7	0	0	14
Alabama (5)	10	10	6	14	40

Team	1	2	3	4	T
North Texas	0	0	7	0	7
Alabama (4)	14	16	14	9	53

Team	1	2	3	4	T
Arkansas	0	0	7	0	7
Alabama (3)	0	14	14	7	35

Team	1	2	3	4	T
Alabama (3)	7	14	17	0	38
Kentucky	6	0	7	7	20

Team	1	2	3	4	T
Alabama (3)	3	13	3	3	22
Ole Miss (20)	0	0	3	0	3

Team	1	2	3	4	T
South Carolina (22)	0	6	0	0	6
Alabama (2)	10	3	0	7	20

Team	1	2	3	4	T
Tennessee	0	3	0	7	10
Alabama (2)	3	6	0	3	12

Team	1	2	3	4	T
LSU (9)	0	7	8	0	15
Alabama (3)	0	3	7	14	24

Team	1	2	3	4	T
Alabama (2)	0	14	3	14	31
Mississippi State	0	0	0	3	3

Team	1	2	3	4	T
Chattanooga	0	0	0	0	0
Alabama (2)	21	14	3	7	45

Team	1	2	3	4	T
Alabama (2)	0	14	6	6	26
Auburn	14	0	7	0	21

Team	1	2	3	4	T
Florida (1)	3	10	0	0	13
Alabama (2)	9	10	7	6	32

Team	1	2	3	4	T
Texas (2)	6	0	7	8	21
Alabama (1)	0	24	0	13	37

2010

Team	1	2	3	4	T
San Jose State	3	0	0	0	3
Alabama (1)	14	17	10	7	48

Team	1	2	3	4	T
Penn State (18)	0	0	0	3	3
Alabama (1)	7	10	0	7	24

Team	1	2	3	4	T
Alabama (1)	28	17	10	7	62
Duke	3	10	0	0	13

Team	1	2	3	4	T
Alabama (1)	7	0	7	10	24
Arkansas (10)	10	7	3	0	20

Team	1	2	3	4	T
Florida (7)	0	3	3	0	6
Alabama (1)	3	21	7	0	31

Team	1	2	3	4	T
Alabama (1)	3	6	5	7	21
South Carolina (19)	14	7	7	7	35

Team	1	2	3	4	T
Ole Miss	0	3	7	0	10
Alabama (8)	10	6	7	0	23

Team	1	2	3	4	T
Alabama (8)	3	10	21	7	41
Tennessee	7	3	0	0	10

Team	1	2	3	4	T
Alabama (6)	0	7	7	7	21
LSU (10)	3	0	7	14	24

Team	1	2	3	4	T
Mississippi State (19)	3	0	0	7	10
Alabama (12)	6	14	7	3	30

Team	1	2	3	4	T
Georgia State	0	7	0	0	7
Alabama (11)	14	28	14	7	63

Team	1	2	3	4	T
Auburn (2)	0	7	14	7	28
Alabama (11)	21	3	3	0	27

Team	1	2	3	4	T
Alabama (16)	7	21	14	7	49
Michigan State (9)	0	0	0	7	7

2011

Team	1	2	3	4	T
Kent State	0	0	7	0	**7**
Alabama (2)	21	3	14	10	**48**

Team	1	2	3	4	T
Alabama (3)	7	10	3	7	**27**
Penn State (23)	3	0	0	8	**11**

Team	1	2	3	4	T
North Texas	0	0	0	0	**0**
Alabama (2)	10	10	7	14	**41**

Team	1	2	3	4	T
Arkansas (14)	7	0	7	0	**14**
Alabama (3)	7	10	21	0	**38**

Team	1	2	3	4	T
Alabama (3)	10	14	0	14	**38**
Florida (12)	10	0	0	0	**10**

Team	1	2	3	4	T
Vanderbilt	0	0	0	0	**0**
Alabama (2)	7	7	13	7	**34**

Team	1	2	3	4	T
Alabama (2)	7	10	28	7	**52**
Ole Miss	7	0	0	0	**7**

Team	1	2	3	4	T
Tennessee	3	3	0	0	**6**
Alabama (2)	3	3	21	10	**37**

Team	1	2	3	4	OT	T
LSU (1)	0	3	0	3	3	**9**
Alabama (2)	0	3	3	0	0	**6**

Team	1	2	3	4	T
Alabama (3)	0	7	3	14	**24**
Mississippi State	0	0	0	7	**7**

Team	1	2	3	4	T
Georgia Southern	0	14	7	0	**21**
Alabama (3)	10	14	14	7	**45**

Team	1	2	3	4	T
Alabama (2)	14	10	3	15	**42**
Auburn (24)	7	0	7	0	**14**

Team	1	2	3	4	T
Alabama (2)	3	6	6	6	**21**
LSU (1)	0	0	0	0	**0**

2012

Team	1	2	3	4	T
Michigan (8)	0	7	7	0	**14**
Alabama (2)	21	10	3	7	**41**

Team	1	2	3	4	T
Western Kentucky	0	0	0	0	**0**
Alabama (1)	14	7	7	7	**35**

Team	1	2	3	4	T
Alabama (1)	7	17	14	14	**52**
Arkansas	0	0	0	0	**0**

Team	1	2	3	4	T
Florida Atlantic	0	0	0	7	**7**
Alabama (1)	14	16	3	7	**40**

Team	1	2	3	4	T
Ole Miss	0	7	7	0	**14**
Alabama (1)	6	21	0	6	**33**

Team	1	2	3	4	T
Alabama (1)	21	7	0	14	**42**
Missouri	0	7	3	0	**10**

Team	1	2	3	4	T
Alabama (1)	7	16	7	14	**44**
Tennessee	3	7	0	3	**13**

Team	1	2	3	4	T
Mississippi State (11)	0	0	0	7	**7**
Alabama (1)	14	10	0	14	**38**

Team	1	2	3	4	T
Alabama (1)	0	14	0	7	**21**
LSU (5)	3	0	7	7	**17**

Team	1	2	3	4	T
Texas A&M (15)	20	0	0	9	**29**
Alabama (1)	0	14	3	7	**24**

Team	1	2	3	4	T
Western Carolina	0	0	0	0	**0**
Alabama (4)	21	21	7	0	**49**

Team	1	2	3	4	T
Auburn	0	0	0	0	**0**
Alabama (2)	14	28	7	0	**49**

Team	1	2	3	4	T
Alabama (2)	0	10	8	14	**32**
Georgia (3)	0	7	14	7	**28**

Team	1	2	3	4	T
Notre Dame (1)	0	0	7	7	**14**
Alabama (2)	14	14	7	7	**42**

2013

Team	1	2	3	4	T
Alabama (1)	14	14	7	0	35
Virginia Tech	7	3	0	0	10

Team	1	2	3	4	T
Alabama (1)	7	21	14	7	49
Texas A&M (6)	14	0	7	21	42

Team	1	2	3	4	T
Colorado State	0	0	6	0	6
Alabama (1)	7	10	0	14	31

Team	1	2	3	4	T
Ole Miss (21)	0	0	0	0	0
Alabama (1)	3	6	7	9	25

Team	1	2	3	4	T
Georgia State	0	0	3	0	3
Alabama (1)	21	17	7	0	45

Team	1	2	3	4	T
Alabama (1)	0	24	10	14	48
Kentucky	0	0	7	0	7

Team	1	2	3	4	T
Arkansas	0	0	0	0	0
Alabama (1)	14	14	17	7	52

Team	1	2	3	4	T
Tennessee	0	0	3	7	10
Alabama (1)	21	14	7	3	45

Team	1	2	3	4	T
LSU (13)	0	14	3	0	17
Alabama (1)	3	14	7	14	38

Team	1	2	3	4	T
Alabama (1)	3	7	7	3	20
Mississippi State	0	0	7	0	7

Team	1	2	3	4	T
Chattanooga	0	0	0	0	0
Alabama (1)	7	21	14	7	49

Team	1	2	3	4	T
Alabama (1)	0	21	0	7	28
Auburn (4)	7	7	7	13	34

Team	1	2	3	4	T
Oklahoma (11)	14	17	0	14	45
Alabama (3)	10	7	7	7	31

2014

Team	1	2	3	4	T
West Virginia	3	14	3	3	23
Alabama (2)	3	17	10	3	33

Team	1	2	3	4	T
Florida Atlantic	0	0	0	0	0
Alabama (2)	21	10	7	3	41

Team	1	2	3	4	T
Southern Mississippi	3	3	3	3	12
Alabama (3)	7	14	14	17	52

Team	1	2	3	4	T
Florida	14	0	7	0	21
Alabama (3)	14	7	14	7	42

Team	1	2	3	4	T
Alabama (3)	0	14	3	0	17
Ole Miss (11)	3	0	7	13	23

Team	1	2	3	4	T
Alabama (7)	0	7	0	7	14
Arkansas	0	6	7	0	13

Team	1	2	3	4	T
Texas A&M (21)	0	0	0	0	0
Alabama (7)	10	35	7	7	59

Team	1	2	3	4	T
Alabama (4)	20	7	7	0	34
Tennessee	0	10	7	3	20

Team	1	2	3	4	OT	T
Alabama (5)	0	10	0	3	7	20
LSU (16)	7	0	3	3	0	13

Team	1	2	3	4	T
Mississippi State (1)	0	3	3	14	20
Alabama (5)	5	14	0	6	25

Team	1	2	3	4	T
Western Carolina	7	7	0	0	14
Alabama (1)	10	28	10	0	48

Team	1	2	3	4	T
Auburn (15)	6	20	10	8	44
Alabama (1)	14	7	13	21	55

Team	1	2	3	4	T
Alabama (1)	7	14	0	21	42
Missouri (16)	0	3	10	0	13

Team	1	2	3	4	T
Alabama (1)	14	7	7	7	35
Ohio State (4)	6	14	14	8	42

2015

Team	1	2	3	4	T
Wisconsin (20)	0	7	3	7	17
Alabama (3)	7	7	14	7	35

Team	1	2	3	4	T
Middle Tennessee State	0	3	0	7	10
Alabama (2)	7	16	14	0	37

Team	1	2	3	4	T
Ole Miss (15)	3	14	13	13	43
Alabama (2)	0	10	7	20	37

Team	1	2	3	4	T
Louisiana Monroe	0	0	0	0	0
Alabama (12)	7	7	10	10	34

Team	1	2	3	4	T
Alabama (13)	3	21	14	0	38
Georgia (8)	0	3	7	0	10

Team	1	2	3	4	T
Arkansas	0	7	0	7	14
Alabama (8)	3	0	7	17	27

Team	1	2	3	4	T
Alabama (10)	14	14	3	10	41
Texas A&M (9)	3	10	7	3	23

Team	1	2	3	4	T
Tennessee	7	0	0	7	14
Alabama (8)	7	0	3	9	19

Team	1	2	3	4	T
LSU (4)	0	10	0	6	16
Alabama (2)	0	13	14	3	30

Team	1	2	3	4	T
Alabama (2)	0	21	3	7	31
Mississippi State (17)	0	3	3	0	6

Team	1	2	3	4	T
Charleston Southern	0	0	0	6	6
Alabama (2)	28	21	0	7	56

Team	1	2	3	4	T
Alabama (2)	3	9	7	10	29
Auburn	6	0	7	0	13

Team	1	2	3	4	T
Florida (18)	0	7	0	8	15
Alabama (2)	2	10	10	7	29

Team	1	2	3	4	T
Michigan State (3)	0	0	0	0	0
Alabama (2)	0	10	21	7	38

Team	1	2	3	4	T
Alabama (2)	7	7	7	24	45
Clemson (1)	14	0	10	16	40

2016

Team	1	2	3	4	T
USC (20)	3	0	3	0	6
Alabama (1)	0	17	21	14	52

Team	1	2	3	4	T
Western Kentucky	3	0	0	7	10
Alabama (1)	10	7	7	14	38

Team	1	2	3	4	T
Alabama (1)	3	14	17	14	48
Ole Miss (19)	7	17	3	16	43

Team	1	2	3	4	T
Kent State	0	0	0	0	0
Alabama (1)	21	20	7	0	48

Team	1	2	3	4	T
Kentucky	3	0	0	3	6
Alabama (1)	3	14	14	3	34

Team	1	2	3	4	T
Alabama (1)	14	21	7	7	49
Arkansas (16)	7	10	7	6	30

Team	1	2	3	4	T
Alabama (1)	14	7	14	14	49
Tennessee (9)	0	7	3	0	10

Team	1	2	3	4	T
Texas A&M (6)	0	7	7	0	14
Alabama (1)	6	7	13	7	33

Team	1	2	3	4	T
Alabama (1)	0	0	0	10	10
LSU (13)	0	0	0	0	0

Team	1	2	3	4	T
Mississippi State	0	0	3	0	3
Alabama (1)	10	20	14	7	51

Team	1	2	3	4	T
Chattanooga	3	0	0	0	3
Alabama (1)	0	14	7	10	31

Team	1	2	3	4	T
Auburn (13)	3	6	3	0	12
Alabama (1)	10	3	14	3	30

Team	1	2	3	4	T
Alabama (1)	16	17	7	14	54
Florida (15)	9	7	0	0	16

Team	1	2	3	4	T
Washington (4)	7	0	0	0	7
Alabama (1)	7	10	0	7	24

Team	1	2	3	4	T
Clemson (2)	0	7	7	21	35
Alabama (1)	7	7	10	7	31

2017

Team	1	2	3	4	T
FSU (3)	0	7	0	0	7
Alabama (1)	3	7	11	3	24

Team	1	2	3	4	T
Fresno State	3	0	0	7	10
Alabama (1)	14	14	3	10	41

Team	1	2	3	4	T
Colorado State	0	10	0	13	23
Alabama (1)	17	7	14	3	41

Team	1	2	3	4	T
Alabama (1)	21	10	21	7	59
Vanderbilt	0	0	0	0	0

Team	1	2	3	4	T
Ole Miss	3	0	0	0	3
Alabama (1)	21	14	24	7	66

Team	1	2	3	4	T
Alabama (1)	7	10	7	3	27
Texas A&M	3	0	7	9	19

Team	1	2	3	4	T
Arkansas	0	0	3	6	9
Alabama (1)	17	7	7	10	41

Team	1	2	3	4	T
Tennessee	0	0	7	0	7
Alabama (1)	7	14	10	14	45

Team	1	2	3	4	T
LSU (19)	0	3	7	0	10
Alabama (2)	7	7	7	3	24

Team	1	2	3	4	T
Alabama (2)	7	7	3	14	31
Mississippi State (16)	7	7	7	3	24

Team	1	2	3	4	T
Mercer	0	0	0	0	0
Alabama (1)	14	21	14	7	56

Team	1	2	3	4	T
Alabama (1)	0	7	7	0	14
Auburn (6)	7	3	10	6	26

Team	1	2	3	4	T
Alabama (4)	10	0	14	0	24
Clemson (1)	0	3	3	0	6

Team	1	2	3	4	OT
Alabama (4)	0	0	10	10	6
Georgia (3)	0	13	7	0	3

2018

Team	1	2	3	4	T
Louisville	0	0	7	7	14
Alabama (1)	14	14	16	7	51

Team	1	2	3	4	T
Arkansas State	0	0	7	0	7
Alabama (1)	19	21	10	7	57

Team	1	2	3	4	T
Alabama (1)	28	21	10	3	62
Ole Miss	7	0	0	0	7

Team	1	2	3	4	T
Texas A&M (22)	7	6	3	7	23
Alabama (1)	14	17	14	0	45

Team	1	2	3	4	T
Louisiana	0	0	0	14	14
Alabama (1)	28	21	7	0	56

Team	1	2	3	4	T
Alabama (1)	21	20	7	17	65
Arkansas	7	7	3	14	31

Team	1	2	3	4	T
Missouri	10	0	0	0	10
Alabama (1)	13	17	2	7	39

Team	1	2	3	4	T
Alabama (1)	28	14	16	0	58
Tennessee	0	14	7	0	21

Team	1	2	3	4	T
Alabama (1)	6	10	6	7	29
LSU (3)	0	0	0	0	0

Team	1	2	3	4	T
Mississippi State (16)	0	0	0	0	0
Alabama (1)	14	7	0	3	24

Team	1	2	3	4	T
Citadel	0	10	0	7	17
Alabama (1)	7	3	27	13	50

Team	1	2	3	4	T
Auburn	7	7	7	0	21
Alabama (1)	7	10	21	14	52

Team	1	2	3	4	T
Alabama (1)	0	14	7	14	35
Georgia (4)	7	14	7	0	28

Team	1	2	3	4	T
Oklahoma (4)	0	10	10	14	34
Alabama (1)	21	10	0	14	45

Team	1	2	3	4	T
Clemson (2)	14	17	13	0	44
Alabama (1)	13	3	0	0	16

2019

Team	1	2	3	4	T
Duke	0	3	0	0	3
Alabama (2)	0	14	21	7	42

Team	1	2	3	4	T
New Mexico State	0	0	7	3	10
Alabama (2)	21	17	24	0	62

Team	1	2	3	4	T
Alabama (2)	14	10	10	13	47
South Carolina	10	0	3	10	23

Team	1	2	3	4	T
Southern Mississippi	0	7	0	0	7
Alabama (2)	14	14	14	7	49

Team	1	2	3	4	T
Ole Miss	10	0	7	14	31
Alabama (2)	7	31	14	7	59

Team	1	2	3	4	T
Alabama (1)	14	10	10	13	47
Texas A&M (24)	7	6	7	8	28

Team	1	2	3	4	T
Tennessee	7	3	3	0	13
Alabama (1)	14	7	7	7	35

Team	1	2	3	4	T
Arkansas	0	0	0	7	7
Alabama (1)	17	24	7	0	48

Team	1	2	3	4	T
LSU (2)	10	23	0	13	46
Alabama (3)	7	6	7	21	41

Team	1	2	3	4	T
Alabama (5)	21	14	3	0	38
Mississippi State	7	0	0	0	7

Team	1	2	3	4	T
Western Carolina	0	0	0	3	3
Alabama (5)	17	21	21	7	66

Team	1	2	3	4	T
Alabama (5)	3	28	7	7	45
Auburn (15)	7	20	13	8	48

Team	1	2	3	4	T
Michigan (14)	10	6	0	0	16
Alabama (8)	7	7	7	14	35

2020

Team	1	2	3	4	T
Alabama (2)	14	14	7	3	38
Missouri	0	3	3	13	19

Team	1	2	3	4	T
Texas A&M (13)	7	7	3	7	24
Alabama (2)	14	21	7	10	52

Team	1	2	3	4	T
Alabama (2)	7	14	21	21	63
Ole Miss	7	14	14	13	48

Team	1	2	3	4	T
Georgia (3)	7	17	0	0	24
Alabama (2)	7	13	14	7	41

Team	1	2	3	4	T
Alabama (2)	14	14	14	6	48
Tennessee	0	10	7	0	17

Team	1	2	3	4	T
Mississippi State	0	0	0	0	0
Alabama (2)	17	10	0	14	41

Team	1	2	3	4	T
Kentucky	3	0	0	0	3
Alabama (1)	7	21	21	14	63

Team	1	2	3	4	T
Auburn (22)	0	3	3	7	13
Alabama (1)	7	14	14	7	42

Team	1	2	3	4	T
Alabama (1)	21	24	7	3	55
LSU	0	14	3	0	17

Team	1	2	3	4	T
Alabama (1)	10	28	7	7	52
Arkansas	3	0	0	0	3

Team	1	2	3	4	T
Alabama (1)	14	21	0	17	52
Florida (7)	10	7	14	15	46

Team	1	2	3	4	T
Notre Dame (4)	0	7	0	7	14
Alabama (1)	14	7	7	3	31

Team	1	2	3	4	T
Ohio State (3)	7	10	7	0	24
Alabama (1)	7	28	10	7	52

2021

Team	1	2	3	4	T
Alabama (1)	10	17	14	3	44
Miami (14)	0	3	10	0	13

Team	1	2	3	4	T
Mercer	0	0	7	7	14
Alabama (1)	14	17	14	3	48

Team	1	2	3	4	T
Alabama (1)	21	0	7	3	31
Florida (11)	3	6	14	6	29

Team	1	2	3	4	T
Southern Miss	0	7	0	7	14
Alabama (1)	21	21	7	14	63

Team	1	2	3	4	T
Ole Miss (12)	0	0	7	14	21
Alabama (1)	7	21	7	7	42

Team	1	2	3	4	T
Alabama (1)	7	3	14	14	38
Texas A&M	17	7	7	10	41

Team	1	2	3	4	T
Alabama (5)	14	7	14	14	49
Mississippi State	3	3	3	0	9

Team	1	2	3	4	T
Tennessee	14	0	3	7	24
Alabama (4)	7	14	3	28	52

Team	1	2	3	4	T
LSU	7	0	7	0	14
Alabama (2)	0	14	6	0	20

Team	1	2	3	4	T
New Mexico State	3	0	0	0	3
Alabama (2)	14	35	0	10	59

Team	1	2	3	4	T
Arkansas (21)	0	14	7	14	35
Alabama (2)	3	21	10	8	42

Team	1	2	3	4	OT	T
Alabama (3)	0	0	0	10	14	24
Auburn	0	7	3	0	12	22

Team	1	2	3	4	T
Georgia (1)	3	14	0	7	24
Alabama (3)	0	24	7	10	41

2022

Team	1	2	3	4	T
Utah State	0	0	0	0	0
Alabama (1)	17	24	14	0	55

Team	1	2	3	4	T
Alabama (1)	10	0	0	10	20
Texas	3	7	3	6	19

Team	1	2	3	4	T
Louisiana Monroe	0	7	0	0	7
Alabama (2)	28	7	14	14	63

Team	1	2	3	4	T
Vanderbilt	3	0	0	0	3
Alabama (2)	14	17	10	14	55

Team	1	2	3	4	T
Alabama (2)	14	14	0	21	49
Arkansas (20)	0	7	16	3	26

Team	1	2	3	4	T
Texas A&M	0	14	3	3	20
Alabama (1)	0	17	7	0	24

Team	1	2	3	4	T
Alabama (3)	7	13	15	14	49
Tennessee (6)	21	7	6	18	52

Team	1	2	3	4	T
Mississippi State (24)	0	0	0	6	6
Alabama (6)	7	17	0	6	30

Team	1	2	3	4	OT	T
Alabama (6)	0	6	3	15	7	31
LSU (10)	0	7	7	10	8	32

Team	1	2	3	4	T
Alabama (9)	0	14	10	6	30
Ole Miss (11)	7	10	7	0	24

Team	1	2	3	4	T
Austin Peay	0	0	0	0	0
Alabama (8)	7	10	10	7	34

Team	1	2	3	4	T
Auburn	7	7	7	6	27
Alabama (7)	14	21	7	7	49

Team	1	2	3	4	T
Alabama (5)	7	14	21	3	45
Kansas State (9)	10	0	3	7	20

2023

Team	1	2	3	4	T
Middle Tennessee State	0	0	7	0	7
Alabama (4)	14	14	14	14	56

Team	1	2	3	4	T
Texas (11)	3	10	0	21	34
Alabama (3)	0	6	10	8	24

Team	1	2	3	4	T
Alabama (10)	0	3	7	7	17
South Florida	3	0	0	0	3

Team	1	2	3	4	T
Ole Miss (15)	7	0	3	0	10
Alabama (13)	3	3	11	7	24

Team	1	2	3	4	T
Alabama (12)	14	17	3	6	40
Mississippi State	0	10	7	0	17

Team	1	2	3	4	T
Alabama (11)	3	7	14	2	26
Texas A&M	3	14	0	3	20

Team	1	2	3	4	T
Arkansas	6	0	7	8	21
Alabama (11)	7	14	3	0	24

Team	1	2	3	4	T
Tennessee (17)	13	7	0	0	20
Alabama (11)	0	7	17	10	34

Team	1	2	3	4	T
LSU (14)	7	14	7	0	28
Alabama (8)	14	7	14	7	42

Team	1	2	3	4	T
Alabama (8)	21	7	7	14	49
Kentucky	7	0	7	7	21

Team	1	2	3	4	T
Chattanooga	0	7	3	0	10
Alabama (8)	21	17	14	14	66

Team	1	2	3	4	T
Alabama (8)	7	10	3	7	27
Auburn	7	7	7	3	24

Team	1	2	3	4	T
Georgia (1)	7	0	3	14	24
Alabama (8)	3	14	3	7	27

Team	1	2	3	4	OT	T
Alabama (4)	7	3	0	10	0	20
Michigan (1)	7	6	0	7	7	27

Postseason Summary

National Championships (6-3)		W/L, Score	Location
2009	Texas	W, 30-24	Rose Bowl
2011	LSU	W, 21-0	Superdome
2012	Notre Dame	W, 42-14	Sun Life Stadium
2015	Clemson	W, 45-40	University of Phoenix Stadium
2016	Clemson	L, 31-35	Raymond James Stadium
2017	Georgia	W, 26-23	Mercedez-Benz Stadium
2018	Clemson	L, 16-44	Levi's Stadium
2020	Ohio State	W, 52-24	AT&T Stadium
2021	Georgia	L, 18-33	Lucas Oil Stadium

SEC Championships (9-1)		W/L, Score	Location
2008	Florida	L, 20-31	Georgia Dome
2009	Florida	W, 32-13	Georgia Dome
2012	Georgia	W, 32-28	Georgia Dome
2014	Missouri	W, 42-13	Georgia Dome
2015	Florida	W, 29-15	Georgia Dome
2016	Florida	W, 54-16	Georgia Dome
2018	Georgia	W, 35-28	Mercedes-Benz Stadium
2020	Florida	W, 52-46	Mercedes-Benz Stadium
2021	Georgia	W, 41-24	Mercedes-Benz Stadium
2023	Georgia	W, 27-24	Mercedes-Benz Stadium

CFP Playoffs (6-2)		W/L, Score	Bowl
2014	Ohio State	L, 35-42	Sugar Bowl
2015	Michigan State	W, 38-0	Cotton Bowl
2016	Washington	W, 24-7	Peach Bowl
2017	Clemson	W, 24-6	Sugar Bowl
2018	Oklahoma	W, 45-34	Orange Bowl
2020	Notre Dame	W, 31-14	Rose Bowl
2021	Cincinnati	W, 27-6	Cotton Bowl
2023	Michigan	L, 20-27	Rose Bowl

Other Bowl games (4-2)		W/L, Score	Bowl
2007	Independence Bowl	W, 30-24	Colorado
2008	Sugar Bowl	L, 17-31	Utah
2010	Capital One Bowl	W, 49-7	Michigan State
2013	Sugar Bowl	L, 31-45	Oklahoma
2019	Citrus Bowl	W, 35-16	Michigan
2022	Sugar Bowl	W, 45-20	Kansas State

Games Grid

Opponent	Rec	07	08	09	10	11	12	13	14	15	16	17	18	19	20	21	22	23
Arkansas	17-0	W	W	W	W	W	W	W	W	W	W	W	W	W	W	W	W	W
Arkansas St.	2-0		W										W					
Auburn	12-5	L	W	W	L	W	W	L	W	W	W	L	W	L	W	W	W	W
Austin Peay	1-0																W	
Charleston So.	1-0									W								
Chattanooga	4-0			W				W			W							W
Cincinnati	1-0															W		
Citadel	1-0												W					
Clemson	3-2		W							W	L	W	L					
Colorado	1-0	W																
Colorado St.	2-0							W				W						
Duke	2-0				W									W				
Florida	8-1		L	W	W	W			W	W	W				W	W		
Florida Atl.	2-0						W		W									
Florida Int'l.	1-0			W														
Florida St.	1-1	L										W						
Fresno St.	1-0											W						
Georgia	8-2	L	W				W		W			W	W		W	W, L		W
Georgia So.	1-0					W												
Georgia St.	2-0			W				W										
Houston	1-0	W																
Kansas St.	1-0																W	
Kent St.	2-0					W						W						
Kentucky	6-0		W	W				W			W				W			W
Louisiana	1-0												W					
LA Monroe	2-1	L							W								W	
Louisville	1-0												W					
LSU	13-5	L	W	W	L	L, W	W	W	W	W	W	W	W	L	W	W	L	W
Mercer	2-0											W				W		
Miami	1-0															W		
Michigan	2-1					W								W				L
Michigan St.	2-0				W				W									
Middle TN St.	2-0								W									W
Mississippi St.	16-1	L	W	W	W	W	W	W	W	W	W	W	W	W	W	W	W	W
Missouri	4-0						W		W				W		W			
New Mexico St.	2-0													W		W		
North Texas	2-0			W		W												
Notre Dame	2-0						W								W			
Oklahoma	1-1						L						W					
Ohio State	1-1							L						W				
Ole Miss	15-2	W	W	W	W	W	W	W	L	L	W	W	W	W	W	W	W	W
Penn State	2-0				W	W												
San Jose St.	1-0				W													
South Carolina	2-1			W	L									W				
South Florida	1-0																	W
Southern Miss.	3-0								W					W		W		
Tennessee	16-1	W	W	W	W	W	W	W	W	W	W	W	W	W	W	W	L	W
Texas	2-1			W													W	L
Texas A&M	10-2						L	W	W	W	W	W	W	W	W	L	W	W
Tulane	1-0		W															
USC	1-0										W							
Utah	0-1		L															
Utah State	1-0																W	
Vanderbilt	4-0	W				W						W					W	
Virginia Tech	2-0			W				W										
Washington	1-0											W						
West Virginia	1-0								W									
Western Carolina	4-0	W					W		W						W			
Western KY	3-0		W				W				W							
Wisconsin	1-0									W								

Coaches

Coach	Position	Alma mater	Years served
Derrick Ansley	Defensive Backs	Troy	2016-17
Major Applewhite	Offensive Coordinator / QBs	Texas	2007
Robert Bala	Safeties / Inside Linebackers	Southern Utah	2023
David Balou	Strength and Conditioning	Indiana	2020-23
Brian Baker	Associate HC / Defensive Line	Maryland	2019
Jeff Banks	Special Teams / Tight Ends	Washington State	2018-20
Greg Brown	Secondary	UTEP	2013
Burton Burns	Associate Head Coach / Running Backs	Nebraska	2007-17
Curt Cignetti	Wide Receivers / Recruiting Coordinator	West Virginia	2007-10
Scott Cochran	Strength and Conditioning	LSU	2007-19
Joe Cox	Tight Ends	Georgia	2022-23
Mario Cristobal	Offensive Line	Miami	2013-16
Brian Daboll	Offensive Coordinator	Rochester	2017
Bo Davis	Defensive Line	LSU	2007-10, 2014-15
Karl Dunbar	Defensive Line	LSU	2016-17
Dan Enos	Quarterbacks	Michigan State	2018
Kyle Flood	Offensive Line	Iona Gaels football	2019-20
Josh Gattis	Co-Offensive Coordinator / WRs	Wake Forest	2018
Robert Gillespie	Running Backs	Florida	2021-23
Pete Golding	Defensive Coordinator / Linebackers	Delta State	2018-22
Mike Groh	Receivers / Recruiting Coordinator	Virginia	2011-12
Charles Huff	Running Backs	Hampton	2019-20
Coleman Hutzler	Outside LBs / Special Teams	Middlebury	2022-23
Charles Kelly	Associate DC / Safeties	Auburn	2019-22
Brent Key	Offensive Line	Georgia Tech	2016-18
Lane Kiffin	Analyst, Offensive Coordinator / QBs	Fresno State	2014-16
Craig Kuligowski	Defensive Line	Toledo	2018
Mike Locksley	Offensive Coordinator	Towson	2016-18
Tosh Lupoi	Linebackers, Defensive Coordinator	California	2015-18
Doug Marrone	Offensive Line	Syracuse	2021
Jim McElwain	Offensive Coordinator / QBs	Eastern Washington	2008-2011
Ron Middleton	Tight Ends / Special Teams	Auburn	2007
Billy Napier	Wide Receivers	Furman	2013-16
Doug Nussmeier	Offensive Coordinator / QBs	Idaho	2012-13
Bill O'Brien	Offensive Coordinator / QBs	Brown	2021-22
Joe Pannunzio	Secondary	Southern Colorado	2017-18
Joe Pendry	Offensive Line	West Virginia	2007-10
Jeremy Pruitt	Secondary, Defensive Coordinator	West Alabama	2010-12, 2016-17
Tommy Rees	Offensive Coordinator / QBs	Notre Dame	2023
Freddie Roach	Asst. Strength and Conditioning, Director of Player Development, DL	Alabama	2008-10, 2015-16, 2020-23
Travaris Robinson	Cornerbacks	Auburn	2022-23
Chris Rumph	Defensive Line	South Carolina	2011-13
Steve Sarkisian	Analyst, Offensive Coordinator / QBs	BYU	2016, 2019-20
Karl Scott	Defensive Backs, Cornerbacks	McMurry University	2018-20
Kirby Smart	Defensive Coordinator	Georgia	2007-15
Kevin Steele	Defensive Line	Tennessee	2007-08, 2014, 2023
Jeff Stoutland	Offensive Line	Southern Connecticut	2011-12
Sal Sunseri	Linebackers	Pittsburgh	2009-11, 2019-21
Lance Thompson	Linebackers	The Citadel	2007-08, 2012-14
Mel Tucker	Defensive Backs	Wisconsin	2015
Jay Valai	Cornerbacks	Wisconsin	2021
Holmon Wiggins	Wide Receivers	New Mexico State	2019-23
Bobby Williams	Tight Ends / Special Teams	Purdue	2008-15
James Willis	Associate HC / Outside Linebackers	Auburn	2009
Eric Wolford	Offensive Line	Kansas State	2022-23

Note: Table data from "Alabama Crimson Tide football under Nick Saban" (471)

Recruits

Name	Year	Pos	Pos Rank	Scout	Rivals	247 Sports	ESPN	ESPN Grade
Cole Adams	2023	WR		N/A	4	4	4	81
Jeremiah Alexander	2022	DE		N/A	5	5	5	90
Antonio Alfano	2019	DT	1	N/A	5	5	4	86
Olaus Alinen	2023	OT		N/A	4	4	4	84
Chris Allen	2017	OLB	4	4	4	4	4	82
Jonathan Allen	2013	DE	3	5	5	5	4	88
Aaron Anderson	2022	WR		N/A	4	4	4	84
Keaton Anderson	2015	OLB	29	3	3	3	3	79
Ryan Anderson	2012	OLB	7	4	4	4	4	80
William Anderson	2020	DE	6	N/A	5	5	4	85
Eyabi Anoma	2018	DE	2	5	5	5	5	94
Jalyn Armour-Davis	2018	CB	28	4	4	4	4	82
Terrion Arnold	2021	S	3	N/A	4	4	4	83
Jonathan Atchison	2009	OLB	14	3	3	3		80
Anthony Averett	2013	ATH	22	4	3	4	4	83
Elliot Baker	2017	OT	1	4	5	4	4	84
Javon Baker	2020	WR	45	N/A	4	4	4	80
Charles Baldwin	2016	OT	1	5	5	4	4	83
Dakota Ball	2012	DT	27		3	3	4	80
Marcus Banks	2019	CB	23	N/A	4	4	4	81
Christian Barmore	2018	DT	4	4	4	4	4	85
Anquin Barnes	2021	DT	25	N/A	3	3	4	80
Blake Barnett	2015	QB	1	5	5	5	5	90
Mark Barron	2008	ATH		5	4	4		80
Cooper Bateman	2013	QB	3	4	4	4	4	87
Jordan Battle	2019	S	4	N/A	4	4	4	84
Christian Bell	2016	DE		3	3	3	4	81
Kenny Bell	2009	WR	49	4	4	4		78
Deion Belue	2010	ATH	40	3	3	3	3	78
	2012	CB		3	3	3	N/A	NR
Malik Benson	2023	WR		N/A	4	4	4	83
Markail Benton	2017	OLB	7	4	4	4	4	85
Jahleel Billingsley	2019	TE	11	N/A	4	4	4	80
Undra Billingsley	2008	DE		3	3	3		74
Chris Black	2012	WR	2	4	4	4	4	83
Kendrick Blackshire	2021	ILB	7	N/A	4	4	4	83
Slade Bolden	2018	ATH	64	3	3	3	3	77
Devonta Bolton	2008	WR		4	4	4		80
Isaiah Bond	2022	WR		N/A	4	4	4	84
Chris Bonds	2009	DT	10	3	3	3		80
Tyler Booker	2022	OT		N/A	4	4	5	91
John Michael Boswell	2008	OT		3	4	3		79
Tanner Bowles	2019	OT	23	N/A	3	4	4	82
Michael Bowman	2009	WR	119	4	4	4		75
Brian Branch	2020	S	3	N/A	4	4	4	84
Chris Braswell	2020	DE	3	N/A	5	5	5	91
Jackson Bratton	2020	ILB	5	N/A	4	4	4	83
James Brockermeyer	2021	OC	1	N/A	4	4	4	84
Tommy Brockermeyer	2021	OT	1	N/A	5	5	5	91
Jacorey Brooks	2021	WR		N/A	4	5	4	86
Deonte Brown	2016	OG	7	4	3	4	4	83
Elijah Brown	2022	TE		N/A	4	4	4	80
Leon Brown	2013	OT	2	4	3	4	4	83
Mekhi Brown	2015	OLB	10	4	4	4	4	83
Tommy Brown	2018	OT	10	4	4	4	4	85
Tony Brown	2014	CB	2	5	5	5	5	92
Isaiah Buggs	2017	DE	1	4	5	4	4	83

Name	Year	Pos	Pos Rank	Scout	Rivals	247 Sports	ESPN	ESPN Grade
Joseph Bulovas	2017	K	6	3	3	3	3	76
Shawn Burgess-Becker	2015	S	7	4	4	4	4	83
Jamil Burroughs	2020	DT	22	N/A	4	4	4	80
Brent Calloway	2011	ATH		4	4	4	4	80
Kadarius Calloway	2021	S	16	N/A	3	4	4	81
Jihaad Campbell	2022	LB		N/A	4	4	4	83
James Carpenter	2009	OT		4	4	4		NR
Ronald Carswell	2010	WR	65	4	3	3	3	78
Ronald Carswell	2011	WR	71		3	3	3	78
Jeffery Carter	2019	CB	4	N/A	4	5	4	86
Shyheim Carter	2016	CB	6	4	4	4	4	86
Joshua Casher	2014	OC	1	3	4	4	4	83
Josh Chapman	2007	DT		3	3	3		71
Daylon Charlot	2015	WR	8	4	4	4	4	85
Caden Clark	2020	TE	6	N/A	3	3	4	80
Ronnie Clark	2014	ATH	7	4	4	4	4	84
Ha Ha Clinton-Dix	2011	S	23	5	5	5	4	84
Terrence Cody	2008	DT		4	3	3		NR
Javion Cohen	2020	OT	56	N/A	4	4	3	79
Jake Coker	2014	QB	18		3	3		
Landon Collins	2012	S	1	5	5	5	5	85
Jonathan Cook	2013	CB	73	3	3	3	3	75
Amari Cooper	2012	WR	7	4	4	4	4	82
David Cornwell	2014	QB	4	4	4	4	4	84
Lester Cotton Sr.	2015	OG	7	4	4	4	4	83
VanDarius Cowan	2017	OLB	4	5	4	4	4	81
Patrick Crump	2007	OL		3	3	3		74
Darrian Dalcourt	2019	OC	3	N/A	4	4	4	84
DJ Dale	2019	DT	14	N/A	3	4	4	83
Marcell Dareus	2008	DT		4	3	4		77
Ben Davis	2016	ILB	1	5	5	5	4	87
Jordan Davis	2018	DE	12	4	4	4	4	84
Luther Davis	2007	DE		4	4	4		79
Raekwon Davis	2016	DT	18	4	4	4	4	82
Skyler DeLong	2018	K	6	3	3	3	3	77
Trey DePriest	2011	OLB	2	5	4	5	4	82
Denzel Devall	2012	DE	22	4	4	4	4	80
Quinton Dial	2009	DT	28	3	4	3		79
Quinton Dial	2011	DT		4	4	4	N/A	NR
Xzavier Dickson	2011	DE	4	4	4	4	4	83
Trevon Diggs	2016	ATH	6	4	4	4	4	83
Travell Dixon	2012	CB		4	4	4	N/A	NR
Aaron Douglas	2011	OT		3	4	4	N/A	NR
Caleb Downs	2023	S		N/A	5	5	5	90
Kenyan Drake	2012	RB	14	4	4	4	4	80
Johnny Dwight	2014	DT	33	4	3	3	4	80
JoJo Earle	2021	WR	10	N/A	4	4	4	86
Justin Eboigbe	2019	DE	5	N/A	4	4	4	86
Kyle Edwards	2020	RB	42	N/A	4	3	3	79
Emil Ekiyor Jr.	2018	OG	3	4	4	4	4	85
Jeremy Elder	2007	DT		3	2	3		73
Phillip Ely	2011	QB	40	3	3	3	3	77
B.J. Emmons	2016	RB	1	4	4	4	4	86
Rashaan Evans	2014	OLB	2	5	5	5	4	84
Malcolm Faciane	2011	TE	4	3	4	4	4	81
Raheem Falkins	2013	WR	41	3	4	3	4	82
LaMichael Fanning	2011	DE	14	4	4	4	4	80
Nick Fanuzzi	2007	QB		3	3	3		78
Tarence Farmer	2007	CB		3	3	3		77

Name	Year	Pos	Pos Rank	Scout	Rivals	247 Sports	ESPN	ESPN Grade
Trequon Fegans	2022	CB		N/A	4	4	4	85
Terrance Ferguson	2021	OT	8	N/A	4	4	4	85
Minkah Fitzpatrick	2015	CB	4	4	4	4	4	88
Thomas Fletcher	2017	LS	3	2	2	2	2	69
Ty Flournoy-Smith	2014	TE	6	3	2	3	3	76
DeSherrius Flowers	2015	RB	10	4	4	4	4	83
D.J. Fluker	2009	OT	1	4	5	5		86
Jerome Ford	2018	RB		3	3	4	4	81
Wilkin Formby	2023	OT		N/A	4	4	4	84
Miller Forristall	2016	TE	11	4	3	3	3	79
Cade Foster	2010	K	12	4	2	3	3	76
Reuben Foster	2013	ILB	1	5	5	5	4	88
Robert Foster	2013	WR	2	3	4	5	4	88
Jalston Fowler	2010	OLB		4	4	4	3	77
Joshua Frazier	2014	DT	10	4	4	4	4	83
Kurt Freitag	2012	TE	13	3	3	3	4	79
John Fulton	2010	CB	4		4	4	4	83
Nick Gentry	2007	DT		3	3	3		78
Damieon George Jr.	2020	OT	30	N/A	3	3	4	80
Brandon Gibson	2007	WR		4	4	4		79
Demetrius Goode	2007	RB		3	4	3		79
Monkell Goodwine	2021	DE	19	N/A	4	4	4	83
Corey Grant	2010	RB	23	4	4	N/A	3	79
Robby Green	2008	CB		4	4	4		80
Brandon Greene	2012	OT	6	4	4	4	4	83
Jeramie Griffin	2007	RB		4	3	3		77
Adam Griffith	2012	K	7	3	3	3	3	78
Caleb Gulledge	2012	OG	69	3	3	3	3	76
Jalen Hale	2023	WR		N/A	4	4	4	86
Agiye Hall	2021	WR	3	N/A	4	4	4	86
Terrell Hall	2016	DE	6	4	5	4	4	85
Jaren Hamilton	2023	WR		N/A	3	4	3	79
Shaun Dion Hamilton	2014	ILB	6	3	4	4	4	83
Da'Shawn Hand	2014	DE	2	5	5	5	5	94
Darius Hanks	2007	WR		3	3	3		71
Glenn Harbin	2008	DE		3	4	3		77
Christian Harris	2019	ATH	6	N/A	4	4	4	84
Damien Harris	2015	RB	2	4	4	4	4	88
Jerrell Harris	2008	OLB		4	4	4		81
Kevin Harris	2019	DE	10	N/A	4	4	4	84
Najee Harris	2017	RB	1	5	5	5	5	90
Ronnie Harrison Jr.	2015	S	25	4	4	4	4	80
Demetrius Hart	2011	RB	8	4	5	4	4	81
J. C. Hassenauer	2014	OC	2	4	4	4	4	83
Isaiah Hastings	2022	DT		N/A	3	3	4	80
Tyler Hayes	2012	OLB	10	4	4	4	4	80
Justice Haynes	2023	RB		N/A	4	5	4	88
DeMarcco Hellams	2019	ATH	10	N/A	4	4	4	84
Emmanuel Henderson	2022	RB		N/A	4	5	4	89
Derrick Henry	2013	ATH	1	5	4	5	5	90
Hale Hentges	2015	TE	3	4	4	4	4	83
Jennings Hester	2007	ILB		2	2	3		72
Dont'a Hightower	2008	DE		4	4	4		79
Brandon Hill	2012	OT	77	3	3	3	3	77
Brandon Hill	2013	OT		3	3	3	3	74
Edric Hill	2023	DT		N/A	4	4	4	80
Grant Hill	2013	OG	1	4	4	4	4	84
Keith Holcombe	2014	OLB	21	3	3	4	4	82
Traeshon Holden	2020	WR	41	N/A	4	4	4	81

Name	Year	Pos	Pos Rank	Scout	Rivals	247 Sports	ESPN	ESPN Grade
Eli Holstein	2023	QB		N/A	4	4	4	88
Destin Hood	2008	WR		3	4	3		80
O.J. Howard	2013	TE	2	5	5	5	4	87
Adrian Hubbard	2010	DE	5	3	3	4	4	82
Brayson Hubbard	2023	ATH		N/A	3	3	4	80
Marlon Humphrey	2014	CB	5	5	5	5	5	90
Jahlili Hurley	2023	CB		N/A	4	4	4	87
Jalen Hurts	2016	QB	13	4	4	4	4	80
Braylen Ingraham	2019	DE	12	N/A	4	4	4	84
Mark Ingram II	2008	RB		3	4	4		81
Brandon Ivory	2010	DT	58	3	3	3	3	77
Chris Jackson	2008	ATH		4	3	4		80
Dominick Jackson	2014	OT	1	4	4	4	4	82
Eddie Jackson	2013	WR	54	3	3	3	4	81
Ian Jackson	2021	OLB	28	N/A	4	4	4	81
Kareem Jackson	2007	CB		3	4	3		40
Khyree Jackson	2021	CB	1	N/A	4	3	4	82
Star Jackson	2008	QB		4	4	4		79
Josh Jacobs	2016	RB	36	3	3	3	3	79
Kedrick James	2017	TE	12	4	4	4	4	80
Justin Jefferson	2023	LB		N/A	4	4	3	79
Anfernee Jennings	2015	DE	28	4	4	4	4	80
Shawn Jennings	2016	S	44	3	3	3	3	78
Jerry Jeudy	2017	WR	3	4	5	4	4	88
Josh Jobe	2018	CB	15	4	4	4	4	84
Nico Johnson	2009	ILB	2	5	5	5		84
Thaiu Jones-Bell	2020	WR	9	N/A	3	4	4	84
Barrett Jones	2008	OT		4	4	4		78
Christion Jones	2011	CB	10	3	4	3	4	80
Cyrus Jones	2012	ATH	4	5	4	4	4	83
Harrison Jones	2010	TE	9	3	3	3	4	80
Julio Jones	2008	WR		5	5	5		95
Kendell Jones	2016	DT	15	5	4	4	4	83
Hootie Jones	2014	S	3	4	4	4	4	86
Mac Jones	2017	QB	18	4	4	4	4	80
Phelon Jones	2009	CB		4	4			
Tyren Jones	2013	RB	8	4	4	4	4	85
Walker Jones	2013	ILB	26	3	3	3	3	79
Chris Jordan	2008	OLB		4	4	4		80
Brandon Kaho	2018	OLB		4	4	5	3	78
Alvin Kamara	2013	RB	4	4	4	4	4	88
Keon Keeley	2023	DE		N/A	5	5	4	89
Tim Keenan	2021	DT	24	N/A	4	3	4	80
Kendall Kelly	2009	WR	7	4	4	4		82
Ryan Kelly	2011	OC	4	4	3	4	3	79
Brandon Kennedy	2015	OG	5	4	4	4	4	83
Demouy Kennedy	2020	OLB	7	N/A	5	4	4	84
Derek Kief	2014	WR	26	4	4	4	4	82
Amari Kight	2019	OT	8	N/A	4	4	4	86
Jamar King	2016	DE	8	3	3	3	3	79
Dre Kirkpatrick	2009	CB	1	5	5	5		92
Korren Kirven	2012	DT	8	4	4	4	4	80
Antonio Kite	2022	ATH		N/A	4	4	4	85
Nigel Knott	2016	CB	5	4	4	4	4	86
Keanu Koht	2021	DE	15	N/A	4	4	4	81
Arie Kouandjio	2010	OG	14	4	4	4	3	79
Cyrus Kouandjio	2011	OT	1	5	5	5	5	87
Eddie Lacy	2009	RB	17	4	4	4		81
Darren Lake	2012	DT	54	3	3	3	3	78

Name	Year	Pos	Pos Rank	Scout	Rivals	247 Sports	ESPN	ESPN Grade
Scott Lashley	2016	OT	15	4	3	4	4	83
JC Latham	2021	OT	2	N/A	5	5	5	90
Jah-Marien Latham	2020	DT	9	N/A	4	4	4	84
Cameron Latu	2018	DE	16	4	4	4	4	83
Kendrick Law	2022	ATH		N/A	4	4	4	83
Alonzo Lawrence	2008	CB		4	4	4		80
Deontae Lawson	2021	OLB	14	N/A	4	4	4	84
Christian Leary	2021	ATH	7	N/A	4	4	4	85
Alex Leatherwood	2017	OT	1	5	5	5	5	90
Dillon Lee	2012	OLB	6	4	4	4	4	81
Shane Lee	2019	ILB	1	N/A	4	4	4	84
Robert Lester	2008	S		3	4	3		80
Chris Lett	2007	S		3	4	3		77
Brandon Lewis	2008	DE		3	4	3		79
	2010	DE		3	3	3	N/A	NR
Danny Lewis	2022	TE		N/A	3	3	4	97
Chad Lindsay	2010	OG	1	3	3	3	4	81
Dee Liner	2013	DT	4	4	4	4	4	88
Earl Little Jr	2022	CB		N/A	4	4	4	82
Ty Lockwood	2023	TE		N/A	4	4	4	83
Dylan Lonergan	2023	QB		N/A	4	4	4	87
Tyler Love	2008	OT		5	5	5		83
Wilson Love	2010	DT	34	3	3	3	3	79
	2011	DT	42		3	N/A	3	79
Isaac Luatua	2011	OG	18	3	3	3	3	79
Keiwone Malone	2010	WR	13	3	4	4	4	81
Mike Marrow	2009	FB	2	3	3	3		80
Ivan Matchett	2008	RB		3	3	3		79
Phidarian Mathis	2017	DT	7	4	4	4	4	86
Jared Mayden	2016	CB	17	4	4	4	4	82
Marquis Maze	2007	WR		3	3	3		79
Cole Mazza	2013	LS	3	2	3	3	2	68
Montel McBride	2014	OG	28	3	3	3	3	79
A.J. McCarron	2009	QB	4	4	4	4		83
Rolando McClain	2007	ILB		4	4	4		79
Jase McClellan	2020	RB	6	N/A	4	4	4	86
Alfred McCullough	2007	DT		3	4	3		76
Kyriq McDonald	2017	CB	45	3	4	3	3	77
RyQueze McElderry	2023	OL		N/A	4	3	3	79
Darius McKeller	2009	OT	30	3	3	3		78
	2010	OT	58		3	3	3	78
Xavier McKinney	2017	S	6	4	4	4	4	84
Kool-Aid McKinstry	2021	ATH	4	N/A	4	5	4	87
Seth McLaughlin	2020	OC	4	N/A	3	3	4	80
Parker McLeod	2013	QB	31	3	3	3	3	78
Joshua McMillon	2015	ILB	5	4	4	4	4	82
Miles McVay	2023	OT		N/A	4	4	4	83
DeQuan Menzie	2010	CB		4	4	4	N/A	NR
John Metchie III	2019	WR	52	N/A	4	4	4	80
Christian Miller	2014	OLB	1	4	4	4	4	84
Jam Miller	2022	RB		N/A	4	4	4	83
Dee Milliner	2010	CB	2	5	5	5	4	84
Jalen Milroe	2021	QB	16	N/A	4	4	4	84
William Ming	2009	DE	19	4	4	4		80
Tony Mitchell	2023	CB		N/A	4	4	4	87
Jaylen Moody	2018	ILB	33	3	2	3	3	75
Brandon Moore	2009	DT	30	4	4	4		79
Malachi Moore	2020	CB	23	N/A	4	4	4	81
Alec Morris	2012	QB	46	3	3	3	3	78

449

Name	Year	Pos	Pos Rank	Scout	Rivals	247 Sports	ESPN	ESPN Grade
Dylan Moses	2017	ATH	1	5	5	5	5	92
C.J. Mosley	2010	OLB	7	4	4	4	4	81
Kerry Murphy	2007	DT		4	4	4		81
	2008	DT		4	4	4		81
	2009	DT			4	4		81
Shawn Murphy	2022	LB		N/A	4	4	4	87
King Mwikuta	2019	DE	19	N/A	4	4	4	83
Evan Neal	2019	OT	2	N/A	5	5	5	91
Wesley Neighbors	2008	S		3	2	3		78
Amari Niblack	2022	TE		N/A	3	3	4	80
Kevin Norwood	2009	WR	66	3	4	3		77
Jaheim Oatis	2022	DT		N/A	4	4	4	87
Anthony Orr	2009	DE	82	3	3	3		76
	2010	OLB	7		3	3	3	76
Hunter Osborne	2023	DE		N/A	4	4	4	82
Robbie Ouzts	2021	TE	11	N/A	3	3	3	79
Chris Owens	2016	OG	3	4	3	4	4	84
Jeoffrey Pagan	2011	DE	8	4	4	4	4	81
Darius Paige	2013	DT	21	4	4	4	4	83
Michael Parker	2018	TE	26	3	3	3	3	76
Jarez Parks	2018	DE	8		4	4	4	83
Tana Patrick	2009	OLB	9	4	4	4		81
Damon Payne	2021	DT	3	N/A	4	5	4	88
Da'Ron Payne	2015	DT	9	4	4	4	4	86
Khurtiss Perry	2022	DT		N/A	4	4	4	86
Nick Perry	2010	S	27	4	4	4	3	79
Richie Petitbon	2015	OG	10	4	4	4	4	82
D.J. Pettway	2011	DE	21	3	4	4	4	80
	2014	DE	2	4	4	4	4	80
Yhonzae Pierre	2023	DE		N/A	4	4	4	82
Ross Pierschbacher	2014	OG	3	4	4	4	4	84
Jake Pope	2022	S		N/A	3	3	4	80
Kobe Prentice	2022	WR		N/A	3	3	4	80
Shazz Preston	2022	WR		N/A	4	4	5	90
Jermaine Preyear	2008	FB		3	3	3		77
	2009	FB	20		3	3		77
Elijah Pritchett	2022	OT		N/A	4	4	4	84
Kadyn Proctor	2023	OL		N/A	5	5	5	90
Pierce Quick	2019	OT	4	N/A	4	4	5	91
Reggie Ragland	2012	ILB	2	5	4	4	4	80
Kendall Randolph	2017	OT	12	4	4	4	4	82
LaBryan Ray	2017	DT	2	4	4	5	4	89
Melvin Ray	2008	WR		4	4	4		80
Jarran Reed	2014	DT	7	4	3	4	3	79
Will Reichard	2019	K	1	N/A	3	3	3	79
Jordan Renaud	2023	DT		N/A	4	4	4	86
Trent Richardson	2009	RB	1	5	5	5		91
Desmond Ricks	2023	CB		N/A	5	5	5	90
Michael Ricks	2007	S		N/A	4	4		NR
Calvin Ridley	2015	WR	1	4	4	5	5	89
Jaeden Roberts	2021	OG	3	N/A	3	4	4	84
A'Shawn Robinson	2013	DT	11	5	5	5	4	84
Aaron Robinson	2016	ATH	18	3	3	3	4	80
Brian Robinson Jr.	2017	RB	8	4	4	4	4	82
Cameron Robinson	2014	OT	1	5	5	5	5	95
Jahquez Robinson	2020	CB	33	N/A	4	4	3	79
Keilan Robinson	2019	RB	12	N/A	4	3	4	82
Quandarrius Robinson	2020	OLB	8	N/A	4	4	4	84
Henry Ruggs III	2017	WR	11	4	4	4	4	82

450

Name	Year	Pos	Pos Rank	Scout	Rivals	247 Sports	ESPN	ESPN Grade
Jaquavious Russaw	2023	LB		N/A	5	5	5	91
Drew Sanders	2020	ATH	4	N/A	4	5	4	86
Trey Sanders	2019	RB	2	N/A	5	5	4	88
Bo Scarbrough	2014	ATH	2	5	5	5	5	90
Bo Scarbrough	2015	ATH	2		5	5	5	90
B.J. Scott	2008	ATH		4	5	5		84
JK Scott	2014	K	5	3	3	3	3	78
Darrington Sentimore	2009	DT	20	4	4	4		79
Tyrell Shavers	2017	WR	12	4	4	4	4	83
Kendall Sheffield	2015	CB	3	5	5	5	5	90
Austin Shepherd	2010	OT	46	3	3	3	3	77
Marvin Shinn	2011	WR	14	4	4	4	4	81
T.J. Simmons	2016	WR	110	4	4	3	3	78
Ty Simpson	2022	QB		N/A	4	5	4	87
Blake Sims	2010	ATH	64	4	4	4	3	78
Cam Sims	2014	WR	8	4	4	4	4	84
Phillip Sims	2010	QB	1	5	4	5	4	83
Brad Smelley	2008	TE		2	3	3		77
Irv Smith Jr.	2016	TE	6	3	3	3	4	80
Corey Smith	2008	K		2	2	3		75
DeVonta Smith	2017	WR	9	4	4	4	4	81
DeVonta Smith	2021	CB	41	N/A	3	4	3	78
Eddie Smith	2018	CB	62	3	3	3	3	78
Geno Smith	2012	CB	2	4	4	4	4	82
James Smith	2023	DT		N/A	5	5	5	90
Maurice Smith	2013	CB	12	4	4	4	4	84
O.J. Smith	2014	DT	18	3	3	3	4	82
Petey Smith	2009	ILB	5	3	3	4		81
Petey Smith	2010	ILB	32		3	4	4	81
Saivion Smith	2018	CB	1	4	4	4	4	84
Timothy Smith	2020	DT	13	N/A	4	4	4	83
Ishmael Sopsher	2019	DT	2	N/A	4	4	4	86
Damion Square	2008	DE		4	3	4		79
Anthony Steen	2009	DT	39	3	3	3		78
ArDarius Stewart	2013	ATH	18	4	4	4	4	83
Ed Stinson	2009	DE	22	3	4	3		80
Kristian Story	2020	ATH	15	N/A	4	4	4	81
Vinnie Sunseri	2011	OLB	18	3	3	3	4	79
Patrick Surtain II	2018	CB	1	5	5	5	5	93
Bradley Sylve	2011	WR	5	4	4	4	4	82
Taulia Tagovailoa	2019	QB	5	N/A	4	4	4	83
Tua Tagovailoa	2017	QB	1	4	4	5	4	85
Conor Talty	2023	PK		N/A	2	3	3	75
Alphonse Taylor	2012	DT	15	4	3	4	4	80
Jamar Taylor	2007	RB		3	3	3		75
Jonathan Taylor	2015	DT	2		3	3	4	81
Major Tennison	2017	TE	9	4	4	4	4	81
Altee Tenpenny	2013	RB	10	4	4	4	4	84
Adonis Thomas	2015	OLB	5	4	4	4	4	85
Deionte Thompson	2015	S	3	4	4	4	4	84
Dalvin Tomlinson	2012	DT	42	4	4	4	3	78
Chadarius Townsend	2017	ATH	5	4	4	4	4	82
Brandon Turnage	2019	CB	6	N/A	4	4	4	84
Dallas Turner	2021	OLB	3	N/A	5	5	5	90
Paul Tyson	2019	QB	14	N/A	4	3	4	80
Chris Underwood	2007	TE		2	2	2		40
Courtney Upshaw	2008	DE		4	4	4		83
William Vlachos	2007	OG		3	3	3		80
Brian Vogler	2010	TE	7	4	4	4	4	81

451

Name	Year	Pos	Pos Rank	Scout	Rivals	247 Sports	ESPN	ESPN Grade
Jaylen Waddle	2018	WR	12	4	5	4	4	85
Chance Warmack	2009	OG	16	3	3	3		79
Dallas Warmack	2015	OG	19	4	4	4	4	81
Jabriel Washington	2011	ATH	29	4	3	4	4	79
Alex Watkins	2007	DE		3	4	3		77
Camar Wheaton	2021	RB	3	N/A	5	5	4	86
DeAndrew White	2010	WR	26	4	4	4	4	80
Chavis Williams	2007	DE		2	3	3		75
Eddie Williams	2012	ATH	2	4	5	5	5	85
Jarrick Williams	2010	S		4	4	4	4	79
Jay Williams	2010	K	9	3	2	3	3	77
Jesse Williams	2011	DT		4	4	4	N/A	NR
Jonah Williams	2016	OT	3	4	5	5	4	87
Kaine Williams	2021	S	7	N/A	4	4	4	83
Kellen Williams	2009	OT	79	3	3	3		75
Michael Williams	2008	DE		4	4	4		79
Quinnen Williams	2016	DE	31	4	4	4	4	81
Ronald Williams	2020	S	3	N/A	4	4	3	79
Roydell Williams	2020	RB	10	N/A	4	4	4	84
Tim Williams	2013	DE	5	4	4	4	4	87
Xavier Williams	2018	ATH	3	4	4	4	4	87
Jedrick Wills	2017	OG	7	4	4	4	4	86
Mack Wilson	2016	OLB	5	4	5	5	4	86
Matt Womack	2015	OT	59	3	3	3	3	78
Danny Woodson Jr.	2011	WR	22	4	4	4	4	80
Daniel Wright	2017	S	16	4	4	4	4	85
Stephon Wynn	2018	DE	9	4	4	4	4	84
T.J. Yeldon	2012	RB	4	4	5	5	4	81
Bryce Young	2020	QB	1	N/A	5	5	5	91
Byron Young	2019	DE	11	N/A	4	4	4	84
Richard Young	2023	RB		N/A	4	4	4	89

	Scout	Rivals	247Sports	ESPN
5 Stars	36	58	66	32
4 Stars	163	260	252	253
3 Stars	91	110	117	59
2 Stars	7	11	2	2

Note: Some recruits are listed in multiple years because they were injured or they were recruited out of high school, went at played at a Community College, then then came back.

Note: Table data from "2007 Alabama Crimson Tide football team" (18), "2008 Alabama Crimson Tide football team" (32), "2009 Alabama Crimson Tide football team" (48), "2010 Alabama Crimson Tide football team" (64), "2011 Alabama Crimson Tide football team" (79), "2012 Alabama Crimson Tide football team" (94), "2013 Alabama Crimson Tide football team" (110), "2014 Alabama Crimson Tide football team" (125), "2015 Alabama Crimson Tide football team" (142), "2016 Alabama Crimson Tide football team" (160), "2017 Alabama Crimson Tide football team" (196), "2018 Alabama Crimson Tide football team" (212), "2019 Alabama Crimson Tide football team" (244), "2020 Alabama Crimson Tide football team" (272), "2021 Alabama Crimson Tide football team" (300), "2022 Alabama Crimson Tide football team" (333), "2023 Alabama Crimson Tide football team" (363)

Players

The list on the left is sorted by last name, and the list on the right is sorted by number. Some players had different numbers in different years. Most players that changed numbers usually started with a number when they joined the team then changed to the one they used more often in later years. I attempted to list the number they used mostly when playing, but if I did not know, I listed the lower number first. In the list sorted by number, I did not duplicate the players - I only listed them one time with the number I felt they wore the most when playing. There are three instances of players that have the same first and last name. To differentiate, I listed their positions in parenthesis beside their names.

Player	Num	Years	Other #s		Num	Player	Years	Other #s
Cole Adams	13	2023			1	Chris Black	2012-2015	5
Connor Adams	86	2018-2019			1	Ben Davis	2016-2020	
Dalton Adkison	37	2018			1	Jahmyr Gibbs	2022	
Edward Aldag	14	2012			1	Dee Hart	2011-2013	
Earl Alexander	82	2007-2010			1	Kool-Aid McKinstry	2021-2023	
Jeremiah Alexander	35	2023			1	B.J. Scott	2008-2010	
Olaus Alinen	73	2023			1	Jameson Williams	2021-2022	
Chase Allen	82	2020-2022			2	Tony Brown	2014-2017	
Christopher Allen	4	2017-2022			2	Simeon Castille	2007	
Jonathan Allen	93	2013-2016			2	Caleb Downs	2023	
Giles Amos	40	2017-2019			2	DeMarcco Hellams	2019-2022	29
Trey Amos	9	2023			2	Derrick Henry	2013-2015	21, 27
Eryk Anders	32	2007-2009			2	Jalen Hurts	2016-2018	
Will Anderson Jr.	31	2020-2022			2	Star Jackson	2008-2009	
Blaine Anderson	41	2015-2016			2	Jase McClellan	2020-2023	21
Keaton Anderson	18	2015-2018			2	Keilan Robinson	2020	
Ryan Anderson	7	2012-2016			2	Patrick Surtain II	2018-2020	
Eyabi Anoma	9	2018			2	DeAndrew White	2010-2014	
Javier Arenas	28	2007-2009			3	Terrion Arnold	2021-2023	12
Jalyn Armour-Davis	5	2018-2022	22		3	Jermaine Burton	2022-2023	
Terrion Arnold	3	2021-2023	12		3	Kareem Jackson	2007-2009	
Noland Asberry	51	2023			3	Trent Richardson	2009-2011	
Jonathan Atchison	49	2009-2012			3	Calvin Ridley	2015-2017	
Anthony Averett	28	2013-2017			3	Vinnie Sunseri	2011-2013	
JD Baird	56	2023			3	Bradley Sylve	2011-2015	16
John Baites	31	2010-2011			3	Xavier Williams	2018-2022	9
Elliot Baker	78	2017-2018			3	Daniel Wright	2017-2022	
Javon Baker	5	2020-2022			4	Christopher Allen	2017-2022	
Dakota Ball	94	2012-2016			4	Mark Barron	2008-2011	
Marcus Banks	26	2019-2022			4	Daylon Charlot	2015	
Braxton Barker	7	2018-2022			4	Eddie Jackson	2013-2016	
Christian Barmore	58	2018-2020			4	Jerry Jeudy	2017-2019	
Anquin Barnest Jr.	59	2021-2023			4	Marquis Maze	2007-2011	
Blake Barnett	8	2015-2016	6		4	Jalen Milroe	2021-2023	2
Matthew Barnhill	53	2020			4	Tyrone Prothro	2007	
Parker Barrineau	87	2012-2015			4	Brian Robinson Jr.	2017-2022	24
Mark Barron	4	2008-2011			4	Saivion Smith	2018	
Diege Barry	13	2011			4	T.J. Yeldon	2012-2014	
Tyler Bass	35	2013			5	Jalyn Armour-Davis	2018-2022	22
Cooper Bateman	18	2013-2016			5	Javon Baker	2020-2022	
Jordan Battle	9	2019-2022			5	Ronald Carswell	2011	
Wes Baumhower	51	2018-2019			5	Shyheim Carter	2016-2019	
Parker Bearden	41	2016-2017	43		5	Ronnie Clark	2014-2018	1
Kenny Bell	7	2009-2013			5	Jerrell Harris	2008-2011	
Upton Bellenfant	98	2023			5	Cyrus Jones	2012-2015	8
Deion Belue	13	2012-2013			5	Taulia Tagovailoa	2019	
Jonathan Bennett	27	2020-2023	25, 26		5	Roy Upchurch	2007-2009	
Alex Benson (LB)	44	2007			5	Roydell Williams	2020-2023	23
Alex Benson (WR)	25	2009			6	Ha Ha Clinton-Dix	2011-2013	
Malik Benson	11	2023			6	Demetrius Goode	2007-2010	33
Markail Benton	36	2017-2019			6	Khyree Jackson	2021-2022	
Mike Bernier	98	2017-2019	97		6	Hootie Jones	2014-2017	
Jerrod Bierbower	31	2011-2014			6	Jaylen Key	2023	
Jahleel Billingsley	19	2019-2022			6	Kobe Prentice	2023	
Melvin Billingsley	46	2019-2022			6	Trey Sanders	2019-2022	24, 26
Undra Billingsley	94	2008-2011			6	Blake Sims	2010-2014	18

Player	Num	Years	Other #s
Brandon Bishop	34	2018	
Cooper Bishop	35	2019-2020	20
Chris Black	1	2012-2015	5
Kendrick Blackshire	40	2021-2023	
David Blalock	69	2010-2011	
Nolan Boatner	61	2015	
Slade Bolden	18	2018-2022	
Bret Bolin	36	2020-2022	
Isaiah Bond	17	2023	
Chris Bonds	93	2009-2012	
Tyler Booker	52	2023	
John Michael Boswell	67	2008-2011	
Landon Bothwell	96	2019-2020	93
Tanner Bowles	51	2019-2022	
Michael Bowman	88	2009-2011	
Jacoby Boykins	84	2021-2022	
Bradley Bozeman	75	2014-2017	
Brian Branch	14	2020-2022	
Hunter Brannon	50	2017-2019	
Chris Braswell	41	2020-2023	
Jackson Bratton	33	2020-2022	
Justin Britt	50	2007	
James Brockermeyer	58	2021-2023	
Tommy Brockermeyer	76	2021-2022	
Ja'Corey Brooks	7	2021-2023	
Deonte Brown	65	2016-2020	
Keith Brown	81	2007	
Leon Brown	72	2013-2014	
Mekhi Brown	48	2015-2017	
Michael Brown	46	2008	
Tommy Brown	75	2018-2022	
Tony Brown	2	2014-2017	
Colin Bryant	56	2021-2022	
Hunter Bryant	45	2015-2017	
Tyler Buchner	8	2023	
Hardie Buck	81	2010-2011	37
Isaiah Buggs	49	2017-2018	
Drew Bullard	87	2008-2010	
Joseph Bulovas	97	2017-2020	
Shawn Burgess-Becker	27	2015	
Logan Burnett	12	2020	
James Burnip	86	2021-2023	
Ryan Burns	57	2017	
Sam Burnthall	43	2007	
Jamil Burroughs	98	2020-2022	
Jermaine Burton	3	2022-2023	
Gussie Busch	43	2014-2015	
Hunter Bush	34	2010-2012	22
Prince Butler	48	2023	
Matt Caddell	11	2007	
Brandon Cade	66	2020	
Antoine Caldwell	59	2007-2008	
Brent Calloway	21	2011-2012	
Miguel Camboia	19	2023	
Jihaad Campbell	30	2023	
Chris Capps	72	2007	
Evan Cardwell	70	2007-2008	
Nate Carlson	20	2010-2011	
James Carpenter	77	2009-2010	
Greg Carroll Jr.	86	2021-2022	
Cade Carruth	16	2023	
Ronald Carswell	5	2011	
Duron Carter	8	2011	
Marcus Carter	20	2007	
Scooby Carter	11	2019	
Shyheim Carter	5	2016-2019	
Joshua Casher	67	2014-2018	
Caleb Castille	33	2010-2012	27, 25

Num	Player	Years	Other #s
6	DeVonta Smith (WR)	2017-2020	
6	Marcel Stamps	2007	
6	William Vandervoort	2007	
7	Ryan Anderson	2012-2016	
7	Braxton Barker	2018-2022	
7	Kenny Bell	2009-2013	
7	Ja'Corey Brooks	2021-2023	
7	Trevon Diggs	2016-2019	
7	Adam Hill	2007	
7	Keiwone Malone	2010	
7	Will Oakley	2007-2008	
7	Elias Ricks	2022	
7	Brandon Turnage	2019-2020	14
8	Blake Barnett	2015-2016	6
8	Tyler Buchner	2023	
8	Duron Carter	2011	
8	Robert Foster	2013-2017	1
8	Tyler Harrell	2022	
8	Christian Harris	2019-2022	
8	Josh Jacobs	2016-2018	25
8	Julio Jones	2008-2010	
8	John Metchie III	2019-2022	
8	Jeoffrey Pagan	2011-2013	
8	Chris Rogers	2007-2009	
8	DeVonta Smith (DB)	2021-2023	27
9	Trey Amos	2023	
9	Eyabi Anoma	2018	
9	Jordan Battle	2019-2022	
9	Amari Cooper	2012-2014	
9	Da'Shawn Hand	2014-2017	
9	Phelon Jones	2009-2011	
9	Bo Scarbrough	2015-2017	
9	Nikita Stover	2007-2008	
9	Heath Thomas	2007-2008	98
9	Nick Williams	2009-2012	18
9	Bryce Young	2020-2022	
10	JoJo Earle	2021-2022	
10	Reuben Foster	2013-2016	2
10	John Fulton	2010-2013	
10	Eli Holstein	2023	
10	Jimmy Johns	2007	
10	Mac Jones	2017-2020	
10	Ale Kaho	2018-2020	
10	J.B. Kern	2010	
10	Justin Martin	2007	
10	A.J. McCarron	2009-2013	
10	Morgan Ogilvie	2008-2011	18
10	Henry To'oTo'o	2021-2022	
11	Malik Benson	2023	
11	Matt Caddell	2007	
11	Scooby Carter	2019	
11	Gehrig Dieter	2016	
11	Brandon Gibson	2007-2011	18
11	Traeshon Holden	2020-2022	
11	Alec Morris	2012-2015	
11	Tana Patrick	2009-2013	2
11	Henry Ruggs III	2017-2019	
11	Kendall Sheffield	2015	
11	Kristian Story	2020-2023	4
11	Ranzell Watkins	2010-2012	49
12	Logan Burnett	2020	
12	Jonathan Cook	2013-2014	15
12	David Cornwell	2014-2016	
12	Skyler DeLong	2018-2020	
12	Phillip Ely	2011-2012	
12	Antonio Kite	2023	
12	Christian Leary	2021-2022	
12	Dylan Lonergan	2023	

Player	Num	Years	Other #s
Simeon Castille	2	2007	
Josh Chapman	99	2007-2011	
Daylon Charlot	4	2015	
Braylon Chatman	52	2023	
MJ Chirgwin	42	2023	
Jamie Christensen	86	2007	
Caden Clark	87	2021-2022	
Ronnie Clark	5	2014-2018	1
Austin Clifford	22	2007	
Ha Ha Clinton-Dix	6	2011-2013	
Terrence Cody	62	2008-2009	
Glen Coffee	38	2007-2008	
Tremayne Coger	23	2007	
Javion Cohen	70	2020-2022	57
Jake Coker	14	2014-2015	
Landon Collins	26	2012-2014	
Matt Collins	56	2007	
Michael Collins	31	2019	
Taylor Conant	43	2011	
Jonathan Cook	12	2013-2014	15
Levi Cook	18	2011-2012	
Amari Cooper	9	2012-2014	
William Cooper	55	2018-2019	
David Cornwell	12	2014-2016	
Lester Cotton Sr.	66	2015-2018	
Zarian Courtney	35	2023	
VanDarius Cowan	43	2017	
Keelan Cox	97	2021-2022	
Robert Cramer	50	2011	
Elijah Crockett	29	2021-2022	
Paden Crowder	39	2013-2015	
Patrick Crump	69	2007	
Joshua Curry	65	2007	
David D'Amico	48	2014-2015	
Darrian Dalcourt	71	2019-2023	
DJ Dale	94	2019-2022	
Marcell Dareus	57	2008-2010	
Thomas Darrah	16	2008-2019	
Ben Davis	1	2016-2020	
Chase Davis	46	2023	
Cody Davis	75	2007	
Drew Davis	79	2007-2009	
Luther Davis	96	2007-2010	
Marlon Davis	76	2007-2008	
Raekwon Davis	99	2016-2019	
Will Davis	62	2014-2016	
Brandon Deaderick	95	2007-2009	51
Trent Dean	37	2007	
Scott Deaton	60	2007-2008	
Sawyer Deerman	36	2023	
Michael DeJohn	51	2008-2010	95
Luke Del Rio	14	2013	
Skyler DeLong	12	2018-2020	
James Denton	16	2007	
Trey DePriest	33	2011-2014	
Denzel Devall	30	2012-2015	
Preston Dial	85	2007-2010	
Quinton Dial	90	2011-2012	
Josh Dickerson	55	2011-2014	
Landon Dickerson	69	2019-2020	
Xzavier Dickson	47	2011-2014	
Gehrig Dieter	11	2016	
Trevon Diggs	7	2016-2019	
CJ Dippre	81	2023	
Joe Donald	57	2018-2020	
DJ Douglas	20	2019-2020	
Caleb Downs	2	2023	
Dillon Drake	98	2012	

Num	Player	Years	Other #s
12	Taylor Morton	2012-2013	23
12	Andy Pappanastos	2016-2017	92
12	Chadarius Townsend	2017-2019	
13	Cole Adams	2023	
13	Diege Barry	2011	
13	Deion Belue	2012-2013	
13	Rob Ezell	2009-2010	
13	Robert Ezell	2008	
13	Nick Fanuzzi	2007-2008	18
13	Nigel Knott	2016-2018	
13	Malachi Moore	2020-2023	
13	Cory Reamer	2007-2009	
13	Ty Reed	2012-2013	
13	ArDarius Stewart	2013-2016	
13	Tua Tagovailoa	2017-2019	
14	Edward Aldag	2012	
14	Brian Branch	2020-2022	
14	Jake Coker	2014-2015	
14	Luke Del Rio	2013	
14	Jalen Hale	2023	
14	Thaiu Jones-Bell	2020-2023	
14	Tyrell Shavers	2017-2019	
14	Phillip Sims	2010-2011	
14	Deionte Thompson	2015-2018	23
14	John Parker Wilson	2007-2008	
15	Darius Hanks	2007-2011	86
15	Ronnie Harrison Jr.	2015-2017	
15	Mark Holt	2010	
15	Alonzo Lawrence	2008	
15	Xavier McKinney	2017-2019	25
15	Parker McLeod	2013	
15	JK Scott	2014-2017	10
15	Ty Simpson	2023	
15	Eddie Smith	2018-2020	25
15	Dallas Turner	2021-2023	
15	Paul Tyson	2019-2022	17
15	Eddie Williams	2012	
16	Cade Carruth	2023	
16	Thomas Darrah	2008-2019	
16	James Denton	2007	
16	Jayden George	2019-2020	
16	Lionel Mitchell	2007	
16	Jamey Mosley	2014-2018	
16	Richard Mullaney	2015	
16	Will Reichard	2019-2023	
16	T.J. Simmons	2016	
17	Isaiah Bond	2023	
17	Kenyan Drake	2012-2015	
17	Trezmen Marshall	2023	
17	Greg McElroy	2007-2010	
17	Parker Philpot	2012	
17	Cam Sims	2014-2017	7
17	Brad Smelley	2008-2011	
17	Adonis Thomas	2015	
17	Jaylen Waddle	2018-2020	
18	Keaton Anderson	2015-2018	
18	Cooper Bateman	2013-2016	
18	Slade Bolden	2018-2022	
18	Levi Cook	2011-2012	
18	Wheeler Harris	2017	
18	Layne Hatcher	2018	
18	Bray Hubbard	2023	
18	Montana Murphy	2016-2017	19
18	Shazz Preston	2023	
18	Reggie Ragland	2012-2015	
18	Rod Woodson	2009	
19	Jahleel Billingsley	2019-2022	
19	Miguel Camboia	2023	

Player	Num	Years	Other #s
Kenyan Drake	17	2012-2015	
Trae Drake	54	2018	
DeMarcus DuBose	40	2009-2011	
Justin Dunn	39	2007	
Johnny Dwight	95	2014-2018	36
Patrick Eades	19	2007	
JoJo Earle	10	2021-2022	
Justin Eboigbe	92	2019-2023	
Jalen Edwards	38	2020-2022	
Kyle Edwards	27	2017-2022	16
Emil Ekiyor Jr.	55	2018-2022	
Jeremy Elder	54	2007	
Cy Ellis	50	2007	
Robert Ellis	43	2020-2023	51
Dustin Ellison	19	2012-2013	36
Phillip Ely	12	2011-2012	
B.J. Emmons	21	2016	
Lawrence Erekosima	43	2015-2016	
Rashaan Evans	32	2014-2017	
Rob Ezell	13	2009-2010	
Robert Ezell	13	2008	
Malcolm Faciane	85	2011-2014	
Raheem Falkins	80	20132016	
Brandon Fanney	98	2007-2008	
LaMichael Fanning	44	2011-2013	
Nick Fanuzzi	13	2007-2008	18
Terrence Ferguson II	69	2021-2023	
P.J. Fitzgerald	97	2007-2009	11
Minkah Fitzpatrick	29	2015-2017	
Kaleb Fleming	39	2023	
Thomas Fletcher	45	2017-2020	
Kyle Flood Jr.	54	2020-2023	
Ty Flournoy-Smith	83	2014-2015	
D.J. Fluker	76	2009-2012	
Jerome Ford	27	2018-2019	
Wilkin Formby	75	2023	
Miller Forristall	87	2016-2020	
Cade Foster	43	2010-2013	
Reuben Foster	10	2013-2016	2
Robert Foster	8	2013-2017	1
Jalston Fowler	45	2010-2014	
Peyton Fox	46	2023	
Joshua Frazier	69	2014-2017	
Kurt Freitag	41	2012-2014	
Andrew Friedman	81	2007-2008	15
John Fulton	10	2010-2013	
Colin Gallagher	95	2010	
JR Gardner	41	2023	
Morgan Garner	57	2007	
Derrick Garnett	46	2015-2016	
Rowdy Garza	63	2019	
A.J. Gates	31	2019	
Daniel Geddes	37	2013-2014	41
Nick Gentry	58	2007-2011	
Damieon George Jr.	74	2020-2022	
Jayden George	16	2019-2020	
Jahmyr Gibbs	1	2022	
Brandon Gibson	11	2007-2011	18
Wallace Gilberry	92	2007	
Chris Golden	85	2018	
Demetrius Goode	6	2007-2010	33
Sean Goodman	48	2017	
Monkell Goodwine	95	2021-2023	
Derrick Gore	27	2015-2016	33
Bo Grant	45	2014-2017	47, 48
Corey Grant	25	2010	
Terry Grant	29	2007-2009	
Austin Gray	68	2010-2011	

Num	Player	Years	Other #s
19	Patrick Eades	2007	
19	Dustin Ellison	2012-2013	36
19	Stone Hollenbach	2019-2022	
19	Chris Jackson	2008	
19	Ronald James	2011	
19	Shawn Jennings	2016	
19	Keanu Koht	2021-2023	
19	Kendrick Law	2023	
19	Xavian Marks	2015-2018	31
19	Jai Miller	2013	
19	Darwin Salaam	2007	
20	Nate Carlson	2010-2011	
20	Marcus Carter	2007	
20	DJ Douglas	2019-2020	
20	Shaun Dion Hamilton	2014-2017	11
20	Tyren Jones	2013-2014	
20	Tyrone King	2007-2009	29
20	Earl Little II	2023	
20	Jonathan Lowe	2007-2008	
20	Drew Sanders	2020-2022	16
20	Jarrick Williams	2010-2014	
21	Brent Calloway	2011-2012	
21	B.J. Emmons	2016	
21	Prince Hall	2007-2008	
21	Ben Howell	2010-2012	25, 34
21	Dre Kirkpatrick	2009-2011	
21	Brylan Lanier	2021-2022	
21	D.J. Lewis	2016-2018	23, 35
21	Jared Mayden	2016-2019	8
21	Jake Pope	2023	
21	Maurice Smith	2013-2015	
22	Austin Clifford	2007	
22	D.J. Hall	2007	
22	Najee Harris	2017-2020	
22	Justice Haynes	2023	
22	Chris Herren Jr.	2021-2022	
22	Mark Ingram II	2008-2010	
22	Christion Jones	2011-2014	
22	Jarelis Owens	2021-2022	
22	Nate Staskelunas	2014-2016	31, 34
22	Ronald Williams Jr.	2020	
23	Tremayne Coger	2007	
23	Robby Green	2008-2010	
23	Jaren Hamilton	2023	
23	Jarez Parks	2018-2020	
23	Aaron Robinson	2016	
23	Jahquez Robinson	2020-2022	21
23	Jabriel Washington	2011-2015	26
24	Clark Griffin	2020-2022	
24	Terrell Hall	2016	
24	Emmanuel Henderson Jr.	2023	
24	Marquis Johnson	2007-2009	
24	Terrell Lewis	2016-2019	
24	Geno Matias-Smith	2015	
24	Nathan McAlister	2010-2012	
24	DeQuan Menzie	2010-2011	
24	Chris Pugh	2007	
24	Geno Smith	2012-2015	
25	Alex Benson (WR)	2009	
25	Corey Grant	2010	
25	Jahlil Hurley	2023	
25	Dillon Lee	2012-2015	
25	Jacobi McBride	2020-2022	47
25	Rolando McClain	2007-2009	1
25	Aaron McDaniel	2007	
25	Buddy Pell	2014	
25	Jordan Tate-Parker	2021-2022	
25	Camar Wheaton	2021-2022	

Player	Num	Years	Other #s
Eric Gray	36	2007	
Hampton Gray	26	2007-2009	33
Stabler Gray	91	2007	
Robby Green	23	2008-2010	
Brandon Greene	89	2012-2016	58
Bobby Greenwood	93	2007-2008	
Clark Griffin	24	2020-2022	
Jeramie Griffin	34	2007-2009	
Adam Griffith	99	2012-2016	
Caleb Gulledge	74	2012-2013	
Jalen Hale	14	2023	
Agiye Hall	84	2021-2022	
D.J. Hall	22	2007	
Jake Hall	59	2019-2022	
Prince Hall	21	2007-2008	
Terrell Hall	24	2016	
Daren Hallman	53	2008	
Jaren Hamilton	23	2023	
Shaun Dion Hamilton	20	2014-2017	11
Da'Shawn Hand	9	2014-2017	
Darius Hanks	15	2007-2011	86
Patrick Hanrahan	30	2007	
Glenn Harbin	54	2008-2010	
Donovan Hardin	67	2020-2022	
Reed Harradine	96	2023	
Rowdy Harrell	48	2010-2012	
Tyler Harrell	8	2022	
Alex Harrelson	58	2013-2015	
Kevin Harris II	44	2019-2020	
Christian Harris	8	2019-2022	
Damien Harris	34	2015-2018	
Jerrell Harris	5	2008-2011	
Najee Harris	22	2017-2020	
Truett Harris	86	2013-2016	
Wheeler Harris	18	2017	
Ronnie Harrison Jr.	15	2015-2017	
Dee Hart	1	2011-2013	
Joseph Harvey	46	2017	
J.C. Hassenauer	63	2014-2017	
Isaiah Hastings	99	2023	
Layne Hatcher	18	2018	
Tyler Hayes	36	2012	
Justice Haynes	22	2023	
DeMarcco Hellams	2	2019-2022	29
Emmanuel Henderson Jr.	24	2023	
Derrick Henry	2	2013-2015	21, 27
Hale Hentges	84	2015-2018	
Mac Hereford	36	2017-2019	
Chris Herren Jr.	22	2021-2022	
Chris Herring	30	2017-2018	41
Jennings Hester	42	2007-2008	
Kneeland Hibbett	48	2021-2023	51
Baker Hickman	66	2023	
Charlie Higginbotham	45	2007-2008	
Dont'a Hightower	30	2008-2011	
Adam Hill	7	2007	
Brandon Hill	73	2013	
Edric Hill	94	2023	
Grant Hill	64	2013-2014	
Wilder Hines	63	2023	
Stephen Hodge	96	2014-2015	
Charles Hoke	89	2007	
Keith Holcombe	42	2014-2017	
Traeshon Holden	11	2020-2022	
Stone Hollenbach	19	2019-2022	
Eli Holstein	10	2023	
Mark Holt	15	2010	
Zach Houston	37	2013-2014	

Num	Player	Years	Other #s
25	Danny Woodson Jr.	2011-2012	
25	Richard Young	2023	
26	Marcus Banks	2019-2022	
26	Landon Collins	2012-2014	
26	Hampton Gray	2007-2009	33
26	Marlon Humphrey	2014-2016	29
26	Alvin Kamara	2013	
26	Kyriq McDonald	2017-2018	
26	Jam Miller	2023	
26	Ali Sharrief	2007-2009	
26	Nick Tinker	2010-2011	
27	Jonathan Bennett	2020-2023	25, 26
27	Shawn Burgess-Becker	2015	
27	Kyle Edwards	2017-2022	16
27	Jerome Ford	2018-2019	
27	Derrick Gore	2015-2016	33
27	Tony Mitchell	2023	
27	Nick Perry	2010-2014	
27	Joshua Robinson	2019-2022	45
27	Justin Woodall	2007-2009	
28	Javier Arenas	2007-2009	
28	Anthony Averett	2013-2017	
28	Justin Jefferson	2023	
28	Josh Jobe	2018-2022	
28	Michael Lorino III	2023	
28	Dee Milliner	2011-2012	
28	Altee Tenpenny	2013-2014	23
29	Elijah Crockett	2021-2022	
29	Minkah Fitzpatrick	2015-2017	
29	Terry Grant	2007-2009	
29	Austin Jones	2018	
29	Will Lowery	2010-2011	
29	Blake Pugh	2021-2022	
29	Dezz Ricks	2023	
29	Caleb Sims	2013	
29	Brandon Turner	2015	
30	Jihaad Campbell	2023	
30	Denzel Devall	2012-2015	
30	Patrick Hanrahan	2007	
30	Chris Herring	2017-2018	41
30	Dont'a Hightower	2008-2011	
30	Rajiv Lundy	2007	
30	King Mwikuta	2019-2022	
30	D.J. Rias	2021-2022	
30	Daniel Skehan	2017	
30	Mack Wilson	2016-2018	
31	Will Anderson Jr.	2020-2022	
31	John Baites	2010-2011	
31	Jerrod Bierbower	2011-2014	
31	Michael Collins	2019	
31	A.J. Gates	2019	
31	Kelly Johnson	2011-2012	
31	Keon Keeley	2023	
31	Ivan Matchett	2008	
31	Bryce Musso	2018	
31	Forress Rayford	2007	
31	Conor Talty	2023	
31	Shatarius Williams	2020-2022	
32	Eryk Anders	2007-2009	
32	Rashaan Evans	2014-2017	
32	Swade Hutchinson	2017	
32	Jalen Jackson	2018-2019	
32	Deontae Lawson	2021-2023	
32	Jay Loper Jr.	2023	
32	Cody Mandell	2010-2013	
32	Dylan Moses	2017-2020	18
32	C.J. Mosley	2010-2013	
32	Trey Roberts	2012-2013	

Player	Num	Years	Other #s
O.J. Howard	88	2013-2016	
Terrance Howard	34	2023	
Ben Howell	21	2010-2012	25, 34
Adrian Hubbard	42	2010-2013	
Bray Hubbard	18	2023	
Baron Huber	40	2007-2009	
Marlon Humphrey	26	2014-2016	29
Richard Hunt	83	2019-2022	82
Jahlil Hurley	25	2023	
Jalen Hurts	2	2016-2018	
Swade Hutchinson	32	2017	
LT Ikner	97	2020-2021	
Braylen Ingraham	52	2019-2022	
Mark Ingram II	22	2008-2010	
Tevin Isom	39	2015	
Jake Ivie	39	2023	
Brandon Ivory	99	2010-2014	62
Chris Jackson	19	2008	
Dominick Jackson	76	2014-2015	
Eddie Jackson	4	2013-2016	
Ian Jackson	36	2021-2023	
Jalen Jackson	32	2018-2019	
Kareem Jackson	3	2007-2009	
Khyree Jackson	6	2021-2022	
Star Jackson	2	2008-2009	
Josh Jacobs	8	2016-2018	25
Kedrick James	44	2017-2018	
Ronald James	19	2011	
Justin Jefferson	28	2023	
Anfernee Jennings	33	2015-2019	
Shawn Jennings	19	2016	
Jerry Jeudy	4	2017-2019	
Josh Jobe	28	2018-2022	
Jimmy Johns	10	2007	
Austin Johnson	38	2015-2017	27
Christian Johnson	58	2021-2022	
Kelly Johnson	31	2011-2012	
Marquis Johnson	24	2007-2009	
Mike Johnson	78	2007-2009	
Nico Johnson	35	2009-2012	
Rashad Johnson	49	2007-2009	
Sam Johnson	98	2020-2022	
Aaron Joiner	57	2010-2012	
Thaiu Jones-Bell	14	2020-2023	
Austin Jones	29	2018	
Barrett Jones	75	2008-2012	
Bernel Jones	89	2013-2015	90
Christion Jones	22	2011-2014	
Cyrus Jones	5	2012-2015	8
Harrison Jones	82	2010-2013	40
Hootie Jones	6	2014-2017	
Jake Jones	84	2007	
Julio Jones	8	2008-2010	
Mac Jones	10	2017-2020	
Phelon Jones	9	2009-2011	
Tyren Jones	20	2013-2014	
Walker Jones	35	2013-2015	
Chris Jordan	36	2008-2011	
Ale Kaho	10	2018-2020	
Alvin Kamara	26	2013	
Kyle Kazakevicius	39	2013-2014	
Sam Kearns	43	2010-2011	
Keon Keeley	31	2023	
Tim Keenan III	96	2021-2023	
Keith Vohn Jr.	50	2016-2017	
Kendall Kelly	81	2009-2010	26
Ryan Kelly	70	2011-2015	
Sean Kelly	38	2018-2019	

Num	Player	Years	Other #s
32	C.J. Williams	2020	
33	Jackson Bratton	2020-2022	
33	Caleb Castille	2010-2012	27, 25
33	Trey DePriest	2011-2014	
33	Anfernee Jennings	2015-2019	
33	Mike Marrow	2009-2010	
33	Joseph Narcisse II	2022	
33	Kendall Norris	2018	
33	Hunter Osborne	2023	
33	Marcus Polk	2012	
33	Walter Sansing	2023	
33	Jack Standeffer	2023	
33	Jeremy Watson	2013	
34	Brandon Bishop	2018	
34	Hunter Bush	2010-2012	22
34	Jeramie Griffin	2007-2009	
34	Damien Harris	2015-2018	
34	Terrance Howard	2023	
34	Coby McNeal	2023	
34	Courtny Moore	2007	
34	Tyler Owens	2012-2014	38
34	Quandarrius Robinson	2020-2023	
35	Jeremiah Alexander	2023	
35	Tyler Bass	2013	
35	Cooper Bishop	2019-2020	20
35	Zarian Courtney	2023	
35	Nico Johnson	2009-2012	
35	Walker Jones	2013-2015	
35	Charlie Kirschman	2007-2008	
35	Shane Lee	2019-2022	
35	De'Marquise Lockridge	2018-2019	
35	Torin Marks	2015-2016	36
35	Austin Owens	2021-2022	
35	Thomas Woods	2015-2016	
36	Markail Benton	2017-2019	
36	Bret Bolin	2020-2022	
36	Sawyer Deerman	2023	
36	Eric Gray	2007	
36	Tyler Hayes	2012	
36	Mac Hereford	2017-2019	
36	Ian Jackson	2021-2023	
36	Chris Jordan	2008-2011	
36	Brandon Wilson	2013	
37	Dalton Adkison	2018	
37	Trent Dean	2007	
37	Daniel Geddes	2013-2014	41
37	Zach Houston	2013-2014	
37	Demouy Kennedy	2020-2022	
37	Robert Lester	2008-2012	
37	Donavan Mosley	2016-2018	
37	Jonathan Rice	2015-2017	
37	Ty Roper	2023	
37	Sam Willoughby	2020-2023	
38	Glen Coffee	2007-2008	
38	Jalen Edwards	2020-2022	
38	Austin Johnson	2015-2017	27
38	Sean Kelly	2018-2019	
38	Zavier Mapp	2017	
38	Alijah May	2023	
38	Joel Nix	2007	
38	Eric Poellnitz	2019	
38	Petey Smith	2010	
38	Jerffrey Stacy Jr.	2017	
38	Jared Watson	2013	
39	Paden Crowder	2013-2015	
39	Justin Dunn	2007	
39	Kaleb Fleming	2023	
39	Tevin Isom	2015	

458

Player	Num	Years	Other #s
Brandon Kennedy	56	2015-2017	
Demouy Kennedy	37	2020-2022	
J.B. Kern	10	2010	
Jaylen Key	6	2023	
Tommy Keys	48	2011	
Derek Kief	81	2014-2018	
Amari Kight	78	2019-2022	
Jamar King	90	2016-2017	
Tyrone King	20	2007-2009	29
Dre Kirkpatrick	21	2009-2011	
Charlie Kirschman	35	2007-2008	
Korren Kirven	78	2012-2016	85
Antonio Kite	12	2023	
Miles Kitselman	88	2023	
Ezekial Knight	47	2007	
Preston Knight	98	2017-2018	
Nigel Knott	13	2016-2018	
Drew Kobayashi	85	2019-2020	
Keanu Koht	19	2021-2023	
Arie Kouandjio	59	2010-2014	
Cyrus Kouandjio	71	2011-2013	
Grant Krieger	89	2019-2022	
Eddie Lacy	42	2009-2012	
Darren Lake	95	2012-2015	
Adrian Lamothe	98	2014	
Brylan Lanier	21	2021-2022	
Joshua Lanier	84	2019-2020	
Scott Lashley	76	2016-2019	
Jah-Marien Latham	93	2020-2023	
JC Latham	65	2021-2023	
Cameron Latu	81	2018-2022	20
Kendrick Law	19	2023	
Alonzo Lawrence	15	2008	
Deontae Lawson	32	2021-2023	
Christian Leary	12	2021-2022	
Alex Leatherwood	70	2017-2020	
Donnie Lee Jr.	85	2016	
Calvin Lee	56	2008	
Dillon Lee	25	2012-2015	
Shane Lee	35	2019-2022	
Issac Leon	40	2013-2014	
Robert Lester	37	2008-2012	
Chris Lett	41	2007	
Danny Lewis Jr.	87	2023	
Brandon Lewis	95	2010-2011	
D.J. Lewis	21	2016-2018	23, 35
Terrell Lewis	24	2016-2019	
Chad Lindsay	78	2010-2013	
Dee Liner	52	2013-2014	
Earl Little II	20	2023	
De'Marquise Lockridge	35	2018-2019	
Ty Lockwood	89	2023	
Dylan Lonergan	12	2023	
Jake Long	51	2014-2016	
Jay Loper Jr.	32	2023	
Michael Lorino III	28	2023	
Tyler Love	72	2008-2011	
Wilson Love	51	2011-2013	
Jonathan Lowe	20	2007-2008	
Julian Lowenstein	54	2019-2022	
Will Lowery	29	2010-2011	
Issac Luatua	68	2011-2015	
Rajiv Lundy	30	2007	
Josh Magee	88	2012	
Keiwone Malone	7	2010	
Preston Malone	52	2018-2019	56
Cody Mandell	32	2010-2013	
Kyle Mann	89	2020-2022	

Num	Player	Years	Other #s
39	Jake Ivie	2023	
39	Kyle Kazakevicius	2013-2014	
39	Kyle Pennington	2008-2010	
39	Loren Ugheoke	2019	
39	Levi Wallace	2014-2017	44
39	Carson Ware	2019-2022	41
39	Peyton Yates	2023	
40	Giles Amos	2017-2019	
40	Kendrick Blackshire	2021-2023	
40	DeMarcus DuBose	2009-2011	
40	Baron Huber	2007-2009	
40	Issac Leon	2013-2014	
40	Joshua McMillon	2015-2020	
41	Blaine Anderson	2015-2016	
41	Parker Bearden	2016-2017	43
41	Chris Braswell	2020-2023	
41	Kurt Freitag	2012-2014	
41	JR Gardner	2023	
41	Chris Lett	2007	
41	Cliff Murphy	2007	
41	Kyle Smoak	2019	
41	Courtney Upshaw	2008-2011	
42	MJ Chirgwin	2023	
42	Jennings Hester	2007-2008	
42	Keith Holcombe	2014-2017	
42	Adrian Hubbard	2010-2013	
42	Eddie Lacy	2009-2012	
42	Jaylen Moody	2018-2022	
42	Jacob Parker	2016-2017	
42	Yhonzae Pierre	2023	
42	Sam Reed	2019-2022	
43	Sam Burnthall	2007	
43	Gussie Busch	2014-2015	
43	Taylor Conant	2011	
43	VanDarius Cowan	2017	
43	Robert Ellis	2020-2023	51
43	Lawrence Erekosima	2015-2016	
43	Cade Foster	2010-2013	
43	Sam Kearns	2010-2011	
43	Shawn Murphy	2023	
43	Daniel Powell	2016-2019	58
43	Jordan Smith	2020-2023	58
43	Matt Tinney	2013	
43	A.J. Walker	2008-2009	
44	Alex Benson (LB)	2007	
44	LaMichael Fanning	2011-2013	
44	Kevin Harris II	2019-2020	
44	Kedrick James	2017-2018	
44	Damon Payne Jr.	2021-2023	
44	Avery Reid	2016	
44	Tonio Ross	2023	
44	Matt Sandlin	2013	
44	Charlie Skehan	2020-2023	56
44	Corey Smith	2008	
44	Jacob Vane	2007, 2009	
44	Demarcus Waldrop	2007	
44	Cole Weaver	2018	
44	Jay Williams	2010-2011	
45	Hunter Bryant	2015-2017	
45	Thomas Fletcher	2017-2020	
45	Jalston Fowler	2010-2014	
45	Bo Grant	2014-2017	47, 48
45	Charlie Higgenbotham	2007-2008	
45	Caleb McDougle	2023	
45	Robbie Ouzts	2021-2023	
45	Cedric Powell	2015	
45	Sam Snider	2008	
45	Reyn Willis	2007	

Player	Num	Years	Other #s
Zavier Mapp	38	2017	
Torin Marks	35	2015-2016	36
Xavian Marks	19	2015-2018	31
Mike Marrow	33	2009-2010	
Trezmen Marshall	17	2023	
Jack Martin	95	2019-2022	
Justin Martin	10	2007	
Malik Martin	60	2016	
Ivan Matchett	31	2008	
Phidarian Mathis	48	2017-2022	93
Geno Matias-Smith	24	2015	
Alijah May	38	2023	
Jared Mayden	21	2016-2019	8
Marquis Maze	4	2007-2011	
Cole Mazza	55	2013-2016	
Nathan McAlister	24	2010-2012	
Jacobi McBride	25	2020-2022	47
Montel McBride	65	2014	
Travis McCall	83	2007-2008	
A.J. McCarron	10	2009-2013	
Corey McCarron	47	2012-2014	
Rolando McClain	25	2007-2009	1
Jase McClellan	2	2020-2023	21
Mike McCoy	80	2007-2009	
Alfred McCullough	52	2007-2011	
Aaron McDaniel	25	2007	
Kyriq McDonald	26	2017-2018	
Caleb McDougle	45	2023	
RyQueze McElderry	-	2023	
Greg McElroy	17	2007-2010	
Xavier McKinney	15	2017-2019	25
Kool-Aid McKinstry	1	2021-2023	
Seth McLaughlin	56	2020-2023	
Parker McLeod	15	2013	
Joshua McMillon	40	2015-2020	
Coby McNeal	34	2023	
Miles McVay	54	2023	
DeQuan Menzie	24	2010-2011	
John Metchie III	8	2019-2022	
Scott Meyer	52	2016-2018	
Christian Miller	47	2014-2018	34
Jai Miller	19	2013	
Jam Miller	26	2023	
Dee Milliner	28	2011-2012	
Jalen Milroe	4	2021-2023	2
William Ming	56	2009-2012	
Lionel Mitchell	16	2007	
Tony Mitchell	27	2023	
Roq Montgomery	55	2023	
Jaylen Moody	42	2018-2022	
Brandon Moore (DL)	59	2009-2010	97
Brandon Moore (OL)	60	2013-2016	64
Courtny Moore	34	2007	
Malachi Moore	13	2020-2023	
Alec Morris	11	2012-2015	
Taylor Morton	12	2012-2013	23
Dylan Moses	32	2017-2020	18
C.J. Mosley	32	2010-2013	
Donavan Mosley	37	2016-2018	
Jamey Mosley	16	2014-2018	
Brian Motley	66	2007-2010	
Richard Mullaney	16	2015	
Cliff Murphy	41	2007	
Kerry Murphy	64	2009-2010	
Montana Murphy	18	2016-2017	19
Shawn Murphy	43	2023	
Tevita Musika	91	2018-2019	
Bryce Musso	31	2018	

Num	Player	Years	Other #s
46	Melvin Billingsley	2019-2022	
46	Michael Brown	2008	
46	Chase Davis	2023	
46	Peyton Fox	2023	
46	Derrick Garnett	2015-2016	
46	Joseph Harvey	2017	
46	Wesley Neighbors	2008-2010	
46	Michael Nysewander	2012-2015	
46	Zach Schreiber	2007	
46	William Strickland	2009-2011	
46	Christian Swann	2020	
46	Wilson Whorton	2012	
47	Xzavier Dickson	2011-2014	
47	Ezekial Knight	2007	
47	Corey McCarron	2012-2014	
47	Christian Miller	2014-2018	34
47	Kolby Peavy	2023	
47	Josh Pugh	2016	
47	James Smith	2023	
47	Logan Thomas	2010	
47	Adam Thorsland	2021-2023	80
47	Byron Young	2019-2022	
48	Mekhi Brown	2015-2017	
48	Prince Butler	2023	
48	David D'Amico	2014-2015	
48	Sean Goodman	2017	
48	Rowdy Harrell	2010-2012	
48	Kneeland Hibbett	2021-2023	51
48	Tommy Keys	2011	
48	Phidarian Mathis	2017-2022	93
48	Hayden Neighbors	2023	
48	Travis Sikes	2007-2009	
49	Jonathan Atchison	2009-2012	
49	Isaiah Buggs	2017-2018	
49	Rashad Johnson	2007-2008	
49	Jax Porter	2023	
49	Qua Russaw	2023	
49	Ed Stinson	2009-2013	47
49	M.K. Taylor	2011-2014	50, 52, 59
49	Conner Warhurst	2023	
49	Kaine Williams	2021-2022	
50	Hunter Brannon	2017-2019	
50	Justin Britt	2007	
50	Robert Cramer	2011	
50	Cy Ellis	2007	
50	Keith Vohn Jr.	2016-2017	
50	Brock O'Quinn	2023	
50	Gabe Pugh	2019-2022	
50	Brian Selman	2007-2009	54
50	Tim Smith	2020-2023	
50	Alphonse Taylor	2012-2016	
51	Noland Asberry	2023	
51	Wes Baumhower	2018-2019	
51	Tanner Bowles	2019-2022	
51	Michael DeJohn	2008-2010	95
51	Jake Long	2014-2016	
51	Wilson Love	2011-2013	
51	Tucker Riddick	2017	
51	Carson Tinker	2008-2012	61
52	Tyler Booker	2023	
52	Braylon Chatman	2023	
52	Braylen Ingraham	2019-2022	
52	Dee Liner	2013-2014	
52	Preston Malone	2018-2019	56
52	Alfred McCullough	2007-2011	
52	Scott Meyer	2016-2018	
52	Alex Rozier	2023	
52	Carter Short	2021-2022	

Player	Num	Years	Other #s
Darren Mustin	57	2007	
King Mwikuta	30	2019-2022	
Joseph Narcisse II	33	2022	
Evan Neal	73	2019-2022	
Hayden Neighbors	48	2023	
Wesley Neighbors	46	2008-2010	
Michael Newsome	64	2012-2013	
Amari Niblack	84	2023	
Harold Nicholson	59	2012-2013	
Joel Nix	38	2007	
Kendall Norris	33	2018	
Kevin Norwood	83	2009-2013	
Michael Nysewander	46	2012-2015	
Brock O'Quinn	50	2023	
Will Oakley	7	2007-2008	
Jaheim Oatis	91	2023	
Morgan Ogilvie	10	2008-2011	18
Anthony Orr	53	2010-2014	
Hunter Osborne	33	2023	
Robbie Ouzts	45	2021-2023	
Austin Owens	35	2021-2023	
Chris Owens	79	2016-2021	84
Jarelis Owens	22	2021-2022	
Tyler Owens	34	2012-2014	38
Jeoffrey Pagan	8	2011-2013	
Darius Paige	91	2013	
Andy Pappanastos	12	2016-2017	92
Jacob Parker	42	2016-2017	
John Parker	83	2018-2019	
Michael Parker	80	2018-2020	
Jarez Parks	23	2018-2020	
Ryan Parris	53	2016-2018	
Tana Patrick	11	2009-2013	2
Da'Ron Payne	94	2015-2017	
Damon Payne Jr.	44	2021-2023	
Alex Pearman	61	2018	
Austin Peavler	61	2013-2014	67
Kolby Peavy	47	2023	
Colin Peek	84	2008-2009	
Buddy Pell	25	2014	
Kyle Pennington	39	2008-2010	
Ty Perine	99	2019-2022	
Vito Perri	53	2023	
Khurtiss Perry	97	2023	
Nick Perry	27	2010-2014	
Davis Peterson	62	2023	
Richie Petitbon	72	2015-2018	
D.J. Pettway	57	2011-2012, 2014-2015	
Taylor Pharr	68	2007-2009	
Parker Philpot	17	2012	
Yhonzae Pierre	42	2023	
Ross Pierschbacher	71	2014-2018	
John Pizzitola	97	2014	
Eric Poellnitz	38	2019	
Marcus Polk	33	2012	
Jake Pope	21	2023	
Jax Porter	49	2023	
Chris Posa	66	2014-2015	
Brad Pounds	57	2008	
Cedric Powell	45	2015	
Daniel Powell	43	2016-2019	58
Kobe Prentice	6	2023	
Shazz Preston	18	2023	
Elijah Pritchett	57	2023	
Jacob Probasco	61	2016	
Kadyn Proctor	74	2023	

Num	Player	Years	Other #s
53	Matthew Barnhill	2020	
53	Daren Hallman	2008	
53	Anthony Orr	2010-2014	
53	Ryan Parris	2016-2018	
53	Vito Perri	2023	
53	Kade Wehby	2021-2023	
54	Trae Drake	2018	
54	Jeremy Elder	2007	
54	Kyle Flood Jr.	2020-2023	
54	Glenn Harbin	2008-2010	
54	Julian Lowenstein	2019-2022	
54	Miles McVay	2023	
54	Russell Raines	2009-2012	
54	Tyler Steen	2022	
54	Dalvin Tomlinson	2012-2016	52
54	Jesse Williams	2011-2012	
55	William Cooper	2018-2019	
55	Josh Dickerson	2011-2014	
55	Emil Ekiyor Jr.	2018-2022	
55	Cole Mazza	2013-2016	
55	Roq Montgomery	2023	
55	Bennett Whisenhunt	2020-2023	59
55	Chavis Williams	2007-2010	
56	JD Baird	2023	
56	Colin Bryant	2021-2022	
56	Matt Collins	2007	
56	Brandon Kennedy	2015-2017	
56	Calvin Lee	2008	
56	Seth McLaughlin	2020-2023	
56	William Ming	2009-2012	
56	Tim Williams	2013-2016	
57	Ryan Burns	2017	
57	Marcell Dareus	2008-2010	
57	Joe Donald	2018-2020	
57	Morgan Garner	2007	
57	Aaron Joiner	2010-2012	
57	Darren Mustin	2007	
57	D.J. Pettway	2011-2012, 2014-2015	
57	Brad Pounds	2008	
57	Elijah Pritchett	2023	
57	Chase Quigley	2021-2023	
57	John Thornton II	2023	
58	Christian Barmore	2018-2020	
58	James Brockermeyer	2021-2023	
58	Nick Gentry	2007-2011	
58	Alex Harrelson	2013-2015	
58	Christian Johnson	2021-2022	
59	Anquin Barnest Jr.	2021-2023	
59	Antoine Caldwell	2007-2008	
59	Jake Hall	2019-2022	
59	Arie Kouandjio	2010-2014	
59	Brandon Moore (DL)	2009-2010	97
59	Harold Nicholson	2012-2013	
59	Mitch Ray	2007	
59	Dallas Warmack	2015-2017	
60	Scott Deaton	2007-2008	
60	Malik Martin	2016	
60	Brandon Moore (OL)	2013-2016	64
60	David Williams	2008-2010	63
61	Nolan Boatner	2015	
61	Alex Pearman	2018	
61	Austin Peavler	2013-2014	67
61	Jacob Probasco	2016	
61	Graham Roten	2021-2023	
61	B.J. Stabler	2007	
61	Anthony Steen	2009-2013	

Player	Num	Years	Other #s
Tyrone Prothro	4	2007	
Blake Pugh	29	2021-2022	
Chris Pugh	24	2007	
Gabe Pugh	50	2019-2022	
Josh Pugh	47	2016	
Armani Purifoye	89	2015-2016	
Pierce Quick	72	2019-2022	
Chase Quigley	57	2021-2023	
Gunnar Raborn	96	2014-2015	
Reggie Ragland	18	2012-2015	
Russell Raines	54	2009-2012	
Kendall Randolph	85	2017-2022	60
LaBryan Ray	89	2017-2022	18
Mitch Ray	59	2007	
Forress Rayford	31	2007	
Cory Reamer	13	2007-2009	
Jarran Reed	90	2014-2015	
Sam Reed	42	2019-2022	
Ty Reed	13	2012-2013	
Gavin Reeder	91	2020	
Will Reichard	16	2019-2023	
Avery Reid	44	2016	
Jordan Renaud	90	2023	
D.J. Rias	30	2021-2022	
Jonathan Rice	37	2015-2017	
Galen Richardson	68	2018	
Trent Richardson	3	2009-2011	
Dezz Ricks	29	2023	
Elias Ricks	7	2022	
Tucker Riddick	51	2017	
Calvin Ridley	3	2015-2017	
Layne Rinks	64	2007	
Jaeden Roberts	77	2021-2023	
Trey Roberts	32	2012-2013	
A'Shawn Robinson	86	2013-2015	
Aaron Robinson	23	2016	
Brian Robinson Jr.	4	2017-2022	24
Cam Robinson	74	2014-2016	
Jahquez Robinson	23	2020-2022	21
Joshua Robinson	27	2019-2022	45
Keilan Robinson	2	2020	
Quandarrius Robinson	34	2020-2023	
Billy Roby	68	2023	
Jackson Roby	62	2018-2022	
Chris Rogers	8	2007-2009	
Ty Roper	37	2023	
David Ross	74	2007-2010	
Tonio Ross	44	2023	
Graham Roten	61	2021-2023	
Alex Rozier	52	2023	
Henry Ruggs III	11	2017-2019	
Qua Russaw	49	2023	
Darwin Salaam	19	2007	
Drew Sanders	20	2020-2022	16
Trey Sanders	6	2019-2022	24, 26
Matt Sandlin	44	2013	
Walter Sansing	33	2023	
Brannon Satterfield	96	2016-2017	98
Keith Saunders	94	2007	
Bo Scarbrough	9	2015-2017	
Zach Schreiber	46	2007	
Reid Schuback	97	2021-2023	
B.J. Scott	1	2008-2010	
Charlie Scott	85	2020	
Chris Scott	86	2008	
JK Scott	15	2014-2017	10
Brian Selman	50	2007-2009	54
Darrington Sentimore	94	2009-2010	
Nick Serpa	99	2023	

Num	Player	Years	Other #s
62	Terrence Cody	2008-2009	
62	Will Davis	2014-2016	
62	Davis Peterson	2023	
62	Jackson Roby	2018-2022	
62	Alex Stadler	2007	
62	Lance Vickers	2007	
63	Rowdy Garza	2019	
63	J.C. Hassenauer	2014-2017	
63	Wilder Hines	2023	
63	Kellen Williams	2010-2013	
64	Grant Hill	2013-2014	
64	Kerry Murphy	2009-2010	
64	Michael Newsome	2012-2013	
64	Layne Rinks	2007	
64	Mac Smith	2023	
65	Deonte Brown	2016-2020	
65	Joshua Curry	2007	
65	JC Latham	2021-2023	
65	Montel McBride	2014	
65	Allen Skelton	2009-2011	71, 74
65	Chance Warmack	2009-2012	
66	Brandon Cade	2020	
66	Lester Cotton Sr.	2015-2018	
66	Baker Hickman	2023	
66	Brian Motley	2007-2010	
66	Chris Posa	2014-2015	
67	John Michael Boswell	2008-2011	
67	Joshua Casher	2014-2018	
67	Donovan Hardin	2020-2022	
67	Alex Shine	2012	
68	Austin Gray	2010-2011	
68	Issac Luatua	2011-2015	
68	Taylor Pharr	2007-2009	
68	Galen Richardson	2018	
68	Billy Roby	2023	
68	Alajujuan Sparks Jr.	2020-2022	
69	David Blalock	2010-2011	
69	Patrick Crump	2007	
69	Landon Dickerson	2019-2020	
69	Terrence Ferguson II	2021-2023	
69	Joshua Frazier	2014-2017	
69	Paul Waldrop	2012-2014	
70	Evan Cardwell	2007-2008	
70	Javion Cohen	2020-2022	57
70	Ryan Kelly	2011-2015	
70	Alex Leatherwood	2017-2020	
71	Darrian Dalcourt	2019-2023	
71	Cyrus Kouandjio	2011-2013	
71	Ross Pierschbacher	2014-2018	
71	Andre Smith	2007-2008	
72	Leon Brown	2013-2014	
72	Chris Capps	2007	
72	Tyler Love	2008-2011	
72	Richie Petitbon	2015-2018	
72	Pierce Quick	2019-2022	
73	Olaus Alinen	2023	
73	Brandon Hill	2013	
73	Evan Neal	2019-2022	
73	William Vlachos	2007-2011	
73	Jonah Williams	2016-2018	
74	Damieon George Jr.	2020-2022	
74	Caleb Gulledge	2012-2013	
74	Kadyn Proctor	2023	
74	Cam Robinson	2014-2016	
74	David Ross	2007-2010	
74	Jedrick Wills Jr.	2017-2019	
75	Bradley Bozeman	2014-2017	
75	Tommy Brown	2018-2022	
75	Cody Davis	2007	

Player	Num	Years	Other #s
Ali Sharrief	26	2007-2009	
Tyrell Shavers	14	2017-2019	
Kendall Sheffield	11	2015	
Jeremy Shelley	90	2009-2012	5, 94
Austin Shepherd	79	2010-2014	
Alex Shine	67	2012	
Marvin Shinn	80	2011-2012	
Carter Short	52	2021-2022	
Travis Sikes	48	2007-2009	
T.J. Simmons	16	2016	
Ty Simpson	15	2023	
Blake Sims	6	2010-2014	18
Caleb Sims	29	2013	
Cam Sims	17	2014-2017	7
Phillip Sims	14	2010-2011	
Charlie Skehan	44	2020-2023	56
Daniel Skehan	30	2017	
Allen Skelton	65	2009-2011	71, 74
Tripp Slyman	93	2019-2020	
Brad Smelley	17	2008-2011	
Irv Smith Jr.	82	2016-2018	
Andre Smith	71	2007-2008	
Corey Smith	44	2008	
DeVonta Smith (WR)	6	2017-2020	
DeVonta Smith (DB)	8	2021-2023	27
Eddie Smith	15	2018-2020	25
Geno Smith	24	2012-2015	
James Smith	47	2023	
Jordan Smith	43	2020-2023	58
Mac Smith	64	2023	
Maurice Smith	21	2013-2015	
O.J. Smith	91	2014-2016	
Petey Smith	38	2010	
Saivion Smith	4	2018	
Tim Smith	50	2020-2023	
Kyle Smoak	41	2019	
Sam Snider	45	2008	
Ishmael Sopsher	95	2019-2020	
Alajujuan Sparks Jr.	68	2020-2022	
Mike Sparks	94	2007	
Damion Square	92	2008-2012	
B.J. Stabler	61	2007	
Jerffrey Stacy Jr.	38	2017	
Alex Stadler	62	2007	
Marcel Stamps	6	2007	
Jack Standeffer	33	2023	
Nate Staskelunas	22	2014-2016	31, 34
Anthony Steen	61	2009-2013	
Tyler Steen	54	2022	
ArDarius Stewart	13	2013-2016	
Cam Stewart	83	2016-2017	
Ed Stinson	49	2009-2013	47
Kristian Story	11	2020-2023	4
Nikita Stover	9	2007-2008	
William Strickland	46	2009-2011	
Vinnie Sunseri	3	2011-2013	
Patrick Surtain II	2	2018-2020	
Christian Swann	46	2020	
Bradley Sylve	3	2011-2015	16
Taulia Tagovailoa	5	2019	
Tua Tagovailoa	13	2017-2019	
Milton Talbert	90	2007-2009	
Conor Talty	31	2023	
Jordan Tate-Parker	25	2021-2022	
Alphonse Taylor	50	2012-2016	
M.K. Taylor	49	2011-2014	50, 52, 59
Major Tennison	88	2017-2022	
Altee Tenpenny	28	2013-2014	23

Num	Player	Years	Other #s
75	Wilkin Formby	2023	
75	Barrett Jones	2008-2012	
76	Tommy Brockermeyer	2021-2022	
76	Marlon Davis	2007-2008	
76	D.J. Fluker	2009-2012	
76	Dominick Jackson	2014-2015	
76	Scott Lashley	2016-2019	
77	James Carpenter	2009-2010	
77	Jaeden Roberts	2021-2023	
77	Byron Walton	2007	
77	Matt Womack	2015-2019	
78	Elliot Baker	2017-2018	
78	Mike Johnson	2007-2009	
78	Amari Kight	2019-2022	
78	Korren Kirven	2012-2016	85
78	Chad Lindsay	2010-2013	
79	Drew Davis	2007-2009	
79	Chris Owens	2016-2021	84
79	Austin Shepherd	2010-2014	
80	Raheem Falkins	20132016	
80	Mike McCoy	2007-2009	
80	Michael Parker	2018-2020	
80	Marvin Shinn	2011-2012	
81	Keith Brown	2007	
81	Hardie Buck	2010-2011	37
81	CJ Dippre	2023	
81	Andrew Friedman	2007-2008	15
81	Kendall Kelly	2009-2010	26
81	Derek Kief	2014-2018	
81	Cameron Latu	2018-2022	20
82	Earl Alexander	2007-2010	
82	Chase Allen	2020-2022	
82	Harrison Jones	2010-2013	40
82	Irv Smith Jr.	2016-2018	
82	Thayer Weaver	2015	
82	JaMichael Willis	2015	
83	Ty Flournoy-Smith	2014-2015	
83	Richard Hunt	2019-2022	82
83	Travis McCall	2007-2008	
83	Kevin Norwood	2009-2013	
83	John Parker	2018-2019	
83	Cam Stewart	2016-2017	
84	Jacoby Boykins	2021-2022	
84	Agiye Hall	2021-2022	
84	Hale Hentges	2015-2018	
84	Jake Jones	2007	
84	Joshua Lanier	2019-2020	
84	Amari Niblack	2023	
84	Colin Peek	2008-2009	
84	Brian Vogler	2010-2014	
85	Preston Dial	2007-2010	
85	Malcolm Faciane	2011-2014	
85	Chris Golden	2018	
85	Drew Kobayashi	2019-2020	
85	Donnie Lee Jr.	2016	
85	Kendall Randolph	2017-2022	60
85	Charlie Scott	2020	
85	Lane Whisenhunt	2023	
86	Connor Adams	2018-2019	
86	James Burnip	2021-2023	
86	Greg Carroll Jr.	2021-2022	
86	Jamie Christensen	2007	
86	Truett Harris	2013-2016	
86	A'Shawn Robinson	2013-2015	
86	Chris Scott	2008	
86	Carl Tucker	2020	
86	Quindarius Watkins	2018-2019	98
87	Parker Barrineau	2012-2015	

Player	Num	Years	Other #s
Adonis Thomas	17	2015	
Heath Thomas	9	2007-2008	98
Logan Thomas	47	2010	
Deionte Thompson	14	2015-2018	23
John Thornton II	57	2023	
Adam Thorsland	47	2021-2023	80
Leigh Tiffin	99	2007-2009	31
Carson Tinker	51	2008-2012	61
Nick Tinker	26	2010-2011	
Matt Tinney	43	2013	
Henry To'oTo'o	10	2021-2022	
Dalvin Tomlinson	54	2012-2016	52
Chadarius Townsend	12	2017-2019	
Carl Tucker	86	2020	
Brandon Turnage	7	2019-2020	14
Brandon Turner	29	2015	
Dallas Turner	15	2021-2023	
Paul Tyson	15	2019-2022	17
Loren Ugheoke	39	2019	
Chris Underwood	87	2007-2011	
Roy Upchurch	5	2007-2009	
Courtney Upshaw	41	2008-2011	
William Vandervoort	6	2007	
Jacob Vane	44	2007, 2009	
Lance Vickers	62	2007	
William Vlachos	73	2007-2011	
Brian Vogler	84	2010-2014	
Jaylen Waddle	17	2018-2020	
Demarcus Waldrop	44	2007	
Paul Waldrop	69	2012-2014	
A.J. Walker	43	2008-2009	
Nick Walker	88	2007-2008	
Levi Wallace	39	2014-2017	44
Byron Walton	77	2007	
Carson Ware	39	2019-2022	41
Conner Warhurst	49	2023	
Chance Warmack	65	2009-2012	
Dallas Warmack	59	2015-2017	
Jabriel Washington	23	2011-2015	26
Lorenzo Washington	97	2007-2009	
Alex Watkins	91	2007-2011	87
Quindarius Watkins	86	2018-2019	98
Ranzell Watkins	11	2010-2012	49
Jared Watson	38	2013	
Jeremy Watson	33	2013	
Cole Weaver	44	2018	
Thayer Weaver	82	2015	
Kade Wehby	53	2021-2023	
Camar Wheaton	25	2021-2022	
Bennett Whisenhunt	55	2020-2023	59
Lane Whisenhunt	85	2023	
DeAndrew White	2	2010-2014	
Wilson Whorton	46	2012	
C.J. Williams	32	2020	
Chavis Williams	55	2007-2010	
David Williams	60	2008-2010	63
Eddie Williams	15	2012	
Jameson Williams	1	2021-2022	
Jarrick Williams	20	2010-2014	
Jay Williams	44	2010-2011	
Jesse Williams	54	2011-2012	
Jonah Williams	73	2016-2018	
Kaine Williams	49	2021-2022	
Kellen Williams	63	2010-2013	
Kieran Williams	89	2013-2014	
Michael Williams	89	2008-2012	
Nick Williams	9	2009-2012	18
Quinnen Williams	92	2016-2018	

Num	Player	Years	Other #s
87	Drew Bullard	2008-2010	
87	Caden Clark	2021-2022	
87	Miller Forristall	2016-2020	
87	Danny Lewis Jr.	2023	
87	Chris Underwood	2007-2011	
88	Michael Bowman	2009-2011	
88	O.J. Howard	2013-2016	
88	Miles Kitselman	2023	
88	Josh Magee	2012	
88	Major Tennison	2017-2022	
88	Nick Walker	2007-2008	
89	Brandon Greene	2012-2016	58
89	Charles Hoke	2007	
89	Bernel Jones	2013-2015	90
89	Grant Krieger	2019-2022	
89	Ty Lockwood	2023	
89	Kyle Mann	2020-2022	
89	Armani Purifoye	2015-2016	
89	LaBryan Ray	2017-2022	18
89	Kieran Williams	2013-2014	
89	Michael Williams	2008-2012	
90	Quinton Dial	2011-2012	
90	Jamar King	2016-2017	
90	Jarran Reed	2014-2015	
90	Jordan Renaud	2023	
90	Jeremy Shelley	2009-2012	5, 94
90	Milton Talbert	2007-2009	
90	Stephon Wynn Jr.	2018-2022	
91	Stabler Gray	2007	
91	Tevita Musika	2018-2019	
91	Jaheim Oatis	2023	
91	Darius Paige	2013	
91	Gavin Reeder	2020	
91	O.J. Smith	2014-2016	
91	Alex Watkins	2007-2011	87
92	Justin Eboigbe	2019-2023	
92	Wallace Gilberry	2007	
92	Damion Square	2008-2012	
92	Quinnen Williams	2016-2018	
93	Jonathan Allen	2013-2016	
93	Chris Bonds	2009-2012	
93	Bobby Greenwood	2007-2008	
93	Jah-Marien Latham	2020-2023	
93	Tripp Slyman	2019-2020	
94	Dakota Ball	2012-2016	
94	Undra Billingsley	2008-2011	
94	DJ Dale	2019-2022	
94	Edric Hill	2023	
94	Da'Ron Payne	2015-2017	
94	Keith Saunders	2007	
94	Darrington Sentimore	2009-2010	.
94	Mike Sparks	2007	
95	Brandon Deaderick	2007-2009	51
95	Johnny Dwight	2014-2018	36
95	Colin Gallagher	2010	
95	Monkell Goodwine	2021-2023	
95	Darren Lake	2012-2015	
95	Brandon Lewis	2010-2011	
95	Jack Martin	2019-2022	
95	Ishmael Sopsher	2019-2020	
96	Landon Bothwell	2019-2020	93
96	Luther Davis	2007-2010	
96	Reed Harradine	2023	
96	Stephen Hodge	2014-2015	
96	Tim Keenan III	2021-2023	
96	Gunnar Raborn	2014-2015	
96	Brannon Satterfield	2016-2017	98
96	Taylor Wilson	2017-2019	68

Player	Num	Years	Other #s		Num	Player	Years	Other #s
Ronald Williams Jr.	22	2020			96	Daniel Wood	2007	
Roydell Williams	5	2020-2023	23		97	Joseph Bulovas	2017-2020	
Shatarius Williams	31	2020-2022			97	Keelan Cox	2021-2022	
Tim Williams	56	2013-2016			97	P.J. Fitzgerald	2007-2009	11
Xavier Williams	3	2018-2022	9		97	LT Ikner	2020-2021	
JaMichael Willis	82	2015			97	Khurtiss Perry	2023	
Reyn Willis	45	2007			97	John Pizzitola	2014	
Sam Willoughby	37	2020-2023			97	Reid Schuback	2021-2023	
Jedrick Wills Jr.	74	2017-2019			97	Lorenzo Washington	2007-2009	
Brandon Wilson	36	2013			97	Jay Woods	2013	
John Parker Wilson	14	2007-2008			98	Upton Bellenfant	2023	
Mack Wilson	30	2016-2018			98	Mike Bernier	2017-2019	97
Taylor Wilson	96	2017-2019	68		98	Jamil Burroughs	2020-2022	
Matt Womack	77	2015-2019			98	Dillon Drake	2012	
Daniel Wood	96	2007			98	Brandon Fanney	2007-2008	
Justin Woodall	27	2007-2009			98	Sam Johnson	2020-2022	
Jay Woods	97	2013			98	Preston Knight	2017-2018	
Thomas Woods	35	2015-2016			98	Adrian Lamothe	2014	
Danny Woodson Jr.	25	2011-2012			99	Josh Chapman	2007-2011	
Rod Woodson	18	2009			99	Raekwon Davis	2016-2019	
Daniel Wright	3	2017-2022			99	Adam Griffith	2012-2016	
Stephon Wynn Jr.	90	2018-2022			99	Isaiah Hastings	2023	
Peyton Yates	39	2023			99	Brandon Ivory	2010-2014	62
T.J. Yeldon	4	2012-2014			99	Ty Perine	2019-2022	
Bryce Young	9	2020-2022			99	Nick Serpa	2023	
Byron Young	47	2019-2022			99	Leigh Tiffin	2007-2009	31
Richard Young	25	2023			-	RyQueze McElderry	2023	

Note: Table data from references 18, 33, 49, 65, 80, 95, 111, 126, 143, 161, 197, 213, 245, 273, 301, 334, 364

465

Transfers

2011	Player	School	Direction
	Demetrius Goode	North Alabama	Outgoing
	Corey Grant	Auburn	Outgoing
	Robby Green	CA Univ of PA	Outgoing
	Keiwone Malone	Memphis	Outgoing
	Brandon Moore	E. MS Comm College	Outgoing
	B.J. Scott	South Alabama	Outgoing
	Petey Smith	Holmes Comm College	Outgoing
2014	Jacob Coker	Florida State	Incoming
	D.J. Pettway	E. MS Comm College	Incoming
	Jarren Reed	E. MS Comm College	Incoming
	Luke Del Rio	Oregon State	Outgoing
	Dee Hart	Colorado State	Outgoing
	Chad Lindsay	Ohio State	Outgoing
2015	Richard Mullaney	Oregon State	Incoming
2016	Gehrig Dieter	Oregon State	Incoming
	Jamar King	Mendocino Comm	Incoming
	Alec Morris	North Texas	Outgoing
2017	Andy Pappanastos	Ole Miss	Incoming
	Blake Barnett	Arizona State	Outgoing
	Cooper Bateman	Utah	Outgoing
	David Cornwell	Nevada	Outgoing
	B.J. Emmons	Hutchinson Comm	Outgoing
	Derrick Gore	Louisiana Monroe	Outgoing
	Aaron Robinson	UCF	Outgoing
2018	Austin Jones	Temple	Incoming
	Saivion Smith	MS Gulf Coast Comm	Incoming
	Mekhi Brown	Tennessee State	Outgoing
	Dallas Warmack	Oregon	Outgoing
2019	Landon Dickerson	FSU	Incoming
	Eyabi Anoma	Houston	Outgoing
	Layne Hatcher	Arkansas State	Outgoing
	Jalen Hurts	Oklahoma	Outgoing
	Kedrick James	SMU	Outgoing
	Kyriq McDonald	Cincinnati	Outgoing
	Scott Meyer	Vanderbilt	Outgoing
	Richie Petitbon	Illinois	Outgoing
2020	Charlie Scott	Air Force	Incoming
	Carl Tucker	North Carolina	Incoming
	Giles Amos	Arkansas State	Outgoing
	Jerome Ford	Cincinnati	Outgoing
	Mac Hereford	Vanderbilt	Outgoing
	Scott Lashley	Mississippi State	Outgoing
	Tyrell Shavers	Mississippi State	Outgoing
	Taulia Tagovailoa	Maryland	Outgoing
2021	Jack Martin	Troy	Incoming
	Henry To'oTo'o	Tennessee	Incoming
	Jameson Williams	Ohio State	Incoming
	Joseph Bulovas	Vanderbilt	Outgoing
	Ben Davis	Texas	Outgoing
	Kevin Harris	Georgia Tech	Outgoing
	Ale Kaho	UCLA	Outgoing
	Joshua Lanier	Jackson State	Outgoing
	Keilan Robinson	Texas	Outgoing
	Eddie Smith	Illinois	Outgoing
	Ishmael Sopsher	USC	Outgoing
	Brandon Turnage	Tennessee	Outgoing
	Ronald Williams Jr.	Michigan State	Outgoing

2022	Player	School	Direction
	Jermaine Burton	Georgia	Incoming
	Jahmyr Gibbs	Georgia Tech	Incoming
	Tyler Harrell	Louisville	Incoming
	Joseph Narcisse II	Alabama A&M	Incoming
	Elias Ricks	LSU	Incoming
	Tyler Steen	Vanderbilt	Incoming
	Javon Baker	UCF	Outgoing
	Marcus Banks	MS State	Outgoing
	Jahleel Billingsley	Texas	Outgoing
	Jackson Bratton	UAB	Outgoing
	Tommy Brown	Colorado	Outgoing
	Caden Clark	Akron	Outgoing
	Keelan Cox	Wyoming	Outgoing
	Kyle Edwards	SE Louisiana	Outgoing
	Agiye Hall	Texas	Outgoing
	Donovan Hardin	LIU	Outgoing
	Stone Hollenbach	W. Michigan	Outgoing
	Brylan Lanier	Indiana	Outgoing
	Shane Lee	USC	Outgoing
	Kyle Mann	Alabama A&M	Outgoing
	King Mwikuta	Arkansas State	Outgoing
	Pierce Quick	Georgia Tech	Outgoing
	DJ Rias	Samford	Outgoing
	Drew Sanders	Arkansas	Outgoing
	Dayne Shor	Uconn	Outgoing
	Paul Tyson	Arizona State	Outgoing
	Camar Wheaton	SMU	Outgoing
	Kaine Williams	Nebraska	Outgoing
	Xavier Williams	Utah State	Outgoing
	Stephon Wynn Jr.	Nebraska	Outgoing
2023	Trey Amos	Louisiana	Incoming
	Tyler Buchner	Notre Dame	Incoming
	CJ Dippre	Maryland	Incoming
	Jaylen Key	UAB	Incoming
	Trezmen Marshall	Georgia	Incoming
	Colby McNeal	Colorado State	Incoming
	Aaron Anderson	LSU	Outgoing
	Tanner Bowles	Kentucky	Outgoing
	Jacoby Boykins	Abilene Ch.	Outgoing
	Tommy Brockermeyer	TCU	Outgoing
	Jamil Burroughs	Miami	Outgoing
	Elijah Brown	Florida Atlantic	Outgoing
	Javion Cohen	Miami	Outgoing
	Elijah Crockett	Cerritos Col.	Outgoing
	JoJo Earle	TCU	Outgoing
	Trequon Fegans	USC	Outgoing
	Damieon George Jr.	Florida	Outgoing
	Tyler Harrell	Miami	Outgoing
	Traeshon Holden	Oregon	Outgoing
	Braylen Ingraham	Syracuse	Outgoing
	Khyree Jackson	Oregon	Outgoing
	Rodney Johnson	Southern Col.	Outgoing
	Demouy Kennedy	Colorado	Outgoing
	Amari Kight	UCF	Outgoing
	Christian Leary	Georgia Tech	Outgoing
	Jack Martin	Houston	Outgoing
	Gabe Pugh	Louisiana Tech	Outgoing
	Jahquez Robinson	Colorado	Outgoing
	Trey Sanders	TCU	Outgoing

Note: Table data from "2011 Alabama Crimson Tide football team" (79), "2014 Alabama Crimson Tide football team" (125), "Richard Mullaney" (144), "Position-by-Position Preview of Alabama's 2016 Roster" (162), "2017 Alabama Crimson Tide Roster" (197) and "Alabama adds Ole Miss kicker transfer" (470), "2018 Alabama Crimson Tide football team" (212), "2019 Alabama Crimson Tide football team" (244), "2020 Alabama Crimson Tide football team" (272), "2021 Alabama Crimson Tide football team" (300), "2022 Alabama Crimson Tide football team" (333), "2023 Alabama Crimson Tide football team" (363)

Awards and Honors

This is not a complete list of awards – it only includes the highlights.

Team

Permanent Team Captains

Player	Year
Jonathan Allen	2016
Will Anderson Jr.	2021
Will Anderson Jr.	2022
Javier Arenas	2009
Mark Barron	2010
Mark Barron	2011
Jordan Battle	2022
Bradley Bozeman	2017
Antoine Caldwell	2008
Jake Coker	2015
Landon Collins	2014
Amari Cooper	2014
Landon Dickerson	2020
Rashaan Evans	2017
Minkah Fitzpatrick	2017
Reuben Foster	2016
Jalston Fowler	2014
Shaun Dion Hamilton	2017
Damien Harris	2018
Derrick Henry	2015
Hale Hentges	2018
Dont'a Hightower	2010
Dont'a Hightower	2011
Eddie Jackson	2016
Anfernee Jennings	2019
Mike Johnson	2009
Rashad Johnson	2008
Barrett Jones	2012
Mac Jones	2020
Ryan Kelly	2015
Alex Leatherwood	2020
Phidarian Mathis	2021
A.J. McCarron	2013
Rolando McClain	2009
Greg McElroy	2010
Xavier McKinney	2019
Christian Miller	2018
Jalen Milroe	2023
Malachi Moore	2023
C.J. Mosley	2013
Evan Neal	2021
Kevin Norwood	2013
Ross Piersbacher	2018
Reggie Ragland	2015
Trent Richardson	2011
Cam Robinson	2016
Blake Sims	2014
DeVonta Smith	2019
DeVonta Smith	2020
Damian Square	2012
Tua Tagovailoa	2019
Dallas Turner	2023
Chance Warmack	2012
John Parker Wilson	2008
Bryce Young	2021
Bryce Young	2022

SEC

91 AP All-SEC First Team
64 AP All-SEC Second Team
8 AP All-SEC Third Team
99 Coaches' All-SEC First Team
69 Coaches' All-SEC Second Team
32 Freshman All SEC Team

Award	Name	Year
Coach of the Year	Nick Saban	2008
Coach of the Year	Nick Saban	2009
Coach of the Year	Nick Saban	2016
Coach of the Year	Nick Saban	2020
Offensive Coordinator of the Year	Lane Kiffin	2016
Offensive Coordinator of the Year	Mike Locksley	2018
Defensive Coordinator of the Year	Jeremy Pruitt	2016
Offensive Player of the Year	Mark Ingram II	2009
Offensive Player of the Year	Trent Richardson	2011
Offensive Player of the Year	Derrick Henry	2015
Offensive Player of the Year	Jalen Hurts	2016
Offensive Player of the Year	Tua Tagovailoa	2018
Offensive Player of the Year	DeVonta Smith	2020
Offensive Player of the Year	Bryce Young	2021
Defensive Player of the Year	Rolando McClain	2009
Defensive Player of the Year	Reggie Ragland	2015
Defensive Player of the Year	Jonathan Allen	2016
Defensive Player of the Year	Patrick Surtain II	2020
Defensive Player of the Year	Will Anderson Jr.	2021
Defensive Player of the Year	Will Anderson Jr.	2022
Defensive Player of the Year	Dallas Turner	2023
Freshman of the Year	Julio Jones	2008
Freshman of the Year	Jalen Hurts	2016
Freshman of the Year (OFF)	Patrick Surtain II	2018
Freshman of the Year (DEF)	Jaylen Waddle	2018
Freshman of the Year	Caleb Downs	2023
AP Offensive Player of the Year	Trent Richardson	2011
AP Player of the Year	Amari Cooper	2014
Co-Defensive Player of the Year	C.J. Mosley	2013
Co-Special Teams Player of the Year	Jameson Williams	2021
Jacobs Blocking Trophy	Barrett Jones	2011
Jacobs Blocking Trophy	Ryan Kelly	2015
Jacobs Blocking Trophy	Cam Robinson	2016
Jacobs Blocking Trophy	Jonah Williams	2018
Jacobs Blocking Trophy	Landon Dickerson	2020
Jacobs Blocking Trophy	Alex Leatherwood	2020
Scholar-Athlete of the Year	Barrett Jones	2011
Scholar-Athlete of the Year	Barrett Jones	2012
Scholar-Athlete of the Year	Ryan Kelly	2015
Scholar-Athlete of the Year	Hale Hentges	2018
Scholar-Athlete of the Year	Mac Jones	2020
Special Teams Player of the Year	Christion Jones	2013
Special Teams Player of the Year	Jaylen Waddle	2019
Special Teams Player of the Year	Will Reichard	2023

National

46x Consensus All-Americans

26x Unanimous All-Americans

Award	Name	Year
Academic All-America of the Year	Barrett Jones	2012
AP Coach of the Year	Nick Saban	2008
AP College Football Player of the Year	Bryce Young	2021
ARA Sportsmanship Award	Barrett Jones	2011
Bednarik Award	Jonathan Allen	2016
Bednarik Award	Minkah Fitzpatrick	2017
Bednarik Award	Will Anderson Jr.	2022
Biletnikoff Award	Amari Cooper	2014
Biletnikoff Award	Jerry Jeudy	2018
Biletnikoff Award	DeVonta Smith	2020
Bronko Nagurski Trophy	Will Anderson Jr.	2021
Bronko Nagurski Trophy	Will Anderson Jr.	2022
Broyles Award	Kirby Smart	2009
Broyles Award	Mike Locksley	2018
Broyles Award	Steve Sarkisian	2020
Butkus Award	Rolando McClain	2009
Butkus Award	C.J. Mosley	2013
Butkus Award	Reuben Foster	2016
Davey O'Brien Award	Mac Jones	2020
Davey O'Brien Award	Bryce Young	2021
Doak Walker Award	Trent Richardson	2011
Doak Walker Award	Derrick Henry	2015
Doak Walker Award	Najee Harris	2020
Eddie Robinson Coach of the Year	Nick Saban	2008
George Munger Award	Nick Saban	2017
Heisman Trophy	Mark Ingram II	2009
Heisman Trophy	Derrick Henry	2015
Heisman Trophy	DeVonta Smith	2020
Heisman Trophy	Bryce Young	2021
Home Depot Coach of the Year	Nick Saban	2008
Jack Lambert Award	Rolando McClain	2009
Jim Thorpe Award	Minkah Fitzpatrick	2017
Johnny Unitas Golden Arm Award	A.J. McCarron	2013
Liberty Mutual Coach of the Year	Nick Saban	2008
Lombardi Award	Will Anderson Jr.	2022
Lott IMPACT Trophy	Will Anderson Jr.	2022
Manning Award	Bryce Young	2021
Maxwell Award	A.J. McCarron	2013
Maxwell Award	Derrick Henry	2015
Maxwell Award	Tua Tagovailoa	2018
Maxwell Award	DeVonta Smith	2020
Maxwell Award	Bryce Young	2021
Nagurski Trophy	Jonathan Allen	2016
Outland Trophy	Andre Smith	2008
Outland Trophy	Barrett Jones	2011
Rimington Trophy	Barrett Jones	2012
Rimington Trophy	Ryan Kelly	2015
Sporting News College Football Coach of the Year	Nick Saban	2008
Sporting News College Football Player of the Year	Bryce Young	2021
Walter Camp Award	Derrick Henry	2015
Walter Camp Award	Tua Tagovailoa	2018
Walter Camp Award	DeVonta Smith	2020
William V. Campbell Trophy	Barrett Jones	2012
Wuerffel Trophy	Barrett Jones	2011

Note: Table data from "2007 Alabama Crimson Tide football team" (18), "2008 Alabama Crimson Tide football team" (32), "2009 Alabama Crimson Tide football team" (48), "2010 Alabama Crimson Tide football team" (64), "2011 Alabama Crimson Tide football team" (79), "2012 Alabama Crimson Tide football team" (94), "2013 Alabama Crimson Tide football team" (110), "2014 Alabama Crimson Tide football team" (125), "2015 Alabama Crimson Tide football team" (142), "2016 Alabama Crimson Tide football team" (160), "2017 Alabama Crimson Tide football team" (196), "2018 Alabama Crimson Tide football team" (212), "2019 Alabama Crimson Tide football team" (244), "2020 Alabama Crimson Tide football team" (272), "2021 Alabama Crimson Tide football team" (300), "2022 Alabama Crimson Tide football team" (333), "2023 Alabama Crimson Tide football team" (363)

NFL

Year drafted	Round	Pick	Overall	Player	Position	Team
2009	1	6	6	Andre Smith	OT	Cincinnati Bengals
2009	3	10	74	Glen Coffee	RB	San Francisco 49ers
2009	3	13	77	Antoine Caldwell	C	Houston Texans
2009	3	31	95	Rashad Johnson	CB	Arizona Cardinals
2010	1	8	8	Rolando McClain	LB	Las Vegas Raiders
2010	1	20	20	Kareem Jackson	CB	Houston Texans
2010	2	18	50	Javier Arenas	DB	Kansas City Chiefs
2010	2	25	57	Terrence Cody	DE	Baltimore Ravens
2010	3	34	98	Mike Johnson	OG	Atlanta Falcons
2010	7	4	211	Marquis Johnson	DB	Los Angeles Rams
2010	7	40	247	Brandon Deaderick	DE	New England Patriots
2011	1	3	3	Marcell Dareus	DT	Buffalo Bills
2011	1	6	6	Julio Jones	WR	Atlanta Falcons
2011	1	25	25	James Carpenter	OT	Seattle Seahawks
2011	1	28	28	Mark Ingram II	RB	New Orleans Saints
2011	7	5	208	Greg McElroy	QB	New York Jets
2012	1	3	3	Trent Richardson	RB	Cleveland Browns
2012	1	7	7	Mark Barron	S	Tampa Bay Buccaneers
2012	1	17	17	Dre Kirkpatrick	CB	Cincinnati Bengals
2012	1	25	25	Dont'a Hightower	LB	New England Patriots
2012	2	3	35	Courtney Upshaw	LB	Baltimore Ravens
2012	5	1	136	Josh Chapman	DT	Indianapolis Colts
2012	5	11	146	Dequan Menzie	CB	Kansas City Chiefs
2012	7	40	247	Brad Smelley	TE	Cleveland Browns
2013	1	9	9	Dee Milliner	CB	New York Jets
2013	1	10	10	Chance Warmack	G	Tennessee Titans
2013	1	11	11	D.J. Fluker	OT	Los Angeles Chargers
2013	2	29	61	Eddie Lacy	RB	Green Bay Packers
2013	4	2	99	Nico Johnson	LB	Kansas City Chiefs
2013	4	16	113	Barrett Jones	C	Los Angeles Rams
2013	5	4	137	Jesse Williams	DT	Seattle Seahawks
2013	5	24	157	Quinton Dial	DE	San Francisco 49ers
2013	7	5	211	Michael Williams	TE	Detroit Lions
2014	1	17	17	C.J. Mosley	LB	Baltimore Ravens
2014	1	21	21	Ha Ha Clinton-Dix	S	Green Bay Packers
2014	2	12	44	Cyrus Kouandjio	OT	Buffalo Bills
2014	4	23	123	Kevin Norwood	WR	Seattle Seahawks
2014	5	20	160	Ed Stinson	DE	Arizona Cardinals
2014	5	24	164	A.J. McCarron	QB	Cincinnati Bengals
2014	5	27	167	Vinnie Sunseri	S	New Orleans Saints
2014	6	1	177	Jeoffrey Pagan	DE	Houston Texans
2015	1	4	4	Amari Cooper	WR	Las Vegas Raiders
2015	2	1	33	Landon Collins	S	New York Giants
2015	2	4	36	T.J. Yeldon	RB	Jacksonville Jaguars
2015	4	9	108	Jalston Fowler	FB	Tennessee Titans
2015	4	13	112	Arie Kouandjio	OG	Washington Commanders
2015	7	11	228	Austin Shepherd	OT	Minnesota Vikings
2015	7	36	253	Xzavier Dickson	LB	New England Patriots
2016	1	18	18	Ryan Kelly	C	Indianapolis Colts
2016	2	10	41	Reggie Ragland	LB	Buffalo Bills
2016	2	14	45	Derrick Henry	RB	Tennessee Titans
2016	2	15	46	A'Shawn Robinson	DT	Detroit Lions
2016	2	18	49	Jarran Reed	DT	Seattle Seahawks
2016	2	29	60	Cyrus Jones	CB	New England Patriots
2016	3	10	73	Kenyan Drake	RB	Miami Dolphins
2017	1	16	16	Marlon Humphrey	CB	Baltimore Ravens
2017	1	17	17	Jonathan Allen	DE	Washington Commanders
2017	1	19	19	O.J. Howard	TE	Tampa Bay Buccaneers

Year drafted	Round	Pick	Overall	Player	Position	Team
2017	1	31	31	Reuben Foster	LB	San Francisco 49ers
2017	2	2	34	Cam Robinson	OT	Jacksonville Jaguars
2017	2	17	49	Ryan Anderson	OLB	Washington Commanders
2017	2	23	55	Dalvin Tomlinson	DT	New York Giants
2017	3	14	78	Tim Williams	DE	Baltimore Ravens
2017	3	15	79	ArDarius Stewart	WR	New York Jets
2017	4	5	112	Eddie Jackson	S	Chicago Bears
2018	1	11	11	Minkah Fitzpatrick	S	Miami Dolphins
2018	1	13	13	Da'Ron Payne	NT	Washington Commanders
2018	1	22	22	Rashaan Evans	LB	Tennessee Titans
2018	1	26	26	Calvin Ridley	WR	Atlanta Falcons
2018	3	29	93	Ronnie Harrison Jr.	S	Jacksonville Jaguars
2018	4	14	114	Da'Shawn Hand	DE	Detroit Lions
2018	4	18	118	Anthony Averett	CB	Baltimore Ravens
2018	5	35	172	JK Scott	P	Green Bay Packers
2018	6	23	197	Shaun Dion Hamilton	LB	Washington Commanders
2018	6	41	215	Bradley Bozeman	C	Baltimore Ravens
2018	7	18	236	Bo Scarbrough	RB	Dallas Cowboys
2018	7	28	246	Joshua Frazier	DT	Pittsburgh Steelers
2019	1	3	3	Quinnen Williams	DT	New York Jets
2019	1	11	11	Jonah Williams	OT	Cincinnati Bengals
2019	1	24	24	Josh Jacobs	RB	Las Vegas Raiders
2019	2	18	50	Irv Smith Jr.	TE	Minnesota Vikings
2019	3	24	87	Damien Harris	RB	New England Patriots
2019	4	13	115	Christian Miller	LB	Carolina Panthers
2019	5	1	139	Deionte Thompson	S	Arizona Cardinals
2019	5	15	153	Ross Pierschbacher	OG	Washington Commanders
2019	5	17	155	Mack Wilson	LB	Cleveland Browns
2019	6	20	192	Isaiah Buggs	DT	Pittsburgh Steelers
2020	1	5	5	Tua Tagovailoa	QB	Miami Dolphins
2020	1	10	10	Jedrick Wills	T	Cleveland Browns
2020	1	12	12	Henry Ruggs III	WR	Las Vegas Raiders
2020	1	15	15	Jerry Jeudy	WR	Denver Broncos
2020	2	4	36	Xavier McKinney	S	New York Giants
2020	2	19	51	Trevon Diggs	CB	Dallas Cowboys
2020	2	24	56	Raekwon Davis	DT	Miami Dolphins
2020	3	20	84	Terrell Lewis	LB	Los Angeles Rams
2020	3	23	87	Anfernee Jennings	LB	New England Patriots
2021	1	6	6	Jaylen Waddle	WR	Miami Dolphins
2021	1	9	9	Patrick Surtain II	CB	Denver Broncos
2021	1	10	10	DeVonta Smith	WR	Philadelphia Eagles
2021	1	15	15	Mac Jones	QB	New England Patriots
2021	1	17	17	Alex Leatherwood	OT	Las Vegas Raiders
2021	1	24	24	Najee Harris	RB	Pittsburgh Steelers
2021	2	5	37	Landon Dickerson	C	Philadelphia Eagles
2021	2	6	38	Christian Barmore	DT	New England Patriots
2021	6	9	193	Deonte Brown	OG	Carolina Panthers
2021	6	38	222	Thomas Fletcher	LS	Carolina Panthers
2022	1	7	7	Evan Neal	OL	New York Giants
2022	1	12	12	Jameson Williams	WR	Detroit Lions
2022	2	12	44	John Metchie III	WR	Houston Texans
2022	2	15	47	Phidarian Mathis	DT	Washington Commanders
2022	3	11	75	Christian Harris	LB	Houston Texans
2022	3	34	98	Brian Robinson	RB	Washington Commanders
2022	4	14	119	Jalyn Armour-Davis	DB	Baltimore Ravens
2023	1	1	1	Bryce Young	QB	Carolina Panthers
2023	1	3	3	Will Anderson Jr.	LB	Houston Texans
2023	1	12	12	Jahmyr Gibbs	RB	Detroit Lions
2023	2	14	45	Brian Branch	CB	Detroit Lions
2023	3	2	65	Tyler Steen	OT	Philadelphia Eagles

Year drafted	Round	Pick	Overall	Player	Position	Team
2023	3	7	70	Byron Young	DT	Las Vegas Raiders
2023	3	32	95	Jordan Battle	S	Cincinnati Bengals
2023	3	38	101	Cameron Latu	TE	San Francisco 49ers
2023	5	32	167	Henry To'oTo'o	LB	Houston Texans
2023	7	7	224	DeMarcco Hellams	S	Atlanta Falcons
2024	1	7	7	JC Latham	OT	Tennessee Titans
2024	1	17	17	Dallas Turner	DE	Minnesota Vikings
2024	1	24	24	Terrion Arnold	CB	Detroit Lions
2024	2	9	41	Kool-Aid McKinstry	CB	New Orleans Saints
2024	2	25	57	Chris Braswell	LB	Tampa Bay Buccaneers
2024	3	16	80	Jermaine Burton	WR	Cincinnati Bengals
2024	4	5	105	Justin Eboigbe	DT	Los Angeles Chargers
2024	6	10	186	Jase McClellan	RB	Atlanta Falcons
2024	6	27	203	Will Reichard	K	Minnesota Vikings
2024	7	37	257	Jaylen Key	S	New York Jets

Round	Picks
1	47
2	26
3	18
4	11
5	12
6	8
7	11
Total	133

Draft Year	Players Drafted
2008	0
2009	4
2010	7
2011	5
2012	8
2013	9
2014	8
2015	7
2016	7
2017	10
2018	12
2019	10
2020	9
2021	10
2022	7
2023	10
2024	10

Team	Players
Arizona Cardinals	3
Atlanta Falcons	5
Baltimore Ravens	8
Buffalo Bills	3
Carolina Panthers	4
Chicago Bears	1
Cincinnati Bengals	6
Cleveland Browns	4
Dallas Cowboys	2
Denver Broncos	2
Detroit Lions	7
Green Bay Packers	3
Houston Texans	7
Indianapolis Colts	2
Jacksonville Jaguars	3
Kansas City Chiefs	3
Las Vegas Raiders	6
Los Angeles Chargers	2
Los Angeles Rams	3
Miami Dolphins	5
Minnesota Vikings	4
New England Patriots	8
New Orleans Saints	3
New York Giants	4
New York Jets	5
Philadelphia Eagles	3
Pittsburgh Steelers	3
San Francisco 49ers	4
Seattle Seahawks	4
Tampa Bay Buccaneers	3
Tennessee Titans	5
Washington Commanders	8

Note: Table data from "2008 Alabama Crimson Tide football team" (32), "2009 Alabama Crimson Tide football team" (48), "2010 Alabama Crimson Tide football team" (64), "2011 Alabama Crimson Tide football team" (79), "2012 Alabama Crimson Tide football team" (94), "2013 Alabama Crimson Tide football team" (110), "2015 NFL Draft" (141), "2015 Alabama Crimson Tide football team" (142), "2016 Alabama Crimson Tide football team" (160), "2017 Alabama Crimson Tide football team" (196), "2018 Alabama Crimson Tide football team" (212), "2019 Alabama Crimson Tide football team" (244), "2020 Alabama Crimson Tide football team" (272), "2022 Alabama Crimson Tide football team" (333), "2023 NFL Draft" (362), "2024 NFL Draft" (395)

References

1. 2007 Alabama Crimson Tide Stats, Sports Reference, https://www.sports-reference.com/cfb/schools/alabama/2007.html
2. 2008 Alabama Crimson Tide Stats, Sports Reference, https://www.sports-reference.com/cfb/schools/alabama/2008.html
3. 2009 Alabama Crimson Tide Stats, Sports Reference, https://www.sports-reference.com/cfb/schools/alabama/2009.html
4. 2010 Alabama Crimson Tide Stats, Sports Reference, https://www.sports-reference.com/cfb/schools/alabama/2010.html
5. 2011 Alabama Crimson Tide Stats, Sports Reference, https://www.sports-reference.com/cfb/schools/alabama/2011.html
6. 2012 Alabama Crimson Tide Stats, Sports Reference, https://www.sports-reference.com/cfb/schools/alabama/2012.html
7. 2013 Alabama Crimson Tide Stats, Sports Reference, https://www.sports-reference.com/cfb/schools/alabama/2013.html
8. 2014 Alabama Crimson Tide Stats, Sports Reference, https://www.sports-reference.com/cfb/schools/alabama/2014.html
9. 2015 Alabama Crimson Tide Stats, Sports Reference, https://www.sports-reference.com/cfb/schools/alabama/2015.html
10. 2016 Alabama Crimson Tide Stats, Sports Reference, https://www.sports-reference.com/cfb/schools/alabama/2016.html
11. 2017 Alabama Crimson Tide Stats, Sports Reference, https://www.sports-reference.com/cfb/schools/alabama/2017.html
12. 2018 Alabama Crimson Tide Stats, Sports Reference, https://www.sports-reference.com/cfb/schools/alabama/2018.html
13. 2019 Alabama Crimson Tide Stats, Sports Reference, https://www.sports-reference.com/cfb/schools/alabama/2019.html
14. 2020 Alabama Crimson Tide Stats, Sports Reference, https://www.sports-reference.com/cfb/schools/alabama/2020.html
15. 2021 Alabama Crimson Tide Stats, Sports Reference, https://www.sports-reference.com/cfb/schools/alabama/2021.html
16. 2022 Alabama Crimson Tide Stats, Sports Reference, https://www.sports-reference.com/cfb/schools/alabama/2022.html
17. 2023 Alabama Crimson Tide Stats, Sports Reference, retrieved 01/30/24 from https://www.sports-reference.com/cfb/schools/alabama/2023.html
18. 2007 Alabama Crimson Tide football team, Wikipedia, retrieved 01/30/24 from https://en.wikipedia.org/wiki/2007_Alabama_Crimson_Tide_football_team
19. Alabama 52-6 Western Carolina (Sep 1, 2007) Box Score, ESPN, https://www.espn.com/college-football/boxscore/_/gameId/272440333
20. Alabama 24-10 Vanderbilt (Sep 8, 2007) Box Score, ESPN, https://www.espn.com/college-football/boxscore/_/gameId/272510238
21. Alabama 41-38 Arkansas (Sep 15, 2007) Box Score, ESPN, https://www.espn.com/college-football/boxscore/_/gameId/272580333
22. Georgia 26-23 Alabama (Sep 22, 2007) Box Score, ESPN, https://www.espn.com/college-football/game/_/gameId/272650333
23. Florida State 21-14 Alabama (Sep 29, 2007) Box Score, ESPN, https://www.espn.com/college-football/boxscore/_/gameId/272720052
24. Alabama 30-24 Houston (Oct 6, 2007) Box Score, ESPN, https://www.espn.com/college-football/boxscore/_/gameId/272790333
25. Alabama 27-24 Ole Miss (Oct 13, 2007) Box Score, ESPN, https://www.espn.com/college-football/boxscore/_/gameId/272860145
26. Alabama 41-17 Tennessee (Oct 20, 2007) Box Score, ESPN, https://www.espn.com/college-football/boxscore/_/gameId/272930333
27. LSU 41-34 Alabama (Nov 3, 2007) Box Score, ESPN, https://www.espn.com/college-football/boxscore/_/gameId/273070333
28. Mississippi State 17-12 Alabama (Nov 10, 2007) Box Score, ESPN, https://www.espn.com/college-football/boxscore/_/gameId/273140344
29. Louisiana Monroe 21-14 Alabama (Nov 17, 2007) Box Score, ESPN, https://www.espn.com/college-football/game/_/gameId/273210333
30. Auburn 17-10 Alabama (Nov 24, 2007) Box Score, ESPN, https://www.espn.com/college-football/boxscore/_/gameId/273280002
31. Alabama 30-24 Colorado (Dec 30, 2007) Box Score, ESPN, https://www.espn.com/college-football/boxscore/_/gameId/273640038
32. 2008 Alabama Crimson Tide football team, Wikipedia, retrieved 01/31/24 from https://en.wikipedia.org/wiki/2008_Alabama_Crimson_Tide_football_team
33. 2008 Alabama Crimson Tide Roster, Sports Reference, https://www.sports-reference.com/cfb/schools/alabama/2008-roster.html
34. Alabama 34-10 Clemson (Aug 30, 2008) Box Score, ESPN, https://www.espn.com/college-football/boxscore/_/gameId/282430228
35. Alabama 20-6 Tulane (Sep 6, 2008) Box Score, ESPN, https://www.espn.com/college-football/boxscore/_/gameId/282500333
36. Alabama 41-7 Western Kentucky (Sep 13, 2008) Box Score, ESPN, https://www.espn.com/college-football/boxscore/_/gameId/282570333
37. Alabama 49-14 Arkansas (Sep 20, 2008) Box Score, ESPN, https://www.espn.com/college-football/boxscore/_/gameId/282640008
38. Alabama 41-30 Georgia (Sep 27, 2008) Box Score, ESPN, https://www.espn.com/college-football/boxscore/_/gameId/282710061
39. Alabama 17-14 Kentucky (Oct 4, 2008) Box Score, ESPN, https://www.espn.com/college-football/boxscore/_/gameId/282780333
40. Alabama 24-20 Ole Miss (Oct 18, 2008) Box Score, ESPN, https://www.espn.com/college-football/boxscore/_/gameId/282920333
41. Alabama 29-9 Tennessee (Oct 25, 2008) Box Score, ESPN, https://www.espn.com/college-football/boxscore/_/gameId/282992633
42. Alabama 35-0 Arkansas State (Nov 1, 2008) Box Score, ESPN, https://www.espn.com/college-football/boxscore/_/gameId/283060333
43. Alabama 27-21 LSU (Nov 8, 2008) Box Score, ESPN, https://www.espn.com/college-football/boxscore/_/gameId/283130099
44. Alabama 32-7 Mississippi State (Nov 15, 2008) Box Score, ESPN, https://www.espn.com/college-football/boxscore/_/gameId/283200333
45. Alabama 36-0 Auburn (Nov 29, 2008) Box Score, ESPN, https://www.espn.com/college-football/boxscore/_/gameId/283340333
46. Florida 31-20 Alabama (Dec 6, 2008) Box Score, ESPN, https://www.espn.com/college-football/boxscore/_/gameId/283410057
47. Utah 31-17 Alabama (Jan 2, 2009) Box Score, ESPN, https://www.espn.com/college-football/boxscore/_/gameId/290020333
48. 2009 Alabama Crimson Tide football team, Wikipedia, retrieved 01/31/24 from https://en.wikipedia.org/wiki/2009_Alabama_Crimson_Tide_football_team
49. 2009 Alabama Crimson Tide Roster, cfbstats, http://www.cfbstats.com/2009/team/8/roster.html
50. Alabama 34-24 Virginia Tech (Sep 5, 2009) Box Score, ESPN, https://www.espn.com/college-football/boxscore/_/gameId/292480259
51. Alabama 40-14 Florida Intl (Sep 12, 2009) Box Score, ESPN, https://www.espn.com/college-football/boxscore/_/gameId/292550333
52. Alabama 53-7 North Texas (Sep 19, 2009) Box Score, ESPN, https://www.espn.com/college-football/boxscore/_/gameId/292620333
53. Alabama 35-7 Arkansas (Sep 26, 2009) Box Score, ESPN, https://www.espn.com/college-football/boxscore/_/gameId/292690333
54. Alabama 38-20 Kentucky (Oct 3, 2009) Box Score, ESPN, https://www.espn.com/college-football/boxscore/_/gameId/292760096
55. Alabama 22-3 Ole Miss (Oct 10, 2009) Box Score, ESPN, https://www.espn.com/college-football/boxscore/_/gameId/292830145
56. Alabama 20-6 South Carolina (Oct 17, 2009) Box Score, ESPN, https://www.espn.com/college-football/boxscore/_/gameId/292900333
57. Alabama 12-10 Tennessee (Oct 24, 2009) Box Score, ESPN, https://www.espn.com/college-football/boxscore/_/gameId/292970333
58. Alabama 24-15 LSU (Nov 7, 2009) Box Score, ESPN, https://www.espn.com/college-football/boxscore/_/gameId/293110333
59. Alabama 31-3 Mississippi State (Nov 14, 2009) Box Score, ESPN, https://www.espn.com/college-football/boxscore/_/gameId/293180344
60. Alabama 45-0 Chattanooga (Nov 21, 2009) Box Score, ESPN, https://www.espn.com/college-football/boxscore/_/gameId/293250333
61. Alabama 26-21 Auburn (Nov 27, 2009) Box Score, ESPN, https://www.espn.com/college-football/boxscore/_/gameId/293310002
62. Alabama 32-13 Florida (Dec 5, 2009) Box Score, ESPN, https://www.espn.com/college-football/boxscore/_/gameId/293390333
63. Alabama 37-21 Texas (Jan 7, 2010) Box Score, ESPN, https://www.espn.com/college-football/boxscore/_/gameId/300070333
64. 2010 Alabama Crimson Tide football team, Wikipedia, retrieved 01/31/24 from https://en.wikipedia.org/wiki/2010_Alabama_Crimson_Tide_football_team
65. 2010 Alabama Crimson Tide Roster, cfbstats, http://www.cfbstats.com/2010/team/8/roster.html
66. Alabama 48-3 San Jose State (Sep 4, 2010) Box Score, ESPN, https://www.espn.com/college-football/boxscore/_/gameId/302470333
67. Penn State 3-24 Alabama (Sep 11, 2010) Box Score, ESPN, https://www.espn.com/college-football/boxscore/_/gameId/302540333
68. Alabama 62-13 Duke (Sep 18, 2010) Box Score, ESPN, https://www.espn.com/college-football/boxscore/_/gameId/302610150
69. Alabama 24-20 Arkansas (Sep 25, 2010) Box Score, ESPN, https://www.espn.com/college-football/boxscore/_/gameId/302680008
70. Alabama 31-6 Florida (Oct 2, 2010) Box Score, ESPN, https://www.espn.com/college-football/boxscore/_/gameId/302750333
71. South Carolina 35-21 Alabama (Oct 9, 2010) Box Score, ESPN, https://www.espn.com/college-football/boxscore/_/gameId/302822579
72. Alabama 23-10 Ole Miss (Oct 16, 2010) Box Score, ESPN, https://www.espn.com/college-football/boxscore/_/gameId/302890333
73. Alabama 41-10 Tennessee (Oct 23, 2010) Box Score, ESPN, https://www.espn.com/college-football/boxscore/_/gameId/302962633

74. LSU 24-21 Alabama (Nov 6, 2010) Box Score, ESPN, https://www.espn.com/college-football/boxscore/_/gameId/303100099
75. Alabama 30-10 Mississippi State (Nov 13, 2010) Box Score, ESPN, https://www.espn.com/college-football/boxscore/_/gameId/303170333
76. Alabama 63-7 Georgia State (Nov 18, 2010) Box Score, ESPN, https://www.espn.com/college-football/boxscore/_/gameId/303220333
77. Auburn 28-27 Alabama (Nov 26, 2010) Box Score, ESPN, https://www.espn.com/college-football/boxscore/_/gameId/303300333
78. Alabama 49-7 Michigan State (Jan 1, 2011) Box Score, ESPN, https://www.espn.com/college-football/boxscore/_/gameId/310010127
79. 2011 Alabama Crimson Tide football team, Wikipedia, retrieved 01/31/24 from
https://en.wikipedia.org/wiki/2011_Alabama_Crimson_Tide_football_team
80. 2011 Alabama Crimson Tide Roster, cfbstats, http://www.cfbstats.com/2011/team/8/roster.html
81. Alabama 48-7 Kent State (Sep 3, 2011) Box Score, ESPN, https://www.espn.com/college-football/boxscore/_/gameId/312460333
82. Alabama 27-11 Penn State (Sep 10, 2011) Box Score, ESPN, https://www.espn.com/college-football/boxscore/_/gameId/312530213
83. Alabama 41-0 North Texas (Sep 17, 2011) Box Score, ESPN, https://www.espn.com/college-football/boxscore/_/gameId/312600333
84. Alabama 38-14 Arkansas (Sep 24, 2011) Box Score, ESPN, https://www.espn.com/college-football/boxscore/_/gameId/312670333
85. Alabama 38-10 Florida (Oct 1, 2011) Box Score, ESPN, https://www.espn.com/college-football/boxscore/_/gameId/312740057
86. Alabama 34-0 Vanderbilt (Oct 8, 2011) Box Score, ESPN, https://www.espn.com/college-football/boxscore/_/gameId/312810333
87. Alabama 52-7 Ole Miss (Oct 15, 2011) Box Score, ESPN, https://www.espn.com/college-football/boxscore/_/gameId/312880145
88. Alabama 6-37 Tennessee (Oct 22, 2011) Box Score, ESPN, https://www.espn.com/college-football/boxscore/_/gameId/312950333
89. LSU 9-6 Alabama (Nov 5, 2011) Box Score, ESPN, https://www.espn.com/college-football/boxscore/_/gameId/313090333
90. Alabama 24-7 Mississippi State (Nov 12, 2011) Box Score, ESPN, https://www.espn.com/college-football/boxscore/_/gameId/313160344
91. Alabama 45-21 Georgia Southern (Nov 19, 2011) Box Score, ESPN, https://www.espn.com/college-football/boxscore/_/gameId/313230333
92. Alabama 42-14 Auburn (Nov 26, 2011) Box Score, ESPN, https://www.espn.com/college-football/boxscore/_/gameId/313300002
93. Alabama 21-0 LSU (Jan 9, 2012) Box Score, ESPN, https://www.espn.com/college-football/boxscore/_/gameId/320090099
94. 2012 Alabama Crimson Tide football team, Wikipedia, retrieved 01/31/24 from
https://en.wikipedia.org/wiki/2012_Alabama_Crimson_Tide_football_team
95. 2012 Alabama Crimson Tide Roster, cfbstats, http://www.cfbstats.com/2012/team/8/roster.html
96. Alabama 41-14 Michigan (Sep 1, 2012) Box Score, ESPN, https://www.espn.com/college-football/boxscore/_/gameId/322450333
97. Alabama 35-0 Western Kentucky (Sep 8, 2012) Box Score, ESPN, https://www.espn.com/college-football/boxscore/_/gameId/322520333
98. Alabama 52-0 Arkansas (Sep 15, 2012) Box Score, ESPN, https://www.espn.com/college-football/boxscore/_/gameId/322590008
99. Alabama 40-7 Florida Atlantic (Sep 22, 2012) Box Score, ESPN, https://www.espn.com/college-football/boxscore/_/gameId/322660333
100. Alabama 33-14 Ole Miss (Sep 29, 2012) Box Score, ESPN, https://www.espn.com/college-football/boxscore/_/gameId/322730333
101. Alabama 42-10 Missouri (Oct 13, 2012) Box Score, ESPN, https://www.espn.com/college-football/boxscore/_/gameId/322870142
102. Alabama 44-13 Tennessee (Oct 20, 2012) Box Score, ESPN, https://www.espn.com/college-football/boxscore/_/gameId/322942633
103. Alabama 38-7 Mississippi State (Oct 27, 2012) Box Score, ESPN, https://www.espn.com/college-football/boxscore/_/gameId/323010333
104. Alabama 21-17 LSU (Nov 3, 2012) Box Score, ESPN, https://www.espn.com/college-football/boxscore/_/gameId/323080099
105. Alabama 24-19 Texas A&M (Nov 10, 2012) Box Score, ESPN, https://www.espn.com/college-football/boxscore/_/gameId/323150333
106. Alabama 49-0 Western Carolina (Nov 17, 2012) Box Score, ESPN, https://www.espn.com/college-football/boxscore/_/gameId/323220333
107. Alabama 49-0 Auburn (Nov 24, 2012) Box Score, ESPN, https://www.espn.com/college-football/boxscore/_/gameId/323290333
108. Alabama 32-28 Georgia (Dec 1, 2012) Box Score, ESPN, https://www.espn.com/college-football/boxscore/_/gameId/323360061
109. Alabama 42-14 Notre Dame (Jan 7, 2013) Box Score, ESPN, https://www.espn.com/college-football/boxscore/_/gameId/330070333
110. 2013 Alabama Crimson Tide football team, Wikipedia, retrieved 01/31/24 from
https://en.wikipedia.org/wiki/2013_Alabama_Crimson_Tide_football_team
111. 2013 Alabama Crimson Tide Roster, cfbstats, http://www.cfbstats.com/2013/team/8/roster.html
112. Alabama 35-10 Virginia Tech (Aug 31, 2013) Box Score, ESPN, https://www.espn.com/college-football/boxscore/_/gameId/332430259
113. Alabama 49-42 Texas A&M (Sep 14, 2013) Box Score, ESPN, https://www.espn.com/college-football/boxscore/_/gameId/332570245
114. Alabama 31-6 Colorado State (Sep 21, 2013) Box Score, ESPN, https://www.espn.com/college-football/boxscore/_/gameId/332640333
115. Alabama 25-0 Ole Miss (Sep 28, 2013) Box Score, ESPN, https://www.espn.com/college-football/boxscore/_/gameId/332710333
116. Alabama 45-3 Georgia State (Oct 5, 2013) Box Score, ESPN, https://www.espn.com/college-football/boxscore/_/gameId/332780333
117. Alabama 48-7 Kentucky (Oct 12, 2013) Box Score, ESPN, https://www.espn.com/college-football/boxscore/_/gameId/332850096
118. Alabama 52-0 Arkansas (Oct 19, 2013) Box Score, ESPN, https://www.espn.com/college-football/boxscore/_/gameId/332920333
119. Alabama 45-10 Tennessee (Oct 26, 2013) Box Score, ESPN, https://www.espn.com/college-football/boxscore/_/gameId/332990333
120. Alabama 38-17 LSU (Nov 9, 2013) Box Score, ESPN, https://www.espn.com/college-football/boxscore/_/gameId/333130333
121. Alabama 20-7 Mississippi State (Nov 16, 2013) Box Score, ESPN, https://www.espn.com/college-football/boxscore/_/gameId/333200344
122. Alabama 49-0 Chattanooga (Nov 23, 2013) Box Score, ESPN, https://www.espn.com/college-football/boxscore/_/gameId/333270333
123. Alabama 28-34 Auburn (Nov 30, 2013) Box Score, ESPN, https://www.espn.com/college-football/boxscore/_/gameId/333340002
124. Alabama 45-31 Oklahoma (Jan 2, 2014) Box Score, ESPN, https://www.espn.com/college-football/boxscore/_/gameId/340020333
125. 2014 Alabama Crimson Tide football team, Wikipedia, retrieved 01/31/24 from
https://en.wikipedia.org/wiki/2014_Alabama_Crimson_Tide_football_team
126. 2014 Alabama Crimson Tide Roster, cfbstats, http://www.cfbstats.com/2014/team/8/roster.html
127. Alabama 33-23 West Virginia (Aug 30, 2014) Box Score, ESPN, https://www.espn.com/college-football/boxscore/_/gameId/400547835\
128. Alabama 41-0 Florida Atlantic (Sep 6, 2014) Box Score, ESPN, https://www.espn.com/college-football/boxscore/_/gameId/400548013
129. Alabama 52-12 Southern Mississippi (Sep 13, 2014) Box Score, ESPN, https://www.espn.com/college-football/boxscore/_/gameId/400548024
130. Alabama 42-21 Florida (Sep 20, 2014) Box Score, ESPN, https://www.espn.com/college-football/boxscore/_/gameId/400548384
131. Alabama 23-17 Ole Miss (Oct 4, 2014) Box Score, ESPN, https://www.espn.com/college-football/boxscore/_/gameId/400548374
132. Alabama 14-13 Arkansas (Oct 11, 2014) Box Score, ESPN, https://www.espn.com/college-football/boxscore/_/gameId/400548365
133. Alabama 59-0 Texas A&M (Oct 18, 2014) Box Score, ESPN, https://www.espn.com/college-football/boxscore/_/gameId/400548364
134. Alabama 34-20 Tennessee (Oct 25, 2014) Box Score, ESPN, https://www.espn.com/college-football/boxscore/_/gameId/400548357
135. Alabama 20-13 LSU (Nov 8, 2014) Box Score, ESPN, https://www.espn.com/college-football/boxscore/_/gameId/400548342
136. Alabama 25-20 Mississippi State (Nov 15, 2014) Box Score, ESPN, https://www.espn.com/college-football/boxscore/_/gameId/400548338
137. Alabama 48-14 Western Carolina (Nov 22, 2014) Box Score, ESPN, https://www.espn.com/college-football/boxscore/_/gameId/400548328
138. Alabama 55-44 Auburn (Nov 29, 2014) Box Score, ESPN, https://www.espn.com/college-football/boxscore/_/gameId/400548323
139. Alabama 42-13 Missouri (Dec 6, 2014) Box Score, ESPN, https://www.espn.com/college-football/boxscore/_/gameId/400609098
140. Alabama 35-42 Ohio State (Jan 1, 2015) Box Score, ESPN, https://www.espn.com/college-football/boxscore/_/gameId/400610178
141. 2015 NFL Draft, Wikipedia, retrieved 01/31/24 from https://en.wikipedia.org/wiki/2015_NFL_Draft
142. 2015 Alabama Crimson Tide football team, Wikipedia, retrieved 01/31/24 from
https://en.wikipedia.org/wiki/2015_Alabama_Crimson_Tide_football_team
143. 2015 Alabama Crimson Tide Roster, cfbstats, http://www.cfbstats.com/2015/team/8/roster.html
144. Richard Mullaney, Wikipedia, retrieved 01/31/24 from https://en.wikipedia.org/wiki/Richard_Mullaney
145. Alabama 35-17 Wisconsin (Sep 5, 2015) Box Score, ESPN, https://www.espn.com/college-football/boxscore/_/gameId/400603827
146. Alabama 37-10 Middle Tennessee (Sep 12, 2015) Box Score, ESPN, https://www.espn.com/college-football/boxscore/_/gameId/400603860
147. Ole Miss 43-37 Alabama (Sep 19, 2015) Box Score, ESPN, https://www.espn.com/college-football/boxscore/_/gameId/400603850

148. Alabama 34-0 Louisiana Monroe (Sep 26, 2015) Box Score, ESPN, https://www.espn.com/college-football/boxscore/_/gameId/400603841
149. Alabama 38-10 Georgia (Oct 3, 2015) Box Score, ESPN, https://www.espn.com/college-football/boxscore/_/gameId/400603879
150. Arkansas 14-27 Alabama (Oct 10, 2015) Box Score, ESPN, https://www.espn.com/college-football/boxscore/_/gameId/400603899
151. Alabama 41-23 Texas A&M (Oct 17, 2015) Box Score, ESPN, https://www.espn.com/college-football/boxscore/_/gameId/400603897
152. Alabama 19-14 Tennessee (Oct 24, 2015) Box Score, ESPN, https://www.espn.com/college-football/boxscore/_/gameId/400603886
153. Alabama 30-16 LSU (Nov 7, 2015) Box Score, ESPN, https://www.espn.com/college-football/boxscore/_/gameId/400603905
154. Alabama 31-6 Mississippi State (Nov 14, 2015) Box Score, ESPN, https://www.espn.com/college-football/boxscore/_/gameId/400603933
155. Alabama 56-6 Charleston Southern (Nov 21, 2015) Box Score, ESPN, https://www.espn.com/college-football/boxscore/_/gameId/400603921
156. Alabama 29-13 Auburn (Nov 28, 2015) Box Score, ESPN, https://www.espn.com/college-football/boxscore/_/gameId/400603913
157. Alabama 29-15 Florida (Dec 5, 2015) Box Score, ESPN, https://www.espn.com/college-football/boxscore/_/gameId/400852681
158. Alabama 38-0 Michigan State (Dec 31, 2015) Box Score, ESPN, https://www.espn.com/college-football/boxscore/_/gameId/400852732
159. Alabama 45-40 Clemson (Jan 11, 2016) Box Score, ESPN, https://www.espn.com/college-football/boxscore/_/gameId/400852743
160. 2016 Alabama Crimson Tide football team, Wikipedia, retrieved 01/31/24 from https://en.wikipedia.org/wiki/2016_Alabama_Crimson_Tide_football_team
161. 2016 Alabama Crimson Tide Roster, cfbstats, http://www.cfbstats.com/2016/team/8/roster.html
162. Position-by-Position Preview of Alabama's 2016 Roster, Bleacher Report, https://bleacherreport.com/articles/2644132-position-by-position-preview-of-alabamas-2016-roster
163. Alabama routs USC 52-6 in season opener, University of Alabama Athletics, https://rolltide.com/news/2016/9/3/football-alabama-routs-usc-52-6-in-season-opener.aspx
164. Alabama 52-6 USC (Sep 3, 2016) Box Score, ESPN, https://www.espn.com/college-football/boxscore/_/gameId/400868969
165. Alabama 38-10 Western Kentucky (Sep 10, 2016) Game Recap, ESPN, https://www.espn.com/college-football/recap/_/gameId/400868980
166. Western Kentucky 10-38 Alabama (Sep 10, 2016) Box Score, ESPN, https://www.espn.com/college-football/boxscore/_/gameId/400868980
167. No. 1 Alabama Football Beats No. 19 Ole Miss, 48-43, In Oxford, University of Alabama Athletics, https://rolltide.com/news/2016/9/17/no-1-alabama-football-beats-no-19-ole-miss-48-43-in-oxford.aspx
168. Alabama 48-43 Ole Miss (Sep 17, 2016) Box Score, ESPN, https://www.espn.com/college-football/boxscore/_/gameId/400868997
169. No. 1 Alabama Football Beats No. 19 Ole Miss, 48-43, In Oxford, University of Alabama Athletics, https://rolltide.com/news/2016/9/17/no-1-alabama-football-beats-no-19-ole-miss-48-43-in-oxford.aspx
170. Alabama 48-0 Kent State (Sep 24, 2016) Box Score, ESPN, https://www.espn.com/college-football/boxscore/_/gameId/400869002
171. No. 1 Alabama Football Earns 34-6 Homecoming Win Over Kentucky, University of Alabama Athletics, https://rolltide.com/news/2016/10/1/no-1-alabama-football-earns-34-6-homecoming-win-over-kentucky.aspx
172. Alabama 34-6 Kentucky (Oct 1, 2016) Box Score, ESPN, https://www.espn.com/college-football/boxscore/_/gameId/400869010
173. No. 1 Alabama Football Knocks Off No. 16 Arkansas, 49-30, in Fayetteville, University of Alabama Athletics, https://rolltide.com/news/2016/10/8/no-1-alabama-football-knocks-off-no-16-arkansas-49-30-in-fayetteville.aspx
174. Alabama 49-30 Arkansas (Oct 8, 2016) Box Score, ESPN, https://www.espn.com/college-football/boxscore/_/gameId/400869018
175. Running Game Shines as Alabama Football Knocks Off Tennessee, 49-10, University of Alabama Athletics, https://rolltide.com/news/2016/10/15/running-game-shines-as-alabama-football-knocks-off-tennessee-49-10.aspx
176. Alabama 49-10 Tennessee (Oct 15, 2016) Box Score, ESPN, https://www.espn.com/college-football/boxscore/_/gameId/400869028
177. No. 1 Alabama Football Beats No. 6 Texas A&M, 33-14, University of Alabama Athletics, https://rolltide.com/news/2016/10/22/no-1-alabama-football-beats-no-6-texas-am-33-14.aspx
178. Alabama 33-14 Texas A&M (Oct 22, 2016) Box Score, ESPN, https://www.espn.com/college-football/boxscore/_/gameId/400869029
179. No. 1 Alabama Wins with Stifling Defense Over No. 15 LSU, 10-0, University of Alabama Athletics, https://rolltide.com/news/2016/11/5/football-no-1-alabama-wins-with-stifling-defense-over-no-15-lsu-10-0.aspx
180. Alabama 10-0 LSU (Nov 5, 2016) Box Score, ESPN, https://www.espn.com/college-football/boxscore/_/gameId/400869044
181. Hurts' Record Day Drives No. 1 Alabama to 51-3 Win over Mississippi State, University of Alabama Athletics, https://rolltide.com/news/2016/11/12/football-hurts-record-day-drives-no-1-alabama-to-51-3-win-over-mississippi-state.aspx
182. Alabama 51-3 Mississippi State (Nov 12, 2016) Box Score, ESPN, https://www.espn.com/college-football/boxscore/_/gameId/400869049
183. No. 1 Alabama Football Beats Chattanooga, 31-3, University of Alabama Athletics, https://rolltide.com/news/2016/11/19/no-1-alabama-football-beats-chattanooga-31-3.aspx
184. Alabama 31-3 Chattanooga (Nov 19, 2016) Box Score, University of Alabama Athletics, https://www.espn.com/college-football/boxscore/_/gameId/400869056
185. No. 1 Alabama Football Beats No. 13 Auburn, 30-12, to Finish Regular Season with Perfect 12-0 Mark, University of Alabama Athletics, https://rolltide.com/news/2016/11/26/no-1-alabama-football-beats-no-13-auburn-30-12-to-finish-regular-season-with-perfect-12-0-mark.aspx
186. Alabama 30-12 Auburn (Nov 26, 2016) Box Score, ESPN, https://www.espn.com/college-football/boxscore/_/gameId/400869068
187. No. 1 Ranked Alabama Earns SEC Title No. 26 with 53-16 Win Over No. 15 Florida, University of Alabama Athletics, https://rolltide.com/news/2016/12/3/football-no-1-ranked-alabama-earns-sec-title-no-26-with-53-16-win-over-no-15-florida.aspx
188. Alabama 54-16 Florida (Dec 3, 2016) Box Score, ESPN, https://www.espn.com/college-football/boxscore/_/gameId/400926943
189. No. 1 Alabama Football Wins 2016 Chick-fil-A Peach Bowl over No. 4 Washington, 24-7, University of Alabama Athletics, https://rolltide.com/news/2016/12/31/no-1-alabama-football-wins-2016-chick-fil-a-peach-bowl-over-no-4-washington-24-7.aspx
190. Alabama 54-16 Florida (Dec 3, 2016) Box Score, ESPN, https://www.espn.com/college-football/boxscore/_/gameId/400876107
191. Alabama Falls, 35-31, to Clemson in CFP National Championship Game, University of Alabama Athletics, https://rolltide.com/news/2017/1/10/football-alabama-falls-35-31-to-clemson-in-cfp-national-championship-game.aspx
192. Clemson 35-31 Alabama (Jan 9, 2017) Box Score, ESPN, https://www.espn.com/college-football/boxscore/_/gameId/400876570
193. Alabama football holds awards banquet, tdalabamamag.com, https://tdalabamamag.com/2016/12/04/alabama-football-holds-awards-banquet/
194. SEC 2016 Season Awards and All-Conference Team, Athlon Sports, https://athlonsports.com/college-football/sec-2016-season-awards-and-all-conference-team
195. Alabama Football: Crimson Tide dominates national player awards, Bama Hammer, https://bamahammer.com/2021/01/07/alabama-football-dominates-player-awards/
196. 2017 Alabama Crimson Tide football team, Wikipedia, retrieved 01/31/24 from https://en.wikipedia.org/wiki/2017_Alabama_Crimson_Tide_football_team
197. 2017 Alabama Crimson Tide Roster, cfbstats, http://www.cfbstats.com/2017/team/8/roster.html
198. Alabama 24-7 Florida State (Sep 2, 2017) Box Score, ESPN, https://www.espn.com/college-football/boxscore/_/gameId/400933827
199. Alabama 41-10 Fresno State (Sep 9, 2017) Box Score, ESPN, https://www.espn.com/college-football/boxscore/_/gameId/400933841
200. Alabama 41-23 Colorado State (Sep 16, 2017) Box Score, ESPN, https://www.espn.com/college-football/boxscore/_/gameId/400933854
201. Alabama 59-0 Vanderbilt (Sep 23, 2017) Box Score, ESPN, https://www.espn.com/college-football/boxscore/_/gameId/400933871
202. Alabama 66-3 Ole Miss (Sep 30, 2017) Box Score, ESPN, https://www.espn.com/college-football/boxscore/_/gameId/400933872
203. Alabama 27-19 Texas A&M (Oct 7, 2017) Box Score, ESPN, https://www.espn.com/college-football/boxscore/_/gameId/400933884
204. Alabama 41-9 Arkansas (Oct 14, 2017) Box Score, ESPN, https://www.espn.com/college-football/boxscore/_/gameId/400933886

205. Alabama 45-7 Tennessee (Oct 21, 2017) Box Score, ESPN, https://www.espn.com/college-football/boxscore/_/gameId/400933893
206. Alabama 24-10 LSU (Nov 4, 2017) Box Score, ESPN, https://www.espn.com/college-football/boxscore/_/gameId/400933904
207. Alabama 31-24 Mississippi State (Nov 11, 2017) Box Score, ESPN, https://www.espn.com/college-football/boxscore/_/gameId/400933916
208. Alabama 56-0 Mercer (Nov 18, 2017) Box Score, ESPN, https://www.espn.com/college-football/boxscore/_/gameId/400933921
209. Alabama 14-26 Auburn (Nov 25, 2017) Box Score, ESPN, https://www.espn.com/college-football/boxscore/_/gameId/400933932
210. Alabama 24-6 Clemson (Jan 1, 2018) Box Score, ESPN, https://www.espn.com/college-football/boxscore/_/gameId/400953413
211. Alabama 26-23 Georgia (Jan 8, 2018) Box Score, ESPN, https://www.espn.com/college-football/boxscore/_/gameId/400953415
212. 2018 Alabama Crimson Tide football team, Wikipedia, retrieved 01/31/24 from https://en.wikipedia.org/wiki/2018_Alabama_Crimson_Tide_football_team
213. 2018 Alabama Crimson Tide Roster, cfbstats, http://www.cfbstats.com/2018/team/8/roster.html
214. Balanced Attack Powers No. 1 Alabama Football to 51-14 Win Over Louisville in Camping World Kickoff, University of Alabama Athletics, https://rolltide.com/news/2018/9/1/balanced-attack-powers-no-1-alabama-football-to-51-14-win-over-louisville-in-camping-world-kickoff.aspx
215. Alabama 51-14 Louisville (Sep 1, 2018) Box Score, ESPN, https://www.espn.com/college-football/boxscore/_/gameId/401012246
216. No. 1 Alabama Football Rolls to 57-7 Victory Over Arkansas State in Home Opener, University of Alabama Athletics, https://rolltide.com/news/2018/9/8/no-1-alabama-football-rolls-to-57-7-victory-over-arkansas-state-in-home-opener.aspx
217. Alabama 57-7 Arkansas State (Sep 8, 2018) Box Score, ESPN, https://www.espn.com/college-football/boxscore/_/gameId/401012260
218. Offense Runs Wild as No. 1 Alabama Football Makes History in 62-7 Road Win Over Ole Miss, University of Alabama Athletics, https://rolltide.com/news/2018/9/15/offense-runs-wild-as-no-1-alabama-football-makes-history-in-62-7-road-win-over-ole-miss.aspx
219. Alabama 62-7 Ole Miss (Sep 15, 2018) Box Score, ESPN, https://www.espn.com/college-football/boxscore/_/gameId/401012277
220. Tagovailoa Continues to Shine as No. 1 Alabama Football Handles No. 22 Texas A&M, 45-23, University of Alabama Athletics, https://rolltide.com/news/2018/9/22/tagovailoa-continues-to-shine-as-no-1-alabama-football-handles-no-22-texas-am-45-23.aspx
221. Texas A&M 23-45 Alabama (Sep 22, 2018) Box Score, ESPN, https://www.espn.com/college-football/boxscore/_/gameId/401012284
222. No. 1 Alabama Football Cruises to 56-14 Victory Over Louisiana, University of Alabama Athletics, https://rolltide.com/news/2018/9/29/no-1-alabama-football-cruises-to-56-14-victory-over-louisiana.aspx
223. Alabama 56-14 Louisiana (Sep 29, 2018) Box Score, ESPN, https://www.espn.com/college-football/boxscore/_/gameId/401012292
224. No. 1 Alabama Football Puts Up Huge Numbers in 65-31 Victory at Arkansas, University of Alabama Athletics, https://rolltide.com/news/2018/10/6/no-1-alabama-football-puts-up-huge-numbers-in-65-31-victory-at-arkansas.aspx
225. Alabama 65-31 Arkansas (Oct 6, 2018) Box Score, ESPN, https://www.espn.com/college-football/boxscore/_/gameId/401012300
226. No. 1 Alabama Posts 39-10 Homecoming Win Over Missouri, University of Alabama Athletics, https://rolltide.com/news/2018/10/13/football-no-1-alabama-posts-39-10-homecoming-win-over-missouri.aspx
227. Alabama 39-10 Missouri (Oct 13, 2018) Box Score, ESPN, https://www.espn.com/college-football/boxscore/_/gameId/401012307
228. No. 1 Alabama Football Beats Tennessee, 58-21, in Knoxville Saturday, University of Alabama Athletics, https://rolltide.com/news/2018/10/20/no-1-alabama-football-beats-tennessee-58-21-in-knoxville-saturday.aspx
229. Alabama 58-21 Tennessee (Oct 20, 2018) Box Score, ESPN, https://www.espn.com/college-football/boxscore/_/gameId/401012318
230. Defense Dominates as No. 1 Alabama Football Clinches SEC West Title With 29-0 Shutout Victory at No. 3 LSU, University of Alabama Athletics, https://rolltide.com/news/2018/11/3/defense-dominates-as-no-1-alabama-football-clinches-sec-west-title-with-29-0-shutout-victory-at-no-3-lsu.aspx
231. Alabama 29-0 LSU (Nov 3, 2018) Box Score, ESPN, https://www.espn.com/college-football/boxscore/_/gameId/401012327
232. No. 1 Alabama Blanks No. 16 Mississippi State, 24-0, University of Alabama Athletics, https://rolltide.com/news/2018/11/10/football-no-1-alabama-blanks-no-16-mississippi-state-24-0.aspx
233. Alabama 24-0 Mississippi State (Nov 10, 2018) Box Score, ESPN, https://www.espn.com/college-football/boxscore/_/gameId/401012331
234. Tagovailoa Breaks Touchdown Record as No. 1 Alabama Downs The Citadel, 50-17, University of Alabama Athletics, https://rolltide.com/news/2018/11/17/football-tagovailoa-breaks-touchdown-record-as-no-1-alabama-downs-the-citadel-50-17.aspx
235. Alabama 50-17 The Citadel (Nov 17, 2018) Box Score, ESPN, https://www.espn.com/college-football/boxscore/_/gameId/401012338
236. No. 1 Alabama Football Closes Regular Season with 52-21 Win over Auburn, University of Alabama Athletics, https://rolltide.com/news/2018/11/24/no-1-alabama-football-closes-regular-season-with-52-21-win-over-auburn.aspx
237. Auburn 21-52 Alabama (Nov 24, 2018) Box Score, ESPN, https://www.espn.com/college-football/boxscore/_/gameId/401012350
238. No. 1 Alabama Football Wins SEC Championship Game with 35-28 Comeback Win over No. 4 Georgia, University of Alabama Athletics, https://rolltide.com/news/2018/12/1/no-1-alabama-football-wins-sec-championship-game-with-35-28-comeback-win-over-no-4-georgia.aspx
239. Alabama 35-28 Georgia (Dec 1, 2018) Box Score, ESPN, https://www.espn.com/college-football/boxscore/_/gameId/401056705
240. No. 1 Alabama Beats No. 4 Oklahoma, 45-34, in College Football Playoff Semifinal, University of Alabama Athletics, https://rolltide.com/news/2018/12/29/no-1-alabama-beats-no-4-oklahoma-45-34-in-college-football-playoff-semifinal.aspx
241. Alabama 45-34 Oklahoma (Dec 29, 2018) Box Score, ESPN, https://www.espn.com/college-football/boxscore/_/gameId/401032078
242. No. 1 Alabama Falls to No. 2 Clemson in 2019 College Football Playoff National Championship Game, 44-16, University of Alabama Athletics, https://rolltide.com/news/2019/1/7/no-1-alabama-falls-to-no-2-clemson-in-2019-college-football-playoff-national-championship-game-44-16.aspx
243. Clemson 44-16 Alabama (Jan 7, 2019) Box Score, ESPN, https://www.espn.com/college-football/boxscore/_/gameId/401032087
244. 2019 Alabama Crimson Tide football team, Wikipedia, retrieved 01/31/24 from https://en.wikipedia.org/wiki/2019_Alabama_Crimson_Tide_football_team
245. 2019 Alabama Crimson Tide Roster, cfbstats, http://www.cfbstats.com/2019/team/8/roster.html
246. Stingy Defense and Tagovailoa's Career Day Propels No. 2 Alabama Football to 42-3 Victory Over Duke in Chick-fil-A Kickoff Game, University of Alabama Athletics, https://rolltide.com/news/2019/8/31/stingy-defense-and-tagovailoas-career-day-propels-no-2-alabama-football-to-42-3-victory-over-duke-in-chick-fil-a-kickoff-game.aspx
247. Alabama 42-3 Duke (Aug 31, 2019) Box Score, ESPN, https://www.espn.com/college-football/boxscore/_/gameId/401110720
248. No. 2 Alabama Football Cruises to 62-10 Win Over New Mexico State, University of Alabama Athletics, https://rolltide.com/news/2019/9/7/no-2-alabama-football-cruises-to-62-10-win-over-new-mexico-state.aspx
249. New Mexico State 10-62 Alabama (Sep 7, 2019) Box Score, ESPN, https://www.espn.com/college-football/boxscore/_/gameId/401110773
250. No. 2 Alabama Football Opens SEC Slate with 47-23 Win at South Carolina, University of Alabama Athletics, https://rolltide.com/news/2019/9/14/no-2-alabama-football-opens-sec-slate-with-47-23-win-at-south-carolina.aspx
251. Alabama 47-23 South Carolina (Sep 14, 2019) Box Score, ESPN, https://www.espn.com/college-football/boxscore/_/gameId/401110794
252. Another Big Day from Tagovailoa Leads No. 2 Alabama Football to 49-7 Win Over Southern Miss, University of Alabama Athletics, https://rolltide.com/news/2019/9/21/another-big-day-from-tagovailoa-leads-no-2-alabama-football-to-49-7-win-over-southern-miss.aspx
253. Alabama 49-7 Southern Mississippi (Sep 21, 2019) Box Score, ESPN, https://www.espn.com/college-football/boxscore/_/gameId/401110797
254. Devonta Smith and Tua Tagovailoa Shatter Records as No. 2 Alabama Beats Ole Miss, 59-31, University of Alabama Athletics, https://rolltide.com/news/2019/9/28/football-devonta-smith-and-tua-tagovailoa-shatter-records-as-no-2-alabama-beats-ole-miss-59-31.aspx
255. Alabama 59-31 Ole Miss (Sep 28, 2019) Box Score, ESPN, https://www.espn.com/college-football/boxscore/_/gameId/401110806
256. Offense and Special Teams Key in No. 1/1 Alabama's 47-28 Win at No. 24/21 Texas A&M, University of Alabama Athletics, https://rolltide.com/news/2019/10/12/football-offense-and-special-teams-key-in-no-1-1-alabamas-47-28-win-at-no-24-21-texas-am.aspx

257. Alabama 47-28 Texas A&M (Oct 12, 2019) Box Score, ESPN, https://www.espn.com/college-football/boxscore/_/gameId/401110822
258. No. 1 Alabama Remains Perfect After Defeating Tennessee, 35-13, Under the Lights in Bryant-Denny Stadium, University of Alabama Athletics, https://rolltide.com/news/2019/10/20/football-no-1-alabama-remains-perfect-after-defeating-tennessee-35-13-under-the-lights-in-bryant-denny-stadium.aspx
259. Alabama 35-13 Tennessee (Oct 19, 2019) Box Score, ESPN, https://www.espn.com/college-football/boxscore/_/gameId/401110824
260. No. 1 Alabama Football Rolls to 48-7 Homecoming Win Over Arkansas Saturday Night, University of Alabama Athletics, https://rolltide.com/news/2019/10/26/no-1-alabama-football-rolls-to-48-7-homecoming-win-over-arkansas-saturday-night.aspx
261. Alabama 48-7 Arkansas (Oct 26, 2019) Box Score, ESPN, https://www.espn.com/college-football/boxscore/_/gameId/401110831
262. No. 3 Alabama Football Comes Up Short in Battle with No. 2 LSU, 46-41, University of Alabama Athletics, https://rolltide.com/news/2019/11/9/no-3-alabama-football-comes-up-short-in-battle-with-no-2-lsu-46-41.aspx
263. LSU 46-41 Alabama (Nov 9, 2019) Box Score, ESPN, https://www.espn.com/college-football/boxscore/_/gameId/401110842
264. Najee Harris, Stout Defense, Leads No. 5 Alabama Past Mississippi State, 38-7, University of Alabama Athletics, https://rolltide.com/news/2019/11/16/football-najee-harris-stout-defense-leads-no-5-alabama-past-mississippi-state-38-7.aspx
265. Alabama 38-7 Mississippi State (Nov 16, 2019) Box Score, ESPN, https://www.espn.com/college-football/boxscore/_/gameId/401110851
266. No. 5 Alabama Football Closes Out its 2019 Home Slate with a 66-3 Win over Western Carolina, University of Alabama Athletics, https://rolltide.com/news/2019/11/23/no-5-alabama-football-closes-out-its-2019-home-slate-with-a-66-3-win-over-western-carolina.aspx
267. Alabama 66-3 Western Carolina (Nov 23, 2019) Box Score, ESPN, https://www.espn.com/college-football/boxscore/_/gameId/401110855
268. No. 5 Alabama Football Falls at No. 16 Auburn, 48-45, to Close the 2019 Regular Season, University of Alabama Athletics, https://rolltide.com/news/2019/11/30/no-5-alabama-football-falls-at-no-16-auburn-48-45-to-close-the-2019-regular-season.aspx
269. Auburn 48-45 Alabama (Nov 30, 2019) Box Score, ESPN, https://www.espn.com/college-football/boxscore/_/gameId/401110865
270. No. 13 Alabama Football Beats No. 14 Michigan in the Vrbo Citrus Bowl 35-16, University of Alabama Athletics, https://rolltide.com/news/2020/1/1/no-13-alabama-football-beats-no-14-michigan-in-the-vrbo-citrus-bowl-35-16.aspx
271. Michigan 16-35 Alabama (Jan 1, 2020) Box Score, ESPN, https://www.espn.com/college-football/boxscore/_/gameId/401135286
272. 2020 Alabama Crimson Tide football team, Wikipedia, retrieved 01/31/24 from https://en.wikipedia.org/wiki/2020_Alabama_Crimson_Tide_football_team
273. 2020 Alabama Crimson Tide Roster, cfbstats, http://www.cfbstats.com/2020/team/8/roster.html
274. No. 2/2 Alabama Football Opens 2020 Season with a 38-19 Win Over Missouri, University of Alabama Athletics, https://rolltide.com/news/2020/9/26/no-2-2-alabama-football-opens-2020-season-with-a-38-19-win-over-missouri.aspx
275. Alabama 38-19 Missouri (Sep 26, 2020) Box Score, ESPN, https://www.espn.com/college-football/boxscore/_/gameId/401236951
276. No. 2/2 Alabama Football Posts 52-24 Victory over No. 13/13 Texas A&M in 2020 Home Opener, University of Alabama Athletics, https://rolltide.com/news/2020/10/3/no-2-2-alabama-football-posts-52-24-victory-over-no-13-13-texas-am-in-2020-home-opener.aspx
277. Alabama 52-24 Texas A&M (Oct 3, 2020) Box Score, ESPN, https://www.espn.com/college-football/boxscore/_/gameId/401237093
278. No. 2/2 Alabama Football Comes Away with 63-48 Win at Ole Miss, University of Alabama Athletics, https://rolltide.com/news/2020/10/11/no-2-2-alabama-football-comes-away-with-63-48-win-at-ole-miss.aspx
279. Alabama 63-48 Ole Miss (Oct 10, 2020) Box Score, ESPN, https://www.espn.com/college-football/boxscore/_/gameId/401237100
280. No. 2/2 Alabama Football Downs No. 3/3 Georgia Saturday Night in Bryant-Denny Stadium, 41-24, University of Alabama Athletics, https://rolltide.com/news/2020/10/17/no-2-2-alabama-football-downs-no-3-3-georgia-saturday-night-in-bryant-denny-stadium-41-24.aspx
281. Alabama 41-24 Georgia (Oct 17, 2020) Box Score, ESPN, https://www.espn.com/college-football/boxscore/_/gameId/401237107
282. No. 2/2 Alabama Football Extends Win Streak over Tennessee with 48-17 Victory in Neyland Stadium, University of Alabama Athletics, https://rolltide.com/news/2020/10/24/no-2-2-alabama-football-extends-win-streak-over-tennessee-with-48-17-victory-in-neyland-stadium.aspx
283. Alabama 48-17 Tennessee (Oct 24, 2020) Box Score, ESPN, https://www.espn.com/college-football/boxscore/_/gameId/401237114
284. No. 2/2 Alabama Football Blanks Mississippi State Saturday Night, 41-0, University of Alabama Athletics, https://rolltide.com/news/2020/10/31/no-2-2-alabama-football-blanks-mississippi-state-saturday-night-41-0.aspx
285. Alabama 41-0 Mississippi State (Oct 31, 2020) Box Score, ESPN, https://www.espn.com/college-football/boxscore/_/gameId/401237119
286. No. 1/1 Alabama Football Beats Kentucky, 63-3, in Bryant-Denny Stadium Saturday, University of Alabama Athletics, https://rolltide.com/news/2020/11/21/no-1-1-alabama-football-beats-kentucky-63-3-in-bryant-denny-stadium-saturday.aspx
287. Alabama 63-3 Kentucky (Nov 21, 2020) Box Score, ESPN, https://www.espn.com/college-football/boxscore/_/gameId/401237135
288. No. 1/1 Alabama Football Downs Auburn, 42-13, in the Crimson Tide's Home Finale Saturday, University of Alabama Athletics, https://rolltide.com/news/2020/11/28/no-1-1-alabama-football-downs-auburn-42-13-in-the-crimson-tides-home-finale-saturday.aspx
289. Alabama 42-13 Auburn (Nov 28, 2020) Box Score, ESPN, https://www.espn.com/college-football/boxscore/_/gameId/401237142
290. No. 1/1 Alabama Football Downs LSU, 55-17, in Baton Rouge Saturday Night, University of Alabama Athletics, https://rolltide.com/news/2020/12/5/no-1-1-alabama-football-downs-lsu-55-17-in-baton-rouge-saturday-night.aspx
291. Alabama 55-17 LSU (Dec 5, 2020) Box Score, ESPN, https://www.espn.com/college-football/boxscore/_/gameId/401265817
292. No. 1/1 Alabama Football Closes Regular Season with a 52-3 Win at Arkansas, University of Alabama Athletics, https://rolltide.com/news/2020/12/12/no-1-1-alabama-football-closes-regular-season-with-a-52-3-win-at-arkansas.aspx
293. Alabama 52-3 Arkansas (Dec 12, 2020) Box Score, ESPN, https://www.espn.com/college-football/boxscore/_/gameId/401267164
294. No. 1/1/1 Alabama Football Downs No. 7/11/11 Florida, 52-46, to Win Its 28th SEC Championship, University of Alabama Athletics, https://rolltide.com/news/2020/12/20/no-1-1-1-alabama-football-downs-no-7-11-11-florida-52-46-to-win-its-28th-sec-championship.aspx
295. Alabama 52-46 Florida (Dec 19, 2020) Box Score, ESPN, https://www.espn.com/college-football/boxscore/_/gameId/401237074
296. No. 1 Alabama Football Wins 2021 College Football Playoff Semifinal, 31-14, over No. 4 Notre Dame, University of Alabama Athletics, https://rolltide.com/news/2021/1/1/no-1-alabama-football-wins-2021-college-football-playoff-semifinal-31-14-over-no-4-notre-dame.aspx
297. Alabama 31-14 Notre Dame (Jan 1, 2021) Box Score, ESPN, https://www.espn.com/college-football/boxscore/_/gameId/401240152
298. No. 1 Alabama Football Wins 2021 CFP National Championship, 52-24, over No. 3 Ohio State, University of Alabama Athletics, https://rolltide.com/news/2021/1/11/football-national-championship.aspx
299. Alabama 52-24 Ohio State (Jan 11, 2021) Box Score, ESPN, https://www.espn.com/college-football/boxscore/_/gameId/401240174
300. 2021 Alabama Crimson Tide football team, Wikipedia, retrieved 01/31/24 from https://en.wikipedia.org/wiki/2021_Alabama_Crimson_Tide_football_team
301. 2021 Alabama Crimson Tide Roster, cfbstats, http://www.cfbstats.com/2021/team/8/roster.html
302. No. 1/1 Alabama Opens 2021 Season with 44-13 Victory over No. 14/16 Miami in Chick-fil-A Kickoff Game, University of Alabama Athletics, https://rolltide.com/news/2021/9/4/football-no-1-1-alabama-opens-2021-season-with-44-13-victory-over-no-14-16-miami-in-chick-fil-a-kickoff-game.aspx
303. Alabama 44-13 Miami (Sep 4, 2021) Box Score, ESPN, https://www.espn.com/college-football/boxscore/_/gameId/401281942
304. No. 1/1 Alabama Football Downs Mercer 48-14 in Saturday's Home Opener at Bryant-Denny Stadium, University of Alabama Athletics, https://rolltide.com/news/2021/9/11/no-1-1-alabama-football-downs-mercer-48-14-in-saturdays-home-opener-at-bryant-denny-stadium.aspx
305. Alabama 48-14 Mercer (Sep 11, 2021) Box Score, ESPN, https://www.espn.com/college-football/boxscore/_/gameId/401282056
306. No. 1/1 Alabama Football Beats No. 11/9 Florida in Gainesville Saturday Afternoon, 31-29, University of Alabama Athletics, https://rolltide.com/news/2021/9/18/no-1-1-alabama-football-downs-no-11-9-florida-in-gainesville-saturday-afternoon-31-29.aspx
307. Alabama 31-29 Florida (Sep 18, 2021) Box Score, ESPN, https://www.espn.com/college-football/boxscore/_/gameId/401282071
308. No. 1/1 Alabama Football Beats Southern Miss, 63-14, Saturday Night in Bryant-Denny Stadium, University of Alabama Athletics, https://rolltide.com/news/2021/9/25/no-1-1-alabama-football-beats-southern-miss-63-14-saturday-night-in-bryant-denny-stadium.aspx

309. Alabama 63-14 Southern Miss (Sep 25, 2021) Box Score, ESPN, https://www.espn.com/college-football/boxscore/_/gameId/401282081
310. No. 1/1 Alabama Football Beats No. 12/12 Ole Miss 42-21 in Bryant-Denny Stadium Saturday, University of Alabama Athletics, https://rolltide.com/news/2021/10/2/no-1-1-alabama-football-beats-no-12-12-ole-miss-42-21-in-bryant-denny-stadium-saturday.aspx
311. Alabama 42-21 Ole Miss (Oct 2, 2021) Box Score, ESPN, https://www.espn.com/college-football/boxscore/_/gameId/401282089
312. No. 1/1 Alabama Football Falls at Texas A&M Saturday Night, 41-38, University of Alabama Athletics, https://rolltide.com/news/2021/10/9/no-1-1-alabama-football-falls-at-texas-am-saturday-night-41-38.aspx
313. Alabama 41-38 Texas A&M (Oct 9, 2021) Box Score, ESPN, https://www.espn.com/college-football/boxscore/_/gameId/401282103
314. No. 5/5 Alabama Football Beats Mississippi State 49-9 Saturday Night in Starkville, University of Alabama Athletics, https://rolltide.com/news/2021/10/16/no-5-5-alabama-football-beats-mississippi-state-49-9-saturday-night-in-starkville.aspx
315. Alabama 49-9 Mississippi State (Oct 16, 2021) Box Score, ESPN, https://www.espn.com/college-football/boxscore/_/gameId/401282107
316. No. 4/4 Alabama Football Wins 15th Straight Over Tennessee Saturday Night, 52-24, University of Alabama Athletics, https://rolltide.com/news/2021/10/23/no-4-4-alabama-football-wins-15th-straight-over-tennessee-saturday-night-52-24.aspx
317. Alabama 52-24 Tennessee (Oct 23, 2021) Box Score, ESPN, https://www.espn.com/college-football/boxscore/_/gameId/401282111
318. No. 2/3 Alabama Football Beats LSU 20-14 Saturday Night in Bryant-Denny Stadium, University of Alabama Athletics, https://rolltide.com/news/2021/11/6/no-2-3-alabama-football-beats-lsu-20-14-saturday-night-in-bryant-denny-stadium.aspx
319. Alabama 20-14 LSU (Nov 6, 2021) Box Score, ESPN, https://www.espn.com/college-football/boxscore/_/gameId/401282120
320. No. 2/3 Alabama Football Beats New Mexico State 59-3 Saturday in Bryant-Denny Stadium, University of Alabama Athletics, https://rolltide.com/news/2021/11/13/no-2-3-2-alabama-football-beats-new-mexico-state-59-3-saturday-in-bryant-denny-stadium.aspx
321. Alabama 59-3 New Mexico State (Nov 13, 2021) Box Score, ESPN, https://www.espn.com/college-football/boxscore/_/gameId/401282127
322. No. 2/2/2 Alabama Football Tops Arkansas 42-35 on Senior Day, University of Alabama Athletics, https://rolltide.com/news/2021/11/20/no-2-2-2-alabama-football-tops-arkansas-42-35-on-senior-day.aspx
323. Arkansas 35-42 Alabama (Nov 20, 2021) Box Score, ESPN, https://www.espn.com/college-football/boxscore/_/gameId/401282135
324. No. 3/3/2 Alabama Football Beats Auburn in First Overtime Game in Series History, 24-22, University of Alabama Athletics, https://rolltide.com/news/2021/11/27/no-3-3-2-alabama-football-beats-auburn-in-first-overtime-game-in-series-history-24-22.aspx
325. Alabama 24-22 Auburn (Nov 27, 2021) Box Score, ESPN, https://www.espn.com/college-football/boxscore/_/gameId/401282146
326. No. 3/4/2 Alabama Football Wins its 29th SEC Championship with a 41-24 Win Over No. 1/1/1 Georgia, University of Alabama Athletics, https://rolltide.com/news/2021/12/4/no-3-4-2-alabama-football-wins-its-29th-sec-championship-with-a-41-24-win-over-no-1-1-1-georgia.aspx
327. Alabama 41-24 Georgia (Dec 4, 2021) Box Score, ESPN, https://www.espn.com/college-football/boxscore/_/gameId/401282154
328. No. 1/1/1 Alabama Advances to CFP Championship Game with 27-6 Win Over No. 4/4/4 Cincinnati, University of Alabama Athletics, https://rolltide.com/news/2021/12/31/football-no-1-1-1-alabama-advances-to-cfp-championship-game-with-27-6-win-over-no-4-4-4-cincinnati.aspx
329. Alabama 27-6 Cincinnati (Dec 31, 2021) Box Score, ESPN, https://www.espn.com/college-football/boxscore/_/gameId/401331235
330. Alabama Football Falls to Georgia in the CFP National Championship Game, 33-18, University of Alabama Athletics, https://rolltide.com/news/2022/1/10/alabama-football-falls-to-georgia-in-the-cfp-national-championship-game-33-18.aspx
331. Georgia 33-18 Alabama (Jan 10, 2022) Box Score, ESPN, https://www.espn.com/college-football/boxscore/_/gameId/401331242
332. Alabama football team awards: Who did Crimson Tide players vote as their MVP?, Tuscaloosa News, https://www.tuscaloosanews.com/story/sports/2021/12/05/alabama-football-names-permanent-captains-team-banquet/8883785002/
333. 2022 Alabama Crimson Tide football team, Wikipedia, retrieved 01/31/24 from https://en.wikipedia.org/wiki/2022_Alabama_Crimson_Tide_football_team
334. 2022 Alabama Crimson Tide Roster, cfbstats, http://www.cfbstats.com/2022/team/8/roster.html
335. No. 1/1 Alabama Football Opens 2022 Season with 55-0 Win Over Utah State, University of Alabama Athletics, https://rolltide.com/news/2022/9/3/no-1-1-alabama-football-opens-2022-season-with-55-0-win-over-utah-state.aspx
336. Alabama 55-0 Utah State (Sep 3, 2022) Box Score, ESPN, https://www.espn.com/college-football/boxscore/_/gameId/401403854
337. Last-Minute Field Goal Lifts No. 1/1 Alabama Football to a 20-19 Victory Over Texas, University of Alabama Athletics, https://rolltide.com/news/2022/9/10/last-minute-field-goal-lifts-no-1-1-alabama-football-to-a-20-19-victory-over-texas.aspx
338. Alabama 20-19 Texas (Sep 10, 2022) Box Score, ESPN, https://www.espn.com/college-football/boxscore/_/gameId/401403868
339. No. 2/1 Alabama Football Rolls Past ULM 63-7, University of Alabama Athletics, https://rolltide.com/news/2022/9/17/no-2-1-alabama-football-rolls-past-ulm-63-7.aspx
340. Alabama 63-7 UL Monroe (Sep 17, 2022) Box Score, ESPN, https://www.espn.com/college-football/boxscore/_/gameId/401403880
341. No. 2/2 Alabama Football Dominant on Both Sides of Ball in a 55-3 Victory Over Vanderbilt, University of Alabama Athletics, https://rolltide.com/news/2022/9/24/no-2-2-alabama-football-dominant-on-both-sides-of-ball-in-a-55-3-victory-over-vanderbilt.aspx
342. Alabama 55-3 Vanderbilt (Sep 24, 2022) Box Score, ESPN, https://www.espn.com/college-football/boxscore/_/gameId/401403892
343. No. 2/2 Alabama Rushes Past No. 20/19 Arkansas, 49-26, University of Alabama Athletics, https://rolltide.com/news/2022/10/1/football-no-2-2-alabama-rushes-past-no-20-19-arkansas-49-26.aspx
344. Alabama 49-26 Arkansas (Oct 1, 2022) Box Score, ESPN, https://www.espn.com/college-football/boxscore/_/gameId/401403902
345. No. 1/1 Alabama Holds Off Texas A&M 24-20, University of Alabama Athletics, https://rolltide.com/news/2022/10/8/football-no-1-1-alabama-holds-off-texas-am-24-20.aspx
346. Alabama 24-20 Texas A&M (Oct 8, 2022) Box Score, ESPN, https://www.espn.com/college-football/boxscore/_/gameId/401403909
347. No. 3/1 Alabama Football Falls on Last-Second Field Goal to No. 6/8 Tennessee in Knoxville, 52-49, University of Alabama Athletics, https://rolltide.com/news/2022/10/15/no-3-1-alabama-football-falls-on-last-second-field-goal-to-no-6-8-tennessee-in-knoxville-52-49
348. No. 52-49 Tennessee (Oct 15, 2022) Box Score, ESPN, https://www.espn.com/college-football/boxscore/_/gameId/401403921
349. No. 6/6 Alabama Overpowers No. 24/24 Mississippi State, 30-6, University of Alabama Athletics, https://rolltide.com/news/2022/10/22/football-no-6-6-alabama-overpowers-no-24-24-mississippi-state-30-6.aspx
350. Alabama 30-6 Mississippi State (Oct 22, 2022) Box Score, ESPN, https://www.espn.com/college-football/boxscore/_/gameId/401403922
351. No. 6 Alabama Football Falls in Overtime at No. 10 LSU, 32-31, University of Alabama Athletics, https://rolltide.com/news/2022/11/6/no-6-alabama-football-falls-in-overtime-at-no-10-lsu-32-31.aspx
352. LSU 32-31 Alabama (Nov 5, 2022) Box Score, ESPN, https://www.espn.com/college-football/boxscore/_/gameId/401403934
353. No. 9/10/11 Alabama Football Uses Second-Half Comeback to Beat No. 11/11/9 Ole Miss, 30-24, University of Alabama Athletics, https://rolltide.com/news/2022/11/12/no-9-10-11-alabama-football-uses-second-half-comeback-to-beat-no-11-11-9-ole-miss-30-24.aspx
354. Alabama 30-24 Ole Miss (Nov 12, 2022) Box Score, ESPN, https://www.espn.com/college-football/boxscore/_/gameId/401403943
355. No. 8/8/8 Alabama Downs Austin Peay, 34-0, University of Alabama Athletics, https://rolltide.com/news/2022/11/19/football-no-8-8-8-alabama-downs-austin-peay-34-0.aspx
356. Alabama 34-0 Austin Peay (Nov 19, 2022) Box Score, ESPN, https://www.espn.com/college-football/boxscore/_/gameId/401403946
357. No. 7/8/7 Alabama Downs Auburn, 49-27, for Third-Straight Iron Bowl Victory, University of Alabama Athletics, https://rolltide.com/news/2022/11/26/football-no-7-8-7-alabama-downs-auburn-49-27-for-third-straight-iron-bowl-victory.aspx
358. Alabama 49-27 Auburn (Nov 26, 2022) Box Score, ESPN, https://www.espn.com/college-football/boxscore/_/gameId/401403957
359. No. 5/5/5 Alabama Cruises to 45-20 Victory over No. 9/11/9 Kansas State in Allstate Sugar Bowl, University of Alabama Athletics, https://rolltide.com/news/2022/12/31/football-no-5-5-5-alabama-cruises-to-45-20-victory-over-no-9-11-9-kansas-state-in-allstate-sugar-bowl.aspx
360. Alabama 45-20 Kansas State (Dec 31, 2022) Box Score, ESPN, https://www.espn.com/college-football/boxscore/_/gameId/401442018

361. Alabama football team awards: Here are permanent captains, team MVP, Tuscaloosa News, https://www.tuscaloosanews.com/story/sports/college/football/2022/12/05/alabama-football-team-awards-captains-nick-saban/69699839007/

362. 2023 NFL Draft, Wikipedia, retrieved 01/31/24 from https://en.wikipedia.org/wiki/2023_NFL_Draft

363. 2023 Alabama Crimson Tide football team, Wikipedia, retrieved 01/31/24 from https://en.wikipedia.org/wiki/2023_Alabama_Crimson_Tide_football_team

364. 2023 Alabama Crimson Tide Roster, cfbstats, http://www.cfbstats.com/2023/team/8/roster.html

365. No. 4/3 Alabama Opens 2023 Campaign with a 56-7 Win Over Middle Tennessee, University of Alabama Athletics, https://rolltide.com/news/2023/9/2/football-no-4-3-alabama-opens-2023-campaign-with-a-56-7-win-over-middle-tennessee.aspx

366. Alabama 56-7 Middle Tennessee (Sep 2, 2023) Box Score, ESPN, https://www.espn.com/college-football/boxscore/_/gameId/401520149

367. No. 3/3 Alabama Falls at Home to No. 11/10 Texas, 34-24, University of Alabama Athletics, https://rolltide.com/news/2023/9/9/football-no-3-3-alabama-falls-at-home-to-no-11-10-texas-34-24.aspx

368. Texas 34-24 Alabama (Sep 9, 2023) Box Score, ESPN, https://www.espn.com/college-football/boxscore/_/gameId/401520183

369. No. 10/10 Alabama Pushes Past South Florida, University of Alabama Athletics, https://rolltide.com/news/2023/9/16/football-no-10-10-alabama-pushes-past-south-florida.aspx

370. Alabama 17-3 South Florida (Sep 16, 2023) Box Score, ESPN, https://www.espn.com/college-football/boxscore/_/gameId/401520244

371. Second Half Surge Pushes No. 13/12 Alabama Past No. 15/16 Ole Miss, 24-10, University of Alabama Athletics, https://rolltide.com/news/2023/9/23/football-second-half-surge-pushes-no-13-12-alabama-past-no-15-16-ole-miss-24-10.aspx

372. Alabama 24-10 Ole Miss (Sep 23, 2023) Box Score, ESPN, https://www.espn.com/college-football/boxscore/_/gameId/401520250

373. No. 12/11 Alabama uses Balanced Attack to Capture a 40-17 Win at Mississippi State, University of Alabama Athletics, https://rolltide.com/news/2023/10/1/football-no-12-11-alabama-uses-balanced-attack-to-capture-a-40-17-win-at-mississippi-state.aspx

374. Alabama 40-17 Mississippi State (Sep 30, 2023) Box Score, ESPN, https://www.espn.com/college-football/boxscore/_/gameId/401520285

375. No. 11/10 Alabama Upends Texas A&M, 26-20, to Remain Unbeaten in SEC Play, University of Alabama Athletics, https://rolltide.com/news/2023/10/7/football-no-11-10-alabama-upends-texas-am-26-20-to-remain-unbeaten-in-sec-play.aspx

376. Alabama 26-20 Texas A&M (Oct 7, 2023) Box Score, ESPN, https://www.espn.com/college-football/boxscore/_/gameId/401520310

377. No. 11/10 Alabama Avoids Upset Bid in 24-21 Victory over Arkansas, University of Alabama Athletics, https://rolltide.com/news/2023/10/14/football-no-11-10-alabama-avoids-upset-bid-in-24-21-victory-over-arkansas.aspx

378. Alabama 24-21 Arkansas (Oct 14, 2023) Box Score, ESPN, https://www.espn.com/college-football/boxscore/_/gameId/401520316

379. No. 11/8 Alabama's Defense Dominates Second Half in 34-20 Victory over No. 17/15 Tennessee, University of Alabama Athletics, https://rolltide.com/news/2023/10/21/football-no-11-8-alabamas-defense-dominates-second-half-in-34-20-victory-over-no-17-15-tennessee.aspx

380. Alabama 34-20 Tennessee (Oct 21, 2023) Box Score, ESPN, https://www.espn.com/college-football/boxscore/_/gameId/401520333

381. Milroe's Four Rushing Touchdowns Leads No. 8/8/8 Alabama Past No. 14/13/13 LSU, 42-28, University of Alabama Athletics, https://rolltide.com/news/2023/11/4/milroe-touchdowns-leads-alabama-past-lsu.aspx

382. Alabama 42-28 LSU (Nov 4, 2023) Box Score, ESPN, https://www.espn.com/college-football/boxscore/_/gameId/401520362

383. Big First Quarter Propels No. 8/8/8 Alabama Past Kentucky, 49-21, University of Alabama Athletics, https://rolltide.com/news/2023/11/11/football-big-first-quarter-propels-no-8-8-8-alabama-past-kentucky-49-21.aspx

384. Alabama 49-21 Kentucky (Nov 11, 2023) Box Score, ESPN, https://www.espn.com/college-football/boxscore/_/gameId/401520386

385. No. 8/8/8 Alabama Defeats Chattanooga, 66-10, on Senior Day, University of Alabama Athletics, https://rolltide.com/news/2023/11/18/football-no-8-8-8-alabama-defeats-chattanooga-66-10-on-senior-day.aspx

386. Alabama 66-10 Chattanooga (Nov 18, 2023) Box Score, ESPN, https://www.espn.com/college-football/boxscore/_/gameId/401520401

387. Late-Game Heroics Lead No. 8/8/8 Alabama to 27-24 Victory at Auburn, University of Alabama Athletics, https://rolltide.com/news/2023/11/25/football-late-game-heroics-lead-no-8-8-8-alabama-to-27-24-victory-at-auburn.aspx

388. Alabama 27-24 Auburn (Nov 25, 2023) Box Score, ESPN, https://www.espn.com/college-football/boxscore/_/gameId/401520427

389. No. 8/8/8 Alabama Upsets No. 1/1/1 Georgia, 27-24, to Capture 30th SEC Championship, University of Alabama Athletics, https://rolltide.com/news/2023/12/2/football-no-8-8-8-alabama-upsets-no-1-1-1-georgia-27-24-to-capture-30th-sec-championship.aspx

390. Alabama 27-24 Georgia (Dec 2, 2023) Box Score, ESPN, https://www.espn.com/college-football/playbyplay/_/gameId/401539483

391. No. 4 Alabama Falls to No. 1 Michigan in Overtime, 27-20, in CFP Semifinal, University of Alabama Athletics, https://rolltide.com/news/2024/1/1/football-no-4-alabama-falls-to-no-1-michigan-in-overtime-27-20-in-cfp-semifinal.aspx

392. Michigan 27-20 Alabama (Jan 1, 2024) Box Score, ESPN, https://www.espn.com/college-football/boxscore/_/gameId/401551786

393. Jumbo Package: Alabama names permanent captains, Roll 'Bama Roll, https://www.rollbamaroll.com/2023/12/4/23987459/alabama-football-nick-saban-names-permanent-captains

394. 2024 Senior Bowl Roster, NFL Mock Draft Database, 2024, https://www.nflmockdraftdatabase.com/senior-bowl-roster-2024

395. 2024 NFL Draft, Wikipedia, retrieved 04/30/24 from https://en.wikipedia.org/wiki/2024_NFL_Draft

396. Jake Coker College Stats, School, Draft, Gamelog, Splits, Sports Reference, https://www.sports-reference.com/cfb/players/jake-coker-1.html

397. Jalen Hurts College Stats, School, Draft, Gamelog, Splits, Sports Reference, https://www.sports-reference.com/cfb/players/jalen-hurts-1.html

398. Mac Jones College Stats, School, Draft, Gamelog, Splits, Sports Reference, https://www.sports-reference.com/cfb/players/mac-jones-1.html

399. A.J. McCarron College Stats, School, Draft, Gamelog, Splits, Sports Reference, https://www.sports-reference.com/cfb/players/aj-mccarron-1.html

400. Greg McElroy College Stats, School, Draft, Gamelog, Splits, Sports Reference, https://www.sports-reference.com/cfb/players/greg-mcelroy-1.html

401. Jalen Milroe College Stats, School, Draft, Gamelog, Splits, Sports Reference, https://www.sports-reference.com/cfb/players/jalen-milroe-1.html

402. Blake Sims College Stats, School, Draft, Gamelog, Splits, Sports, Reference, https://www.sports-reference.com/cfb/players/blake-sims-2.html

403. Tua Tagovailoa College Stats, School, Draft, Gamelog, Splits, Sports Reference, https://www.sports-reference.com/cfb/players/tua-tagovailoa-1.html

404. John Parker Wilson College Stats, School, Draft, Gamelog, Splits, Sports Reference, https://www.sports-reference.com/cfb/players/john-parker-wilson-1.html

405. Bryce Young College Stats, School, Draft, Gamelog, Splits, Sports Reference, https://www.sports-reference.com/cfb/players/bryce-young-1.html

406. Glen Coffee College Stats, Sports Reference, https://www.sports-reference.com/cfb/players/glen-coffee-1.html

407. Kenyan Drake College Stats, Sports Reference, https://www.sports-reference.com/cfb/players/kenyan-drake-1.html

408. Jalston Fowler College Stats, Sports Reference, https://www.sports-reference.com/cfb/players/jalston-fowler-1.html

409. Jahmyr Gibbs College Stats, Sports Reference, https://www.sports-reference.com/cfb/players/jahmyr-gibbs-1.html

410. Terry Grant College Stats, Sports Reference, https://www.sports-reference.com/cfb/players/terry-grant-1.html

411. Damien Harris College Stats, Sports Reference, https://www.sports-reference.com/cfb/players/damien-harris-1.html

412. Najee Harris College Stats, Sports Reference, https://www.sports-reference.com/cfb/players/najee-harris-1.html

413. Derrick Henry College Stats, Sports Reference, https://www.sports-reference.com/cfb/players/derrick-henry-2.html

414. Mark Ingram College Stats, Sports Reference, https://www.sports-reference.com/cfb/players/mark-ingram-1.html

415. Joshua Jacobs College Stats, Sports Reference, https://www.sports-reference.com/cfb/players/joshua-jacobs-1.html
416. Jimmy Johns College Stats, Sports Reference, https://www.sports-reference.com/cfb/players/jimmy-johns-1.html
417. Eddie Lacy College Stats, Sports Reference, https://www.sports-reference.com/cfb/players/eddie-lacy-1.html
418. Jase McClellan College Stats, Sports Reference, https://www.sports-reference.com/cfb/players/jase-mcclellan-1.html
419. Trent Richardson College Stats, Sports Reference, https://www.sports-reference.com/cfb/players/trent-richardson-1.html
420. Brian Robinson Jr. College Stats, Sports Reference, https://www.sports-reference.com/cfb/players/brian-robinson-jr-1.html
421. Bo Scarbrough College Stats, Sports Reference, https://www.sports-reference.com/cfb/players/bo-scarbrough-1.html
422. Roy Upchurch College Stats, Sports Reference, https://www.sports-reference.com/cfb/players/roy-upchurch-1.html
423. Roydell Williams College Stats, Sports Reference, https://www.sports-reference.com/cfb/players/roydell-williams-2.html
424. T.J. Yeldon College Stats, Sports Reference, https://www.sports-reference.com/cfb/players/tj-yeldon-1.html
425. Kenny Bell College Stats, Sports Reference, https://www.sports-reference.com/cfb/players/kenny-bell-1.html
426. Jahleel Billingsley College Stats, Sports Reference, https://www.sports-reference.com/cfb/players/jahleel-billingsley-1.html
427. Chris Black College Stats, Sports Reference, https://www.sports-reference.com/cfb/players/chris-black-2.html
428. Slade Bolden College Stats, Sports Reference, https://www.sports-reference.com/cfb/players/slade-bolden-1.html
429. Isaiah Bond College Stats, Sports Reference, https://www.sports-reference.com/cfb/players/isaiah-bond-1.html
430. Ja'Corey Brooks College Stats, Sports Reference, https://www.sports-reference.com/cfb/players/jacorey-brooks-1.html
431. Jermaine Burton College Stats, Sports Reference, https://www.sports-reference.com/cfb/players/jermaine-burton-1.html
432. Amari Cooper College Stats, Sports Reference, https://www.sports-reference.com/cfb/players/amari-cooper-1.html
433. Preston Dial College Stats, Sports Reference, https://www.sports-reference.com/cfb/players/preston-dial-1.html
434. Gehrig Dieter College Stats, Sports Reference, https://www.sports-reference.com/cfb/players/gehrig-dieter-1.html
435. Miller Forristall College Stats, Sports Reference, https://www.sports-reference.com/cfb/players/miller-forristall-1.html
436. Robert Foster College Stats, Sports Reference, https://www.sports-reference.com/cfb/players/robert-foster-1.html
437. D.J. Hall College Stats, Sports Reference, https://www.sports-reference.com/cfb/players/dj-hall-1.html
438. Darius Hanks College Stats, Sports Reference, https://www.sports-reference.com/cfb/players/darius-hanks-1.html
439. Hale Hentges College Stats, Sports Reference, https://www.sports-reference.com/cfb/players/hale-hentges-1.html
440. Traeshon Holden College Stats, Sports Reference, https://www.sports-reference.com/cfb/players/traeshon-holden-1.html
441. O.J. Howard College Stats, Sports Reference, https://www.sports-reference.com/cfb/players/oj-howard-1.html
442. Jerry Jeudy College Stats, Sports Reference, https://www.sports-reference.com/cfb/players/jerry-jeudy-1.html
443. Christion Jones College Stats, Sports Reference, https://www.sports-reference.com/cfb/players/christion-jones-1.html
444. Julio Jones College Stats, Sports Reference, https://www.sports-reference.com/cfb/players/julio-jones-1.html
445. Cameron Latu College Stats, Sports Reference, https://www.sports-reference.com/cfb/players/cameron-latu-1.html
446. Kendrick Law College Stats, Sports Reference, https://www.sports-reference.com/cfb/players/kendrick-law-1.html
447. Marquis Maze College Stats, Sports Reference, https://www.sports-reference.com/cfb/players/marquis-maze-1.html
448. John Metchie College Stats, Sports Reference, https://www.sports-reference.com/cfb/players/john-metchie-1.html
449. Richard Mullaney College Stats, Sports Reference, https://www.sports-reference.com/cfb/players/richard-mullaney-1.html
450. Amari Niblack College Stats, Sports Reference, https://www.sports-reference.com/cfb/players/amari-niblack-1.html
451. Kevin Norwood College Stats, Sports Reference, https://www.sports-reference.com/cfb/players/kevin-norwood-1.html
452. Colin Peek College Stats, Sports Reference, https://www.sports-reference.com/cfb/players/colin-peek-1.html
453. Kobe Prentice College Stats, Sports Reference, https://www.sports-reference.com/cfb/players/kobe-prentice-1.html
454. Calvin Ridley College Stats, Sports Reference, https://www.sports-reference.com/cfb/players/calvin-ridley-1.html
455. Henry Ruggs III College Stats, Sports Reference, https://www.sports-reference.com/cfb/players/henry-ruggs-iii-1.html
456. Cam Sims College Stats, Sports Reference, https://www.sports-reference.com/cfb/players/cam-sims-1.html
457. Brad Smelley College Stats, Sports Reference, https://www.sports-reference.com/cfb/players/brad-smelley-1.html
458. DeVonta Smith College Stats, Sports Reference, https://www.sports-reference.com/cfb/players/devonta-smith-1.html
459. Irv Smith Jr. College Stats, Sports Reference, https://www.sports-reference.com/cfb/players/irv-smith-jr-1.html
460. Ardarius Stewart College Stats, Sports Reference, https://www.sports-reference.com/cfb/players/ardarius-stewart-1.html
461. Jaylen Waddle College Stats, Sports Reference, https://www.sports-reference.com/cfb/players/jaylen-waddle-1.html
462. Deandrew White College Stats, Sports Reference, https://www.sports-reference.com/cfb/players/deandrew-white-1.html
463. Jameson Williams College Stats, Sports Reference, https://www.sports-reference.com/cfb/players/jameson-williams-1.html
464. Michael Williams College Stats, Sports Reference, https://www.sports-reference.com/cfb/players/michael-williams-3.html
465. Alabama Crimson Tide football statistical leaders, Wikipedia, retrieved 01/30/24 from
https://en.wikipedia.org/wiki/Alabama_Crimson_Tide_football_statistical_leaders
466. University of Alabama Football Team Summary, College Poll Archive,
http://www.collegepollarchive.com/football/ap/teams/summary.cfm?teamid=25
467. Nick Saban's legendary college coaching career: By the numbers, Fox Sports, https://www.foxsports.com/stories/college-football/nick-saban-legendary-college-coaching-career-by-the-numbers
468. Alabama Crimson Tide football under Nick Saban, Wikipedia, retrieved 01/30/24 from
https://en.wikipedia.org/wiki/Alabama_Crimson_Tide_football_under_Nick_Saban
469. Football, 247Sports, https://247sports.com/Season/2023-Football/CompositeTeamRankings/
470. Alabama adds Ole Miss kicker transfer, AL.com, https://www.al.com/alabamafootball/2016/03/alabama_adds_ole_miss_kicker_t.html
471. Alabama Crimson Tide football under Nick Saban, Wikipedia, retrieved 01/30/24 from
https://en.wikipedia.org/wiki/Alabama_Crimson_Tide_football_under_Nick_Saban
472. Brad Edwards, Dynasty by the Numbers (2021), 10
473. Brad Edwards, Dynasty by the Numbers (2021), 11
474. Brad Edwards, Dynasty by the Numbers (2021), 61
475. Christopher Allen College Stats, Sports Reference, https://www.sports-reference.com/cfb/players/christopher-allen-1.html
476. Jonathan Allen College Stats, Sports Reference, https://www.sports-reference.com/cfb/players/jonathan-allen-1.html
477. Eryk Anders College Stats, Sports Reference, https://www.sports-reference.com/cfb/players/eryk-anders-1.html
478. Ryan Anderson College Stats, Sports Reference, https://www.sports-reference.com/cfb/players/ryan-anderson-1.html
479. Will Anderson Jr. College Stats, Sports Reference, https://www.sports-reference.com/cfb/players/will-anderson-jr-1.html
480. Javier Arenas College Stats, Sports Reference, https://www.sports-reference.com/cfb/players/javier-arenas-1.html
481. Jalyn Armour-Davis College Stats, Sports Reference, https://www.sports-reference.com/cfb/players/jalyn-armour-davis-1.html
482. Terrion Arnold College Stats, Sports Reference, https://www.sports-reference.com/cfb/players/terrion-arnold-1.html
483. Anthony Averett College Stats, Sports Reference, https://www.sports-reference.com/cfb/players/anthony-averett-1.html
484. Christian Barmore College Stats, Sports Reference, https://www.sports-reference.com/cfb/players/christian-barmore-1.html
485. Mark Barron College Stats, Sports Reference, https://www.sports-reference.com/cfb/players/mark-barron-1.html
486. Jordan Battle College Stats, Sports Reference, https://www.sports-reference.com/cfb/players/jordan-battle-1.html
487. Deion Belue College Stats, Sports Reference, https://www.sports-reference.com/cfb/players/deion-belue-1.html
488. Brian Branch College Stats, Sports Reference, https://www.sports-reference.com/cfb/players/brian-branch-1.html
489. Chris Braswell College Stats, Sports Reference, https://www.sports-reference.com/cfb/players/chris-braswell-1.html

490. Tony Brown College Stats, Sports Reference, https://www.sports-reference.com/cfb/players/tony-brown-8.html
491. Isaiah Buggs College Stats, Sports Reference, https://www.sports-reference.com/cfb/players/isaiah-buggs-1.html
492. Jihaad Campbell College Stats, Sports Reference, https://www.sports-reference.com/cfb/players/jihaad-campbell-1.html
493. Shyheim Carter College Stats, Sports Reference, https://www.sports-reference.com/cfb/players/shyheim-carter-1.html
494. Simeon Castille College Stats, Sports Reference, https://www.sports-reference.com/cfb/players/simeon-castille-1.html
495. Josh Chapman College Stats, Sports Reference, https://www.sports-reference.com/cfb/players/josh-chapman-1.html
496. Ha Ha Clinton-Dix College Stats, Sports Reference, https://www.sports-reference.com/cfb/players/ha-ha-clinton-dix-1.html
497. Terrence Cody College Stats, Sports Reference, https://www.sports-reference.com/cfb/players/terrence-cody-1.html
498. Landon Collins College Stats, Sports Reference, https://www.sports-reference.com/cfb/players/landon-collins-1.html
499. DJ Dale College Stats, Sports Reference, https://www.sports-reference.com/cfb/players/dj-dale-1.html
500. Marcell Dareus College Stats, Sports Reference, https://www.sports-reference.com/cfb/players/marcell-dareus-1.html
501. Raekwon Davis College Stats, Sports Reference, https://www.sports-reference.com/cfb/players/raekwon-davis-1.html
502. Brandon Deaderick College Stats, Sports Reference, https://www.sports-reference.com/cfb/players/brandon-deaderick-1.html
503. Trey DePriest College Stats, Sports Reference, https://www.sports-reference.com/cfb/players/trey-depriest-1.html
504. Denzel Devall College Stats, Sports Reference, https://www.sports-reference.com/cfb/players/denzel-devall-1.html
505. Quinton Dial College Stats, Sports Reference, https://www.sports-reference.com/cfb/players/quinton-dial-1.html
506. Xzavier Dickson College Stats, Sports Reference, https://www.sports-reference.com/cfb/players/xzavier-dickson-1.html
507. Trevon Diggs College Stats, Sports Reference, https://www.sports-reference.com/cfb/players/trevon-diggs-1.html
508. Caleb Downs College Stats, Sports Reference, https://www.sports-reference.com/cfb/players/caleb-downs-1.html
509. Justin Eboigbe College Stats, Sports Reference, https://www.sports-reference.com/cfb/players/justin-eboigbe-1.html
510. Rahsaan Evans College Stats, Sports Reference, https://www.sports-reference.com/cfb/players/rashaan-evans-1.html
511. Brandon Fanney College Stats, Sports Reference, https://www.sports-reference.com/cfb/players/brandon-fanney-1.html
512. Minkah Fitzpatrick College Stats, Sports Reference, https://www.sports-reference.com/cfb/players/minkah-fitzpatrick-1.html
513. Reuben Foster College Stats, Sports Reference, https://www.sports-reference.com/cfb/players/reuben-foster-1.html
514. Nick Gentry College Stats, Sports Reference, https://www.sports-reference.com/cfb/players/nick-gentry-1.html
515. Wallace Gilberry College Stats, Sports Reference, https://www.sports-reference.com/cfb/players/wallace-gilberry-1.html
516. Robby Green College Stats, Sports Reference, https://www.sports-reference.com/cfb/players/robby-green-1.html
517. Bobby Greenwood College Stats, Sports Reference, https://www.sports-reference.com/cfb/players/bobby-greenwood-1.html
518. Prince Hall College Stats, Sports Reference, https://www.sports-reference.com/cfb/players/prince-hall-1.html
519. Da'Shawn Hand College Stats, Sports Reference, https://www.sports-reference.com/cfb/players/dashawn-hand-1.html
520. Shaun Dion Hamilton College Stats, Sports Reference, https://www.sports-reference.com/cfb/players/shaun-dion-hamilton-1.html
521. Christian Harris College Stats, Sports Reference, https://www.sports-reference.com/cfb/players/christian-harris-3.html
522. Jerrell Harris College Stats, Sports Reference, https://www.sports-reference.com/cfb/players/jerrell-harris-1.html
523. Ronnie Harrison College Stats, Sports Reference, https://www.sports-reference.com/cfb/players/ronnie-harrison-1.html
524. DeMarcco Hellams College Stats, Sports Reference, https://www.sports-reference.com/cfb/players/demarcco-hellams-1.html
525. Dont'a Hightower College Stats, Sports Reference, https://www.sports-reference.com/cfb/players/donta-hightower-1.html
526. Keith Holcombe College Stats, Sports Reference, https://www.sports-reference.com/cfb/players/keith-holcombe-1.html
527. Adrian Hubbard College Stats, Sports Reference, https://www.sports-reference.com/cfb/players/adrian-hubbard-1.html
528. Marlon Humphrey College Stats, Sports Reference, https://www.sports-reference.com/cfb/players/marlon-humphrey-1.html
529. Brandon Ivory College Stats, Sports Reference, https://www.sports-reference.com/cfb/players/brandon-ivory-1.html
530. Eddie Jackson College Stats, Sports Reference, https://www.sports-reference.com/cfb/players/eddie-jackson-6.html
531. Kareem Jackson College Stats, Sports Reference, https://www.sports-reference.com/cfb/players/kareem-jackson-1.html
532. Anfernee Jennings College Stats, Sports Reference, https://www.sports-reference.com/cfb/players/anfernee-jennings-1.html
533. Josh Jobe College Stats, Sports Reference, https://www.sports-reference.com/cfb/players/josh-jobe-1.html
534. Marquis Johnson College Stats, Sports Reference, https://www.sports-reference.com/cfb/players/marquis-johnson-2.html
535. Nico Johnson College Stats, Sports Reference, https://www.sports-reference.com/cfb/players/nico-johnson-1.html
536. Rashad Johnson College Stats, Sports Reference, https://www.sports-reference.com/cfb/players/rashad-johnson-1.html
537. Cyrus Jones College Stats, Sports Reference, https://www.sports-reference.com/cfb/players/cyrus-jones-1.html
538. Hootie Jones College Stats, Sports Reference, https://www.sports-reference.com/cfb/players/laurence-hootie-jones-1.html
539. Jaylen Key College Stats, Sports Reference, https://www.sports-reference.com/cfb/players/jaylen-key-1.html
540. Dre Kirkpatrick College Stats, Sports Reference, https://www.sports-reference.com/cfb/players/dre-kirkpatrick-1.html
541. Ezekial Knight College Stats, Sports Reference, https://www.sports-reference.com/cfb/players/ezekial-knight-1.html
542. Deontae Lawson College Stats, Sports Reference, https://www.sports-reference.com/cfb/players/deontae-lawson-1.html
543. Dillon Lee College Stats, Sports Reference, https://www.sports-reference.com/cfb/players/dillon-lee-1.html
544. Shane Lee College Stats, Sports Reference, https://www.sports-reference.com/cfb/players/shane-lee-1.html
545. Robert Lester College Stats, Sports Reference, https://www.sports-reference.com/cfb/players/robert-lester-1.html
546. Terrell Lewis College Stats, Sports Reference, https://www.sports-reference.com/cfb/players/terrell-lewis-2.html
547. Will Lowery College Stats, Sports Reference, https://www.sports-reference.com/cfb/players/will-lowery-1.html
548. Trezmen Marshall College Stats, Sports Reference, https://www.sports-reference.com/cfb/players/trezmen-marshall-1.html
549. Phidarian Mathis College Stats, Sports Reference, https://www.sports-reference.com/cfb/players/phidarian-mathis-1.html
550. Jared Mayden College Stats, Sports Reference, https://www.sports-reference.com/cfb/players/jared-mayden-1.html
551. Rolando McClain College Stats, Sports Reference, https://www.sports-reference.com/cfb/players/rolando-mcclain-1.html
552. Xavier McKinney College Stats, Sports Reference, https://www.sports-reference.com/cfb/players/xavier-mckinney-1.html
553. Kool Aid McKinstry College Stats, Sports Reference, https://www.sports-reference.com/cfb/players/kool-aid-mckinstry-1.html
554. Dequan Menzie College Stats, Sports Reference, https://www.sports-reference.com/cfb/players/dequan-menzie-1.html
555. Christian Miller College Stats, Sports Reference, https://www.sports-reference.com/cfb/players/christian-miller-2.html
556. Dee Milliner College Stats, Sports Reference, https://www.sports-reference.com/cfb/players/dee-milliner-1.html
557. Jaylen Mooody College Stats, Sports Reference, https://www.sports-reference.com/cfb/players/jaylen-moody-1.html
558. Malachi Moore College Stats, Sports Reference, https://www.sports-reference.com/cfb/players/malachi-moore-2.html
559. Dylan Moses College Stats, Sports Reference, https://www.sports-reference.com/cfb/players/dylan-moses-1.html
560. C.J. Mosley College Stats, Sports Reference, https://www.sports-reference.com/cfb/players/cj-mosley-1.html
561. Darren Mustin College Stats, Sports Reference, https://www.sports-reference.com/cfb/players/darren-mustin-1.html
562. Jaheim Oatis College Stats, Sports Reference, https://www.sports-reference.com/cfb/players/jaheim-oatis-1.html
563. Jeoffrey Pagan College Stats, Sports Reference, https://www.sports-reference.com/cfb/players/jeoffrey-pagan-1.html
564. Da'Ron Payne College Stats, Sports Reference, https://www.sports-reference.com/cfb/players/daron-payne-1.html
565. Nick Perry College Stats, Sports Reference, https://www.sports-reference.com/cfb/players/nick-perry-2.html
566. D.J. Pettway College Stats, Sports Reference, https://www.sports-reference.com/cfb/players/dj-pettway-1.html
567. Reggie Ragland College Stats, Sports Reference, https://www.sports-reference.com/cfb/players/reggie-ragland-1.html
568. Labryan Ray College Stats, Sports Reference, https://www.sports-reference.com/cfb/players/labryan-ray-1.html
569. Cory Reamer College Stats, Sports Reference, https://www.sports-reference.com/cfb/players/cory-reamer-1.html

570. Jarran Reed College Stats, Sports Reference, https://www.sports-reference.com/cfb/players/jarran-reed-1.html
571. Eli Ricks College Stats, Sports Reference, https://www.sports-reference.com/cfb/players/eli-ricks-1.html
572. A'Shawn Robinson College Stats, Sports Reference, https://www.sports-reference.com/cfb/players/ashawn-robinson-1.html
573. Drew Sanders College Stats, Sports Reference, https://www.sports-reference.com/cfb/players/drew-sanders-1.html
574. Ali Sharrief College Stats, Sports Reference, https://www.sports-reference.com/cfb/players/ali-sharrief-1.html
575. Geno Smith College Stats, Sports Reference, https://www.sports-reference.com/cfb/players/geno-smith-2.html
576. Saigon Smith College Stats, Sports Reference, https://www.sports-reference.com/cfb/players/saivion-smith-2.html
577. Tim Smith College Stats, Sports Reference, https://www.sports-reference.com/cfb/players/tim-smith-8.html
578. Damion Square College Stats, Sports Reference, https://www.sports-reference.com/cfb/players/damion-square-1.html
579. Ed Stinson College Stats, Sports Reference, https://www.sports-reference.com/cfb/players/ed-stinson-1.html
580. Vinnie Sunseri College Stats, Sports Reference, https://www.sports-reference.com/cfb/players/vinnie-sunseri-1.html
581. Patrick Surtain II College Stats, Sports Reference, https://www.sports-reference.com/cfb/players/patrick-surtain-ii-1.html
582. Denote Thompson College Stats, Sports Reference, https://www.sports-reference.com/cfb/players/deionte-thompson-1.html
583. Henry To'oto'o College Stats, Sports Reference, https://www.sports-reference.com/cfb/players/henry-tootoo-1.html
584. Dalvin Tomlinson College Stats, Sports Reference, https://www.sports-reference.com/cfb/players/dalvin-tomlinson-1.html
585. Dallas Turner College Stats, Sports Reference, https://www.sports-reference.com/cfb/players/dallas-turner-1.html
586. Courtney Upshaw College Stats, Sports Reference, https://www.sports-reference.com/cfb/players/courtney-upshaw-1.html
587. Levi Wallace College Stats, Sports Reference, https://www.sports-reference.com/cfb/players/levi-wallace-1.html
588. Lorenzo Washington College Stats, Sports Reference, https://www.sports-reference.com/cfb/players/lorenzo-washington-1.html
589. Jarrick Williams College Stats, Sports Reference, https://www.sports-reference.com/cfb/players/jarrick-williams-1.html
590. Jesse Williams College Stats, Sports Reference, https://www.sports-reference.com/cfb/players/jesse-williams-3.html
591. Quinnen Williams College Stats, Sports Reference, https://www.sports-reference.com/cfb/players/quinnen-williams-1.html
592. Tim Williams College Stats, Sports Reference, https://www.sports-reference.com/cfb/players/tim-williams-7.html
593. Mack Wilson College Stats, Sports Reference, https://www.sports-reference.com/cfb/players/mack-wilson-1.html
594. Justin Woodall College Stats, Sports Reference, https://www.sports-reference.com/cfb/players/justin-woodall-1.html
595. Daniel Wright College Stats, Sports Reference, https://www.sports-reference.com/cfb/players/daniel-wright-1.html
596. Byron Young College Stats, Sports Reference, https://www.sports-reference.com/cfb/players/byron-young-1.html
597. What was Nick Saban's 'most humiliating' defeat?, al.com, https://www.perplexity.ai/search/how-do-i-VXljbP9USmWroqc9A9hETg

About the Author

Brad Beard was born an Alabama fan. Both of his parents were born in Tuscaloosa, AL and attended the University of Alabama (Kay, 1956-1960 and Jerry, 1956-1961), and that's where they met. His dad was a running back and played football for Coach Paul Bear Bryant, and his uncle, Gene, played basketball and baseball for the university. His grandfather on his mother's side, William Henderson Jones, co-founded the Alabama Bookstore (currently operating as Bamastuff) in 1938 which moved to the strip in 1942. His uncle, David, now owns it, and it was added to the National Register of Historic Places in 2020. Legend has it that his grandfather either created or had a hand in creating the logo of the elephant coming out of the Alabama "A", but since it was not copyrighted at the time, we'll never know for sure.

When Brad was young, he often traveled to Tuscaloosa with his family to visit his grandparents, aunts, uncles, and cousins. He has fond memories of everyone watching Alabama football games together, his grandfather listening to the radio commentary instead of the TV, and playing with his cousins.

Brad attended the University of Alabama from 1994-1998 and received a Bachelor of Science degree with a major in Management Information Systems and minor in Computer Science. He met his wife, Jill (she was on the Alabama Dance Team), in a class on campus in 1996. They got married in 2002. They have three wonderful children who were all born in National Championship years (Brooklyn - 2009, Jaclyn - 2012, and Goldie - 2015).

He was fortunate enough to have been able to attend every National Championship game in the Saban era. He also attended every playoff game since the inception in 2014. He attended all but one SEC Championship game, only missing the one that occurred in 2009. He made some wonderful memories attending many other great games and witnessing history.